FEDERAL INCOME TAXATION

How to use your Connected Casebook

Step 1: Go to **www.CasebookConnect.com** and redeem your access code to get started.

Access Code:

Step 2: Go to your **BOOKSHELF** and select your Connected Casebook to start reading, highlighting, and taking notes in the margins of your e-book.

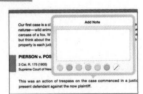

Step 3: Select the **STUDY** tab in your toolbar to access a variety of practice materials designed to help you master the course material. These materials may include explanations, videos, multiple-choice questions, flashcards, short answer, essays, and issue spotting.

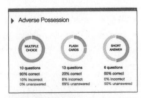

Step 4: Select the **OUTLINE** tab in your toolbar to access chapter outlines that automatically incorporate your highlights and annotations from the e-book. Use the My Notes area for copying, pasting, and editing your book notes or creating new notes.

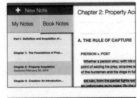

Step 5: If your professor has enrolled your class, you can select the **CLASS INSIGHTS** tab and compare your own study center results against the average of your classmates.

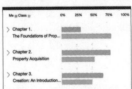

Is this a used casebook? Access code already scratched off?

You can purchase the Digital Version and still access all of the powerful tools listed above. Please visit CasebookConnect.com and select Catalog to learn more.

PLEASE NOTE: Each access code can only be used once. This access code will expire one year after the discontinuation of the corresponding print title and must be redeemed before then. CCH reserves the right to discontinue this program at any time for any business reason. For further details, please see the Casebook Connect End User Agreement.

ASPEN CASEBOOK SERIES

FEDERAL INCOME TAXATION

Eighteenth Edition

JOSEPH BANKMAN

Ralph M. Parsons Professor of Law and Business
Stanford University

DANIEL N. SHAVIRO

Wayne Perry Professor of Taxation
New York University School of Law

KIRK J. STARK

Barrall Family Professor of Tax Law and Policy
University of California, Los Angeles

EDWARD D. KLEINBARD

Ivadelle and Theodore Johnson Professor of Law and Business
USC Gould School of Law

Wolters Kluwer

Published by Wolters Kluwer in New York.

Wolters Kluwer Legal & Regulatory U.S. serves customers worldwide with CCH, Aspen Publishers, and Kluwer Law International products. (www.WKLegaledu. com)

To contact Customer Service, e-mail customer.service@wolterskluwer.com, call 1-800-234-1660, fax 1-800-901-9075, or mail correspondence to:

> Wolters Kluwer
> Attn: Order Department
> PO Box 990
> Frederick, MD 21705

Printed in the United States of America.

2 3 4 5 6 7 8 9 0

ISBN 978-1-5438-0149-1

Library of Congress Cataloging-in-Publication Data

Names: Bankman, Joseph, 1955- author. | Shaviro, Daniel N., author. | Stark, Kirk J., author. | Kleinbard, Edward D., author.
Title: Federal income taxation / Joseph Bankman, Ralph M. Parsons Professor of Law and Business, Stanford University; Daniel N. Shaviro, Wayne Perry Professor of Taxation, New York University School of Law; Kirk J. Stark, Barrall Family Professor of Tax Law and Policy, University of California, Los Angeles; Edward D. Kleinbard, Ivadelle and Theodore Johnson Professor of Law and Business, USC Gould School of Law.
Description: Eighteenth edition. | New York : Wolters Kluwer, [2019] | Series: Aspen casebook series | Includes bibliographical references and index.
Identifiers: LCCN 2018042501 | ISBN 9781543801491
Subjects: LCSH: Income tax—Law and legislation—United States. | LCGFT: Casebooks (Law)
Classification: LCC KF6369 .B265 2019 | DDC 343.7305/2—dc23
LC record available at https://lccn.loc.gov/2018042501.

About Wolters Kluwer Legal & Regulatory U.S.

Wolters Kluwer Legal & Regulatory U.S. delivers expert content and solutions in the areas of law, corporate compliance, health compliance, reimbursement, and legal education. Its practical solutions help customers successfully navigate the demands of a changing environment to drive their daily activities, enhance decision quality and inspire confident outcomes.

Serving customers worldwide, its legal and regulatory portfolio includes products under the Aspen Publishers, CCH Incorporated, Kluwer Law International, ftwilliam.com, and MediRegs names. They are regarded as exceptional and trusted resources for general legal and practice-specific knowledge, compliance and risk management, dynamic workflow solutions, and expert commentary.

SUMMARY OF CONTENTS

CONTENTS

1

INTRODUCTION   1

3

THE PRIVATE SPHERE AND THE PUBLIC SPHERE   133

4

WHEN IS IT INCOME?   189

5

DEBT AND CERTAIN OTHER FINANCIAL INSTRUMENTS 317

6

WHOSE INCOME IS IT?   387

7

| **EXPENSES OF EARNING INCOME** | **415** |

8

TAX SHELTERS AND TAX PLANNING   481

9

MIXED BUSINESS AND PERSONAL EXPENSES — 519

10

PERSONAL DEDUCTIONS, EXEMPTIONS, AND CREDITS — 573

11

TAX AND POVERTY: THE EARNED INCOME TAX CREDIT 611

12

CAPITAL GAINS AND LOSSES 619

PREFACE

Boris Bittker and William Klein, our predecessors on the first few editions of this book, had a unique gift for presenting complex material in an easy-to-understand way. We have tried to preserve that quality, despite the unceasing efforts of Congress (aided at times by taxpayers, their advisors, and the courts) to make the tax law incomprehensible.

Many of the changes made in recent editions reflect an ongoing shift in the direction of legal scholarship in the field of income taxation. While this book is fundamentally a text designed for law school courses, we have endeavored, where appropriate, to incorporate perspectives on taxation from fields other than law—including history, economics, finance, and political science. In addition, because of the continuing significance of globalization and its impact on the study of law, we have begun to incorporate some materials relating to the tax systems of other countries. We also, however, emphasize the underlying practical issues that can make particular doctrinal issues especially important.

Finally, as part of our ongoing effort to keep pace with an ever-changing field of law, we have eliminated some cases and materials less relevant to the practice of tax law in the 21st century. The current edition incorporates data and materials available as of the date of publication. Annual (or more frequent) supplements will be sent to adopters.

As with each of the prior editions, the overall objective has been to give students a basic framework for understanding federal income tax law and policy. While tax may be a field famous for its ever-changing legal details, our hope is that this book will help students develop a durable and adaptive knowledge base that will serve them well beyond future amendments to the tax code.

Joseph Bankman
Daniel N. Shaviro
Kirk J. Stark
Edward D. Kleinbard

November 2018

ACKNOWLEDGMENTS

The authors gratefully acknowledge the permission granted from the following publishers to reprint excerpts and cartoons from their publications:

Cotham, Frank, The New Yorker Collection/The Cartoon Bank; © Condé Nast.

Maremont, "Mark Silicon Valley's Mouthwatering Tax Break," The Wall Street Journal, April 7, 2013. Copyright © 2013 The Wall Street Journal by Dow Jones & Co. News Corporation. Reproduced with permission of Dow Jones Company via Copyright Clearance Center.

Shanahan, Danny, The New Yorker Collection/The Cartoon Bank; © Condé Nast.

Simons, Henry C., Personal Income Taxation, University of Chicago Press, 1938, pp. 80-88. Reproduced with permission of University of Chicago Press via Copyright Clearance Center.

Stevens, Matt and Taylor Goldenstein, Los Angeles Times, "Residents May Have To Pay Taxes On Their Turf Rebate Money," published September 22, 2015. Reprinted by permission of The Los Angeles Times.

Williams, Roberton C., Tax Policy Center, "Federal Taxes Are Very Progressive," Tax Policy Vox Blog, Aug. 11, 2016. Copyright © 2016 Tax Analysts. Reprinted with permission.

EDITORIAL NOTICE

The original author of this casebook was Boris I. Bittker of Yale Law School, who has earned the admiration and affection of generations of teachers and students. Much of his original structure and choice of materials remains in the current edition. Bittker was joined in later editions by Lawrence M. Stone and William A. Klein, both of whom contributed immeasurably to the content and direction of the book. The current authors are deeply indebted to Professors Bittker, Stone, and Klein for the many wise choices and valuable insights that have survived.

All omissions from cases and other materials, except omissions of footnotes, are indicated either by substitution of new material in brackets or, more often, by an ellipsis (...). Thus, omissions of citations, as well as omissions of text, are generally indicated by the insertion of the ellipsis. Citations have been excised ruthlessly on the theory that for the most part they are of no use to students and that the rare student who might have some interest in them can easily look them up in the original report. There is no notation of omitted footnotes, and all footnotes, including those in cases and other materials, are numbered consecutively from the beginning of each chapter.

FEDERAL INCOME TAXATION

1

INTRODUCTION

The art of taxation consists in so plucking the goose as to obtain the largest possible amount of feathers with the smallest possible amount of hissing.

— Jean Baptiste Colbert (1619-83),
Finance Minister to King Louis XIV of France

A. TAXING AND SPENDING

Welcome to the world of taxation. If you are like most law students, chances are that the course for which you are reading this book marks your first formal introduction to tax law. Most law students show up for their first tax class thinking it's going to be dull and dry, dense and difficult. We would like to use this introductory chapter to offer an alternative view of tax as a field of study to lay the groundwork for what follows.

Tax law informs many choices we make over the course of our lives, such as how to finance the purchase of a home, what career to pursue, or even whether to get married. It also is central to structuring business deals and to virtually every other business decision. But, notwithstanding the importance of tax law, you should not put the cart before the horse. As former Congressman Barney Frank was fond of saying, in our democracy (and unlike the France of Louis XIV), government is simply the things we choose to do together. Government instantiates those collective activities by paying salaries (for example, to military personnel), purchasing goods and services from the private sector, and spending money to improve the welfare of our citizens, whether by providing "in kind" services or cash assistance, as, for example, through Social Security payments.

In short, government exists to spend, not to tax.[1] Government spends on all of us, through programs selected by the democratic process the money obtains

---

1. As you will learn, all general statements about taxation always have exceptions. Some taxes, for example, are designed to correct private market failures rather than to fund spending. Even in a hypothetical world of barebones government, such taxes might still be employed to help private markets more accurately allocate goods through the price mechanism.

1

from us (presumably in differing proportions) through mandatory contributions whose terms again are set through the democratic process—that is, through taxation. Not even your least favorite political party would impose taxes just for fun and then burn the money in a giant bonfire.

The impact of government cannot be measured by looking solely at the pain we feel when paying taxes; it must also take into account the goods and services that those taxes have purchased. Too often, whether in popular discourse or among academics, we debate tax policy when what we really mean to address is *fiscal policy*: the net effects of government taxing and spending on our lives.

Intuitively, most of us recognize that choosing how we share the costs of government is a subtler art than splitting the check four ways at the local pizzeria. Some citizens, for example, appear to have greater "ability to pay" (a phrase to which we will often return)—they're just plain richer, to put it bluntly—than other citizens. Designing a tax system necessarily entails asking how the allocation of the burdens of financing government should reflect that fact.

Looking more generally at fiscal policy, we can ask what (if anything) are the obligations that each of us owes to others? What are we entitled to keep for ourselves? These are big, important questions at the heart of the social contract.

Theorists across many disciplines have struggled for centuries to answer these sorts of questions, employing in the modern era primarily the tools of economics and moral philosophy. Sir James Mirrlees, for example, won a Nobel Prize in economics for his work on "optimal tax" theory, which begins by positing a social consensus on how important egalitarianism is to a society, and then builds from that a tax-rate schedule that minimizes what Jean Baptiste Colbert would call the hissing of the geese or what modern economists would call the deadweight loss of taxation. Approaching these issues from the vantage point of moral philosophy, thinkers from Hobbes and Locke to Rawls and Nozick have debated the morality of taxation and its implications for the relationship between the individual and the broader community.

But more importantly, these same questions regularly stoke debate among ordinary citizens. Everyone has an opinion about taxes. Are they too high? Are they too low? Who pays too much? Who pays too little? Tax policy ultimately is not an academic exercise, but one in which all citizens have an immediate interest and in which policy decisions are resolved through the political process.

This casebook is an introduction to understanding and working with the federal personal income tax as it exists at the time of writing. As you will see, this is a large challenge, and in reducing the material to a digestible size we are not always able to address the larger economic or philosophical issues underlying the design of the income tax. The casebook necessarily is full of cases and laws that address, sometimes with almost overbearing specificity, how we go about calculating our tax liabilities, as well as the enforcement tools available to government. In studying these rules, with all their exceptions and exceptions to exceptions, it is easy to lose sight of the ultimate purpose of the federal income tax (raising money, efficiently and fairly), but whenever possible you should try to take a step back and ask, what policy does this rule serve?

In a democracy, the success of any tax system rests on citizens' understanding of its purpose as well as on its operational details. If tax and fiscal policy intrigue you, we hope you will search out more advanced courses that build on the technical foundations to which this casebook is addressed, or read further on your own.[2]

B.   SOME DATA ON TAXES AND THE DISTRIBUTION OF INCOME

1.   Income Tax Data

Income taxes dominate the American tax structure. As can be seen from Table 1-1 below, for 2015, income taxes, corporate and individual, produced 58 percent of total federal revenues.[3] Income taxes are also an important source of revenue for most state governments. In 2015, approximately 149 million federal income tax returns were filed by individuals.[4] Nearly all individuals will at some time file a federal income tax return—the infamous Form 1040. While this book emphasizes the development and operation of tax law and policy, rather than how and when to file forms with the IRS, you may find it useful to consult Form 1040 from time to time to see how specific provisions from the statute, regulations, and case law are reflected on the tax return.

TABLE 1-1
Sources of Federal Revenue for FY 2015

	Amount (billions)	Percentage of total
Individual income taxes	$1,541	47
Corporation income taxes	344	11
Social insurance taxes and contributions	1,065	33
Excise taxes	98	3
Estate and gift taxes	19	1
Other (incl. deposits by Fed Reserve)	183	6
Total	$3,250	100

2. One very accessible (if a bit long in the tooth) textbook on tax policy is Slemrod and Bakija, *Taxing Ourselves: A Citizen's Guide to the Debate over Taxes* (4th ed. 2008). Sir James Mirrlees, referenced in the text, led a blue-ribbon panel of experts to review in depth the operation of the UK's tax system, which has many similarities to our own. The panel produced a summary of its findings for general readers under the title *Tax by Design: The Mirrlees Review*. It is available for free online at http://www.ifs.org.uk/publications/5353. Other recent books intended for nonspecialist audiences include Bruce Bartlett, *The Benefit and the Burden: Tax Reform—Why We Need It and What It Will Take* (2013), and Edward Kleinbard, *We Are Better Than This: How Government Should Spend Our Money* (2014).

3. Staff of the Joint Committee on Taxation, *Overview of the Federal Tax System as in Effect for 2016*, JCX-43-16, May 10, 2016, available at www.jct.gov.

4. IRS 2015 Data Book, available at https://www.irs.gov/pub/irs-soi/15databk.pdf.

FIGURE 1-1.
Federal Receipts by Source as Share of Total Receipts, 1950-2015

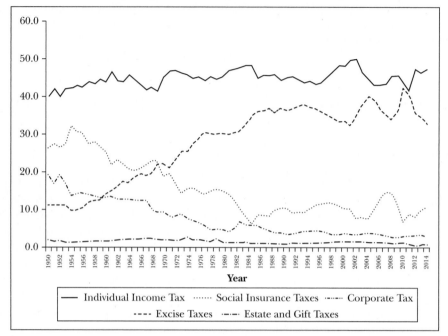

Source: Office of Management and Budget, Historical Tables, Budget of the United States Government, Fiscal Year 2017, and Joint Committee on Taxation calculations.

Over the last 65 years, the personal income tax has remained a relatively stable percentage of total federal receipts. The largest changes have been the dramatic increase in the importance of payroll taxes (Social Security and Medicare contributions) and the declining share of the corporate income tax and excise taxes as percentages of the total.

Despite these fluctuations in relative contributions among the sources of federal revenues, total federal revenues have stayed within a relatively narrow band when measured against the relevant benchmark, Gross Domestic Product (for this purpose, a fair approximation of national income). There is no natural law of government revenue collections at work here, but rather an active Congress, which constantly tinkers with tax rates and the size of government programs. The modern high point for tax collections as a percentage of GDP was 2000; the recession of 2008-2010 led to a significant temporary drop in revenues:

FIGURE 1-2.
Federal Receipts as a Percentage of GDP, 1942-2015

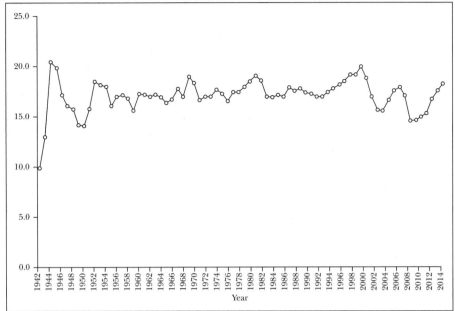

Source: Office of Management and Budget, Historical Tables, Budget of the United States Government, Fiscal Year 2017, and Joint Committee on Taxation calculations.

Within the individual income tax base, wage income is by far the largest component, accounting for roughly 68 percent of total gross income in 2016. Capital gains (gain, for example, from selling stock held as an investment) and dividend income make up only 8 percent of the total:

FIGURE 1-3.
Sources of Gross Income for All Individual Taxpayers, 2016

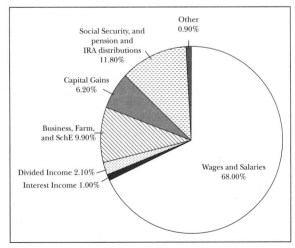

Source: Office of Management and Budget, Historical Tables, Budget of the United States Government, Fiscal Year 2017, and Joint Committee on Taxation calculations.

At the same time, long-term capital gains and dividend income, which are taxed at a preferential rate compared to "ordinary" income, are highly concentrated within the incomes of the highest-income taxpayers. The IRS annually publishes data on the 400 highest-income taxpayers. In 2012, it took an adjusted gross income (for our purposes now, gross income less business expenses) of $140 million to join this elite club; the average income for the members of the fortunate 400 in this one year was $336 million. This income was overwhelmingly comprised of capital gains and dividends taxed at preferential rates. As a result, the average federal income tax rate paid by the top 400 taxpayers in that year was about 17 percent—less than the average rate that a married couple with no dependents, and earning around $100,000 in wages, would have paid in combined income tax and social security contributions in that year.[5] Section D.5, *infra*, offers some more detail as to how the preferential tax rate on capital gains (and, to a lesser extent, dividends) affects the tax burdens of the most affluent taxpayers.

None of this answers the question uppermost on the minds of many Americans, which is, are we taxed too heavily? One useful approach in answering that question involves comparing tax burdens across different countries. When the United States is benchmarked against other major economies around the world, the results may be surprising: The United States is the *lowest* taxed large developed economy in the world (including all subnational taxes, which must be done for the sake of comparability). In 2013, for example, Danes paid about 48 percent of their GDP in taxes; Americans, by contrast, paid about 25 percent of U.S. GDP in federal, state, and local taxes. Within the Organization for Economic Cooperation and Development, an organization of thirty-six member countries, including all the major economies in the world other than the "BRICs" (Brazil, Russia, India, and China), the total tax burden in the United States as a percentage of GDP was the fourth lowest: Only South Korea, Chile, and Mexico took in less tax revenues as a percentage of their GDPs. The simple (unweighted) average tax rate across the OECD in 2013 was 34 percent of GDP.[6]

But, as emphasized at the outset, this is an incomplete picture. Danes pay a great deal more in tax than do Americans, but by the same token Danes receive the benefits of many government programs not available in the United States. Whatever your political convictions tell you about what tax burdens ought to be, the data show the United States to be a low-tax, small-government country

---

5. The wage base against which Social Security contributions are measured is capped (in 2012, at about $110,000), so that Social Security contributions are an inconsequential portion of the tax liabilities of taxpayers in the top 400 but very much a concern to more ordinary wage earners. The text assumes that the standard deduction was claimed by the hypothetical married couple.

Note also that 2012 saw a surge in capital gains realizations, because the tax rate on capital gains increased on January 1, 2013. This by itself is an interesting window into a fundamental problem in tax system design, which is that taxpayers adjust their behavior (in this case, the timing of stock sales) in light of the tax rules applicable from year to year. Nonetheless, the average tax rate for the top 400 from 2006 to 2011 was closely comparable to that in 2012. The rate increased in 2013 because capital gains realizations were down (as a result of accelerating capital gains realizations into 2012) and because the tax rate on capital gains and dividend income increased as of January 1, 2013.

6. The OECD data are available at http://www.oecd.org/tax/tax-policy/revenue-statistics-ratio-change-previous-year.htm.

when compared with other developed economies. The two areas where the United States outspends other governments (again, as a percentage of GDP) are defense spending and healthcare. The former represents a conscious policy choice, with which you may agree or not. The second—a phenomenon that long predates the Affordable Care Act—is largely the result of the fragmented systems through which healthcare is delivered in the United States and the large tax subsidy for healthcare provided through one's employer. (See Chapter 10.) Whether life in Denmark or the United States leads to a happier citizenry is exactly the sort of fraught question that the political process is meant to answer.

2.   Distributional Data

No tax policy issue is more likely to lead to heated arguments than the question of the distribution of tax burdens relative to incomes. The problem is that the data can be sliced to make almost any case. For example, it is sometimes observed that a significant percentage of Americans (about 34 percent of income tax filers in 2016) do not owe any federal income tax in a given year.[7] But there are many reasons why this is true, including the fact that income tax filers include both older Americans with modest incomes primarily comprised of Social Security payments on which they owe no income tax, as well as low-income wage earners who receive a targeted form of income assistance called the "earned income tax credit," or EITC. Depending on income level and number of dependents, the EITC can not only wipe out one's income tax liability but lead to a substantial "refund" (more neutrally, a government check), which is why so many low-income wage earners file tax returns in the first place. The EITC is discussed in detail in Section D.2. If the EITC were instead called a separate "welfare program," and not run through the tax system, more individuals might be taxpayers, but they would receive separate earned income welfare checks that offset their tax liability; nothing would change but the labels (and the duplication of costs to the government).

Very generally, a "progressive" income tax system is one where the average tax rate rises with income. (Section D.3, *infra*, expands on this.) A "proportional" income tax is one where the same tax rate applies regardless of income. A proportional tax does not mean that everyone pays the same tax, but rather that the tax *rate* stays constant as incomes rise; a $200,000 tax bill on $1 million of income is a great deal more money than a $20,000 tax bill on $100,000 of income, but the tax rate is identical, in this case, 20 percent. A tax under which $100,000 of income is associated with a $20,000 tax bill but $1 million of income incurs a $300,000 tax bill employs a progressive rate structure; the tax rate is 20 percent in the former case, and 30 percent in the latter. Finally, a "regressive" tax is one where the average tax rate goes down as income goes up. Social Security contributions function as a regressive tax, because the wage

---

7. Tax Policy Center Table T15-0138. For an introduction to the topic, see Rachel Johnson et al., *Why Some Tax Units Pay No Income Tax*, Tax Policy Center, July 2011, available online at http://www. taxpolicycenter.org/publications/url.cfm?ID=1001547. See also the discussion at http://www.taxpolicy center.org/taxvox/new-estimates-how-many-households-pay-no-federal-income-tax.

base on which tax is imposed is capped: For 2016, the cap was $118,500. Higher wages (as well as nonwage income) are untaxed under the Social Security tax.

As we will see, the individual income tax is progressive, but whether it is highly progressive or only modestly so is a trickier question. The very bottom of the income distribution shows negative income tax liabilities because of the EITC, which again is a form of targeted income support run through the income tax system, because that actually is the most efficient way to deliver the program. Removing the EITC from measures of income tax progressivity and treating it as a separate income security spending program (as would be true in many other countries) would reduce the apparent progressivity of the income tax. And at the very top of the pyramid, the average tax rate paid by the top 400 taxpayers actually is much lower than the average rate paid by the merely highly successful, because such a large percentage of the income of the top 400 is in the form of tax-favored capital gains and divided income.

More fundamentally, the federal income tax is one of just a suite of taxes to which Americans are subject. At the federal level, payroll taxes are regressive, and start with the first dollar of wage income. So too are federal excise taxes (for example, the excise tax on gasoline), because purchases subject to those taxes constitute a larger percentage of a poor person's income than they do for an affluent individual. The same is true for state and local sales taxes and other subnational taxes.[8]

To our knowledge, no federal agency tracks the distribution of national and subnational taxes, but both the nonpartisan Congressional Budget Office (CBO) and the nonpartisan Staff of the Joint Committee on Taxation (JCT) regularly undertake work on the distribution of federal taxes. For example, the JCT staff begins with all "tax units" (that is, 173 million potential tax filers, including individuals with no income or who otherwise are nonfilers, of whom about 145 million actually file income tax returns) and places those tax units into different income categories based on their "expanded incomes."[9]

For 2016, the JCT Staff estimates that tax units in the $30,000 to $40,000 expanded income category face a tax rate of −1.9 percent (that is, they are entitled to receive cash back from the IRS, in most cases through the operation of the EITC, although in a few cases by virtue of operating a business at a loss in that year). Expanded incomes in the over $1 million category, by contrast, face an average tax rate of 26.7 percent. This certainly sounds highly progressive. But if instead one looks at the JCT Staff data for all federal taxes, the range narrows somewhat, from 9 percent for tax units in the $30,000 to $40,000 range to 32 percent for the over $1 million bracket. And if one were to

8. State and local income taxes are generally progressive, but less so than the federal income tax. Frank Sammartino and Norton Francis, *Federal-State Income Tax Progressivity*, Tax Policy Center, June 2016.

9. "Expanded income" is not a tax term; rather, it indicates an effort to define a broader measure of income than that captured by the Internal Revenue Code. It includes, for example, nontaxable Social Security benefits and the annual insurance value of Medicare for all tax units that qualify for the latter program. As in the case of the CBO's concept of "before-tax income" (see below), expanded income thus includes nontaxable benefits funded by the tax system, including those funded by prior years' taxes imposed on the same tax unit (as when a tax unit ages into Social Security). The JCT data concerning expanded incomes comes from Staff of the Joint Committee on Taxation, *Overview of the Federal Tax System as in Effect for 2016*, JCX-43-16, May 10, 2016, Table A-6.

FIGURE 1-4.
Effective Federal Tax Rates, by Income Percentile

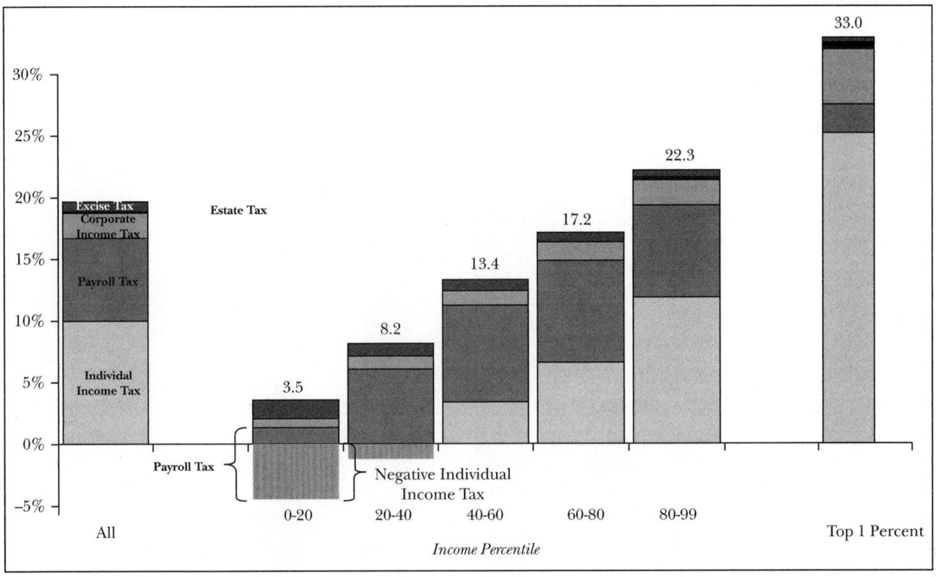

Source: Roberton C. Williams, Tax Policy Center, Federal Taxes Are Very Progressive, Tax Policy Vox Blog, Aug. 11, 2016.

refine the top of the income ladder further, then the over $100 million income crowd would show a lower rate than 32 percent.[10]

Another way of parsing the same JCT Staff data is to observe that tax units with over $1 million in income accounted for 19 percent of all federal taxes: But they also accounted for 13 percent of all income. Whether this is highly progressive or not is exactly the sort of question that you will have to answer for yourself.

The Tax Policy Center, a well-respected nonpartisan organization based in Washington, has published a helpful graphical summary of the progressivity of all federal taxes, relying on raw data from the IRS and other government sources. You can see here how important the EITC is in any discussion of tax rate progressivity. But even in a chart like this, the EITC's reduction in affected taxpayers' income tax to zero (as opposed to cash refunds) is invisible, as is the decline in tax rates at the most stratospheric levels of income, by virtue of the preferential tax rate on capital gains (discussed later in this chapter).

Another nonpartisan organization, Citizens for Tax Justice, has estimated how the progressivity of the U.S. tax system looks when taking into account state and local taxes, which, as noted earlier, are generally less progressive or even regressive in effect.

---

10. Because the JCT Staff includes an allocation of corporate income taxes to individuals, its data are not strictly comparable to the IRS top 400 data, which includes only individual taxes.

FIGURE 1-5.
Shares of Total Taxes Paid by Each Income Group Compared to Shares of Total Income in 2016

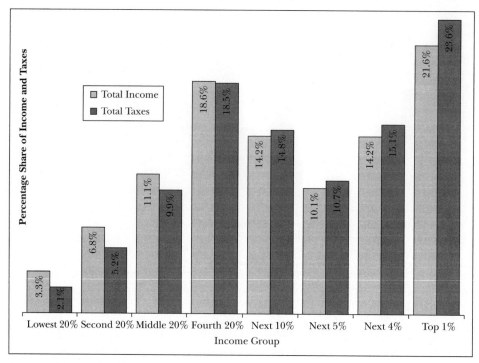

Source: Citizens for Tax Justice, Institute on Taxation and Economic Policy (ITEP) Tax Model, April 2016.

As you can see, distributional analysis is not a simple matter.

The CBO produces from time to time a comprehensive review of the distribution of income and taxes; the most recent publication covers 2013.[11] The CBO's work is broader in scope in one important respect than the JCT Staff's, in that it seeks to offer insight not simply into who pays how much tax, but also into how income concentration (income inequality, in other words) has evolved over time. In determining the concentration of incomes, the CBO works with "market incomes" and also with a concept called "before-tax income." This latter concept includes government transfer payments received.

Comparing market incomes to after-tax incomes arguably presents the clearest picture of the totality of the federal fiscal system in application, because it compares pure market outcomes, on the one hand, with individuals' positions after paying taxes and also after receiving federal benefits, on the other. (All the data presented prior to this point looked at the tax system in the abstract, rather than the impact of the fiscal system as a whole.) This is a snapshot of the comparison for 2013:

11. Congressional Budget Office, *The Distribution of Household Income and Federal Taxes, 2013* (June 2016), available at www.cbo.gov.

FIGURE 1-6.
Shares of Market and After-Tax Income, by Market Income Group, 2013

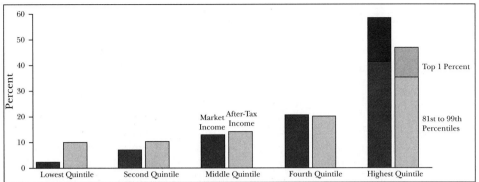

Source: Congressional Budget Office.

Market income consists of labor income, business income, capital gains (profits realized from the sale of assets), capital income excluding capital gains, income received in retirement for past service, and other sources of income.

After-tax income is market income plus government transfers minus federal taxes. Government transfers are cash payments and in-kind benefits from social insurance and other government assistance programs. Those transfers include payments and benefits from federal, state, and local governments. Federal taxes include individual income taxes, payroll taxes, corporate income taxes, and excise taxes.

The tax law was significantly amended in 2017. Among the most noticeable changes were significant reductions in the effective rate on various forms of capital investment. All else being equal, this might be thought to disproportionately benefit wealthier taxpayers, who overwhelmingly own such investments. However, the new law also increased the standard deduction, described below, which reduces the tax owed by middle- and low-income taxpayers. Preliminary estimates by the Joint Committee on Taxation show that, on balance, the new law is expected to reduce taxes by 5 to 10 percent for most income classes.[12] (Note, however, that since the federal income tax is progressive, an equal percentage reduction would increase disparities in after-tax wealth.[13]) The reason why the new law could reduce taxes for nearly all income classes is that it is not revenue neutral; the Joint Committee on Taxation estimated that it will reduce net revenues, and increase the deficit, by over a trillion dollars in its ten-year budget window.[14]

12. Joint Committee on Taxation, Distributional Effects of the Conference Agreement for H.R. 1, the "Tax Cuts and Jobs Act," December 19, 2017, available at www.jct.gov/publications/html.

13. The intuition behind this statement can be gleaned by imagining a 100 percent reduction in the federal income tax for all taxpayers. The percentage reduction would be equal — but since the federal income tax helps reduce inequality in after-tax income, its elimination would increase disparities in wealth.

14. Joint Committee on Taxation, *Macroeconomic Analysis of the Conference Agreement for H.R. 1, the "Tax Cuts and Jobs Act,"* JCX-69-17, December 22, 2017. This document can also be found on the Joint Committee on Taxation website at www.jct.gov.

C. WHY IS TAX LAW SO COMPLICATED?

1. A Model of Economic Activity

This casebook uses the toolkit of a lawyer to approach the technical, policy, and economic issues raised by our federal income tax system as it applies to individuals. The subject can seem daunting, frankly for good reason. For many students, this course will be your first introduction to a subject dominated by statutory analysis—by a close reading of an enormously complex and precise set of laws (the Internal Revenue Code)[15] and administrative interpretations, totaling many thousands of pages. (A code differs from simple legislation in that laws enacted at different times are reassembled into a logical order when codified; old legislation that has subsequently been repealed is deleted and new material added in the correct place, so that one need not thumb through 100 years of tax legislation to ascertain the rules applicable today.)

Reading and working with a complex statute like the Internal Revenue Code is an enormously important skill for any lawyer, and like other skills it requires a great deal of practice. At the same time, the application of that complex statute to actual fact patterns often requires judgment and recourse to common law principles. Perverse literal mindedness is the right place for a lawyer to begin parsing a tax problem, but it is rarely the only analytical tool required. This in fact is good news for aspiring lawyers, because it means that the study of tax law is both intellectually challenging and irreducible to purely mechanical analysis. Such irreducibility is the very essence of law as a discipline.

The income tax is of special interest to lawyers because it affects so many other branches of law. The tax lawyer, perhaps above all else, is a planner: a person who advises clients on how to structure transactions so as to ensure compliance with the tax laws and minimize tax liability. Lawyers who do not specialize in tax law must know at least enough about it to recognize when a tax specialist must be consulted. By the same token, the practitioner or the legal scholar who wants to understand economic and legal institutions such as the sale and leaseback method of financing the purchase of property, the family-controlled charitable foundation, or the use of limited liability companies must understand the tax reasons for the use of such devices.

The Internal Revenue Code is very long and complex because it offers a model that must apply to all purposive economic activity. Whatever might happen in the sphere of public economic activity—whether earning a salary,

---

15. Practitioners in the area often refer to the governing statute simply as "the Code"—almost as if to say, "What other statutory code of interest could there possibly be?" Regardless, it is incorrect to refer to the statute as "the IRS Code." The Internal Revenue Service (IRS) is the administrative agency (technically, a part of the Treasury Department) principally responsible for administering the federal tax system, but it has no responsibility for the design of the statute itself. That onus falls squarely on the shoulders of Congress. Some scholars have argued that the term "IRS Code" has been consciously applied in recent years as a rhetorical device to incite citizens to believe that the IRS was responsible for unpopular tax laws, although plenty of inadvertent uses of the term certainly also occur. See Sheldon Pollack, "The Politics of Taxation," *in Handbook of Government Budgeting*, Roy T. Meyers, ed. (San Francisco: Jossey-Bass Publishers, 1999), pp. 332-354.

being a self-employed plumber, starting your own software company, buying the stock of an established corporation, operating a tuna boat, or entering the timber business—has corresponding rules inside the model. Events in the real world turn dials and pull levers in the model, and out spits a tax bill. Fortunately for law students and lawyers, this model, unlike the models built by social scientists, relies on ordinary words rather than Greek letters and exotic symbols.

The federal income tax's modeling of economic reality is made more complex by the fact that wherever feasible the income tax model takes commercial behavior as the model finds it and seeks to fashion a tax outcome that comports with the underlying commercial understanding. State and local property and sales taxes raise about 35 percent of the amount raised by federal and state income taxes. Yet because sales and property taxes are generally based on simpler concepts and rules, and cover far fewer types of commercial relationships, they produce far less business for lawyers, relative to the amounts involved, than does the income tax.

This idea of the Internal Revenue Code as a model, with economic activity as its inputs and tax bills as its outputs, encapsulates a vitally important goal of the U.S. tax system, which is that the methodologies applied to calculate our respective tax obligations (but not our specific tax bills) should be transparent to all and should apply uniformly to all similarly situated citizens. We do not rely on the local tax inspector to set our tax liabilities based on her intuitions. (This is why tax preparation software can function!)

Every model has an owner: a party responsible for writing and updating it and that controls modifications to it. In the case of the Internal Revenue Code, Congress is the owner. Congress sets the terms under which we are taxed, including the tax rates applicable to our taxable incomes. The Internal Revenue Service is an executive agency charged with administering the tax law, but despite all the heated rhetoric that sometimes surrounds that agency, it is Congress that is ultimately responsible for the Internal Revenue Code. And to emphasize, Congress does not work in broad brushstrokes in establishing the operation of the Internal Revenue Code. The Code is enormously precise and specific, both because it must address thousands of different forms of economic activity and relations, and to ensure that its operation is ultimately transparent (if sometimes difficult to parse). If you think that the Internal Revenue Code stinks, complain to your representatives in Congress, not to the hapless Commissioner of Internal Revenue.

Because the Internal Revenue Code uses ordinary words to define its operation, its rules theoretically are accessible to any perspicacious citizen or legislator. But, with this accessibility sometimes comes ambiguity. As the examples a bit later demonstrate, even a word as basic as "income" can be difficult to apply in some cases.

This high level picture is incomplete in at least one very important respect: As a general matter, the tax system does not invade what might be called the private sphere of our lives. To an economist, housework or child care by a parent is demonstrably economic activity, as is painting one's own home. But the tax system generally does not take cognizance of these vitally important economic activities unless they cross the barrier to the public side of our lives, as, for example, when you hire a housepainter to fix up the bungled job you did when trying to paint your home on your own. (Chapter 3 develops this important theme further.)

So the Internal Revenue Code is complex and ambitious, in that it attempts to establish transparent and objective rules for calculating the tax consequences of all economic activities within its scope. Its application involves not only a close reading of highly interconnected rules, but also consideration of general principles of statutory interpretation, as further refined for use in this specific context. Moreover, much of the model's core system-architecture was established many decades ago; many (but certainly not all) contemporary observers believe that the core architecture requires wholesale revision. These are reasons enough to find federal income taxation a challenging subject.

In addition, the Internal Revenue Code has suffered from more than 100 years of mission creep. Many tax provisions are designed to deliver some sort of social or economic incentive or compensation (or, more rarely, a monetary penalty) that in theory could be offered outside the tax system. Policymakers often call these provisions "tax expenditures," in recognition of the fact that they have been placed into the Code for reasons extrinsic to the revenue-raising function of taxes.[16] Some of these government subsidies are placed into the Code because the criteria on which the subsidies are based depend on information already collected by the tax system (such as income, working status, and family size). The EITC is an important example. Others are there because legislators and citizens alike often see "tax cuts" as qualitatively superior to "new spending programs," even when they have the same economic effect. By one common definition, in 2014 tax expenditures (that is, government spending programs baked into the Internal Revenue Code) exceeded in amount all the revenue raised by the personal income tax.

Our point here is not to criticize tax expenditures or to enter the unending debate over how they should be defined. Rather, we intend only to observe that their existence enormously complicates the study of the federal income tax, even in a survey course like this. An economist describing an "ideal" income tax might reasonably claim that in his imagined system personal consumption expenses cannot be "deducted" (i.e., subtracted) in calculating taxable income (the base on which tax is imposed), but in the real world millions of citizens know otherwise, because the Internal Revenue Code allows them, for example, to deduct certain expenses incurred in owning their own homes.

The Internal Revenue Code actually imposes many taxes, but this book addresses only the personal income tax — the largest single tax in terms of revenues and the one with which all of you either are or soon will become familiar in your individual capacities. (You participate already in other federal tax systems as well, such as the federal gasoline excise (sales) tax, but the collection of these taxes is imposed on others.) In addition to numerous non-income-related taxes, such as the estate tax or the fishing tackle excise tax, individual

---

16. For a more complete discussion of this fraught issue, including a summary of much of the academic debate on the point, see Staff of the Joint Committee on Taxation, *A Reconsideration of Tax Expenditure Analysis,* JCX-37-08, May 12, 2008, https://www.jct.gov/publications.html?func=startdown&id=1196.

Social Security and other "contribution" schemes operate in a manner similar to the personal income tax, in that your liability goes up with your income, at least to a point. These "payroll taxes," as they often are called, are described in a little more detail below.

2.   How Hard Can It Be?

Since this casebook is devoted to the personal income tax, it might be useful to offer an example of the complexity—and also the fun—of working through tax problems. Consider the definition of the word "income." Although the statutory framework is developed in much more detail throughout this book, start for now with the simple idea that a taxpayer initially earns "gross income"—for example, her salary from her full-time job, plus the profit from selling 100 shares of stock that she owned.[17] (The technical term "gross income" is what many people have in mind when they use the term "income" in ordinary speech.) The taxpayer "deducts" (subtracts) various specified expenses, costs, and statutory allowances from her gross income to determine her "taxable income," which is the point from which her tax liability can be calculated.

One important issue which this simple summary has elided is what does it mean to be a "taxpayer"? Is each individual a separate taxpayer? Are married spouses to be treated as a single combined taxpayer? What about an extended family, with three generations living under one roof? Chapter 6 returns to this, but for the moment let's just concentrate on what we mean by "gross income."

If the Internal Revenue Code is the refined clockwork model that we have implied, you would expect that at its absolute core you would find a precise definition of the phrase "gross income." But read Code §61, which defines this irreducible starting point for all income tax calculations. In relevant part, it states that "gross income means all income from whatever source derived, including (but not limited to) the following items . . . ." There follows what seems to be a pretty complete list of fifteen items, including salaries, gains from dealings in property (the stock sale profit in our example above), alimony received, interest income, and dividends received, to name a few. But, on closer examination, we can see two interesting points. The first phrase—which by itself actually is the definition—is completely tautological (gross income means all income—how helpful is that?). Second, the laundry list of fifteen items is offered only by way of example of what is included within the tautologically defined phrase—that's what the statute means when it says that those fifteen items are included in "gross income" but that gross income is not limited to them.

Look at the laundry list of fifteen items. Can you think of an activity that arguably gives rise to a category of gross income *not* identified in the list? Admittedly, it's not easy to do so.

---

17. We return to the point throughout the book, but do not assume that cash coming in always equals gross income. A gift, we will learn, is not gross income. As another example, if you sell today 100 shares of stock for $4,000 ($40/share), and those shares cost you $25/share a few years ago, you have $4,000 in "gross *receipts*" [$40 × 100] but $1,500 in "gross *income*" (i.e., profit) from this one transaction [$4,000 gross receipts less $2,500 original cost].

Now consider a 21-year-old baseball fan from New York named Matt Murphy. The date is August 7, 2007, and Murphy (a Mets fan, as it happens) has arranged his travel to Australia to allow for a layover day in San Francisco so that he can take a seat in the bleachers of Giants Stadium. He's done so, of course, in the hopes of seeing, and perhaps even catching, the 756th career home run hit by Giants star Barry Bonds, which would make Bonds the all-time career home-run leader.

Murphy's dream came true: Bonds hit number 756, and Murphy caught the ball. More remarkably, he held onto it, despite suffering bruises from the other denizens of the bleachers trying to claw it out of his hands. The newspapers trumpeted his accomplishment, and the ball's value was estimated at up to $500,000. About a month later, in September, Murphy sold the ball at auction for about $750,000.

Did Matt Murphy recognize gross income on that fateful August day? He went to a ball game, and he caught a home-run ball. Under the rules of Major League Baseball and the stadium, fans may keep any ball hit into the stands. Murphy received no spendable cash from his catch, and in fact he left the stadium covered in bruises. Where's the income in that?

Should we nonetheless conclude that Murphy recognized gross income the moment he caught the ball? After all, it was plainly very valuable, and he left the ballpark richer than when he came into it. But home-run baseballs don't appear anywhere on that list in §61 of the fifteen examples of gross income, and it's difficult to see a home-run ball as closely analogous to any of them. The issue had never before come up in a court case, and indeed it has not to this date.

Nor is there much administrative guidance on the point. Read, however, Treas. Reg. §1.61-14, which in relevant part states that "Treasure trove, to the extent of its value in United States currency, constitutes gross income for the taxable year in which it is reduced to undisputed possession." Is a home-run baseball treasure trove? Do we look to admiralty law circa 1913 (the year the modern Internal Revenue Code was first enacted) to find out what "treasure trove" means? Should it be relevant that this baseball had no intrinsic value: that is, it did not constitute gems or jewels or gold doubloons, whose values in the marketplace depend only a little, if at all, on the circumstance surrounding their acquisition?

In circumstances like these, all lawyers like to fashion analogies from known outcomes to the novel facts before them. Tax lawyers know, for example, that §74(a) mandates that "gross income includes amounts received as prizes and awards." Thus, lottery payouts constitute gross income, as does the cash award given in connection with the Nobel Prize. In some ways, Matt Murphy might remind you of a lottery winner, given how fortuitous it was that the fateful home run came down within his reach. Does this analogy seem apt to you? Are you swayed by the fact that Matt Murphy did not win $500,000, or any other amount of currency, but rather a small sphere of no intrinsic value, but worth some speculative (but in all probability large) number of dollars by virtue of the circumstances under which it was obtained? In considering your response, bear in mind that if you appear on a television quiz show and win a new car, you will discover that the market value of that car does fall squarely within §74(a).

From another direction, §102 of the Code provides that "Gross income does not include the value of property acquired by gift." Can you construct an argument that the baseball that came to Matt Murphy was a gift? From Barry Bonds? From the gods? Is it relevant that Murphy had gone to the ballpark in the hope of catching this very ball? Conversely, does it matter that Murphy was simply a fan and not a professional baseball memorabilia scrounger and reseller? Would the result have been different had the ball dropped into the lap of a bored father keeping his young son company? In this regard, how should we think about §102? That it signals that value that falls into our lap without much effort on our part is not income? Or alternatively, should we construe "gifts" narrowly, to avoid conflict with prizes and awards? What should be the criteria for drawing the distinction? Does §102's appearance in the Code signal that gifts would be gross income but for Code §102 or, alternatively, that the drafters of the Code were looking to remove the slightest doubt around a point that would have appeared obvious to any reasonable person?

From still another direction, when a taxpayer purchases property at a bargain price, whether shares of stock, her own home, or a collectible baseball, she does not recognize any gross income at that moment. Suppose that because of your superior philatelical knowledge, you purchase at a garage sale for $10 a rare stamp with a readily ascertainable market value of $1,000. You are $990 wealthier at that moment. Yet even in an extreme case like this, the tax system treats you as simply buying a piece of property for $10; it waits until you "realize" your gain, typically through a sale, to take cognizance of your increased wealth. In tax lingo, your "unrealized" gain does not by itself constitute gross income, because you must have a realization event—a sale, for example—to crystallize that gain as gross income. In this regard, look at §61(a)(3), which includes in gross income "gains from dealings in property" but not increases in value of property. (See Section D.8 for a discussion of the central role of the "realization" doctrine in defining gross income from dealings in property.)

Murphy paid a few dollars for his seat in the bleachers, which gave him the opportunity to catch Bonds's home run ball. When Murphy caught the ball, why wasn't that just a purchase transaction, in which Murphy's purchase price for the ball equals the price he paid for his bleacher seat? In other words, why should Murphy be treated worse than a canny investor? He went to the ballpark investing a few dollars and some time, and did not crystallize his gain until he sold the ball at auction.

On the other hand, every fan in the bleachers who didn't catch the ball also paid for his seat: Actually catching the home-run ball was not part of the entertainment for which the admission price was paid. So perhaps the purchase analogy is a bit strained?

If catching a record-setting home-run ball indeed does constitute gross income at that moment, how would Murphy go about valuing the amount of his income? There were no direct comparables to look to, and the numbers bandied about in the newspapers were largely guesses. Does the fact that the home run ball was very difficult to value precisely on August 7, 2007, militate against declaring it to be income on that date?

What if Murphy had wanted to keep the ball as a treasured souvenir? A rule concluding that catching a record-setting home-run ball constituted immediate income of hundreds of thousands of dollars would have effectively compelled Murphy to sell the ball, regardless of his actual desires. Is this why he sold it only a month later?

And what's the rush in arguing that Murphy had income in August 2007? The "unrealized" (or "built-in") gain that Murphy enjoyed wasn't going anywhere: It was there waiting to be measured precisely, and reduced to cash, through the medium of the auction or another sales transaction. At that moment, both the precise amount of gain and the means of paying the resulting tax would have been resolved. But, on the other hand, Murphy could then have postponed any tax bill for years, or even decades. And would we then need to take into account the later steroid-related scandals that materially reduced the value of this very home-run ball?

If you are confused as to what the right answer here is, that is appropriate. You have not yet read the cases and other authorities that have tried to put some meat on the bones of these arguments. Moreover, tax academics have written articles debating the correct outcome in this very case. We hope, however, that you can see from this small example that the income tax is simultaneously a very complex statute and an exercise in applied metaphysics. It is intellectually far richer than its enormous, technical verbiage might imply, but it also is much more rigorous in its internal rules than are many purely normative inquiries.

D.   FUNDAMENTAL TAX TERMINOLOGY AND CONCEPTS

As is true for most law school courses, especially those that survey an entire field of law, the basic federal income tax class effectively requires you to learn a new language. Some of the terminology will already be familiar to you, but much of it may not be. This section briefly introduces some of the most important terminology. If you choose to read only one section of this chapter, make it this one.

1.   The Tax Base: From Gross Income to Tax Payable

The term *"tax base"* is not part of the specialized vocabulary of the Internal Revenue Code. It refers to a general concept used by lawyers and economists to describe the items to be taxed under whatever system of taxation is adopted: that is, it represents the determination of the amount to which the appropriate tax rate is applied.

The starting point for calculating the tax base of an individual under our income tax is the taxpayer's *gross income.* Gross income is defined by an elaborate set of rules found in the Internal Revenue Code, the case law, and other sources of tax law. The statutory centerpiece is §61. Take a look at it, if you haven't already. As described in the last section, it consists of a general, all-inclusive (and completely circular) description of what is to be included ("all income from whatever source derived"), plus a list of nonexclusive exemplars. For most individuals the major items covered will be wages, salaries, interest, dividends, and rents. Sections 71 to 85 list various items included in gross income but requiring special treatment. These sections also, however, identify certain receipts, such as child-support payments,[18] that are excluded from gross income. Sections 101 to 127 exclude from gross income a number of receipts such as gifts,[19] interest on state and local bonds[20] and damages received on account of personal physical injury or physical sickness.[21]

The result of these various statutory and other exclusions is that a substantial difference exists between any generally accepted economic concept of gross income and the tax concept. Chapter 2 returns to this. At this point, however, it is important to emphasize that the term "gross income" is primarily a creature of statute, not of natural law or economics. As we stress throughout this book, Congress has tremendous leeway to define accessions to wealth as gross income, or not, as it sees fit. Gifts are just one of many examples: Their exclusion from the definition of gross income cannot be intuited by simple introspection, or, as we will see, by reference to any economic norm.

As a recent example, consider the Olympics. During the course of 2016, Congress was deadlocked on almost every issue of importance to the country. Yet one new tax law did emerge, carried from bill to law in a few months on a tide of bipartisan enthusiasm. The new statute was the "United States Appreciation for Olympians and Paralympians Act of 2016," signed into law by President Obama in October 2016. The substance of the law is captured by its title: it amended §74 to provide that cash awards made by the United States Olympic Committee to Olympic and Paralympic medalists, as well as the value of the medals themselves, are excludible from gross income, commencing in 2016.

If you are a diehard sports fan, you might think this new law to be eminently fair, but ask yourself, how are the cash payments made to Olympic athletes different from cash payments made to factory workers for their services? Both are plainly the result of personal efforts, knowingly applied to a goal whose financial and more intangible returns are clearly spelled out. And more poignantly, imagine how you will feel when you win a Nobel Prize, only to discover that the cash received in respect of your extraordinary contribution in your field is fully taxable to you?

Just by way of preview, courts and the IRS also play a role in the definition of "gross income." We will discuss at length in Chapter 3 the mischief caused by the Supreme Court's decision many decades ago in Eisner v. Macomber, to the effect that "unrealized" gain (an accession to wealth not yet crystallized through a sale or other disposition of the property) could not be taxed as a constitutional matter, because it fell outside the definition of "income." And Congress has been content to allow the IRS to create a "general welfare" exception to the definition of gross income, under which payments made under many government income assistance programs are excluded from the definition of gross income for tax purposes. See Notice 99-3, 1999-1 C.B. 271.

Gross income is not identical to *gross receipts*, for two important reasons. First is all the statutory exceptions and exclusions just mentioned. Second, when a business holds inventories of goods to sell to customers, its "gross income" in

---

18. §71(b).
19. §102.
20. §103.
21. §104(a)(2).

respect of those sales basically means its gross profit from those sales. So, for example, if you operate a hardware store in which you sell to customers for $20 hammers that cost you $12, your gross receipts from the sale of two hammers would be $40, but your gross income would be $16.

Gross income does not include any deductions (subtractions) for the costs of earning income or to satisfy any other social objective. This is the role of *taxable income*,[22] another statutory term that is narrower than one would expect if one started with the notion that economic income is the appropriate base. Under the income tax, the tax base is taxable income. Your income tax bill is the sum of the tax rates applicable to your taxable income.

Taxable income has some rough, intuitive overlap with the accounting concept of net pretax income, but it cannot be emphasized too strongly that relying on intuition is very dangerous in working with the federal income tax, particularly at the beginning of your study. In every case you should read the statute first and foremost, and you should do so with a literal mindedness that you would not bring to other forms of reading.

Corporations are subject to income tax just as individuals are (but under a different rate structure). The face of the corporate income tax return (Form 1120) actually is much simpler than that of the Form 1040 filed by millions of individuals. The reason is simply that corporations are presumed to exist solely to advance their business objectives, and so the taxable income of a corporation comprises simply its gross income minus the expenses of earning that income (its various business deductions and losses).

Individuals, however, have a personal sphere to their existence as well as a commercial sphere. Moreover, Congress has always made many refinements to the tax base to reflect social norms of "ability to pay" and the like (for example, the idea that a big family with an income of $50,000 should pay less tax than an unmarried individual with the same income). And so the drafters of the Internal Revenue Code invented a halfway house: *adjusted gross income*.[23] You can think of an individual's adjusted gross income for the moment as similar in some respects to "taxable income" in the corporate context (although adjusted gross income is not the tax base for individuals); it comprises gross income, minus the costs of earning that income, and also minus some miscellaneous expenses that Congress felt should be treated the same as if they were costs of earning income, even if that is not technically true.[24] (An example would be school supplies that teachers voluntarily buy because they care about their students.) To emphasize, though, adjusted gross income is a way station on the path to calculating an individual's tax base: that is, her taxable income.

Expenses that are not strictly necessary to earn gross income but that nonetheless reduce the tax base (e.g., home mortgage interest deductions), as well as arbitrary adjustments to the tax base (the standard deduction, discussed

---

22. §63.

23. §63.

24. If you look carefully at the Form 1040 and its related schedules you will see that business expenses appear there for individuals, just as they do for corporations, but they are difficult to find on the face of the return, because most individuals are wage earners, not independent entrepreneurs. Take a look at line 12 of the form, plus Schedule C.

below) are subtracted from an individual's adjusted gross income (invariably abbreviated to *AGI*) to get to her *taxable income*. Very generally, the Code treats expenses that are allowable (i.e., that may be deducted) in getting from gross income to AGI more favorably than expenses allowable in going from AGI to taxable income: This is why the AGI concept is needed.[25]

Practitioners refer to deductions that are allowable in getting from gross income to AGI as *above the line* expenses. (The "line" is AGI.) Expenses that reduce AGI to get to taxable income, which as noted generally are subject to stricter limits, are called *below the line* expenses. Both terms are terms of convenience, not technical ones employed by the Code. Again, as a way of orienting yourself, think of "above the line" expenses as those that relate directly to earning gross income, plus some specially favored deductions, and "below the line" expenses as items that are closer in nature to personal consumption expenses.[26]

Moving from AGI to *taxable income* involves deducting the greater of (i) the *standard deduction* or (ii) *personal itemized deductions*. By virtue of the 2017 tax law, the standard deduction for 2018 tax returns is $24,000 for a married couple and $12,000 for a single person.[27] This represents a large increase over prior years. At the same time, however, the 2017 law eliminated "personal exemptions" (basically a deduction for the taxpayer, her spouse if filing a joint return, and dependent children), and limited some personal itemized deductions. Like many features of the 2017 act's amendments affecting individuals, these new rules "sunset" after 2025.

25. More completely, the concept of AGI has three functions. First, AGI is used to separate those deductions that can be claimed by all taxpayers, regardless whether they claim the standard deduction, from those that cannot. Essentially, one must choose between the standard deduction and certain other deductions (mostly personal) but not between the standard deduction and those deductions allowable in arriving at AGI. Second, AGI is for some tax policy purposes considered a better measure of income than is taxable income. Thus, it is used in shaping the rule for deduction of medical expenses, where the amount deductible is the excess of such expenses over 10 percent of AGI. §213(a). Similarly, AGI is used in calculating the maximum amount that can be deducted for contributions to charity. §170(b). Third, people using tax statistics in analysis of tax and economic policy issues find AGI to be more useful for many purposes than taxable income, since AGI corresponds more closely to economic income.

26. The outlier here is any expense incurred by a wage earner in respect of her job that is not reimbursed by her employer. Logically one might expect these to be above the line deductions. For many years prior to the 2017 tax law, however, Code treated them as below the line deductions—and what is worse, as "miscellaneous itemized deductions," which were deductible only to the extent that the sum of such deductions exceeded 2 percent of a taxpayer's AGI. This disfavoring of unreimbursed employee trade or business expenses was motivated in part by a need to find revenues to pay for a specific legislation, but also perhaps by a general skepticism that, if certain expenses really were necessary for the performance of a job, the employer would require the employee to pay them. The 2017 act suspended the deductibility of unreimbursed employee expenses, and indeed of *all* miscellaneous itemized deductions, for the period 2018-2025. The general theory of the 2017 act here was that the increased standard deduction should obviate the need for miscellaneous itemized deductions and personal exemptions, but some taxpayers will be disadvantaged by the trade.

27. §63. As in all tax matters, other exceptions and special categories occur, including an extra standard deduction available to taxpayers over the age of 65. The standard deduction for taxpayers who may be claimed as a dependent on another individual's tax return is subject to its own special limitations. §63(c)(5).

A taxpayer cannot claim both a standard deduction and personal itemized deductions; you choose each year one or the other, depending on which is larger. The functions of the standard deduction include both relieving people with modest incomes of the nuisance of keeping track of outlays covered by the itemized deduction and ensuring that people with incomes below a certain level pay no tax.

Personal itemized deductions include home mortgage interest, non-business state and local taxes (since 2017, limited to $10,000/year), disaster-related casualty losses above 10 percent of AGI, medical expenses above 7.5 percent of AGI, charitable contributions, and certain other expenses (most notably, unreimbursed employee business expenses) to the extent they exceed 2 percent of AGI.

Every individual filing a Form 1040 can claim the standard deduction applicable to his or her filing status, so itemized deductions are valuable only to the extent they exceed the standard deduction. When the realtor tells you (as a single taxpayer) that your $12,700 in mortgage interest expense on your first home is fully deductible, remind the realtor that no, if this is your only itemized deduction, its value as a deduction to you is only $700 (the excess of the expense over the standard deduction of $12,000). And, in turn, any deduction ultimately saves you money only to the extent that it reduces your tax bill, which means that a deduction is valuable only to the extent of the tax rate that would have applied to your last dollars of income in the absence of the deduction. If your top tax rate in this example were 33 percent, the incremental $700 deduction would save you about $231.

Applying the rate schedule to taxable income is almost the end of the process, but not quite. The final step is to offset the tax with any *credits* that may be available and to determine whether a minimum tax must be paid. A credit is a direct offset to the tax. It is to be contrasted with a deduction, which reduces taxable income and thereby reduces the tax payable by the amount of the deduction multiplied by the relevant rate of tax. For example, there is a credit for "expenses for household and dependent care services necessary for gainful employment," sometimes referred to (somewhat inaccurately) as the child-care credit.[28] Other credits are found at §§21 to 41. The most important, and most obviously appropriate, is the credit for the amount of your income tax that your employer has withheld from your wages.[29]

Finally, there is an *alternative minimum tax* for individuals, the details of which are set forth in §§55 et seq.[30] For 2018, the tax is imposed on a special base at a rate of 26 percent of the first $95,750 of income in the AMT base and 28 percent on higher amounts. The special base is AGI plus various "preferences" and exclusions, reduced, for individuals, by certain non-§62 deductions and by a special AMT exemption ($109,400 for joint returns in 2018, subject to its own exotic phaseouts). This tax is in lieu of, and is payable only if it is greater than, the tax computed under the normal rules. Prior to the 2017 act, the AMT had been the bane of many affluent households; the 2017 amendments have greatly reduced the scope of its application.

---

28. §21.
29. §31.
30. For further discussion of §55, see Chapter 10, *infra*.

2.   Deduction, Exemption, Exclusion, and Credit

The previous subsection touched on various deductions and credits. It is worth going through some of the terminology more slowly to help ensure that you approach the substantive tax rules correctly.

A *deduction* is just a number that gets subtracted from your gross income or AGI in getting to taxable income. In terms of money in (or out of) your pocket, a deduction reduces your tax bill by the amount of tax the deduction saves you, which in turn means your *marginal* tax rate multiplied by the amount of the deduction—because the deduction offsets your topmost layer of income. For example, if you are in the 39.6 percent tax bracket (the highest), a $100 deduction saves you $39.60 in cash that you otherwise would send to the government. If you don't owe any taxes before taking a deduction into account, then you're generally out of luck, at least for the year in question: The government does not send you a check for having negative income.[31]

By contrast, a tax *credit* is like a voucher or gift certificate: You can use it instead of cash to pay your taxes. A $100 tax credit is worth $100 to you—so long as you have a tax liability against which to apply your credit. Think of it like a gift certificate at a store: It will be useful only as long as the store stays in business.

The earned income tax credit (EITC) for the working poor has the unusual property of being "refundable"; that is, the government mails you a check if your EITC is greater than your income tax bill. (This is unusual, in that most credits can only be applied to reduce a tax liability, and, as previously noted, deductions are not generally refundable if they exceed income.)

The EITC is the federal government's principal low-income assistance program, with a cost of over $40 billion each year. The EITC creates a great deal of progressivity in the very low end of the income spectrum. For example, a family of four with earned income of $51,492 in 2018 would pay no income tax; rather, the family would get a check from the government for almost $5,716. While payroll taxes are not directly refundable, this hypothetical family would receive an EITC refund check that exceeded the sum of the employee and employer halves of the family's Social Security contributions for the year.

The Code also offers *exemptions* and *exclusions*. The term "*exemption*" is used in two senses. It often is used colloquially to refer to taxpayers or types of income (in an economic sense) that are not subject to tax: a tax-exempt charity, for example, or tax-exempt municipal bonds. An *exclusion* is some identifiable category of economic income that is not taken into account for tax purposes. It is essentially a synonym for the first sense of exemption. So, we might say, colloquially, "this item is tax exempt," or alternatively that the item is excluded from income. Gifts are an easy example: Take a look at §102.

Excluding/exempting an item from income has the same economic effect as including it in gross income but then giving an equal deduction. Assuming no other limits are triggered, excluding $50 of economic income from your gross

---

31. Of course, every general statement in tax turns out to have an exception. If a business that you operate incurs a loss for a year, that business loss can be "carried back" to offset taxable income from earlier years; the result would be a refund for the taxes paid in those earlier years.

(and therefore taxable) income leads to the same tax liability as including the $50 in your gross income but then providing an offsetting $50 deduction.

The effect of the standard deduction is to create the economic equivalent of a zero-rate bottom tax bracket: a bottom layer of economic income that is subject to a 0 percent tax rate, even though this is not explicitly stated in §1 of the Code (which sets out the tax rates applicable to individuals). For example, a married couple filing jointly for the 2018 taxable year would get a $24,000 standard deduction. This means that the family needs to have $24,001 in economic income before the family has $1 in taxable income.

The Code could have been drafted to phrase amounts equal to these two arbitrary deductions as income exclusions, but instead it employs the terminology of deductions, mostly for reasons of history. In fact, many years ago Congress briefly replaced the standard deduction with a "zero bracket amount," but that produced a great deal of taxpayer confusion, so engrained was the idea that taxpayers are entitled to a standard deduction.

3. Tax Brackets, Progressive Tax Structures, and Effective and Marginal Tax Rates

As briefly mentioned in Section B, a *progressive* income tax is one with average tax rates that rise as income rises. Under a progressive rate structure, the tax on a person with a high income is not just a greater *amount* than the tax on a person with a lower income; it is a greater *proportion* of income. A *regressive* income tax is one where average tax rates decline with income. The personal income tax has a progressive rate structure, and Social Security payroll taxes have a regressive structure.[32]

The table below shows the distribution of tax burdens in three different income tax systems: one with proportional rates (System A), one with progressive rates (System B), and one with regressive rates (System C). Note that in each system the *amount* of tax owed increases with income.

TABLE 1-2

Taxpayer	Income	Type of Tax and Total Tax Owed (Average Tax Rate)		
		System A: *Proportional*	*System B:* *Progressive*	*System C:* *Regressive*
Akira	$20,000	$2,000 (10%)	$2,000 (10%)	$5,000 (25%)
Benito	$50,000	$5,000 (10%)	$10,000 (20%)	$10,000 (20%)
Cora	$100,000	$10,000 (10%)	$30,000 (30%)	$15,000 (15%)

32. More accurately, one should measure the progressivity of Social Security by looking not just at the tax rate structure (which is regressive) but rather at the combination of the tax rate and benefits ultimately received. When the two are considered together, the totality of the Social Security system operates in a progressive fashion, because benefits do not scale up in strict proportion to "contributions" (taxes) paid into the system. This is another example of how focusing on the tax side alone can produce a distorted picture of citizens' actual relationship with government.

The personal income tax implements its progressive tax-rate structure in two basic ways. First, the standard deduction and the earned income tax credit all operate to push down the average tax rate imposed on lower-income individuals, and even to lead to negative tax rates (refunds). Second, once a taxpayer has positive taxable income, that income is sliced horizontally into layers of income that sit on top of one another, like a layer cake. Each layer is termed a *tax bracket*, and each bracket has its own tax rate associated with it; in our personal income tax, income in each higher tax bracket incurs a higher tax rate. This by itself makes the income tax progressive, because the more income you have in the higher tax brackets, the greater your average (blended) tax rate on all your income.

The key thought is that earning additional income does not change the tax burden on the lower brackets (lower layers of the cake)—it simply determines the tax rate to be imposed on that incremental income. As an arbitrary example, if the tax rate schedule imposes tax at a 20-percent rate on the first $50,000 of taxable income and 40 percent on amounts above that, a taxpayer with exactly $50,000 in taxable income pays $10,000 in tax. If she earns $10 more, the bottom layer of $50,000 is unaffected, but that last $10 in income is taxed at 40 percent (i.e., $4.00 in tax), for a total bill of $10,004.

The personal income tax's use of tax-rate brackets with increasing rates in each higher bracket illustrates the importance of distinguishing between *marginal* and *average* tax rates. A marginal tax rate is the rate applied to your last (top) dollar of income; an average tax rate is your tax bill divided by your income. Under the stylized example offered in the last paragraph, a taxpayer with $60,000 in taxable income would pay $14,000 in tax, for an average tax rate of about 23 percent. (Note that this rate corresponds to neither tax rate bracket, because the average represents a blending of the different rates applied to different quanta of income.) Her marginal tax rate, however, is 40 percent, because that is the tax rate she would pay on her next dollar of income.

If this taxpayer then had the opportunity to claim a new $1,000 deduction, she would save $400, not $230, in tax, because the deduction would reduce her highest-taxed income. So, marginal rates are relevant not only to the cost of earning incremental income, but also to the value of incremental deductions.

To complicate matters further, economists and other policy analysts often distinguish between *statutory* and *effective* tax rates. *Statutory* rates are the tax rates actually specified in §1 of the Internal Revenue Code, as applied to the different tax brackets also specified there. Depending on context, we can describe either an average or a marginal statutory tax rate.

Economists use the word "effective" to signal more complete measures of income or taxes than those evident through the application of the rates listed in §1 to the Code's definition of taxable income. For example, you can calculate an average tax rate in two ways. You can divide your actual tax bill by your *taxable income*, as determined by the Code or other tax statute (as we did in the above stylized tax rate example), or you can divide your actual tax bill by your true *economic income*, as determined by a gaggle of economists. Scholarships and gifts are economic income, but they are not included in taxable income. So your taxable income and economic income will be different, and your average tax rate, accordingly, will be different depending on which measure of income you use. The former might technically be called your statutory average tax rate and the latter your effective average tax rate. In practice, however, most analysts simply use "effective tax rate" to refer to an average rate where the denominator is a broader definition of income than the statutory measure of "taxable income."

The same point is true of marginal tax rates: An *effective marginal tax rate* is one that reflects economic considerations not evident on the face of the Code.[33] For example, the earned income tax credit and other income support mechanisms are phased out as a taxpayer's income increases. So, too, are the benefits of certain itemized deductions (via PEP). A policy analyst looking at the marginal costs faced by a taxpayer in the phase-out range of income will take into account not only the marginal statutory tax bracket into which the next dollar of the taxpayer's income falls, but also the forgone tax credit or other benefit that results from the phase-out rule in question. The result on some bands of income can be very high effective marginal tax rates—much higher than the statutory marginal tax rate—until income rises above the phase-out range. This can lead to surprising claims of marginal tax burdens imposed on lower income taxpayers, but it should be remembered that these effective marginal rates may apply to only a narrow band of income, depending on the interaction of all the relevant rules.

The Code itself never defines or uses the terms "average," "marginal," or "effective" tax rates. The concepts simply are not relevant to the mechanical calculation of your tax bill. They are, however, very important for those struggling to understand the practical economic effects of tax structures.

The marginal tax rate in particular is relevant for purposes of tax planning and for understanding incentive effects. For example, suppose a couple with an income of $50,000 and a marginal rate of 15 percent contemplates a gift of $1,000 to charity. As you will learn (or perhaps already knew), taxpayers are generally permitted to deduct such gifts in calculating the amount of their income subject to taxation. By making the gift they would reduce their taxable income by $1,000 and save $150 in taxes.[34] In other words, the net cost to the couple of making the gift would not be $1,000 but rather $850. By contrast, for a couple with a taxable income of $150,000 and a marginal rate of 30 percent, the net cost of a $1,000 gift is $700. As these examples illustrate, the bottom line value of a deduction depends on the marginal tax rate at which the taxpayer's income would have been taxed.

In addition, it is the taxpayer's marginal rate that is relevant for purposes of evaluating the incentive effects of the income tax. For example, it is commonly argued that the income tax discourages work by taxing people on their labor income. Consider a taxpayer, Neela, who currently earns $80,000 and is subject to a marginal tax rate of 25 percent. Should Neela work Saturday

33. Analysts use "effective marginal tax rate" and "marginal effective tax rate" interchangeably. The authors believe that the former is more appropriate.

34. The example, of course, assumes that the taxpayers would be able fully to deduct the $1,000 because they already had other personal itemized deductions equal to or larger than the standard deduction. If, by contrast, this were the couple's only potential personal itemized deduction, the net cost of the gift would be $1,000: The gift effectively would give rise to no marginal tax savings at all.

FIGURE 1-7.
Effective Income Tax Rate on U.S. Taxpayers with Incomes Over
$1 Million, 1996-2013

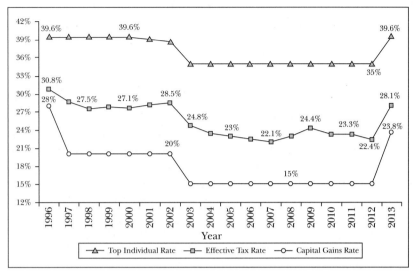

Source: Martin Sullivan, *U.S. Income Tax Still Isn't Progressive at the High End*, Tax Notes, Aug. 18, 2016, pp. 903-905. Copyright 2016 Tax Analysts. Reprinted with permission.

afternoons to earn an additional salary of $10,000 per year? In making her decision, Neela will of course want to think about how she would otherwise spend her Saturday afternoons and what value that activity has to her. But she shouldn't compare her subjective value of that experience to $10,000 but rather to her after-tax wage, which would be $7,500, after accounting for the income taxes she will owe on the additional earnings.

By way of demonstrating the care that must be taken when discussing effective tax rates, this figure compares the *statutory* effective tax rates paid by taxpayers with incomes over $1 million in the period 1996-2013 to the top statutory marginal rates and capital gains rates in effect in each year. If the denominator were instead a broader economic measure of income, including "unrealized" appreciation in value of capital assets, effective tax rates could be expected to be lower.

4.   Tax Incidence

Tax policy analysts typically use the term "incidence" to describe the ultimate economic burden of a tax. The person bearing the ultimate economic burden of a tax may not be the same person that remitted the tax to the government. To be clear, you do not need to be an expert on tax incidence to practice tax law, even at a high level, but it is a vitally important concept in policy discussions of who pays tax in America and how taxes affect our behaviors.

For example, if a tax is imposed on a refrigerator manufacturer and the manufacturer is able to raise prices and pass the tax on to consumers, the tax is said to have been shifted, and the incidence is on consumers rather than on manufacturers. A more commonplace example is the federal gasoline excise tax, which is tacked onto the price you pay at the pump. The party required actually to remit the tax is far "upstream" in the gasoline distribution process, but because it is passed through to you, you bear the economic incidence of the tax.

To determine the incidence of a tax, or the burden or effect of particular provisions of a tax system, one must compare the world with the tax or provision and the world without it. This is a difficult task, even for the best economists.

It is generally assumed that the burden of the individual income tax, so far as it falls on income from wages, salaries, and other earnings from services, is, not shifted from the individuals on whom it is imposed. There is much less consensus as to the incidence of the tax on corporate income and on individual income from investments. In the end, individuals, not abstract legal entities, bear all taxes. So which individuals ultimately bear the burden of the corporate income tax? Stockholders? Owners of all investment capital? Employees? Customers? There is no unanimity on this. The nonpartisan Congressional Budget Office and the Staff of the Joint Committee on Taxation assume for purposes of their analyses that over the long term owners of all investment capital shoulder about three-quarters of the corporate tax burden and employees the remainder, but other economists come to different conclusions.

5.   Capital Gain and Dividend Income; Ordinary Income; Losses and Expenses

During almost the entire history of our income tax, capital gain has been taxed at a lower rate than most other income. Currently, most forms of capital gain of noncorporate taxpayers, as well as most dividends received from corporations, are subject to a maximum rate of 20 percent, about half the maximum rate on other forms of income, although the effective rate may be higher in certain income ranges because of the 3.8 percent net investment income tax introduced by the 2013 "fiscal cliff" tax package, as well as the alternative minimum tax (AMT).

Observers sometimes refer to "the capital gains tax" and contrast that with "the income tax," but this is a misnomer. There is one federal income tax.[35] Some types of income (certain types of capital gain or dividend income, for example) are taxed at different rates from other types, but the proper formulation is to think of this as income taxed at capital gain rates, not as a capital gain tax. The distinction is important, because many of the general rules of the Code are relevant to calculating tax liability with respect to "net capital gain" (the term of art that opens the gateway to lower tax rates), and because the two categories are not watertight compartments: An operating

---

35. Persnickety readers might object that there actually are two, the other being the alternative minimum tax.

loss incurred in a trade or business conducted in one's personal capacity can reduce net capital gain otherwise eligible for the preferential 20 percent rate.

A taxpayer who earns $100,000 in wages and who sells for $50,000 Apple stock purchased for $20,000 as an investment many years ago has gross income of $130,000 (the wage income plus the gross profit, not the gross receipts, from the sale of the stock). She also can be said to have $100,000 of *ordinary income* and $30,000 of capital gains. *Ordinary income* is defined, obliquely, by §64, but basically it means all gross income that does not qualify for the preferential rates afforded certain capital gains and dividends.

The definition of capital gain (or loss) depends on a large and complex body of law, reflecting both uncertainties in the underlying concept and provisions enacted to combat taxpayer efforts to transform ordinary income into capital gain. Capital losses can be used only to offset capital gain, except that individuals may use up to $3,000 of capital losses to offset ordinary income. This means that it is important in some instances to be able to distinguish between *capital* gain and loss and *ordinary* gain and loss.

Briefly, capital gain or loss is gain or loss from the "sale or exchange of a capital asset."[36] The term "capital asset" is statutorily defined as "property," with a number of exceptions, most notably for "inventory" or "property held by the taxpayer primarily for sale to customers in the ordinary course of his trade or business."[37] For example, a person who invests in a corporation, like Apple or GE, by buying common stock or bonds issued by the corporation, has acquired a capital asset. So too has an individual who buys a home, although special tax rules apply to both gains and losses from the sale of a personal residence.

Gain on the sale of a capital asset held for one year or less is *short-term* capital gain. Gain from the sale of a capital asset held for more than a year is *long-term* capital gain. After a netting process, only "net capital gain" (i.e., the excess of net long-term capital gain over net short-term capital loss) is subject to the preferential rate. Chapter 8 explores both the complex definitional issues in the capital gains area and the conceptual issues raised by the lower rate for long-term capital gains and by the capital loss limitation.

It is a mistake to use the phrase "capital gain" to mean gain eligible for preferential tax rates. Any gain from the sale of a capital asset constitutes capital gain. Technically only "net capital gain" qualifies for preferential tax rates, although in practice many simplify that to "long-term gain" or the like.

If a taxpayer sells an asset (whether a capital asset or not) for less than her cost, the shortfall is a *loss*. The principal rule for the deductibility of losses is found in §165; capital losses are further addressed in §1211. The day-to-day costs of running a business are usually referred to as *expenses*; thus, §162 permits the deduction of ordinary and necessary business expenses. Depending on the circumstances, losses and expenses may both give rise to tax deductions, but the point is that losses and expenses follow different analytical pathways. It will save you much confusion if you consistently distinguish between the two.

---

36. §1222.
37. §1221.

Recent joint work by the nonpartisan Congressional Budget Office and the nonpartisan Staff of the Joint Committee on Taxation estimates that in 2010 U.S. families directly held about $50 trillion in gross value in capital assets, including housing stock.[38] (Retirement accounts and cash balances at banks add another $20 trillion to that total; note, however, that the figures do not reflect mortgage debt or other debt encumbering such assets.) Seventy percent of families own at least some capital assets; in most cases, this comprises a personal residence. Unsurprisingly, gains from the sale of financial assets (corporate stocks and bonds, for example) are very top-weighted. Only 15 percent of families in 2010 held any corporate stock as a capital asset (that is, outside retirement accounts). Taxpayers with incomes in that year of $1 million or more earned about half of the total gross capital gains (gains unreduced by losses) from the sale of corporate stock.

As Section A of this chapter suggested, capital gains are not evenly distributed across the income spectrum. This is not surprising, given that capital gains are a property of owning capital, which by definition means that the rich will have more of them than the poor, but the extent to which capital gains are so highly concentrated, and their effect on overall tax rates, is still surprising.

FIGURE 1-8.
Capital Gains and Qualified Dividends as a Percentage of AGI by Income Category, 2013

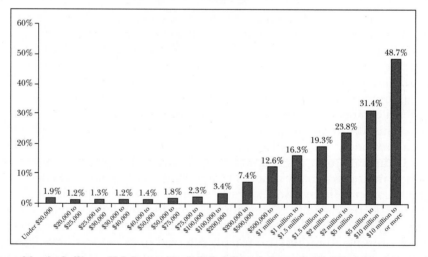

Source: Martin Sullivan, *U.S. Income Tax Still Isn't Progressive at the High End*, Tax Notes, Aug. 18, 2016, pp. 903-905. Copyright 2016 Tax Analysts. Reprinted with permission.

38. *The Distribution of Asset Holdings and Capital Gains,* Aug. 2016, available at https://www.cbo.gov/publication/51831.

Working with IRS data for the 2013 tax year, economist Martin Sullivan developed the following chart showing the percentage of different income groups' AGI that comprised capital gains and dividend income. One particularly useful aspect of this work is that it provides a picture of what is happening at the very top of the income distribution. Much official data on income and tax distributions still lumps all taxpayers with incomes over $200,000, or the top 20 percent, into one bucket for purposes of income distribution analysis, but this obfuscates a great deal of what actually goes on at the top end.[39]

In Figure 1-9, Sullivan again relies on IRS data. This data source is extremely accurate, but only in respect of those items that are relevant to calculating taxable income on a tax return. This means that Sullivan's construction of effective tax rates looks only to income reported on tax returns and therefore includes only the effect of *recognized* capital gains. A broader construction of the income denominator in the effective tax-rate calculation that included economic income from investments on a "mark-to-market" basis (i.e., showing unrealized appreciation in the value of capital assets) — were the data available — could be expected to show a materially lower tax rate than those in Sullivan's figures.

FIGURE 1-9.
Effective Income Tax Rates by Income Category, 2013

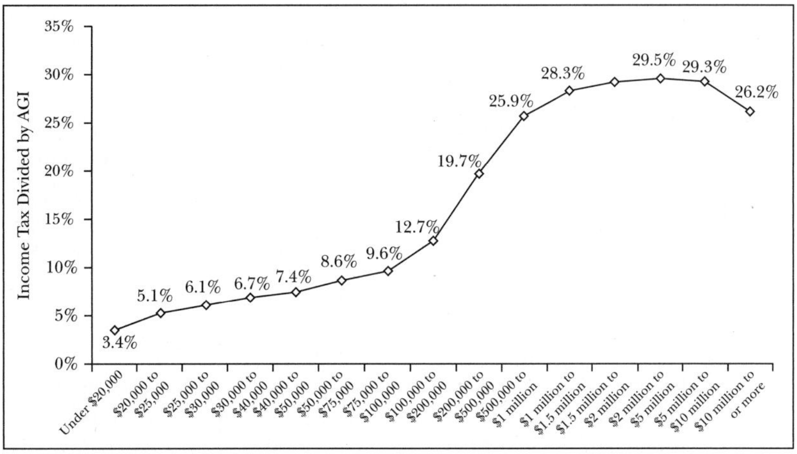

Source: Martin Sullivan, *U.S. Income Tax Still Isn't Progressive at the High End,* Tax Notes, Aug. 18, 2016, pp. 903-905. Copyright 2016 Tax Analysts. Reprinted with permission.

---

39. It might not seem that the choice of income groupings in a distributional analysis would have a political dimension, but it does. Coarser gradations tend to understate the effect of the preferential tax rate on the incomes of those who recognize a preponderance of those gains.

6.   Tax Accounting

The rules of accounting for income-tax purposes mainly follow the basic approaches of financial accounting, although with some important differences. The two basic methods of tax accounting are the *cash method* and the *accrual method*. Under the cash method, speaking very generally, amounts are treated as income when received in cash (or cash equivalent) and are deductible when paid. Under the accrual method, subject to some important exceptions, items are included in gross income when earned, regardless of whether payment has been received, and items of expense are deductible when the obligation to pay is incurred, regardless of when payment is made. Tax liabilities are computed on an annual, as opposed to a transactional, basis.

For example, suppose that an accountant, A, performs services in connection with the law practice of a lawyer, L. The services are performed on December 5, 2015; three days later L receives a bill for $500; L does not dispute his obligation to pay the full amount but does not pay until January 10, 2016. If A and L both use the cash method, L is entitled to a deduction (if otherwise allowable) in 2016, and A should report the item as income in the same year, since 2016 is the year of payment by L and of receipt by A. If both A and L used the accrual method, L would be entitled to the deduction in 2015, when the obligation was incurred, and A would include the $500 in income in 2015, when it was earned.[40] Most individuals use the cash method (because it is simple), and most businesses use the accrual method (because it more accurately reflects economic realities). Section 448 requires certain taxpayers to employ the accrual method.

Capital expenditure. An important limitation on the cash method is that the costs of capital investments may not be deducted when the cash outlay is made, but only as the asset is used or when it is sold, exchanged, or abandoned. For example, suppose a farmer who uses the cash method buys forty acres of farm land, to be used in his farming business, for $400,000. The $400,000 is called a capital expenditure and may not be deducted at the time of the purchase. Generally speaking, capital expenditures are amounts spent for assets that have a useful life of more than a year. In the case of land, a record is kept of the cost, and gain or loss is computed and reported for tax purposes only on disposition of the land. Suppose the farmer buys a tractor for $50,000. Again, the $50,000 outlay is a capital expenditure and cannot be treated as a current expense. Subsection 7 describes how tax investment is recovered over time.

---

40. Under rules added to the Code in 1984, the deduction for L in 2015 would be allowed under the accrual method, but the result would depend not only on principles of accrual accounting but also on the fact that the obligation meets the requirements of §461(h)(4) (the "all events" test) and §461(h)(2)(a)(i) (the "economic performance" test).

7.   Recovery of Cost, Depreciation, and Basis

Suppose *T* is a retail seller of widgets. In a particular year, *T* buys 1,000 widgets for $10 each and sells them all for $15 each. Assuming no other expenses, *T* has a profit of $5,000, which is arrived at simply by deducting her cost of $10,000 from her receipts of $15,000. Since the federal income tax is a tax on the net income of $5,000, not on the gross receipts of $15,000, *T* must be allowed to recover her cost of $10,000 in arriving at her taxable income.

Now suppose *T* decides to manufacture widgets and buys widget-making machinery at a cost of $100,000. How does *T* take account of the cost incurred in buying the machinery? Even if she uses the "cash method" of accounting, *T* will not be allowed an immediate deduction, given that the machinery continues to have economic value. Instead, *T* must recover her investment gradually over time by taking what are commonly called depreciation deductions under the Code's *cost recovery* rules.[41] Under these rules, the cost of the machine generally is spread out over a number of years (less than the expected life) according to formulas provided in the Code. The effect of the formulas is to bunch cost recovery deductions in the early years of the use of the machine relative to its economic depreciation (wear and tear).[42] This treatment is accelerated in comparison with normal methods of financial accounting, under which the amount of the allowance is designed to correspond better to the actual decline in the value of the asset and costs are spread out over a period roughly equivalent to the expected useful life of the asset.

The depreciation expense for certain expenditures is further accelerated under the Code's bonus depreciation rules. Qualifying capital expenses can be depreciated on an accelerated basis, thereby maximizing the present value of the tax deduction that would otherwise be spread out over the usable life of the asset. In 2017, bonus depreciation allowed qualifying expenses to be depreciated up to 40 percent in the first year. From 2018 until the end of 2022, first-year bonus depreciation will be 100 percent for qualifying purchases of property placed into service that year—that is, a business will now "expense" the cost of the widget-making machinery in the above example in the year the machinery is acquired.

The Code uses the term "*basis*" to mean the taxpayer's cost for an asset. Depreciation deductions on depreciable investments reduce a taxpayer's basis, and additional cash invested in improving the property increases basis. The technical term for a taxpayer's basis after taking into account all such adjustments is *adjusted basis*, although it must be admitted that this term (but not the underlying concept) is more honored in the breach than the observance.

8.   Realization and Recognition

Realization and *recognition* are important terms of art in tax law, particularly with respect to sales of property. A gain or loss is said to be *realized* when there has been some change in circumstances such that the gain or loss would ordinarily

41. §168.
42. See Chapter 7 *infra.*

be taken into account for tax purposes. The classic realization event is a sale or exchange of the underlying property. A realized gain or loss is said to be *recognized* when no applicable provision calls for nonrecognition, that is, temporary or permanent (and either partial or complete) disregard of the fact that a realization event occurred. Thus, where realization occurs, there may or may not be recognition, but where recognition occurs, there must have been realization.

For example, suppose a taxpayer buys undeveloped land for $1 million, and the land's value increases to $5 million. The economic gain from this appreciation is not realized. Now suppose that the taxpayer exchanges this land for an apartment building also worth $5 million. The taxpayer has realized a gain of $4 million. However, the transaction will probably qualify as an exchange of like-kind property, the subject of a statutory "nonrecognition" rule, so the $4 million gain will not be recognized until the apartment building is sold.[43]

9.   Types of Entities

A *sole proprietor* is a person who owns a business solely and directly, with no partners or other co-owners and no use of a corporation or other such legal device. All items of business income and expense are treated for tax purposes as belonging directly to the sole proprietor. There are separate schedules attached to the Form 1040 on which these items may be netted out, but the use of these forms does not negate the direct relationship between the sole proprietor and each and every one of the transactions occurring in his or her business.

A *partnership* is a combination of two or more people (or entities) who have agreed to carry on a business for profit as co-owners. The partnership is to some extent reified for tax purposes: "It" files a tax return. (That is, some person files a tax return covering the joint activities of the partners.) On the partnership tax return, income and expenses are netted out, but the partnership pays no tax. (That is, the partners' jointly held funds are not used to pay a tax.) Instead, the partners report on their individual tax returns their pro rata share of whatever net profit or loss was calculated by the partnership. This treatment of partners and partnerships is sometimes called *pass-through* taxation. (Outside the United States, such arrangements often are described as fiscal transparencies.)

The *limited liability company* (*LLC*) is a form of business organization with many similarities outside the tax arena to a corporation, including in particular limited liability for all investors therein. For purposes of this introductory casebook, however, you can treat an LLC as a type of partnership, so that LLC members enjoy pass-through tax treatment in respect of the LLC's income.

A *trust* is a legal device by which one person, the trustee, holds and invests property for the benefit of another person, the beneficiary. The rules for taxation of trusts are too complex for development here. It is enough for now to say that the general effect is to achieve a pass-through or conduit result, but since there may be a delay between the time income is earned and the time a beneficiary becomes entitled to it, and since the identity of the beneficiary may be

---

43. See §1031.

undetermined, the trust may be required to pay a tax; this is generally treated like a withholding tax paid by an employer on the wages of an employee, but it is sometimes the final tax on the income.

Corporations, although merely legal devices for organizing economic activity, are treated as separate taxpaying entities. They pay a flat rate of 21 percent on their income. Payments of income by a corporation to its shareholders are called dividends;[44] these constitute taxable income to shareholders (although at present they generally are taxed at the same preferential rates applicable to net capital gain). Thus, distributed income is to a degree doubly taxed, once at the corporate level and again at the individual level, while income that is retained is subject only to the corporate tax. When a corporation retains income, if the amount is wisely invested, the value of the corporation and of its common shares should rise (all other things being equal). Thus, retained income should result in an increase in shareholder wealth in the form of increased share values. Such gain is not realized by the shareholders; it is not taxed until the shares are sold. Shareholders, unlike partners, cannot take into account their pro rata share of corporate losses. Losses can only be used by the corporation to offset income in other years.

The Code distinguishes between "C" corporations taxed in the manner just described, and "S" corporations. An S corporation is a hybrid, generally taxed as a pass through entirely (so that shareholders pay tax on their share of the S corporation's income), but subject to various constraints not applicable to partnerships.[45] The partnership structure is far more flexible, but S corporations remain a very popular form of business entity.

10. Inflation

Inflation makes it difficult to levy the right amount of tax on investment income. To illustrate, suppose a taxpayer purchases property for $100 on January 1. The inflation rate during the year is 5 percent, and the property is sold on the following January 1 for $105. The property transaction does not leave the taxpayer any wealthier: The $105 sales proceeds purchase the same basket of goods that cost $100 a year earlier. A tax imposed only on real increases in economic well-being would not measure gain or loss by the difference in investment cost (or basis) and sales proceeds; instead, such a tax would increase basis, or investment cost, by the inflation rate. In this hypothetical example, that would require an increase in the $100 cost by 5 percent, to give an inflation-adjusted cost of $105. If that were done, no gain would be recognized on the sale of the property for $105. (The same result could be reached by leaving the investment cost at $100 but reducing the sales proceeds by the inflation rate, to $100.) This adjustment would also be required in other areas. For example, suppose the taxpayer had loaned out her $100 and received that sum back, plus $5 interest. The transaction would leave the taxpayer no wealthier (and the counterparty

44. *See* §316.
45. S corporations are so named because their rules are found in Subchapter S of Chapter 1 of the Code (§§1361 to 1379).

who pays the interest no poorer). The taxpayer receives $5 characterized as interest but made no real economic (or inflation-adjusted) profit on the loan transaction. Increasing the taxpayer's investment in the loan by the inflation rate, to $105, yields the correct result. Now the entire $105 can be treated as tax-free recovery of investment. Unfortunately, the tax system does not allow this cost or basis adjustment and, as a result, systemically overtaxes investment income in this regard, unless there is no inflation.

Inflation also poses a problem for determining the proper rate at which to tax income. To illustrate, suppose that our tax law initially provides that the marginal rate for taxable income of $25,000 is 15 percent, and that the marginal rate for an income of $50,000 is 30 percent. Now suppose that ten years pass and inflation reduces the value of money by half. A person currently earning $50,000 is in the same real economic position as a person earning $25,000 ten years earlier. If no automatic adjustment expands the rate brackets to take account of the economic reality, even without any increase in real (that is, inflation-adjusted) income, people will pay higher percentages of their real income as taxes, and government revenues will increase (in real terms) even though Congress did not explicitly change the tax brackets. In 1981, Congress added §1(f) and §151(f) requiring increases in the standard deduction and in the rate schedule dollar-amount brackets (the layers of the layer cake) to reflect increases in the Consumer Price Index. In 2018, the government amended the inflation adjustment from a traditional Consumer Price Index (CPI) measure to a chained-CPI calculation, which adjusts for substitution bias in consumer purchasing activity and is understood to more slowly recognize price increases, thereby slightly increasing the real amount of taxes paid over the traditional CPI measure.

E.   CONVERSION AND DEFERRAL

As a wise man once observed, it generally is better to be rich and healthy than poor and sick. This casebook does not address the secrets of good health, but it does look at the principal ways by which individual taxpayers can reduce their tax liabilities, and thereby increase their wealth. These opportunities revolve around two themes: *conversion* and *deferral.*

"Conversion" is another term often used by tax lawyers and analysts that is not employed by the Code itself. It refers to arrangements by which activity that would be expected to give rise to ordinary income instead generates long-term capital gains taxed at more favorable rates. The tax shelters of the 1970s and 1980s often relied on real or imagined conversion strategies. To take a simple example with more continuing relevance, imagine that you work very hard for your own start-up firm, and as a result of your great intelligence and the long hours you invest, the firm is a success. The start-up required very little capital to get going. Two years after starting the business, you sell the firm for an enormous sum of money. Your gain generally will be long-term capital gain, even though from an economic perspective your newfound wealth is attributable to a return on your labor, which when expressed as wage income is taxed at ordinary income rates.

"Deferral" refers to the fact that, so long as interest rates are positive, taxpayers generally find it advantageous to defer their tax liability to future years. The intuitive advantage of deferral is straightforward, although measuring the benefit is a bit more complex: A tax liability deferred from the present to the future gives the taxpayer the use in the interim of the amount that would otherwise have been paid in taxes.

Here is the crucial takeaway on deferral: *If* investment opportunities and returns are the same inside the deferral vehicle as they are outside, tax rates remain constant over time, and interest rates are positive, then deferral of tax liability will always benefit taxpayers. What is sometimes forgotten is that deferring a 20 percent tax today in order to pay a 40 percent tax tomorrow is not necessarily a smart idea: In every case, the tax advisor and the taxpayer need to think through all the moving pieces.

Deferral and realization work together, because an increase in an asset's value is not taken into account for tax purposes until that gain is realized and recognized, as by a sale of an asset. This means that if you buy an asset and hold onto it for twenty years, any tax on its increase in value automatically is deferred until you sell the asset.

Moreover, the tax benefits of deferral in this common circumstance can be turbocharged in several ways. First, under §1014, all income tax is forgiven with respect to unrealized (or built-in) gain attributable to assets held at the time of death. (See Chapter 3.) What is more, heirs get a "step-up" (another common nontechnical term) in their tax basis in the inherited property to fair market value, so the forgone income tax is never collected. This is an extraordinary reward for taking the long view of things: The tax rate goes to zero if you can resist the urge to sell during your lifetime and instead leave the selling to your heirs.

Second, as Chapter 4 explores, a taxpayer can use appreciated property as collateral for a loan that the taxpayer takes out, thereby extracting cash for current consumption, and those loan proceeds are not taxable income, even if the loan is nonrecourse to the taxpayer's other assets and the loan principal exceeds the taxpayer's tax basis in the asset. This means that the patient taxpayer who out of the kindness of her heart is playing the long game, so that neither she nor her estate will be burdened by income tax on the appreciation in value of her investments by virtue of §1014, nonetheless can live it up during her lifetime. One professor has summed up this fundamental strategy as "buy, borrow, die."[46]

But deferral opportunities are not limited to gain from asset sales. Consider the following example:

---

46. J. McCaffery, *A New Understanding of Tax*, 103 Mich. L Rev. 807, 891-894 (2004).

T is a high-income taxpayer subject to a marginal rate of 40 percent. Assume that he earns $100,000 this year and is permitted to put $10,000 of those earnings into a retirement fund and to deduct that contribution from his gross income. The result is that he will have only $90,000 of income this year. The same result would be reached if we were to say that, for whatever reason, $10,000 of his earnings were tax-exempt.

The rule is that once put into the retirement fund, earnings on the $10,000 from the present to whenever it is drawn out on retirement are not taxed. In other words, *T* has received the $10,000 income, in cash; he has the cash to use and has chosen to set it aside to fund his retirement, but taxation is deferred until retirement on both the $10,000 and the earnings on it. Suppose *T* invests the $10,000 for ten years at 10 percent, compounded annually, and then retires. By that time, the $10,000 will have increased to $25,937. If *T* then pays a tax at the rate of 40 percent, he will have $15,562 left to spend.

In contrast, suppose that the law is different and makes no special provision for deferral. In this situation, *T* must pay taxes on any money he earns and wants to set aside for retirement as well as on his earnings on the amount set aside. In other words, assume normal current taxation rather than deferral. In the first year, the $10,000 of earnings would be reduced by taxes to $6,000. In turn, that $6,000, if invested to produce interest at the same rate of 10 percent per year as posited in the first part of the hypothetical, would earn, after tax, only 6 percent. At the end of ten years, at 6 percent, the $6,000 would have increased to $10,745. This amount would be tax-paid and fully spendable, but it is still only 69 percent of the tax-paid, fully spendable amount ($15,562) available with deferral. As the number of years of deferral increases, the gap between the two amounts becomes even more dramatic. If the number of years to retirement is twenty rather than ten, the relative after-tax amounts are $40,365 with deferral and $19,243 without.

The process of calculating the present value of a future amount is called *discounting to present value*, and the present value is sometimes redundantly called the discounted present value.[47]

---

47. The algebraic formulas for the relationships between present and future value are simple. For computing future value,

$$FV = PV(1 + r)^n,$$

where *FV* is future value (or future amount), *PV* is present value (or amount), *r* is the interest rate, and *n* is the number of years. Thus, in the first example in which $10,000 is invested at 15 percent for ten years,

$$FV = \$10,000(1.15)^{10} = \$40,456.$$

To determine present value, we do a minor transposition, and the formula is

$$PV = FV/(1 + r)^n$$

Thus, using the same numbers,

$$PV = \$40,456/(1.15)^{10} = \$10,000.$$

TABLE 1-3
Present Value of $1: What a Dollar at End of Specified Future Year Is Worth Today

Year	3%	4%	5%	6%	7%	8%	10%	12%	15%	20%	Year
1	.971	.962	.952	.943	.935	.926	.909	.893	.870	.833	1
2	.943	.925	.907	.890	.873	.857	.826	.797	.756	.694	2
3	.915	.889	.864	.840	.816	.794	.751	.712	.658	.579	3
4	.889	.855	.823	.792	.763	.735	.683	.636	.572	.482	4
5	.863	.822	.784	.747	.713	.681	.620	.567	.497	.402	5
6	.837	.790	.746	.705	.666	.630	.564	.507	.432	.335	6
7	.813	.760	.711	.665	.623	.583	.513	.452	.376	.279	7
8	.789	.731	.677	.627	.582	.540	.467	.404	.327	.233	8
9	.766	.703	.645	.592	.544	.500	.424	.361	.284	.194	9
10	.744	.676	.614	.558	.508	.463	.386	.322	.247	.162	10
11	.722	.650	.585	.527	.475	.429	.350	.287	.215	.135	11
12	.701	.625	.557	.497	.444	.397	.319	.257	.187	.112	12
13	.681	.601	.530	.469	.415	.368	.290	.229	.163	.0935	13
14	.661	.577	.505	.442	.388	.340	.263	.205	.141	.0779	14
15	.642	.555	.481	.417	.362	.315	.239	.183	.123	.0649	15
16	.623	.534	.458	.394	.339	.292	.218	.163	.107	.0541	16
17	.605	.513	.436	.371	.317	.270	.198	.146	.093	.0451	17
18	.587	.494	.416	.350	.296	.250	.180	.130	.0808	.0376	18
19	.570	.475	.396	.331	.277	.232	.164	.116	.0703	.0313	19
20	.554	.456	.377	.312	.258	.215	.149	.104	.0611	.0261	20
25	.478	.375	.295	.233	.184	.146	.0923	.0588	.0304	.0105	25
30	.412	.308	.231	.174	.131	.0994	.0573	.0334	.0151	.00421	30
40	.307	.208	.142	.0972	.067	.0460	.0221	.0107	.00373	.000680	40
50	.228	.141	.087	.0543	.034	.0213	.00852	.00346	.000922	.000109	50

Table 1-3 gives relationships between present and future amounts. Present values can be derived by multiplying the future amount by the appropriate number. Thus, for the present value of $1 ten years hence, at 10 percent, the multiplier is 0.386. The present value of $10,000 ten years hence, at 10 percent, is 0.386 ($10,000) or $3,860. The present value of $25,907 ten years hence, at 10 percent, is 0.386 ($25,907) or about $10,000. (These figures are slightly inaccurate because of rounding off in the table.)

As the materials in this book unfold, it will become clear just how important it is to understand the relationships between present and future value. Deferral is a major element in tax planning and tax analysis.

F.   COMPLIANCE AND ADMINISTRATION

1.   Self-Assessment, Audits, and Tax Litigation

Our income tax relies on initial self-assessment, which means that once each year each individual or entity subject to the tax makes a calculation of the amount of tax owed. The calculation is based on information supplied by the taxpayer on forms, sometimes called tax returns, devised and provided by the Internal Revenue Service. The Internal Revenue Service, often called the Service or the IRS, is the branch of the Treasury Department, headed by a person called the Commissioner of Internal Revenue, responsible for the administration of the tax laws. The Service makes available some limited amount of assistance in preparing returns, but no government approval or other involvement is required before a return is filed. Before the taxpayer files the annual return, some amount approximating the tax owed will probably have been paid to the government either through withholding from wages by an employer[48] or by special quarterly returns for estimated taxes for people whose income is from sources not subject to withholding (like income from self-employment) or for whom the amount withheld is less than the amount of tax that will be payable.[49] When the annual return is filed, the taxpayer takes a credit against the tax computed on that return for any taxes paid by withholding or as estimated tax and will be entitled to a refund of any overpayment or will be required to pay the amount of any shortfall.

A person who fails to file an income tax return may be subject to both civil and criminal penalties.[50] No statutory limit applies on the time within which civil penalties must be sought,[51] and a six-year limitation applies on criminal prosecution.[52] The risk of being caught for failure to file is high, in large part because employers and other payors of income are required to file "information" returns[53] that report wages, dividends, interest, and various other kinds of payments and benefits.

The IRS reviews all income tax returns for computational error and selects a relatively small number of them for a more complete review, called an audit. Some returns are selected for audit at random, but most are selected on the basis of some evidence, either in the return itself or from some other source (e.g., information returns), indicating a greater-than-average probability of error. The Service ordinarily has three years to assert a "deficiency"[54]—that is, to assert that the taxpayer owes more tax by virtue of an error in the return. The amount owed is called an "underpayment," and the taxpayer must pay

---

48. §3402.

49. §§6015, 6153.

50. The basic provisions are §6651(a) (civil) and §7201 (criminal).

51. §6501(c)(3).

52. §6531.

53. §§6031-6058.

54. §6501(a). The period is extended to six years if the taxpayer omits from gross income more than "25 percent of the amount of the gross income stated in the return." §6501(e). See also §6229(c)(2) (similar rule for partnerships).

interest on all underpayments.[55] The interest rate is set quarterly and is equal to the rate on U.S. Treasury short-term obligations plus 3 percent.[56]

If a taxpayer's return is audited and the taxpayer and the employee who initially reviews the return for the IRS cannot agree on one or more items, the return can be reviewed at higher levels within the IRS. Most disputes are ultimately settled within the IRS, often after considerable bargaining and with compromise on both sides. If the taxpayer and the IRS cannot reach agreement, the IRS will order the taxpayer to pay the deficiency, plus interest and any applicable penalties, and the taxpayer must either do so or go to court.

Three different options are available to the taxpayer for judicial review. One option is to decline to pay the tax and to file a petition for review with the Tax Court (formerly the Board of Tax Appeals). The Tax Court is available only if the tax has not been paid as of the date of the petition. (The tax can be paid thereafter to stop the running of interest.) Tax Court judges typically have tax backgrounds and try only tax cases. Tax Court has no jury trials. Tax Court judgments are reviewable by the federal circuit courts of appeals in the circuit where the taxpayer resides and ultimately by the Supreme Court (but only on certiorari). If the taxpayer loses, the tax must be paid with interest to the date of payment, so an important factor in deciding whether to follow the Tax Court route is the current interest rate charged by the government on deficiencies, as compared with what the taxpayer must pay or can earn elsewhere.

The second option is to pay the tax and sue for a refund in the federal *district court* where the taxpayer resides. The judge in the district court is not likely to be a tax expert and a jury trial is available. Appeal is, as usual, to the circuit courts of appeals, with the possibility of review by the Supreme Court on certiorari.

The final option is to pay the tax and sue for a refund in the United States Court of Federal Claims. Its decisions are reviewable by the United States Court of Appeals for the Federal Circuit and by the Supreme Court (on certiorari). If an issue is first litigated by a taxpayer who obtains a favorable legal ruling in the Claims Court, and that ruling is upheld on appeal, all other taxpayers may then take their cases to that court and foreclose the possibility of a conflict among the circuits. By contrast, if a taxpayer wins a favorable ruling in a court of appeals in a circuit other than the Federal Circuit, the government may have the opportunity to litigate that issue with other taxpayers in other circuits.

2.   Penalties for Noncompliance

In a tax system based on self-assessment, it is necessary to provide incentives for taxpayers to comply with the law. In the U.S. income tax, these incentives take the form of penalties for noncompliance. Taxpayers must pay a penalty equal to 20 percent of the amount of any underpayment due to negligence.[57] Even in the absence of negligence, a penalty equal to 20 percent of the amount

---

55. §601.
56. §6621.
57. §6662(a), (c).

of any underpayment is levied on taxpayers who substantially understate their income tax.[58] A substantial understatement is one that exceeds the greater of 10 percent of the proper tax or $5,000 ($10,000 for corporations).[59] Significantly, the amount of the understatement is reduced by amounts attributable to treatment for which there was "substantial authority" or amounts "with respect to which the relevant facts affecting the item's tax treatment are adequately disclosed . . . and [for which] there is a reasonable basis."[60] The penalty "may" be waived by the Service if the taxpayer demonstrates "reasonable cause" and "good faith."[61] An underpayment that fits within more than one category (for example, an understatement that is substantial and negligent) is subject to only one 20 percent penalty. A penalty of 5 percent per month, not to exceed 25 percent, is also imposed for failure to file a return, and a penalty of 0.5 percent per month, not to exceed 25 percent, is imposed for failure to pay a tax shown on a return when it is due or for failure to pay, within ten days, a tax assessed and demanded by the IRS.[62] Notwithstanding the seemingly inclusive array of penalty provisions, in the ordinary case of underpayment, all the taxpayer stands to lose, in addition to the amount of the tax owed, is interest on that amount.

An error may be attributable to what is loosely referred to as "fraud." An underpayment attributable to fraud subjects the taxpayer to a civil penalty of 75 percent of the amount of the fraudulent underpayment.[63] While fraud seems to be a familiar concept and one that could sensibly be applied to a large number of taxpayer returns, in fact the courts have developed a narrow definition, and even the civil penalty is imposed only in the most egregious cases. Criminal fraud, or, to be more precise, any "willful attempt to evade or defeat any tax imposed by this title or the payment thereof," is a felony carrying a penalty of not more than $100,000 ($500,000 for corporations) or five years in prison, or both.[64] For criminal prosecution the statute of limitations is six years.[65]

G.   THE SOURCES OF FEDERAL TAX LAW IN A NUTSHELL

Taxes are imposed only by statute. Although the lawyer who fails to look beyond the statute will often err, the statute should almost always be the starting point.

At the same time, some parts of federal tax law, especially where statutory pronouncements were absent, vague, or confused, have been influenced by

---

58. §6662(a), (d).

59. §6662(d).

60. §6662(d)(2)(B).

61. §6664(c).

62. §6651(a). The penalty percentages for failure to file are increased to 15 percent and 75 percent if the failure is "fraudulent." §6651(f).

63. §6663.

64. §7201.

65. §6531.

judicial doctrines of a common-law character, created by the courts as case after case came before them. In these areas, the lawyer must be attuned to the judiciary's signals even more than to those of Congress. Moreover, the detail of the statute is often deceptive, since the courts may exercise their traditional power to disregard form for substance and to hold that an arrangement that complies with the literal terms of the statute is not within its spirit, just as a deed absolute on its face may be shown to be a mortgage. One of the fascinations of federal tax law is the interplay between the detail of a statute and the creative spirit of the courts; even the tax attorney who cannot pause to enjoy this interplay must understand it.

Although the congressional debates ordinarily do not illuminate technical problems of federal taxation, there are occasional exceptions, and then recourse to the Congressional Record is necessary. The committee reports, on the other hand, are frequently helpful, and it is common for the courts to rely heavily on them. The importance of the committee reports increases with the complexity of the statute, since difficult drafting problems frequently are "taken care of" in the committee report.[66] They are prepared by the staff of the relevant committees, working with the nonpartisan staff of the Joint Committee on Taxation.

The Joint Committee on Taxation, one of four joint committees in Congress, comprises senior members of the two tax-writing committees, the House Ways and Means Committee and the Senate Finance Committee. The Joint Committee only rarely engages in any kind of official substantive work (because the authority for that belongs to the two tax-writing committees), but it does house its staff, who operate as a kind of legislative civil service of tax experts, composed of lawyers, economists, and accountants. In addition to its work helping to draft statutes and legislative history, the Staff of the Joint Committee is the official "scorekeeper" for tax proposals. That is, the Staff determines the official estimates of the impact of tax law changes on projected tax revenues for the ten-year period following the change in law. These estimates have an enormous influence on the shape of tax legislation, given the resource constraints under which any government must operate.

The Staff of the Joint Committee on Taxation also prepare very helpful summaries of tax legislation after the fact. These summaries are colloquially known as "blue books." They are drawn largely from earlier Committee and Conference reports, but occasionally include observations as to problems that might require "technical corrections" legislation, or last-minute instructions to the Treasury on how the new statute is to be interpreted.

Second only to the statute and the legislative materials in importance are the Treasury regulations. Code §7805 authorizes the Secretary of the Treasury or his delegate to prescribe "all needful rules and regulations for the enforcement" of the Code. In addition, the secretary is expressly instructed to issue regulations to cover more specific areas, e.g., under §3 to prescribe tax tables for individuals and under §472 to set rules governing use of the last-in-first-out

---

66. Occasionally, the Committee Report is used to direct the Treasury to modify, institute, or abandon a regulation or other administrative practice. Often these directions, the result of understandings between Treasury staff and the committees, are followed by the Internal Revenue Service. Some view this as abuse of the process, others as an efficient way of doing business.

method of accounting for inventories. In the 2011 *Mayo* case,[67] the Supreme
Court held that Treasury regulations should receive what is commonly called
"*Chevron* deference," from the leading administrative law case,[68] holding that
when congressional intent is unclear regarding a particular issue raised by a
statute, the administrative agency responsible for interpreting the statute has
broad discretion to adopt whichever interpretation it prefers, subject only to the
requirement that its interpretation be reasonable. However, while this may offer
Treasury regulations significant protection from judicial challenge, Congress
has in recent years frequently intervened in the Treasury's regulation function.
Regulations or rulings dealing with fringe benefits, travel and entertainment,
deduction of expenses for commuting to work, treatment of deferred compensation, and imputed interest on related party transactions have been blocked
either by formal legislation or by agreement with congressional committees.[69]

Treasury regulations bear the key numeral "1" if related to the income tax
provisions of the Code, and "20" or "25" if related to the estate or the gift
tax provisions, respectively. Thus, "Reg. §1.170-1" denotes a regulation having
to do with §170 (income tax consequences of charitable contributions); and
"Reg. §20.2041-1" is concerned with §2041 (estate tax treatment of powers of
appointment). Other series exist for more specialized subjects. Changes in the
regulations are issued as Treasury Decisions. The Administrative Procedure
Act requires proposed regulations (with certain exceptions) to be published
in the Federal Register to permit interested parties to file their objections or
suggestions for consideration before adoption.[70] The proposed regulations are
prepared by the Service in consultation with the Treasury staff.

In addition to the regulations, which are issued by authority of the Secretary
of the Treasury, a steady supply of rulings, instructions, releases, and other
lesser pronouncements flows from the Internal Revenue Service. Not bearing
the imprimatur of the secretary, these documents are less authoritative than
the regulations, but they are of great importance in the day-to-day administration of the tax laws, and often they are persuasive to the courts. The most
important are Revenue Rulings (Rev. Rul.) and Revenue Procedures (Rev.
Proc.). Revenue Rulings are opinions on matters of law arising in particular
fact settings. Often they are based on requests by taxpayers for advice about a
specific legal issue with which they are confronted. Revenue Procedures are
statements describing procedures affecting the rights or duties of taxpayers or
other information. Both Revenue Rulings and Revenue Procedures are published by the government and by unofficial commercial services that keep tax
specialists apprised of new developments.

Also of importance is advice given to taxpayers in "private letter rulings'"
(PLR). These rulings are issued (in letter form) to taxpayers in response to
requests for advice about their own specific fact situations. Some of these
ultimately are developed into Revenue Rulings, which set forth the official

---

67. *Mayo Foundation for Medical Education and Research v. United States*, 562 U.S. 44 (2011).

68. *Chevron, U.S.A., Inc. v. Natural Resources Defense Council, Inc.*, 467 U.S. 837 (1984).

69. *See* Parnell, *Congressional Interference in Agency Enforcement: The IRS Experience*, 89 Yale L.J. 1360
(1980).

70. 5 U.S.C. §553.

position of the IRS on which all taxpayers are entitled to rely. In the case of a PLR that has not become a Revenue Ruling, the government is not bound to follow the legal position that it adopts except as it is applied to the individual taxpayer to whom the advice is directed. PLRs are published by commercial publishers[71] and, while they lack precedential force,[72] practitioners find them useful as a guide to the IRS's likely view of the issues covered.

As we have seen, tax litigation may begin in the Tax Court, in the various federal district courts, or in the Claims Court. The opinions of the Tax Court fall into two categories: "regular" decisions, which are published by the court itself, and "memorandum" decisions, which are not officially reported but are published commercially by Research Institute of America and by Commerce Clearing House.

When the IRS loses a case in the Tax Court, it often announces, in the Internal Revenue Bulletin, whether it acquiesces (acq. or A) or does not acquiesce (nonacq. or NA) in the decision. Acquiescence operates as advice to the staff of the IRS on whether to rely on the decision in the disposition of other cases. Nonacquiescence indicates that the IRS, whether it appeals the decision or not, will not accept the principle enunciated in disposing of other cases (though of course the decision is binding as to the taxpayer in the case itself, unless reversed on appeal), and that the IRS may litigate the same issue when it arises again. Because decisions of the Tax Court are reviewed by thirteen courts of appeals, the government may eventually succeed in obtaining a reversal of the Tax Court, even though the decision in the nonacquiesced case was affirmed by a court of appeals; indeed, the principal way for the Treasury to get a conflict among the circuits (as a basis for a petition for certiorari) when the Tax Court decides in favor of the taxpayer is to stick to its guns and relitigate the same issue in one or more other cases. After announcing its nonacquiescence, the Treasury may be discouraged by a series of losses in the courts of appeals, or it may reconsider its views for other reasons and substitute an acquiescence for nonacquiescence.[73]

H.   WALZ TAX RETURN

Students often find it useful to look at an actual tax return while reading the material in this book. For this reason, the editors have always included the most recent publicly available tax return of the current president of the United States. President Trump has not released his tax returns. As an alternative, we include the first publicly released tax return of U.S. Representative Tim Walz. This tax return was chosen because it was the first that appeared in a keyword search of the subject.

---

71. Letter rulings first became public information in 1976, with the adoption of §6110.

72. §6110(j)(3). *See* Rev. Proc. 79-45, 1979-2 C.B. 508, §17.01.

73. The Tax Court will normally apply the rule of the court of appeals with jurisdiction over an appeal in the particular case before it even if it disagrees with the court of appeals. Golsen v. Commissioner, 54 T.C. 742 (1970).

Form 1040 Department of the Treasury—Internal Revenue Service (99) **U.S. Individual Income Tax Return** | **2017** | OMB No. 1545-0074 | IRS Use Only—Do not write or staple in this space.

For the year Jan. 1–Dec. 31, 2017, or other tax year beginning , 2017, ending 20 — See separate instructions.

Your first name and initial — TIMOTHY J	Last name — WALZ
If a joint return, spouse's first name and initial — GWEN L	Last name — WALZ

Your social security number

Spouse's social security number

Home address (number and street). If you have a P.O. box, see instructions.   Apt. no.

Make sure the SSN(s) above and on line 6c are correct.

City, town or post office, state, and ZIP code. If you have a foreign address, also complete spaces below (see instructions).
Mankato   MN   56001-2500

Foreign country name   Foreign province/state/county   Foreign postal code

Presidential Election Campaign Check here if you, or your spouse if filing jointly, want $3 to go to this fund. Checking a box below will not change your tax or refund. [X] You [X] Spouse

Filing Status Check only one box.
1. [ ] Single
2. [X] Married filing jointly (even if only one had income)
3. [ ] Married filing separately. Enter spouse's SSN above and full name here.
4. [ ] Head of household (with qualifying person). (See instructions.) If the qualifying person is a child but not your dependent, enter this child's name here.
5. [ ] Qualifying widow(er) (see instructions)

Exemptions
6a [X] Yourself. If someone can claim you as a dependent, do not check box 6a
b [X] Spouse
} Boxes checked on 6a and 6b **2**

c Dependents:

(1) First name Last name	(2) Dependent's social security number	(3) Dependent's relationship to you	(4) ✓ if child under age 17 qual. for child tax credit (see inst.)
▓▓▓▓▓▓▓▓	▓▓▓▓▓▓▓	Daughter	X
▓▓▓▓▓▓▓▓	▓▓▓▓▓▓▓	Son	X

No. of children on 6c who:
• lived with you **2**
• did not live with you due to divorce or separation (see instructions)
Dependents on 6c not entered above

If more than four dependents, see instructions and check here [ ]

d Total number of exemptions claimed

Add numbers on lines above **4**

Income

Attach Form(s) W-2 here. Also attach Forms W-2G and 1099-R if tax was withheld.

If you did not get a W-2, see instructions.

7	Wages, salaries, tips, etc. Attach Form(s) W-2	7	206,642
8a	Taxable interest. Attach Schedule B if required	8a	
b	Tax-exempt interest. Do not include on line 8a	8b	
9a	Ordinary dividends. Attach Schedule B if required	9a	
b	Qualified dividends	9b	
10	Taxable refunds, credits, or offsets of state and local income taxes	10	31
11	Alimony received	11	
12	Business income or (loss). Attach Schedule C or C-EZ	12	
13	Capital gain or (loss). Attach Schedule D if required. If not required, check here [ ]	13	
14	Other gains or (losses). Attach Form 4797	14	
15a	IRA distributions 15a	b Taxable amount	15b	
16a	Pensions and annuities 16a	b Taxable amount	16b	
17	Rental real estate, royalties, partnerships, S corporations, trusts, etc. Attach Schedule E	17	1,276
18	Farm income or (loss). Attach Schedule F	18	
19	Unemployment compensation	19	
20a	Social security benefits 20a	b Taxable amount	20b	
21	Other income. List type and amount 1099/Hogan Lovells US LLP	21	3,750
22	Combine the amounts in the far right column for lines 7 through 21. This is your **total income**	22	211,699

Adjusted Gross Income

23	Educator expenses	23	
24	Certain business expenses of reservists, performing artists, and fee-basis government officials. Attach Form 2106 or 2106-EZ	24	
25	Health savings account deduction. Attach Form 8889	25	
26	Moving expenses. Attach Form 3903	26	
27	Deductible part of self-employment tax. Attach Schedule SE	27	265
28	Self-employed SEP, SIMPLE, and qualified plans	28	
29	Self-employed health insurance deduction	29	
30	Penalty on early withdrawal of savings	30	
31a	Alimony paid b Recipient's SSN	31a	
32	IRA deduction	32	
33	Student loan interest deduction	33	
34	Tuition and fees. Attach Form 8917	34	
35	Domestic production activities deduction. Attach Form 8903	35	
36	Add lines 23 through 35	36	265
37	Subtract line 36 from line 22. This is your **adjusted gross income**	37	211,434

For Disclosure, Privacy Act, and Paperwork Reduction Act Notice, see separate instructions.
DAA   Form **1040** (2017)

Form 1040 (2017)   **TIMOTHY J & GWEN L WALZ**

Page 2

	38	Amount from line 37 (adjusted gross income)		38	211,434

Tax and Credits

39a	Check if: { You were born before January 2, 1953, ☐ Blind. } Total boxes checked ▸ 39a				
	Spouse was born before January 2, 1953, ☐ Blind.				
b	If your spouse itemizes on a separate return or you were a dual-status alien, check here ▸ 39b ☐				

Standard Deduction for—

- People who check any box on line 39a or 39b or who can be claimed as a dependent, see instructions.
- All others:

Single or Married filing separately, $6,350

Married filing jointly or Qualifying widow(er), $12,700

Head of household, $9,350

40	Itemized deductions (from Schedule A) or your standard deduction (see left margin)			40	29,857
41	Subtract line 40 from line 38			41	181,577
42	Exemptions. If line 38 is $156,900 or less, multiply $4,050 by the number on line 6d. Otherwise, see instructions			42	16,200
43	Taxable income. Subtract line 42 from line 41. If line 42 is more than line 41, enter -0-			43	165,377
44	Tax (see instr.). Check if any from: a ☐ Form(s) 8814 b ☐ Form 4972 c ☐			44	33,190
45	Alternative minimum tax (see instructions). Attach Form 6251			45	
46	Excess advance premium tax credit repayment. Attach Form 8962			46	
47	Add lines 44, 45, and 46		▸	47	33,190
48	Foreign tax credit. Attach Form 1116 if required	48			
49	Credit for child and dependent care expenses. Attach Form 2441	49			
50	Education credits from Form 8863, line 19	50			
51	Retirement savings contributions credit. Attach Form 8880	51			
52	Child tax credit. Attach Schedule 8812, if required	52			
53	Residential energy credits. Attach Form 5695	53			
54	Other credits from Form a ☐ 3800 b ☐ 8801 c ☐	54			
55	Add lines 48 through 54. These are your total credits			55	
56	Subtract line 55 from line 47. If line 55 is more than line 47, enter -0-		▸	56	33,190

Other Taxes

57	Self-employment tax. Attach Schedule SE			57	530
58	Unreported social security and Medicare tax from Form: a ☐ 4137 b ☐ 8919			58	
59	Additional tax on IRAs, other qualified retirement plans, etc. Attach Form 5329 if required			59	
60a	Household employment taxes from Schedule H			60a	
b	First-time homebuyer credit repayment. Attach Form 5405 if required			60b	
61	Health care: individual responsibility (see instructions) Full-year coverage ☒			61	
62	Taxes from: a ☐ Form 8959 b ☐ Form 8960 c ☐ Instructions; enter code(s)			62	
63	Add lines 56 through 62. This is your total tax		▸	63	33,720

Payments

If you have a qualifying child, attach Schedule EIC.

64	Federal income tax withheld from Forms W-2 and 1099	64	31,953		
65	2017 estimated tax payments and amount applied from 2016 return	65			
66a	Earned income credit (EIC)	66a			
b	Nontaxable combat pay election	66b			
67	Additional child tax credit. Attach Schedule 8812	67			
68	American opportunity credit from Form 8863, line 8	68			
69	Net premium tax credit. Attach Form 8962	69			
70	Amount paid with request for extension to file	70			
71	Excess social security and tier 1 RRTA tax withheld	71			
72	Credit for federal tax on fuels. Attach Form 4136	72			
73	Credits from Form: a ☐ 2439 b ☐ Reserved c ☐ 8885 d ☐	73			
74	Add lines 64, 65, 66a, and 67 through 73. These are your total payments		▸	74	31,953

Refund

Direct deposit? See instructions.

75	If line 74 is more than line 63, subtract line 63 from line 74. This is the amount you overpaid			75	
76a	Amount of line 75 you want refunded to you. If Form 8888 is attached, check here ▸ ☐			76a	
b	Routing number ▯	c	Type: ☐ Checking ☐ Savings		
d	Account number ▯				
77	Amount of line 75 you want applied to your 2018 estimated tax ▸	77			

Amount You Owe

78	Amount you owe. Subtract line 74 from line 63. For details on how to pay, see instructions		▸	78	1,767
79	Estimated tax penalty (see instructions)	79			

Third Party Designee

Do you want to allow another person to discuss this return with the IRS (see instructions)? ☒ Yes. Complete below. ☐ No

Designee's name ▸	Phone no. ▸
	Personal identification number (PIN) ▸ 12345

Sign Here

Joint return? See instructions. Keep a copy for your records.

Under penalties of perjury, I declare that I have examined this return and accompanying schedules and statements, and to the best of my knowledge and belief, they are true, correct, and accurately list all amounts and sources of income I received during the tax year. Declaration of preparer (other than taxpayer) is based on all information of which preparer has any knowledge.

Your signature	Date	Your occupation
Spouse's signature. If a joint return, both must sign.	Date	Spouse's occupation

Daytime phone number

If the IRS sent you an Identity Protection PIN, enter it here (see inst.)

Paid Preparer Use Only

Print/Type preparer's name	Preparer's signature	Date
		Check ☐ if self-employed PTIN
Firm's name ▸		Firm's EIN ▸
Firm's address ▸		Phone no.

Go to www.irs.gov/Form1040 for instructions and the latest information.

DAA

Form **1040** (2017)

2

THE WHY AND THE WHAT
OF TAXING INCOME

*"I'm sure you're a nice man, but I'm not interested in
hearing your plan for a flat tax."*

A.   WHY TAX *INCOME*?

1.   The Tax Base and Ability to Pay

There are many different paths by which the federal government can finance its operations—which is to say, to tax its citizens to fund the government spending and investment programs chosen through the legislative process. For its fiscal year ending September 30, 2017, the federal government raised about $3.3 trillion in tax revenues and spent $4.0 trillion. (The $700 billion excess of spending over tax revenues represents the deficit incurred in that year; the deficit is financed by government borrowing.) The magnitude of these amounts makes it obvious that whatever tax system we choose, in the end it must rely on a relatively broad tax base. Government cannot raise trillions of dollars per year only by taxing luxury yachts or private planes. But what should the tax base be? In particular, why has the United States chosen to rely on taxing *income* as the principal object of the tax base?[1]

Perhaps the simplest approach to taxation would be to levy a "head tax"—a tax of an equal dollar amount on everyone, or at least on each person above a certain age. In 2015, we could have funded the federal government by imposing a head tax on every American, regardless of age, of about $10,000. A simpler tax system is hard to imagine. It would eliminate the need for tax returns, tax lawyers, and all tax planning (apart from finding the money to pay the tax). Moreover, a head tax would be highly *efficient*, in the sense that it would not distort economic behavior, beyond requiring some minimum engagement with the market economy to raise the funds to pay the tax. After all, the same amount of tax would be owed regardless of hours worked, money spent, etc.

Despite the advantages of a head tax, most people would regard a tax system that charged everyone the same amount as unfair, even unthinkable. Unpacking the intuition behind that natural reaction goes a long way toward explaining the allure of income taxes. At bottom, most people believe that a highly compensated CEO should pay more tax than a schoolteacher, who in turn should pay more tax than someone who is unable to find work. The reason for this belief is usually that those with higher earnings are thought to be "better off" and therefore have a greater "ability to pay."

Tax scholars have long used the term "ability to pay" to describe the attribute that might justify requiring some people to pay more tax than others. But what does it mean? While the phrase might superficially imply convenience in paying, with relative tax burdens turning on the availability of cash or other liquid assets, a moment's reflection reveals the shortcomings of such an approach. Among other things, it would encourage people to lower their tax bills by accepting payment in illiquid assets, like artwork or real estate, arguably to no good purpose. As we will see, taxpayer liquidity has sometimes

---

1. The personal income tax and the corporate income tax have income as their tax base, as their names imply. So do payroll taxes, except that in the case of payroll taxes the income that forms the tax base is limited to labor income only. Capital income (income from investments, for example) is excluded from the payroll tax base.

influenced the development of our tax rules; however, most commentators view this as a concession to administrative practicalities rather than a determination regarding taxpayers' relative abilities.

The intention behind a progressive tax rate structure—the idea that the rich should pay more than the average rate of tax, and the poor less or none at all—might rest on a notion of *declining marginal utility of income.* That is, the wealthier you are, the less each dollar lost to the tax collector diminishes your well-being. But even if you accept this approach, further reflection might lead you to question whether your earnings are the right metric to use in applying it. As an example, compare Dora, who works fifty hours per week and brings home a $1,000 weekly paycheck, to Felix, who works ten hours per week for the same $1,000 paycheck and spends forty hours per week taking leisurely walks on the beach as the sun disappears into the ocean. Their tax returns will show identical annual wages of $52,000, but are Felix and Dora equally well-off? After all, Felix has just as much money as Dora plus considerably more free time, an important fact that the earnings measure ignores.

A broader view might encompass what economists sometimes call "endowment" or "wage rate" (the rate per hour at which one can earn money, as opposed to one's absolute earnings): the *opportunity* to earn wealth whether or not exercised (and indeed whether or not developed through education and experience). In the example above, one might note that Dora's wage rate is $20 per hour, while Felix's is $100 per hour. Should these differences be taken into account in allocating tax burdens? While few would claim that the tax system should cast quite so broad a net, the basic argument for taxing endowment is similar to that for moving beyond a simple liquidity-based view of ability to pay. Taxing only those who exercise their earning power may discourage such exercise (presumably not a deliberate goal of the tax system) and mistakenly classify people who earn and spend at a given level as "better off" than those who have the same opportunities but just happen to prefer to work and earn less.

2. Alternative Measures of Ability to Pay

Once one accepts that some variant of ability to pay ought to serve as the touchstone for allocating tax burdens, the question becomes how to implement it. Since the thing we might really want to tax (endowment) is not directly observable, we must rely on some proxy measure. There are numerous possibilities. Historically, the main contenders have been income, consumption, and wealth, although one could imagine a host of other alternatives, such as an amalgam based on looks, height, schooling, intelligence, and family connections. It is important to keep in mind that the argument for taxing any of these alternatives depends on its properties as indirect evidence or a signal of whatever attributes (for example, ability to pay) we really care about in distributing tax burdens.

Most countries, including the United States, rely on some combination of income, consumption, and wealth taxes. While this casebook addresses the federal income tax, the federal estate tax is an indirect tax on wealth, measured at the time of death, and the federal government also employs many

consumption taxes, such as the gasoline excise tax. State and local governments also employ multiple tax instruments, although they typically rely more
heavily on property (wealth) taxes and sales (consumption) taxes than does
the federal government.

Income, wealth, and consumption may sound like three very different tax
bases, but in fact they overlap a great deal. A more formal economic definition
of income helps to illustrate this important point. The Haig-Simons definition
of income, named in honor of two early proponents, provides as follows:

> Personal income may be defined as the algebraic sum of (1) the market value of
> rights exercised in consumption and (2) the change in the value of the store of
> property rights between the beginning and the end of the period in question.[2]

This can be phrased in simple algebraic terms:

$$Y = C + S$$

where Y is income, C is consumption, and S is saving. The underlying idea is
that people can do one of two things with their income, spend it or save it. And
the amount they end up having saved can be defined as equaling the amount
by which their net worth changes. Thus, one could equivalently define income
as follows:

$$Y = C + \Delta W$$

where ΔW denotes change in net worth. In the legal and economic literature,
this equation underlies the prevalent "Haig-Simons" definition of income as
the sum of the taxpayer's consumption plus change in net worth, each defined
in terms of market value during some specified accounting period (such as a
taxable year). See H. Simons, *Personal Income Taxation* 50 (1938).

Consider some simple examples. If you have $10,000 in wage income for
a year, spend $9,000 on beer and iTunes, and put $1,000 in the bank, your
income (ignoring anything else) for the year is $10,000: Your personal con-
sumption for the year is $9,000, and your wealth has gone up by $1,000 from
the beginning to the end of the year. If instead you spend $11,000 on beer and
iTunes, the question must be, from where did that $1,000 of spending in excess
of your salary come? It must have come from preexisting savings or from borrowing. This means that your wealth has gone down by $1,000 from the begin-
ning to the end of the year, and your income therefore must again be $10,000:
$11,000 in personal consumption minus $1,000 decrease in wealth (smaller
savings in the bank or a new liability).

Among other things, the above formulas reveal that *an income tax contains within it a consumption tax.* For those who spend exactly what they earn,
there is no difference. The chief difference between the two taxes concerns
those amounts that are *not* spent in the year they are earned or otherwise
acquired—that is, those amounts that are saved and invested. In other words,

---

2. H. Simons, *Personal Income Taxation* 50 (1938).

the debate between an income tax and a consumption tax is principally a debate about the proper tax treatment of savings and investment—more particularly, whether the "return to waiting," the basic economic return to deferring consumption from this year to a future year, should be subject to tax.

At one time, many experts thought that a consumption tax would be hopelessly difficult to administer because of problems of measuring consumption outlays and implementing progressive rate schedules. In an article published in 1974, however, Professor William D. Andrews of Harvard Law School demonstrated that this fear was unfounded both conceptually and practically and that, apart from other possible virtues, a consumption tax could even (depending on the form it took) be *easier* to compute than an income tax. Working from the insight conveyed by the formula above, Andrews showed that a consumption tax is simply an income tax with a deduction for savings and with the inclusion in the tax base of amounts drawn down from savings and used for consumption, as well as amounts borrowed for current consumption. The type of consumption tax Andrews had in mind is called a "cash-flow tax." Like the income tax, a cash-flow tax can employ progressive tax rates in respect of the tax base, in this case, annual consumption rather than annual income.

The practical operation of a cash-flow tax is best illustrated by reference to the *individual retirement account* (IRA). Amounts set aside in an IRA for retirement are currently deductible in computing the amount subject to taxation, and amounts withdrawn from the IRA account are included in income in the year of withdrawal. For example, if a taxpayer earns $40,000 each year and contributes $4,000 to an IRA, the amount subject to income taxation is $36,000 (assuming no other deductions). Later, if the taxpayer earns $10,000 and withdraws from the IRA a retirement benefit of, say, $5,000, the amount subject to income taxation is $15,000. This is entirely consistent with a consumption tax and entirely inconsistent with a straightforward income tax. If one simply imagines a vastly expanded IRA account, with no limits on the amount or purpose of contributions to the account, rules treating borrowing as a form of consumption, and repayment of a loan as form of savings, and no limits on the time of or reasons for withdrawal, one has a consumption tax of the cash-flow tax variety.

One feature that income, consumption, and wealth taxation share is the use of a relatively objective measure of ability to pay. All tend to measure cash flows or the market value of specific items. This tends to reduce government officials' discretion, which could potentially be abused if all factors pertinent to "ability to pay" were legally relevant, as well as the costs of running a more subjective and personalized system.

A preference for relying on observable transactions implies disregarding much or all of what economists call "imputed income," or the value of goods and services one provides to oneself. Examples include living in one's own home rather than paying rent, raising one's own children rather than paying for child care, and enjoying leisure rather than working for a wage. Here at the beginning of the book, you may well be wondering how on earth any sane person could ever entertain the idea of including in taxable income the value of goods and services provided to oneself. While your apprehension is understandable, we urge you to keep an open mind about these things. As we hope to illustrate in the following chapter, our failure to tax imputed income—however understandable—has concrete economic consequences for society, many of them arguably unfortunate.

3.   Efficiency of an Income Tax

Economists and policy makers often talk about how taxation affects work or savings and whether a tax is efficient. This section provides a brief overview of those topics. It is useful to begin this discussion with the simplest tax imaginable: the "head tax" described at the start of this chapter. The head tax is a lump-sum, must-be-paid-no-matter-what tax. It reduces wealth or income—just like any other expense. All else equal, this tends to increase work effort, as individuals try to regain their prior standard of living. For example, before the tax, an individual might have a *reservation price*, or rate at which she will work, of $25 an hour. After the head tax, the individual is poorer and so values income more. As a result, she might reduce her reservation price to $20. This means that she might accept an offer to work overtime that she would not have accepted prior to the tax. This effect is called the *income effect* (or sometimes the *wealth effect*) of the tax. It generally leads to an increase in work effort and other behavioral responses.

Economists do not regard the change in behavior due to the income effect as inefficient. Instead, it is a rational response to changing circumstances: The taxpayer is poorer and so decides to work more.[3] The taxpayer would do the same if his or her home were damaged by a storm or she encountered other unanticipated expenses. Of course, the tax may be spent in efficient or inefficient ways, but that side of the ledger is typically ignored when talking about the efficiency of a tax.

Since a head-tax must be paid no matter what, its only effect on behavior is that described by the income effect, and (ignoring the costs of collection and so on) it is always perfectly efficient.

A practical market income or consumption tax has an income effect, just as a head tax does. In response to being made poorer by an income tax, the taxpayer might again choose to work more to earn more money. However, an income or consumption tax affects your behavior in ways that go beyond just making you poorer, because *for all practical taxes you can change your tax liability by changing your behavior,* through substituting other goods or activities that are less heavily taxed.[4] If apples are taxed and pears are not, you might increase your pear consumption relative to apples; if mobile phone services are subject to new excise taxes, you might rely more on email or Skyping from your desktop computer, and so on.

---

3. Note that a tax might lead to a welfare payment to an individual. The income or wealth effect might then lead to that person working less, since he may now be a little less desperate for cash. His reservation price might increase from, say, $8 an hour to $12 an hour. This too would be considered a rational response to changing circumstances.

4. Jonathan Gruber, *Public Finance and Public Policy* 620 (New York: Worth Publishers, 4th ed. 2007).

This is the *substitution effect*—the idea that individuals change their behavior away from what is taxed more highly to something that is taxed more lightly. A head tax does not offer this opportunity, because wherever you go, there you are: a taxpayer with a fixed liability to the government.

In the case of even the most comprehensive income tax, one important endeavor that is necessarily taxed lightly is the one other use to which you can put your time besides participating in the market economy: leisure. An income tax might cause you to substitute leisure for labor, just as the tax on apples might cause you to substitute pears for apples. One way to understand this effect is to imagine an individual with a reservation price of $20 an hour who is offered a job that pays $24 an hour. If the wages were tax free, the individual takes the job. If the wages are taxed at 50 percent, the after-tax wage rate is only $12, and the individual substitutes leisure for labor.

The substitution effect leads to inefficiencies. In the example immediately above, the individual loses the surplus she would have gotten from the job (which paid $4 above her reservation price), and the government has gotten no tax revenue. This loss is referred to as the *excess burden* or *deadweight loss* of the tax.

An income tax on wages will produce an income and substitution effect. One way to think about this combination is first to imagine the income effect. This reduces wealth. In order to regain at least part of that wealth, a representative taxpayer reduces her reservation price. As noted, that is a rational response. The taxpayer then decides, as against her new, lower reservation price, whether a job is worth taking. If the tax causes the individual to reject the job, the substitution effect is at work. In that event, the individual is poorer, the government no wealthier, and an efficiency cost arises in the form of deadweight loss. At the extreme, a tax could be high enough for the substitution effect to dominate the income effect and preclude any work effort. Imagine, for example, a 100 percent tax on labor within a jurisdiction. (In practice, of course, a tax like that would not get adopted or, if adopted, survive.)

In sum, efficiency loss occurs when tax causes an individual to change his behavior to avoid the tax. The change in behavior reduces taxpayer wealth, and the government collects no revenue. When the tax is actually paid, it simply transfers wealth. The government activity may be wise or foolish, but the tax is efficient. We can think of a perfectly efficient tax as one that carries water from one spot to another in a watertight bucket. Deadweight loss is the measure of trying to do the same job with a leaky bucket.[5] That is, taxpayers suffer greater economic burdens in respect of their tax liabilities than the cash that gets delivered to other citizens, through the intermediation of government, at the other hand.

In practice, the income and substitution effects of a tax will differ from activity to activity and from subgroup to subgroup. For example, most studies of work effort show that the substitution effect (and consequent efficiency loss) is relatively small among men in their prime working years but larger among married women, who are more likely to be "second-wage earners," although this effect has diminished over time.

---

5. Arthur Okun is credited with first using this metaphor. Arthur M. Okun, *Equality and Efficiency: The Big Trade Off* (Washington, D.C.: Brookings Institution, 1975).

From this very brief description, you can begin to see why it is so challenging to model the economic consequences of a change in tax law.

4. Allocative and Distributive Effects

The previous two subsections' discussions of economic efficiency and ability to pay, or the more formal concept of the declining marginal utility of income, implicate the *allocative* and *distributive* effects of government fiscal policies. *Allocative effects* refer to the fact that government policies often change the mix of goods and services produced in the economy, when compared to a pure private market economy, through the various levers available to government (subsidies, government purchases of goods or services, regulation, favorable or onerous taxation, etc.). For example, the deductions for home mortgage interest and for property taxes and the nontaxation of imputed rental income from home own-ership[6] encourage people (especially those with high incomes) to buy homes rather than rent them. At one time, very substantial tax breaks benefited the oil industry, thereby encouraging the production of oil and reducing the price of gasoline; even today, the tax laws treat the oil industry more favorably in some respects than other industries. It is by no means implausible to suppose that these tax provisions played an important role in encouraging the shift of popula-tions to the suburbs and in the problems of pollution and energy management.

Other kinds of tax provisions may have allocative effects that most people would view as more benign. For example, as discussed later in this book, the deduction for charitable contributions seems to have played a significant role in raising the level of support for private colleges and universities, museums and symphony orchestras, as well as religious organizations. The charitable contribution deduction is very decentralized, in that support for cultural insti-tutions, for example, effectively operates through all of us (through the media-tion of government) co-contributing to your favorite charity. That, after all, is what it means for you to reduce your tax liability by the amount of your chari-table contribution. On the other hand, it also means that you have no choice but to support your professor's oddball tastes in cultural matters.

Even when the use of the tax system in this way is less effective than direct government expenditure, politicians and voters often prefer it to direct expen-diture because it looks different. Suppose that a company is paying income taxes of $10 million per year, and some members of Congress propose a subsidy for a particular type of investment that has a value to that company of $6 mil-lion a year. Using the tax system to deliver the subsidy permits its advocates to label it a "tax cut" rather than a "spending increase." This may be politically advantageous, even though the company's net payment to the government is $4 million either way. In part for this reason, the tax system is used to deliver an enormous range of incentive provisions for various activities and investments.

The term "*distributive effects*" refers to the use of government mechanisms, including the tax system, to "redistribute" income (or wealth) from rich to

---

6. Imputed income is discussed further in Chapter 3, Section A.

poor.[7] In practice allocative and distributive effects are not neat categories: Allocative initiatives can have distributive effects. Neither economists nor moral philosophers have ever come to a consensus on how distributive issues should be evaluated and resolved. Instead, addressing this is one of the core functions of the political process. Political processes in large developed economies have reached different conclusions on this question.

As noted in Chapter 7, allocative and distributive consequences properly should be measured in respect of the totality of the fiscal system, not the tax side by itself. Even regressive tax systems can fund progressive fiscal systems, because the spending side dominates the tax structure. This underlies the Nordic countries' fiscal policies. Their tax systems, measured in the abstract, are more regressive than those of the United States, but their tax shares of GDP are much higher, and the ways in which those revenues are spent are very progressive in their economic impact (lower income citizens benefit disproportionately more). The resulting net fiscal systems thereby become highly progressive.[8]

As a general observation, most tax provisions that serve allocative purposes and that are not tailored to respond to some market failure introduce deadweight loss beyond the irreducible minimum inherent in any practical tax, for the simple reason that prices, and therefore choices, are distorted from what they would have been in the absence of those provisions. Tax provisions designed to embody distributional goals also introduce deadweight loss, because the higher marginal tax rates that form part of the redistribution mechanism are thought to exacerbate the fundamental labor-leisure tradeoff.

In addition, many features of the income tax are deliberately designed to have allocative effects, which is to say, to change the relative prices of goods or services when compared to a market economy supported by the narrowest possible government.

B. WHAT IS "INCOME" ANYWAY?

1. What *Do* We Tax?

Given the title of this book, the answer to the question "What do we tax?" might seem completely obvious: income. By the time you reach the end of the book, however, we suspect you may have some doubts that the U.S. "income" tax truly deserves that label. After all, just calling something an income tax does not make it so.

Thus, consider again the "Haig-Simons" definition of income as the sum of the taxpayer's consumption plus change in net worth during the taxable year,

---

7. The term "redistribution" is itself a loaded one, in that it assumes an unencumbered normative claim to market income, but this points toward questions of moral philosophy, not the law of income taxation.

8. Edward Kleinbard, *We Are Better Than This: How Government Should Spend Our Money*, ch. 12 (2014).

each defined in terms of market value. This is a far broader definition than any that has ever been implemented or even seriously proposed. What is more, many of the items that Haig-Simons income would embrace, but that the actual tax system does not—for example, unrealized appreciation (the increase in value of one's assets such as a home or shares of corporate stock)—relate to saving or changes in net worth. So do the rules for IRAs that eliminate any current taxation of retirement saving.

Given the extensive departures of our actual income tax from the Haig-Simons idea, especially with regard to the tax treatment of investment returns, many commentators assert that our system is closer to a consumption tax than to an income tax.

The references to income "from whatever source derived" in both the Sixteenth Amendment and §61 of the Internal Revenue Code suggest that the United States follows a comprehensive approach to income taxation. Over the years, however, Congress has incorporated various schedular features in the U.S. income tax, including, for example, preferential tax rates for capital gains and dividend income and limitations on the deductibility of capital losses and of what are called passive activity losses. In addition, taxpayers calculate certain of these items on separate "schedules" attached to their tax returns (e.g., Schedule D for capital gains and losses), leading some commentators to view the U.S. income tax as a global system built on a schedular foundation.

Even insofar as we have an income tax, defining income in terms of consumption plus change in net worth merely begins, rather than ends, the process of identifying income in practice. For example, does "consumption" include the cost of dinner with a business client who is also a friend? Should it include medical expenses incurred to recover from an illness? What about the cost of a gift to a charity or a family member? Surely the answer to such questions is not a matter of parsing dictionary definitions, but rather of deciding how we want to allocate tax burdens, based on ability to pay (however defined) and all other relevant considerations.

The remainder of this chapter seeks to put meat on these bones by examining how some important questions along these lines have been resolved. In practice, U.S. federal income tax liability depends on the statutory concept of "taxable income," rather than on any abstract definition. This concept, in turn, reflects a welter of competing objectives and myriad compromises between them.

2. The Limits of Intuition

So, what is income? Chances are that you already have some well-developed intuitions about the answer to that question. For example, if you read Harper Lee's novel, *To Kill a Mockingbird*, you probably weren't stumped by the sentence near the start, "Atticus derived a reasonable income from the law." Like most people, you probably imagined Atticus Finch receiving cash from his clients for the various legal services he rendered. For the most part, you will find that your everyday intuitions about what is and isn't income are a useful guide in thinking about the meaning of the term for legal purposes as well.

At times, however, your intuition may not be enough. Take the case of Walter Cunningham, the poor Maycomb County farmer Atticus helped in connection with an entailment on his land. What "income" did Finch recognize when Cunningham, lacking cash, instead left a sack of hickory nuts and turnip greens at the Finches' back door in partial satisfaction of his legal fees? Does it make any difference to Finch or to Cunningham that payment was made in kind rather than in cash? Would it matter if Finch's usual fee for legal work far exceeded the value of the hickory nuts and turnip greens? What if Finch had accepted an ownership interest in Cunningham's land instead? At the risk of spoiling one of America's greatest novels with talk of federal taxes, we'd like to suggest that intuition alone may not have equipped you to offer professional tax guidance on these questions. One of the objectives of this chapter, therefore, is to provide you with a framework for thinking about the definition of income from a legal perspective.

As a legal matter, income is simply whatever the Internal Revenue Code is authoritatively (and constitutionally) interpreted to say that it is. Although this initial response may seem curt and not particularly helpful, it reflects the fact that federal income tax liability is determined, not by reference to first principles or the whims of a tax inspector, but rather through the application of a highly specified model of economic activity, written and owned by Congress. In turn, Congress has found that in a complex and rapidly evolving society, the contours of a fundamental term like "income" resist precise specification. Rather than constant revisions to the Code to deal with every new application, Congress here relies on generalities and vagueness as an ally, by defining income in the broadest possible terms; Congress then largely confines its statutory amendments to exclusions from its broad definition of the term.

The 2016 law described in Chapter 1 that excludes Olympic and Paralympic prizes from the definition of income is one example. Similarly, no simple or intuitive conception of income could yield the result that interest earned on bonds issued by a state (or any political subdivision thereof), unlike other interest income, is excludable from the bondholder's gross income. And as a third example, no amount of logic, intuition, or other abstract reasoning will reveal that income does not include gain from the sale of one's principal residence, but only to the extent that such gain does not exceed $250,000 ($500,000 in the case of married couples filing a joint return) and only if the taxpayer has owned and occupied the residence for at least two out of the last five years.

Clearly these rules derive not from logic or intuition but rather from the fact that the U.S. Congress, in accordance with the powers conferred upon it by Article I and the Sixteenth Amendment of the U.S. Constitution, enacted legislation defining income in this manner. Nonetheless, intuition has a role to play here, by reason of the fact that the Internal Revenue Code defines "gross income" through the (at first glance) inscrutably circular statement that it "means *all income* from whatever source derived" (§61(a)) (emphasis added). Moreover, before listing some of the most obvious sources of income (wages, interest, etc.), the statute indicates that the term is "not limited to" the enu-merated items. Thus, from the very outset, the statutory language strongly implies that the term "income" has some meaning beyond that which Congress has expressly given it. In addition, both courts and the Internal Revenue Service—in some cases, with explicit statutory encouragement—may regard accurate measurement of "income" as among the principles that should guide decisions when persuasive authority on the point is lacking. But even if we accept that the term "income" has some general, common meaning to which we can turn, what is that meaning? And where does it come from?

Judicial opinions provide some guidance. An early Supreme Court decision, Eisner v. Macomber, 252 U.S. 189, 207 (1920) (*infra*), defined income as "the gain derived from capital, from labor, or from both combined." As we will see, this definition excludes windfalls, so that a person who works to earn money is taxed on it, while a person who stumbles across the same amount lying in the street would not be. One could criticize this narrowness as producing unfairness (because people with similar ability to pay are not taxed similarly) or inefficiency (because some kinds of gain-producing activities are favored over others). In any event, by 1955 the Supreme Court had developed a much broader under-standing of the term, concluding instead that "Congress applied no limitations as to the source of taxable receipts, nor restrictive labels as to their nature" (Commissioner v. Glenshaw Glass, 348 U.S. 426, 429-430 (1955) (*infra*)).

Support for an even broader definition of income can be found in the Haig-Simons definition, discussed in the preceding section. With its reference to algebra and the market value of rights, this definition sounds at once both precise and capacious. Yet a moment's reflection reveals that the Haig-Simons approach, if fully implemented, would likely encounter political resistance, as well as some practical problems of implementation. Among other things, it would require taxation of such items as unrealized asset appreciation, imputed income from the ownership of homes and other assets, and the value of gov-ernment services such as education at a state-supported low-tuition university. Moreover, it would leave difficult questions of when certain expenses consti-tuted consumptions, or instead a cost of earnings income.

Realistic observers understand that a workable tax, particularly one that relies on self-assessment, must be an administrable one. Administrative consid-erations are thought to require relying most of the time on observable market transactions, such as the actual sale of an asset, not just its appreciation, or on the actual earning of a wage, not just the opportunity to earn a wage. In practice, therefore, even those who favor a Haig-Simons approach concede the importance of workable accounting rules that emphasize observable inflows and outflows of cash and other valuable assets. As a result, key design ques-tions arise at the implementation stage regarding how to account for a given inflow or outflow. Should a particular item be included or deducted at all, rather than ignored? Should inclusion or deduction occur now or later? As is almost always the case in tax, the devil is in the details.

Putting it in terms of people rather than things, designing a tax system is about deciding how to share burdens. So every decision about what is or isn't income may have important implications for whom among us pays more, and who pays less.

C. BACK TO THE BALLPARK

"Found meat is income."

Chapter 1 asked you to think about whether, and when, Matt Murphy recognized income when he caught Barry Bonds's record-setting home run. At the moment of his catch? When he sold the ball a few months later? What if he hadn't sold the ball?

Similar issues were raised in 1998 in connection with the historic home-run balls of Mark McGwire and Sammy Sosa, who were in a heated race to break the record of 61 home runs in a single season held by Roger Maris. After the fan who caught McGwire's 61st home run ball handed it back to McGwire, an IRS spokesman was quoted as saying that the fan might owe federal gift taxes on the transfer. The statement did not mention federal income tax consequences, but arguably those could have followed as well from viewing the events as significant for tax purposes. Various commentators noted that McGwire's upcoming 62nd home run ball, which would set the new single-season record, was likely to be worth at least $1 million.

Congressional critics of the IRS had a field day. Senate Finance Committee Chair Roth called "even the possibility of Mark McGwire's historic 62nd baseball being taxed . . . a prime example of what is wrong with our current tax code." Senator Christopher Bond demanded corrective legislation and said: "If the IRS wants to know why they are the most hated federal agency in America, they need look no further than this assault on America's baseball fans."

The IRS promptly backed off, issuing a press release in which it stated that a fan who catches and returns a home-run ball does not have taxable income "based on an analogy to principles of tax law that apply when someone immediately declines a prize or returns unsolicited merchandise." It cautioned that the tax implications "may be different" if the fan retained the ball for sale. As it turned out, McGwire's 62nd home run ball was retrieved by a groundskeeper at the stadium, rather than a fan. The groundskeeper promptly (and arguably in his capacity as a baseball team employee) gave it to McGwire. The IRS apparently decided not to explore the possibility that McGwire had taxable income from the transfer.

The IRS's practical stance notwithstanding, what can be said about the underlying meaning of income here? We can be confident that Henry Simons would have treated Matt Murphy as recognizing income when Murphy caught the ball, because Murphy had an undeniable (if uncertain) accession to wealth at that time. Is there some constitutional law constraint here? Does the Sixteenth Amendment really countenance treating lucky fans as recognizing income when valuable baseballs fall in their laps?

The case that follows, Commissioner v. Glenshaw Glass, Inc., is one of the most famous and important Supreme Court opinions in the tax field. We suspect, however, that you may find its holding to be somewhat unremarkable. To fully appreciate its significance requires an understanding of its historical context; we'll have more to say about that in the notes following the case. For now, we'd like to draw your attention to the reference in the first paragraph of Chief Justice Warren's opinion to the fact that the taxpayers prevailed in both the Tax Court and the U.S. Court of Appeals. Both of those tribunals based their holdings on a much earlier Supreme Court opinion, Eisner v. Macomber (1920), which, as you will recall from earlier in this chapter, narrowly defined the term "income" as "the gain derived from capital, from labor, or from both combined." Under Eisner v. Macomber, the IRS presumably would have been required to argue that Matt Murphy's efforts to catch the ball, and to hold onto it in the resulting scrum, constituted the labor to which his gain (the value of the ball) related.[9]

Glenshaw Glass technically addresses whether punitive damages constitute income, but its continued importance relates not to this narrow question but rather the continuing vitality (or lack thereof) of Eisner v. Macomber, as well as the extent to which the Supreme Court plays a role in policing the contours of the term "income."

---

9. One of the authors, older in years if not in tax wisdom than the others, remembers when he was a boy and his maternal grandmother, who had been a flapper in the Roaring '20s, explained tax policy to him. She related how in her time as a young woman going out to fashionable nightclubs, one club adopted a popular gimmick of releasing helium-filled balloons to drift above the diners. An occasional balloon had a $100 bill placed inside it. Over time the helium would leak out, and a balloon would come within reach of the club goers. Each table was equipped with a pin for such occasions, and guests would prick the balloon, squealing with delight at the loud pop and hoping that a $100 bill would fall to the table. If one did, she explained, it was income, because the habitués of the club had supplied labor by reaching up to prick the balloon. The author now realizes that she was channeling Eisner v. Macomber. Sadly, the author does not remember how the subject came up in the first place.

COMMISSIONER v. GLENSHAW GLASS CO.
348 U.S. 426 (1955)

Mr. Chief Justice WARREN delivered the opinion of the Court.

This litigation involves two cases with independent factual backgrounds yet presenting the identical issue. The two cases were consolidated for argument before the Court of Appeals for the Third Circuit and were heard en banc. The common question is whether money received as exemplary damages for fraud or as the punitive two-thirds portion of a treble-damage antitrust recovery must be reported by a taxpayer as gross income under §22(a) of the Internal Revenue Code of 1939 [the predecessor of §61 of the 1954 Code]. In a single opinion, 211 F.2d 928, the Court of Appeals affirmed the Tax Court's separate rulings in favor of the taxpayers. . . .

The facts of the cases were largely stipulated and are not in dispute. So far as pertinent they are as follows:

Commissioner v. Glenshaw Glass Co. The Glenshaw Glass Company, a Pennsylvania corporation, manufactures glass bottles and containers. It was engaged in protracted litigation with the Hartford-Empire Company, which manufactures machinery of a character used by Glenshaw. Among the claims advanced by Glenshaw were demands for exemplary damages for fraud and treble damages for injury to its business by reason of Hartford's violation of the federal antitrust laws. In December 1947, the parties concluded a settlement of all pending litigation, by which Hartford paid Glenshaw approximately $800,000. Through a method of allocation which was approved by the Tax Court, 18 T.C. 860, 870-872, and which is no longer in issue, it was ultimately determined that, of the total settlement, $324,529.94 represented payment of punitive damages for fraud and antitrust violations. Glenshaw did not report this portion of the settlement as income for the tax year involved. The Commissioner determined a deficiency claiming as taxable the entire sum less only deductible legal fees. As previously noted, the Tax Court and the Court of Appeals upheld the taxpayer.

Commissioner v. William Goldman Theatres, Inc. William Goldman Theatres, Inc., a Delaware corporation operating motion picture houses in Pennsylvania, sued Loew's, Inc., alleging a violation of the federal antitrust laws and seeking treble damages. After a holding that a violation had occurred, William Goldman Theatres, Inc. v. Loew's, Inc., 150 F.2d 738, the case was remanded to the trial court for a determination of damages. It was found that Goldman had suffered a loss of profits equal to $125,000 and was entitled to treble damages in the sum of $375,000. William Goldman Theatres, Inc. v. Loew's, Inc., 69 F. Supp. 103, aff'd, 164 F.2d 1021, cert. denied, 334 U.S. 811. Goldman reported only $125,000 of the recovery as gross income and claimed that the $250,000 balance constituted punitive damages and as such was not taxable. The Tax Court agreed, 19 T.C. 637, and the Court of Appeals, hearing this with the Glenshaw case, affirmed. 211 F.2d 928.

It is conceded by the respondents that there is no constitutional barrier to the imposition of a tax on punitive damages. Our question is one of statutory construction: Are these payments comprehended by §22(a)?

The sweeping scope of the controverted statute is readily apparent:

Sec. 22. Gross Income

(a) *General Definition.* "Gross income" includes gains, profits, and income derived from salaries, wages, or compensation for personal service . . . of whatever kind and in whatever form paid, or from professions, vocations, trades, businesses, commerce, or sales, or dealings in property, whether real or personal, growing out of the ownership or use of or interest in such property; also from interest, rent, dividends, securities, or the transaction of any business carried on for gain or profit, *or gains or profits and income derived from any source whatever. . . .*

(Emphasis added.)

This Court has frequently stated that this language was used by Congress to exert in this field "the full measure of its taxing power." Helvering v. Clifford [309 U.S. 331]; Helvering v. Midland Mutual Life Ins. Co., 300 U.S. 216, 223; Douglas v. Willcuts, 296 U.S. 1, 9; Irwin v. Gavit, [268 U.S. 161]. Respondents contend that punitive damages, characterized as "windfalls" flowing from the culpable conduct of third parties, are not within the scope of the section. But Congress applied no limitations as to the source of taxable receipts, nor restrictive labels as to their nature. And the Court has given a liberal construction to this broad phraseology in recognition of the intention of Congress to tax all gains except those specifically exempted. . . . Thus, the fortuitous gain accruing to a lessor by reason of the forfeiture of a lessee's improvements on the rented property was taxed in Helvering v. Bruun [*infra* page 247]. Cf. Robertson v. United States, 343 U.S. 711; Rutkin v. United States, 343 U.S. 130; United States v. Kirby Lumber Co. [*infra* page 321]. Such decisions demonstrate that we cannot but ascribe content to the catchall provision of §22(a), "gains or profits and income derived from any source whatever." The importance of that phrase has been too frequently recognized since its first appearance in the Revenue Act of 1913 to say now that it adds nothing to the meaning of "gross income."

Nor can we accept respondents' contention that a narrower reading of §22(a) is required by the Court's characterization of income in Eisner v. Macomber, 252 U.S. 189, 207 [*infra* page 232], as "the gain derived from capital, from labor, or from both combined."[10] The Court was there endeavoring to determine whether the distribution of a corporate stock dividend constituted a realized gain to the shareholder, or changed "only the form, not the essence," of his capital investment. *Id.* at 210. It was held that the taxpayer had "received nothing out of the company's assets for his separate use and benefit." *Id.* at 211. The distribution, therefore, was held not a taxable event.

---

10. The phrase was derived from Stratton's Independence, Ltd. v. Howbert, 231 U.S. 399, 415, and Doyle v. Mitchell Bros. Co., 247 U.S. 179, 185, two cases construing the Revenue Act of 1909, 36 Stat. 11, 112. Both taxpayers were "wasting asset" corporations, one being engaged in mining, the other in lumbering operations. The definition was applied by the Court to demonstrate a distinction between a return on capital and "a mere conversion of capital assets." Doyle v. Mitchell Bros. Co., *supra* at 184. The question raised by the instant case is clearly distinguishable.

In that context—distinguishing gain from capital—the definition served a useful purpose. But it was not meant to provide a touchstone to all future gross income questions. . . .

Here we have instances of undeniable accessions to wealth, clearly realized, and over which the taxpayers have complete dominion. The mere fact that the payments were extracted from the wrongdoers as punishment for unlawful conduct cannot detract from their character as taxable income to the recipients. Respondents concede, as they must, that the recoveries are taxable to the extent that they compensate for damages actually incurred. It would be an anomaly that could not be justified in the absence of clear congressional intent to say that a recovery for actual damages is taxable but not the additional amount extracted as punishment for the same conduct which caused the injury. And we find no such evidence of intent to exempt these payments. . . .

Reversed.

Mr. Justice DOUGLAS dissents.

Mr. Justice HARLAN took no part in the consideration or decision of this case.

NOTES AND QUESTIONS

1. *Why is this case important?* As previously indicated, the thrust of the Court's opinion is in the language, "But Congress applied no limitations as to the source of taxable receipts, nor restrictive labels as to their nature." The significance of this statement derives not so much from its conclusion regarding whether Congress applied "limitations" or "restrictive labels" in the definition of income, but rather from its premise that it is *Congress* that decides how narrow or broad "income" should be. In this regard, *Glenshaw Glass* marks a complete and final repudiation of the Supreme Court's earlier approach, which had characterized much of the first four decades of the modern U.S. income tax. During that earlier era, courts had actively scrutinized legislative and regulatory decisions for consistency with their views regarding the meaning of "income" under the Sixteenth Amendment. That approach, typified by the famous decision in Eisner v. Macomber (1920), viewed the Supreme Court as the ultimate arbiter of the scope of legislative power, thus sharing a jurisprudential heritage with famous nontax cases like Lochner v. New York (1905). As with the "Lochner era," the Court's "Macomber era" began to pass with the advent of the New Deal Court in the late 1930s. *Glenshaw Glass* was the final nail in the coffin.

2. Glenshaw Glass *and the modern (broad) conception of income.* In many ways, Chief Justice Warren's opinion in *Glenshaw Glass* is consistent with the broad definition of income reflected in the Haig-Simons formulation, and it is favored by most modern tax experts. The facts of the case nicely illustrate the appeal of that definition. As the Court argues, it would be anomalous indeed to tax a recovery of lost profits but not a treble-damages windfall arising from the same events. Similarly, it might offend one's sense of fairness to tax wages a person earns by hard work but not money a person happens to find lying on the street.

The facts in *Glenshaw Glass* are not strictly comparable to those facing Matt Murphy. And the fact that the IRS could have argued that Murphy had income in a constitutional sense does not determine whether this is the result Congress contemplated. Does this next case shed additional light?

CESARINI v. UNITED STATES
296 F. Supp. 3 (N.D. Ohio 1969), aff'd per curiam, 428 F.2d 812 (6th Cir. 1970)

YOUNG, District Judge:

This is an action by the plaintiffs as taxpayers for the recovery of income tax payments made in the calendar year 1964. Plaintiffs contend that the amount of $836.51 was erroneously overpaid by them in 1964, and that they are entitled to a refund in that amount, together with the statutory interest from October 13, 1965, the date which they made their claim upon the Internal Revenue Service for the refund.

Plaintiffs and the United States have stipulated to the material facts in the case, and the matter is before the Court for final decision. The facts necessary for a resolution of the issues raised should perhaps be briefly stated before the Court proceeds to a determination of the matter. Plaintiffs are husband and wife, and live within the jurisdiction of the United States District Court for the Northern District of Ohio. In 1957, the plaintiffs purchased a used piano at an auction sale for approximately $15.00, and the piano was used by their daughter for piano lessons. In 1964, while cleaning the piano, plaintiffs discovered the sum of $4,467.00 in old currency, and since have retained the piano instead of discarding it as previously planned. Being unable to ascertain who put the money there, plaintiffs exchanged the old currency for new at a bank, and reported the sum of $4,467.00 on their 1964 joint income tax return as ordinary income from other sources. On October 18, 1965, plaintiffs filed an amended return with the District Director of Internal Revenue in Cleveland, Ohio, this second return eliminating the sum of $4,467.00 from the gross income computation, and requesting a refund in the amount of $836.51, the amount allegedly overpaid as a result of the former inclusion of $4,467.00 in the original return for the calendar year of 1964. On January 18, 1966, the Commissioner of Internal Revenue rejected taxpayers' refund claim in its entirety, and plaintiffs filed the instant action in March of 1967.

* * * *

The starting point in determining whether an item is to be included in gross income is, of course, *Section 61(a) of Title 26 U.S.C.*, and that section provides in part:

> "Except as otherwise provided in this subtitle, *gross income means all income from whatever source derived*, including (but not limited to) the following items: . . ."

Subsections (1) through (15) of Section 61(a) then go on to list fifteen items specifically included in the computation of the taxpayer's gross income, and Part II of Subchapter B of the 1954 Code (*Sections 71 et seq.*) deals with *statutory reasoning* (handwritten margin note)

other items expressly included in gross income. While neither of these listings expressly includes the type of income which is at issue in the case at bar, Part III of Subchapter B (Sections 101 *et seq.*) deals with items specifically *excluded* from gross income, and found money is not listed in those sections either. This absence of express mention in any of the code sections necessitates a return to the "all income from whatever source" language of Section 61(a) of the code, and the express statement there that gross income is "not limited to" the following fifteen examples. [Treas. reg. §1.61-1(a)] . . . reiterates this broad construction of gross income, providing in part:

> "Gross income means all income from whatever source derived, unless excluded by law. *Gross income includes income realized in any form*, whether in money, property, or services. * * *"

The decisions of the United States Supreme Court have frequently stated that this broad all-inclusive language was used by Congress to exert the full measure of its taxing power under the 16th Amendment. *Commissioner of Internal Revenue v. Glenshaw Glass Co., 348 U.S. 426.* . . .

In addition, the Government in the instant case cites and relies upon an I.R.S. Revenue Ruling which is undeniably on point:

> The finder of treasure trove is in receipt of taxable income, for Federal income tax purposes, to the extent of its value in United States currency, for the taxable year in which it is reduced to undisputed possession. Rev. Rul. 61, 1953-1, Cum. Bull. 17.

The plaintiffs argue that the above ruling does not control this case for two reasons. The first is that subsequent to the Ruling's pronouncement in 1953, Congress enacted Sections 74 and 102 of the 1954 Code, §74 expressly *including* the value of prizes and gifts in gross income in most cases, and §102 specifically *exempting* the value of gifts received from gross income. From this, it is argued that Section 74 was added because prizes might otherwise be construed as nontaxable gifts, and since no such section was passed expressly taxing treasure trove, it is therefore a gift which is non-taxable under Section 102. This line of reasoning overlooks the statutory scheme previously alluded to, whereby income from all sources is taxed unless the taxpayer can point to an express exemption. Not only have the taxpayers failed to list a specific exclusion in the instant case, but also the Government *has* pointed to express language covering the found money, even though it would not be required to do so under the broad language of Section 61(a) and the foregoing Supreme Court decisions interpreting it.

[The argument] that found money must be construed to be a gift under Section 102 of the 1954 Code since it is not expressly included as are prizes in Section 74 of the Code, would not even be effective were it being urged at a time prior to 1953, when the ruling had not yet been promulgated. In addition to the numerous cases in the Supreme Court which uphold the broad sweeping construction of Section 61(a) found in Treas. reg. §1.61-1(a), other courts and commentators writing at a point in time before the ruling came down took the position that windfalls, including found monies, were properly includable in gross income under Section 22(a) of the 1939 Code, the predecessor of Section 61(a) in the 1954 Code.

* * * *

Although not cited by either party, and noticeably absent from the Government's brief, the following Treasury Regulation appears in the 1964 Regulations, the year of the return in dispute:

§1.61-14 Miscellaneous items of gross income.

(a) In general. In addition to the items enumerated in Section 61(a), there are many other kinds of gross income. . . . *Treasure trove, to the extent of its value in United States currency, constitutes gross income for the taxable year in which it is reduced to undisputed possession.*

Identical language appears in the 1968 Treasury Regulations, and is found in all previous years back to 1958. This language is undoubtedly an attempt to codify [Rev. Rul. 61] into the Regulations which apply to the 1954 Code. This Court is of the opinion that Treas. Reg. §1.61-14(a) is dispositive of the major issue in this case. . . .

NOTES AND QUESTIONS

1. Is there any argument rooted in principles of taxation, other than fairness, for excluding windfalls? Are windfalls "income" as that word is normally used outside the tax system?[11] Examine the language of §61. Can you make a "strict constructionist" or "plain language" argument for exclusion? Bear in mind, this is a tax code that we interpret, not a constitution. Is there virtue in a "government of laws," even if the laws produce results we would not otherwise find appealing?

2. You are the lawyer for Matt Murphy, who in this hypothetical did not sell the home-run ball but rather continues to own it to this day. What argument(s) can you construct for distinguishing or disagreeing with *Cesarini*? Traditionally, the IRS has not sought to tax the income of commercial fishermen, big game hunters, prospectors, miners, and salvors who raise sunken treasure from ships until they turn their bounty into cash (or its equivalent). However, this practice seemingly contradicts Reg. §1.61-14, quoted in *Cesarini*.

3. If the home-run ball was income in the year it was caught, and there was no sale, how much income should Murphy report?

4. Academics and practitioners struggle just as much as students do with some of the questions posed by Murphy's good fortune. See, for example, Andrew Appleby, *Ball-Busters: How the IRS Should Tax Record-Setting Baseballs and Other Found Property Under the Treasure Trove Regulation*, 33 Vt. L. Rev. 43

---

11. Suppose that last year you earned $20,000 as a law clerk and won $5,000 in a lottery and someone now asks you, "How much did you earn last year?" What would you say? Suppose the question is, "What was your income last year?"

(2008); Joseph M. Dodge, *Accessions to Wealth, Realization of Gross Income, and Dominion and Control: Applying the "Claim of Right Doctrine" to Found Objects, Including Record-Setting Baseballs*, 4 Fla. Tax Rev. 685, 691 (2000); Lawrence A. Zelenak and Martin J. McMahon, Jr., *Taxing Baseballs and Other Found Property*, 84 Tax Notes 1299 (Aug. 30, 1999).

5. Examine the cartoon at the start of this section. Common sense tells us that "found meat" is not income. What authority would you cite for that proposition? See Note 1, above.

D.   PAYING ANOTHER'S BILLS

Example 1

Baseball raised yet another "what is taxable" question, when Derek Jeter's 3,000th hit bounced into the left field bleachers and was picked up by 23-year-old Christian Lopez. Lopez became a hero to millions of fans when he gave the ball back to Jeter, rather than sell it to a collector. Lopez told reporters that he believed the ball belonged to Jeter and he had never considered keeping it. Experts estimate the ball might have sold for as much as $250,000.

Lopez didn't walk away entirely empty-handed. The Yankees gave Mr. Lopez bats, balls, and jerseys with an estimated resale value of approximately $4,500. They also gave him four tickets to the remaining home games, with an estimated value of approximately $50,000.

Tax experts contacted by the media suggested that Lopez might be taxed on the value of the merchandise and tickets. The possibility that Lopez's act of generosity nonetheless would leave him stuck with a tax bill was prevented when Miller Brewing Company announced it would pay any taxes Lopez might owe.

NOTES AND QUESTIONS

1. Assume Lopez has no tax liability from merely picking up the ball. Does Lopez owe tax on the merchandise? The tickets? If Miller Brewing Company winds up paying his tax liability, would Lopez be taxed on Miller Brewing's payment of Lopez's tax bill?

2. The leading case in this area is Old Colony Trust Co. v. Commissioner, 279 U.S. 716, 729 (1929), holding that an employer's payment of federal income taxes on behalf of its employee constituted income to the employee. The Court found it "immaterial that the taxes were directly paid over [by the employer] to the Government. The discharge by a third person of an obligation to him is equivalent to receipt by the person taxed." This case preceded the adoption of federal income tax withholding. Due to withholding, it is now routine for the employer to make federal (along with state and local) income tax payments on the employee's behalf and yet for these payments to be included in the employee's gross income.

Example 2

Alice is a computer programmer who works for Unitek. Ignoring tax planning considerations, Unitek would pay her a salary of $5,000 per month ($60,000 per year). Every month she would spend $1,000 of this amount on rent.

Suppose (counterfactually) that Alice's gross income under §61 from working for Unitek included only the amount of her paycheck. Alice and Unitek could agree that it would directly pay her only $4,000 per month, but that the company would also pay her rent. Unitek would still be paying $5,000 per month, and Alice would still have $4,000 per month left before tax after payment of her rent. Thus, in a sense, nothing would have changed. Yet Alice's income for tax purposes would have declined by $1,000 per month, or $12,000 per year. Assuming a marginal tax rate of 30 percent, Alice would potentially have reduced her annual federal income tax liability by $3,600.

If this worked, perhaps the next step would be for Unitek to reduce Alice's paycheck still more, substituting payments to the grocery stores, restaurants, dry cleaners, health clubs, and the like that she patronizes, to be credited to her account in these establishments. Suppose Unitek and Alice could work out a way to convert an additional $2,500 per month of her compensation into this indirect form, without any change in her patronage of these establishments. Thus, her paycheck would be down to $1,500 per month ($18,000 per year). She would be taxed like someone who was really making that amount annually, rather than like someone who was really making the same $60,000 but had not structured the cash flows as cleverly.

NOTES AND QUESTIONS

1. Why would Unitek agree to such a deal? Might Alice and Unitek end up splitting the tax savings? What would this involve?

2. To allow Alice's rent to be excluded from her income when Unitek pays it has the same effect as permitting her a deduction if she pays it. Thus, suppose that rent were deductible from income. Alice's income would be the same, $4,000, whether (a) Unitek directly paid her $5,000 and she then paid and deducted $1,000 of rent; or (b) Unitek paid $4,000 to Alice and $1,000 to her landlord and Alice was then permitted to exclude the latter amount.

3. Why doesn't it make sense to let Alice and Unitek reduce her income tax liability through these arrangements?

4. Moving from the counterfactuals in Example 2 to the law under *Old Colony Trust*, Alice would in fact have income in the amount of Unitek's rental (and other) payments on her behalf. So don't propose this to your employer on the basis that you will split the tax savings with them.

The rule of the *Old Colony Trust* case comes up routinely in negotiating commercial settlements and the like, when one party agrees to pay to another a fixed sum, "net of taxes"—that is, after taking into account the recipient's income tax liability in respect of that payment. The payor must increase the nominal net-of-tax amount to reflect not only the recipient's apparent tax liability but also the tax due on the payment of the recipient's tax. In practice, these arrangements are called "gross-ups."

For example, assume that an employee has a salary of $50,000 and that income is taxed at a flat 40 percent rate: that is, $20,000 of tax on an income of $50,000. Now the employee moves to a new employer that promises to pay the same $50,000 salary but, as an inducement, agrees to pay the salary such that the employee will receive the $50,000 "net of income tax."

Paying the employee $70,000 ($50,000 plus her $20,000 tax bill at the old job) won't do the trick, because after tax she would have only $42,000 left. The reason is that the $20,000 extra payment to cover the employee's tax bill is itself income under *Old Colony* and therefore is subject to an incremental income tax of $8,000.

In cases like this, elementary algebra comes to the rescue. What one needs to do is figure out some amount X such that, after reducing X by 40 percent, the remaining amount equals $50,000. In other words, we need 0.6X [that is, X, after taxes] = $50,000, or (X = $50,000 ÷ 0.6) = $83,333. You can check by taking 40 percent away from that number and seeing what you are left with. The "gross up" here to the $50,000 salary is $33,333. Sometimes people like to think of this as a $20,000 gross-up for taxes on the first $50,000, plus "gross-up on the gross-up," over and over.

The generic formulation is that the *total payment to be made* [X, above] = *the after tax amount to be received* ÷ (1-T), where T is recipient's tax rate.

E.   NONCASH BENEFITS

Our detailed investigation of the contours of the term "income" continues with what may seem to be, at least initially, an unlikely place: the income tax treatment of *noncash* benefits received in connection with employment. It bears noting that the reason for focusing on these fact patterns is not because of the overall significance of noncash benefits to the federal revenue structure. In fact, the vast majority of total U.S. income tax receipts comes from taxes on various types of cash payments, most notably cash salaries and wages. We focus on noncash benefits to introduce you to one of the great challenges engendered by interacting with the tax law—namely, the importance of analyzing transactions according to both their economic substance and their form. We have already seen that the Internal Revenue Code, in its definition of "gross income" as "all income from whatever source derived," makes no distinction whatsoever between cash and noncash transactions. Likewise, under longstanding Treasury regulations, "[g]ross income includes income realized in any form, whether in money, property, or services." Reg. §1.61-1(a). For example, "if services are paid for in property, the fair market value of the property taken in payment must be included in income as compensation." Reg. §1.61-2(d)(1). Thus, what matters is not the form that one's income takes but rather the fact that the taxpayer has received an economic benefit.

Some may find these rules troubling. After all, payment of taxes must be made in cash, check, money order, or by other "commercially acceptable means" (such as electronic funds transfers) deemed appropriate by the Internal

Revenue Service. §6311(a). However, one can easily appreciate the need to include noncash benefits in income if the outcomes under a contrary rule are imagined. (See Example 2 in Section D, *supra*.) Although not all taxpayers could readily barter work for noncash benefits, many could—for example, a lawyer might draft a will for a carpenter in exchange for work on her home, or the employees of a supermarket might accept part of their pay in groceries. To the extent that some people could take advantage of such arrangements more freely than others, tax burdens to some degree would, at least initially, fall in a haphazard manner, depending on the practicality of compensation in kind in a particular kind of activity. That might reduce fairness. As people respond by moving to tax-favored jobs, the wages in such jobs would tend to fall. Industries providing such jobs would, for no good reason, tend to benefit as compared with industries that did not. That might reduce efficiency. Moreover, people would be encouraged to take compensation in the form of goods and services instead of taking it in cash and spending the cash on goods and services that they might value more highly; again, that might reduce efficiency—it would be wasteful.

On the other hand, taxing noncash benefits raises problems of administrative feasibility or practicality. Often it is difficult to know whether a noncash benefit (e.g., free air travel) has any significant value to the taxpayer and, if so, how much. Sometimes it may be best, for reasons of practicality, to wait until some later time to impose the tax (e.g., where the benefit consists of an item of property that will not be sold until sometime in the future and whose present value is uncertain). Sometimes it may be difficult to separate the business from the personal aspects of such noncash benefits as the use of a well-furnished office or a company limousine.

The cases and other materials that follow in this section reveal how the law has reacted to the competing dictates of fairness, efficiency, and practicality. One background factor must be kept in mind: Use of noncash benefits may make enforcement difficult. The amounts involved tend to be modest; the IRS has bigger fish to fry. Cheating is often difficult to detect. Taxpayers begin to realize that they can get away with certain kinds of cheating—for example, with not reporting the value of the personal use of a company car. They may rely on that disturbing but common defense, "everyone is doing it." The IRS must ever be alert to the dangers inherent in enforcement policies that tend to encourage such attitudes, not so much because the amounts may grow over time (if they do, the IRS can crack down), but because of adverse effects on general taxpayer morale and because, after a sufficiently long period of non-enforcement, taxpayers may begin to rely on, and to feel that they are entitled to continue to enjoy, the tax benefits they have claimed; and Congress may agree.

1. Meals and Lodging Provided to Employees

Suppose that, for federal income tax purposes, a worker's gross income from a job consisted solely of the amount of all paychecks received during the year. Employers and workers would find that they could generate substantial tax savings by changing the form of their transactions, without making any change (the use of the tax savings aside) in how much the employer paid or what the employee got.

Example 1

<u>SILICON VALLEY'S MOUTHWATERING TAX BREAK</u>
Mark Maremont, *Wall St. Journal,* April 7, 2013

When outsiders visit Silicon Valley, the first thing they often notice is the food: Cafeterias brimming with free gourmet meals and snacks offered to employees of Google Inc., Facebook Inc., and other technology firms.

But not all is as it seems in the buffet line. There is growing controversy among tax experts about how to treat these coveted freebies. The Internal Revenue Service also has been focusing on the topic, according to attorneys who practice in the area, examining whether the free food is a fringe benefit on which employees should pay additional tax.

Tax rules around fringe benefits are complex, but in general they categorize meals regularly provided by an employer as a taxable perk, similar to personal use of a company car. That leads several tax experts to wonder if some companies providing free food may be skirting the rules.

* * * *

[Some] lawyers point to an exception that allows meals to remain untaxed if they are served for a "noncompensatory" reason for the "convenience of the employer." The exception generally has been applied to workers in remote locations or in professions where reasonable lunch breaks aren't feasible. But these lawyers argue that some technology firms could qualify, in part because free food encourages longer work hours and is a crucial part of Silicon Valley's collaborative culture.

* * * *

Google has more than 120 cafes world-wide serving over 50,000 meals a day, according to its website, which says the aim is to foster collaboration and healthy eating. A spokeswoman declined to comment on the tax treatment of employee meals. Several former employees who recently left Google said the company didn't include the value of the meals in their paystubs or in W-2 tax statements.

* * * *

Although collectively hundreds of millions of dollars in taxes could be involved, some experts say the more significant issue is fairness. If some employers are allowed to offer tax-free perks, they argue, that puts other employers and employees at a disadvantage, and if left unchecked could spread.

"I buy my lunch with after-tax dollars," said [Professor X], "and I have to pay taxes to support free meals for those Google employees."

Still, an IRS crackdown could raise hackles in the influential technology industry, and generate concerns that the federal government is interfering—for relative pocket change—with a culture that has made Silicon Valley a world leader.

"There are real benefits for knowledge workers in having unplanned, face to face interaction," and free food helps facilitate that, said [Professor Y], who argues that aggressive enforcement of tax laws might be poor public policy in this case.

Although some employers long have been providing free lunches for their executives or even ordinary workers, Silicon Valley has taken the practice to a new level.

A *Gourmet* magazine article last year raved about the "mouthwatering free food" at Google's headquarters in Mountain View, Calif. The article cited dishes such as porcini-encrusted grass-fed beef and noted that nearly half the produce was organic.

* * * *

Facebook's headquarters in nearby Menlo Park, Calif., has two main cafes, plus a barbecue shack, a pizza shop, a burrito bar, and a 50's-style burger joint. Recent menu options at Facebook's Café Epic, which dishes up free food from morning until night, included spicy she-crab soup and grilled steak with chimichurri sauce.

Both Twitter Inc. and Zynga Inc. offer three free meals a day in their San Francisco offices. A Zynga spokeswoman had no comment, and a Twitter spokesman confirmed the free meals policy but otherwise didn't comment.

NOTES AND QUESTIONS

1. Until 2018, companies such as Google deducted all of the cost of providing meals. Thus, non-taxation of employees was accompanied by an employer deduction. The 2017 act limits the employer deduction in the above cases to 50 percent of cost. (These expenses are not deductible at all for years after 2025.) This obviously reduces the tax advantage of employer-provided meals.

2. An employee of Google earning $60,000 per year and receiving free meals along the lines suggested in the *Wall Street Journal* article likely will have lower grocery store bills than an employee of Acme Tool Works with the same salary and nothing but an occasional stale donut in the break room. Would the principle of "horizontal equity"—that taxpayers facing similar economic situations should be taxed similarly—argue that the Google employee has taxable gross income in respect of the value of those meals?

3. How would it affect your thinking to learn that Acme Tool Works is located in a bucolic corner of the country where the living is easy and apartment rentals go for one-third the price of those in Silicon Valley?

4. How would you weigh the idea that Google wants to keep its employees on campus as much of the time as possible, to foster collaboration and to extract as much value as possible from them? In other words, is Google's strong business purpose here relevant to the employees' income?

5. If you do think that the Google employee has gross income, how would you go about measuring it? Would every employee be required to keep a food

diary? If not, how could the IRS collect the tax? Hint: Google and the other employers described in the article deduct the costs of providing the free meals in calculating their corporate incomes, just as they deduct cash salaries.

6. A real-life Google employee, Brandon S., took Google's corporate largesse one step further, and set up living in a box truck in Google's parking lot. Yanan Wan, Life Inside the Box: A Google Engineer's Home in a Truck at Company Headquarters, *Wash. Post,* Oct. 21, 2015. Brandon relies on the company's free food for most meals, showers at the corporate gym, and so on. He has documented his alternative lifestyle on his blog, Thoughts from Inside the Box, https://frominsidethebox.com/. As of August 2016, Brandon estimates that his unusual arrangements have saved him about $21,000 in cash living expenses, net of the cost of the truck. Do you think Brandon should be reporting some of his savings on consumption expenses as income, or is living in a box truck punishment enough?

Example 2

Unitek makes a single $10,000 payment to an insurance company that agrees in return to pay $50,000 to Alice when she reaches the age of 70. Her legal rights to this money are fully vested. That is, she will get the $50,000 at age 70 even if Unitek fires her or goes bankrupt in the interim. She is not entitled to receive any cash payment until she reaches age 70. If she dies before reaching this age, her estate or heirs become entitled to the money on the date when she would have reached age 70. As it turns out, Alice lives to age 70 and receives the $50,000 payout from the insurance company.

QUESTIONS

1. Under *Old Colony,* the Internal Revenue Service argues that Alice has $10,000 of taxable income in the year Unitek paid that amount to the insurance company. In the absence of specific statutory rules concerning retirement benefits, are the issues here identical to those presented by Google's free food?

2. What should be Alice's taxable income upon receiving the $50,000 distribution if the $10,000 employer contribution was included in her income? If it was not?

3. Each year, as Alice grows older, the value of her right to receive the $50,000 increases. How, if at all, should this economic gain be reflected on her annual income tax returns?

BENAGLIA v. COMMISSIONER
36 B.T.A. 838 (1937), acq. 1940-1 C.B. 1

FINDINGS OF FACT

The petitioners are husband and wife, residing in Honolulu, Hawaii, where they filed joint income tax returns for 1933 and 1934.

The petitioner has, since 1926 and including the tax years in question, been employed as the manager in full charge of the several hotels in Honolulu owned and operated by Hawaiian Hotels, Ltd., a corporation of Hawaii, consisting of the Royal Hawaiian, the Moana and bungalows, and the Waialae Golf Club. These are large resort hotels, operating on the American plan. Petitioner was constantly on duty, and, for the proper performance of his duties and entirely for the convenience of his employer, he and his wife occupied a suite of rooms in the Royal Hawaiian Hotel and received their meals at and from the hotel.

Petitioner's salary has varied in different years, being in one year $25,000. In 1933 it was $9,625, and in 1934 it was $11,041.67. These amounts were fixed without reference to his meals and lodging, and neither petitioner nor his employer ever regarded the meals and lodging as part of his compensation or accounted for them.

OPINION

STERNHAGEN, J.

The Commissioner has added $7,845 each year to the petitioner's gross income as "compensation received from Hawaiian Hotels, Ltd.," holding that this is "the fair market value of rooms and meals furnished by the employer." In the deficiency notice he cites article 52 [53], Regulations 77,[12] and holds inapplicable Jones v. United States, 60 Ct. Cls. 552; I.T. 2232; G.C.M. 14710; and G.C.M. 14836. The deficiency notice seems to hold that the rooms and meals were not in fact supplied "merely as a convenience to the hotels" of the employer.

From the evidence, there remains no room for doubt that the petitioner's residence at the hotel was not by way of compensation for his services, not for his personal convenience, comfort or pleasure, but solely because he could not otherwise perform the services required of him. The evidence of both the employer and employee shows in detail what petitioner's duties were and why his residence in the hotel was necessary. His duty was continuous and required his presence at a moment's call. He had a lifelong experience in hotel management and operation in the United States, Canada, and elsewhere, and testified that the functions of the manager could not have been performed by one living outside the hotel, especially a resort hotel such as this. The demands and requirements of guests are numerous, various, and unpredictable, and affect the meals, the rooms, the entertainment, and everything else about the hotel. The manager must be alert to all these things day and night. He would not consider undertaking the job and the owners of the hotel would not consider employing a manager unless he lived there. This was implicit throughout his employment and when his compensation was changed from time to time no

---

12. ["Where services are paid for with something other than money, the fair market value of the thing taken in payment is the amount to be included as income. . . . When living quarters such as camps are furnished to employees for the convenience of the employer, the ratable value need not be added to the cash compensation of the employees, but where a person receives as compensation for services rendered a salary and in addition thereto living quarters, the value to such person of the quarters furnished constitutes income subject to tax."—EDS.]

mention was ever made of it. Both took it for granted. The corporation's books carried no accounting for the petitioner's meals, rooms, or service.

Under such circumstances, the value of meals and lodging is not income to the employee, even though it may relieve him of an expense which he would otherwise bear. In Jones v. United States, *supra*, the subject was fully considered in determining that neither the value of quarters nor the amount received as commutation of quarters by an Army officer is included within his taxable income. There is also a full discussion in the English case of Tennant v. Smith, H.L. (1892) App. Cas. 150, III British Tax Cases 158. A bank employee was required to live in quarters located in the bank building, and it was held that the value of such lodging was not taxable income. The advantage to him was merely an incident of the performance of his duty, but its character for tax purposes was controlled by the dominant fact that the occupation of the premises was imposed upon him for the convenience of the employer. The Bureau of Internal Revenue has almost consistently applied the same doctrine in its published rulings.

The three cases cited by the respondent, Ralph Kitchen, 11 B.T.A. 855; Charles A. Frueauff, 30 B.T.A. 449; and Fontaine Fox, 30 B.T.A. 451, are distinguishable entirely upon the ground that what the taxpayer received was not shown to be primarily for the need or convenience of the employer. Of course, as in the *Kitchen* case, it can not be said as a categorical proposition of law that, where an employee is fed and lodged by his employer, no part of the value of such perquisite is income. If the Commissioner finds that it was received as compensation and holds it to be taxable income, the taxpayer contesting this before the Board must prove by evidence that it is not income. In the *Kitchen* case the Board held that the evidence did not establish that the food and lodging were given for the convenience of the employer. In the present case the evidence clearly establishes that fact, and it has been so found.

The determination of the Commissioner on the point in issue is reversed.

Reviewed by the Board.

Judgment will be entered under Rule 50.

MURDOCK, J., concurs only in the result.

ARNOLD, J., dissenting.

I disagree with the conclusions of fact that the suite of rooms and meals furnished petitioner and his wife at the Royal Hawaiian Hotel were entirely for the convenience of the employer and that the cash salary was fixed without reference thereto and was never regarded as part of his compensation.

Petitioner was employed by a hotel corporation operating two resort hotels in Honolulu — the Royal Hawaiian, containing 357 guest bed rooms, and the Moana, containing 261 guest bed rooms, and the bungalows and cottages in connection with the Moana containing 127 guest bed rooms, and the Waialae Golf Club. His employment was as general manager of both hotels and the golf club.

His original employment was in 1925, and in accepting the employment he wrote a letter to the party representing the employer, with whom he conducted the negotiations for employment, under date of September 10, 1925, in which he says:

> Confirming our meeting here today, it is understood that I will assume the position of general manager of both the Royal Waikiki Beach Hotel (now under construction) and the Moana Hotel in Honolulu, at a yearly salary of $10,000.00, payable monthly, together with living quarters, meals, etc., for myself and wife. In addition I am to receive $20.00 per day while travelling, this however, not to include any railroad or steamship fares, and I [am] to submit vouchers monthly covering all such expenses.

While the cash salary was adjusted from time to time by agreement of the parties, depending on the amount of business done, it appears that the question of living quarters, meals, etc., was not given further consideration and was not thereafter changed. Petitioner and his wife have always occupied living quarters in the Royal Hawaiian Hotel and received their meals from the time he first accepted the employment down through the years before us. His wife performed no services for the hotel company.

This letter, in my opinion, constitutes the basic contract of employment and clearly shows that the living quarters, meals, etc., furnished petitioner and his wife were understood and intended to be compensation in addition to the cash salary paid him. Being compensation to petitioner in addition to the cash salary paid him, it follows that the reasonable value thereof to petitioner is taxable income. Cf. Ralph Kitchen, 11 B.T.A. 855; Charles A. Frueauff, 30 B.T.A. 449.

Conceding that petitioner was required to live at the hotel and that his living there was solely for the convenience of the employer, it does not follow that he was not benefited thereby to the extent of what such accommodations were reasonably worth to him. His employment was a matter of private contract. He was careful to specify in his letter accepting the employment that he was to be furnished with living quarters, meals, etc., for himself and wife, together with the cash salary, as compensation for his employment. Living quarters and meals are necessities which he would otherwise have had to procure at his own expense. His contract of employment relieved him to that extent. He has been enriched to the extent of what they are reasonably worth.

The majority opinion is based on the finding that petitioner's residence at the hotel was solely for the convenience of the employer and, therefore, not income. While it is no doubt convenient to have the manager reside in the hotel, I do not think the question here is one of convenience or of benefit to the employer. What the tax law is concerned with is whether or not petitioner was financially benefited by having living quarters furnished to himself and wife. He may have preferred to live elsewhere, but we are dealing with the financial aspect of petitioner's relation to his employer, not his preference. He says it would cost him $3,600 per year to live elsewhere.

It would seem that if his occupancy of quarters at the Royal Hawaiian was necessary and solely for the benefit of the employer, occupancy of premises at the Moana would be just as essential so far as the management of the Moana was concerned. He did not have living quarters or meals for himself and wife at the Moana and he was general manager of both and both were in operation during the years before us. Furthermore, it appears that petitioner was absent from Honolulu from March 24 to June 8 and from August

19 to November 2 in 1933, and from April 8 to May 24 and from September 3 to November 1 in 1934—about 5 months in 1933 and 3 months in 1934. Whether he was away on official business or not we do not know. During his absence both hotels continued in operation. The $20 per day travel allowance in his letter of acceptance indicates his duties were not confined to managing the hotels in Honolulu, and the entire letter indicates he was to receive maintenance, whether in Honolulu or elsewhere, in addition to his cash salary.

At most the arrangement as to living quarters and meals was of mutual benefit, and to the extent it benefited petitioner it was compensation in addition to his cash salary, and taxable to him as income.

The Court of Claims in the case of Jones v. United States, relied on in the majority opinion, was dealing with a governmental organization regulated by military law where the compensation was fixed by law and not subject to private contract. The English case of Tennant v. Smith, involved the employment of a watchman or custodian for a bank whose presence at the bank was at all times a matter of necessity demanded by the employer as a condition of the employment.

The facts in both these cases are so at variance with the facts in this case that they are not controlling in my opinion.

SMITH, TURNER, and HARRON agree with this dissent.

NOTES AND QUESTIONS

1. Why should it matter whether the reason for giving Benaglia free room and board was the "convenience of the employer"? Wasn't paying him a cash salary also convenient for the employer, since otherwise he would have declined to take the job? Should the court have focused on the value to Benaglia of the free room and board?

2. How does the "convenience of the employer" claim undermine the government's position that the room and board were worth their market price of $7,845? Does it support arguing that the free room and board had zero value to Benaglia?

3. Judge Arnold's dissent notes that Benaglia "says it would cost him $3,600 per year to live elsewhere." Would this provide a good measure of the value of the room and board in this case? In future cases? What about the cost to the employer (including opportunity costs if other paying customers were turned away) of providing the meals and lodging to Benaglia? What if there had been credible evidence either that Benaglia disliked hotel accommodations notwithstanding his choice of career or that he had written a letter to the employer during the wage negotiations in which he offered to find housing within a few blocks of the hotel if his salary were increased by $5,000?

4. Even if one agreed that Benaglia's free room and board should be excluded from income, what about that provided to his wife? Since there is no claim that she was providing hotel management services, should some amount have been included in the Benaglias' income for the benefits to her?

STATUTORY AFTERMATH TO BENAGLIA

Section 119, enacted in 1954, ended the common-law realm of "convenience of the employer" cases such as *Benaglia* by adopting a specific version of their general approach. You can see this by reading §119(a), which states a general rule quite close to the outcome in *Benaglia* (although not resting on the parties' intent). The rest of §119 provides additional detail, including an array of special rules for particular taxpayers, such as employees of educational institutions (§119(d)).

Section 119 is a good example of how the tax law evolves. In this instance, for many years courts were compelled to resolve controversies through application of judge-made principles, resting primarily on common-sense commercial intuitions. With §119, Congress properly took ownership of the issue. In many analogous circumstances, taxpayers have responded to new legislative rules by developing new strategies to avoid them, which in turn lead courts to layer on new common law glosses or Congress to amend the original rule. This iterative process explains much of the Code's complexity.

While §119(a) may look simple on its face, it stands as a good example of how a seemingly minor provision, in terms of revenue and general applicability, can foster an inordinate amount of judicial interpretation and administrative complexity, not to mention repeated congressional intervention. (It has been amended four times since the beginning of 1978.) A key part of the problem is that even, or perhaps especially, a simple English word such as "meal" or "employee" can be ambiguous in practice. Here are some of the terms in §119(a) that a good tax lawyer might immediately spot as potentially ambiguous, followed by a brief account of their litigation history:

(a) *"Meals."* While this term may initially appear unambiguous, what about groceries that the employee selects in the employer's commissary and takes home? Tougher v. Commissioner, 51 T.C. 737 (1969), aff'd per curiam, 441 F.2d 1148 (9th Cir.), cert. denied, 404 U.S. 856 (1971), held that groceries were not within the term "meals." On the other hand, Jacob v. United States, 493 F.2d 1294 (3d Cir. 1974), held that groceries were within the meals exclusion, and also held toilet tissue, soap, and other nonfood items to be excludable under §119 as an integral part of meals and lodging.

(b) *"Furnished."* Is a meal "furnished" by the employer if the employer provides cash to purchase it rather than directly (i.e., through the use of its employees) by supplying the food? In Commissioner v. Kowalski, 434 U.S. 77 (1977), the Court, resolving a conflict among the circuits, held that meal allowance payments to state highway patrol troopers were not excludable under §119 due to failure to satisfy the "furnished" requirement. Thus, in effect, to meet the terms of the statute, the state would need to open its own version of McDonald's or Pizza Hut at various convenient points along the highway, rather than relying on the private sector to supply its troopers with fast food. Subsequent cases have applied Kowalski in seemingly inconsistent ways.

(c) *"Convenience of the employer."* This term presumably refers to business reasons other than compensatory intent for having the employee accept free or below-cost meals and lodging. The difficulty lies in determining how strong the nontax motives must be and how they are to be demonstrated. Section 119(b)(1) sheds some light by stating that "the provisions of an employment contract . . . shall not be taken as determinative of whether the meals or lodging are intended as compensation." Thus, one cannot satisfy the standard simply by adding a contract clause that says, in effect, "Take this free room and board, please," although such a clause may still be legally relevant. In practice, the requisite employer's convenience is most often established by proof that the employee is "on call" outside of business hours. See Rev. Rul. 71-411, 71-2 C.B. 103.

(d) *"Business premises of the employer."* The circuits have split on what constitutes "business premises of the employer" for state police. United States v. Barrett, 321 F.2d 911 (5th Cir. 1963), held that every state road and highway, and evidently adjacent restaurants as well, constitute the business premises of their employer, the state. Accord: United States v. Keeton, 383 F.2d 429 (10th Cir. 1967); United States v. Morelan, 356 F.2d 199 (8th Cir. 1966). Contra: Wilson v. United States, 412 F.2d 694 (1st Cir. 1969). In *Kowalski, supra,* the Supreme Court did not reach the "business premises" issue because it was able to dispose of the case on the basis of the "furnished" language.

In Lindeman v. Commissioner, 60 T.C. 609 (1973), acq., the business premises of a beachfront hotel were held to include a house across the street from it occupied by the hotel's manager and his family. But in Commissioner v. Anderson, 371 F.2d 59 (6th Cir. 1966), cert. denied, 387 U.S. 906 (1967), a house that was two blocks away from the employer's motel and was occupied by its manager was held not to be part of the employer's business premises.

Official residences of the governors of the states, and presumably the White House, also qualify under §119. Rev. Rul. 75-540, 1975-2 C.B. 53.

(e) *"Employee."* Section 119's exclusion is for "an employee," which rules out self-employed persons such as farmers who own and operate their own farms or persons classified as independent contractors (such as a lawyer who does work for various clients). But a person may be treated as the employee of a corporation even if she or he owns all the shares of that corporation and thus in a practical (as opposed to a legal) sense appears to be self-employed. And since corporations are themselves taxpayers, they can potentially deduct the costs of providing meals and lodging to owner-employees who receive these benefits tax free.

In J. Grant Farms, Inc. v. Commissioner, 49 T.C.M. 1197 (1985), Mr. Grant had since 1949 owned and operated a farm. In 1976 he formed a corporation, all the shares of which were owned by himself and his wife. Mr. Grant transferred or leased to the corporation all of the assets used in the farming business, and the corporation formally became the operator of the farm. The corporation hired Mr. Grant as its employee in the role of manager of the farm, and he continued to manage and operate the farm as he had been doing in the past. One of the assets transferred to the corporation was the house in which the Grants and their children lived; the house thus became a business asset of the corporation instead of a personal asset of the Grants. The corporation (remember, it was owned and controlled by the Grants) required Mr. Grant to live in the house as a condition of his employment, and the Tax Court found that there were sound business reasons for this requirement. Accordingly, the corporation was allowed deductions for depreciation and utility costs for the house (which had not previously been allowable to anyone), and Mr. Grant was not required to include any amount in his gross income by virtue of its use by himself and his family.

(f) *University presidents.* Waggish students may enjoy pondering how the official residence of their university president (or law school dean) is treated for purposes of §119, considering both the convenience of the employer test and (in many cases) the business premises of the employer test. See Winchell v. United States, 564 F. Supp. 131 (1983). This will give you something to talk about when you meet the president (or dean) at an official function.

UNITED STATES v. GOTCHER
401 F.2d 118 (5th Cir. 1968)

THORNBERRY, Circuit Judge.

In 1960, Mr. and Mrs. Gotcher took a twelve-day expense-paid trip to Germany to tour the Volkswagen facilities there. The trip cost $1372.30. His employer, Economy Motors, paid $348.73, and Volkswagen of Germany and Volkswagen of America shared the remaining $1023.53. Upon returning, Mr. Gotcher bought a twenty-five percent interest in Economy Motors, the Sherman, Texas Volkswagen dealership, that had been offered to him before he left. Today he is President of Economy Motors in Sherman and owns fifty percent of the dealership. Mr. and Mrs. Gotcher did not include any part of the $1372.30 in their 1960 income. The Commissioner determined that the taxpayers had realized income to the extent of the $1372.30 for the expense-paid trip and asserted a tax deficiency of $356.79, plus interest. Taxpayers paid the deficiency, plus $82.29 in interest, and thereafter timely filed suit for a refund. The district court, sitting without a jury, held that the cost of the trip was not income or, in the alternative, was income and deductible as an ordinary and necessary business expense. *259 F. Supp. 340.* We affirm the district court's determination that the cost of the trip was not income to Mr. Gotcher ($686.15); however, Mrs. Gotcher's expenses ($686.15) constituted income and were not deductible.

Section 61 defines gross income as income from whatever source derived and specifically includes fifteen items within this definition. The court below reasoned that the cost of the trip to the Gotchers was not income because an economic or financial benefit does not constitute income under section 61 unless it is conferred as compensation for services rendered. This conception of gross income is too restrictive since it is well-settled that section 61 should be broadly interpreted and that many items, including noncompensatory gains, constitute gross income.[13]

Sections 101-123 specifically exclude certain items from gross income. Appellant argues that the cost of the trip should be included in income since it is not specifically excluded by sections 101-123, reasoning that Section 61 was drafted broadly to subject all economic gains to tax and any exclusions should

---

13. See *Commissioner of Internal Revenue v. Glenshaw Glass Co.* 348 U.S. 426 (1955).

be narrowly limited to the specific exclusions. This analysis is too restrictive since it has been generally held that exclusions from gross income are not limited to the enumerated exclusions.

In determining whether the expense-paid trip was income within section 61 we must look to the tests that have been developed under this section. The concept of economic gain to the taxpayer is the key to section 61. H. Simons, Personal Income Taxation 51 (1938). This concept contains two distinct requirements: There must be an economic gain, and this gain must primarily benefit the taxpayer personally. In some cases, as in the case of an expense-paid trip, there is no direct economic gain, but there is an indirect economic gain inasmuch as a benefit has been received without a corresponding diminution in wealth. Yet even if expense-paid items, as meals and lodging, are received by the taxpayer, the value of these items will not be gross income, even though the employee receives some incidental benefit, if the meals and lodging are primarily for the convenience of the employer. See section 119.

In two cases, *Rudolph v. United States, 5th Cir. 1961, 291 F.2d 841,* and *Patterson v. Thomas, 5th Cir. 1961, 289 F.2d 108,* this Court has examined expense-paid trips and held that the value of these trips constituted income. Both of these cases involved conventions for insurance salesmen, and in both it was evident that the trip was awarded as compensation for past services. The instant case differs from *Rudolph* and *Patterson* in that there is no evidence in the record to indicate that the trip was an award for past services since Mr. Gotcher was not an employee of VW of Germany and he did nothing to earn that part of the trip paid by Economy Motors.

The trip was made in 1959 when VW was attempting to expand its local dealerships in the United States. The "Buy American" campaign and the fact that the VW people felt they had a "very ugly product" prompted them to offer these tours of Germany to prospective dealers. . . . In 1959, when VW began to push for its share of the American market, its officials determined that the best way to remove the apprehension about this foreign product was to take the dealer to Germany and have him see his investment first-hand. It was believed that once the dealer saw the manufacturing facilities and the stability of the "new Germany" he would be convinced that VW was for him.

* * * *

The question, therefore, is what tax consequences should follow from an expense-paid trip that primarily benefits the party paying for the trip. In several analogous situations the value of items received by employees has been excluded from gross income when these items were primarily for the benefit of the employer. Section 119 excludes from gross income of an employee the value of meals and lodging furnished to him for the convenience of the employer. Even before these items were excluded by the 1954 Code, the Treasury and the courts recognized that they should be excluded from gross income. Thus it appears that the value of any trip that is paid by the employer or by a businessman primarily for his own benefit should be excluded from gross income of the payee on similar reasoning.

* * * *

Here, although taxpayer was not forced to go, there is no doubt that in the reality of the business world he had no real choice. The trial judge reached the same conclusion. He found that the invitation did not specifically order the dealers to go, but that as a practical matter it was an order or directive that if a person was going to be a VW dealer, sound business judgment necessitated his accepting the offer of corporate hospitality. So far as Economy Motors was concerned, Mr. Gotcher knew that if he was going to be a part-owner of the dealership, he had better do all that was required to foster business relations with VW. Besides having no choice but to go, he had no control over the schedule or the money spent. One does not realize taxable income when he is serving a legitimate business purpose of the party paying the expenses. VW did all the planning. In cases involving noncompensatory economic gains, courts have emphasized that the taxpayer still had complete dominion and control over the money to use it as he wished to satisfy personal desires or needs. Indeed, the Supreme Court has defined income as accessions of wealth over which the taxpayer has complete control. *Commissioner of Internal Revenue v. Glenshaw Glass Co., supra.* Clearly, the lack of control works in taxpayers' favor here.

[T]he cases involving corporate officials who have traveled or entertained clients at the company's expense are apposite. Indeed, corporate executives have been furnished yachts, *Challenge Mfg. Co. v. Commissioner, 1962, 37 T.C. 650,* taken safaris as part of an advertising scheme, *Sanitary Farms Dairy, Inc., 1955, 25 T.C. 463,* and investigated business ventures abroad, but have been held accountable for expenses paid only when the court was persuaded that the expenditure was primarily for the officer's personal pleasure. . . . [T]his trip was not given as a pleasurable excursion through Germany or as a means of teaching taxpayer the skills of selling. He had been selling cars since 1949. The personal benefits and pleasure were incidental to the dominant purpose of improving VW's position on the American market and getting people to invest money.

The corporate-executive decisions indicate that some economic gains, though not specifically excluded from section 61, may nevertheless escape taxation. They may be excluded even though the entertainment and travel unquestionably give enjoyment to the taxpayer and produce indirect economic gains. When this indirect economic gain is subordinate to an overall business purpose, the recipient is not taxed. We are convinced that the personal benefit to Mr. Gotcher from the trip was merely incidental to VW's sales campaign.

As for Mrs. Gotcher, the trip was primarily a vacation. She did not make the tours with her husband to see the local dealers or attend discussions about the VW organization. This being so the primary benefit of the expense-paid trip for the wife went to Mr. Gotcher in that he was relieved of her expenses. He should therefore be taxed on the expenses attributable to his wife.

NOTES AND QUESTIONS

1. You are offered a "call back" job interview at Dewey, Cheatem, and Howe, located in New York City. You are flown to New York in business class, put up at a four-star hotel, and wined and dined the evenings before and after your on-site interviews. Explain why you have no income from this trip.

2. The court in *Gotcher* concluded that the portion of costs attributable to Mrs. Gotcher's participation constituted income to the couple. Imagine that Mrs. Gotcher had no particular interest in touring Germany, or VW factories, or meeting VW executives and their spouses, but did so solely to accommodate Mr. Gotcher's business interests. Should Mrs. Gotcher be taxed on her share of the costs? Wouldn't a medal be the more appropriate response?

2. Other Fringe Benefit Statutes

Meals and lodging are only two examples of fringe benefits, meaning noncash benefits provided at no charge or at a below-market price by an employer to an employee. Among the most important of such benefits are life insurance, medical insurance and payments, discounts on merchandise, parking, company cars, airline travel, club memberships, and tuition remissions. In many cases these benefits substitute for cash; they relieve employees of expenses they would otherwise incur and are intended as compensation. Yet often they have not been taxed, which explains in part why over the years they became an increasingly important part of employee compensation. Fringe benefits raise problems of valuation, enforcement, and political acceptance.

The problems of valuation are similar to those we have already examined in this chapter. The value of a particular benefit to the person receiving it may depend on the circumstances of that person. Consider, for example, airline employees who are permitted to fly free, or at reduced cost, on their employers' flights. Would it make sense to include in income the amount that ordinary passengers would be required to pay for the same flight? Even if employees are required to fly on a standby basis? Or what about life insurance supplied to a single person with no dependents? Or a government-owned limousine that drives the Commissioner of Internal Revenue from home to the office in the morning, to meetings around town during the day, and back home at night? Is it relevant if the limousine has a reading lamp and a telephone?

Through the years, some fringe benefits were excluded as a result of the Service's inaction (e.g., parking supplied or paid for by an employer and air travel by airline employees) or acquiescence (e.g., tuition remission). Others were excluded by express statutory provisions, including $50,000 worth of group term life insurance (§79), medical insurance and payments (§§105(b), 106), and dependent care assistance (§129). Finally, in 1984 Congress enacted §132, providing comprehensive coverage of fringe benefits. We next discuss certain statutory exclusions, followed by the state of the law where no such exclusion applies.

SECTION 132 FRINGE BENEFITS

The basic approach taken in §132 was to offer taxpayers and the Internal Revenue Service a "ceasefire in place": statutory exclusion for well-established taxpayer practices (or those supported by significant political clout), in exchange for forestalling further expansion of such practices. To the latter end, §61(a)(1), specifying that gross income includes compensation for services, was amended to include a specific mention of fringe benefits. The main fringe benefits that §132 presently makes excludable are:

(1) "no-additional cost services," such as free seating for airline employees on flights that would not otherwise have sold out (§132(b));

(2) "qualified employee discounts," such as when a department store permits its employees to purchase at a modest discount items that are sold to customers (§132(c));

(3) "working condition fringes," such as the business use of a company car or a free subscription to a magazine that relates to the employee's job (e.g., where a brokerage house buys a financial publication for its brokers) (§132(d));

(4) "de minimis fringes," or those of sufficiently low value to make accounting for them "unreasonable or administratively impractical" (§132(e)(1)). A special rule extends the reach of this provision to certain eating facilities (§132(e)(2)), without regard to whether they would otherwise qualify;

(5) "qualified transportation fringes," such as employer-provided parking or mass transit passes (§132(f)). Note, however, that under the 2017 act, these expenses are no longer deductible to employers.

(6) "qualified retirement planning services" (§132(m)); and

(7) certain "on-premises gyms and other athletic facilities" (§132(j)(4)).

No-additional cost services and qualified employee discounts, but not the other items on this list, are subject to two further restrictions. First, in order to claim either exclusion, one must work in a line of business of the employer in which the item at issue is ordinarily offered for sale to customers (§§132(b)(1) and (c)(4)). Thus, if the same corporation operated both an airline and a department store, airline workers would be taxed on receiving discount department store goods, and department store workers would be taxed on receiving free airline flights. Second, neither of these two exclusions applies to "highly compensated employees" if the employer discriminates in favor of such employees in determining to whom a given fringe benefit is available (§132(j)(1)).

"No-additional cost services" and "qualified employee discounts," as well as "qualified tuition reduction" (§117(d)), may be provided tax free to an employee's spouse, surviving spouse, or dependent children (§132(h)) but not to others such as same-sex domestic partners. See Private Letter Ruling 200137041.

QUESTIONS

1. Suppose that an airline offers free seating to its employees on a standby basis (i.e., only for seats that are not sold as of boarding time), qualifying for exclusion as a no-additional-cost service. Can the exclusion be defended on the ground that, if the employees were taxed on the value of the seating, they would simply decline to go, leading to pointless waste as the seats stayed vacant and the Commissioner got no revenue from attempting to impose a tax? Or is the point simply that overvaluation, like undervaluation, can result in mismeasuring ability to pay and/or distorting economic decisions?

2. Why limit tax-free no-additional-cost services and qualified employee discounts to employees in the line of business of the employer in which the item at issue is ordinarily offered for sale to customers?

3. Why deny the exclusion for a no-additional-cost service or a qualified employee discount to highly compensated employees when the employer discriminates in favor of such employees in determining to whom the item is available? Even if the employer disdains its rank-and-file employees, is its self-interest served by offering them these benefits if excludable?

4. Review the various subsections of §132 that include "special rules" for air transportation (e.g., §132(h)(3), §132(j)(5)). Can you think of any principled reason why the exclusion of a no-additional-cost service should extend to the parents of employees in the airline industry (§132(h)(3)) but not to the parents of those employed in other industries? Although the Internal Revenue Code is a highly technical compendium of rules, it is important to keep in mind that it is, at bottom, a political document. When reviewing this and other provisions of the tax code, be on the lookout for "special rules" like these. If you do a little independent digging, you will find that each one has its own unique political history. But before joining the chorus of critics who decry the extension of special interest favors for the well-connected, ask yourself whether some other provision that you like would have been enacted without the political "grease" furnished by these "special rules." Then decide: Are you a tax code purist or a political realist? Can you be both?

FURTHER NOTES ON FRINGE BENEFITS

1. *Valuation: The regulations.* The Treasury has published detailed regulations on fringe benefits. Reg. §1.61-21 and §1.132-1 to -8. These regulations include rules for valuation of certain fringe benefits, most significantly the personal use of employer-provided aircraft and automobiles. The basic valuation rule is that the amount to be included is "fair market value." Reg. §1.61-21(b). Special optional "safe-harbor" valuation formulas are provided, however, for aircraft and automobiles, and it can be expected that most employers and employees will use these formulas. While the rules are lengthy and detailed, individual employers and employees will generally be able to focus on the relatively few rules relevant to them. A reading of the regulations will provide a good sense of the interplay between the need to impose fair tax burdens and prevent tax avoidance and the need to have common-sense, workable rules.

2. *Cafeteria plans.* A "cafeteria plan" is a plan under which an employee may choose to designate a specified amount of his future salary to be applied instead to one or more noncash nontaxable benefits. In other words, an employee may elect to swap taxable salary for noncash benefits. This makes it possible for an employer to provide nontaxable fringe benefits to those employees who want them without disfavoring employees who have no need for them. For example, suppose an employer has two employees, each earning $35,000 a year. One employee has children and pays $5,000 a year to babysitters while he is at work. The other employee has no children. Under a cafeteria plan, the employer

can allow the employee with children to take his compensation in the form of $30,000 worth of taxable salary and $5,000 worth of child-care payments (nontaxable under §129). Meanwhile, the other employee can elect to take the entire $35,000 in salary; all of this is taxable, but he is no worse off than he would be if there were no cafeteria plan. The employer is allowed to deduct the full $35,000 for each employee.

Section 125 expressly authorizes cafeteria plans. Were it not for that provision, the doctrine of constructive receipt (discussed later) would result in an employee being taxed on the cash that he or she could have received by not putting money into the cafeteria plan, notwithstanding that the employee elected a benefit that would have been nontaxable if it were mandatorily made available to all employees without any ability to opt out. Section 125 greatly increases the potential use of nontaxable fringe benefits by removing the element of employee envy that would restrain an employer from offering fringe benefits for which some employees have no use.

Section 125 limits the fringe benefits that can be included in a cafeteria plan and imposes a nondiscrimination rule. The permissible benefits include group-term life insurance (up to $50,000) (§79); dependent care assistance (§129); adoption assistance (§137); excludable accident and health benefits, subject to a cap of $2,500/year for health flexible spending accounts (§105 and §106(a)); and elective contributions under a qualified cash or deferred arrangement under §401(k).

One important aspect of cafeteria plans is the so-called use-it-or-lose-it rule. See §125(d)(2)(A) and Proposed Reg. §1.125-1. Under this rule, if, for example, an employee elects at the beginning of the year to take $5,000 worth of child-care reimbursement instead of the same amount of cash compensation or other benefits, any part of the $5,000 not used for child care will be lost to the employee. The unused portion cannot at the end of the year be paid out to the employee as additional taxable compensation or carried forward to the next year. An exception allows a change in election of benefits or cash during the year on account of, and consistent with, a change in family status (e.g., marriage, divorce, or death of a child). The rationale offered by the Treasury in support of the use-it-or-lose-it rule is that nontaxable benefits under cafeteria plans are supposed to be in the nature of insurance. Why so? Some evidence in testimony by Treasury officials before Congress indicates their concern about the substantial loss of revenue associated with increasing use of cafeteria plans.

The use-it-or-lose-it rule presents a good example of how the income tax laws often try to limit the extent to which taxpayers can take advantage of favorable planning opportunities. The rule imposes burdens on taxpayers that in some respects seem pointless and wasteful. In order to get the maximum benefit from the exclusion, employees must engage up front in relatively precise forecasting and planning of their expected expenses. If they aim too high, they risk losing some of their salary for the year. Or, they may end up purchasing medical or other covered services at year's end that they do not really need or value very highly. Healthcare providers, among others, have found that §125 is great for business in December!

3. *Frequent flyer credits.* Most airlines now have "frequent flyer" programs, under which passengers can earn credits that can be accumulated and traded in for tickets or for upgrades. (Credits may also be earned from hotel stays and car rentals.) When these credits are earned from personal travel they can best be thought of as reductions in the price of the flights (or hotel stays or car rentals) from which they are earned — as if the ticket cost consists of a package of a flight plus credits — and there should be, and is, no tax consequence. For business trips, however, clearly there is a tax issue. Suppose, for example, that Ada, an employee of Baker Co., takes a flight for Baker Co.'s business purposes. Baker Co. pays for the ticket, but Ada receives the frequent flyer credits in her own name. Baker Co.'s cost for the ticket plainly should be, and is, a deductible business expense. If Ada flies frequently enough to accumulate entitlement to a free ticket, and if she uses the free ticket for a business flight, Baker Co. is not properly chargeable with taxable gain. Again, the free ticket is just a reduction in Baker Co.'s cost of earlier tickets.

Suppose, however, that Ada uses the credits for a ticket or an upgrade for a purely personal trip (with or without Baker Co.'s acquiescence). Ada has plainly received a benefit, and most tax experts would agree that she has income in some amount. But how much? Generally, use of frequent flyer credits has some limitations; often, for example, they cannot be used during peak travel periods. Moreover, for all we know, if Ada had not had the credit she might not have taken the flight or the upgrade. And, given the fact that airlines charge many different fares for the same flight, who knows what Ada's ticket would have cost? Beyond that, she may have used credits from a combination of personal trips for which she paid and business trips for which Baker Co. paid. Keeping track of the relative amounts might be difficult. What is more, treating the use of the business-derived credits as income would impose significant administrative costs on the IRS.

For many years the IRS, although well aware of the tax issue, made no effort to impose tax liability, despite some criticism (largely from academics and other spoilsports). Business travelers became accustomed to using the credits for personal purposes without including any amount in income. Finally, in 2002, the IRS officially threw in the towel, issuing Announcement 2002-18 (2002-10 I.R.B. 621), which stated:

> Consistent with prior practice, the IRS will not assert that any taxpayer has understated his federal tax liability by reason of the receipt or personal use of frequent flyer miles or other in-kind promotional benefits attributable to the taxpayer's business or official travel. . . .

This relief does not apply to travel or other promotional benefits that are converted to cash, to compensation that is paid in the form of travel or other promotional benefits, or in other circumstances where these benefits are used for tax avoidance purposes.

If you had been Commissioner of Internal Revenue, would you have authorized the issuance of this Announcement? Bear in mind that as Commissioner you would be a high-level political appointee, probably from private tax practice. You might want to think about the fact that members of Congress are frequent flyers.

Suppose that a respected member of your staff had proposed that, rather than adopt a policy of no taxation, the Announcement should impute a value of $100 per flight (round trip) for free tickets received by an employee using miles earned from travel for the employer. The $100 value would presumably be lower than the fair market value of the flight and lower than the value placed upon the flight by nearly all frequent fliers. What would your reaction be? Which of the problems mentioned above would be eliminated?

4. *Employer deduction.* One of the barriers to taxing employees on fringe benefits is that often the value to each employee is small and difficult to determine, for example, the value of meals supplied to employees at a company cafeteria. One way to respond to this problem is to ignore the income to the employees but deny the employer a deduction for the amount of the subsidy, that is, the amount by which the cost of the meals exceeds the payments received from employees. The effect is to treat the employer, for taxpaying purposes, as a surrogate for the employees. Another possibility is to impose a special tax on the amount of the subsidy, using a rate intended to approximate the rate at which the employees would be taxed.

5. *Benefits from other than employer.* Suppose that a school principal receives unsolicited sample books from the publishers. Even if the books could be sold, it would not seem proper to include the value of the books in the gross income of the principal. After all, they are not items for personal consumption, nor do they provide the wherewithal to acquire consumption items, except by trade or barter. And even if the value of the books were included in income, an offsetting deduction for the same amount, as a business expense (§162), might seem appropriate. Accordingly, exclusion seems sensible. On the other hand, if the books are sold, the proceeds surely should be included in income. If the taxpayer gives the books to a charity (e.g., the school's library) and claims their value as a deduction, it is as if they had been sold and the proceeds given to charity. Any amount allowed as a charitable deduction should be included in income. It was so held in Haverly v. United States, 513 F.2d 224 (7th Cir.), cert. denied, 423 U.S. 912 (1975). In Rev. Rul. 70-498, 1970-2 C.B. 6, the Service ruled that sample books (received by a book reviewer for a newspaper) would be taxable only if the taxpayer donated them to charity and claimed a deduction for that donation.

QUESTIONS

What tax treatment is required by §132 in each of the following situations?

1. *F*, a flight attendant in the employ of *A*, an airline company, and *F*'s spouse decide to spend their annual vacation in Europe. *A* has a policy whereby any of its employees, along with members of their immediate families, may take a number of personal flights annually for a nominal charge, on a standby basis. *F* and *F*'s spouse take advantage of this policy and fly to and from Europe.

2. *P* is the president of *C*, a corporation that has its executive offices situated in New York City. *P* is planning a week-long business trip to Los Angeles and

will fly there and back on *C*'s corporate jet. *P*'s spouse intends to accompany *P* on the round-trip flight for personal reasons.

3. *S*, a senior vice president of *D*, a retail department store, purchases a refrigerator from *D*'s appliance department. *D* has a policy whereby all employees are entitled to a 20 percent discount from the ticketed sales price of any item sold by the store so long as the resulting sales price, on average, approximately covers *D*'s costs. See §132(c), Reg. §1.132-3(c).

4. The facts are the same as in Question 3 except that *D*'s profit margin on ticketed items is only 10 percent, so the resultant sales price does not cover *D*'s costs.

5. The facts are the same as in Question 3 except that the discount is available only to *S* and other officers of *D*.

6. *A*, an assistant manager in the employ of *D*, a department store, is occasionally required to work overtime to help mark down merchandise for special sales. On those occasional instances, *D* pays for the actual cost of *A*'s evening meal. Such payment is pursuant to company policy whereby *D* will pay the actual, reasonable meal expense of a management-level employee when such an expense is incurred in connection with the performance of services either before or after such an employee's regular business hours.

7. *S*, a senior partner of *L*, a law firm, is provided free parking by the law firm. This benefit is provided by *L* to all partners, associates, and other employees. The parking privilege has a value of $75 per month. See §132(f)(5)(E).

8. *A*, an attorney in the employ of *C*, a corporation, works at *C*'s national headquarters. *C* maintains an on-site gymnasium that is available to all employees during normal business hours. *A* uses the gymnasium each working day.

3. Health Insurance

The most important of all employee noncash benefits is health insurance provided by one's employer, the annual value of which can exceed $10,000 per employee. Under current law, employers are allowed to deduct the cost of medical insurance they buy for their employees. At the same time, the benefits received by employees are excluded from their gross income. §106(a). The exclusion extends to an employee's spouse or dependents. See Reg. §1.106-1. The benefits are also excluded from wages for the purposes of determining payroll tax (e.g., Social Security and Medicare). We discuss the exclusion in connection with the limited deduction given medical expenses that are not covered by employer-provided health insurance.

4. Another Approach to Valuation

As the prior three sections showed, the employment setting has mainly been characterized by an all-or-nothing approach to including in-kind benefits. Items tend either to be wholly excludable (as under §§119 and 132), or else included at their fair market value without regard to any argument that they were worth less to the taxpayer. The following case adopts a different approach in the setting of a quiz-show award.

TURNER v. COMMISSIONER
13 T.C.M. 462 (1954)

MEMORANDUM FINDINGS OF FACT AND OPINION

The Commissioner determined a deficiency of $388.96 in the income tax of the petitioners for 1948. The only question for decision is the amount which should be included in income because of the winning by Reginald of steamship tickets by answering a question on a radio program.

FINDINGS OF FACT

The petitioners are husband and wife who filed a joint return for 1948 with the collector of internal revenue for the District of North Carolina. They reported salary of $4,536.16 for 1948.

Reginald, whose name had been selected by chance from a telephone book, was called on the telephone on April 18, 1948 and was asked to name a song that was being played on a radio program. He gave the correct name of the song and then was given the opportunity to identify a second song and thus to compete for a grand prize. He correctly identified the second song and in consideration of his efforts was awarded a number of prizes, including two round trip first-class steamship tickets for a cruise between New York City and Buenos Aires. The prize was to be one ticket if the winner was unmarried, but, if he was married, his wife was to receive a ticket also. The tickets were not transferable and were good only within one year on a sailing date approved by the agent of the steamship company.

The petitioners reported income on their return of $520, representing income from the award of the two tickets. The Commissioner, in determining the deficiency, increased the income from this source to $2,220, the retail price of such tickets.

Marie was born in Brazil. The petitioners had two sons. Reginald negotiated with the agent of the steamship company, as a result of which he surrendered his rights to the two first-class tickets, and upon payment of $12.50 received four round-trip tourist steamship tickets between New York City and Rio de Janeiro. The petitioners and their two sons used those tickets in making a trip from New York City to Rio de Janeiro and return during 1948.

The award of the tickets to Reginald represented income to him in the amount of $1,400.

OPINION

Persons desiring to buy round trip first-class tickets between New York and Buenos Aires in April 1948, similar to those to which the petitioners were entitled, would have had to pay $2,220 for them. The petitioners, however, were not such persons. The winning of the tickets did not provide them with something which they needed in the ordinary course of their lives and for which they would have made an expenditure in any event, but merely gave them an opportunity to enjoy a luxury otherwise beyond their means. Their value to the petitioners was not equal to their retail cost. They were not transferable and not salable and there were other restrictions on their use. But even had the petitioner been permitted to sell them, his experience with other more salable articles indicates that he would have had to accept substantially less than the cost of similar tickets purchased from the steamship company and would have had selling expenses. Probably the petitioners could have refused the tickets and avoided the tax problem. Nevertheless, in order to obtain such benefits as they could from winning the tickets, they actually took a cruise accompanied by their two sons, thus obtaining free board, some savings in living expenses, and the pleasure of the trip. It seems proper that a substantial amount should be included in their income for 1948 on account of the winning of the tickets. The problem of arriving at a proper fair figure for this purpose is difficult. The evidence to assist is meager, perhaps unavoidably so. The Court, under such circumstances, must arrive at some figure and has done so.

NOTES AND QUESTIONS

1. The court's decision seems to imply that $2,200 was the price for tickets that were identical to the taxpayers' but transferable. Suppose there had been evidence that nonrefundable, nontransferable tickets, precisely identical to those awarded to the Turners had a retail price of $1,900. Would this have made it an open-and-shut case, with $1,900 clearly the amount includable? Or would the Turners' argument that the tickets' value to them was less than the retail price have remained as relevant as in the actual case?

2. Why exactly could the Turners argue (persuasively, as it turned out) that the tickets' value to them was less than the retail price? Should it have mattered that they were able to exchange two first-class tickets to Buenos Aires for four tourist-class tickets to Rio de Janeiro, thus permitting them to take their children and visit the country where Mrs. Turner was born?

3. How do you think the court determined that the value of the tickets to the Turners was $1,400? Might it have averaged the opposing "bids" ($520 + $2,220 = $2,740/2 = $1,370) and then rounded off this number to the nearest $100 increment?

4. It is useful to keep in mind exactly what matters about the arbitrariness of the court's precise finding as to value. Despite the lack of any evident basis for the court's precise determination, the $1,400 value it selected may conceivably have come closer to measuring the tickets' value accurately than either the Commissioner's or the taxpayer's position (although, how would one know this?). The problem with the arbitrariness of the court's determination is less that it was unlikely to be exactly correct than that it provided little guidance as to what value taxpayers in similar circumstances should report in the future.

5. Another subjective valuation case is McCoy v. Commissioner, 38 T.C. 841 (1962), acq., in which the taxpayer won a new Lincoln car in a sales contest. The car's cost to the employer ($4,453) was more than half of the taxpayer's income for the year (about $7,500), and he did not own another car. He drove the Lincoln for ten days and then traded it in for a Ford station wagon (with a dealer's price of $2,600) plus $1,000 cash. The court, exercising its "best judgment" where the "evidence adduced does not permit of an exact determination of . . . fair market value," held that the amount includable in income was $3,900 (38 T.C. at 844). On the other hand, in Rooney v. Commissioner, 88 T.C. 523 (1988), the court required members of an accounting firm who had reluctantly accepted payment in the form of goods and services in payment of fees to include these items at their market prices. The court approvingly quoted the following language from an earlier case: "[T]he use of any such subjective measure of value as is suggested is contrary to the usual way of valuing either services or property, and would make the administration of the tax laws in this area depend upon a knowledge by the Commissioner of the state of mind of the individual taxpayer. We do not think that tax administration should be based upon anything so whimsical" (88 T.C. at 528).

6. Carla, a contestant on a game show, wins a new car. The show's producer received the car free from the manufacturer because of the advertising value of its use on the show. The ordinary dealer cost of the car is $20,000 and the "sticker" price is $25,000. Carla tries to sell the car, but the best offer she gets is $16,000, and she therefore decides to keep it. She hires you for professional tax advice concerning the amount, if any, that she must include as income on her federal income tax return. Her exact words to you are "Just tell me the answer." What sort of advice should you give her? How should you frame your response? In thinking about how you'll approach the situation, assume that you'll be up for partner next year at your law firm and that Carla owns a business that could provide lots of fees for the firm.

F.   PRICE ADJUSTMENT OR INCOME?

Consider these hypotheticals:

1. You walk by a boutique and see in the window a pair of Manolo Blahnik shoes that you are desperate to own, but you are put off by the price: $800. Two weeks later you walk by the same boutique, see a "Going Out of Business" sign, and are able to buy the shoes for $350. It's still an extravagant price, but you love them, and besides, you can tell your friends how you saved $450. Is the $450 you saved income to you?

The answer is no. You purchased shoes for $350, and that's an end to it. Not spending money to buy something is not income. If it were, then having the good sense not to buy the shoes at all would mean that you had income of $800.

2. Now this case: You buy a new big screen TV for $1,000 at a local retailer and receive from the retailer a $200 debit card as a "free gift" for your purchase. Income of $200 or an $800 TV?

In Generic Legal Advice Memorandum 2014-004, the IRS summarized the principle at work in this and similar cases as follows:

> As established in case law, the test for whether a payment, credit, allowance or rebate is a purchase price adjustment is what the parties intend and for what purpose the payment, credit, allowance, or rebate was paid. If the purpose was to adjust the price of the item between the parties, then the consideration given, in whatever form, is a purchase price adjustment and is not a separate item of gross income. The seminal case addressing purchase price adjustments is Pittsburgh Milk v. Commissioner, 26 T.C. 707 (1956). There the Tax Court concluded that allowances that a milk producer paid to buyers lowered the sales price of the milk for income tax purposes. The Tax Court held that only the net price was includable in the seller's gross income, even though the discounts were illegal. The Tax Court stated:
>
> > It does not follow, of course, that all allowances, discounts, and rebates made by a seller of property constitute adjustments to the selling prices. Terminology, alone, is not controlling; and each type of transaction must be analyzed with respect to its own facts and surrounding circumstances. Such examination may reveal that a particular allowance has been given for a separate consideration—as in the case of rebates made in consideration of additional purchases of specified quantity over a specified subsequent period; or as in the case of allowances made in consideration of prepayment of an account receivable, so as to be in effect a payment of interest. The test to be applied, as in the interpretation of most business transactions, is: What did the parties really intend, and for what purpose or consideration was the allowance actually made? Where, as here, the intention and purpose of the allowance was to provide a formula for adjusting a specified gross price to an agreed net price, and where the making of such adjustment was not contingent upon any subsequent performance or consideration from the purchaser, then, regardless of the time or manner of the adjustment, the net selling price agreed upon must be given recognition for income tax purposes.

26 T.C. at 716-717.

3. In Rev. Proc. 2000-30, 2000-2 C.B. 113, the IRS concluded that "gifts" or "premiums" for opening a bank account constitute gross income, unless they are de minimis in amount. Why might the analysis be different for this case than in the case of the debit card received when one purchases a TV?

4. In the United States, automobiles generally are sold to retail purchasers by independent dealers. Indeed, many states require this business structure (an issue being contested by Tesla Motors in particular). As a result, retail purchasers have no privity with the manufacturer. It is common, however, for manufacturers to offer cash rebates directly to retail purchasers. Should those be treated as purchase price adjustments, notwithstanding the lack of privity? See Rev. Rul. 76-96, 1976-1 C.B. 23. If you were Commissioner of Internal Revenue, what administrative and practical concerns might be relevant to you here?

5. What would your advice be to an affected taxpayer in this case of even more attenuated privity?

RESIDENTS MAY HAVE TO PAY TAXES ON THEIR TURF
REBATE MONEY
Matt Stevens and Taylor Goldenstein, *Los Angeles Times,*
September 22, 2015

Thousands of Southern Californians who received checks to tear out their lawns and replace them with more drought-friendly landscapes may have to pay taxes on the rebate money they received.

To prepare for that possibility, officials from the Metropolitan Water District of Southern California—which funded a $340-million incentive program—say they have begun collecting tax identification numbers and other information from program participants who received rebates of more than $600.

Those customers may be receiving 1099s from the MWD by the end of the year, said Deven Upadhyay, an MWD manager. But Upadhyay emphasized that the agency has "not made a decision" about whether the forms will be sent.

"There is a bit of lack of clarity on this," he said.

California provides a tax exemption for turf removal rebates, Upadhyay said, but the federal tax code only provides an exemption for rebates related to energy efficiency. The state Franchise Tax Board has asked the IRS to clarify whether the exemption also applies to water-efficiency rebates, Upadhyay said.

MWD is awaiting a response. The agency would be supportive of an exemption, Upadhyay said.

In the meantime, people in the process of getting a rebate must now provide their tax identification numbers online. MWD officials are also emailing customers who have already received their rebate checks and asking them to provide the information that the agency needs.

MWD has already been providing 1099s to commercial customers that got more than $600 in rebate money, "so it is something that's been on our minds," Upadhyay said. There has always been language "about the potential tax liability," in signup agreements, he added.

"We're only a few weeks into this, so who knows if this becomes an issue or not," Upadhyay said. "Is it something that people are going to be concerned with that would affect their participation? I don't know."

So far, more than 24,000 homeowners have already received or have been approved to receive a rebate of $600 or more, according to MWD records.

In some cases, residents received rebates of more than $70,000. The average residential rebate totals about $3,000, according to the MWD data.

The $340 million in program funding ran dry in July.

"We're certainly not in a position to be providing tax advice," Upadhyay said, though he added, "if it is something they're going to report on their taxes, the larger the amount, the more potential tax liability they would have."

Since the date of this article the Metropolitan Water District in fact has issued Form 1099-MISC (the form used by payers of miscellaneous income) to taxpayers receiving turf rebates over $600.

6. The following is a comment posted on a website on which taxpayers ventilated about the turf-rebate issue. What would you tell this individual if she asked you to confirm her proposed tax return position?

What a scam! I spent close to $5,000 on the installation of synthetic turf and when I had an appraisal done on my home it didn't even raise the property value a cent! They added $0 in improvements to the home. Now on top of being out $5,000 I am now going to have to pay taxes on $1,500 in rebates. Had I known I would have never removed the turf. I was under the impression it would add value to my home or at least what I paid out since I got a decent deal on it but the only reason I did it was because I figured with the added home value and the rebate I would about break even. . . . Why did they bother to even run the program? They knew that if they had informed people ahead of time that this would be taxed that very few would have bothered to remove the grass and replace it with synthetic turf. If they are going to tax me on $1,500 then I'm writing off the $5,000 I paid since I received no added value in my home and there is no guarantee of water savings.

G. RECOVERY OF CAPITAL

Income includes interest, rents, dividends, and other returns *on* one's capital or cost or investment. It also includes gains from the sale (or other disposition) of that capital. But it does not include returns or recoveries *of* one's capital. That is, if you lend a friend $500 for a few weeks, and get back $500, you have no income, because all that has been returned to you is your own money.[14]

The materials in this section and in Chapter 5, which explores a variety of financial arrangements, are concerned with the recovery-of-capital exclusion, which has always been a part of fundamental tax doctrine. The rules tend to reflect the ever-present conflict between practicality and accuracy. In general, the Code errs on the side of accuracy when it comes to explicit financial transactions, such as the loan just described.

If a taxpayer buys one hundred shares of common stock of a corporation for $1,000 and later sells forty of those shares for $700, the tax calculation is simple. Since the shares are homogeneous, the total cost is allocated equally among them. Thus, the cost of the forty shares that were sold is $400, and the gain for tax purposes is $300. But suppose that the taxpayer buys one hundred acres of land for $1,000, that forty acres are wooded and sixty acres are tillable, and that the forty wooded acres are sold for $700. It is not reasonable to assume that the value of wooded acres is necessarily the same as the value of tillable acres. An allocation of the total cost will require judgment based on experience. Despite the difficulties, an allocation of cost will be required. Suppose, for example, that experts determine that at the time of purchase, the wooded acres had been worth $450 and the tillable acres had been worth $550. The gain on the sale of the wooded acres for $700 would then be $250. See Reg. §1.61-6 and cases cited in Heiner v. Mellon, 304 U.S. 271, 275 n.3 (1938).

illustration

---

14. No simple claim about the income tax can be made without qualification. Code §7872 "imputes" interest income to a lender in respect of certain gratuitous (no-interest) loans made in a gift setting. Fortunately for the text's example, these rules do not apply to gift loans of less than $10,000. Students may wish to ponder how you should handle for tax purposes the case of beer your friend later buys you by way of saying thank you.

For movie buffs, the next case should ring a bell. It involves one small part of the saga told from a fictional perspective in the movie *Chinatown*, starring Jack Nicholson, concerning the efforts of the City of Los Angeles to secure a water supply for the city from the Sierra Nevada mountains, several hundred miles away.

1.   Sale of Easements

INAJA LAND CO. v. COMMISSIONER
9 T.C. 727 (1947), acq. 1948-1 C.B. 2

[In 1928, the taxpayer paid $61,000 for 1,236 acres of land on the banks of the Owens River in Mono County, California, together with certain water rights, for use primarily as a private fishing club. In 1934, the City of Los Angeles constructed a tunnel nearby and began to divert "foreign waters" into the Owens River upstream from the taxpayer's property. These foreign waters contained "concrete dust, sediment, and foreign matter," which adversely affected the fishing on the taxpayer's preserve and, by substantially increasing the flow of water, caused flooding and erosion. In 1939, after the taxpayer threatened legal action, a settlement was reached under which the city paid the taxpayer $50,000 to "release and forever discharge" the city from any liability for the diversion and for an easement to continue to divert foreign waters into the Owens River. In settling its claim, the taxpayer incurred attorneys' fees and costs of $1,000.]

LEECH, Judge.

The question presented is whether the net amount of $49,000 received by petitioner in the taxable year 1939 under a certain indenture constitutes taxable income under [§61(a)], or is chargeable to capital account. The respondent contends: (a) That the $50,000, less $1,000 expenses incurred, which petitioner received from the city of Los Angeles under the indenture of August 11, 1939, represented compensation for loss of present and future income and consideration for release of many meritorious causes of action against the city, constituting ordinary income; and, (b) since petitioner has failed to allocate such sum between taxable and nontaxable income, it has not sustained its burden of showing error. Petitioner maintains that the language of the indenture and the circumstances leading up to its execution demonstrate that the consideration was paid for the easement granted to the city of Los Angeles and the consequent damage to its property rights; that the loss of past or future profits was not considered or involved; that the character of the easement rendered it impracticable to attempt to apportion a basis to the property affected; and, since the sum received is less than the basis of the entire property, taxation should be postponed until the final disposition of the property. . . .

[margin note: taxpayer arg]

Upon this record we have concluded that no part of the recovery was paid for loss of profits, but was paid for the conveyance of a right of way and easements, and for damages to petitioner's land and its property rights as riparian owner. Hence, the respondent's contention has no merit. Capital recoveries in excess of cost do constitute taxable income. Petitioner has made no attempt to allocate a basis to that part of the property covered by the easements. It is conceded that all of petitioner's lands were not affected by the easements conveyed. Petitioner does not contest the rule that, where property is acquired for a lump sum and subsequently disposed of a portion at a time, there must be an allocation of the cost or other basis over the several units and gain or loss computed on the disposition of each part, except where apportionment would be wholly impracticable or impossible. . . . Petitioner argues that it would be impracticable and impossible to apportion a definite basis to the easements here involved, since they could not be described by metes and bounds; that the flow of the water has changed and will change the course of the river; that the extent of the flood was and is not predictable; and that to date the city has not released the full measure of water to which it is entitled. In Strother v. Commissioner, 55 Fed.(2d) 626, the court says: " . . . A taxpayer . . . should not be charged with gain on pure conjecture unsupported by any foundation of ascertainable fact." See Burnet v. Logan [*infra* page 276].

This rule is approved in the recent [case of] Raytheon Prod. Corp. [v. Commissioner, 144 F.2d 110 (1st Cir.), cert. denied, 323 U.S. 779 (1944)]. Apportionment with reasonable accuracy of the amount received not being possible, and this amount being less than petitioner's cost basis for the property, it can not be determined that petitioner has, in fact, realized gain in any amount. Applying the rule as above set out, no portion of the payment in question should be considered as income, but the full amount must be treated as a return of capital and applied in reduction of petitioner's cost basis. Burnet v. Logan [*infra* page 276].

Reviewed by the Court.

NOTES AND QUESTIONS

1. *All or nothing at all?* Given the difficulty of allocating basis or cost, why not treat the entire $49,000 as gain? What about some sort of arbitrary rule of allocation? What justification, if any, is there for in effect allocating the entire basis, up to the amount received, to the interest conveyed? Rev. Rul. 70-510, 1970-2 C.B. 104, covering a situation remarkably similar to that in *Inaja*, follows the same allocation-of-basis rule. No explanation is given.

2. *Drawing the line.* The 1,236 acres owned by the taxpayer included 419 acres of "rocky hill lands." Suppose that this part of the property had been sold for $2,000. How would gain or loss be determined? See the beginning paragraphs of Section G. See also Williams v. McGowan, *infra* page 625 (taxpayer selling hardware business is treated as selling various individual assets, not one aggregate asset, and must allocate price among the various components to determine tax consequences, where the sale of some assets produces ordinary gain or loss and the sale of others produces capital gain or loss).

3. *Effect in later years.* Suppose that in a later year Inaja sells the entire property for $25,000. What tax consequences? Suppose that in 1939 the city had

paid Inaja $65,000 instead of $49,000 (net). What tax result in that year and in a later year when the entire property is sold for $25,000?

4. *The forgone income issue.* (a) What characteristics of the transaction justify treatment of the $50,000 as payment for part of the taxpayer's property rather than rent or the like? Is it possible for a payment to be for "loss of profits" and still be proceeds from the sale of a capital asset?

(b) Suppose that negotiations between the city and Inaja had reached a point where the city offered to pay a fee of $2,500 a year forever for the discharge and easement, but Inaja was more interested in a lump-sum payment. Suppose that at this point a financial expert pointed out that for an annual interest cost of $2,500 the city could issue a bond for $50,000 and use the proceeds to pay off Inaja and that an agreement was thereupon reached under which Inaja received the $50,000 instead of the $2,500 per year. Plainly, the $2,500 per year would have been fully taxable: There would be no recovery-of-cost offset. Does it follow that the $50,000 should be fully taxable? Why?

2.   Gains and Losses from Gambling

The basic rule. By definition, every bet that has a winner also has a loser. Thus, in an economy-wide sense, monetary gains from gambling transactions must always equal monetary losses, leading to net gambling income of zero. Under the federal income tax, however, we tax more than aggregate "income" in this financial sense: All gains are taxable, but losses are deductible only to the extent of gains from the same taxable year; in addition, for non-professional gamblers, losses from different gambling sessions are deductible only the taxpayer forgoes the standard deduction and itemizes. §165(d). Itemized deductions are discussed in Chapter 10. Thus, in theory, although, one suspects, not very often in practice, if two friends bet $50 on the outcome of the Super Bowl and make no other bets for the year, the winner has $50 of taxable income while the loser has no deduction.

To illustrate this basic rule, suppose that a taxpayer goes to a casino on January 5 and bets $10 a hand on one hundred hands of blackjack. She wins sixty and loses forty. Since the gains and losses come from the same session, she does not have to itemize to reduce her gains by her losses. She has a net gain of twenty winning hands, for $200. Suppose she comes back to the casino on February 5 and loses $200. She can deduct the $200 loss on February 5 against her $200 gain on January 5 only if she itemizes.[15]

It may be that this seemingly adverse treatment of gambling transactions reflects a moral condemnation of them, although for lawful betting and, in particular, for state-sponsored lotteries, this position seems difficult to defend.

---

15. The 2017 act expanded the scope of wagering losses to include ancillary expenses incurred in connection with wagering activity where those ancillary expenses otherwise would be deductible as business expenses. Thus, travel expenses incurred by a professional gambler to reach her favorite casino are now wagering losses. This change in law actually was disadvantageous to professional gamblers. Can you see why?

There is another possible rationale, however. Consider gambling at a casino, racetrack, or other organized consumer business that provides gambling opportunities to its patrons as a form of entertainment for which they are willing to pay. One typically knows, or at least ought to know, that on average one is likely to lose. If one gambles anyway, this may be due to the fun and excitement of the process, along with the special satisfaction that winning would provide. How is a night at the casino that on average costs, say, $100 any different than (nondeductibly) spending $100 on dinner and a movie?

From this perspective, one could in theory have taxable income reflect the undeniable fact that someone who gambles and wins is better off than someone who gambles and loses, without having to allow the deduction of consumption expenditures. The way to do this would be to treat the expected cost of one's gambling (given the amount wagered and the odds) as a nondeductible consumption expense, with an inclusion or deduction to the extent one did better or worse than this. Thus suppose that someone "ought" to have lost $100 given her bets. If she actually lost $150, she would deduct $50; if she broke even she would have taxable income of $100. Obviously, however, this approach is utterly impractical.

The actual statutory approach of allowing gambling losses to be deducted only against gambling gains is an example of an approach that could be called "basketing" or "scheduling" and that is quite common in the tax law. In effect, gambling transactions are placed in a separate "basket" from all of the taxpayer's other transactions to ensure that no net loss from the "basket" will be deductible. Other prominent "basketing" rules that cause particular deductions to be allowable only against related income and that are discussed *infra* pertain to investment interest (§163(d)), capital losses (§1211), personal casualty losses (§165(h)), hobby losses (§183), and passive losses (§469).

Whatever their overall merits, "basketing" rules give unfortunate prominence to the question of what transactions fit in the basket. The allowance of gains and losses in a single session as comprising one basket answers one of the questions, but others remain. Thus, in Boyd v. United States, 762 F.2d 1369 (9th Cir. 1985), the manager of a poker room at a casino unsuccessfully argued that his losses from playing poker there were business expenses rather than gambling losses because he played in order to attract customers. He also lost his alternative argument, that compensation in the form of a part of the house's take from poker games constituted gambling income against which he could deduct these losses if they were from gambling. In Jasinski v. Commissioner, 37 T.C.M. 1 (1978), the taxpayer had bought risky subordinated corporate debentures—"junk bonds" in common parlance—that yielded interest income but an eventual loss. The court gave short shrift to the taxpayer's argument that the entire high-risk transaction amounted to gambling and that the loss should therefore be deductible against the interest income instead of being treated as a capital loss. Precisely what is the difference between a person who legally bets the horses (but only after many hours studying all available information) and one who trades in the commodities market? Is there an assumption (not necessarily always correct) that the former activity, but not the latter, involves enjoyable consumption and thus is done for its own sake?

Enforcement. Since gambling is a cash business, enforcement is a problem. For relatively large transactions, §3402(q) requires that the race track or other payor withhold taxes at a rate of 20 percent. Withholding is not required for most gambling winnings of lesser amounts, although the payor is often required to send the payee and the IRS an information return indicating the amount won. In general, this information reporting obligation is only triggered for winnings of $600 or more, leading some gamblers to believe that the law allows individuals to receive up to $600 in gambling winnings tax free. This is of course not true (all gambling winnings are taxable; the $600 refers only to the reporting threshold), but it illustrates the importance of understanding how reporting obligations influence the public's perceptions regarding tax rules.

Recall that gambling losses are deductible to the extent of gambling winnings. How would a taxpayer prove losses to offset such gambling winnings? In Parchutz v. Commissioner, 1988-327 T.C. Memo., the court had this to say about evidence of race-track gambling losses:

> Gambling loss tickets are of slight, if any, evidentiary weight where no corroboration is offered of petitioner's own testimony that each ticket was purchased by him. . . . In the instant case, petitioner offered only his own uncorroborated testimony that the losing tickets were his. We have no way of knowing whether petitioner purchased these tickets or received them from acquaintances at the track or acquired them by resorting to stooping, that is, stooping down and picking up the discarded stubs of other bettors. . . . Moreover, the credibility of petitioner's testimony that he purchased each of the losing tickets has been undermined since some of the losing tickets were purchased during a two-week period within the first two months of 1982, when he was confined to a hospital and unable to go to the track.

The preceding cases and materials on recovery of cost have focused on judicial and legislative reactions to problems of practicality. The case that follows is concerned with the somewhat more perplexing question of what we mean, for tax purposes, by a "recovery of capital."

3.   Recovery of Loss

CLARK v. COMMISSIONER
40 B.T.A. 333 (1939), acq. 1957-1 C.B. 4

LEECH, J.

This is a proceeding to redetermine a deficiency in income tax for the calendar year 1934 in the amount of $10,618.87. The question presented is whether petitioner derived income by the payment to him of an amount of $19,941.10, by his tax counsel, to compensate him for a loss suffered on account of erroneous advice given him by the latter. The facts were stipulated and are so found. The stipulation, so far as material, follows:

> 3. The petitioner during the calendar year 1932, and for a considerable period prior thereto, was married and living with his wife. He was required by

the Revenue Act of 1932 to file a Federal Income Tax Return of his income for the year 1932. For such year petitioner and his wife could have filed a joint return or separate returns.

4. Prior to the time that the 1932 Federal Income Tax return or returns of petitioner and/or his wife were due to be filed, petitioner retained experienced tax counsel to prepare the necessary return or returns for him and/or his wife. Such tax counsel prepared a joint return for petitioner and his wife and advised petitioner to file it instead of two separate returns. In due course it was filed with the Collector of Internal Revenue for the First District of California.

5. Thereafter on or about the third day of February, 1934, a duly appointed revenue agent of the United States audited the aforesaid 1932 return and recommended an additional assessment against petitioner in the sum of $34,590.27, which was subsequently reduced to $32,820.14. This last mentioned sum was thereafter assessed against and was paid by petitioner to the Collector of Internal Revenue for the First District of California.

6. The deficiency of $32,820.14 arose from an error on the part of tax counsel who prepared petitioner's 1932 return. The error was that he improperly deducted from income the total amount of losses sustained on the sale of capital assets held for a period of more than two years instead of applying the statutory limitation required by Section 101(b) of the Revenue Act of 1932.

7. The error referred to in paragraph six above was called to the attention of the tax counsel who prepared the joint return of petitioner and his wife for the year 1932. Recomputations were then made which disclosed that if petitioner and his wife had filed separate returns for the year 1932 their combined tax liability would have been $19,941.10 less than that which was finally assessed against and paid by petitioner.

8. Thereafter, tax counsel admitted that if he had not erred in computing the tax liability shown on the joint return filed by the petitioner, he would have advised petitioner to file separate returns for himself and his wife, and accordingly tax counsel tendered to petitioner the sum of $19,941.10, which was the difference between what petitioner and his wife would have paid on their 1932 returns if separate returns had been filed and the amount which petitioner was actually required to pay on the joint return as filed. Petitioner accepted the $19,941.10.

9. In his final determination of petitioner's 1934 tax liability, the respondent included the aforesaid $19,941.10 in income.

10. Petitioner's books of account are kept on the cash receipts and disbursements basis and his tax returns are made on such basis under the community property laws of the State of California.

The theory on which the respondent included the above sum of $19,941.10 in petitioner's gross income for 1934, is that this amount constituted taxes paid for petitioner by a third party and that, consequently, petitioner was in receipt of income to that extent. The cases of Old Colony Trust Co. v. Commissioner, 279 U.S. 716; United States v. Boston & Maine Railroad, 279 U.S. 732, are cited as authority for his position. Petitioner, on the contrary, contends that this payment constituted compensation for damages or loss caused by the error of tax counsel, and that he therefore realized no income from its receipt in 1934.

We agree with petitioner. The cases cited by the respondent are not applicable here. Petitioner's taxes were not paid for him by any person—as rental, compensation for services rendered, or otherwise. He paid his own taxes.

When the joint return was filed, petitioner became obligated to and did pay the taxes computed on that basis. . . . In paying that obligation, he sustained a loss which was caused by the negligence of his tax counsel. The $19,941.10 was paid to petitioner, not qua taxes . . . , but as compensation to petitioner for his loss. The measure of that loss, and the compensation therefor, was the sum of money which petitioner became legally obligated to and did pay because of that negligence. The fact that such obligation was for taxes is of no moment here.

It has been held that payments in settlement of an action for breach of promise to marry are not income. . . . Compromise payments in settlement of an action for damages against a bank on account of conduct impairing the taxpayer's good will by injuring its reputation are also not taxable. . . . The same result follows in the case of payments in settlement for injuries by libel and slander. . . . Damages for personal injury are likewise not income. . . .

The theory of those cases is that recoupment on account of such losses is not income since it is not "derived from capital, from labor or from both combined." . . . And the fact that the payment of the compensation for such loss was voluntary, as here, does not change its exempt status. . . . It was, in fact, compensation for a loss which impaired petitioner's capital.

Moreover, so long as petitioner neither could nor did take a deduction in a prior year of this loss in such a way as to offset income for the prior year, the amount received by him in the taxable year, by way of recompense, is not then includable in his gross income. . . .

Decision will be entered for the petitioner.

CURRENT LEGAL STATUS OF CLARK

The apparent ultimate ground for the holding in *Clark*, that the payment the taxpayer received from his tax counsel was not "derived from capital, from labor, or from both combined," is no longer good law. See Glenshaw Glass Co. v. Commissioner, *supra*. Nonetheless, the holding in *Clark* remains good law, as shown by its occasional invocation in private letter rulings issued by the Internal Revenue Service in response to taxpayer requests for advice about their own specific fact situations. According to the Internal Revenue Service, *Clark* does not apply to a reimbursement by one's tax advisor unless it compensates one for having paid more than the minimum amount of tax that was actually due given all relevant facts. For example, there is no exclusion if, in connection with a business transaction, Sam tells Betty that her tax will be $100 and it turns out that Betty is required to pay $110 (the true amount payable) and recovers $10 from Sam. Similarly, there is no exclusion if Sam pays Betty $10 because he told her to structure a business transaction one way, resulting in tax liability of $110, and it turns out that if only he had given her better advice regarding how to structure the transaction she could, at zero practical inconvenience, have been in a position to owe only $100 of tax.

NOTES AND QUESTIONS

1. The problem presented by *Clark* is subtler and more puzzling than it may initially appear. The core of the dilemma that it poses can be shown through the following hypothetical:

Suppose that in Year 1 Tom, Dick, and Harry all have identical economic circumstances (and thus would have had the same taxable income and income tax liabilities) except that, of the tax accountants they hire to prepare their federal income tax returns, only Harry's is competent. As a result, for Year 1 Tom and Dick end up paying $5,000 more of federal income tax than does Harry. As in *Clark*, suppose that the error cannot be corrected by filing an amended return for Year 1.

Plainly, once the dust has settled Harry is $5,000 better off than Tom and Dick. His bank account is that much higher after paying the tax, and their circumstances otherwise remain the same. It is not as if Tom and Dick received an extra $5,000 of valuable government services by reason of paying more tax. However, because federal income tax payments are nondeductible, the difference in economic well-being is ignored in the measurement of their respective taxable incomes (except insofar as, in future years, Harry has more income due to investing the $5,000).

Now suppose that, before the end of Year 2, Tom receives a $5,000 payment from his tax accountant as compensation for the error that resulted in his overpayment of that amount in Year 1. Dick, however, learns that no compensation will be forthcoming at any time from *his* accountant, who has permanently moved to Patagonia to search for dinosaur fossils. This changes the three taxpayers' relative positions as follows: Rather than Harry being $5,000 better off than Tom and Dick, Tom and Harry are $5,000 better off than Dick. In other words, Tom has moved up from the "Dick" level to the "Harry" level of relative well-being.

Should Tom's $5,000 recovery be taxed? If we compare him to Dick, the answer is clearly yes. He is $5,000 better off than Dick due to the recovery, and this ought to be recognized in an income tax that aims to apportion tax liability based on a measure of relative well-being. By contrast, if we compare Tom to Harry, the answer is clearly no. Recovering the $5,000 that he needlessly overpaid merely places him on a par with Harry and the result should not be that he has $5,000 *more* of taxable income (as would result from including the recovery).

Accordingly, the question posed by *Clark* is, in effect, whether Tom should be undertaxed relative to Dick via exclusion of the recovery, or overtaxed relative to Harry via its inclusion. We cannot avoid committing one or the other of these two "errors" (of the overall tax system, not the decision maker) given that Dick and Harry are not being taxed correctly relative to each other. The court in *Clark* chose to impose the first error rather than the second.

2. How would you resolve this conundrum and decide the *Clark* case?

3. How did the court determine how the unavoidable dilemma was best resolved? Perhaps the best clue, apart from its now-dated theorizing about what the payment was "derived from," is its statement that the taxpayer merely

received "compensation for a loss which impaired [his] capital." In short, in organizing the facts, the court seems (perhaps quite logically) to have conceived of
an overall "transaction" in which *Clark* first needlessly overpaid federal income
tax and then was reimbursed for the overpayment. It then determined that a
transaction yielding no overall gain should have no overall income tax consequences. What, if anything, makes this "transactional" view an appealing one?

4. In effect, the court in *Clark* treats the taxpayer as having a kind of partial
or quasi-basis as a result of the nondeductible tax overpayment of $19,941.10.
In general, an asset's true or full basis can be used to offset inclusion of the
gross proceeds realized when the asset is sold. For example, if you buy an acre
of land for $20,000, it has a $20,000 basis. Thus, if you sell it for $25,000 you
will offset the basis from the amount realized and report only $5,000 of gross
income (gain). The overpayment in *Clark* seems to work the same way. Thus,
had the taxpayer's counsel made his apology even fuller by throwing in an
extra $5,000 and paying Clark $24,941.10, the extra $5,000 would presumably
have been taxable income.

True or full basis, however, can often (although with important exceptions
and qualifications) be deducted when it turns out to be unrecoverable. For
example, if the acre of land that you bought for $20,000 turns out to contain
a toxic waste dump and you therefore transfer it for zero consideration, then,
subject to various special rules that we can ignore for now, you could deduct
the $20,000 loss from the transaction. By contrast, in a *Clark* situation the tax-
payer gets no deduction for the overpayment if there is no recovery.

HYPOTHETICAL

Suppose that on December 29, 2016, Tom picks up his pay envelope containing $300. When he arrives home he finds a hole in his pocket and no pay
envelope. He retraces his steps and cannot find it. He reports his loss to the
police, but they offer him no encouragement. He checks with the police again
on December 31 and still receives no encouragement.

1. What are the income tax consequences for 2016? (a) Is the $300 exclud-
able from income, on the basis that Tom never had the opportunity to use the
money? (b) Alternatively, can Tom deduct the $300 as a loss? (See §165(c)(3);
disregard the limitations in §165(h).)

2. Assume that Tom was entitled to and claimed a deduction of $300 in 2016
but that in 2017 he once more retraces his steps and, by a stroke of remarkable
good fortune, finds his lost pay envelope with the $300 still in it. (a) Should
he file an amended return for 2016? (b) Assuming that it would not be appropriate to file an amended return for 2016, should he treat the $300 as income
in 2017? If your intuition tells you that he should, congratulations—it is consistent with rules referred to as the "tax benefit doctrine," which is considered
later in this chapter.

3. Assume again that in 2017, he finds his lost pay envelope with the $300,
but that in 2016 he had not been entitled to and did not claim a loss deduction.
How should he treat the $300 in 2017? The *Clark* case provides the answer to
this question. Is that answer correct? Is it not clear that Tom is better off than

an otherwise identical person who does not find his pay envelope in 2017? To achieve fairness, if Tom can exclude the $300, should that other person not be allowed a deduction? When?

4. Assume, as in Note 3, that Tom was not entitled to and did not claim a deduction in 2016, and in 2017 he finds a pay envelope with $300 but it is someone else's rather than his own. Assume further that efforts to find the owner prove unavailing, and Tom is advised by a lawyer in 2017 that he is entitled to treat the $300 as his own. Must he report that amount as income? See *Glenshaw Glass, supra.* Can you reconcile your answer to this question with your answer to the questions in Note 3? What would Henry Simons say?

5. Suppose that Tom was entitled to a deduction in 2011 but neglected to claim it. (a) He finds his $300 in 2012. Should he include it in income? (b) He finds his $300 in 2016, after the statute of limitations has run on 2011. Now, how should he treat the $300?

H.   RECOVERIES FOR PERSONAL AND BUSINESS INJURIES

1.   The Basic Rules

Tax lawyers often are asked to describe the tax treatment of amounts received as damages for injuries of one kind or another. For taxpayers other than individuals, the tax treatment is straightforward. Damage awards for lost profits are taxed in the year received. Thus a company that sues and recovers for lost profits is taxed on the amount received just as if it had earned that amount as profit in the year the recovery is made. Punitive damages are also taxed in the year received. Suppose a company recovers damages in recompense for destroyed or damaged property. The recovery is taxable in the year received to the extent it exceeds the basis of the property, just as if the property were sold for that amount. Section 1033, however, allows a taxpayer to defer taxation provided the amounts are reinvested in similar property or property related in use. To understand the treatment of amounts received for damaged or destroyed property, suppose a company's building is destroyed by a contractor's negligence. The building has a basis of $600,000 and a fair market value of $700,000. The company sues and in the same year collects $700,000. The company is taxable on $100,000—just as if it had sold the building for $700,000.[16] However, the tax will be deferred if the company uses the proceeds to build or buy a similar building. In the above examples, the awards were court ordered. The result would be the same if the recoveries were received through settlement or through insurance.

---

16. The result would be different if the company had deducted the $600,000 as a loss in one year and then did not recover the amount until a subsequent year. In that case, the so-called tax benefit rule would require the taxpayer to treat the entire amount as gain in the year received. In effect, the taxpayer would not only recognize the $100,000 income but would also have to "give back" the $600,000 loss that, in retrospect, was erroneously deducted.

In the case of individual taxpayers, awards (or settlements or insurance proceeds) are generally tax free—provided the payment is attributable to a personal injury. §104. The tax-free treatment does not extend, however, to punitive damages arising out of a personal injury. §104(a)(2). Some years ago, a surprising amount of litigation arose concerning the definition of "personal injury." The term clearly encompasses physical injuries, but what about amounts received for nonphysical injuries, such as libel or discrimination? The issue led to two Supreme Court decisions, and scores of lower court decisions and controversies, before Congress finally resolved the issue in 1996. Section 104(a)(2) now excludes only amounts arising from personal physical injuries or sickness.

In some cases, the nontaxation of recoveries on account of physical injuries is arguably correct. Suppose, for example, someone is hit by a car and recovers amounts for uninsured medical expenses, pain, and suffering. The victim may seem to be no better off (at least if the court got the award right) after the award than prior to the accident. If this is the comparison (the same individual prior to the accident and after the award), nontaxation seems appropriate. There simply has not been an increase in well-being. Nontaxation also seems appropriate if we compare the victim after the award to those who did not suffer an accident. Again, the combination of accident and award have not produced an increase in wealth. (Note, however, that the individual after the award will be better off than someone who suffers from the same accident and does not recover. If this is the most relevant comparison, and we do not allow a deduction for the victim who does not recover, nontaxation seems incorrect. See *Clark, supra.*)

We could, in theory, treat the damage to the individual from the accident in the same manner as damage to business property: taxable to the extent that the award exceeds basis. That approach, however, would require us to attribute basis to the human body or treat the entire award as taxable. For obvious reasons, no one has ever seriously suggested such treatment. In other cases, the nontaxation of physical injuries seems flawed. For example, suppose an individual is hit by a car and misses a month of work. Some portion of her recovery is attributable to lost wages. The wages would be taxed; why not the amounts received in lieu of the wages?

Suppose an individual receives an award for a nonpersonal injury. In that case, the treatment described above, for taxpayers other than individuals, applies. Amounts received in recompense for lost profits are taxed as profits in the year received. Amounts received as damages to property are taxed to the extent such amounts exceed basis. Thus, an individual who recovers $200,000 for the destruction of property with a basis of $150,000 is taxed on $50,000. As in the case of business taxpayers, special nonrecognition rules will allow deferral of gain if the proceeds are reinvested in similar property.

Consider, finally, the effect of the 1996 legislation that limited personal injury to *physical injuries*. A is injured in an automobile accident and recovers $100,000 for pain and suffering; B recovers the same amount for damages to reputation from libel, or perhaps as compensation for emotional distress. A's recovery is tax free, because the pain and suffering relates to a physical injury. B's recovery is taxed in its entirety. How, if at all, can this difference in outcome be justified? A's exclusion is justified on the grounds that she is simply being made whole. At an intuitive level, the $100,000 recovery seems to constitute "income" no more than the $7.01 change you get after giving the cashier a $20 bill for a $12.99 DVD. But doesn't the same argument apply to *B*? If so, then why tax *B*'s recovery?

MURPHY v. UNITED STATES

493 F.3d 170 (D.C. Cir. 2007), cert. denied, 553 U.S. 1004 (2008)

On Rehearing.

GINSBURG, Chief Judge: Marrita Murphy brought this suit to recover income taxes she paid on the compensatory damages for emotional distress and loss of reputation she was awarded in an administrative action she brought against her former employer. Murphy contends that under *§104(a)(2)*, her award should have been excluded from her gross income because it was compensation received "on account of personal physical injuries or physical sickness." She also maintains that, in any event, her award is not part of her gross income as defined by *§61*. Finally, she argues that taxing her award subjects her to an unapportioned direct tax in violation of Article I, Section 9 of the Constitution of the United States.

We reject Murphy's argument in all aspects. We hold, first, that Murphy's compensation was not "received . . . on account of personal physical injuries" excludable from gross income under *§104(a)(2)*. Second, we conclude gross income as defined by *§61* includes compensatory damages for non-physical injuries. Third, we hold that a tax upon such damages is within the Congress's power to tax.

I.   BACKGROUND

In 1994 Marrita Leveille (now Murphy) filed a complaint with the Department of Labor alleging that her former employer, the New York Air National Guard (NYANG), in violation of various whistle-blower statutes, had "blacklisted" her and provided unfavorable references to potential employers after she had complained to state authorities of environmental hazards on a NYANG airbase. The Secretary of Labor determined the NYANG had unlawfully discriminated and retaliated against Murphy, ordered that any adverse references to the taxpayer in the files of the Office of Personnel Management be withdrawn, and remanded her case to an Administrative Law Judge "for findings on compensatory damages."

On remand Murphy submitted evidence that she had suffered both mental and physical injuries as a result of the NYANG's blacklisting her. A psychologist testified that Murphy had sustained both "somatic" and "emotional" injuries, basing his conclusion in part upon medical and dental records showing Murphy had "bruxism," or teeth grinding often associated with stress, which may cause permanent tooth damage. Noting that Murphy also suffered from other "physical manifestations of stress" including "anxiety attacks, shortness of breath, and dizziness," and that Murphy testified she "could not concentrate, stopped talking to friends, and no longer enjoyed 'anything in life,' " the ALJ recommended compensatory damages totaling $70,000, of which $45,000 was for "past and future emotional distress," and $25,000 was for "injury to [Murphy's] vocational reputation" from having been blacklisted. None of the award was for lost wages or diminished earning capacity.

In 1999 the Department of Labor Administrative Review Board affirmed the ALJ's findings and recommendations. On her tax return for 2000, Murphy included the $70,000 award in her "gross income." As a result, she paid $20,665 in taxes on the award.

Murphy later filed an amended return in which she sought a refund of the $20,665 based upon *§104(a)(2)*, which provides that "gross income does not include . . . damages . . . received . . . on account of personal physical injuries or physical sickness." In support of her amended return, Murphy submitted copies of her dental and medical records. Upon deciding Murphy had failed to demonstrate the compensatory damages were attributable to "physical injury" or "physical sickness," the Internal Revenue Service denied her request for a refund.

Murphy thereafter sued the . . . United States [for a refund] in the district court.

B.   *SECTION 104(A)(2)* OF THE IRC

Section 104(a) ("Compensation for injuries or sickness") provides that "gross income does not include the amount of any damages (other than punitive damages) received . . . on account of personal physical injuries or physical sickness." Since 1996 it has further provided that, for purposes of this exclusion, "emotional distress shall not be treated as a physical injury or physical sickness." *Id. §104(a)*. The version of *§104(a)(2)* in effect prior to 1996 had excluded from gross income monies received in compensation for "personal injuries or sickness," which included both physical and nonphysical injuries such as emotional distress. . . . In *Commissioner v. Schleier, 515 U.S. 323, 115 S. Ct. 2159, 132 L. Ed. 2d 294 (1995)*, the Supreme Court held that before a taxpayer may exclude compensatory damages from gross income pursuant to *§104(a)(2)*, he must first demonstrate that "the underlying cause of action giving rise to the recovery [was] 'based upon tort or tort type rights.' " *Id. at 337.* The taxpayer has the same burden under the statute as amended.

Murphy contends *§104(a)(2)*, even as amended, excludes her particular award from gross income. First, she asserts her award was "based upon . . . tort type rights" in the whistle-blower statutes the NYANG violated—a position the Government does not challenge. Second, she claims she was compensated for "physical" injuries, which claim the Government does dispute. Murphy points both to her psychologist's testimony that she had experienced "somatic" and "body" injuries "as a result of NYANG's blacklisting [her]," and to the American Heritage Dictionary, which defines "somatic" as "relating to, or affecting the body, especially as distinguished from a body part, the mind, or the environment." Murphy further argues the dental records she submitted to the IRS proved she has suffered permanent damage to her teeth. . . . Murphy contends that "substantial physical problems caused by emotional distress are considered physical injuries or physical sickness."

Murphy further contends that neither *§104 of the IRC* nor the regulation issued thereunder "limits the physical disability exclusion to a physical stimulus." . . .

For its part, the Government argues Murphy's focus upon the word "physical" in *§104(a)(2)* is misplaced; more important is the phrase "on account of." In *O'Gilvie v. United States, 519 U.S. 79, 117 S. Ct. 452, 136 L. Ed. 2d 454 (1996)*, the Supreme Court read that phrase to require a "strong[] causal connection," thereby making *§104(a)(2)* "applicable only to those personal injury lawsuit damages that were awarded by reason of, or because of, the personal injuries." *Id. at 83.* The Court specifically rejected a "but-for" formulation in favor of a "stronger causal connection." *Id. at 82-83.* The Government therefore concludes Murphy must demonstrate she was awarded damages "because of" her physical injuries, which the Government claims she has failed to do.

* * * *

Murphy responds that it is undisputed she suffered both "somatic" and "emotional" injuries, and the ALJ and Board expressly cited to the portion of her psychologist's testimony establishing that fact. She contends the Board therefore relied upon her physical injuries in determining her damages, making those injuries a direct cause of her award in spite of the Board's labeling the award as one for emotional distress.

Although the pre-1996 version of *§104(a)(2)* was at issue in *O'Gilvie*, the Court's analysis of the phrase "on account of," which phrase was unchanged by the 1996 Amendments, remains controlling here. Murphy no doubt suffered from certain physical manifestations of emotional distress, but the record clearly indicates the Board awarded her compensation only "for mental pain and anguish" and "for injury to professional reputation." Although the Board cited her psychologist, who had mentioned her physical ailments, in support of Murphy's "description of her mental anguish," we cannot say the Board, notwithstanding its clear statements to the contrary, actually awarded damages because of Murphy's bruxism and other physical manifestations of stress. At best—and this is doubtful—at best the Board and the ALJ may have considered her physical injuries indicative of the severity of the emotional distress for which the damages were awarded, but her physical injuries themselves were not the reason for the award. The Board thus having left no room for doubt about the grounds for her award, we conclude Murphy's damages were not "awarded by reason of, or because of, . . . [physical] personal injuries." Therefore, *§104(a)(2)* does not permit Murphy to exclude her award from gross income.

C.   *SECTION 61* OF THE IRC

Murphy and the Government agree that for Murphy's award to be taxable, it must be part of her "gross income" as defined by *§61(a)*, which states in relevant part: "gross income means all income from whatever source derived." The Supreme Court has interpreted the section broadly to extend to "all economic gains not otherwise exempted." *Comm'r v. Banks, 543 U.S. 426, 433, (2005); see also, e.g., James v. United States, 366 U.S. 213, 219, (1961)* (*Section 61* encompasses "all accessions to wealth") (internal quotation mark omitted); *Comm'r v. Glenshaw*

Glass Co., 348 U.S. 426, 430, ("the Court has given a liberal construction to ['gross income'] in recognition of the intention of Congress to tax all gains except those specifically exempted"). "Gross income" in *§61(a)* is at least as broad as the meaning of "incomes" in the *Sixteenth Amendment. See Glenshaw Glass, 348 U.S. at 429, 432 n.11* (quoting H.R. Rep. No. 83-1337, at A18 (1954) . . . .

Murphy argues her award is not a gain or an accession to wealth and there- fore not part of gross income. Noting the Supreme Court has long recognized "the principle that a restoration of capital [i]s not income; hence it [falls] out- side the definition of 'income' upon which the law impose[s] a tax," Murphy contends a damage award for personal injuries—including nonphysical inju- ries should be viewed as a return of a particular form of capital —"human capital," as it were. *See* Gary S. Becker, HUMAN CAPITAL (1st ed. 1964); Gary S. Becker, The Economic Way of Looking at Life, Nobel Lecture (Dec. 9, 1992), *in* NOBEL LECTURES IN ECONOMIC SCIENCES 1991-1995, at 43-45 (Torsten Persson, ed., 1997). In her view, the Supreme Court in *Glenshaw Glass* acknowledged the relevance of the human capital concept for tax pur- poses. There, in holding that punitive damages for personal injury were "gross income" under the predecessor to *§61*, the Court stated:

> The long history of . . . holding personal injury recoveries nontaxable on the theory that they roughly correspond to a return of capital cannot support exemption of punitive damages following injury to property. . . . Damages for personal injury are by definition compensatory only. Punitive damages, on the other hand, cannot be considered a restoration of capital for taxation purposes.

348 U.S. at 432 n.8. By implication, Murphy argues, damages for personal in- jury are a "restoration of capital."

As further support, Murphy cites various administrative rulings issued shortly after passage of the *Sixteenth Amendment* that concluded recoveries from personal injuries were not income, such as this 1918 Opinion of the Attorney General:

> Without affirming that the human body is in a technical sense the "capital" invested in an accident policy, in a broad, natural sense the proceeds of the policy do but substitute, so far as they go, capital which is the source of future periodical income. They merely take the place of capital in human ability which was destroyed by the accident. They are therefore "capital" as distinguished from "income" receipts.

31 Op. Att'y Gen. 304, 308; *see* T.D. 2747, 20 Treas. Dec. Int. Rev. 457 (1918); Sol. Op. 132, I-1 C.B. 92, 93-94 (1922) ("[M]oney received . . . on account of . . . defamation of personal character . . . does not constitute income within the meaning of the *sixteenth amendment* and the statutes enacted thereunder"). She also cites a House Report on the bill that became the Revenue Act of 1918. H.R. Rep. No. 65-767, at 9-10 (1918) ("Under the present law it is doubt- ful whether amounts received . . . as compensation for personal injury . . . are required to be included in gross income").

* * * *

The Government disputes Murphy's interpretation on all fronts. First, noting "the definition [of gross income in the IRC] extends broadly to all economic gains," *Banks, 543 U.S. at 433*, the Government asserts Murphy "undeniably had economic gain because she was better off financially after receiving the damages award than she was prior to receiving it." Second, the Government argues that the case law Murphy cites does not support the proposition that the Congress lacks the power to tax as income recoveries for personal injuries. In its view, to the extent the Supreme Court has addressed at all the taxability of compensatory damages, *see, e.g.,* O'Gilvie, 519 U.S. at 86; *Glenshaw Glass, 348 U.S. at 432 n.8,* it was merely articulating the Congress's rationale at the time for not taxing such damages, not the Court's own view whether such damages could constitutionally be taxed.

Finally, the Government argues that even if the concept of human capital is built into *§61*, Murphy's award is nonetheless taxable because Murphy has no tax basis in her human capital. Under the IRC, a taxpayer's gain upon the disposition of property is the difference between the "amount realized" from the disposition and his basis in the property, *§1001*, defined as "the cost of such property," *§1012*, adjusted "for expenditures, receipts, losses, or other items, properly chargeable to [a] capital account," *§1016(a)(1)*. The Government asserts, "The Code does not allow individuals to claim a basis in their human capital"; accordingly, Murphy's gain is the full value of the award. *See Roemer v. Commissioner, 716 F.2d 693, 696 n.2 (9th Cir. 1983)* ("Since there is no tax basis in a person's health and other personal interests, money received as compensation for an injury to those interests might be considered a realized accession to wealth") (dictum).

Although Murphy and the Government focus primarily upon whether Murphy's award falls within the definition of income first used in *Glenshaw Glass*, coming within that definition is not the only way in which *§61(a)* could be held to encompass her award. Principles of statutory interpretation could show [that] *§61(a)* includes Murphy's award in her gross income regardless whether it was an "accession to wealth," as *Glenshaw Glass* requires. For example, if *§61(a)* were amended specifically to include in gross income "$100,000 in addition to all other gross income," then that additional sum would be a part of gross income under *§61* even though no actual gain was associated with it. In other words, although the "Congress cannot make a thing income which is not so in fact," *Burk-Waggoner Oil Ass'n v. Hopkins, 269 U.S. 110, 114, (1925)*, it can *label* a thing income and tax it, so long as it acts within its constitutional authority, which includes not only the *Sixteenth Amendment* but also Article I, Sections 8 and 9. *See Penn Mut. Indem. Co. v. Comm'r, 277 F.2d 16, 20 (3d Cir. 1960)* ("Congress has the power to impose taxes generally, and if the particular imposition does not run afoul of any constitutional restrictions then the tax is lawful, call it what you will") (footnote omitted). Accordingly, rather than ask whether Murphy's award was an accession to her wealth, we go to the heart of the matter, which is whether her award is properly included within the definition of gross income in *§61(a)*, to wit, "all income from whatever source derived."

Looking at *§61(a)* by itself, one sees no indication that it covers Murphy's award unless the award is "income" as defined by *Glenshaw Glass* and later cases. Damages received for emotional distress are not listed among the examples of income in *§61* and, as Murphy points out, an ambiguity in the meaning of a revenue-raising statute should be resolved in favor of the taxpayer. As noted above, in 1996 the Congress amended *§104(a)* to narrow the exclusion to amounts received on account of "personal physical injuries or physical sickness" from "personal injuries or sickness," and explicitly to provide that "emotional distress shall not be treated as a physical injury or physical sickness," thus making clear that an award received on account of emotional distress is not excluded from gross income under *§104(a)(2)*. [T]his amendment, which narrows the exclusion, would have no effect whatsoever if such damages were not included within the ambit of *§61*, and as we must presume that "[w]hen Congress acts to amend a statute, . . . it intends its amendment to have real and substantial effect," *Stone v. INS, 514 U.S. 386, 397(1995)*, the 1996 amendment of *§104(a)* strongly suggests *§61* should be read to include an award for damages from nonphysical harms. Although it is unclear whether *§61* covered such an award before 1996, we need not address that question here; even if the provision did not do so prior to 1996, the presumption indicates the Congress implicitly amended *§61* to cover such an award when it amended *§104(a)*. . . .

For the 1996 amendment of *§104(a)* to "make sense," gross income in *§61(a)* must, and we therefore hold it does, include an award for nonphysical damages such as Murphy received, regardless whether the award is an accession to wealth. . . .

D.   THE CONGRESS'S POWER TO TAX

The taxing power of the Congress is established by Article I, Section 8 of the Constitution: "The Congress shall have power to lay and collect taxes, duties, imposts and excises." There are two limitations on this power. First, as the same section goes on to provide, "all duties, imposts and excises shall be uniform throughout the United States." Second, as provided in Section 9 of that same Article, "No capitation, or other direct, tax shall be laid, unless in proportion to the census or enumeration herein before directed to be taken." *See also U.S. CONST. art. I, §2, cl. 3* ("direct taxes shall be apportioned among the several states which may be included within this union, according to their respective numbers").[17] We now consider whether the tax laid upon Murphy's award violates either of these two constraints.

[Murphy here is arguing that the tax on her is "direct," in the constitutional sense, but not apportioned, and therefore is unconstitutional. An "apportioned" direct tax in general is a practical impossibility; it would require that the same tax be collected from each state, adjusted only for population size, but not any other attribute relevant to the tax base. For example, a federal wealth tax would require residents of a poorer state to pay a higher rate of tax on their wealth than residents of a richer state.—EDS.]

1.   A Direct Tax?

Over the years, courts have considered numerous claims that one or another nonapportioned tax is a direct tax and therefore unconstitutional. Although

---

17. Although it is unclear whether an income tax is a direct tax, the *Sixteenth Amendment* definitively establishes that a tax upon income is not required to be apportioned. *See Stanton v. Baltic Mining Co., 240 U.S. 103, 112-13, 36 S. Ct. 278, 60 L. Ed. 546 (1916).*

these cases have not definitively marked the boundary between taxes that must be apportioned . . . , some characteristics of each may be discerned.

Only three taxes are definitely known to be direct: (1) a capitation, U.S. CONST. art. I, §9, (2) a tax upon real property, and (3) a tax upon personal property. *See Fernandez v. Wiener, 326 U.S. 340, 352 (1945)* ("Congress may tax real estate or chattels if the tax is apportioned"); *Pollock v. Farmers' Loan & Trust Co., 158 U.S. 601, 637, (1895) (Pollock II)*.[18] Such direct taxes are laid upon one's "general ownership of property," *Bromley, 280 U.S. at 136*, as contrasted with excise taxes laid "upon a particular use or enjoyment of property or the shifting from one to another of any power or privilege incidental to the ownership or enjoyment of property." *Fernandez, 326 U.S. at 352; see also Thomas v. United States, 192 U.S. 363, 370, (1904)* (excises cover "duties imposed on importation, consumption, manufacture and sale of certain commodities, privileges, particular business transactions, vocations, occupations and the like"). More specifically, excise taxes include, in addition to taxes upon consumable items, *see Patton v. Brady, 184 U.S. 608, 617-18, (1902)*, taxes upon the sale of grain on an exchange, *Nicol v. Ames, 173 U.S. 509, 519 (1899)*, the sale of corporate stock, *Thomas, 192 U.S. at 371*, doing business in corporate form, *Flint, 220 U.S. at 151*, gross receipts from the "business of refining sugar," *Spreckels, 192 U.S. at 411*, the transfer of property at death, *Knowlton v. Moore, 178 U.S. 41, 81-82 (1900)*, gifts, *Bromley, 280 U.S. at 138*, and income from employment, *see Pollock v. Farmers' Loan & Trust Co., 157 U.S. 429, 579, (1895) (Pollock I* (citing *Springer v. United States, 102 U.S. 586, 26 L. Ed. 253 (1881))*.

* * * *

We find it . . . appropriate to analyze this case based upon the precedents and therefore to ask whether the tax laid upon Murphy's award is more akin, on the one hand, to a capitation or a tax upon one's ownership of property, or, on the other hand, more like a tax upon a use of property, a privilege, an activity, or a transaction, *see Thomas, 192 U.S. at 370*. Even if we assume one's human capital should be treated as personal property, it does not appear that this tax is upon ownership; rather, as the Government points out, Murphy is taxed only after she receives a compensatory award, which makes the tax seem to be laid upon a transaction. *See Tyler v. United States, 281 U.S. 497, 502* ("A tax laid upon the happening of an event, as distinguished from its tangible fruits, is an indirect tax which Congress, in respect of some events . . . undoubtedly may impose"); *Simmons v. United States, 308 F.2d 160, 166 (4th Cir. 1962)* (tax upon receipt of money is not a direct tax); *cf. Penn Mut., 277 F.2d at 20*. Murphy's situation seems akin to an involuntary conversion of assets; she was forced to surrender some part of her mental health and reputation in return for monetary damages. *Cf. 26 U.S.C. §1033* (property involuntarily converted into money is taxed to extent of gain recognized).

At oral argument Murphy resisted this formulation on the ground that the receipt of an award in lieu of lost mental health or reputation is not a

---

18. *Pollock II* also held that a tax upon the income of real or personal property is a direct tax. *158 U.S. at 637*. Whether that portion of *Pollock* remains good law is unclear. *See Graves v. New York ex rel. O'Keefe, 306 U.S. 466, 480, 59 S. Ct. 595, 83 L. Ed. 927, 1939-1 C.B. 129 (1939)*.

transaction. This view is tenable, however, only if one decouples Murphy's injury (emotional distress and lost reputation) from her monetary award, but that is not beneficial to Murphy's cause, for then Murphy has nothing to offset the obvious accession to her wealth, which is taxable as income. Murphy also suggested at oral argument that there was no transaction because she did not profit. Whether she profited is irrelevant, however, to whether a tax upon an award of damages is a direct tax requiring apportionment; profit is relevant only to whether, if it is a direct tax, it nevertheless need not be apportioned because the object of the tax is income within the meaning of the *Sixteenth Amendment. Cf. Spreckels, 192 U.S. at 412-13* (tax upon gross receipts associated with business of refining sugar not a direct tax); *Penn Mut., 277 F.2d at 20* (tax upon gross receipts deemed valid indirect tax despite taxpayer's net loss).

So we return to the question: Is a tax upon this particular kind of transaction equivalent to a tax upon a person or his property? *Cf. Bromley, 280 U.S. at 138* (assuming without deciding that a tax "levied upon all the uses to which property may be put, or upon the exercise of a single power indispensable to the enjoyment of all others over it, would be in effect a tax upon property"). Murphy did not receive her damages pursuant to a business activity, *cf. Flint, 220 U.S. at 151; Spreckels, 192 U.S. at 411,* and we therefore do not view this tax as an excise under that theory. *See Stratton's Independence, Ltd. v. Howbert, 231 U.S. 399, (1913)* ("The sale outright of a mining property might be fairly described as a mere conversion of the capital from land into money"). On the other hand, as noted above, the Supreme Court several times has held a tax not related to business activity is nonetheless an excise. And the tax at issue here is similar to those.

Bromley, in which a gift tax was deemed an excise, is particularly instructive: The Court noted it was "a tax laid only upon the exercise of a single one of those powers incident to ownership," *280 U.S. at 136,* which distinguished it from "a tax which falls upon the owner merely because he is owner, regardless of the use or disposition made of his property," *id. at 137.* A gift is the functional equivalent of a below-market sale; it therefore stands to reason that if, as *Bromley* holds, a gift tax, or a tax upon a below-market sale, is a tax laid not upon ownership but upon the exercise of a power "incident to ownership," then a tax upon the sale of property at fair market value is similarly laid upon an incidental power and not upon ownership, and hence is an excise. Therefore, even if we were to accept Murphy's argument that the human capital concept is reflected in the *Sixteenth Amendment,* a tax upon the involuntary conversion of that capital would still be an excise and not subject to the requirement of apportionment. *But see Nicol, 173 U.S. at 521* (indicating pre-*Bromley* that tax upon "every sale made in any place . . . is really and practically upon property").

In any event, even if a tax upon the sale of property is a direct tax upon the property itself, we do not believe Murphy's situation involves a tax "upon the sale itself, considered separate and apart from the place and the circumstances of the sale." *Id. at 520.* Instead, as in *Nicol,* this tax is more akin to "a duty upon the facilities made use of and actually employed in the transaction." *Id. at 519.* To be sure, the facility used in *Nicol* was a commodities exchange whereas the facility used by Murphy was the legal system, but that hardly seems a significant distinction. The tax may be laid upon the proceeds received when one vindicates a statutory right, but the right is nonetheless a "creature of law," which *Knowlton* identifies as a "privilege" taxable by excise. *178 U.S. at 55* (right to take property by inheritance is granted by law and therefore taxable as upon a privilege);[19] *cf. Steward, 301 U.S. at 580-81* ("[N]atural rights, so called, are as much subject to taxation as rights of less importance. An excise is not limited to vocations or activities that may be prohibited altogether. . . . It extends to vocations or activities pursued as of common right") (footnote omitted).

* * * *

III. CONCLUSION

For the foregoing reasons, we conclude (1) Murphy's compensatory award was not received on account of personal physical injuries, and therefore is not exempt from taxation pursuant to *§104(a)(2) of the IRC*; (2) the award is part of her "gross income," as defined by *§61 of the IRC*; and (3) the tax upon the award is an excise and not a direct tax subject to the apportionment requirement of Article I, Section 9 of the Constitution. The tax is uniform throughout the United States and therefore passes constitutional muster. The judgment of the district court is accordingly
Affirmed.

NOTES AND QUESTIONS

1. *Section 104's policy.* The *Murphy* case makes clear that damages received for pain and suffering, or for emotional illness, resulting directly from a physical injury are excludable from income under §104, but that damages received for physical illnesses resulting from emotional injury are not. Do you see a policy rationale for this result?

2. *Helpful diagnoses.* Perhaps the genesis of the amendment to §104 in 1996 was a suspicion that damage claims for emotional injury or pain and suffering are inherently suspect. But isn't that the job of the triers of fact on the underlying substantive claim? Rules like that now contained in §104 lead sympathetic physicians and courts to search for a physical injury kernel at the heart of damage claims for emotional and pain and suffering injuries, on the theory that it helps the plaintiff and no one else is hurt in the process. Is that right?

3. *Is §61 circular?* In *Murphy II* (the case excerpted above), Chief Judge Ginsburg wrote, "For example, if *§61(a)* were amended specifically to include in gross income '$100,000 in addition to all other gross income,' then that additional sum would be a part of gross income under *§61* even though no actual gain was associated with it. In other words, although the 'Congress cannot make a thing income which is not so in fact,' . . . it can *label* a thing income and tax it, so long as it acts within its constitutional authority, which includes not only the *Sixteenth Amendment* but also Article I, Sections 8 and 9." But adding

---

19. For the same reason, we infer from *Knowlton* that a tax laid upon an amount received in settlement of a suit for a personal nonphysical injury would also be an excise. *See 178 U.S. at 55.*

$100,000 to every taxpayer's income is tantamount to simply adjusting the tax rate brackets. What is relevant in this case is that one taxpayer (Murphy) got a type of cash inflow (damages for emotional injuries) that others did not.

4. You receive compensation of $60,000 per year working at a job you hate, resenting every minute of it. You might view the paycheck you receive as a fair exchange for your loss of free time and for the way the job makes you feel stressed and bad about yourself. Your friend earns $60,000 per year at a job she loves, which makes her feel empowered and a meaningful contributor to society. How should the income tax reflect these two circumstances?

5. *Constitutional kerfuffle.* The *Murphy* case might strike you as overwrought and tortured in its constitutional analysis, which would be a fair assessment. The case's history is even more complex. The D.C. Circuit Court of Appeals originally held that Murphy's damages were not includable in income, because the 1996 amendment to §104 led to an unconstitutional outcome in taxing as income damages that were unrelated to lost wages or earnings. Instead, concluded the court, the damages constituted a pure return of (human) capital. Murphy v. I.R.S., 460 F.3d 79 (D.C. Cir. 2006) ("Murphy I") (Ginsburg, Chief J., opinion):

> Broad though the power granted in the *Sixteenth Amendment* is, the Supreme Court, as Murphy points out, has long recognized "the principle that a restoration of capital [i]s not income; hence it [falls] outside the definition of 'income' upon which the law impose[s] a tax.

* * * *

> As we have seen, it is clear from the record that the damages were awarded to make Murphy emotionally and reputationally "whole" and not to compensate her for lost wages or taxable earnings of any kind. The emotional well-being and good reputation she enjoyed before they were diminished by her former employer were not taxable as income. Under this analysis, therefore, the compensation she received in lieu of what she lost cannot be considered income and, hence, it would appear the *Sixteenth Amendment* does not empower the Congress to tax her award.

The opinion in *Murphy I* was unprecedented. No court of appeals had found a component of the personal income tax to be an unconstitutional overreach of the Sixteenth Amendment or Congress's general power to tax in the previous several decades. The case triggered a firestorm of academic criticism (and some defense). Stratton, *Experts Ponder Murphy Decision's Many Flaws*, 112 Tax Notes 822 (Sept. 4, 2006) (" 'We law professors must not be doing our jobs right if three federal judges and their clerks can reach a conclusion like this one,' [Professor George] Yin said"); Kenney, Murphy a Boon for Protesters, Critics Say, 112 Tax Notes 832 (Sept. 4, 2006).

Most of the criticism centered around *Murphy I's* failure to consider whether Murphy had any tax basis to recover in her own human capital. That is, all freely bargained exchanges are for like *value*; the question for taxation is whether there is a difference between that value and the taxpayer's cost (basis) in the asset surrendered. See, e.g., Dodge, Murphy and the Sixteenth

Amendment in Relation to the Taxation of Non-Excludable Personal Injury Awards, 8 Fla. Tax Rev. 369 (2007); Geier, Murphy and the Evolution of "Basis," 113 Tax Notes 576 (Nov. 6, 2006). For a defense of a narrow reading of the Sixteenth Amendment and Congress's power to tax more generally, see Jensen, Did the Sixteenth Amendment Ever Matter? Does It Matter Today?, 108 Nw. U. L. Rev. 799 (2014).

The D.C. Circuit granted a rehearing, and Chief Judge Ginsburg again wrote the opinion, which required him to come to the opposite conclusions from those he reached in *Murphy I* while grappling with the same precedents.

PEREZ v. COMMISSIONER
144 T.C. 51 (2015)

HOLMES, Judge:

Nichelle Perez received $20,000 under contracts that she signed with a clinic before she underwent a prolonged series of painful injections and operations to retrieve her unfertilized eggs for transfer to infertile couples. The contracts said that she was being paid in compensation for her pain and suffering. The Code says that *damages* for pain and suffering are not taxable.

Was the $20,000 Perez received "damages"?

FINDINGS OF FACT

Perez is a 29-year-old single woman from Orange County, California. She is a high-school graduate and worked as a full-time sales associate for Sprint. In her early 20s Perez learned about egg donation. Her Internet search soon led her to the website of the Donor Source International, LLC—an egg-donation agency in Orange County that matches egg donors with women and couples struggling to conceive on their own.

* * * *

This [procedure] is all called egg "donation," but the term is a misnomer—the participant in the egg-stimulation and retrieval is compensated. . . .

* * * *

Perez signed one contract with the Donor Source in February 2009. It promised her money:

> Donor Fee: Donor and Intended Parents will agree upon a Donor Fee for Donor's time, effort, inconvenience, pain, and suffering in donating her eggs. This fee is for Donor's good faith and full compliance with the donor egg procedure, not in exchange for or purchase of eggs and the quantity or quality of eggs retrieved will not affect the Donor Fee.

This meant that if Perez kept her side of the deal, but produced unusable eggs or no eggs at all, she would still be paid the contract price. The contract plainly provides that it is not for the sale of body parts:

> The Parties acknowledge and agree that the funds provided to the Donor shall not in any way constitute payment to Donor for her eggs.

It also allocates foreseeable risk. It states that the donor assumes "all medical risks and agree[s] to hold The Donor Source harmless from any and all liability for any and all physical or medical harm to herself * * *." The Donor Source takes its deals seriously, and its representative credibly testified that the company could sue Perez for breach of contract if she did not strictly comply with all the requirements.

* * * *

[U]p until March 27, 2009—the egg-retrieval date—Perez underwent a series of intrusive physical examinations. She frequently had to travel to a fertility clinic, submit to pregnancy tests, endure invasive internal ultrasound examinations, and have a syringe stuck into her arm to draw four to five vials of blood.

The needlework followed Perez home. She had to self-administer hormonal injections using a one-inch needle. Perez injected herself with 10 units of Lupron each morning from March 7 to March 11, and she had to take the shots right into her stomach, which often bruised and hurt her. With complete credibility Perez said that these procedures were "actually very painful * * * it was burning the entire time you were injecting it."

As the retrieval date approached, the injection schedule increased. Between March 16 and 25, she had to self-administer anywhere from one to three daily injections of Lupron, Follistim, and Menopur. She made around 22 injections into her stomach during this period. Every time she had to administer another dose of the hormones, she had to search for a part of her stomach not already covered in bruises.

Then on March 25 Perez administered to herself—under the observation of a professional at a fertility clinic—the final "trigger shot" of hCG. This is an intramuscular injection in the lower hip that goes through a two-inch needle. The shots caused Perez significant physical pain deep in her muscles as well as extreme abdominal bloating.

On the retrieval date, Perez was required to undergo anesthesia for the procedure. Doctors informed her that anesthesia carries with it a risk of possible death, and so she had to sign another liability waiver just before she went under. Egg removal is a type of surgery, during which the doctor worked his way into an anesthetized Perez with an ultrasound needle, and then penetrated her ovaries to harvest any viable eggs. The unnatural amount of hormones she'd taken had done their job, and the doctors were able to retrieve between 15 and 20 eggs—rather than the body's normal production of just one—from her. After it was over, Perez felt cramped and bloated; she had mood swings, headaches, nausea, and fatigue.

But she'd kept the promises she made and got a check for $10,000. [She then repeated the process later in the year.]

* * * *

The Donor Source sent a Form 1099 to Perez for $20,000 for tax year 2009. After consulting other egg donors online, Perez concluded that the money was not taxable because it compensated her only for pain and suffering; therefore, she left it off her tax return. The Commissioner disagreed and sent her a notice of deficiency. Perez timely filed a petition, and we tried the case in California, where Perez still lives.

OPINION

We acknowledge that this case has received some publicity in tax and nontax publications, which is why it is important to state clearly what it does not concern. It does not require us to decide whether human eggs are capital assets. It does not require us to figure out how to allocate basis in the human body, or the holding period for human-body parts, or the character of the gain from the sale of those parts.[20]

A.   NATURE OF THE COMPENSATION

So what is this case about? Both parties agree that payments Perez received were not for the sale of her eggs. Perez argues that they were in exchange for the pain, suffering, and physical injuries she endured as part of the egg-retrieval process; the Commissioner, on the other hand, argues Perez was simply compensated for services rendered. The only two cases we have found that are anywhere near this issue are *Green v. Commissioner,* 74 T.C. 1229 (1980) and *United States v. Garber,* 607 F.2d 92 (5th Cir. 1979). Both involved the exchange of blood plasma for compensation. In *Green,* the taxpayer was paid by the pint, and we found her to be engaged in the sale of tangible property rather than the performance of services. *Green,* 74 T.C. at 1234. In *Garber,* the Fifth Circuit suggested the taxpayer might be engaged in the sale of property because the extent of her compensation was directly related to the concentration of antibodies in the plasma she produced. *Garber,* 607 F.2d at 97. . . . But because the appeal was from a criminal conviction, the court concluded that it didn't have to solve this puzzle, and could instead decide the case on the ground that a criminal prosecution for tax evasion was "an inappropriate vehicle for pioneering interpretations of tax law." *Id.* at 100.

Both of Perez's 2009 contracts with the Donor Source specify that her compensation is in exchange for her "good faith and compliance with the donor egg procedure." Unlike the taxpayers in *Green* and *Garber,* who were paid by the quantity and the quality of plasma produced, Perez's compensation depended on neither the quantity nor the quality of the eggs retrieved, but solely on how far into the egg-retrieval process she went. On this key point, the testimony of

---

20. For a thorough discussion of the sale of human-body parts, see Bridget J. Crawford, "Our Bodies, Our (Tax) Selves," 31 Va. Tax Rev. 695 (2012), and Lisa Milot, "What Are We — Laborers, Factories or Spare Parts? The Tax Treatment of Transfers of Human Body Materials," 67 Wash. & Lee L. Rev. 1053 (2010).

both parties to the contracts agrees with the contract language. We have to find that Perez was compensated for services rendered and not for the sale of property.

And, as we know, "gross income means all income from whatever source derived, including * * * compensation for services." Sec. 61(a)(1). But this general rule of inclusion has many exceptions, and the one that Perez points us to is section 104(a)(2). . . .

Before the regulations were amended, section 1.104-1(c) used to require payments excluded under section 104(a)(2) be "received * * * through prosecution of a legal suit or action based upon tort or tort type rights, or through a settlement agreement entered into in lieu of such prosecution." Sec. 1.104-1(c), Income Tax Regs. (former regulations), *amended by* T.D. 9573, 77 Fed. Reg. 3106-01, 3107 (Jan. 23, 2012). There were thus two separate requirements for a taxpayer to exclude income under section 104(a)(2): (1) the underlying cause of action giving rise to the recovery had to be based on tort or tort-type rights; and (2) the taxpayer had to receive the payment on account of his or her personal injuries or sickness.

But the Secretary has amended these regulations and abandoned the . . . language requiring a "tort or tort-type right.". . . The regulation now states:

> Section 104(a)(2) excludes from gross income the amount of any damages (other than punitive damages) received (whether by suit or agreement and whether as lump sums or as periodic payments) on account of personal physical injuries or physical sickness.

* * * *

Perez very clearly has a legally recognized interest against bodily invasion. But we must hold that when she forgoes that interest—and consents to such intimate invasion for payment—any amount she receives must be included in her taxable income. Had the Donor Source or the clinic exceeded the scope of Perez's consent, Perez may have had a claim for damages. But the injury here, as painful as it was to Perez, was exactly within the scope of the medical procedures to which she contractually consented. Twice. Her physical pain was a byproduct of performing a service contract, and we find that the payments were made not to compensate her for some unwanted invasion against her bodily integrity but to compensate her for services rendered.

But what is one to make of the regulation's amendment to remove the "tort and tort-type right" requirement? One should always pause before holding that an amendment didn't change anything. But here the reason is clear—the amendment *did* change the law—it just didn't change the law for people like Perez. In 1992 the Supreme Court decided *United States v. Burke*, 504 U.S. 229 (1992). It held that title VII backpay settlement awards were not excludable from income under section 104(a)(2). *Id.* at 242. At the time the statute read "damages received * * * on account of personal injuries," and the taxpayer pounced on the argument that her settlement with the Tennessee Valley Authority for unlawfully discriminating against her because she was a woman fit that requirement. Not so, said the Supreme

Court. The Court emphasized that since the 1960s the Commissioner has formally linked the section 104(a)(2) exclusion to "tort or tort-type rights." *Id.* at 234. It pronounced:

> "The essential element of an exclusion under section 104(a)(2) is that the income involved must derive from some sort of tort claim against the payor. . . . As a result, common law tort concepts are helpful in deciding whether a taxpayer is being compensated for a 'personal injury'" * * *

* * * *

Congress amended the Code in the Small Business Job Protection Act of 1996, and the Secretary in 2009 rewrote his regulations. This amended Code section and regulation let taxpayers who recovered under no-fault statutes exclude the "damages" that they received, even if they did not receive them for a "tort-type" claim.

The change in the section 104 regulation reflected a profusion of remedies for persons who are physically injured and recover under no-fault statutes, so that they are treated like those who are physically injured and recover through more traditional actions in tort. But that regulation still addresses situations where a taxpayer settles a claim for physical injuries or physical sickness before — or at least in lieu of — seeing litigation through to its conclusion.

This small change just helped tax regulation keep up with a bit of a shift in American law toward administrative or statutory remedies and away from common-law tort for some kinds of personal injuries. It is not at all arbitrary, capricious, or manifestly contrary to the Code. But it also doesn't help Perez. We completely believe Perez's utterly sincere and credible testimony that the series of medical procedures that culminated in the retrieval of her eggs was painful and dangerous to her present and future health. But what matters is that she voluntarily signed a contract to be paid to endure them. This means that the money she received was not "damages."

We conclude by noting that the result we reach today by taking a close look at the language and history of section 104 is also a reasonable one. We see no limit on the mischief that ruling in Perez's favor might cause: A professional boxer could argue that some part of the payments he received for his latest fight is excludable because they are payments for his bruises, cuts, and nosebleeds. A hockey player could argue that a portion of his million-dollar salary is allocable to the chipped teeth he invariably suffers during his career. And the same would go for the brain injuries suffered by football players and the less-noticed bodily damage daily endured by working men and women on farms and ranches, in mines, or on fishing boats. We don't doubt that some portion of the compensation paid all these people reflects the risk that they will feel pain and suffering, but it's a risk of pain and suffering that they agree to before they begin their work. And that makes it taxable compensation and not excludable damages.

Because Perez's compensation was not "damages" under section 104(a)(2), we must rule against her on the main issue in the case.

2. Deferred Payments and Structured Settlements

In 1983, Congress codified an earlier revenue ruling and added to §104(a)(2) the language that reads "and whether as a lump sum or periodic payments." Under that provision, as amended, a tort victim who is able to defer current payment in return for a series of later payments can exclude the entire amount of the later payments as recovery for personal injury. The complete exclusion is available even though the deferred payments will invariably contain an interest component.

The nontaxation of the interest component creates an incentive for tort victims to structure settlements to provide deferred periodic payments. After all, if one received a lump-sum payment and invested it, the interest returns would presumably be taxable.

In many circumstances, the tax advantage to the tort victim may be offset by a disadvantage to the tortfeasor. Suppose, for example, that the tortfeasor is an individual who cannot deduct the amount to be paid. If the tortfeasor retains for a while a portion of the principal that is due to the victim, she presumably will earn taxable interest income, and receive no deduction for whatever payments of principal plus interest she ultimately makes. The arrangement may, however, reduce the overall tax paid on the interest income if the tortfeasor pays tax for the relevant period at a lower marginal tax rate than the tort victim.

Now suppose that the tortfeasor is a business firm and is allowed to deduct the payment, although not until it is made. Once again, the tax advantage to the tort victim from delaying the transfer of the funds may be offset by a disadvantage to the tortfeasor, since deduction of the loan principal is deferred until the payment is made. Deferral of the deduction can be avoided, however, if the business tortfeasor enters into a somewhat complex set of transactions with an insurance company, which in turn transacts with another company that specializes in "structured settlements" (that is, settlements providing for deferred payments). Consequently, deferred payments are now commonly used to settle tort cases involving large sums of money. The victim might prefer to take an immediate payment and invest it herself or himself, but the tax advantage of deferred payment — the ability to avoid tax on interest earned on the lump-sum amount — provides a powerful incentive to use the somewhat complex, costly, and restrictive structured settlement technique.

3. Medical Expenses and Other Recoveries and Benefits

As discussed earlier, employees are not taxed on the value of employer-provided health insurance, nor are they taxed on the value of services or other recoveries received from that insurance policy. What about insurance that is purchased directly by employees? As discussed in Chapter 10, medical expenses, including premiums paid for medical insurance, are deductible only to the extent that in the aggregate they exceed, for the taxable year, 7.5 percent of adjusted gross income. §213. Recoveries under an individual's medical insurance policy are excluded, even if those recoveries exceed the cost of medical care (for example, where the insured has two policies covering the same outlay and is permitted to recover under both). See §104(a)(3). Assuming that the premium was not deducted (as part of expenses in excess of 7.5 percent of adjusted gross income), this rule of no deduction of premiums/no income from payments is consistent with the rule for taxation of term life insurance; in the aggregate, disregarding insurance company costs and profits, nondeductible payments equal nontaxable benefits.

Section 104(a)(1) excludes workers' compensation. Recoveries under disability insurance policies financed by taxpayer (rather than employer) payments are excluded under §104(a)(3); but the premiums are not deductible.

I. ILLEGAL INCOME

GILBERT v. COMMISSIONER
552 F.2d 478 (2d Cir. 1977)

Lumbard, Circuit Judge.

The taxpayer Edward M. Gilbert appeals from a determination by the tax court that he realized taxable income on certain unauthorized withdrawals of corporate funds made by him in 1962. We reverse.

Until June 12, 1962, Gilbert was president, principal stockholder, and a director of the E. L. Bruce Company, Inc., a New York corporation which was engaged in the lumber supply business. In 1961 and early 1962 Gilbert acquired on margin [that is, in large part with borrowed money] substantial personal and beneficial ownership of stock in another lumber supply company, the Celotex Corporation, intending ultimately to bring about a merger of Celotex into Bruce. To this end, he persuaded associates of his to purchase Celotex stock, guaranteeing them against loss, and also induced Bruce itself to purchase a substantial number of Celotex shares. In addition, on March 5, 1962, Gilbert granted Bruce an option to purchase his Celotex shares from him at cost. By the end of May 1962, 56% of Celotex was thus controlled by Gilbert and Bruce, and negotiations for the merger were proceeding; agreement had been reached that three of the directors of Bruce would be placed on the board of Celotex. It is undisputed that this merger would have been in Bruce's interest.

The stock market declined on May 28, 1962, however, and Gilbert was called upon to furnish additional margin [that is, individual funds] for the Celotex shares purchased by him and his associates. Lacking sufficient cash of his own to meet this margin call, Gilbert instructed the secretary of Bruce to use corporate funds to supply the necessary margin. Between May 28 and June 6 a series of checks totalling $1,958,000 were withdrawn from Bruce's accounts and used to meet the margin call. $5,000 was repaid to Bruce on June 5. According to his testimony in the tax court, Gilbert from the outset intended to repay all the money and at all times thought he was acting in the corporation's best interests as well as his own. He promptly informed several other Bruce officers and directors of the withdrawals; however, some were not notified until June 11 or 12.

On about June 1, Gilbert returned to New York from Nevada, where he had been attending to a personal matter. Shortly thereafter he consulted with Shearman, Sterling & Wright, who were outside counsel to Bruce at the time, regarding the withdrawals. They, he, and another Bruce director initiated negotiations to sell many of the Celotex shares to Ruberoid Company as a way of recouping most of Bruce's outlay.

On June 8, Gilbert went to the law offices of Shearman, Sterling & Wright and executed interest-bearing promissory notes to Bruce for $1,953,000 secured by an assignment of most of his property. The notes were callable by Bruce on demand, with presentment and notice of demand waived by Gilbert. The tax court found that up through June 12 the net value of the assets assigned for security by Gilbert substantially exceeded the amount owed.

After Gilbert informed other members of the Bruce board of directors of his actions, a meeting of the board was scheduled for the morning of June 12. At the meeting the board accepted the note and assignment but refused to ratify Gilbert's unauthorized withdrawals. During the meeting, word came that the board of directors of the Ruberoid Company had rejected the price offered for sale of the Celotex stock. Thereupon, the Bruce board demanded and received Gilbert's resignation and decided to issue a public announcement the next day regarding his unauthorized withdrawals. All further attempts on June 12 to arrange a sale of the Celotex stock fell through and in the evening Gilbert flew to Brazil, where he stayed for several months. On June 13 the market price of Bruce and Celotex stock plummeted, and trading in those shares was suspended by the Securities and Exchange Commission.

On June 22 the Internal Revenue Service filed tax liens against Gilbert based on a [claim of tax liability of] $1,720,000 for 1962. Bruce, having failed to file the assignment from Gilbert because of the real estate filing fee involved,[21] now found itself subordinate in priority to the IRS and, impeded by the tax lien, has never since been able to recover much of its $1,953,000 from the assigned assets.[22] For the fiscal year ending June 30, 1962, Bruce claimed a loss deduction on the $1,953,000 withdrawn by Gilbert. Several years later Gilbert pled guilty to federal and state charges of having unlawfully withdrawn the funds from Bruce.

On these facts, the tax court determined that Gilbert realized income when he made the unauthorized withdrawals of funds from Bruce, and that his efforts at restitution did not entitle him to any offset against this income.

---

21. When attempting to file in the New York County Clerk's office on June 13 or 14, Bruce was told that it would have to pay a mortgage tax of at least $10,000 because the assignment included real property. Since the net value of the real property was negligible, Bruce sought to perfect only the personal property portion, but the clerk still demanded the mortgage tax on the ground that the real property assignment and the personal property assignment were contained in the same document.

22. As of the date of trial in the tax court, less than $500,000 had been raised through sales of the assigned assets. Pursuant to an agreement reached between Bruce and the government in 1970, 35% of these proceeds have been paid over to the government pending the outcome of this lawsuit.

The starting point for analysis of this case is James v. United States, 366 U.S. 213 (1961), which established that embezzled funds can constitute taxable income to the embezzler.

> When a taxpayer acquires earnings, lawfully or unlawfully, without the consensual recognition, express or implied, of an obligation to repay and without restriction as to their disposition, "he has received income which he is required to return, even though it may still be claimed that he is not entitled to the money, and even though he may still be adjudged liable to restore its equivalent." . . .

Id. at 219.

The Commissioner contends that there can never be "consensual recognition . . . of an obligation to repay" in an embezzlement case. He reasons that because the corporation—as represented by a majority of the board of directors—was unaware of the withdrawals, there cannot have been *consensual* recognition of the obligation to repay at the time the taxpayer Gilbert acquired the funds. Since the withdrawals were not authorized and the directors refused to treat them as a loan to Gilbert, the Commissioner concludes that Gilbert should be taxed like a thief rather than a borrower.

In a typical embezzlement, the embezzler intends at the outset to abscond with the funds. If he repays the money during the same taxable year, he will not be taxed. See James v. Commissioner, *supra* at 220; Quinn v. Commissioner, 524 F.2d 617, 624-625 (7th Cir. 1975); Rev. Rul. 65-254, 1965-2 Cum. Bul. 50. As we held in Buff v. Commissioner, 496 F.2d 847 (2d Cir. 1974), if he spends the loot instead of repaying, he cannot avoid tax on his embezzlement income simply by signing promissory notes later in the same year. See also *id.* at 849-850 (Oakes, J., concurring).

This is not a typical embezzlement case, however, and we do not interpret *James* as requiring income realization in every case of unlawful withdrawals by a taxpayer. There are a number of facts that differentiate this case from *Buff* and *James*. When Gilbert withdrew the corporate funds, he recognized his obligation to repay and intended to do so.[23] The funds were to be used not only for his benefit but also for the benefit of the corporation; meeting the margin calls was necessary to maintain the possibility of the highly favorable merger. Although Gilbert undoubtedly realized that he lacked the necessary authorization, he thought he was serving the best interests of the corporation and he expected his decision to be ratified shortly thereafter. That Gilbert at no time intended to retain the corporation's funds is clear from his actions.[24] He immediately informed several of the corporation's officers and directors, and he made a complete accounting to all of them within two weeks. He also disclosed his actions to the corporation's outside counsel, a reputable law firm, and followed its instructions regarding repayment. In signing immediately payable

23. Quinn v. Commissioner, relied on by the Commissioner, involved taxation of funds received without any contemporaneous recognition of the obligation to repay, and it is therefore distinguishable from the present case.

24. If Gilbert had been intending to abscond with the $1,953,000, it is difficult to see how he could have hoped to avoid detection in the long run. Since his equity in the corporation itself was worth well over $1,953,000, it would have been absurd for him to attempt such a theft.

promissory notes secured by most of his assets, Gilbert's clear intent was to ensure that Bruce would obtain full restitution. In addition, he attempted to sell his shares of Celotex stock in order to raise cash to pay Bruce back immediately.

When Gilbert executed the assignment to Bruce of his assets on June 8 and when this assignment for security was accepted by the Bruce board on June 12, the net market value of these assets was substantially more than the amount owed. The Bruce board did not release Gilbert from his underlying obligation to repay, but the assignment was nonetheless valid and Bruce's failure to make an appropriate filing to protect itself against the claims of third parties, such as the IRS, did not relieve Gilbert of the binding effect of the assignment. Since the assignment secured an immediately payable note, Gilbert had as of June 12 granted Bruce full discretion to liquidate any of his assets in order to recoup on the $1,953,000 withdrawal. Thus, Gilbert's net accretion in real wealth on the overall transaction was zero: he had for his own use withdrawn $1,953,000 in corporate funds but he had now granted the corporation control over at least $1,953,000 worth of his assets.

We conclude that where a taxpayer withdraws funds from a corporation which he fully intends to repay and which he expects with reasonable certainty he will be able to repay, where he believes that his withdrawals will be approved by the corporation, and where he makes a prompt assignment of assets sufficient to secure the amount owed, he does not realize income on the withdrawals under the *James* test. When Gilbert acquired the money, there was an express consensual recognition of his obligation to repay: the secretary of the corporation, who signed the checks, the officers and directors to whom Gilbert gave contemporaneous notification, and Gilbert himself were all aware that the transaction was in the nature of a loan. Moreover, the funds were certainly not received by Gilbert "without restriction as to their disposition" as is required for taxability under *James*; the money was to be used solely for the temporary purpose of meeting certain margin calls and it was so used. For these reasons, we reverse the decision of the tax court.

NOTES AND QUESTIONS

1. *Analysis.* The court says, "In a typical embezzlement, the embezzler intends at the outset to abscond with the funds." That may well be true, but in many instances the embezzler fully intends to repay, as soon as his or her horse, lottery ticket, or high-tech stock investment pays off. If misfortune becomes evident within two weeks and an embezzler confesses, and promises repayment, are the proceeds of the embezzlement nontaxable?

2. *The special status of embezzlers.* The decision of the Supreme Court in James v. United States, relied on by the court in *Gilbert*, overruled an earlier decision of the Court in Commissioner v. Wilcox, 327 U.S. 404 (1946), in which it had held that embezzled funds were not income because of the obligation to restore the funds to the victim. This decision was at odds with a later decision in Rutkin v. United States, 343 U.S. 130 (1952), in which the Court held an extortionist liable for tax on the amount extorted, but the *Rutkin* Court had

expressly refused to overrule *Wilcox*. *James* was thought to have laid to rest the confusion and inconsistency created by the *Rutkin-Wilcox* distinction. Does the *Gilbert* decision revive the confusion and uncertainty to some degree?

3. *Dirty business?* Is it unseemly for the government, by taxing the proceeds of an embezzlement, to share in the profits of an illegal activity? This was the view expressed by Judge Martin T. Manton of the Second Circuit Court of Appeals in a concurring opinion in Steinberg v. United States, 14 F.2d 564, 569 (1926). Judge Manton also expressed his dismay over the thought of the government allowing deductions for bribes. In an O. Henry ending, Judge Manton was convicted in 1939 of accepting bribes of more than $66,000 over a three-year period when he was senior circuit judge of the Second Circuit and in 1948, after his death, was held liable for fraud penalties for failing to report the bribes on his tax returns. 7 T.C.M. 937.

4. *Borrowing versus swindling.* A taxpayer who purports to borrow funds, or to receive them as investments, may in fact be a swindler. The line between the two possibilities may in some instances be difficult to draw. See In re Diversified Brokers Co., 487 F.2d 355 (8th Cir. 1973) (receipts in "Ponzi" pyramiding scheme treated as loans to corporate borrower rather than as embezzled funds); Moore v. United States, 412 F.2d 974 (5th Cir. 1969) (money received in complex scheme involving purported purchase of equipment that did not exist held to be the fruits of a swindle, not a loan). Would it be best in situations of this sort to wait and see how a person uses the funds, instead of examining the circumstances of receipt?

5. *Nontax objectives.* The use of selective tax enforcement to punish political enemies is plainly intolerable. But what about selective enforcement against "known" crime figures who cannot be convicted of other crimes? Al Capone, the Chicago mob leader who was reportedly guilty of a host of serious crimes, was ultimately sent to jail for tax evasion. Is it wrong to use the tax system deliberately to punish people like Capone?

6. *Adding injury to injury.* As the *Gilbert* case illustrates, the taxes collected from an embezzler (or other wrongdoer) by the IRS generally will come from funds that otherwise would be returned (or paid) to the victim; generally the IRS's claim for taxes comes before the victim's claim for recovery of the stolen money.[25]

An interesting example of the IRS attitude toward victims of embezzlement is found in Letter Ruling 8604003. The embezzler, a bank employee, had disguised his defalcation by making false book entries showing wage payments (in amounts reaching a total of about $1 million). As part of his scheme he paid Social Security taxes (FICA) and withholding taxes. The bank, on discovering that it had been victimized, sought to recover the taxes. The IRS refused. It defended this result by arguments in the alternative. On the one hand, it

---

25. Under §6321 the United States has a lien for unpaid taxes after demand for the tax owed. The lien is against all the property of the taxpayer, which, in the case of an embezzler, will include the embezzled funds. This lien will take priority over any claim of the victim unless the victim is able to file a judgment lien (that is, obtain a judgment against the embezzler and then file a lien on the embezzled funds) before the IRS files its lien. See §6323. As a practical matter, the IRS will be able to file its lien before the victim will be able to file its lien.

reasoned, if the amounts were wages to the embezzler, the taxes were properly withheld. On the other hand, if the wage payments and the corresponding tax payments were unauthorized, then the bank did not make any payments, the embezzler did; so the bank is not entitled to a recovery on the theory of a mistaken payment. Moreover, the IRS is entitled to keep the money as long as the amount does not exceed what the embezzler owes. As far as the IRS is concerned, once money is stolen, that money belongs to the thief and the thief must pay his or her taxes before returning anything to the victim.

J.   GAIN ON THE SALE OF A HOME

According to the U.S. Census Bureau, more than three-fifths of Americans own their homes. The homeownership rate has, however, declined significantly in the past few years, from 69 percent in 2004 to 62.9 percent in 2016.

For the typical American family, the principal residence is by far the most valuable asset they own, dominating the household's investment portfolio. It is perhaps not surprising, therefore, that Congress has turned to the tax code to curry favor with America's homeowners. Chapter 3 considers in detail how the nontaxation of imputed rental income is one of the key benefits available for owner-occupied housing. We now turn to a more explicit benefit available for the American homeowner: the exclusion of gain from the sale of one's principal residence.

Section 121 excludes from income certain gain on the sale or exchange of a home. For the exclusion to apply, the taxpayer must have owned the home and used it as a principal residence for periods aggregating at least two years over the five-year period ending on the date the taxpayer sold it. §121(a). Thus, the sale of a vacation home generally would not qualify for the exclusion.

The amount of gain that §121 excludes from income on a given home sale is generally limited to $250,000 for a single taxpayer. §121(b)(1). Thus, suppose a single taxpayer sold for $400,000 a home that she had bought for $100,000. Assuming that the sale otherwise qualified under §121, $50,000 of the gain (the excess of the overall gain of $300,000 over the exclusion limit) would be taxable.

For married taxpayers filing a joint return, the exclusion limit is $500,000 rather than $250,000, so long as both spouses have used the home as a principal residence for two of the prior five years. §121(b)(2). Exclusion at the $500,000 level is also available for surviving spouses, provided that the sale takes place within two years of the date of death of the deceased spouse and the ownership and holding period requirements were satisfied as of that date. §121(b)(4).

Section 121 generally cannot apply to any taxpayer more than once every two years. §121(b)(3)(A). Thus, if on January 25 of Year 1 a taxpayer made a qualifying sale of a principal residence for an amount that was at least 1 cent greater than her basis for the property, the exclusion could not apply again until January 25 of Year 3.[26] However, this limitation is called off if the sale or exchange was "by reason of a change in place of employment, health, or, to the extent provided in regulations, unforeseen circumstances." §121(c)(2)(B).

These same grounds also permit exclusion up to a reduced dollar ceiling for taxpayers who failed to meet the two-year use requirement. For example, if an unmarried taxpayer lived in a principal residence for exactly one year before moving, due to a transfer from the New York to the California office of her employer, §121 would permit exclusion of up to $125,000 of gain upon its sale.

NOTES AND QUESTIONS

1. Section 121 was added to the Code in 1997. Prior to its enactment, gain upon the sale of a home could be "rolled over" (and thus not currently included in income) to the extent that the sale proceeds were reinvested within a two-year period through the purchase of a new home. (§1034, repealed in 1997.) In addition, a repealed prior version of §121 provided a limited one-time exclusion of gain on the sale of a principal residence to taxpayers who were age 55 or older. This rule was apparently designed to help "empty-nesters," who sold their homes and bought smaller ones (thus potentially failing to reinvest fully) when their children moved out.

2. What policy arguments, if any, support the current version of §121? Is the exclusion supported by the fact that losses on the sale of a home are considered personal in character and thus are not deductible? If so, should the exclusion be unlimited? And should gambling gains be excluded from income on the same rationale?

3. Section 121 arguably creates various incentives for taxpayers to alter their behavior so they can take full advantage of it. For example, if you have a vacation home that has appreciated significantly and that you plan to sell soon, the provision can motivate using it as a principal residence for two years, even if you otherwise would not have chosen to do so. Or, if your home has appreciated to about the full statutory limit and you expect homes in general to continue appreciating, the provision creates an incentive to sell now and buy a new home so that you can start excluding appreciation all over again.

Are these incentives likely to have much effect on people's behavior? Even if not, do the disparities in tax treatment that give rise to them tell you anything about §121?

4. Some commentators believe that §121 contributed to the 2008 financial crisis by encouraging home investment (and periodic sale), thereby helping to feed the real-estate "bubble" that abruptly and spectacularly collapsed.

---

26. This limitation is not merely redundant of the two-year use requirement because taxpayers can move into new principal residences before selling previous ones.

3

THE PRIVATE SPHERE AND THE PUBLIC SPHERE

The previous chapter examined some aspects of the question, "What is income?" Whether your role is advising a client or advocating tax reform, understanding the scope of the tax base obviously is important.

In working through the materials in Chapter 2, you should already have noticed a fundamental problem in tax system design: The Code, like any other practical tax system, is a great deal more adept at handling transactions that take place in markets among third parties than it is peering into how we conduct ourselves in nonmarket contexts. For convenience, we can think of these two realms as the public sphere and the private sphere of our lives.

In general, visible transactions in the public sphere can be expected to have some tax effect—to pull some lever or push some button in the large model of economic activity that we call the Code. By contrast, the Code ignores much of what transpires in the private sphere of our lives and often makes a muddle of those private matters that it does try to identify and tax. Some of the issues relate to matters like "imputed income," discussed below, when work that could be done in the commercial sphere of life takes place behind the curtain of our private time. Others relate to the impossibility of unraveling the relationships within a household or family. In many contexts, it is a closer approximation of reality to see the family or household as a single entity, rather than as multiple individuals negotiating with each other at arm's length.

This chapter explores this tension between the private sphere and the public sphere of our lives, focusing on three principal areas: imputed income, gifts, and transfers incident to marriage or divorce. The problems, however, are much more endemic than that, and their resolution necessarily relies more on administrative feasibility than it does on a Haig-Simons definition of income. Chapter 6 returns to another aspect of this tension, when it considers whether married spouses should be treated as one taxpayer or two.

For example, if Professor Abbott hires a housekeeper, the salary the housekeeper receives is taxable income to the housekeeper. But how then do we treat the parents who pay their child a $20 per week allowance and in return expect the child to perform a set schedule of chores? Do we expect the child to file a tax return to report his labor income? The answer in practice is obvious, even if the theory is not always so clear.

A.   IMPUTED INCOME

1.   Imputed Income, Psychic Income, In-Kind Income

The concept of imputed income is poorly defined in much of the tax literature. For our purposes, we will employ "imputed income" to mean activities that theoretically *could have* taken place in the public sphere of your life but that in fact take place in the private sphere. More specifically, imputed income comprises (i) services you perform for yourself or your household that could have been provided in ordinary commercial transactions, or (ii) capital you invest to fund durable personal consumption goods whose consumption you enjoy, thereby forgoing a financial return on that capital. We will use a related concept, psychic income, to refer either to activities you engage in that give you pleasure or to the pleasure you get from passively enjoying an hour of leisure.[1]

Painting your own apartment, cutting your own hair, and putting together an IKEA bookshelf are examples of imputed income, because they take place in the personal sphere, but they could just as easily have been commercial transactions. In a Haig-Simons sense, you have an accession to wealth or personal consumption, but it should be apparent that no practical tax administration can be expected to inspect your apartment for telltale signs of fresh paint or recently constructed furniture. Of necessity, imputed income here falls squarely on the side of the private sphere of your life, and it remains invisible to the tax system.

The tax treatment of the at-home spouse is a far more serious example. In effect, the tax law treats a stay-at-home spouse as earning tax-exempt income (because his or her value added through services to the household is not taxed); when that spouse enters the workforce, and perhaps (as in the case of Professor Abbott) hires others to help out around the house, that tax-exempt imputed income suddenly becomes fully taxable income (with no deduction for most of those personal services now contracted out to third parties).[2] That

---

1. In practice, these two concepts will often overlap. For example, suppose you plant a garden. We could consider this imputed income on the ground that you could have worked longer hours to hire a gardener. But suppose you just love gardening, so that hiring someone to do it for you would remove all of the benefit?

2. Students often are confused into thinking that every taxable labor income inclusion must have an offsetting deductible expense, but this is simply incorrect. Payments for services for personal consumption goods, like housekeeping in the example here, are nondeductible. Some see this as a form of double taxation, in which Professor Abbott pays tax on her salary and again (through the denial of a deduction) when she hires a housekeeper to enable her to concentrate on her university work, but this confuses consumption decisions with the costs of earning income. We all have to keep house, at least to some minimal extent, and the decision to preserve one's time by paying another to do it is

is, the tax system sees that the stay-at-home spouse has moved his or her activities from the private sphere to the commercial sphere, so the tax system now takes cognizance of the spouse's efforts—while the spouse says, hey, I was working my tail off before, too![3]

The sudden appearance of a tax cost to what might be viewed as just different forms of work can be a big impediment that keeps the stay-at-home spouse from moving into the official workforce. The tax system in fact responds to this problem through such mechanisms as the standard deduction, personal exemptions, low tax rates on the bottom brackets of income, the earned income tax credit, and the child tax credit. In other words, the tax system cannot as a practical matter tax the Haig-Simons income attributable to household work, so it addresses the enormous discontinuity between work in the private sphere and work in the public sphere by driving down the effective marginal tax rate on the first dollars of labor income earned in the public sphere.

The biggest example of imputed income in the real world, outside of household work, is the rental value of owner-occupied housing. Professor Zelig could earn a return on his investment in his home by renting it out to a tenant and then going out to rent a place for himself, but instead Professor Zelig combines those two theoretical transactions into one by investing in a home and then occupying it himself. Zelig gets no actual annual cash return on his investment, and therefore the rental value of his home disappears below the surface of the tax ocean: It becomes part of the private sphere of his life. Unlike the household work case, we *could* break this transaction apart, by treating Professor Zelig as simultaneously wearing a landlord's hat and a tenant's hat—the valuation issues are not insurmountable—but we do not. (Norway did just this for a period of time, but unsurprisingly it found that political meddling substantially interfered with the tax authority's efforts to measure the rental value of owner-occupied housing.)

The role of imputed income puts into sharper relief the magnitude of the subsidies currently directed to owner-occupied housing. The Code allows Professor Zelig to deduct many expenses that would be relevant if he were a commercial landlord, such as interest expense and local property tax expenses (but not depreciation), and on top of that §121 offers the professor a tax exclusion—tax-free profits—on a substantial amount of any gain ultimately realized on the sale of his home. But the Code does not require any inclusion on the other side of the ledger: Professor Zelig's imputed income is not included

---

precisely the sort of personal tradeoff that falls within the meaning of "consumption" in the Haig-Simons equation; it is therefore not sufficient to justify a deduction. The same is true for grocery bills. Were this not the case, we would turn consumption taxes on their head, because the only remaining component of the tax base would be savings. See further Note 3 in Section B.1, *infra*.

The housekeeping example also lies at the heart of the hoary joke generally attributed to the great English economist Arthur Pigou about the professor who married her housekeeper and by doing so wrecked the economy. The joke, such as it is, is that the same housekeeping services presumably are performed by the couple after their marriage as were performed by the housekeeper in her role as employee before the marriage, but that work has now become invisible for purposes of official statistics, like measuring gross national product.

3. The same sort of inefficient behavioral effect occurs if we assume that the stay-at-home spouse is trading off psychic income from leisure against monetary rewards in the formal workplace.

in the real-world tax base. Again, this is not ultimately because the measurement of the income side of the hypothetical transaction is impossible.

Henry Simons outlined arguments both for and against treating imputed income as part of a theoretical income tax base, but even he would have drawn the line at what we have labelled *psychic income*.[4] When Henry Simons defined income as the algebraic sum of your consumption plus your change in wealth, we should understand him to have meant "consumption," for purposes of a practical income tax, to refer to the things that money can buy—not happiness, pleasure, "flows of satisfaction," or "utility." The pleasure you might derive in listening to a Mozart concerto while sitting in a sylvan glade, far away from the toils of life as a law student, is not income in this sense. Psychic income operates entirely in the personal sphere and is ignored for practical income tax purposes.

This is another important limitation on the construct of "income," because it restricts our field of interest to measuring things that could go to one's real-life ability to write a check to the IRS, not who is the most spiritually evolved. Putting to one side the fundamental obtrusiveness of a government attempting to measure your emotional state, we can probably agree that psychic income is so personal as to defy consistent measurement across individuals. Note, however, that ignoring the psychic income from leisure has important real-world consequences, leading taxpayers to substitute untaxed leisure for labor performed in the public sphere, where it is subject to tax.

To be clear, however, the public sphere of our lives plainly does include *in-kind* income. As Chapter 2 demonstrated through its long discussion of employer-provided housing, healthcare, and other benefits, these items are forms of in-kind income obtained in the public sphere of our lives, although in the case of employer-provided healthcare, for example, the Code makes a conscious decision to exclude that item from the tax base. Your income is not synonymous with the cash payments you receive for your labor.

In-kind income simply describes the case where (for example), instead of getting paid for your labor in cash, you get paid in property that has a commercial value, other than a handful of dollar bills. You still have income, because you have something with monetary value, but you can't directly pay your tax bill with it. If you have a job where you get paid in parsnips and rutabagas, you have at the end of each week "income"—and a big pile of vegetables.

In-kind income is not commensurate with "fringe benefits." Fringe benefits are just one cluster of in-kind income. Fringe benefits often involve items that the recipients might not conceive to be income at all, like employee discounts or even, we suspect, free food at Google's world headquarters. This reflects a failure in the recipients' imaginations, and does not alter the item's status as clear economic value transferred to an individual in the commercial sphere of her life.

As Chapter 2 showed, the Code excludes from the definition of gross income fringe benefits or their sibling, food/lodging provided for the convenience of the employer, but the Code does so by explicit rule (e.g., §§119 and 132);

---

4. Henry Simons, *The Personal Income Tax* 51-52, 110-113 (1938).

in the absence of such a rule, the item is plainly gross income for purposes of §61. Congress crafted many of these exclusions for a number of reasons: because you cannot run a tax system in which every taxpayer is an outlaw, because the benefits often are differentially valued by payer and recipient, because it is difficult in many cases to apportion the value among employees, and because members of Congress don't have very rarified understandings of what the word "income" really means. Because an item of in-kind income is excluded from the definition of gross income under §61 does not mean that it really constitutes psychic income or the like: It just means that it is tax-exempt in-kind income.

If you babysit your own child and I paint my living room, we each have imputed income. Those pseudo-commercial activities reside completely within the private sphere of our lives, and the tax law does not peek into our windows to try to tax that.

But if you babysit *my* child and, in exchange, I paint *your* living room, we *both* have *in-kind* income. If you imagine that the market value of each bundle of services is $100, then we each have $100 in income (and no corresponding deductions, of course, for buying these personal consumption items): $200 total. By virtue of our negotiated exchange we have moved our activities from the private sphere into the public (commercial) sphere, and that triggers the sudden materialization of "gross income" from nothing. The laws of conservation of matter and energy do not apply to the income tax.

Getting a set of golf clubs from your employer as a bonus is another example of "in-kind" income. But what happens if the employer gives you a couple of extra vacation days next year as a bonus instead?

The basic answer is that the extra vacation days are like getting tax-exempt income. The income tax (or any other real-world tax, besides a "head" tax) does not tax imputed income. What has happened here is that your *wage rate* has gone up: You are now effectively getting paid more per hour (by virtue of being paid the same amount to work fewer hours), but the income tax law does not tax your wage *rate*, it taxes the wages you receive. The extra free time just slides over into the personal sphere of your life and gets ignored for tax purposes.

Imagine that you are trying to choose between two job offers. They both pay $60,000 per year and otherwise look equally attractive, except that one offers three weeks of vacation and the other two weeks. If you are rational, you choose the first job: You'll get the same cash salary and one more week of personal time. How does the tax law handle that? By saying that the two jobs are identical in terms of the things the tax law measures: that is, in terms of the things that money can buy. If you earn $60,000 in forty-nine work weeks, you have the same "income" as if you earn $60,000 in fifty work weeks, even though you plainly are richer in leisure in the first case.

The tax law does not generally enter the domain of the private sphere, which means that *the tax law does not tax "leisure."* The tax law does not even attempt to measure your imputed income from painting your own living room, *and* further does not take cognizance of how much more cash you could have earned had you worked fifty weeks instead of forty-nine (or, phrasing the same thing from another perspective, the value to you of an extra week of leisure time).

As we previously noted, much of the early material in this casebook can use-fully be analyzed by posing four questions to yourself:

1. Is it income at all?
2. If it is income, when is it income?
3. If it is income this year, how much income is it?
4. And if we know how much the income is this year, whose income is it?

Imputed income is a good example of a conceptual "is it income at all" issue, while the exclusion from your income for the compensation you receive in the form of a health insurance policy purchased for you by your employer is an example of in-kind income that happens to be excluded from gross income by virtue of a Code rule to that effect.

In practice, and as Chapter 4 elaborates, many issues along the lines just discussed get resolved through *accounting conventions*, not through grand con-cepts. On New Year's Eve a professional artist paints a new painting, which she reasonably anticipates selling to her gallery in the next year for $10,000. Does she have income this year of $10,000? If not, is it because this is imputed income, which exists only in the personal sphere of her life, until she actually sells it? That seems a bit strained; she is a professional after all and created the painting wearing that hat.

If the artist were instead a dealer and bought for $10,000 a painting she anticipated reselling for $20,000, she has no income until the sale takes place. Once again, an advantageous purchase is not "income."

We resolve this hypothetical in favor of the view that the artist has no cur-rent-year income. But what is the most convincing reason for that? And would your answer change if we were instead dealing with a professional treasure hunter hauling up a chest of gold doubloons from the ocean floor?

QUESTIONS

1. Which, if any, of the following raise issues of imputed or psychic income?

(a) buying a car
(b) buying a tuxedo
(c) renting a tuxedo
(d) buying a washing machine
(e) repairing one's own car
(f) enjoyment of leisure
(g) enjoyment of work

2. In what way does the nontaxation of imputed income from housing create problems of fairness? Of economic efficiency?

3. Is a rent deduction for people who do not own their own homes a good solution to the problems created by the nontaxation of the imputed income from owner-occupied housing?

4. Suppose the tax rate on earned income is lowered and a special tax is added to the price of leisure-time activities such as sporting events, concerts, movies, and nonbusiness travel. Would these two changes be a sensible way to reduce the problems caused by the nontaxation of the psychic value of leisure?

2.   Drawing the Line

The Revenue Ruling reproduced below concerns an application of in-kind, rather than imputed, income. The taxpayers in the ruling perform services for strangers, not themselves or members of their households. But the difference may not be so clear in other situations.

REVENUE RULING 79-24
1979-1 C.B. 60

FACTS

Situation 1. In return for personal legal services performed by a lawyer for a housepainter, the housepainter painted the lawyer's personal residence. Both the lawyer and the housepainter are members of a barter club, an organization that annually furnishes its members a directory of members and the services they provide. All the members of the club are professional or trades persons. Members contact other members directly and negotiate the value of the services to be performed.

Situation 2. An individual who owned an apartment building received a work of art created by a professional artist in return for the rent-free use of an apartment for six months by the artist.

LAW

The applicable sections of the Internal Revenue Code of 1954 and the Income Tax Regulations thereunder are 61(a) and 1.61-2, relating to compensation for services.

Section 1.61-2(d)(1) of the regulations provides that if services are paid for other than in money, the fair market value of the property or services taken in payment must be included in income. If the services were rendered at a stipulated price, such price will be presumed to be the fair market value of the compensation received in the absence of evidence to the contrary.

HOLDINGS

Situation 1. The fair market value of the services received by the lawyer and the housepainter are includable in their gross incomes under section 61 of the Code.

Situation 2. The fair market value of the work of art and the six months' fair rental value of the apartment are includable in the gross incomes of the apartment-owner and the artist under section 61 of the Code.

QUESTIONS

1. Suppose Betty owns the right, under a time share, to the use of an apartment at the beach for a week in July and exchanges that right for the right of another time-share owner, Stan, to the use of an apartment at a ski resort for a week in December. Should each person report income by virtue of the exchange?

2. Suppose that two couples exchange babysitting services on weekends. Should both report income? Code §6045 requires information reporting by any "barter exchange." Reg. §1.6045-1(a)(4) provides that "the term 'barter exchange' . . . does not include arrangements that provide solely for the informal exchange of similar services on a noncommercial basis."

3. Suppose that one couple joins a cooperative day-care center that maintains a limited professional staff and requires each parent to supply two hours of day care a week. Parents who do not wish to supply day care may buy out of the obligation for $50 a month. However, parents are encouraged to provide child care and not buy their way out of the obligation. Should parents who provide child care pay tax on $50 of monthly income?

4. Attorney Ann joins a barter club. In return for services as an attorney, Ann receives credits that she can use to obtain other professional services, such as carpentry or dentistry. Taxable? See Rev. Rul. 80-52, 1980-1 C.B. 100, holding people taxable on credits earned in a barter club. As noted above, §6045 requires information returns to the IRS from "barter exchanges."

5. One hundred people pool their resources and buy land in Colorado, where they set up a commune. They perform various tasks for each other according to their skills. Any income for tax purposes?

6. A bank offers its customers the option of earning interest on the money in their checking accounts or of receiving free checking services. Any income to the customers who take the free checking services? The Service has never sought to tax the value of such services. Does this help to explain the prevalence of "free checking," relative to charging a fee for each check but paying depositors more (taxable) interest?

3.   Imputed Income, Implicit Income, Substitute Taxation

To identify a stream of Haig-Simons income as imputed income arising entirely within the private sphere of a person's life may resolve first-order practical income tax questions, but it is not necessarily the end of the economic analysis. If some forms of ownership are tax-favored, then capital will pour into those arrangements, which will have the effect of driving down the yield (economic return) on them. This is the phenomenon of *implicit taxation*, or *tax capitalization* in prices, whichever term you prefer (they are the same thing viewed from different perspectives).[5] This is a vitally important concept in modeling how people respond to asymmetrical tax rules.

For example, we have just seen that the phenomenon of imputed income means that owner-occupied housing is heavily tax-subsidized. As another example, state and local governments sell bonds (publicly traded debt instruments), the interest on which is exempt from federal income tax by virtue of §103. Why would anyone looking for an investment yielding a fixed return ever invest in anything other than tax-exempt bonds? Isn't this just like getting tax-free compensation income in the form of employer-provided healthcare insurance?

Not exactly. The income is exempt, but markets are not stupid, and it turns out that assets like tax-exempt bonds are bought and sold *at prices that reflect their favorable tax attributes.* That is what the term "implicit taxation" tries to capture: No tax may be owed to a tax authority, but the instrument's price is inflated (and therefore its yield reduced) to reflect its special tax status.

As an example, imagine that fully taxable normal returns on U.S. Treasury bonds are 10 percent, and a high grade tax-exempt municipal bond yields 6 percent, so that both a $1,000 principal amount taxable bond with a 10 percent coupon and a $1,000 principal amount tax-exempt municipal bond with the same maturity and a 6 percent coupon trade for $1,000. In this case one can say that the different tax burdens have been capitalized into prices, or that the municipal bond's owner bears an implicit tax of 40 percent, because she accepts a 6 percent rather than 10 percent coupon.

If tax capitalization is perfect, investors should face the same after-tax risk-adjusted rate of return on all their investments and suffer the same tax burden, where "tax" for this particular purpose is understood to include both explicit and implicit taxes.

Explicit taxes yield genuine transfers to governments. By contrast, implicit taxes can be viewed as a form of government subsidy, when measured from a hypothetical baseline (in this example, a baseline in which investors are fully taxed on state and local bond income). In the case of tax-exempt state and local bonds, to which party in the transaction is the subsidy primarily aimed? What alternative ways of delivering that subsidy might occur to you?

The same point can be made about home ownership. If the tax subsidies are perfectly reflected in home prices, then those prices will be inflated relative to what they would be in a world of more neutral taxation. Again you should consider, if that is the case, who benefits from the subsidy?

Finally, because it often is infeasible or impossible to tax directly many forms of imputed income (as well as everyday examples of in-kind income, like free coffee in the break room at work), an alternative tax system design strategy is to "overtax" the other side of the transaction. For example, we could impose a special national sales tax on sales of furniture that require assembly by the purchaser. This would seem doubly perverse to individuals struggling

5. Myron S. Scholes, Mark A. Wolfson, Merle Erickson, Edward L. Maydew, and Terry Shevlin, *Taxes and Business Strategy: A Planning Approach*, ch. 5 (4th ed. 2009); Stanley Koppelman, *Tax Arbitrage and Interest Deduction*, 61 S. Cal. L. Rev. 1143, 1172-1173.

to put their kit furniture together, but it would be a way of taxing indirectly the Haig-Simons income created by the application of one's own labor in the private sphere of one's life. This strategy is termed *substitute taxation*.

More realistic examples might be found in the workplace. Imagine, for example, that as a member of Congress you are troubled by the Silicon Valley practice of offering lavish food service to employees for three meals a day, seven days a week. At the same time, you have no interest in requiring thousands of employees to keep food logs to measure the subsidies they receive. If we assume for purposes of simplicity that the employer and its employees all are taxed at the same rate, and if we think it administratively complex to tax all the employees on some item of in-kind compensation income, or we think it politically expedient to hide the ball, we can get to the same economic result by just denying a tax deduction to the employer. In fact, the Code does that already, at least in part, by denying 50 percent of an employer's deduction for meal expenses.

Another kind of substitute taxation is fundamental to the Code. This is the idea of "carryover basis" transactions.[6] As the next section elaborates, when mom gives daughter stock worth $100,000, but with a basis of $10,000, neither mom nor daughter has immediate income. Instead, daughter takes the stock with a $10,000 carryover basis, and the built-in gain is preserved in daughter's hands for recognition at some future date. The daughter is stepping into the shoes of mom from a tax point of view, so you can say that daughter is substituting for mom. This is less interesting than the first use of the term, because the technique of disallowing a deduction as a substitute for current income to the recipient is both less obvious than the second usage and has powerful applications in the taxation of all sorts of arrangements that otherwise would be impossible to reach as practical matter.

B.   GIFTS

1.   Gift: The Basic Concept

What should be the income tax consequences of receiving a gift? In the words of *Glenshaw Glass*, an outright gift—say, of cash, with no strings attached—would appear to be an "undeniable accession to wealth, clearly realized, and over which the [recipient] has complete dominion." Even if it is a gift of some sort of property, such as a birthday gift of an item of clothing, one would think that only its value to the recipient (which might conceivably be less than its cost or market price), as opposed to whether it is income to begin with, could seriously be contested.

---

6. The Code technically refers to transferred basis (the gift case) and exchanged basis property; the two together comprise substituted basis property. See §7701(a)(42)-(44). Most practitioners elide over the differences and refer simply to carryover basis transactions.

The economist Henry Simons (of Haig-Simons income fame) came to just this theoretical conclusion in his landmark book *Personal Income Taxation* (1936). He wrote there:

> Our [Haig-Simons] definition of income perhaps does violence to traditional usage in specifying implicitly a calculation which would include gratuitous receipts. To exclude gifts . . . , however, would be to introduce additional arbitrary distinctions; it would be necessary to distinguish among an individual's receipts according to the intentions of second parties [i.e. donors] . . . if the distinctions may be avoided, the income concept will thus be left more precise and more definite.[7]

Nonetheless, from the beginning of the federal income tax, gifts have always been excluded from taxable income. The exclusion today is found in §102. What is more, this exclusion extends to gifts (such as cash) that involve no valuation difficulty, and as it applies to large gifts as well as small, it is not simply a de minimis rule of administrative convenience.[8]

Henry Simons lived in the real world, and even he understood the problems inherent in applying a Haig-Simons definition of income in a literal sense. The theoretical answer—that gifts should constitute gross income—runs headlong into the fundamental problem adverted to at the outset of this chapter, which is that gifts occur in the private sphere of our lives. By definition they are not market transactions, or even substitutes for market transactions (that is, imputed income). No one wants to have the government looking over one's shoulder every time one receives some benefit. Having repeated his theoretical point, Simons continued:

> It would obviously be folly for an income to try to reach all gifts. It is unthinkable that taxpayers should be obliged to account in their returns for the value of all dinners and entertainments which they enjoy as guests, and even for cigars. . . . Besides the overwhelming administrative difficulties, one faces here all the problems of [different perspectives on valuation].[9] How should one value things obtained by gift which one would never purchase for one's self? What is the pecuniary equivalent of a Corona-Corona [an expensive cigar] to a poor pedagog?[10]

---

7. Simons, *Personal Income Taxation* 56-57 (1936).

8. It is important here to distinguish between the federal income tax, which is the subject of this casebook, and the federal estate and gift tax, which is an excise tax on certain gratuitous transfers. Gifts in excess of $14,000 per year by a given donor to a given donee may give rise to gift tax liability. Essentially, the gift tax is a backup to the estate tax, since the latter would be too easy to avoid if transfers before one died were excluded. However, if one believes that both the income tax and the estate and gift tax should be levied, then taxing a transaction under one system presumably should not rule out taxing it under the other system.

9. Simons here actually uses the word *Flügeladjutant*, a German military term referring to an aide-de-camp to a high-ranking official. This is reference to a conundrum posed by a German scholar, F. Kleinwächter, about the measure of income to a *Flügeladjutant* who receives many fringe benefits from his elevated status, such as attending opera and going hunting with his sovereign, but who detests opera and hunting. Simons, *supra note 7*, at 53. How would §132 address these fringe benefits?

10. *Id. at* 135.

In short, even Simons recognized that his theoretical answer—that gifts should constitute gross income—runs headlong into the fundamental problem adverted to at the outset of this chapter, which is that gifts occur in the private sphere of our lives, and the value of privacy alone, without regard to all the practical issues that would be raised, argues that most routine gifts should not be reached by any tax system. By definition these gifts are not market transactions, or even substitutes for market transactions (that is, imputed income). It would be intolerable to have the government looking over one's shoulder every time one received some minor benefit from a relative or friend, and different valuations of gifts in kind from the perspectives of donor and donee would exacerbate the practical problems. (The gift tax deals with this by adopting a relatively high de minimis rule, under which gifts from one donor to any one donee are ignored for gift tax purposes if the gifts total less than $14,000 in a year.)

But Simons's arguments here can be expanded still further, by returning again to the point made at the outset of this chapter that for a great many policy reasons it often is better to view a family or household as a single "tax unit." From such a viewpoint, transfers within the family or household no more give rise to income than does moving your wallet from your left jeans pocket to your right. (The gift tax, by contrast, does take cognizance of such transfers if they exceed the annual exclusion, but the gift tax does so primarily because its purpose is to backstop the estate tax.)

Simons thought that a pragmatic resolution of this conflict between two important principles would be to ignore the cigars he received from his host at dinner, but to treat gifts of money, real estate, investment assets, and consumer durables (yachts, houses, artwork, etc.) as gross income to the donee.

What do you think of Simons's proposed compromise?

In thinking about the tax consequences of gifts, it is important to consider both sides of the gift transaction: that is, the income tax treatment of the donor as well as of the donee.

Example

Donna earns $100,000 per year, and her adult son Edward earns nothing. Out of love, Donna gives Edward $30,000 per year. Nothing else with federal income tax consequences happens to either of them. (Ignore the federal gift tax here; that is not the object of this casebook.) There would appear to be three main ways in which the federal income tax could treat them in light of the gift transaction:

(a) income to Edward, deduction to Donna. Thus, Edward's annual taxable income would be $30,000, and Donna's would be $70,000.

(b) income to Edward, no deduction to Donna. Thus, Edward's annual taxable income would be $30,000, and Donna's would be $100,000.

(c) no income to Edward, no deduction to Donna. This is the rule that the federal income tax actually follows, and under it Edward's taxable income is zero and Donna's is $100,000.

NOTES AND QUESTIONS

1. What do you think of the hypothetical rule in (a) above? Does it inappropriately permit Donna a deduction for a voluntary personal consumption expense akin to buying food? What tax planning opportunities would this rule open up for related parties, such as Donna and Edward, who are in different income tax rate brackets?

2. What do you think of the hypothetical rule in (b) above? Note that it describes the actual tax treatment that would apply if Edward were Donna's employee rather than (or in addition to being) her son, and he received $30,000 for rendering nondeductible personal services such as cooking, cleaning, mowing the lawn, and so forth. What, if anything, makes the gift case relevantly different from the case of compensation for personal services?

3. Many students instinctively recoil at the hypothetical rule in (b) above, and for that matter they also are discomfited by the thought that income seems to be duplicated in the case of the employee who performs personal services for Donna, because the employee has income but Donna has no deduction. Henry Simons wrote particularly cogently about this false reasoning:

> It has been argued that the inclusion [into the definition of income] of gratuities introduces an objectionable sort of double-counting. . . .
> The very notion of double-counting implies, indeed, the familiar, and disastrous, misconception that personal income is merely a share in some undistributed, separately measurable whole [such as national income].
>
> * * * *
>
> Income taxes are levies upon persons, not upon parts of the social income; their proper objective is that of imposing equitable relative levies upon [persons]. . . . Considerations of equity surely afford little ground for excluding (or including) particular receipts according to the intentions of second parties. Gifts are very much like earnings, and earnings are often quite like gifts.[11]

In more modern phrasing, the overarching goal of the federal income tax is to measure an individual's ability to pay, not to divide up national income into individual shares. As a result, the double counting argument is "meaningless." Simons, *id.* at 134. The gift clearly increases the donee's ability to pay, and at the same time it does not reduce the donor's ability to pay, because the donor voluntarily chose to spend her after-tax income in a specific form of consumption: giving. The definition of "income" should be implemented with a view to advancing that overarching goal, and from this perspective a gift enhances the donee's ability to pay as much as do earnings, arguably, even more so, since a gift ordinarily involves little sacrifice in leisure. And from the other direction, neither the donor nor the employer of an employee performing personal services should obtain a deduction. Neither cost is an expense of earning income; instead they represent decisions about how to dispose of income, that is, consumption.

11. *Id.* at 56-57, 134.

4. Rule (c), which the federal income tax actually follows, has administrative advantages even apart from whether it levies the right amount of tax on the participants in a gift transaction. Under it, no need generally arises under the income tax to report gift transactions or to determine the value of property received as a gift.

5. Rule (c), which, to repeat, encapsulates current law, requires determining whether a given transfer received by the taxpayer from another person, constitutes a gift under §102 and thus can be excluded from taxable income. To do so requires deciding how much weight to give the donee's understanding of the purpose behind the gift, as compared to the donor's subjective intent. In many cases these can be different. (See Harris v. Commissioner, *infra*.) The difficulty of making this determination was one of the arguments advanced by Simons for taxing gifts as income. As the following case shows, such determinations can be particularly difficult when transfers arguably constituting gifts occur in a commercial rather than a family setting.

COMMISSIONER v. DUBERSTEIN
363 U.S. 278 (1960)

Mr. Justice BRENNAN delivered the opinion of the Court.

These two cases concern [§102(a)] which excludes from the gross income of an income taxpayer "the value of property acquired by gift." . . .

No. 376, Commissioner v. Duberstein. The taxpayer, Duberstein, was president of the Duberstein Iron & Metal Company, a corporation with headquarters in Dayton, Ohio. For some years the taxpayer's company had done business with Mohawk Metal Corporation, whose headquarters were in New York City. The president of Mohawk was one Berman. The taxpayer and Berman had generally used the telephone to transact their companies' business with each other, which consisted of buying and selling metals. The taxpayer testified, without elaboration, that he knew Berman "personally" and had known him for about seven years. From time to time in their telephone conversations, Berman would ask Duberstein whether the latter knew of potential customers for some of Mohawk's products in which Duberstein's company itself was not interested. Duberstein provided the names of potential customers for these items.

One day in 1951 Berman telephoned Duberstein and said that the information Duberstein had given him had proved so helpful that he wanted to give the latter a present. Duberstein stated that Berman owed him nothing. Berman said that he had a Cadillac as a gift for Duberstein, and that the latter should send to New York for it; Berman insisted that Duberstein accept the car, and the latter finally did so, protesting however that he had not intended to be compensated for the information. At the time Duberstein already had a Cadillac and an Oldsmobile, and felt that he did not need another car. Duberstein testified that he did not think Berman would have sent him the Cadillac if he had not furnished him with information about the customers. It appeared that Mohawk later deducted the value of the Cadillac as a business expense on its corporate income tax return.

Duberstein did not include the value of the Cadillac in gross income for 1951, deeming it a gift. The Commissioner asserted a deficiency for the car's value against him, and in proceedings to review the deficiency the Tax Court affirmed the Commissioner's determination. It said that "The record is significantly barren of evidence revealing any intention on the part of the payor to make a gift. . . . The only justifiable inference is that the automobile was intended by the payor to be remuneration for services rendered to it by Duberstein." The Court of Appeals for the Sixth Circuit reversed. 265 F.2d 28.

No. 506, Stanton v. United States. The taxpayer, Stanton, had been for approximately 10 years in the employ of Trinity Church in New York City. He was comptroller of the Church corporation, and president of a corporation, Trinity Operating Company, the church set up as a fully owned subsidiary to manage its real estate holdings, which were more extensive than simply the church property. His salary by the end of his employment there in 1942 amounted to $22,500 a year. Effective November 30, 1942, he resigned from both positions to go into business for himself. The Operating Company's directors, who seem to have included the rector and vestrymen of the church, passed the following resolution upon his resignation:

> *BE IT RESOLVED* that in appreciation of the services rendered by Mr. Stanton . . . a gratuity is hereby awarded to him of Twenty Thousand Dollars, payable to him in equal installments of Two Thousand Dollars at the end of each and every month commencing with the month of December, 1942; provided that, with the discontinuance of his services, the Corporation of Trinity Church is released from all rights and claims to pension and retirement benefits not already accrued up to November 30, 1942.

The Operating Company's action was later explained by one of its directors as based on the fact that,

> Mr. Stanton was liked by all of the Vestry personally. He had a pleasing personality. He had come in when Trinity's affairs were in a difficult situation. He did a splendid piece of work, we felt. Besides that . . . he was liked by all of the members of the Vestry personally.

And by another:

> [W]e were all unanimous in wishing to make Mr. Stanton a gift. Mr. Stanton had loyally and faithfully served Trinity in a very difficult time. We thought of him in the highest regard. We understood that he was going in business for himself. We felt that he was entitled to that evidence of good will.

On the other hand, there was a suggestion of some ill-feeling between Stanton and the directors, arising out of the recent termination of the services of one Watkins, the Operating Company's treasurer, whose departure was evidently attended by some acrimony. At a special board meeting on October 28, 1942, Stanton had intervened on Watkins' side and asked reconsideration of the matter. The minutes reflect that "resentment was expressed as to the 'presumptuous' suggestion that the action of the Board, taken after long deliberation, should be changed." The Board adhered to its determination that Watkins be separated from employment, giving him an opportunity to resign rather than be discharged. At another special meeting two days later it was revealed that Watkins had not resigned; the previous resolution terminating his services was then viewed as effective; and the Board voted the payment of six months' salary to Watkins in a resolution similar to that quoted in regard to Stanton, but which did not use the term "gratuity." At the meeting, Stanton announced that in order to avoid any such embarrassment or question at any time as to his willingness to resign if the Board desired, he was tendering his resignation. It was tabled, though not without dissent. The next week, on November 5, at another special meeting, Stanton again tendered his resignation which this time was accepted.

The "gratuity" was duly paid. So was a smaller one to Stanton's (and the Operating Company's) secretary, under a similar resolution, upon her resignation at the same time. The two corporations shared the expense of the payments. There was undisputed testimony that there were in fact no enforceable rights or claims to pension and retirement benefits which had not accrued at the time of the taxpayer's resignation, and that the last proviso of the resolution was inserted simply out of an abundance of caution. The taxpayer received in cash a refund of his contributions to the retirement plans, and there is no suggestion that he was entitled to more. He was required to perform no further services for Trinity after his resignation.

. . . The trial judge, sitting without a jury, made the simple finding that the payments were a "gift," and judgment was entered for the taxpayer. The Court of Appeals for the Second Circuit reversed. 268 F.2d 727. . . .

The exclusion of property acquired by gift from gross income under the federal income tax laws was made in the first income tax statute passed under the authority of the Sixteenth Amendment, and has been a feature of the income tax statutes ever since. The meaning of the term "gift" as applied to particular transfers has always been a matter of contention. Specific and illuminating legislative history on the point does not appear to exist. Analogies and inferences drawn from other revenue provisions, such as the estate and gift taxes, are dubious. . . . The meaning of the statutory term has been shaped largely by the decisional law. With this, we turn to the contentions made by the Government in these cases.

First. The Government suggests that we promulgate a new "test" in this area to serve as a standard to be applied by the lower courts and by the Tax Court in dealing with the numerous cases that arise.[12] We reject this invitation. We are of opinion that the governing principles are necessarily general and have already been spelled out in the opinions of this Court, and that the problem is one which, under the present statutory framework, does not lend itself to any more definitive statement that would produce a talisman for the solution of

12. [The government's test would have generally ruled out gift treatment for transfers from employers to employees. — Eds.]

concrete cases. The cases at bar are fair examples of the settings in which the problem usually arises. They present situations in which payments have been made in a context with business overtones—an employer making a payment to a retiring employee; a businessman giving something of value to another businessman who has been of advantage to him in his business. In this context, we review the law as established by the prior cases here.

The course of decision here makes it plain that the statute does not use the term "gift" in the common-law sense, but in a more colloquial sense. This Court has indicated that a voluntary executed transfer of his property by one to another, without any consideration or compensation therefor, though a common-law gift, is not necessarily a "gift" within the meaning of the statute. For the Court has shown that the mere absence of a legal or moral obligation to make such a payment does not establish that it is a gift. Old Colony Trust Co. v. Commissioner, 279 U.S. 716, 730. And, importantly, if the payment proceeds primarily from "the constraining force of any moral or legal duty," or from "the incentive of anticipated benefit" of an economic nature, Bogardus v. Commissioner, 302 U.S. 34, 41, it is not a gift. And, conversely, "[w]here the payment is in return for services rendered, it is irrelevant that the donor derives no economic benefit from it." Robertson v. United States, 343 U.S. 711, 714. A gift in the statutory sense, on the other hand, proceeds from a "detached and disinterested generosity," Commissioner v. LoBue, 351 U.S. 243, 246; "out of affection, respect, admiration, charity or like impulses." Robertson v. United States, *supra* at 714. And in this regard, the most critical consideration, as the Court was agreed in the leading case here, is the transferor's "intention." Bogardus v. Commissioner, 302 U.S. 34, 43. "What controls is the intention with which payment, however voluntary, has been made." *Id.,* at 45 (dissenting opinion).

The Government says that this "intention" of the transferor cannot mean what the cases on the common-law concept of gift call "donative intent." With that we are in agreement, for our decisions fully support this. Moreover, the *Bogardus* case itself makes it plain that the donor's characterization of his action is not determinative—that there must be an objective inquiry as to whether what is called a gift amounts to it in reality. 302 U.S., at 40. It scarcely needs adding that the parties' expectations or hopes as to the tax treatment of their conduct in themselves have nothing to do with the matter. . . .

Second. The Government's proposed "test," while apparently simple and precise in its formulation, depends frankly on a set of "principles" or "presumptions" derived from the decided cases, and concededly subject to various exceptions; and it involves various corollaries, which add to its detail. Were we to promulgate this test as a matter of law, and accept with it its various presuppositions and stated consequences, we would be passing far beyond the requirements of the cases before us, and would be painting on a large canvas with indeed a broad brush. The Government derives its test from such propositions as the following: That payments by an employer to an employee, even though voluntary, ought, by and large, to be taxable; that the concept of a gift is inconsistent with a payment's being a deductible business expense; that a gift involves "personal" elements; that a business corporation cannot properly make a gift of its assets. The Government admits that there are exceptions and qualifications to these propositions. We think, to the extent they are correct, that these propositions are not principles of law but rather maxims of experience that the tribunals, which have tried the fact of cases in this area have enunciated in explaining their factual determinations. Some of them simply represent truisms: it doubtless is, statistically speaking, the exceptional payment by an employer to an employee that amounts to a gift. Others are overstatements of possible evidentiary inferences relevant to a factual determination on the totality of circumstances in the case: it is doubtless relevant to the over-all inference that the transferor treats a payment as a business deduction, or that the transferor is a corporate entity. But these inferences cannot be stated in absolute terms. Neither factor is a shibboleth. The taxing statute does not make nondeductibility by the transferor a condition on the "gift" exclusion; nor does it draw any distinction, in terms, between transfers by corporations and individuals, as to the availability of the "gift" exclusion to the transferee. The conclusion whether a transfer amounts to a "gift" is one that must be reached on a consideration of all the factors.

Specifically, the trier of fact must be careful not to allow trial of the issue whether the receipt of a specific payment is a gift to turn into a trial of the tax liability, or of the propriety, as a matter of fiduciary or corporate law, attaching to the conduct of someone else. . . . The major corollary to the Government's suggested "test" is that, as an ordinary matter, a payment by a corporation cannot be a gift, and, more specifically, there can be no such thing as a "gift" made by a corporation which would allow it to take a deduction for an ordinary and necessary business expense. As we have said, we find no basis for such a conclusion in the statute; and if it were applied as a determinative rule of "law," it would force the tribunals trying tax cases involving the donee's liability into elaborate inquiries into the local law of corporations or into the peripheral deductibility of payments as business expenses.[13]

Third. Decision of the issue presented in these cases must be based ultimately on the application of the fact-finding tribunal's experience with the mainsprings of human conduct to the totality of the facts of each case. The nontechnical nature of the statutory standard, the close relationship of it to the data of practical human experience, and the multiplicity of relevant factual elements, with their various combinations, creating the necessity of ascribing the proper force to each, confirm us in our conclusion that primary weight in this area must be given to the conclusions of the trier of fact. . . .

This conclusion may not satisfy an academic desire for tidiness, symmetry, and precision in this area, any more than a system based on the determinations of various fact-finders ordinarily does. But we see it as implicit in the present statutory treatment of the exclusion for gifts, and in the variety of forums in which federal income tax cases can be tried. If there is fear of undue

---

13. Justice Cardozo once described in memorable language the inquiry into whether an expense was an "ordinary and necessary" one of a business: "One struggles in vain for any verbal formula that will supply a ready touchstone. The standard set up by the statute is not a rule of law; it is rather a way of life. Life in all its fullness must supply the answer to the riddle." Welch v. Helvering, 290 U.S. 111, 115. The same comment well fits the issue in the cases at bar.

uncertainty or overmuch litigation, Congress may make more precise its treatment of the matter by singling out certain factors and making them determinative of the matter, as it has done in one field of the "gift" exclusion's former application, that of prizes and awards. Doubtless diversity of result will tend to be lessened somewhat since federal income tax decisions, even those in tribunals of first instance turning on issues of fact, tend to be reported, and since there may be a natural tendency of professional triers of fact to follow one another's determinations, even as to factual matters. But the question here remains basically one of fact, for determination on a case-by-case basis.

One consequence of this is that appellate review of determinations in this field must be quite restricted. Where a jury has tried the matter upon correct instructions, the only inquiry is whether it cannot be said that reasonable men could reach differing conclusions on the issue. . . . Where the trial has been by a judge without a jury, the judge's findings must stand unless "clearly erroneous." Fed. Rules Civ. Proc., 52 (a). . . .

Fourth. A majority of the Court is in accord with the principles just outlined. And, applying them to the *Duberstein* case, we are in agreement, on the evidence we have set forth, that it cannot be said that the conclusion of the Tax Court was "clearly erroneous." It seems to us plain that as trier of the facts it was warranted in concluding that despite the characterization of the transfer of the Cadillac by the parties and the absence of any obligation, even of a moral nature, to make it, it was at bottom a recompense for Duberstein's past services, or an inducement for him to be of further service in the future. We cannot say with the Court of Appeals that such a conclusion was "mere suspicion" on the Tax Court's part. To us it appears based in the sort of informed experience with human affairs that fact-finding tribunals should bring to this task.

As to *Stanton,* we are in disagreement. To four of us, it is critical here that the District Court as trier of fact made only the simple and unelaborated finding that the transfer in question was a "gift." To be sure, conciseness is to be strived for, and prolixity avoided, in findings; but, to the four of us, there comes a point where findings become so sparse and conclusory as to give no revelation of what the District Court's concept of the determining facts and legal standard may be. . . . Such conclusory, general findings do not constitute compliance with Rule 52's direction to "find the facts specially and state separately . . . conclusions of law thereon." While the standard of law in this area is not a complex one, we four think the unelaborated finding of ultimate fact here cannot stand as a fulfillment of these requirements. It affords the reviewing court not the semblance of an indication of the legal standard with which the trier of fact has approached his task. For all that appears, the District Court may have viewed the form of the resolution or the simple absence of legal consideration as conclusive. While the judgment of the Court of Appeals cannot stand, the four of us think there must be further proceedings in the District Court looking toward new and adequate findings of fact. In this, we are joined by Mr. Justice Whittaker, who agrees that the findings were inadequate, although he does not concur generally in this opinion.

Accordingly, in No. 376, the judgment of this Court is that the judgment of the Court of Appeals is reversed, and in No. 546, that the judgment of the

District Court of Appeals is vacated, and the case is remanded to the District Court for further proceedings not inconsistent with this opinion.

It is so ordered.

Mr. Justice HARLAN concurs in the result in No. 376. In No. 546, he would affirm the judgment of the Court of Appeals for the reasons stated by Mr. Justice FRANKFURTER.

Mr. Justice WHITTAKER agreeing with Bogardus that whether a particular transfer is or is not a "gift" may involve "a mixed question of law and fact," 302 U.S., at 39, concurs only in the result of this opinion.

Mr. Justice DOUGLAS dissents, since he is of the view that in each of these two cases there was a gift under the test which the Court fashioned nearly a quarter of a century ago in Bogardus v. Commissioner, 302 U.S. 34.

[Mr. Justice BLACK concurred in *Duberstein* and dissented in *Stanton*, on the ground that the trial court's finding in each case was "not clearly erroneous."]

[Mr. Justice FRANKFURTER said that "in the two situations now before us the business implications are so forceful that I would apply a presumptive rule placing the burden upon the beneficiary to prove the payment wholly unrelated to his services to the enterprise" and that the Court's emphasis on the fact-finding tribunal's "experience with the mainsprings of human conduct" would set them "to sail on an illimitable ocean of individual beliefs and experiences." He concluded that Duberstein was properly taxed, and that Stanton's payment should have been taxed because it was not "sheer benevolence but in the nature of a generous lagniappe, something extra thrown in for services received though not legally nor morally required to be given."]

NOTES AND QUESTIONS

1. To correct a common misunderstanding, "disinterested" does not mean "bored," "indifferent," or "neutral." Donors invariably have a keen interest in the welfare of their donees. "Disinterested" here means that the donor is not motivated by the anticipation of receiving a commercial quid pro quo in return for the gift.

2. *Aftermath.* (a) On the remand of the *Stanton* case, the district court made detailed findings of fact and again concluded that the payments to Stanton were gifts. 186 F. Supp. 393 (E.D.N.Y. 1960). On appeal the Court of Appeals affirmed on the ground that the findings were not "clearly erroneous," Chief Judge Lumbard concurring because of the restricted character of appellate review, although he thought a "contrary inference should have been drawn from the undisputed basic facts." 287 F.2d 876, 877 (2d Cir. 1961).

(b) Section 102(c), added in 1986, alters the result in *Stanton* by a categorical rule precluding gift treatment in the case of any transfer by an employer to an employee. There is, however, a modest and carefully circumscribed exclusion for "employee achievement awards." See §74(c).

3. *Analysis.* (a) The Court says that it cannot find any "specific and illuminating legislative history." Accordingly, it interprets "gift" in the "colloquial sense." In other words, it adopts a "plain language" approach to the statute. From there, it defines "gift" by reference to a state of mind. What is the required state of mind? In a case like *Stanton*, whose state of mind counts? How does the trier of fact find that state of mind?

(b) Can a part of the message that the Supreme Court was really sending in *Duberstein* be fairly summarized as follows: "We don't ever want to review another gift case, so within limits finders of fact can do whatever they like"?

(c) The Court refuses to accept as a "shibboleth" that "nondeductibility by the transferor [is] a condition on the 'gift' exclusion" (*supra* page 89). How can a transfer simultaneously proceed from the "detached and disinterested generosity" of the transferor and yet generate a business deduction on the ground that it was a cost of earning income?

(d) Is the Court letting itself off too easily when it concludes that its broad focus on "the mainsprings of human conduct" will not satisfy "a desire for academic tidiness"? What would happen to the career of a law firm associate who, when asked to provide helpful guidance regarding whether a given transfer qualified as a gift, replied, quoting Justice Cardozo from the Court's approving footnote, that "[l]ife in all its fullness must supply the answer to the riddle"?

4. *Business versus family transfers.* (a) Would an inquiry into the policy reasons for excluding gifts from gross income have been useful? Henry Simons argued that gifts ought to be included in income because "surely it is hard to defend exclusion of certain receipts merely because one has done nothing or given nothing in return." *Personal Income Taxation* 135 (1938). Simons would not have allowed a deduction for the donor. *Id.* at 136. Thus, Simons would have followed Rule (b) from the example that precedes *Duberstein*. Simons's position has been criticized on two main grounds: for insufficient sensitivity to notions of the family or household as an economic unit and for overly harsh treatment of socially desirable altruistic transfers. Does this perspective on the gift exclusion shed any light on what the outcome ought to be under the *Duberstein* and *Stanton* facts?

(b) People who are supported by members of their family do not have gross income in the amount of the support they receive. This rule is without express statutory authority; it is simply part of the accepted definition of "income" and has never been questioned by the Service or by tax theorists. It reflects the point made earlier, that even without a statutory basis, many transactions within a family or household are ignored, because it is appropriate to treat that tax unit as a single entity when dealing with exchanges or transfers not expressly part of the public sphere of our lives. By contrast, parents with a small business sometimes do hire the ne'er-do-well son-in-law to work in the family firm in an expressly commercial transaction best analyzed as falling within the public sphere of our lives.

Often it may be difficult to distinguish between support payments and gifts—for example, where a parent buys an automobile for his or her child. Does this help explain the gift exclusion? If so, how does it bear on the decision in *Duberstein*?

5. *Congressional reaction and the payor's deduction for business gifts.* Section 274(b), added in 1962, allows persons such as Berman, in the *Duberstein* case,

to deduct as an ordinary and necessary business expense the first $25 of any business gift. That section seems to accept implicitly the notion that there can be "business gifts": that is, transfers that, although business motivated for the transferor, are gifts to the transferee. Of course, if the business motivation is strong enough, the transfer will not be a gift, the transferee will be required to treat the value of the item received as an addition to adjusted gross income; and §274(b)'s limitation will not operate to deny a deduction to the transferor. Where the item is treated as a gift to the transferee and, under §274(b), the deduction above $25 is denied to the transferor, the net effect can be thought of as a good example of substitute taxation, where the tax burden of one person (here, the transferor) is increased to offset what is regarded as an improper tax benefit to another person (here, the payee).

6. *Later development: §83.* Section 83 was adopted after the decision in *Duberstein*, with different, more sophisticated kinds of transactions in mind. Would it make a difference in a case like *Duberstein*? Under the decision in *Duberstein* is it possible for a transfer of property to be a "gift" within the meaning of §102 and still be made "in connection with the performance of services" within the contemplation of §83? If so, which provision governs?

UNITED STATES v. HARRIS
942 F.2d 1125 (7th Cir. 1991)

Eschbach, Senior Circuit Judge.

David Kritzik, now deceased, was a wealthy widower partial to the company of young women. Two of these women were Leigh Ann Conley and Lynnette Harris, twin sisters. Directly or indirectly, Kritzik gave Conley and Harris each more than half a million dollars over the course of several years. For our purposes, either Kritzik had to pay gift tax on this money or Harris and Conley had to pay income tax. The United States alleges that, beyond reasonable doubt, the obligation was Harris and Conley's. In separate criminal trials, Harris and Conley were convicted of willfully evading their income tax obligations regarding the money,[14] and they now appeal. . . .

INSUFFICIENCY OF THE EVIDENCE AS TO CONLEY

Conley was convicted on each of four counts for violating 26 U.S.C. §7203, which provides,

> Any person . . . required . . . to make a [tax] return . . . who willfully fails to . . . make such return . . . shall, in addition to other penalties provided by law, be guilty of a misdemeanor. . . .

_____

14. Harris was sentenced to ten months in prison, to be followed by two months in a halfway house and two years of supervised release. She was also fined $12,500.00 and ordered to pay a $150.00 special assessment. Conley was sentenced to five months in prison, followed by five months in a halfway house and one year supervised release. She was also fined $10,000.00 and ordered to pay a $100.00 assessment.

Conley was "required . . . to make a return" only if the money that she received from Kritzik was income to her rather than a gift. Assuming that the money was income, she acted "willfully," and so is subject to criminal prosecution, only if she knew of her duty to pay taxes and "voluntarily and intentionally violated that duty." Cheek v. United States 498 U.S. 192 (1991). The government met its burden of proof if the jury could have found these elements beyond a reasonable doubt, viewing the evidence in the light most favorable to the government.

The government's evidence was insufficient to show either that the money Conley received was income or that she acted in knowing disregard of her obligations. "Gross income" for tax purposes does not include gifts, which are taxable to the donor rather than the recipient. §§61, 102(a), 2501(a). In Commissioner v. Duberstein, 363 U.S. 278 (1960), the Supreme Court stated that in distinguishing between income and gifts the "critical consideration . . . is the transferor's intention." A transfer of property is a gift if the transferor acted out of a "detached and disinterested generosity, . . . out of affection, respect, admiration, charity, or like impulses." *Id.* By contrast, a transfer of property is income if it is the result of "the constraining force of any moral or legal duty, constitutes a reward for services rendered, or proceeds from the incentive of anticipated benefit of an economic nature."

Regarding the "critical consideration" of the donor's intent, the only direct evidence that the government presented was Kritzik's gift tax returns. On those returns, Kritzik identified gifts to Conley of $24,000, $30,000, and $36,000 for the years 1984-6, respectively, substantially less than the total amount of money that Kritzik transferred to Conley. This leaves the question whether Kritzik's other payments were taxable income to Conley or whether Kritzik just underreported his gifts. The gift tax returns raise the question, they do not resolve it.[15]

This failure to show Kritzik's intent is fatal to the government's case. . . .

The government's remaining evidence consisted of a bank card that Conley signed listing Kritzik in a space marked "employer" and testimony regarding the form of the payments that Conley received. The bank card is no evidence of Kritzik's intent and even as to Conley is open to conflicting interpretations—she contends that she listed Kritzik as a reference and no more. As to the form of payments, the government showed that Conley would pick up

---

15. Our discussion assumes that the gift tax returns were admissible as evidence because the parties have not raised the issue. We note, however, that the returns appear on their face to be hearsay. The government used the returns (out of court statements) to prove that Kritzik's gifts were the amount that he reported (that is, to prove the truth of the matter asserted). . . . Along these lines, the United States tried to present direct evidence of Kritzik's intent in the form of an affidavit that he provided IRS investigators before his death. In the affidavit, Kritzik stated that he regarded both Harris and Conley as prostitutes. But Kritzik had an obvious motive to lie to the investigators—he could have been subject to civil or criminal penalties for failure to pay gift taxes if he failed to shift the tax burden to the sisters. The District Court was correct to exclude this affidavit under the hearsay rule and under the confrontation clause. In general, evidentiary difficulties such as this will often be insurmountable in trying to prove a willful tax violation that hinges on the intent of a dead person. The civil remedies available to the IRS will almost always lead to surer justice in such cases than criminal prosecution.

a regular check at Kritzik's office every week to ten days, either from Kritzik personally or, when he was not in, from his secretary. According to the government, this form of payment is that of an employee picking up regular wages, but it could just as easily be that of a dependent picking up regular support checks.

We will "not permit a verdict based solely upon the piling of inference upon inference." United States v. Balzano, 916 F.2d 1273, 1284 (7th Cir. 1990). . . .

THE ADMISSIBILITY OF KRITZIK'S LETTERS

Harris was convicted of two counts of willfully failing to file federal income tax returns under §7203 (the same offense for which Conley was convicted) and two counts of willful tax evasion under §7201. At trial, Harris tried to introduce as evidence three letters that Kritzik wrote, but the District Court excluded the letters as hearsay. The District Court also suggested that the letters would be inadmissible under Fed. R. Evid. 403 because the possible prejudice from the letters exceeded their probative value. We hold that the letters were not hearsay because they were offered to prove Harris' lack of willfulness, not for the truth of the matters asserted. We further hold that the critical nature of the letters to Harris' defense precludes their exclusion under Rule 403, and so reverse her conviction.

The first of the letters at issue was a four page, handwritten letter from Kritzik to Harris, dated April 4, 1981. In it, Kritzik wrote that he loved and trusted Harris and that, "so far as the things I give you are concerned — let me say that I get as great if not even greater pleasure in giving than you get in receiving." Def. Ex. 201, p.2. He continued, "I love giving things to you and to see you happy and enjoying them." *Id.* In a second letter to Harris of the same date, Kritzik again wrote, "I . . . love you very much and will do all that I can to make you happy," and said that he would arrange for Harris' financial security. Def. Ex. 202, p.3. In a third letter, dated some six years later on May 28, 1987, Kritzik wrote to his insurance company regarding the value of certain jewelry that he had "given to Ms. Lynette Harris as a gift." Kritzik forwarded a copy of the letter to Harris.

These letters were hearsay if offered for the truth of the matters asserted — that Kritzik did in fact love Harris, enjoyed giving her things, wanted to take care of her financial security, and gave her the jewelry at issue as a gift. But the letters were not hearsay for the purpose of showing what Harris believed, because her belief does not depend on the actual truth of the matters asserted in the letters. Even if Kritzik were lying, the letters could have caused Harris to believe in good faith that the things he gave her were intended as gifts. . . . This good faith belief, in turn, would preclude any finding of willfulness on her part. . . .

THE TAX TREATMENT OF PAYMENTS TO MISTRESSES

Our conclusion that Harris should have been allowed to present the letters at issue as evidence would ordinarily lead us to remand her case for retrial. We further conclude, however, that current law on the tax treatment of payments to mistresses provided Harris no fair warning that her conduct was criminal. Indeed, current authorities favor Harris' position that the money she received from Kritzik was a gift. We emphasize that we do not necessarily agree with these authorities, and that the government is free to urge departure from them in a *non*criminal context. But new points of tax law may not be the basis of criminal convictions. For this reason, we remand with instructions that the indictment against Harris be dismissed. Although we discuss only Harris' case in this section, the same reasoning applies to Conley and provides an alternative basis for dismissal of the indictment against her.

Again, the definitive statement of the distinction between gifts and income is in the Supreme Court's *Duberstein* decision, which applies and interprets the definition of income contained in §61. But as the Supreme Court described, the *Duberstein* principles are "necessarily general." It stated, " 'One struggles in vain for any verbal formula that will supply a ready touchstone. The standard set up . . . is not a rule of law; it is rather a way of life. Life in all its fullness must supply the answer to the riddle.' " *Id.,* quoting Welch v. Helvering, 290 U.S. 111 (1933). Along these lines, Judge Flaum's concurrence properly characterizes *Duberstein* as "eschew[ing] . . . [any] categorical, rule-bound analysis" in favor of a "case-by-case" approach.

Duberstein was a civil case, and its approach is appropriate for civil cases. But criminal prosecutions are a different story. These must rest on a violation of a clear rule of law, not on conflict with a "way of life." If "defendants [in a tax case] . . . could not have ascertained the legal standards applicable to their conduct, criminal proceedings may not be used to define and punish an alleged failure to conform to those standards." United States v. Mallas, 762 F.2d 361, 361 (4th Cir. 1985). . . .

We do not doubt that *Duberstein*'s principles, though general, provide a clear answer to many cases involving the gift versus income distinction and can be the basis for civil as well as criminal prosecutions in such cases. We are equally certain, however, that *Duberstein* provides no ready answer to the taxability of transfers of money to a mistress in the context of a long-term relationship. The motivations of the parties in such cases will always be mixed. The relationship would not be long term were it not for some respect or affection. Yet, it may be equally clear that the relationship would not continue were it not for financial support or payments. . . .

The most pertinent authority lies in several civil cases from the Tax Court, but these cases *favor* Harris' position. At its strongest, the government's case against Harris follows the assertions that Harris made, but now repudiates, in a lawsuit she filed against Kritzik's estate. According to her sworn pleadings in that suit, "all sums of money paid by David Kritzik to Lynette . . . were made . . . in pursuance with the parties' express oral agreement." Government Exhibit 22, p.4. As Harris' former lawyer testified at her trial, the point of this pleading was to make out a "palimony" claim under the California Supreme Court's decision in Marvin v. Marvin, 18 Cal. 3d 660, 134 Cal. Rptr. 815, 557 P.2d 106 (1976). Yet, the Tax Court has likened *Marvin*-type claims to amounts paid under antenuptial agreements. Under this analysis, these claims are *not* taxable income to the recipient:

In an antenuptial agreement the parties agree, through private contract, on an arrangement for the disposition of their property in the event of death or separation. *Occasionally, however, the relinquishment of marital rights is not involved. These contracts are generally enforceable under state contract law. See* Marvin v. Marvin, 18 Cal. 3d 660 [134 Cal. Rptr. 815], 557 P.2d 106 (1976). Nonetheless, transfers pursuant to an antenuptial agreement are generally treated as gifts between the parties, because under the gift tax law the exchanged promises are not supported by full and adequate consideration, in money or money's worth.

Green v. Commissioner, T.C. Memo 1987-503 (emphasis added).[16] We do not decide whether *Marvin*-type awards or settlements are or are not taxable to the recipient. The only point is that the Tax Court has suggested they are not. Until contrary authority emerges, no taxpayer could form a willful, criminal intent to violate the tax laws by failing to report *Marvin*-type payments. Reasonable inquiry does not yield a clear answer to the taxability of such payments.

Other cases only reinforce this conclusion. Reis v. Commissioner, T.C. Memo 1974-287, is a colorful example. The case concerned the tax liability of Lillian Reis, who had her start as a 16-year-old nightclub dancer. At 21, she met Clyde "Bing" Miller when he treated the performers in the nightclub show to a steak and champagne dinner. As the Tax Court described it, Bing passed out $50 bills to each person at the table, on the condition that they leave, until he was alone with Reis. Bing then offered to write a check to Reis for any amount she asked. She asked for $1,200 for a mink stole and for another check in the same amount so her sister could have a coat too.

The next day the checks proved good; Bing returned to the club with more gifts; and "a lasting friendship developed" between Reis and Bing. For the next five years, she saw Bing "every Tuesday night at the [nightclub] and Wednesday afternoons from approximately 1:00 p.m. to 3:00 p.m. . . . at various places

---

16. [The Court's use of the *Green* decision may be misleading. Note that the last sentence of the excerpt from the case refers to the gift tax, not the income tax. It is settled that the definition of "gift" is different for gift-tax purposes than for income-tax purposes. For nine years, taxpayer Green, and a man named Richmond, who was a stockbroker, had been "inseparable." Among other things, Green had traveled with Richmond on his business trips and had "watched his diet and health, cared for him when he was ill, kept track of his appointments and concerned herself with his personal needs." Though he declined to marry Green, Richmond promised to leave his large estate to her. He died without having kept the promise and Green sued the estate, under a theory of quantum meruit, for the value of services rendered. After Green was successful at trial, the suit was settled for a payment of $900,000 by the estate to her. The Tax Court sustained the IRS's determination that the settlement amount was income to Green. The court, in rejecting Green's effort to analogize her rights to a claim under an antenuptial agreement, stated that there was in fact no antenuptial agreement and that, in her state-court action, Green had relied on a theory of quantum meruit—that is, on claimed entitlement to payment for services rendered. On the other hand, in Reynolds v. Commissioner, T.C. Memo. 1999-62, the court concluded that cash payments received by a woman were nontaxable compensation for relinquishment of her interests in property (consisting mainly of a house and a large boat). The man and woman had lived together for twenty-five years, unmarried but in a marriage-like relationship. Despite the fact that the property had been bought by the man and was held solely in his name, the court accepted the woman's claim that the man had given her an interest in the property, as gifts, during their years together. The court emphasized that although the woman, in the legal action filed against the man, had referred to various household services that she had provided, she had not made any claim based on those services.—Eds.]

including . . . a girl friend's apartment and hotels where [Bing] was staying." He paid all of her living expenses, plus $200 a week, and provided money for her to invest, decorate her apartment, buy a car, and so on. The total over the five years was more than $100,000. The Tax Court held that this money was a gift, not income, despite Reis' statement that she "earned every penny" of the money. Similarly, in Libby v. Commissioner, T.C. Memo 1969-184 (1969), the Tax Court accorded gift treatment to thousands of dollars in cash and property that a young mistress received from her older paramour. And in Starks v. Commissioner, T.C. Memo 1966-134, the Tax Court did the same for another young woman who received cash and other property from an older, married man as part of "a very personal relationship."

The Tax Court did find that payments were income to the women who received them in Blevins v. Commissioner, T.C. Memo 1955-211, and in Jones v. Commissioner, T.C. Memo 1977-329. But in *Blevins*, the taxpayer was a woman who practiced prostitution and "used her home to operate a house of prostitution" in which six other women worked. Nothing suggested that the money at issue in that case was anything other than payments in the normal course of her business. Similarly in *Jones*, a woman had frequent hotel meetings with a married man, and on "*each* occasion" he gave her cash (emphasis added). Here too, the Tax Court found that the relationship was one of prostitution, a point that was supported by the woman's similar relationships with other men.

If these cases make a rule of law, it is that a person is entitled to treat cash and property received from a lover as gifts, as long as the relationship consists of something more than specific payments for specific sessions of sex. What's more, even in *Blevins*, in which the relationship was one of raw prostitution, the Tax Court rejected the IRS' claim that a civil fraud penalty should be imposed. Nor was a fraud penalty applied in *Jones*, the other prostitution case, although there the issue apparently was not raised. The United States does not allege that Harris received specific payments for specific sessions of sex, so *Reis, Libby,* and *Starks* support Harris' position. . . .

Besides Harris' prior suit, the United States also presented evidence regarding the overall relationship between Harris and Kritzik. Testimony showed that Harris described her relationship with Kritzik as "a job" and "just making a living." She reportedly complained that she "was laying on her back and her sister was getting all the money," described how she disliked when Kritzik fondled her naked, and made other derogatory statements about sex with Kritzik.

This evidence still leaves Harris on the favorable side of the Tax Court's cases. Further, this evidence tells us only what Harris thought of the relationship. Again, the Supreme Court in *Duberstein* held that the *donor's* intent is the "critical consideration" in determining whether a transfer of money is a gift or income. Commissioner v. Duberstein, 363 U.S. 278, 285 (1960). If Kritzik viewed the money he gave Harris as a gift, or if the dearth of contrary evidence leaves doubt on the subject, does it matter how mercenary Harris' motives were? *Duberstein* suggests that Harris' motives may not matter, but the ultimate answer makes no difference here. As long as the answer is at least a close call, and we are confident that it is, the prevailing law is too uncertain to support Harris' criminal conviction. . . .

In short, criminal prosecutions are no place for the government to try out "pioneering interpretations of tax law." United States v. Garber, 607 F.2d 92, 100 (5th Cir. 1979) (en banc). The United States has not shown us, and we have not found, a single case finding tax liability for payments that a mistress received from her lover, absent proof of specific payments for specific sex acts. Even when such specific proof is present, the cases have not applied penalties for civil fraud, much less criminal sanctions. The broad principles contained in *Duberstein* do not fill this gap. Before she met Kritzik, Harris starred as a sorceress in an action/adventure film. She would have had to be a real life sorceress to predict her tax obligations under the current state of the law.[17]

CONCLUSION

For the reasons stated, we reverse Harris and Conley's convictions and remand with instructions to dismiss the indictments against them.

FLAUM, Circuit Judge, concurring.

The majority has persuasively demonstrated why Leigh Ann Conley's conviction is infirm and why the district court abused its discretion in excluding the Kritzik letters. I therefore join that portion of its opinion.

I further agree that Lynnette Harris' conviction must be reversed as well. . . .

I am troubled, however, by the path the majority takes to reach this result, and thus concur only in the court's judgment with respect to the reversal of Harris' conviction. I part company with the majority when it distills from our gift/income jurisprudence a rule that would tax only the most base type of cash-for-sex exchange and categorically exempt from tax liability all other transfers of money and property to so-called mistresses or companions. . . . Consider the following example. *A* approaches *B* and offers to spend time with him, accompany him to social events, and provide him with sexual favors for the next year if *B* gives her an apartment, a car, and a stipend of $5,000 a

---

17. Harris and Conley have already served most of the sentences under the convictions that we now reverse. This is an injustice, and requires at least a brief explanation. To be released pending appeal of a criminal conviction, a defendant must show "by clear and convincing evidence that the person is not likely to flee or pose a danger to the safety of any other person" *and* "that the appeal is not for the purpose of delay and raises a substantial question of law or fact likely to result in reversal or an order for a new trial." 18 U.S.C. §3143(b). This is an exacting standard. Harris and Conley's counsel performed well, but failed in their petitions for release pending appeal to draw the Court's attention to the unique nature of Harris and Conley's convictions under the prevailing tax cases. In Orders dated September 25, 1990, and October 26, 1990, the Court denied those petitions. We vacated those Orders on May 10, 1991, the day after oral argument, and ordered Harris and Conley's immediate release. In the future, counsel who believe that the Court should have granted a petition for release can assist the Court by renewing the petition in their main appellate briefs. Also, this Court's warnings to counsel against the "buckshot" approach of raising as many issues as possible . . . are particularly applicable to motions for release pending appeal. Finally, the district courts can assist us by stating in detail their reasons for denying a petition for release pending appeal, especially in a case like the present one in which the defendants posed no danger to the community and apparently negligible threat of flight. Necessarily, a district court's thorough knowledge of the merits of a case puts it in a better position to evaluate petitions for release than our Court, at least until the issues have been fully presented to the Court through briefing and oral argument.

month. *B* agrees to *A*'s terms. According to the majority, because this example involves a transfer of money to a "mistress in the context of a long-term relationship," *A* could never be charged with criminal tax evasion if she chose not to pay taxes on *B*'s stipend. I find this hard to accept; what *A* receives from *B* is clearly income as it is "in return for services rendered." 363 U.S. at 285. To be sure, there will be situations—like the case before us—where the evidence is insufficient to support a finding that the transferor harbored a "cash for services" intent; in such cases, criminal prosecutions for willful tax evasion will indeed be impossible as a matter of law. That fact does not, however, condemn as overly vague the analysis itself.

I am thus prompted to find Harris' conviction infirm because of the relative scantiness of the record before us, not because mistresses are categorically exempt from taxation on the largess they receive. . . .

NOTES

1. *The private sphere and the public sphere.* Harris vividly demonstrates how awkward things become when the tax law wades into intimate relationships in the private sphere of our lives.

2. *The stakes in* Harris. A government victory in *Harris* would have increased income tax revenue by the amount of tax due on the income; there would have been no offsetting deduction for the payor, Kritzik. (A government victory would, however, lessen the gift tax liability due the government from Kritzik's estate.) In contrast, cases involving business-related transfers (as in *Duberstein*) usually involve a tradeoff for the government. If the transfers do not constitute gifts, they are taxable to the recipient but generally deductible by the payor. If the two parties are in the same tax bracket, tax revenues will not be affected by whether the transfer is characterized as a gift or a business payment.

3. *Criminal tax evasion.* Harris is a criminal tax case; it is the only such case in this casebook. The statutes under which Harris was convicted, §7201 and §7203, apply to "willful" failures to pay tax or file a return, respectively. In order to obtain a conviction, the government had to prove not only that the transfers constituted income to Harris but that Harris *knew* the transfers constituted income and willfully failed to file returns or pay tax due. The mens rea requirement for the crime is knowledge or intent. Note that no mens rea is required for civil tax liability. (Or, to put the matter somewhat differently, the tax law is in general a strict liability statute.) An individual who receives income is liable for tax on that income regardless of whether she realizes she has income or, for that matter, realizes she must pay tax on that income.

Would the court have reached a similar decision if the issue had been solely one of civil tax liability?

4. *Transfers in and out of marriage.* Had Kritzik and Harris married, the transfers of money to Harris would have been tax free under §1041, discussed in Section C of this chapter. The tax law would not inquire as to the motives for the marriage or the transfers. Because Kritzik and Harris were not married, the taxability of the transfers hinged on the application of the "detached and disinterested generosity" test of *Duberstein*.

5. *Taxes and morality.* Relationships like the one in *Harris* may be inherently exploitative. It may be that the tax law does not want to make it easy for couples to structure this kind of relationship in a tax-favored manner. Certainly, at the extreme, the tax law would not want to exempt wages from prostitution.

On the other hand, transfers may be made between two individuals in a committed relationship who choose not to marry. Assume the low-wage earner in the couple wants to assure himself the right to support payments in the event the relationship ends. He cannot rely on alimony: It is reserved for transfers incident to the breakup of a marriage. He could perhaps establish a right to "palimony" by insisting on a contract that assured him support in the event of a breakup. The consideration for the contract might include the services he provides to the relationship. Would the receipt of property pursuant to such a contract be taxable? Should it be taxable?

2.   Gift: Some Applications

The scope of the gift exclusion, and the taxability of various gratuitous transfers even if they do not constitute gifts under §102, has varied over time and with the type of transfer involved. Here are some of the main areas in which the issue has arisen:

1. *Ordinary tips.* Ordinary tips are includable in income on the theory that they are payments for services rendered. See Reg. §1.61-2(a)(1). The problem with tips is enforcement. Section 6053, enacted in 1982, contains complex and stiff rules requiring employer information returns on actual or putative tip income in the case of restaurants and cocktail lounges employing more than ten persons. The apparent burdensomeness of the reporting requirement is testimony to the seriousness of the Service's enforcement problems.

More unusual payments, analogous (at least) to tips, have led to clever, but unsuccessful, arguments. For example, United States v. McCormick, 67 F.2d 867 (2d Cir. 1933), cert. denied, 291 U.S. 662 (1934), holds that "contributions" received by a city clerk after marriage ceremonies from bridegrooms who were fearful of being accused of stinginess were taxable; and see Reg. §1.61-2(a)(1), to the effect that "marriage fees and other contributions received by a clergyman for services" are taxable.

In Olk v. United States, 536 F.2d 876 (9th Cir.), cert. denied, 429 U.S. 920 (1976), the court required inclusion of money given to a craps dealer in a casino by gamblers who the trial court determined were acting out of "impulsive generosity or superstition." The court rejected as a mere conclusion of law the trial court's further finding of "detached and disinterested generosity." It deemed this conclusion to be erroneous because of the gamblers' hope of a benefit of some sort.

2. *Prizes, awards, scholarships, and fellowships.* Before 1954, the forerunner of §102 was used by the courts and the Service to provide a broad exclusion for scholarships and fellowships and a limited exclusion for prizes and awards. The 1954 act added provisions that modified and attempted to clarify the existing law in this area but, at least in the case of scholarships and fellowships, left enough uncertainty to generate a seemingly endless stream of litigation

(e.g., over whether stipends to graduate students or interns were compensation for services rather than fellowships). The 1986 act excised the portion of the provision relating to prizes and awards (§74) that allowed a limited exclusion. In doing so it left in place a rule requiring inclusion of such benefits in gross income (with a few minor exceptions relating to charitable contributions).[18]

The 1986 act also drastically modified the provision relating to scholarships and fellowships (§117), leaving only a limited exclusion for scholarships provided to degree candidates. The limited exclusion is for that portion of a scholarship required to be used for tuition, fees, books, supplies, and equipment required for courses. The new law retained the previous rule that the exclusion does not apply to any portion of a scholarship that represents payment for teaching, research, or other services. This rule has given rise to disputes between students (who proved to be an exceptionally litigious lot) and the Service in the past and will no doubt continue to do so in the future, but the stakes will be much smaller (because the exclusion is more limited). Does the distinction between a "pure" scholarship and one that requires the performance of services seem to you consistent with sound principles of taxation? Why should scholarships be excluded at all? Are they like gifts? (And if so, so what?) Or does the exclusion reflect the notion that a tuition remission has no significant value? If it is fair to exclude tuition scholarships from gross income, should students who work their way through school and pay full tuition be allowed a deduction for their tuition payments? Should students who pay relatively low tuition at state universities and colleges be required to include in income the value of the subsidy they receive? What about the argument that scholarship students generally receive barely enough for survival and therefore should not be expected to pay taxes?

3. *Bequest.* Under §102, bequests are excluded from income along with gifts. Problems have arisen in distinguishing between bequests and belated compensation for services rendered to the decedent during his or her lifetime. In Wolder v. Commissioner, 493 F.2d 608 (2d Cir.), cert. denied, 419 U.S. 828 (1974), a "bequest" to a lawyer pursuant to a formal agreement under which he rendered legal services without charge was held to be income. On the other hand, in McDonald v. Commissioner, 2 T.C. 840 (1943), a bequest "in appreciation" of services as the decedent's nurse, dietitian, secretary, and driver during his declining years was held to be excluded under §102.

A payment received in settlement of a will contested by a person claiming rights as an heir has been held to be a bequest within the contemplation of §102. Lyeth v. Hoey, 305 U.S. 188 (1938).

4. *Welfare.* Traditional welfare payments and various other government payments, such as those for relief of disaster (Rev. Rul. 76-144, 1976-1 C.B. 17) and for victims of crime (Rev. Rul. 74-74, 1974-1 C.B. 18), have long been treated by the Service as excludable not under §102 but rather as not within the contemplation of §61. The label attached has been payments "for the general welfare," or something similar. Unemployment payments were also excluded (Rev. Rul. 76-63, 1976-1 C.B. 14), but now, under §85, are fully includable.

---

18. The 1986 act also added §74(c), which provides a narrowly circumscribed exclusion for certain noncash awards to employees for length of service or for safety achievements.

In 1996, Congress replaced the basic federal welfare program, Aid to Families with Dependent Children (AFDC), with a program called Temporary Assistance for Needy Families (TANF). TANF places a substantially increased emphasis on forcing welfare recipients to perform "work services"—essentially by imposing time limits to cut off benefits of people who do not perform such services. The program thus gave prominence to a difficult tax issue—how to distinguish between excludable welfare payments and taxable pay for work. The type of work services contemplated by TANF as a condition for continued entitlement to benefits included unsubsidized private-sector employment, subsidized public-sector employment, on-the-job training, community service, and certain school attendance. Most benefit recipients will not earn enough to reach the threshold for paying income taxes, but some might do so if, for example, they had a good job before qualifying for benefits or got a good job after doing so. More importantly, compensation for work, unlike welfare benefits, is subject to Social Security taxes and may entitle the worker to receive payments from the §32 Earned Income Tax Credit (EITC).

In Notice 99-3, 1999-1 C.B. 271, the IRS offered the following guideline:

> In cases where the following three conditions are satisfied, TANF payments will be treated as made for the promotion of the general welfare and therefore will not be includible in an individual's gross income; will not be earned income for EIC purposes; and will not be wages for employment tax purposes:
>
> (1) The only payments received by the individual with respect to the work activity are received directly from the state or local welfare agency (for this purpose, an entity with which a state or local welfare agency contracts to administer the state TANF program on behalf of the state will be treated as the state or local welfare agency);
>
> (2) The determination of the individual's eligibility to receive any payment is based on need and the only payments received by the individual with respect to the work activity are funded entirely under a TANF program (including any payments with respect to qualified state expenditures (as defined in §409(a)(7)(B)(i)(1) of the Social Security Act) and the Food Stamp Act of 1977)); and
>
> (3) The size of the individual's payment is determined by the applicable welfare law, and the number of hours the individual may engage in the work activity is limited by the size of the individual's payment (as determined by applicable welfare law) divided by the higher of the federal or state minimum wage.

Is there a sound policy argument for drawing a distinction between wages and welfare benefits for purposes of imposing an income tax (assuming total income above the exemption threshold)?[19] For purposes of imposing

---

19. Both the income tax and welfare benefits have distributional aims. In theory, the two need to be viewed in a coordinated fashion; otherwise, two families with identical incomes in the tax sense, but with different benefits, will be taxed quite differently. It is difficult for Congress to do this in a comprehensive way, because responsibilities for different programs are placed in different committees. In practice, however, the problem is militated by the standard deduction, personal allowances, the earned income tax credit, and other income support programs embedded in the Code, all of which operate to make it very improbable that families receiving any level of explicit welfare benefits are also subject to the federal income tax.

a Social Security (FICA) tax, with a corresponding right to receive benefits at retirement age or upon permanent and total disability? If so, what is it? If not, which way would you go: tax both or tax neither? Would your answer to these questions be different under the old AFDC law, which had much weaker provisions for inducing benefit recipients to go to work (or prepare to go to work)?

5. *Social Security.* Before 1983, the entire amount of Social Security retirement benefits was excluded from income, by longstanding IRS fiat. See Rev. Rul. 70-217, 1970-1 C.B. 13. Under current law, the treatment of Social Security benefits depends on the taxpayer's adjusted gross income, augmented by one-half the benefits received, tax-exempt interest, and other items. §86. Married couples filing joint returns with adjusted gross income (augmented by items stated above) less than $32,000 may continue to exclude Social Security benefits from taxation. Married couples with adjusted gross income in excess of $32,000 but below $44,000 must take into income the lesser of one-half of Social Security benefits or one-half the amount by which adjusted gross income exceeds $32,000. The treatment of benefits received by married couples with adjusted gross income between $44,000 and about $60,000 is computationally somewhat complex. Essentially, as adjusted gross income rises above $44,000, the couple must take into income 85 percent of the amount of Social Security benefits. The intent behind all this complexity is to phase out the exclusion as income rises. As is the case when any benefit is phased out as income rises, this approach ensures substantially higher effective marginal tax rates (and corresponding disincentives to work) for taxpayers over a certain income range.

QUESTIONS

1. Orthopedic surgeon Sandy successfully performs a difficult operation on accident victim Wendy. Therapist Teresa helps Wendy recover the full use of her damaged muscles. Wendy pays her bill and then, unexpectedly, offers both Sandy and Teresa free use of her ski condominium. Sandy and Teresa each accept Wendy's offer and each spends two weeks at the condominium. Suppose that Sandy and Teresa ask your advice on whether they must, or should, report the value of their use of the condominium as income. What do you say?

2. The facts are the same as in Question 1 except that instead of giving the use of the condominium, Wendy gives Sandy and Teresa each a check for $2,000. Are Sandy and Teresa taxable on the amounts they received? Is it important to know whether Wendy claimed a deduction for the payments as medical expenses? Suppose Wendy did deduct the payments as medical expenses, that the deduction was challenged by the IRS, and that the Tax Court, after observing that Wendy's opinion about the nature of the payments is irrelevant, upheld the IRS's denial of the deduction. Would these additional facts relating to the deduction by Wendy strengthen or weaken Sandy's and Teresa's claim that the payments were gifts?

3.   Transfer of Unrealized Gain by Gift While the Donor Is Alive

The following case is not part of our examination of gifts and windfalls as they affect the concept of income for tax purposes. Instead, it illustrates the effects of a gift transaction on the ultimate taxation of any unrealized (colloquially, "built-in") gain in respect of appreciated property (property that has increased in value) at the time the gift is made. The basic rule, as you will see, is that the built-in gain is not forgiven, but instead is reflected in the donee's measure of gain when she ultimately sells the property received as gift.

The principal purpose of putting the case here is to introduce the concept of basis, which we will examine at various points in this casebook and which is vital to an understanding of income taxation. In this instance, basis operates as the accounting mechanism by which unrealized gain is preserved in a gift transaction.

But the case may also be thought of as touching on all four of the questions that we suggested earlier are helpful in organizing one's thoughts. First, does the transaction give rise to income today? The answer under current law is no; the donee has no income from the receipt of a gift, and the donor likewise has no income on disposing of an asset with built-in gain: that is, the gift of appreciated property is not treated as if the donor sold the property and then gave the proceeds (or reinvested them in identical property and gave that). Note that the donor's side of the transaction is not logically necessary even in a world where donees receive gifts free of income tax, and it raises none of the conflict between the private sphere and the public sphere of our lives that taxing the donee would implicate. And, in turn, the built-in gain can in fact disappear, never constituting income, if the donee holds the appreciated property until her or his death. §1014.

Second, when is the built-in gain included in income? As the previous sentences suggested, under current law, gain is deferred until the donee sells the property or engages in another recognition transaction.

What happens if property depreciates in value from the time of a gift, but some built-in gain remains? The last question goes to the third of the four analytical tools: How much income is recognized?

Finally, whose income is it? Should the income attributable to pre-gift appreciation be assigned to the donor or the donee? This issue is squarely presented in the next case. Without meaning to spoil the surprise, the donee pays the tax on all the gain, including pre-gift gain. This can be seen as an illustration of a subset of substitute taxation, in this case through a "surrogate" taxpayer, a person who is taxed on the income of another person. As such, the case is another example of the conflict between accuracy (which argues in this setting for taxing the person to whom the income accrued, ideally at the time of gift, but as a second best at the time of sale) and practicality (which argues here for taxing the person who triggers the tax liability by selling the property and who has the proceeds from which to pay the tax).

The present statutory background is this: Section 61(a)(3) includes in gross income "gains from dealings in property." Section 1001 provides that the amount of the gain is the "excess of the amount realized . . . over the adjusted basis." The adjusted basis is the basis, defined under §1012 as "cost" (with certain exceptions), "adjusted as provided in section 1016." However, there is an exception in §1015 for property acquired by gift. Generally, the donee's basis (which word is used in §1015 to refer to adjusted basis) is the same as the donor's basis; in other words, the donee takes a "transferred basis" (§7701(a)(43)) from the donor. (Tax experts often simplify matters by using the word "basis" to refer either to an asset's cost basis or its adjusted basis, whichever is appropriate, and commonly use the phrase "carryover basis" to refer either to transferred basis or what the Code now calls "substituted basis." See *supra* note 6.) There is, however, an exception: If at the time of the gift the donor's basis is greater than the fair market value of the property (so that the donor would have a loss if he or she sold the property), then for purposes of computing the donee's loss (but not gain) on any subsequent sale, the donee's basis is the fair market value at the time of the gift. This rule was added to the statute in 1934.

The same basic statutory scheme (minus the 1934 revision) was in effect at the time the case below arose. The taxpayer challenged its application on constitutional grounds.

TAFT v. BOWERS
278 U.S. 470 (1929)

Mr. Justice McREYNOLDS delivered the opinion of the Court. . . .
Abstractly stated, this is the problem:

In 1916 *A* purchased 100 shares of stock for $1,000, which he held until 1923 when the fair market value had become $2,000. He then gave them to *B* who sold them during the year 1923 for $5,000. The United States claim that under the Revenue Act of 1921 *B* must pay income tax upon $4,000, as realized profits. *B* maintains that only $3,000—the appreciation during her ownership—can be regarded as income; that the increase during the donor's ownership is not income assessable against her within intendment of the Sixteenth Amendment.

The District Court ruled against the United States; the Circuit Court of Appeals held with them. . . .

We think the manifest purpose of Congress expressed in [§1015] was to require the petitioner to pay the enacted tax.[20]

The only question subject to serious controversy is whether Congress had power to authorize the exaction.

---

20. [Before the enactment of the predecessor of §1015, the Service had ruled that the basis to the donee of property received by gift was its fair market value at the time of the transfer. In 1921, the House Committee on Ways and Means reported: "This rule has been the source of serious evasion and abuse. Taxpayers having property which has come to be worth far more than it cost give such property to wives or relatives by whom it may be sold without realizing a gain unless the selling price is in excess of the value of the property at the time of the gift." To cure this practice, Congress enacted what is now the first clause of §1015(a). At the same time, it endorsed the administrative rule for pre-1921 gifts. §1015(c). See H.R. Rep. No. 350, 67th Cong., 1st Sess., 1939-1 (Pt. 2) C.B. 175.—Eds.]

It is said that the gift became a capital asset of the donee to the extent of its value when received and, therefore, when disposed of by her no part of that value could be treated as taxable income in her hands.

The Sixteenth Amendment provides—

The Congress shall have power to lay and collect taxes on incomes from whatever source derived, without apportionment among the several States, and without regard to any census or enumeration.

Income is the thing which may be taxed—income from any source. The Amendment does not attempt to define income or to designate how taxes may be laid thereon, or how they may be enforced.

Under former decisions here the settled doctrine is that the Sixteenth Amendment confers no power upon Congress to define and tax as income without apportionment something which theretofore could not have been properly regarded as income.

Also, this Court has declared—"Income may be defined as the gain derived from capital, from labor, or from both combined, provided it be understood to include profit gained through a sale or conversion of capital assets." Eisner v. Macomber, 252 U.S. 189, 207. The "gain derived from capital," within the definition, is "not a gain accruing to capital, nor a growth or increment of value in the investment, but a gain, a profit, something of exchangeable value proceeding from the property, severed from the capital however invested, and coming in, that is, received or drawn by the claimant for his separate use, benefit and disposal." United States v. Phellis, 257 U.S. 156, 169.

If, instead of giving the stock to petitioner, the donor had sold it at market value, the excess over the capital he invested (cost) would have been income therefrom and subject to taxation under the Sixteenth Amendment. He would have been obliged to share the realized gain with the United States. He held the stock—the investment—subject to the right of the sovereign to take part of any increase in its value when separated through sale or conversion and reduced to his possession. Could he, contrary to the express will of Congress, by mere gift enable another to hold this stock free from such right, deprive the sovereign of the possibility of taxing the appreciation when actually severed, and convert the entire property into a capital asset of the donee, who invested nothing, as though the latter had purchased at the market price? And after a still further enhancement of the property, could the donee make a second gift with like effect, etc.? We think not.

In truth the stock represented only a single investment of capital—that made by the donor. And when through sale or conversion the increase was separated therefrom, it became income from that investment in the hands of the recipient subject to taxation according to the very words of the Sixteenth Amendment. By requiring the recipient of the entire increase to pay a part into the public treasury, Congress deprived her of no right and subjected her to no hardship. She accepted the gift with knowledge of the statute and, as to the property received, voluntarily assumed the position of her donor. When she sold the stock she actually got the original sum invested, plus the entire appreciation and out of the latter only was she called on to pay the tax demanded.

The provision of the statute under consideration seems entirely appropriate for enforcing a general scheme of lawful taxation. . . .

The power of Congress to require a succeeding owner, in respect of taxation, to assume the place of his predecessor is pointed out by United States v. Phellis, 257 U.S. 156, 171:

> Where, as in this case, the dividend constitutes a distribution of profits accumulated during an extended period and bears a large proportion to the par value of the stock, if an investor happened to buy stock shortly before the dividend, paying a price enhanced by an estimate of the capital plus the surplus of the company, and after distribution of the surplus, with corresponding reduction in the intrinsic and market value of the shares, he was called upon to pay a tax upon the dividend received, it might look in his case like a tax upon his capital. But it is only apparently so. In buying at a price that reflected the accumulated profits, he of course acquired as a part of the valuable rights purchased the prospect of a dividend from the accumulations—bought "dividend on," as the phrase goes—and necessarily took subject to the burden of the income tax proper to be assessed against him by reason of the dividend if and when made. He simply stepped into the shoes, in this as in other respects, of the stockholder whose shares he acquired, and presumably the prospect of a dividend influenced the price paid, and was discounted by the prospect of an income tax to be paid thereon. In short, the question whether a dividend made out of company profits constitutes income of the stockholder is not affected by antecedent transfers of the stock from hand to hand.

There is nothing in the Constitution which lends support to the theory that gain actually resulting from the increased value of capital can be treated as taxable income in the hands of the recipient only so far as the increase occurred while he owned the property. And Irwin v. Gavit, 268 U.S. 161, 167, is to the contrary.

The judgments below are affirmed.

NOTES AND QUESTIONS

1. *Gift versus compensation.* The stock received by the taxpayer in this case was plainly a gift. As such it was excluded from income under §102(a). If the transfer had been compensatory, the basis rule would have been different. For example, suppose that L (a lawyer) performs services for C (a client) and bills C for $2,000. C admits she owes the $2,000 but offers to pay by transferring to L shares of stock of IBM that C had bought for $1,000 and that presently are worth $2,000. L accepts, and the shares are transferred. L has income of $2,000, and her basis for the shares is $2,000. The basis is arrived at under §1012, which refers to "cost"; "cost" has a special meaning for tax purposes. The results are, as they should be, the same as they would be if C had paid L $2,000 cash and L had used the cash to buy the shares. If L subsequently sells the shares for $5,000, she will have a gain for tax purposes of $3,000. By virtue of the transfer of the shares to L, C has a taxable gain of $1,000, just as

if she had sold the shares and paid L cash. Would it be better in this situation to follow the approach used in the case of gifts? That is, would it be sensible to ignore the gain on the stock at the time of the transfer from C to L and to tax L on $4,000 gain at the time of sale? Would your answer be different if the property transferred were not shares of stock of a publicly traded corporation but rather property that was difficult to value (for example, a work of art)?

2. *Pity the donee?* The taxpayer made the following argument (278 U.S. at 474): "The person acquiring property can never tell what liability he assumes in the way of income tax if any basis entirely foreign to him can be arbitrarily adopted for determining his gain." How would you respond? Is it relevant that Ms. Taft, the donee, happened to be the daughter of the donor? Is this relationship a surprising element in the case? Why should the donee's basis not be zero?

3. *Estoppel?* The Court says that Ms. Taft "accepted the gift with knowledge of the statute." Would the result be different in another case if the taxpayer were able to prove total ignorance of the statute? What if the taxpayer were six months old at the time of the gift?

4. *Tax the donor?* Would it be better to tax the gain (or allow a deduction for the loss) on property at the time of a transfer by gift? In other words, should such a transfer be a recognition event? The Code could implement this by treating the occasion of a gift as a time to settle up tax accounts with the donor, by "deeming" a sale to have occurred at the property's fair market value at the time of gift, in order to determine how much income tax the donor owed. See §84, treating the transfer of appreciated property to a political organization as a sale. See also §644, taxing a trust at the donor's rates where property is sold by the trust within two years of the transfer to it. And finally, note that §475 uses the deemed sale metaphor (here usually called "mark-to-market" taxation) to calculate the annual income of certain dealers and traders in securities. Wouldn't this approach be both constitutionally acceptable and closer to a Haig-Simons notion of income? What arguments can you make in opposition to a legislative proposal along these lines?

5. *Broader implications.* In *Taft*, the taxpayers (there were two cases, consolidated) relied heavily on Eisner v. Macomber's definition of income, but they lost. (*Macomber* is presented in the next chapter.) This case therefore can be seen as a limitation on, or partial rejection of, the concept of income for which *Macomber* is authority and symbol. (Note, by the way, that where a tax case is to be referred to by one of two names in its caption, the name used should be that of the taxpayer, e.g., Macomber, not that of the tax collector, e.g., Eisner, since the tax collector's name is likely to appear in many cases.)

6. *Adjustment for gift tax.* Section 1015(d) provides an upward adjustment of the donee's basis to reflect any federal gift tax paid by the donor.[21] For gifts made before 1977 the adjustment is for the entire amount of the gift tax paid by the donor, but the basis as adjusted may not exceed the value of the

---

21. The gift tax is a tax on the act of transfer by gift and is imposed on the donor with secondary liability on the donee if the donor does not pay. For the most part, the gift tax, and the estate tax (which is a tax on the act of transfer by reason of death), should be thought of as entirely separate from, and not relevant to, the income tax.

property at the time of the gift. For post-1977 gifts, the adjustment is limited to the gift tax attributable to the net appreciation in the value of the gift property. §1016(d)(6). The congressional rationale for the adjustment is that the gift tax is part of the cost of the property. The post-1977 rule reflects a sense that the prior rule was too generous, but, in any event, the congressional rationale is unsatisfactory. See 2 B. Bittker, *Federal Income, Estate and Gift Taxation* ¶41.3.23 (1981). The adjustment perhaps reflects the fact that the gift tax may have been excessive since that tax is based on the full value of the property instead of the value reduced by the liability for a future income tax.

4. Transfers at Death

1. *Inherited property.* Under §1014, the basis of property acquired by reason of death is the fair market value on the date of death or, at the election of the executor or administrator under §2032, on the optional valuation date (six months after death).[22] For simplicity we will, as most practitioners do, sometimes use "date-of-death" value to refer to whichever date is applicable. The effect of §1014 is that the basis is either "stepped up" or "stepped down" from the decedent's basis to the date-of-death value. What one encounters in practice is mostly stepped-up basis, because of inflation and because holders of property will find it profitable to sell their loss property before death, to take advantage of a deduction for the loss, and to retain their gain property, enabling their heirs to take advantage of the step-up.

To be clear, §1014 leads to the forgiveness of income tax on the gain inherent in property held at death, while well-advised (and prescient) taxpayers trigger loss deductions on depreciated properties by selling them prior to death. The mechanism for forgiving the tax is to give the donee a "stepped up" basis in property: that is, there is no Code section excluding the built-in gain from the donee's income, but by not treating death as an income tax realization even to the decedent (which would close the books on the decedent's lifetime tax history), and by revising the donee's tax basis to date of death fair market value, the Code accomplishes the same result.

Section 1014 is a very important exception to a rule of thumb you should keep in mind in thinking about the relationship between gain recognition and basis. Outside of §1014, your first intuition should be that if gain is taxed, basis is reset. If gain on property is deferred, gain is preserved in the hands of the donee, as surrogate taxpayer, through carryover basis.[23] Remember as well that Congress can be mean spirited, by providing a different rule for unrealized

---

22. In community-property states, the basis of the entire amount of property held by husband and wife as community property is stepped up (or down) (see §1014(b)(6)), whereas in common-law property states, there is a basis step up (or down) for only half of property held in joint tenancy. Under either property-law regime, the basis of the separate property of the decedent spouse is stepped up (or down), but not that of the survivor.

23. As a reminder, the Code technically refers to "transferred basis" (the gift case) and "exchanged basis" property; the two together comprise "substituted basis" property. See §7701(a)(42)-(44). Most practitioners elide over the differences and refer simply to carryover basis transactions.

loss than it does for unrealized gain. It is not the only example in the Code of such asymmetrical tax results!

It is true, of course, that the full value of the property may be subject to an estate tax. However, this tax (which reaches only very large estates) applies without regard to previously unrealized appreciation. Thus, a person who sells property before death pays an income tax on any gain plus an estate tax on the property remaining in the estate after payment of the income tax. An otherwise identical person who holds onto the property until death pays only the estate tax, though on a larger amount, because the estate has not been reduced by the income tax.

The effect of §1014 is to encourage people to hold onto appreciated property until death, which results in some degree of immobility of capital. Economists often refer to this incentive as the "lock-in" effect, because affluent elderly individuals with warm feelings towards their future heirs feel pressure not to sell appreciated assets that they otherwise would prefer to sell, either to fund consumption or to optimize their investment portfolios. They thereby enhance the size of their future estates by the income taxes not paid. Economists find the lock-in phenomenon troubling, because the tax system has in this respect imposed an artificial inducement to hold onto assets that the owner would sell in a world where built-in gains were taxed at death. This deadweight loss is unrelated to the $171 billion tax expenditure estimate mentioned below; the former reflects the consequences of economic decisions that would be different in a world with a consistent tax burden, while the latter measures forgone government revenues.

The fact that a person must hold onto the property until death does not necessarily mean that that person will be unable to enjoy the benefit of its increased value. Often, the owner will be able to borrow against the appreciation, and loans do not result in recognition of gain, even when they exceed basis. The proceeds of the loan can be used for any purpose, including consumption, and property sold to pay off the loan after death has produced a stepped-up basis, so that the sale will not generate taxable income. At the same time, the loan obligation will reduce the value of the estate for estate tax purposes.

In 2016, the Staff of the Joint Committee on Taxation estimated that §1014 will reduce government revenues by $171 billion over the five-year period 2017-2021. What principle of tax policy justifies this rule?

In 1970, Stanley Surrey (Harvard Law School professor and, from 1961 to 1969, Assistant Secretary of the Treasury for Tax Policy) and Jerome Kurtz (tax practitioner, formerly Tax Legislative Counsel and later Commissioner of Internal Revenue) wrote that "the failure of the income tax to reach the appreciation in value of assets transferred at death" is "the most serious defect in our federal tax structure today." *Reform of Death and Gift Taxes: The 1969 Treasury Proposals, The Criticisms, and a Rebuttal,* 70 Colum. L. Rev. 1365, 1381. In 1976, Congress enacted §1023, which provided for a substituted (carryover, in the more colloquial use adopted in this chapter) basis for property acquired by reason of death; however, this provision proved to be surprisingly complicated, and (perhaps more importantly from a political perspective) it was extremely unpopular. In response to these complaints, Congress postponed the effective date of the new substituted basis rule and ultimately repealed it, with a grandfather clause to protect reliance interests. The new rule thus never took effect.

QUESTIONS

1. Suppose *A* purchases stock for $1,000 and gives the stock to his son, *B*, at a time when the fair market value of the stock is $2,500.
   (a) How much gain does *B* recognize if he sells the stock for $3,500?
   (b) How much gain does *B* recognize if he sells the stock for $1,500?
2. Suppose *C* purchases stock for $2,000 and gives the stock to her daughter, *D*, at a time when the fair market value of the stock is $1,000. What amount of gain or loss (if any) is recognized by *D* on a sale for the following amounts?
   (a) $2,500
   (b) $500
   (c) $1,500
3. During the next four years, Ernesto's daughter, Ana, will require a total of $80,000 for college tuition and expenses. In each of the following settings, advise Ernesto as to the best means of transferring wealth to his daughter so that she may go to college. Ernesto is in the maximum marginal tax bracket, and Ana has no income.
   (a) Ernesto has a single asset, stock with a basis of $20,000 and a fair market value of $80,000.
   (b) Ernesto has a single asset, stock with a basis of $120,000 and a fair market value of $80,000.
   (c) Ernesto has stock with a basis of $20,000 and a fair market value of $80,000, plus $80,000 in a savings account.
   (d) Ernesto has stock with a basis of $20,000 and a fair market value of $80,000, plus stock with a basis of $120,000 and a fair market value of $80,000.
   (e) The facts are the same as in (a) except that Ernesto is 88 years old and is in poor health.

C. TRANSFERS INCIDENT TO MARRIAGE AND DIVORCE

1. Introduction

As we observed at the outset, it often is appropriate to view a family or household as a single tax unit for income tax purposes, because this best reflects the constant stream of instances of formal and informal support that each member provides the others. In this view, the income tax should ignore these commonplaces of family affection and unity and instead take cognizance only of the most conspicuously commercial forms of interaction (as when the parents who own a small business hire an adult child as a genuine employee). The explicit issue of the definition of the tax unit—that is, the nature of marriage and the treatment of a married couple as a single taxpayer for many purposes — is discussed in Chapter 6.

In fact, the income tax law more or less follows this viewpoint. But from the other direction, the Code is replete with anti-abuse rules that would be unnecessary if all intrafamily or household transactions were ignored. For example, the Code contains several provisions aimed at preventing tax avoidance through sales of property at a loss from one family member to another.

Transfers incident to marriage and divorce raise an interesting set of issues along these lines. In the case of divorce, for example, should transfers of property between the divorcing couple be analyzed as falling outside the private sphere of their lives, as the arrangement often is intensely negotiated, in many states with the assistance of lawyers and under the ultimate supervision of a court?

Suppose, for example, that pursuant to a divorce, Linda transfers to her ex-spouse, Martin, stock with a basis of $40,000 and a fair market value of $100,000. One question raised by such a transfer is whether, by virtue of the transfer, Martin should be required to include $100,000 in his income and Linda should be allowed to deduct $100,000. That is the "alimony" issue, to which we will return later in this section. (The answer under current law is that Linda would not be entitled to a deduction, and Martin would not be required to include any amount in his income, but it is by no means obvious that that result is consistent with sound principles of tax policy.) At this point we address the narrower question — the "recognition" question — of whether the transfer should be treated as a realization event for Linda, that is, an appropriate time at which to recognize Linda's gain of $60,000. Should Linda be treated as if she had sold the property and transferred the proceeds? Should it matter whether the transfer is of community property? Whether the transfer is made pursuant to a divorce decree or an antenuptial agreement?

2. Property Settlements

The next two cases, *Davis* and *Farid-Es-Sultaneh*, are included because of their historical importance and usefulness in setting forth some of the key issues raised by property transfers incident to marriage and divorce. As we will see, their current legal significance is affected, and in some respects eliminated, by the subsequent enactment of §1041.

a. Transfers Incident to a Divorce or Separation Agreement

UNITED STATES v. DAVIS
370 U.S. 65 (1962)

Mr. Justice CLARK delivered the opinion of the Court.

These cases involve the tax consequences of a transfer of appreciated property by Thomas Crawley Davis to his former wife pursuant to a property settlement agreement executed prior to divorce. . . .

In 1954 the taxpayer and his then wife made a voluntary property settlement and separation agreement calling for support payments to the wife and minor child in addition to the transfer of certain personal property to the wife. Under Delaware law all the property transferred was that of the taxpayer, subject to certain statutory marital rights of the wife including a right of intestate succession and a right upon divorce to a share of the husband's property. Specifically, as a "division in settlement of their property" the taxpayer agreed to transfer to his wife, inter alia, 1,000 shares of stock in the E. I. duPont de Nemours & Co. The then Mrs. Davis agreed to accept this division "in full settlement and satisfaction of any and all claims and rights against the husband whatsoever (including but not by way of limitation, dower and all rights under the laws of testacy and intestacy). . . ."

I

The determination of the income tax consequences of the stock transfer described above is basically a two-step analysis: (1) Was the transaction a taxable event? (2) If so, how much taxable gain resulted therefrom? Originally the Tax Court (at that time the Board of Tax Appeals) held that the accretion to property transferred pursuant to a divorce settlement could not be taxed as capital gain to the transferor because the amount realized by the satisfaction of the husband's marital obligations was indeterminable and because, even if such benefit were ascertainable, the transaction was a nontaxable division of property. . . . However, upon being reversed in quick succession by the Courts of Appeals of the Third and Second Circuits, . . . the Tax Court accepted the position of these courts and has continued to apply these views in appropriate cases since that time. . . . [T]he Courts of Appeals reasoned that the accretion to the property was "realized" by the transfer and that this gain could be measured on the assumption that the relinquished marital rights were equal in value to the property transferred. The matter was considered settled until the Court of Appeals for the Sixth Circuit, in reversing the Tax Court, ruled that, although such a transfer might be a taxable event, the gain realized thereby could not be determined because of the impossibility of evaluating the fair market value of the wife's marital rights. . . . In so holding that court specifically rejected the argument that these rights could be presumed to be equal in value to the property transferred for their release. This is essentially the position taken by the Court of Claims in the instant case.

II

We now turn to the threshold question of whether the transfer in issue was an appropriate occasion for taxing the accretion to the stock. There can be no doubt that Congress, as evidenced by its inclusive definition [in §61(a)] of income subject to taxation, that is, "all income from whatever source derived, . . . [g]ains derived from dealings in property," intended that the economic growth of this stock be taxed. The problem confronting us is simply when is such accretion to be taxed. Should the economic gain be presently assessed against taxpayer, or should this assessment await a subsequent transfer of the property by the wife? The controlling statutory language, which provides [§1001] that gains from dealings in property are to be taxed upon "sale or other disposition," is too general to include or exclude conclusively the transaction presently in issue. Recognizing this, the Government and the taxpayer argue by analogy with transactions more easily classified as within or without the ambient [sic] of taxable events. The taxpayer asserts that the present disposition is comparable to a nontaxable division of property between two co-owners,[24] while the Government contends it more resembles a taxable transfer of property in exchange for the release of an independent legal obligation. Neither disputes the validity of the other's starting point.

In support of his analogy the taxpayer argues that to draw a distinction between a wife's interest in the property of her husband in a common-law jurisdiction such as Delaware and the property interest of a wife in a typical community property jurisdiction would commit a double sin; for such differentiation would depend upon "elusive and subtle casuistries which . . . possess no relevance for tax purposes," Helvering v. Hallock, 309 U.S. 106, 118 (1940), and would create disparities between common-law and community property jurisdictions in contradiction to Congress' general policy of equality between the two. The taxpayer's analogy, however, stumbles on its own premise, for the inchoate rights granted a wife in her husband's property by the Delaware law do not even remotely reach the dignity of co-ownership. The wife has no interest—passive or active—over the management or disposition of her husband's personal property. Her rights are not descendable, and she must survive him to share in his intestate estate. Upon dissolution of the marriage she shares in the property only to such extent as the court deems "reasonable." 13 Del. Code Ann. §1531(a). What is "reasonable" might be ascertained independently of the extent of the husband's property by such criteria as the wife's financial condition, her needs in relation to her accustomed station in life, her age and health, the number of children and their ages, and the earning capacity of the husband. See, e.g., Beres v. Beres, 52 Del. 133, 154 F.2d 384 (1959).

This is not to say it would be completely illogical to consider the shearing off of the wife's rights in her husband's property as a division of that property, but we believe the contrary to be the more reasonable construction. Regardless of the tags, Delaware seems only to place a burden on the husband's property rather than to make the wife a part owner thereof. In the present context the rights of succession and reasonable share do not differ significantly from the husband's

24. Any suggestion that the transaction in question was a gift is completely unrealistic. Property transferred pursuant to a negotiated settlement in return for the release of admittedly valuable rights is not a gift in any sense of the term. To intimate that there was a gift to the extent the value of the property exceeded that of the rights released not only invokes the erroneous premise that every exchange not precisely equal involves a gift but merely raises the measurement problem discussed in Part III [of this opinion]. Cases in which this Court has held transfers of property in exchange for the release of marital rights subject to gift taxes are based not on the premise that such transactions are inherently gifts but on the concept that in the contemplation of the gift tax statute they are to be taxed as gifts. Merrill v. Fahs, 324 U.S. 308 (1945); Commissioner v. Wemyss, 324 U.S. 303 (1945); see Harris v. Commissioner, 340 U.S. 106 (1950). In interpreting the particular income tax provisions here involved, we find ourselves unfettered by the language and considerations ingrained in the gift and estate tax statutes. See Farid-Es-Sultaneh v. Commissioner.

obligations of support and alimony. They all partake more of a personal liability of the husband than a property interest of the wife. The effectuation of these marital rights may ultimately result in the ownership of some of the husband's property as it did here, but certainly this happenstance does not equate the transaction with a division of property by co-owners. Although admittedly such a view may permit different tax treatment among the several States, this Court in the past has not ignored the differing effects on the federal taxing scheme of substantive differences between community property and federal taxing systems. E.g., Poe v. Seaborn. To be sure Congress has seen fit to alleviate this disparity in many areas, . . . but in other areas the facts of life are still with us. . . .

III

Having determined that the transaction was a taxable event, we now turn to the point on which the Court of Claims balked, viz., the measurement of the taxable gain realized by the taxpayer. The Code defines the taxable gain from the sale or disposition of property as being the "excess of the amount realized therefrom over the adjusted basis. . . ." §1001(a). The "amount realized" is further defined as "the sum of any money received plus the fair market value of the property (other than money) received." §1001(b). In the instant case the "property received" was the release of the wife's inchoate marital rights. The Court of Claims, following the Court of Appeals for the Sixth Circuit, found that there was no way to compute the fair market value of these marital rights and that it was thus impossible to determine the taxable gain realized by the taxpayer. We believe this conclusion was erroneous.

It must be assumed, we think, that the parties acted at arm's length and that they judged the marital rights to be equal in value to the property for which they were exchanged. There was no evidence to the contrary here. Absent a readily ascertainable value it is accepted practice where property is exchanged to hold, as did the Court of Claims in Philadelphia Park Amusement Co. v. United States, 130 Ct. Cl. 166, 172, 126 F. Supp. 184, 189 (1954), that the values "of the two properties exchanged in an arm's-length transaction are either equal in fact, or are presumed to be equal." . . . To be sure there is much to be said of the argument that such an assumption is weakened by the emotion, tension, and practical necessities involved in divorce negotiations and the property settlements arising therefrom. However, once it is recognized that the transfer was a taxable event, it is more consistent with the general purpose and scheme of the taxing statutes to make a rough approximation of the gain realized thereby than to ignore altogether its tax consequences. . . .

Moreover, if the transaction is to be considered a taxable event as to the husband, the Court of Claims' position leaves up in the air the wife's basis for the property received. In the context of a taxable transfer by the husband,[25] all

---

25. Under the present administrative practice, the release of marital rights in exchange for property or other consideration is not considered a taxable event as to the wife. For a discussion of the difficulties confronting a wife under a contrary approach, see Taylor and Schwartz, *Tax Aspects of Marital Property Agreements*, 7 Tax L. Rev. 19, 30 (1951); *Comment, The Lump Sum Divorce Settlement as a Taxable Exchange*, 8 U.C.L.A. L. Rev. 593, 601-602 (1961).

indicia point to a "cost" basis for this property in the hands of the wife [under §1012]. Yet under the Court of Claims' position her cost for this property, that is, the value of the marital rights relinquished therefor, would be indeterminable, and on subsequent disposition of the property she might suffer inordinately over the Commissioner's assessment which she would have the burden of proving erroneous. . . . Our present holding that the value of these rights is ascertainable eliminates this problem; for the same calculation that determines the amount received by the husband fixes the amount given up by the wife, and this figure, that is, the market value of the property transferred by the husband, will be taken by her as her tax basis for the property received.

Finally, it must be noted that here, as well as in relation to the question of whether the event is taxable, we draw support from the prior administrative practice and judicial approval of that practice. See *supra*. We therefore conclude that the Commissioner's assessment of a taxable gain based upon the value of the stock at the date of its transfer has not been shown erroneous.

IV

[Discussion of attorney fee question omitted.]
Reversed in part and affirmed in part.

Mr. Justice FRANKFURTER took no part in the decision of these cases.

Mr. Justice WHITE took no part in the consideration or decision of these cases.

NOTES AND QUESTIONS

1. *Analysis of* Davis. (a) As described in more detail below, the 2017 tax law made a fundamental change in the taxation of alimony. For almost the entire history of the income tax, alimony payments had been deductible to the payor and includible in the income of the recipient ex-spouse. For divorces finalized after 2018, however, alimony payments will not be deductible/includible. The result is to tax the income from which the alimony is paid at the tax brackets applicable to the payor ex-spouse. (This restores a 1917 Supreme Court ruling that the Code had long since overruled.) If *Davis* were decided in 2019, how (if at all) would the 2017 Act's treatment of alimony affect the Court's analysis?

(b) Assume that the general approach of the Court was correct and that the outcome of *Davis* should turn on whether Mrs. Davis owned an "interest" in property held in Mr. Davis's name, as opposed to a "mere expectancy"; that is, on whether Mrs. Davis received property that she previously owned in some sense, as opposed to a payment in discharge of a debt owed to her by Mr. Davis. How should the issue be decided? By reference to one's common-sense judgment about how married people in Delaware are likely to think of the property rights of husbands and wives? By reference to what sociologists can tell us about the question? By trying to count the ways in which Delaware marital-property law is like or unlike community-property law? Or by reference to rules of law defining what is an interest in property for purposes of resolving other legal issues? Which approach did the Court adopt?

(c) Compare the outcome of this case with the rules adopted by Congress in provisions such as §§1031, 1033, and 109. What does this comparison tell you about the wisdom and fairness of the rule applied in the case?

(d) What was Mrs. Davis's basis in the property received? What is the conceptual foundation for that result? If the Court had held that the transfer did not result in the realization of gain by Mr. Davis, what should Mrs. Davis's basis have been? Under what Code provision can that result be reached?

2. *Belated congressional response.* (a) The *Davis* decision gave rise to a substantial amount of litigation and complexity in the law. Ultimately, Congress altered the result in *Davis* and simplified the law by adopting §1041. Section 1041 provides that no gain or loss shall be recognized on transfers of property between spouses or incident to a divorce. Thus, most spousal transfers of appreciated or depreciated property are not treated as sales that generate gain or loss to the transferor. Consistent with nonrecognition treatment, the property transferred has a substituted basis in the hands of the transferee. Section 1041 works together with the alimony rule, in §71(b)(1), discussed below, that provides that only cash transfers are considered alimony. Alimony is deductible by the payor and included in the income of the payee; other transfers incident to divorce are not deductible by the payor or included in the income of the payee. The results are that a transfer of property, other than cash, incident to divorce (a) does not result in the recognition of gain, and (b) does not give rise to a deduction by the transferor or income to the transferee. This combination of rules may offend other goals of the tax system, but it does simplify administration.

(b) By what authority can Congress overrule a Supreme Court decision in this manner?

3. *The limits of §1041.* In Rev. Rul. 87-112, 87-2 C.B. 207, the taxpayer, *A*, transferred to the taxpayer's former spouse, *B*, U.S. Series E and EE savings bonds that had been bought in an earlier year entirely with *A*'s separate funds. *A*, pursuant to §454(c) and Reg. §1.454-1(a), had not included in income the interest on these bonds; taxpayers are allowed to defer tax on such interest until the bonds are cashed in. The Ruling holds that §1041(a) does not apply to the gain from the accrued interest and that the deferred, accrued interest from the date of original issuance of the bonds to the date of transfer of the bonds to *B* is includable in *A*'s gross income.

4. *Unmarried couples.* Section 1041 substantially reduces the problems of dividing the economic interests of married couples. It is not available to unmarried couples who split up, no matter how long they have lived together, how deep and sincere their sharing and mutual commitment has been, and how tangled and intertwined their economic interests.

PROBLEMS

1. Henry and Wilma, when they were married, jointly owned a house with a fair market value of $400,000 and a basis of $100,000. Pursuant to their recent

divorce, Henry took title to the house and executed a promissory note for $200,000 payable to Wilma and secured by the house.

(a) What amount of gain, if any, is recognized by Wilma? What is Wilma's basis for the note?

(b) What is Henry's basis for the house?

(c) What would your answer to the above questions be in the absence of §1041?

2. Herb and Wanda were divorced six years ago. Herb was awarded custody of their two children. The decree of divorce provided that Herb was to remain in the family home until the younger child reached age 18 and that the house would then be sold, with the proceeds equally divided between Herb and Wanda. Last month, when the younger child turned 18, the house was sold for $400,000. Its basis was $100,000. Can Wanda, who currently lives in an apartment, exclude the $150,000 from income under §121?

b.   Antenuptial Settlements ("Prenups")

FARID-ES-SULTANEH v. COMMISSIONER
160 F.2d 812 (2d Cir. 1947)

Before SWAN, CHASE, and CLARK, Circuit Judges.

CHASE, Circuit Judge. . . .

[In 1924, S. S. Kresge, in contemplation of his marriage to taxpayer (petitioner) Farid-Es-Sultaneh, transferred to her some shares of stock of the S. S. Kresge Co. worth a total of about $800,000. Shortly thereafter they entered into an antenuptial agreement under which she acknowledged receipt of the shares "as a gift . . . pursuant to this indenture, and as an antenuptial settlement" and in consideration thereof released all her dower and other marital rights, including the right to support. Kresge and Farid-Es-Sultaneh were married in 1924 and divorced in 1928. She did not claim or receive alimony. Kresge's basis for the shares transferred in 1924 was fifteen cents per share; their value at that time was about $10 per share. In 1938, Farid-Es-Sultaneh sold some of the shares for $19 per share].[26]

When the petitioner and Mr. Kresge were married he was 57 years old with a life expectancy of 16 years. She was then 32 years of age with a life expectancy of 33 years. He was then worth approximately $375,000,000 and owned real estate of the approximate value of $100,000,000.

The Commissioner determined [a deficiency for the year 1938] on the ground that the petitioner's stock . . . was acquired by gift . . . and [that under

---

26. [After her divorce from Kresge (her second husband), the taxpayer "sailed in luxury to Europe. An extremely attractive woman who just missed beauty," she met and married Prince Farid of Sadri-Azam, a nephew of a former Shah of Iran, and acquired the title Princess Farid-Es-Sultaneh. Her marriage to the prince ended in 1936, but for the rest of her life she continued to use the name Farid-Es-Sultaneh and, despite the published declaration of the prince that she was not entitled to do so, the title 'princess.' " *N.Y. Times,* Aug. 13, 1963, at 31, col. 3 (obituary).—EDS.]

§1015(a) she must thus use] as the basis for determining the gain on her sale of it the basis it would have had in the hands of the donor. This was correct if [§1015(a)] is applicable, and the Tax Court held it was on the authority of Wemyss v. Commissioner, 324 U.S. 303 (1945) and Merrill v. Fahs, 324 U.S. 308 (1945).

The issue here presented cannot, however, be adequately dealt with quite so summarily. The *Wemyss* case determined the taxability to the transferor as a gift, under [§§2511(a) and 2512(b)], of property transferred in trust for the benefit of the prospective wife of the transferor pursuant to the terms of an antenuptial agreement. It was held that the transfer, being solely in consideration of her promise of marriage, and to compensate her for loss of trust income which would cease upon her marriage, was not for an adequate and full consideration in money or money's worth within the meaning of [§2512(b)], the Tax Court having found that the transfer was not one at arm's length made in the ordinary course of business. But we find nothing in this decision to show that a transfer, taxable as a gift under the gift tax, is ipso facto to be treated as a gift in construing the income tax law.

In Merrill v. Fahs [*supra*], it was pointed out that the estate and gift tax statutes are in pari materia and are to be so construed. . . . Although Congress in 1932 also expressly provided that the release of marital rights should not be treated as a consideration in money or money's worth in administering the estate tax law [see §2043(b)] and failed to include such a provision in the gift tax statute, it was held that the gift tax law should be construed to the same effect.

We find in this decision no indication, however, that the term "gift" as used in the income tax statute should be construed to include a transfer which, if made when the gift tax were effective, would be taxable to the transferor as a gift merely because of the special provisions in the gift tax statute defining and restricting consideration for gift tax purposes.[27]

In our opinion the income tax provisions are not to be construed as though they were in pari materia with either the estate tax law or the gift tax statutes. They are aimed at the gathering of revenue by taking for public use given percentages of what the statute fixes as net taxable income. Capital gains and losses are . . . factors in determining net taxable income. What is known as the basis for computing gain or loss on transfers of property is established by statute in those instances when the resulting gain or loss is recognized for income tax purposes. . . . When Congress provided that gifts should not be treated as taxable income to the donee, there was, without any correlative provisions fixing the basis of the gift to the donee, a loophole which enabled the donee to . . . take as the basis for computing gain or loss its value when the gift was made. Thus it was possible to exclude from taxation any increment in value during the donor's holding and the donee might take advantage of any shrinkage in such increment after the acquisition by gift in computing gain

---

27. [See the suggestion of Judge Jerome N. Frank that the terms "gift," "gaft," and "geft" be used, depending upon whether the gift, income, or estate tax meaning is implied. Commissioner v. Beck's Estate, 129 F.2d 243 (2d Cir. 1942).—EDS.]

or loss upon a subsequent sale or exchange. It was to close this loophole that Congress provided that the donee should take the donor's basis when property was transferred by gift. . . . Because of this we think that a transfer which would be classed as a gift under the gift tax law is not necessarily to be treated as a gift income-tax-wise. Though such a consideration as this petitioner gave for the shares of stock she acquired from Mr. Kresge might not have relieved him from liability for a gift tax, had the present gift tax then been in effect, it was nevertheless a fair consideration which prevented her taking the shares as a gift under the income tax law since it precluded the existence of a donative intent.

Although the transfers of the stock made . . . to this taxpayer are called a gift in the antenuptial agreement later executed and were to be for the protection of his prospective bride if he died before the marriage was consummated, the "gift" was contingent upon his death before such marriage, an event that did not occur. Consequently, it would appear that no absolute gift was made before the antenuptial contract was executed and that she took title to the stock under its terms, viz.: in consideration for her promise to marry him coupled with her promise to relinquish all rights in and to his property which she would otherwise acquire by the marriage. Her inchoate interest in the property of her affianced husband greatly exceeded the value of the stock transferred to her. It was a fair consideration under ordinary legal concepts of that term for the transfers of the stock by him. . . . She performed the contract under the terms of which the stock was transferred to her and held the shares not as a donee but as a purchaser for a fair consideration. . . .

Decision reversed.

CLARK, Circuit Judge (dissenting). . . .
It is true that Commissioner v. Wemyss and Merrill v. Fahs, *supra,* which would require the transactions here to be considered a gift, dealt with estate and gift taxes. But no strong reason has been advanced why what is a gift under certain sections of the Revenue Code should not be a gift under yet another section. . . . The Congressional purpose would seem substantially identical — to prevent a gap in the law whereby taxes on gifts or on capital gains could be avoided or reduced by judicious transfers within the family or intimate group.

But decision on that point might well be postponed. . . . Kresge transferred the stock to petitioner more than three months before their marriage. Part was given when Kresge was married to another woman. At these times petitioner had no dower or other rights in his property. If Kresge died before the wedding, she could never secure dower rights in his lands. Yet she would nevertheless keep the stock. Indeed the specifically stated purpose of the transfer was to protect her against his death prior to marriage. It is therefore difficult to perceive how her not yet acquired rights could be consideration for the stock. . . .

If the transfer be thus considered a sale, as the majority hold, it would seem to follow necessarily that this valuable consideration (equivalent to one-third for life in land valued at one hundred million dollars) should have yielded sizable taxable capital gains to Kresge, as well as a capital loss to petitioner when eventually she sold. I suggest these considerations as pointing to the unreality of holding as a sale what seems clearly only intended as a stimulating cause to eventual matrimony.

QUESTIONS

1. What were the tax consequences to Kresge in 1924? Note the court's statement (last paragraph of majority opinion) about the value of the rights released by Farid-Es-Sultaneh.

What would have been the tax consequences of the transfer in 1924 if §1041 had been enacted? What if the antenuptial agreement provided that the transfer would not be made until after the marriage? What do these questions suggest about negotiating and drafting antenuptial settlements?

2. Was Farid-Es-Sultaneh taxable in 1924? If not, on what theory? Whatever your theory, is it better than viewing the transfer as a gift?

3. In Marvin v. Marvin, 18 Cal. 3d 660, 557 F.2d 106, 134 Cal. Rptr. 815 (1976), the plaintiff alleged an agreement with the defendant by which they would live together as husband and wife and the plaintiff would "devote her full time to defendant . . . as a companion, homemaker, housekeeper and cook" and in return defendant would "provide for all of plaintiff's financial support and needs for the rest of her life." 18 Cal. 3d at 666. The court held that the complaint stated a cause of action. What is the proper tax treatment of any amount ultimately recovered by the plaintiff? Is the defendant entitled to a deduction? If the final judgment were to order the defendant to transfer a house to the plaintiff, what would be the tax consequences to the defendant? See Green v. Commissioner and Reynolds v. Commissioner, described *supra* page 97. In the *Reynolds* case, the court assumed, without much evidence, that the property received as gifts by the woman during the years of cohabitation, and relinquished by her in return for a cash settlement, had a basis equal at least to the amount that she received, so she did not realize any gain. The court noted that the woman did not claim a loss deduction (which probably would have been useless to her); thus, there was no need to determine the actual basis.

3.   Alimony, Child Support, and Property Settlements

a.   *Transfers Pursuant to Agreements Entered into After 2018*

Transfers occurring pursuant to marriage, separation, and divorce are commonly separated into prenuptial agreements, divorce or separation property settlements, alimony, and child care. Transfers pursuant to agreements entered into after 2018 are all treated in the same manner: There is no deduction to the transferor and no income to the transferee. If property is transferred, its basis remains unchanged. These rules were enacted in two main tax reform acts. First, in 1986, the realization/recognition rule of *Davis* and

Farid was overturned. Thus, payments that fell into the category of "property settlements" were nontaxable, whether or not the transfers were made in community or separate property states. Payments that fell into the category of alimony, however, were deductible to the payor and included in income to the payee. Thus, the law distinguished (and with respect to transfers pursuant to agreements entered into prior to 2019, still distinguishes) between alimony and property settlements. Second, the 2017 act placed all transferors made pursuant to agreements entered into after 2018 into the same category: nonrealization events that are not deductible by the payor and not includable in income by the payee.

Taxpayers who entered into agreements prior to 2019 can elect to have the new rules apply to them. The election must be made by both the payor and payee.

To illustrate the new law, suppose that in 2019 Leslie and Sam divorce. As part of the divorce agreement, Sam receives stock with a basis of $50,000 and fair market value of $500,000. In addition, Leslie agrees to provide $10,000 a month to Sam as alimony and $5,000 a month in child support. No payment is taxable to Sam or deductible to Leslie. Sam assumes the existing basis of $50,000 for the property.

b.   *Transfers Pursuant to Agreements Entered into Before 2019*

"Alimony," and "separate maintenance payments," are payments that meet certain conditions specified in §71. First, the payment must be in cash. §71(b)(1). This rule jibes with the rule of §1041, *supra*, that no gain or loss is recognized on certain transfers of property between spouses and former spouses. The two rules together serve the goal of simplicity. Putting aside that goal, it is difficult to see why a transfer of property in satisfaction of periodic support-type obligations should not be treated as alimony.

Second, the payment must be received under an "instrument" of divorce or separate maintenance. §§71(b)(1)(A), 71(b)(2). Oral agreements will not do. Unmarried couples are not covered.

Third, the parties must not have agreed that the payment will be nontaxable to the payee and nondeductible by the payor. This rule simply gives the parties an election as to payments that would, but for the election, be treated as alimony. Note, however, that the election goes only one way. No election is available to treat as deductible by the payor and taxable to the payee payments that are not alimony or separate maintenance within the rules of §71.

Fourth, the parties must not be members of the same household. §71(b)(1)(C). This rule will remove some or all of the tax incentive for friendly divorces by couples who seek to take advantage of the favorable single-person (or head-of-household) rates. A tax advantage will still be available to unmarried couples (either never-married or divorced from one another) whose marginal rates on their individual incomes would be about the same. But for couples with unequal incomes the advantage of the more favorable rates for single taxpayers will be offset by the disadvantage of having more income taxed at the higher end of the rate structure, and they will not be able to equalize the individual incomes by alimony payments—unless they are prepared to live apart.

Fifth, the payments cannot continue after the death of the payee spouse. §71(b)(1)(D). This rule is consistent with a notion that alimony and separate maintenance are payments for support of the payee. If the payments continue after the death of the payee, they cannot have been intended purely as support; they must be in the nature of a property settlement or, at least in part, for the support of some other person. The nondeductibility of property settlements seems to be based on the idea that because such payments do not represent a diversion of income nothing justifies a deduction.

Sixth, the payments must not be for child support. The relevant provision, §71(c), attempts to ensure that substance prevails over form. Thus, a payment that is called "alimony" but terminates when a child of the marriage dies or reaches age 18 will be treated as child support. This is an important change from prior law. The idea behind the denial of a deduction for child support is that if the payor had custody of, and supported, the children, the cost of the support would not be deductible, so nothing justifies the deduction of similar amounts when paid to a former spouse. Obviously, this rule does not take account of the expense of maintaining two households. Perhaps the lack of sympathy for that circumstance is a reflection of a moral (or moralistic) sense that people should not expect the tax system to relieve them of burdens of their own making.

Finally, a set of rules deals broadly, and arbitrarily, with the problem of distinguishing between alimony and cash "property settlements." Roughly speaking, §71(f) provides that only payments that are substantially equal for the first three years will be treated as alimony. This requirement of "periodicity" reflects a long-held notion of a distinction between, on the one hand, once-and-for-all settlements ("property settlements"), in one payment or a few installments, and, on the other hand, regular support payments (alimony).

Under §71(f)'s arbitrary implementation of this distinction, if the first three yearly payments are "front-loaded"—that is, unequal, with larger amounts in the first or second year—some portion of the amount paid will not be treated as alimony. (Section 71(f) does not recharacterize unequal but "back-loaded" alimony payments—that is, payments that increase in size over the first three years.)

4. Child-Support Obligations in Default

Regardless of whether child support is part of an agreement entered into before 2019, it is not deductible by the payor and is not taxed to the payee (usually the custodial parent). Suppose that child-support payments are not made, and the expense of child support is borne entirely by the custodial parent. The custodial parent is clearly poorer. Should the tax burden of the custodial parent reflect the loss?

DIEZ-ARGUELLES v. COMMISSIONER
48 T.C.M. 496 (1984)

FINDINGS OF FACT . . .

In 1972, petitioner, Christina Diez-Arguelles ("Christina"), was divorced from her former husband, Kevin Baxter, and was granted custody of their two minor children. Pursuant to a property settlement agreement, which was incorporated into the divorce decree, Mr. Baxter agreed to pay Christina $300 per month for child support. Mr. Baxter failed to make full payment of his obligation for child support during the years 1972 through 1978 and by the end of 1978 he was in arrears by the amount of $4,325.00. During 1979 he paid only $600.00 in child support and consequently at the end of 1979 was in arrears by another $3,000.00. On their 1978 return the petitioners treated the $4,325.00 then due from Mr. Baxter as a nonbusiness bad debt and deducted the amount from their gross income as a short-term capital loss. On their 1979 return they deducted the $3,000.00 in the same manner. Respondent disallowed both deductions in their entirety.

Because of Mr. Baxter's failure to meet his support obligations, the petitioners had to bear the entire support of the two children from the date of the divorce in 1972 through 1979. The amount of such support borne by the petitioners through the end of 1978 exceeded the support payments made by Mr. Baxter during that period by at least $4,325.00. The amount of such support borne by them during 1979 exceeded the support payments made by Mr. Baxter in that year by more than $3,000.00.

Over the years Christina has diligently attempted to collect the support payments from Mr. Baxter. She has returned to the divorce court on several occasions and has received judgments and supplemental orders against him but to the date of trial she had been unable to collect the amount deducted on the joint returns for 1978 and 1979.

OPINION . . .

Under §166(d) a noncorporate taxpayer may deduct nonbusiness bad debts as a short-term capital loss in the year such debts become completely worthless. However, the nonbusiness bad debts are deductible only to the extent of the taxpayer's basis in the debts. Section 166(b); Long v. Commissioner, 35 B.T.A. 479 (1937), affd., 96 F.2d 270 (9th Cir. 1938), cert. denied, 305 U.S. 616 (1938). In Long v. Commissioner, *supra,* the Board of Tax Appeals held that the uncollectible obligation of a taxpayer's ex-husband to pay her a fixed amount for maintenance was not deductible as a bad debt because the taxpayer was not "out of pocket" anything as the result of the ex-husband's failure to pay the support obligation. In other words, the taxpayer had no basis in the debt. Swenson v. Commissioner, 43 T.C. 897 (1965).

In the case before us, petitioners argue that they are "out of pocket" the amounts they expended for the support of Christina's children in excess of the support payments received from Mr. Baxter. We have considered and rejected this argument in similar cases. Swenson v. Commissioner, *supra;* Imeson v.

Commissioner, T.C. Memo. 1969-180, affd., 487 F.2d 319 (9th Cir. 1973), cert. denied, 417 U.S. 917 (1974).

In *Imeson* the Ninth Circuit affirmed our decision but stated by way of dictum that the taxpayer might have a basis in the debt up to the amount she had expended from her capital or income to support the children, 487 F.2d at 321. Because of this dictum we subsequently reexamined our position on this issue and concluded that the cases cited by the Ninth Circuit were distinguishable. Williford v. Commissioner, T.C. Memo. 1975-65. Consequently, our position on this issue is still the same as set forth in Swenson v. Commissioner, *supra,* and Imeson v. Commissioner, *supra.* Respondent's determination that the amounts due Christina by Mr. Baxter for child support are not deductible under section 166 as nonbusiness bad debts is sustained.

NOTES AND QUESTIONS

1. *Analysis.* Is the result in *Diez-Arguelles* consistent with principles of taxation previously examined? Does it seem fair? In answering these questions, consider the following hypotheticals. What are the tax consequences to Ann and Bob in each? Why? In each of the hypotheticals, assume that Ann is obligated to pay Bob $10,000 pursuant to a court order for child support issued on their divorce.

(a) Ann pays Bob $10,000. Two days later, pleading a medical emergency, Ann borrows the $10,000 back from Bob. Shortly thereafter, Ann dies, totally destitute (though she had a good job at the time of her death).

(b) Ann, having failed to pay Bob the $10,000 child support obligation when it became due, executes and delivers to Bob a negotiable promissory note, payable in three months and bearing interest at the market rate of 1 percent per month. Shortly thereafter, Ann dies, totally destitute.

(c) What are the implications of the court's statement that "the taxpayer had no basis in the debt"? Suppose, again, that Ann owes Bob $10,000 for child support. If she pays him the $10,000, it is excluded from Bob's gross income under §71(c). Basis seems to be irrelevant because of the statutory exclusion. But what if Bob sells or assigns his claim against Ann to a third party for $9,000?

2. *Public policy.* In Perry v. Commissioner, 92 T.C. 470 (1989), aff'd, 912 F.2d 1466 (5th Cir. 1990), the Tax Court again rejected a claim for a bad-debt deduction for nonpayment of child support. After addressing a variety of legal arguments, the court concluded with the following:

> Petitioner insists that she ought to be allowed to deduct the shortfall in Perry's support payment obligations. If this were to be viewed as an appeal to public policy, that is, the public failed to see to it that Perry satisfied his legal obligations and so the public ought to make up for this to some extent by reducing petitioner's tax obligations, then we have two responses.
>
> Firstly, the statute for the years in issue does not embody that policy; to get that policy into the law, petitioner should go to the Congress, in which has been "vested" "All legislative Powers herein granted." U.S. Const., art. 1, §1.

Secondly, since the tax benefit of such a deduction relates directly to the taxpayer's marginal tax bracket, it would appear that this claimed public policy would provide the greatest relief to those who have the greatest amount of other income and little or no relief to those who truly depended on the fulfillment of the support obligations. The Congress, of course, may enact any public policy it chooses (unless otherwise limited by the Constitution), but the policy that would be advanced by allowing such a deduction may fairly be viewed as topsy-turvy.

In any event, this Court will not so legislate in the guise of filling in gaps in the statute, or whatever other judicial power it is that petitioner would have us exercise.

3. *A bad trip.* Compare Garber v. Commissioner, 48 T.C.M. 959 (1984), in which the taxpayer signed up for a two-year, around-the-world sailing trip with seven other people. Each of the eight contributed $16,000 toward the cost of the boat. Their agreement with the captain provided that if any of them were required to leave, there would be no refund, but if the boat were destroyed there would be a pro rata refund. The taxpayer became ill and left the boat for several months. He recovered from his illness and would have returned to the boat for the remainder of the cruise, but it was destroyed by fire. He was unable to obtain a refund and claimed a deduction for a bad debt. The court denied the deduction, relying on Reg. §1.166-1(c), which requires a "valid and enforceable obligation to pay a fixed or determinable sum of money." The court said, "Generally, a claim which arises out of breach of contract prior to being reduced to judgment does not create a debtor-creditor relationship because the injured party has only an unliquidated claim to damages." Suppose the captain had written a letter to the taxpayer saying, "I have collected insurance proceeds from the loss of the boat and clearly I owe you $5,000. I will put a check in the mail tomorrow." Suppose the check never arrives and the captain dies following a drunken binge on which he spent all the insurance money. What if the captain had sent a check for $5,000, but it bounced (i.e., proved uncollectible)?

Was the claim in the *Diez-Arguelles* case a "valid and enforceable obligation to pay a fixed or determinable sum of money"?

4. *Legal fees.* In McClendon v. Commissioner, T.C. Memo. 1986-416, legal fees incurred to obtain child-support payments were held to be nondeductible personal expenses. The court relied on United States v. Gilmore, discussed in Chapter 10.

4

WHEN IS IT INCOME?

Chapter 2 examined some fundamental aspects of the question, "What is income?"—not as a matter of metaphysics, but from the perspective of how we should go about defining the tax base we call "taxable income." Chapter 3 continued in this vein by stressing the fundamental limits that any practical tax faces in reaching the private spheres of our lives. These practical constraints introduce largely unavoidable economic distortions, often compounded rather than militated by special tax rules, as in the case of home ownership.

But as we have indicated already, defining what constitutes income is only the first of several related questions that you should pose to yourself. This chapter considers the second of these basic questions—"*When* is it income?" Indeed, the question of when a tax liability arises is one of the most significant issues in all of tax law. Its importance is such that we have divided the topic into two chapters. This chapter focuses on basic timing issues involving "real" (non-financial) transactions. Chapter 5 introduces the taxation of common financial transactions and instruments; timing lies at the heart of many of the issues that these present.

This casebook does not have a chapter devoted specifically to the third question—How much income?—but the issue is implicated in many cases along the way, including Turner v. Commissioner. Nonetheless, you should be aware that valuation questions are not trivial matters to taxpayers or the IRS. For example, at the time of writing the IRS is engaged in litigation with several public U.S. corporations that ultimately center on valuations of intangible assets and in each of which billions of dollars of tax are at stake.

The fourth basic question—Whose income is it?—has already appeared in Chapter 3 in our discussion of whether alimony payments should be treated as deductible to the payor (thereby splitting taxable income between the two ex-spouses), or instead (as mandated by the 2017 act) treated as taxable entirely to the payor (thereby treating those payments closer to payments within an intact marriage, but for the unavailability of married filing joint return status). The issue is much broader than this, however. For example, should a married couple be treated as one taxpayer or two, keeping in mind all the problems attendant on trying to prise apart arrangements made entirely in the private sphere of our lives? Chapter 6 focuses on this.

Timing is important for at least two reasons. First, tax rates may vary from year to year. One source of tax rate variation is the system of progressive marginal tax rates. For example, consider a farmer with fluctuating income who is subject to a top marginal tax rate of 37 percent in Year 1 and 12 percent in Year 2. Any set of tax rules that allows taxpayers the flexibility to manipulate the timing of income recognition will obviously give the farmer an incentive to shift income to Year 2 to enjoy the benefit of the lower tax rate. In this example, shifting the timing of income recognition by one year is the equivalent of avoiding a 25 percent tax. More commonly, a taxpayer may anticipate a steep drop in income following retirement. Where possible, deferring income until then offers the taxpayer the opportunity to pay tax at lower marginal rates.

Tax rate variation may also arise from legislative changes in the tax rate schedule. Historically, year-over-year variation in tax rates has been a significant feature of the U.S. tax system. The 2017 act, for example, changed a tax rate structure that had been in effect only since 2013, and the tax rate tables of the 2017 act by their terms will sunset at the end of 2025.

Even leaving aside tax rate variation, however, timing issues are important because of the time value of money. Chapter 1 introduced the theme that tax deferral has a quantifiable value, subject to the sometimes countervailing incentive to respond to marginal tax rate differentials that taxpayers may face in different years, due to fluctuating incomes or different statutory rate structures. (For example, in late 2012 many affluent taxpayers sold appreciated financial assets, thereby accelerating capital gains recognitions, to avoid what they correctly predicted would be higher capital gain tax rates from 2013 forward.)

The time value of money has varying implications in different fact patterns, and you must be careful to think through the facts of any case you have under consideration. For example, a tax bill is simply a liability. If in some entirely hypothetical world you were given the opportunity to pay your $10,000 tax bill in respect of your 2018 income in 2023, without any additional cost, you should accept the option, because you will have the use of that $10,000—the ability to earn a return on it—for that time period. This is a pure time value of money benefit that is not affected by fluctuations in tax rates from 2018 to 2023.

Consider the issue from the perspective of a taxpayer who knows that she must include $5,000 in income at some point and that, no matter which year the amount is included in income, the tax rate will be 20 percent, meaning a tax liability of $1,000. If she can earn interest at an after-tax rate of, say, 5 percent, then postponing a $1,000 tax liability for one year reduces its cost in present value terms from $1,000 to $952. That is, she would need to set aside (and invest at 5 percent) only $952 today in order to have $1,000 to pay in a year, whereas it would obviously cost her $1,000 to pay $1,000 of tax today. Permit the deferral of a $1,000 tax liability to last for, say, ten years instead of one, and its present value declines to $641.

In the real world, however, one rarely is given such opportunities on a silver platter. Instead, taxpayers look to approximate this result synthetically, by accelerating into the current year deductions that economically relate to future years, or by deferring the recognition of income, while getting the cash today (or at least very quickly).

This last point trips up many students at first: There is no time value of money benefit in simply not getting paid! That is, if Dr. Zhivago is in the 37 percent marginal tax bracket, and a patient offers to cut the good doctor's 2018 tax bill by not paying the doctor's $500 fee until 2023, the doctor should decline—unless the patient also is willing to pay an additional sum in 2023 that, after tax, puts the doctor in a better position than receiving the fee today, paying tax, and investing the after-tax proceeds.

On the other hand, and as discussed in detail later in this chapter, if Dr. Zhivago bills a patient $500 in December, and the patient pays only in January of the following year, Dr. Zhivago might be content, because at the price of deferring his use of the cash income for a week or two, he has gained a year's deferral on the tax liability associated with it.[1] This example hints at the many opportunities for tax gaming inherent in the cash method of accounting, where taxable income follows the receipt of cash, rather than the time the services giving rise to the income were performed.

When we or other authors write about the time value of deferral, we usually have in mind cases like the Investment Retirement Account (IRA) example in Chapter 2, where the deferral in question is the deferral of tax on current income from this year to some future date. In such a case, the income is not escaping tax permanently: It is not ultimately exempt or excludable from income. Authors often colloquially refer to the time value of deferring income when what they mean is the time value of deferring the tax on that income.

When students are introduced to the time value of money, the emphasis is on how the value of money compounds over time through the interest that can be earned on it. Discounting to present value is the same exercise, in the reverse direction. The time value of "deferring income" is a little trickier, because, to repeat, the income in fact will be taxed at some point; what really is deferred is not the income, but rather the tax on the income. In thinking about the benefit of deferral, then, it is important not to confuse it with permanent exemption of the amount in question from tax, or with some simple compounding of the income that is deferred. The example in the box illustrates this point.

Value of Deferral

Imagine that Rufus T. Firefly earns $50,000 in salary income in 2018 and gets the cash each week as he goes along. Ordinarily, that income would be taxable in 2018. But by depositing $2,000 into a "regular" IRA, Firefly reduces his taxable income to $48,000 and simultaneously acquires a new investment asset: the $2,000 IRA. The entire proceeds in the IRA ultimately will be taxable when Firefly withdraws them to fund his retirement (*including* the original $2,000), but Firefly obtains a time value of money benefit through deferring his 2018 tax on the $2,000 income he in fact received and in turn invested in the IRA.

---

1. For simplicity this example ignores the effect of estimated tax payments.

Continuing with the example, assume that Firefly is subject to a constant 35 percent marginal tax rate, earns 8 percent pretax compounded annually on his money, and has the benefit of the IRA (that is, income deferral) for ten years. At the end of ten years, he withdraws the entirety of his IRA account—$4,318 ($2,000 compounded annually at 8 percent for ten years)—pays 35 percent tax on that amount ($1,511), and is left with $2,807. Again, note that both the original amount deferred ($2,000) and the compound interest accruing on that amount are included in the tax base at the end of Year 10.

By contrast, if Firefly did not use an IRA, he would have had only $1,300 to invest, after paying $700 in tax (35 percent of $2,000). His annual interest income (8 percent) would be subject to tax at well, reducing his return to 5.2 percent per annum (8 percent less a 35 percent tax on that 8 percent). After ten years, Firefly would have $2,158.

Plainly, having $2,807 to consume at the end of Year 10, after all taxes have been paid, is better than having $2,158, so the IRA has a positive payoff—a time value in deferring income (to use the colloquial expression). But how can we measure that payoff?

The answer is that the deferral is just as valuable as a hypothetical world in which the $2,000 is taxed in Year 1 but then earns interest tax free (or at the pretax rate) for the life of the investment. Had Firefly been taxed in Year 1 then, as noted above, he would have $1,300, rather than $2,000 to invest. Had he then been able to invest that $1,300 tax free, at the pretax 8 percent rate of return, he would end up with $2,807. That is the same amount he ended up with through deferral.

We can generalize this result: *The value of income deferral (really, deferral of the tax on income in hand in Year 1) is equal to paying the tax in Year 1 and then earning interest at the pretax rate (e.g., tax free) for the life of the deferral.* If we take paying the tax at year one as the "normal" rule, we can say the value of deferral is as great as not paying tax on the annual interest income for the life of the deferral.

So, by taking advantage of the IRA, Firefly is left in the same position as if he paid tax in 2016 on the $2,000 and put the after-tax proceeds ($1,300, if Firefly were in the 35 percent tax bracket) into a special account under the terms of which interest income is tax-exempt and the proceeds could be withdrawn at retirement free of any further tax. (Indeed, such a mechanism exists today, called the Roth IRA.)[2]

2. The text's example tees up the question, what advantage is there in a Roth IRA when compared to a regular one, given that the two can be equated by changing the amount invested ab initio to reflect the current year's tax? The answers are, first, taxpayers concerned that tax rates will trend up will prefer the Roth IRA, because once tax-paid income is set aside into a Roth IRA, no further tax is due. More interestingly, Congress built in a poorly appreciated preference for Roth IRAs when Congress set the annual contribution limits for both at the same dollar amount. As a result, while the deferral mechanism operates identically, the amounts that can be deferred are systematically greater in a Roth IRA—assuming that the taxpayer has the resources to take advantage of it.

As the materials that follow demonstrate, U.S. tax law provides ample opportunity for taxpayers to shift the timing of their tax liabilities from one year to another. The tax lawyer who understands the importance of timing will always be a step ahead of those who do not.

A. ANNUAL ACCOUNTING AND ITS CONSEQUENCES

The issues and principles to be examined in this section have traditionally been thought of as stemming from problems of "accounting." Nonetheless, they are the starting point for taking up the broader problems of income timing and recognition.

1. The Use of Hindsight

BURNET v. SANFORD & BROOKS CO.
282 U.S. 359 (1931)

Mr. Justice STONE delivered the opinion of the Court. . . .

From 1913 to 1915, inclusive, respondent, a Delaware corporation engaged in business for profit, was acting for the Atlantic Dredging Company in carrying out a contract for dredging the Delaware River, entered into by that company with the United States. In making its income tax returns for the years 1913 and 1916, respondent added to gross income for each year the payments made under the contract that year, and deducted its expenses paid that year in performing the contract. The total expenses exceeded the payments received by $176,271.88. The tax returns for 1913, 1915, and 1916 showed net losses. That for 1914 showed net income.

In 1915 work under the contract was abandoned, and in 1916 suit was brought in the Court of Claims to recover for a breach of warranty of the character of the material to be dredged. Judgment for the claimant, 53 Ct. Cls. 490, was affirmed by this Court in 1920. . . . It held that the recovery was upon the contract and was "compensatory of the cost of the work, of which the government got the benefit." From the total recovery, petitioner received in that year the sum of $192,577.59, which included the $176,271.88 by which its expenses under the contract had exceeded receipts from it, and accrued interest amounting to $16,305.71. Respondent having failed to include these amounts as gross income in its tax returns for 1920, the Commissioner made the deficiency assessment here involved, based on the addition of both items to gross income for that year.

The Court of Appeals ruled that only the item of interest was properly included, holding, erroneously as the government contends, that the item of $176,271.88 was a return of losses suffered by respondent in earlier years and hence was wrongly assessed as income. Notwithstanding this conclusion, its judgment of reversal and the consequent elimination of this item from gross income for 1920 were made contingent upon the filing by respondent of amended returns for the years 1913 to 1916, from which were to be omitted the deductions of the related items of expenses paid in those years. Respondent insists that as the Sixteenth Amendment and the Revenue Act of 1918, which was in force in 1920, plainly contemplate a tax only on net income or profits, any application of the statute which operates to impose a tax with respect to the present transaction, from which respondent received no profit, cannot be upheld.

If respondent's contention that only gain or profit may be taxed under the Sixteenth Amendment be accepted without qualification, . . . the question remains whether the gain or profit which is the subject of the tax may be ascertained, as here, on the basis of fixed accounting periods, or whether, as is pressed upon us, it can only be net profit ascertained on the basis of particular transactions of the taxpayer when they are brought to a conclusion.

All the revenue acts which have been enacted since the adoption of the Sixteenth Amendment have uniformly assessed the tax on the basis of annual returns showing the net result of all the taxpayer's transactions during a fixed accounting period, either the calendar year, or, at the option of the taxpayer, the particular fiscal year which he may adopt. . . .

That the recovery made by respondent in 1920 was gross income for that year within the meaning of these sections cannot, we think, be doubted. The money received was derived from a contract entered into in the course of respondent's business operations for profit. While it equaled, and in a loose sense was a return of, expenditures made in performing the contract, still, as the Board of Tax Appeals found, the expenditures were made in defraying the expenses incurred in the prosecution of the work under the contract, for the purpose of earning profits. They were not capital investments, the cost of which, if converted, must first be restored from the proceeds before there is a capital gain taxable as income. . . .

That such receipts from the conduct of a business enterprise are to be included in the taxpayer's return as a part of gross income, regardless of whether the particular transaction results in net profit, sufficiently appears from the quoted words of §213(a) and from the character of the deductions allowed. Only by including these items of gross income in the 1920 return would it have been possible to ascertain respondent's net income for the period covered by the return, which is what the statute taxes. The excess of gross income over deductions did not any the less constitute net income for the taxable period because respondent, in an earlier period, suffered net losses in the conduct of its business which were in some measure attributable to expenditures made to produce the net income of the later period. . . .

But respondent insists that if the sum which it recovered is the income defined by the statute, still it is not income, taxation of which without apportionment is permitted by the Sixteenth Amendment, since the particular transaction from which it was derived did not result in any net gain or profit. But we do not think the amendment is to be so narrowly construed. A taxpayer may be in receipt of net income in one year and not in another. The net result of the two years, if combined in a single taxable period, might still be a loss; but it has never been supposed that that fact would relieve him from a tax on the first, or that it affords any reason for postponing the assessment of the tax until the end of a lifetime, or for some other indefinite period, to ascertain more precisely whether the final outcome of the period, or of a given transaction, will be a gain or a loss.

The Sixteenth Amendment was adopted to enable the government to raise revenue by taxation. It is the essence of any system of taxation that it should produce revenue ascertainable, and payable to the government, at regular intervals. Only by such a system is it practicable to produce a regular flow of income and apply methods of accounting, assessment, and collection capable of practical operation. It is not suggested that there has ever been any general scheme for taxing income on any other basis. The computation of income annually as the net result of all transactions within the year was a familiar practice, and taxes upon income so arrived at were not unknown, before the Sixteenth Amendment. . . . It is not to be supposed that the amendment did not contemplate that Congress might make income so ascertained the basis of a scheme of taxation such as had been in actual operation within the United States before its adoption. While, conceivably, a different system might be devised by which the tax could be assessed, wholly or in part, on the basis of the finally ascertained results of particular transactions, Congress is not required by the amendment to adopt such a system in preference to the more familiar method, even if it were practicable. It would not necessarily obviate the kind of inequalities of which respondent complains. If losses from particular transactions were to be set off against gains in others, there would still be the practical necessity of computing the tax on the basis of annual or other fixed taxable periods, which might result in the taxpayer being required to pay a tax on income in one period exceeded by net losses in another. . . .

NOTES AND QUESTIONS

1. *Relationship with recovery-of-cost principles.* How can the decision in this case be reconciled with the decision in Clark v. Commissioner?

2. *Implications. Sanford & Brooks* is often cited for the proposition that our income tax system uses annual, as opposed to transactional, accounting. Transactional accounting as a general proposition would present the practical problem of separating out the costs of, and returns from, every significant transaction. For example, in *Sanford & Brooks,* it would require allocation of the taxpayer's general overhead cost (e.g., the salary of its president and the costs of its headquarters facilities) among all of its projects. At the time of the decision in *Sanford & Brooks* such allocation would probably have been considered a daunting task. In the current era accountants are more familiar with the required techniques. In fact, allocations of overhead and other such costs among various projects are now required for the purpose of determining the costs of assets that a taxpayer produces for itself. See §263A, which is described *infra.*

3. *Relief from harshness: Whose job?* The Court's insistence on strict application of annual accounting produces a harsh, basically unfair outcome in this case. Should the Court have figured out some device for providing relief? Or is

the problem one that should be left to Congress? Consider the forms of relief from the harshness of annual accounting that are discussed in the rest of this section.

4. *"Refundable" or negative taxes.* The reason annual accounting produced such harsh results in this case is that losses do not result in negative taxes. That is, the tax on income of, say, negative $1 million, or for that matter negative $100 million, like the tax on income of zero, is zero. Under an income tax system that provided for negative taxes (sometimes called a "refundable" system), negative taxable income would trigger payments from the government, ideally using the same rate tables as those used to determine positive tax liability on positive taxable income. Thus, if the tax on income of positive $1 million were $200,000, then the government might pay $200,000 to taxpayers with a loss of $1 million. In practice, this would mainly matter to businesses (including but not limited to those that are operated in corporate form), since one who is primarily a wage earner generally will not have taxable income below zero.

Why aren't losses refundable in this way under the federal income tax? Would the case for refundability be strengthened if we were more confident that taxable income roughly equaled economic income, and thus that government payments were not going to taxpayers who had merely engaged in clever tax planning to generate noneconomic tax losses? Or is the underlying concern that Congress does not want to subsidize every crazy business idea that comes along, by sharing in the resulting losses?

How does nonrefundability influence a taxpayer's decision whether to enter a risky business (one that might either make a lot or lose a lot of money)?

5. *Loss carryovers.* The harshness of annual accounting as applied to fact patterns like *Sanford & Brooks* is mitigated by §172, which allows a deduction in a profitable year of a net operating loss (NOL) arising in an earlier loss year (an NOL carryover). In addition, under pre-2018 law losses could be carried back to certain earlier profitable years (an NOL carryback). Losses that may be carried over or back under §172 are primarily losses incurred in a trade or business. There is a separate provision for carryover of capital losses, in §1212.

Before the 2017 act, business losses giving rise to an NOL could be carried back two years and forward for twenty. Thus, if a firm lost $1 million in 2015 and earned $1 million in 2017 after all deductions other than the §172 deduction, the firm could use that 2015 loss to reduce its 2017 taxable income to zero. As a result of the availability of NOL carrybacks, a taxpayer could achieve a form of income averaging over a three-year period (the current year and the two previous ones), thereby obtaining an immediate refund of taxes paid in respect of the previous two years. Any remaining NOL could be carried forward to use against future income. If by the end of the twentieth year following the loss year any NOL was unused, it simply expired.

For post-2017 business losses, §172 now eliminates the two-year carryback but allows indefinitely long carryovers of losses. At least as important, post 2017-NOLs will be utilizable only to offset 80 percent of a taxpayer's income. This is not a "haircut" to a firm's available NOL carryovers, but rather to the rate at which those NOLs can be applied against subsequent income. For example, if a business loses $1 million in 2020 and then earns $1 million in 2021 after all deductions other than the §172 deduction, the taxpayer will be able to reduce its 2021 taxable income to $200,000 (not, as under prior law, to zero). The remaining $200,000 in NOL carryovers will be available to use in future years, again subject each year to the same 80 percent of income cap. Because the NOL carryover period is now infinitely long, a firm that loses money and then at some future date becomes profitable will eventually use up all its NOLs.

Which do you think is the fairer system here, pre-2018 law (two-year carryback/twenty-year carryover period but NOLs available against 100 percent of future years' income) or post-2017 law (zero carrybacks/infinitely long carryover period, but NOL limited in each year to 80 percent of income in that year)? Is it relevant to your analysis that the 2017 amendment to §172 was estimated to raise over $200 billion in tax (i.e., cost taxpayers the same amount) relative to pre-2018 law?

Although not strictly speaking a timing of income rule, the 2017 act introduced another provision relating to the use by individuals of business losses. Imagine a highly compensated individual who has $1 million in salary income and a business that loses $600,000. Under prior law, the taxpayer could net her business loss against her salary income. After the 2017 act, however, the taxpayer can use only $250,000 of her business loss against nonbusiness income (including salary) ($500,000 if married filing joint). The excess business loss is then treated as an NOL carryover to future years.

A related Code provision, §382, provides complex rules designed to limit the use of NOLs following the acquisition of a business. These rules, aimed at limiting "trafficking" in loss carryovers, are not covered in this book.

PROBLEMS

1. Aerospace Corp. was formed and began operations selling flying toasters in 2019. It incurred a net taxable loss (i.e., an excess of deductions over gross income) of $100,000 from its business operations in that first year. In 2020, Aerospace Corp. earned net taxable income of the same amount, prior to considering §172. Must Aerospace Corp. pay tax on all or any of its $100,000 income in 2020? See §172(a), (c).

2. In 2020, Bob earns $100,000 as an associate in a law firm, but also suffers an ordinary (that is, noncapital) loss of $120,000 from his wholly owned business. His itemized nonbusiness deductions, comprising charitable contributions, are $15,000, and he claims itemized rather than the standard deduction. In 2021, Bob again earns a salary of $100,000 and has no other income or business loss. He has a deduction for itemized nonbusiness deductions of $20,000, so his taxable income for 2021 is $80,000. How much is Bob's 2020 NOL carryover to 2021, and what is Bob's taxable income in 2021? See §172(c) and (d)(4).

2. Capital Expenditures, Depreciation, and Expensing

A fundamental theme of all business accounting, developed originally in financial accounting but imported into the income tax from the beginning, is that an accurate calculation of a business's taxable income (or net income, in financial accounting terminology) requires a *matching* between gross income and the expenses incurred to earn that gross income. For example, this is the theory underlying the idea that businesses in general should employ the accrual rather than the cash method of accounting. (See below.) It also is the theory behind traditional tax and financial accounting treatments of a capital expenditure (or capital investment) — the purchase of a business asset that is used by the taxpayer in its business operations to generate income, and which asset has a useful life in the business extending over several years. See §167.

Sanford & Brooks could have been decided on matching grounds, but that would have conflicted with another principle, which is the practical necessity of closing a business's books once a year to determine its annual income and tax liability. The case stands in this respect for the proposition that the annual accounting period takes priority. In turn, Congress has developed many tax accounting rules whose underlying motivations are better matching of long-term investments or liabilities with the income to which they relate, but within the framework of the annual accounting period. Some of these (e.g., §461(h)) are discussed later in this chapter.

If a taxpayer buys a robotic machine tool or a truck for use in her business, the cost is treated as a capital expenditure, because those assets are used to generate business income and have useful lives extending over several years. How should the cost of such an investment be "recovered" (i.e., deducted against gross income)? This is where the concept of depreciation comes in.

The underlying aim of classic accounting for the cost of a capital investment through depreciation is to match annual income and expense by treating an appropriate portion of the cost of a capital investment as attributable to each year that the asset contributes to the firm's income. As a simple example, if Acme Manufacturing buys for $10,000 a machine that it will use five years to produce the goods it sells, after which time the machine will be worthless, the matching principle holds that the $10,000 cost should be matched against the income that will be generated over the entire five-year period in which the machine is employed.

It is helpful to think about the treatment of the $10,000 cost in the simple example above by comparing it to the rental expense that Acme would incur if, instead of buying the machine, it rented the same kind of machine from year to year, for the sake of simplicity at $2,000/year. (This leaves no profit for the lessor, but this nonetheless illustrates the point being made here.) The idea is that, without more, the rental case does achieve a matching of revenues and costs: This year's rental charge is a component of generating this year's revenues.

Compared to an annual rental expense of $2,000, deducting the entire $10,000 cost in the first year would understate that year's income and overstate future years' incomes (thereby working a tax deferral). Conversely, delaying the deduction until the machine is useless and discarded understates the expenses in the earlier years and concomitantly overstates taxable income.

To accomplish this matching of gross income and expenses, traditional accounting principles require that the cost of an asset that contributes to earning income for more than one year, and which wears out over time, must be depreciated: that is, a fraction of the cost must be deducted each year, until the entire cost is recovered. Acme Manufacturing has spent $10,000 on a depreciable asset that has a five-year "useful life" and a "salvage value" of zero. Assume for the moment that it depreciates the machine on a "straight-line" schedule over its useful life, that is, ratably over the five-year useful life ($2,000/year). (This is called "straight-line" depreciation.) Each year's depreciation expense is a noncash cost: Acme laid out the cash at inception, when it bought the machine. As such, the depreciation expense "shelters" or "shields" (the informal terminology employed) an equivalent amount of gross income from inclusion as taxable income.

Acme can set aside those pretax cash flows into a piggybank, and at the end of five years Acme will have $10,000 in the piggybank with which to replace the machine.[3] Depreciation thus serves to separate gross income from the goods Acme sells into two streams: a return *of* principal (the $10,000 investment) and a return on principal. In doing so, depreciation measures more accurately Acme's annual taxable income from one period to the next than would immediate expensing or deferral of any deduction until the machine's useful life is exhausted.

The matching principle is still the agenda of financial accounting for depreciation. As we will see in the paragraphs that follow, however, the tax law in this area has evolved to advance a separate agenda, which is to encourage business investment through offering depreciation deductions on an "accelerated" schedule relative to the actual economic wear and tear on a capital expenditure. In other words, tax law has consciously abandoned the principle of matching in order to provide subsidies (relative to an idealized matching norm) for business capital investment.[4]

For many years, tax depreciation was an intensely fact-specific exercise, and therefore a constant source of controversy. Congress eliminated most of the points of friction when it adopted the Accelerated Cost Recovery System (ACRS). See §168. ACRS sets out statutory depreciation periods for different kinds of property and further assumes a salvage value of zero.

---

3. Readers sensitized to time value of money considerations will note that Acme's piggybank actually will contain more than $10,000 at the end of five years, because Acme will get a return on investing the cash in the piggybank during that time. "Samuelson" depreciation is designed to adjust the depreciation claimed to reflect this fact, but it is not followed in tax or financial accounting. See P. Samuelson, *Tax Deductibility of Economic Depreciation to Insure Invariant Valuations*, 72 J. Pol. Econ. 604 (1964).

4. A system that allows deductions for depreciation at a rate faster than the actual decline in the value of the asset will favor investment in long-lived assets over short-lived assets and investment in capital (plant, machinery, etc.) over investment in current labor inputs. In other words, if an income tax is to be neutral among different types of investments and inputs, it must be accurate in its measurement of income. This is not to say, however, that an income tax is to be preferred to a consumption tax, even though a consumption tax allows an immediate write-off of all investments. It is merely a statement about neutrality once the decision has been made to adopt an income tax. Some economists believe that an income tax unduly burdens all investment and that a consumption tax is preferable for that reason. If one accepts this position, then it is the consumption tax that produces neutrality among investments, as well as between investment and consumption. In any event, all arguments based on the desirability of a neutral tax system are confounded by the reality of pervasive tax and nontax governmental intervention in the allocation of resources.

What is more, in the case of tangible equipment (but not real estate), Congress used the ACRS system to enshrine subsidies (relative to a pure income tax norm) for manufacturers and other businesses that rely heavily on depreciable property to earn income, by adopting depreciation schedules that are very accelerated (the deductions are "front-loaded") when compared to a straight-line schedule.

The 2017 act made radical changes to the ACRS system, and did so with complicated sunset provisions to boot. Very generally, if a taxpayer acquires tangible personal property, as well as most real property other than buildings (e.g., a sewage treatment plant), or certain film and other entertainment intangible assets, for use in the taxpayer's trade or business, and the taxpayer places the property in service before 2023, the taxpayer may now claim 100 percent of the cost as an immediate deduction. See §168(k). This rule is known colloquially as "bonus depreciation," or more generally as "expensing" of a capital expenditure. Expensing is available for the purchase of used as well as new qualifying property. From 2023 onwards the bonus depreciation percentage declines from 100 percent on a schedule set in the statute. Assets not described in §168(k) fall under pre-2017 act ACRS.

The 2017 act also expanded a parallel expensing rule for "small business" (§179). The §179 rule now allows a "small" business to expense up to $1 million in capital expenditures each year, provided that its total cost of §179 property placed in service during the year does not exceed $2.5 million. (A dollar-for-dollar phase-out rule applies above the $2.5 million figure.) The principal advantage of §179 over §168(k) is that the former is a permanent provision of the Code (to the extent that any provision can be said to be permanent), while the latter by design begins to phase down in 2023.

Expensing of many capital expenditures is a profound change from the rules applicable throughout most of the Code's history, with important economic, commercial, and revenue collection implications.

Expensing of tangible property places the corporation in the same position as Rufus T. Firefly and his IRA contribution, as described earlier in this chapter, once one adjusts the latter case to make an apples-to-apples comparison.[5] The corporation can deduct what would otherwise be a capitalized investment (subject to depreciation). Like Rufus, will be taxed when quits reinvesting in tangible machinery and the like and instead withdraws cash, for example to

---

5. There is one important difference between the Rufus T. Firefly case and a corporation investing in tangible business assets, which is that when Firefly sets aside money in an IRA that money he is investing pretax rather than after-tax income. (The box earlier in this chapter addressing the Firefly case develops this point.) When a corporation invests, by contrast, it is using its own after-tax dollars to make that investment. The general rule just expressed in the text applies to the corporate investment case. To extend it to Firefly, one must first treat the economic effect of the IRA contribution as if it were subject to tax up-front: Firefly then will earn the economic equivalent of a pretax return on that hypothetical after-tax initial contribution. Thus, if Firefly's marginal tax rate is 30 percent, and returns on investment earn 6 percent pretax, Firefly's contribution of $2,000 to his "regular" IRA will have the same aggregate after-tax effect returns as if he made an investment of $1,400 (the after-tax amount he would have were he simply to have $2,000 in income) and then earned a tax-free and compounding return of 6 percent per annum, starting from that $1,400 base. In other words, when you work through the next few paragraphs, bear in mind that they address a case where a taxpayer invests its after-tax cash in a new asset. That presentation can be applied to Firefly and other instances of deferring *income* by first tax-effecting the income that is set aside to make it an after-tax equivalent.

fund a dividend. And as the next few paragraphs demonstrate, the net economic effect to the corporation of immediately expensing capital investment is to put the corporation in the same place as if it received the compounding returns from its investment free of tax. In other words, just as in the IRA case, expensing the investment is the same as exempting the yield on the investment from income tax.

The 2017 amendments to §179 and §168(k) were estimated to lose about $110 billion in tax revenue over the next ten years, relative to pre-2017 act laws.

The gradual shift in tax policy from depreciating capital expenditures over their economic life, to ACRS, to expensing, has somewhat blunted our sensitivity to the dramatic importance of expensing in economic and tax policy. In economic terms, expensing turns a business income tax into a species of consumption tax—a cash-flow tax—because in simple cases at least the one business cost not immediately expensed in a traditional income tax is a business capital expenditure, and bonus depreciation/expensing reverses that result.

Chapter 2 introduced the idea of a consumption tax as a tax system that does not burden the "return to waiting," and further used as an example an IRA, where amounts set aside in an IRA account along with the investment returns within the IRA remain free of tax during the period assets are kept in the IRA. The result sometimes is phrased as deferring any tax until income is withdrawn from savings (the IRA account) and used to fund consumption—hence the term "consumption" tax. But what on earth does this have to do with expensing rather than depreciating capital investment? Drawing the connection requires pivoting in one's thinking from the individual saver to the business firm as investor of capital in its business operations.

To simplify things, imagine that all businesses earn the same basic return on the capital (money) invested in them—say 6 percent per annum, and that there are lots of opportunities around to invest more capital (so that incremental investments do not change the returns on investment). Assume for a moment a world without taxes.

If a business in this world were to buy a new machine to use in its operations, it would expect to earn 6 percent on that investment. If the machine were perpetual in life and the cost were $1,000, the business would earn an incremental $60 every year in perpetuity from having made the investment. Think of this as the most extreme sort of depreciation case—a depreciation allowance of zero, because the asset never declines in its productivity.[6] (Raw land is treated in this way.)

---

6. In real life, machines are not perpetual in life, and instead decline in value until they become worthless—they depreciate. For simplicity, assume that the machine declines in value (depreciates) by a fixed $200 each year. In Year 1, the firm will expect to generate $260 in cash flow from that incremental machine, but that $260 is not all income. Of the $260 in cash flow, $200 constitutes cash received by the firm that simply offsets the loss to the firm in the value of the machine (from $1,000 to $800). That, of course, is what a depreciation deduction does—it sets aside some of the cash flow received by a firm as a "return of capital," rather than as income (a return *on* capital). The firm is left with $60 in income in Year 1. In Year 2, the firm would expect to earn $248, not $260. Again $200 would represent an offset to the annual decline in value of the machine, but now the firm's investment at the start of the year is only $800. And so on. Taking depreciation into account does not change the point in the text, which is only to contrast a cash-flow tax with an income tax, but it does introduce more numbers to keep track of.

Now introduce an income tax into the mix. The 6 percent return each year (after depreciation deductions) becomes subject to tax—let's say at a 25 percent rate. Each year, the firm's after-tax income is reduced by the tax, so that its after-tax return on its remaining capital investment becomes 4.5 percent. The firm would earn $45 after-tax every year, because the machine never declines in value. Simple enough.

Let's contrast the income tax result with a cash-flow tax, which in this respect is not hypothetical at all—it is the result achieved under §168(k) after the 2017 act. Under a cash-flow tax, the firm would "expense" its $1,000 investment in the machine immediately. This $1,000 deduction means a $250 reduction in the firm's tax bill. Think of that as a new-found pot of cash (although of course it is the firm's own money). Imagine that the firm takes the $250 in tax savings and uses it to buy a new mini-machine, identical to the first except in cost. That also will throw off a 6 percent pretax return ($15) and a 4.5 percent after-tax return ($11.25). But—and here is the fun part—that new $250 machine also will be expensed, thereby producing an immediate tax savings of $62.50 (25 percent of $250). This $62.50 could be used to buy still another machine, and so on, like a set of nesting Russian Matryoshka dolls.

When you tote up all those Matryoshka dolls ($1,000 + $250 + $62.50 . . .), you end up with the firm able to use the tax savings from expensing to buy at the outset machines having a total value of $1,333. (The general formula is $1/1 - T$, where T is the tax rate.) The returns will be the same 6 percent pretax, and 4.5 percent after-tax—but now applied to a larger investment, such that the aggregate returns are $80/year pretax, and $60/year after-tax.

Look what's happened—by virtue of expensing, the taxpayer has earned $60/year after-tax, which is exactly the same as its $60/year return in a world without tax (or of course its pretax return under an income tax).The more general formulation of this important insight is that expensing a business investment is the same as exempting the investment's yield from taxation.[7] This of course exactly describes how a cash-flow tax operates: By expensing all investments, therefore, it is said that a cash-flow tax exempts from tax the normal return on those investments.

This is a profound result. It means that, without more, expensing offers a business a zero rate of tax on ordinary ("marginal") business investments. The nominal tax rate on business income is irrelevant—the "scaling-up" strategy just described works the same, assuming that the investment in question is replicable. Alternatively, one could say that in a tax system that employs expensing,

---

7. E. Cary Brown, "Business-Income Taxation and Investment Incentives," *in Income, Employment and Public Policy* 300, 309-310 (1948). In honor of Brown's contribution, this insight today often is called the Cary Brown Theorem.

The Cary Brown Theorem requires a number of technical assumptions, all of which have been explored in a large economic literature that has sprouted from this original tax acorn; the authors of this casebook have all contributed to this literature. See, e.g., Bankman and Griffith, *Is the Debate Between an Income Tax and a Consumption Tax a Debate About Risk? Does It Matter?*, 47 Tax L. Rev. 377 (1992); Shaviro, *Replacing the Income Tax with a Progressive Consumption Tax*, 103 Tax Notes 91, 99-101 (2004). For recent summaries and references to the literature, see Kleinbard, *Capital Taxation in an Age of Inequality*, 90 S. Cal. L. Rev. 593, 605-608, 624-626, 645-649, 675-678 (2017), and Kleinbard, *The Right Tax at the Right Time*, 21 Fla. Tax Rev. 208, 267-271 (2017).

these sorts of ordinary business investments operate in a consumption tax environment, because so long as profits are reinvested in more machines, the returns on these investments remains zero.[8]

Many economists strongly endorse cash-flow business taxes, because such a system means that a taxpayer faces the same tax burden on an ordinary ("marginal") investment inside the system as it would face in a world without taxation at all—namely, zero. To an economist, this means that businesses will make capital investments in a world with a cash-flow tax to exactly the same extent as they would if there were no tax at all, which in turn means that the tax system does not distort the scale of investment. These conclusions also imply, however, that in a well-constructed cash-flow tax firms would not obtain any interest expense deduction, because they already face a zero rate of tax on their marginal investments. The U.S. income tax (which by now you have come to realize is not necessarily an income tax in a theoretical sense) offers firms both expensing and interest deductibility, which is to say that it significantly subsidizes business capital investments relative to either an ideal income tax or an ideal cash-flow tax.

Chapter 7 continues the discussion of depreciation.

3.   Claim of Right

In North American Oil Consolidated v. Burnet, 286 U.S. 417 (1932), the Supreme Court addressed the case of a taxpayer operating an oil well property. In 1916, the United States claimed that it, not the taxpayer, owned the land in question. In the first stage of the resulting litigation the United States succeeded in having a receiver appointed to operate the property, and to which the income from the property was paid, pending the final resolution of the litigation. The following year (1917) the taxpayer prevailed on the merits (although the case continued until 1922), and the amounts that had accumulated during the term of the receivership were paid over to the taxpayer.

The question was, did the taxpayer have income in 1916, as the oil was pumped and sold, or in 1917, when the competing claims to the property (and therefore its income) were resolved? The Court concluded that the right answer was 1917:

> [T]he company was not required in 1916 to report as income an amount which it might never receive. See Burnet v. Logan. Compare Lucas v. American Code Co., 280 U.S. 445, 452; Burnet v. Sanford & Brooks Co. There was no constructive receipt of the profits by the company in that year, because at no time

---

8. The term "consumption tax" is not very intuitive when applied at the level of a business tax; a better term would be a "profits" tax, where the word "profits" is used in the economists' sense of special supersized returns ("economic rents") over and above the returns on ordinary business investments. In addition, one must remember that tax imposed on a business enterprise such as a corporation is not an end to the tax burdens on the capital invested in that firm: One must also consider shareholder/creditor taxes. One can combine a consumption or profits tax at the business firm level with a complementary tax at the shareholder/investor level that taxes only ordinary returns to yield a single income tax on capital investment, when viewed from the integrated perspective of the two levels of taxation. The articles by Kleinbard, *supra* note 7, develop both these points.

during the year was there a right in the company to demand that the receiver pay over the money. Throughout 1916 it was uncertain who would be declared entitled to the profits. It was not until 1917, when the District Court entered a final decree vacating the receivership and dismissing the bill, that the company became entitled to receive the money.

The case gave rise to the "claim of right" doctrine. As formulated in that case, the doctrine contemplates that:

> If a taxpayer receives earnings under a claim of right and without restriction as to its disposition, he has received income which he is required to return [i.e., report], even though it may still be claimed that he is not entitled to retain the money, and even though he may still be adjudged liable to restore its equivalent.

NOTES AND QUESTIONS

1. *The proper taxable year.* (a) In *North America Oil Consolidated*, there was no finding as to whether the taxpayer was on the cash or the accrual method of accounting. Assume that the taxpayer was on the accrual method. (For a brief description, see Section B *infra*.) What was it that stood in the way of taxation in 1916, the dispute or the receivership?

(b) If the latter, can the result be reconciled with principles of accrual accounting?

(c) If the former, why was the receipt taxable in 1917, when the dispute was still alive?

(d) Could the taxpayer have protected itself from liability in 1917 by treating the receipt as a trust fund pending outcome of the appeal, for example, by depositing it in a special account and labeling it as a trust fund on its books? No, per Commissioner v. Alamitos Land Co., 112 F.2d 648 (9th Cir.), cert. denied, 311 U.S. 679 (1940), and Rev. Rul. 55-137, 1955-1 C.B. 215. See also Commissioner v. Brooklyn Union Gas Co., 62 F.2d 505 (2d Cir. 1933), acq. (amount under dispute but received before final judicial determination taxable despite the fact that taxpayer was required to post bond to secure repayment if dispute ultimately were resolved against it).

2. *More on the "claim of right" doctrine.* In Illinois Power Co. v. Commissioner, 792 F.2d 683 (7th Cir. 1986), the taxpayer, an electric company, was ordered by the Illinois Commerce Commission to raise its rates. The Commission made it clear, however, that its purpose was to discourage the consumption of electricity and that the taxpayer would not be allowed to keep the extra revenue resulting from the increase, or any interest on it. The money was not kept in any separate account or trust. The IRS argued that the money was taxable under *North American Oil*. The court, in rejecting this position, likened the taxpayer to "a custodian, . . . with no greater beneficial interest in the revenues collected than a bank has in the money deposited with it." Generalizing, the court stated, "The underlying principle is that the taxpayer is allowed to exclude from his [sic] income money received under an unequivocal contractual, statutory, or regulatory duty to repay it, so that he really is just the custodian of the money." Thus, in this case there was no dispute; the taxpayer never claimed a right to the funds at issue. Note that during the time the power company held the money, it earned interest on that money. How should that interest be taxed?

4. The Tax Benefit Rule

In claim of right cases, the taxpayer includes something in income in an earlier year and then has an offsetting deduction[9] in a later year when the income is lost. What are called "tax benefit" cases involve the opposite problem. The taxpayer claims a deduction in an earlier year and then in a later year the deducted amount is in some sense recovered or regained. This may happen, for example, where there have been deductions for bad debts, taxes, losses by theft, worthless assets, expropriation losses, or other calamities and later, to the surprise and delight of the taxpayer, part or all of the amount written off is recovered. As it turns out, the tax benefit doctrine has two aspects, one exclusionary and one inclusionary.

Exclusionary aspect of the tax benefit rule. Suppose initially that the taxpayer received no tax benefit (in the sense of a reduction of tax liability) for any year by reason of the earlier year's deduction. Thus, in the year when the deduction arose, the taxpayer may have had negative taxable income even without regard to this deduction, and thus owed the same tax of zero with it as without it. Or the deduction may simply have increased the taxpayer's net capital loss for the year that was disallowed under §1211. However, since excess deductions that create net operating losses, excess capital losses, and the like typically give rise to carryovers that can be deducted in other taxable years, the possibility of tax benefit from a given deduction cannot be foreclosed until any such carryovers have expired.

Under §111, to the extent that a deduction did not reduce the taxpayer's tax liability for any year *and* any loss carryovers resulting from it have expired without being used, the recovery of the amount deducted need not be included in income. In effect, §111 protects the taxpayer against adverse marginal tax rate swings that result from claiming the deduction at a zero percent rate and then including the recovery at a positive rate.

Inclusionary aspect of the tax benefit rule. The distinct "inclusionary" aspect of the tax benefit rule arises when the taxpayer has indeed received a tax benefit from a deduction and the includability or amount of the subsequent offsetting gain is not otherwise clear-cut. Under these circumstances, the rule requires that income in the amount of the prior deduction be included, thus moving toward transactional rather than strict annual accounting.

In illustration, in Alice Phelan Sullivan Corp. v. United States, 381 F.2d 399 (Ct. Cl. 1967), the taxpayer had made a charitable gift of property, subject to the condition that the property be used for either a religious or an educational purpose, and claimed a charitable deduction that it used in full. Nearly twenty years later, the charity decided not to so use the property and therefore returned it to the taxpayer. This recovery was held to generate taxable income in the amount of the earlier deduction, as distinct from the value of the property in the year when it was returned.

---

9. The text throughout this chapter ignores the complex and rarely encountered rules of §1341, which when relevant gives taxpayers the benefit of the tax rates applicable to the year of the original income inclusion that is now being undone.

The most difficult cases for determining the applicability of the inclusionary aspect of the tax benefit rule are those where the event that "matches" the earlier deduction is not a "recovery" of property in the most direct and literal sense. In Hillsboro National Bank v. Commissioner, 460 U.S. 370 (1983), the Supreme Court considered two such cases (*Hillsboro* itself and the consolidated case of United States v. Bliss Dairy, Inc.). In *Hillsboro*, a corporation had been allowed, under §164(e), to deduct certain state taxes that were imposed on its shareholders but that it paid. (Without §164(e), such payments would be treated as nondeductible dividends to the shareholders whose state tax liabilities were thereby satisfied.) However, due to a state law dispute about whether the taxes were lawfully imposed, the payments went to a state-administered escrow fund. The taxes were subsequently struck down under state law, whereupon state authorities repaid the contested payments to the shareholders rather than to the bank itself. The Commissioner claimed that the bank had taxable income by reason of the refund, even though it had not literally recovered the amounts paid, on the ground that payment of the disputed amount to the shareholders was "inconsistent" with the earlier deduction, which had been premised on the view that a state tax liability was owed. The taxpayer argued that a literal recovery was necessary in order for inclusion to be mandated by the tax benefit rule.

In *Bliss Dairy*, a corporation had deducted the cost of buying cattle feed, under since-repealed rules permitting farming businesses to use the cash method of accounting. In a later year, however, rather than using the cattle feed in its operations, the corporation liquidated and distributed its assets, including the unused cattle feed, to its shareholders. Here again, the government argued that inclusion by the corporation was required by the tax benefit rule under its "inconsistent event" theory, while the taxpayer pointed to the lack of a literal "recovery" of the deducted cattle feed by the liquidating corporation.

The Supreme Court began by rejecting the taxpayer's view of the tax benefit rule:

> An examination of the purpose and accepted applications of the tax benefit rule reveals that a "recovery" will not always be necessary to invoke the tax benefit rule. The purpose of the rule is not simply to tax "recoveries." On the contrary, it is to approximate the results produced by a tax system based on transactional rather than annual accounting. . . . It has long been accepted that a taxpayer using accrual accounting who accrues and deducts an expense in a tax year before it becomes payable and who for some reason eventually does not have to pay the liability must then take into income the amount of the expense earlier deducted. . . . The bookkeeping entry canceling the liability, though it increases the balance sheet net worth of the taxpayer, does not fit within any ordinary definition of "recovery." Thus, the taxpayers' formulation of the rule neither serves the purpose of the rule nor accurately reflects the cases that establish the rule. Further, the taxpayer's proposal would introduce an undesirable formalism into the application of the tax benefit rule. . . . Imposition of a requirement that there be a recovery would, in many cases, simply require the Government to cast its argument in different and unnatural terminology, without adding anything to the analysis.

However, the Court also rejected the government's proposed test, which it described as "requir[ing] the inclusion of amounts previously deducted if later events are inconsistent with the deductions," on the following ground:

> The basic purpose of the tax benefit rule is to . . . protect the Government and the taxpayer from the adverse effects of reporting a transaction on the basis of assumptions that an event in a subsequent year proves to have been erroneous. Such an event, unforeseen at the time of an earlier deduction, may in many cases require the application of the tax benefit rule. We do not, however, agree that this consequence invariably follows. Not every unforeseen event will require the taxpayer to report income in the amount of his earlier deduction. On the contrary, the tax benefit rule will "cancel out" an earlier deduction only when a careful examination shows that the later event is indeed *fundamentally* inconsistent with the premise on which the deduction was initially based. [Emphasis added.]

The Court then decided, on somewhat confusing and technical grounds, that the tax benefit rule required inclusion in *Bliss Dairy* but not in *Hillsboro.*

NOTES AND QUESTIONS

1. By applying solely when the marginal tax rate in the year of the deduction was in effect zero, does §111 do too little to address tax rate differences between the year of deduction and of recovery? Or does it do too much? Does it matter to the merits of this rule that the government gets no relief in cases where the taxpayer received a tax benefit from the deduction but gets no "tax detriment" (in the form increased tax liability for any year) from including the recovery?

2. Can the inclusionary aspect of the tax benefit rule reduce the amount that a taxpayer must include in income? Consider *Alice Phelan Sullivan Corp.* where the taxpayer received back property that it had contributed to a charity. Is it possible, in the absence of the tax benefit rule, that the taxpayer would have had income in the full amount of the property's value, rather than the amount of the earlier deduction? In the words of *Glenshaw Glass, supra,* could one argue that this was taxable as an "undeniable accession to wealth, clearly realized, and over which the taxpayer had complete dominion"?

Does it matter in this regard that the taxpayer in *Alice Phelan Sullivan* technically had never given away the right to hold the property if it ceased to be used for religious or educational purposes? If so, does it matter that the taxpayer had claimed a charitable deduction for the property's full value at the time of the gift, rather than treating itself as having made only a partial gift (akin to a term interest) through its retention of a valuable, albeit conditional, right of reversion?

3. The Supreme Court in *Hillsboro* declined to broaden the term "recovery" to cover all cases where the inclusionary aspect of the tax benefit rule ought to apply, on the ground that this would "simply require the Government to cast its argument in different and unnatural terminology, without adding anything to the analysis." In retrospect, might such an approach have provided greater clarity than what the Court actually did? For example, the Court could perhaps have developed a notion of "constructive" or "equitable" recovery, to

cover at least two types of cases: (a) those where assets are converted from deductible to nondeductible use and (b) cases where the recovery is by parties closely related to the taxpayer, such as a corporation's shareholders or an individual taxpayer's children. How would the *Hillsboro* and *Bliss Dairy* cases come out under such a rule?

B.   CASH AND ACCRUAL METHODS OF ACCOUNTING FOR INCOME

1.   Introduction to Accounting Methods

The two major systems of annual accounting for income are the cash method and the accrual method. The cash method focuses on actual receipts and disbursements, while the accrual method focuses on amounts earned (though not necessarily received) and obligations incurred (though not necessarily paid). The differences between the two can be relevant even to an employee. For example, is the 2018 performance bonus awarded to an employee in December 2018 but paid in January 2019 included in 2018 or 2019 income? For an accrual method taxpayer, the answer is 2018, because the bonus is earned in that year, but for a cash method taxpayer (the normal state of affairs), the answer is 2019, because that is the earliest year in which she can pick up the bonus check. The differences become even more acute in the measure of income from business operations.

The accrual method looks less to cash in and out the door and more to connecting the activities through which receipts are earned to the costs of those activities, subject to the constraints of the annual accounting period. As such it continues the matching theme introduced above in our discussion of depreciation. Financial statements prepared under "Generally Accepted Accounting Principles" generally must be prepared under the accrual method of accounting, because by doing a better job of implementing the matching principle it yields a measure of annual income that is superior to the cash method in three critical respects. First, by aligning gross receipts with the costs of earning those receipts, it simply is more accurate than the cash method. Second, it is more consistent from year to year, because the accrual method eliminates the lumpiness in income from year to year that otherwise occurs by virtue of the accidents (or planning) of when receivables (money owed a business for goods sold or services performed) are reduced to cash and when the taxpayer pays its bills. Third, as just implied, it is much less susceptible to gaming. Cash method business taxpayers with adequate financial resources have every reason to pay every conceivable tax-deductible bill in December and to be diffident about collecting receivables until January 2nd. Each year, the cycle repeats, creating a permanent deferral of income rolled forward from one year to the next in perpetuity.

You might expect from this that the accrual method of accounting is the norm for income tax purposes as well, but that is not the case when dealing with the personal income tax. The problem is that the greater accuracy of the accrual method requires somewhat more sophisticated bookkeeping and accounting than does the cash method—although it might fairly be questioned just how large a problem that is in the modern world of inexpensive software accounting packages. Both for this reason and for the gaming opportunities that the cash method offers, most individuals use the cash method of accounting whenever permitted. Unless you are a very unusual person, if you have filed tax returns, you have done so using the cash method, even though you probably were not even aware of it.

Section 446(a) provides that an individual's tax accounting method generally is the same as "the method of accounting on the basis of which the taxpayer regularly computes his income in keeping his books."[10] This formulation reflects the belief that business people should be free to adopt methods of accounting that best reflect the nature of their businesses,[11] and also the fact that the income tax did not begin its existence in 1913 operating with a blank canvas. Businesses had kept accounts that would be recognizable to a modern financial accountant for the previous 600 years, and the federal income tax, rather than reinventing every principle of income accounting, built on this foundation, and implicitly assumed that sound accounting judgment would dominate any inclination for tax hanky-panky.

Section 448 limits the availability of the cash method of accounting. Generally, taxable corporations (so-called C corporations) or partnerships with C corporations as partners and having gross receipts greater than $25 million/year must use the accrual method. Personal services corporations are exempted from this rule. So for that matter are partnerships all of whose partners are individuals or personal services corporations. The partners of a law partnership with gross revenues exceeding $1 billion annually are permitted to employ the cash method of accounting on their individual tax returns. (As a reminder, partnerships are not themselves subject to income tax; instead a partnership's income flows up to its partners for inclusion on their returns.)

Section 446(b) imposes an important limitation on taxpayer flexibility, which is that an accounting method must "clearly reflect income." As often is the case with some of the Code's most elemental rules, this provision is circular, in that it uses the concept of income to define those methods of calculating income which are impermissible, but the IRS has vigorously applied its authority here in many cases, essentially arguing that a particular method of accounting as applied to a particular fact pattern yields outcomes that diverge unacceptably from what business people might adopt by way of an accounting method in a world without income taxes.

Section 451 imposes specific rules for when certain instances of gross income must be included. Section 461 addresses the other side of calculating taxable income, by imposing important limitations on the deductibility of expenses to prevent gaming of both cash and accrual methods.

---

10. It is an incomplete response to the inevitable objection to this form of statutory drafting, but §7701(p), by cross reference to 1 U.S.C. 1, does provide that the masculine pronoun includes the feminine.

11. Reg. §1.446-1(a)(2) ("It is recognized that no uniform method of accounting can be prescribed for all taxpayers. Each taxpayer shall adopt such forms and systems as are, in his judgment, best suited to his needs").

The general rule of §461 is that cash method taxpayers report deductible expenses when paid, and accrual method taxpayers do so when "all events" have taken place to fix the liability. This test stems from early case law, and was codified by §461(h)(1) and (h)(4). The "all events test" does not require mathematical certitude as to amount, but it does require that all conditions precedent to the liability being fixed have occurred, so that it is "fixed and determinate."

In United States v. General Dynamics Corp., 481 U.S. 239 (1987), the taxpayer provided medical benefits to its employees by reimbursing qualifying medical expenses that they incurred. It claimed deductions for its obligations to pay for medical services that, as of the close of the taxable year, had been rendered but as to which the employee had not yet submitted a claim. These deductions were based on estimates from past experience. The Supreme Court (by a six-to-three vote) denied the deductions on the ground that the all events test was not satisfied until employees actually submitted their reimbursement claims. Such filing was not a "mere technicality," because some employees might fail to submit claims for reimbursement to which they were plainly entitled out of "oversight, procrastination, confusion over the coverage provided, or fear of disclosure to the employer of the extent or nature of the services received" (481 U.S. at 244).

Section 461(h), added in 1984, is an important limitation on the all events test. It provides that an accrual method taxpayer may not deduct an expense until "economic performance" of the undertaking giving rise to the expense has taken place. In general, economic performance occurs as the property or services to which an obligation relates are provided. Thus, a fixed and determinate obligation to pay a lessor for the use of property next year generally cannot be deducted this year.

Financial accounting, as used for example for the financial statements prepared by a public corporation, and the accrual method of accounting for tax purposes have similar foundations but can diverge in practice. For example, financial accounting permits the use of estimates of liabilities in instances when tax accrual accounting does not, and, as just noted, §461(h) can require that certain expenses that are recognized in the current year for financial accounting purposes can be deducted for tax purposes only in future years when "economic performance" takes place.

In both of the examples just given, specific Code provisions require that the accrual method of tax accounting diverge from the results obtained under financial accounting. The 2017 act added another important gloss on the intersection of the two concepts, this time requiring that the accrual method of tax accounting for certain *income* (but not expense) items *conform* to the timing of recognition of those items for financial accounting purposes. Section 451(b), as added by that act, now provides that in the case of an accrual method taxpayer, the "all events" test with respect to an item of gross income shall be deemed to be satisfied no later than the year the income item is recognized for financial accounting purposes. (Exceptions are provided for cases where other specific income inclusion rules are mandated by the Code.) The Senate Report accompanying the legislation described the rule as motivated in part by the theory that "conformity will create a healthy tension between a taxpayer's desire to have high book income and its desire to have low taxable income," but the practical implications of the new rule are very uncertain.[12]

QUESTIONS

1. Does the suggestion by the Supreme Court in *General Dynamics* that procrastinators might never file claims to reimbursable medical expenses seem a bit strained? Other language in the decision suggests that the Court was partly motivated by its discomfort with deduction claims based on mere estimates, "no matter how statistically certain" or defensible as an "appropriate conservative accounting measure" (481 U.S. at 244, 246).

2. The taxable year at issue in *General Dynamics* predated the enactment of the economic performance requirement. How would this test have applied to the case if the taxpayer had satisfied the all events test?

The next case was decided after §461(h) was enacted, but deals with a tax year prior to the effective date of §461(h). Its fact pattern was widely known at the time §461(h) was considered and in fact served as an impetus to its enactment. The case illustrates the power of the time value of money in tax planning, the operation of §446(b), and the delicate dance among the IRS, Congress, and the courts, in which taxpayers' stratagems precipitated both a change to the Code for years after the year at issue, and an effort by the IRS to reach similar results for earlier years, without appearing to simply apply the new law retroactively.

FORD MOTOR CO. v. COMMISSIONER
71 F.3d 209 (6th Cir. 1995)

MILBURN, Circuit Judge. Petitioner Ford Motor Company ("Ford") appeals the decision of the United States Tax Court upholding respondent Commissioner of Internal Revenue's ("Commissioner") reduction of petitioner's deductions for its obligations under agreements it entered into in settlement of tort lawsuits against it. On appeal, the issue is whether respondent Commissioner abused her discretion in determining that petitioner's method of accounting for its structured settlements was not a clear reflection of income under 26 U.S.C. §446(b) and in ordering petitioner to limit its deduction in 1980 to the cost of the annuity contracts it purchased to fund the settlements. For the reasons that follow, we affirm.

I.

A.

Petitioner Ford Motor Company is engaged in a number of businesses, including the manufacture of cars and trucks, and it maintains its books and

---

12. Sheppard, *Fahrenheit 451(b)*, 158 Tax Notes 1161 (Feb. 26, 2018).

records and files its income taxes using the accrual method of accounting. In the years preceding 1980, some of Ford's cars and trucks were involved in automobile accidents, and in 1980, Ford entered into 20 structured settlement agreements in settlement of personal injury or accidental death claims with persons who were injured in the accidents and with survivors of persons who died as a result of the accidents. In these structured settlement agreements, Ford agreed to make periodic payments of tort damages, yearly or monthly, in exchange for a release of all claims against it. The payments were to be made over various periods of time, the longest of which was 58 years. All but three of the settlements provided for payments over a period of 40 years or more. The agreements were of three types: (I) those that required petitioner to make periodic payments for a period certain ("Type I settlements"); (II) those that required petitioner to make periodic payments for the remainder of a claimant's life ("Type II settlements"); and (III) those that required petitioner to make periodic payments for the longer of a period certain or the remainder of a claimant's life ("Type III settlements"). In total, the structured settlement agreements provided for payments of $24,477,699.[13]

To provide it with funds to cover the periodic payments, Ford purchased [from life insurance companies] single premium annuity contracts at a cost of $4,424,587. The annuity contracts were structured so that the yearly annuity payments would equal the yearly amount owed to the claimants under the structured settlement agreements. None of the settlement agreements released petitioner from liability following the purchase of the annuity contract, and, in the event of a default on an annuity, petitioner would be required to pay the remaining balance owed to the tort claimants. The parties stipulated that the present value of the deferred payments that petitioner agreed to make to the claimants did not exceed the cost of the annuity contracts.

On its 1980 tax return, petitioner claimed deductions for the various types of structured settlements as follows: for the Type I settlements, it claimed the total amount of all periodic payments due; for the Type II settlements, it claimed the amounts it actually paid during 1980; and for the Type III settlements, it claimed the total amount of all payments due for the period certain portion of the settlement. These deductions totaled $10,636,994, which petitioner included as part of a product liability loss that it carried back to its 1970 taxable year pursuant to §172(b)(1)(I). It also reported the annuity income on its 1980 federal income tax return under §72. For financial accounting purposes, petitioner reported the 1980 structured settlements by expensing the cost of the annuity in the year of the settlement. . . .

Respondent Commissioner determined that Ford's method of accounting for its structured settlements did not clearly reflect income under §446(b) and disallowed the deductions petitioner claimed in excess of the cost of the annuities petitioner purchased. Respondent also excluded from petitioner's income the amounts required to be reported as income from annuity contracts, which was $323,340 in 1980. As a result, respondent determined a deficiency in petitioner's 1970 federal income tax liability of $3,300,151.

---

13. In order to reach this figure, petitioner presumed that the claimants receiving payments for life would survive to their life expectancies.

B.

Petitioner Ford challenged this deficiency determination by filing a petition in the United States Tax Court. In its amended petition, Ford claimed that it was entitled to deduct in 1980 the full amount of all payments to be made under the structured settlements, basing its valuation of the life settlements on the life expectancies of the claimants. The total deduction Ford claimed was $24,477,699.

The parties submitted the case to the United States Tax Court with all facts fully stipulated. A divided court upheld the Commissioner's position. . . . This timely appeal followed.

II.

A.

Section 446 of the Internal Revenue Code provides the general rule governing use of methods of accounting by taxpayers. Section 446(b) provides that, if the method of accounting used by the taxpayer to compute income does not clearly reflect income, "the computation of taxable income shall be made under such method as, in the opinion of the Secretary or his delegate, does clearly reflect income." The Commissioner has broad discretion under §446(b) to determine whether a particular method of accounting clearly reflects income. *Thor Power Tool Co. v. Commissioner*, 439 U.S. 522 (1979). "Since the Commissioner has 'much latitude for discretion,' his interpretation of the statute's clear-reflection standard 'should not be interfered with unless clearly unlawful.'" 439 U.S. at 532 [internal citations omitted]. Once the Commissioner has determined that a method of accounting does not clearly reflect income, she may substitute a method that, in her opinion, does clearly reflect income.

Petitioner appeals the tax court's holding that respondent correctly determined that petitioner's accrual method of accounting for its tort obligations did not clearly reflect income and its resulting disallowance of a portion of petitioner's deductions for such obligations by imposing a different accounting method on petitioner. . . .

B.

There are three stages to our analysis in this case: first, we decide whether the application of §446(b) was appropriate; second, we decide whether the tax court correctly determined that petitioner's method of accounting did not clearly reflect income; and third, we address the appropriateness of the method of accounting that the Commissioner imposed in its place.

First, petitioner argues that the tax court erred in allowing the Commissioner to require Ford to change its method of accounting because, in the absence of abuse or manipulation, an accrual method taxpayer clearly reflects its income when its reporting satisfies the "all events" test. Therefore, it argues that, because its accrual of deductions satisfied the all events test, the Commissioner had no authority to invoke §446(b).

Ford Motor Company is an accrual method taxpayer. The accrual method of accounting takes income into account when the right to payment is earned, even if payment is not received until later, and expenses into account when they are incurred, even if payment is not made until a later time. Financial accounting systems differ regarding the time that an expense is "incurred" and therefore should be accrued, but, under the tax law, the standard for determining when an expense is "incurred" is the "all events" test. Treas. Reg. §1.466-1(c)(1)(ii); *United States v. Hughes Properties, Inc.*, 476 U.S. 593, 600 (1986). This test provides that an accrual method taxpayer must deduct an expense in the taxable year when all the events have occurred that establish the fact of liability giving rise to the deduction and the amount of the liability can be determined with reasonable accuracy. *Id.* The tax court assumed for purposes of discussion that Ford's deductions satisfied the all events test, and for purposes of our review, we will make this assumption as well.

It is a well-established principle that the Commissioner may not invoke her authority under §446(b) to require a taxpayer to change from an accounting method that clearly reflects income, even if she believes that a second method might more clearly reflect income. . . . However, we hold that satisfaction of the all events test by an accrual method taxpayer does not preempt the Commissioner's authority under §446(b) to determine that a taxpayer's method of accounting does not clearly reflect income.

Section 446(c) of the Internal Revenue Code provides that, *subject to the provisions of subsections (a) and (b)*, a taxpayer may compute taxable income under the accrual method of accounting. 26 U.S.C. §446(c)(2). The all events test, which is merely a means devised to define the years in which income and deductions accrue, clearly is subordinate to the clear reflection standard contained in subsection (b). The Tax Court stated:

> The provisions of section 446 make it clear that a taxpayer's ability to use one or more of the methods of accounting listed in 446(c) is contingent upon the satisfaction of subsections 446(a) and (b). The statute does not limit the Commissioner's discretion under section 446(b) by the taxpayer's mere compliance with the methods of accounting generally permitted under section 446(c). . . . In short, the statute clearly provides that the taxpayers may use an accrual method so long as it clearly reflects income.

The language of §446 is clear on its face, and we agree with the tax court's interpretation of the statute. See *Mooney Aircraft, Inc. v. United States*, 420 F.2d 400, 406 (5th Cir. 1969) ("The 'all events test', however, is not the only basis upon which the Commissioner can disallow a deduction. Under 446(b) he has discretion to disallow any accounting method which does not clearly reflect income").

Petitioner argues that Congress acknowledged that the Commissioner's discretion under §446(b) does not extend to situations such as the present case when it changed the Internal Revenue Code, effective in 1984, to provide in §461(h)(2)(c) that accrual method taxpayers cannot deduct tort liabilities until the year in which payment is made. . . . Section 461(h) was a Congressional effort to remedy an accounting distortion by placing *all* accrual method taxpayers on the cash method of accounting for tort liabilities, regardless of the length of the payout period and without any consideration of whether accrual of an expense in an earlier year would distort income. Its enactment does not preclude the Commissioner from applying the clear reflection standard of §446(b) on a case-by-case basis to taxpayers in tax years prior to 1984.

C.

Having determined that expenses that satisfy the all events test can be disallowed when accrual would not result in a clear reflection of income, we now examine the correctness of the Commissioner's determination that Ford's method of accounting for its tort obligations did not clearly reflect income. In its opinion, the tax court used an example to "highlight the distortion [of petitioner's income] about which respondent complains." It utilized the numbers from one settlement agreement under which Ford agreed to pay the claimant $504,000 in 42 equal, annual installments of $12,000. The annuity contract that Ford purchased to fund the payments cost $141,124, demonstrating an implicit rate of return of 8.19 percent. Ford claimed a deduction in 1980 in the amount of $504,000 for this obligation. The tax court used these numbers to create three scenarios, assuming that but for the settlement agreement in question, petitioner would have had taxable income in 1980 of at least $504,000.

In the first scenario, the tax court assumed that the accident in question did not occur and that, as a result, petitioner received an additional $504,000 of currently taxable income. The tax court further assumed that petitioner would have been subject to a 40 percent marginal tax rate, leaving it with $302,400. The tax court then noted that, if the after tax proceeds were invested over 42 years at a rate of 8.19 percent, the $302,400 would grow to $8,249,751.

In the second scenario, the tax court assumed that the accident occurred but that Ford discharged its liability in full by paying and deducting $141,124 and investing the remainder over 42 years. Its current deduction of the $141,124 it paid for the annuity would leave it with $362,876 of taxable income on which it would pay tax of $145,150, leaving $217,726. If it invested the $217,726 over the 42-year period at a 8.19 percent rate of return, it would grow to $5,939,756.

In the third scenario, the tax court assumed that the events occurred as they did in the present case, with Ford deducting the full $504,000 it was required to pay the tort claimants and paying no tax. Investing the $504,000 at a rate of return of 8.19 percent and taking into account the annual payments of $12,000, the tax court found that petitioner would have $9,898,901 remaining after 42 years.

The tax court pointed out that Ford is claiming scenario three treatment and that comparing scenario three to scenario one demonstrates that petitioner is better off with the accidents than if they never occurred. The tax court held that fully deducting payments extending over a long period of time leads to a distortion of income and "the incongruous result that the greater a taxpayer's nominal liability for negligence, the more it benefits." It therefore concluded that petitioner's method of accounting did not clearly reflect income.

Petitioner challenges the tax court's approval of the Commissioner's determination that its accounting method did not clearly reflect income on several grounds. First, it argues that the tax court's numerical example was flawed by its use of a 8.19 percent rate of return. It asserts that the 8.19 percent rate of return that the tax court found implicit in one of the annuity contracts is a pre-tax rate of return because Ford is required to pay tax on amounts received as an annuity under 26 U.S.C. §72 and that the tax court instead should have used the after-tax rate of 4.91 percent. . . . In her brief, respondent acknowledges the flaw in the tax court's numerical example and presents an example of her own, arguing that Ford was in a 46 percent tax bracket rather than a 40 percent tax bracket. In respondent's example, petitioner again fares better under scenario three treatment than under scenario one.

Petitioner's brief suggests that the tax court's determination that its accounting method did not clearly reflect income was based solely on the fact that, in the tax court's example, petitioner fared better with the accident than without. We conclude, however, that this factor was not determinative, and that, even viewing petitioner's numerical example as correct, the gross distortion of income that it demonstrates between the economic and tax results persuades us that the tax court's decision was not improper. Given the length of the payment periods, allowing a deduction for the full amount of liability in 1980 could lead to the result that the tax benefit from the deduction would fund the full amounts due in future years and leave petitioner with a profit. Such a result extends the accrual method of accounting beyond its inherent limitations.

Our task on appeal is to determine whether there is an adequate basis in law for the Commissioner's conclusion that Ford's method of accounting did not clearly reflect income. We find several cases from other circuits that support our finding that the Commissioner's exercise of her discretion was proper. First, in *Mooney Aircraft, Inc. v. United States*, 420 F.2d 400 (5th Cir. 1969), the Fifth Circuit upheld the Commissioner's denial of the taxpayer's use of an accounting method based on his §446(b) authority. In that case, Mooney manufactured airplanes, and each purchaser of an airplane received a "Mooney Bond," redeemable for $1,000 when the airplane was permanently retired from service. Retirement of the aircraft usually occurred 20 or more years from the date of purchase. Mooney, an accrual method taxpayer, argued that the sale of an aircraft and corresponding issuance of a bond satisfied the all events test for the liability, and, therefore, it attempted to deduct the $1,000 redemption price of the bonds in the year of sale. Conversely, the government argued that the all events test was not satisfied until the aircraft was retired and that the deduction was improper prior to such time. The Fifth Circuit disagreed with the government, holding that the all events test was satisfied at the time of sale. However, it concluded that the taxpayer's method of accounting did not clearly reflect income, emphasizing that the long time period between the deduction for the bonds and their date of redemption was problematic and caused a distortion of income.

* * * *

Petitioner also argues that the tax court's decision that petitioner's method of accounting did not clearly reflect income was improper because it "authorizes arbitrary and unprincipled use of the Commissioner's section 446(b) power." It asserts that the tax court failed to provide any principles "to delineate the scope of section 446(b)," and that, in doing so, it created an "arbitrary system . . . that requires all accrual taxpayers to account for their liabilities when they become fixed, yet makes the validity of that reporting method subject to the unconstrained whim of the Commissioner."

We are not persuaded by this policy-based argument. The tax court concluded its opinion stating:

> Finally, we want to make clear that the mere fact that a deduction which accrues prior to the time payment is made (the timing factor) does not, by itself, cause the accrual to run afoul of the clear reflection of income requirement. Inherent in the use of an accrual method is the fact that a deduction may be allowed in advance of payment. Our holding in the instant case is not intended to draw a bright line that can be applied mechanically in other circumstances. We decide only the ultimate question of fact in the instant case; namely, whether, for tax purposes, petitioner's method of accounting for its obligations under the structured settlements clearly reflects income. We hold that it does not and that the Government did not abuse its discretion in making that determination.

As the tax court observed, "the issue of whether the taxpayer's method of accounting clearly reflects income is a question of fact to be determined on a case-by-case basis." We find the tax court's language sufficient to limit its holding to extreme cases such as this one in which the economic results are grossly different from the tax results and therefore conclude that the tax court's decision does not allow the Commissioner arbitrary or unprincipled discretion.

D.

Given that a change was necessary because Ford's accrual of its settlement obligations in 1980 did not clearly reflect income, Ford argues that the method of accounting that the Commissioner imposed in its place was improper. . . .

The method of accounting that the Commissioner imposed was to allow Ford a deduction for the amount that it paid for the annuities with no further deductions for the future payments that Ford will make to the claimants. To offset her disallowance of future deductions, the Commissioner will permit Ford to exclude its income from the annuity contracts. Petitioner asserts that this scheme violates established tax law for several reasons and forces Ford to use a tax treatment that it could not have adopted on its own.

First, petitioner argues that the Commissioner is imposing on it a present value method of accounting which should only be imposed in the presence of a directive by Congress to do so. Ford additionally argues that this method impermissibly allows it only to deduct the approximately $4 million it paid for the annuities without ever allowing a deduction for the additional approximately $20 million it will pay to the claimants and that the Commissioner's method is arbitrary because it is not a method that Ford could have adopted on its own.

Respondent counters that its method of accounting is a modified cash basis method that allows Ford "a dollar for dollar deduction, albeit in the form of an offset against its annuity income, for the full face amount of its future payments of approximately $24 million." Respondent points out that, because she allowed Ford to deduct the full cost of the annuity contracts in 1980, it has no basis in the contracts and would be fully taxable on the annuity income of $24,477,699 as it is received. However, the payments Ford is required to make to the tort claimants, which correspond exactly to the amount of its annuity income, give rise to deductions that offset the income and create a wash. Respondent argues that, because she has relieved taxpayer of the obligation to report the annuity income as it is received, she should not allow Ford any deductions for the required payments.

We find no merit in petitioner's assertion that this methodology is improper because it reduces the amount of the deductions to the present value of the payments petitioner is obligated to make. The Commissioner reduced petitioner's deduction to the cost of the annuity contracts. The stipulated facts provided only that the present value of the payments petitioner is obligated to make *did not exceed* this amount. There is no indication that respondent was imposing a present value method of accounting on petitioner.

Furthermore, we find no authority that prohibits the tax accounting treatment that the Commissioner and the tax court imposed here. The Commissioner's discretion to impose an alternate method of accounting under §446(b) is not limited to methods that Ford could have adopted on its own. While we recognize that to require Ford to account for its tort obligations on the cash method might have been a more logical alternative, we cannot find that the Commissioner's exercise of her discretion was arbitrary because it resulted in an accounting treatment more favorable to Ford than a straight cash method would be. The only difference between the Commissioner's method of accounting and the cash basis method is that petitioner receives an immediate deduction for the cost of its annuities rather than recovering that cost over the terms of the annuities under §72, and this difference inures to Ford's benefit. We therefore conclude that the tax court's decision regarding the accounting method the Commissioner imposed was proper.

III.

For the reasons stated, the judgment of the tax court is AFFIRMED.

NOTES AND QUESTIONS

1. In the absence of §104, which presumably excluded from gross income all or most of the payments received by plaintiffs in the structured tort settlements described in the case, when would cash method individual plaintiffs have reported income from the arrangement?

2. Ford Motor Co. "hedged" (in a colloquial sense) its obligations to make annual payments to plaintiffs for the duration of their lives by buying annuity policies on their lives. This eliminated Ford's "mortality risk" (the risk that a plaintiff would live longer than expected). Why didn't Ford and the plaintiffs just agree that Ford would settle these cases by Ford buying annuity contracts and giving those contracts to the plaintiffs?

3. One of Ford Motor Co.'s arguments essentially went to a notion of fair play. It structured unusual tort settlement arrangements to obtain a tax advantage; Congress responded by shutting down the stratagem as of 1984, and that should have been an end to it. The IRS should not have employed the blunt instrument of §446(b) to do retroactively what Congress fixed prospectively. What do you think of this argument? Note that corporate taxpayers in particular often find themselves litigating cases many years (in this case fifteen years) after the year in which an issue arises. Tax directors of large companies frequently articulate the concern that they are unable to plan the affairs of their companies when important questions of interpretation can go unresolved for years.

4. Section 461(h) now basically defines the "economic performance" of a tort settlement like those at issue in this case to occur when payment is made. In other words, in this respect accrual method taxpayers are placed on the cash method. Was the accounting method that Ford was required to adopt for pre-1984 years similar or different in economic terms from this cash method approach? Why as a tactical matter might the IRS have preferred the accounting method that it compelled Ford to adopt?

There are many other methods of accounting in the Code besides the cash and accrual methods. The taxation of installment sales, *infra*, technically is an instance of a special method of accounting. Similarly, taxpayers who perform work under long-term contracts for construction or the manufacture of property must account for profit under the percentage-of-completion method. See §460. Under this method, a portion of the gross contract price is included in income as work progresses, with the portion determined on the basis of cost of work performed. See Reg. §1.451-3. And firms that hold inventories for sale to customers must follow the specialized accounting rules for inventories contained in §§471-474.

Securities dealers must use a "mark-to-market" method of accounting, under which all their securities (other than those identified as held for investment) are deemed to be sold at fair market value at the end of each year, and immediately repurchased at that same price. Certain taxpayers that are in the business of trading securities but that do not hold securities for sale to customers (e.g., many hedge funds) may elect to use the mark-to-market method.

NOTES AND QUESTIONS

1. You are the chief financial officer of Wynken, Blynken, and Nod, one of America's largest and most successful law firms. What are some strategies you might propose to the Management Committee to defer the partners' taxable incomes without dramatically affecting their economic incomes?

2. Economists and many tax law professors view mark-to-market accounting as the best the income tax system can do by way of measuring capital income (income from investments), because it comes closest to encapsulating the Haig-Simons definition of income, as consumption plus changes in wealth.

(a) Do you agree? What counterarguments might be made?

(b) How would you handle private investments, such as those with no visible year-end prices or liquid markets in which to convert such an investment to cash?

2.   Delay in Receiving Cash

GEORGIA SCHOOL-BOOK DEPOSITORY v. COMMISSIONER
1 T.C. 463 (1943)

KERN, Judge.

The question is whether petitioner, which was on an accrual basis, should have accrued certain school book commissions at the time the books were sold by the publishers to the state, or should have returned them as income only when the books were paid for by the state, as petitioner contends.

Petitioner was a broker which received an 8 percent commission on all school books purchased by the State of Georgia through it. For this commission it performed certain services of advantage to both parties, such as executing the contracts of the state board of education with various publishers, taking care of the books as a central depository until final distribution, seeing that enough were on hand to meet the state's demands, distributing them, and collecting the moneys in payment from the state and holding them in trust until paid over to the publishers. It was responsible for the return in salable condition of any books not used. It had no title to the books at any time, and (except in the case of one publisher) posted a bond with each publisher to guarantee performance of its duties. Petitioner also carried on a somewhat similar business as a book broker of college books not on the state list and under these contracts was responsible for the collection of all accounts.

Petitioner did not accrue its commissions on the state books but did accrue its commissions on the college books at the same time that its liability for the books to the publishers was accrued. Under the contracts for state school books it was provided that petitioner should receive its brokerage "at the time of settlement" and this term is explained by the provision that the petitioner shall make quarterly reports "so as to show the exact balance due" the publisher by the petitioner, and shall remit "its pro rata share of all cash received from the collection of warrants issued by the State of Georgia for books sold to the state when and as such warrants are received."

The publishers could look for payment from the state, and, consequently, petitioner could look for its commissions only from the "Free Textbook Fund," which was renewed only from the excise laid on beer.[14] During the taxable

---

14. [The court's findings of fact describe the textbook fund as follows:

   On March 4, 1937, the State of Georgia enacted a Free Textbook Act, under which the state board of education was directed to inaugurate and administer a system of free textbooks for the public schools of Georgia, and to execute contracts therefor. The act provides that the cost of administering the free textbook system and purchasing the books shall be paid by the state from such funds as may be provided by the General Assembly for that purpose. . . . The Legislature thereupon created a free textbook fund, made up solely from excise taxes on the sale of malt beverages in the state. The act provides that funds derived from taxes on malt beverages shall be apportioned as follows: Not over 3 percent shall be paid to the revenue commission for enforcing the malt beverage act and "the remainder shall be set aside and devoted for the support of the common schools of the state and used for the purpose of furnishing free textbooks to the children attending the common schools, any excess to be used for other school purposes."—EDS.]

years 1938 and 1939 this fund was insufficient to pay the petitioner in full. The state, in its accounting, did not treat these large deficits as present liabilities except to the extent that funds were already on hand to meet them, the remainder being considered an encumbrance on the textbook fund in the next year. The "accounts ripen," the auditor reported, "for payment when and as funds become available in the Textbook Fund."

Petitioner contends, first, that the brokerage was not earned until payment, and, secondly, that there was no reasonable expectancy that payment ever would be made; and for these reasons, it urges its ultimate contention that the commissions here involved were not properly accruable in the respective taxable years.

In so far as appears, all acts which were required of petitioner to earn its brokerage, save one, had been done in the taxable year. It had received the books from the publishers, stored them, and later distributed them to the several schools. All it had not done was to receive the money from the state and pay it out to the publishers. On this account the actual payment of the brokerage may not have been due to petitioner until this money was received, but the right to it had accrued by the performance of its duties. United States v. Anderson, 269 U.S. 422. It is the *right* to receive money which in accrual accounting justifies the accrual of money receivable and its return as accrued income.

The Supreme Court said in Spring City Foundry Co. v. Commissioner, 292 U.S. 182 (p.184):

> . . . Keeping accounts and making returns on the accrual basis, as distinguished from the cash basis, import that it is the right to receive and not the actual receipt that determines the inclusion of the amount in gross income. When the right to receive an amount becomes fixed, the right accrues. . . .

The receipt of the money from the state, the deduction of petitioner's commission, and the transmission of the balance to the publishers were the least of its duties and can not be made the criterion of the arisal of the right. Paragraph 9 of the contract assumes that the publisher's right to payment had arisen, for it requires that the quarterly reports which petitioner was to submit should "show the exact balance due the first party by the second party [petitioner]. . . ."

We pass, then, to the second question, whether there was a reasonable expectancy that the claim would ever be paid. Where there is a contingency that may preclude ultimate payment, whether it be that the right itself is in litigation or that the debtor is insolvent, the right need not be accrued when it arises. This rule is founded on the old principle that equity will not require a suitor to do a needless thing. The taxpayer need not accrue a debt if later experience, available at the time that the question is adjudged, confirms a belief reasonably held at the time the debt was due, that it will never be paid. . . . On the other hand, it must not be forgotten that the alleviating principle of "reasonable expectancy" is, after all, an exception, and the exception must not be allowed to swallow up the fundamental rule upon which it is engrafted requiring a taxpayer on the accrual basis to accrue his obligations, Spring City

Foundry Co. v. Commissioner, *supra*. If this were so, the taxpayer might at his own will shift the receipt of income from one year to another as should suit his fancy. . . . To allow the exception there must be a definite showing that an unresolved and allegedly intervening legal right makes receipt contingent or that the insolvency of his debtor makes it improbable. Postponement of payment without such accompanying doubts is not enough. . . .

Applying these principles to the instant case, we must conclude that, despite the condition of the treasury of the State of Georgia when the free schoolbook fund was inaugurated and for several years thereafter, there was no reasonable expectation that the sums owed by the state to petitioner's publishers and, consequently, the commissions to petitioner itself, would not ultimately be paid. It would naturally take a few years to establish in full working order a system of such magnitude, but a comparison of the two years before us shows that Georgia was gradually reducing its schoolbook obligations. Georgia is a state possessing great resources and a fine record of fiscal probity, and undoubtedly it can and will meet its obligations. The fact that petitioner, on behalf of its principals, continued to sell and deliver school books to the state indicates that there was no serious doubt as to the ultimate collection of the accounts here involved.

We conclude, therefore, that petitioner's commissions on all books purchased by the state through it in the taxable years should have been accrued and returned as income in those years.

Judgment will be entered for the respondent.

NOTES AND QUESTIONS

1. *Analysis.* (a) Under *Georgia School-Book Depository*, delay in the receipt of cash in the absence of doubt about ultimate payment is not enough to prevent accrual of income. Collectibility has nothing to do with accruability unless the obligor is insolvent. The "reasonable expectancy" language in *Georgia School-Book Depository* goes to the issue of solvency. It is important to distinguish between a contingent receivable, which will not accrue since it is uncertain whether the taxpayer has earned it as yet, and an earned determinable amount, which must be accrued even if there is some question as to whether it will ultimately be collected. In defense of its rule, the court says that if "reasonable expectancy" is interpreted too favorably to taxpayers, "a taxpayer might at his own will shift the receipt of income from one year to another as should suit his fancy." Do you agree? See §446(b).

(b) In Hallmark Cards, Inc. v. Commissioner, 90 T.C. 26 (1988), Hallmark, to maintain a level production schedule and to avoid warehousing costs, shipped Valentine cards to retailers in December. After the customers objected to including the cards in their inventory (which resulted, among other things, in their becoming liable for personal property taxes), Hallmark adopted a policy under which it retained title to the cards until January 1. The court held that Hallmark was not required to accrue income from the sale of the cards in December, because the "all events" test was not satisfied until title passed in January.

2. *Other accrual methods.* Section 446(c) speaks of "the" cash receipts and disbursements method of accounting for taxable income, but in sanctioning accrual accounting, it uses the more expansive phrase "an accrual method." The principal variations are the installment method of reporting income from installment sales (*infra* page 256) and the "completed-contract" and "percentage-of-completion" methods of reporting income from building, installation, construction, or manufacturing contracts not completed within one taxable year.

3.   Prepaid Income

The following case involves income of an automobile club operated by the American Automobile Association. For purposes of analysis it may be helpful to refer to the following hypothetical facts.

Suppose that the club is on the calendar year and that a particular member joins on October 1 of 1982 for one year and pays upon joining a fixed fee of $60. The member is entitled, among other things, to towing services and maps, on demand. The club has hundreds of thousands of members and has kept good records of its costs. Its fixed costs (for offices, staff, etc.) are $3 per month per member and vary only insignificantly from month to month and year to year. Its variable costs (for towing, etc.) are (on average) $3 per month per member in the six months of October through March and $1 per month per member in the other six months, but they vary from member to member.

How was AAA reporting these kinds of receipts and outlays before being challenged? How was it required to report under the decision in the case? Why?

AMERICAN AUTOMOBILE ASSOCIATION v. UNITED STATES
367 U.S. 687 (1961)

Mr. Justice CLARK delivered the opinion of the Court.

In this suit for refund of federal income taxes the petitioner, American Automobile Association, seeks determination of its tax liability for the years 1952 and 1953. Returns filed for its taxable calendar years were prepared on the basis of the same accrual method of accounting as was used in keeping its books. The Association reported as gross income only that portion of the total prepaid annual membership dues, actually received or collected in the calendar year, which ratably corresponded with the number of membership months covered by those dues and occurring within the same taxable calendar year. The balance was reserved for ratable monthly accrual over the remaining membership period in the following calendar year as deferred or unearned income reflecting an estimated future service expense to members. The Commissioner contends that petitioner should have reported in its gross income for each year the entire amount of membership dues actually received in the taxable calendar year without regard to expected future service expense in the subsequent year. The sole point at issue, therefore, is in what year the prepaid dues are taxable as income.

In auditing the Association's returns for the years 1952 through 1954, the Commissioner, in the exercise of his discretion under [§446(b)], determined not to accept the taxpayer's accounting system. As a result, adjustments were made for those years principally by adding to gross income for each taxable year the amount of prepaid dues which the Association had received but not recognized as income, and subtracting from gross income amounts recognized in the year although actually received in the prior year. . . .

The Association is a national automobile club organized as a nonstock membership corporation with its principal office in Washington, D.C. It provides a variety of services to the members of affiliated local automobile clubs and those of ten clubs which taxpayer itself directly operates as divisions, but such services are rendered solely upon a member's demand. Its income is derived primarily from dues paid one year in advance by members of the clubs. Memberships may commence or be renewed in any month of the year. For many years, the association has employed an accrual method of accounting and the calendar year as its taxable year. It is admitted that for its purposes the method used is in accord with generally accepted commercial accounting principles. The membership dues, as received, were deposited in the Association's bank accounts without restriction as to their use for any of its corporate purposes. However, for the Association's own accounting purposes, the dues were treated in its books as income received ratably[15] over the 12-month membership period. The portions thereof ratably attributable to membership months occurring beyond the year of receipt, that is, in a second calendar year, were reflected in the Association's books at the close of the first year as unearned or deferred income. Certain operating expenses were chargeable as prepaid membership cost and deducted ratably over the same periods of time as those over which dues were recognized as income.

The Court of Claims bottomed its opinion on Automobile Club of Michigan v. Commissioner, 1957, 353 U.S. 180, finding that "the method of treatment of prepaid automobile club membership dues employed [by the Association here was,] . . . for Federal income tax purposes, 'purely artificial.' " 181 F. Supp. 255, 258. It accepted that case as "a rejection by the Supreme Court of the accounting method advanced by plaintiff in the case at bar." Ibid. The Association does not deny that its accounting system is substantially identical to that used by the petitioner in *Michigan*. It maintains, however, that *Michigan* does not control this case because of a difference in proof, that is, that in this case the record contains expert accounting testimony indicating that the system used was in accord with generally accepted accounting principles; that its proof of cost of member service was detailed; and that the correlation between that cost and the period of time over which the dues were credited as income was shown and

---

15. In 1952 and 1953 dues collected in any month were accounted as income to the extent of one-twenty-fourth for that month (on the assumption that the mean date of receipt was the middle of the month), one-twelfth for each of the next eleven months, and again one-twenty-fourth in the anniversary month. In 1954, however, guided by its own statistical average experience, the Association changed its system so as to more simply reach almost the same result by charging to year of receipt, without regard to month of receipt, one-half of the entire dues payment and deferring the balance to the following year.

justified by proof of experience. The holding of *Michigan*, however, that the system of accounting was "purely artificial" was based upon the finding that "substantially all services are performed only upon a member's demand and the taxpayer's performance was not related to fixed dates after the tax year." 353 U.S. 180, 189, note 20. That is also true here. . . .

Whether or not the Court's judgment in *Michigan* controls our disposition of this case, there are other considerations requiring our affirmance. . . . In 1954 the Congress found dissatisfaction in the fact that

> as a result of court decisions and rulings, there have developed many divergencies between the computation of income for tax purposes and income for business purposes as computed under generally accepted accounting principles. The areas of difference are confined almost entirely to questions of when certain types of revenue and expenses should be taken into account in arriving at net income.

House Ways and Means Committee Report, H.R. Rep. No. 1337, 83d Cong., 2d Sess. 48. As a result, it introduced into the Internal Revenue Code of 1954 §452 and §462 which specifically permitted essentially the same practice as was employed by the Association here. Only one year later, however, in June, 1955, the Congress repealed these sections retroactively. . . . [T]he repeal of the section the following year, upon insistence by the Treasury that the proposed endorsement of such tax accounting would have a disastrous impact on the Government's revenue, was . . . clearly a mandate from the Congress that petitioner's system was not acceptable for tax purposes. . . . We are further confirmed in this view by consideration of the even more recent action of the Congress in 1958, subsequent to the decision in *Michigan*, *supra*. In that year §455 was added to the Internal Revenue Code of 1954. It permits publishers to defer receipt as income of prepaid subscriptions of newspapers, magazines, and periodicals. An effort was made in the Senate to add a provision in §455 which would extend its coverage to prepaid automobile club membership dues. However, in conference the House Conferees refused to accept this amendment . . . .

The validity of the long established policy of the Court in deferring, where possible, to congressional procedures in the tax field is clearly indicated in this case. Finding only that, in light of existing provisions not specifically authorizing it, the exercise of the Commissioner's discretion in rejecting the Association's accounting system was not unsound, we need not anticipate what will be the product of further "study of this entire problem."

Affirmed.

Mr. Justice STEWART, whom Mr. Justice DOUGLAS, Mr. Justice HARLAN, and Mr. Justice WHITTAKER join, dissenting. . . .

The effect of the Court's decision is to allow the Commissioner to prevent an accrual basis taxpayer from making returns in accordance with the accepted and clearly valid accounting practice of excluding from gross income amounts received as advances until the right to such amounts is earned by rendition of the services for which the advances were made. To permit the Commissioner to do this, I think, is to ignore the clear statutory command that a taxpayer must be allowed to make his returns in accord with his regularly employed method of accounting, so long as that method clearly reflects his income. . . .

I can find nothing in *Automobile Club of Michigan* which controls disposition of this case. And the legislative history upon which the Court alternatively relies seems to me upon examination to be singularly unconvincing.

In *Michigan* there was no offer of proof to show the rate at which the taxpayer fulfilled its obligations under its membership contracts. The deferred reporting of prepaid dues was, therefore, rejected in that case simply because there was no showing of a correlation between the amounts deferred and the costs incurred by the taxpayer in carrying out its obligations to its members. Until today, that case has been recognized as one that simply held that, in the absence of proof that the proration used by the taxpayer reasonably matched actual expenses with the earning of related revenue, the Commissioner was justified in rejecting the taxpayer's proration. . . .

As to the enactment and repeal of §452 and §462, upon which the Court places so much reliance, . . . I think that the enactment and subsequent repeal of §452 and §462 give no indication of Congressional approval of the position taken by the Commissioner in this case. If anything, the legislative action leads to the contrary impression. . . .

To my mind, this legislative history shows that Congress made every effort to dissuade the courts from doing exactly what the Court is doing in this case—drawing from the repeal of §452 an inference of Congressional disapproval of deferred reporting of advances. But even if the legislative history on this point were hazy, the same conclusion would have to be reached upon examination of Congressional purpose in repealing §452 and §462. . . . Sections 452 and 462 were repealed *solely* because of a prospective loss of revenue during the first year in which taxpayers would take advantage of the new sections. Insofar as the reporting of advances was concerned, that loss of revenue would have occurred solely as a consequence of taxpayers changing their method of reporting, without the necessity of securing the Commissioner's consent, to that authorized under §452 and §462. The taxpayer who shifted his basis for reporting advances would have been allowed what was commonly termed a "double deduction" during the transitional year. Under §462, deductions could be taken in the year of change for expenses attributable to advances taxed in prior years under a claim of right theory, as well as for reserves for future expenditures attributable to advances received and reported during that year. Similarly, under §452, pre-payments received during the year of transition would be excluded from gross income while current expenditures attributable to past income would still be deductible.

The Congressional purpose in repealing §452 and §462—maintenance of the revenues—does not, however, require disapproval of sound accounting principles in cases of taxpayers who, like the petitioner, have customarily and regularly used a sound accrual accounting method in reporting advance payments. No transition is involved, and no "double deduction" is possible. Moreover, taxpayers formerly reporting advances as income in the year of receipt can now shift to a true accrual system of reporting only with the approval of the Commissioner. See . . . §446(e). Before giving his approval the

Commissioner can be expected to insist upon adjustments in the taxpayer's transition year to forestall any revenue loss which would otherwise result from the change in accounting method. . . .

The net effect of compelling the petitioner to include all dues in gross income in the year received is to force the petitioner to utilize a hybrid accounting method—a cash basis for dues and an accrual basis for all other items. Schlude v. Commissioner, 8 Cir., 283 F.2d 234, 239. Cf. Commissioner of Internal Revenue v. South Texas Lumber Co., 333 U.S. 496, 501. For taxpayers generally the enforcement of such a hybrid accounting method may result in a gross distortion of actual income, particularly in the first and last years of doing business. On the return for the first year in which advances are received, a taxpayer will have to report an unrealistically high net income, since he will have to include unearned receipts, without any offsetting deductions for the future cost of earning those receipts. On subsequent tax returns, each year's unearned prepayments will be partially offset by the deduction of current expenses attributable to prepayments taxed in prior years. Even then, however, if the taxpayer is forbidden to correlate earnings with related expenditures, the result will be a distortion of normal fluctuations in the taxpayer's net income. For example, in a year when there are low current expenditures because of fewer advances received in the preceding year, the result may be an inflated adjusted gross income for the current year. Finally, should the taxpayer decide to go out of business upon fulfillment of the contractual obligations already undertaken, in the final year there will be no advances to report and many costs attributable to advances received in prior years. The result will be a grossly unrealistic reportable net loss.

The Court suggests that the application of sound accrual principles cannot be accepted here because deferment is based on an estimated rate of earnings, and because this estimate, in turn, is based on average, not individual, costs. It is true, of course, that the petitioner cannot know what service an individual member will require or when he will demand it. Accordingly, in determining the portion of its outstanding contractual obligations which have been discharged during a particular period (and hence the portion of receipts earned during that period), the petitioner can only compare the total expenditures for that period against estimated average expenditures for the same number of members over a full contract term. But this use of estimates and averages is in no way inconsistent with long-accepted accounting practices in reflecting and reporting income. . . .

Finally, it is to be noted that the regulations under both the 1939 and 1954 Codes permit various methods of reporting income which require the use of estimates.[16] In the absence of any showing that the estimates used here were faulty, I think the law did not permit the Commissioner to forbid the use of standard accrual methods simply upon the ground that estimates were necessary to determine what the rate of deferral should be. . . .

16. See, e.g., Treas. Reg. §1.451-3 (1975) (providing for the percentage of completion method of reporting income on long-term contracts); Treas. Reg. §1.451-4 (1957) (providing for [a] deduction for redemption of trading stamps based upon "the rate, in percentage, which the stamps redeemed in each year bear to the total stamps issued in such year"). . . .

NOTES AND QUESTIONS

1. *The deduction side.* One of the principal objectives of accrual accounting is to match income with the costs of producing that income. The good sense of such an approach is obvious in the case of a firm like American Automobile Association. Imagine the first year of its operations. If it reports as income the fees received during the year from members, without taking into account the cost of the services that it will be required to render to those members in the following year, it will overstate its income. Thus, assuming that the decision in the *AAA* case is controlling as to income, should the taxpayer be allowed to claim a deduction for the expected costs of providing services?

2. *Other cases.* The *AAA* case is but one of many that consider the includability of prepaid income upon receipt. In Schlude v. Commissioner, 372 U.S. 128 (1963), the Supreme Court, relying on *AAA* along with the limited scope of the subsequently enacted §456, held (five to four) that a dancing school was taxable in the year of receipt on amounts paid by students for lessons to be provided in the future. However, some appellate decisions reflect greater sympathy for the use of accrual principles (requiring deferral of prepaid but unearned income).

For example, Artnell Co. v. Commissioner, 400 F.2d 981 (7th Cir. 1968), rev'g 48 T.C. 411 (1967), permits income recognition to be deferred for prepaid admissions to baseball games to be played in the following taxable year. The court stated that, where the time and extent of the future services are sufficiently specific, the Commissioner would abuse his discretion under §446 by refusing to permit deferral. The three Supreme Court decisions (*Automobile Club of Michigan, American Automobile Association*, and *Schlude*) were distinguished as involving greater uncertainty.

One wag has explained the difference in outcomes between *Artnell* and *Schlude* as resting on the fact that everyone goes to the ball games for which they've purchased tickets, and no one shows up for all the prepaid dance lessons for which they've signed up. Do you have a better theory?

A similar sympathy for accrual principles is found in Boise Cascade Corp. v. United States, 530 F.2d 1367 (Ct. Cl.), cert. denied, 429 U.S. 867 (1976), where the taxpayer had performed engineering services. In *Boise Cascade*, the taxpayer sometimes performed services before being paid, and other times was paid before performing services. It followed a consistent practice of reporting the income when services were performed. The Commissioner sought to require that the income be reported when the services were performed or when the payment was collected, whichever came first. This was too much for the court to swallow. It concluded that "the inconsistency within the Commissioner's method is strident," and that "his method would appear to the ordinary mind to distort income instead of clearly reflecting it" (530 F.2d at 1378). *American Automobile Association* and *Schlude* were distinguished—although how convincingly is open to dispute—on the ground that here the services to be performed by the taxpayer were "fixed and definite," and "in no sense . . . dependent solely upon the demand or request of its clientele" (530 F.2d at 1377).

3. *The legislative sequel to the AAA case.* Following the decision in *American Automobile Association*, Congress enacted §456 to permit membership

organizations reporting on the accrual method to elect to spread prepaid dues over the period of responsibility for the performance of services. The provision has much in common with §455 (prepaid subscription income), to which both the majority and the dissenters in the *AAA* case referred.

4. *Relief provided by §451(c)*. Modest relief from the full force of the all events test—and from the divergence between financial (nontax) accounting and tax accounting—is made available by §451(c), as added by the 2017 act. This essentially codifies longstanding administrative practice, as reflected in Revenue Procedure 2004-34 and Reg. §1.451-5. Section 451(c) applies to advance payments for certain services, sales of goods, and other specified types of payments. Section 451(c) is elective: If its conditions are met, and a taxpayer elects to apply it, then advance payments received in one year but attributable to future years may be reported as taxable income in the following year, provided that this is consistent with the taxpayer's financial reporting. To illustrate, drawing on Examples 1 and 2 of the Revenue Procedure, suppose that in 2004 Taxpayer (*T*), which is in the business of providing dance lessons, receives $6,000 as full advance payment for 100 lessons. The expectation is that there will be twenty lessons in 2004, forty in 2005, and forty in 2006. Assuming consistency with its financial reports, and assuming that in fact twenty lessons are provided in 2004, *T* may report for tax purposes, in 2004, $1,200, rather than the entire $6,000. The remaining $4,800 must be reported in 2005, even if a total of only sixty lessons have been provided by the end of that year.

5. Under the all events test and substantial performance requirement, would the American Automobile Association be able to claim deductions for the expected cost of providing future services to members whose fees were currently includable?

4. Deposits Versus Advance Payments

When is an advance payment not an advance payment? This question will naturally occur to any taxpayer that is paid in advance of performing services and wishes to avoid the *American Automobile Association* line of cases. One answer is to characterize and structure the payment as merely a security deposit made in advance to protect the recipient against the risk of being paid late or not at all.

In Commissioner v. Indianapolis Power & Light Co., 493 U.S. 203 (1990), the taxpayer (IPL), an electrical utility, succeeded on this ground in avoiding inclusion upon receipt of advance payments that it demanded from customers whose credit it determined was suspect. In practice, these payments usually ended up being credited against the customers' monthly electric bills. Customers earned interest on the payments, but at what the Court noted was a relatively modest rate, below what IPL could expect to earn by investing the money. IPL did not place the deposits in escrow or segregate them from its other funds, and thus could use the money without restriction.

Under these circumstances, the Supreme Court held for IPL, finding that the payments were analogous to loans by the customers rather than to advance payments of the sort discussed in *AAA*. The Court mainly relied on the fact that customers could demand repayment of the deposits if service was terminated or upon establishing good credit. Earlier Tax Court decisions had come out the same way for lease deposits that secure the tenant's obligations under a lease. The main difference from prepaid rent, apparently, was the landlord's legal obligation to return lease deposits if the tenant met all its obligations, such as by paying all rent when due and not damaging the premises.

QUESTIONS

1. Suppose you have just bought a rental apartment building. In accordance with local practice, you expect that at the time you rent an apartment you will collect the first month's rent in advance plus an amount equal to the last month's rent, with the latter intended to provide security for any damages to the apartment and for the payment of the rent. Is it possible to contract with your lessees so that the "last month's rent" will be treated as a security deposit rather than as advance rent? What might you do, both at the outset of the lease and thereafter?

2. Suppose you are counsel to the American Automobile Association, which wants to know if it can restructure its membership practices to take advantage, if possible, of the cases concerning the tax treatment of security deposits. What, if anything, would you suggest?

C.   THE REALIZATION DOCTRINE: THE ROOT OF MANY TAX EVILS

In general, gain or loss resulting from a change in the value of an asset held by the taxpayer is not taken into account under the income tax until a "realization" event occurs (such as sale). Think of the tax law in this respect as a sleeping dog that slumbers through fluctuations in values until some specific event, like a sale, startles the dog into waking and barking.

Many tax scholars believe that the realization doctrine is the original sin of the federal income tax. It stands in diametric opposition to a Haig-Simons construction of income as including annual increases in wealth, without regard to whether those increases have been crystallized through a sale or exchange. As this section develops, it offers endless opportunities to engage in tax planning (including through simple indolence) that collectively have the effect, when compared to a Haig-Simons measure of income, of reducing the effective tax rate on capital income (income from investments) far below even the preferential tax rates available for long-term capital gains.

It is true that the purpose of the federal income tax is not simply to instantiate the Haig-Simons definition of income, but rather to use income as a proxy for ability to pay. But the realization doctrine arguably stands in the way of measuring ability to pay in any real sense, as this section's later discussion of nonrecourse borrowing shows.

To illustrate, consider taxpayer *A* who buys for $100,000 an asset that rises in value by $20,000 during the year. The asset is not sold, so the gain is not "realized" and is not taxed. Taxpayer *B* buys for $100,000 a similar asset that also rises in value; he sells for a profit of $20,000. Under the realization approach, *B*'s profit is taxable, even if *B* reinvests the $20,000, along with the $100,000, in some other asset. Taxpayer *C* receives a salary of $20,000, which he invests, along with $100,000 previously saved, in a third asset. Like *B*'s profit, *C*'s $20,000 salary will be fully taxed. In the end, each taxpayer experiences a similar $20,000 increase in wealth, yet *B* and *C* are taxed, while *A* escapes taxation (at least for now). Moreover, *A* can obtain the use of that $20,000 to fund current consumption by borrowing, secured by the asset. Fairness and economic rationality argue for treating all three taxpayers the same.

Practicality is generally thought to argue for nontaxation of *A*'s gain, on three grounds. First, the gain may be difficult to measure, particularly if the asset is not publicly traded. Second, the asset may not be liquid: *A* may not be able to reduce the asset to cash with which to pay a tax. The second argument often is expressed intuitively as the idea that the tax law should not force people to sell assets to pay their tax: The same intuition may motivate some objectors to the estate tax. What counterarguments might be offered? (A third argument, sounding more in fairness than practicality, is that this year's appreciation might be followed by next year's decline in value.)

Gain that has been *realized* through a sale or exchange must in turn generally be *recognized*: that is, actually reported on one's tax return. §1001. However, the Code contains a number of important nonrecognition rules governing specified forms of exchanges. If applicable, a *nonrecognition* rule generally provides that realized gain is not recognized in the year of the nonrecognition transaction. Instead, the unrealized gain generally is preserved for later taxation through the mechanism of preserving the taxpayer's basis in the old asset in some fashion. Gifts are one example of a nonrecognition transaction. "Like-kind exchanges," discussed later in this chapter, are another. Nonrecognition rules also are at the center of much corporate tax law practice, as they are necessary, for example, to permit a "tax-free" (more accurately, tax-deferred) merger between two companies. Section E, *infra*, returns to this.

1.   Legal Origins of the Realization Doctrine

Our first case, Eisner v. Macomber, is one of the most famous and significant decisions in the history of U.S. tax law. As noted in Chapter 1, the opinion's notoriety derives in part from its definition of income as comprising only "the gain derived from capital, from labor, or from both combined." In fairness, however, the United States Treasury raises relatively little tax revenue from home-run balls, cash found inside pianos, treasure trove, or treble damages in antitrust cases. This much-maligned definition by itself does less damage than is sometimes asserted, and in any event arguably it was dictum in the case, as the issue there was whether stock dividends in fact constituted gain derived from capital, an issue that could be resolved without concluding that only gain derived from labor or capital constituted "income" in the constitutional sense.

The case is much more important for its enthusiastic adoption of the requirement, as a condition for taxing gain, that the gain be "realized," that is, that there be something more than a mere increase in value. The Court holds, in fact, that the realization requirement is embedded in the Sixteenth Amendment.

The case was not decided in a vacuum. Following the case appear excerpts from an article written by Edwin Seligman, the dominant figure in tax theory at the time of the adoption of the income tax. Seligman had written his article in the hope that he would influence the court's reasoning—in which, as you will see, he plainly succeeded.

EISNER v. MACOMBER
252 U.S. 189 (1920)

Mr. Justice PITNEY delivered the opinion of the Court.

This case presents the question whether, by virtue of the Sixteenth Amendment, Congress has the power to tax, as income of the stockholder and without apportionment, a stock dividend made lawfully and in good faith against profits accumulated by the corporation since March 1, 1913.

It arises under the Revenue Act of September 8, 1916, c.463, 39 Stat. 756, et seq., which, in our opinion . . . plainly evinces the purpose of Congress to tax stock dividends as income.[17]

[In 1916, the taxpayer, Mrs. Myrtle H. Macomber, owned 2,200 shares of the common stock of Standard Oil Company of California. Each of her shares had a "par value" of $100 per share. In the era in which this case arose, par value was a significant financial and accounting concept; generally, it reflected the amount initially paid to the company for each share, or at least a minimum amount that could be paid; in the aggregate, the amounts paid as par value were labeled, on the company's books, "capital" or "capital stock," with any excess paid, over par value, called "capital surplus" or "paid in surplus" or something of the sort. The company over the years had earned profits substantially in excess of the amounts paid out as dividends on the common stock. Such retained earnings are recorded on the books of a company under a heading such as "earned surplus." By strict accounting convention, the company must show on its books assets corresponding in value to the par value plus the earned surplus (though this book value might be different from market value). Generally, dividends can be paid only to the extent of the earned surplus. In 1916, the company declared a 50 percent stock dividend. This meant that the company issued to each and every existing shareholder one new share for each two old shares, without cost to the shareholders. Accordingly, Mrs. Macomber

---

17. TITLE I. INCOME TAX *Part I. On Individuals.* Sec. 2(a) That, subject only to such exemptions and deductions as are hereinafter allowed, the net income of a taxable person shall include gains, profits, and income derived . . . , also from interest, rent, dividends, securities, or the transaction of any business carried on for gain or profit, or gains or profits and income derived from any source whatever: Provided, that the term "dividends" as used in this title shall be held to mean any distribution made or ordered to be made by a corporation, . . . out of its earnings or profits accrued since March first, nineteen hundred and thirteen, and payable to its shareholders, whether in cash or in stock of the corporation, . . . which stock dividend shall be considered income, to the amount of its cash value.

received 1,100 new shares to add to her 2,200 original shares. The issuance of the new shares required a bookkeeping adjustment by the company: For each new share issued, the par value of that share, $100, was transferred from the earned surplus account to the par value, or capital, account. That amount of earned surplus (undistributed profits) was then said to have been "capitalized." In some instances, such an adjustment might improve the creditworthiness of the company by limiting its freedom to pay dividends, though lenders of large sums can bargain for contractual limitations on dividend payments. Otherwise, the adjustment is purely a matter of changing bookkeeping labels. It has no effect whatsoever on underlying economic values or on operations.

According to the record in the case (at pages 4-5), the market value of Mrs. Macomber's shares before the stock dividend was $360 to $382 per share and after the stock dividend was $234 to $268 per share. In other words, the price of each share fell by about 30 to 35 percent, so that Mrs. Macomber's wealth was not significantly altered by the stock dividend. This is what one would expect, since the total value of the company, and her pro rata share of that total value, both remained the same. (Modern studies confirm the hypothesis that stock dividends do not increase wealth.)

The government sought to impose a tax on Mrs. Macomber based on the par value of the new shares, rather than the market value. However, of the amounts transferred by the company from earned surplus to capital, only 18.07 percent had arisen after the imposition of an income tax in 1913, and it was only this portion of the total that the government claimed to be taxable. Accordingly, the amount the government included in income was 18.07 percent of $100 multiplied by 1,100 shares, or $19,877. — Eds.]

[The Sixteenth Amendment states]:

The Congress shall have power to lay and collect taxes on incomes, from whatever source derived without apportionment among the several States, and without regard to any census or enumeration.

As repeatedly held, this did not extend the taxing power to new subjects, but merely removed the necessity which otherwise might exist for an apportionment among the States of taxes laid on income. . . .

A proper regard for its genesis, as well as its very clear language, requires also that this Amendment shall not be extended by loose construction, so as to repeal or modify, except as applied to income, those provisions of the Constitution that require an apportionment according to population for direct taxes upon property, real and personal. This limitation still has an appropriate and important function, and is not to be overridden by Congress or disregarded by the courts.

In order, therefore, that the clauses cited from Article I of the Constitution may have proper force and effect, save only as modified by the Amendment, and that the latter also may have proper effect, it becomes essential to distinguish between what is and what is not "income," as the term is there used; and to apply the distinction, as cases arise, according to truth and substance, without regard to form. Congress cannot by any definition it may adopt conclude the matter, since it cannot by legislation alter the Constitution, from which alone it derives its power to legislate, and within whose limitations alone that power can be lawfully exercised.

The fundamental relation of "capital" to "income" has been much discussed by economists, the former being likened to the tree or the land, the latter to the fruit or the crop; the former depicted as a reservoir supplied from springs, the latter as the outlet stream, to be measured by its flow during a period of time. For the present purpose we require only a clear definition of the term "income," as used in common speech, in order to determine its meaning in the Amendment; and, having formed also a correct judgment as to the nature of a stock dividend, we shall find it easy to decide the matter at issue.

After examining dictionaries in common use (Bouv. L.D.; Standard Dict.; Webster's Internat. Dict.; Century Dict.), we find little to add to the succinct definition adopted in two cases arising under the Corporation Tax Act of 1909 (Stratton's Independence v. Howbert, 231 U.S. 399, 415; Doyle v. Mitchell Bros. Co., 247 U.S. 179, 185) — "income may be defined as the gain derived from capital, from labor, or from both combined," provided it be understood to include profit gained through a sale or conversion of capital assets, to which it was applied in the *Doyle* case (pp. 183, 185).

Brief as it is, it indicates the characteristic and distinguishing attribute of income essential for a correct solution of the present controversy. The Government, although basing its argument upon the definition as quoted, placed chief emphasis upon the word "gain," which was extended to include a variety of meanings; while the significance of the next three words was either overlooked or misconceived. "*Derived—from—capital*"; — "the *gain—derived—from—capital*," etc. Here we have the essential matter: not a gain accruing to capital, not a *growth* or *increment* of value in the investment; but a gain, a profit, something of exchangeable value *proceeding from* the property, *severed from* the capital however invested or employed, and *coming in*, being "*derived*," that is, *received or drawn by* the recipient (the taxpayer) for his *separate use*, benefit and disposal; — *that is* income derived from property. Nothing else answers the description.

The same fundamental conception is clearly set forth in the Sixteenth Amendment — incomes *from* whatever *source derived* — the essential thought being expressed with a conciseness and lucidity entirely in harmony with the form and style of the Constitution.

Can a stock dividend, considering its essential character, be brought within the definition? To answer this, regard must be had to the nature of a corporation and the stockholder's relation to it. We refer, of course, to a corporation such as the one in the case at bar, organized for profit, and having a capital stock divided into shares to which a nominal or par value is attributed.

Certainly the interest of the stockholder is a capital interest, and his certificates of stock are but the evidence of it. They state the number of shares to which he is entitled and indicate their par value and how the stock may be transferred. . . . Short of liquidation, or until dividend declared, he has no right to withdraw any part of either capital or profits from the common enterprise; on the contrary, his interest pertains not to any part, divisible or indivisible, but to the entire assets, business, and affairs of the company. Nor is it the interest of an owner in the assets themselves, since the corporation has full title, legal and equitable, to the whole. The stockholder has the right to have the assets employed in the enterprise, with the incidental rights mentioned;

but, as stockholder, he has no right to withdraw, only the right to persist, subject to the risks of the enterprise, and looking only to dividends for his return. If he desires to dissociate himself from the company he can do so only by disposing of his stock.

For bookkeeping purposes, the company acknowledges a liability in form to the stockholders equivalent to the aggregate par value of their stock, evidenced by a "capital stock account." If profits have been made and not divided they create additional bookkeeping liabilities under the head of "profit and loss," "undivided profits," "surplus account," or the like. None of these, however, gives to the stockholders as a body, much less to any one of them, either a claim against the going concern for any particular sum of money, or a right to any particular portion of the assets or any share in them unless or until the directors conclude that dividends shall be made and a part of the company's assets segregated from the common fund for the purpose. The dividend normally is payable in money, under exceptional circumstances in some other divisible property; and when so paid, then only (excluding, of course, a possible advantageous sale of his stock or winding-up of the company) does the stockholder realize a profit or gain which becomes his separate property, and thus derive income from the capital that he or his predecessor has invested.

In the present case, the corporation had surplus and undivided profits invested in plant, property, and business, and required for the purposes of the corporation, amounting to about $45,000,000, in addition to outstanding capital stock of $50,000,000. In this the case is not extraordinary. The profits of a corporation, as they appear upon the balance sheet at the end of the year, need not be in the form of money on hand in excess of what is required to meet current liabilities and finance current operations of the company. Often, especially in a growing business, only a part, sometimes a small part, of the year's profits is in property capable of division; the remainder having been absorbed in the acquisition of increased plant, equipment, stock in trade, or accounts receivable, or in decrease of outstanding liabilities. . . .

A "stock dividend" shows that the company's accumulated profits have been capitalized, instead of distributed to the stockholders or retained as surplus available for distribution in money or in kind should opportunity offer. Far from being a realization of profits of the stockholder, it tends rather to postpone such realization, in that the fund represented by the new stock has been transferred from surplus to capital, and no longer is available for actual distribution.

The essential and controlling fact is that the stockholder has received nothing out of the company's assets for his separate use and benefit; on the contrary, every dollar of his original investment, together with whatever accretions and accumulations have resulted from employment of his money and that of the other stockholders in the business of the company, still remains the property of the company, and subject to business risks which may result in wiping out the entire investment. Having regard to the very truth of the matter, to substance and not to form, he has received nothing that answers the definition of income within the meaning of the Sixteenth Amendment. . . .

We are clear that not only does a stock dividend really take nothing from the property of the corporation and add nothing to that of the shareholder, but that the antecedent accumulation of profits evidenced thereby, while indicating that the shareholder is the richer because of an increase of his capital, at the same time shows he has not realized or received any income in the transaction.

It is said that a stockholder may sell the new shares acquired in the stock dividend; and so he may, if he can find a buyer. It is equally true that if he does sell, and in doing so realizes a profit, such profit, like any other, is income, and so far as it may have arisen since the Sixteenth Amendment is taxable by Congress without apportionment. The same would be true were he to sell some of his original shares at a profit. But if a shareholder sells dividend stock he necessarily disposes of a part of his capital interest, just as if he should sell a part of his old stock, either before or after the dividend. What he retains no longer entitles him to the same proportion of future dividends as before the sale. His part in the control of the company likewise is diminished. Thus, if one holding $60,000 out of a total $100,000 of the capital stock of a corporation should receive in common with other stockholders a 50 percent stock dividend, and should sell his part, he thereby would be reduced from a majority to a minority stockholder, having six-fifteenths instead of six-tenths of the total stock outstanding. A corresponding and proportionate decrease in capital interest and in voting power would befall a minority holder should he sell dividend stock; it being in the nature of things impossible for one to dispose of any part of such an issue without a proportionate disturbance of the distribution of the entire capital stock, and a like diminution of the seller's comparative voting power—that "right preservative of rights" in the control of a corporation. Yet, without selling, the shareholder, unless possessed of other resources, has not the wherewithal to pay an income tax upon the dividend stock. Nothing could more clearly show that to tax a stock dividend is to tax a capital increase, and not income, than this demonstration that in the nature of things it requires conversion of capital in order to pay the tax. . . .

We have no doubt of the power or duty of a court to look through the form of the corporation and determine the question of the stockholder's right, in order to ascertain whether he has received income taxable by Congress without apportionment. But, looking through the form, we cannot disregard the essential truth disclosed; ignore the substantial difference between corporation and stockholder; treat the entire organization as unreal; look upon stockholders as partners, when they are not such; treat them as having in equity a right to a partition of the corporate assets, when they have none; and indulge the fiction that they have received and realized a share of the profits of the company which in truth they have neither received nor realized. We must treat the corporation as a substantial entity separate from the stockholder, not only because such is the practical fact but because it is only by recognizing such separateness that any dividend—even one paid in money or property—can be regarded as income of the stockholder. Did we regard corporation and stockholders as altogether identical, there would be no income except as the corporation acquired it; and while this would be taxable against the corporation as income under appropriate provisions of law, the individual stockholders could not be separately and additionally taxed with respect to their several shares even when divided, since if there were entire identity between them and the company they could not be regarded as receiving anything from it, any more than if one's money were to be removed from one pocket to another.

Conceding that the mere issue of a stock dividend makes the recipient no richer than before, the Government nevertheless contends that the new certificates measure the extent to which the gains accumulated by the corporation have made him the richer. There are two insuperable difficulties with this: In the first place, it would depend upon how long he had held the stock whether the stock dividend indicated the extent to which he had been enriched by the operations of the company; unless he had held it throughout such operations the measure would not hold true. Secondly, and more important for present purposes, enrichment through increase in value of capital investment is not income in any proper meaning of the term.

The complaint contains averments respecting the market prices of stock such as plaintiff held, based upon sales before and after the stock dividend, tending to show that the receipt of the additional shares did not substantially change the market value of her entire holdings. This tends to show that in this instance market quotations reflected intrinsic values—a thing they do not always do. But we regard the market prices of the securities as an unsafe criterion in an inquiry such as the present, when the question must be, not what will the thing sell for, but what is it in truth and in essence.

It is said there is no difference in principle between a simple stock dividend and a case where stockholders use money received as cash dividends to purchase additional stock contemporaneously issued by the corporation. But an actual cash dividend, with a real option to the stockholder either to keep the money for his own or to reinvest it in new shares, would be as far removed as possible from a true stock dividend, such as the one we have under consideration, where nothing of value is taken from the company's assets and transferred to the individual ownership of the several stockholders and thereby subjected to their disposal.

Upon the second argument,[18] the Government, . . . virtually abandoning the contention that a stock dividend increases the interest of the stockholder or otherwise enriches him, insisted as an alternative that by the true construction of the Act of 1916 the tax is imposed not upon the stock dividend but rather upon the stockholder's share of the undivided profits previously accumulated by the corporation; the tax being levied as a matter of convenience at the time such profits become manifest through the stock dividend. If so construed, would the act be constitutional?

That Congress has power to tax shareholders upon their property interests in the stock of corporations is beyond question; and that such interest might be valued in view of the condition of the company, including its accumulated and undivided profits, is equally clear. But that this would be taxation of property because of ownership, and hence would require apportionment under the provisions of the Constitution, is settled beyond peradventure by previous decisions of this court. . . .

---

18. [Eisner v. Macomber was argued in 1919 and reargued by order of the Court in 1920.—EDS.]

Thus, from every point of view, we are brought irresistibly to the conclusion that neither under the Sixteenth Amendment nor otherwise has Congress power to tax without apportionment a true stock dividend made lawfully and in good faith, or the accumulated profits behind it, as income of the stockholder. The Revenue Act of 1916, in so far as it imposes a tax upon the stockholder because of such dividend, contravenes the provisions of Article I, §2, cl. 3, and Article I, §9, cl. 4, of the Constitution, and to this extent is invalid notwithstanding the Sixteenth Amendment.

Judgment affirmed.

Mr. Justice HOLMES, dissenting. . . .

I think that the word "incomes" in the Sixteenth Amendment should be read in "a sense most obvious to the common understanding at the time of its adoption." . . . For it was for public adoption that it was proposed. McCulloch v. Maryland, 4 Wheat. 316, 407. The known purpose of this Amendment was to get rid of nice questions as to what might be direct taxes, and I cannot doubt that most people not lawyers would suppose when they voted for it that they put a question like the present to rest. I am of opinion that the Amendment justifies the tax. . . .

Mr. Justice DAY concurs in this opinion.

Mr. Justice BRANDEIS, dissenting, delivered the following opinion, in which Mr. Justice CLARKE concurred.

Financiers, with the aid of lawyers, devised long ago two different methods by which a corporation can, without increasing its indebtedness, keep for corporate purposes accumulated profits, and yet, in effect, distribute these profits among its stockholders. One method is a simple one. The capital stock is increased; the new stock is paid up with the accumulated profits; and the new shares of paid-up stock are then distributed among the stockholders pro rata as a dividend. If the stockholder prefers ready money to increasing his holding of the stock in the company, he sells the new stock received as a dividend. The other method is slightly more complicated. Arrangements are made for an increase of stock to be offered to stockholders pro rata at par and, at the same time, for the payment of a cash dividend equal to the amount which the stockholder will be required to pay to the company, if he avails himself of the right to subscribe for his pro rata of the new stock. If the stockholder takes the new stock, as is expected, he may endorse the dividend check received to the corporation and thus pay for the new stock. In order to ensure that all the new stock so offered will be taken, the price at which it is offered is fixed far below what it is believed will be its market value. If the stockholder prefers ready money to an increase of his holdings of stock, he may sell his right to take new stock pro rata, which is evidenced by an assignable instrument. In that event the purchaser of the rights repays to the corporation, as the subscription price of the new stock, an amount equal to that which it had paid as a cash dividend to the stockholder.

Both of these methods of retaining accumulated profits while in effect distributing them as a dividend had been in common use in the United States for many years prior to the adoption of the Sixteenth Amendment. They were recognized equivalents. Whether a particular corporation employed one or the other method was determined sometimes by requirements of the law under which the corporation was organized; sometimes it was determined by preferences of the individual officials of the corporation; and sometimes by stock market conditions. Whichever method was employed the resultant distribution of the new stock was commonly referred to as a stock dividend. . . .

It is conceded that if the stock dividend paid to Mrs. Macomber had been made by the more complicated method . . . , that is, issuing rights to take new stock pro rata and paying to each stockholder simultaneously a dividend in cash sufficient in amount to enable him to pay for this pro rata of new stock to be purchased—the dividend so paid to him would have been taxable as income, whether he retained the cash or whether he returned it to the corporation in payment for his pro rata of new stock. But it is contended that, because the simple method was adopted of having the new stock issued direct to the stock-holders as paid-up stock, the new stock is not to be deemed income, whether she retained it or converted it into cash by sale. If such a different result can flow merely from the difference in the method pursued, it must be because Congress is without power to tax as income of the stockholder either the stock received under the latter method or the proceeds of its sale; for Congress has, by the provisions in the Revenue Act of 1916, expressly declared its purpose to make stock dividends, by whichever method paid, taxable as income. . . .

It surely is not clear that the enactment exceeds the power granted by the Sixteenth Amendment. And, as this court has so often said, the high prerogative of declaring an act of Congress invalid, should never be exercised except in a clear case. "It is but a decent respect due to the wisdom, the integrity and the patriotism of the legislative body, by which any law is passed, to presume in favor of its validity, until its violation of the Constitution is proved beyond all reasonable doubt." Ogden v. Saunders, 12 Wheat. 213, 270.

Mr. Justice CLARKE concurs in this opinion.

NOTES AND QUESTIONS

1. *Introduction.* The government sought to justify the taxation of Mrs. Macomber's stock dividend on at least three related grounds. First, the government argued that the distribution of the stock dividend increased Mrs. Macomber's wealth. Second, the government argued that the company's accumulation of profits increased Mrs. Macomber's wealth and that part of that increase was realized through the distribution of the stock dividend. Finally, the government argued that the company's accumulation of profits increased Mrs. Macomber's wealth and that the increase in wealth could be taxed at any time. Broadly construed, the last argument would allow an annual tax on all property appreciation, whether or not such appreciation had been realized in the form of a sale or a cash distribution.

Most of the Court's opinion deals with the first two arguments, which are explored in Notes 2 and 3. The larger question raised by the case—the possibility of an annual tax on unrealized appreciation—is discussed in Note 5.

(a) You and your two friends are about to enjoy a pizza cut into six slices — two slices for each of you. Suddenly three more hungry friends arrive and stare longingly at the pizza. "Not to worry!" you exclaim, "I'll just slice the pizza into twelve slices, and we can all still enjoy two slices." Are you as satiated as you would have been if the three interlopers had not arrived?

(b) How is a stock dividend different from the pizza cut into smaller slices? Imagine that three of you own all the stock of a corporation in equal shares, 200 shares each. You three started the company by each investing $20/share ($4,000 total). The company is now worth $18,000 in total.

The corporation pays a stock dividend of 100 shares to each of you. You have pieces of paper labeled "300 shares," but what matters is not the number of share certificates or number of shares, but rather the fact that you owned one-third of the company before the stock dividend, and one-third of the company afterwards. How are you better off for the stock dividend? More specifically, how much was each share worth before the stock dividend? How much is each share worth after the dividend? How has the aggregate value of your invest-ment changed by virtue of the stock dividend?

(c) Perhaps the answer to (b) lies in the fact that it is asking the wrong ques-tion. Of course a stock dividend without more does not create income, any more than slicing the pizza into twelve slices creates more pizza. But perhaps a stock dividend is just a convenient time for the sleeping dog of taxation to wake up and bark that there has been income all along, in the form of the increasing value of the stock, and the stock dividend is simply the occasion to tax that increase in wealth, to that extent.

(d) Did the government make the argument suggested in (c)?

(e) The court assumes that a cash dividend is taxable income to the share-holder who receives it. That is, because corporations were by the early twen-tieth century understood to be juridical persons separate from their owners, it must follow that corporate income cannot be taxed directly to corporate owners, but only to the corporation itself. Similarly, dividends are income to a shareholder, even though she is not one dollar richer in fact for having received them. That is, cash dividends just move existing wealth from one of your pockets to another. The dividend does not create wealth, although it does separate some of your wealth from your continuing investment.

2. *Analysis of stock dividends.* (a) If the government had prevailed in Eisner v. Macomber, what effect do you suppose the decision would have had on the policies of corporations on the issuance of stock dividends? What do you sup-pose Justice Brandeis, who, in his days as a practitioner, had been an expert on matters of this sort, would have advised his corporate clients? If he had been asked how to advise Congress on the advisability of taxing stock dividends, what do you suppose he would have said?

(b) One reason sometimes given for issuing stock dividends is to provide shareholders with tangible evidence of the success of the corporation. Would a piece of parchment entitled "declaration of success," with a gold seal and a blue ribbon, do just as well?

(c) The Court refers to the fact that if Mrs. Macomber had sold her dividend shares she would have reduced her fractional voting power (control) in the company. How important do you suppose this would have been to her?

3. *Stock dividends versus cash dividends.* Treating a cash dividend as invariably income to a shareholder in fact can create taxable income where no economic income exists. Imagine that you buy 100 shares of Alphabet Soup Corp. for $50 per share ($5,000 total). The very next day the company declares a dividend of $2 per share, and you receive a check for $200. No income has accrued in an economic sense during your brief holding period; because markets are rational, the price of Alphabet Soup Corp. stock will drop to $48 immediately after the dividend, and so the sum of your investments remains $50, but from Eisner v. Macomber to the present it has been assumed that you have a taxable $200 dividend. See §§61(a)(7) and 316(a). Is this fair? Again, perhaps this is because the wrong question is being asked?

As an incidental matter, overlooking the fact that stock prices decline to reflect the consequences of a dividend is one of the many conceptual errors embedded in Seligman's influential article set out *infra*.

4. *Depreciation.* Neither the Eisner v. Macomber Court nor any other case has thought that the realization doctrine was an impediment to deducting the "inchoate" or "unseparated" *diminution* in value represented by depreciation. That is, an asset may be depreciated (whether under the old facts and circumstances test or modern ACRS) without the requirement of a realization event, like a sale. Indeed, a taxpayer can claim tax depreciation deductions even if the asset in fact is increasing in value. As a result, realization is vitally important when it comes to taxing increases in an asset's value, but not at all necessary to provide what in substance are loss deductions (depreciation) for declines in value of "real" (non-financial) assets that under ACRS are arbitrary in amount and that may be wholly counterfactual. Can you explain this asymmetry in outcomes?

5. *Policy: Taxing unrealized appreciation.* (a) What are the objections to taxing shareholders on amounts earned by the corporation, regardless of distribution? This is how partners are taxed. In a partnership, the decision whether to distribute profits is one that is made by a majority of the partners, but in the absence of an agreement to the contrary, any partner can withdraw from the partnership (and be paid his or her pro rata share of the value of the partnership) at any time. Should this freedom to withdraw matter? If so, what if the partnership agreement makes withdrawal very costly? If the law were to provide for taxation of shareholders on corporate profits regardless of distribution of dividends, how do you suppose corporations would adjust?

(b) Another possibility would be to tax people like Mrs. Macomber every year on their "paper" profits—that is, on the unrealized appreciation in the market value of their shares of stock at year-end—with a corresponding deduction for unrealized losses. (Today this generally is described as "move to market" taxation.) The principal objections to taxing unrealized gains have been (i) the potential difficulties of valuation, and (ii) the fact that the taxpayer might have difficulty raising the cash to pay the tax. How forceful are these objections as applied to Mrs. Macomber and people like her? Would it have been difficult to value the appreciation in her holdings? Do you think she would have found it difficult to obtain the cash to pay the tax?

(c) The principle that unrealized appreciation should not be taxed is no longer thought to be embedded in the Constitution, but it is thoroughly embedded in present tax rules. Those rules, which will be examined in the remainder of this chapter, create serious problems of tax fairness, or equity, of economic incentive, and of administration. The problem of horizontal equity is illustrated by comparison of a person whose wealth increases by $100,000 from receipt of a salary, and who must pay a tax on that amount, with a person whose wealth increases by the same amount through a rise in the value of her property holdings and who pays no tax on that increase. The discrepancy in tax treatment is particularly disturbing where the property can easily be sold or can serve as collateral for a loan. Nontaxation of appreciation may also distort investment decisions. At the margin, taxpayers will prefer investments that produce gain in the form of unrealized appreciation. Finally, the current regime raises serious definitional issues: At what point has appreciation been realized? As you read the cases in this chapter you may find it useful to think about how a regime that taxed unrealized appreciation might simplify the law.

6. *The present law.* The rule of Eisner v. Macomber is now embodied in §305(a) ("Gross income does not include the amount of any distribution of the stock of a corporation made by such corporation to its shareholders with respect to its stock"), with several important limitations set forth in §305(b). The most easily understood limitation is that a stock dividend is taxable if the shareholder had the option to take cash or other property in lieu of that dividend. §305(b)(1). Other rules in §305(b) cover situations in which the distribution results in some change in the nature of the shareholder's initial investment or proportional interest. These statutory provisions are covered in detail in more advanced courses on the taxation of corporations and their shareholders.

7. *Basis and holding period.* Under Reg. §1.307-1(a), the taxpayer's total basis of the old shares is allocated between the old and the new shares in accordance with relative fair market values after the distribution of the stock dividend. In a case like *Macomber* (where the new shares were identical to the old shares), this means simply that the total basis is allocated equally to all shares, so each share, old and new, winds up with the same basis. The holding period is important in distinguishing between long-term and short-term capital gains. The rule, under §1223(5), is that the new shares will be deemed to have been acquired at the time when the old shares were acquired.

A special rule (Reg. §1.307-2) provides that if the fair market value of a stock dividend is less than 15 percent of the fair market value of the old stock, the new stock takes a tax basis of zero, unless the shareholder elects to apportion her basis. In distant days, affluent shareholders regularly relied on this rule to gift zero basis stock to children and grandchildren; small scale stock dividends are unusual, however, in the modern capital markets.

8. *The "realization" concept today.* Notwithstanding general rejection of the constitutional principle of Eisner v. Macomber, the realization requirement remains important in our tax law. We do not generally tax unrealized gains in property values, perhaps because annual property appraisals are difficult; or because the taxpayer may not have the money to pay the tax on such gains; or because unrealized gains in one year may turn into unrealized losses in another year. For better or for worse, the current U.S. income tax depends on

"transactions" or "taxable events" and thus is not strictly a tax on "income" as an economist might define that term.

ARE STOCK DIVIDENDS INCOME?
Edwin Seligman, 9 Am. Econ. Rev. 517 (1919)

Among the difficult problems raised by our income tax is that of the nature of stock dividends. . . . The question now arises [in Eisner v. Macomber, under consideration] whether the act of 1916 is constitutional in declaring stock dividends to be income. . . . We have accordingly deemed it wise to consider the problem purely from the economic point of view. . . .

The most natural definition of income is all wealth that comes in. This, however, obviously is entirely too vague. The things that come in are fundamentally utilities and services. Income is the inflow of satisfactions from services and utilities. . . .

[Income] denotes a flow or succession of such satisfactions, expressed in money or money's worth, during a period of time. . . . But whether there be one or many, we think of their coming in during a period of time. The quality of periodicity is essential. . . .

Since the real wealth of an individual . . . consists of this inflow of satisfactions that we call income, it is clear that the satisfaction must be realized before we can predicate of it the quality of income. . . . [U]nrealized or imaginary income is not an income at all. . . . Realization is a necessary attribute of income. . . .

The next characteristic of income is that it is something distinct and separate from the person or thing that affords the income. . . . [T]he fruit separated from the tree is the income from the tree. . . .

[As opposed to] the income, which, as we have seen, is the satisfaction afforded by services or utilities, is the capital. . . . [Capital] is a store of such future or inchoate satisfactions. . . . The capital possesses a value which reflects our estimate of the succession of anticipated utilities or income. . . .

The real distinction between income and capital as the embodiment or the measurement of wealth, therefore, is that income represents a flow or stream of utilities or money, and capital represents a fund or stock of utilities and money. The flow or stream is periodic; it represents a succession of utilities or income during a period of time. The fund or stock is the accumulation of such utilities or money at an instant of time. . . .

[T]he owner of a herd of cattle may decide not to sell his yearlings [sic]. Although they may be merged with the herd, however, they are none the less separate; for it makes no difference whether he keeps them in a distinct enclosure or lets them pasture with their mothers. The increment in the value of the herd is income, because it is both realized and separated. . . .

The income of a forest is the annual yield of timber. The trees of a certain size may be cut yearly, leaving the forest intact. . . . If the trees are not cut, the forest becomes more valuable—up to a certain point at least. What would have been income has been converted into capital increment. But this capital increment is not income, because it has not been separated and because it is not capable of separation if uncut. When the trees are ultimately cut, the gain undoubtedly becomes income. Up to that time, however, the increase in the value of the forest is only inchoate income. What is done with the particular trees therefore determines whether they are income or capital. To the owner of the forest there is an increment of wealth in each case; but from the economic point of view there is a distinction between the increase in the form of income and the increase in the form of capital. . . .

If the income has been actually realized and separated and then again added to, or reconverted into, the capital, it remains none the less income although called capital increment. But if the income is simply unconsumed or postponed, without being actually realized and separated, the resulting capital increment is not income. What we are dealing with in such a case is inchoate, not real, income. Realizability is not realization; separability is not separation.

It would not be fair to give Seligman his due without offering his nemesis, Henry Simons, the opportunity to offer his response to the arguments of Seligman and the Court in Eisner v. Macomber. The excerpt that follows is highly compacted; the complete discussion is much funnier and less kind than this selection might suggest.

EXCERPT FROM *PERSONAL INCOME TAXATION*
Henry Simons (1938) (pp. 80-88)

We turn now to brief consideration of the familiar criterion of realization. A standard manual on our federal income tax quotes Professor Haig's definition of income and then remarks: "It should include the word realized"— as though the omission were only a careless oversight! This view is widely held by accountants, by the courts, and even by some economists. It derives clearly enough from the conventional practices of financial accounting. The accountant, faced with problems of valuation for which data are often meager, has developed and followed religiously a rule-of-thumb procedure which sacrifices relevance to "accuracy." Instead of attempting the best estimates which can be made, he is usually content to employ figures already available in his accounts and thus to minimize demands upon mere judgment. . . .

If all business ventures were initiated and completed within the fiscal period, the realization criterion would lead to no serious confusion. But, in a world where ventures often have neither beginning nor end within the lives of interested parties, it is hard to argue that one may grow richer indefinitely without increasing one's income. . . .

One realizes on assets; one converts assets from one form into another; and one may "realize" cash, potatoes, or chicken pox. But gain simply is not something which may be delivered at one's doorstep. One may gain without realizing and realize without gaining; and, if either is essential to the existence of income, the other must be excluded. Common sense and established usage suggest that gain is the true *sine qua non;* but much of the current discussion of the income concept, especially by the courts, may be regarded as emphasizing realization to the exclusion of gain. If a corporation has undistributed income, then [dividend] distributions are treated as income to shareholders on that evidence alone.

In emphasis upon the necessity of realization, Professor Seligman has out-done even the accountants. Seeking to show how an economist would dispose of the stock-dividend problem—and his assistance evidently was not spurned by the Supreme Court—he proceeds to define income in such manner as to exclude stock dividends and then moves merrily to his conclusion. Professor Seligman's definition appears to be both original and unique; but he has evi-dently no misgivings as to the finality of his contribution, for he says:

> When income taxes were first introduced, economic science was only in its infancy and the above analysis of the relations between capital and income had not yet been worked out. We therefore find a considerable confusion. . . .

He begins by defining income as satisfactions. "Income is therefore fun-damentally pleasure or benefit income." On the next page, "Income denotes any inflow of satisfactions which can be parted with for money." So far income would seem to be consumption. Before long, however, income becomes some-thing more familiar—savings being slipped in quite unceremoniously.

Seligman's differentiation between the growth of a herd and the growth of a forest is one of the less obscure features of his argument. . . . Thus, the gain [in the value of the forest], because not separated, becomes capital; yet the capital, in turn, becomes income when the separation is finally effected. Income depends upon the number of trees cut—but only provided they do not cut too many! Certainly the phrase "inchoate income" deserves a prominent place among the curiosities of economic terminology.

Professor Seligman's insistence both upon "realization" and upon deprecia-tion deductions seems to involve serious logical difficulties. All credit items must be realized; but the requirements for admission on the debit side are much less exacting. Surely no definition of income which admits "mere value changes" only in one direction can well escape the fate of appearing ridicu-lous. . . . Of course, it goes without saying that, after dragging in an amazing variety of income concepts and choosing useful attributes from different ones at will, Seligman finds little difficulty in throwing out an item like stock divi-dends, which was almost defenseless from the start.

2.   Some Implications of the Realization Doctrine in Practice

One important implication of the realization doctrine is the "lock-in" effect. Because we use realization to define income, an investor with unrealized gains on an investment can defer his tax liability by choosing not to sell. The result in practice is that investors hold onto stock that they really would prefer to sell, in order to reduce the present value of their tax liability on sale. And by holding to their death, affluent taxpayers with a fondness for their heirs can escape income tax entirely. As pointed out earlier, this leads to a deadweight loss—people are induced to behave in a way that is contrary to how they would behave in a world without taxes.

The realization doctrine thus turns capital gains taxation into a wholly volun-tary tax. In practice, taxpayers often adopt as a rule of thumb selling the losers at year-end, and letting the winners ride into the next year ("loss harvesting"). The more general term for this phenomenon of taxpayers minimizing their tax liabilities through control over the timing of gains and losses is "cherry picking."

In response, Congress has been required to develop all sorts of rules to limit the payoff to cherry picking. The most important of these is that capital losses from selling investments cannot be used as deductions against ordinary income (like salary). In the field of financial products taxation, the anti-cherry picking rules get more and more abstruse.

The capital gains tax is not simply a voluntary tax, it is effectively an *excise tax*, because the nominal tax rate stays constant once the long-term holding period is satisfied. That is, a taxpayer's annual effective tax rate goes down the longer she holds a capital asset, because the same tax rate is applied to more taxable years. Imagine that you can invest in a corporation that itself pays no corporate income tax, and which is profitable. The longer you hold the investment, the more dramatically your annual effective tax rate declines, because the value of the firm is compounding annually at a tax-free rate, while the ultimate tax cost of extracting your economic gain remains a fixed percentage of that compounded growth. As seen in our earlier discussion of the time value of money, your after-tax annual profits compound at a tax-free rate of return.

Mark-to-market taxation eliminates the lock-in effect as effectively as does a world without the income tax, because realization is irrelevant to income measurement under mark-to-market taxation (except to the extent of it eliminates valuation disputes). Many academics have written articles urging Congress to make mark-to-market taxation mandatory for all taxpayers in respect of publicly traded financial instruments like stocks and bonds. The idea is that this eliminates all gaming, more neatly accords with Haig-Simons principles, and is not troublesome from a liquidity perspective because the instruments are publicly traded, and so can always be sold to pay a tax bill. Such a rule has its own issues, however, because it would create new tensions between mark-to-market and realization-based investments, particularly when one was used to hedge the other.[19] Further, it would encourage successful start-up firms to remain privately held, to avoid coming within the strictures of shareholder mark-to-market taxation. To date, Congress has shown little interest in following up on this, except in respect of securities dealers and professional traders.

Finally, and as discussed in subsection 4, *infra*, the realization barrier is not an impediment to current consumption, once opportunities to borrow are taken into account. So current law facilitates the ability of sophisticated taxpayers quite literally to eat their cake and have it too.

3.   The Decline of Realization as a Constitutional Requirement

Understanding the role of the realization requirement in the U.S. tax system requires understanding the interplay between Congress and the

---

19. Kleinbard and Evans, *The Role of Mark-to-Market Taxation in a Realization Based Tax System*, 75 Taxes 788 (1997).

judiciary, as well as having some sense of the political history of the U.S. Supreme Court. In the same way that the New Deal Court in the late 1930s began chipping away at the Court's more conservative constitutional jurisprudence from the *Lochner* era, so too did the Court begin to depart from its restrictive understanding of "income" within the meaning of the Sixteenth Amendment. The case reproduced below, Helvering v. Bruun, was decided at a time when a majority of the Court's members had been appointed by President Franklin Roosevelt. It marks an important midway point in the Court's march away from its constitutional holding in Eisner v. Macomber (1920) and toward the view of congressional primacy in tax matters endorsed in *Glenshaw Glass* (1955). Significantly, however, the decline of realization *as a constitutional requirement* did not translate into a decline of realization principles in U.S. tax law. Indeed, as is further discussed in Note 6 following the case, two years after the Court's decision Congress passed legislation overruling *Bruun*.

HELVERING v. BRUUN
309 U.S. 461 (1940)

Mr. Justice ROBERTS delivered the opinion of the Court.

The controversy had its origin in the petitioner's [the tax collector's] assertion that the [taxpayer/lessor] realized taxable gain from the forfeiture of a leasehold, the tenant having erected a new building upon the premises. The court below held that no income had been realized. . . .

The Board of Tax Appeals made no independent findings. The cause was submitted upon a stipulation of facts. From this it appears that on July 1, 1915, the respondent, as owner, leased a lot of land and the building thereon for a term of ninety-nine years.

The lease provided that the lessee might, at any time, upon giving bond to secure rentals accruing in the two ensuing years, remove or tear down any building on the land, provided that no building should be removed or torn down after the lease became forfeited, or during the last three and one-half years of the term. The lessee was to surrender the land, upon termination of the lease, with all buildings and improvements thereon.

In 1929 the tenant demolished and removed the existing building and constructed a new one which had a useful life of not more than fifty years. July 1, 1933, the lease was cancelled for default in payment of rent and taxes and the respondent regained possession of the land and building.

The parties stipulated

> that as at said date, July 1, 1933, the building which had been erected upon said premises by the lessee had a fair market value of $64,245.68 and that the [lessor's] unamortized cost of the old building, which was removed from the premises in 1929 to make way for the new building, was $12,811.43, thus leaving a net fair market value [net "gain"] as at July 1, 1933, of $51,434.25, for the aforesaid new building erected upon the premises by the lessee.

On the basis of these facts, the petitioner determined that in 1933 the respondent realized a net gain of $51,434.25. The Board overruled his determination and the Circuit Court of Appeals affirmed the Board's decision.

The course of administrative practice and judicial decision in respect of the question presented has not been uniform. In 1917 the Treasury ruled that the adjusted value of improvements installed upon leased premises is income to the lessor upon the termination of the lease. The ruling was incorporated in two succeeding editions of the Treasury Regulations. In 1919 the Circuit Court of Appeals for the Ninth Circuit held in Miller v. Gearin, 258 F. 225, that the regulation was invalid as the gain, if taxable at all, must be taxed as of the year when the improvements were completed.

The regulations were accordingly amended to impose a tax upon the gain in the year of completion of the improvements, measured by their anticipated value at the termination of the lease and discounted for the duration of the lease. Subsequently the regulations permitted the lessor to spread the depreciated value of the improvements over the remaining life of the lease, reporting an aliquot part each year, with provision that, upon premature termination, a tax should be imposed upon the excess of the then value of the improvements over the amount theretofore returned.

In 1935 the Circuit Court of Appeals for the Second Circuit decided in Hewitt Realty Co. v. Commissioner, 76 F.2d 880, that a landlord received no taxable income in a year, during the term of the lease, in which his tenant erected a building on the leased land. The court, while recognizing that the lessor need not receive money to be taxable, based its decision that no taxable gain was realized in that case on the fact that the improvement was not portable or detachable from the land, and if removed would be worthless except as bricks, iron, and mortar. . . .

This decision invalidated the regulations then in force.

In 1938 this court decided M. E. Blatt Co. v. United States, 305 U.S. 267. There, in connection with the execution of a lease, landlord and tenant mutually agreed that each should make certain improvements to the demised premises and that those made by the tenant should become and remain the property of the landlord. The Commissioner valued the improvements as of the date they were made, allowed depreciation thereon to the termination of the leasehold, divided the depreciated value by the number of years the lease had to run, and found the landlord taxable for each year's aliquot portion thereof. His action was sustained by the Court of Claims. The judgment was reversed on the ground that the added value could not be considered rental accruing over the period of the lease; that the facts found by the Court of Claims did not support the conclusion of the Commissioner as to the value to be attributed to the improvements after a use throughout the term of the lease; and that, in the circumstances disclosed, any enhancement in the value of the realty in the tax year was not income realized by the lessor within the Revenue Act.

The circumstances of the instant case differentiate it from the *Blatt* and *Hewitt* cases; but the petitioner's contention that gain was realized when the respondent, through forfeiture of the lease, obtained untrammeled title, possession and control of the premises, with the added increment of value added by the new building, runs counter to the decision in the *Miller* case and to the reasoning in the *Hewitt* case.

The respondent insists that the realty—a capital asset at the date of the execution of the lease—remained such throughout the term and after its expiration; that improvements affixed to the soil became part of the realty indistinguishably blended in the capital asset; that such improvements cannot be separately valued or treated as received in exchange for the improvements which were on the land at the date of the execution of the lease; that they are, therefore, in the same category as improvements added by the respondent to his land, or accruals of value due to extraneous and adventitious circumstances. Such added value, it is argued, can be considered capital gain only upon the owner's disposition of the asset. The position is that the economic gain consequent upon the enhanced value of the recaptured asset is not gain derived from capital or realized within the meaning of the Sixteenth Amendment and may not, therefore, be taxed without apportionment.

We hold that the petitioner was right in assessing the gain as realized in 1933.

We might rest our decision upon the narrow issue presented by the terms of the stipulation. It does not appear what kind of a building was erected by the tenant or whether the building was readily removable from the land. It is not stated whether the difference in the value between the building removed and that erected in its place accurately reflects an increase in the value of land and building considered as a single estate in land. On the facts stipulated, without more, we should not be warranted in holding that the presumption of the correctness of the Commissioner's determination has been overborne.

The respondent insists, however, that the stipulation was intended to assert that the sum of $51,434.25 was the measure of the resulting enhancement in value of the real estate at the date of the cancellation of the lease. The petitioner seems not to contest this view. Even upon this assumption we think that gain in the amount named was realized by the respondent in the year of repossession.

The respondent cannot successfully contend that the definition of gross income in [§61(a) of the 1986 Code] is not broad enough to embrace the gain in question. That definition follows closely the Sixteenth Amendment. Essentially the respondent's position is that the Amendment does not permit the taxation of such gain without apportionment amongst the states. He relies upon what was said in Hewitt Realty Co. v. Commissioner, supra, and upon expressions found in the decisions of this court dealing with the taxability of stock dividends to the effect that gain derived from capital must be something of exchangeable value proceeding from property, severed from the capital, however invested or employed, and received by the recipient for his separate use, benefit, and disposal. He emphasizes the necessity that the gain be separate from the capital and separately disposable. These expressions, however, were used to clarify the distinction between an ordinary dividend and a stock dividend. They were meant to show that in the case of a stock dividend, the stockholder's interest in the corporate assets after receipt of the dividend was the same as and inseverable from that which he owned before the dividend was declared. We think they are not controlling here.

While it is true that economic gain is not always taxable as income, it is settled that the realization of gain need not be in cash derived from the sale of an asset. Gain may occur as a result of exchange of property, payment of the taxpayer's indebtedness, relief from a liability, or other profit realized from the completion of a transaction. The fact that the gain is a portion of the value of property received by the taxpayer in the transaction does not negate its realization.

Here, as a result of a business transaction, the respondent received back his land with a new building on it, which added an ascertainable amount to its value. It is not necessary to recognition of taxable gain that he should be able to sever the improvement begetting the gain from his original capital. If that were necessary, no income could arise from the exchange of property; whereas such gain has always been recognized as realized taxable gain.

Judgment reversed.

THE CHIEF JUSTICE concurs in the result in view of the terms of the stipulation of facts.

Mr. Justice MCREYNOLDS took no part in the decision of this case.

NOTES AND QUESTIONS

1. *The original lease transaction.* When Mr. Bruun leased the land in 1915, did he have rental income in the amount of the present value of the expected future rental payments to be made during the entire term of the lease?

2. *The events of 1929.* When the tenant in 1929 tore down the old building and constructed the new one, why did Bruun not have income for tax purposes in an amount equal to the difference between the value of the new building and his basis in the old one? Apart from taxes, is it likely that the construction of the building increased the value of his investment?

3. *Buildings intended as rent.* (a) Suppose that the owner of land agrees to allow a tenant to occupy the land "rent free" for ten years if the tenant constructs a building with an expected life of twenty years, a value at the completion of construction of $400,000, and an expected value at the end of the ten-year lease of $200,000. If income is realized in this situation, when and how much? Which of the possibilities discussed by the Court in *Bruun* makes the most sense? See Reg. §1.61-8(c). Cf. Code §109.

(b) If an owner of land enters into a lease under which an oil company is permitted to drill for oil, in return for a royalty on any oil that is discovered and sold, does the landowner have income at the time the oil company constructs a rig and begins drilling? When oil is found?

4. *The events of 1933.* The Court holds that Bruun realized a big chunk of income in 1933. (a) Does this accord with economic reality? Though the tenant no doubt added considerable value to the property by constructing the new building in 1929, presumably this added value was not reflected in the rent, since the lease did not require the tenant to build and the cost was borne by the tenant. Thus, as of 1929, presumably the rental value of the property,

with its new building, was higher than the amount of rent that the tenant was required to pay to Bruun. (b) If so, why do you suppose that the tenant "forfeited" the lease in 1933? (c) What do you suppose had happened to the value of the land? (d) If the value of the land fell, does it follow that Bruun had a loss in a tax sense? See §1001(a). (e) Even if he did have a loss, was it realized? See Trask v. Hoey, 177 F.2d 940 (2d Cir. 1949) (lessor taxed on fair market value at the time of forfeiture of tenant's improvements but can claim no offsetting loss for decline in value of lessor's improvements; taxable gain or loss with respect to lessor's improvements will be realized only on a disposition of the property).

5. *Realization doctrine.* (a) Considering the reasons that might be given for the result in *Macomber,* and for the requirement of realization in general, does Mr. Bruun seem to have a stronger or a weaker case for nonrealization than Mrs. Macomber? The Court in *Bruun* says that "it does not appear . . . whether the building was readily removable from the land." The building was in Kansas City, Missouri, where, one presumes, buildings have basements and are firmly attached to the ground. Note the interesting discussion of the nature of the taxpayer's stipulation as to the amount of gain at issue. What's this all about? If you had represented Bruun, how would you have written the stipulation?

(b) Simplifying, in Helvering v. Bruun, an individual leased real estate, and at the end of the arrangement got back the same real estate, yet he had income, because the tenant built a nice building on the real estate. But buildings are not fruit—they cannot be separated from the land on which they sit. So the landlord just got back "his" realty: How is that different from a lease of timberland where the tenant returns the land without having cut any trees, yet the trees have increased in value? And yet without even mentioning Eisner v. Macomber by name, the Supreme Court concluded that the increase in wealth had to be included in income when the tenant defaulted and returned the property.

(c) How did Helvering v. Bruun reach its conclusion without explicitly overruling Eisner v. Macomber? Perhaps it helps to analogize the case to a windfall. The landlord did not expect ever to get the value of the new building, because it would have declined in value to zero by the time the land was returned to him in 2014. (That is why he had no income in 1929, when the tenant built the new building.) But when the tenant unexpectedly defaulted in 1933, the landlord got a windfall, by getting back a spanking new building he could lease out (presumptively) for a higher rent than the old tenant had been paying, and for which the landlord had not bargained in the original lease. But underneath this explanation lurks the fact the Court simply was backpedalling furiously from Eisner v. Macomber.

6. *Statutory relief.* Congress ultimately accepted the arguments for nontaxation in cases like *Bruun* with legislation enacted in 1942. See §§109 and 1019. Note that the effect of the statutory relief is not to exclude or exempt income but to defer or postpone its recognition. Suppose, for example, that in 1933, when the lease was abandoned by the tenant, the building was worth $50,000 and had a ten-year remaining life and that Mr. Bruun was able to lease the property to a new tenant for $7,000 per year net of all expenses, beginning in 1933. Disregard any unrecovered cost of the demolished building. Under the

decision in the case, Bruun would have income of $50,000 in 1933. This means that he would have a basis in the building of $50,000; for tax purposes it is as if he had received $50,000 in cash and had used that money to buy the building. Thus, he would have been entitled to a depreciation deduction. If we assume that he would have used straight-line depreciation, the deduction would have been $5,000 per year. Thus, the income to be reported from the new rental of the property for the period 1933 through 1942 would have been $2,000 per year, or a total of $20,000. The total income would have been $50,000 in 1933 from the abandonment plus the $20,000 from 1933 through 1942 from the rental, or a total of $70,000. If §§109 and 1019 had been applied, there would have been no income from the abandonment in 1933. Since Bruun paid nothing for the building, his basis in it would have been zero, so there would have been no depreciation deduction. His rental income would therefore have been $7,000 per year or a total of $70,000 over the ten-year term of the new lease. Table 4-1 summarizes this illustration.

TABLE 4-1
Illustration of Mr. Bruun's Income Under *Bruun*
and Under §§109 and 1019

Outcome Under Bruun	
Income from abandonment in 1933	$50,000
Income from rental, 1933-1942	$20,000
Total	$70,000
Outcome Under §§109 and 1019	
Income from abandonment in 1933	$-0-
Income from rental, 1933-1942	$70,000
Total	$70,000

4. The Limits of Realization: Nonrecourse Borrowing in Excess of Basis

The tax law has developed to treat a broad range of transactions as "realization" events. It is now widely understood that any sale or other disposition of an asset will be regarded as a realization event, thus requiring the taxpayer (in the absence of an applicable nonrecognition provision) to report any gain or loss from the sale on her federal income tax return. But *why* should a sale of an asset be regarded as a realization event? Common sense suggests that there must be something about the change in the taxpayer's economic circumstances that makes it an appropriate time for the tax system to take account of the taxpayer's gain or loss. But what if the taxpayer's economic circumstances change in some manner very closely approximating a sale but the taxpayer has not actually parted with legal title to the property? Keep this question in mind when reading the following case.

WOODSAM ASSOCIATES, INC. v. COMMISSIONER
198 F.2d 357 (2d Cir. 1952)

CHASE, Circuit Judge.

OPINION

The petitioner paid its income . . . taxes for 1943 as computed upon returns it filed which included as part of its gross income . . . gain realized upon the mortgage foreclosure sale in that year of improved real estate which it owned and which was bid in by the mortgagee for a nominal sum. It filed a timely claim for refund on the ground that its adjusted basis for the property had been understated and its taxable gain, therefore, was less than that reported. The refund claim was denied and a deficiency . . . was determined which was affirmed, without dissent, in a decision reviewed by the entire Tax Court. The decisive issue now presented is whether the basis for determining gain or loss upon the sale or other disposition of property is increased when, subsequent to the acquisition of the property, the owner receives a loan in an amount greater than his adjusted basis which is secured by a mortgage on the property upon which he is not personally liable. If so, it is agreed that part of the income taxes . . . paid for 1943 should be refunded.

A comparatively brief statement of the admitted facts and their obvious, and conceded, tax consequences will suffice by way of introduction.

On December 29, 1934, Samuel J. Wood and his wife organized the petitioner and each transferred to it certain property in return for one-half of its capital stock. One piece of property so transferred by Mrs. Wood was the above mentioned parcel of improved real estate consisting of land in the City of New York and a brick building thereon divided into units suitable for use, and used, in retail business. The property was subject to a $400,000 mortgage on which Mrs. Wood was not personally liable and on which the petitioner never became personally liable. [Under applicable statutory nonrecognition rules] the petitioner took the basis of Mrs. Wood for tax purposes. . . . Upon the final disposition of the property at the foreclosure sale there was still due upon the mortgage the principal amount of $381,000. . . .

Turning now to the one item whose effect upon the calculation of the petitioner's adjusted basis is disputed, the following admitted facts need to be stated. Mrs. Wood bought the property on January 20, 1922, at a total cost of $296,400. [The acquisition was partly financed by mortgage debt, which she increased through further mortgage borrowing post-acquisition. The various mortgages were then refinanced into a single consolidated mortgage debt in the amount of $325,000. Up to this point, Mrs. Wood had been personally liable to repay the mortgage debt. In 1931, however, she borrowed an additional $75,000 from the bank that now held the mortgage and refinanced again to create a second, replacement consolidated mortgage in the amount of $400,000. This second consolidated mortgage was nonrecourse; she was not personally liable to repay it upon default even if the value of the property was insufficient to pay it off in full.]

The contention of the petitioner may now be stated quite simply. It is that, when the borrowings of Mrs. Wood subsequent to her acquisition of the property became charges solely upon the property itself [in 1931], the cash she received for the repayment of which she was not personally liable was a gain then taxable to her as income to the extent that the mortgage indebtedness exceeded her adjusted basis in the property. That being so, it is argued that her tax basis was, under familiar principles of tax law, increased by the amount of such taxable gain. . . .

While this conclusion would be sound if the premise on which it is based were correct, we cannot accept the premise. It is that the petitioner's transferor made a taxable disposition of the property . . . when the second consolidated mortgage was executed, because she had, by then, dealt with it in such a way that she had received cash, in excess of her basis, which, at that time, she was freed from any personal obligation to repay. Nevertheless, whether or not personally liable on the mortgage, "The mortgagee is a creditor, and in effect nothing more than a preferred creditor, even though the mortgagor is not liable for the debt. He is not the less a creditor because he has recourse only to the land." . . . Mrs. Wood merely augmented the existing mortgage indebtedness when she borrowed each time and, far from closing the venture, remained in a position to borrow more if and when circumstances permitted and she so desired. And so, she never "disposed" of the property to create a taxable event which [§1001(a)] makes a condition precedent to the taxation of gain. "Disposition," within the meaning of [§1001(a)], is the "getting rid, or making over, of anything; relinquishment." . . . Nothing of that nature was done here by the mere execution of the second consolidated mortgage; Mrs. Wood was the owner of this property in the same sense after the execution of this mortgage that she was before. As was pointed out in our decision in the *Crane* case, [a nonrecourse borrower] . . . has all the income from the property; he manages it; he may sell it; any increase in its value goes to him; any decrease falls on him, until the value goes below the amount of the lien. Realization of gain was, therefore, postponed for taxation until there was a final disposition of the property at the time of the foreclosure sale. . . . Therefore, Mrs. Wood's borrowings did not change the basis for the computation of gain or loss.

Affirmed.

NOTES AND QUESTIONS

1. How could Mrs. Wood have persuaded the mortgage lender (a bank that was an unrelated party) to execute a $400,000 nonrecourse mortgage on land that she had purchased for only $296,400? Was there any reason for the bank to care about her original purchase price? Why would it have agreed to waive her personal liability to repay the mortgage in the event that the land's value declined to less than the amount of the outstanding loan?

2. Under the taxpayer's theory, executing a $400,000 nonrecourse mortgage in 1931 with respect to property that had a basis of $296,400 (ignoring, for simplicity, any depreciation deductions with respect to the building) was

tantamount, for income tax purposes, to selling the property for the amount of the mortgage. Thus, the taxpayer argued that in 1931 Mrs. Wood should have reported taxable gain in the amount of $103,600 (the excess of the "sale price" over basis), whereupon the basis increased to $400,000—just as if she had received that amount outright and used it to purchase new property—so that the property's appreciation from the sale price to the amount she borrowed would not be taxed twice. This argument was to her benefit because the 1931 taxable year, unlike 1943, was no longer open to review due to the statute of limitations.

3. To understand the taxpayer's theory in *Woodsam Associates*, you need to ask: Why is the mere appreciation of property generally not taxed in the absence of an event such as a sale or exchange? The usual rationales for not taxing unrealized appreciation are threefold: It is hard to measure; the taxpayer may not have the cash in hand to pay the tax; and the taxpayer still faces a risk of loss if the property subsequently declines in value. Upon the execution of a nonrecourse mortgage in excess of basis, are these rationales still persuasive?

4. (a) The court rejects the taxpayer's theory on straight statutory interpretation grounds: A nonrecourse loan is not a sale or exchange under the existing Code, particularly in the aftermath of cases such as *Crane* (Chapter 5, *infra*) that, in other settings, ignore nonrecourse debt's arguably distinctive features.

(b) Plainly, there is no constitutional issue regarding whether Congress *could* tax appreciation in these circumstances. Congress can if it chooses retain the realization doctrine in general but treat borrowing in excess of basis as a deemed sale.

(c) What industry might be expected to be particularly vocal in lobbying against the adoption of the rule suggested in (b)?

5. Would accepting the taxpayer's theory in *Woodsam Associates* have been in the government's long-run revenue interest even though, in this case, it was too late to reopen the 1931 taxable year? Why?

6. Would a rule treating the execution of a nonrecourse mortgage in excess of basis as a taxable event be difficult to enforce? How easy or hard would taxpayers find the challenge of avoiding the realization of taxable gain under such a rule?

5. Contemporary Understandings of the Realization Doctrine

The following case, Cottage Savings Association v. Commissioner, shows these dynamics at play in the context of so-called Memorandum R-49 transactions entered into by thrift institutions at the height of the savings and loan crisis in the 1980s. Motivating these transactions was the dramatic increase in interest rates during the 1970s. The rise in interest rates reduced the value of existing fixed-rate mortgages held by thrift institutions. To understand why this is so, imagine that a thrift institution had made a $100,000 loan in 1965 at 7 percent annual interest. Assume (somewhat unrealistically) that the loan required the borrower to make interest payments only for thirty years and then to repay the full amount of the principal. In 1980, the thrift would hold an asset — the mortgage — that amounted to a promise to repay $100,000 in fifteen years and in the meantime to pay interest of $7,000 a year. The prevailing interest rate on home loans in 1980, however, was approximately 14 percent. No one in 1980 would pay $100,000 for a debt obligation that paid only 7 percent interest. Why invest at 7 percent when you could make a similar investment at 14 percent? The fair market value of the 7 percent mortgage as of 1980 might be as low as $60,000. That is, the thrift would be holding an asset with a basis of $100,000 (the amount originally extended as a loan) and fair market value of $60,000 — that is, an asset with a built-in loss of $40,000.

By 1980, when the events at issue in *Cottage Savings* took place, the fair market value of mortgages held by the nation's savings and loan institutions had declined by more than one trillion dollars. Recognizing these losses for tax purposes would generate valuable loss deductions for the thrifts, but an outright sale of the mortgages was off the table for accounting reasons. To have their cake and eat it too, the thrifts would have to find a way to "sell" their mortgages for tax purposes without "selling" their mortgages for accounting purposes.

COTTAGE SAVINGS ASSOCIATION v. COMMISSIONER
499 U.S. 554 (1991)

Justice MARSHALL delivered the opinion of the Court.

The issue in this case is whether a financial institution realizes tax-deductible losses when it exchanges its interests in one group of residential mortgage loans for another lender's interests in a different group of residential mortgage loans. We hold that such a transaction does give rise to realized losses.

I

Petitioner Cottage Savings Association (Cottage Savings) is a savings and loan association (S&L) formerly regulated by the Federal Home Loan Bank Board (FHLBB). Like many S&L's, Cottage Savings held numerous long-term, low-interest mortgages that declined in value when interest rates surged in the late 1970's. These institutions would have benefited from selling their devalued mortgages in order to realize tax-deductible losses. However, they were deterred from doing so by FHLBB accounting regulations, which required them to record the losses on their books. Reporting these losses consistent with the then-effective FHLBB accounting regulations would have placed many S&L's at risk of closure by the FHLBB.

The FHLBB responded to this situation by relaxing its requirements for the reporting of losses. In a regulatory directive known as "Memorandum R-49," dated June 27, 1980, the FHLBB determined that S&L's need not report losses associated with mortgages that are exchanged for "substantially identical" mortgages held by other lenders.[20] The FHLBB's acknowledged purpose for Memorandum R-49 was to facilitate transactions that would generate tax losses but that would not substantially affect the economic position of the transacting S&L's.

This case involves a typical Memorandum R-49 transaction. On December 31, 1980, Cottage Savings sold "90% participation" in 252 mortgages to four S&L's. It simultaneously purchased "90% participation interests" in 305 mortgages held by these S&L's. All of the loans involved in the transaction were secured by single-family homes, most in the Cincinnati area. The fair market value of the package of participation interests exchanged by each side was approximately $4.5 million. The face value of the participation interests Cottage Savings relinquished in the transaction was approximately $6.9 million.

On its 1980 federal income tax return, Cottage Savings claimed a reduction for $2,447,091, which represented the adjusted difference between the face value of the participation interests that it traded and the fair market value of the participation interests that it received. As permitted by Memorandum R-49, Cottage Savings did not report these losses to the FHLBB. After the Commissioner of Internal Revenue disallowed Cottage Savings' claimed deduction, Cottage Savings sought a redetermination in the Tax Court. The Tax Court held that the deduction was permissible.

On appeal by the Commissioner, the Court of Appeals reversed. 890 F.2d 848 (C.A.6 1989). The Court of Appeals agreed with the Tax Court's determination that Cottage Savings had realized its losses through the transaction. See *id.*, at 852. However, the court held that Cottage Savings was not entitled to a deduction because its losses were not "actually" sustained during the 1980 tax year for purposes of §165(a). See 890 F.2d at 855.

Because of the importance of this issue to the S&L industry and the conflict among the Circuits over whether Memorandum R-49 exchanges produce deductible tax losses, we granted certiorari. We now reverse.

II

Rather than assessing tax liability on the basis of annual fluctuations in the value of a taxpayer's property, the Internal Revenue Code defers the tax

---

20. Memorandum R-49 listed ten criteria for classifying mortgages as substantially identical. Record, Exh. 72-BT.

1) involve single-family residential mortgages,
2) be of similar type (e.g., conventionals for conventionals),
3) have the same stated terms to maturity (e.g., 30 years),
4) have identical stated interest rates,
5) have similar seasoning (i.e., remaining terms to maturity),
6) have aggregate principal amounts within the lesser of 2-1/2% or $100,000 (plus or minus) on both sides of the transaction, with any additional consideration being paid in cash,
7) be sold without recourse,
8) have similar fair market values,
9) have similar loan-to-value ratios at the time of the reciprocal sale, and
10) have all security properties for both sides of the transaction in the same state.

Record, Exh. 72-BT

consequences of a gain or loss in property value until the taxpayer "realizes the gain or loss." The realization requirement is implicit in §1001(a) of the Code, which defines "[t]he gain [or loss] from the sale or other disposition of property" as the difference between "the amount realized" from the sale or disposition of the property and its "adjusted basis." As this Court has recognized, the concept of realization is "founded on administrative convenience." Helvering v. Horst, 311 U.S. 112, 116 (1940). Under an appreciation-based system of taxation, taxpayers and the Commissioner would have to undertake the "cumbersome, abrasive, and unpredictable administrative task" of valuing assets on an annual basis to determine whether the assets had appreciated or depreciated in value. See 1 B. Bittker & L. Lokken, *Federal Taxation of Income, Estates and Gifts* ¶5.2, pp. 5-16 (2d ed. 1989). In contrast, "[a] change in the form or extent of an investment is easily detected by a taxpayer or an administrative officer." R. Magill, *Taxable Income* 79 (rev. ed. 1945).

Section 1001(a)'s language provides a straightforward test for realization: to realize a gain or loss in the value of property, the taxpayer must engage in a "sale or other disposition of [the] property." The parties agree that the exchange of participation interests in this case cannot be characterized as a "sale" under §1001(a); the issue before us is whether the transaction constitutes a "disposition of property." The Commissioner argues that an exchange of property can be treated as a "disposition" under §1001(a) only if the properties exchanged are materially different. The Commissioner further submits that, because the underlying mortgages were essentially economic substitutes, the participation interests exchanged by Cottage Savings were not materially different from those received from the other S&L's. Cottage Savings, on the other hand, maintains that any exchange of property is a "disposition of property" under §1001(a), regardless of whether the property exchanged is materially different. Alternatively, Cottage Savings contends that the participation interests exchanged were materially different because the underlying loans were secured by different properties.

We must therefore determine whether the realization principle in §1001(a) incorporates a "material difference" requirement. If it does, we must further decide what that requirement amounts to and how it applies in this case. We consider these questions in turn.

A

Neither the language nor the history of the Code indicates whether and to what extent property exchanged must differ to count as a "disposition of property" under §1001(a). Nonetheless, we readily agree with the Commissioner that an exchange of property gives rise to a realization even under §1001(a) only if the properties exchanged are "materially different." The Commissioner himself has by regulation construed §1001(a) to embody a material difference requirement:

> Except as otherwise provided . . . the gain or loss realized from the conversion of property into *cash, or from the exchange of property for other property differing materially either in kind or in extent,* is treated as income or as loss sustained.

* * * *

B

Precisely what constitutes a "material difference" for purposes of §1001(a) of the Code is a more complicated question. The Commissioner argues that properties are "materially different" only if they differ in economic substance. To determine whether the participation interests exchanged in this case were "materially different" in this sense, the Commissioner argues, we should look to the attitudes of the parties, the evaluation of the interests by the secondary mortgage market, and the views of the FHLBB. We conclude that §1001(a) embodies a much less demanding and less complex test.

Unlike the question *whether* §1001(a) contains a material difference requirement, the question of *what constitutes* a material difference is not one on which we can defer to the Commissioner. For the Commissioner has not issued an authoritative, prelitigation interpretation of what property exchanges satisfy this requirement. Thus, to give meaning to the material difference test, we must look to the case law from which the test derives and which we believe Congress intended to codify in enacting and reenacting the language that now comprises §1001(a). . . .

We start with the classic treatment of realization in Eisner v. Macomber [*supra*]. In *Macomber,* a taxpayer who owned 2,200 shares of stock in a company received another 1,100 shares from the company as part of a pro rata stock dividend meant to reflect the company's growth in value. At issue was whether the stock dividend constituted taxable income. We held that it did not, because no gain was realized. . . . We reasoned that the stock dividend merely reflected the increased worth of the taxpayer's stock, . . . and that a taxpayer realizes increased worth of property only by receiving "something of exchangeable value *proceeding from* the property." . . .

In three subsequent decisions—United States v. Phellis, [257 U.S. 156 (1921)]; Weiss v. Stearn, [265 U.S. 242 (1924)]; and Marr v. United States, [268 U.S. 536 (1925)]—we refined *Macomber*'s conception of realization in the context of property exchanges. In each case, the taxpayer owned stock that had appreciated in value since its acquisition. And in each case, the corporation in which the taxpayer held stock had reorganized into a new corporation, with the new corporation assuming the business of the old corporation. While the corporations in *Phellis* and *Marr* both changed from New Jersey to Delaware corporations, the original and successor corporations in *Weiss* both were incorporated in Ohio. In each case, following the reorganization, the stockholders of the old corporation received shares in the new corporation equal to their proportional interest in the old corporation.

The question in these cases was whether the taxpayers realized the accumulated gain in their shares in the old corporation when they received in return for those shares stock representing an equivalent proportional interest in the new corporations. In *Phellis* and *Marr,* we held that the transactions were realization events. We reasoned that because a company incorporated in one State has "different rights and powers" from one incorporated in a different State, the taxpayers in *Phellis* and *Marr* acquired through the transactions property that was "materially different" from what they previously had. . . . In contrast, we held that no realization occurred in *Weiss.* By exchanging stock in the predecessor corporation for stock in the newly reorganized corporation, the taxpayer did not receive "a thing really different from what he theretofore had." Weiss v. Stearn, *supra*, 265 U.S., at 254. As we explained in *Marr*, our determination that the reorganized company in *Weiss* was not "really different" from its predecessor turned on the fact that both companies were incorporated in the same State. . . .

Obviously, the distinction in *Phellis* and *Marr* that made the stock in the successor corporations materially different from the stock in the predecessors was minimal. Taken together, *Phellis, Marr,* and *Weiss* stand for the principles that properties are "different" in the sense that is "material" to the Internal Revenue Code so long as their respective possessors enjoy legal entitlements that are different in kind or extent. Thus, separate groups of stock are not materially different if they confer "the same proportional interest of the same character in the same corporation." Marr v. United States, 268 U.S., at 540. However, they *are* materially different if they are issued by different corporations, id., at 541; United States v. Phellis, supra, 257 U.S., at 173, or if they confer "differen[t] rights and powers" in the same corporation, Marr v. United States, *supra*, 268 U.S., at 541. No more demanding a standard than this is necessary in order to satisfy the administrative purposes underlying the realization requirement in §1001(a). . . . For, as long as the property entitlements are not identical, their exchange will allow both the Commissioner and the transacting taxpayer easily to fix the appreciated or depreciated values of the property relative to their tax bases.

In contrast, we find no support for the Commissioner's "economic substitute" conception of material difference. According to the Commissioner, differences between properties are material for purposes of the Code only when it can be said that the parties, the relevant market (in this case the secondary mortgage market), and the relevant regulatory body (in this case the FHLBB) would consider them material. Nothing in *Phellis, Weiss,* and *Marr* suggests that exchanges of properties must satisfy such a subjective test to trigger realization of a gain or loss.

* * * *

Finally, the Commissioner's test is incompatible with the structure of the Code. Section 1001(c) provides that a gain or loss realized under §1001(a) "shall be recognized" unless one of the Code's nonrecognition provisions applies. One such nonrecognition provision withholds recognition of a gain or loss realized from an exchange of properties that would appear to be economic substitutes under the Commissioner's material difference test. This provision, commonly known as "like kind" exception, withholds recognition of a gain or loss realized "on the exchange of property held for productive use in a trade or business or for investment . . . for property of like kind which is to be held either for productive use in a trade or business or for investment." §1031. If Congress had expected that exchanges of similar properties would not count as realization events under §1001(a), it would have had no reason to bar recognition of a gain or loss realized from these transactions.

c

Under our interpretation of §1001(a), an exchange of property gives rise to a realization event so long as the exchanged properties are "materially different"—that is, so long as they embody legally distinct entitlements. Cottage Savings' transactions at issue here easily satisfy this test. Because the participation interests exchanged by Cottage Savings and the other S&L's derived from loans that were made to different obligors and secured by different homes, the exchanged interests did embody legally distinct entitlements. Consequently, we conclude that Cottage Savings realized its losses at the point of the exchange.

The Commissioner contends that it is anomalous to treat mortgages deemed to be "substantially identical" to the FHLBB as "materially different." The anomaly, however, is merely semantic; mortgages can be substantially identical for Memorandum R-49 purposes and still exhibit "differences" that are "material" for purposes of the Internal Revenue Code. Because Cottage Savings received entitlements different from those it gave up, the exchange put both Cottage Savings and the Commissioner in a position to determine the change in the value of Cottage Savings' mortgages relative to their tax bases. Thus, there is no reason not to treat the exchange of these interests as a realization event, regardless of the status of the mortgages under the criteria of Memorandum R-49.

III

Although the Court of Appeals found that Cottage Savings' losses were realized, it disallowed them on the ground that they were not sustained under §165(a) of the Code. Section 165(a) states that a deduction shall be allowed for "any loss sustained during the taxable year and not compensated for by insurance or otherwise." Under the Commissioner's interpretation of §165(a).

To be allowable as a deduction under section 165(a), a loss must be evidenced by closed and completed transactions, fixed by identifiable events, and, except as otherwise provided in section 165(h) and §1.165-11, relating to disaster losses, actually sustained during the taxable year. Only a bona fide loss is allowable. Substance and not mere form shall govern in determining a deductible loss. Treas. Reg. §1.165-1(b).

The Commissioner offers a minimal defense of the Court of Appeals' conclusion. The Commissioner contends that the losses were not sustained because they lacked "economic substance," by which the Commissioner seems to mean that the losses were not bona fide. We say "seems" because the Commissioner states the position in one sentence in a footnote in his brief without offering further explanation. The only authority the Commissioner cites for this argument is Higgins v. Smith, 308 U.S. 473 (1940).

In *Higgins*, we held that a taxpayer did not sustain a loss by selling securities below cost to a corporation in which he was the sole shareholder. We found that the losses were not bona fide because the transaction was not conducted at arm's length and because the taxpayer retained the benefit of the securities through his wholly owned corporation. . . . Because there is no contention that the transactions in this case were not conducted at arm's length, or that Cottage Savings retained de facto ownership of the participation interests it traded to the four reciprocating S&L's, *Higgins* is inapposite. In view of the Commissioner's failure to advance any other arguments in support of the Court of Appeals' ruling with respect to §165(a), we conclude that, for purposes of this case, Cottage Savings sustained its losses within the meaning of §165(a).

IV

For the reasons set forth above, the judgment of the Court of Appeals is reversed, and the case is remanded for further proceedings consistent with this opinion.

So ordered.

Justice BLACKMUN with whom Justice WHITE joins . . . dissenting. . . .

The exchanges, as the Court acknowledges, were occasioned by the Federal Home Loan Bank Board's (FHLBB) Memorandum R-49 of June 27, 1980, and by that Memorandum's relaxation of theretofore-existing accounting regulations and requirements, a relaxation effected to avoid placement of "many S&L's at risk of closure by the FHLBB" without substantially affecting the "economic position of the transacting S&L's." . . . But the Memorandum, the Court notes, also had as a purpose "the facilit[ation of] transactions that would generate tax losses. . . ." I find it somewhat surprising that an agency not responsible for tax matters would presume to dictate what is or is not a deductible loss for federal income tax purposes. I had thought that that was something within the exclusive province of the Internal Revenue Service, subject to administrative and judicial review. Certainly, the Bank Board's opinion in this respect is entitled to no deference whatsoever. . . .

That the mortgage participation partial interests exchanged in these cases were "different" is not in dispute. The materiality prong is the focus. A material difference is one that has the capacity to influence a decision. . . .

The application of this standard leads, it seems to me, to only one answer—that the mortgage participation partial interests released were not materially different from the mortgage participation partial interests received. Memorandum R-49, as the Court notes, . . . lists 10 factors that, when satisfied, as they were here, serve to classify the interests as "substantially identical." These factors assure practical identity; surely, they then also assure that any difference cannot be of consequence. Indeed, nonmateriality is the full purpose of the Memorandum's criteria. The "proof of the pudding" is in the fact of its complete accounting acceptability to the FHLBB. Indeed, as has been noted, it is difficult to reconcile substantial identity for financial accounting purposes with a material difference for tax accounting purposes.

This should suffice and be the end of the analysis. Other facts, however, solidify the conclusion: The retention by the transferor of 10% interests, enabling it to keep on servicing its loans; the transferor's continuing to collect the payments due from the borrowers so that, so far as the latter were concerned, it was business as usual, exactly as it had been; the obvious lack of concern or dependence of the transferor with the "differences" upon which the Court relies (as transferees, the taxpayers made no credit checks and no appraisals of collateral . . .); the selection of the loans by computer programmed to match mortgages in accordance with the Memorandum R-49 criteria; the absence of even the names of the borrowers in the closing schedules attached to the agreements; Centennial's receipt of loan files only six years after its exchange; the restriction of the interests exchanged to the same State; the identity of the respective face and fair market values; and the application by the parties of common discount factors to each side of the transaction — all reveal that any differences that might exist made no difference whatsoever and were not material. This demonstrates the real nature of the transactions, including nonmateriality of the claimed differences.

We should be dealing here with realities and not with superficial distinctions. As has been said many times, and as noted above, in income tax law we are to be concerned with substance and not with mere form. When we stray from that principle, the new precedent is likely to be a precarious beacon for the future.

I respectfully dissent on this issue.

NOTES

1. The taxpayer in *Cottage Savings* was able to eat its cake and have it too, because it could have just sold the assets in question (a pool of mortgages) and realized its loss, but if it did so it also would be required to realize the loss for purposes of its income and balance sheet statements that it furnished its financial regulator (the FHLBB). Critically important, the FHLBB, like the tax code, followed a realization-based accounting system in figuring out the health of the S&Ls that it regulated.

The FHLBB wanted to help the S&L industry avoid tax on the interest income each S&L earned on the mortgages it owned, without recognizing losses for regulatory purposes (which would wipe out the S&L's regulatory capital, thereby rendering them instantly insolvent and requiring that they be shut down). The FHLBB therefore constructed the Memorandum R-49 trade to permit swaps of commercially identical mortgage portfolios that would not trigger a loss for regulatory purposes, but would trigger a loss, it was hoped, for tax purposes.

In other words, what really was going on was a plot by one federal agency and the taxpayers it regulated to minimize their tax liability to the federal government. What arguments could the IRS make in response? There was (and is) an important anti-abuse rule in the Code, the "wash sale" rules of §1091. These limit the optionality of loss recognition available to taxpayers by providing that if a taxpayer sells stocks or bonds at a loss and then buys the same (technically, "substantially identical") property back within thirty days, the loss will not be recognized (will not be available to be claimed on the tax return for the year of the wash sale). But the wash sale rules are very narrowly written, and do not apply to sales of individual mortgages (or portfolios of many individual mortgages, for that matter). So the IRS essentially tried to invent a "common law of wash sales"—a rule that said, if the taxpayer takes back property that is designed to be commercially and economically indistinguishable from the property it gives up, then a loss cannot be recognized. It is this argument that the Supreme Court rejected.

2. Although the subject of the *Cottage Savings* litigation was the tax treatment of S&L mortgage portfolio swaps, the opinion, like most court decisions, had much broader and far-reaching consequences. Most commentators came to view the case as establishing a "hair-trigger" standard for interpreting §1001. As a result, certain transactions not considered as triggering realization prior to *Cottage Savings* were regarded, after the decision, as taxable events. Perhaps the most important impact of the Court's decision was in the area of debt workouts, where distressed borrowers and their creditors agreed to certain modifications of the underlying debt instruments. Post-*Cottage Savings*, the question arose whether debt modifications would require the parties to such transactions to treat the modification as a "sale or other disposition" of the original obligation, triggering recognition of gain or loss by investor and, in some cases, of income to the obligor from cancellation of indebtedness. Reg. §1.1001-3.

In response, the IRS issued the so-called *Cottage Savings* regulations, which cover a wide variety of possible modifications. In general, the key is whether a "significant modification" has occurred in yield, timing or amounts of payments, the obligor, or the nature of the instrument. Some of the rules are specific. For example, if the interest rate is changed by more than of 1 percent, the change is significant and a recognition event has occurred, but in the case of a variable-rate obligation, a change in the rate resulting from a change in the index used to compute the rate is not a modification. Regs. 1.1001-3(e)(1). An extension of the final maturity date is significant if it is greater than the lesser of five years or 50 percent of the original term. Regs. 1.1001-3(e)(2). Other rules are stated more generally. For example, a change in the collateral is "a significant modification if a substantial portion of the collateral is released or replaced with other property," but not where fungible property is replaced by similar property (for example, "government securities of a particular type and rating"). Regs. 1.1001-3(e)(3)(iv).

The result of modifying a debt instrument can be a surprising potential tax liabilities for taxpayers who buy distressed debt at a discount and thereafter modify the terms. Bear in mind that a significant modification results in an exchange—a recognition event—for both the debtor and the holder of the debt. Suppose, for example, that debt owed by Debtor Co. has a face amount of $10 million and an interest rate of 10 percent, but that Debtor Co., subsequent to the issuance of the debt, has experienced financial reverses. Because of an increased risk of default, the market value of the debt has declined. Suppose Holder buys the debt for $7 million and shortly thereafter, seeking to give Debtor Co. an improved chance of survival, reduces the interest rate to 9 percent. This is a significant modification. Suppose the applicable federal rate of interest (which is, essentially, the market rate for debt with comparable terms) is 8 percent. Debtor Co. will not have any cancellation of debt income. See §108(e)(10). Holder, on the other hand, despite having no economic gain, will be treated as having exchanged a debt instrument with a basis of $7 million for a new debt instrument with a value of $10 million and will realize a gain of $3 million.

QUESTIONS

1. Before the swap described in *Cottage Savings*, had the taxpayer experienced a true economic loss on the loans that it swapped? If so, when was that loss incurred?

2. If the taxpayer had a true economic loss (with or without the swap), why did the FHLBB not require that the loss be recognized for nontax accounting purposes?

3. Should the fact that the FHLBB did not recognize the loss for nontax accounting purposes have had any bearing on whether the loss was recognized for tax purposes? Why?

4. If the taxpayer had a true economic loss, was there any tax policy justification for the Commissioner's resistance to allowing the loss to be recognized once the swap occurred?

5. What is the legal test for recognition of loss? What is meant by "legal entitlements"? Is it fair to describe the test as "formalistic"? If so, what is the advantage, if any, of such a test?

6. Was there any reason for the taxpayer in *Cottage Savings* to enter into a Memorandum R-49 transaction other than a reduction in its federal income tax liability? If not, should the Court's opinion be viewed as support for the proposition that taxpayer efforts to structure transactions for the sake of tax benefits should be respected even if the taxpayer has no independent business purpose for undertaking the transaction?

PROBLEMS

1. Jim and Barbara, both cotton dealers, are business acquaintances. Each is in the business of buying cotton from farmers and selling it to manufacturers. Recently each bought large quantities of cotton and stored it in a warehouse in the town where both of them live. The cotton was all grown in the same area and is considered to be identical in grade and quality. The end of the year is approaching. The price of cotton has fallen and Jim and Barbara both have substantial unrealized losses on the cotton they hold in storage. Jim and Barbara both believe that the price of cotton will rise in a month or so and would like to avoid selling, but each has large gains from transactions earlier in the year and would like to be able to deduct their losses. Will each of them be entitled to recognize his or her loss if they swap their cotton holdings? (Ignore pre-2017 act §1031.)

2. Susan and Josh both deal in high-priced, high-performance, "exotic" sports cars. Susan has her showroom and office in New York City, and Josh has his showroom and office in Miami. Two years ago Machorari Automobile Company, which is located in Italy, announced that it had plans to build a new sports car, to be called the Streaker, and that it would take orders at $500,000 each, with $100,000 payable on placing the order. Only thirty of the cars were

to be built. Susan and Josh each placed orders. Machorari's cars are essentially hand made. When an order is placed, a particular car is assigned to the buyer. Susan was assigned Streaker No. 13 and Josh was assigned Streaker No. 14. The cars were recently finished, paid for by Susan and Josh, and shipped to them. Unfortunately, a mistake was made in the shipping and Susan's Streaker No. 13 was shipped to Miami while Josh's Streaker No. 14 was shipped to New York. Susan and Josh each have documents establishing their ownership of their cars. The cars are as close to being identical as cars can be when they are not made on an assembly line. Demand is so intense that the cars can be sold without effort for $750,000. Susan has several potential buyers in New York at that price. In Miami, several people have come to Josh's showroom with suitcases full of cash ($750,000), seeking to buy a Streaker. Certain modifications must be made, however, before the cars can meet federal regulations and be sold. The modifications will take several months. Josh calls Susan and suggests that they swap titles, which can be accomplished easily, so they don't need to ship cars to each other. If they do so, must they recognize their gain at the time of the swap? Would it matter if the colors of the cars were different and colors were of great importance to particular buyers?

D.   STATUTORY NONRECOGNITION PROVISIONS

Section 1001(c) of the Internal Revenue Code reads as follows: "Except as otherwise provided in this subtitle, the entire amount of the gain or loss, determined under this section, on the sale or exchange of property shall be recognized." As previously explained, in most cases this language ensures an automatic connection between realization and recognition. That is, a taxpayer who *realizes* a gain or loss from the disposition of property must *recognize* such gain or loss for tax purposes. The Code's nonrecognition provisions, however, trump the general rule of §1001(a), by providing that certain realized gains and losses will not be recognized for federal tax purposes. Students who go on to take advanced tax courses, especially those relating to the taxation of corporations and partnerships, typically devote a great deal of time to mastering highly sophisticated nonrecognition provisions in subchapters C (relating to corporations and their shareholders) and K (relating to partnerships and their partners).

1.   Introduction to Nonrecognition Rules

The chief function of a nonrecognition rule is to ensure that a taxpayer disposing of property in a manner that would otherwise be a taxable event will not recognize gain or loss on the disposition of the property. Nonrecognition rules typically do not provide for the permanent exclusion of gain or disallowance of loss but rather defer that gain or loss for recognition at some later time. In most transactions involving nonrecognition provisions, the taxpayer maintains some sort of property interest following the disposition upon which nonrecognition treatment has been conferred. Thus, preservation of any realized but unrecognized gain or loss is accomplished through adjustments to the basis of the taxpayer's ongoing property interest.

To illustrate, imagine a provision allowing for the tax-free exchange of baseball memorabilia. Gianna owns a vintage New York Yankees jersey worth $1,000 that she bought several years ago for $300. She plans to exchange it for a Los Angeles Dodgers jersey, also worth $1,000, which Nora purchased for $800. It should be clear that, in the absence of a nonrecognition provision, the jersey exchange would trigger $700 of gain for Gianna and $200 of gain for Nora. Both taxpayers have experienced a realization event. Under §1001(c), any gain from the sale or other disposition of an asset must generally be recognized and reported on the taxpayer's federal income tax returns for the year of the exchange. Assuming that a nonrecognition rule applies, however, neither taxpayer would be required to recognize gain from the exchange. In order to preserve each taxpayer's realized but unrecognized gain from the transaction, Gianna would take a basis in her newly acquired Dodgers jersey equal to her basis in the Yankees jersey ($300), while Nora would take a basis in her newly acquired Yankees jersey equal to her basis in the Dodgers jersey ($800).

What is the rationale for nonrecognition rules? Consider the following arguments: (a) Gain should not be recognized if the transaction does not generate cash with which to pay the tax. (b) Gain or loss should not be recognized if the transaction is one in which the gain or loss is or might be difficult to measure, that is, in which there is or might be a serious problem of valuation. (c) Gain or loss should not be recognized if the nature of the taxpayer's investment does not significantly change. (d) Gain should not be recognized in order to avoid discouraging mobility of capital (that is, the movement of investments from less valuable to more valuable uses).

Arguments (a) and (b) respond to the goal of practicality or administrative feasibility in the operation of the tax system. As noted earlier, the realization concept is rooted, at least in part, in precisely such practical considerations. Perhaps nonrecognition rules are justified in those transactions where a realization event has occurred yet liquidity and valuation concerns still obtain because of the nature of the transaction. Argument (c) seems to respond to the goal of fairness; it compares the taxpayer who sells and reinvests, or who swaps, with an otherwise similar taxpayer who holds on to an existing investment. If continuity of investment justifies not taxing those who simply hold on to existing investments, then perhaps the same rationale justifies extending nonrecognition treatment to those who continue in a similar investment. Finally, argument (d) speaks to economic considerations. To the extent that the realization doctrine discourages the transfer of property that has appreciated in value, then perhaps nonrecognition rules can be justified as a means of mitigating that lock-in effect.

2.   Like-Kind Exchanges

For purposes of the material covered in this casebook, the most prominent nonrecognition rule in the Code is §1031, which applies to exchanges of certain business or investment property that are held to be "of a like kind." Before the 2017 act, §1031 applied to exchanges of real estate and certain personal property held for investment or used in a trade or business, but *not* to exchanges of financial instruments, such as stocks and bonds.

The 2017 act radically narrowed the scope of the like-kind exchange rules, so that they now apply only to real estate exchanges. Nonetheless, it probably is the case that real estate exchanges have always accounted for the bulk of the dollar value of like-kind exchanges. Moreover, and somewhat surprisingly, exchanges of tangible personal property, whether or not of like kind, are now effectively tax free by virtue of the "expensing" of capital expenditures, as also provided in the 2017 act.[21]

Taxpayers have relied upon §1031 across a broad range of business and investment settings. Indeed, an entire industry has grown up around this one provision of the Internal Revenue Code. To get some sense of the players in this industry and the types of transactions being done, take a moment and Google "section 1031 like-kind exchanges." The sources you will discover are no substitute for actually reading the statute and regulations (and this casebook!). Nonetheless, spending ten minutes online—perhaps reviewing the IRS website or the National Association of Realtors' "Field Guide to 1031 Exchanges"—can give you a quick "lay of the land" that will help put the materials that follow into context.

Section 1031(a)(1) provides that "[n]o gain or loss shall be recognized on the exchange of real property held for productive use in a trade or business or for investment if such property is exchanged solely for real property of a like kind which is to be held either for productive use in a trade or business or for investment." At first blush, this provision seems extraordinarily broad, potentially conferring nonrecognition treatment on all property exchanges other than those involving personal use assets. However, §1031(a)(2) sets forth several important exceptions. Read these provisions and consider the tax consequences of the following transactions.

(a) Long ago *A* bought shares of stock of Texaco for $10,000. He swaps them for shares of stock of Exxon worth $60,000. Is the swap covered by §1031?

(b) Long ago *B* bought *X* Farm for $10,000 and has held it as an investment. He swaps *X* Farm for *Y* Farm, worth $60,000. Is the swap covered by §1031?

(c) Long ago *C* bought *M* Farm for $10,000 and has held it as an investment. She sells it for $60,000 and uses the proceeds to buy *N* Farm the next week. Is the sale covered by §1031?

(d) Long ago *D* bought *S* Farm for $10,000 and has used it in his farming business. He swaps it for a fleet of tractors worth $60,000 that he will also use in his farming business. Is the sale covered by §1031?

Is it possible to reconcile the outcomes in the hypotheticals (a) through (d) by reference to the alternative rationales for nonrecognition treatment discussed above?

---

21. That is, a nominally taxable exchange by Taxpayer 1 of Asset 1 for Taxpayer 2's Asset 2 becomes effectively nontaxable to both taxpayers in a world where each taxpayer recognizes income on the asset given up, but can expense the value of the asset acquired.

a.   *The Like-Kind Requirement*

As noted above, §1031(a) applies only if qualifying property is exchanged "for property of a *like-kind*" (emphasis added), but the statute itself offers no guidance whatsoever regarding how to make the like-kind determination, beyond limiting the term "property" to mean only real property. As a result, the taxpayer must turn to other sources of legal authority to glean the meaning of the term. Reg. §1.1031(a)-1(b) notes that "the words 'like-kind' have reference to the nature or character of the property and not to its grade or quality." The following private letter ruling illustrates the application of that standard.

PLR 200203033
Internal Revenue Service

Private Letter Ruling
January 18, 2002

Dear _____:

This responds to the letter written in your behalf, dated January 26, 2001, requesting a ruling on the proper treatment of an exchange, under §1031 of the Internal Revenue Code, of a Perpetual Conservation Easement (PCE) in real property for a fee interest in other real estate that will also be burdened with a PCE upon receipt. These are the applicable facts:

. . .

Taxpayers and other co-owners wish to engage in a like-kind exchange with ConOrg, a §501(c)(3) organization. Under an agreement entered into by Taxpayers and the other co-owners with ConOrg, Taxpayers and the other co-owners will convey a PCE on the Old Ranch to ConOrg in exchange for the fee estate of New Ranch, in State X, which will also be burdened with a PCE when received by Taxpayers and the other co-owners.

The planned transaction will be a simultaneous, two-sided exchange (i.e., involving no accommodation parties, third-party sellers of replacement property or third-party buyers of relinquished property). Following the exchange, New Ranch will be held by Taxpayers and the other co-owners in the exact same proportions as the interests they now hold and will retain in Old Ranch burdened with the PCE.

The State X Civil Code provides at Citation X.1 that the purpose of a conservation easement is to retain land predominantly in its natural, scenic, historical, agricultural, forested, or open space condition. Citation X.2 provides that a conservation easement is an interest in real property voluntarily created and freely transferable in whole or in part for the purposes stated in Citation X.1 by any lawful method for the transfer of interest in real property in State X. Citation X.2 further provides that a conservation easement shall be perpetual in duration and shall constitute an interest in real property notwithstanding the fact that it is negative in character.

Section 1031(a)(1) of the Code provides generally that no gain or loss shall be recognized on the exchange of property held for productive use in a trade or business or for investment if such property is exchanged solely for property of like kind which is to be held either for productive use in a trade or business or for investment.

Section 1031(b) states that if an exchange would be within the provisions of section 1031(a) if it were not for the fact that the property received in exchange consists not only of property permitted by such provisions to be received without the recognition of gain, but also of other property or money, then the gain, if any, to the recipient shall be recognized, but in an amount not in excess of the sum of such money and the fair market value of such other property.

Section 1.1031(a)-1(b) of the Income Tax Regulations provides that, as used in section 1031(a), the words "like kind" have reference to the nature or character of the property and not to its grade or quality. One kind or class of property may not, under that section, be exchanged for property of a different kind or class. The fact that any real estate involved is improved or unimproved is not material, for that fact relates only to the grade or quality of the property and not to its kind or class. Unproductive real estate held by one other than a dealer for future use or future realization of the increment in value is held for investment and not primarily for sale.

Section 1.1031(a)-1(c) of the regulations, as an example, provides that no gain or loss is recognized if a taxpayer who is not a dealer in real estate exchanges city real estate for a ranch or farm, or exchanges a leasehold of a fee with 30 years or more to run for real estate, or exchanges improved real estate for unimproved real estate.

Rev. Rul. 55-749, 1955-2 C.B. 295 holds that where, under applicable state law, water rights are considered real property rights, the exchange of perpetual water rights for a fee interest in land constitutes a nontaxable exchange of property of like kind within the meaning of §1031(a).

Rev. Rul. 72-549, 1972-2 C.B. 472, holds that an easement and right-of-way, which were permanent, granted to an electric power company, were properties of like kind with real property with nominal improvements and real property improved with an apartment building.

Under the regulations cited, the types of real estate interests that are within the same kind or class as fee interests in real estate is broad. Both revenue rulings cited demonstrate that perpetual easements in the form of water rights and right-of-ways are of the same kind or class of property to which a fee interest in real estate belongs. The PCE at issue is also an easement. Under State X law, a PCE is an interest in real estate which, like a fee, is of a perpetual nature.

Therefore, based upon the above authorities and the facts and representations submitted, and assuming the proposed PCE is, by virtue of state law, an interest in real property, Taxpayers' exchange of a PCE in real property, under §1031(a), for a fee interest in other real estate that is also subject to a PCE will qualify as a tax deferred exchange of like-kind property, provided that the properties are held for productive use in a trade or business or for investment. If Taxpayers receive money or other nonlike-kind property in the exchange, gain will be recognized to the extent of such money received and the fair market value of such other property. Also, Taxpayers (and each of the co-owners) must recognize whatever gain is realized with respect to the fair market value of the replacement property received attributable to the transfer of the PCE as to that portion of the Old Ranch used for residential purposes and not for use in a trade or business or for investment.

No determination is made by this letter as to whether the described transaction otherwise qualifies for deferral of gain realized under §1031. Except as specifically ruled above, no opinion is expressed as to the federal tax treatment of the transaction under any other provisions of the Code and the Income Tax Regulations that may be applicable or under any other general principles of federal income taxation. No opinion is expressed as to the tax treatment of any conditions existing at the time of, or effects resulting from, the transaction that are not specifically covered by the above ruling.

This ruling is directed only to the taxpayer(s) who requested it. Section 6110(k)(3) of the Code provides that it may not be cited as precedent.

Sincerely yours,

Office of Associate Chief Counsel (Income Tax & Accounting)

This document may not be used or cited as precedent. Section 6110(j)(3) of the Internal Revenue Code.

NOTES AND QUESTIONS

1. PLR 200203033 is the first and only "private letter ruling" included in this casebook. Among alternative sources of legal authority, the private letter ruling is perhaps the weakest. Indeed, as you can see from the final sentence of this ruling, the IRS expressly notes that it "may not be used or cited as precedent." Still, tax attorneys regularly consult IRS letter rulings for guidance regarding the tax effects of various transactions, especially in the absence of clear answers from the statute, regulations, court decisions, or revenue rulings. The procedures for requesting a letter ruling are set forth in the first

revenue procedure (also known as a "Rev. Proc.") of each calendar year. Rev. Proc. 2012-1 defines a "letter ruling" as "a written determination issued to a taxpayer by an Associate office in response to the taxpayer's written inquiry, filed prior to the filing of returns or reports that are required by the tax laws, about its status for tax purposes or the tax effects of its acts or transactions." The user fee charged for providing a letter ruling varies depending on the nature of the question asked and the gross income of the requesting taxpayer. Standard user fees can range from $10,000 on up. These fees are typically set forth in an Appendix to the Revenue Procedure containing the procedures for requesting a ruling. For example, see Appendix A, Rev. Proc. 2012-1.

2. Suppose that when ConOrg initially approached the owners of Old Ranch, ConOrg had proposed paying cash for the PCE. Suppose further that the owners had in turn proposed that ConOrg buy New Ranch and then exchange it with them for the PCE. Would the result be the same?

3. Section 1033 provides for nonrecognition where real or personal property is compulsorily or involuntarily converted (e.g., by theft, destruction, or condemnation) and is replaced with property that is "similar or related in service or use." Nonrecognition of gain is mandatory where there is a direct conversion. Where the taxpayer receives cash and then buys the replacement property, nonrecognition is optional. The period in which replacement must occur is generally two years. Note the contrasts with §1031. Under §1033, (a) the replacement property must be "similar or related in service or use" as opposed to "like kind" (but see §1033(g), allowing reliance on the "like kind" standard in the case of certain conversions of real property); (b) if cash is received, the taxpayer has two years in which to find replacement property; (c) if cash is received, the taxpayer may choose to recognize gain; and (d) losses are recognized.

b. *Boot and Basis in Like-Kind Exchanges*

Boot. As you might suspect, most transactions qualifying as like-kind exchanges involve the transfer of property without identical values. Unless the party transferring the more valuable property is willing to accept property of a lesser value (which is very unlikely), the other party to the exchange will have to pay some additional amount to even out the deal. Tax lawyers use the word "boot" to refer to money and property other than money that, under a provision like §1031, is transferred as part of the like-kind exchange but is not like-kind property. The transfer of boot will affect basis and may result in the recognition of gain.

For example, if a farmer exchanges a farm for another farm and receives some cash and a tractor to boot (that is, in addition), the amount of the money plus the value of the tractor is the boot. The transaction qualifies for nonrecognition despite the boot, but if there is gain, it is recognized to the extent of the boot. See §1031(b). Thus, the amount of gain recognized is the lesser of the amount of gain realized or the amount of the boot. See also §1031(c), relating to loss situations. Note that if there is no gain to be recognized, the boot is not taxable; it is only gain that is recognized (and taxable), to the extent of boot, not the boot itself. For example, suppose that *S* exchanges *X* Farm, with a basis of $10,000, for *Y* Farm, which is worth $100,000, and that in addition *S* receives $15,000 cash and a tractor worth $8,000, or a total of $123,000 in property and cash. His total *gain* would be $113,000, the difference between his proceeds ($123,000) and his basis ($10,000). Of this realized gain of $113,000, $23,000, the fair market value of the boot, would be recognized. The remaining $90,000 gain would not be recognized. What amount of gain or loss would be recognized if the basis for *X* Farm had been $110,000? $130,000?

Basis. Section 1031(d) sets forth the rule for determining the basis of property received in an exchange covered by §1031. Generally, there will be a "substituted" basis (see §7701(a)(42)) — that is, the basis for the property received will be the same as the basis of the property relinquished. The rule becomes slightly more complicated when there is boot. The calculation of basis when there is boot involved can be made by following the directions in §1031(d) mechanically, but the following principles should explain why those directions produce a correct result. First, in a simple exchange of like-kind properties with no boot, the property received must take on the basis of the property relinquished so that when the property received is ultimately disposed of in a recognition transaction, any previously realized but unrecognized gain or loss will be taken into account for tax purposes. For example, if *S* exchanges *X* Farm, with a basis of $10,000, for *Y* Farm, worth $100,000, and there is no boot, and no gain is recognized, *S*'s basis for *Y* Farm must be $10,000 so that if it is later sold for $100,000 the previously unrecognized gain of $90,000 will be recognized.

Second, when gain is recognized because of boot, basis must be increased in the amount recognized so that that gain will not be taxed again; the basis of the like-kind property received plus the basis of the boot must therefore equal the basis of the original property plus the amount of gain recognized. For example, if *S* exchanges his *X* Farm, with a basis of $10,000, for *Y* Farm, worth $100,000, and receives $15,000 cash to boot, he must recognize his gain to the extent of the $15,000, and his basis must be increased by that amount. The basis of the property received plus the basis of the cash must therefore be $25,000.

Third, of the total basis thus calculated, a portion equal to the fair market value of the boot must be allocated to that boot, with the remainder being allocated to the like-kind property received. Thus, in the immediately preceding example, $15,000 of the total basis must be allocated to the cash (which always must receive a basis equal to its face amount). If the boot had consisted of a tractor worth $15,000, rather than cash, $15,000 of basis would be allocated to the tractor; because there is no justification for attaching nonrecognition basis attributes to the tractor, *S* is treated as if he had received cash equal to the tractor's fair market value and had used that cash to buy the tractor.

Fourth, if boot is *paid*, rather than received, the amount of the boot is added to basis. See Reg. §1.1031(d)-1(a). For example, if *T* owns *Y* farm, with a basis of $10,000, and exchanges it, plus $15,000 cash, for X farm, in an exchange that qualifies under §1031, T's basis in the X farm will be $25,000.

The rules described above can be expressed algebraically—though we emphasize that algebra is hardly necessary to understand the basic approach just described. Nevertheless, for those who are algebraically inclined, note that where A is the original basis, B is the amount of gain recognized, and C is the total basis to be allocated between the like-kind property received and the boot,

$$(1) \; A + B = C.$$

Where D is the portion of the basis allocated to the boot (which always receives a basis equal to its fair market value (FMV), so D is the fair market value of the boot) and E is the new, or substituted, basis of the like-kind property received,

$$(2) \; C - D = E.$$

Thus, if there is no boot (B and D are both zero), the like-kind property received will have the same basis as the property surrendered ($E = A$). If there is boot, the first step is to increase the original basis by the amount of the gain recognized to determine the total basis to be allocated (see equation (1) above). Then the boot receives a basis equal to its fair market value ($D = \text{FMV}$) and the basis left for the like-kind property received (E) is the total basis (C) reduced by the basis allocated to the boot (D), so $E = C - D$. If the gain recognized is equal to the amount of the boot ($B = D$), then the basis of the like-kind property received equals the basis of the like-kind property surrendered.

c.   Multiparty Transactions

Section 1031 is an important element in the planning of transactions involving real estate investments, from family farms to billion-dollar commercial towers. Many transactions have taken the form of complex three-party or four-party exchanges. By its terms, §1031 (unlike §1033) would seem to be available only in the relatively unusual circumstance where owners of two like-kind properties happen to want to swap with one another, but it has been extended beyond that situation, in a series of cases dealing with complex, multiparty transactions. These cases offer valuable insights into a basic problem in tax, and other, law: the problem of distinguishing between substance and form and of deciding when outcomes should be governed by form and when by substance.

Suppose that S (seller) owns the X Farm, which has risen in value because of its potential for residential real estate development. B (buyer) offers to buy the farm for $1 million in cash. S would be happy to sell and use the proceeds to buy a bigger and better farm, but his basis is only $10,000 and he can't stand the thought of sharing any of his gain with the Treasury. (He has held the farm so long that he thinks of it as entirely his, almost as part of his person. He has come to think of himself as a person worth $1 million and has forgotten, or never recognized, that for years he has managed to escape tax on his gradual increase in wealth.) *R*, a real estate broker, who will earn a commission of $60,000 if the sale is made, proposes that the tax barrier to the transaction can be avoided if the parties are prepared to pay a modest fee for a lawyer to construct a somewhat complex, and obviously artificial, legal arrangement. Following *R*'s advice, *S* finds another farm, the *Y* Farm, whose owner, *O*, is willing to sell for $1 million. The lawyer then devises the following transaction: *B* will buy the *Y* Farm for $1 million cash. Since *B* does not want to be stuck with that farm, there will be a previous agreement between *S* and *B* that will require *S* to swap the *X* Farm for the *Y* Farm once *B* has acquired the *Y* Farm. *S*, *B*, and *O* all follow the plan. *B* buys the *Y* Farm from *O* for $1 million and swaps it with *S* for the *X* Farm. *S* winds up with the *Y* Farm, *B* with the *X* Farm, and *O* with $1 million. *S* is so happy that he scarcely quibbles over the $70,000 that he must borrow in order to be able to pay $60,000 to *R* and $10,000 to the lawyer. The relationships and transactions may be depicted as in Figure 4-1.

(a) What is the substance of the transactions? Bear in mind that *B* never wanted the *Y* Farm. He wanted to buy the *X* Farm for cash and bought the *Y* Farm only to help *S* exchange his farm for another farm he wanted. In fact, his purchase of the *Y* Farm is contingent on *S*'s agreement to swap the *X* Farm for it. In the end, *B* winds up paying out cash and owning the *X* Farm. If tax considerations had played no role in the transactions, the easy, natural way for the three parties to have accomplished their objective would have been for *B* to pay $1 million for the *X* Farm and for *S* to use the $1 million to buy the *Y* Farm. We know as much not just from logic but from experience as well. Thus, one might argue that while the form of the transaction was a swap, the substance was a sale for cash and a reinvestment of the cash (though perhaps that is true to some degree of all swaps). Beyond that, the argument for granting relief under §1031 is weakened by the fact that the calculation of the gain to *S* is not a problem, and cash was available to him. Given the substance versus form issue and the policy considerations, will the effort to achieve nonrecognition succeed? Many tax lawyers, if confronted with this question, in the absence of any authority on which to rely, might predict that it would not. The Service is quite capable of seeing through artificially devised transactions and taxing them according to their underlying substance. And the courts often uphold the

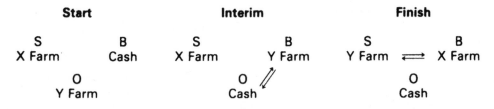

FIGURE 4-1
Illustration of Three-Party Transactions Under §1031 (Part I)

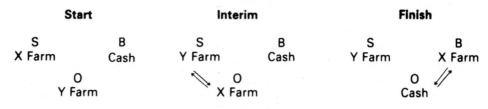

FIGURE 4-2
Illustration of Three-Party Transactions Under §1031 (Part II)

Service in this kind of effort. But not always, and the three-corner exchange is one instance where they did not. See, e.g., Alderson v. Commissioner, 317 F.2d 790 (9th Cir. 1963), where the court held in favor of the taxpayer, even though he had initially agreed to sell for cash and later modified the agreement to follow the three-corner-exchange model.

E.   OPEN TRANSACTIONS AND INSTALLMENT SALES

1.   Open Transaction Doctrine

The case that follows, Burnet v. Logan, has little if any remaining importance for the rule it adopts. The case continues to be of interest, however, because it establishes what one may think of as one end of a spectrum of possible recovery-of-basis rules and because of its discussion of the justification for the approach it adopts.

BURNET v. LOGAN
283 U.S. 404 (1931)

Mr. Justice McREYNOLDS delivered the opinion of the Court.

[The facts in the case are complicated and confusing. The following simplified and modified version of the facts reveals the essence of the transaction and the issues raised.

Mrs. Logan, the taxpayer, owned 1,000 shares of stock of Andrews and Hitchcock Mining Company. Her basis in these shares was $180,000. Andrews and Hitchcock owned the right to a part of the ore mined from a rich iron deposit. In 1916, Youngstown Sheet & Tube Company bought all the shares of Andrews and Hitchcock owned by Mrs. Logan and her fellow shareholders. As consideration for the purchase, Youngstown made a cash payment and agreed to make additional payments in the future based on the amount of ore that it would receive as a result of its acquisition of the Andrews and Hitchcock rights in the iron mine. There was considerable uncertainty about what the amount of the future payments would turn out to be.

Mrs. Logan's share of the cash payment was $120,000. The government estimated that she would receive future payments, based on the amount of ore going to Youngstown, of $9,000 per year for twenty-five years, with a present value of $100,000.

The position taken by the government was that in 1916 Mrs. Logan sold her shares for $220,000 (the cash of $120,000 plus the present value of the promise of future payments, $100,000) and should have reported a gain of $40,000. In other words, the government claimed that the transaction was a "closed transaction" in 1916. Mrs. Logan would then have a basis of $100,000 in the right to receive the future payments and, according to the government, would be allowed to recover this basis at the rate of $4,000 per year over the twenty-five years in which she expected to receive payments.

Mrs. Logan argued for "open transaction" treatment. There were two separate aspects to her position. The first was that the promise to make future payments did not have an ascertainable value in 1916 and should be ignored in that year. The second aspect of Mrs. Logan's tax position was that she should be allowed to recover her entire basis before reporting any gain. Thus, she claimed that she was not required to report any gain in 1916, since she received only $120,000 in cash and her basis was $180,000, and that she was not required to treat any of the future payments from Youngstown as income until the total of such payments had exceeded her remaining basis ($60,000).

The Court, without separating the two aspects of Mrs. Logan's position, held in her favor. Its opinion follows.]

The 1916 transaction was a sale of stock—not an exchange of property. We are not dealing with royalties or deductions from gross income because of depletion of mining property. Nor does the situation demand that an effort be made to place according to the best available data some approximate value upon the contract for future payments. This probably was necessary in order to assess the mother's estate. As annual payments on account of extracted ore come in they can be readily apportioned first as return of capital and later as profit. The liability for income tax ultimately can be fairly determined without resort to mere estimates, assumptions, and speculation. When the profit, if any, is actually realized, the taxpayer will be required to respond. The [total] consideration for the sale [realized by all the shareholders] was $2,200,000.00 in cash and the promise of future money payments wholly contingent upon facts and circumstances not possible to foretell with anything like fair certainty. The promise was in no proper sense equivalent to cash. It had no ascertainable fair market value. The transaction was not a closed one. Respondent might never recoup her capital investment from payments only conditionally promised. Prior to 1921, all receipts from the sale of her shares amounted to less than their value on March 1, 1913. She properly demanded the return of her capital investment before assessment of any taxable profit based on conjecture.

"In order to determine whether there has been gain or loss, and the amount of the gain if any, we must withdraw from the proceeds an amount sufficient to restore the capital value that existed at the commencement of the period under consideration." Doyle v. Mitchell Bros. Co., 247 U.S. 179, 184, 185. . . . Ordinarily, at least, a taxpayer may not deduct from gross receipts a supposed loss which in fact is represented by his outstanding note. . . . And, conversely, a promise to pay indeterminate sums of money is not necessarily taxable income.

"Generally speaking, the income tax law is concerned only with realized losses, as with realized gains." Lucas v. American Code Co., 280 U.S. 445, 449.

From her mother's estate, Mrs. Logan obtained [by inheritance] the right to [additional payments from Youngstown Steel by virtue of the mother's ownership of Andrews and Hitchcock stock]. The value of this [right] was assumed [for estate tax purposes] to be $277,164.50. . . . Some valuation—speculative or otherwise—was necessary in order to close the estate. It may never yield as much, it may yield more. If a sum equal to the value thus ascertained had been invested in an annuity contract, payments thereunder would have been free from income tax until the owner had recouped his capital investment.[22] We think a like rule should be applied here. The statute definitely excepts bequests from receipts which go to make up taxable income. . . .

The judgments below are affirmed.

NOTES AND QUESTIONS

1. *The "open transaction."* Burnet v. Logan is said to stand for the "open transaction" concept or doctrine—the notion that where the total value of the consideration to be received by a taxpayer is sufficiently uncertain (not "equivalent to cash" because of "no ascertainable fair market value") that gain is not recognized until the payments actually received exceed basis. The key sentence in the opinion is, "The transaction was not a closed one." The case may be compared with Inaja Land Co. v. Commissioner, *supra,* where the taxpayer sold an easement affecting a river that crossed its property and the court treated the entire proceeds as a recovery of basis. There the uncertainty related to what was sold, and in Burnet v. Logan it related to what was received. In both cases the courts adopted a "wait and see" attitude. This is highly favorable to the taxpayer, much more so in an era of high interest rates than in the era of low interest rates when these cases were decided.

The taxpayer had another, unused string to her bow in Burnet v. Logan. Even if the value of the expected payments in the case had been ascertainable, the taxpayer might have argued that the transaction should not result in recognition or gain because what she received was a "mere" promise to pay, which is not treated as a receipt for cash-method taxpayers. For example, if a lawyer performs services for a client and the client agrees to pay $1,000 to the lawyer next year, the lawyer (assuming she or he uses the cash method) is not required to report the $1,000 until received. If, on the other hand, the promise to pay takes the form of negotiable promissory notes, such notes generally are considered "property," the value of which be included in income.

2. *Three possible approaches.* Consider three possible approaches to recognition of gain or loss and recovery of basis where property has been sold in return for the right to a series of cash payments (installments) to be received in the future. For present purposes, let us assume that each installment payment is to bear interest at the market rate, so we need not be concerned about

---

22. [This was the rule for annuities before 1934.—EDS.]

the rules relating to unstated interest or original issue discount. (1) One possible rule for recovery of basis is the *open transaction* approach. In Burnet v. Logan this was combined with a rule under which all payments received were treated as recovery of basis until the full amount of the basis was recovered and then all payments are treated as gain. Thus, the case may be said to reflect a *basis-first* rule. (2) A second possibility is to determine the *present value* of the expected payments and treat this sum as if it were cash received on the date of the sale. Gain or loss is then determined by comparing this amount with basis.[23] This is the *closed transaction* approach. (3) A third possibility is to use an open transaction approach but to allocate some portion of basis to each expected payment received, so that some portion of the gain or loss is recognized as each payment is received. This is the approach of the *installment method.*

What are the advantages of and objections to each approach? What are the circumstances to which each approach may be best suited?

3. *The present rule.* (a) In 1980, Congress expanded the availability of the installment method of reporting, under which gain or loss is reported as payments are received. See *infra* subsection 3. In explaining the revised rules, the Senate Finance Committee Report (No. 96-1000, 96th Cong., 2d Sess. (1980)) had this to say:

> The creation of a statutory deferred payment option for all forms of deferred payment sales significantly expands the availability of installment reporting to include situations where it has not previously been permitted. By providing an expanded statutory installment reporting option, the Committee believes that in the future there should be little attempt to obtain deferred reporting. In any event, the effect of the new rules is to reduce substantially the justification for treating transactions as "open" and permitting the use of the cost-recovery method sanctioned by Burnet v. Logan. Accordingly, it is the Committee's intent that the cost-recovery method not be available in the case of sales for a fixed price (whether the seller's obligation is evidenced by a note, contractual promise, or otherwise), and that its use be limited to those rare and extraordinary cases involving sales for a contingent price where the fair market value of the purchaser's obligation cannot reasonably be ascertained.

(b) Even before 1980, the Regulations relating to gain or loss on disposition of property had provided that "only in rare and extraordinary cases will property be considered to have no fair market value." Reg. §1.1001-1(a).

(c) In Warren Jones Co. v. Commissioner, 524 F.2d 788 (9th Cir. 1975), the taxpayer sold a building by land sale contract for $153,000, receiving $20,000 in cash and a contract calling for payment of the balance, $133,000, over fifteen years. In the year of sale, the taxpayer received $24,000, and since it had a basis of $61,913.34, it deferred reporting gain until it recovered its basis. Evidence was presented that the $133,000 contract could have been sold in the marketplace for only $76,980. The Tax Court held that the taxpayer

---

23. If the payments bear interest at the market rate, the present value will be equal to the total stated amount of the payments, before interest.

properly deferred reporting gain, that the contract was not "property (other than money)" under §1001(b), and that it was not the equivalent of cash since, with a fair market value of $76,980, it could not be sold for anywhere near its $133,000 face amount. The circuit court reversed, interpreting the legislative history of §1001(b) to mean that Congress intended to establish a definite rule that if the fair market value received in an exchange can be ascertained, the fair market value must be reported as the amount realized, rejecting the argument that cash equivalency close to face amount of an obligation was an element to be considered in determining whether fair market value could be ascertained. The court reasoned that §453, providing for installment reporting was Congress's way of providing relief from the rigors of §1001(b). Compare material on economic benefit and cash equivalents supra.

(d) Cf. Bolles v. Commissioner, 69 T.C. 342 (1977), where members of the Piper family agreed in 1969 to an exchange offer of their shares of Piper Corp. stock for Bangor Punta Corp. stock if Bangor Punta could acquire more than half of the Piper Corp. outstanding shares, with the consideration to be determined by a third party. During 1969, Bangor Punta had not acquired the requisite number of shares and the final price had not been set by the third party. The court, following Burnet v. Logan, held that due to the contingencies involved, the rights had no ascertainable fair market value and the taxpayer need not recognize any gain from receipt of the rights in 1969. Should the reason for deferral in this case be the lack of ascertainable value or the inappropriateness of the time to tax, given the substantial contingencies still unresolved? Can't everything be valued if necessary?

4. *The capital gain issue.* Under present law, whenever we are confronted with deferred payments we must be concerned about unstated interest (§483) or original issue discount (OID). The §483 and OID rules have the important effect of ensuring that the interest element in any deferred payment is treated as ordinary income rather than capital gain. Before §483 and the OID rules were adopted, and to some extent even now, judicially developed rules relating to open versus closed transactions affected the characterization of gain as ordinary or capital and the timing of the recognition of gain. If, as in Burnet v. Logan, a transaction was treated as open, payments received were treated as nontaxable recovery of basis until basis was exhausted and, if, as in that case, the transaction involved the sale of a capital asset, all subsequent payments were treated as capital gain. Thus, the seller had two advantages, maximum deferral and maximum capital gain treatment.

If the transaction had been treated as closed, the seller not only would have lost the advantage of deferral but also could have lost some of the benefit of capital gain treatment. For example, in Waring v. Commissioner, 412 F.2d 800 (3d Cir. 1969), the taxpayer in 1946 had in effect sold a license to use the name "Waring" on the Waring blender, in return for royalties. In his 1946 tax return, he treated the transaction as closed. He valued the right to the royalties at $300,000, deducted his basis of $93,000, and reported a capital gain of $207,000. This meant that his basis for the right to receive the royalties became $300,000. As royalties were received in subsequent years, he treated them as recovery of capital, reducing basis.[24] By the end of 1952, all the basis was exhausted and at that point all subsequent payments were treated as ordinary income (since they were not received as a result of a "sale or exchange"). In time, Waring obviously realized that he would have been better off if, in 1946, he had treated the transaction as open, under Burnet v. Logan. If he had done so, after recovery of basis, all payments would have been treated as capital gain as long as he received them. In 1960 and 1961, he filed returns claiming capital gain treatment for the royalties received in those years; his position was that his original decision to treat the transaction as closed was an error as to a continuing transaction and that he was entitled to correct that error as it affected years not closed by the statute of limitations. Unfortunately for him, open-transaction treatment depends on the taxpayer's ability to establish that the value of the rights received is not ascertainable. In light of the fact that in 1946 his accountant had valued the rights at $300,000, the court had little difficulty in concluding that no error had been made in treating the transaction as closed in 1946.

2.   Executory Contract or Completed Sale?

The open transaction doctrine of Burnet v. Logan is now highly disfavored, and, as stated in Reg. §1.1001-1(a), will be available "only in rare and extraordinary cases." As a result, almost all common commercial sales transactions today are treated as closed transactions for tax purposes, which means that their tax consequences must be reflected on the seller's tax return for the year of the sale (subject to the discussion of the installment sale method of accounting, in the next subsection).

But when exactly does a sale take place for tax purposes? This is not always obvious. If seller and buyer enter into a definitive sale and purchase agreement for appreciated property in 2016, and the deal "closes" in 2017 (title is transferred and the buyer pays for the property), in which year does the seller report the gain? Does the answer change depending on whether the seller is on the cash or accrual method of accounting?

The following case is one of the leading common-law analyses of the question.

---

24. Note that the taxpayer treated the initial sale as a closed transaction. The result was that he had a basis of $300,000 in the right to receive the royalty payments. The standard treatment then would have been to amortize this basis over the expected duration of the payments. For example, if that expected duration was ten years, the taxpayer should have deducted $30,000 per year. Instead, he was allowed to follow the basis-first approach of Burnet v. Logan, allocating basis to the payments thereafter received until all of his basis was recovered, with subsequent payments fully taxed. That basis-first approach was justified in Burnet v. Logan by the difficulty of determining the duration and amount of the payments. In *Waring*, however, the valuation difficulties were not considered too serious to prevent treating the original transaction as closed. That being so, it seems inconsistent to use basis-first cost recovery, which can be thought of as a form of open-transaction treatment. In other words, in *Waring* the open-transaction issue arises not just once but twice. The first time we get closed-transaction treatment, and the second time we get open-transaction treatment on the same facts.

LUCAS v. NORTH TEXAS LUMBER
281 U.S. 11 (1930)

Mr. Justice BUTLER delivered the opinion of the Court.

The respondent, a Texas corporation, for some time prior to 1917 was engaged in operating a sawmill, selling lumber and buying and selling timber lands. December 27, 1916, it gave to the Southern Pine Company a ten-day option to purchase its timber lands for a specified price. The latter was solvent and able to make the purchase. On the same day title was examined and found satisfactory to the Pine Company. It arranged for the money needed and December 30, 1916, notified respondent that it would exercise the option. On that day respondent ceased operations and withdrew all employees from the land. January 5, 1917, the papers which were required to effect the transfer were delivered, the purchase price was paid and the transaction was finally closed.

Respondent kept its accounts on the accrual basis and treated the profits derived from the sale as income in 1916. The Commissioner of Internal Revenue determined that the gain had been realized in, and was taxable for, 1917. The Board of Tax Appeals sustained his finding. 11 B. T. A. 1193. The Circuit Court of Appeals reversed the Board. 30 F.2d 680.

The gain derived from this sale was taxable income. If attributed to 1916 the tax would be much less than if made in 1917. Section 13 (d) of the Revenue Act of 1916 provided that a corporation keeping its accounts upon any basis other than that of actual receipts and disbursements [i.e., the cash method], unless such other basis failed clearly to reflect income, might make return upon the basis upon which its accounts were kept and have the tax computed upon the income so returned.

An executory contract of sale was created by the option and notice, December 30, 1916. In the notice the purchaser declared itself ready to close the transaction and pay the purchase price "as soon as the papers were prepared." Respondent did not prepare the papers necessary to effect the transfer or make tender of title or possession or demand the purchase price in 1916. The title and right of possession remained in it until the transaction was closed. Consequently unconditional liability of vendee for the purchase price was not created in that year. . . . The entry of the purchase price in respondent's accounts as income in that year was not warranted. Respondent was not entitled to make return or have the tax computed on that basis, as clearly it did not reflect 1916 income.

Judgment reversed.

NOTES AND QUESTIONS

1. The result in Lucas v. North Texas Lumber did not depend on the taxpayer's method of accounting, but rather the meaning of "sale." In the court's view, a contract to sell was a bilateral executory contract, not a completed sale, and as a result income could not accrue in 1916.

2. Would the result have been different if North Texas Lumber had prepared all the necessary papers in 1916 and the parties had scheduled a closing for January 1917? The next case addresses this question.

COMMISSIONER v. SEGALL
114 F. 2d 706 (6th Cir. 1940)

ARANT, Circuit Judge.

[On October 2, 1931, the Timken-Detroit Company, a Michigan corporation, entered into a "plan and agreement of merger, consolidation and reorganization" with the Silent Automatic Company, another Michigan corporation. The parties believed that the transaction was a tax-free reorganization, in which the assets of Silent Automatic were transferred to Timken-Detroit in a transaction in which gain was realized but not recognized. In the first part of the opinion the court concluded that the parties' analysis was incorrect, and the transaction in fact was a taxable sale of assets.]

We think the transactions involved herein constituted a sale, and the Board of Tax Appeals erred in holding otherwise.

The Board of course did not consider when the sale took place, having erroneously reached the conclusion that there was none; and that question remains to be determined.

There are no hard and fast rules of thumb that can be used in determining, for taxation purposes, when a sale was consummated, and no single factor is controlling; the transaction must be viewed as a whole and in the light of realism and practicality. Passage of title is perhaps the most conclusive circumstance. . . . Transfer of possession is also significant. . . . A factor often considered is whether there has been such substantial performance of conditions precedent as imposes upon the purchaser an unconditional duty to pay. . . .

* * * *

The situation in Lucas v. North Texas Lumber Co., 281 U.S. 11, is analogous in the instant case. An executory contract was made on October 2, 1931. Some of the purchase price was then paid and a promissory note for broker's commission given, but the Timken Company did not have an unconditional right to the execution of the documents transferring title until it delivered or tendered the promised debentures on January 2, 1932; nor had Silent Automatic an unconditional right to the debentures until it had delivered or tendered the bills of sale contemplated. It follows, we think, under the doctrine of the Lucas case, that for taxation purposes the sale herein did not occur until January 2, 1932.

Moreover, we think this conclusion accords with the intention of the parties. An examination of the contract reveals that Silent Automatic agreed to transfer and Timken to acquire all of the former's assets, including those of the Sales Corporation "as of January 2, 1932." These concurrent obligations were to be performed "on January 2, 1932, or as soon thereafter as possible." Silent Automatic also agreed that it would "diligently conduct its business in the usual manner" until delivery, and Timken agreed to assume all notes and accounts payable as shown by the consolidated balance sheet of Silent Automatic and the Sales Corporation dated August 31, 1931, "together with those currently accruing from August 31, 1931, to the effective date of delivery." The common stockholders of Silent Automatic were informed that Timken would acquire the assets of Silent Automatic as of January 2, 1932, subject to its liabilities. The stockholders of the Timken-Detroit Axle Company were notified not only that Timken and Silent Automatic would merge on January 2, 1932, but that they would continue to operate separately until that time. We think the parties themselves have interpreted this agreement as contemplating consummation on January 2, 1932. Their interpretation is entitled to great, if not controlling, weight. . . .

NOTES

1. The holding of Commissioner v. Segall, that a sale takes place on the transfer by the seller of title and possession, remains a useful starting point in analyzing transactions. Thus, a buyer's "prepayment" or "deposit" of cash does not turn an executory contract into a completed sale. Conversely, when the seller delivers title and possession, against the buyer's promise to pay in the future, a sale has taken place, even though the seller has received no cash. Such a sale may fall under the special rules for installment sales, covered in the next subsection.

2. The "constructive sale" rules of §1259, discussed in Chapter 5, can override common law and treat an executory contract for the sale of stock or certain other financial assets as a current disposition. Section 1259 was added as an anti-abuse rule, and contains an important exception for an executory contract to sell non-publicly traded stock that closes within one year from the date of the executory contract. §1259(c)(2).

3. Every stock sale on the New York Stock Exchange (or other exchanges with similar rules) actually creates a short-term executory contract. The date on which you direct your broker to sell your 100 shares of Apple stock is the "trade date." The contract settles three business days later, on the "settlement date." (This is shortened to "T+3" or "regular way" settlement among traders.) Shares actually are delivered against payment for them on the settlement date. Many years ago, cash-method taxpayers could sell stock for a gain on December 31st (that is, enter into a trade on that date) and report the income the following year. Under current law (the elimination of the installment sale method in the case of publicly traded securities and the constructive sale rules acting as belt and suspenders here), gain or loss is recognized by both cash method and accrual method taxpayers on the trade date.

4. What are the tax consequences of terminating or amending an executory contract? There is surprisingly little authority on the question, but the case usually cited for the proposition that amending or terminating an executory contract has no tax consequences is Commissioner v. Olmsted Inc. Life Agency, 304 F.2d 16 (8th Cir. 1962).

3.   The Installment Method

As developed in the preceding subsections, a sale of property ordinarily is a closed transaction, and the seller must include her gain or loss on her tax return for the year of sale. This is true whether the taxpayer employs the cash or accrual method of accounting.

But what does this mean for a cash method taxpayer who sells property that is not of a type that is publicly traded, where the seller provides seller financing? "Seller financing" (in slang terms, "taking back paper") refers to sales of property where part or all of the consideration received by the seller takes the form of promissory notes from the buyer. In this way, the seller finances the buyer's purchase of property from the seller. Seller financing is common in real estate transactions in particular.

Here, the label *cash* method may confuse. A cash-method seller includes in her receipts in the year of sale the *value* of any consideration received from buyer on the sale, whether cash, government bonds, piglets, or promissory notes of the buyer.[25] This should not surprise you. If, for example, you receive a bonus from your employer in the form of a new BMW automobile, its value is compensation income to you.

This means that in general the value of any buyer promissory notes received by a cash-method seller are included in calculating the seller's gain from the sale in the year thereof, even if the notes are not repayable for many years. This presents a cash flow problem for many sellers, as well as a sense that a seller may be reporting gain that will never materialize, because the buyer may default. The installment sale method was a response to this problem, and in fact was relied on by Congress in 1980 when it simultaneously liberalized the installment sale rules and aggressively narrowed the scope of the open transactions doctrine. (See subsection 2, *supra*.)

The installment method (§§453, 453A, and 453B) is an accounting method, like the cash or the accrual method of accounting. The installment method can be understood as accepting that a sale of property with seller financing is a closed transaction, but then adopting a special regime for the seller's recognition of gain that matches gain recognition against the receipt of principal on the seller financing. If the buyer borrows from third parties and pays in cash, the sale is entirely outside the scope of the installment sale rules. The installment sales method is relevant only to gains and does not apply to sales at a loss; these are simply closed transactions, and the loss arises in the year of sale.

Installment sale accounting is attractive, when compared with a closed transaction, for two reasons. First, it operates to defer tax liability, which conveys a time value of money benefit. The time value of money advantage of deferral can be seen here as equivalent to an interest-free loan from the government (in the amount of the tax). Second, it addresses the seller's cash flow problems,

---

25. As always, an issue may arise over how to value unusual consideration received: cost to buyer (if recently acquired)? Wholesale market price at which seller could convert the asset to cash? Retail value? But that issue is independent of the "When is it income?" question explored here.

because the government in effect becomes a lender to the seller, financing the seller's tax liability.

The basic approach is simple. Assume for this illustration that the buyer's promissory notes, however denominated, constitute debt for tax purposes, and further bear interest at an adequate rate. In such a case, the seller computes a ratio of gain to total expected payments and applies this ratio to each payment. For example, suppose a taxpayer sells property with a basis of $100,000 in return for a total stated amount of $300,000 in the form of payments to be received at the end of each of the subsequent five years of $30,000, $60,000, $30,000, $60,000, and $120,000 (plus adequate interest on each payment). Since the basis is $100,000 and the total to be received is $300,000, two-thirds of each payment received is treated as gain; the other one-third is a recovery of basis.

The installment sale method of accounting was once very important, but since 1980 Congress has repeatedly narrowed its scope to near the vanishing point (without revisiting the open transaction doctrine). It is today a very complex regime relevant principally to relatively small transactions.

Specifically, the installment method is not available for sales of personal property under a revolving credit plan, for sales of publicly traded property including exchange-trade securities, or for sales of inventory items by dealers in real or personal property. §453(b)(2), (k)(1).

Moreover, sales of nonfarm property where the sales price is greater than $150,000 lose the time value of money benefit of the installment method, *if* the aggregate face amount of all installment obligations derived from such sales in any year exceeds $5 million. See §453A. In that case, tax that is deferred on the excess is subject to an interest charge. This means that sellers are permitted to use the installment method, but when payment is received they must pay the government interest on the amount of tax deferred. Thus, any cash-flow problems are solved, but the tax advantage of deferral is eliminated.

Since the installment method is designed to provide relief where the taxpayer has not received cash, it is not available where the consideration received is thought to be readily convertible into cash. Thus, demand notes and publicly tradable debt obligations are treated the same as cash payments (in an amount equal to their fair market value). See §453(f)(4).

In the case of certain installment obligations, if a seller uses the buyer's obligation to secure a loan to the seller, the loan is treated as payment of the installment obligation. §453A(d).

F.   CONSTRUCTIVE RECEIPT AND RELATED DOCTRINES

Earlier sections of this chapter reviewed some of the special timing issues relevant to accrual method taxpayers. The materials that follow cover some of the most significant exceptions relevant to cash method taxpayers. (See, e.g., *Ford Motor Co., supra.*)

1. Basic Principles

Under case law and longstanding Treasury regulations, cash-method tax-payers must take income into account in the first year in which it is either actu-ally or constructively received. Treasury regulations provide that "[i]ncome although not actually reduced to a taxpayer's possession is constructively received by him in the taxable year during which it is credited to his account, set apart for him, or otherwise made available so that he may draw upon it at any time, or so that he could have drawn upon it during the taxable year if notice of intention to withdraw had been given." Treas. Reg. §1.451-2(a). A key to understanding some of the subtler aspects of the doctrine of constructive receipt is to remember that constructive receipt results in taxation of amounts that are set aside or available—amounts to which the taxpayer has a legal claim—not amounts that would have been available if the taxpayer had made some other deal. The following case nicely illustrates this point.

AMEND v. COMMISSIONER
13 T.C. 178 (1949), acq., 1950-1 C.B. 1

BLACK, Judge.

We have two taxable years before us for decision, 1944 and 1946. . . .

In each of the taxable years there is one common issue and that is whether the doctrine of constructive receipt should be applied to certain payments which petitioner received from the sale of his wheat. There is no controversy as to the amounts which petitioner received or as to the time when he actually received them. Petitioners, being on the cash basis, returned these amounts as part of their gross income in the years when petitioner actually received them. . . .

In applying the doctrine of constructive receipt, the Commissioner relies upon Regulations 111, section 29.42-2. . . .[26]

In Loose v. United States, 74 Fed. (2d) 147, the rule providing for the taxa-tion of income constructively received is stated as follows:

> the strongest reason for holding constructive receipt of income to be within the statute is that for taxation purposes income is received or realized when it is made subject to the will and control of the taxpayer and can be, except for his own action or inaction, reduced to actual possession. So viewed, it makes no dif-ference why the taxpayer did not reduce to actual possession. The matter is in no wise dependent upon what he does or upon what he fails to do. It depends solely upon the existence of a situation where the income is fully available to him. . . .

---

26. "Sec. 29.42-2. *Income Not Reduced to Possession.* Income which is credited to the account of or set apart for a taxpayer and which may be drawn upon by him at any time is subject to tax for the year during which so credited or set apart, although not then actually reduced to possession. To constitute receipt in such a case the income must be credited or set apart to the taxpayer without any substantial limitation or restriction as to the time or manner of payment or condition upon which payment is to be made, and must be made available to him so that it may be drawn at any time, and its receipt brought within his own control and disposition. . . ."

Respondent, in his brief, relies upon the *Loose* case, from which the above quotation is taken, and several other cases which deal with the doctrine of constructive receipt. Needless to say, each of those cases depends upon its own facts. In the *Loose* case, for example, interest coupons had matured prior to the decedent's death. The decedent had not presented them for payment because of his physical condition. It was held that, even though the decedent had not cashed them, the interest coupons represented income to him in the year when they matured, under the doctrine of constructive receipt.

It seems clear to us that the facts in the instant case do not bring it within the doctrine of Loose v. United States, *supra,* and the other cases cited by respondent dealing with constructive receipt.

In discussing the situation which we have in the instant case, we turn our attention first to the contract of sale which petitioner made of his 1944 wheat crop to Burrus. The testimony was that 1944 was a bumper wheat crop year and that petitioner produced and harvested about 30,000 bushels, some of which was lying out on the ground and some of which was stored on the farm. Petitioner, through his attorney in fact, Paul Higgs, sold his wheat to Burrus for January 1945 delivery at $1.57 per bushel. It was the understanding that petitioner would ship his wheat to Burrus at once and that Burrus would pay him for it in January of the following year. The contract was carried out. Some time during the month of August 1944, after August 2, petitioner shipped the 30,000 bushels to Burrus. Burrus received it, put it in its elevator, and paid petitioner for it by check dated January 17, 1945.

Respondent's contention seems to be based primarily on the fact that petitioner could have sold Burrus the wheat at the same price for immediate cash payment in August 1944 and that although he did not do so, he should be treated in the same manner as if he had and the doctrine of constructive receipt should be applied to the payments received. We do not think the doctrine of constructive receipt goes that far. Porter Holmes, who was the manager of the Burrus Panhandle Elevator in Amarillo at the time of the 1944 transaction, testified at the hearing. He testified that it was the usual custom of Burrus to pay cash for wheat soon after it was delivered and that the transaction between Burrus and petitioner for January 1945 delivery and settlement was unusual and that he telephoned the manager at Dallas, Texas, for authority to make the deal that way and secured such authority and the deal was made. He testified that when Burrus' check for $40,164.08 was mailed to petitioner January 17, 1945, it was done in pursuance of the contract. So far as we can see from the evidence, petitioner had no legal right to demand and receive his money from the sale of his 1944 wheat until in January 1945. Both petitioner and Burrus understood that to be the contract. Such is the substance of the testimony of both petitioner, who was the seller of the wheat, and Holmes, who acted for the buyer. Such also is the testimony of Paul Higgs, who represented the seller in the negotiations for the sale. During 1944 all that petitioner had in the way of a promise to pay was Burrus' oral promise to pay him for that wheat in January 1945. Burrus was a well-known and responsible grain dealer and petitioner who testified that he had not the slightest doubt that he would receive his money in January 1945, as had been agreed upon in the contract. Such a situation, however, does not bring into play the doctrine of constructive receipt. See Bedell v. Commissioner, 30 Fed. (2d) 622, wherein the court said:

> While, therefore, we do not think that the case is like a promise to pay in the future for a title which passes at the time of contract, we would not be understood as holding by implication that even in that case the profit is to be reckoned as of the time of sale. If a company sells out its plant for a negotiable bond issue payable in the future, the profit may be determined by the present market value of the bonds. But if land or a chattel is sold, and title passes merely upon a promise to pay money at some future date, to speak of the promise as property exchanged for the title appears to us a strained use of language, when calculating profits under the income tax. . . . [I]t is absurd to speak of a promise to pay in the future as having a "market value," fair or unfair. . . .

The doctrine that a cash basis taxpayer can not be deemed to have realized income at the time a promise to pay in the future is made was reiterated by the Circuit Court of Appeals for the Eighth Circuit in the more recent case of Perry v. Commissioner, 152 Fed. (2d) 183. In that case it was stated:

> These cases seem to be predicated upon the fact that in a contract of sale of property containing a promise to pay in the future, but not accompanied by notes or other unqualified obligations to pay a definite sum on a day certain, the obligation to pay and the obligation to pass title both being in the future, there is an element of uncertainty in the transaction and the promise has no "market value," fair or unfair. This theory is supported by the decision of the Supreme Court in Lucas v. North Texas Co. . . .

The Commissioner in the instant case is not contending that Burrus' contract to pay petitioner for his wheat in January 1945 had a fair market value equal to the agreed purchase price of the wheat when the contract was made in August 1944. What he is contending is that petitioner had the unqualified right to receive his money for the wheat in 1944; that all he had to do to receive his money was to ask for it; and that, therefore, the doctrine of constructive receipt applies as defined in section 29.42-2, Regulations 118.

For reasons already stated, we do not think the Commissioner's determination to this effect can be sustained. If petitioner had begun this method of selling his wheat in 1944, when he had a bumper crop, there might be reason to doubt the bona fides of the contract, but what we have said about the 1944 transaction between Burrus and petitioner is based upon the finding that the contract between Burrus and petitioner was bona fide in all respects, though it was initiated by petitioner, and each party was equally bound by its terms. Petitioner did not begin this method of selling his wheat in 1944—he began it in 1942 and continued it through 1946. No doubt his taxes were more in some years and less in others than they would have been if petitioner had sold and delivered his wheat for cash in the year when it was produced. To illustrate this we need only point out that under the method which petitioner used he reported income in 1945 upon which he paid a tax of $2,672.64. His wife Eva also reported income and paid a tax of about the same amount. By treating petitioner's proceeds from the sale of his 1944 wheat as constructively received in 1944, the Commissioner determined over-assessments as to each petitioner for 1945 and deficiencies against each petitioner for 1944.

Petitioner was asked at the hearing why he adopted the manner of selling his wheat which has been detailed in our findings of fact. His answer was as follows:

> Well, that had been my practice, to handle that wheat that way since 1942 and I have handled my wheat that way, '42, '43, '44, '45, '46, '47 and into 1948. It is still my practice to do that and there have been some years in that interval that I would certainly have paid less income had I handled it the other way, but that is a semi-arid country and we are uncertain about our wheat crops and our expenses are always pretty well set and we know they are going to be high and we need our own protection to carry part of this wheat forward. . . .
>
> As I have already explained, it's been a matter of making my income more uniform and even; about five of those years had it all been set back and sold in the year that it was supposed to have been sold in, my income tax would have been less and in the other two it would have been more. I merely emphasize that to show the consistency of my policy and not as a matter of paying any tax.

Whether the reasons advanced by petitioner in his testimony quoted above are good or bad as a business policy, we do not undertake to decide. The question we think we have to decide is whether the contracts detailed in our findings of fact were bona fide arm's-length transactions and whether under them the petitioner had the unqualified right to receive the money for his wheat in the year when the contracts were made and whether petitioner's failure to receive his money was of his own volition. Our conclusion, as already stated, is that the contracts were bona fide arm's-length transactions and petitioner did not have the right to demand the money for his wheat until in January of the year following its sale. This being true, we do not think the doctrine of constructive receipt applies. See Howard Veit, first point decided, 8 T.C. 809.

Petitioner, in each of the years before us, returned as a part of his gross income the checks which he actually received in payment for his wheat. This being so, we think he complied with the income tax laws governing a taxpayer who keeps his accounts and makes his returns on the cash basis. . . .

NOTES

1. *Installment sales.* Assuming that his total sales in a year were below $5 million, could Amend today rely on the installment method of accounting?

The court wrote:

> While, therefore, we do not think that the case is like a promise to pay in the future for a title which passes at the time of contract, we would not be understood as holding by implication that even in that case the profit is to be reckoned as of the time of sale. If a company sells out its plant for a negotiable bond issue payable in the future, the profit may be determined by the present market value of the bonds. But if land or a chattel is sold, and title passes merely upon a promise to pay money at some future date, to speak of the promise as property exchanged for the title appears to us a strained use of language, when

calculating profits under the income tax. . . . [I]t is absurd to speak of a promise to pay in the future as having a "market value," fair or unfair. . . .

(a) In what way wasn't this a promise to pay in the future (1945) for a title which passes at the time of the contract (1944)?

(b) The court seems to distinguish negotiable bonds of a buyer from a contractual promise by buyer to pay for property. Is that consistent with your understanding of the current state of the open transaction doctrine?

2. *Consistency and clear reflection of income.* Note the court's reference to the fact that the taxpayer had been consistent in his practice. Thus, there was no distortion of income. Had there been such distortion, the Service could have invoked the forerunner of §446(b), which allows the Service to impose a method of accounting if the taxpayer's method does not "clearly reflect income."

The next case tests the distinction between constructive receipt and economic benefit.

PULSIFER v. COMMISSIONER
64 T.C. 245 (1975)

HALL, Judge.

Respondent determined a deficiency of $2,449.41 against each of the three petitioners for 1969. The sole issue for decision is whether petitioners, who were minors in 1969, must include in gross income in 1969 their winnings from the 1969 Irish Hospital Sweepstakes which were deposited with the Irish court.

FINDINGS OF FACT

All of the facts have been stipulated and are so found.

The petitioners, Stephen W. Pulsifer, Susan M. Pulsifer, and Thomas O. Pulsifer, are brothers and sister who lived in Medford, Mass., when they filed their petitions. . . . They are the minor children of Gordon F. Pulsifer and Theodora T. Pulsifer of Medford, Mass., who together are petitioners' counsel herein.

Mr. Pulsifer acquired an Irish Hospital Sweepstakes ticket in his name and the names of his three minor children. On March 21, 1969, he and petitioners received a telegram from the Hospital Trust advising them that their ticket would be represented by Saratoga Skiddy, a horse which would run on their behalf in the Lincolnshire Handicap. Saratoga Skiddy placed second, winning $48,000.

When he applied for the winnings, Mr. Pulsifer was advised that three-fourths of the amount would not be released to him because the ticket stub reflected three minor co-owners. He was further advised that, pursuant to Irish law, the withheld portion together with interest earned to date would be deposited with the Bank of Ireland at interest to the account of the Accountant of the Courts of Justice for the benefit of each of the petitioners. The money would not be released until petitioners reached 21 or until application on their behalf was made by an appropriate party to the Irish court for release of the funds. Mr. Pulsifer was sent his share of the prize.

The amounts paid over and credited to each of the petitioners were principal of $11,925 plus interest of $250.03, or $12,175.03. Mr. Pulsifer, as petitioners' next friend and legal guardian, has since filed for release of those funds, and he has an absolute right to obtain them.[27]

OPINION

Both parties agree the prize money is income to the petitioners. The only question is in what year must it be included in income. Petitioners contend that they should not be required to recognize the Irish Hospital Sweepstakes winnings held for them by the Irish court in 1969. They reason that neither the constructive-receipt nor the economic-benefit doctrines apply, and that all they had in 1969 was a nonassignable choice in action. Respondent argues that the economic-benefit doctrine applies, thereby dictating recognition of the prize money in 1969. . . . We agree with respondent.

Under the economic-benefit theory, an individual on the cash receipts and disbursements method of accounting is currently taxable on the economic and financial benefit derived from the absolute right to income in the form of a fund which has been irrevocably set aside for him in trust and is beyond the reach of the payor's [creditors]. E. T. Sproull, 16 T.C. 244 (1951), affd. per curiam, 194 F.2d 541 (6th Cir. 1952). Petitioners had an absolute, nonforfeitable right to their winnings on deposit with the Irish court. The money had been irrevocably set aside for their sole benefit. All that was needed to receive the money was for their legal representative to apply for the funds, which he forthwith did. See Orlando v. Earl of Fingall, Irish Reports 281 (1940). We agree with respondent that this case falls within the legal analysis set out in *E. T. Sproull*, supra.

In the *Sproull* case the employer-corporation unilaterally and irrevocably transferred $10,500 into a trust in 1945 for taxpayer's sole benefit in consideration for prior services. In 1946 and 1947, pursuant to the trust document, the corpus was paid in its entirety to taxpayer. In the event of his death the funds were to have been paid to his administrator, executor, or heirs. The Court held that the entire $10,500 was taxable in 1945 because Sproull derived an economic benefit from it in 1945. The employer had made an irrevocable transfer to the trust, relinquishing all control. Sproull was given an absolute right to the funds which were to be applied for his sole benefit. The funds were beyond the reach of the employer's creditors. Sproull's right to those funds was not contingent, and the trust agreement did not contain any restrictions on his right to assign or otherwise dispose of that interest.

The record does not show whether the right to the funds held by the Bank of Ireland was assignable. Petitioner claims they were not, but cites no authority for

---

27. The record does not disclose whether he had already received the funds at the time of trial.

his position. However, the result is the same whether or not the right to the funds is assignable. See Renton K. Brodie, 1 T.C. 275 (1942) (deferred annuity contract held currently taxable even though nonassignable and without surrender value).

In order to reflect our conclusion, decisions will be entered for the respondent.

QUESTION

Could the court have reached the same result under the doctrine of constructive receipt? What if the funds could not be obtained until the person entitled to them reached age 21?

G. NONQUALIFIED DEFERRED COMPENSATION

1. Background

This book covers a great deal of material, but arguably the taxation of "nonqualified deferred compensation" has as much importance to the life of a practicing lawyer, particularly one without the resources of specialist colleagues on whom to rely, as any other area that we cover. The reason is that the subject is vitally important to senior executives in structuring their compensation arrangements, and the rules in this area are even less intuitive than are most other tax regimes.

The types of arrangements covered by this section are referred to as *nonqualified* deferred compensation plans, to distinguish them from *qualified* deferred compensation plans, which are discussed in the next section. Nonqualified plans have essentially no limit on the amount of current compensation that can be deferred to, and become taxable in, future years. Qualified plans, as we shall see, generally must be made available to all employees and are limited in the amounts that can be deferred. On the other hand, the tax advantages of qualified plans are greater.

"Nonqualified" does not mean fatally flawed or defective in any way. It simply means that the deferred compensation plan does not constitute a qualified pension plan or the like. A nonqualified deferred compensation plan is one that defers an employee's income without violating the *funding* or *constructive receipt* principles applicable to the deferred compensation arrangements described in subsection 2, *infra*.

Every arrangement to pay money in the future for work done today is an "employee plan" for purposes of §404, even if the plan covers only one employee. See §404(a). This means in particular that the employer's tax deduction for the employee's compensation attributable to a nonqualified deferred compensation deal will always be governed by the matching rule of §404(a)(5). As a result, if an employee's income is deferred for four years under a nonqualified deferred compensation plan, so too is the employer's deduction.

The taxation of nonqualified deferred compensation directly implicates the constructive receipt doctrine introduced in Section F. However, §409A, added to the Code in 2004, along with the regulations promulgated thereunder, have greatly modified common law constructive receipt principles.[28] Nonqualified deferred compensation in the form of property (most commonly stock of the employer) adds the specific rules of §83 to the analysis. Finally, nonqualified employee stock options exist in their own mildly bizarre world; as we will see, despite the fact that they constitute property in any ordinary sense of the word, and valuable property at that, they are treated as tax nothings: essentially the same as a mere promise to pay deferred compensation in cash, in amounts tied to the value of the employer's stock. This means that nonqualified "restricted stock" and nonqualified stock options are analyzed differently—much to the confusion of clients and lawyers alike.

In Revenue Ruling 60-31, 1960-1 C.B. 174, the IRS established some basic rules for the taxation of nonqualified deferred cash compensation (that is, compensation whose receipt is deferred to a future taxable year). One important principle stated in Revenue Ruling 60-31 is that a cash-method employee is not taxable currently by virtue of an employer's "mere promise to pay" some amount of compensation in the future, even if the promise is unqualified (that is, without contingencies). (Practitioners in the area *always* preface the phrase "promise to pay" with the adjective "mere.")

Citing the *Amend* case (*supra*), the ruling observes that "the statute cannot be administered by speculating whether the payor would have been willing to agree to an earlier payment." In other words—and subject to the discussion of §409A that follows—the IRS does not apply constructive receipt principles by speculating that perhaps the employer would have been just as willing to pay the deferred amount this year rather than in the future.

On the other hand, where money is set aside in an independent trust or an escrow account for the benefit of the employee, out of the control of the employer, the employee is taxed at the time when the money is paid by the employer to the trustee or escrow agent, if at that time the employee is not at risk of losing the money by failing to continue his employment or some other act. (In the terminology used later, the employee's claim is both vested and funded.) The case that follows applies these principles.

MINOR v. UNITED STATES
772 F.2d 1472 (9th Cir. 1985)

The government appeals a tax refund judgment holding that contributions to a deferred compensation plan are not currently taxable. We affirm.

Ralph H. Minor is a physician practicing in Snohomish County, Washington. In 1959, he entered into an agreement with the Snohomish County Physicians Corporation (Snohomish Physicians) under which he agreed to render medical services to subscribers of Snohomish Physicians'

---

28. Section 409A is not the same as §409(a). Section 409A comes after §409.

prepaid medical plan in exchange for fees to be paid by Snohomish Physicians according to its fee schedule.

In 1967, Snohomish Physicians adopted a deferred compensation plan for its participating physicians. Under the voluntary plan, a physician who desired deferred compensation entered into a "Supplemental Agreement" in which the physician and Snohomish Physicians agree that for future services the physician would be paid a designated percentage of the fee he or she would receive under the fee schedule if not participating in the plan. The physician could elect any percentage from 10 per cent to 90 per cent. The balance would go into the deferred compensation fund. Minor's agreement with Snohomish Physicians provided that he would be paid 50 per cent of the scheduled fees through November 30, 1971, and 10 per cent thereafter.

To provide for its obligations under the Supplemental Agreement, Snohomish Physicians established a trust. Snohomish Physicians was the settlor, three physicians, including Minor, were trustees, and Snohomish Physicians was the beneficiary. The trustees, pursuant to instructions from Snohomish Physicians, purchased retirement annuity policies to provide for the payment of benefits under the plan. These benefits would become payable to the physician or to his beneficiaries when he or she retires, dies, becomes disabled, or leaves the Snohomish Physicians service area to practice medicine elsewhere. The physician agrees to continue to provide services to Snohomish Physicians patients until the benefits become payable, to limit his or her practice after retirement, to continue to provide certain emergency and consulting services at Snohomish Physicians' request, and to refrain from providing medical services to competing groups.

On his federal income tax returns for 1970, 1971, and 1973, Minor included in gross income only the 10 per cent of the scheduled fees which he actually received. The remaining 90 per cent, which Minor did not receive, went into the deferred compensation plan trust.

The IRS argues that Minor should have included in his gross income that portion of the fees Snohomish Physicians placed in trust for his future benefit. The IRS relies on the economic benefit doctrine, which is an exception to the well-settled rule that a taxpayer pays income tax only on income which is actually or constructively received by him. In this case, Minor did not actually receive the income the IRS attributes to him nor, the IRS has conceded, did he constructively receive the income. The IRS argues, however, that the economic benefit doctrine applies here because an economic benefit was presently conferred on Minor, although he did not receive and had no right to receive the deferred compensation benefits during the tax year.

Minor argues that the participants in the deferred compensation plan have no right to compel Snohomish Physicians to execute the trust agreement, or even to cause it to be created, implemented, or continued. The participants have no right, title, or interest in the trust agreement or any asset held by the trust. He argues that his right to receive payments of currently earned compensation in the future is contingent, and therefore does not vest any interest in him.

Recent cases from a number of courts provide useful guidelines for determining when a taxpayer is entitled to defer his tax obligations by participating in a deferred compensation plan. The cases fall into two general groups.

(1) *Constructive Receipt.* The constructive receipt doctrine holds that income, although not actually reduced to the taxpayer's possession, is constructively received by the taxpayer during any year in which it is credited to his account or otherwise set apart so that it is available to him without "substantial limitations or restrictions." Regs. §1.451-2(a) (1985). . . . If a corporation merely credits funds to an employee on its books but does not make those funds available to the employees, there has been no constructive receipt. [Regs.] §1.451-2(a). Similarly, an employer's mere promise to pay funds, not represented by notes or otherwise secured, cannot constitute constructive receipt by the employee to whom the promise is made. Rev. Rul. 60-31, 1960-1 C.B. 174, 177.

The IRS has conceded that Minor did not constructively receive the proceeds of Snohomish Physicians' deferred compensation plan. Because the IRS has acknowledged that the doctrine does not apply, we need not decide whether, under the constructive-receipt doctrine, Snohomish Physicians' promise to pay deferred compensation is anything more than a "naked, unsecured promised to pay compensation in the future." Goldsmith v. United States, 586 F.2d 810, 816, 218 Ct. Cl. 387 (1978).

(2) *Economic Benefit.* Although taxation of deferred compensation plans is generally analyzed under the constructive receipt doctrine, the economic benefit doctrine provides an alternate method of determining when a taxpayer receives taxable benefits. Under that doctrine, an employer's promise to pay deferred compensation in the future may itself constitute a taxable economic benefit if the current value of the employer's promise can be given an appraised value. The concept of economic benefit is quite different from that of constructive receipt because the taxpayer must actually receive the property or currently receive evidence of a future right to property. . . .

The economic benefit doctrine is applicable only if the employer's promise is capable of valuation. . . . A current economic benefit is capable of valuation where the employer makes a contribution to an employee's deferred compensation plan which is nonforfeitable, fully vested in the employee and secured against the employer's creditors by a trust arrangement.

In cases where courts or the IRS have found a current economic benefit to have been conferred, the employer's contribution has always been secured or the employee's interest has been nonforfeitable. See United States v. Basye, 410 U.S. 441, 445-446 (1973) (because trust was established, partnership's interest was nonforfeitable even though individual partner's share of the trust monies was not capable of valuation); *Goldsmith,* 586 F.2d at 821 (life insurance benefits were a nonforfeitable current economic benefit although other unsecured elements of deferred compensation plan did not constitute currently taxable economic benefit); Reed v. Commissioner, 723 F.2d 138, 147 (1st Cir. 1983) (economic benefit for a cash basis taxpayer requires that taxpayer's contractual right to future payment be evidenced by an instrument which is not only nonforfeitable but also readily assignable); United States v. Drescher, 179 F.2d 863, 865 (2d Cir.) (non-assignable annuity confers an economic benefit because annuity was nonforfeitable), cert. denied, 340 U.S. 821 (1950), McEwen v. Commissioner, 6 T.C. 1018, 1026 (1946) (deferred compensation secured by trust in which employee was the beneficiary). If the employee's interest is unsecured or not otherwise protected from the employer's creditors, the employee's interest is not taxable property, see [Regs.] §1.83-3(e) (1985), so the forfeitability of the employee's interest is irrelevant.

Superficially, the Snohomish Physicians' deferred compensation plan establishes a trust arrangement which protects the plan against Snohomish Physicians' creditors but also establishes conditions upon Minor's receipt of the deferred compensation which makes his benefits forfeitable. We examine separately the trust arrangement and risk of forfeiture.

Trust Arrangement. Neither Minor nor any other participants in the deferred compensation plan has any right, title, or interest in the trust which holds the annuity contract. The trust, which was established to hold the assets of the deferred compensation plan, was not established pursuant to Minor's Supplemental Agreement, but was created at the initiative of Snohomish Physicians which is both the settlor and beneficiary of the trust. Although Minor incidentally benefits from the trust, he is not a beneficiary. See Restatement (Second) of Trusts §126 (1959). Because Snohomish Physicians has not established any trust in favor of Minor or the other participants, the assets of the trust remain solely those of Snohomish Physicians and subject to the claims of its general creditors. . . .

Minor has pointed out several provisions of the trust agreement which show that the participating physicians had no vested, funded right to the assets of the trust. The IRS in response has cited Sproull v. Commissioner, 16 T.C. 244 (1951), aff'd, 194 F.2d 541 (6th Cir. 1952), in which a corporation paid over to a trustee compensation for past services rendered by petitioner. The trustee was directed to hold, invest, and pay over this sum to petitioner or his estate in two installments. The Tax Court held the entire trust fund was income to the petitioner in the year it was paid to the trustee. In *Sproull*, the settlor of the trust was the corporation and the beneficiary was the petitioner or his estate. The petitioner exercised substantial control over the money because he could assign or otherwise alienate the trust, had standing to bring an action against the trustee, if needed, and other powers under the trust. See *id.* at 247-248. In this case Snohomish Physicians is both the settlor and the beneficiary of the trust. Minor's only involvement is as one of the trustees. Because Snohomish Physicians' trust was not established in favor of Minor or the other plan participants, the deferred compensation plan is unfunded. Unfunded plans do not confer a present taxable economic benefit. . . .

Risk of Forfeiture. Minor's receipt of benefits under the deferred compensation plan is contingent upon his agreement to limit his practice after retirement to consulting services and to refrain from competing with Snohomish Physicians if he leaves its practice. The district court found that this restriction subjected Minor's benefits to a risk of forfeiture. The Code requires a taxpayer to include in his gross income any property transferred in connection with the performance of services unless the taxpayer's rights in such property are subject to a "substantial risk of forfeiture." §83(a) (1982). The district court did not enter a finding on the substantiality of the risk that Minor's benefits could be forfeited. See §83(c)(1) (1982).

If a recipient must perform or refrain from performing further acts as a condition to payment of benefits, the recipient's rights are regarded as forfeitable. . . . If Minor's Supplemental Agreement requires him to perform substantial post-retirement services or imposes substantial conditions upon his receipt of benefits, the economic benefit doctrine is inapplicable. . . .

From the record before us, we are unable to determine whether the restrictions on Minor's receipt of benefits satisfy the substantiality requirement of §83. We need not, however, invade the province of the trial court by inferring either substantiality or insubstantiality. We conclude that the deferred compensation plan is unsecured from Snohomish Physicians' creditors and therefore incapable of valuation. Thus, Minor's benefits do not constitute property under §83 (1982) and [Regs.] §1.83-3.

While Minor's deferred compensation plan severely stretches the limits of a non-qualified deferred compensation plan, we conclude that the Snohomish Physicians' plan is an unfunded, unsecured plan subject to a risk of forfeiture. We need not examine the substantiality of that risk.

Affirmed.

NOTES

1. *Constructive receipt.* In *Minor,* it was clear that the taxpayer could have contracted for payment to him of the amounts that were in fact, pursuant to the actual contract, credited to his account in the deferred compensation fund. This being so, why was the amount set aside for the taxpayer not constructively received?

2. *The importance of looking at both sides of the transaction.* The attractiveness of deferred compensation plans of the sort approved by Rev. Rul. 60-31 is limited by the fact that the employer will not receive a deduction for the amount to be paid in the future until the year in which the employee recognizes income. See §404(a)(5). If, in a given situation, a deferred payment is not taxed to the employee until ten years from now, the deferred payment will not generate a deduction for the employer until ten years from now. If the parties are in the same tax bracket, the advantage to the employee of deferral of the income will be exactly offset by the disadvantage to the employer of deferral of the deduction for the amount to be paid.

This is an extremely important point, but one that has less impact in practice than might be expected. It can be argued that the abundant use of non-qualified deferred compensation arrangements even in instances where the tax advantages are small or nonexistent suggests that corporate employers, particularly large public ones, are willing to use these structures to subsidize their senior executives' economic compensation in ways that are somewhat less visible than current cash compensation.

2. Nonqualified Deferred Compensation: Current Practice Overview

To make sense of nonqualified deferred compensation in general, it helps to organize the analysis according to three related but ultimately distinct concepts: vesting, funding, and constructive receipt.

The first concept is that of *vesting*. That term is not used on the face of the Code, but it is commonly employed in practice. Practitioners mean by it that an employee's claim to deferred compensation is "vested" if the employee has satisfied all the conditions precedent under her control to be entitled to receive the deferred compensation. As such, vesting looks at a deferred compensation arrangement from the employee's perspective and asks whether there is anything more she must do or refrain from doing (e.g., not working for a competitor) for her claim to the compensation to ripen fully, but for the passage of time. Vesting in practice is a concept unique to deferred compensation settings.

As an example of vesting, if you are recruited in 2016 to become the general counsel of World Wide Sprockets, Inc., and as part of your compensation package WWS promises to pay you $100,000 in 2021 without any conditions, your claim to the $100,000 vests in 2016. As it happens, you have received in 2016 a "mere promise to pay" you in the future (that is, no property has been transferred to you in 2016), and therefore, subject to §409A, discussed below, you do not have income in 2016, because your claim is not *funded*.

On the other hand, if WWS promises in 2016 to pay you $100,000 in 2021, but only if you work for WWS through 2019, you have no claim to the money until you satisfy the condition precedent: working through 2019. This arrangement vests in 2019, and it cannot be included in income prior to that date. But again, in 2019 all you possess is a mere promise on the part of WWS to pay you in 2021, and again that would not give rise to income in 2019, absent more facts.

Vesting may occur simultaneously with payment. If WWS promises to pay you $100,000 on June 30, 2021, if you are employed continuously by WWS from July 1, 2016, to that future date, then your entitlement to the money (vesting) and payment of it both occur on June 30, 2021.

The Code invokes the vesting concept by phrasing matters in the negative. Section 83 is the special Code section providing that any transfer of property to an individual in connection with the performance of services by that individual (or, technically, by anyone else, thus obviating avoidance schemes) must be included in the income of the person providing those services in the first year that the property is transferable by the recipient, or is not subject to "a substantial risk of forfeiture." Properly drafted nonqualified deferred compensation plans generally do not permit employees to transfer property before it is awarded outright to them.[29] As a result, §83 in practice requires the inclusion of deferred compensation income when (i) property is (ii) transferred by the employer beyond the reach of the employer or its creditors and (iii) the transferred property is not subject to a substantial risk of forfeiture by the employee.

"Vesting" is a shorthand way of saying that an employee's claim is not subject to a substantial risk of forfeiture, often because an existing substantial risk of forfeiture has lapsed. Tweaking the previous example, imagine that you are

---

29. The remainder of this section ignores the possibility that property subject to a substantial risk of forfeiture (unvested) nonetheless is transferable by the employee. Employers want to make sure they can in fact get the property back if the employee does not satisfy the conditions precedent to her entitlement to the property.

promised 50,000 shares of WWS stock in 2021, but only if you work for WWS from 2016 through 2019, continuously, under §83 there is a substantial risk of forfeiture until the end of 2019, at which time it lapses. The lapsing of the substantial risk of forfeiture is what is meant by vesting.

Section 83 thus can be understood as indirectly defining "vesting" and further as codifying the old economic benefit cases. To rephrase the critical point, the idea underlying §83 is that if an employee receives *property* from her employer, the fair market value of that property (minus anything employee is required to pay for the property) is immediately includable in the employee's income, *unless* the property is subject to a *substantial risk of forfeiture*—that is, unless it has not vested.

In the real world, the "property" to which §83 applies often is employer stock. For example, imagine that World Wide Sprockets on June 1, 2017, grants an employee 100 shares of WWS stock, subject to the condition that employee work for WWS until May 31, 2020. The stock actually is issued and held by a trustee for the benefit of the employee. The employee is not permitted to sell the stock during this term. This is a "restricted stock" arrangement. The employee really owns the stock for corporate law purposes. He gets to vote it, he gets dividends on it, and so on. But he does not yet own the stock for tax purposes. When the forfeiture condition lapses (2020), then he becomes the owner for tax purposes, and then he has income on the value of the stock, measured by the fair market value of the stock at that time (2020).

Technically, and very confusingly, money is not property for §83 purposes (although it is for most every other purpose in the Code). That is, employer's promise to pay you cash compensation in the future is not itself treated as property: The *promise* is not analyzed as if it were a standalone debt instrument (property) issued by the employer to you. So a "mere" promise to pay compensation in the future technically is simply outside the reach of §83. However, if the employer takes cash and puts it into a trust for the employee's benefit, then the employee's *interest in that trust* is property to which §83 can apply. Reg. §1.83-3(e) provides:

> For purposes of section 83 and the regulations thereunder, the term "property" includes real and personal property other than either money or an unfunded and unsecured promise to pay money or property in the future. The term also includes a beneficial interest in assets (including money) which are transferred or set aside from the claims of creditors of the transferor, for example, in a trust or escrow account.

In practice, if you apply §83 principles by analogy to pure deferred cash compensation, you are unlikely to go wrong, both because those principles themselves reflect preexisting common law, and because complex promises to pay cash in the future often are wrapped inside some sort of trust. A mere promise to pay, for example, implies that nothing has been transferred, because the promise itself is deemed not to constitute property. So the mere promise to pay by itself cannot constitute an immediate income inclusion. Similarly, vesting can be relevant, although when combined with a mere promise to pay the latter usually swallows the former.

Example: Employer agrees in December 2016 to pay Adam in January 2021 $1,000, plus notional "interest" on that $1,000 from January 1, 2017, to the payment date, if Adam works for Employer until the end of 2018. The $1,000 is not put into a trust beyond the reach of Employer's creditors or otherwise segregated from Employer's other assets. The payment cannot be accelerated for any reason. The deal is a one-off arrangement with Adam.

Result. There is an unfunded (or "mere," or "naked") promise to pay Adam. Adam's claim will *vest* on December 31, 2018: He will have satisfied the conditions set by the arrangement then. Adam will not have constructive or actual receipt of any income in respect of the arrangement until 2021. It does not matter whether Adam or Employer proposed the arrangement, or whether Employer would have been willing to pay $1,000 in cash in December 2016. Adam has income in 2021, and Employer has a deduction in 2021. The amount of the income and the deduction is the same: It is whatever is paid, that is, not $1,000, but $1,000 plus the notional "interest" credited to Adam.

The notional "interest" credited to Adam is a red herring: It is just a way of expressing the total amount of contingent compensation payable to Adam in 2021. Adam does not include the "interest" in income earlier, because it in fact is not interest for tax purposes, in that Adam has not actually lent capital to Employer. The same would be true if Employer instead promised to pay Adam in 2021 the total return on $1,000 notionally invested in the S&P 500 from January 1, 2017, until January 2021. Again, this is just a way of expressing the contingent amount of compensation that Adam will receive.

The second fundamental concept is *funding.* Funding looks at a deferred compensation arrangement from the employer's perspective, and it asks whether property has been irrevocably set aside for the benefit of the employee beyond the reach of the employer's creditors. It is the converse of a "mere promise to pay." "Funding" means that there has been an irrevocable transfer of property set aside for the benefit of an employee beyond the reach of creditors.

One might intuitively think that if a deferred compensation arrangement is funded—if property has irrevocably been set aside for an employee, beyond the reach of creditors—the employee must have immediate income, but that ignores the role of vesting. Again, go back to the restricted stock example above: Funding *plus* vesting is the usual trigger for income inclusion in a properly drafted plan. One without the other usually is insufficient.

For employers to enforce their rights to claw back property that has been transferred to an employee before the property has vested (e.g., a restricted stock plan), employers typically use some sort of trust vehicle. This was the case in *Minor,* for example. But placing property in trust by itself does not answer the question of whether the property has been transferred to the employee—that is, whether the arrangement has been funded, to use this section's term. Property is transferred only if it is beyond the reach of the employer's creditors. In *Minor,* the court concluded that the trust's assets had not been transferred beyond the reach of the employer's creditors, and therefore the employee (Minor) had not received any property interest to which §83 could apply; notwithstanding the trust, all that Minor had was a mere promise to be paid.

Deferred compensation specialists have a sense of humor, after a fashion, which they evidence by regularly referring to "Rabbi trusts." In doing so they are not expressing any religious preferences, but rather referring to a famous IRS ruling of many years ago in which a trust was carefully structured to be defective, in the sense that the trust assets were not beyond the reach of the creditors of the employer (a synagogue). To say that an employee has an interest in a Rabbi trust is to say that the deferred compensation arrangement is unfunded for §83 purposes. To complete the knee slapping, a "secular trust" is one where the assets are beyond the reach of employer's creditors.

In modern practice a Rabbi trust is used not only to achieve a tax objective, but also to bridge a credibility gap. It often is the case that a high-income employee—a new CEO, for example, brought in to right a listing ship—does not fully trust her new employer to pay her what she is owed in the future, even though the employer can afford to do so, because the CEO knows the employer can be vindictive when things do not work out, and it will have much deeper pockets to fund litigation than will the CEO. So the incoming CEO may insist that the employer set aside her deferred cash compensation in a trust for her benefit. At the same time, the CEO wants to defer her income until she gets the cash. The resolution is that the employer will put the money into a trust, to give the CEO confidence that the employer will not hassle her in the future, but the trust instrument will explicitly provide that the trust's assets are fully within the reach of creditors of the employer.

Section 83(b) offers employees an interesting opportunity to gamble. As previously discussed, long-term capital gains are taxed at much lower rates than is ordinary income (including compensation income). The normal rule of §83 is that the receipt of unrestricted property is ordinary compensation income. The property can be employer stock, or real estate, or kumquats, or cash held in trust. Section 83(b), however, permits an employee who receives a current transfer of property (i.e., the arrangement is *funded*) but whose interest has *not* yet vested (i.e., it is subject to a substantial risk of forfeiture), to ignore the forfeiture risk and to declare the current value (on grant) of the property as income. From that point forward, the employee is treated as the tax owner of the property. This means the employee will enjoy preferential capital gains rates on the subsequent appreciation (once the one-year holding period has been satisfied). But if the stock collapses in value, then the employee will have recognized ordinary compensation income on the original value of the stock and an offsetting capital loss, which often has less value to the employee.

Executives of start-up companies are heavy users of §83(b) elections in respect of restricted stock arrangements. On information and belief, the ordinary income/capital loss whipsaw risk often is handled by executives adopting the position that the restricted stock has extremely low value at the time of the §83(b) election.

As developed in subsection 4, *infra*, the most common nonqualified employee stock options are *not* eligible for §83(b) elections. This point deserves stressing, because it is counterintuitive, and because so many people get it wrong.

PROBLEM

Suppose you represent a superstar college football player who was selected first in the National Football League draft by a newly established team (an "expansion" team). The team has offered to pay your client a signing bonus of $1 million, payable at the end of five years. This is in addition to salary and performance bonuses, and it is not contingent on any aspect of performance other than signing the contract. You are satisfied with the amount of the signing bonus, but you are concerned about the financial ability of the team to continue to pay the $1 million at the end of the five years, since it will presumably operate at a loss for at least five years, and the losses may turn out to be greater than expected. The team is operated as a corporation. All the shares of the corporation's stock are held by a real-estate tycoon who is active in the team's management and who is extremely anxious that your client sign. Your client is anxious not to pay tax on money that he has not received and wants to avoid any substantial risk of not being paid. What is your advice about each of the following possible ways of structuring the deal?

(a) The corporation buys an annuity policy from an insurance company. The policy names the player as the annuitant and provides for payment of $1 million to the player at the end of five years. The corporation pays $600,000 for the policy. It is nonassignable, and the payment cannot be accelerated.

(b) The corporation contributes $600,000 to a trust. The trustee is directed to invest the $600,000 in U.S. Treasury bonds. The interest earned on these bonds (and on the interest received) over the next five years will total $400,000. The trustee is directed to pay the player $1 million at the end of five years. The corporation retains no interest in the trust.

(c) The facts are the same as in (b) except that at the end of the five years the $1 million is to be paid to the corporation to provide funds it can use to meet its own contractual obligation to the player.

(d) The corporation signs an unconditional agreement to pay $1 million to the player at the end of five years. The real-estate tycoon who owns all the shares of the corporation signs a guarantee of its obligation.

The third fundamental concept is constructive receipt. Because of its reinvigorated importance, it is the subject of the next subsection.

3.   Nonqualified Deferred Compensation: Constructive Receipt and §409A

Prior to the adoption of §409A in 2004, the concept of constructive receipt had a relatively modest role in nonqualified deferred compensation practice. The idea, best summarized in Reg. §1.451-2(a), was that a taxpayer could not turn his back on compensation income made available to him:

> Income although not actually reduced to a taxpayer's possession is constructively received by him in the taxable year during which it is credited to his account, set apart for him, or otherwise made available so that he may draw upon

it at any time, or so that he could have drawn upon it during the taxable year if notice of intention to withdraw had been given. However, income is not constructively received if the taxpayer's control of its receipt is subject to substantial limitations or restrictions. Thus, if a corporation credits its employees with bonus stock, but the stock is not available to such employees until some future date, the mere crediting on the books of the corporation does not constitute receipt.

For example, Otis B. Driftwood is the CEO of World Wide Sprockets. On December 1, 2016, the Board of Directors of WWS awards him a $100,000 bonus for his exemplary work in 2016, payable on December 15th. Driftwood proposes that the award be deferred and paid to him (with an interest factor) in December 2021. Even before §409A, most practitioners would have agreed that this deferral would fail the application of the constructive receipt doctrine and therefore would be taxable to Driftwood in 2016, even though the contract was unfunded and unvested.

Section 409A is often referred to as "constructive receipt on steroids." It was adopted in 2004 as an anti-abuse rule, as explained below. For purposes of these materials, §409A can be viewed as implementing new standards for applying constructive receipt principles in a much more rigorous fashion than prior practice and case law countenanced.

For example, a deferred compensation plan that allows employees to accelerate their right to deferred income, but at the cost of a significant "haircut" in the amount to be paid, arguably would not have been a constructive receipt problem before 2004, but most advisors would agree that such a plan violates §409A today.

In general, §409A provides that amounts payable in the future are taxable when bargained for if the plan allows employees to accelerate benefits or provides that upon a deterioration of the employer's financial health assets are shielded from outside creditors. Section 409A applies, with some significant exceptions, to grants of restricted stock and stock options. It does not apply to qualified deferred compensation plans, discussed in the next section.[30]

---

30. Under Code §409A, distributions to employees of deferred compensation may not occur earlier than the earliest to occur of the following:

- separation from service (except distributions to key employees of publicly traded corporations may not be made before the date which is six months after the date of separation from service (or, if earlier, the date of death of the key employee)). Key employee generally includes persons who are officers having an annual compensation greater than $130,000, adjusted for cost of living ($160,000 for 2009 and limited to fifty employees), 5 percent owners and 1 percent owners having annual compensation greater than $150,000;
- the date the participant becomes disabled;
- death;
- a specified time (or pursuant to a fixed schedule) specified under the plan at the date of the deferral of such compensation (note that this literally requires a specified time and not a specified event; would not cover an event like a payout due upon meeting a performance target);
- to the extent provided by the Secretary, a change in the ownership or effective control of the corporation, or in the ownership of a substantial portion of the assets of the corporation; or
- the occurrence of an unforeseeable emergency.

Provisions that would permit distributions earlier than that outlined above cause a deferred compensation plan to violate §409A. The consequence of violating §409A is that all compensation,

Section 409A may represent good tax policy but was adopted in response to a failure in corporate governance. A prime example was Enron Corporation, a large natural resources and trading company that had enjoyed great success with investors, based in large part on phony transactions and misleading accounting. Enron eventually collapsed, with huge losses to investors and employees. By late 2001, top executives in Enron had claims to over $150 million in nonqualified deferred compensations plans. Under those plans, executives were allowed to petition for acceleration of payment in the event of financial hardship. As the collapse of Enron became more and more likely, executives petitioned the plan administrator (another Enron executive) for acceleration of payment, and the administrator granted the petitions. In the weeks before bankruptcy, over $50 million of previously deferred compensation left the company in the form of accelerated payments to executives.

Bad facts make hard law. In the words of two eminent scholars in this area: "We think §409A basically gets it backward. Taxpayers now face extremely complicated rules that are focused on the least important considerations and that overlook the most important." Daniel Halperin and Ethan Yale, *Deferred Compensation Revisited*, 114 *Tax Notes* 939 (2007).

4. Nonqualified Deferred Compensation: Stock Options

One very popular form of deferred compensation is the nonqualified employee stock option. (Incentive Stock Options are a form of qualified compensation, and are discussed in the next section.) In the ordinary case involving an established publicly traded company, an employee stock option will be nonassignable by the option holder, and its exercise price will be set no lower than the current trading price for the employer's stock on the date of grant.

The tax treatment of employee stock options along the lines just outlined is simple, once one suspends disbelief. Such stock options generally are *not* treated as property at all for §83 purposes, by virtue of §83(e)(3), Reg. §1.83-7, and decades of administrative practice. Technically, those regulations adopt the position that a nonqualified option falls within §83 only if it has a "readily ascertainable fair market value," and that, while options of course have value when granted, that value is not "readily ascertainable" unless the option itself "is actively traded on an established market" or certain other conditions are satisfied, the first of which is that the option be assignable.[31]

---

including past contributions by the employer, become immediately taxable. Moreover, the tax for the year is increased by an amount equal to 20 percent of the compensation required to be included in gross income, plus an interest charge—actually an additional tax—at the underpayment rate plus 1 percentage point on the underpayments that would have occurred had the deferred compensation been includable in gross income for the taxable year in which first deferred or, if later, the first taxable year in which such deferred compensation is not subject to a substantial risk of forfeiture.

31. It is theoretically possible to deliberately design stock options to have a readily ascertainable fair market value, for the purpose of enabling a §83(b) election to be made, but the same result can be reached through other means, and is not what ordinarily is understood by the term nonqualified stock option.

This means that an employee does *not* have income on the *grant* of properly drafted nonqualified employee stock options, even with *no* risk of forfeiture. Instead, the option is viewed as identical in tax impact to a mere promise to pay cash in the future. Neither the grant nor (if relevant) vesting of a nonqualified employee stock option triggers tax, because the option is viewed as a "tax nothing." Tax is triggered only when the employee *exercises* the option, at which time the employee has ordinary compensation income equal to the "spread" between the then-market value of the stock and the employee's exercise price.

For example, imagine that World Wide Sprockets stock on March 1, 2017, trades at $200 per share, and that Driftwood is awarded fifty nonassignable nonqualified stock options on that date exercisable at $200 per share. The options vest on March 1, 2020, if Driftwood has been employed continually from the grant date until that date, and can be exercised (if vested) at any time thereafter until February 28, 2025.

The grant of this option has no tax consequences. On March 1, 2020, when WWS stock trades for $300 per share, the options vest. Driftwood's option still has no tax consequences, even though in any ordinary sense of the words Driftwood has both vesting and funding (the receipt of "property" in the form of the stock options).

In 2024, when WWS stock trades for $450 per share, Driftwood exercises ten of his stock options by tendering $2,000 to WWS; in return, he gets back ten shares worth $4,500. Driftwood has $2,500 of ordinary compensation income in 2024, and WWS has a compensation expense deduction of $2,500 in 2024.

Because a nonqualified employee stock option is a tax nothing from the start, *there is nothing in respect of which the employee can make a §83(b) election.* As a result, the "spread" ($2,500 in this example) is always ordinary compensation income.

5.   Nonqualified Deferred Compensation: Qualified Equity Grants

The 2017 act added a new category of nonqualified deferred compensation, confusingly termed "qualified equity grants." See §83(i). This category applies only to privately held corporations (i.e., a corporation whose stock is not readily tradable on an established securities market). The general idea is that a "qualified employee" who receives "qualified stock" on the exercise of a stock option may elect to defer the income inclusion associated with the exercise of the option from the date the stock is vested (typically, on exercise) to a date five years later, or, if earlier, the date on which the stock becomes publicly traded, the employee becomes a 1 percent or greater shareholder of the company, or certain other events occur. (The provision also can apply to a form of notional stock called a "restricted stock unit.") Section 83(i) is available only if at least 80 percent of the company's employees receive stock options on the same terms. In light of this requirement of broad participation, and the fact that holders of 1 percent or more of a firm's stock cannot make the §83(i) election, the new rule seems to be aimed at plans offered to rank-and-file employees of private firms, particularly, one would imagine, in the start-up arena.

6.   Nonqualified Deferred Compensation: Shortcuts

This material is difficult, but important. Here is a summary that might be useful.[32]

Fundamental Operating Rules

No vesting = No current income to employee (*generally; see next rule*)

No vesting + Funding = Transfer of property "subject to substantial risk of forfeiture" = Possibility of §83(b) *election by employee*

Vesting + Funding = Immediate income to employee

Vesting + Constructive receipt = Immediate income to employee

Vesting + No funding + No constructive receipt = Deferral = Happy employee

Employer deduction for wage expense = Amount and timing of employee's inclusion

---

Nonqualified Stock Options

(Solely in deferred compensation context; assumes the option is not tradable)
Employee stock option = *Tax nothing*
                     = No transfer of "property"
                     = No possibility of §83(b) election
                     = Vesting by itself not problematic
                     = Tax equivalent of "mere promise to pay" contingent compensation in amount of bargain element of option (value — exercise price) *when employee exercises option*

---

7.   Nonqualified Deferred Compensation: Policy

Under §404(a)(5), an employer may claim a tax deduction for compensation paid only when (and in the same amount as) the employee includes the compensation as income. (A special rule enables accrual method employers to deduct compensation paid in the first two and a half months of the succeeding taxable year.) If, in a given situation, a deferred payment is not taxed to the employee until ten years from now, the deferred payment will not generate a deduction for the employer until ten years from now. This rule adopts a

---

32. This ignores §§457 and 457A.

matching principle that is extremely important in thinking about the real cost to the Treasury of deferred compensation arrangements.

If the parties to a deferred compensation arrangement are in the same tax bracket, the advantage to the employee of deferral of the income will be exactly offset by the disadvantage to the employer of deferral of the deduction for the amount to be paid.

If the employer is in a lower tax bracket than the employee, deferral can be advantageous. To understand why this is so, imagine an employee who works for a tax-exempt employer, such as a private university. Suppose the employee's marginal tax rate is 40 percent, and she is able to earn a 10 percent before-tax rate of return on her money. Her after-tax rate of return is 6 percent. The employer, on the other hand, pays no tax and is able to earn a before-tax and after-tax rate of return of 10 percent. The employee obviously would be better off if she were able to invest a portion of her salary at her employer's after-tax rate of return.

In the past, employees who worked for tax-exempt institutions managed to achieve this result through deferred compensation arrangements. The amount of currently deferred compensation would be invested by the employer and would increase in value at the employer's after-tax (that is, no-tax) rate — in our example, 10 percent. Eventually, the deferred funds, together with the interest earned on the funds, would be distributed to the employee.

Concern over the use of such plans led to the adoption of §457, which places dollar limitations on the plans when used by tax-exempt organizations like state agencies, charities, and universities. But §457 does not apply to a nominally taxable corporation with large NOL carryovers. Employees of such a company may therefore find it advantageous to defer unlimited amounts of their income and share, in effect, the tax shield of the company's NOLs.

More recently, Congress became aware that many hedge funds were organized as offshore partnerships, while their managers are domiciled in the United States. These entities compensated managers using deferred compensation arrangements in which the deferred compensation was reinvested in the hedge fund. Congress responded in 2008 by enacting §457A, which imposes a special penalty tax on amounts received from such arrangements.

The matching principle underlying §404(a)(5) is a very imperfect implementation of what more usefully can be approached by thinking of the deferred deductibility afforded the employer as a form of *substitute taxation*. That is, the real question is, are employer and employee in fact taxed at the same rate? Sometimes they are, and sometimes they are not, but by focusing on this question, it becomes apparent that matching by itself is an imperfect tool, if the goal is not to subsidize deferred compensation over current compensation.[33]

---

33. In fact, tax rates faced by employer and employee in deferred compensation plans always do diverge in one important respect that consistently works to the benefit of the combined incomes of employer and employee. As we have seen, many deferred compensation arrangements involve future payouts in the form of the employer's stock or in cash measured by the value of that stock. At the same time, companies, particularly publicly traded ones, wish to control the stock dilution that will follow on paying out compensation in future years in the form of their stock or in cash tied to the value of their stock. The obvious strategy is for the employer to buy back some of its outstanding stock today, to "hedge," in a colloquial sense, its future stock-based deferred compensation costs.

H.   QUALIFIED EMPLOYEE PLANS AND INCENTIVE STOCK OPTIONS

1.   Qualified Employee Plans

a.   *Basic Choices and Rules*

As the last section suggested, employers have many incentives to offer special deferred compensation or retirement plans for senior executives—particularly when one remembers that the "employer" acts only through senior management, as mediated by the Board of Directors. These plans usually offer the tax benefit of deferral to the employee (at the cost of deferring deductions to the employer, as just explained) and, in some cases, the ability for an employee to take a significant portion of compensation income as capital gain (through the §83(b) election available for "restricted stock," but not nonqualified stock options).

These plans are not as attractive from a pure tax perspective, however, as the "qualified plans" discussed in this section. The basic tension is that qualified plans offer tax turbocharging, but must be broadly offered and not "top heavy" in their benefit structure. So employers have two basic retirement or deferred compensation choices: highly targeted nonqualified plans and broadly offered tax-subsidized qualified ones.

Even without tax considerations, employers might have good reason to establish qualified employee retirement plans. For example, such plans may increase employee loyalty if benefits are subjects to forfeiture upon leaving the employer prematurely or moving to a competing firm. Or the plans may be thought to improve employees' incentives to increase shareholder value if the benefits are linked to the value of company stock. Well-run retirement plans may also simply be a benefit that prospective employees value in deciding where to work.

The overall trend, however, has been for firms to be more and more parsimonious in the qualified retirement plans they offer. Many reasons have been suggested for this, including global competition, smaller employee expectations for retirement plans in light of greater job insecurity, and shifts in the relative bargaining power of employers and employees (concomitant with the decline of unions in most industries).

Qualified employee retirement plans generally take one of two forms. First, they may be defined benefit plans, in which the employer agrees to provide fixed retirement benefits to each employee based on factors such as the employee's preretirement salary and number of years of employment. Second, they may be defined contribution plans, in which the employer's annual contribution

---

Under corporate tax law principles, if a corporation buys back its own stock, it pays no tax on the gain when it "resells" that stock in the future by delivering it to an employee. The employer thus has a zero tax rate on investing in its own stock, which means that the substitute taxation principle is always violated in this very common case. The matching principle here is honored, but the real issue is completely obfuscated.

to the plan, rather than the amount of ultimate benefit, is fixed by a formula, and the amount a retiree ultimately gets depends on the investment return earned on the contributions. Most qualified plans today are defined contribution plans.

Qualified plans are subject not only to abstruse tax rules, but also to regulation by the Department of Labor. The so-called ERISA rules (after the Employee Retirement Income Security Act of 1974) impose obligations designed to ensure the safety of investments by the plan and impose vesting requirements. The vesting rules are designed to ensure that after specified periods of service an employee's retirement benefit becomes nonforfeitable (that is, it is not lost if the employee quits or is fired). See §§401(a)(7), 411.

The relevant tax and ERISA rules are only hinted at in the material that follows. The role of adviser on qualified plans is a full-time specialty, and it would not be difficult to write a book as long as this one on that field.

Qualified pension (i.e., retirement), profit-sharing, or stock bonus plans have the following set of highly attractive features:

(i) Amounts that an employer pays into the plan (technically, pays to the plan's independent trustee) are not taxed to those employees who become entitled to future benefits by virtue of such payments, even if the employee rights are vested. Employees are taxed only when they actually receive payments on retirement.[34]

(ii) Employers are entitled to an immediate deduction for amounts paid into the plan. Thus, disregarding the tax and nontax effects on the employee, the employer should be indifferent as between a payment into a plan and a payment of an equal amount as part of the employee's current wage or salary; the employer gets the same deduction either way.

(iii) Earnings on funds paid into the plan and invested by it are not taxed as those investment earnings accrue and compound inside the plan. Instead, the earnings are taxed to employees only as and when paid to them.

(iv) A special type of plan termed a "cash or deferred arrangement," or more colloquially a "401(k) plan" (after Code §401(k), which provides its legal authority), permits employees to elect before the beginning of each year the amount of their upcoming year's income they wish to set aside into a retirement plan, up to $18,000 per year (for 2016). Additional "catch-up contributions" may be made, in limited amounts, by people age 50 or over.

(v) Employers are also allowed to provide "Roth 401(k)" plans. Under these plans, the employee is taxed on amounts paid into the retirement fund by the employer, but distributions are tax free — including earnings on the initial contributions. Thus, the tax advantage of deferral in the traditional 401(k) plan is sacrificed in return for the later advantage of tax-free distributions. The most important reason for these plans is that they effectively raise the annual cap on contributions, because taxpayers can set

---

34. At retirement, the employee normally receives payments spread over his or her remaining life, but in some circumstances the employee may be allowed to choose a single lump-sum payment.

aside $18,000 per year (for 2016) in after-tax dollars, rather than in pretax dollars (i.e., dollars ultimately subject to an income tax claim). See further description below.

b.   *Amount of Tax Benefit*

The following hypothetical figures illustrate the tax advantage of qualified plans (including traditional, tax-deferred 401(k) plans). Suppose that an employer pays into a qualified defined-contribution plan, on behalf of an employee, $10,000 per year for twenty-five years, and these funds earn an annual return of 10 percent. At the end of twenty-five years, on these assumptions, the total of the contributions and the earnings will be $983,471. Assume that at this point the employee retires and begins to collect benefits for life; that his life expectancy is fifteen years; and that the amounts to be paid to him are calculated on the assumption that the funds held in the plan will continue to earn 10 percent per year. The annual payment to the employee will be $129,301,[35] all of which is taxable. Assume that the employee pays a tax on this amount at a rate of 35 percent on the entire amount. The amount left after tax will be $84,045.

Now consider what happens if we remove all the tax benefits. The employer pays $10,000 each year to the employee as a bonus. Assume that the employee is taxed on this amount at a rate of 35 percent. After tax, the amount available for investment is $6,500. Assume that this sum is invested each year at 10 percent before tax. The after-tax rate of return will be 6.5 percent. Assuming, then, an investment of $6,500 per year with a return of 6.5 percent per year, the total accumulated at the end of twenty-five years will be $382,770. Assume that this fund is used to buy an annuity whose payout is calculated based on an assumption of a rate of return of 10 percent. Again, assume a life expectancy of fifteen years. The annual payment will be $50,324. Of this, $24,810 will be taxed.[36] Assuming a tax rate of 35 percent, the tax will be $8,684, leaving, after tax, $41,640 per year. This is 49.5 percent of the after-tax amount ($84,045) available where the qualified plan is used.[37]

35. This figure is not quite accurate. In calculating it, the assumption was made that each year of life expectancy is weighed equally. In the real world this assumption is not true. The deviation from reality is not important for our purposes, however, since it is relatively minor and since the same method of calculation is used in the next paragraph.

36. See §72(e). The exclusion ratio is the investment in the contract ($382,770) divided by the expected return ($50,324 × 15 = $754,860), or 0.507. The amount excluded is 0.507 × $50,324, which is $25,514. The amount taxed is the $50,324 received, less the $25,524 excluded under §72(e), or $24,810.

37. The calculation ignores Social Security taxes, which would be relevant for a taxpayer whose other income is below the Social Security maximum. For such taxpayers, the cash bonus will be subject to the Social Security tax, but neither contributions to qualified plans nor retirement benefits received from such plans are. The additional Social Security taxes will, however, result in increased Social Security retirement benefits.

Note that in this hypothetical a constant tax rate of 35 percent has been assumed and that consequently the entire advantage of the qualified plan is from deferral. In one respect, the comparison probably overstates somewhat the advantage of the use of qualified plans, however, because it assumes that a taxpayer whose salary and investment returns are not sheltered by such a plan would fail to find some form of investment with its own tax advantage (e.g., investment in common stocks with growth potential, where there is deferral on unrealized appreciation). From the other direction, this hypothetical understates the benefits, because individuals often drop back to lower tax brackets following retirement.

c. Antidiscrimination Rules

Congress has conditioned the availability of the tax benefits associated with qualified plans on compliance with certain rules. The most important of these are rules prohibiting discrimination in favor of highly paid employees. The purpose of the antidiscrimination rules may be understood by first examining the interests of highly compensated and of rank-and-file employees. Rank-and-file employees are generally in the lower tax brackets and benefit less than do highly compensated employees from the tax savings associated with qualified pension plans. Moreover, rank-and-file employees generally are inclined to save only a small portion of their salaries. Highly compensated employees, on the other hand, benefit more substantially from the tax savings associated with qualified plans and generally are more inclined to save a higher portion of their salaries than are low-paid employees. Absent a rule to the contrary, highly compensated employees might bargain with employers to receive a large percentage of their salaries in the form of tax-favored pension benefits, while rank-and-file employees might bargain with employers for higher cash wages and low pension benefits or none at all, or might not be offered the option of taking a pension benefit in lieu of wages.

The antidiscrimination rules prevent this outcome by requiring that qualified plans must provide reasonably comparable benefits to all employees. At the heart of the antidiscrimination rules is the requirement that, in general, the ratio of pension benefits to salary for highly compensated employees must be no greater than the ratio of such benefits to the wages of rank-and-file employees. Thus, if highly paid employees receive benefits equal to 50 percent of their immediate preretirement salary, rank-and-file employees must also receive benefits equal to 50 percent of their preretirement wages. This requirement tends to limit the use of qualified plans by highly compensated employees while at the same time helping to ensure that rank-and-file employees receive some form of pension benefits. It is important to understand, however, that the benefits do not necessarily represent a "gift" to rank-and-file employees. Some portion of the benefits is most likely paid for by a reduction in the cash wages received by those employees.

The rules on qualified plans also contain provisions designed to protect the interest of an employee's spouse in the retirement benefits earned by the employee. See §§401(a)(11), 417.

d.   Individuals

There are special rules under which self-employed individuals are permitted to set up qualified plans, called H.R. 10 (formerly "Keogh") plans. For many years, self-employed doctors, lawyers, actors, and other highly paid individuals formed corporations, of which they became the sole (or at least the major) employee, to take advantage of the more generous rules available to employees (as compared to self-employed individuals). The Tax Equity and Fiscal Responsibility Act of 1982 (TEFRA) removed most of the advantage of this artificial use of the corporate form, partly by increasing the maximum amount that can be set aside each year by self-employed individuals and partly by reducing to the same level the maximum amount that can be set aside in corporate plans.

Individuals may also set up for themselves qualified plans called individual retirement accounts (IRAs). See §408. An individual may set aside in the IRA account, and claim as a deduction, up to $5,000 ($6,000 for a person over 50 years of age), with inflation adjustments after 2008, but not more than the amount of his or her compensation. Additional "catch-up contributions" may be made, in limited amounts, by people age 50 or over. The income earned on IRAs is not taxed as long as it is accumulated. The amounts put into the account each year are deductible if the taxpayer is not covered by an employer plan or, if covered, has adjusted gross income below certain limits, with a phaseout as income rises above these levels. Amounts ultimately withdrawn as retirement benefits are included in income, with an exclusion to take account of amounts for which there was no deduction.

Instead of contributing funds to a "regular" IRA, described above, individuals filing a joint return whose adjusted gross income is below certain thresholds can elect to contribute to a "Roth IRA." §408A. Contributions to a Roth IRA are nondeductible, but there is no annual tax on the income earned by funds in a Roth IRA and "qualified distributions" are tax free. A "qualified distribution" is a distribution that takes place more than five years after the year of contribution, is made after age 59½, is made after the contributor becomes disabled or dies, or is made for certain first-time home-buyer expenses. Any other distribution, to the extent that it (along with prior distributions) exceeds the nondeductible contributions to the Roth IRA, is taxable as ordinary income and is subject to a 10 percent penalty.

A Roth IRA will be more advantageous than a "regular" IRA for taxpayers who wish to save for qualifying first-time home-purchase expenses or who are in a lower tax bracket in the time of contribution than in the time of withdrawal. Otherwise, under reasonable assumptions, the value of deducting the contribution (as in the case of a "regular" IRA) is exactly equal to the value of not paying tax on the distribution (as in the case of a Roth IRA).

Since the Roth IRA is established with after-tax dollars, however, the amount sheltered from taxation, as compared with a "regular" IRA, in effect includes the amount of tax already paid. That is, if an individual in a 40 percent bracket puts $100 into a "regular" IRA, she effectively has set aside $60 of her after-tax money (and the earnings thereon) for her ultimate retirement. If her counterpart can afford the current out-of-pocket tax expense, a $100 contribution to a Roth IRA means that all $100 is going to work in a tax-deferred account to fund the second individual's retirement. Roth IRAs and Roth 401(k)'s thus offer a hidden subsidy to those who need it least—those with plenty of current-year liquidity.

Another tax-favored saving provision is §530, which provides for tax-exempt education IRAs. These IRAs are trusts created for the purpose of paying a beneficiary's higher education expenses. Contributions to the trust are nondeductible, cannot exceed $500 per year, and must be made before the beneficiary reaches age 18. No tax is payable on income by the trust, and distributions from the trust are tax free to the extent of the beneficiary's higher education expenses in the year of distribution. Again, the education IRA is phased out as income rises above certain statutorily specified income levels.

e.   Penalty for Early Withdrawal

Amounts withdrawn from a qualified plan before reaching age 59½, in addition to being includable in gross income, are subject to a penalty of 10 percent. §72(t). The penalty does not apply if the employee has retired after age 55, has died, or has become disabled; or if the distribution is one of a series of periodic payments for the life of the employee or the joint lives of the employee and a designated beneficiary; or if the distribution does not exceed deductible medical expenses; or to distributions used, after separation from employment, to pay medical insurance premiums; or, in the case of an IRA (normal or Roth), if the distribution is used for higher education or a limited amount (typically, $10,000) of first-time home-purchase costs. The penalty tax is consistent with the purpose of the favorable treatment of retirement plans—encouraging saving for retirement. Some of the exceptions, however, have the effect of transforming retirement plans into college, home-buying, or medical savings plans and move the income tax in the direction of a consumption tax.

f.   Mandatory Distributions

Since the purpose of the favorable treatment of retirement plans is to encourage or support saving for retirement, not to allow accumulation of wealth for future generations, qualified plans are subject to rules specifying minimum distributions, which generally must begin in the calendar year following the year in which the employee reaches age 70½.

g.   *Limitations on Contributions and Benefits*

The Code imposes limitations on contributions to and benefits from qualified plans, including a rule under which the maximum "annual benefit" (itself a very technical term) under any plan may not exceed $210,000 (in 2016). See §415.

2.   Incentive Stock Options

Section 422 covers what are called "incentive stock options" (ISOs). It is important not to confuse these with nonqualified stock options, discussed in the previous section. Nonqualified stock options are more important to the compensation packages of senior management. ISOs are limited in their size, as described below, and are subject to other limitations.

The holder of an ISO does not recognize income when she receives her option (also true of a nonqualified stock option). She also does not recognize income when she exercises an ISO (the opposite rule to a nonqualified stock option, where exercise triggers ordinary compensation income). Finally, the ISO holder takes as her tax basis (cost) in the stock she acquires through exercising her ISO whatever she pays under the terms of that option; from that point forward, and assuming that the special holding period rules described below are satisfied, the stock is a capital asset the gains from which can qualify for long-term capital gain treatment.

The employer obtains no deduction in respect of the grant or exercise of an ISO. Instead, the employer effectively is treated as if the employee were an investor buying a capital markets stock option from the employer.

An ISO plan must require the employee to retain the stock she receives on exercise of her ISO for at least two years after the grant of the option and one year after receiving the stock under the option (§422(a)(1)). Also, the option price must be no less than the fair market value of the stock at the time the option is granted (§422(b)(4)). Moreover, the option must be granted pursuant to a plan that stockholders of the granting corporation approve after receiving information about how many shares and which employees the plan covers (§422(b)(1)).

A final important limitation on application of the ISO rules is that, for each individual, there is a $100,000 ceiling on the value of the stock that as yet unexercised options constituting ISOs can cover (§422(d)). The value of the stock is determined as of the time the option is granted. In illustration, suppose that, on each of five consecutive days, an employer issues a stock option to a given employee for the purchase of stock that, as of the issue date, was worth $25,000, and otherwise meets all the terms of §422. Given the $100,000 ceiling, only the first four days' options receive ISO treatment. The $100,000 ceiling makes the ISO rules relatively insignificant as a factor in the overall compensation of senior executives.

QUESTIONS

1. Do corporations need a special tax incentive to provide compensation in whatever form most favors superior management performance? Or should one expect corporations to make the best compensation decisions for themselves? For that matter, might they be if anything *too* inclined to use incentive compensation, which may make it easier to pay executives staggering salaries without shareholder protest?

2. Given the fact that §422 results in the denial of any corporate deduction for compensation provided through incentive stock options, is it really an incentive provision? In circumstances where it is not tax favorable, might there be any other reasons why companies would prefer to provide compensation this way, despite (or because of) the lack of any tax deduction?

5

<hr>

DEBT AND CERTAIN OTHER
FINANCIAL INSTRUMENTS

A. FINANCIAL INSTRUMENTS AND THE INCOME TAX

Financial instruments are real or virtual documents representing legal agreements that involve some sort of monetary value. The best-known types of financial instruments are debt and equity. Debt, in the simplest case, represents an amount of money that one legal person owes to another, such as by reason of a direct loan of that amount. Debt issued by a legal entity, such as a corporation or a government, is sometimes called a bond. Equity, in the simplest case, represents an ownership interest in an asset or set of assets. Equity interests in a corporation or similar legal entity are sometimes called stocks, or shares of stock. There also are numerous other kinds of financial instruments, such as insurance contracts and annuity contracts, which we cover briefly towards the end of this chapter, along with others that are mainly reserved for more advanced tax classes, such as options, swaps and forward contracts.[1]

The simplest financial instruments include two-party contracts in which each party has payment obligations at distinct times. For example, in a classic debt instrument, the lender transfers money to (or on behalf of) the borrower at the start of the associated loan transaction. The borrower is expected to repay the amount borrowed (i.e., the loan principal) at the end of the transaction. In addition, the borrower owes interest, computed on a per-period (such as annual) basis, as a percentage of the loan principal. Such interest may be paid periodically during the term of the loan, and/or at the end. Debt, of

<hr>

1. The distinctions between different types of financial instrument, as defined by the tax system, are often formalistic and unclear. One could spend an entire law school semester—or, for that matter, much of one's legal career—focusing on the debt-equity line, among others. This, too, however, is best reserved for more advanced tax classes.

course, is an asset to the lender and a liability to the borrower—increasing the former's net worth, but commensurately reducing the latter's net worth.

The economic values associated with financial instruments greatly exceed the values of currently existing real assets, such as buildings, factories, and land.[2] As of 2014, U.S. households (along with nonprofit entities) held financial assets with a gross value of about $70 trillion, and a net value (subtracting their debt liabilities) of about $55 trillion. By contrast, the total value of all real estate in the United States was only about $25 trillion. The large numbers associated with financial instruments can give them enormous effects, not just on particular persons' net worth, but also on the income tax system.

In this chapter, we will mainly examine selected issues that relate to debt instruments, first concerning loan principal and then interest. We will then focus briefly on life insurance and annuity contracts, which we will see are in some ways debt-like. For example, like conventional debt, they may involve an investor making an up-front payment to a counterparty that agrees in return to make future payments back.

B. LOANS AND CANCELLATION OF INDEBTEDNESS INCOME

1. The Exclusion of Loan Proceeds from Income

Suppose the tax system used a pure cash flow measure of gross income, under which all cash payments (or their noncash equivalents) that one received were automatically includable. Under such an approach, loan proceeds would automatically be taxable when received by the borrower and presumably would be deductible when repaid. Thus, for example, if you took out a $10,000 loan in Year 1 and repaid the full loan principal in Year 5, then—ignoring all interest payments—such an approach would cause you to have $10,000 of gross income in Year 1 and an offsetting $10,000 reduction to gross income in Year 5.

Instead, however, the income tax ignores flows of loan principal. You don't generally have $X of income (or indeed, any income) by reason of borrowing $X in an arm's-length transaction, and you don't get a deduction for repaying the principal.

Rationale for excluding loan proceeds from income. Why doesn't the tax system treat loan proceeds as taxable income? And, for that matter, why might a contrary rule treating them as income seem intuitively—not just, as it happens, legally—incorrect?

---

2. A second reason why net financial instruments are worth more than net real assets is that the former can derive value from conveying claims to the fruits of expected future economic activity. Suppose, for example, that an entrepreneur issues stock in a new start-up company. The stock may be valuable because people anticipate that the company will earn large profits in the future, even if it has not actually done anything yet.

If you were asked why you shouldn't have $10,000 of taxable income in Year 1 by reason of borrowing that amount, you might say that it didn't make you any richer, because you anticipate having to repay the loan. By contrast, if you had gotten a $10,000 service fee—or, for that matter, a $10,000 gift (even though gifts are excluded from income under Code §102)—you actually would have been $10,000 richer.

The underlying intuition can be expressed in terms of the loan's effect (or rather, non-effect) on your Haig-Simons income. Again, if $Y = C + \Delta W$, the loan has given you both $10,000 in cash and a $10,000 liability.[3] Thus, if you saved or invested the cash, both C and ΔW are the same as previously. And even if you spent some of the loan proceeds on personal consumption—say, a vacation—then the increase in C and the decline in ΔW should be identical.

Accordingly, the result of excluding loan proceeds from gross income is generally accepted, both legally and as a policy matter, even though it is not spelled out in any express provision of the Code. In some cases, however, the receipt of loan proceeds tax free may enable a taxpayer to convert into cash (albeit, subject to a repayment obligation) economic value that has not yet been taxed under our realization-based system.

To illustrate how this is true for some loans, but not for others, consider the following three cases:

(a) *A* earns a good salary and accumulates $50,000 in after-tax savings. She uses this entire amount to buy Microsoft stock. At a time when her Microsoft stock is still worth exactly $50,000, she uses it as collateral to secure a $25,000 loan.

Here the lender's willingness to give *A* $25,000 in cash evidently reflects *A*'s having earned income in the past that the income tax system has already reached. Note that she would not have been taxable upon selling any of the Microsoft stock for its cost basis.

(b) *B*'s circumstances are the same as *A*'s, except that he bought Amazon stock for $50,000, and it is now worth $200,000. *B* uses this stock as collateral securing a $100,000 loan. While the tax system treats this case identically to case (a) above—i.e., he is not currently taxed[4]—one could view this transaction as enabling *B* to convert some of the value of his unrealized stock appreciation into cash, on a tax-free basis.

(c) *C* has just completed a surgical residency and is about to begin her medical practice, at which point she expects to start earning a high salary. A bank loans her $50,000, even though she has no current assets, based on her expected future earnings. Here, as in (b) above, she has acquired current cash without facing any current tax liability. Indeed, she has turned her future earning ability into current cash even before it has become current Haig-Simons income. The Haig-Simons concept generally is thought not to

---

3. While the present value of a $10,000 receipt today exceeds the present value of an obligation to repay that amount in the future, the obligation to pay interest, presumably at a market rate (in an arm's-length transaction), should keep at zero the loan's net effect on one's net worth.

4. See Woodsam Associates, Inc., v. Commissioner, discussed *supra* in Chapter 4, holding that even nonrecourse borrowing against property for more than its tax basis does not generate currently taxable gain.

reach the appreciation of "human capital" (i.e., increases in the present value of one's expected future earnings).

Importance of keeping in mind the rationale for excluding loan proceeds from income. Again, whether one receives loan proceeds by reason of (a) past income that has already been taxed, (b) past economic income that has not yet been taxed, or (c) expected future economic income that has not even been earned yet, the rationale for excluding the proceeds from gross income is in each case the same. One gets the loan proceeds tax free by reason of the fact that one is expected to repay them in the future. But what happens if this expectation is subsequently falsified?

Returning to the initial example where you received $10,000 tax free because it consisted of loan proceeds that you were expected to repay, let's consider what happens if, for some reason — let's hold off on asking why — it turns out that you will get to keep the money. Now it is clear that, at some point, you really were enriched by the amount received. Since you were not taxed upon getting the cash, the inclusion must occur later — i.e., at the time when the repayment obligation disappeared (or is deemed to have done so).

The Code therefore provides — subject to express statutory exceptions — for the inclusion in gross income of what §61(a)(12) calls "income from discharge of indebtedness." A more colloquial term is cancellation of indebtedness income (or "CODI," for cancellation of debt income).

The separation in time between when a taxpayer receives loan proceeds and when CODI arises can create problems for the tax system, given its use of annual accounting. In particular, when a taxpayer borrows money in one year, and the expectation of repayment disappears only later, the events in the later year may not intuitively look as if they involve income realization. Suppose, for example, that the reason you end up not having to repay a loan is that you have become insolvent, or alternatively, that the property securing the loan has lost significant value. This hardly looks like an event characterized by economic gain. Yet, if one is trying to tax income consistently over time, one must keep in mind the reason for not imposing tax in the year of the loan, which is that you were expected to repay it, but now (as it turns out) you will not be doing so.

Do we really want to tax people on CODI, if the reason for the debt discharge is that bad things have happened to them? The answer that Congress has reached is: not necessarily. For this reason, it has addressed CODI not just in §61(a)(12), which defines it as a category of gross income, but also under §108, which provides rules permitting its exclusion under specified circumstances and subject to particular conditions.

2.   True Discharge of Indebtedness

Why would a taxpayer be able to avoid fully repaying outstanding debts? Subsequent economic distress that undermines the expectation of repayment is only one possible ground. Another possibility is that interest rates may have increased since the time of the loan.

Suppose that, in the middle of Year 1, *T* borrows $100,000 for five years, at 5 percent per year, and uses the money to finance a trip around the world. He returns from his trip early in Year 2, and finds that interest rates have risen drastically in his absence. As *T* now happens to have cash available, he offers to repay the loan for $90,000. The bank accepts, based on calculating that it will come out ahead after relending this amount to a new borrower at the current interest rate.

As a result of this agreement, *T* gets to retain $10,000 out of the borrowed amount. Thus, he should have $10,000 of taxable CODI. Yet there are two distinct ways of rationalizing this result. The first looks at the transaction as a whole: Year 1 plus Year 2. *T* got $100,000 tax free and then repaid only $90,000. The second looks just at Year 2. *T* had an outstanding $100,000 obligation, which he discharged for only $90,000. This means that, if *T* was keeping a current year balance sheet based on historical cost figures, *T*'s recorded net worth or net equity would have gone up by $10,000 when the bank agreed to the discounted repayment.

Why might it matter which of these two explanations one uses? Often, it does not matter. However, to see why it can potentially matter, consider the following case.

UNITED STATES v. KIRBY LUMBER CO.
284 U.S. 1 (1931)

Mr. Justice HOLMES delivered the opinion of the Court.

In July, 1923, the plaintiff, the Kirby Lumber Company, issued its own bonds for [$12,000,000] for which it received their par value. Later in the same year it purchased in the open market [$1,000,000 face amount] of the same bonds at [$862,000], the difference of price being [$138,000]. The question is whether this difference is a taxable gain or income of the plaintiff for the year 1923. By the Revenue Act of 1921, gross income includes "gains or profits and income derived from any source whatever" [§61(a), 1954 Code] and by the Treasury Regulations . . . that have been in force through repeated reenactments, "If the corporation purchases and retires any of such bonds at a price less than the issuing price or face value, the excess of the issuing price or face value over the purchase price is gain or income for the taxable year." . . . We see no reason why the Regulations should not be accepted as a correct statement of the law.

In . . . [the present case, there] was no shrinkage of assets and the taxpayer made a clear gain. As a result of its dealings it made available [$138,000 worth of] assets previously offset by the obligation of bonds now extinct. We see nothing to be gained by the discussion of judicial definitions. The [taxpayer] has realized within the year an accession to income, if we take words in their plain popular meaning, as they should be taken here. . . .

Judgment reversed.

NOTES AND QUESTIONS

1. *What's the problem?* Justice Holmes's reasoning in *Kirby Lumber* is characteristically terse, and apparently clear. Unfortunately, however, it caused problems

down the road, as described in the following passages from 1 B. Bittker, *Federal Taxation of Income, Estates and Gifts* ¶¶6-31 to 6-32 (1981):

> A particularly troublesome legacy of the above passage has been the tendency of some courts to read *Kirby Lumber* as holding that the *freeing of assets* on the cancellation of indebtedness, rather than the cancellation itself, results in a taxable gain. In actuality, income results from the discharge of indebtedness because the taxpayer has received more than is paid back, not because assets are freed of offsetting liabilities on the balance sheet. . . .
>
> [T]he tax treatment of below-face debt discharges would have been much simplified if it had been based at the outset on the fact that borrowed funds are excluded from gross income because of the assumption that they will be repaid in full and on the simple corollary that a tax adjustment is required when this assumption proves erroneous, regardless of the use to which the taxpayer put the borrowed funds.

2. *Why does it matter?* In *Kirby Lumber*, it appears to make no difference whether one uses a "freeing of assets" rationale or one based on the difference between what a taxpayer initially receives tax free and what it subsequently pays back. Either way, in this case, the result is taxable income of $138,000 in the year of debt discharge.

With different facts, however, the choice of rationale may make a difference. Suppose, for example, that the taxpayer in *Kirby Lumber* had been insolvent. In that case, there arguably would have been no "freeing of assets," as all of its assets would have remained encumbered by outstanding debt. But there still would have been a $138,000 difference between the amounts received for the bonds and subsequently repaid.

Or suppose that the $1 million loan in *Kirby Lumber* had been nonrecourse—that is, that the bondholders' only recourse in case of default had been against particular assets that were pledged as security for the bonds but that had declined in value since the date of bond issuance. If the repayment discount had reflected such a decline in value—rather than, as was apparently the case, reflecting a rise in interest rates—then, once again, there at least arguably would have been no "freeing of assets."

As we will shortly see, the tax law now expressly addresses the tax consequences both of borrower insolvency and of borrowing nonrecourse against assets that decline in value. In each case, however, the starting point for legal analysis has been to reject any possible implication, from the language in *Kirby Lumber*, to the effect that, without "freeing of assets," there is no gross income to begin with, under §61(a)(12), from the cancellation of indebtedness.

3.   Relief Provisions

a.   *Insolvent Debtors*

Section 108 contains elaborate rules relating to discharge of the indebtedness of insolvent debtors. Generally, these rules reflect the notion, previously embodied in judicially developed doctrines, that one should not hit a person who is down, or that one cannot squeeze blood from a turnip (so to speak), or both. Or it could reflect the interests of insolvent debtors' other creditors, who may get to collect more if the government doesn't have a tax claim based on CODI.

Under the relevant provision, if, at the time of discharge, the taxpayer was insolvent or was the debtor in a proceeding under the Bankruptcy Act, the income from discharge of indebtedness is excluded. However, certain tax attributes (such as net operating loss carryovers) must be reduced, if possible in the same net amount as that of the excluded CODI. See §108(b). Such reduction of tax attributes may subsequently increase taxable income by the full amount of the CODI that was excluded under this rule, if the taxpayer is sufficiently profitable.

For example, suppose that, in Year 1, a company with $3 million of NOLs becomes insolvent, leading to debt write-downs that give it $1 million of CODI excluded from income under §108(b). This causes the amount of its NOLs to be reduced to $2 million. However, the company manages to stay in business, and in Year 2 it makes a $7 million profit. Given the reduction in its NOLs by reason of the Year 1 CODI, this amount is reduced by the company's NOLs to only $5 million, rather than to $4 million.

b. Solvent Farmers

The relief provided under §108 for insolvent debtors is also available to solvent farmers if they are able to discharge "qualified farm indebtedness," which is debt incurred in the operation of a farm by a person who, during the three preceding taxable years, derived more than 50 percent of his or her annual gross receipts from farming. §108(g).

c. Adjustment of Purchase Money Debt

Section 108(e)(5) provides that the reduction of debt incurred to purchase property and owed to the seller is treated as a reduction in sale price, rather than income to the purchaser. To illustrate this provision, suppose you buy a used car from a dealership, in exchange for $6,000 in cash plus $24,000 in seller financing. The car's basis to you is therefore $30,000. You subsequently get the debt reduced from $24,000 to $15,000. In the absence of §108(e)(5), should this give rise to $9,000 of cancellation of indebtedness income?

Suppose initially that this was a true debt renegotiation, based, say, on changes in interest rates. Then under standard income tax reasoning, dating back to *Kirby Lumber,* you should indeed have $9,000 of taxable income. The car's basis continues to be $30,000.

Now suppose instead that you got the debt reduced by complaining that the car has various defects that were not disclosed to you at purchase. The dealer responds by taking $9,000 off the price, which he implements by agreeing to a reduction in the outstanding debt. In effect, then, the debt reduction was "actually" a purchase price adjustment. In this scenario, there is no cancellation of indebtedness income, but the car's basis is reduced to $21,000.

In effect, §108(e)(5) mandates taking the latter view of the facts, rather than the former view, whenever "the debt of a [solvent] purchaser of property to the seller of such property which arose out of the purchase of such property is reduced." §108(e)(5)(A). In effect, it doesn't matter if this is what "actually" happened. Thus, the purchaser avoids having cancellation of indebtedness income and instead gets basis reduction for the purchased asset. However, since the provision only applies to solvent debtors, it does not stand in the way of having cancellation of indebtedness income that is excludable by reason of §108(b).

Ordinarily, reducing the basis of property may cause the owner to have higher taxable income in the future. For example, a lower basis may increase the gain, or reduce the loss, that the owner realizes upon subsequent sale of the property. However, for an item such as a car or home appliance that one buys for personal consumption use, and that one does not subsequently sell for as much as the original purchase price (even as adjusted), the basis reduction may have no effect on subsequent taxable income. In such a case, §108(e)(5) permanently reduces taxable income, relative to treating the transaction as involving true debt forgiveness.

d.   Student Loan Forgiveness

Section 108(f)(2) excludes from income any cancellation or repayment of a student loan, provided the cancellation or repayment is contingent upon work for a charitable or educational institution.

e.   Mortgage Forgiveness

Section 108(h)(2) provides relief for taxpayers who would otherwise recognize income from the discharge of indebtedness when mortgage lenders foreclose on the taxpayer's principal residence. In addition to foreclosure situations, the exclusion applies to mortgage workouts, where the lender renegotiates the terms of the taxpayer's mortgage indebtedness in such a manner as would normally result in the recognition of income from the discharge of indebtedness. The statute provides for an exclusion of up to $2 million of forgiven "qualified principal residence indebtedness." The taxpayer must reduce her basis in the principal residence (but not below zero) by the amount excluded. The reduction in basis may increase the likelihood that the taxpayer will recognize gain upon a subsequent disposition of the property. Recall, however, that, under §121, up to $250,000 ($500,000 for married couples filing a joint return) of any gain upon the sale of a principal residence is excluded from income.

4.   Contested or Uncertain Liabilities

Suppose that a debt is repaid for less than the amount the lender had claimed was due, and that the repayment discount reflects a good faith dispute as to (a) the entire debt's legal enforceability, (b) the amount that had actually been borrowed, and/or (c) the amount due from the borrower, given the debt instrument's particular repayment terms. How might this affect the analysis of whether CODI exists, and if so, how much it is?

ZARIN v. COMMISSIONER
916 F.2d 110 (3d Cir. 1990)

COWEN, Circuit Judge.

David Zarin ("Zarin") appeals from a decision of the Tax Court holding that he recognized $2,935,000 of income from discharge of indebtedness resulting from his gambling activities, and that he should be taxed on the income. . . . After considering the issues raised by this appeal, we will reverse.

I

Zarin was a professional engineer who participated in the development, construction, and management of various housing projects. A resident of Atlantic City, New Jersey, Zarin occasionally gambled, both in his hometown and in other places where gambling was legalized. To facilitate his gaming activities in Atlantic City, Zarin applied to Resorts International Hotel ("Resorts") for a credit line in June, 1978. Following a credit check, Resorts granted Zarin $10,000 of credit. Pursuant to this credit arrangement with Resorts, Zarin could write a check, called a marker,[5] and in return receive chips, which could then be used to gamble at the casino's tables.

Before long, Zarin developed a reputation as an extravagant "high roller" who routinely bet the house maximum while playing craps, his game of choice. Considered a "valued gaming patron" by Resorts, Zarin had his credit limit increased at regular intervals without any further credit checks, and was provided a number of complimentary services and privileges. By November, 1979, Zarin's permanent line of credit had been raised to $200,000. Between June, 1978, and December, 1979, Zarin lost $2,500,000 at the craps table, losses he paid in full.

Responding to allegations of credit abuses, the New Jersey Division of Gaming Enforcement filed with the New Jersey Casino Control Commission a complaint against Resorts. Among the 809 violations of casino regulations alleged in the complaint of October, 1979, were 100 pertaining to Zarin. Subsequently, a Casino Control Commissioner issued an Emergency Order, the effect of which was to make further extensions of credit to Zarin illegal.

Nevertheless, Resorts continued to extend Zarin's credit limit through the use of two different practices: "considered cleared" credit and "this trip only"

---

5. A "marker" is a negotiable draft payable to Resorts and drawn on the marker's bank.

credit.[6] Both methods effectively ignored the Emergency Order and were later found to be illegal.[7]

By January, 1980, Zarin was gambling compulsively and uncontrollably at Resorts, spending as many as sixteen hours a day at the craps table.[8] During April, 1980, Resorts again increased Zarin's credit line without further inquiries. That same month, Zarin delivered personal checks and counterchecks to Resorts which were returned as having been drawn against insufficient funds. Those dishonored checks totaled $3,435,000. In late April, Resorts cut off Zarin's credit.

Although Zarin indicated that he would repay those obligations, Resorts filed a New Jersey state court action against Zarin in November, 1980, to collect the $3,435,000. Zarin denied liability on grounds that Resort's claim was unenforceable under New Jersey regulations intended to protect compulsive gamblers. Ten months later, in September, 1981, Resorts and Zarin settled their dispute for a total of $500,000.

The Commissioner of Internal Revenue ("Commissioner") subsequently determined deficiencies in Zarin's federal income taxes for 1980 and 1981, arguing that Zarin recognized $3,435,000 of income in 1980 from larceny by trick and deception. After Zarin challenged that claim by filing a Tax Court petition, the Commissioner abandoned his 1980 claim, and argued instead that Zarin had recognized $2,935,000 of income in 1981 from the cancellation of indebtedness which resulted from the settlement with Resorts.

Agreeing with the Commissioner, the Tax Court decided, eleven judges to eight, that Zarin had indeed recognized $2,935,000 of income from the discharge of indebtedness, namely the difference between the original $3,435,000 "debt" and the $500,000 settlement. Zarin v. Commissioner, 92 T.C. 1084 (1989). Since he was in the seventy percent tax bracket, Zarin's deficiency for 1981 was calculated to be $2,047,245. With interest to April 5, 1990, Zarin allegedly owes the Internal Revenue Service $5,209,033.96 in additional taxes. Zarin appeals the order of the Tax Court.

II

The sole issue before this Court is whether the Tax Court correctly held that Zarin had income from discharge of indebtedness.[9] Sections 108 and 61(a)(12)

---

6. Under the "considered cleared" method, Resorts would treat a personal check as a cash transaction, and would therefore not apply the amount of the check in calculating the amount of credit extended Zarin. "This trip only" credit allows Resorts to grant temporary increases of credit for a given visit, so long as the credit limit was lowered by the next visit.

7. On July 8, 1983, the New Jersey Casino Control Commission found that Resorts violated the Emergency Order at least thirteen different times, nine involving Zarin, and fined Resorts $130,000.

8. Zarin claims that at the time he was suffering from a recognized emotional disorder that caused him to gamble compulsively.

9. Subsequent to the Tax Court's decision, Zarin filed a motion to reconsider, arguing that he was insolvent at the time Resorts forgave his debt, and thus, under section 108(a)(1)(B), could not have income from discharge of indebtedness. He did not, however, raise that issue before the Tax Court until after it rendered its decision. The Tax Court denied the motion for reconsideration. By reason of our resolution of this case, we do not need to decide whether the Tax Court abused its discretion in denying Zarin's motion.

of the Code set forth "the general rule that gross income includes income from the discharge of indebtedness." §108(e)(1). The Commissioner argues, and the Tax Court agreed, that pursuant to the Code, Zarin did indeed recognize income from discharge of gambling indebtedness.

Under the Commissioner's logic, Resorts advanced Zarin $3,435,000 worth of chips, chips being the functional equivalent of cash. At that time, the chips were not treated as income, since Zarin recognized an obligation of repayment. In other words, Resorts made Zarin a tax-free loan. However, a taxpayer does recognize income if a loan owed to another party is cancelled, in whole or in part. I.R.C. §§61(a)(12), 108(e). The settlement between Zarin and Resorts, claims the Commissioner, fits neatly into the cancellation of indebtedness provisions in the Code. Zarin owed $3,435,000, paid $500,000, with the difference constituting income. Although initially persuasive, the Commissioner's position is nonetheless flawed for two reasons.

III

Initially, we find that sections 108 and 61(a)(12) are inapplicable to the Zarin/Resorts transaction. Section 61 does not define indebtedness. On the other hand, section 108(d)(1), which repeats and further elaborates on the rule in section 61(a)(12), defines the term as any indebtedness "(A) for which the taxpayer is liable, or (B) subject to which the taxpayer holds property." §108(d)(1). In order to bring the taxpayer within the sweep of the discharge of indebtedness rules, then, the IRS must show that one of the two prongs in the section 108(d)(1) test is satisfied. It has not been demonstrated that Zarin satisfies either.

Because the debt Zarin owed to Resorts was unenforceable as a matter of New Jersey state law,[10] it is clearly not a debt "for which the taxpayer is liable." §108(d)(1)(A). Liability implies a legally enforceable obligation to repay, and under New Jersey law, Zarin would have no such obligation.

Moreover, Zarin did not have a debt subject to which he held property as required by section 108(d)(1)(B). Zarin's indebtedness arose out of his

---

10. The Tax Court held that the Commissioner had not met its burden of proving that the debt owed Resorts was enforceable as a matter of state law. *Zarin*, 92 T.C. at 1090. There was ample evidence to support that finding. In New Jersey, the extension of credit by casinos "to enable [any] person to take part in gaming activity as a player" is limited. N.J. Stat. Ann. §5:12-101(b) (1988). Under N.J. Stat. Ann. §5:12-101(f), any credit violation is "invalid and unenforceable for the purposes of collection. . . ." In Resorts Int'l Hotel, Inc. v. Salomone, 178 N.J. Super. 598, 429 A.2d 1078 (App. Div. 1981), the court held that "casinos must comply with the Legislature's strict control of credit for gambling purposes. Unless they do, the debts reflected by players' checks will not be enforced. . . ." *Id.* at 607, 429 A.2d at 1082.

With regards to the extension of credit to Zarin after the Emergency Order of October, 1979, was issued, Resorts did not comply with New Jersey regulations. The Casino Control Commission specifically stated in 1983 "that Resorts was guilty of infractions, violations, improprieties, with the net effect that [Zarin] was encouraged to continue gambling long after, one, his credit line was reached, and exceeded; two, long after it became apparent that the gambler was an addicted gambler; three, long after the gambler had difficulty in paying his debts; and four, Resorts knew the individual was gambling when he should not have been gambling." Appendix at 325-326. It follows, therefore, that under New Jersey law, the $3,435,000 debt Zarin owed Resorts was totally unenforceable.

acquisition of gambling chips. The Tax Court held that gambling chips were not property, but rather, "a medium of exchange within the Resorts casino" and a "substitute for cash." Alternatively, the Tax Court viewed the chips as nothing more than "the opportunity to gamble and incidental services. . . ." *Zarin*, 92 T.C. at 1099. We agree with the gist of these characterizations, and hold that gambling chips are merely an accounting mechanism to evidence debt.

Gaming chips in New Jersey during 1980 were regarded "solely as evidence of a debt owed to their custodian by the casino licensee and shall be considered at no time the property of anyone other than the casino licensee issuing them." N.J. Admin. Code tit. 19k, §19:46-1.5(d) (1990). Thus, under New Jersey state law, gambling chips were Resorts' property until transferred to Zarin in exchange for the markers, at which point the chips became "evidence" of indebtedness (and not the property of Zarin).

Even were there no relevant legislative pronouncement on which to rely, simple common sense would lead to the conclusion that chips were not property in Zarin's hands. Zarin could not do with the chips as he pleased, nor did the chips have any independent economic value beyond the casino. The chips themselves were of little use to Zarin, other than as a means of facilitating gambling. They could not have been used outside the casino. They could have been used to purchase services and privileges within the casino, including food, drink, entertainment, and lodging, but Zarin would not have utilized them as such, since he received those services from Resorts on a complimentary basis. In short, the chips had no economic substance.

Although the Tax Court found that theoretically, Zarin could have redeemed the chips he received on credit for cash and walked out of the casino, *Zarin*, 92 T.C. at 1092, the reality of the situation was quite different. Realistically, before cashing in his chips, Zarin would have been required to pay his outstanding IOUs. New Jersey state law requires casinos to "request patrons to apply any chips or plaques in their possession in reduction of personal checks or Counter Checks exchanged for purposes of gaming prior to exchanging such chips or plaques for cash or prior to departing from the casino area." N.J. Admin. Code tit. 19k, §19:45-1.24(s) (1979) (currently N.J. Admin. Code tit. 19k, §19:45-1.25(o) (1990) (as amended)). Since his debt at all times equalled or exceeded the number of chips he possessed, redemption would have left Zarin with no chips, no cash, and certainly nothing which could have been characterized as property.

Not only were the chips non-property in Zarin's hands, but upon transfer to Zarin, the chips also ceased to be the property of Resorts. Since the chips were in the possession of another party, Resorts could no longer do with the chips as it pleased, and could no longer control the chips' use. Generally, at the time of a transfer, the party in possession of the chips can gamble with them, use them for services, cash them in, or walk out of the casino with them as an Atlantic City souvenir. The chips therefore become nothing more than an accounting mechanism, or evidence of a debt, designed to facilitate gambling in casinos where the use of actual money was forbidden. Thus, the chips which Zarin held were not property within the meaning of §108(d)(1)(B).

In short, because Zarin was not liable on the debt he allegedly owed Resorts, and because Zarin did not hold "property" subject to that debt, the cancellation of indebtedness provisions of the Code do not apply to the settlement between Resorts and Zarin. As such, Zarin cannot have income from the discharge of his debt.

Instead of analyzing the transaction at issue as cancelled debt, we believe the proper approach is to view it as disputed debt or contested liability. Under the contested liability doctrine, if a taxpayer, in good faith, disputed the amount of a debt, a subsequent settlement of the dispute would be treated as the amount of debt cognizable for tax purposes. The excess of the original debt over the amount determined to have been due is disregarded for both loss and debt accounting purposes. Thus, if a taxpayer took out a loan for $10,000, refused in good faith to pay the full $10,000 back, and then reached an agreement with the lendor that he would pay back only $7,000 in full satisfaction of the debt, the transaction would be treated as if the initial loan was $7,000. When the taxpayer tenders the $7,000 payment, he will have been deemed to have paid the full amount of the initially disputed debt. Accordingly, there is no tax consequence to the taxpayer upon payment.

The seminal "contested liability" case is N. Sobel, Inc. v. Commissioner, 40 B.T.A. 1263 (1939). In *Sobel*, the taxpayer exchanged a $21,700 note for 100 shares of stock from a bank. In the following year, the taxpayer sued the bank for recision, arguing that the bank loan was violative of state law, and moreover, that the bank had failed to perform certain promises. The parties eventually settled the case in 1935, with the taxpayer agreeing to pay half of the face amount of the note. In the year of the settlement, the taxpayer claimed the amount paid as a loss. The Commissioner denied the loss because it had been sustained five years earlier, and further asserted that the taxpayer recognized income from the discharge of half of his indebtedness.

The Board of Tax Appeals held that since the loss was not fixed until the dispute was settled, the loss was recognized in 1935, the year of the settlement, and the deduction was appropriately taken in that year. Additionally, the Board held that the portion of the note forgiven by the bank "was not the occasion for a freeing of assets and that there was no gain. . . ." *Id*. at 1265. Therefore, the taxpayer did not have any income from cancellation of indebtedness.

There is little difference between the present case and *Sobel*. Zarin incurred a $3,435,000 debt while gambling at Resorts, but in court, disputed liability on the basis of unenforceability. A settlement of $500,000 was eventually agreed upon. It follows from *Sobel* that the settlement served only to fix the amount of debt. No income was realized or recognized. When Zarin paid the $500,000, any tax consequence dissolved.[11]

Only one other court has addressed a case factually similar to the one before us. In United States v. Hall, 307 F.2d 238 (10th Cir. 1962), the taxpayer owed an unenforceable gambling debt alleged to be $225,000. Subsequently,

---

11. Had Zarin not paid the $500,000 settlement, it would be likely that he would have had income from cancellation of indebtedness. The debt at that point would have been fixed, and Zarin would have been legally obligated to pay it.

the taxpayer and the creditor settled for $150,000. The taxpayer then transferred cattle valued at $148,110 to his creditor in satisfaction of the settlement agreement. A jury held that the parties fixed the debt at $150,000, and that the taxpayer recognized income from cancellation of indebtedness equal to the difference between the $150,000 and the $148,110 value affixed to the cattle. Arguing that the taxpayer recognized income equal to the difference between $225,000 and $148,000, the Commissioner appealed.

The Tenth Circuit rejected the idea that the taxpayer had any income from cancellation of indebtedness. Noting that the gambling debt was unenforceable, the Tenth Circuit said, "The cold fact is that taxpayer suffered a substantial loss from gambling, the amount of which was determined by the transfer." *Id.* at 241. In effect, the Court held that because the debt was unenforceable, the amount of the loss and resulting debt cognizable for tax purposes were fixed by the settlement at $148,110. Thus, the Tenth Circuit lent its endorsement to the contested liability doctrine in a factual situation strikingly similar to the one at issue.[12]

The Commissioner argues that *Sobel* and the contested liability doctrine only apply when there is an unliquidated debt; that is, a debt for which the amount cannot be determined. . . . Since Zarin contested his liability based on the unenforceability of the entire debt, and did not dispute the amount of the debt, the Commissioner would have us adopt the reasoning of the Tax Court, which found that Zarin's debt was liquidated, therefore barring the application of *Sobel* and the contested liability doctrine. *Zarin*, 92 T.C. at 1095 (Zarin's debt "was a liquidated amount" and "[t]here is no dispute about the amount [received]").

We reject the Tax Court's rationale. When a debt is unenforceable, it follows that the amount of the debt, and not just the liability thereon, is in dispute. Although a debt may be unenforceable, there still could be some value attached to its worth. This is especially so with regards to gambling debts. In most states, gambling debts are unenforceable, and have "but slight potential. . . ." United States v. Hall, 307 F.2d 238, 241 (10th Cir. 1962). Nevertheless, they are often collected, at least in part. For example, Resorts is not a charity; it would not have extended illegal credit to Zarin and others if it did not have some hope of collecting debts incurred pursuant to the grant of credit.

Moreover, the debt is frequently incurred to acquire gambling chips, and not money. Although casinos attach a dollar value to each chip, that value, unlike money's, is not beyond dispute, particularly given the illegality of

---

12. The Commissioner argues that the decision in *Hall* was based on United States Supreme Court precedent since overruled, and therefore *Hall* should be disregarded. Indeed, the *Hall* court devoted a considerable amount of time to Bowers v. Kerbaugh-Empire Co., 271 U.S. 170 (1926), a case whose validity is in question. We do not pass on the question of whether or not *Bowers* is good law. We do note that *Hall* relied on *Bowers* only for the proposition that "'a court need not in every case be oblivious to the net effect of the entire transaction.'" United States v. Hall, 307 F.2d at 242, quoting Bradford v. Commissioner, 233 F.2d 935, 939 (6th Cir. 1956). *Hall*'s reliance on *Bowers* did not extend to the issue of contested liability, and even if it did, the idea that "Courts need not apply mechanical standards which smother the reality of a particular transaction," *Id.* at 241, is hardly an exceptional concept in the tax realm. See Commissioner v. Tufts, 461 U.S. 300 (1983); Hillsboro Nat'l Bank v. Commissioner, 460 U.S. 370 (1983).

gambling debts in the first place. This proposition is supported by the facts of the present case. Resorts gave Zarin $3.4 million dollars of chips in exchange for markers evidencing Zarin's debt. If indeed the only issue was the enforceability of the entire debt, there would have been no settlement. Zarin would have owed all or nothing. Instead, the parties attached a value to the debt considerably lower than its face value. In other words, the parties agreed that given the circumstances surrounding Zarin's gambling spree, the chips he acquired might not have been worth $3.4 million dollars, but were worth something. Such a debt cannot be called liquidated, since its exact amount was not fixed until settlement.

To summarize, the transaction between Zarin and Resorts can best be characterized as a disputed debt, or contested liability. Zarin owed an unenforceable debt of $3,435,000 to Resorts. After Zarin in good faith disputed his obligation to repay the debt, the parties settled for $500,000, which Zarin paid. That $500,000 settlement fixed the amount of loss and the amount of debt cognizable for tax purposes. Since Zarin was deemed to have owed $500,000, and since he paid Resorts $500,000, no adverse tax consequences attached to Zarin as a result.

In conclusion, we hold that Zarin did not have any income from cancellation of indebtedness for two reasons. First, the Code provisions covering discharge of debt are inapplicable since the definitional requirement in I.R.C. section 108(d)(1) was not met. Second, the settlement of Zarin's gambling debts was a contested liability. We reverse the decision of the Tax Court and remand with instructions to enter judgment that Zarin realized no income by reason of his settlement with Resorts.

STAPLETON, Circuit Judge, dissenting.

I respectfully dissent because I agree with the Commissioner's appraisal of the economic realities of this matter.

Resorts sells for cash the exhilaration and the potential for profit inherent in games of chance. It does so by selling for cash chips that entitle the holder to gamble at its casino. Zarin, like thousands of others, wished to purchase what Resorts was offering in the marketplace. He chose to make this purchase on credit and executed notes evidencing his obligation to repay the funds that were advanced to him by Resorts. As in most purchase money transactions, Resorts skipped the step of giving Zarin cash that he would only return to it in order to pay for the opportunity to gamble. Resorts provided him instead with chips that entitled him to participate in Resorts' games of chance on the same basis as others who had paid cash for that privilege.[13] Whether viewed as a one- or two-step transaction, however, Zarin received either $3.4 million in cash or an entitlement for which others would have had to pay $3.4 million.

---

13. I view as irrelevant the facts that Resorts advanced credit to Zarin solely to enable him to patronize its casino and that the chips could not be used elsewhere or for other purposes. When one buys a sofa from the furniture store on credit, the fact that the proprietor would not have advanced the credit for a different purpose does not entitle one to a tax-free gain in the event the debt to the store is extinguished for some reason.

Despite the fact that Zarin received in 1980 cash or an entitlement worth $3.4 million, he correctly reported in that year no income from his dealings with Resorts. He did so *solely* because he recognized, as evidenced by his notes, an offsetting obligation to repay Resorts $3.4 million in cash. . . . In 1981, with the delivery of Zarin's promise to pay Resorts $500,000 and the execution of a release by Resorts, Resorts surrendered its claim to repayment of the remaining $2.9 million of the money Zarin had borrowed. As of that time, Zarin's assets were freed of his potential liability for that amount and he recognized gross income in that amount. . . .[14]

The only alternatives I see to this conclusion are to hold either (1) that Zarin realized $3.4 million in income in 1980 at a time when both parties to the transaction thought there was an offsetting obligation to repay or (2) that the $3.4 million benefit sought and received by Zarin is not taxable at all. I find the latter alternative unacceptable as inconsistent with the fundamental principle of the Code that anything of commercial value received by a taxpayer is taxable unless expressly excluded from gross income.[15] Commissioner v. Glenshaw Glass Co., 348 U.S. 426 (1955); United States v. Kirby Lumber Co., *supra*. I find the former alternative unacceptable as impracticable. In 1980, neither party was maintaining that the debt was unenforceable and, because of the settlement, its unenforceability was not even established in the litigation over the debt in 1981. It was not until 1989 in this litigation over the tax consequences of the transaction that the unenforceability was first judicially declared. Rather than require such tax litigation to resolve the correct treatment of a debt transaction, I regard it as far preferable to have the tax consequences turn on the manner in which the debt is treated by the parties. For present purposes, it will suffice to say that where something that would otherwise be includable in gross income is received on credit in a purchase money transaction, there should be no recognition of income so long as the debtor continues to recognize an obligation to repay the debt. On the other hand, income, if not earlier recognized, should be recognized when the debtor no longer recognizes an obligation to repay and the creditor has released the debt or acknowledged its unenforceability.

---

14. This is not a case in which parties agree subsequent to a purchase money transaction that the property purchased has a value less than thought at the time of the transaction. In such cases, the purchase price adjustment rule is applied and the agreed-upon value is accepted as the value of the benefit received by the purchaser; see e.g., Commissioner v. Sherman, 135 F.2d 68 (6th Cir. 1943); N. Sobel, Inc. v. Commissioner, 40 B.T.A. 1263 (1939). Nor is this a case in which the taxpayer is entitled to rescind an entire purchase money transaction, thereby to restore itself to the position it occupied before receiving anything of commercial value. In this case, the illegality was in the extension of credit by Resorts and whether one views the benefit received by Zarin as cash or the opportunity to gamble, he is no longer in a position to return that benefit.

15. As the court's opinion correctly points out, this record will not support an exclusion under §108(a) which relates to discharge of debt in an insolvency or bankruptcy context. Section 108(e)(5) of the Code, which excludes discharged indebtedness arising from a "purchase price adjustment" is not applicable here. Among other things, §108(e)(5) necessarily applies only to a situation in which the debtor still holds the property acquired in the purchase money transaction. Equally irrelevant is §108(d)'s definition of "indebtedness" relied upon heavily by the court. Section 108(d) expressly defines that term solely for the purposes of §108 and not for the purposes of §61(a)(12).

In this view, it makes no difference whether the extinguishment of the creditor's claim comes as a part of a compromise. Resorts settled for 14 cents on the dollar presumably because it viewed such a settlement as reflective of the odds that the debt would be held to be enforceable. While Zarin should be given credit for the fact that he had to pay 14 cents for a release, I see no reason why he should not realize gain in the same manner as he would have if Resorts had concluded on its own that the debt was legally unenforceable and had written it off as uncollectible.[16]

I would affirm the judgment of the Tax Court.

NOTES

1. The dissent in *Zarin*, as well as the majority opinion in the Tax Court decision, treated the taxpayer as having CODI under the holding of *Kirby Lumber, supra*. But the majority in *Zarin* ruled for the taxpayer on the basis of a judicially created "contested liability" doctrine, under which the amount of a disputed debt is held to be the amount for which the debt is settled. In the majority's view, there never was a valid debt for $2,935,000, so there could be no relief from cancellation of indebtedness income when the debt was settled for $500,000.

Central to the majority's holding in *Zarin* was the fact that New Jersey law cast doubt on the enforceability of debts incurred by compulsive gamblers such as Zarin. Suppose that such debts were clearly enforceable under state law. Would it then be clear that Zarin had taxable income equal to the difference between the debt incurred and the settlement amount? Does someone who borrows approximately $3.4 million from a casino, loses the sum in a matter of hours, and settles the debt for $500,000, really have $2.9 million of income? The Tax Court opinion indicated that, at the time when the debt was incurred, Zarin was gambling twelve to sixteen hours a day, seven days a week, and wagering $15,000 on each roll of the dice. Is that relevant? Why do you suppose the casino allowed Zarin to keep on gambling with what was now, given the enforceability problem, likely to be its money (or chips)?

2. In Preslar v. Commissioner, 167 F.3d 1323 (10th Cir. 1999), the court rejected the Third Circuit's conclusion in *Zarin* that contested liability doctrine can apply merely because the enforceability of an asserted debt is being contested in good faith. According to *Preslar*, contested liability doctrine should not apply unless the amount that was initially transferred under the loan is in dispute, because only then is the IRS "unaware of the exact consideration initially received in a transaction." 167 F.3d at 1329. By contrast, "[i]f the parties initially treated the transaction as a loan when the loan proceeds were received, thereby not declaring the receipt as income, then the transaction

---

16. A different situation exists where there is a bona fide dispute over the amount of a debt and the dispute is compromised. Rather than require tax litigation to determine the amount of income received, the Commission treats the compromise figure as representing the amount of the obligation. I find this sensible and consistent with the pragmatic approach I would take.

should be treated consistently when the loan is discharged and income should be declared in the amount of the discharge." *Id.*

Preslar therefore concludes that the Third Circuit erred in *Zarin* when it asserted that, "[w]hen a debt is unenforceable, it follows that the amount of the debt, and not just the liability thereon, is in dispute." *Zarin*, 916 F.2d at 116. This disagreement between the Third and Tenth Circuits remains unresolved.

3. One of the dissents in the Tax Court decision in *Zarin* took the view that the taxpayer qualified for relief under §108(e)(5). As noted earlier, that provision treats the reduction of seller-financed debt that was incurred to purchase property as a reduction in the property's purchase price. This argument was rejected by a majority in both the Tax Court and the Third Circuit, on the ground that the chips did not represent "property," but instead were merely an "accounting mechanism" for purchasing gambling services. Is there any good reason why §108(e)(5) should not cover debt incurred to purchase services?

4. A bailment relationship exists when you temporarily transfer the control or possession of personal property for a specifically designated purpose. An example is leaving your car with the valet in a parking garage. Could it be argued that Zarin held the chips under a bailment relationship with the casino, that is, under the implicit understanding (even if unconscious on his part) that he would use them just in the casino and gradually give them back via gambling losses? How would this affect the legal analysis of the case?

5. Zarin's losses occurred in 1980, and he settled with Resorts in 1981. Section 165(d) provides: "Losses from wagering transactions shall be allowed only to the extent of the gains from such transactions." Reg. §1.165-10 provides: "Losses sustained during the taxable year on wagering transactions shall be allowed as a deduction but only to the extent of the gains *during the taxable year* from such transactions" (emphasis supplied). If Zarin had settled with Resorts in 1980, could he have prevailed on the ground that any gain from cancellation was offset by his losses from gambling?

C.   TRANSFERS OF PROPERTY SUBJECT TO DEBT

1.   The Basic Rules

When a taxpayer's acquisition of property is debt-financed, the debt is included in basis. Another way of stating this is to say that the taxpayer's basis is her cost, even if she used the proceeds of a loan to make the purchase. For this purpose, it generally makes no difference whether the debt is (a) newly incurred and owed directly to the seller, (b) newly incurred and owed to a third party, such as a bank, or (c) a preexisting lien or mortgage to which the property is subject. For now, however, suppose that, in each of these cases, the acquirer is personally liable to repay the debt. As we will see shortly, if the debt is nonrecourse—i.e., if the lender's only remedy in the case of default is against the property, not against the taxpayer personally—then, in certain limited situations, this may affect the legal analysis.

To illustrate the above rule including debt in basis, suppose that Alice acquires Blackacre for $2 million. Her initial cost basis for Blackacre is $2 million, whether she acquired it solely for cash, solely for debt, or for a combination of cash and debt adding up to $2 million. For this purpose, it generally does not matter which of the three scenarios describes the debt's origin.

One can describe the above rule as treating debt like cash. Incurring or assuming liability upon acquisition of property is generally treated the same as paying cash in the face amount of the debt.[17] This cash-equivalent approach likewise applies when one transfers property partly or wholly for debt, including in the case where the property is subject to a mortgage or lien that travels with the property to its new owner. Upon such a transfer, the amount realized generally includes the amount of the debt, just as if that amount had been paid to the seller in cash (which she then might have used to repay the debt).

Returning to Alice and Blackacre, suppose that she sells Blackacre for either (a) $3 million in cash, (b) $3 million in debt, or (c) $1 million in cash plus $2 million in debt (whether or not this is the same debt that may have financed her acquisition of the property). In each of these scenarios, her amount realized is $3 million.

Suppose that Alice's basis for Blackacre was still $2 million when she sold it for $3 million. Then her gain upon the sale is $1 million. This is the right answer, in terms of transactional consistency over time, given that she paid $2 million and then received $3 million (treating debt liabilities as equivalent to cash on both ends of the transaction).

Now let's add a further complication. Suppose that Blackacre consists of a building plus the surrounding land. In addition, suppose that Alice uses Blackacre in a business, for example, as the site for a restaurant or a shop. Then she may be allowed depreciation deductions with respect to the building and any equipment or other items of property that are part of Blackacre.

Depreciation deductions are intended as an allowance for the decline in the value of business property, due to wear and tear and/or obsolescence. They are not allowed with respect to land, as it is not thought to have a finite useful life or to be subject to predictable loss of value. However, for all depreciable property, depreciation deductions are allowed even if in fact there is no decline in the value of the property. They are computed under specific arithmetic formulas, generally, for each item of property in a particular category. The formulas specify what percentage of basis can be deducted each year, starting with when the taxpayer placed the particular item in service.

When depreciation deductions are allowed, they reduce the basis of the property to which they relate. This prevents "double counting" of the tax-free cost recovery that results from making use of basis. In illustration, suppose you buy property for $100, claim depreciation deductions of $60, and then sell the property for $35. The deductions reduce your basis for the property to $40, and therefore the sale yields only a $5 loss ($35 amount realized minus $40

---

17. We ignore for now the possibility, discussed later in this chapter, that the interest rate on the debt varies sufficiently from a reasonable market rate to require adjusting the stated principal amount.

adjusted basis). Given, however, that you also deducted $60 of depreciation, the tax system accurately measured your overall loss of $65 (i.e., $100 paid up front minus $35 received at the end).

Now let's return to Alice and Blackacre. Suppose that, during the period when she owned Blackacre, with its overall $2 million cost basis, she had been entitled to depreciation deductions in an amount equal to one-fifth of this amount, or $400,000. This would have reduced its basis to $1.6 million. Accordingly, upon selling it for $3 million, she would have had gain of $1.4 million (i.e., $3 million amount realized minus $1.6 million in adjusted basis). Overall, however, given the $400,000 in depreciation deductions that she was entitled to claim, her net income from the transaction as a whole would still be $1 million, just as in the case where no depreciation was allowable (e.g., if Blackacre consisted solely of land).

By reason of the time value of money, Alice is probably better off by reason of the depreciation deductions than she would have been if they were not allowed. They permit her to deduct $400,000, instead of zero, during her period of ownership, in exchange for including an additional $400,000 later on, when she sells Blackacre. Suppose that the marginal tax rate she faces at all times is 25 percent. Then, in effect, she got to reduce her tax liability by $100,000 (i.e., 25 percent of $400,000) during her period of ownership, in exchange for increasing it by $100,000 at the back-end. This is like getting a $100,000 interest-free loan (albeit, with the $100,000 being spread out over the period when she was claiming depreciation deductions), which has value to her given that (a) she would have had to pay interest on an actual $100,000 loan, and (b) she can earn a positive return on the $100,000 that she effectively "borrows" from the government (relative to the no-depreciation case) while holding Blackacre.

With all this in mind, suppose that the tax system treated debt differently than in fact it does. (Our reason for mentioning this scenario relates to the tax issues posed by nonrecourse debt, which we discuss next.) Suppose that, when a taxpayer acquired property partly or solely for debt, the debt was excluded from the basis of the property until she actually repaid it with her own cash. This would not affect the overall measure of gain or loss from holding property so long as the debt was treated symmetrically upon sale, i.e., excluded from the amount realized. But it would affect allowable depreciation deductions.

To illustrate, suppose that Alice acquired Blackacre solely for $2 million of debt and then transferred it to a purchaser for that same debt plus $1 million cash. Under our hypothetical and counterfactual rule excluding debt both from basis and from the amount realized, she would still have gain of $1 million. Only, here it would come from treating the amount realized as $1 million, rather than $3 million, and the original cost basis as zero rather than as $2 million.

This hypothetical rule would, however, generally be worse for Alice, in a time value of money sense, if Blackacre included depreciable property. With a basis for Blackacre of zero rather than $2 million, her depreciation deductions would be zero rather than any positive amount (such as $400,000). Indeed, even if she had paid *some* cash along with debt for Blackacre and thus had some positive basis for it (even under our hypothetical rule in which debt is excluded

from basis), excluding the debt from basis would lower her allowable depreciation deductions, since they are computed relative to basis.

2.   Nonrecourse Debt, Part I: *Crane* and *Tufts*

Some debt is nonrecourse. That is, the lender's only remedy in the case of
default is against the property, and the borrower is not personally liable for the
shortfall if the property's value is less than that of the debt.

Why would lenders be willing to lend nonrecourse? Presumably, it's usually some combination of (a) expecting the property's value to be adequate
to repay the loan, and/or (b) charging a higher interest rate to compensate
for the risk of a decline in the property's value that reduces the amount
that is ultimately collected. Plus, in some cases the lender may be pessimistic
about the prospects for getting great collection value out of the borrower's
personal liability, which may make agreeing to a nonrecourse loan a small
sacrifice.

Now let's turn to the tax consequences of using nonrecourse debt. In general, or at least as a starting point for analysis, the above-described rules for
transfers of property subject to debt still apply. However, nonrecourse debt can
create important complications, pertaining both to the purchase and to the
sale of debt-encumbered property by a given taxpayer.

These complications relate to the fact that, if the debt is nonrecourse, its
collection value is (by definition) limited to the property's value, even if that
is less than the debt's face amount. This raises issues regarding (a) whether
nonrecourse debt should always be fully included in the basis of property that
one acquires subject to it, (b) whether it should always be fully included in the
amount realized from the sale of property that is subject to it, and (c) how such
debt's treatment upon acquisition should affect its subsequent treatment upon
sale, given the issue of transactional consistency (i.e., the aim of correctly measuring overall gain or loss from holding the property).

These problems took decades for the tax system to figure out, and indeed
there are open questions still. The two leading cases, which follow below, are
Crane v. Commissioner, from 1947, and *Commissioner v. Tufts*, from 1983.

CRANE v. COMMISSIONER
331 U.S. 1 (1947)

Mr. Chief Justice VINSON delivered the opinion of the Court.

The question here is how a taxpayer who acquires depreciable property subject to an unassumed mortgage, holds it for a period, and finally sells it still so
encumbered, must compute her taxable gain.

[In 1932, Mrs. Beulah Crane inherited land and a building from her husband. The property was subject to a nonrecourse mortgage, or one that she
was not personally liable to repay, with an unpaid balance of $262,042.50. An
appraisal conducted for federal estate tax purposes determined that the property's value was also exactly $262,042.50.

Between 1932 and 1938, Mrs. Crane claimed depreciation deductions for the building in the amount of $25,500. In 1938, with the lender threatening foreclosure, Mrs. Crane transferred the property, still subject to the mortgage, to a third party in return for a cash payment (net of sale expenses) of $2,500.

In reporting this transaction, Mrs. Crane took the position that, for income tax purposes, the "property" she acquired in 1932 and sold in 1938 consisted only of the "equity," or excess in value of the land plus building over the mortgage that encumbered them. Thus, her amount realized on the sale was $2,500 and her basis was zero. This suggested that she had previously erred in claiming that the building had a depreciable basis, but the statute of limitations prevented any adjustment.

The government argued that her "property" was not limited to her "equity" interest. It thus recomputed her basis as $233,997.40 (the original appraised value of the land and building minus a slightly revised measure of the proper depreciation). And it included in her amount realized the principal amount of the mortgage to which the property remained subject, thus increasing the amount realized to $257,500.

Accordingly, under the government's approach, Mrs. Crane's gain from selling the property was $23,502.60, rather than $2,500 as reported. The difference was mainly attributable to the fact that, under its view but not hers, depreciation deductions that reduced the basis of the property had been properly allowable between 1932 and 1938.

[Section 1001(a)] defines the gain from "the sale or other disposition of property" as "the excess of the amount realized therefrom over the adjusted basis provided in section [1011(a)]. . . ." It proceeds, [§1001(b)], to define "the amount realized from the sale of other disposition of property" as "the sum of any money received plus the fair market value of the property (other than money) received." Further, in [§1016(a)(2)], the "adjusted basis for determining the gain or loss from the sale or other disposition of property" is declared to be "the basis determined under subsection (a), adjusted . . . for exhaustion, wear and tear, obsolescence, amortization . . . to the extent allowed (but not less than the amount allowable). . . ." The basis under subsection (a) "if the property was acquired by . . . devise . . . or by the decedent's estate from the decedent," [§1014], is "the fair market value of such property at the time of such acquisition."

Logically, the first step under this scheme is to determine the unadjusted basis of the property, under [§1014], and the dispute in this case is as to the construction to be given the term "property." If "property," as used in that provision, means the same thing as "equity," it would necessarily follow that the basis of petitioner's property was zero, as she contends. If, on the contrary, it means the land and building themselves, or the owner's legal rights in them, undiminished by the mortgage, the basis was $262,042.50.

We think that the reasons for favoring one of the latter construction are of overwhelming weight. In the first place, the words of statutes—including revenue acts—should be interpreted where possible in their ordinary, everyday senses. The only relevant definitions of "property" to be found in the principal standard dictionaries are the two favored by the Commissioner, that is, either that "property" is the physical thing which is a subject of ownership, or that it is the aggregate of the owner's rights to control and dispose of that thing. "Equity" is not given as a synonym, nor do either of the foregoing definitions suggest that it could be correctly so used. Indeed, "equity" is defined as "the value of a property . . . above the total of the liens. . . ." The contradistinction could hardly be more pointed. Strong countervailing considerations would be required to support a contention that Congress, in using the word "property," meant "equity," or that we should impute to it the intent to convey that meaning.

In the second place, the Commissioner's position [accorded with longstanding administrative practice]. . . .

Moreover, in the many instances in other parts of the Act in which Congress has used the word "property," or expressed the idea of "property" or "equity," we find no instances of a misuse of either word or of a confusion of the ideas. In some parts of the Act other than the gain and loss sections, we find "property" where it is unmistakably used in its ordinary sense. On the other hand, where either Congress or the Treasury intended to convey the meaning of "equity," it did so by the use of appropriate language.

A further reason why the word "property" in [§1001(a)] should not be construed to mean "equity" is the bearing such construction would have on the allowance of deductions for depreciation and on the collateral adjustments of basis.

Section [167(a)] permits deduction from gross income of "a reasonable allowance for the exhaustion, wear and tear of property. . . ." Section [167(i)] declare[s] that the "basis upon which exhaustion, wear and tear . . . are to be allowed" is the basis "provided in section [1001] for the purpose of determining the gain upon the sale" of the property, which is the [§1001(a)] basis "adjusted . . . for exhaustion, wear and tear . . . to the extent allowed (but not less than the amount allowable). . . ."

Under these provisions, if the mortgagor's equity were the [§1001(a)] basis, it would also be the original basis from which depreciation allowances are deducted. If it is, and if the amount of the annual allowances were to be computed on that value, as would then seem to be required, they will represent only a fraction of the cost of the corresponding physical exhaustion, and any recoupment by the mortgagor of the remainder of that cost can be effected only by the reduction of his taxable gain in the year of sale. If, however, the amount of the annual allowances were to be computed on the value of the property, and then deducted from an equity basis, we would in some instances have to accept deductions from a minus basis or deny deductions altogether.[18] The Commissioner also argues that taking the mortgagor's equity as the [§1001(a)] basis would require the basis to be changed with each payment on the mortgage, and that the attendant problem of repeatedly recomputing basis and annual allowances would be a tremendous accounting burden on

18. So long as the mortgagor remains in possession, the mortgagee can not take depreciation deductions, even if he is the one who actually sustains the capital loss, as [§167(a)] allows them only on property "used in the trade or business."

both the Commissioner and the taxpayer. Moreover, the mortgagor would acquire control over the timing of his depreciation allowances.

Thus it appears that the applicable provisions of the Act expressly preclude an equity basis, and the use of it is contrary to certain implicit principles of income tax depreciation, and entails very great administrative difficulties. It may be added that the Treasury has never furnished a guide through the maze of problems that arise in connection with depreciating an equity basis, but, on the contrary, has consistently permitted the amount of depreciation allowances to be computed on the full value of the property, and subtracted from it as a basis. Surely, Congress' long-continued acceptance of this situation gives it full legislative endorsement.

We conclude that the proper basis under [§1014] is the value of the property, undiminished by mortgages thereon, and that the correct basis here was $262,042.50. The next step is to ascertain what adjustments are required under [§1016]. As the depreciation rate was stipulated, the only question at this point is whether the Commissioner was warranted in making any depreciation adjustments whatsoever.

Section [1016] provides that "proper adjustment in respect of the property *shall in all cases be made* . . . for exhaustion, wear and tear . . . to the extent allowed (but not less than the amount allowable). . . ." (Italics supplied.) The Tax Court found on adequate evidence that the apartment house was property of a kind subject to physical exhaustion, that it was used in taxpayer's trade or business, and consequently that the taxpayer would have been entitled to a depreciation allowance under [§167], except that, in the opinion of that Court, the basis of the property was zero, and it was thought that depreciation could not be taken on a zero basis. As we have just decided that the correct basis of the property was not zero, but $262,042.50, we avoid this difficulty, and conclude that an adjustment should be made as the Commissioner determined.

Petitioner urges to the contrary that she was not entitled to depreciation deductions, whatever the basis of the property, because the law allows them only to one who actually bears the capital loss, and here the loss was not hers but the mortgagee's. We do not see, however, that she has established her factual premise. There was no finding of the Tax Court to that effect, nor to the effect that the value of the property was ever less than the amount of the lien. Nor was there evidence in the record, or any indication that petitioner could produce evidence, that this was so. The facts that the value of the property was only equal to the lien in 1932 and that during the next six and one-half years the physical condition of the building deteriorated and the amount of the lien increased, are entirely inconclusive, particularly in the light of the buyer's willingness in 1938 to take subject to the increased lien and pay a substantial amount of cash to boot. Whatever may be the rule as to allowing depreciation to a mortgagor on property in his possession which is subject to an unassumed mortgage and clearly worth less than the lien, we are not faced with that problem and see no reason to decide it now.

At last we come to the problem of determining the "amount realized" on the 1938 sale. Section [§1001(b)], it will be recalled, defines the "amount realized" from "the sale . . . of property" as "the sum of any money received plus the fair market value of the property (other than money) received," and [§1001(a)] defines the gain on "the sale . . . of property" as the excess of the amount realized over the basis. Quite obviously, the word "property," used here with reference to a sale, must mean "property" in the same ordinary sense intended by the use of the word with reference to acquisition and depreciation in [§1014], both for certain of the reasons stated heretofore in discussing its meaning in [§1014], and also because the functional relation of the two sections requires that the word mean the same in one section that it does in the other. If the "property" to be valued on the date of acquisition is the property free of liens, the "property" to be priced on a subsequent sale must be the same thing.

Starting from this point, we could not accept petitioner's contention that the $2,500.00 net cash was all she realized on the sale except on the absurdity that she sold a quarter-of-a-million dollar property for roughly one percent of its value, and took a 99 percent loss. Actually, petitioner does not urge this. She argues, conversely, that because only $2,500.00 was realized on the sale, the "property" sold must have been the equity only, and that consequently we are forced to accept her contention as to the meaning of "property" in [§1014]. We adhere, however, to what we have already said on the meaning of "property," and we find that the absurdity is avoided by our conclusion that the amount of the mortgage is properly included in the "amount realized" on the sale.

Petitioner concedes that if she had been personally liable on the mortgage and the purchaser had either paid or assumed it, the amount so paid or assumed would be considered a part of the "amount realized" within the meaning of [§1001(b)]. The cases so deciding have already repudiated the notion that there must be an actual receipt by the seller himself of "money" or "other property," in their narrowest senses. It was thought to be decisive that one section of the Act must be construed so as not to defeat the intention of another or to frustrate the Act as a whole, and that the taxpayer was the "beneficiary" of the payment in "as real and substantial [a sense] as if the money had been paid it and then paid over by it to its creditors."

Both these points apply to this case. The first has been mentioned already. As for the second, we think that a mortgagor, not personally liable on the debt, who sells the property subject to the mortgage and for additional consideration, realizes a benefit in the amount of the mortgage as well as the boot.[19] If a purchaser pays boot, it is immaterial as to our problem whether the mortgagor is also to receive money from the purchaser to discharge the mortgage prior to sale, or whether he is merely to transfer subject to the mortgage—it may make a difference to the purchaser and to the mortgagee, but not to the mortgagor. Or put in another way, we are no more concerned with whether the mortgagor is, strictly speaking, a debtor on the mortgage, than we are with whether the benefit to him is, strictly speaking, a receipt of money or property. We are rather concerned with the reality that an owner of property, mortgaged at a figure less than that at which the property will sell, must and will treat the conditions of the mortgage exactly as if they were his personal obligations. If he transfers subject to the mortgage, the benefit to him is as real and

---

19. [This is the well-known footnote 37 in the original opinion.—EDS.] Obviously, if the value of the property is less than the amount of the mortgage, a mortgagor who is not personally liable cannot realize a benefit equal to the mortgage. Consequently, a different problem might be encountered where a mortgagor abandoned the property or transferred it subject to the mortgage without receiving boot. That is not this case.

substantial as if the mortgage were discharged, or as if a personal debt in an equal amount had been assumed by another.

Therefore we conclude that the Commissioner was right in determining that petitioner realized $257,500.00 on the sale of this property. . . .

Petitioner contends that the result we have reached taxes her on what is not income within the meaning of the Sixteenth Amendment. If this is because only the direct receipt of cash is thought to be income in the constitutional sense, her contention is wholly without merit. If it is because the entire transaction is thought to have been "by all dictates of common sense . . . a ruinous disaster," as it was termed in her brief, we disagree with her premise. She was entitled to depreciation deductions for a period of nearly seven years, and she actually took them in almost the allowable amount. The crux of this case, really, is whether the law permits her to exclude allowable deductions from consideration in computing gain. We have already showed that, if it does, the taxpayer can enjoy a double deduction, in effect, on the same loss of assets. The Sixteenth Amendment does not require that result any more than does the Act itself.

Affirmed.

Mr. Justice JACKSON, dissenting.

The Tax Court concluded that this taxpayer acquired only an equity worth nothing. The mortgage was in default, the mortgage debt was equal to the value of the property, any possession by the taxpayer was forfeited and terminable immediately by foreclosure, and perhaps by a receiver pendente lite. Arguments can be advanced to support the theory that the taxpayer received the whole property and thereupon came to owe the whole debt. Likewise it is argued that when she sold she transferred the entire value of the property and received release from the whole debt. But we think these arguments are not so conclusive that it was not within the province of the Tax Court to find that she received an equity which at that time had a zero value. The taxpayer never became personally liable for the debt, and hence when she sold she was released from no debt. The mortgage debt was simply a subtraction from the value of what she did receive, and from what she sold. The subtraction left her nothing when she acquired it and a small margin when she sold it. She acquired a property right equivalent to an equity of redemption and sold the same thing. It was the "property" bought and sold as the Tax Court considered it to be under the Revenue Laws. We are not required in this case to decide whether depreciation was properly taken, for there is no issue about it here.

We would reverse the Court of Appeals and sustain the decision of the Tax Court.

Mr. Justice FRANKFURTER and Mr. Justice DOUGLAS join in this opinion.

NOTES AND QUESTIONS

1. The events described in *Crane* can be portrayed visually through this chart. As it shows, the property assertedly had a basis and value slightly over $250,000 in 1932, was sold for the initial debt plus $2,500 in 1938, and in the interim was the subject of depreciation deductions of about $25,500.

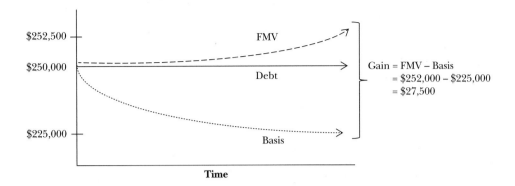

2. Whose view of how to treat acquisitions and dispositions of property subject to nonrecourse debt is more favorable to taxpayers in the long run: that of Mrs. Crane or that of the Commissioner? Note that under Mrs. Crane's view, if applied consistently throughout her period of ownership, she acquired the property with a zero basis, should not have deducted any depreciation, and then sold it for $2,500. The Commissioner's view gives her a higher basis and amount realized, by reason of including on both sides the amount of the nonrecourse debt. In practice, the main difference between the two views is that the Commissioner permits the taxpayer to claim depreciation deductions, which are then offset by recapture gain upon disposition of the property. Why does this matter?

3. *Basis and tax shelters.* Despite its somewhat homely facts, the *Crane* decision turned out to be highly significant to the development of U.S. tax law. Boris Bittker, the original author of this casebook, once observed that *Crane* "laid the foundation stone of most tax shelters." The term "tax shelter" is typically used to describe certain investments entered into largely for the sake of their tax benefits, such as by reason of their generating large tax losses that exceed any actual economic losses. The idea is to deduct these losses against items of positive taxable income that would otherwise trigger significant tax liability, thereby "sheltering" such income.

While we will extensively discuss tax shelters, along with various rules that were enacted to address them, in Chapter 7, a simple example here may help to demonstrate how *Crane* might (in the absence of those rules) be used to generate tax shelter losses, at least by unscrupulous taxpayers who were willing to structure bogus transactions that they were hoping would not be audited carefully. This example, which we call the "paper clip tax shelter," is both fictional and extreme—but it may help to dramatize the underlying issue.

Suppose (counterfactually) that people who used paper clips in their businesses were allowed to expense the cost of buying them—that is, to deduct it immediately and in full—even while the items remained on hand and in use. If acquisition nonrecourse debt was always, and automatically, fully included in the basis of property even if it substantially exceeded the property's value—and if various other rules impeding or penalizing the suggested transaction did not exist—then a tax shelter promoter could offer the following deal to a taxpayer who wanted to create a $1 million tax loss:

> "Here is a paper clip. How would you like to buy it for $1 million nonrecourse debt? That way [supposing counterfactually that paper clips could be expensed], you get an immediate $1 million deduction.
>
> "And don't worry about actually repaying the debt. When it comes due, you can simply refuse to pay. Since the debt is nonrecourse, all I can do is take back the paper clip, or another one just like it.
>
> "When that happens, at worst you'll have a $1 million amount realized. [And even this wasn't entirely clear prior to the *Tufts* case, which we discuss next.] But not to worry—in the interim you will have gotten the time value of the money from the up-front deduction. Plus, at that point I can sell you another million-dollar paper clip, and we'll start all over again.
>
> "Finally, don't worry about the fact that, in *Crane*, the property was worth as much as the nonrecourse debt on the date when Mrs. Crane acquired it. We have found a valuation 'expert' who is willing to write a report stating that the paper clip we are selling you is actually worth $1 million. So you can use this report in support of the claim that *Crane* is directly on point."

Exaggerated? Perhaps, not to mention fraudulent. What's more, under present law (as discussed in Chapter 7), the taxpayer would face overvaluation penalties (since the paper clip is presumably worth pennies at most, rather than $1 million),[20] and the deduction might not even be usable against the taxpayer's positive income.[21] Nonetheless, transactions of this general type—if less extreme—were widespread during the 1970s and 1980s. They made use of nonrecourse debt both because it permitted overvaluation of the depreciable property that was being "sold," and because purchasers liked the assurance it offered that their potential cash liabilities to the transactions' promoters and "lenders" were limited.

What's in it for the tax shelter promoter? Presumably, the transaction also includes substantial fees that the promoter can pocket.

4. *Alternatives to nonrecourse debt.* When a mortgage is nonrecourse, the lender rather than the borrower bears the risk that, on the maturity date, the security's value will be less than the amount due. For example, suppose Beulah owes a bank $1 million under a nonrecourse mortgage on Blackacre that is due in ten years. If, on the maturity date, Blackacre is worth, say, $850,000, Beulah can default, leaving the bank with no further right to repayment on its million-dollar loan.

However, the use of nonrecourse debt provides only one of an array of distinctive legal forms that can be used to make the bank, rather than Beulah, bear this risk of loss. Alternatively, the parties could, for example:

- Make Beulah personally liable to repay the loan but have the bank give her the legal right to require it to buy Blackacre from her for $1 million on the loan maturity date. How can this lead to the same result as the use of

---

20. See, e.g., §6662.
21. See §469 (passive loss rules).

a nonrecourse mortgage if Blackacre is worth only $850,000 on the loan maturity date?

- Structure the transaction so that the bank, rather than Beulah, is Blackacre's legal owner during the ten-year period, but give her the legal right to require the bank to sell her Blackacre for $1 million at the end of this period.

Can you think of any other ways (e.g., with "default insurance") to replicate the economic substance of a *Crane*-style transaction, without formally using nonrecourse debt? What does the variety of ways in which the same economic transaction can be arranged tell you about the wisdom of (as Mrs. Crane proposed) treating nonrecourse debt differently from recourse debt?

5. *Whose depreciation?* If nonrecourse borrowers were denied depreciation deductions, by reason of a hypothetical rule excluding nonrecourse debt from basis, might Congress decide that such deductions should go to the lender? Critics of the *Crane* rule sometimes argue that this is the correct result, on the ground that the lender, rather than the owner, bears the economic loss if the property's value declines to less than the face amount of the outstanding nonrecourse debt. In fact, however, this is not entirely correct, even to the extent that the deductions correctly measure an actual decline in value of the property. Rather, if the property's value is volatile (e.g., it might go back up) or, if its annual rental or use value to the owner declines along with its sale value, the economic loss is split between the owner and lender. As for depreciation that exceeds any real economic decline in the property's value, it does not represent an economic loss that *anyone* has actually suffered. Thus, there arguably is no "correct" taxpayer to claim the deduction to that extent. See Shaviro, *Risk and Accrual: The Tax Treatment of Nonrecourse Debt*, 44 Tax L. Rev. 401, 433-437 (1989).

6. *Crane*'s famous footnote 37 (appearing in this chapter as footnote 19) expressly reserves the question of how to treat a sale of property that is worth less than the amount of a nonrecourse mortgage to which it is subject. Thus, suppose a taxpayer purchases depreciable property for $1 million of nonrecourse debt, over time claims $1 million of depreciation deductions (reducing adjusted basis to zero), and then abandons the property. If the property is worth zero upon abandonment, the footnote seems to suggest that the taxpayer need not include any gain to offset the previously deducted loss, although the last paragraph of the Court's opinion is seemingly to the contrary.

For many years, a belief among taxpayers that they were entitled to rely upon the favorable implications of footnote 37 helped to make tax shelters even more appealing than otherwise. After all, if one never has an offsetting inclusion for the depreciation that one deducted, despite never bearing it economically, that is better still than the mere deferral described above with regard to the "paper clip tax shelter." This practice, and the correct tax treatment of situations described in footnote 37, finally received the Supreme Court's attention in the following case.

COMMISSIONER v. TUFTS
461 U.S. 300 (1983)

Justice BLACKMUN delivered the opinion of the Court.

Over 35 years ago, in Crane v. Commissioner, 331 U.S. 1 (1947), this Court ruled that a taxpayer, who sold property encumbered by a nonrecourse mortgage (the amount of the mortgage being less than the property's value), must include the unpaid balance of the mortgage in the computation of the amount the taxpayer realized on the sale. The case now before us presents the question whether the same rule applies when the unpaid amount of the nonrecourse mortgage exceeds the fair market value of the property sold.

I

On August 1, 1970, respondent Clark Pelt, a builder, and his wholly owned corporation, respondent Clark, Inc., formed a general partnership. The purpose of the partnership was to construct a 120-unit apartment complex in Duncanville, Tex., a Dallas suburb. Neither Pelt nor Clark, Inc., made any capital contribution to the partnership. Six days later, the partnership entered into a mortgage loan agreement with the Farm & Home Savings Association (F&H). Under the agreement, F&H was committed for a $1,851,500 loan for the complex. In return, the partnership executed a note and a deed of trust in favor of F&H. The partnership obtained the loan on a nonrecourse basis: neither the partnership nor its partners assumed any personal liability for repayment of the loan. Pelt later admitted four friends and relatives, respondents Tufts, Steger, Stephens, and Austin, as general partners. None of them contributed capital upon entering the partnership.

The construction of the complex was completed in August 1971. During 1971, each partner made small capital contributions to the partnership; in 1972, however, only Pelt made a contribution. The total of the partners' capital contributions was $44,212. In each tax year, all partners claimed as income tax deductions their allocable shares of ordinary losses and depreciation. The deductions taken by the partners in 1971 and 1972 totalled $439,972. Due to these contributions and deductions, the partnership's adjusted basis in the property in August 1972 was $1,455,740.

In 1971 and 1972, major employers in the Duncanville area laid off significant numbers of workers. As a result, the partnership's rental income was less than expected, and it was unable to make the payments due on the mortgage. Each partner, on August 28, 1972, sold his partnership interest to an unrelated third party, Fred Bayles. As consideration, Bayles agreed to reimburse each partner's sale expenses up to $250; he also assumed the nonrecourse mortgage.

On the date of transfer, the fair market value of the property did not exceed $1,400,000. Each partner reported the sale on his federal income tax return and indicated that a partnership loss of $55,740 had been

sustained.[22] The Commissioner of Internal Revenue, on audit, determined that the sale resulted in a partnership capital gain of approximately
$400,000. His theory was that the partnership had realized the full amount
of the nonrecourse obligation.[23]

Relying on Millar v. Commissioner, 577 F.2d 212, 215 (C.A.3), cert. denied,
439 U.S. 1046 (1978), the United States Tax Court, in an unreviewed decision, upheld the asserted deficiencies. 70 T.C. 756 (1978). The United States
Court of Appeals for the Fifth Circuit reversed. 651 F.2d 1058 (1981). That
court expressly disagreed with the *Millar* analysis, and, in limiting Crane v.
Commissioner, supra, to its facts, questioned the theoretical underpinnings of
the *Crane* decision. We granted certiorari to resolve the conflict. . . .

II

Section 752(d) of the Internal Revenue Code of 1954 specifically provides
that liabilities incurred in the sale or exchange of a partnership interest are
to "be treated in the same manner as liabilities in connection with the sale
or exchange of property not associated with partnerships." Section 1001 governs the determination of gains and losses on the disposition of property.
Under §1001(a), the gain or loss from a sale or other disposition of property
is defined as the difference between "the amount realized" on the disposition
and the property's adjusted basis. Subsection (b) of §1001 defines "amount
realized." "The amount realized from the sale or other disposition of property
shall be the sum of any money received plus the fair market value of the property (other than money) received." At issue is the application of the latter provision to the disposition of property encumbered by a nonrecourse mortgage
of an amount in excess of the property's fair market value.

A

In Crane v. Commissioner, supra, this Court took the first and controlling
step toward the resolution of this issue. . . .

[T]he Court concluded that Crane obtained an economic benefit from the
purchaser's assumption of the mortgage identical to the benefit conferred by
the cancellation of personal debt. Because the value of the property in that
case exceeded the amount of the mortgage, it was in Crane's economic interest
to treat the mortgage as a personal obligation; only by so doing could she
realize upon sale the appreciation in her equity represented by the $2,500
boot. The purchaser's assumption of the liability thus resulted in a taxable

---

22. The loss was the difference between the adjusted basis, $1,455,740, and the fair market value
of the property, $1,400,000. On their individual tax returns, the partners did not claim deductions
for their respective shares of this loss. In their petitions to the Tax Court, however, the partners did
claim the loss.

23. The Commissioner determined the partnership's gain on the sale by subtracting the adjusted
basis, $1,455,740, from the liability assumed by Bayles, $1,851,500. . . .

economic benefit to her, just as if she had been given, in addition to the boot, a sum of cash sufficient to satisfy the mortgage.

In a footnote, pertinent to the present case, the Court observed:

> Obviously, if the value of the property is less than the amount of the mortgage, a mortgagor who is not personally liable cannot realize a benefit equal to the mortgage. Consequently, a different problem might be encountered where a mortgagor abandoned the property or transferred it subject to the mortgage without receiving boot. That is not this case.

Id., at 14, n.37.

B

This case presents that unresolved issue. We are disinclined to overrule *Crane*, and we conclude that the same rule applies when the unpaid amount of the nonrecourse mortgage exceeds the value of the property transferred. *Crane* ultimately does not rest on its limited theory of economic benefit; instead, we read *Crane* to have approved the Commissioner's decision to treat a nonrecourse mortgage in this context as a true loan. This approval underlies *Crane*'s holdings that the amount of the nonrecourse liability is to be included in calculating both the basis and the amount realized on disposition. That the amount of the loan exceeds the fair market value of the property thus becomes irrelevant.

When a taxpayer receives a loan, he incurs an obligation to repay that loan at some future date. Because of this obligation, the loan proceeds do not qualify as income to the taxpayer. When he fulfills the obligation, the repayment of the loan likewise has no effect on his tax liability.

Another consequence to the taxpayer from this obligation occurs when the taxpayer applies the loan proceeds to the purchase price of property used to secure the loan. Because of the obligation to repay, the taxpayer is entitled to include the amount of the loan in computing his basis in the property; the loan, under §1012, is part of the taxpayer's cost of the property. Although a different approach might have been taken with respect to a nonrecourse mortgage loan,[24] the Commissioner has chosen to accord it the same treatment he gives to a recourse mortgage loan. The Court approved that choice in *Crane*, and the respondents do not challenge it here. The choice and its resultant

---

24. The Commissioner might have adopted the theory, implicit in Crane's contentions, that a nonrecourse mortgage is not true debt, but, instead, is a form of joint investment by the mortgagor and the mortgagee. On this approach, nonrecourse debt would be considered a contingent liability, under which the mortgagor's payments on the debt gradually increase his interest in the property while decreasing that of the mortgagee. . . . Because the taxpayer's investment in the property would not include the nonrecourse debt, the taxpayer would not be permitted to include that debt in basis. . . .

We express no view as to whether such an approach would be consistent with the statutory structure and, if so, and *Crane* were not on the books, whether that approach would be preferred over *Crane*'s analysis. We note only that the *Crane* Court's resolution of the basis issue presumed that when property is purchased with proceeds from a nonrecourse mortgage, the purchaser becomes the sole owner of the property. . . .

benefits to the taxpayer are predicated on the assumption that the mortgage will be repaid in full.

When encumbered property is sold or otherwise disposed of and the purchaser assumes the mortgage, the associated extinguishment of the mortgagor's obligation to repay is accounted for in the computation of the amount realized. . . . Because no difference between recourse and nonrecourse obligations is recognized in calculating basis,[25] *Crane* teaches that the Commissioner may ignore the nonrecourse nature of the obligation in determining the amount realized upon disposition of the encumbered property. He thus may include in the amount realized the amount of the nonrecourse mortgage assumed by the purchaser. The rationale for this treatment is that the original inclusion of the amount of the mortgage in basis rested on the assumption that the mortgagor incurred an obligation to repay. Moreover, this treatment balances the fact that the mortgagor originally received the proceeds of the nonrecourse loan tax-free on the same assumption. Unless the outstanding amount of the mortgage is deemed to be realized, the mortgagor effectively will have received untaxed income at the time the loan was extended and will have received an unwarranted increase in the basis of his property.[26] The Commissioner's interpretation of §1001(b) in this fashion cannot be said to be unreasonable.

C

The Commissioner in fact has applied this rule even when the fair market value of the property falls below the amount of the nonrecourse obligation. Treas. Reg. §1.1001-2(b); Rev. Rul. 76-111, 1976-1 Cum. Bull. 214. Because the theory on which the rule is based applies equally in this situation, . . . we have no reason, after *Crane*, to question this treatment.[27]

---

25. The Commissioner's choice in *Crane* "laid the foundation stone of most tax shelters," Bittker, *Tax Shelters, Nonrecourse Debt, and the Crane Case*, 33 Tax L. Rev. 277, 283 (1978), by permitting taxpayers who bear no risk to take deductions on depreciable property. Congress recently has acted to curb this avoidance device by forbidding a taxpayer to take depreciation deductions in excess of amounts he has at risk in the investment. . . . §465(a) [see infra 596]. . . . Although this congressional action may foreshadow a day when nonrecourse and recourse debts will be treated differently, neither Congress nor the Commissioner has sought to alter *Crane*'s rule of including nonrecourse liability in both basis and the amount realized.

26. Although the *Crane* rule has some affinity with the tax benefit rule; . . . the analysis we adopt is different. Our analysis applies even in the situation in which no deductions are taken. It focuses on the obligation to repay and its subsequent extinguishment, not on the taking and recovery of deductions. . . .

27. Professor Wayne G. Barnett, as amicus in the present case, argues that the liability and property portions of the transaction should be accounted for separately. Under his view, there was a transfer of the property for $1.4 million, and there was a cancellation of the $1.85 million obligation for a payment of $1.4 million. The former resulted in a capital loss of $50,000, and the latter in the realization of $450,000 of ordinary income. Taxation of the ordinary income might be deferred under §108 by a reduction of respondents' bases in their partnership interests. [Deferral under §108 was broadly available at the time this case was decided. It is now available only for insolvent debtors and farmers and the relief mechanism is slightly different from the one applied under the now-repealed provision referred to by the Court. —Eds.]

Respondents received a mortgage loan with the concomitant obligation to repay by the year 2012. The only difference between that mortgage and one on which the borrower is personally liable is that the mortgagee's remedy is limited to foreclosing on the securing property. This difference does not alter the nature of the obligation; its only effect is to shift from the borrower to the lender any potential loss caused by devaluation of the property. If the fair market value of the property falls below the amount of the outstanding obligation, the mortgagee's ability to protect its interests is impaired, for the mortgagor is free to abandon the property to the mortgagee and be relieved of his obligation.

This, however, does not erase the fact that the mortgagor received the loan proceeds tax-free and included them in his basis on the understanding that he had an obligation to repay the full amount. . . . When the obligation is canceled, the mortgagor is relieved of his responsibility to repay the sum he originally received and thus realizes value to that extent within the meaning of §1001(b). From the mortgagor's point of view, when his obligation is assumed by a third party who purchases the encumbered property, it is as if the mortgagor first had been paid with cash borrowed by the third party from the mortgagee on a nonrecourse basis, and then had used the cash to satisfy his obligation to the mortgagee.

Moreover, this approach avoids the absurdity the Court recognized in *Crane*. Because of the remedy accompanying the mortgage in the nonrecourse situation, the depreciation in the fair market value of the property is relevant economically only to the mortgagee, who by lending on a nonrecourse basis remains at risk. To permit the taxpayer to limit his realization to the fair market value of the property would be to recognize a tax loss for which he has suffered no corresponding economic loss. Such a result would be to construe "one section of the Act . . . so as . . . to defeat the intention of another or to frustrate the Act as a whole." 331 U.S., at 13.

In the specific circumstances of *Crane*, the economic benefit theory did support the Commissioner's treatment of the nonrecourse mortgage as a personal obligation. The footnote in *Crane* acknowledged the limitations of that theory when applied to a different set of facts. *Crane* also stands for the broader proposition, however, that a nonrecourse loan should be treated as a true loan. We therefore hold that a taxpayer must account for the proceeds of obligations he has received tax-free and included in basis. Nothing in either §1001(b) or in the Court's prior decisions requires the Commissioner to permit a taxpayer to treat a sale of encumbered property asymmetrically, by including the proceeds of the nonrecourse obligation in basis but not accounting for the proceeds upon transfer of the encumbered property. . . .

Justice O'CONNOR, concurring.

I concur in the opinion of the Court, accepting the view of the Commissioner. I do not, however, endorse the Commissioner's view. Indeed, were we writing

---

Although this indeed could be a justifiable mode of analysis, it has not been adopted by the Commissioner. Nor is there anything to indicate that the Code requires the Commissioner to adopt it. We note that Professor Barnett's approach does assume that recourse and nonrecourse debt may be treated identically. . . .

on a slate clean except for the *Crane* decision, I would take quite a different approach — that urged upon us by Professor Barnett as amicus.

Crane established that a taxpayer could treat property as entirely his own, in spite of the "coinvestment" provided by his mortgagee in the form of a nonrecourse loan. That is, the full basis of the property, with all its tax consequences, belongs to the mortgagor. That rule alone, though, does not in any way tie nonrecourse debt to the cost of property or to the proceeds upon disposition. I see no reason to treat the purchase, ownership, and eventual disposition of property differently because the taxpayer also takes out a mortgage, an independent transaction. In this case, the taxpayer purchased property, using nonrecourse financing, and sold it after it declined in value to a buyer who assumed the mortgage. There is no economic difference between the events in this case and a case in which the taxpayer buys property with cash; later obtains a nonrecourse loan by pledging the property as security; still later, using cash on hand, buys off the mortgage for the market value of the devalued property; and finally sells the property to a third party for its market value.

The logical way to treat both this case and the hypothesized case is to separate the two aspects of these events and to consider, first, the ownership and sale of the property, and, second, the arrangement and retirement of the loan. Under *Crane*, the fair market value of the property on the date of acquisition — the purchase price — represents the taxpayer's basis in the property, and the fair market value on the date of disposition represents the proceeds on sale. The benefit received by the taxpayer in return for the property is the cancellation of a mortgage that is worth no more than the fair market value of the property, for that is all the mortgagee can expect to collect on the mortgage. His gain or loss on the disposition of the property equals the difference between the proceeds and the cost of acquisition. Thus, the taxation of the transaction in *property* reflects the economic fate of the *property*. If the property has declined in value, as was the case here, the taxpayer recognizes a loss on the disposition of the property. The new purchaser then takes as his basis the fair market value as of the date of the sale. . . .

In the separate borrowing transaction, the taxpayer acquires cash from the mortgagee. He need not recognize income at that time, of course, because he also incurs an obligation to repay the money. Later, though, when he is able to satisfy the debt by surrendering property that is worth less than the face amount of the debt, we have a classic situation of cancellation of indebtedness, requiring the taxpayer to recognize income in the amount of the difference between the proceeds of the loan and the amount for which he is able to satisfy his creditor. 26 U.S.C. §61(a)(12). The taxation of the financing transaction then reflects the economic fate of the loan.

The reason that separation of the two aspects of the events in this case is important is, of course, that the Code treats different sorts of income differently. A gain on the sale of the property may qualify for capital gains treatment, while the cancellation of indebtedness is ordinary income, but income that the taxpayer may be able to defer. Not only does Professor Barnett's theory permit us to accord appropriate treatment to each of the two types of income or loss present in these sorts of transactions, it also restores continuity to the system by making the taxpayer-seller's proceeds on the disposition of property equal to the purchaser's basis in the property. Further, and most important, it allows us to tax the events in this case in the same way that we tax the economically identical hypothesized transaction.

Persuaded though I am by the logical coherence and internal consistency of this approach, I agree with the Court's decision not to adopt it judicially. We do not write on a slate marked only by *Crane*. The Commissioner's long-standing position, Rev. Rul. 76-111, 1976-1 C.B. 214, is now reflected in the regulations. Treas. Reg. §1.1001-2, 26 C.F.R. §1.1001-2 (1982). In the light of the numerous cases in the lower courts including the amount of the unrepaid proceeds of the mortgage in the proceeds on sale or disposition, . . . it is difficult to conclude that the Commissioner's interpretation of the statute exceeds the bounds of his discretion. As the Court's opinion demonstrates, his interpretation is defensible. . . .

NOTES AND QUESTIONS

1. The events described in *Tufts* can be portrayed visually through this chart. As it shows, the property was subject to a nonrecourse loan in the amount of about $1.85 million, but when transferred to Bayles had a basis of about $1.45 million and was worth no more than $1.4 million.

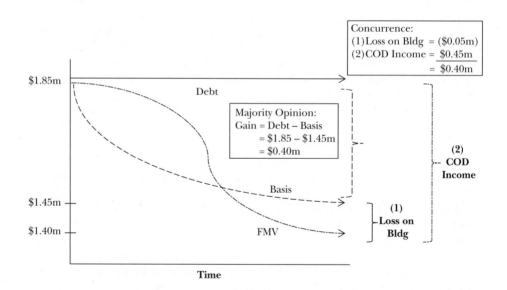

2. *Taking debt into account on disposition of property.* (a) The Court in *Tufts* requires the taxpayer to recognize income upon the disposition of the apartment complex. The following simplified version of the facts in the case should help illuminate the logic behind that aspect of the decision. Assume Tufts put up $45,000 of his own funds and used $1,850,000 of borrowed funds to acquire an apartment complex for $1,895,000. Tufts deducted $440,000 depreciation

and then "sold" the complex for a nominal sum (which we will ignore). Tufts's total dollar loss, then, was $45,000. His prior tax loss, however, was $440,000. Clearly, something is amiss here. Tufts deducted $440,000 depreciation but lost only the cash contribution of $45,000. For the tax consequences to match the economic consequences, the taxpayer must, in effect, "give back" the $395,000 of depreciation that represented a loss he did not incur.

The Court in *Tufts* reaches the correct result (as to income recognized) by including the buyer's assumption of the nonrecourse debt as part of the sales proceeds. The taxpayer is thus treated as having received $1,850,000 upon sale of the property. The depreciation reduced the taxpayer's basis in the property from $1,895,000 (the invested loan proceeds plus the $45,000 of the taxpayer's own funds) to $1,455,000 (basis less depreciation). The difference between that basis and the $1,850,000 sales proceeds yields a gain of $395,000. The Court derives the proper result with a nice symmetry: If nonrecourse debt is treated as cash for the purposes of determining basis, perhaps it should be treated as cash for the purposes of determining sales proceeds.

3. *Bifurcation: The approach not taken.* The approach described in Justice O'Connor's concurrence reaches the same result (as to amount recognized), but by a different means. Under that approach, property is treated as sold for its fair market value. If property purchased with, and secured by, a nonrecourse loan declines in value to zero and is abandoned (or foreclosed upon by the lender, or deeded over to the lender in lieu of foreclosure) the sales proceeds are zero. The taxpayer recognizes no property gain and, depending on the basis of the property at the time the proposed is disposed of, may well recognize a loss. The taxpayer does, however, recognize cancellation of indebtedness income equal to the difference between the amount of outstanding debt secured by the property and its fair market value at time of disposal. The intuition behind this "bifurcated" approach is that the taxpayer has not repaid the full amount it has borrowed and must recognize cancellation of indebtedness income under *Kirby Lumber, supra.*

If the Supreme Court had adopted a bifurcation approach in *Tufts*, then taxpayers would have to determine the value of the property in nonrecourse debt discharge cases, whereas, under the actual approach followed, this was not necessary. One reason it could make a difference is that the CODI potentially created under a bifurcation approach will invariably be treated as ordinary income, whereas its inclusion in the amount realized may affect the amount of capital gain or capital loss. A second possible implication goes to the rules in §108 that may permit CODI, in particular cases, to be excluded from income.

Bifurcation is the rule with respect to transactions in which property is transferred to a creditor in satisfaction of *recourse* debt. See Reg. §1.1001-2(a)(2), (b), and Ex. 8; Gehl v. Commissioner, 102 T.C. 784 (1994), aff'd without op., 50 F.3d 12 (8th Cir. 1995). In such cases, however, one would expect the parties to determine the property's value, irrespective of tax considerations, given its effect on the amount due from the borrower.

4. *Comparison to the tax benefit rule. Tufts* provides a kind of tax benefit rule whereby "a taxpayer must account for the proceeds of obligations he has received tax free and included in basis." Is inclusion in basis necessary for its tax benefit rationale to apply? Suppose one owned property with a basis and

value of $1 million, and then borrowed $900,000 in cash under a nonrecourse mortgage of the property. If the property's value subsequently declined below $900,000 and one abandoned the property rather than repay the loan, *Tufts* presumably would require treating the abandonment as a sale of the property for $900,000. Here, however, it is the receipt of $900,000 in cash tax free, rather than inclusion in basis, that triggers application of the tax benefit rationale.

3.   Nonrecourse Debt, Part II: Property Worth Less at Acquisition Than the Face Amount of the Debt

In *Crane*, it was stipulated that, when the taxpayer acquired the property, the face amount of the nonrecourse debt precisely equaled the value of the property. In *Tufts*, we can presume that, at the start of the transaction, the property was worth at least the face amount of the nonrecourse debt, given that a third-party lender (F&H) made the loan in that amount on a nonrecourse basis.

But what if the face amount of the loan is greater than the value of the property when initially acquired by the taxpayer? Here are two distinct scenarios in which this might happen:

a.   Seller Financing

When the seller, rather than a third party lender such as an independent bank, is the party offering nonrecourse financing to the buyer of property, it may have nothing to lose on balance economically from making an "excessive" loan. After all, if a nonrecourse loan that exceeds the property's value is part of the sale transaction, then the seller/lender is also benefiting from an "excessive" sale price.

For an extreme example, consider again the "paper-clip tax shelter." If a tax shelter promoter purports to sell you a paper clip for $1 million in nonrecourse debt, then, while it is true she will never collect on the loan, the money she thus "loses" was never realistically available to her anyway, given the impossibility of truly selling a paper clip for $1 million.

b.   Mid-Stream Acquisition of "Distressed" Property

Recall that in *Tufts*, Fred Bayles, an unrelated third party, agreed to take over property that was worth $1.4 million, even though it was subject to $1.85 million in nonrecourse debt. Indeed, he even agreed to reimburse each partner's sale expenses up to $250.

Was this a foolish blunder on his part? Not necessarily. After all, if F&H demanded full repayment on the due date, he could simply walk away from the property, like the partners before him. (The court's statement that he "assumed the nonrecourse mortgage" presumably does not mean that he accepted personal liability.) Indeed, if the property was still worth $1.4 million and he offered that amount in full settlement of the debt, F&H might have good reason to accept this offer. So Bayles acquired not only title to the property, but a chance to become its owner permanently, without overpaying, if he and F&H could agree regarding settlement of the loan.

Indeed, if the property's value subsequently rebounded to the point that it exceeded the loan balance, Bayles, rather than F&H, would be the party that reaped the gain. Suppose, for example, that Duncanville, where the property was located, experienced an employment boom, causing workers who needed housing to flood in, and that this caused the property's value to rise to $2 million. The gain from its appreciation over the face amount of the non-recourse loan would accrue to Bayles, rather than to F&H, since he, by fully repaying the loan, would extinguish its financial claim.

Whatever the underlying cause, in any case where a taxpayer acquires property subject to nonrecourse debt in excess of the value of the property, one must determine how this acquisition should be treated for tax purposes. Indeed, there really are two questions, pertaining to (1) the consequences for basis when the taxpayer acquires the property, and (2) the amount realized if the taxpayer subsequently transfers the property, still subject to the non-recourse debt. While the answers to these two questions are related to each other—as we saw in *Tufts*, where the amount realized depended on how basis had been computed at the front end—they are best analyzed separately.

(i) Basis consequences of acquiring property subject to "excess" nonrecourse debt. The "paper-clip tax shelter" transaction looks like a sham, whereas Bayles's acquisition of the *Tufts* property looks like a genuine business decision. But telling apart these two types of transactions in practice may not always be so simple, especially given that seller nonrecourse financing does not automatically establish that a transaction is a sham. And even in the case of an apparently bona fide purchase like that by Bayles, it does not automatically follow that the basis of the property should include the full face amount of the nonrecourse debt. After all, this might seem to fly in the face of the apparent unlikelihood (given the property's current value) that the taxpayer will ever repay the debt in full. Thus, giving the taxpayer in Bayles's position basis for the full face amount of the nonrecourse debt might be viewed as unduly increasing the tax shelter advantages of the investment, by creating "extra" depreciation deductions.

In Estate of Franklin v. Commissioner, 544 F.2d 1045 (9th Cir. 1976), *infra*, the taxpayer had purchased a motel (which was simultaneously leased back to the seller/lender) for nonrecourse debt in an amount that substantially exceeded the hotel's fair market value. The court held that the nonrecourse debt lacked economic substance since it was unlikely ever to be repaid, and that the purported buyer was not the owner of the property for tax purposes. Even had ownership been transferred for tax purposes, the court's analysis suggests that the nonrecourse debt might have been completely excluded from the new owner's basis.

By contrast, in Pleasant Summit Land Corp. v. Commissioner, 863 F.2d 263 (3d Cir. 1988), cert. denied, 493 U.S. 901 (1989), the court permitted nonrecourse debt that exceeded the value of the property to be included in basis to the extent of such value at the time of acquisition. The case involved preexisting nonrecourse debt, provided by a third-party lender rather than by the seller, to which the property was subject when acquired by the taxpayer. The court defended its departure from the approach in *Estate of Franklin* by noting the possibility that the taxpayer might end up agreeing with the lender to settle the debt for this amount.

Subsequent cases have generally either rejected *Pleasant Summit* in favor of *Estate of Franklin*, or else have reconciled the two on the ground that *Pleasant Summit* applies in nonabusive situations, such as those involving preexisting or third-party financing, rather than seller financing and a sale-leaseback as in *Estate of Franklin*. Lukens v. Commissioner, 945 F.2d 92 (5th Cir. 1991); Regents Park Partners v. Commissioner, 63 T.C.M. 3131 (1992).

Thus, if one paid $5,000 in cash for property that was worth $400,000 and subject to a $1 million nonrecourse debt, one's basis for the property would be either $5,000 under *Estate of Franklin* or $405,000 under *Pleasant Summit*. However, it plainly would not be $1,005,000, as seemingly would result from treating *Crane* as applicable.

(ii) Subsequent transfer of property subject to "excess" nonrecourse debt. Suppose that a taxpayer acquires property subject to "excess" nonrecourse debt, or that exceeding the contemporaneous fair market value of the property, and that the taxpayer subsequently transfers the property, still subject to the debt. What should be the effect on the taxpayer's amount realized?

Under the tax benefit-like reasoning of the Supreme Court in *Tufts*, this may depend on how the nonrecourse debt was treated upon the acquisition. Thus, consider the above example, in which one acquired property was worth $400,000 and was subject to a $1 million nonrecourse debt. If the nonrecourse debt was wholly excluded from basis under *Estate of Franklin*, then presumably it would also contribute zero to the amount realized. By contrast, if, under *Pleasant Summit*, the nonrecourse debt had been treated up front as if its face amount were $400,000, then presumably that same amount would also be its deemed value for purposes of determining the amount realized upon disposition.

(iii) Repayment of "excess" nonrecourse debt. Suppose again that a taxpayer acquires property subject to "excess" nonrecourse debt, the face amount of which is either wholly (under *Estate of Franklin*) or partly (under *Pleasant Summit*) excluded from the property's basis. What should be the tax consequences for basis (and subsequently for the amount realized) if the taxpayer ends up repaying the debt, in part or in full?

Taking once again the above case in which a $1 million nonrecourse debt is either fully or partly excluded from basis, suppose that the taxpayer actually repays the debt in full. In such a case, it would seem clear that the taxpayer's basis for the property should now include the debt's full $1 million face amount.

But what if the repayment was only partial? Thus, suppose that *Pleasant Summit* applied, causing the nonrecourse debt to be treated as if its face amount had been $400,000 and that the taxpayer subsequently repaid $450,000 to the lender—without discharge of the remaining loan balance (i.e., $550,000). Should the taxpayer's basis for the property increase by (a) $450,000 or

(b) only $50,000? (The latter amount is the excess of the amount newly repaid over the $400,000 amount that had previously been treated as the taxpayer's expected repayment.)

4. Gift Tax Liability Created by the Transfer

The following case, Diedrich v. Commissioner, considers the tax consequences of a transfer of property subject to a liability that arose, not by reason of a prior loan, but due to the imposition of federal gift tax liability on the transfer itself. Should this make any difference to the tax treatment? After all, in the case of a loan the transferor previously got cash (or indirect value that was equivalent to getting cash). By contrast, in the gift tax scenario, the liability only arises because the transferor is giving away the property.

As we will see, *Diedrich* is also noteworthy for a second reason. The Supreme Court seems to have gotten confused in its determination of exactly how gain to the transferor on the sale should be computed. However, since it is the Supreme Court (and since Congress has not subsequently acted), its apparent confusion created authoritative law.

DIEDRICH v. COMMISSIONER
457 U.S. 191 (1982)

Chief Justice BURGER delivered the opinion of the Court.

We granted certiorari to resolve a circuit conflict as to whether a donor who makes a gift of property on condition that the donee pay the resulting gift tax receives taxable income to the extent that the gift tax paid by the donee exceeds the donor's adjusted basis in the property transferred. 454 U.S. 813 (1981). The United States Court of Appeals for the Eighth Circuit held that the donor realized income. 643 F.2d 499 (1981). We affirm.

I

In 1972 petitioners Victor and Frances Diedrich made gifts of approximately 85,000 shares of stock to their three children, using both a direct transfer and a trust arrangement. The gifts were subject to a condition that the donees pay the resulting federal and state gift taxes. There is no dispute concerning the amount of the gift tax paid by the donees. The donors' basis in the transferred stock was $51,073; the gift tax paid in 1972 by the donees was $62,992. . . .

II

A

Pursuant to its Constitutional authority, Congress has defined "gross income" as income "from whatever source derived," including "[i]ncome from discharge of indebtedness." §61 (1976).[28] This Court has recognized that "income" may be realized by a variety of indirect means. In Old Colony Tr. Co. v. Commissioner, 279 U.S. 716 (1929), the Court held that payment of an employee's income taxes by an employer constituted income to the employee. Speaking for the Court, Chief Justice Taft concluded that "[t]he payment of the tax by the employer was in consideration of the services rendered by the employee and was a gain derived by the employee from his labor." *Id.*, at 729. The Court made clear that the substance, not the form, of the agreed transaction controls. "The discharge by a third person of an obligation to him is equivalent to receipt by the person taxed." *Ibid.* The employee, in other words, was placed in a better position as a result of the employer's discharge of the employee's legal obligation to pay the income taxes; the employee thus received a gain subject to income tax. . . .

B

The principles of *Old Colony* . . . control.[29] A common method of structuring gift transactions is for the donor to make the gift subject to the condition that the donee pay the resulting gift tax, as was done in each of the cases now before us. When a gift is made, the gift tax liability falls on the donor under §2502(d).[30] When a donor makes a gift to a donee, a "debt" to the United States for the amount of the gift tax is incurred by the donor. Those taxes are as much the legal obligation of the donor as the donor's income taxes; for these purposes they are the same kind of debt obligation as the income taxes of the employee in *Old Colony, supra.* Similarly, when a donee agrees to discharge an indebtedness in consideration of the gift, the person relieved of the tax liability realizes an economic benefit. In short, the donor realizes an immediate economic benefit by the donee's assumption of the donor's legal obligation to pay the gift tax.

An examination of the donor's intent does not change the character of this benefit. Although intent is relevant in determining whether a gift has been

---

28. The United States Constitution provides that Congress shall have the power to lay and collect taxes on income "from whatever source derived." Art. I, §8, cl. 1; Amendment XVI.

In Helvering v. Bruun, [*supra*], the Court noted: "While it is true that economic gain is not always taxable as income, it is settled that the realization of gain need not be in cash derived from a sale of an asset. Gain may occur as a result of exchange of property, *payment of the taxpayer's indebtedness, relief from a liability*, or other profit realized from the completion of a transaction." (Emphasis supplied.)

29. Although the Commissioner has argued consistently that payment of gift taxes by the donee results in income to the donor, several courts have rejected this interpretation. . . . It should be noted that the *gift* tax consequences of a conditional gift will be unaffected by the holding in this case. When a conditional "net" gift is given, the gift tax attributable to the transfer is to be deducted from the value of the property in determining the value of the gift at the time of transfer. . . .

30. "The tax imposed by section 2501 shall be paid by the donor." Section 6321 imposes a lien on the personal property of the donor when a tax is not paid when due. The donee is secondarily responsible for payment of the gift tax should the donor fail to pay the tax. §6324(b). The donee's liability, however, is limited to the value of the gift. *Ibid.* This responsibility of the donee is analogous to a lien or security. *Ibid.*

made, subjective intent has not characteristically been a factor in determining whether an individual has realized income. Even if intent were a factor, the donor's intent with respect to the condition shifting the gift tax obligation from the donor to the donee was plainly to relieve the donor of a debt owed to the United States; the choice was made because the donor would receive a benefit in relief from the obligation to pay the gift tax.[31]

Finally, the benefit realized by the taxpayer is not diminished by the fact that the liability attaches during the course of a donative transfer. It cannot be doubted that the donors were aware that the gift tax obligation would arise immediately upon the transfer of the property; the economic benefit to the donors in the discharge of the gift tax liability is indistinguishable from the benefit arising from discharge of a preexisting obligation. Nor is there any doubt that had the donors sold a portion of the stock immediately before the gift transfer in order to raise funds to pay the expected gift tax, a taxable gain would have been realized. §1001. The fact that the gift tax obligation was discharged by way of a conditional gift rather than from funds derived from a pregift sale does not alter the underlying benefit to the donors.

C

Consistent with the economic reality, the Commissioner has treated these conditional gifts as a discharge of indebtedness through a part gift and part sale of the gift property transferred. The transfer is treated as if the donor sells the property to the donee for less than the fair market value. The "sale" price is the amount necessary to discharge the gift tax indebtedness; the balance of the value of the transferred property is treated as a gift. The gain thus derived by the donor is the amount of the gift tax liability less the donor's adjusted basis in the entire property. Accordingly, income is realized to the extent that the gift tax exceeds the donor's adjusted basis in the property. This treatment is consistent with §1001 of the Internal Revenue Code, which provides that the gain from the disposition of property is the excess of the amount realized over the transferor's adjusted basis in the property.

III

We recognize that Congress has structured gift transactions to encourage transfer of property by limiting the tax consequences of a transfer. See, e.g., §102 (gifts excluded from donee's gross income). Congress may obviously provide a similar exclusion for the conditional gift. Should Congress wish to encourage "net gifts," changes in the income tax consequences of such gifts lie

---

31. The existence of the "condition" that the gift will be made only if the donee assumes the gift tax consequences precludes any characterization that the payment of the taxes was simply a gift from the donee back to the donor. A conditional gift not only relieves the donor of the gift tax liability, but also may enable the donor to transfer a larger sum of money to the donee than would otherwise be possible due to such factors as differing income tax brackets of the donor and donee.

within the legislative responsibility. Until such time, we are bound by Congress' mandate that gross income includes income "from whatever source derived." We therefore hold that a donor who makes a gift of property on condition that the donee pay the resulting gift taxes realizes taxable income to the extent that the gift taxes paid by the donee exceed the donor's adjusted basis in the property.

The judgment of the United States Court of Appeals for the Eighth Circuit is affirmed.

[The dissenting opinion of Mr. Justice REHNQUIST is omitted.]

NOTES AND QUESTIONS

1. *Treatment of the gift tax liability as a debt like any other.* The taxpayer's "net gift" argument, which the Court rejected, would likewise have applied had the donors borrowed money against the value of the property and then required the donees to repay the loan. In that case, however, the donors would have received a more tangible benefit than merely the satisfaction of making a gift (which, under the actual facts, gave rise to a liability that would not otherwise have existed). However, the Court declines to view this distinction as legally relevant.

2. *The amount of the gain.* (a) At the end of the opinion the Court states that the amount of gain to be taxed is the excess of "the gift taxes paid by the donee [over] the donor's adjusted basis in the property." Is this formula for computing the amount of gain consistent with the theory of the case? Consider the following hypothetical facts: *P* owns 1,000 shares of common stock with a basis of $15,000 and a fair market value of $100,000. She transfers the shares to *C*, who agrees to pay the gift tax of $20,000. Under the *Diedrich* formula the gain recognized is $5,000. What would the gain have been if *P* had sold enough shares to pay the tax herself?

Likewise, suppose that the basis of the shares had been $25,000. The Court's reasoning in *Diedrich* seems to suggest that *P* should be allowed to claim a loss of $5,000. Would this make sense? Reg. §1.1001-1(e) holds that the loss would not be allowed.

(b) By way of comparison, in the case of a transfer to a charitable organization that is part sale and part gift (that is, where the transfer is for an amount less than the fair market value of the property), the basis of the property is allocated between the portion deemed to have been sold and the portion deemed to have been given. §1011(b). For example, suppose that *T* transfers to a charitable organization property with a basis of $20 and a fair market value of $100, in return for a payment of $20. The transaction is treated as if *T* had sold $20 worth, or one-fifth, of the property and had given the other $80 worth. Thus, one-fifth of the basis, or $4, is allocated to the sale, and *T* has a taxable gain of $16. *T* will also be entitled to a charitable deduction of $80, to the extent allowed by §170.

3. *Donor's liability.* As the Court in *Diedrich* points out, the gift tax is imposed on the donor. Would the result have been different if the tax had been imposed solely on the donee?

D. INTEREST INCOME AND ORIGINAL ISSUE DISCOUNT

1. Compounding and the Economic Accrual of Interest Income

So far, this chapter has looked mainly at loan principal—covering, for example, the tax consequences of non-repayment and of acquiring or transferring property subject to debt. Now, however, we turn to certain issues pertaining to the interest charged on a loan.

In general, interest earned is includable by the lender. It may also be deductible by the borrower, although this depends on further issues discussed in Chapters 7 through 9. The topic for now, however, is *when* the tax system takes interest into account, whether for purposes of includability, deductibility, or otherwise.

When interest on a loan is fully payable in cash on a current basis (or at least within the taxable year in which it accrues), no distinctive timing issues arise. Economic accrual and "follow the money" yield the same answer, so there is no need to choose between them or to fuss about measurement issues. However, loans need not, and often do not, require that the borrower pay the lender all of the economically accruing interest on a current basis. Instead, such payment may be deferred. At the limit, *no* interest is paid in cash until the loan's maturity date, when repayment of the principal is also due.

To illustrate that case, suppose you pay $100 for a bond and that under the bond's terms the issuer (i.e., the borrower) will pay you $121 when the bond matures, exactly two years after the purchase date, but nothing until that time. Such a bond may be called an original issue discount (OID) bond, reflecting that it is sold for a "discount" (here, $100) relative to the amount due at maturity (here, $121). Economically, the "discount," that is, the excess of the amount due at maturity over the issue price, constitutes interest.

At what rate does the interest accrue on an OID bond (or any other bond in which not all interest is payable currently)? For the above-described instrument with its $100 issue price, suppose that you had instead deposited $100 in a bank account that paid interest at an annual 10 percent rate. After a year, you would have had $110 in the account. After two years, you would have had $121: the same as under the above OID bond.

This example helps to show two things. First, the bond must also be accruing interest at a 10 percent annual rate, since it likewise appreciates to $121 after two years.[32] Second, under the bond, no less than the bank

---

32. The above statement is not precisely correct due to the term structure of interest rates—that is, the fact that long-term interest rates are generally higher than short-term rates, reflecting that investors may demand greater compensation per period in exchange for locking up their funds for a longer term.

account, your economic accrual of interest was $10 in the first year and $11 in the second year.[33]

Why is the economic accrual of interest income, such as in each of the above two cases, back-loaded, meaning higher in later years than in earlier ones? The answer is that accrued but unpaid interest compounds. After the first year (or any other period), the borrower now owes the lender any accrued but as yet unpaid interest, in addition to owing the loan principal. Thus, in an arm's-length transaction, the unpaid interest must itself accrue further interest.

The compounding of unpaid interest can be quite economically significant. For example, suppose a $100 loan keeps accruing interest (none due until maturity) at a 10 percent annual rate for thirty years. While the annual interest accrual is only $10 in the first year and $11 in the second year, by year 30 it is $158.63, and the full amount due at the end of that year is $1,744.94.

As we will see, the tax system now generally uses the compound interest model to measure the accrual of interest on loans, such as OID bonds. However, it took quite a while to get there. Until 1954, a bondholder or other lender who generally used cash accounting could not only defer the inclusion of any income until the bond's maturity date (or the occurrence of any earlier realization event, such as a sale of the bond), but it could even treat the accrued interest as capital gain, which generally is taxed at a lower rate than ordinary income. While Congress in 1954 required treating OID bond interest as interest, rather than as capital gain, it did not get around to requiring accrual of the interest over the period of the loan until 1969.

However, the rule enacted in 1969 provided for straight-line accrual, rather than economic accrual in light of compounding. Thus, in the above example involving a two-year OID bond that was issued for $100 and redeemed for $121, the deemed annual interest amounts for tax purposes would have been $10.50 each year, rather than $10 followed by $11. In the above example involving a 30-year bond that paid 10 percent annual interest, the tax system would have deemed the interest accrual to be $54.83 annually (i.e., $1,744.94 due at maturity minus $100 issue price, divided by thirty years), rather than rising gradually from $10 to $158.63.

In 1982, Congress finally enacted a set of detailed rules that require current economic accrual of OID interest based on compounding. These rules apply to cash method taxpayers, no less than to those who use the accrual method of accounting. However, before offering an overview of these rules' basic mechanics and scope, we first discuss why it proved so important for the tax system to get economic accrual "right." In short, straight-line accrual proved to be so highly exploitable by tax planners as to convince Congress that it was not, as the saying goes, "close enough for government work."

---

33. Suppose the market interest rate fell from 10 percent to 5 percent in the year after the above OID bond's issuance for $100. This might be expected to increase the bond's market value from $110 to $115.24; i.e., the amount that would grow to $121 in a year at a 5 percent interest rate. However, questions about market value are distinct from that about how interest accrues economically over time when there is a fixed yield to maturity that implies a determinate interest rate.

2.   When and Why It Matters: Counterparty Effects

Consider again the two-year OID bond that has an issue price of $100 and a redemption price of $121. Again, the interest that accrues economically (and, as we will see, for tax purposes under current law) is $10 in the first year and $11 in the second year. By contrast, straight-line accrual, such as that which applied between 1969 and 1982, would have deemed the annual interest amounts to be $10.50 in each of the two years.

In considering why it proved so important to measure annual interest accrual accurately, one's first question might be: Wasn't the straight-line method less favorable to taxpayers than economic accrual? After all, by ignoring compounding, it overmeasures interest income in early years, while undermeasuring it in later years. It therefore seemingly accelerates taxable income relative to the economic method, thus causing the straight-line method to penalize taxpayers, rather than benefiting them.

The answer to this point is that, so long as the interest amounts are deductible by the borrower, in addition to being includable by the lender, the straight-line method creates deferral, as well as acceleration, of income. In the above example, while the lender would suffer a detriment from being required to include $10.50, rather than just $10, in income in the first year, the borrower would enjoy a symmetric benefit.

This, however, might lead to the following second question: Why does the tax system need to get right the annual interest amounts, if straight-line accrual yields symmetric overmeasurement of income in early years for lenders and undermeasurement for borrowers? Thus, suppose that both the borrower and the lender have marginal tax rates of 30 percent. Then, in the above example, while in Year 1 the borrower would pay 15 cents "too little" tax by reason of deducting $10.50 rather than $10 under the straight-line method, the tax system would break even overall, by reason of the lender's paying 15 cents "too much."[34] Doesn't this mean that the tax system should be indifferent? Shouldn't it let lenders and borrowers sort out for themselves the question of how to adjust for the symmetric mismeasurement?

This would be an important and powerful point if borrowers and lenders always had the same marginal tax rates. Suppose, however, that in many cases tax-exempt investors—for example, universities, pension funds, and foreigners who do not pay U.S. tax—are lending to U.S. taxpayers in high rate brackets who *do* get to deduct annual interest expense, as measured by the tax system. In that case, overmeasuring interest amounts in the early years of a loan, as would happen if taxpayers could use straight-line accrual in lieu of economic accrual based on compounding, could be used to create significant deferral of tax liability by borrowers, without commensurate offsetting effects on the lender side.

---

34. In this scenario, should we be concerned about the seeming unfairness of overtaxing the lender and undertaxing the borrower? The answer is no, not if they can be expected to adjust the pretax terms of the transaction to reflect their comparative treatment. If taxable interest amounts are symmetrically overmeasured in the early years for lenders and undermeasured for borrowers, the pretax interest rate may adjust so that both sides will come out the same, on an after-tax basis, as in the scenario where both sides were being taxed accurately.

Does it still seem too trivial to matter enormously? Not if taxpayers can take sufficient advantage of predictable mismeasurements of income by the tax system. Thus, suppose that you wanted to defer significant amounts of taxable income for a year just by using offsetting loan transactions. With a tax-exempt counterparty, if the tax system used straight-line accrual on OID bonds, this might be incredibly easy.

Consider again two-year OID bonds where the interest rate is 10 percent. Suppose you issued a $10 million bond that would pay the buyer $12.1 million in two years. And suppose you placed the $10 million that you got for the bond in a regular bank account that paid 10 percent annual interest. When the bond matured in two years, you could use the bank account (which would have grown to $12.1 million) to pay off the bond in full. Thus, you would have broken even before-tax.

For tax purposes, however, while your interest income from the bank account would be $1 million in Year 1 and $1.1 million in Year 2, straight-line accrual (if allowed) would cause you to have interest deductions of $1.05 million for each year. Thus, you would get to report a net loss of $50,000 (i.e., $.05 million) in Year 1, followed by a net gain of $50,000 in Year 2. If your marginal tax rate was, say, 40 percent, this would be the equivalent of getting a one-year interest-free loan in the amount of $20,000.

Add a zero to the dollar amount on each side—borrowing and lending $10 million, instead of $1 million—and the interest-free loan grows to $200,000. Add another zero, and it becomes $2 million, and so forth indefinitely.[35] For a sufficiently liquid and well-heeled taxpayer, especially given the economic offset between the two sides to the transaction, the ability to keep on adding zeroes could theoretically have no real limit, until the point where one has eliminated enough current year income to have no further use for net deductions that permit income deferral.

This helps to show why use of the straight-line method, to compute the annual interest amounts on OID bonds, most definitely was *not* "close enough for government work." Aggressive tax planning has been compared to taking a pinprick of economic inaccuracy in the rules and finding ways to drive a truck through it. The "truck" often relies on—or the trick often involves—pairing tax-exempts with high-rate taxpayers and on arranging reciprocal cash flows that offset each other economically but are measured for tax purposes under inconsistent timing rules. This can result in large net income deferrals (the tax benefit from which we discuss at the start of Chapter 3).

3.   Mechanics of the OID Rules

The rules on original issue discount (OID) provide that, to the extent that a "debt instrument" does not provide for current payment of an adequate

---

35. The advantages of this scheme would grow considerably if the time period were lengthened, as the interest would compound each year, making the straight-line method increasingly inaccurate.

amount of interest, interest must be accrued (that is, included currently in income) by the obligee, regardless of whether the obligee is a cash-method or accrual-method taxpayer. See §§1272-1275. The obligor is entitled to deduct the amount that the obligee is required to accrue. The OID rules apply to debt instruments issued for cash or for property, with certain exceptions for relatively small transactions.

The concept of original issue discount (OID) refers to the unstated interest in a deferred payment, even if some interest is payable currently. When a bond is sold for cash, the OID is the difference between the issue price (that is, the price at which the bond is sold) and the redemption price (the price required to be paid by the issuer/borrower when the term of the loan ends and the bond must be paid off (redeemed)).

For example, suppose that a bond is issued (sold) for $600,000 and that it is to be redeemed five years later for $1 million, with no interest payments in the interim. The amount of the OID is the difference between the redemption price ($1 million) and the issue price ($600,000), or $400,000. §1273(a). This amount is treated as interest earned ratably over the five-year term of the loan, with semi-annual compounding. The amount of interest to be reported by the lender and deducted by the borrower each year is shown below:

Redemption price	$1,000,000
Issue price	600,000
OID	400,000
Term	5 years

	Annual interest amounts:	*New basis (end of year):*
Year 1	$64,540	$664,540
Year 2	71,482	736,022
Year 3	79,171	815,193
Year 4	87,687	902,880
Year 5	97,120	1,000,000
Total	$400,000	

Here the effect of the OID rules is to treat the purchaser of the bond as if she had simply placed the $600,000 issue price in a bank or money market account that paid interest at a rate sufficient to generate the redemption price in five years. Each year the amount in the account would rise, and the interest income would increase. Section 1275(a)(1)(A) provides that "the term 'debt instrument' means a bond, debenture, note, or certificate or other evidence of indebtedness."

The application of the OID concept in the above example of a sale of a bond for cash is relatively simple and straightforward, since there is no question about the amount of the original issue discount: It is simply the difference between the price paid for the bond at the time of issuance and the redemption price. Where a promissory obligation is issued in return for property, the application of the OID rules is more complex because there is no readily determinable issue price. The counterpart of the receipt and payment of an issue price is the transfer of property. However, the value of the property may be hard to determine.

The approach of the OID rules is to apply discount rates to the expected payments. In other words, the issue price is determined by discounting the expected payments to present value. Obviously, the key element in the process is the selection of an appropriate interest rate. The Code calls for the Treasury to publish periodically interest rates for obligations of various durations. §1274(d). These interest rates, called the "applicable federal rates," are based on the current rates paid on U.S. Treasury obligations. If the amount of interest stated by the parties is adequate, as compared with the applicable federal rate, then that stated rate is accepted in determining the amount of interest deducted by the obligor and reported by the obligee. Otherwise, the applicable federal rate is used.

To illustrate, assume that on January 1 of Year 1, T buys an apartment building for an amount stated to be $5 million. T pays no cash but instead executes a promissory note for $5 million, due ten years later, with interest payable at the rate of 8 percent per year. Assume that the annualized "applicable federal rate" at the time the note is issued is 10 percent.[36] The payments of $400,000 per year for nine years, plus $5,400,000 in the tenth year, are discounted to present value using the 10 percent rate. The result is a present value, or "imputed principal amount" (§1274(b)(1)), of $4,385,543, which is treated as the issue price. The difference between this amount and the $5,000,000 redemption price is $614,457, which is the OID. A portion of this total amount of OID must be reported each year along with the $400,000 annual cash payment called for in the obligation.

How much OID is recognized each year? In the first year, the total interest earned on the note is equal to the present value of the amount owed ($4,385,543) multiplied by the applicable federal rate of 10 percent. That comes to $438,554. The stated interest is only $400,000, so the OID is the difference, $38,554. This $38,554, along with the $400,000 cash payment, is reported as income by the holder of the obligation and is deducted by the obligor in the first year. The $38,554 has not in fact been paid, however, and is in effect added to the principal amount owed, which produces a principal amount at the beginning of the second year of $4,424,097 (with an error of $1 due to rounding). (The same result is reached by discounting the remaining payments to present value.) The interest on the debt in the second year is equal to the new principal amount ($4,424,097) multiplied by the applicable federal rate of 10 percent, or $442,410. Again, the stated interest is $400,000, so the OID is $42,410. These numbers and the corresponding numbers for the remaining years are shown in Table 5-1.

---

36. The rates published by the Treasury include rates with a slight upward adjustment that may be used for compounding on an annual, rather than semiannual, basis to achieve the same annual result that would be reached using the semiannual rate with semiannual compounding.

TABLE 5-1

Year	Value of debt obligation[a]	Total interest earned	Annual stated interest	Annual OID[b]	Principal payment
1	$4,385,543	$438,554	$400,000	$38,554	
2	4,424,098	442,410	400,000	42,410	
3	4,466,507	446,651	400,000	46,651	
4	4,513,158	451,316	400,000	51,316	
5	4,564,474	456,447	400,000	56,447	
6	4,620,921	462,092	400,000	62,092	
7	4,683,013	468,301	400,000	68,301	
8	4,751,315	475,131	400,000	75,131	
9	4,826,446	482,645	400,000	82,645	
10	4,909,091	490,909	400,000	90,909	$5,000,000

[a]Principal and interest payments discounted at applicable federal rate of 10 percent.
[b]This amount is added to principal.

There are also rules for taxation of "market discount." These rules do not alter the normal rules on timing of recognition of gain. Their purpose and function was to prevent the conversion of ordinary income into capital gain. To illustrate their operation, suppose a bond was issued many years ago and bears interest at a rate of 3 percent on a face value of $1,000 (this being the amount that must be paid at maturity), with four years remaining until maturity. If the present market rate of interest is 12 percent, the present value of the bond is $727. A buyer of such a bond would receive annual interest payments of $30. These would be taxable and received as ordinary income. At maturity, the buyer would receive $1,000 and would report a gain of $273. This $273 is called "market discount"; under §§1276 and 1278 the gain is treated as ordinary income, rather than as capital gain (which is the way it was treated before the adoption of these provisions in 1984). If the bond is sold before the maturity date, a ratable portion of the market discount (determined on a linear daily basis) is treated as ordinary income.

Some exceptions to the application of the OID rules include sales of principal residences, sales of farms for less than $1 million, and sales for payments totaling less than $250,000. §1274(c)(3). In these situations, where the OID rules do not apply, §483 applies. Section 483 does not affect the timing of the recognition of the imputed interest income, but it ensures that that income is treated as ordinary income rather than as capital gain. In other words, §483 determines the character or nature of the gain from certain sales transactions, whereas the OID rules determine not just the character of the gain but the time of its recognition.

For example, suppose that a personal residence with a basis of $400,000 is sold for a single payment of $1 million to be made at the end of five years, and that the applicable federal rate is 10 percent. At the time of sale, the present value of the future payment is $620,921, and the "unstated interest" is the difference between that present value amount and the $1 million payment, or $379,079. When the $1 million is collected at the end of five years, the seller will report a total gain of $600,000, the difference between the basis, $400,000, and the amount received, $1 million. Of the $600,000, $379,079 is reported as ordinary interest income, and the remaining $220,921 is capital gain. Section 121, permitting certain gain upon the sale of a primary residence to be excluded from income, can only apply to the latter amount, not to the amount that is treated as interest income.

E.   INTEREST ON STATE AND LOCAL BONDS

1.   Basic Concepts

Section 103 exempts from taxation the interest on certain debt obligations issued by state governments or their political subdivisions, such as local governments. This provision is often colloquially called the exclusion for municipal bond interest.

At one time, retention of the municipal bond interest exclusion reflected beliefs as to comity between different levels of government in the U.S. federal system. Even though a tax on municipal bond interest would be paid by the bondholders, it was deemed substantively equivalent to having the federal government tax the state and local government issuers directly, which was thought to be inappropriate, or even unconstitutional. Today, however, the exclusion is mainly rationalized as a deliberate subsidy from the federal government to state and local governments that issue municipal bonds, permitting them to borrow more cheaply than they could if the interest were taxable to bond purchasers.

The mechanism for the subsidy is a broader economic phenomenon sometimes called "implicit taxation." Tax-exempt bonds pay a lower rate of interest than taxable bonds, because purchasers of the former are willing to accept a lower pretax rate in order to obtain the exemption. The relationship between the taxable and the tax-exempt rate varies from time to time, but the tax-exempt rate should always be lower than the taxable rate (all else being equal).

Suppose that the interest rate for taxable bonds is 10 percent, and that the rate for comparable tax-exempt bonds is 8 percent. A holder of the latter bonds may be viewed as paying an implicit tax of 20 percent. That is, the holder enjoys the same after-tax return as she would have if (a) the bond interest were taxable, and (b) her marginal tax rate on this interest was 20 percent.

With an implicit tax of 20 percent, taxpayers in the 20 percent marginal tax bracket should be indifferent between otherwise identical taxable and tax-exempt alternatives. However, taxpayers whose marginal rates are higher than the implicit tax rate implied by municipal bond yields should prefer them (all else being equal) to otherwise similar, but taxable, bonds. For example, if one's marginal tax rate is 30 percent, a taxable bond that pays 10 percent interest yields only 7 percent after-tax, as distinct from the 8 percent return that we have posited is available on the municipal bonds.

By contrast, a taxpayer whose marginal tax rate is lower than the implicit tax rate implied by municipal bond yields should prefer the taxable bonds. In the above scenario, for example, a tax-exempt investor would earn 10 percent, both before-tax and after-tax, on bonds that yield generally taxable interest. Such an investor should therefore prefer the taxable bonds, all else being equal.

In the case where the implicit tax equals the marginal tax rate, the exemption for municipal bond interest yields a result that is economically equivalent to the case where the federal government directly pays a subsidy to the state or local government issuer. Thus, suppose that such a government issues $100 million of municipal bonds and gets to pay 8 percent interest, rather than 10 percent interest, by reason of the exclusion. This saves the issuer $2 million per year, relative to the case where it issued bonds of the same value but had to offer the same rate as issuers of taxable bonds. Likewise, assuming a 20 percent marginal tax rate for all of the municipal bondholders, the federal government loses $2 million of revenue, relative to the case where the bonds had paid aggregate annual interest of $10 million (rather than $8 million) and where this amount was taxable to the bondholders. So the end result in this hypothetical case is the same as it would have been if (a) the bonds had paid 10 percent interest, creating $10 million of interest income that yielded $2 million in federal income tax revenues, and (b) the federal government had paid $2 million to the issuer.

Suppose, however, that all of the bonds end up being held by individuals in the 30 percent marginal rate bracket. Then the federal government loses $3 million in tax revenues, relative to the case where the state or local government had issued $100 million of bonds that paid 10 percent interest. Yet the issuer still saves just $2 million in interest costs. So what happens to the extra $1 million revenue cost to the federal government in this comparison? The answer is that it is captured by the bondholders, who get to earn a total of $8 million after-tax, rather than just $7 million, by reason of the difference between the implicit tax and their actual marginal tax rates.

NOTES AND QUESTIONS

1. *Why might the implicit tax be lower than some bondholders' marginal tax rates?* A key part of the answer is that the issuers cannot tailor the interest rates that they offer to the marginal rates of particular investors. Thus, suppose that some prospective bondholders face 20 percent marginal tax rates, while others face 30 percent marginal tax rates. State and local government issuers might find that they cannot sell enough bonds unless they limit the pretax discount on the interest rate that they offer to 20 percent, rather than 30 percent. They then have no choice but to offer the bonds to prospective investors in both federal marginal tax rate brackets.

2. *Who is intended to benefit from the municipal bond exclusion: issuers or bondholders?* In the above example, the federal government's hypothetical revenue cost, by reason of the bond exclusion, was $3 million, yet the benefit to the governmental issuer was only $2 million, with the remaining $1 million of

benefit being captured by bondholders. This is inefficient as a matter of subsidy design, relative to paying the state and local governments directly, if one posits that benefiting them is the goal. In practice, however, if Congress were to consider repealing §103, it might hear complaints both from state and local governments and from investors.

3. *In the above example, is the revenue cost of the exclusion likely to be the full $3 million that was posited?* In describing the cost of the exclusion as $3 million in the preceding example, we assumed that the issuer would still have issued $100 million in bonds, even if the annual interest cost was $10 million, rather than $8 million. In practice, however, it is possible that state and local governments would engage in lower levels of bond issuance if not for the federal tax subsidy. Indeed, encouraging them to issue more bonds (and thus to fund greater outlays) might even be the main reason for offering them the subsidy. It also is possible that investor demand for the bonds would have been lowered if the after-tax return was reduced from 8 percent to 7 percent for investors in the 30 percent bracket.

Does this mean that the example is potentially "incorrect"? The answer would be yes, if one were treating it as a literal prediction of how much more income tax revenue the federal government would raise in this instance, if it repealed §103. The answer is no, however, if one is merely using the hypothetical transaction, in the absence of the interest exclusion, as a device for understanding the main effects of §103.

4. *Why subsidize state and local governments indirectly, via the exclusion for municipal bond interest, rather than directly through federal cash grants?* The inefficiency of the municipal bond exclusion as a means of subsidizing state and local governments, if the implicit tax often is significantly less than the bondholders' marginal tax rates, has been widely noticed. Then why not replace it with a direct subsidy (assuming that one still wants to benefit the state and local governments)? Many commentators do indeed take this view. State and local governments, however, may view the exclusion for municipal bond interest as more politically durable than a program under which Congress would annually decide how much it wanted to pay them. Use of the bond exclusion, in lieu of a direct cash subsidy, may also reduce the extent to which the federal government makes its own judgments about how state and local governments ought to spend their borrowing proceeds (and their available funds more generally). Legislation enacted in 2009 during the Great Recession included a new type of municipal bond—i.e., "Build America Bonds" or BABs—the interest on which was fully taxable under the federal income tax. Two types of BABs were available under the legislation, "Tax Credit BABs" (which granted for bondholders a credit equal to 35 percent of interest payable under the bonds) and "Direct Payment BABs" (which granted state and local issuers a direct payment equal to 35 percent of the interest paid). Note that both approaches unhitch the intended subsidy from the bondholder's marginal tax rate, consistent with the approach suggested by many tax reform advocates. Significantly, the BABs program supplemented (rather than replaced) the exclusion under §103. The program was popular among issuers while it lasted, but it expired at the end of 2010.

5. *Implicit taxes more generally.* The above observations regarding implicit taxation may also be relevant to other tax-favored investments. People who make

other types of tax-favored investments may likewise find that the pretax rate of return is bid down by reason of the tax benefits, potentially causing the after-tax returns from such investments to be no greater than those otherwise available.

Implicit taxes also can lead to what are sometimes called "clientele effects." Consider the case in which taxable investments offer a 10 percent pretax rate of return, but a given tax-favored investment offers only 8 percent before tax. All else being equal, this will cause investors facing marginal tax rates above 20 percent to seek out this investment, and it will be shunned by those facing lower marginal tax rates (such as tax-exempt investors).

This can cause at least two types of nontax problems for investors. First, those who wish to diversify their investment portfolios, so as to minimize their exposure to risk if one type of investment or another ends up doing poorly, may face a tradeoff between this diversification objective and that of maximizing their expected after-tax returns. Second, suppose that a given asset, such as an oil well, can be operated more efficiently if it is owned by Taxpayer *A* than Taxpayer *B*, for example, because *A* knows more about the oil business. From the standpoint of such efficiency concerns, clientele effects may cause particular tax-favored assets to be held, for tax reasons, by the "wrong" taxpayers.

2. Limitations on Exempt Status

In recent decades, state and local governments started using their ability to borrow at low rates to finance projects having little or nothing to do with traditional governmental activities. The most important manifestation of this trend was the "industrial revenue bond" (IRB),[37] a bond whose proceeds were used to finance private investment, generally in an effort to lure industry to a community (in competition, often, with other communities offering the same financial incentive). The payment of interest and principal on such bonds is solely the responsibility of the user of the property bought or built with the proceeds; the local government unit that is the purported borrower is strictly an intermediary, with no financial risk.

Congress responded by imposing limitations on the use of tax-exempt financing for private purposes. For example, some limitations are based on the purpose for which the proceeds are used and require specific provisions defining permissible purposes. The result is that the law, once simple, has become detailed and complex. See §§103, 142-151. Exemption continues to be available, without limit, for bonds whose proceeds are used for traditional governmental purposes such as financing schools, roads, and sewers. All other bonds are called "private-activity bonds" and are not exempt unless they fit within a specific exception. One major exception is for "exempt-facility bonds." These include bonds used to finance airports, docks and wharves, mass commuting facilities, water and sewage disposal facilities, qualified hazardous

---

37. Also sometimes referred to as industrial development bonds (IDBs).

waste facilities, and certain electric and gas facilities. Other categories of private-activity bonds that qualify for exemption include qualified mortgage bonds (for financing home purchases by middle- and low-income people) and qualified veterans' mortgage bonds, qualified small-issue (not more than $1 million) bonds, and bonds used for certain charitable purposes. The income on certain private-activity bonds, though exempt from the regular tax, may be subject to the alternative minimum tax. Congress also enacted an overall, or aggregate, dollar volume limit, or "cap," on most categories of newly issued private-activity bonds for which exemption is available. See §146. The states may allocate the total among their subdivisions and agencies. If they fail to do so, the allocation is made according to rules set forth in the Code.

3.   Constitutional Barrier?

In South Carolina v. Baker, 485 U.S. 505 (1988), the Court upheld the requirement (now in §149(a)) that interest on otherwise qualifying bonds is not tax exempt unless the bonds are registered and subject to certain reporting requirements. In so holding, the Court rejected the notion that a constitutional barrier exists to the imposition of a federal income tax on the interest earned on obligations issued by a state or by one of its instrumentalities. In a study published in 1989, economist James Poterba showed that municipal bond futures prices dropped sharply in the hour following the announcement of the Supreme Court's decision in South Carolina v. Baker, presumably because of the new legal risk that the tax-exemption might actually be repealed. As Poterba noted, however, "[i]n the hours immediately following the decision, key Congressional leaders indicated support for retaining tax-exempt treatment for interest . . . and by the end of the trading day the rapid decline in municipal bond prices had been reversed." See James Poterba, *Tax Reform and the Market for Tax-Exempt Debt,* 19 *Regional Science and Urban Economics* 537, 556 (1989).

4.   Tax Arbitrage

Economists define arbitrage as buying and selling (or borrowing and lending), without cost, the same item at different prices so that one is guaranteed a positive payoff. An arbitrage opportunity therefore provides the equivalent of a risk-free "money pump" for as long as it lasts. The idea that arbitrage is impossible at equilibrium is a central unifying concept in modern financial theory.

The tax policy literature has developed a notion of "tax arbitrage" that is broader than the standard finance concept. It refers to holding positions that are at least approximately opposite to each other—for example, borrowing and lending, or buying and selling, similar assets—but that are treated by the tax system asymmetrically. An example would be combining borrowing that generates deductible interest expense with investing that generates tax-free income. Tax arbitrage can generate tax losses in excess of any economic losses.

It thus can motivate deliberately generating pretax losses, because after-tax one comes out ahead.

Tax-exempt bonds offer a useful illustration. Suppose that (a) you can borrow at a 10 percent interest rate, (b) tax-exempt bonds pay interest at 8 percent, and (c) your marginal rate is 30 percent. Then, assuming no tax rules got in the way, it might make sense for you to borrow lots of money and invest in tax-exempt bonds. Indeed, there might be no obvious point at which this strategy ceased to make sense for you—leaving aside its associated economic risks, if any—until you had generated sufficient tax losses to reduce taxable income to the point where your marginal tax rate was no longer 30 percent.

Thus, suppose that you could deduct up to $100,000 without reducing your marginal tax rate to below 30 percent. Suppose further that you could borrow as much as $1 million at 10 percent interest and could use the funds to buy $1 million worth of municipal bonds that paid 8 percent interest. Each year, before tax, you would pay $100,000 of interest and earn $80,000 of interest, generating a $20,000 loss. Given, however, our presumption of interest deductibility, along with the excludability of municipal bond interest, the loss you reported for tax purposes would be $100,000. Given your presumed marginal tax rate of 30 percent, this would reduce your income tax liability for the year by $30,000. Thus, after tax, you would actually come out $10,000 ahead.

While the discussion thus far has focused on municipal bondholders, state and local governments might also want to take advantage. Only, in their case, since they are not taxpayers, it would be a kind of economic arbitrage, rather than a straightforward tax arbitrage. They might be able to make a lot of money by issuing bonds that paid 8 percent interest and using the proceeds to hold investments that paid 10 percent interest.

However, the Code attempts to prevent such arbitrages by both issuers and bondholders. For issuers, §148 aims to prevent a state or local government from borrowing at tax-exempt rates, and investing in taxable obligations with the expectation of profiting on the spread in interest rates. This provision does not, however, prevent such governments from issuing bonds for exempt purposes and collecting the proceeds before they are ready to start making the intended outlays. In the interim the proceeds will, of course, be invested at the highest available rate.

For bondholders, §265(a)(2) denies interest deductions for interest on indebtedness that was "incurred or continued to purchase or carry" tax-exempt bonds. While we defer until Chapter 8 discussion of how this provision operates in practice to identify disallowed interest expense, suppose for now that it is reasonably effective in limiting the feasibility of tax arbitrage transactions involving municipal bonds, like that described above.

What would happen if §265(a)(2), despite its presumed effectiveness, was repealed? One possible consequence is that prospective bondholders' demand for tax-free municipal bonds would increase substantially. But suppose that the increase in demand allowed issuers to start paying lower pretax interest rates.

In terms of the earlier example, suppose it meant that issuers could reduce the return they offered to 7 percent, having found they were now able to sell enough bonds at this interest rate. In effect, this would raise the implicit tax to 30 percent, causing the disappearance of the tax arbitrage opportunity that we described above for investors in the 30 percent bracket. While all this might increase the revenue cost to the federal fisc of the exclusion for municipal bond interest, it also would address the misdirection of the subsidy, if we posit that it is meant to benefit issuers but that at present, to some extent, it instead benefits investors in high marginal tax brackets.

Does this line of analysis suggest that §265(a)(2) should be repealed? Some tax experts believe so. However, whether they are right or not, the crucial point about their analysis is that it rests on positing that the prospective supply of municipal bonds is limited, given that only state and local governments can issue them (subject to their own arbitrage restrictions).

For the ultimate in tax arbitrage, suppose that you were allowed to borrow and lend to yourself for tax purposes and then to exclude the interest "income" while deducting the interest "expense." (Perhaps this would involve establishing two bank accounts and endlessly recycling "loans" and "repayments of interest and principal" through them.) It is easy to see that this would permit everyone who could do this to eliminate all income tax liability. In Chapter 8, we will see how real a danger this is to the income tax system (at least, when dressed up with a few fig leaves, as a literal form of the transaction would not work) and how the system responds to the danger.

5. U.S. Treasury Bonds

Section 135 exempts from taxation the interest on certain U.S. Treasury savings bonds if the proceeds of the redemption of the bonds do not exceed tuition and fees for higher education for the taxpayer and her or his spouse or dependents. The exclusion is phased out as income rises, with the phase-out levels being annually adjusted for inflation. As of 2016, the exclusion is phased out as income rises from $116,300 to $146,300 for joint returns and from $77,550 to $92,550 for single returns.

Funds are not traced, so even if other funds are in fact used to pay the education expenses, the exemption is available. (Then again, why should it matter which funds one uses for a particular purpose? After all, money is fungible.) One also may wonder why education is singled out, as compared, for example, with medical expenses or the down payment on a house. Further questions that one might ask include:

(1) What percentage of the taxpayers who are eligible for this benefit would you guess are even aware of it?

(2) What percentage of the taxpayers who are eligible for this benefit would you guess have sufficient savings to take advantage of it?

(3) Why should eligibility for the exclusion depend on one's holding U.S. Treasury savings bonds?

Our point in asking these questions is less to direct attention to this particular tax benefit, which is not especially important in the big picture, than to draw attention to the seeming randomness of "micro-provisions" like this one, even when they at least arguably serve good purposes.

F.   CERTAIN OTHER FINANCIAL INSTRUMENTS

Debt typically involves an initial cash flow from the lender to the borrower, followed by cash flows in the other direction later on. In an arm's-length transaction between unrelated parties, the market values of the expected cash flows in each direction should be the same, taking account of both (a) expected present value at the start of the transaction, and (b) risk, which may reduce market value below expected present value in the presence of risk aversion.

Various other types of financial instruments share with debt this basic feature of having offsetting cash flows between two parties that occur at different times but have the same market value up front, along with the same expected present value insofar as risk does not affect market valuations. Such financial instruments are therefore inherently debt-like in certain respects, even if they also have important distinctive features not found in a standard debt instrument. Yet their income tax treatment often differs from that of debt in ways that one might view as failing to take account of the instruments' common elements. This, in turn, can significantly influence tax planning.

In this section, we will examine the rules for two such instruments: life insurance contracts and annuities. In each case, a failure to extend OID-like treatment to holders creates opportunities to replicate some of the economics of holding a debt instrument, while being taxed more favorably. However, the tax rules for these two types of financial instruments do this to different extents and by different means.

1.   Life Insurance

Basic analysis. Section 101(a) excludes "amounts received . . . under a life insurance contract, if such amounts are paid by reason of the death of the insured." This exclusion applies to all types of life insurance policies. Under §264(a), premiums paid for life insurance are nondeductible. To understand the combined effect of these two rules, one must consider each of the two basic elements of life insurance policies: (a) mortality protection or "pure" insurance, and (b) saving through life insurance policies.

Let us begin with the pure insurance element of protection against mortality losses. One example of this kind of insurance is trip insurance covering air travel. These policies pay off if the insured dies as a result of an airplane crash. Suppose that a person, just prior to boarding, pays $10 for $100,000 of such coverage. If the plane crashes and the insured dies, the beneficiary receives the $100,000, which can be thought of as consisting of a $10 recovery of cost plus a mortality gain of $99,990. The entire amount is excluded under §101(a). On the other hand, if the plane arrives safely at its destination, the insurance company gets to keep the $10 insurance premium. The insured has a $10 economic loss, as measured ex post, for which there is no deduction.

This mortality gamble—in which the taxpayer, in effect, bets on her own death—has both "winners" and "losers." You "win" by dying (thus earning, on behalf of the beneficiary, the right to receive a cash payment), and you "lose" by surviving. In the aggregate, however, the amounts paid out will equal the amounts paid in (disregarding amounts that fund the costs and profits of the insurer). Thus, the tax system in effect breaks even by reason of its ignoring both mortality gains and mortality losses.

Would it be better to tax the "winners" (i.e., the life insurance contract beneficiaries) and allow deductions to the "losers" (i.e., those who fail to collect on their life insurance contracts)? Even leaving aside the question of whether these two groups really are best thought of as "winners" and "losers"—given that one "wins" by dying—the question arises of whether doing this would serve any good purpose.

To illustrate, suppose that you and your heirs are both in the hypothetical 50 percent marginal rate bracket (which we use here for arithmetic convenience). Suppose that, in the actual state of the world in which life insurance proceeds are excludable and premium payments are nondeductible, you would pay $10 for $100,000 of coverage. But then the rules are changed so that life insurance proceeds are taxable but the payments are deductible (giving rise to an allowable loss if one fails to collect). Suppose that you learn of this change just before you would buy the contract and board the plane.

In effect, the hypothetical change in the tax rules has cut the true size of your life insurance contract in half (so far as after-tax amounts are concerned). Now, if you "lose" the bet by surviving, you will be out only $5 after tax, rather than $10. But if you "win" the bet by dying in a plane crash, the beneficiary will end up with only $4,995 (i.e., 50 percent of the pretax mortality gain of $9,990).

How might you respond to the change in tax rules? What you actually *will* do may depend on your psychology and motivations for buying life insurance, how well you understand the change, and so forth. But what you *should* do, if your goal is simply to make the same true mortality bet as before, is clear. In that event, you should simply double the size of the life insurance contract, paying $20 for a payout to your beneficiary, if you die, of $200,000. Now, on an after-tax basis, you have restored the prior state of affairs, in which either you would lose $10 or your beneficiary would gain $9,990 (i.e., $20,000 payout minus $20 return of capital, divided by 50 percent).

Would, should, and could people actually do this? All three questions may be debatable. But at a minimum the hypothetical should raise doubt concerning any assumption that one might otherwise have made that, simply by analogy to the treatment of loans or any other investments, life insurance gains should be taxed and losses (barring some other argument to the contrary) deducted.

The analysis so far, however, has looked only at the pure insurance element of life insurance contracts, not at the savings element that they also commonly have. In this example, the payout or loss was almost instantaneous, requiring just the completion of a single plane flight before it would be resolved.

Suppose you have instead a life insurance contract that will pay your beneficiaries, say, $1 million whenever you die. In one sense, this "bet" is a sure thing (at least, barring default or defalcation by the life insurance company). After all, whether or not death and taxes are *both* sure things, we certainly know that death is an eventual certainty. But given present value considerations, you are still "betting," on behalf of the beneficiaries, that you will die sooner rather than later. After all, $1 million today or tomorrow is worth a lot more financially than $1 million in ten or fifty or seventy years. And the life insurance company, just like in the airplane flight insurance example, is making the opposite bet. (Or more precisely, it makes enough such bets, with distinct insured individuals facing idiosyncratic personal risks, to make its expected payouts fairly predictable.)

Thus, under a life insurance contract that will pay off whenever you die (called whole life insurance), there is still a mortality bet, leading to a pure insurance element. But there is also a savings element. After all, you presumably don't expect to die immediately. If your remaining life expectancy is, say, fifty years, then, in a well-functioning market where buyers get fair value, the life insurance company must promise to pay you more, in nominal cash terms, than you are paying it, because its payment to you will likely be significantly deferred.

Suppose you purchase a single-premium life insurance policy, under which you make just one payment up front, and the company will then pay out $1 million to your designated beneficiaries whenever you die. Suppose further that your remaining life expectancy, as determined actuarially by the life insurance company, is fifty years. If the interest rate is 5 percent, that expected future payment is worth roughly $80,000 today. Under §101(a), your beneficiaries will be able to exclude the $1 million payout from income. Thus, your and their combined net gain—$920,000, or the excess of the payout over your premium—is a type of saving that, unlike a bank account or an OID bond, wholly escapes taxation.

We have thus far discussed only the two extremes, within the spectrum of life insurance contracts: (a) those that are resolved instantaneously, and thus are pure mortality bets with almost no savings element, and (b) whole life insurance contracts, which still contain a mortality bet but have very substantial savings elements, especially if the insured has a long remaining life expectancy. For an intermediate case, consider term life insurance contracts, or those that apply for, say, one year or ten or twenty. They have a mortality bet, not only from the timing element that even whole life insurance presents, but also from the possibility (unless the term is simply too long, relative to the insured's life expectancy) that the contract will expire without any payments being due. But they also have a savings element, the value of which depends on the expected time when a payout, if any, would be made.

While these various types of life insurance contracts may vary along a continuum, so far as the relative significance of their mortality bet and savings elements are concerned, all are taxed the same way under §§101(a) and 264(a). In each case, payouts are excluded and premiums are nondeductible. In consequence, not only mortality bets but also the savings derived through life insurance contracts are excluded from tax.

In the absence of any mortality bet, however, one will not have life insurance as defined by the Code, and therefore the exclusion under §101(a) will not apply. This limitation arises under §7702, which defines life insurance contracts for tax purposes. While this provision is too complicated to merit examination here, it would unambiguously matter in a case such as the following.

Suppose that you pay $100,000 for a supposed life insurance contract, but the amount due to your beneficiaries is simply $100,000 plus whatever interest accrued at a specified interest rate between the contract date and your death. Thus, if the interest rate and you died exactly a year later, they would receive $110,000; if you died in exactly two years they would get $121,000, and so forth.

In substance, this would not be much different from an OID bond that happened to be due on the date of your death. It would involve no mortality bet, except as a byproduct of its containing, like any OID bond with a fixed interest rate, an implicit bet on future interest rates.[38] However, given the absence of a true mortality bet, it would end up failing to qualify as life insurance under §7702.

Policy questions. Why does Congress allow returns on investments with insurance companies to escape taxation while investments with banks or in mutual funds are taxed? Consider the two elements of tax avoidance—the deferral and the ultimate exemption—in the case of the single-premium policy. Each year, as the insured gets older, the policy increases in value. Would it be appropriate to tax this annual increment or allocate the insurance company's investment income each year to policyholders based on the company's calculations of amounts required for necessary reserves for future payments? Is the policyholder's gain more like the increase in the value of farm land held for investment, or like the annual interest earned on a savings account? (Note that, because of commissions and other costs, if a life insurance policy is cashed in too soon after its purchase, the insured person generally will lose money. Life insurance generally is not a good short-term investment.) If annual taxation of policyholders is not sensible, would it be appropriate to tax the insurance company on the investment returns set aside for policyholders?

Perhaps the aim is to encourage people to hold adequate life insurance on behalf of their heirs. But if that is so, should there be a ceiling on the amount that can be excluded? Does it matter that the value of the exclusion is highest for taxpayers in high rate brackets, who may be the least in need of having the tax system induce greater life insurance coverage?

Employee coverage. Suppose that a corporation buys one-year term insurance on the life of one of its key executives, with itself as the beneficiary. Here the premium seems to be part of the cost of doing business, and seemingly it should be deductible like any other business expense (under §162). But §264(a)(1) expressly denies the deduction. Correspondingly, the proceeds, if any, are excluded under §101(a). On the other hand, if the beneficiary under the policy on the life of the executive were his or her spouse, or if the corporation were to buy group term life insurance for its employees, §264(a)(1) would not apply and the premiums would be deductible (as a form of compensation to such employees). The premiums would be taxable to the executive or other

---

38. In an OID bond with a fixed interest rate, the holder is in effect betting that interest rates will decline. This would increase the bond's value, as it would now offer a higher payout than new bonds with the same face amount that were paying interest based on current rates. The issuer is in effect betting that interest rates will rise.

employees, except for the portion allocable to the first $50,000 of group-term coverage. See §79.

Transferees. The exclusion in §101(a)(1) generally is not available to a person who acquired the policy for valuable consideration. For many such people there will be no statutory basis for deduction of premiums, and for some, even if there is such a basis in §162, deduction will be barred by §264(a)(1). The congressional rationale for the §101(a)(2) limitation was that the exclusion might "result in abuse by encouraging speculation on the death of the insured." S. Rep. No. 1622, 83d Cong., 2d Sess. 14 (1954). Consistent with this rationale, certain policies that were transferred for consideration remain eligible for the exclusion: policies transferred to a person with a substituted, or carryover, basis (e.g., a successor corporation in a tax-free merger or a corporation resulting from a tax-free incorporation of a partnership) and transfers to the insured or to his or her partner, partnership, or corporation. Both these exceptions were enacted to overrule adverse judicial decisions. No exemption from the "transfer for valuable consideration" restriction is needed for transfers of insurance policies by gift or bequest, since no consideration is paid for such transfers.

Accelerated benefits for the terminally ill and chronically ill. If a life insurance policy is sold to an authorized "viatical settlement provider" by a person who is "chronically ill" (as defined in §7702B(c)(2)) or "terminally ill" (as defined in §101(g)(4)(A)), the payments received are treated as having been received by reason of the death of the insured and are excluded from gross income under §101(a). See §101(g).

2. Annuities

Deferral benefits for annuity income. In common usage, an annuity is a contract that entitles the holder (the "annuitant") to receive the payment of a specified amount at specified regular intervals, such as monthly or yearly. Under a term annuity, the exact period for receiving these payments is specified. Under a life annuity, one receives the payments until one dies. (Thus, Social Security in effect pays life annuities to retirees, although Social Security benefits get separate tax treatment under §86.)

Annuities are vehicles for saving. A life annuity also contains a mortality bet, although here, in contrast to life insurance, the annuitant is betting that she will live a long time, rather than die sooner, and thus will receive more payments than the insurance company anticipates. Insurance companies, of course, use life expectancy estimates in determining how they should price life annuities, just as they do (with respect to the opposite mortality bet) in pricing life insurance contracts.

Suppose that *A* is 60 years old, plans to retire at age 70, and has $100,000 to invest. She purchases a life annuity from an insurance company that agrees to start paying her when she turns 70. Suppose further that, given her life expectancy and prevailing interest rates, the annual payment to her, starting at age

70, to which the insurance company agrees is $20,000 per year. How should she be taxed?

If annuities were taxed like OID bonds—using life expectancy tables (see Reg. §1-72-9) to determine the expected payout from a life annuity—then *A* would start being taxed immediately on the annuity contract, even before she received any payments. After all, its value would be appreciating, all else being equal, from the date when the payments grew nearer. In addition, by reason of compounding, she presumably would be treated as having more taxable income each year than she had the year before.

However, for *A*'s tax treatment under the annuity to be treated neutrally relative to the tax treatment of debt instruments, once she started getting cash payments under the annuity, she would have to be granted cost recovery. That is, not all of the amounts she ultimately received would be "interest" as an economic matter. She would also be receiving repayment of "principal" on the "loan," which would have to be excluded from income.

Under §72, which covers the tax treatment of annuities to annuitants, the rules are more favorable than those for debt instruments, albeit less favorable than the rules for life insurance contracts under §101. Annuity payments, unlike life insurance proceeds, are indeed taxable. However, the applicable timing rules for annuitants are in a key respect more favorable than those for OID bondholders. Annuitants are generally only taxable upon the receipt of annuity payments, whereas OID bondholders are taxable purely by reason of the passage of time. Even without such deferral, however, annuitants are treated more favorably than the application of compounding interest would suggest.

To apply §72 to a given annuity, one must compute the "exclusion ratio." §72(b). This is the ratio of the investment in the contract to the expected return. Returning to the above case of *A*, suppose that, given her life expectancy as determined under Reg. §1-72-9, she is expected to receive ten years of payments, for a total gross return of $200,000. Given her $100,000 investment in the contract, her exclusion ratio is $100,000 / $200,000, or fifty percent. This ratio will apply to each payment she receives. Thus, starting at age 70, when *A* begins receiving annuity payments, each annual receipt of $20,000 will cause her to have taxable income of $10,000.

Let's compare this to true economic accrual in an example where, unlike with *A*, no period of tax-free investment buildup occurs before annual annuity payments begin to be made. Thus, suppose *B* spends $100,000 on an annuity that will immediately (i.e., in a year) start paying her $15,000 per year for ten years. (This would require an annual interest rate of slightly above 10 percent.) *B*'s exclusion rate would be $100,000 / $150,000, or 66.67 percent, and thus she would have taxable income of $5,000 per year.

By contrast, suppose *C* deposited $100,000 in a new bank account that paid the same interest rate as that earned by *B* in the above example, thus permitting *C* to withdraw $15,000 per year for the next ten years, starting in a year, with the last withdrawal reducing her account balance to zero. *C*, of course, would be taxed each year on her interest accrual from the bank account, wholly without regard to how much cash she happened to withdraw. However, each withdrawal, by reducing her bank account balance, would reduce the amount of money in the account earning interest the next year.

Over the entire ten-year period, given that *C* would have withdrawn a total of $150,000 from an account that started at $100,000 from her initial (and only) deposit, we know that she would have a total of $50,000 of taxable income (just like *B*). However, rather than having taxable income of exactly $5,000 each year, like *B*, she would have taxable income of more than $10,000 in the first year, gradually declining to less than $1,500 in the final year. Accordingly, *B*, by purchasing a term annuity instead of simply putting her initial investment stake in the bank and then withdrawing it in equal increments, gets the benefit of significant tax deferral, even without a significant buildup period (like that enjoyed by *A*) before the first payment is made.

Life annuities in which the annuitant does not live for exactly the expected period. In the above example concerning *A*, we noted that the exclusion ratio, for the purchaser of a life annuity, depends on the expected number of payments, which is determined using the life expectancy tables in Reg. §1-72-9. In most real-world examples, however, the annuitant, rather than living for *exactly* the projected amount of time, will die either sooner or later than was projected, causing her to receive either fewer payments or more payments than the applicable tax rules assumed. *A*, for example, would receive only five annual payments of $20,000 if she died right after reaching 75, and she would receive fifteen such payments if she lived to age 85 (or thirty payments if she lived to be 100).

With respect to *A*'s cost recovery deductions, what happens then? The answer is that she will nonetheless get exactly the right overall amount of cost recovery. If she dies before full cost recovery of her $100,000 investment in the annuity contract, then the unrecovered amount will be allowed as a deduction in her final year's tax return. §72(b)(3). If she receives more than ten annual payments, then, once full cost recovery has been completed, all subsequent payments under the annuity will be fully included in her gross income. §72(b)(2).

The use of annuities in tax planning. For many years, deferred annuities, given their substantial tax advantage by reason of the exclusion before periodic payments start, have been an important product from the standpoint of insurance companies and an important tax-reduction tool for individuals. Insurance companies have enhanced the attraction of deferred annuities by designing them so that investors can choose the type of investment (for example, a choice from among a number of different mutual funds, including common stock funds, bond funds, etc.) and thus can choose a "variable" return or buildup in value, depending on their investment choice. Moreover, investors can be allowed to change their minds from time to time (for example, by switching from one type of mutual fund to another).

Tax planners sought further to increase the attractiveness of deferred annuities by allowing annuitants to borrow against the instruments' time value appreciation. At one time, such loans did not trigger recognition of gain, except to the extent that the amount of the loan exceeded the investment in the contract. Today, however, under §72(e), a taxpayer who receives a loan against an annuity policy will recognize income equal to the lesser of (a) the amount of the loan, and (b) the increase in the value of the policy. Moreover, under §72(q), taxpayers who are under the age of 59½ generally must pay a penalty tax equal to 10 percent of the amount of the income otherwise recognized.

Section 72(q) applies not just to amounts received by loan but also to any "premature distribution." A premature distribution includes any distribution that is not part of a series of substantially equal periodic payments for life. Absent §72(q), a taxpayer might purchase a deferred annuity that did not pay out for the annuitant's lifetime, but that instead provided only a few annual payments beginning at a designated future date. Such an annuity would offer tax-deferred savings and a quick withdrawal of the investment at maturity; it would be much like a bond issued by a corporation or certificate of deposit issued by a bank. Under §72(q), unless the recipient is age 59½ or older, the distributions on such nonperiodic annuities are subject to the 10 percent penalty tax. For people over 59½, and for younger people who do not need access to their savings until they reach that age, the deferred annuity offers a tax-favored alternative to direct investment in a mutual fund or savings account.

This tax advantage cannot be achieved without some cost. The insurance companies that sell annuities charge fees for their services. Still, in many situations deferred annuities will produce better long-run returns than will direct investments that are essentially identical except for tax considerations. The annuity with an underlying investment in a mutual fund and a direct investment in the same mutual fund are, financially, "perfect substitutes," with different tax characteristics. Taxpayers are therefore encouraged to select the tax-favored investment over the direct investment, as long as the tax saving exceeds the fees paid to achieve that tax saving. A question emerges from these observations: If Congress is willing to allow people to escape tax on their investments, why not let them do so directly so they can save the administrative costs of an intermediary? The answer to that question may have something to do with the exercise of political influence by insurance companies and their agents.

G.   DEEMED REALIZATIONS: CONSTRUCTIVE SALES

In late 1996, the *New York Times* published a front-page special report titled "Wealthy, Helped by Wall St., Find New Ways to Escape Tax on Profits." The article described "several exotic Wall Street strategies" designed to allow large shareholders "to raise cash and lock in their stock market profits without actually selling their shares." Among the numerous transactions described in the article was the so-called short-against-the-box strategy that members of the Estée Lauder family had reportedly used to avoid paying $95 million in federal income taxes that would have been owed had they chosen to simply sell their stock. The article quoted then Deputy Treasury Secretary Lawrence H. Summers as saying, "What are functionally capital gains realizations should be taxed." Congress agreed, adopting the administration's "constructive sale" provision—now §1259—as part of the Taxpayer Relief Act of 1997. The story behind §1259 provides a fascinating illustration of our tax system's ongoing struggle to manage the realization concept.

The transactions at which §1259 was aimed were designed principally for individuals with large blocks of low basis, high value stock—typically company founders. In most cases, these individuals had a disproportionately large share of their overall net worth invested in a single company. Absent tax consider-ations, the desired strategy would be to sell the company stock and reinvest the proceeds in a diversified pool of assets to minimize exposure to company-specific risk. However, that approach would clearly trigger a realization event for tax purposes, causing the taxpayer to recognize a large amount of taxable gain. The trick then was to devise transactions that would allow the taxpayer to monetize her appreciated financial position without triggering a realization event. One such transaction was the so-called short against the box.

To understand how these transactions work, imagine that Eileen owns 1,000 shares of ABC stock with a basis of $10,000 ($10 per share) and a fair market value of $90,000 ($90 per share). Eileen obviously cannot sell the stock without recognizing gain. Suppose, however, that Eileen borrows 1,000 shares of ABC from Bob for a period of one year and then immediately sells those shares. The sale of borrowed stock is called a "short sale." It is a strategy com-monly used by investors who believe the stock is going to decline in value. For example, assume that Jake borrows 1,000 shares of ABC stock from his broker, agreeing to deliver the same number of ABC shares a year later, and sells those borrowed shares for $90,000 cash ($90 per share). If ABC drops to $50 per share, it will cost Jake only $50,000 to come up with the replacement shares, leaving him with a $40,000 profit.

In Eileen's case, however, the short sale serves a somewhat different func-tion. Like Jake, Eileen will benefit from a decline in value of the ABC stock because that decline will reduce the cost of acquiring the shares she must deliver to Bob a year later. But because Eileen still owns her original ABC shares, a decline in the value of ABC stock also hurts her. In fact, any benefit she enjoys with respect to her short position is precisely offset by the loss she suffers with respect to her long position, and vice versa. In other words, by entering into a short sale of ABC stock, Eileen (i) gets $90,000 cash up front, and (ii) completely insulates herself from fluctuations in value of the ABC stock. Is it accurate to say that Eileen still "owns" the ABC stock? In a superfi-cial legal sense, the answer is yes; after all, she still has title to her ABC stock. In an economic sense, however, these transactions have a great deal in common with an outright sale. As is true for an outright sale, Eileen has completely transformed her economic exposure to fluctuations in value of the ABC stock.

Section 1259 now treats this transaction as a sale. More precisely, the statute provides that if there is a "constructive sale" of an "appreciated financial posi-tion" the taxpayer must "recognize gain as if such position were sold. . . ." §1259(a)(1). A taxpayer is treated as having made a constructive sale of an appreciated financial position if she "enters into a short sale of the same or sub-stantially identical property." §1259(c)(1)(A). Thus, the statute directly targets the "short-against-the-box transaction" described above. However, the statute doesn't stop there. It also treats certain other transactions—including "offset-ting notional principal contracts" (§1259(c)(1)(B)) and "futures or forward contracts" (§1259(c)(1)(C))—as constructive sales.

As is often the case in the development of the tax law, §1259 has not put an end to the types of transactions it targeted but rather has turned attention to whether particular transactions not expressly described by the statute should be treated as "constructive sales." The ongoing ambiguity of §1259's scope is per-haps best illustrated by reference to a transaction known as a "zero-cost collar."

Like the short-against-the-box transaction, the zero-cost collar is designed to allow investors to replicate the economic effects of a sale without parting with legal title to the appreciated stock. For example, assume that XYZ founder Ahmed owns XYZ stock with a basis of $10,000 and a value of $500 million. In a typical collar transaction, Ahmed might (i) sell a call option (i.e., an option to purchase the shares from him on some future date for, say $510 million), and (ii) buy a put option (i.e., an option to sell the shares on some future date for, say, $490 million). By entering into these two transactions—called a *zero-cost* collar because the cost of acquiring the put option can be financed by the proceeds of the sale of the call option—Ahmed has effectively eliminated his exposure to upside potential over and above $510 million as well as any downside risk should the stock decline in value below $490 million.

Should Ahmed's zero-cost collar be treated as a "constructive sale" within the meaning of §1259? As a first cut, note that these transactions are not described in §1259(c)(1)(A), (B), (C), or (D). However, this is not the end of the analysis. The statute further provides that a taxpayer will be treated as having made a constructive sale of an appreciated financial position if he, or a related person, "to the extent prescribed by the Secretary in regulations, enters into one or more other transactions (or acquires one or more positions) that have substantially the same effect as" any of the other constructive sale transactions described in the statute. §1259(c)(1)(E). Given this language, it might be tempting to examine the Treasury regulations under §1259. As of 2016, however, regulations under §1259 have not yet been promulgated.

The absence of regulatory guidance leaves taxpayers and their advisors with some uncertainty regarding the appropriate tax treatment of the transaction in question. Often, tax lawyers will consult legislative history in an effort to get some comfort with a particular transaction. With respect to collar transactions, consider the following passage from the "General Explanation of Tax Legislation Enacted in 1997" prepared by the staff of the Joint Committee on Taxation (December 17, 1997):

JOINT COMMITTEE ON TAXATION GENERAL EXPLANATION OF TAX LEGISLATION ENACTED IN 1997

December 17, 1997

. . .

TITLE X. REVENUE-INCREASE PROVISIONS

A.   FINANCIAL PRODUCTS

1. Require Recognition of Gain on Certain Appreciated Financial Positions in Personal Property (sec. 1001(a) of the Act and sec. 1259 of the Code)

. . .

Treasury Guidance

The Act provides regulatory authority to the Treasury to treat as constructive sales certain transactions that have substantially the same effect as those specified (i.e., short sales, offsetting notional principal contracts and futures or forward contracts to deliver the same or substantially similar property).

. . .

The Congress anticipated that the Treasury regulations, when issued, will provide specific standards for determining whether several common transactions will be treated as constructive sales. One such transaction is a "collar." In a collar, a taxpayer commits to an option requiring him to sell a financial position at a fixed price (the "call strike price") and has the right to have his position purchased at a lower fixed price (the "put strike price"). For example, a shareholder may enter into a collar for a stock currently trading at $100 with a put strike price of $95 and a call strike price of $110. The effect of the transaction is that the seller has transferred the rights to all gain above the $110 call strike price and all loss below the $95 put strike price; the seller has retained all risk of loss and opportunity for gain in the price range between $95 and $110. A collar can be a single contract or can be effected by using a combination of put and call options. In order to determine whether collars have substantially the same effect as the transactions specified in the provision, the Congress anticipated that Treasury regulations will provide specific standards that take into account various factors with respect to the appreciated financial position, including its volatility. It is expected that several aspects of the collar transaction will be relevant, including the spread between the put and call prices, the period of the transaction, and the extent to which the taxpayer retains the right to periodic payments on the appreciated financial position (e.g., the dividends on collared stock). The Congress intended that the Treasury regulations with respect to collars will be applied prospectively, except in cases to prevent abuse.

QUESTIONS

1. Recall that Company XYZ founder Ahmed is considering entering into a zero-cost collar transaction. His basis in the XYZ stock is $10,000. The fair market value of the stock is $500 million. Under the terms of the proposed transaction, Ahmed will (i) sell to a third party an option to purchase his XYZ shares on December 31, 2015, for $510 million, and (ii) buy from a third party an option to sell his XYZ shares on December 15, 2015, for $490 million. Based on your understanding of §1259 and the foregoing legislative history, what advice would you give Ahmed regarding the federal income tax treatment of the proposed transaction? Are there any changes to the proposed transaction that you might suggest in order to minimize the likelihood that it will be treated as a constructive sale?

2. Woodsam Associates, Inc. v. Commissioner, discussed in Chapter 4, held that a taxpayer who borrows money on a nonrecourse basis, pledging appreciated property as security for the loan, does not experience a realization event for tax purposes. In what sense is borrowing nonrecourse against appreciated property any different from the types of transactions covered by §1259? Should the statute be amended to treat borrowing nonrecourse against appreciated property as a constructive sale?

6

WHOSE INCOME IS IT?

The preceding chapters have addressed certain fundamental questions relating to the federal tax treatment of income. What exactly must a taxpayer include as taxable income? Under what circumstances may a taxpayer exclude income from the tax base? What does the law require regarding the timing of the taxpayer's inclusion of income on a tax return? In this chapter, we turn to an equally fundamental issue lurking behind all of these questions: *Whose income is it?*

At the level of first principles in devising a tax system, one might put this question slightly differently: What is the appropriate taxpaying unit? Should the tax system require all individuals to separately report their own income? Should married couples be allowed (or perhaps required) to report their income as a single filing unit? Should "households" file a single tax return? If so, how should we define that term? If other groups of individuals share economic resources on terms similar to married couples and households, should they too be allowed (or perhaps required) to file a single tax return? Whatever approach is used, how exactly should federal law define the parameters of a filing unit? For example, should state law determine who is married and who is not? Or should we rely instead on a federal definition of the taxpaying unit to ensure uniform application of the income tax nationwide?

To appreciate how our tax system has approached these questions, it is essential to understand the influence of the rate structure on taxpayer incentives. Recall that the U.S. federal income tax is progressive. That is, as an individual's taxable income rises, her tax liability also increases—not only in absolute terms but as a percentage of income as well. To be more precise, we can say that average tax rates (i.e., total tax owed as a percentage of total income) generally rise with income. Our tax system accomplishes this outcome through the use of progressive marginal tax rates. If you haven't already done so, now would be a good time to review the basic arithmetic of the rate structure of the U.S. income tax. The 2018 tax rate table for single individuals is shown below:

If taxable income is	The tax is
Not over $9,525	10% of the taxable income
Over $9,525 but not over $38,700	$952.50 plus 12% of the excess over $9,525
Over $38,700 but not over $82,500	$4,453.50 plus 22% of the excess over $38,700
Over $82,500 but not over $157,500	$14,089.50 plus 24% of the excess over $82,500
Over $157,500 but not over $200,000	$32,089.50 plus 32% of the excess over $157,500
Over $200,000 but not over $500,000	$45,689.50 plus 35% of the excess over $200,000
Over $500,000	$150,689.50 plus 37% of the excess over $500,000

Because marginal tax rates increase with income, an increase of taxable income of, say, $10,000, will lead to a greater tax liability for a high-income taxpayer (subject to higher marginal tax rates) than for a low-income taxpayer (subject to lower marginal tax rates). If these two taxpayers share economic resources, and thus don't really care which of them receives the $10,000 of additional income, then it will be advantageous for the low-income taxpayer to report the income rather than the high-income taxpayer. Put differently, in a tax system featuring progressive marginal tax rates, there is an incentive for taxpayers who share economic resources to get as many "starts from the bottom" (of the rate structure) as possible to minimize the amount of income subject to the higher rates at higher income levels.

This effort is often referred to as the "splitting" or "assignment" of income. To take a simple example, consider two sisters, Meg and Jo, with aggregate taxable income of $200,000, which for 2018 is the breakpoint 32 percent and 35 percent tax brackets shown in the table above. If Jo reports the entire $200,000 amount herself, her total tax liability would be $45,689.50. However, if Meg and Jo each report $100,000 then each would have a tax liability of $18,289.50 for a total tax liability of $36,579. For these two hypothetical sisters, how their total income is reported on their tax returns means the difference between $45,689.50 of taxes owed (if one of them reports the entire $200,000) or $36,579 in taxes owed (if they each report $100,000). The $9,110.50 difference between those two figures represents the tax savings derived from getting "two starts from the bottom" of the progressive rate structure.

The incentive to split income is of course greatest where two taxpayers face a large marginal tax rate differential. Under today's statutory tax rates, the gains from shifting income can sometimes be significant, especially if replicated year after year, but historically the tax savings from income splitting were much larger. For example, in 1940 the spread between the top and bottom tax rates was 76.7 percent (i.e., top rate of 81.1 percent and a bottom rate of 4.4 percent). These large tax-rate differences not only influenced planning behavior, encouraging taxpayers to shift income to minimize tax liability, they also help explain certain key features of our tax system, such as the emergence of the income-splitting joint return for married couples in 1948. We will examine the joint return in further detail below. We begin, however, with a pair of landmark U.S. Supreme Court decisions on income splitting that are essential to understanding this important corner of the tax law.

A. INCOME FROM SERVICES: DIVERSION BY PRIVATE AGREEMENT

Our first case, Lucas v. Earl, arose at a time when there was only one rate schedule used by all taxpayers and when husband and wife were treated as separate taxpayers. Since 1948, we have had a system of joint returns and split income for husband and wife, and as a result no advantage can be achieved (except in rare circumstances) by shifting income from one spouse to another. The legal principles developed in early husband/wife cases are still relevant to efforts to shift income to other family members and to entities, however. In addition, this case and the one that follows (Poe v. Seaborn) are essential to understanding contemporary controversies over the "marriage penalty" and broader issues of how to tax the family unit.

LUCAS v. EARL
281 U.S. 111 (1930)

Mr. Justice HOLMES delivered the opinion of the Court.

This case presents the question whether the respondent, Earl, could be taxed for the whole of the salary and attorney's fees earned by him in the years 1920 and 1921, or should be taxed for only a half of them in view of a contract with his wife which we shall mention. The Commissioner of Internal Revenue and the Board of Tax Appeals imposed a tax upon the whole, but their decision was reversed by the Circuit Court of Appeals, 30 F.2d 898. . . .

By the contract, made in 1901, Earl and his wife agreed

> that any property either of us now has or may hereafter acquire . . . in any way, either by earnings (including salaries, fees, etc.), or any rights by contract or otherwise, during the existence of our marriage, or which we or either of us may receive by gift, bequest, devise, or inheritance, and all the proceeds, issues, and profits of any and all such property shall be treated and considered, and hereby is declared to be received, held, taken, and owned by us as joint tenants, and not otherwise, with the right of survivorship.

The validity of the contract is not questioned, and we assume it to be unquestionable under the law of the State of California,[1] in which the parties lived. Nevertheless we are of opinion that the Commissioner and Board of Tax Appeals were right.

The Revenue Act of 1918 . . . imposes a tax upon the net income of every individual including "income derived from salaries, wages, or compensation for

---

1. [Under the community property law of California at the time this case arose, Mrs. Earl's rights in Mr. Earl's salary and fees were less substantial than the rights she acquired under the contract. In 1927, in response to the U.S. Supreme Court's 1926 decision in United States v. Robbins, California changed its law to give wives greater community-property rights. — EDS.]

personal service . . . of whatever kind and in whatever form paid," [§61(a)]. . . . A very forcible argument is presented to the effect that the statute seeks to tax only income beneficially received, and that taking the question more technically the salary and fees became the joint property of Earl and his wife on the very first instant on which they were received. We well might hesitate upon the latter proposition, because however the matter might stand between husband and wife he was the only party to the contracts by which the salary and fees were earned, and it is somewhat hard to say that the last step in the performance of those contracts could be taken by anyone but himself alone. But this case is not to be decided by attenuated subtleties. It turns on the import and reasonable construction of the taxing act. There is no doubt that the statute could tax salaries to those who earned them and provide that the tax could not be escaped by anticipatory arrangements and contracts however skillfully devised to prevent the salary when paid from vesting even for a second in the man who earned it. That seems to us the import of the statute before us and we think that no distinction can be taken according to the motives leading to the arrangement by which the fruits are attributed to a different tree from that on which they grew.

Judgment reversed.

NOTES AND QUESTIONS

1. *Fruit and tree.* The fruit-and-tree metaphor in the last sentence of Justice Holmes's opinion is widely known among tax experts and is frequently cited but, like many metaphors, it is more colorful than helpful. For example, if two unrelated lawyers form a partnership and agree to split equally any net income, the income will be taxed according to the rights created by the agreement, regardless of whose efforts happen to generate the income. The fruit-and-tree metaphor is simply inaccurate as applied to such a case. In other cases, it is often more puzzling to try to figure out what is tree and what is fruit than to reach a decision by using more direct analysis.

2. *Mrs. Earl's tax status.* Was Mrs. Earl also taxable on the income in question? Why (not)?

3. *Tax avoidance.* Was *Earl* a tax avoidance case?

4. *Theory of the case.* (a) Is it fair to say that in the era in which this case arose, Mr. Earl probably gave up nothing of significance when he entered into the contract with Mrs. Earl? Would the result have been different if the agreement had been for the life of Mr. Earl rather than "during the existence of [the] marriage"? If the income in question had gone into a trust for the benefit of impoverished relatives of Mrs. Earl, to be selected by her, would it still have been taxable to Mr. Earl?

(b) What if Mrs. Earl had paid for Mr. Earl's legal education, his law library, etc., in return for an assignment of 50 percent of his professional earnings either for a stated period or for life? Would the income then be taxed to Mr. Earl? See Hundley v. Commissioner, 48 T.C. 339 (1967), in which the taxpayer, a teenager, agreed in 1958 in exchange for his father's coaching, business management, and agent services, to share with his father equally any bonus he might receive for signing a professional baseball contract. The taxpayer signed with a professional team in 1960 and was allowed to deduct as a business expense $55,000 (one-half of his $110,000 bonus) paid to his father. But compare Allen v. Commissioner, 50 T.C. 466 (1968), aff'd per curiam, 410 F.2d 398 (3d Cir. 1969), where a similar effort failed since the taxpayer shared his bonus with his mother, whom the Tax Court found to be ignorant of baseball.

(c) In some instances splitting may be attempted by creation of a partnership between, say, a father and his sons. This possibility is explored later in this chapter.

5. *Gratuitous performance of services.* Suppose that a famous actress plays the lead role in a movie produced by her son and is not paid for her services. Should and would the mother be taxed on some reasonable compensation? How would you determine the appropriate amount? It may be difficult to draw the line between this kind of service performed for one's child and other, presumably nontaxable, benefits that a parent may bestow on a child, such as investment advice by an investment advisor or legal advice by a lawyer.

When it comes to services performed for charities, the rules are more generous to taxpayers than the rules relating to services performed for an employer, customer, or client. Ordinarily any income that might be attributed to a taxpayer from performance of services for a charity would be offset by a deduction of the same amount. The issue becomes significant, however, where the deduction would be limited in some manner, such as by the percentage limitations on the deductibility of charitable contributions in §170(b). The regulations provide that no income arises where services are rendered directly to a charitable organization (Reg. §1.61-2(c)), and this includes services rendered to a charity as promoter of public entertainment (G.C.M. 27026, 1951-2 C.B. 7). But despite the scorn expressed by Justice Holmes for "attenuated subtleties," the regulations distinguish between services rendered directly to the charity and services rendered to a third person with payment going to the charity. This is the kind of distinction that invites manipulation of the forms of transactions to achieve desirable tax results.

It may be difficult to work up concern about the shifting of income to charities. The principles applied to charities have been extended, however, to services rendered for the benefit of political organizations. See Rev. Rul. 68-503, 1968-2 C.B. 44, issued during the heat of the 1968 presidential campaign and holding that a featured performer at a political fund-raising event, for which admission was charged, was not taxable on any amount of income. Is this result consistent with *Earl*? With sound principles of taxation? With sound principles of campaign funding? If income should be taxed to the performer at a political fund-raising event, what if a famous actor appears in a television "spot" on behalf of a candidate (with no direct effort to raise money)?

B.   INCOME FROM SERVICES: DIVERSION BY OPERATION OF LAW

Lucas v. Earl dealt with private agreements to divert income from the person who earned it to someone else. But what about situations where income is diverted not via some "skillfully devised" arrangement but rather by operation of law?

The following case, decided approximately eight months after Lucas v. Earl, deals with the division of income between a couple whose rights are determined under state community property law. As noted in Justice Roberts's opinion, *Earl* presented "quite a different question" from Poe v. Seaborn. See if you agree.

POE v. SEABORN
282 U.S. 101 (1930)

Mr. Justice ROBERTS delivered the opinion of the Court.

Seaborn and his wife, citizens and residents of the State of Washington, made for the year 1927 separate income tax returns. . . .

During and prior to 1927 they accumulated property comprising real estate, stocks, bonds, and other personal property. While the real estate stood in [the husband's] name alone, it is undisputed that all of the property real and personal constituted community property and that neither owned any separate property or had any separate income.

The income comprised Seaborn's salary, interest on bank deposits and on bonds, dividends, and profits on sales of real and personal property. He and his wife each returned one-half the total community income as gross income and each deducted one-half of the community expenses to arrive at the net income returned.

The Commissioner of Internal Revenue determined that all of the income should have been reported in the husband's return. . . .

The case requires us to construe Sections 210(a) and 211(a) of the Revenue Act of 1926,[2] and apply them, as construed, to the interests of husband and wife in community property under the law of Washington. These sections lay a tax upon the net income of every individual. The Act goes no farther, and furnishes no other standard or definition of what constitutes an individual's income. The use of the word "of" denotes ownership. . . .

The Commissioner concedes that the answer to the question involved in the cause must be found in the provisions of the law of the State, as to a wife's ownership of or interest in community property. What, then, is the law of Washington as to the ownership of community property and of community income including the earnings of the husband's and wife's labor?

The answer is found in the statutes of the State, and the decisions interpreting them.

These statutes provide that, save for property acquired by gift, bequest, devise or inheritance, all property however acquired after marriage, by either husband or wife, or by both, is community property. On the death of either spouse his or her interest is subject to testamentary disposition, and failing that, it passes to the issue of the decedent and not to the surviving

2. [These sections provided that the normal tax and the surtax "shall be levied, collected, and paid for each taxable year upon the net income of every individual." Substantially the same language now appears in §1(a) of the Code. — EDS.]

spouse. While the husband has the management and control of community personal property and like power of disposition thereof as of his separate personal property, this power is subject to restrictions which are inconsistent with denial of the wife's interest as co-owner. The wife may borrow for community purposes and bind the community property. . . . Since the husband may not discharge his separate obligation out of community property, she may, suing alone, enjoin collection of his separate debt out of community property. . . . She may prevent his making substantial gifts out of community property without her consent. . . . The community property is not liable for the husband's torts not committed in carrying on the business of the community. . . .

Without further extending this opinion it must suffice to say that it is clear the wife has, in Washington, a vested property right in the community property, equal with that of her husband; and in the income of the community, including salaries or wages of either husband or wife, or both. . . .

The taxpayer contends that if the test of taxability under Sections 210 and 211 is ownership, it is clear that income of community property is owned by the community and that husband and wife have each a present vested one-half interest therein.

The Commissioner contends, however, that we are here concerned not with mere names, nor even with mere technical legal titles; that calling the wife's interest vested is nothing to the purpose, because the husband has such broad powers of control and alienation, that while the community lasts, he is essentially the owner of the whole community property, and ought so to be considered for the purposes of Sections 210 and 211. He points out that as to personal property the husband may convey it, make contracts affecting it, may do anything with it short of committing a fraud on his wife's rights. And though the wife must join in any sale of real estate, he asserts that the same is true, by virtue of statutes, in most States which do not have the community system. He asserts that control without accountability is indistinguishable from ownership, and that since the husband has this, quoad community property and income, the income is that "of" the husband under Sections 210, 211 of the income tax law.

We think, in view of the law of Washington above stated, this contention is unsound. The community must act through an agent. . . .

The reasons for conferring such sweeping powers of management on the husband are not far to seek. Public policy demands that in all ordinary circumstances, litigation between wife and husband during the life of the community should be discouraged. Law-suits between them would tend to subvert the marital relation. The same policy dictates that third parties who deal with the husband respecting community property shall be assured that the wife shall not be permitted to nullify his transactions. The powers of partners, or of trustees of a spendthrift trust, furnish apt analogies.

The obligations of the husband as agent of the community are no less real because the policy of the State limits the wife's right to call him to account in a court. Power is not synonymous with right. Nor is obligation coterminous with legal remedy. The law's investiture of the husband with broad powers, by no means negatives the wife's present interest as a co-owner.

We are of opinion that under the law of Washington the entire property and income of the community can no more be said to be that of the husband, than it could rightly be termed that of the wife. . . .

The Commissioner urges that we have, in principal [sic], decided the instant question in favor of the Government. He relies on United States v. Robbins, 269 U.S. 315; Corliss v. Bowers, 281 U.S. 376; and Lucas v. Earl.

In the *Robbins* case, we found that the law of California, as construed by her own courts, gave the wife a mere expectancy and that the property rights of the husband during the life of the community were so complete that he was in fact the owner. . . .

The *Corliss* case raised no issue as to the intent of Congress, but as to its power. We held that where a donor retains the power at any time to revest himself with the principal of the gift, Congress may declare that he still owns the income. While he has technically parted with title, yet he in fact retains ownership, and all its incidents. But here the husband never has ownership. That is in the community at the moment of acquisition.

In the *Earl* case a husband and wife contracted that any property they had or might thereafter acquire in any way, either by earnings (including salaries, fees, etc.), or any rights by contract or otherwise, "shall be treated and considered and hereby is declared to be received held taken and owned by us as joint tenants. . . ." We held that, assuming the validity of the contract under local law, it still remained true that the husband's professional fees, earned in years subsequent to the date of the contract, were his individual income, "derived from salaries, wages, or compensation for personal services." . . . The very assignment in that case was bottomed on the fact that the earnings would be the husband's property, else there would have been nothing on which it could operate. That case presents quite a different question from this, because here, by law, the earnings are never the property of the husband, but that of the community. . . .

The District Court was right in holding that the husband and wife were entitled to file separate returns, each treating one-half of the community income as his or her respective income, and its judgment is affirmed.

NOTES AND QUESTIONS

1. *Reconciliation with Lucas v. Earl.* What do you think of the Court's effort to distinguish Lucas v. Earl?

2. *The congressional response.* After the decision in Poe v. Seaborn, couples in community property states enjoyed a significant tax advantage compared with couples in common-law property states. Spouses in common-law property states could split income by transfers of income-producing property but not by diversions of earnings from the performance of services. In the years following the decision in *Seaborn*, particularly as rates rose before and during World War II, some common-law states reacted by adopting the community-property system. Congress could have eliminated most of the disparity among the states by rejecting *Seaborn* and taxing spouses in both community and common-law states on their own salaries, wages, fees, etc. *Seaborn* was based on statutory

language, not on the Constitution. But rejecting *Seaborn* would have meant taking away from couples in community-property states a benefit to which they had become accustomed, and Congress followed the more politically palatable course of extending the benefit of income splitting to all married couples. It did this, in 1948, by allowing married couples in all states to file joint returns and compute the total tax by first computing a tax on half of the total and then doubling that amount, thereby providing two starts at the bottom of the rate structure, regardless of how income was earned and regardless of legal claims to it. As a result, marriage reduced tax liability for all but the (then very unusual) family in which both spouses earned the same amount of income. This phenomenon is typically called a "marriage bonus," but an equally accurate term is "singles penalty." The 1948 regime remained in force until 1969, when Congress responded to complaints of unfair treatment from unmarried individuals. The story is continued in Section C below.

3. *Who is "married" for federal income tax purposes?* The federal income tax generally relies on state law in determining who is married. In 1996, however, Congress passed and President Bill Clinton signed into law the "Defense of Marriage Act" (DOMA), which defined "marriage" for purposes of federal law as "a legal union between one man and one woman as husband and wife" and "spouse" as "a person of the opposite sex who is a husband or a wife." Because of this provision, only opposite-sex couples were permitted to file joint returns or otherwise be treated as spouses under the numerous provisions of the Internal Revenue Code where marriage is relevant. In 2013, the U.S. Supreme Court struck down DOMA as unconstitutional. United States v. Windsor, 570 U.S. 744 (2013). Exactly two years later, the Court issued its landmark decision in Obergefell v. Hodges, 576 U.S. ____ (2015), concluding that the right to marry is a fundamental right in our constitutional order and, therefore, that states cannot deny marriage licenses to same-sex couples or refuse to recognize marriages performed in other states. As a result of these decisions, all persons who are married for purposes of state law—whether they be same-sex or opposite-sex couples—are considered to be married for purposes of the federal income tax. In September 2016, the IRS issued final regulations to this effect. *See* Reg. §301.7701-18(a)-(b).

4. *Application of Poe v. Seaborn to domestic partners.* As noted above, the adoption of the joint return and income splitting in 1948 essentially rendered moot the distinction, established in Lucas v. Earl and Poe v. Seaborn, between married couples living in common-law and community property jurisdictions. In 2003, however, California adopted AB205, known as the California Domestic Partner Rights and Responsibilities Act. The stated purpose of this legislation, which was enacted before the state's recognition of same-sex marriage, was to extend to same-sex couples (and certain heterosexual couples) "the same rights, protections, and benefits" as well as "the same responsibilities, obligations, and duties" as those granted to married individuals under state law. Accordingly, among other things, AB205 extended the state's community property regime to those who registered as domestic partners, treating them for state property law purposes the same as married persons subject to the state's community property law regime. This raised the question of whether such individuals should, for federal income tax purposes, separately report the amounts that

each taxpayer earns (as indicated by Lucas v. Earl) or combine and split their income (as indicated by Poe v. Seaborn). The issue was presented to the Office of the Chief Counsel of the IRS, which concluded in 2010 that "a California registered domestic partner must report one-half of the community income, whether received in the form of compensation for personal services or income from property, on his or her federal income tax return." California first began recognizing same-sex marriages in 2008 and of course states are now constitutionally prohibited from denying same-sex couples the right to marry. *See* Obergefell v. Hodges, 576 U.S. ____ (2015). Because AB205 does not concern the state law definition of marriage, its operation is not affected by the *Obergefell* decision. *See* Reg. §301.7701-18(c). Thus, domestic partnership remains available as an alternative to marriage for California couples who meet the statutory criteria and the IRS's 2010 ruling continues to apply to such couples.

C.   THE MARRIAGE PENALTY (AND BONUS)

1. The Legislative "Solution": The Income-Splitting Joint Return

In 1948, Congress amended the tax law to allow married couples to split their incomes by filing a joint return, regardless of how the income was earned and regardless of whether the couple lived in a community-property state or a common-law jurisdiction. The result was a system of universal marriage bonuses since all married couples would effectively get two "starts from the bottom" of the progressive rate structure. For example, if Don earned a $100,000 salary while Betty stayed home to care for their children, the couple would be taxed as though each earned $50,000. Meanwhile, Dick, who earns the same $100,000 salary but is not married, would get only one start from the bottom of the rate structure. Predictably, single individuals complained that they were paying more than their fair share of the tax burden.

In 1969, Congress responded to the complaints of singles by adjusting the rate structure to reduce, but not completely eliminate, the singles penalty. The net effect of this change was approximately the same as having the single individual rate structure apply to every taxpayer, and to allow some but not complete income shifting within marriage. From 1969 onward, the tax consequences of marriage would depend upon the composition of the couple's total income between the two spouses. Couples with only one wage earner were still better off with marriage, since the effect of the new schedules was to assume that some (though less than half) of the income was earned by the non-wage earner, and thus (with respect to that income), it would give the couple two starts at the bottom of the rate structure. The change produced the worst outcome for couples where the income was earned evenly by the two spouses, since the two starts from the bottom they enjoyed while single would no longer be available to them when married. Thus, while there remained a "marriage bonus" for some couples, it was reduced, and there was now a "marriage penalty" for many couples with two wage earners.

Present law contains both marriage bonuses and marriage penalties. In 2018, a single individual with taxable income of $200,000 would pay a tax of $45,689.50. The tax liability for that same amount of taxable income earned by a married couple filing jointly would be $36,579. In other words, if an individual earning $200,000 were to marry someone with no taxable income, there would be a "marriage bonus" of $9,110.50. Marriage bonuses for couples with one wage earner occur at almost any level of income. By contrast, there is sometimes a marriage *penalty* for families with two wage earners with substantial incomes. The penalty has been eliminated for the lower brackets. Thus, if two individuals who each have taxable income of $100,000 married, their total tax liability would remain the same (at $36,579) whether single or married. There is no marriage penalty. However, if two individuals who each have taxable incomes of $500,000 get married, their combined tax liability increases by $8,000 (from $301,379 to $309,379), again based on 2018 tax rates. In effect, this couple must pay an annual surtax by virtue of their decision to wed.

2. Addressing the Marriage Penalty/Bonus

It is sometimes noted that it is mathematically impossible for a tax system to satisfy all three of the following principles: (1) marriage neutrality (i.e., no penalties or bonuses), (2) couple equality (i.e., couples with the same aggregate income bear the same tax burden), and (3) progressivity. As the examples above illustrate, current law sacrifices marriage neutrality to ensure both couple equality and progressivity. If all income were taxed at a single rate, say 20 percent, then it would be possible to have both marriage neutrality and couple equality, but at the expense of progressivity. Alternatively, a system of individual filing and rising marginal tax rates would ensure marriage neutrality and progressivity, but at the expense of couple equality.

There is one way that a tax system can satisfy all three principles described above. For example, imagine a system of individual filing in which everyone is subject to a flat rate of 20 percent but also entitled to a refundable tax credit of $5,000. Now consider how this regime would apply to Couple A, which consists of one taxpayer with $100,000 of income and another taxpayer with zero income. The taxpayer with $100,000 of income would owe $15,000 in tax for an average tax rate of 15 percent. The taxpayer with no income would owe no tax but would receive a $5,000 check from the government. Unmarried, Couple A would face a total tax liability of $10,000. Married, they would pay the same amount. Thus, the principle of marriage neutrality is satisfied. Now consider Couple B, where each spouse earns $50,000. Like Couple A, this couple would pay a total of $10,000 in federal income taxes ($5,000 each), with the result that the principle of couple equality is also satisfied.

As for progressivity, note that our hypothetical tax regime features rising *average* tax rates. That is, as an individual's income rises, so does the percentage of income that she must pay in taxes. The taxpayer with $50,000 in income has an average tax rate of 10 percent, the taxpayer with $100,000 in income has an average tax rate of 15 percent, the taxpayer with $200,000 in income has an average tax rate of 17.5 percent, and so on. What this system lacks, of course, is rising *marginal* tax rates. In fact, every taxpayer faces the same marginal tax rate of 20 percent. This is where the mathematical impossibility comes in: It is indeed mathematically impossible to have a tax system that features marriage neutrality, couple equality, and *marginal* tax rate progressivity.

Our tax system has opted for couple equality and marginal tax rate progressivity at the expense of marriage neutrality. It bears noting, however, that even within that framework there remains a question of precisely how marriage will influence a couple's income tax liability. As shown by our experience with the income-splitting joint return between 1948 and 1969, it is possible to eliminate marriage penalties completely, though doing so necessarily entails conferring large marriage bonuses (aka "singles penalties"). The 1969 changes to the rate structure sought to steer a middle course by reducing the marriage bonuses, but doing so necessarily introduced some marriage penalties. In recent years, more attention has been given to reducing the effect of the marriage penalty. In 2001, Congress eliminated the marriage penalty completely by adjusting the lowest brackets so that the breakpoints for the married filing jointly rates are exactly twice the amounts for single individuals. Congress extended this treatment through all but the highest bracket in legislation enacted in 2017. The result of these changes has been an increase in marriage bonuses for many couples across the income distribution. For all but the highest earning couples, the rate structure sends a very clear signal in favor of marriage and against remaining single.

3.   Filing Status: Summary and Data

When filing Form 1040 with the Internal Revenue Service, taxpayers must select the appropriate "filing status" based on their personal circumstances. Not surprisingly, the two most common filing statuses are (1) unmarried individuals, and (2) married individuals filing jointly. Of the 150,493,263 individual income tax returns filed with the IRS in 2015, just over 71 million returns were filed by unmarried individuals, while another 54 million returns were filed by married individuals filing jointly. Thus, those two filing statuses account for roughly 83 percent of all individual income tax returns filed. The remaining returns consisted of (1) head of households (22 million returns), (2) married individuals filing separate returns (3 million returns), and (3) surviving spouses (fewer than 100,000 returns).

As the "married filing separate" moniker suggests, there is a separate rate structure for married persons filing separate returns. It is important to emphasize, however, that this special filing status generally offers no tax savings and therefore does not enable those couples subject to the marriage penalty to avoid the additional tax burden created by being married. Individuals who use the "married filing separate" status may be separated but not yet divorced. In addition, a spouse may wish to use the married filing separate status in order to avoid the joint and several liability that one is normally subject to when filing a joint return with one's spouse. Finally, there may be some rare instances (e.g., where one spouse incurs large medical expenses) where using this filing status may allow a couple to reduce its overall tax liability.

There is also a separate rate schedule for "heads of households." This schedule may be used by taxpayers who are not married but whose household includes certain dependents, such as children or parents. This schedule has brackets that are more favorable than those for single people but less favorable than those for married couples filing jointly. In other words, heads of house-hold receive some but not all of the advantage of the married persons' joint return schedule. The reasons for this favorable treatment are perhaps easiest to understand in the case of a surviving spouse with continuing obligations to care for young children.

D.   TRANSFERS OF PROPERTY AND INCOME FROM PROPERTY

Generally, income from property—such as interest, dividends, or rent—is treated for tax purposes as having been received by the owner of the property and thus is taxed to that person, at that person's rate. One notable exception to that rule is the so-called kiddie tax, which provides that the unearned income of a child under age 18 is taxed at his or her parents' marginal rate. §1(g). Putting that aside, in applying the principle that income from property is taxed to the owner of that property we are confronted with the question of what is meant by "property." As the materials that follow demonstrate, courts have sometimes answered this question in legalistic and even metaphysical ways.

The next two cases can be viewed from a formalistic perspective as efforts to distinguish between gifts of property and gifts of income from property. From a more realistic perspective the two cases can be seen as efforts to draw a line between diversions of income from property that are respected for tax purposes and those that are not, which should depend, in large part at least, on the economic characteristics of what was given away and what was retained. In the first case (*Blair*), the taxpayer had a limited interest (a life estate), but gave away a portion for its entire duration (i.e., part of the income for his life). In the second (*Horst*), the taxpayer owned the entire property (a bond), and gave away a limited interest (the interest income for a brief period of time); he gave away what has come to be called a "carved out" income interest.[3] The challenge in reading the cases is to figure out why the first taxpayer won and the second lost.

BLAIR v. COMMISSIONER
300 U.S. 5 (1937)

Mr. Chief Justice HUGHES delivered the opinion of the Court.

This case presents the question of the liability of a beneficiary of a testamen-tary trust for a tax upon the income which he had assigned to his children. . . .

The trust was created by the will of [the petitioner's (taxpayer's) father and called for payment of all income to petitioner during his life]. In 1923, . . .

---

3. An assigned interest that is coextensive in time with the assignor's interest is sometimes called a "horizontal" division or "horizontal slice," as contrasted with an interest for a fixed number of years shorter than the assignor's interest, called a "vertical slice." This assumes that money flows from side to side rather than up and down—or, if you will, west to east rather than south to north.

petitioner assigned to his daughter . . . an interest amounting to $6,000 for the remainder of that calendar year, and to $9,000 in each calendar year thereafter, in the net income. . . . At about the same time, he made like assignments of interest, amounting to $9,000 in each calendar year, in the net income of the trust to [two other children]. . . . In later years, by similar instruments, he assigned to these children additional interests. . . . The trustees accepted the assignments and distributed the income directly to the assignees. . . .

[After holding that a judgment in an earlier proceeding involving the same trust was not conclusive in this proceeding as res judicata and that the assignments were valid under local law, the Supreme Court turned to the third issue in the case.]

Third. The question remains whether, treating the assignments as valid, the assignor was still taxable upon the income under the federal income tax act. That is a federal question.

Our decisions in Lucas v. Earl and Burnet v. Leininger, 285 U.S. 136, are cited. In the *Lucas* [*sic*] case . . . [w]e were of the opinion that the case turned upon the construction of the taxing act. We said that "the statute could tax salaries to those who earned them and provide that the tax could not be escaped by anticipatory arrangements and contracts however skillfully devised to prevent the same when paid from vesting even for a second in the man who earned it." That was deemed to be the meaning of the statute as to compensation for personal service and the one who earned the income was held to be subject to the tax. In Burnet v. Leininger, a husband, a member of a firm, assigned future partnership income to his wife. We found that the revenue act dealt explicitly with the liability of partners as such. The wife did not become a member of the firm; the act specifically taxed the distributive share of each partner in the net income of the firm; and the husband by the fair import of the act remained taxable upon his distributive share. These cases are not in point. The tax here is not upon earnings which are taxed to the one who earns them. Nor is it a case of income attributable to a taxpayer by reason of the application of the income to the discharge of his obligation. . . . There is here no question of evasion or of giving effect to statutory provisions designed to forestall evasion; or of the taxpayer's retention of control. . . .

The Government points to the provisions of the revenue acts imposing upon the beneficiary of a trust the liability for the tax upon the income distributable to the beneficiary.[4] But the term is merely descriptive of the one entitled to the beneficial interest. . . . If under the law governing the trust the beneficial interest is assignable, and if it has been assigned without reservation, the assignee thus becomes the beneficiary and is entitled to rights and remedies accordingly. We find nothing in the revenue acts which denies him that status.

The decision of the Circuit Court of Appeals turned upon the effect to be ascribed to the assignments. The court held that the petitioner had no interest in the corpus of the estate and could not dispose of the income until he received it. Hence it was said that "the income was *his*" and his assignment

---

4. [The provisions stated in general terms that the "beneficiary" of a trust was taxable on the income distributable to him. See §§652(a) and 662(a). —Eds.]

was merely a direction to pay over to others what was due to himself. The question was considered to involve "the date when the income became transferable." 83 F.(2d), p.662. The Government refers to the terms of the assignment,—that it was of the interest in the income "which the said party of the first part now is, or may hereafter be, entitled to receive during his life from the trustees." From this it is urged that the assignments "dealt only with a right to receive the income" and that "no attempt was made to assign any equitable right, title or interest in the trust itself." This construction seems to us to be a strained one. We think it apparent that the conveyancer was not seeking to limit the assignment so as to make it anything less than a complete transfer of the specified interest of the petitioner as the life beneficiary of the trust, but that with ample caution he was using words to effect such a transfer. That the state court so construed the assignments appears from the final decree which described them as voluntary assignments of interests of the petitioner "in said trust estate," and it was in that aspect that petitioner's right to make the assignments was sustained.

The will creating the trust entitled the petitioner during his life to the net income of the property held in trust. He thus became the owner of an equitable interest in the corpus of the property. . . . By virtue of that interest he was entitled to enforce the trust, to have a breach of trust enjoined and to obtain redress in case of breach. The interest was present property alienable like any other, in the absence of a valid restraint upon alienation. . . . The beneficiary may thus transfer a part of his interest as well as the whole. See Restatement of the Law of Trusts, §§130, 132 et seq. The assignment of the beneficial interest is not the assignment of a choice in action but of the "right, title, and estate in and to property." . . . See Bogert, Trusts and Trustees, vol. 1, 183, pp. 516, 517; 17 Columbia Law Review, 269, 273, 289, 290.

We conclude that the assignments were valid, that the assignees thereby became the owners of the specified beneficial interests in the income, and that as to these interests they and not the petitioner were taxable for the tax years in question. . . .

HELVERING v. HORST
311 U.S. 112 (1940)

Mr. Justice STONE delivered the opinion of the Court.

The sole question for decision is whether the gift, during the donor's taxable year, of interest coupons detached from the bonds, delivered to the donee and later in the year paid at maturity, is the realization of income taxable to the donor.[5]

---

5. [Coupon bonds, which were far more common in earlier days than they are now, are "bearer" obligations (that is, payable to the bearer, or holder). The obligation is reflected in a large, sturdy piece of paper, part of which states the borrower's obligation to pay the principal amount on a given date and part of which is divided into segments called coupons, each of which states the borrower's obligation to pay a fixed amount of money, the interest payment, on a particular interest-payment date, with one coupon for each interest payment. Each coupon is a separate negotiable instrument.

In 1934 and 1935 respondent, the owner of negotiable bonds, detached from them negotiable interest coupons shortly before their due date and delivered them as a gift to his son who in the same year collected them at maturity. The Commissioner ruled that under [§61(a)], the interest payments were taxable, in the years when paid, to the respondent donor who reported his income on the cash receipts basis. . . .

The court below thought that as the consideration for the coupons had passed to the obligor, the donor had, by the gift, parted with all control over them and their payment, and for that reason the case was distinguishable from Lucas v. Earl and Burnet v. Leininger, 285 U.S. 136, where the assignment of compensation for services had preceded the rendition of the services, and where the income was held taxable to the donor.

The holder of a coupon bond is the owner of two independent and separable kinds of right. One is the right to demand and receive at maturity the principal amount of the bond representing capital investment. The other is the right to demand and receive interim payments of interest on the investment in the amounts and on the dates specified by the coupons. Together they are an obligation to pay principal and interest given in exchange for money or property which was presumably the consideration for the obligation of the bond. Here respondent, as owner of the bonds, had acquired the legal right to demand payment at maturity of the interest specified by the coupons and the power to command its payment to others which constituted an economic gain to him.

Admittedly not all economic gain of the taxpayer is taxable income. From the beginning the revenue laws have been interpreted as defining "realization" of income as the taxable event rather than the acquisition of the right to receive it. And "realization" is not deemed to occur until the income is paid. But the decisions and regulations have consistently recognized that receipt in cash or property is not the only characteristic of realization of income to a taxpayer on the cash receipts basis. Where the taxpayer does not receive payments of income in money or property realization may occur when the last step is taken by which he obtains the fruition of the economic gain which has already accrued to him. . . .

In the ordinary case the taxpayer who acquires the right to receive income is taxed when he receives it, regardless of the time when his right to receive payment accrued. But the rule that income is not taxable until realized has never been taken to mean that the taxpayer, even on the cash receipts basis, who has fully enjoyed the benefit of the economic gain represented by his right to receive income, can escape taxation because he has not himself received payment of it from his obligor. The rule, founded on administrative convenience, is only one of postponement of the tax to the final event of enjoyment

---

Ordinarily, the holder of the bond collects interest by cutting off ("clipping") coupons as they mature and cashing them in, usually at a bank, but, as this case reveals, any other holder of the coupons can cash them in on their due date. These days, most corporate bonds are registered; the owner's name is registered with the debtor company, and the interest payment goes in the mail by check to the registered owner. Since 1983, most bonds are in effect required to be registered. See §§103(d), 163(f), 165(j), 1232(d), and 4701.—Eds.]

of the income, usually the receipt of it by the taxpayer, and not one of exemption from taxation where the enjoyment is consummated by some event other than the taxpayer's personal receipt of money or property. . . . This may occur when he has made such use of disposition of his power to receive or control the income as to procure in its place other satisfactions which are of economic worth. The question here is whether because one who in fact receives payment for services or interest payments is taxable only on his receipt of the payments, he can escape all tax by giving away his right to income in advance of payment. If the taxpayer procures payment directly to his creditors of the items of interest or earnings due him, see Old Colony Trust Co. v. Commissioner, 279 U.S. 716; Bowers v. Kerbaugh-Empire Co., 271 U.S. 170; United States v. Kirby Lumber Co., or if he sets up a revocable trust with income payable to the objects of his bounty, Corliss v. Bowers, 281 U.S. 376, he does not escape taxation because he did not actually receive the money. . . .

Underlying the reasoning in these cases is the thought that income is "realized" by the assignor because he, who owns or controls the source of the income, also controls the disposition of that which he could have received himself and diverts the payment from himself to others as the means of procuring the satisfaction of his wants. The taxpayer has equally enjoyed the fruits of his labor or investment and obtained the satisfaction of his desires whether he collects and uses the income to procure those satisfactions, or whether he disposes of his right to collect it as the means of procuring them. . . .

Although the donor here, by the transfer of the coupons, has precluded any possibility of his collecting them himself he has nevertheless, by his act, procured payment of the interest, as a valuable gift to a member of his family. Such a use of his economic gain, the right to receive income, to procure a satisfaction which can be obtained only by the expenditure of money or property, would seem to be the enjoyment of the income whether the satisfaction is the purchase of goods at the corner grocery, the payment of his debt there, or such non-material satisfactions as may result from the payment of a campaign or community chest contribution, or a gift to his favorite son. Even though he never receives the money he derives money's worth from the disposition of the coupons which he has used as money or money's worth in the procuring of a satisfaction which is procurable only by the expenditure of money or money's worth. The enjoyment of the economic benefit accruing to him by virtue of his acquisition of the coupons is realized as completely as it would have been if he had collected the interest in dollars and expended them for any of the purposes named. . . .

In a real sense he has enjoyed compensation for money loaned or services rendered and not any the less so because it is his only reward for them. To say that one who has made a gift thus derived from interest or earnings paid to his donee has never enjoyed or realized the fruits of his investment or labor because he has assigned them instead of collecting them himself and then paying them over to the donee, is to affront common understanding and to deny the facts of common experience. Common understanding and experience are the touchstones for the interpretation of the revenue laws.

The power to dispose of income is the equivalent of ownership of it. The exercise of that power to procure the payment of income to another is the enjoyment and hence the realization of the income by him who exercises it. We have had no difficulty in applying that proposition where the assignment preceded the rendition of the services, Lucas v. Earl; Burnet v. Leininger, for it was recognized in the *Leininger* case that in such a case the rendition of the service by the assignor was the means by which the income was controlled by the donor and of making his assignment effective. But it is the assignment by which the disposition of income is controlled when the service precedes the assignment and in both cases it is the exercise of the power of disposition of the interest or compensation with the resulting payment to the donee which is the enjoyment by the donor of income derived from them.

This was emphasized in Blair v. Commissioner, on which respondent relies, where the distinction was taken between a gift of income derived from an obligation to pay compensation and a gift of income-producing property. In the circumstances of that case the right to income from the trust property was thought to be so identified with the equitable ownership of the property from which alone the beneficiary derived his right to receive the income and his power to command disposition of it that a gift of the income by the beneficiary became effective only as a gift of his ownership of the property producing it. Since the gift was deemed to be a gift of the property the income from it was held to be the income of the owner of the property, who was the donee, not the donor, a refinement which was unnecessary if respondent's contention here is right, but one clearly inapplicable to gifts of interest or wages. Unlike income thus derived from an obligation to pay interest or compensation, the income of the trust was regarded as no more the income of the donor than would be the rent from a lease or a crop raised on a farm after the leasehold or the farm has been given away. . . .

The dominant purpose of the revenue laws is the taxation of income to those who earn or otherwise create the right to receive it and enjoy the benefit of it when paid. . . . The tax laid by the 1934 Revenue Act upon income "derived from . . . wages, or compensation for personal service, of whatever kind and in whatever form paid . . . ; also from interest . . ." therefore cannot fairly be interpreted as not applying to income derived from interest or compensation when he who is entitled to receive it makes use of his power to dispose of it in procuring satisfactions which he would otherwise procure only by the use of the money when received.

It is the statute which taxes the income to the donor although paid to his donee. Lucas v. Earl; Burnet v. Leininger. True, in those cases the service which created the right to income followed the assignment and it was arguable that in point of legal theory the right to the compensation vested instantaneously in the assignor when paid although he never received it; while here the right of the assignor to receive the income antedated the assignment which transferred the right and thus precluded such an instantaneous vesting. But the statute affords no basis for such "attenuated subtleties." The distinction was explicitly rejected as the basis of decision in Lucas v. Earl. It should be rejected here, for no more than in the *Earl* case can the purpose of the statute to tax the income to him who earns, or creates and enjoys it be escaped by "anticipatory arrangements . . . however skillfully devised" to prevent the income from vesting even for a second in the donor.

Nor is it perceived that there is any adequate basis for distinguishing between the gift of interest coupons here and a gift of salary or commissions. The owner of a negotiable bond and of the investment which it represents, if not the lender, stands in the place of the lender. When, by the gift of the coupons, he has separated his right to interest payments from his investment and procured the payment of the interest to his donee, he has enjoyed the economic benefits of the income in the same manner and to the same extent as though the transfer were of earnings and in both cases the import of the statute is that the fruit is not to be attributed to a different tree from that on which it grew. See Lucas v. Earl.

Reversed.

The separate opinion of Mr. Justice MCREYNOLDS.

. . . The unmatured coupons given to the son were independent negotiable instruments, complete in themselves. Through the gift they became at once the absolute property of the donee, free from the donor's control and in no way dependent upon ownership of the bonds. No question of actual fraud or purpose to defraud the revenue is presented. . . .

THE CHIEF JUSTICE and Mr. Justice ROBERTS concur in this opinion.

NOTES AND QUESTIONS

1. *Rationale:* Blair. The Court says that Mr. Blair was "the owner of an equitable interest in the corpus of the property." So what? Is the characterization relevant because of language in the Code? Because of tax policy objectives? Does it help make the law more predictable? If so, at what cost?

2. *Rationale:* Horst. (a) Is realization a problem in *Horst?* (b) What is the relevance of the fact that Mr. Horst may have obtained some satisfaction from the enjoyment of the income by the son? If Mr. Horst had given the entire bond to the son, would his satisfaction in the son's enjoyment of the income over the next several years have been less? Would the father have been taxed on the interest payments received by the son? (c) What if the father had removed some of the coupons and given them to the son and given the rest of the coupons and the bond itself (that is, the claim to the terminal payment at maturity) to his daughter? Who would be taxed on what? (d) Suppose that the father had cut off all the coupons and given them to the son and had at the same time given the bond itself to his daughter; suppose, too, that thereafter the son had given all the coupons to his son (the grandson). Now who is taxed on the interest: son, daughter, or grandson? Should it matter whether the coupons are called "property" or "an equitable interest in the corpus of the property"? (e) What *is* the proper rationale for *Horst?*

3. Horst, *economic substance, and interest stripping.* Recall that accrual method taxpayers take income into account as it is earned, regardless of when it is received. If Horst senior had been on the accrual method of accounting, he would have included interest income in respect of the bond every day. The gift of the coupon just before its collection date would not have had any income tax

significance at all (although it would of course be a gift for gift tax purposes), because all the income would already have been accounted for. Under this scenario, the receipt of the coupon payment would simply have been a nontaxable receipt of cash attributable to previously taxed income. This approach arguably would have better reflected economic reality. Here the father as bondholder (lender) earned the interest by holding the bond for a period of time, over which interest income accrued, in an amount corresponding to the coupon payment (less a few days). On this view, the outcome of *Horst* is correct (i.e., Horst senior is taxed) but for the wrong reasons. The Court's reliance on the fruit/tree metaphor only obscures matters: The reason the donor properly should be taxed on the interest coupon is not that the coupon represents "income" while the "corpus" (the promise to repay principal at maturity) constituted property, but rather that interest is simply compensation for the use of another's money for a period of time. In other words, the result of the case simply corrected a distortion introduced by the cash method of accounting. If the case reached the right result, why should we care that its reasoning was unsophisticated? The reason is that the false equation of "coupons" with income led to many tax shelters, in the form of "interest stripping" transactions. For example, a taxpayer might buy a bond for $1,000, strip all the negotiable coupons representing future interest payments from the bond, retain the coupons, and finally sell the "naked corpus" for, say, $700. The naked corpus by itself simply represented a promise to pay a fixed lump sum at some future date; in other words, it was a zero coupon bond bearing original issue discount in economic substance, and by itself could not be worth as much as the bond with coupons attached. The taxpayer then would claim a loss deduction of $300, on the premise that only the naked corpus was property, and therefore the entire original $1,000 investment was the basis of the naked corpus. The same point could be made about each negotiable coupon: As a standalone instrument each constituted a mini-zero coupon bond. Congress eventually adopted just this reasoning in 1982, by enacting §1286. That provision treats interest stripping as the occasion to apportion the taxpayer's original investment (basis) among all the stripped coupons and corpus, based on their respective values as mini-zero coupon bonds, and then requires taxpayers to accrue income under the original issue discount rules. For a more complete description, with examples, see Peter Canellos and Edward Kleinbard, *The Miracle of Compound Interest: Interest Deferral and Discount After 1982*, 38 Tax L. Rev. 4 (1983).

4. *Unrealized appreciation.* Can the result in *Horst* be reconciled with the rule reflected in §1015, that the donee, rather than the donor, is taxed on the unrealized gain on property transferred by gift?

E.   SERVICES TRANSFORMED INTO PROPERTY

Consider what you've learned so far from the foregoing materials. Lucas v. Earl indicates that income from the provision of personal services should generally be taxed to the person who provided those services. In the previous section, we saw that income from property is generally taxed to the owner of that property. The obvious next question may have already occurred to you: What happens when one person's services result in the creation of property that is then transferred to another person? The following two cases speak to this issue.

HELVERING v. EUBANK
311 U.S. 122 (1940)

Mr. Justice STONE delivered the opinion of the Court.

This is a companion case to Helvering v. Horst, and presents issues not distinguishable from those in that case.

Respondent, a general life insurance agent, after the termination of his agency contracts and services as agent, made assignments in 1924 and 1928 respectively of renewal commissions to become payable to him for services which had been rendered in writing policies of insurance under two of his agency contracts.[6] The Commissioner assessed the renewal commissions paid by the companies to the assignees in 1933 as income taxable to the assignor in that year under [§61].

No purpose of the assignments appears other than to confer on the assignees the power to collect the commissions, which they did in the taxable year. The Government and respondent have briefed and argued the case here on the assumption that the assignments were voluntary transfers to the assignees of the right to collect the commissions as and when they became payable, and the record affords no basis for any other.

For the reasons stated at length in the opinion in the *Horst* case, we hold that the commissions were taxable as income of the assignor in the year when paid. The judgment below is reversed.

The separate opinion of Mr. Justice MCREYNOLDS. . . .
The court below declared—

In the case at bar the petitioner owned a right to receive money for past services; no further services were required. Such a right is assignable. At the time of assignment there was nothing contingent in the petitioner's right, although the amount collectible in future years was still uncertain and contingent. But this may be equally true where the assignment transfers a right to income from investments, as in Blair v. Commissioner and Horst v. Commissioner, 107 F.2d 906 (C.C.A. 2), or a right to patent royalties, as in Nelson v. Ferguson, 56 F.2d 121 (C.C.A. 3), certiorari denied, 286 U.S. 565. By an assignment of future earnings a taxpayer may not escape taxation upon his compensation in the year when he

---

6. [The commissions were assigned to a corporate trustee. The opinion of the Supreme Court and of the lower courts and the record before the Supreme Court all fail to reveal the purposes of the trust or the relationship of the beneficiaries to Mr. Eubank. The record (at page 6) does, however, establish that the assignment was gratuitous. For purposes of analysis, it seems reasonable to treat the case as if the assignee had been Mr. Eubank's wife or children. —EDS.]

earns it. But when a taxpayer who makes his income tax return on a cash basis assigns a right to money payable in the future for work already performed, we believe that he transfers a property right, and the money, when received by the assignee, is not income taxable to the assignor.

Accordingly, the Board of Tax Appeals was reversed; and this, I think, is in accord with the statute and our opinions.

The assignment in question denuded the assignor of all right to commissions thereafter to accrue under the contract with the insurance company. He could do nothing further in respect of them; they were entirely beyond his control. In no proper sense were they something either earned or received by him during the taxable year. The right to collect became the absolute property of the assignee without relation to future action by the assignor.

A mere right to collect future payments, for services already performed, is not presently taxable as "income derived" from such services. It is property which may be assigned. Whatever the assignor receives as consideration may be his income; but the statute does not undertake to impose liability upon him because of payments to another under a contract which he had transferred in good faith, under circumstances like those here disclosed. . . .

The general principles approved in Blair v. Commissioner, . . . are controlling and call for affirmation of the judgment under review.

THE CHIEF JUSTICE and Mr. Justice ROBERTS concur in this opinion.

HEIM v. FITZPATRICK
262 F.2d 887 (2d Cir. 1959)

Before SWAN and MOORE, Circuit Judges, and KAUFMAN, District Judge.
SWAN, Circuit Judge.

This litigation involves income taxes of Lewis R. Heim, for the years 1943 through 1946. On audit of the taxpayer's returns, the Commissioner of Internal Revenue determined that his taxable income in each of said years should be increased by adding thereto patent royalty payments received by his wife, his son and his daughter. . . .

Plaintiff was the inventor of a new type of rod end and spherical bearing. In September 1942 he applied for a patent thereon. On November 5, 1942 he applied for a further patent on improvements of his original invention. Thereafter on November 17, 1942 he executed a formal written assignment of his invention and of the patents which might be issued for it and for improvements thereof to The Heim Company.[7] This was duly recorded in the Patent Office and in January 1945 and May 1946 plaintiff's patent applications were acted on favorably and patents thereon were issued to the Company. The assignment to the Company was made pursuant to an oral agreement, subsequently

---

7. The stock of The Heim Company was owned as follows: plaintiff 1%, his wife 41%, his son and daughter 27% each, and his daughter-in-law and son-in-law 2% each.

reduced to a writing dated July 29, 1943, by which it was agreed (1) that the Company need pay no royalties on bearings manufactured by it prior to July 1, 1943; (2) that after that date the Company would pay specified royalties on 12 types of bearings; (3) that on new types of bearings it would pay royalties to be agreed upon prior to their manufacture; (4) that if the royalties for any two consecutive months or for any one year should fall below stated amounts, plaintiff at his option might cancel the agreement and thereupon all rights granted by him under the agreement and under any and all assigned patents should revert to him, his heirs and assigns; and (5) that this agreement is not transferable by the Company.

In August 1943 plaintiff assigned to his wife "an undivided interest of 25 per cent [sic] in said agreement with The Heim Company dated July 29, 1943, and in all his inventions and patent rights, past and future, referred to therein and in all rights and benefits of the First Party [plaintiff] thereunder. . . ." A similar assignment was given to his son and another to his daughter. Plaintiff paid gift taxes on the assignments. The Company was notified of them and thereafter it made all royalty payments accordingly. As additional types of bearings were put into production from time to time the royalties on them were fixed by agreement between the Company and the plaintiff and his three assignees. . . .

The appellant contends that the assignments to his wife and children transferred to them income-producing property and consequently the royalty payments were taxable to his donees, as held in Blair v. Commissioner. Judge Anderson, however, was of opinion that [151 F. Supp. 576]: "The income-producing property, i.e., the patents, had been assigned by the taxpayer to the corporation. What he had left was a right to a portion of the income which the patents produced. He had the power to dispose of and divert the stream of this income as he saw fit." Consequently he ruled that the principles applied by the Supreme Court in Helvering v. Horst, and Helvering v. Eubank, required all the royalty payments to be treated as income of plaintiff. . . .

In the present case more than a bare right to receive future royalties was assigned by plaintiff to his donees. Under the terms of his contract with The Heim Company he retained the power to bargain for the fixing of royalties on new types of bearings, i.e., bearings other than the 12 products on which royalties were specified. This power was assigned and the assignees exercised it as to new products. Plaintiff also retained a reversionary interest in his invention and patents by reason of his option to cancel the agreement if certain conditions were not fulfilled. This interest was also assigned. The fact that the option was not exercised in 1945, when it could have been, is irrelevant so far as concerns the existence of the reversionary interest. We think that the rights retained by plaintiff and assigned to his wife and children were sufficiently substantial to justify the view that they were given income-producing property.

In addition to Judge Anderson's ground of decision appellee advances a further argument in support of the judgment, namely, that the plaintiff retained sufficient control over the invention and the royalties to make it reasonable to treat him as owner of that income for tax purposes. Commissioner v. Sunnen, 333 U.S. 591, is relied upon. There a patent was licensed under a royalty contract with a corporation in which the taxpayer-inventor held 89% of the stock. An assignment of the royalty contract to the taxpayer's wife was held ineffective to shift the tax, since the taxpayer retained control over the royalty payments to his wife by virtue of his control of the corporation, which could cancel the contract at any time. The argument is that, although plaintiff himself owned only 1% of The Heim Company stock, his wife and daughter together owned 68% and it is reasonable to infer from depositions introduced by the Commissioner that they would follow the plaintiff's advice. Judge Anderson did not find it necessary to pass on this contention. But we are satisfied that the record would not support a finding that plaintiff controlled the corporation whose active heads were the son and son-in-law. No inference can reasonably be drawn that the daughter would be likely to follow her father's advice rather than her husband's or brother's with respect to action by the corporation. . . .

For the foregoing reasons we hold that the judgment should be reversed and the cause remanded with directions to grant plaintiff's motion for summary judgment.

So ordered.

NOTES AND QUESTIONS

1. *Analysis.* (a) In *Eubank*, the majority relied on *Horst*. Was there a better case to rely on? The dissent relied on *Blair*. As between *Blair* and *Horst*, which seems more in point?

(b) In *Heim*, the lower court relied on *Horst* and *Eubank*. Again, was there a better case?

(c) In Commissioner v. Olmsted Incorporated Life Agency, 304 F.2d 16 (8th Cir. 1962) the taxpayer surrendered rights to renewal commissions in return for an annuity of $500 per month for fifteen years. The court rejected the Commissioner's argument that the exchange should have been treated as a taxable disposition. It relied heavily on Commissioner v. Oates, 207 F.2d 711 (7th Cir. 1953). In that case the taxpayer had been entitled to renewal commissions and exchanged that right for a right to payments extending over a longer period of time than the expected duration of the renewal commissions. The Commissioner in *Oates* relied in part on Lucas v. Earl, on Helvering v. Horst, and on *Eubank*. The court distinguished those cases by observing that in each of them the "taxpayer had effectually received the income" in that "by assigning it, he took dominion over it, converted it to his own use and treated it as a property right, thus realizing its full economic benefit." What was the economic benefit in *Earl*, in *Horst*, and in *Eubank*? Why was there no similar economic benefit in *Blair* or in *Heim*?

2. *The pattern.* (a) *A*, an engineer who spends all her time working for herself on ideas for inventions, creates and patents an invention, then gives (assigns) the patent to her son, who licenses it and receives royalties. As is clear from *Heim*, the son, not the mother, is taxable on the royalties.

(b) *B*, an investor, buys a patent from the inventor and gives the patent to her son, who licenses it and receives the royalties. Plainly, the son, not the mother, is taxable on the royalties.

(c) *C*, a lawyer, assists *N*, an inventor, in obtaining financing for *N*'s invention, which *N* patents. *N* licenses the patent to *X* and, in return for *C*'s services, assigns to *C* a portion of the royalties to be paid by *X. C* then assigns her rights to the royalties to her son. In a closely analogous case, the Second Circuit, relying on *Earl* and *Eubank*, and on the fact that the assignor (the *C* counterpart) did not receive any part of the patent itself or any right to control its disposition, held that the royalties were taxable to the assignor. Strauss v. Commissioner, 168 F.2d 441 (2d Cir. 1948), cert. denied, 335 U.S. 858, rehearing denied, 335 U.S. 888 (1948).

(d) *D*, an author, copyrights her book and then assigns the copyright to her son, who licenses it and receives royalties. The royalties are taxable to the son. See Rev. Rul. 54-599, 1954-2 C.B. 52.

(e) Do the outcomes in these hypothetical cases form a consistent pattern? A sensible one?

(f) *F*, an architect, agrees with a client to design a building but refuses to set a price for the job. When the plans are completed, *F* gives them to her son, who sells them to the client for a share of the rents from the building for the next twenty years. Who is taxable on the share of the rents received by the son? When?

3. *The interest element.* In *Eubank*, the commissions received by the assignees were a form of deferred compensation and must have included an element of interest on the amount initially earned. Suppose that immediately after writing a group of policies, Mr. Eubank had assigned the renewal commissions to a person who paid him the full market value of the rights, $1,000. How would Mr. Eubank have been taxed? What about the assignee? What, if anything, does this tell us about how the amounts collected by the assignee in the actual situation in *Eubank* should be taxed? Should the *amount* taxable to Mr. Eubank be the value of the renewal commissions at the time of the assignment? If so, at what *time* should this amount be taxed, and how should the assignee be taxed?

F. SHIFTING INCOME THROUGH LEGAL ENTITIES

Issues regarding the splitting or shifting of income sometimes arise when taxpayers utilize legal entities such as partnerships, limited liability companies (which are generally treated as partnerships for federal income tax purposes), and corporations. These legal entities face very different treatment under the federal income tax. In a nutshell, neither partnerships nor LLCs are treated as separate taxable entities. Rather, a partnership return must be filed for the Treasury's information, reporting all partnership income and deductions, but the firm's net income is taxed to the partners individually, whether withdrawn or not, in accordance with their respective interests. §§701-704. Losses and credits of the firm are similarly allocated among the partners and deducted by them on their individual returns. By contrast, corporations are treated as separate taxable entities. They must pay federal income tax calculated under the corporate tax rate structure. §11. Distributions to shareholders are taxed to the extent of the corporations' earnings and profits.

1. Family Partnerships and S Corporations

Income-splitting issues have arisen most prominently in the case of family partnerships. In a typical arrangement, the head of the family, doing business as an individual proprietor, would make gifts of portions of his business capital to children or other relatives. Then a partnership would be formed with these relatives, usually with the income of the enterprise to be distributed among the partners according to their interests in the firm's capital. Ordinarily, the new partners took no part in the management of the firm, though occasionally they served in clerical or other minor capacities. Sometimes the donor would reserve a salary for his or her own services, to be deducted before the profits accruing to capital were calculated. The highwater mark in this area is Tinkoff v. Commissioner, 120 F.2d 564 (7th Cir. 1941), involving an accountant who took his son into his accounting firm as a partner on the day the boy was born.

In Commissioner v. Culbertson, 337 U.S. 733 (1949), the Supreme Court attempted to resolve the problematic use of family partnerships to shift income by issuing a set of criteria with which to determine whether a partnership "is real within the meaning of the federal revenue laws." These criteria included relationship of the parties, their respective abilities and capital contributions, and the actual control of income. The *Culbertson* criteria produced considerable uncertainty as to the treatment of any given partnership, leading Congress in 1951 to adopt what is now §704(e).

Under §704(e), a partner in a partnership in which capital is a material income-producing factor is free to give some or all of his interest in the partnership to a family member. The family member, not the donor, will be taxed on the income attributable to that interest. Thus, a parent who owns a hotel may give a partnership interest to his or her child, and the child will be taxed on his or her partnership income. This result is consistent with the tax principles discussed earlier in this chapter. As noted above, taxpayers may shift income from property by transferring ownership of the property. The gift of a partnership interest in which capital is a material income-producing factor represents a gift of the underlying capital of the partnership. On the other hand, suppose a parent gives his or her newborn infant an interest in his or her law partnership in the hope of shifting the income from that partnership. The attempt will fail because capital is not a material income-producing factor in a law partnership. Here it is income from services, rather than property, that the taxpayer is attempting to shift.

Even in cases in which capital is a material income-producing factor, the amount of income shifted is limited by the requirement that the donor receive reasonable compensation for services rendered to the partnership. The statute and accompanying regulations also contain rules designed to ensure that a partner is able to shift partnership income only by making an actual transfer of the partnership interest that is the source of that income. An individual may not, for example, retain voting rights or other indicia of ownership with respect to a partnership interest and succeed in shifting income from that interest through a putative transfer of the interest to a low-bracket family member.

Taxpayers sometimes conduct business affairs through so-called S corporations; that is, corporations governed by Subchapter S of the Code.

S corporations, like partnerships, report income but do not pay tax. Instead, S corporation income, like partnership income, is taxed directly to the entity owners—here, the shareholders. The rules governing family S corporations are similar to those governing family partnerships. Section 1366 requires each family member to receive reasonable compensation for services rendered, and thus prevents a high-bracket family member from using an S corporation to shift personal service income.

2. Income Splitting Through Corporations

If one concentrates on economic substance rather than on legal forms, it is hard to see why efforts to shift income to children or other dependents by use of ordinary corporations should be dealt with differently from similar efforts involving partnerships or S corporations. But the intellectual tradition of treating corporations as separate entities has exerted a strong influence on tax law. Moreover, a taxpayer who uses the ordinary corporation as a vehicle for shifting income must pay a price: a tax at the corporate level.

For example, suppose that a person operates in corporate form a business that generates a net income of $250,000 per year, $200,000 of which is attributable to her services; gives 40 percent of the shares of stock of the corporation to her children, retaining the other 60 percent; and takes no compensation for her services. In effect, $80,000 worth of income from the performance of services (40 percent of $200,000) is diverted to the children, in apparent violation of the principle of Lucas v. Earl that income from the performance of services must be taxed to the one who earns it. The income ultimately realized by the children may take the form of dividends and at a highly conceptual level one might argue that their income is from "property" (the shares of common stock that they own) rather than from services. This ignores the underlying economic reality, but in the case of ordinary corporations the reality is likely to be ignored; the income is not likely to be attributed to the parent. As suggested, however, the price of achieving the shift in income in our example is a corporation income tax, not just on the $80,000 diverted to the children but on the entire $250,000, plus the individual income tax on dividends paid by the corporation from the amount of corporate earnings left after the corporation income tax. The corporate-level tax can be reduced by paying a deductible salary to the parent, but to that extent the objective of shifting income is defeated.

Notwithstanding the presence of the corporate income tax, individuals sometimes attempt to shift income through corporations and then to family members. A corporation might have an unusable net operating loss and thus not face any corporate tax liability. In the past, corporate rates were sometimes significantly below individual rates, so that an advantage to income shifting remained even after the payment of the corporate income tax. In recent years, the top rate of the corporate income tax has not varied significantly from the top rate of the individual income tax. In 2017, however, Congress reduced the corporate rate from 35 percent to 21 percent, thus potentially reintroducing the incentive to shift income to corporations in some circumstances.

7

EXPENSES OF EARNING INCOME

A. INTRODUCTION

1. Expenses and the Net Income Concept

The first six chapters focused primarily on questions relating to the definition of gross income, including when it arises and to whom it accrues. In this chapter, we will turn our attention to the various deductions allowed in arriving at taxable income.

As you well might imagine, certain deductions are necessary to ensure that what is ultimately taxed is indeed "income" and not something else, like "revenue" or "gross receipts." Thus, suppose that the owner of a grocery store sells $1 million worth of goods, but that, in the course of doing so, she spends (a) $600,000 for the items that were sold to customers, plus (b) $140,000 in salaries to employees, plus (c) $160,000 for on-site rent and utilities. Clearly, her net income is $100,000 (i.e., $1 million minus $600,000 minus $140,000 minus $160,000); this is the same amount that she would have earned had she simply been someone's employee for a $100,000 salary, if we assume for simplicity that, as an employee, she would have incurred no deductible expenses.[1]

Recall that, under an economic definition of income:

$$Y = C + S$$

where Y is income, C is consumption, and S is saving. Only one's net income, after paying the expenses of earning it, is available to be spent on consumption or saving. It is important, therefore, to distinguish between (a) expenses of earning income, which must be deducted in order to measure income accurately, and (b) consumption expenses, which merely reflect how one has spent

---

1. As we will see in Chapter 8, however, employees may potentially incur deductible expenses of earning income.

one's income and therefore should not be deducted if accurate income measurement is the goal. As we will see in Chapter 9, often it is not so easy to distinguish between the two categories, as either a theoretical or a practical matter.

Now recall the Haig-Simons definition of income:

$$Y = C + \Delta W$$

where ΔW denotes change in net worth. This is identical to the immediately prior economic definition, if one defines the amount one has saved as equal to the change in one's net worth. However, the Haig-Simons formulation conveniently brings to mind that, on the deduction side no less than on the gross income inclusion side, important timing questions may need to be addressed. Even taking it as given that a particular expenditure was incurred purely to generate future income, *when* does it reduce one's net worth? Thus, in the above grocery store example, there is a difference between the amount paid for last month's rent—which is now over and done with—and that paid for inventory, such as boxes of pasta and cans of soup, that remain on the shelves, and will thus generate future revenue when and if they are sold.

2.   Deduction Mechanics

While this chapter focuses on expenses of earning income—leaving for Chapter 10 the question of when "personal" deductions may be allowable under the existing federal income tax,[2] even if they concededly are not expenses of earning income—it is useful briefly to consider here the overall structure of an individual's income tax return. It can be depicted as follows:

Gross Income (§61)

minus

Above the Line Deductions (§62(a))

equals

—Adjusted Gross Income (§62)**—**

minus

Below the Line Deductions

(i.e., either the standard deduction, §63(c), or itemized deductions, §63(d))

and

Deduction for Personal Exemptions (§151)

equals

---

2. The 2017 act eliminated personal and dependent exemptions from 2018 through 2025, while nearly doubling the standard deduction during the same period.

Taxable Income (§63)

For the most part, expenses of earning income are allowed as above the line deductions and thus are allowable in determining adjusted gross income (AGI). As we noted in Chapter 1, AGI is a kind of halfway house between gross income and taxable income, reducing gross income by the costs of earning it, as well as by some additional expenses that Congress wished to treat similarly to such costs. As we will see later, however, certain items that are allowed only below the line, as itemized deductions, clearly are, at least in some circumstances, expenses of earning income. The allowance of some such items only below the line reflects a mix of (a) responses to classification ambiguities, (b) accidents of history, (c) tax simplification concerns (since not everyone claims, and thus must keep track of, itemized deductions), and (d) the inevitably chaotic nature of the tax legislative process. To complicate things further, the §199A pass-through deduction added by the 2017 act is, in effect, between the lines (see Section B, *infra*).

When one is filing an actual federal income tax return—Schedule 1040, for individuals—only a few specified deductions, many of which are not, at least unambiguously, expenses of earning income, actually appear on the face of Schedule 1040 itself. Others appear on separate attachments or "schedules" that must also be filed with the return. For example, Schedule C, "Profit or Loss from Business," covers deductions pertaining to business owners who operate sole proprietorships, as distinct from businesses operated in corporate or partnership form. By contrast, itemized deductions appear on Schedule A, capital losses (along with capital gains) appear on Schedule D, Schedule E covers "Supplemental Income and Loss" (such as from rental real estate, royalties, and partnerships), and Schedule F covers one's profit or loss from farming. Often, however, the choice of schedule on which to report a particular item—as distinct from the question of whether it is allowable above or below the line—makes no significant difference regarding the overall amount of one's taxable income.

B.   THE PASS-THROUGH DEDUCTION FOR QUALIFYING BUSINESS INCOME

The 2017 act added a new deduction for 20 percent of the "Qualifying Business Income" (QBI) earned by an individual taxpayer, whether through a trade or business conducted directly by the taxpayer (a sole proprietorship) or as the taxpayer's share of income from a pass-through vehicle (partnership, limited liability company, or S corporation). §199A. A taxpayer need not actively participate in a pass-through business to obtain the benefit of the 20 percent QBI deduction. Thus, if a taxpayer's qualifying income totaled $1 million, and the rule fully applied, the taxpayer would get a $200,000 deduction (unrelated to any actual expense), and include in net income only $800,000. Wages received by an employee cannot under any circumstances qualify as QBI. Investment-type income (dividends, investment interest income, capital gains, gains from commodity, foreign currency, and derivatives transactions) are also disqualified. These are absolute limitations that apply in all cases; in addition, two other important conditional restrictions apply to taxpayers whose income exceeds a specified threshold, as described below. Nonetheless, and despite the fact that they are direct investment substitutes for other less-favored forms of investment, income derived from an investment in a real estate investment trust (REIT) or publicly traded investment partnership (a "master limited partnership," or MLP) always constitute QBI, regardless of the taxpayer's income level. In essence, the QBI deduction can be seen as a 20 percent discount on the marginal tax rates applicable to qualifying income. Thus, for example, if the taxpayer in the above example would otherwise have faced a 37 percent marginal rate on the entire $1 million, increasing the tax-payer's tax liability by $370,000, the 20 percent deduction lowers such liability to $296,000 (i.e., 37 percent of $800,000), and hence the effective marginal tax rate for such income to 29.6 percent.

This provision is commonly called the "pass-through rule," reflecting that many of its beneficiaries earn their income through legal entities, such as partnerships, that are called "pass-throughs" because their income is "passed through" and taxed directly to the owners, rather than at the entity level. As noted, however, the pass-through deduction can also apply to sole proprietors, such as an Uber driver or a consultant (but see below on income caps), provided that they properly are classified as independent contractors. Section 199A imposes two important conditional constraints (described in the next paragraphs) on the amount of a taxpayer's income that can qualify as QBI beyond the two absolute rules that wage and most investment income never qualify. (To repeat, these conditional constraints are not imposed on income derived from REITs or MLPs, so that affluent investors have available to them unlimited new streams of tax-privileged income.)

We describe these two further constraints as "conditional" because neither applies to taxpayers whose total income (from all sources, not just QBI) falls below a threshold amount. For 2018, the threshold was set at $157,500 for single individuals ($315,000 for married taxpayers). Thus, for example, a solo law practitioner, who otherwise would be barred from using the QBI deduction under the first constraint described immediately below, nonetheless would qualify if her total income was below the threshold. These thresholds phase out over the next $100,000 of income above the threshold (married filing joint).

The first constraint on the QBI deduction is that it is not available to (a) "any trade or business involving the performance of services in the fields of health, law, accounting, actuarial science, performing arts, consulting, athletics, financial services, brokerage services, or any trade or business where the principal asset of such trade or business is the reputation or skill of 1 or more of its employees or owners," or (b) involves the performance of services that consist of investing and investment management, trading, or dealing in securities. (To repeat, this is not relevant to taxpayers below the income threshold in respect of their total incomes.) Architects and engineers, displaying a level of lobbying clout that surprised many, are exempt from this constraint, even though engineering and architecture are included in the existing Code provision, §1202(e)(3)(A), from which the above list was otherwise derived verbatim.

The second conditional constraint on the QBI deduction is that the amount of qualifying income cannot exceed the greater of two sums that relate in whole or part to the wages paid by the business. (Again, this is not relevant to taxpayers below the income threshold, or to income derived from REITs or MLPs.) The first sum is 50 percent of the wage base paid by the qualifying business; the second sum, inserted into the law at the last moment, is (a) 25 percent of the wage base paid by the qualifying business plus (b) 2.5 percent per year of the original cost of all tangible property acquired by the business, continuing for the life of most real property investments (forty-year depreciation equals 2.5 percent per year), and for ten years in the case of most personal property acquired by the firm. This alternative measure was widely understood to facilitate the availability of the QBI deduction to real estate developers and real estate investment firms, which typically have very small payrolls compared to the amount they invest. Note that the 2.5 percent of original cost per year includes that portion of any asset acquisition that is debt-financed.

It is difficult to explain the rationale for the QBI deduction, as none comes clearly to mind and Congress offered little by way of explanation. By reason of it, two employees working side by side for the same company, doing the same job, for the same hours and the same money will pay different amounts of tax if one, but not the other, is formally classified as an employee. The QBI deduction was perhaps motivated by a desire to "do something" for "small business" in light of the sharp cut in corporate tax rates. The top QBI tax rate (29.6 percent) is about seven percentage points lower than the sum of the new corporate tax rate and a 20 percent tax on dividends received from a corporation. But there is no strong correlation between small businesses and pass-through businesses, nor is the QBI rule limited to firms below a certain size. Moreover, there is no sound economic reason why independent contractors should be privileged over wage earners; in the modern world it simply is not correct to assert that wage earners have all traded for job security rather than entrepreneurial risk and reward, while independent contractors have taken the opposite side of that bet. More directly, the QBI deduction is available to completely passive investors in pass-through businesses. As applied to REITs and MLPs, the results are particularly paradoxical, because both are publicly traded financial instruments that compete for investors' funds against mutual funds and taxable corporations.

Due to the threshold amount, it may sometimes be the case that law firm associates, but not law firm partners, can benefit from the pass-through deduction—but only if they cease to be classified as "employees" for tax purposes. This might involve their being formally turned into a state law partnership of associates that offers its members' services to the "true" law firm partnership in exchange for specified payments (no longer called salary). The partners in a law firm, meanwhile, may consider each separately incorporating—and then forming a new partnership between all these corporations—since, under the 2017 act, the tax rate for corporations is only 21 percent. Alternatively, or additionally, personal services partnerships might spin off their real estate into a separate partnership that leases back to the professional partnership the premises that it occupies.

C.   CURRENT EXPENSES VERSUS CAPITAL EXPENDITURES

Costs of earning income from a business generally are deductible under §162 of the Internal Revenue Code. This provision can come into conflict not only with §262, which disallows deductions for "personal, family, and living expenses," but also with §263, which disallows deductions for "any amount paid out for new buildings or for permanent improvements or betterments made to increase the value of any property or estate." Here the issue is timing, rather than ultimate allowability, given that the items thus targeted are concededly expenses of earning income. Thus, a company cannot currently deduct the amount that it pays for a new factory. The idea behind disallowing the deduction is that a new factory is more in the nature of an investment than a current expense. Hence, the amount thus paid is "capitalized" under §263, essentially a fancy way of saying that the company keeps track of the amount thus spent, which may become tax-relevant later.

In many cases, costs that must be capitalized under §263 will be "recovered" (i.e., deducted) via some other provision, such as §§167-168 concerning the allowance for depreciation. Thus, unlike §262, the effect of §263 is typically not complete disallowance, but rather a spreading of the cost recovery over a longer period of time or perhaps even postponement until a sale of the asset.

The rationale for capitalization, followed by cost recovery over a multi-year period, can be expressed in terms of the *matching* principle that was discussed in Chapter 4. Thus, recall the example in which Acme Manufacturing would either (1) spend $10,000 to buy a machine that would last for five years, or (2) rent such a machine for $2,000 in each of the same five years. Matching would arise automatically in Case (2), as the rental expense was deducted against the gross income yielded by using the machine. Extending the same treatment to Case (1), by matching the $10,000 outlay against the gross income that it produced over the five-year period, would require capitalization, followed by cost recovery over the period.

1.   Which Expenditures Must Be Capitalized?

Controversies abound regarding which expenditures can be currently deducted and which must be capitalized. For example, suppose that a company spends $1 million not on a factory but on a product, such as an atlas or encyclopedia, with a long useful life. Is the cost deductible? Does it matter whether the product is developed in-house, and the $1 million is paid out as salaries to employees, or whether the developed product is purchased from another company? Consider the following case.

ENCYCLOPAEDIA BRITANNICA v. COMMISSIONER
685 F.2d 212 (7th Cir. 1982)

Posner, Circuit Judge.

Section 162(a) of the Internal Revenue Code allows the deduction of "all the ordinary and necessary expenses paid or incurred during the taxable year in carrying on any trade or business . . . ," but this is qualified (see §161) by section 263(a) of the Code, which forbids the immediate deduction of "capital expenditures" even if they are ordinary and necessary business expenses. We must decide in this case whether certain expenditures made by Encyclopaedia Britannica, Inc. to acquire a manuscript were capital expenditures.

Encyclopaedia Britannica decided to publish a book to be called The Dictionary of Natural Sciences. Ordinarily it would have prepared the book in-house, but being temporarily shorthanded it hired David-Stewart Publishing Company "to do all necessary research work and to prepare, edit and arrange the manuscript and all illustrative and other material for" the book. Under the contract David-Stewart agreed "to work closely with" Encyclopaedia Britannica's editorial board "so that the content and arrangement of the Work (and any revisions thereof) will conform to the idea and desires of [Encyclopaedia Britannica] and be acceptable to it"; but it was contemplated that David-Stewart would turn over a complete manuscript that Encyclopaedia Britannica would copyright, publish, and sell, and in exchange would receive advances against the royalties that Encyclopaedia Britannica expected to earn from the book.

Encyclopaedia Britannica treated these advances as ordinary and necessary business expenses deductible in the years when they were paid, though it had not yet obtained any royalties. The Internal Revenue Service disallowed the deductions and assessed deficiencies. Encyclopaedia Britannica petitioned the Tax Court for a redetermination of its tax liability, and prevailed. The Tax Court held that the expenditures were for "services" rather than for the acquisition of an asset and concluded that therefore they were deductible immediately rather than being, as the Service had ruled, capital expenditures. "The agreement provided for substantial editorial supervision by [Encyclopaedia Britannica]. Indeed, David-Stewart's work product was to be the embodiment of [Encyclopaedia Britannica's] ideas and desires. David-Stewart was just the vehicle selected by [Encyclopaedia Britannica] to assist . . . with the editorial phase of the Work." Encyclopaedia Britannica was "the owner of the Work at all stages of completion" and "the dominating force associated with the Work." The Service petitions for review of the Tax Court's decision pursuant to §7482.

As an original matter we would have no doubt that the payments to David-Stewart were capital expenditures regardless of who was the "dominating force" in the creation of The Dictionary of Natural Sciences. The work was intended to yield Encyclopaedia Britannica income over a period of years. The object of sections 162 and 263 of the Code, read together, is to match up expenditures with the income they generate. Where the income is generated over a period of years the expenditures should be classified as capital, contrary to what the Tax Court did here. From the publisher's standpoint a book is just another rental property; and just as the expenditures in putting a building into shape to be rented must be capitalized, so, logically at least, must the expenditures used to create a book. It would make no difference under this view whether Encyclopaedia Britannica hired David-Stewart as a mere consultant to its editorial board, which is the Tax Court's conception of what happened, or bought outright from David-Stewart the right to a book that David-Stewart had already published. If you hire a carpenter to build a tree house that you plan to rent out, his wage is a capital expenditure to you. See Commissioner of Internal Revenue v. Idaho Power Co., 418 U.S. 1, 13 (1974).[3]

We are not impressed by Encyclopaedia Britannica's efforts to conjure up practical difficulties in matching expenditures on a book to the income from it. What, it asks, would have been the result if it had scrapped a portion of the manuscript it received from David-Stewart? Would that be treated as the partial destruction of a capital asset, entitling it to an immediate deduction? We think not. The proper analogy is to loss or breakage in the construction of our hypothetical tree house. The effect would be to increase the costs of construction, which are deductible over the useful life of the asset. If the scrapped portion of the manuscript was replaced, the analogy would be perfect. If it was not replaced, the tax consequence would be indirect: an increase or decrease in the publisher's taxable income from the published book.

What does give us pause, however, is a series of decisions in which authors of books have been allowed to treat their expenses as ordinary and necessary business expenses that are deductible immediately even though they were incurred in the creation of long-lived assets—the books the authors were writing. The leading case is Faura v. Commissioner, 73 T.C. 849 (1980); it was discussed with approval just recently by a panel of the Tenth Circuit in Snyder v. United States, 674 F.2d 1359, 1365 (10th Cir. 1982), and was relied on heavily by the Tax Court in the present case.

We can think of a practical reason for allowing authors to deduct their expenses immediately, one applicable as well to publishers though not in the circumstances of the present case. If you are in the business of producing a series of assets that will yield income over a period of years—which is the situation of most authors and all publishers—identifying particular expenditures with particular books, a necessary step for proper capitalization because the useful lives of the books will not be the same, may be very difficult, since the expenditures of an author or publisher (more clearly the latter) tend to be joint among several books. Moreover, allocating these expenditures among the different books is not always necessary to produce the temporal matching of income and expenditures that the Code desiderates, because the taxable income of the author or publisher who is in a steady state (that is, whose output is neither increasing nor decreasing) will be at least approximately the same whether his costs are expensed or capitalized. Not the same on any given book—on each book expenses and receipts will be systematically mismatched—but the same on average. Under these conditions the benefits of capitalization are unlikely to exceed the accounting and other administrative costs entailed in capitalization.

Yet we hesitate to endorse the *Faura* line of cases: not only because of the evident tension between them and *Idaho Power, supra,* where the Supreme Court said that expenses, whatever their character, must be capitalized if they are incurred in creating a capital asset, but also because *Faura,* and cases following

---

3. [In *Idaho Power,* the taxpayer claimed current deductions for depreciation on the trucks and other such equipment it used in constructing capital assets such as transmission lines. The Court upheld the Commissioner's disallowance of such deductions, reasoning that the cost of the trucks was simply part of the cost of creating the capital asset itself. — Eds.]

it such as *Snyder,* fail in our view to articulate a persuasive rationale for their result. *Faura* relied on cases holding that the normal expenses of authors and other artists are deductible business expenses rather than nondeductible personal expenses, and on congressional evidence of dissatisfaction with the Internal Revenue Service's insistence that such expenses be capitalized. See 73 T.C. at 852-861. But most of the cases in question (including all those at the court of appeals level), such as Doggett v. Burnett, 65 F.2d 191 (D.C. Cir. 1933), are inapposite, because they consider only whether the author's expenditures are deductible at all—not whether, if they are deductible, they must first be capitalized. . . .

[But] we need not decide whether *Faura* is good law, and we are naturally reluctant to precipitate a conflict with the Tenth Circuit. The Tax Court interpreted *Faura* too broadly in this case. As we interpret *Faura* its principle comes into play only when the taxpayer is in the business of producing a series of assets that yield the taxpayer income over a period of years, so that a complex allocation would be necessary if the taxpayer had to capitalize all his expenses of producing them. This is not such a case. The expenditures at issue are unambiguously identified with The Dictionary of Natural Sciences. We need not consider the proper tax treatment of any other expenses that Encyclopaedia Britannica may have incurred on the project—editorial expenses, for example—as they are not involved in this case. Those expenses would be analogous to author Faura's office and travel expenses; they are the normal, recurrent expenses of operating a business that happens to produce capital assets. This case is like *Idaho Power, supra.* The expenditure there was on transportation equipment used in constructing capital facilities that Idaho Power employed in its business of producing and distributing electricity, and was thus unambiguously identified with specific capital assets, just as Encyclopaedia Britannica's payment to David-Stewart for the manuscript of The Dictionary of Natural Sciences was unambiguously identified with a specific capital asset.

It is also relevant that the commissioning of the manuscript from David-Stewart was somewhat out of the ordinary for Encyclopaedia Britannica. Now the word "ordinary" in section 162 of the Internal Revenue Code has two different uses: To prevent the deduction of certain expenses that are not normally incurred in the type of business in which the taxpayer is engaged ("ordinary" in this sense blends imperceptibly into "necessary"), . . . and to clarify the distinction between expenses that are immediately deductible and expenses that must first be capitalized. . . . (A merging of these two distinct senses of the word is a possible explanation for the result in *Faura.*) Most of the "ordinary," in the sense of recurring, expenses of a business are noncapital in nature and most of its capital expenditures are extraordinary in the sense of nonrecurring. Here, as arguably in *Idaho Power* as well—for Idaho Power's business was the production and distribution of electricity, rather than the construction of buildings—the taxpayer stepped out of its normal method of doing business. In this particular project Encyclopaedia Britannica was operating like a conventional publisher, which obtains a complete manuscript from an author or in this case a compiler. The conventional publisher may make a considerable contribution to the work both at the idea stage and at the editorial stage but the deal is for a manuscript, not for services in assisting the publisher to prepare the manuscript itself. Yet we need not consider whether a conventional publisher should be permitted to deduct royalty advances made to its authors as current operating expenses, merely because those advances are for its recurring business expenses because its business is producing capital assets. *Idaho Power*, though factually distinguishable, implies one answer to this question (no), [and] *Faura* another (yes). . . . But the principle of *Faura*, whatever its soundness, comes into play only when the expenditure sought to be immediately deducted is a normal and recurrent expense of the business, as it was not here. . . .

There is another point to be noted about the distinction between recurring and nonrecurring expenses and its bearing on the issue in this case. If one really takes seriously the concept of a capital expenditure as anything that yields income, actual or imputed, beyond the period (conventionally one year . . .) in which the expenditure is made, the result will be to force the capitalization of virtually every business expense. It is a result courts naturally shy away from. . . . It would require capitalizing every salesman's salary, since his selling activities create goodwill for the company and goodwill is an asset yielding income beyond the year in which the salary expense is incurred. The administrative costs of conceptual rigor are too great. The distinction between recurring and nonrecurring business expenses provides a very crude but perhaps serviceable demarcation between those capital expenditures that can feasibly be capitalized and those that cannot be. Whether the distinction breaks down where, as in the case of the conventional publisher, the firm's entire business is the production of capital assets, so that it is literally true that all of its business expenses are capital in nature, is happily not a question we have to decide here, for it is clear that Encyclopaedia Britannica's payments to David-Stewart were of a nonnormal, nonrecurrent nature.

In light of all that we have said, the contention that really what David-Stewart did here was to render consulting services to Encyclopaedia Britannica no different from the services of a consultant whom Encyclopaedia Britannica might have hired on one of its in-house projects, which if true would make the payments more "ordinary" in the *Faura* sense, is of doubtful relevance. But in any event, if that is what the Tax Court meant when it said that David-Stewart was not the "dominating force," its finding was, we think, clearly erroneous. We deprecate decision by metaphor. If the concept of a dominating force has any relevance to tax law, which we doubt, an attempt should have been made to operationalize it, as by computing the ratio of Encyclopaedia Britannica's in-house expenditures on The Dictionary of Natural Sciences to its payments to David-Stewart. If the ratio was greater than one, then Encyclopaedia Britannica could fairly be regarded as the dominant force in the enterprise. Although this computation was never made, we have no doubt that Encyclopaedia Britannica was dominant in the sense that, as the buyer, it was calling the tune; and it was buying a custom-made product, built to its specifications. But what it was buying was indeed a product, a completed manuscript. This was a turnkey project, remote from what is ordinarily understood by editorial consultation. While maybe some creators or buyers of capital goods—some authors and publishers—may deduct as current expenses what realistically are capital expenditures, they may not do so . . . when the expense is tied to producing or acquiring a specific capital asset.

Encyclopaedia Britannica urges, as an alternative ground for sustaining the Tax Court's decision, that the payments to David-Stewart were immediately deductible as research and experimental expenditures under §174(a). This ground was not considered by the Tax Court, and it would be premature for us to consider it without the benefit of that court's views. The Tax Court can on remand consider it and any other unresolved issues.

Reversed and remanded.

NOTES AND QUESTIONS

1. *True reflection of income.* As the court in *Encyclopaedia Britannica* observes, "The object of sections 162 and 263 of the Code, read together, is to match up expenditures with the income they generate." This objective, though often ignored both by Congress and by the courts in shaping the rules of tax accounting, is consistent with the basic goal of sound accrual accounting principles, which is to provide a true reflection of income. To appreciate the importance of the point, imagine that the contract in the *Encyclopaedia Britannica* case had represented a large part of the total operations of Encyclopaedia Britannica for the year at issue. If the entire cost of the contract had been treated as an expense of the year in which the payment was made, the result could well have been a huge loss for that year. Surely it would be misleading for the managers or the shareholders of the company to conclude that in fact they had a very bad year and that drastic changes might be required. The amounts spent are obviously the price of acquiring a capital asset, not money down the drain. It seems quite likely, therefore, that for the purposes of making investment decisions and of reporting to shareholders (assuming the item was significant), the outlay was not treated as an offset to current income.

Corporate scandals in the early 2000s help to illustrate, from the financial accounting side, the importance of the distinction between expensing and capitalization. In June 2002, WorldCom, a leading telecommunications company with more than 20 million customers and $100 billion of assets, disclosed that, for accounting purposes, it had improperly capitalized nearly $4 billion of expenditures that ought to have been expensed, thereby inflating its reported earnings. The market reaction was so intense that, within a month, WorldCom was forced to file for bankruptcy.

2. *Capitalization of inventory, construction, and development costs.* The court in *Encyclopaedia Britannica* states that "if you hire a carpenter to build a tree house that you plan to rent out, his wage is a capital expenditure to you." The court cites Commissioner v. Idaho Power Co., 418 U.S. 1 (1974), which is described in footnote 3, *supra*. The principle underlying the court's tree-house metaphor, and *Idaho Power,* is now generalized in §263A, which was adopted in 1986 and is described in further detail below.

3. *Depreciation and amortization.* When an outlay is treated as the cost of acquiring a capital asset, traditional accounting principles require that that cost be recovered over the useful life of the asset—that is, over the time

in which the asset is expected to contribute to the production of the firm's income. In the case of an intangible asset like a copyright for a book, the label given to the annual deductions is "amortization." In the case of a tangible asset like a factory building or a truck, the deduction has traditionally been called "depreciation." See §167. Under the present Code, the deduction is called "ACRS" (accelerated cost recovery system). See §168, which is discussed later in this chapter. Under ACRS, the time over which deductions are claimed in some cases is shorter than the expected useful lives of the assets. This favorable tax treatment may be the result of a conscious decision to use the tax system to encourage investments in plant and equipment.

4. *Scrapping part of the manuscript.* If a taxpayer buys four trucks in a single transaction, the cost is allocated among them. If one is destroyed in a fire, the cost of that truck is deductible as a loss under §165(a). On the other hand, if Encyclopaedia Britannica had scrapped a portion of the manuscript that it had acquired, presumably, as the court suggests, there would be no loss deduction. The amount paid for the original manuscript would be treated as the cost of what was ultimately used. What if a publisher commissions the preparation of a set of four books and ultimately decides to sell only three of them?

5. *Cash method versus accrual method of accounting.* Note that §263 applies to both cash method and accrual method taxpayers. Thus, it is irrelevant that individual authors are likely to use the cash method, while Encyclopaedia Britannica no doubt used the accrual method.

6. *The value of deferral.* In distinguishing the *Faura* case, the court in *Encyclopaedia Britannica* observes that "the taxable income of the author or publisher who is in a steady state . . . will be at least approximately the same whether his costs are expensed or capitalized." This is true only in the long run. Imagine an author, with income from other sources, who begins to write books in 2011 and to receive royalties in 2012. Suppose he is allowed to begin deducting research expenses in 2011, rather than in 2012, and continues this practice until he retires forty years later. He will have the advantage of deferral to the extent of one year's deductions not just for one year but for forty. That is, he will reduce his income in 2011 and the effects will not catch up with him until forty years later. To put that still another way, he has the advantage of a premature deduction of expense attributable to the next year's income not just in the first year (2011) but in every year until retirement. What is the relative burden of a tax paid now as compared with one paid forty years from now? What does this tell you about the significance of the *Encyclopaedia Britannica* decision?

7. *Economic consequences.* How do you suppose the holding in *Encyclopaedia Britannica* affected the decisions of firms like Encyclopaedia Britannica about contracting out manuscript-preparation work to other firms? Was that a sensible economic outcome?

8. *Research and development expenses.* Before the 2017 act, one important exception to the requirement of capitalization of expenditures expected to produce revenues in future years was §174, covering research and development (R&D) expenditures. Taxpayers used to have the option to deduct R&D expenditures when paid or incurred. The 2017 act eliminated the exception by requiring taxpayers, starting in 2022, to amortize R&D expenditures over

a period of five years (for domestic R&D) or fifteen years (for foreign R&D). R&D expenditures must continue to be amortized over the remainder of the period even if the research project is retired or abandoned. The 2017 act also specifies that software development expenses are R&D expenditures.

9. *Exceptions to the requirement of capitalization.* One exception that still exists is the rule permitting current deductions for "marketing, selling, advertising, and distribution costs." Reg. §1.263A-1(e)(3)(iii)(A). Advertising may in some cases aim primarily at increasing current sales, but in other cases it may mainly serve to enhance the advertiser's general goodwill so as to increase its expected future income.

10. *Prepaid expenses.* In Commissioner v. Boylston Market Association, 131 F.2d 966 (1st Cir. 1942), a cash basis taxpayer was required to capitalize prepaid insurance premiums covering a three-year period. The court cited similar results in cases involving prepaid rent, bonuses for the acquisition of leases, and commissions for negotiating leases. Under §461(g), a taxpayer must capitalize most forms of prepaid interest. Note, however, the special treatment of "points" in §461(g)(2).

2.   The Uniform Capitalization Rules of §263A

Before 1986, the rules governing capitalization of costs incurred in creating inventory or other long-lived assets produced by the taxpayer were inconsistent. This inconsistency is apparent on a careful reading of the *Encyclopaedia Britannica* case. In that case, the court held that the cost of purchasing a completed manuscript from an unrelated company must be capitalized and amortized against sales. The court noted, however, that the in-house costs of producing such a manuscript would be currently deductible. One reason why in-house publishing expenses have in the past been deductible is administrative. An in-house employee's time may be spent on many different projects. Allocating that time among projects may be quite difficult. As the court in *Encyclopaedia Britannica* concluded, "[t]he administrative costs of conceptual rigor are too great." (Note, however, that allocation of costs may be vital to making sound business decisions. How can a business person decide whether a project will be or has been profitable without knowing what it cost?)

In 1986, Congress decided that conceptual rigor and, probably more importantly, revenue needs outweighed administrative concerns in this area, and adopted §263A, the uniform capitalization (UNICAP) rules. Under that provision, the costs of producing inventory and other self-created assets, such as the in-house production of a manuscript, must be capitalized. See §263A(b). These costs include not only the salaries of people writing the manuscript, but such indirect expenses as the allocable share of the salaries of supervisory and administrative people.

The UNICAP rules extend to virtually all manufacturers. All the costs of producing the goods to be sold, including such items as the cost of insurance on the manufacturing plant, must be added to the cost of the inventory and deducted at the time the inventory is sold. Reg. §1.263A-1(e). Similar rules apply to large wholesalers and retailers of inventory. For example, the salaries of purchasing agents must be allocated to inventory and recovered at the time the inventory is sold.

Costs incurred by sellers or producers of long-lived assets that do not require capitalization include marketing and advertising costs and costs of general and administrative expenses that do not relate to sale or production. In this latter category are costs of general business planning, costs of shareholder or public relations, and other costs removed from sale or production. Reg. §1.263A-1(e)(4).

As is perhaps evident from the preceding discussion, the rules governing uniform capitalization under §263A are complicated and require many difficult determinations. For example, it will often be unclear whether a particular employee's time is spent on matters that relate to production or to general business planning. Congress has limited the scope of §263A somewhat by excluding from its ambit retailers and wholesalers with annual gross receipts of less than $10 million. §263A(b)(2)(B). Congress has also excluded from §263A costs incurred by freelance writers, artists, and photographers. §263A(h). Other producers and sellers will have to learn to live with the complexity (and conceptual rigor) of UNICAP.

3. The *INDOPCO* Decision and the Capitalization Regulations

Section 263A applies only to real or tangible personal property produced or acquired by the taxpayer or to inventory or property acquired for resale. See §263A(b). After the adoption of §263A, uncertainty and litigation persisted over intangibles that produce long-term benefits. In a landmark decision in 1992, INDOPCO, Inc. v. Commissioner, 503 U.S. 79, the Supreme Court, resolving a conflict among the circuits, held that investment banking fees incident to a merger must be capitalized. Prior case law had left open the possibility that such fees could be currently deducted since they typically did not "create or enhance . . . a separate and distinct additional asset." See Commissioner v. Lincoln Savings & Loan Ass'n, 403 U.S. 345, 354 (1971).

The *INDOPCO* Court rejected the taxpayer's argument that capitalization was required only in instances involving the creation or enhancement of a separate and distinct asset, holding instead that "the realization of benefits beyond the year in which the expenditure is incurred is undeniably important in determining whether the appropriate tax treatment is immediate deduction or capitalization." Since the fees at issue in the case generated a host of long-term benefits for the taxpayer, the Supreme Court concluded that the amounts could not be deductions under §162 as ordinary and necessary business expenses.

The highly general language of the Court in *INDOPCO* left considerable uncertainty, which gave rise to controversy and litigation over tax-accounting practices of widespread and significant impact. The Treasury responded by proposing and ultimately, in 2004, adopting lengthy, detailed regulations under §263 (as distinguished from §263A).

These so-called *INDOPCO* regulations cover a broad range of expenses, including amounts incurred in creating or acquiring various intangibles, such as goodwill, customer lists, covenants not to compete, an assembled workforce, an ownership interest in a corporation or partnership, or a license to practice law. The regulations eschew the approach of stating general principles and concepts; instead, they are replete with highly detailed rules for specific types of expenditures. For example, Reg. §1.263(a)-4(e)(5) (Ex. 8), states that a commercial bank "is not required to capitalize any portion of the compensation paid to the employees in its loan acquisition department or any portion of its overhead allocable to the loan acquisition department." Reg. §1.263(a)-5 covers "amounts paid or incurred to facilitate an acquisition of a trade or business, a change in the capital structure of a business entity, and certain other transactions," such as bankruptcy reorganization costs. Under Reg. §1.167(a)-3, many capitalized expenses are amortizable over a fifteen-year period.

The rules found in the *INDOPCO* regulations are in some respects more favorable to taxpayers than the more stringent rules that might have been imposed under existing precedent, leading one commentator to suggest that a more apt moniker would be the "anti-*INDOPCO* regulations."[4] The Treasury's explanation states that the "regulations strike an appropriate balance between the capitalization provisions of the Code and the ability of taxpayers and IRS personnel to administer the law." T.D. 9107, 68 Fed. Reg. 436, 436-437 (2004). One important general principle is that expenses must be capitalized if they create, or facilitate the creation of, a "separate and distinct intangible": One that has a "measurable value in money's worth" is legally protected and is "capable of being sold, transferred or pledged . . . separate and apart from a trade or business." §1.263(a)-4(b)(3). A de minimis rule (excluding expenses under $5,000) provides an interesting cell-phone example: Where a telecommunications company provides a "free" telephone worth $300 to induce a customer to sign a multi-year contract, the company may deduct the $300 currently under the de minimis rule. In another concession to practicality, expenses for benefits that extend beyond the current year may be deducted currently if they provide benefits that do not extend beyond twelve months. The regulations' detailed rules and extensive examples quite plainly respond to issues raised in the administrative process by particular industries and types of business activity.

The broader lesson of *INDOPCO* and its regulatory aftermath is that administrative practicalities often set the basic parameters for the development of the law. Even if correct on the merits, the Supreme Court's *INDOPCO* decision triggered an avalanche of new legal controversies. According to a GAO study published in 1995, within a few years of the Supreme Court's opinion the *INDOPCO* issue had come to dominate the portfolio of cases involving large corporate taxpayers before the IRS Office of Appeals, accounting "for about 42 percent of the issues they contested" and "$1.1 billion of the total $1.9 billion in proposed adjustments."[5] In some ways, then, the final regulations may be viewed as a white flag of sorts, with the government surrendering its victory in *INDOPCO* for greater certainty in the law and a reduced likelihood of perpetual litigation.

---

4. See Ethan Yale, *The Final INDOPCO Regulations*, Tax Notes (Oct. 25, 2004).

5. Government Accounting Office, *Tax Administration: Recurring Issues in Tax Disputes Over Business Expense Deductions* 2 (Sept. 1995) (available at http://www.gao.gov/archive/1995/gg95232.pdf).

D.   REPAIR AND MAINTENANCE EXPENSES

Another area of frequent controversy concerns the tax treatment of repair and maintenance expenses. As a general rule, taxpayers may take a current deduction for amounts spent on repair and maintenance of property, whereas the cost of improvements to property must typically be capitalized (i.e., added to the basis of the property and recovered through depreciation deductions). This divergent treatment, along with the often fuzzy line between what constitutes a repair and what constitutes an improvement, has spawned decades of litigation. The case that follows illustrates the difficulties involved in resolving these disputes.

MIDLAND EMPIRE PACKING CO. v. COMMISSIONER
14 T.C. 635 (1950), acq., 1950-2 C.B. 3

ARUNDELL, Judge.

The issue in this case is whether an expenditure for a concrete lining in petitioner's basement to oil-proof it against an oil nuisance created by a neighboring refinery is deductible as an ordinary and necessary expense under [§162(a)], on the theory it was an expenditure for a repair, or, in the alternative, whether the expenditure may be treated as the measure of the loss sustained during the taxable year and not compensated for by insurance or otherwise within the meaning of [§165(a)].

The respondent has contended, in part, that the expenditure is for a capital improvement and should be recovered through depreciation charges and is, therefore, not deductible as an ordinary and necessary business expense or as a loss.

[Reg. §1.162-4] is helpful in distinguishing between an expenditure to be classed as a repair and one to be treated as a capital outlay. In Illinois Merchants Trust Co., Executor, 4 B.T.A. 103, at p.106, we discussed this subject in some detail and in our opinion said:

> It will be noted that the first sentence of the article [now Reg. §1.162-4] relates to repairs, while the second sentence deals in effect with replacements. . . . To repair is to restore to a sound state or to mend, while a replacement connotes a substitution. A repair is an expenditure for the purpose of keeping the property in an ordinarily efficient operating condition. It does not add to the value of the property, nor does it appreciably prolong its life. It merely keeps the property in an operating condition over its probable useful life for the uses for which it was acquired. Expenditures for that purpose are distinguishable from those for replacements, alterations, improvements, or additions which prolong the life of the property, increase its value, or make it adaptable to a different use. The one is a maintenance charge, while the others are additions to capital investment which should not be applied against current earnings.

It will be seen from our findings of fact that for some 25 years prior to the taxable year petitioner had used the basement rooms of its plant as a place for the curing of hams and bacon and for the storage of meat and hides. The basement had been entirely satisfactory for this purpose over the entire period in spite of the fact that there was some seepage of water into the rooms from time to time. In the taxable year it was found that not only water, but oil, was seeping through the concrete walls of the basement of the packing plant and, while the water would soon drain out, the oil would not, and there was left on the basement floor a thick scum of oil which gave off a strong odor that permeated the air of the entire plant, and the fumes from the oil created a fire hazard. It appears that the oil which came from a nearby refinery had also gotten into the water wells which served to furnish water for petitioner's plant, and as a result of this whole condition the Federal meat inspectors advised petitioner that it must discontinue the use of the water from the wells and oil-proof the basement, or else shut down its plant.

To meet this situation, petitioner during the taxable year undertook steps to oil-proof the basement by adding a concrete lining to the walls from the floor to a height of about four feet and also added concrete to the floor of the basement. It is the cost of this work which it seeks to deduct as a repair. The basement was not enlarged by this work, nor did the oil-proofing serve to make it more desirable for the purpose for which it had been used through the years prior to the time that the oil nuisance had occurred. The evidence is that the expenditure did not add to the value or prolong the expected life of the property over what they were before the event occurred which made the repairs necessary. It is true that after the work was done the seepage of water, as well as oil, was stopped, but, as already stated, the presence of the water had never been found objectionable. The repairs merely served to keep the property in an operating condition over its probable useful life for the purpose for which it was used.

While it is conceded on brief that the expenditure was "necessary," respondent contends that the encroachment of the oil nuisance on petitioner's property was not an "ordinary" expense in petitioner's particular business. But the fact that petitioner had not theretofore been called upon to make a similar expenditure to prevent damage and disaster to its property does not remove that expense from the classification of "ordinary" for, as stated in Welch v. Helvering, *infra:*

> ordinary in this context does not mean that the payments must be habitual or normal in the sense that the same taxpayer will have to make them often. . . . [T]he expense is an ordinary one because we know from experience that payments for such a purpose, whether the amount is large or small, are the common and accepted means of defense against attack. . . . The situation is unique in the life of the individual affected, but not in the life of the group, the community, of which he is a part.

Steps to protect a business building from the seepage of oil from a nearby refinery, which had been erected long subsequent to the time petitioner started to operate its plant, would seem to us to be a normal thing to do. . . .

In *American Bemberg Corporation*, 10 T.C. 361, we allowed as deductions, on the ground that they were ordinary and necessary expenses, extensive expenditures made to prevent disaster, although the repairs were of a type which had never been needed before and were unlikely to recur. In that case the taxpayer, to stop cave-ins of soil which were threatening destruction of its manufacturing plant, hired an engineering firm which drilled to the bedrock and injected grout to fill the cavities where practicable. . . . We found that the cost [of the drilling and grouting] did not make good the depreciation previously allowed, and stated in our opinion:

> [T]he . . . program was intended to avert a plant-wide disaster and avoid forced abandonment of the plant. The purpose was not to improve, better, extend or increase the original plant, nor to prolong its original useful life. Its continued operation was endangered; the purpose of the expenditures was to enable petitioner to continue the plant in operation not on any new or better scale, but on the same scale and, so far as possible, as efficiently as it had operated before.

The petitioner here made the repairs in question in order that it might continue to operate its plant. Not only was there danger of fire from the oil and fumes, but the presence of the oil led the Federal meat inspectors to declare the basement an unsuitable place for the purpose for which it had been used for a quarter of a century. After the expenditures were made, the plant did not operate on a changed or larger scale, nor was it thereafter suitable for new or additional uses. The expenditure served only to permit petitioner to continue the use of the plant, and particularly the basement for its normal operations.

In our opinion, the expenditure of $4,868.81 for lining the basement walls and floor was essentially a repair and, as such, it is deductible as an ordinary and necessary business expense. This holding makes unnecessary a consideration of petitioner's alternative contention that the expenditure is deductible as a business loss. . . .

NOTES AND QUESTIONS

1. *The Treasury Department's new "repair regulations."* Under Treasury regulations that took effect in January 2012, "a taxpayer may deduct amounts paid for repairs and maintenance to tangible property if the amounts paid are not otherwise required to be capitalized." Treas. Reg. §1.162-4T. This rule, along with 68 pages of additional detail, replaces regulations that had governed the federal income tax treatment of repairs for over half a century.[6] Although the Treasury Decision incorporating the new rules indicates a desire to clarify legal standards and provide certain bright-line tests for applying those standards, some commentators have expressed concern that the new rules may be difficult to comply with in practice. Such reactions are not uncommon upon the issuance of new regulations, especially among practitioners tasked with deciphering the new rules for anxious clients.

---

6. T.D. 9564, Department of the Treasury, Internal Revenue Service (December 27, 2011). The new rules, which were issued as both temporary and proposed regulations, replace proposed regulations issued in 2008.

The new regulations specify a two-step inquiry with regard to repair and maintenance expenses. First, the taxpayer must determine the "unit of property" to which an expense relates. As a general rule, a unit of property will be either (i) a building, or (ii) real and personal property other than buildings. Determining whether multiple items should constitute separate units or property or a single unit of property requires an assessment of the functional interdependence of those items in the taxpayer's trade or business, which turns on whether the items could only be placed in service together. For example, a printer and computer are separate units of property because placing either item in service is not dependent on the other item being in service, while a locomotive consisting of several components (e.g., engine, generators, batteries) is considered a single unit of property.

Identifying the unit of property to which an expense relates is relevant because of the second part of the inquiry: i.e., determining whether the expense results in a "betterment" to the unit of property, a "restoration," or an "adaptation to new or different use." The regulations are clear that expenses having any of these effects must be capitalized, though uncertainty persists regarding how to determine whether an expense has had the specified effect. For example, the regulations indicate that when determining "whether an amount paid results in a betterment . . . it is appropriate to consider all the facts and circumstances including, but not limited to, the purposes of the expenditure, the physical nature of the work performed, the effect of the expenditure on the unit of property, and the taxpayer's treatment of the expenditure on its applicable financial statement." Treas. Reg. §1.263(a)-3T(h)(3). Likewise, determining whether a "restoration" has occurred turns on numerous factors, including, inter alia, whether the expense "returns the unit of property to its ordinarily efficient operating condition if the property has deteriorated to a state of disrepair and is no longer functional for its intended use." Treas. Reg. §1.263-3T(i)(1)(iv).

2. *Midland Empire and the 2011 repair regulations.* The regulations just described incorporate an example based on the facts of *Midland Empire.* Treas. Reg. §1.263-3T(h)(4) (Ex. 12). The regulations indicate that "the event necessitating the expenditure was the seepage of the oil" and conclude that the taxpayer "is not required to treat the expenditure as a betterment . . . because it does not result in a material addition or material increase in capacity, productivity, efficiency, strength or quality of the building structure or its output compared to the condition of the structure prior to the seepage." *Id.* This reasoning is consistent with the rationale for current deductibility offered by the Court. Oftentimes a taxpayer needing to repair property is faced with a choice regarding how to repair the item. For example, consider an owner of a small retail shop that suffers damage during a storm. Faced with the decision of replacing wooden shingles displaced by the storm, the owner could (a) purchase wooden shingles identical to those damaged by the storm, (b) purchase asphalt shingles comparable to the wooden shingles damaged by the storm, or (c) purchase shingles made of lightweight composite materials that are maintenance-free, do not absorb moisture, and come with a fifty-year warranty and a Class A fire rating. Under which circumstances is the expense

for replacement shingles deductible as a repair versus required to be capitalized? See Treas. Reg. §1.263-3T(h)(4) (Ex. 13-15).

3. *Repairs and losses.* (a) An interesting aspect of the *Midland Empire* opinion is its reference at the beginning and end to the possible alternative of a deduction for a loss, which would be claimed under §165(a). A problem with deductions for losses is that they must be "realized." There must be some identifiable event that justifies a current accounting. A decline in value due to wear and tear, to changes in the economic environment, or to other circumstances does not give rise to a loss deduction; such a decline is recognized only through ACRS (formerly, and for nontax purposes, called depreciation) or as a loss when the property is sold. Does the oil-seepage problem confronted by the taxpayer in *Midland Empire* seem to you to justify a loss deduction? If so, what is the best way to measure the amount of the loss? If no loss deduction is available, is a deduction for repair a sensible substitute?

(b) If a deduction for a loss is allowed, a deduction for any repair to restore the property to the pre-loss condition must be denied. See Reg. §1.161-1 ("Double deductions are not permitted").[7] To illustrate this principle, suppose a farmer builds a new barn for $50,000. The cost is a capital expenditure, even for a cash method farmer. See Reg. §1.162-12(a). The basis for the barn is its cost, $50,000. This cost is deducted over time through ACRS. Suppose that in the first year of its existence, the roof of the barn is destroyed by a tornado and is replaced at a cost of $10,000. The farmer has two tax alternatives. One alternative is to claim a deduction for a loss. The amount, quite plainly, would be $10,000. The loss deduction would reduce basis by $10,000, to $40,000. §1016(a)(1). The cost of the replacement, or repair, would not be deducted. It would be treated as a capital cost, increasing basis by $10,000, back to $50,000. §1016(a)(1). The other alternative is to forgo any deduction for a loss and deduct instead the cost of the repair, $10,000, as a current expense. The basis of the barn would not change. Under either alternative we get the same net result: a current deduction of $10,000 and a basis of $50,000, which properly reflects what happened. The 2011 regulations reflect this treatment by requiring capitalization.

(c) But what if the roof wears out over a period of several years, because of shoddy initial construction or because of some unusually harsh weather, or both? Is a loss deduction still available? Should the replacement be treated as a repair or as a capital expenditure? What if the barn had been fully depreciated and thus had a basis of zero?

In Mt. Morris Drive-In Theatre Co. v. Commissioner, 238 F.2d 85 (6th Cir. 1956), a taxpayer, whose actions in clearing land to build a drive-in theater caused substantial increase of water drainage onto an adjacent landowner's property, installed a correction drainage system under threat of litigation. The cost of the drainage system had to be capitalized since the need for it was foreseeable and was part of the process of completing taxpayer's initial investment for its original intended use.

---

7. The same conclusion seems to be supported by §263(a)(2), but Reg. §1.263(a)-1(a)(2) refers only to deductions for "depreciation, amortization, or depletion."

TREATMENT OF ENVIRONMENTAL REMEDIATION EXPENSES UNDER SECTION 263A

Revenue Ruling 2004-18 2004-8 I.R.B. 509

. . .

ISSUE

Are costs incurred to clean up land that a taxpayer contaminated with hazardous waste by the operation of the taxpayer's manufacturing plant includible in inventory costs under §263A of the Internal Revenue Code?

FACTS

X, a corporation using an accrual method of accounting, owns and operates a manufacturing plant that produces property that is inventory in *X*'s hands. *X*'s manufacturing operations discharge hazardous waste. In the past, *X* buried this waste on portions of *X*'s land. The land was not contaminated by hazardous waste when purchased by *X*.

In order to comply with applicable federal, state, and local environmental requirements, *X* incurs costs (within the meaning of §461(h)) to remediate the soil and groundwater that had been contaminated by the hazardous waste, and to establish an appropriate system for the continued monitoring of the groundwater to ensure that the remediation removes all hazardous waste. The costs *X* incurs are not research and experimental expenditures within the meaning of §174 or environmental management policy costs. The soil remediation and groundwater treatment restores *X*'s land to essentially the same physical condition that existed prior to the contamination. During and after the remediation and treatment, *X* continues to use the land and operate the plant in the same manner as *X* did prior to the cleanup except that *X* disposes of any hazardous waste in compliance with environmental requirements.

LAW

Section 263A(a) provides that the direct costs and indirect costs properly allocable to property that is inventory in the hands of the taxpayer shall be included in inventory costs.

Section 1.263A-1(a)(3)(ii) of the Income Tax Regulations provides, in part, that taxpayers that produce tangible personal property must capitalize (1) all direct costs of producing the property, and (2) the property's allocable share of indirect costs.

Section 1.263A-1(e)(3)(i) provides, in part, that indirect costs are properly allocable to property produced when the costs directly benefit or are incurred by reason of the performance of production activities. Cost recovery, production facility repair and maintenance costs, and scrap and spoilage costs, such as waste removal costs, are examples of indirect costs that must be capitalized to the extent the costs are properly allocable to produced property. See §1.263A-1(e)(3)(ii)(I), (O) and (Q).

Section 1.263A-1(e)(4)(iv)(I) provides that costs incurred for environmental management policy generally are not allocated to production or resale activities (except to the extent that the costs of any system or procedure benefit a particular production or resale activity).

. . .

Rev. Rul. 94-38, 1994-1 C.B. 35, analyzes whether costs incurred to clean up land and to treat groundwater that a taxpayer contaminated with hazardous waste from the taxpayer's manufacturing business are capital expenditures. The ruling holds that the costs to clean up land used in the taxpayer's manufacturing process and to treat groundwater are not capital expenditures because these costs do not prolong the useful life of the land or adapt the land to a new or different use. Therefore, costs incurred to clean up land and to treat groundwater that a taxpayer contaminated with hazardous waste from the taxpayer's business are deductible by the taxpayer as business expenses under §162. Costs properly allocable to constructing groundwater treatment facilities, however, are capital expenditures under §263.

Rev. Rul. 98-25, 1998-1 C.B. 998, holds that costs incurred to replace underground storage tanks containing waste by-products under the circumstances in the ruling are not capital expenditures under §263, but are ordinary and necessary expenses under §162.

ANALYSIS

The discussion in Rev. Rul. 94-38 of Plainfield-Union Water Co. v. Commissioner, 39 T.C. 333 (1962), nonacq., 1964-2 C.B. 8, demonstrates that the revenue ruling was intended to address whether the costs to clean up the land and to treat the groundwater are capital expenditures that must be capitalized into the basis of the land under §263(a) or whether the costs are ordinary and necessary repair expenses under §162. Rev. Rul. 94-38 does not address the treatment of these costs as inventory costs under §263A. Similarly, Rev. Rul. 98-25 does not address whether amounts incurred to replace underground storage tanks must be included in inventory costs under §263A.

The holdings of Rev. Rul. 94-38 that the costs to construct a groundwater treatment facility must be capitalized under §§263(a) and 263A rather than deducted under §162 demonstrates the distinction between capital expenditures and costs that are more in the nature of repairs than capital improvements. As with other types of deductible business costs, such as labor costs, taxes, rent, and supplies, once repair costs are determined to be deductible under §162, a taxpayer with inventories must still apply the rules of §263A to determine whether the repair costs must be included in inventory. . . . In addition, if repair costs must be capitalized under §§263(a) and 263A to a depreciable asset, a taxpayer with inventories must still apply the rules of §263A to determine whether the depreciation expenses must be included in inventory. . . .

In this situation, X incurs environmental remediation costs to clean up land that was contaminated as part of the ordinary business operations of X's manufacturing of inventory. X's environmental remediation costs are incurred by reason of X's production activities within the meaning of §1.263A-1(e)(3)(i). The costs are properly allocable to property produced by X that is inventory in X's hands under §1.263A-1(e)(3)(i). Accordingly, X must capitalize the otherwise deductible environmental remediation costs by including the costs in inventory costs in accordance with §1.263A-1(c)(3). Similarly, costs incurred to replace underground storage tanks and depreciation cost recoveries of the groundwater treatment facility must be included in inventory costs to the extent properly allocable to inventory.

HOLDING

Environmental remediation costs are subject to capitalization under §263A. Therefore, costs incurred . . . to clean up land that a taxpayer contaminated with hazardous waste by the operation of the taxpayer's manufacturing plant must be included in inventory costs under §263A. . . .

E.   INVENTORY ACCOUNTING

If a taxpayer buys machinery that will produce income over several years, its costs must be capitalized and depreciated over such period. If a taxpayer buys pencils, stationery, and other supplies, they are usually currently deductible even if some may last beyond the present tax year. But what about goods that the taxpayer sells to the public? What if the owner of a clothing store buys dresses, suits, and other goods during the year, sells some, and has some on hand at the end of the year? Or what if a manufacturer of clothing buys cloth, thread, and other materials, some of which is on hand at the end of the year in its original form and some of which has been embodied in finished product that has not yet been shipped out? Inventory accounting methods are used to match costs with revenues in such cases.

The underlying problem is that the taxpayer may simultaneously be (a) selling goods to the public, and (b) buying (or manufacturing) replacement goods—its inventories. If the inventory items are fungible, it may make little or no practical difference which of them the taxpayer sells to a particular customer. Yet the items may have cost the taxpayer different amounts to buy or manufacture. Thus, individually tracking the items' cost basis would create pointless tax planning or compliance burdens, and/or encourage selling the high-basis (though fungible) items first, simply to reduce current-year taxable income by increasing the amount that could be charged against the sales price as the cost of goods sold.

To mitigate such problems, taxpayers generally must keep track of overall inventory accounts, rather than operating purely on an item-by-item basis. This means, for example, that a retailer does not simply deduct the costs of producing or acquiring inventory during the year. Instead, such costs are treated as capital expenditures that must be added to "inventory." Then, when inventory items are sold, arbitrary conventions are used to determine what should be treated as the cost of goods sold.

To determine which among the fungible items in a taxpayer's inventory should be deemed to have been sold, the general rule is that a first-in-first-out

(FIFO) assumption, or method, applies. This involves assuming that the goods first acquired were sold first, and thus that the items in the closing inventory are those most recently purchased. However, last-in-first-out (LIFO) may be used if the taxpayer so elects under §472. Under this method, the items purchased last are deemed to have been sold first, and closing inventory is thus measured as if it consisted of the earlier-purchased items.

If inventory prices are generally rising over time, LIFO tends to defer reported taxable income, relative to FIFO. However, while this commonly makes it tax-advantageous, publicly traded companies often prefer using FIFO for financial accounting purposes, as this may cause their reported profits to be higher. Section 472(c) provides that taxpayers cannot use LIFO for tax purposes if they are not also using it in reports or statements to shareholders or creditors. In practice, however, taxpayers may be able to use LIFO for tax purposes while calling shareholders' and creditors' attention to both FIFO-based and LIFO-based computations.

PROBLEM

In December 2017, Products Inc. begins business and buys 100,000 widgets for $200,000. It has no sales in 2017. In January 2018, Products Inc. buys another 100,000 widgets for $300,000. In June 2018, Products Inc. sells 100,000 widgets for $350,000. Assume no costs are allocable to the widget inventory under §263A. (a) Assume Products Inc. uses the LIFO method of inventory valuation. What is the cost of the goods sold and the gross profit on the June 2018 sale? (b) What is the answer to the same question if Products Inc. uses FIFO instead of LIFO?

F.   "ORDINARY AND NECESSARY"

In reading the language of §162, one is immediately struck by the use of the words "ordinary and necessary." What is meant by these words? Is the limitation designed to prevent deductions for unusual or needless expenses? Or do these words serve some other function? The following two cases touch on these questions.

1.   Payments for "Goodwill" and Other Assets

WELCH v. HELVERING
290 U.S. 111 (1933)

Mr. Justice CARDOZO delivered the opinion of the Court.

The question to be determined is whether payments by a taxpayer, who is in business as a commission agent, are allowable deductions in the computation of his income if made to the creditors of a bankrupt corporation in an endeavor to strengthen his own standing and credit.

In 1922, petitioner was the secretary of the E. L. Welch Company, a Minnesota corporation, engaged in the grain business. The company was adjudged an involuntary bankrupt, and had a discharge from its debts. Thereafter, the petitioner made a contract with the Kellogg Company to purchase grain for it on a commission. In order to reestablish his relations with customers whom he had known when acting for the Welch Company and to solidify his credit and standing, he decided to pay the debts of the Welch business so far as he was able. In fulfillment of that resolve, he made payments of substantial amounts during five successive years. In 1924, the commissions were $18,000;[8] the payments $4,000; in 1925, the commissions $31,000, the payments $12,000; in 1926, the commissions $21,000, the payments $13,000; in 1927, the commissions $22,000, the payments $7,000; and in 1928, the commissions $26,000, the payments $11,000. The Commissioner ruled that these payments were not deductible from income as ordinary and necessary expenses, but were rather in the nature of capital expenditures, an outlay for the development of reputation and goodwill. . . . [The Tax Court and Eighth Circuit sustained the Commissioner.]

We may assume that the payments to creditors of the Welch Company were necessary for the development of the petitioner's business, at least in the sense that they were appropriate and helpful. . . . He certainly thought they were, and we should be slow to override his judgment. But the problem is not solved when the payments are characterized as necessary. Many necessary payments are charges upon capital. There is need to determine whether they are both necessary and ordinary. Now, what is ordinary, though there must always be a strain of constancy within it, is none the less a variable affected by time and place and circumstance. Ordinary in this context does not mean the payments must be habitual or normal in the sense that the same taxpayer will have to make them often. A lawsuit affecting the safety of a business may happen once in a lifetime. The counsel fees may be so heavy that repetition is unlikely. None the less, the expense is an ordinary one because we know from experience that payments for such a purpose, whether the amount is large or small, are the common and accepted means of defense against attack. . . . The situation is unique in the life of the individual affected, but not in the life of the group, the community, of which he is a part. At such times there are norms of conduct that help to stabilize our judgment, and make it certain and objective. The instance is not erratic, but is brought within a known type.

The line of demarcation is now visible between the case that is here and the one supposed for illustration. We try to classify this act as ordinary or the opposite, and the norms of conduct fail us. No longer can we have recourse to any fund of business experience, to any known business practice. Men do at times pay the debts of others without legal obligation or the lighter obligation imposed by the usages of trade or by neighborly amenities, but they do not do so ordinarily, not even though the result might be to heighten their reputation for generosity and opulence. Indeed, if language is to be read in its natural and common meaning . . . we should have to say that payment in

---

8. [Amounts have been rounded.—EDS.]

such circumstances, instead of being ordinary, is in a high degree extraordinary. There is nothing ordinary in the stimulus evoking it, and none in the response. Here, indeed, as so often in other branches of the law, the decisive distinctions are those of degree and not of kind. One struggles in vain for any verbal formula that will supply a ready touchstone. The standard set up by the statute is not a rule of law; it is rather a way of life. Life in all its fullness must supply the answer to the riddle.

The Commissioner of Internal Revenue resorted to that standard . . . and found that the payments in controversy came closer to capital outlays than to ordinary and necessary expenses in the operation of a business. His ruling has the support of a presumption of correctness, and the petitioner has the burden of proving it to be wrong. . . . Unless we can say from facts within our knowledge that these are ordinary and necessary expenses according to the ways of conduct and the forms of speech prevailing in the business world, the tax must be confirmed. But nothing told us by this record or within the sphere of our judicial notice permits us to give that extension to what is ordinary and necessary. Indeed, to do so would open the door to many bizarre analogies. One man has a family name that is clouded by thefts committed by an ancestor. To add to his own standing he repays the stolen money, wiping off, it may be, his income for the year. The payments figure in his tax return as ordinary expenses. Another man conceives the notion that he will be able to practice his vocation with greater ease and profit if he has an opportunity to enrich his culture. Forthwith the price of his education becomes an expense of the business, reducing the income subject to taxation. There is little difference between these expenses and those in controversy here. Reputation and learning are akin to capital assets, like the good will of an old partnership. . . . For many, they are the only tools with which to hew a pathway to success. The money spent in acquiring them is well and wisely spent. It is not an ordinary expense of the operation of a business.

Many cases in the federal courts deal with phases of the problem presented in the case at bar. To attempt to harmonize them would be a futile task. They involve the appreciation of particular situations, at times with border-line conclusions. . . .

The decree should be affirmed.

NOTES AND QUESTIONS

1. *Analysis. Welch* is a famous and often-cited decision. This reflects its showy, relentless phrasemaking and the fame of its author rather than its capacity to aid in the analysis of subsequent fact patterns, which (to put it as kindly as possible) is extremely limited. Pompous and needlessly Delphic, it has generated considerable confusion. The issue presented by the Commissioner was simply whether the payments were capital expenditures or current expenses. This being so, what is the relevance, if any, of "uniqueness" (of litigation expenses) or of payments to establish "reputation for generosity and opulence," to "protect a family name," or to "enrich [one's] culture"? Does Justice Cardozo confuse the distinction between capital and current with the distinction between

personal and business?[9] Is it clear that "one struggles in vain for any verbal formula that will apply a ready touchstone"? See the opinion in the *Encyclopaedia Britannica* case, *supra*. If your authorities were limited to the principal cases in this chapter, on which one would you place your principal reliance if you were representing Mr. Welch? What facts would you emphasize?

2. *Other debt-repayment cases.* In Dunn & McCarthy v. Commissioner, 139 F.2d 242 (2d Cir. 1943), a corporation was permitted to deduct amounts it paid to certain employees who had lent funds to its former president; he had lost the money gambling at the race track and had died insolvent. The court did not think the payments were "extraordinary": "It was the kind of outlay which we believe many corporations would make, and have made, under similar circumstances." The *Welch* case was distinguished: "Welch made a capital outlay to acquire goodwill for a new business. In the present case the payment was an outlay to retain an existing goodwill, that is, to prevent loss of earnings that might result from destroying such goodwill by failing to recognize the company's moral obligation." In M.L. Eakes Co. v. Commissioner, 686 F.2d 217 (4th Cir. 1982), the court allowed a current deduction of the debts of a predecessor corporation that had become insolvent. The court concluded that the payments were made to establish credit and thereby preserve an existing business rather than to establish a new one and, after quoting extensively from the *Welch* discussion of "ordinary and necessary," referred to testimony to the effect that the repayment of debts of a liquidated corporation was not unusual in the business in which the taxpayer was engaged.

3. *Recovery of cost of goodwill.* As suggested in Note 1, *supra,* the holding in *Welch* is best justified on the rationale that the expenditure at issue produced benefits beyond the current year and for that reason was capital in nature. If the cost of acquiring goodwill is a capital expenditure, can a taxpayer receive a deduction for amortization of that cost over the expected life of the asset? Historically, the answer to this question has been "no." Amounts paid to produce goodwill have been recoverable for tax purposes only upon sale or other taxable disposition of the business. The same treatment has applied to the portion of the purchase price paid for a business that is allocable to goodwill: no current deduction, no amortization, recovery only upon disposition of the business. Understandably, taxpayers have gone to great length to avoid characterizing expenditures as having been for goodwill. Section 197, added to the tax law in 1993, provides for a fifteen-year amortization of goodwill acquired through purchase. Self-created goodwill, such as that at issue in *Welch*, is still unamortizable. See §197(c)(2)(B), (d)(1)(A), (d)(1)(C)(iv), (d)(1)(C)(v), (d)(2), (d)(3). See also discussion of "Goodwill and Other Intangibles," *infra*.

In Steger v. Commissioner, 113 T.C. 227 (1999), the taxpayer, a lawyer who had just retired from practice, paid $3,168 for a malpractice policy that had an indefinite duration but covered only malpractice that occurred before

---

9. In Commissioner v. Tellier, 383 U.S. 687, 689-690 (1966), see infra, the Court said,

The principal function of the term ordinary in §162(a) is to clarify the distinction, often difficult, between those expenses that are currently deductible and those that are in the nature of capital expenditures, which, if deductible at all, must be amortized over the useful life of the asset. Welch v. Helvering. . . .

the date of retirement. The IRS took the position that Steger was entitled to deduct only 10 percent of the cost of the policy each year for ten years; there is no explanation in the Tax Court opinion of where the 10 percent came from. The Tax Court—relying on language from INDOPCO, Inc. v. Commissioner, *supra*—held that Steger was entitled to deduct the entire amount in the year of purchase, reasoning that even if the policy was a capital asset (as opposed to a current cost of closing the business), the cost was deductible in full on dissolution of his business.

4. *Advertising.* The Regulations under §263A allow current deductions for "marketing, selling, advertising, and distribution costs." Reg. §1.263A-1(e)(3)(iii)(A). Would this rule change the outcome in Welch v. Helvering?

2.   Extraordinary Behavior

GILLIAM v. COMMISSIONER
51 T.C.M. 515 (1986)

When the petition was filed in the instant case, petitioners Sam Gilliam, Jr. (hereinafter sometimes referred to as "Gilliam"), and Dorothy B. Gilliam, husband and wife, resided in Washington, D.C.

Gilliam was born in Tupelo, Mississippi, in 1933, and raised in Louisville, Kentucky. In 1961, he received a master of arts degree in painting from the University of Louisville.

Gilliam is, and was at all material periods, a noted artist. His works have been exhibited in numerous art galleries throughout the United States and Europe, including the Corcoran Gallery of Art, Washington, D.C., the Philadelphia Museum of Art, Philadelphia, Pennsylvania, the Karl Solway Gallery, Cincinnati, Ohio, the Phoenix Gallery, San Francisco, California, and the University of California, Irvine, California. His works have also been exhibited and sold at the Fendrick Gallery, Washington, D.C. In addition, Gilliam is, and was at all material periods, a teacher of art. On occasion, Gilliam lectured and taught art at various institutions.

Gilliam accepted an invitation to lecture and teach for a week at the Memphis Academy of Arts in Memphis, Tennessee. On Sunday, February 23, 1975, he flew to Memphis to fulfill this business obligation.

Gilliam had a history of hospitalization for mental and emotional disturbances and continued to be under psychiatric care until the time of his trip to Memphis. In December 1963, Gilliam was hospitalized in Louisville; Gilliam had anxieties about his work as an artist. For periods of time in both 1965 and 1966, Gilliam suffered from depression and was unable to work. In 1970, Gilliam was again hospitalized. In 1973, while Gilliam was a visiting artist at a number of university campuses in California, he found it necessary to consult an airport physician; however, when he returned to Washington, D.C., Gilliam did not require hospitalization.

Before his Memphis trip, Gilliam created a 225-foot painting for the Thirty-fourth Biennial Exhibition of American Painting at the Corcoran Gallery of Art (hereinafter sometimes referred to as "the Exhibition"). The Exhibition opened on Friday evening, February 21, 1975. In addition, Gilliam was in the process of preparing a giant mural for an outside wall of the Philadelphia Museum of Art for the 1975 Spring Festival in Philadelphia. The budget plans for this mural were due on Monday, February 24, 1975.

On the night before his Memphis trip, Gilliam felt anxious and unable to rest. On Sunday morning, Gilliam contacted Ranville Clark (hereinafter sometimes referred to as "Clark"), a doctor Gilliam had been consulting intermittently over the years, and asked Clark to prescribe some medication to relieve his anxiety. Clark arranged for Gilliam to pick up a prescription of the drug Dalmane on the way to the airport. Gilliam had taken medication frequently during the preceding 10 years. Clark had never before prescribed Dalmane for Gilliam.

On Sunday, February 23, 1975, Gilliam got the prescription and at about 3:25 he boarded American Airlines flight 395 at Washington National Airport, Washington, D.C., bound for Memphis. Gilliam occupied a window seat. He took the Dalmane for the first time shortly after boarding the airplane.

About one and one-half hours after the airplane departed Washington National Airport, Gilliam began to act in an irrational manner. He talked of bizarre events and had difficulty in speaking. According to some witnesses, he appeared to be airsick and held his head. Gilliam began to feel trapped, anxious, disoriented, and very agitated. Gilliam said that the plane was going to crash and that he wanted a life raft. Gilliam entered the aisle and, while going from one end of the airplane to the other, he tried to exit from three different doors. Then Gilliam struck Seiji Nakamura (hereinafter sometimes referred to as "Nakamura"), another passenger, several times with a telephone receiver. Nakamura was seated toward the rear of the airplane, near one of the exits. Gilliam also threatened the navigator and a stewardess, called for help, and cried. As a result of the attack, Nakamura sustained a one-inch laceration above his left eyebrow which required four sutures. Nakamura also suffered ecchymosis of the left arm and pains in his left wrist. Nakamura was treated for these injuries at Methodist Hospital in Memphis.

On arriving in Memphis, Gilliam was arrested by Federal officials. On March 10, 1975, Gilliam was indicted. He was brought to trial in the United States District Court for the Western District of Tennessee, Western Division, on one count of violation of 49 U.S.C. §1472(k) (relating to certain crimes aboard an aircraft in flight) and two counts of violating 49 U.S.C. §1472(j) (relating to interference with flight crew members or flight attendants). Gilliam entered a plea of not guilty to the criminal charges. The trial began on September 9, 1975, and ended on September 10, 1975. After Gilliam presented all of his evidence, the district court granted Gilliam's motion for a judgment of acquittal by reason of temporary insanity.

Petitioners paid $9,250 and $9,600 for legal fees in 1975 and 1976, respectively, in connection with both the criminal trial and Nakamura's civil claim. In 1975, petitioners also paid $3,900 to Nakamura in settlement of the civil claim.

Petitioners claimed deductions for the amounts paid in 1975 and 1976 on the appropriate individual income tax returns. Respondent disallowed the amounts claimed in both years attributable to the incident on the airplane.

Gilliam's trip to Memphis was a trip in furtherance of his trades or businesses. Petitioners' expenses for the legal fees and claim settlement described, *supra,* are not ordinary expenses of Gilliam's trades or businesses.

OPINION

Petitioners contend that they are entitled to deduct the amounts paid in defense of the criminal prosecution and in settlement of the related civil claim under section 162.[10] Petitioners maintain that the instant case is directly controlled by our decision in Dancer v. Commissioner, 73 T.C. 1103 (1980). According to petitioners, "[t]he clear holding of *Dancer* is . . . that expenses for litigation arising out of an accident which occurs during a business trip are deductible as ordinary and necessary business expenses." Petitioners also contend that Clark v. Commissioner, 30 T.C. 1330 (1958), is to the same effect as *Dancer.*

Respondent maintains that *Dancer* and *Clark* are distinguishable. Respondent contends that the legal fees paid are not deductible under either section 162 or section 212 because the criminal charges against Gilliam were neither directly connected with nor proximately resulted from his trade or business and the legal fees were not paid for the production of income. Respondent maintains that "the criminal charges which arose as a result of . . . [the incident on the airplane], could hardly be deemed 'ordinary,' given the nature of [Gilliam's] profession." Respondent contends "that the provisions of section 262 control this situation." As to the settlement of the related civil claim, respondent asserts that since Gilliam committed an intentional tort, the settlement of the civil claim constitutes a nondeductible personal expense.

We agree with respondent that the expenses are not ordinary expenses of Gilliam's trade or business.

Section 162(a) allows a deduction for all the ordinary and necessary expenses of carrying on a trade or business. In order for the expense to be deductible by a taxpayer, it must be an ordinary expense, it must be a necessary expense, and it must be an expense of carrying on the taxpayer's trade or business. If any one of these requirements is not met, the expense is not deductible under section 162(a). Deputy v. du Pont, 308 U.S. 488 (1940); Welch v. Helvering [*supra*]; Kornhauser v. United States, 276 U.S. 145 (1928). In Deputy v. du Pont, the Supreme Court set forth a guide for application of the statutory requirement that the expense be "ordinary," as follows (308 U.S. at 494-497):[11]

---

10. At trial, petitioners asserted that the amounts paid were deductible under section 162 and section 212. On brief, petitioners do not address the deductibility of the amounts paid under section 212. Whether this constitutes a concession by petitioners is unclear; however, it does not affect the analysis herein, since the same criteria apply to the deduction of expenses under section 162 and section 212. . . .

11. [In Deputy v. du Pont, the taxpayer had claimed a deduction for certain expenses arising from his sale of stock in the du Pont Corporation to a group of young executives. The purpose of the sale was to give these executives a financial interest in the corporation; because the corporation was prevented by legal restrictions from doing so, the taxpayer stepped in "to the end that his beneficial stock ownership in the du Pont Company might be conserved and enhanced."—EDS.]

In the second place, these payments were not "ordinary" ones for the conduct of the kind of business in which, we assume arguendo, respondent was engaged. The District Court held that they were "beyond the norm of general and accepted business practice" and were in fact "so extraordinary as to occur in the lives of ordinary business men not at all" and in the life of the respondent "but once." Certainly there are no norms of conduct to which we have been referred or of which we are cognizant which would bring these payments within the meaning of ordinary expenses for conserving and enhancing an estate. We do not doubt the correctness of the District Court's finding that respondent embarked on this program to the end that his beneficial stock ownership in the du Pont Company might be conserved and enhanced. But that does not make the cost to him an "ordinary" expense within the meaning of the Act. Ordinary has the connotation of normal, usual, or customary. To be sure, an expense may be ordinary though it happen but once in the taxpayer's lifetime. Cf. Kornhauser v. United States, *supra.* Yet the transaction which gives rise to it must be of common or frequent occurrence in the type of business involved. Welch v. Helvering, *supra.* Hence, the fact that a particular expense would be an ordinary or common one in the course of one business and so deductible under [§162(a)] does not necessarily make it such in connection with another business. . . . As stated in Welch v. Helvering, *supra,* pp.113-114: ". . . What is ordinary, though there must always be a strain of constancy within it, is none the less a variable affected by time and place and circumstance." One of the extremely relevant circumstances is the nature and scope of the particular business out of which the expense in question accrued. The fact that an obligation to pay has arisen is not sufficient. It is the kind of transaction out of which the obligation arose and its normalcy in the particular business which are crucial and controlling.

Review of the many decided cases is of little aid since each turns on its special facts. But the principle is clear. And on application of that principle to these facts, it seems evident that the payments in question cannot be placed in the category of those items of expense which a conservator of an estate, a custodian of a portfolio, a supervisor of a group of investments, a manager of wide financial and business interests, or a substantial stockholder in a corporation engaged in conserving and enhancing his estate would ordinarily incur. We cannot assume that they are embraced within the normal overhead or operating costs of such activities. There is no evidence that stockholders or investors, in furtherance of enhancing and conserving their estates, ordinarily or frequently lend such assistance to employee stock purchase plans of their corporations. And in absence of such evidence there is no basis for an assumption, in experience or common knowledge, that these payments are to be placed in the same category as typically ordinary expenses of such activities, e.g., rental of safe deposit boxes, cost of investment counsel or of investment services, salaries of secretaries and the like. Rather these payments seem to us to represent most extraordinary expenses for that type of activity. Therefore, the claim for deduction falls, as did the claim of an officer of a corporation who paid its debts to strengthen his own standing and credit. Welch v. Helvering, *supra.* And the fact that the payments might have been necessary in the sense that consummation of the transaction with the Delaware Company was beneficial to respondent's estate is of no aid. For Congress has not decreed that all necessary expenses may be deducted. Though plainly necessary they cannot be allowed unless they are also ordinary. Welch v. Helvering, *supra.*

Petitioners bear the burden of proving entitlement to a deduction under section 162. Welch v. Helvering, 290 U.S. at 115; Rule 142(a), Tax Court Rules of

Practice & Procedure. Gilliam is a noted artist and teacher of art. It undoubtedly is ordinary for people in Gilliam's trades or businesses to travel (and to travel by air) in the course of such trades or businesses; however, we do not believe it is ordinary for people in such trades or businesses to be involved in altercations of the sort here involved in the course of any such travel. The travel was not itself the conduct of Gilliam's trades or businesses. Also, the expenses here involved are not strictly a cost of Gilliam's transportation. Finally, it is obvious that neither the altercation nor the expenses were undertaken to further Gilliam's trades or businesses.

We conclude that Gilliam's expenses are not ordinary expenses of his trades or businesses.

It is instructive to compare the instant case with Dancer v. Commissioner, *supra,* upon which petitioners rely. In both cases, the taxpayer was travelling on business. In both cases, the expenses in dispute were not the cost of the travelling, but rather were the cost of an untoward incident that occurred in the course of the trip. In both cases, the incident did not facilitate the trip or otherwise assist the taxpayer's trade or business. In both cases, the taxpayer was responsible for the incident; in neither case was the taxpayer willful. In *Dancer,* the taxpayer was driving an automobile; he caused an accident which resulted in injuries to a child. The relevant expenses were the taxpayer's payments to settle the civil claims arising from the accident. 73 T.C. at 1105. In the instant case, Gilliam was a passenger in an airplane, he apparently committed acts which would have been criminal but for his temporary insanity, and he injured a fellow passenger. Gilliam's expenses were the costs of his successful legal defense, and his payments to settle Nakamura's civil claim.

In *Dancer,* we stated as follows (73 T.C. at 1108-1109):

> It is true that the expenditure in the instant case did not further petitioner's business in any economic sense; nor is it, we hope, the type of expenditure that many businesses are called upon to pay. Nevertheless, neither factor lessens the direct relationship between the expenditure and the business. Automobile travel by petitioner was an integral part of this business. *As rising insurance rates suggest, the cost of fuel and routine servicing are not the only costs one can expect in operating a car. As unfortunate as it may be, lapses by drivers seem to be an inseparable incident of driving a car.* . . . Costs incurred as a result of such an incident are just as much a part of overall business expenses as the cost of fuel. [Emphasis supplied.]

Dancer is distinguishable.

In Clark v. Commissioner, *supra,* also relied on by petitioners, the expenses consisted of payments of (a) legal fees in defense of a criminal prosecution and (b) amounts to settle a related civil claim.[12] In this regard, the instant case

---

12. [In *Clark,* the taxpayer, as branch manager of a company that solicited magazine subscriptions, was responsible for hiring people to go out and do the soliciting. "If an applicant for an outside solicitor's job was a married female, [taxpayer's] policy was always to interview the applicant's husband, have him understand the conditions under which the wife would be working, and get his approval before employing the applicant." Pursuant to this policy, the taxpayer made an appointment with an applicant to interview the applicant's husband at the applicant's and her husband's home at 8 A.M., before the husband went to work. When the taxpayer arrived for the interview, the husband was not

is similar to *Clark*. In *Clark*, however, the taxpayer's activities that gave rise to the prosecution and civil claim were activities directly in the conduct of Clark's trade or business. In the instant case, Gilliam's activities were not directly in the conduct of his trades or businesses. Rather, the activities merely occurred in the course of transportation connected with Gilliam's trades or businesses. And, as we noted in Dancer v. Commissioner, 73 T.C. at 1106, "in cases like this, where the cost is an adjunct of and not a direct cost of transporting an individual, we have not felt obliged to routinely allow the expenditure as a transportation costs deduction."

Petitioners also rely on Commissioner v. Tellier, 383 U.S. 687 (1966), in which the taxpayer was allowed to deduct the cost of an unsuccessful criminal defense to securities fraud charges. The activities that gave rise to the criminal prosecution in *Tellier* were activities directly in the conduct of Tellier's trade or business. Our analysis of the effect of Clark v. Commissioner, applies equally to the effect of Commissioner v. Tellier.

In sum, Gilliam's expenses were of a kind similar to those of the taxpayers in *Tellier* and *Clark*; however the activities giving rise to Gilliam's expenses were not activities directly in the conduct of his trades or businesses, while Tellier's and Clark's activities were directly in the conduct of their respective trades or businesses. Gilliam's expenses were related to his trades or businesses in a manner similar to those of the taxpayer in *Dancer;* however Gilliam's actions giving rise to the expenses were not shown to be ordinary, while Dancer's were shown to be ordinary. *Tellier, Clark,* and *Dancer* all have similarities to the instant case, however, *Tellier, Clark,* and *Dancer* are distinguishable in important respects. The expenses are not deductible under section 162(a).

We hold for respondent.

NOTES AND QUESTIONS

1. *Precedent.* The court in *Gilliam* relies on Welch v. Helvering, *supra,* and Deputy v. du Pont (quoted at length in the court's opinion). Disregarding the language of those two cases, how might they be distinguished?

2. *Appropriate time and place?* Suppose Gilliam's anxiety attack had occurred while he had been lecturing to a room full of students, and he had injured one of them. Would his expenses then have been deductible?

---

at home. The taxpayer spent a few minutes in the house and left. According to the tax court, the taxpayer "did not assault the . . . applicant." Nonetheless, the applicant later the same day "swore out a warrant against [the taxpayer] charging him with assault with intent to rape," and this was followed by a warrant served by the county sheriff. Nine days later a court order was issued stating that "after hearing evidence [it appears] that the offense is Assault and Battery instead of Assault with Intent to Rape." Thereafter the criminal action was dismissed "upon the request of the prosecutrix." The taxpayer thereafter paid $1,250 as fees to his lawyers and "turned over to them $1,500 which they paid over to [the] applicant and her husband in consideration for a release to [the taxpayer] of any claim of civil liability which might arise." The Tax Court allowed deductions for both the $1,250 and the $1,500. As to the $1,500, the court relied on the statement of doctrine, "Expenditures incurred by a taxpayer to protect his business reputation or avoid unfavorable business or commercial publicity have been regarded as deductible."—EDS.]

3. *Causation.* (a) Is it the assumption of the court that the anxiety attack was brought on by the business trip—that is, that it would not have occurred but for the pressures associated with that trip? Or is the assumption that it was only a coincidence that the attack occurred while Gilliam was on a business trip? Should it matter?

(b) Suppose that Gilliam had hired an attendant to accompany him on the trip, to soothe and, if necessary, restrain him. Would the cost have been deductible?

(c) If the above hypothetical assistant had an anxiety attack on the airline flight and assaulted a passenger, who then sued Gilliam, would Gilliam be able to deduct the costs of the settlement? If this question has a different answer than that with respect to the costs of settlement for Gilliam's own attack, does the word "ordinary" help us to understand the difference? Why or why not?

4. *The scrupulous lawyer and other extraordinary taxpayers.* (a) In Friedman v. Delaney, 171 F.2d 269 (1st Cir. 1948), cert. denied, 336 U.S. 936 (1949), the taxpayer, Friedman, was a lawyer. After one of his clients had become insolvent, Friedman met with creditors to work out a settlement and finally reached an agreement under which the client would pay $5,000 to the creditors. Friedman, relying on prior representations by the client, gave his word that this money would be forthcoming, but when Friedman asked for it, the client (who had anticipated cashing in an insurance policy to produce the money) had a change of heart and refused. Thereupon, Friedman paid the $5,000 himself. Claiming that the ethics of his profession and his own conscience required that he keep his word, he deducted the $5,000 as a business loss. The court denied the deduction on the ground that the payment was "voluntary." The court said that "it is obviously no part of a lawyer's business to take on a personal obligation to make payments which should come from his client, unless in pursuance of a previous understanding or agreement to do so."

(b) On the other hand, in Pepper v. Commissioner, 36 T.C. 886 (1961), another lawyer paid up when his client misbehaved and a deduction was allowed. The taxpayer had helped a client find financing for a business by approaching other clients, friends, and business acquaintances and by drafting the necessary loan and security arrangements. On discovering that the client was engaged in fraudulent manipulations and that the business was bankrupt, the taxpayer and his law partner paid about $65,000 to the victims after concluding that the payments were "imperative" in order to save their law practice. Welch v. Helvering, *supra,* was distinguished on the ground that there the expenditures were made to *acquire,* and not to *retain or protect,* the taxpayer's business. *Friedman* was distinguished on the ground that in that case "there was no contention that the money involved was paid to protect or promote Friedman's business." Does this mean that if Friedman had proved that his conduct had been a response not to moral scruple, but rather to profit-maximization goals, the deduction would have been allowed? If a payment is not unlawful, if its deduction would not contravene public policy in some fashion and if it is made in a taxpayer's business judgment for profit-making reasons, should a deduction be denied merely because it is unusual, extraordinary, or unique?

In Goedel v. Commissioner, 39 B.T.A. 1, 12 (1939), a stock dealer was denied a deduction for premiums paid on insurance on the life of the President of the United States, whose death, he feared, would disrupt the stock market:

> Where, as here, the expenditure is so unusual as never to have been made, so far as the record reveals, by other persons in the same business, *when confronted with similar conditions*, . . . then we do not think the expenditure was ordinary or necessary, so as to be a deductible business expense within the intendment and meaning of the statute.

In Trebilcock v. Commissioner, 64 T.C. 852 (1975), aff'd, 557 F.2d 1226 (6th Cir. 1977), a deduction was denied for the cost of hiring an ordained minister "to minister spiritually to petitioner and his employees [and to conduct] prayer meetings, at which he tried to raise the level of spiritual awareness of the participants." The court said that such "benefits . . . are personal in nature." Suppose an employer who is a physical-fitness addict hires a physical education instructor to come to her place of business each morning and lead her employees in exercises. "Ordinary"? Deductible? If not, what if the employer hates all forms of physical exercise but thinks it might make her employees work better? What if an employer hires a yoga instructor to lead his employees in meditation each morning?

3. Reasonable Compensation

Section 162(a)(1) provides expressly for the deduction of a "reasonable allowance for salaries or other compensation for personal services actually rendered." In the past, the IRS often challenged deductions taken by closely held C corporations for payments made to owner-employees. The IRS argued the payments were unreasonably large, and were best characterized as nondeductible dividends. Today, most closely held corporations have elected to be taxed as so-called S corporations. An S corporation is treated very much like a partnership for tax purposes. It pays no tax; instead, its income is taxed to its shareholders. Whether a payment is characterized as a dividend or salary makes no difference to an S corporation, which pays no tax, and little difference to its shareholders, who are taxed on both dividends and salary.[13]

In addition to the reasonable compensation limit of §162(a)(1), deductions for compensation are subject to a number of additional limitations. Under §162(m), added to the Code in 1993, publicly held corporations cannot deduct more than $1 million a year in pay to "covered employees," namely, a chief executive officer or any other of its four highest paid employees. Before 2018, §162(m)(4) included an exception for "performance-based compensation," such as stock options and other stock appreciation rights. Performance-based compensation paid to covered employees could be deducted without regard

---

13. The characterization may matter for reasons unrelated to the reasonable compensation limitation of §162. For example, amounts paid as salary are subject to Social Security and related payroll taxes.

to the $1 million limit. The 2017 act removed this exception, and clarified the definition of covered employees to include the chief financial officer. The 2017 act also introduced a tainting rule, such that "once a covered employee, always a covered employee."

Of somewhat lesser importance, §§280G and 4999 restrict deductions for so-called golden parachute payments and impose an excise tax on such payments. Roughly speaking, golden parachute payments are substantial bonuses paid to corporate executives on termination of employment following a change in control of the corporation.

4. Sexual Harassment Settlements

Employers commonly settle sexual harassment lawsuits with a requirement that the claim and resolution are subject to nondisclosure and confidentiality. Before 2018, employers could treat these settlements as a cost of doing business and deduct the settlement payments as an "ordinary and necessary" business expense under §162. Perhaps as a reaction to the 2017 #MeToo movement against sexual harassment and abuse, especially in the workplace, Congress included an amendment in the 2017 act that added a new subsection to §162. Section 162(q) disallows any deduction for any payment or settlement related to sexual harassment or sexual abuse that is subject to a nondisclosure or confidentiality provision, as well as any attorney's fees related to such settlement or payment.

G. DEPRECIATION AND AMORTIZATION

1. Significance of the Timing of Cost Recovery

Things that seem trivial at first can sometimes have large consequences. The depreciation rules, which determine the rate of cost recovery for capital assets, are a case in point. Initially, one might think that the question of just how fast, and over what period, taxpayers can claim depreciation deductions might make only a modest difference. In fact, however, it can potentially make a large difference—especially, as we will see, when interest rates are high.

To explain why this might matter significantly, consider two benchmarks. The first is economic depreciation, or allowing a deduction precisely equal to the asset's actual decline in value during the year. In practice, this amount would often be hard or even impossible to determine, but we can ignore this problem for treating it as a conceptual benchmark.

At the other extreme, suppose that taxpayers could actually expense the costs of purchasing capital assets, rather than having to capitalize such costs and only get depreciation deductions over time. The reason for using this benchmark is that, in practice, allowable depreciation deductions often are accelerated relative to economic depreciation, causing them to vary from it in the direction of expensing.

Under the first benchmark, the use of economic depreciation means, by definition, that we are accurately measuring economic income from the use of the asset (assuming accurate measurement in all other respects). Thus, the normal return to capital is being taxed (plus or minus the variation between this asset's actual return and that normal return.)[14] By contrast, under the second benchmark, expensing, as we saw in Chapter 4, the normal rate of return to capital would be effectively tax-exempt. Thus, only the above-normal component of the taxpayer's economic return from using the asset would face a positive tax burden.

For this reason, accelerated depreciation (i.e., that which is faster than economic depreciation) leans towards effectively exempting the normal return to capital, as under a consumption tax, as distinct from taxing it, as under a Haig-Simons income tax. How much of a difference this makes, however, depends on whether the normal rate of return—which presumably is reflected in contemporary market interest rates—is low or high, relatively speaking.

2. Overview of Depreciation Rules

A departure from strict realization accounting. If only realization events had tax consequences, and prior fluctuations in asset value never had tax consequences, then taxpayers would not get depreciation deductions. To claim the losses, they would actually have to dispose of assets that have lost value. Given, however, that assets with finite useful lives can generally be expected to lose value over time—based on the passage of time, independently of whether market prices for new or used assets go up or down—this would predictably result in overmeasurement of the economic income earned by taxpayers using such assets. Thus, considerable logic supports allowing cost recovery deductions for assets with finite useful lives without awaiting the occurrence of a conventional realization event.

Absent realization, however, it is hard to determine how much depreciation should be allowed. Again, the actual change in a given asset's market value is likely to be difficult, or even impossible, to observe. The depreciation rules therefore prescribe allowable deductions, based on the type of asset and its initial cost or other basis, without regard to actual market values.

The effort to provide investment incentives. Even if one assumes that economic depreciation is unobservable (or, at least, that trying to observe it accurately in each case would be unduly costly), one could imagine the depreciation rules being designed with an eye towards replicating it on average. For many decades, however, attempting to replicate economic depreciation has not been a goal of the tax system. Instead, the depreciation provisions are designed to

---

14. In general, one would not expect the taxpayer to acquire and use the asset, absent an advance expectation that it would earn at least the normal return. Otherwise, some other investment choice presumably would have been preferable.

overstate the decline in value of business property—i.e., to be accelerated relative to economic depreciation—leading to the expectation that they will result in undermeasurement of the taxable income earned by using depreciable assets. The rationale for this approach is to encourage business investment.

The "building blocks" of depreciation rules. Any depreciation system revolves around the spreading, or allocation, of cost over time and has three elements: (a) determining useful life; (b) taking account of salvage value; and (c) applying a method of allocating the cost, in excess of salvage value, over the useful life. For example, if a farmer buys a tractor for $10,000, expects to use it for five years before selling it for scrap for $2,000, the tractor's useful life is five years, its salvage value is $2,000, and the amount to be allocated over the five years is $8,000. One possible method of allocation would be to assign equal amounts of $1,600 to each year. This would be an example of what is called the "straight-line" method. Other methods, generally resulting in larger early-year deductions than straight-line, along with smaller late-year deductions, are described below.

Useful lives and salvage value in practice. One way the depreciation rules are designed to be more favorable than economic depreciation is by specifying shorter useful lives, for cost recovery purposes, than one might anticipate would be the asset's likely actual useful life. A second way is by specifying a salvage value of zero, making the entire asset cost recoverable during the tax useful life, even if this exceeds the actual decline in asset value, given the prospect of recovering something at the end.

Rate of cost recovery. As noted above, under the *straight-line* method an equal portion of the total cost of the asset is allocated to each year. The deduction can be expressed as an annual percentage. For example, this would be 20 percent per year of the asset's original cost or other basis for an asset with a useful life of five years or 10 percent per year for an asset with a useful life of ten years.

Under various accelerated methods greater amounts are allocated to early years than to later years.[15] Again, taxpayers generally prefer such methods to straight-line depreciation, since the effect is to increase deductions, and reduce income, in the early years of the life of an asset, at the price of reduced deductions, and increased income, in the later years. Relative to the straight-line method, this results in deferral of taxable income.

The currently most significant accelerated method is the *declining balance* method. Under this method, the straight-line percentage is determined, and then this percentage is increased by a specified factor. The resulting percentage is applied to the cost of the asset, reduced by the amounts previously deducted. For example, suppose an asset costs $10,000 and has an expected life of ten years and a zero salvage value. Under the straight-line method, the annual deduction would be 10 percent of $10,000, or $1,000. Suppose the

---

15. Of course, the fact that a given depreciation method is accelerated relative to the straight-line method does not automatically tell us whether, in any given case, it is accelerated relative to true economic depreciation.

declining balance factor is 200 percent (which is referred to as the 200 percent or double-declining balance method). The amount of the deduction in the first year would be double that under the straight-line method, or 20 percent: here, $2,000. The next year the same percentage is used, but it is applied to the balance of the original $10,000 cost after subtracting the $2,000 already deducted. The balance would be $8,000, and the deduction would be $1,600. The balance the next year would be $6,400, and 20 percent of that would be $1,280. And so forth. At some point, this method produces a deduction less than would be produced by straight-line; and it never reaches zero. Under the present system, however, when the point is reached where the straight-line amount exceeds the declining balance amount, the taxpayer switches to straight-line.

It would be possible, of course, to use a method under which deductions are lower in the early years of an asset than in the later years. In fact, if an asset produces a steady stream of income over its useful life, the method that corresponds with economic depreciation has this characteristic (that is, the characteristic of rising each year). The possibility of a "decelerated" (sometimes referred to as "sinking fund") method as a basic or general method of cost recovery is only of theoretical importance, given that there has been little public political discussion of using it.

Other methods are also possible, including the "income forecast" method, under which the current year's depreciation deduction is derived from a projection of future income: specifically, that portion of basis equal to a fraction of which the numerator is the current year's income and the denominator is the estimated total income to be derived from the asset for its entire useful life. See Rev. Rul. 60-358, 1960-2 C.B. 68. This method is used for films, sound recordings, and video recordings. See Rev. Rul. 89-62, 1989-1 C.B. 62.

Rapid amortization and current deduction. The Code allows rapid amortization for certain investments (e.g., §169 relating to pollution control facilities) and current deductions for various other investments (e.g., §263(a) relating to intangible drilling costs).

The first year of service. A practical problem arises over how much of a deduction to allow for an asset that is first used during a taxable year but is not used for the whole year. The question is just how accurate does one want to be? One possibility would be to prorate the deduction on a daily basis, but that could be more trouble than it is worth. The practical compromise under present law, which is further described below, mainly involves using a half-year convention (i.e., assuming that the item was placed in service exactly halfway through the taxable year).

Component depreciation. Another problem of practicality is how far to go in allowing, or requiring, different rates of depreciation for different components of an asset. For example, in the case of a building, should separate rates apply for the structure, the roof, the elevators, the plumbing and wiring, the air-conditioning equipment, etc.?

Basis and gain or loss on disposition. The deduction for depreciation, or cost recovery, results, for tax purposes, in a reduction of basis. In fact, the basis is reduced if depreciation is allowable, even if the deduction is not taken. See §1016(a)(2). If the depreciation deduction happens to correspond exactly with economic reality, adjusted basis will correspond exactly with market value. Otherwise a gain or loss will be reported on disposition of the asset.

Recapture. Generally, as we discuss in Chapter 12, when a business asset is disposed of, any gain is treated as capital gain. But the depreciation deduction is an offset to ordinary income. For example, suppose that a farmer buys a tractor for $10,000 and, over the first three years of its use, claims depreciation deductions of $6,000, leaving an adjusted basis of $4,000. Now suppose the tractor is sold for $5,000. The gain is $1,000. But for the "recapture" rule, adopted in 1962, that gain would be treated as capital gain. However, capital gain treatment may seem wrong, given the gain is in a sense a recovery of what turned out to be an excess reduction of ordinary income by virtue of depreciation deductions.

In the case of personal property such as tractors (and other equipment and machinery), the Code now provides that any gain on disposition is treated as ordinary income to the extent of prior deductions for depreciation. §1245. Thus, in our example, the gain of $1,000 would be treated as ordinary income. If the tractor had been sold for $11,000, the gain would consist of $6,000 of ordinary income (the amount of depreciation previously taken) and $1,000 of capital gain. For real property, depreciation recapture is at a 25 percent rate.

Investment tax credit. The depreciation deduction has been supplemented, from time to time, by a series of investment tax credits. As the term implies, an investment tax credit gives a taxpayer a one-time credit upon purchase of a qualifying asset. Perhaps the most important investment tax credit was adopted in 1981 and generally applied to tangible depreciable property other than real estate. Taxpayers purchasing such property received a tax credit equal to 10 percent of the purchase price. In effect, the government paid 10 percent of the cost of all qualifying property. (Recall that while a deduction simply reduces taxable income, a credit produces a dollar-for-dollar reduction in taxes owed.) This was repealed in 1986 and has not generally been restored since, although doing so is sometimes discussed.

3. The Current System

a. *Tangible Assets Depreciable Under §168*

Tangible assets placed in service after 1980 are depreciated under the rules of §168, described below.

Recovery period. The useful life or (to use the statutory term) recovery period for many assets is stated directly in the statute. For example, automobiles are subject to a five-year recovery period. §168(e)(3). Cost recovery begins not when property is acquired but when it is "placed in service." The useful life for more specialized assets is determined by reference to class life tables published by the IRS. §168(e). Note that under the 2017 act, qualified leasehold, restaurant, and retail improvements are no longer included under the §168(e) fifteen-year recovery period. Instead, under §179, all qualified improvement property, in addition to being eligible for bonus depreciation, is apparently meant to have a fifteen-recovery period (although a drafting error has placed this result in doubt).

Personal property: Basic recovery periods. Personal property now has recovery periods for six different classes: three-year property (e.g., certain special tools and racehorses more than two years old when placed in service); five-year property (e.g., computers, typewriters, copiers, trucks, cargo containers, and semiconductor manufacturing equipment); seven-year property (e.g., office furniture, fixtures and equipment, railroad tracks, and single-purpose agricultural and horticultural structures); ten-year property (e.g., assets used in petroleum refining); fifteen-year property (e.g., sewage treatment plants and telephone distribution plants); and twenty-year property (e.g., municipal sewers).

Personal property: Basic method. The method prescribed for personal property is 200 percent or double declining balance for three-, five-, seven-, and ten-year property and 150 percent for fifteen- and twenty-year property, shifting to straight-line when that produces larger deductions.

As noted above, a half-year convention generally is used for the first year of service. That is, for the first year the rate is half of what it would be for a full year (as if the asset had been placed in service exactly in the middle of the year, without regard to when it was actually placed in service). If, however, more than 40 percent of all property is placed in service in the last quarter of the taxable year, a mid-quarter convention applies.

In general, a half-year's deduction is allowed in the year of disposition. Special rules, however, apply for automobiles and other "listed" property; for patents and copyrights (straight-line under Reg. §1.167(a)(6)); and for films, sound recordings, and certain other assets (§168(f)(3) and (4)).

Personal property: Bonus depreciation. Since 2001, §168(k) has allowed taxpayers to take an immediate first-year deduction of 50 percent of the acquisition cost of qualifying assets. This bonus depreciation was set to be phased out starting in 2018. However, the 2017 act instead doubled the bonus, by providing full 100 percent expensing for most eligible property placed in service after September 27, 2017 and before January 1, 2023. §168(k)(2). In addition, used property was made eligible for bonus depreciation. The 100 percent depreciation will be phased out from 2024 to 2027.

The allowance of 100 percent expensing for eligible property represents an important step in the direction of making the existing federal income tax more consumption tax-like, and less income tax-like. In a pure consumption tax model, however, *all* business outlays would be expensed—including, for example, amounts paid to acquire land or real property, inventory, and intangible assets. By retaining capitalization in many contexts, as well as in various other respects (such as generally retaining interest deductibility), the 2017 act ensured that the tax system would continue to be a kind of hybrid, blending "true" income tax and consumption tax features, albeit on balance closer to the latter than previously.

Personal property: Optional recovery periods and method. Taxpayers have the option of using certain recovery periods and methods that tend to delay deductions.

Real property: Basic recovery periods. The recovery periods for real property are 27.5 years for residential rental property and 39 years for other real property.

Real property: Basic method. The method for real property is straight-line. The first-year applicable convention is that the full-year deduction is prorated according to the number of months during which the property is in service during the year. Similarly, in the year of disposition, the deduction is prorated according to months of service. Component depreciation is not permitted; the recovery period and method used for a building as a whole must be used for all its components that are real property.

Real property: Optional recovery periods and method. Taxpayers may use optional longer useful lives.

Limited expensing. Up to $1 million of the cost of certain property (roughly, all personal property and certain real estate investments) used in a trade or business may be treated as a current expense. §179. This deduction may not exceed the income from the business and is phased out, dollar for dollar, as total investment exceeds $2.5 million. The $1 million and $2.5 million amounts are to be adjusted for inflation. Section 179 may seem irrelevant in light of the 2017 act's general extension of expensing to investments by firms regardless of size, but in theory at least the §179 amendments are permanent and the general extension of 100 percent bonus depreciation phases out after 2022.

Intangible assets. Intangible assets, such as patents and copyrights, are subject to §167 and are not eligible for the accelerated statutory methods of depreciation described above. In general, such assets must be depreciated on a straight-line basis. Intangible assets that are purchased rather than created "in-house" are generally subject to §197, discussed immediately below.

COMPARATIVE FOCUS:
The UK "Industrial Buildings Allowance"

Recall that under U.S. law, depreciation deductions are allowed with respect to the "exhaustion, wear and tear" of "property used in the trade or business" or "property held for the production of income." §167(a). In the United Kingdom, the scope of tax depreciation is substantially narrower, especially with respect to buildings.

As part of the Income Tax Act of 1945, the UK adopted what came to be known as the "industrial buildings allowance" (IBA) as a means of encouraging post-war reconstruction by certain industries. Under the original IBA scheme, depreciation deductions were allowed for the cost of constructing buildings and structures, but only for firms engaged in manufacturing and processing. Over time, the buildings allowance was broadened to incorporate depreciation for certain other types of structures (e.g., qualifying hotels, tunnels, and bridges); however, the IBA regime was never extended to buildings and structures used in connection with a retail establishment. The distinction naturally resulted in litigation, especially in cases where the taxpayer had constructed a building used for both qualifying and nonqualifying purposes (see, e.g., Kilmarnock Equitable Co-operative Society Ltd. v. CIR, 42 TC 675).

Beginning in April 2008, the UK initiated a "phased withdrawal" of the industrial buildings allowance regime over four years. The change, which was adopted as part of a broader package of business tax reforms, was motivated in part by a desire to eliminate the preferential treatment of industrial buildings. Despite a storm of protest over the IBA repeal, the government stuck to its guns, noting that IBAs had become a "poorly focused subsidy" and that "the tax system already recognises the depreciation of buildings and structures in other ways: through tax relief for the costs of repairs and insurance, and by directly recognising any actual depreciation (or appreciation) through the capital gains tax system at the point of a building's sale." For more information, see *HM Revenue & Customs, Business Tax Reform: Capital Allowance Changes*, Technical Note (Dec. 2007) (available at http://www.hmrc.gov.uk/legislation/pu451.pdf).

4. Goodwill and Other Intangibles

An individual who acquires more than one asset in a single transaction must allocate a portion of the purchase price to each asset. The allocation is made on the basis of the relative fair market value of the assets as of the date of purchase. Under this rule, the purchase of a business is treated as the purchase of the individual assets of the business. In many cases, tangible assets and intangible assets such as copyrights or patents will account for the entire purchase price. In some cases, however, some portion of the purchase price will be attributable to a different sort of intangible, such as the enterprise's reputation, loyal customers, or skilled work force. These sorts of intangibles are sometimes referred to collectively as the enterprise's going concern value or goodwill. A business with a high going concern value may be worth far more than the sum of its tangible assets and discrete intangible assets, such as copyrights.

The treatment of going concern value, goodwill, and similar intangibles for purposes of depreciation has long been a bone of contention. For many years, the government has contended that such assets are non-depreciable goodwill. Taxpayers, on the other hand, have estimated useful lives for some of these assets and have depreciated the portion of the purchase price allocated to them over their useful lives. In 1993, the Supreme Court attempted to resolve a conflict among the circuits over the treatment of such assets in its decision in Newark Morning Ledger Co. v. United States, 507 U.S. 546 (1993). The taxpayer in that case had paid $328 million to acquire a chain of newspapers and had allocated $67.8 million of that amount to an intangible asset denominated "paid subscribers." The $67.8 million was the taxpayer's estimate of the present value of future profits to be derived from the newspaper's current subscribers, most of whom were expected to continue to subscribe after the acquisition. The taxpayer presented experts who testified that, using generally accepted statistical techniques, they were able to estimate how long the average subscriber would continue to subscribe. The taxpayer then depreciated the $67.8 million on a straight-line basis over the estimated life of the asset. The government denied the deduction on the ground that the concept of "paid subscribers" was indistinguishable from goodwill, which had long been treated as non-depreciable. The Court (in a five-to-four decision) held that the taxpayer had in fact shown the asset had a determinable useful life and allowed the deduction.

The decision in *Newark Morning Ledger Co.* threatened to embroil taxpayers, the Service, and the courts in a never-ending wave of fact-specific litigation. To understand why this is so, suppose you represent a client who in 1992 paid $2,000,000 for a well-regarded and highly successful restaurant. The restaurant's tangible assets were worth only $500,000; the remaining value was attributable to the reputation and skill of the current employees, the presumed loyalty of the current clientele, and the restaurant's reputation apart from its current employees. Under *Newark Morning Ledger Co.*, the remaining $1,500,000 is in theory depreciable. But how would one go about assigning values to the different intangibles described above? And how would one determine the useful life of those intangibles?

To end unproductive litigation, and to limit the damage to the fisc from aggressive taxpayer positions, Congress in 1993 passed §197, which provides for a fifteen-year amortization of a long list of intangibles. These intangibles include goodwill, going concern value, the value of work force in place, and the value of current relationships with customers or suppliers, provided that such assets are acquired by purchase rather than self-created. Under §197, then, it no longer matters whether the premium paid in connection with a business is called by a general term such as goodwill or going concern value or is divided among its component parts and allocated to work force in place or to customer relationships. The premium will in any event be depreciable over fifteen years.

Section 197 applies to purchased patents, copyrights, films, sound recordings, etc. (but only if they are acquired as part of the acquisition of a trade or business or a substantial portion thereof) (§197(e)(4)). What about self-created assets? Certain assets, such as trademarks and covenants not to compete, qualify for fifteen-year amortization under §197. The assets in these categories that are not covered by §197 are subject to the various other tax rules relating to capitalization (see, e.g., §263(a)) and are depreciable under §167 rather than under the fifteen-year, straight-line rule of §197.

H.   DEPLETION AND INTANGIBLE DRILLING COSTS

Cost and percentage depletion. Although the Court in Stanton v. *Baltic Mining Co.*, 240 U.S. 103 (1916), stated that an "adequate allowance . . . for the exhaustion of the ore body" resulting from mining operations is not required by the Constitution, Congress has always allowed depletion to be deducted in computing taxable income from mining and other extractive activities.

Originally, the deduction was based on the cost of the property being depleted, and cost depletion is still authorized. §611. When this method is employed, the taxpayer allocates adjusted basis equally among the estimated recoverable units and deducts an appropriate amount as the units are sold. Thus, if the cost to be allocated is $100,000, and there are 100,000 recoverable tons, the depletion allowance will be $1 per ton, deducted as the ore is sold. This method of depletion, cost depletion, may simply be viewed as another method of depreciation. The provision considered in the *Baltic Mining Co.* case, providing that the depletion allowance might not in any circumstances exceed 5 percent of gross income, was repealed in 1916.

The second method available for recovering the cost of most depletable deposits is percentage depletion. The percentage depletion method ignores both the taxpayer's cost and the number of recoverable units. Instead, the taxpayer is permitted to deduct a given percentage of gross income (but not to exceed 50 percent of taxable income calculated before depletion is taken) as a depletion allowance. This method avoids the problem in cost depletion of estimating the number of recoverable units in the deposit—an estimate that may be only the wildest of guesses.[16] For the taxpayer, percentage depletion has the special attraction of an increasing depletion allowance as income rises, which ordinarily is when the deduction will save most in taxes. But percentage depletion just keeps rolling along, even after the taxpayer's full cost has been recovered. This is not an essential feature of percentage depletion, since the total depletion deductions could have been limited to the tax cost of the deposit, but the statute does not contain such a limitation.

Percentage depletion rates. The percentage of annual gross income that may be deducted as depletion ranges from 22 percent for certain minerals (such as sulfur and uranium) to 5 percent for other minerals (such as clay used in the manufacture of drainage and roofing tile). §613(b). The percentage depletion rates reflect the political clout of the various extractive industries. As the political influence of an industry changes, the percentage depletion rates sometimes change. For example, soon after the oil blockade was carried out by Arab members of OPEC, percentage depletion was eliminated for major oil and gas producers but was retained for the relatively small, independent producers and royalty owners (though even for them it was reduced from 22 percent to 15 percent). Many explanations have been given for these changes, but

---

16. Despite this, the taxpayer may have to compute depletion on a cost basis for some purposes (e.g., for purposes of the alternative minimum tax, discussed *infra* in Chapter 9), even though percentage depletion is used in determining taxable income.

the most cogent appears to be that independent producers and royalty owners were an effective lobbying group and were not as unpopular as the major oil and gas producers, whose images were tarnished by charges of collaboration with the blockading OPEC nations.

The concept of an "economic interest" in the depletable mineral. Many problems arise in determining which of the many persons with a financial stake in the extraction of a mineral are entitled to a deduction for depletion. Since the grant of depletion rights to one taxpayer may deny them to another in the chain of production, many cases have been litigated. The Supreme Court early formulated the notion of an economic interest in the mineral extracted as the touchstone. To have an economic interest, the taxpayer must have acquired an interest in the mineral in place and must look only to the mineral for return of his or her capital. Palmer v. Bender, 287 U.S. 551 (1933). For example, a landowner who allows another the right to drill for and extract oil in exchange for a royalty based on production has such an economic interest. See Thomas v. Perkins, 301 U.S. 655 (1937), and Kirby Petroleum Co. v. Commissioner, 326 U.S. 599 (1946). Thus, if the gross income is $100 and the royalty is 16 percent, the operator uses $83.50 as the base for percentage depletion while the landowner takes percentage depletion on the $16.50.

Income subject to percentage depletion. The appropriate percentage depletion rate for a mineral (other than oil or gas) is applied to the "gross income from mining" to determine the taxpayer's percentage depletion deduction. In United States v. Cannelton Sewer Pipe Co., 364 U.S. 76 (1960), the taxpayer mined clay, processed it, and manufactured clay pipes and other related products. It claimed percentage depletion on its gross income from the sale of manufactured sewer pipe. The Court found that it was entitled to a percentage depletion only on the value of the clay up to the cutoff point of processes used by a nonintegrated miner before sale. The range of choice in *Cannelton* was from $1.60 (the going price for fire clay) to $40 per ton, the value of the finished pipe product, but for some other minerals the range is even more dramatic; for example, salt worth $10 at an early point in the extractive process might be worth $1,800 after it has been purified for table use and packaged in small containers for sale to consumers.

Today, gross income from mining is defined in §613(c) to include income from certain technical processes and from transportation. Section 613(c)(4)(G) now contains an explicit statement of the processes that qualify for sewer pipe clay.

Limits on percentage depletion. Section 613 limits the percentage depletion deduction to 50 percent of the taxable income from the property. The importance of this limitation may be illustrated as follows: Suppose that *X* Corp. sells 10,000 tons of a certain mineral for $100,000; that *X* Corp. has labor and other mining costs (exclusive of depletion) of $90,000; and that the depletion percentage for the mineral is 22 percent. *X* Corp.'s gross income from mining is $100,000, and its depletion deduction would therefore be 22 percent of that amount, or $22,000. But *X* Corp.'s taxable income from mining is only $10,000, and its percentage depletion deduction is limited to half of that amount, or $5,000.

Intangible drilling costs. Section 263(c) allows taxpayers that develop an oil, gas, or geothermal deposit (as opposed to buying a deposit from someone else) to deduct as current expenses the "intangible drilling and development costs."[17] These costs, roughly speaking, include materials used up in the drilling or development process and labor. See Reg. §1.612-4. Section 263(c) is a dramatic exception to the general rule that the costs of acquiring a capital asset must be treated as a capital expenditure; it is an important element in the economics of the extractive industries and in tax shelter planning. To the same general effect as §263(c) are §§616 and 617, applying to other deposits.[18]

Percentage depletion is particularly beneficial to taxpayers who take advantage of §263(c). Such taxpayers will have deducted virtually all the costs of development before production of the mineral deposit and will have a cost basis in the deposit of zero (or close to it). Cost depletion will therefore be of no value. Percentage depletion, however, will be unaffected by the low basis.

Foreign natural resource interest. While the tax benefits provided to the natural resource industries are often justified on the ground that they stimulate increased supplies of such resources in the United States, the benefits in the past normally applied to foreign activities also. Increasingly, this has changed. See, for example, limitations to U.S. deposits in §613(b)(1)(B) and (b)(2); §613A(c); §616(d); §617(h)(1); §901(e).

The environment and natural resource tax benefits. It is interesting to speculate on the effect on some of our current environmental problems of the tax benefits available to our natural resource industries. For example, have these benefits led to a lower price for gasoline, encouraging the use of more and larger automobiles than would otherwise have been the case? If so, has this contributed to the demise or stillbirth of public transportation in many parts of our country and substantial reliance on automobile transportation, to the detriment of the quality of our air? Has this contributed to or created patterns of suburban living that might otherwise not have occurred? Does the fact that new metals and some virgin oil receive percentage depletion make recycling of used metals or used oil relatively less economical, thereby accelerating the exhaustion of natural resources and exacerbating waste disposal problems? Federal income tax benefits for home ownership, which we discuss in Chapter 9, may also have played a significant role. In addition, the federal and state highway trust funds direct gasoline tax and other revenues into highway construction, also likely affecting living patterns.

I. OTHER LOSS DEDUCTION ISSUES

One could think of depreciation, amortization, and other such cost recovery deductions as being allowed, despite the lack of a conventional realization

17. For large, "integrated" producers, however, 30 percent of intangible drilling and development costs must be amortized over a five-year period. See §291(b).

18. In the case of foreign mines, however, exploration and development costs are recovered by either (a) ten-year straight-line amortization, or (b) at the election of the taxpayer, as part of basis for cost depletion. See §616(d).

event such as a sale or exchange, because the underlying assets' finite useful lives make plausible the hypothesis of declining market value, by reason of the passage of time. However, some observed circumstances may take the place of a conventional realization event in indicating reliably that the taxpayer has incurred an economic loss. In such circumstances, denying the loss until there has been a sale or exchange might unduly disadvantage either taxpayers, if such a transaction is hard to arrange, or the government, if taxpayers have too much flexibility in deciding when it should occur. (For example, taxpayers might choose to wait for a year in which the tax rate is scheduled to increase.) For this reason, certain rules permit, and may require, deductions to be claimed under specified circumstances, even if no conventional realization event has occurred.

For example, §165(a) allows as a deduction "any loss sustained during the taxable year and not compensated for by insurance or otherwise," subject to exceptions that are stated later in §165. Section 166 allows deductions, under specified circumstances, for debts that have "become[] worthless during the taxable year." §166(a)(1). In short, both rules focus on particular value changes—the occurrence of a "loss" and a debt's becoming "worthless"—rather than expressly relying on the occurrence of conventional realization events.

The issues raised by such rules include the following: (1) When should a loss be allowed, even without a sale or exchange, or disallowed, even if there has been one? (2) Was a given loss incurred in the course of seeking to earn income? (3) How should the amount of an allowable loss be determined?[19]

1.   Timing of Loss Allowance

On its face, §165(a) is quite broad. It refers to "any loss sustained during the taxable year," if not insured or otherwise compensable. If one read this language out of context—that is, without regard either to applicable regulations and case law or to the history of the U.S. income tax law's general reliance on realization—one might think it potentially applied, say, to the case where the value of publicly traded stock that one owns happen to decline during the taxable year. After all, that is economically a "loss," and it has in a general economic sense been "sustained," even if it might subsequently be reversed via subsequent stock appreciation. (To be sure, even wholly out of context like this, one would need to give further attention to the question of whether the word "sustained" might require something more definite and irreversible.)

As it happens, however—both unsurprisingly and uncontroversially, given the historical centrality of the realization concept—the regulations eliminate any prospect that §165(a) could validly be so interpreted. Reg. §1.165-4(a) provides that "[n]o deduction shall be allowed under section 165(a) solely on account of a decline in the value of stock owned by the taxpayer when the

---

19. A further issue is whether a given loss should be classified as capital or ordinary. See Chapter 12, *infra,* regarding capital gains and losses generally.

decline is due to a fluctuation in the market price of the stock or to other similar cause. A mere shrinkage in the value of stock owned by the taxpayer, even though extensive, does not give rise to a deduction under section 165(a) if the stock has any recognizable value on the date claimed as the date of loss."

In addition, to explain §165(a)'s scope more generally, Reg. §1.165-1(b) provides that "[t]o be allowable as a deduction under section 165(a), a loss must be evidenced by closed and completed transactions, fixed by identifiable events, and . . . [subject to specified exceptions], actually sustained during the taxable year." This generally requires a decisive change of some kind, such as from the taxpayer's abandoning an asset or business or its becoming irreversibly worthless. "Assets may not be considered worthless, even when they have no liquidated value, if there is a reasonable hope and expectation that they will become valuable in the future." Rev. Rul. 2004-58, 2004-1 C.B. 1043.

Section 166, allowing deductions that become wholly or partially worthless during the taxable year, similarly does not apply merely by reason of a debt's fluctuation in value "such as by reason of a rise in interest, or a growing possibility that the debtor will eventually have to default." The regulations provide that, in assessing worthlessness, the IRS "will consider all pertinent evidence, including the value of the collateral, if any, securing the debt and the financial condition of the debtor." Reg. §1.166-2(a). Legal action to enforce payment is not required "[w]here the surrounding circumstances indicate that a debt is worthless and uncollectible" and that such action "would in all probability not result in the satisfaction of execution on a judgment." Reg. §1.166-2(b). Bankruptcy proceedings against the debtor are "generally an indication of the worthlessness of at least part of an unsecured and unpreferred debt," Reg. §1.166-2(c)(1), and a determination of worthlessness need not await such proceedings' termination. Reg. §1.166-2(c)(2).

For theft losses sustained by a taxpayer, the year in which the theft occurred may differ from that in which the taxpayer discovered it. Given the obvious difficulties that would result from requiring the taxpayer to determine when a freshly discovered theft had actually occurred—and then from needing to file an amended return, if still permissible, for that earlier year—Reg. §1.165-8(a)(2) provides that a theft loss generally is treated as sustained in the year when the taxpayer discovers the loss.

Losses not currently allowable despite the occurrence of a sale or exchange. The above-discussed rules concern cases where a loss with respect to an asset may be currently allowed, despite the lack of a sale or exchange. The other side of the coin involves rules providing that, even though a sale or exchange at a loss has occurred, no loss deduction is currently permissible. The apparent rationale may be either that there is reason to doubt the occurrence of an overall economic loss, or that the sale, when viewed in a larger context, did not sufficiently change the taxpayer's relationship to the property to justify current loss recognition.

Under §1092, taxpayers who have straddles, or "offsetting positions with respect to personal property," cannot currently deduct any loss with respect to such positions, except to the extent that such loss exceeds the unrecognized gain with respect to the offsetting positions. §1092(a)(1)(A). For this purpose, "offsetting positions" arise "if there is a substantial diminution of the taxpayer's risk of loss from holding any position with respect to personal property by reason of his holding one or more other positions with respect to personal property (whether or not of the same kind)." §1092(c)(2)(A).

A simple example would be as follows. Suppose that a taxpayer holds both (a) a share of Microsoft stock, currently worth $60, and (b) a put option, entitling the taxpayer to sell a share of Microsoft stock for $60. These are offsetting positions, each of which reduces the taxpayer's risk of loss from holding the other position. After all, if Microsoft's stock price declines, reducing the value of the share, the put option will become more valuable, thus reducing the taxpayer's risk of loss with respect to the stock. By the same token, if Microsoft's stock price increases, causing the put option to lose value, the taxpayer will have offsetting gain from the rise in share value.[20]

Absent §1092, this would (and at one time did) create an easy opportunity for taxpayers selectively to realize and recognize losses, while not doing the same for gains. The first step would be to create a straddle by acquiring offsetting positions. In general, the value of such positions would be expected to "travel" in opposite directions, so long as there is any price volatility whatsoever. Thus, in the above case, the taxpayer would be confident of generating a tax loss whether Microsoft's stock price went up or down. If it went up, she would continue to hold the stock and would sell the put option for a loss. If it went down, she would continue to hold the put and would sell the stock for a loss. Section 1092 addresses this tax planning opportunity by disallowing the loss, to the extent of unrecognized gain from offsetting positions. However, since the unrecognized loss is carried over to the next taxable year (see §1092(a)(1)(B)), it will be allowed when the offsetting gain is recognized.

Section 1091, addressing "wash sales" of stock and securities, may frustrate a different type of tax planning gambit. Suppose a taxpayer owns a share of stock that has declined substantially in value. This gives her a tax reason to sell the stock, even if she would otherwise have continued holding it, so long as the loss will in fact be currently allowable.[21] Sometimes, however, taxpayers don't actually want to sell a given financial asset, even if it has declined in value — for example, because they believe that its long-term prospects remain good.

Thus, in the absence of §1091, taxpayers could seek convenient loss realization and recognition, without actually having to change their economic positions substantially, by purchasing the same (or similar) items close in time to the date of sale. In terms of the above example, involving Microsoft stock that is currently trading at $60 per share, suppose that its stock price had once been as high as $100. A taxpayer who had bought it at that price, and still

---

20. A simpler example still, causing the two positions to be even more precisely offsetting, would involve the taxpayer's holding both a call option to buy Microsoft (or other) stock for a specified price and a put option to buy such stock at a specified price (even if it is not exactly the same price).

21. One possible reason why the loss might not be currently allowable, even without regard to §1091, applies if the stock is a capital asset for tax purposes. Under §1211, capital losses are generally deductible only to the extent of capital gains (plus $3,000, for individuals). We address the definition of capital assets, and the application of §1211, in Chapter 12, *infra.*

wanted to hold it despite the price drop to $60, might simply buy a new share, shortly before or after selling the old one. When all the dust settled, the taxpayer's economic position would be unchanged, except for its having borne price risk for the short period between the sale and the new purchase.

Section 1091 addresses this tax planning gambit by disallowing losses on the sale of stock or securities if, "within a period beginning 30 days before the date of such sale or disposition and ending 30 days after such date, the taxpayer has acquired . . . or has entered into a contract or option so to acquire, substantially identical stock or securities." §1091(a). However, the result of the loss disallowance generally is only its deferral, rather than permanent disallowance. The basis of the replacement stock or securities in the "wash sale" generally is the same as that for the item that was sold. However, such basis is increased to the extent that the new purchase price exceeded the sale price or reduced to the extent that the sale price was the higher of the two. §1091(d).[22]

In illustration, suppose again that a taxpayer had earlier purchased Microsoft stock for $100 and now, within a thirty-day period, both buys and sells shares of such stock for $60. The basis of the newly acquired stock is $100, just like that of the stock that was sold. Thus, if the new stock is now sold for $60, and there is no further wash sale aspect, a $40 loss will indeed be allowable. If the old stock was sold for $60, and the new stock was purchased for $61, there will be a $1 increase in its basis, to $101. And if the old stock was sold for $60, while the new one is purchased for $59, there will be instead a $1 reduction in its basis, to $99.

2.   Was the Taxpayer Seeking to Earn Income?

A second issue that may affect the tax treatment of losses that did not involve a sale or exchange is that of whether the taxpayer held the item that generated the loss in connection with seeking to earn income. Under §165, individuals can generally deduct losses, as defined by the provision, that were incurred either in a trade or business or in any transaction entered into for profit. §165(c)(1) and (2). However, for losses of property not connected with a trade or business or a transaction entered into profit—i.e., for personal assets, such as consumer goods—such losses are disallowed unless they resulted from "fire, storm, shipwreck, or other casualty, or from theft," and even in those instances certain further limitations apply. §165(c)(3) and (h). Under the 2017 act, from 2018 to 2025, personal casualty losses are only deductible to the extent that they arise from or are attributable to a federally declared disaster. (Personal casualty losses not incurred in a federally declared disaster can still be used to offset personal casualty gains.) §165(h). We further discuss such "personal casualty losses" in Chapter 10. In addition, Reg. §1.165-9 provides that a loss

---

22. This is generally equivalent to giving the newly acquired stock a cost basis, increased by the amount of the disallowed loss with respect to the old stock.

on selling one's home is not deductible under §165 (or generally otherwise),[23] notwithstanding that one might view home ownership as serving both investment and personal consumption objectives.[24]

3.   Determining the Amount of Allowable Loss

A further issue concerns the measurement of a loss allowable under §165 or §166. Under the former provision, the loss property's adjusted basis is used to determine the amount of the loss. §165(b). Thus, for example, suppose a building that the taxpayer used in a business was destroyed in a hurricane and that no insurance or other compensation was available. If the building's basis was $100,000, while its value was $1 million, only $100,000 would be deductible under §165. This rule generally prevents unrealized appreciation, which has not been taxed, from nonetheless triggering deductible losses.[25]

4.   Section 165 in Action: The Madoff Fraud

The following Revenue Ruling was issued by the IRS to address issues pertaining to taxpayers who had been victimized by the infamous Madoff fraud. In this fraud, Bernard Madoff, the founder and chairman of a prominent Wall Street investment firm, was purportedly profitably investing tens of billions of dollars on behalf of his many clients; as it turned out, however, he was found to have been running a Ponzi scheme, issuing fraudulent profit reports and using deposits to pay off investors who wanted to withdraw their cash. When the fraud was finally discovered in 2008 — after a more than thirty-year run — Madoff went to prison on a 150-year sentence, leaving investors with more than $50 billion of losses, relative to the money they had thought they had.

---

23. More specifically, §1.165-9(a) disallows a "loss sustained on the sale of residential property purchased or constructed by the taxpayer for use as his personal residence and so used by him up to the time of the sale." Where such property is converted from personal use to a business or income-producing use prior to its sale, such as in the case where the taxpayer starts using it instead as a rental property, economic loss occurring after the conversion may end up being allowable. See §1.165-9(b).

24. Section 166 distinguishes between business and nonbusiness bad debts. Here, however, the distinction only affects whether the loss from worthlessness is an ordinary loss or a capital loss. (As we discuss in Chapter 12, capital losses generally cannot be deducted against ordinary income under §1211.) Nonbusiness debts of taxpayers other than corporations generally give rise to capital, rather than ordinary, losses upon the occurrence of worthlessness. §166(d)(1) and (2). A nonbusiness debt is defined as any debt other than one that the taxpayer created or acquired in the course of a trade or business, or the loss from the worthlessness of which was incurred in the taxpayer's trade or business. §166(d)(2).

25. However, just as generally happens upon a sale of property, unrealized appreciation that has entered into the taxpayer's basis by reason of §1014 (allowing basis step-up with respect to property acquired by bequest from a decedent) can increase the amount deductible under §165.

REVENUE RULING 2009-9
2009-1 C.B. 735

ISSUES

(1) Is a loss from criminal fraud or embezzlement in a transaction entered into for profit a theft loss . . . under §165 of the Internal Revenue Code?

(2) Is such a loss subject to . . . the personal loss limits in §165(h) . . . ?

(3) In what year is such a loss deductible?

(4) How is the amount of such a loss determined?

. . .

FACTS

A is an individual who uses the cash receipts and disbursements method of accounting and files federal income tax returns on a calendar year basis. B holds himself out to the public as an investment advisor and securities broker.

In Year 1, A, in a transaction entered into for profit, opened an investment account with B, contributed $100x to the account, and provided B with power of attorney to use the $100x to purchase and sell securities on A's behalf. A instructed B to reinvest any income and gains earned on the investments. In Year 3, A contributed an additional $20x to the account.

B periodically issued account statements to A that reported the securities purchases and sales that B purportedly made in A's investment account and the balance of the account. B also issued tax reporting statements to A and to the Internal Revenue Service that reflected purported gains and losses on A's investment account. B also reported to A that no income was earned in Year 1 and that for each of the Years 2 through 7 the investments earned $10x of income (interest, dividends, and capital gains), which A included in gross income on A's federal income tax returns.

At all times prior to Year 8 and part way through Year 8, B was able to make distributions to investors who requested them. A took a single distribution of $30x from the account in Year 7.

In Year 8, it was discovered that B's purported investment advisory and brokerage activity was in fact a fraudulent investment arrangement known as a "Ponzi" scheme. Under this scheme, B purported to invest cash or property on behalf of each investor, including A, in an account in the investor's name. For each investor's account, B reported investment activities and resulting income amounts that were partially or wholly fictitious. In some cases, in response to requests for withdrawal, B made payments of purported income or principal to investors. These payments were made, at least in part, from amounts that other investors had invested in the fraudulent arrangement.

When B's fraud was discovered in Year 8, B had only a small fraction of the funds that B reported on the account statements that B issued to A and other investors. A did not receive any reimbursement or other recovery for the loss in Year 8. The period of limitation on filing a claim for refund under §6511 has not yet expired for Years 5 through 7, but has expired for Years 1 through 4.

B's actions constituted criminal fraud or embezzlement under the law of the jurisdiction in which the transactions occurred. At no time prior to the discovery did A know that B's activities were a fraudulent scheme. . . .

LAW AND ANALYSIS

ISSUE 1. THEFT LOSS

Section 165(a) allows a deduction for losses sustained during the taxable year and not compensated by insurance or otherwise. For individuals, §165(c)(2) allows a deduction for losses incurred in a transaction entered into for profit, and §165(c)(3) allows a deduction for certain losses not connected to a transaction entered into for profit, including theft losses. Under §165(e), a theft loss is sustained in the taxable year the taxpayer discovers the loss. . . .

For federal income tax purposes, "theft" is a word of general and broad connotation, covering any criminal appropriation of another's property to the use of the taker, including theft by swindling, false pretenses and any other form of guile. . . . A taxpayer claiming a theft loss must prove that the loss resulted from a taking of property that was illegal under the law of the jurisdiction in which it occurred and was done with criminal intent. . . . However, a taxpayer need not show a conviction for theft. . . .

The character of an investor's loss related to fraudulent activity depends, in part, on the nature of the investment. For example, a loss that is sustained on the worthlessness or disposition of stock acquired on the open market for investment is a capital loss, even if the decline in the value of the stock is attributable to fraudulent activities of the corporation's officers or directors, because the officers or directors did not have the specific intent to deprive the shareholder of money or property. . . .

In the present situation . . . B specifically intended to, and did, deprive A of money by criminal acts. B's actions constituted a theft from A, as theft is defined for §165 purposes. Accordingly, A's loss is a theft loss, not a capital loss. . . .

ISSUE 2. DEDUCTION LIMITATIONS

Section 165(h) imposes [certain] limitations on casualty loss deductions, including theft loss deductions, for property not connected either with a trade or business or with a transaction entered into for profit. . . .

In opening an investment account with B, A entered into a transaction for profit. A's theft loss therefore is deductible under §165(c)(2).

. . .

ISSUE 3. YEAR OF DEDUCTION

Section 165(e) provides that any loss arising from theft is treated as sustained during the taxable year in which the taxpayer discovers the loss. Under §§1.165-8(a)(2) and 1.165-1(d), however, if, in the year of discovery, there exists a claim for reimbursement with respect to which there is a reasonable prospect of recovery, no portion of the loss for which reimbursement may be received is sustained until the taxable year in which it can be ascertained with reasonable certainty whether or not the reimbursement will be received, for example, by a settlement, adjudication, or abandonment of the claim. Whether a reasonable prospect of recovery exists is a question of fact to be determined upon examination of all facts and circumstances.

A may deduct the theft loss in Year 8, the year the theft loss is discovered, provided that the loss is not covered by a claim for reimbursement or other recovery as to which A has a reasonable prospect of recovery. To the extent that A's deduction is reduced by such a claim, recoveries on the claim in a later taxable year are not includible in A's gross income. If A recovers a greater amount in a later year, or an amount that initially was not covered by a claim as to which there was a reasonable prospect of recovery, the recovery is includible in A's gross income in the later year under the tax benefit rule, to the extent the earlier deduction reduced A's income tax. See §111; §1.165-1(d)(2)(iii). Finally, if A recovers less than the amount that was covered by a claim as to which there was a reasonable prospect of recovery that reduced the deduction for theft in Year 8, an additional deduction is allowed in the year the amount of recovery is ascertained with reasonable certainty.

ISSUE 4. AMOUNT OF DEDUCTION

Section 1.165-8(c) provides that the amount deductible in the case of a theft loss is determined consistently with the manner described in §1.165-7 for determining the amount of a casualty loss, considering the fair market value of the property immediately after the theft to be zero. Under these provisions, the amount of an investment theft loss is the basis of the property (or the amount of money) that was loss, less any reimbursement or other compensation.

The amount of a theft loss resulting from a fraudulent investment arrangement is generally the initial amount invested in the arrangement, plus any additional investments, less amounts withdrawn, if any, reduced by reimbursements or other recoveries and reduced by claims as to which there is a reasonable prospect of recovery. If an amount is reported to the investor as income in years prior to the year of discovery of the theft, the investor includes the amount in gross income, and the investor reinvests the amount in the arrangement, this amount increases the deductible theft loss.

Accordingly, the amount of A's theft loss for purposes of §165 includes A's original Year 1 investment ($100x) and additional Year 3 investment ($20x). A's loss also includes the amounts that A reported as gross income on A's federal income tax returns for Years 2 through 7 ($60x). A's loss is reduced by the amount of money distributed to A in Year 7 ($30x). If A has a claim for reimbursement with respect to which there is a reasonable prospect of recovery, A may not deduct in Year 8 the portion of the loss that is covered by the claim.

. . .

HOLDINGS

(1) A loss from criminal fraud or embezzlement in a transaction entered into for profit is a theft loss, not a capital loss, under §165.

(2) A theft loss in a transaction entered into for profit is deductible under §165(c)(2), not §165(c)(3). . . .

(3) A theft loss in a transaction entered into for profit is deductible in the year the loss is discovered, provided that the loss is not covered by a claim for reimbursement or recovery with respect to which there is a reasonable prospect for recovery.

(4) The amount of a theft loss in a transaction entered into for profit is generally the amount invested in the arrangement, less amounts withdrawn, if any, reduced by reimbursements or recoveries, and reduced by claims as to which there is a reasonable prospect of recovery. Where an amount is reported as income to the investor prior to discovery of the arrangement and the investor includes that amount in gross income and reinvests this amount in the arrangement, the amount of the theft loss is increased by the purportedly reinvested amount.

    . . .

NOTES AND QUESTIONS

1. The Madoff investors clearly invested in his fund in pursuit of profit. Thus, if their losses were theft losses covered by §165(c), there could be no serious dispute that §165(c)(2), rather than §165(c)(3) (concerning personal casualty losses) was the operative provision. However, prior to the issuance of the Revenue Ruling, it had been considered less certain that the IRS would agree that the losses qualified as theft losses, rather than as capital losses. This made an important difference because, as we discuss in Chapter 12, capital losses generally are limited to the amount of capital gains for the year, plus (for individuals) $3,000.

2. To illustrate the importance of this difference, suppose that, consistent with the stated facts in the ruling, a given taxpayer had (a) invested a total of $120,000 with Madoff, (b) reported a total of $60,000 of taxable income from her Madoff account, and (c) withdrawn from the account $30,000 that was treated as a tax-free return of capital (like withdrawing money from a bank account). Her basis in the account would therefore have been $150,000 (i.e., $120,000 + $60,000 − $30,000). If she then collected zero when the Madoff fraud was discovered, and never had any other capital gains, a capital loss classification would have meant that she could only deduct $3,000 per year (for the next fifty years!).[26] By contrast, under the Ruling, the full theft loss deduction of $150,000 would be allowable immediately.

3. While the above consideration provides a strong equitable argument in favor of the Ruling's conclusion, could it be questioned on purely semantic

---

26. If she died sooner than this, the unused capital losses would expire and could not be used by her estate or any other taxpayer. See Rev. Rul. 74-175, 1974-1 C.B. 52.

grounds? Even if we agree that the investor was a theft victim with respect to her net $90,000 (i.e., $120,000 minus $30,000) cash investment in the account, could one argue that the $60,000 in fictitious profits that she reported could not actually have been stolen from her, since (albeit unbeknownst to her) it never actually existed to begin with?

J. INVESTMENTS IN HUMAN CAPITAL

1. Educational Expenses in Theory

Human capital can be defined as the present value of one's remaining lifetime earning ability. Common usage of the term (at least by economists) reflects that one's ability to work and earn income has economic value. Thus, each of us, unless incapable of productive labor, effectively owns a productive asset. What is more, this asset presents its owner with many of the same choices and issues as other assets. For example, one can try to increase its value through investment, such as in education and job training. In addition, just as with other assets that have finite useful lives, one faces the inevitable prospect of its depreciating over time. One also faces the risk that its market value will unpredictably fluctuate, due either to events in one's own life or to external forces that change market prices.

Human capital and other capital, of course, have important differences. For example, human capital is not tradable, at least in the same ways as are both physical assets and many intangible assets. In addition, we all think of our personal human endowments as not limited to the ability to earn money in market transactions. Our nonmarket capabilities may include, for example, enjoying our own lives, engaging in leisure activities, and helping other people. The use and development of these capabilities may compete with our using and developing our capacities to engage in remunerated market production.

Even when thought of purely in a market sense, human capital is by far the most important asset class in America. For example, labor income, as officially measured by the government, is always well over half of gross domestic product (GDP). This finding persists even though much of what the government officially classifies as capital income, rather than as labor income, derives from labor in an economic sense. Suppose, for example, that you form a new Internet start-up, which is so successful that you are able to sell its stock for $1 billion in the initial public offering. While official statistics would likely classify this as capital income, rather than labor income, it might in fact have been the product of your (and any colleagues') personal effort.

PRESENT LAW AND ANALYSIS RELATING TO
TAX BENEFITS FOR HIGHER EDUCATION

Staff of the Joint Committee on Taxation

July 21, 2004

JCX-52-04

. . .

B.   TREATMENT OF EDUCATION EXPENSES UNDER AN INCOME TAX

EDUCATIONAL EXPENDITURES

Students and their families incur direct educational expenses when they pay tuition and fees. Federal, State, and local governments and private persons make expenditures on behalf of students by funding State and local and private educational institutions. Such expenditures by governments or private persons are equivalent to the government or private person transferring funds to the student which the student subsequently pays over to the educational institution. Lastly, students incur implicit expenditures for education by choosing schooling over the alternative of taking a job and earning a wage. The time spent in school means forgone income. Alternatively viewed, it is as if the student worked, was paid, and used the wages to purchase education. Analysts have concluded that the largest cost of obtaining an education comes from forgone wages.

Post-secondary education helps individuals develop general analytic and reasoning skills (e.g., problem solving) and often job specific skills (e.g., nursing training) that enhance the student's ability to earn a future income. In this way, expenditures on education are like an investment in a capital good: an outlay is made in the present for a machine that will produce income over a number of years in the future. It is because of this similarity that economists often refer to expenditures on education as investment in "human capital." However, some part of expenditures on post-secondary education are not as obviously investments in human capital but are more like consumption. For example, the chemical engineering student who takes an elective course in the history of music probably would not find her future earning potential increased by that particular elective. It is difficult to determine what portion of post-secondary education represents consumption for any given student and what portion represents investment in human capital. . . .

EDUCATIONAL EXPENSES UNDER A THEORETICAL INCOME TAX

Under a theoretical income tax, any expenditures undertaken in the present for returns that are expected in the future should be capitalized and recovered as the future returns are earned. Consumption expenditures are neither deductible nor amortizable under a theoretical income tax. Thus, certain expenditures on education should be capitalized by the taxpayer and recovered against future earnings. As discussed above, the relevant expenditures to be capitalized would only be those that represent investments in human capital, not those related to consumption. Of course, making such decisions would be quite difficult in practice. For example, the would-be chemical engineer of the example above may not know whether her future employment will be in the chemical industry or perhaps as a chanteuse, making it difficult to know how to account for the costs of the chemical engineering courses and the music course. Many educational expenses are paid by a parent on behalf of a student. In such case, the theoretical income tax would permit amortization only by the student.

EDUCATIONAL EXPENSES UNDER THE PRESENT-LAW INCOME TAX

As discussed above, there are three types of expenditures made by students on their education: (1) payment via implicit or explicit transfers received from governments or private persons; (2) forgone wages; and (3) direct payment of tuition and other educational expenses by the student.

By not including the transfers from governments or private persons in the income of the student, present law offers the equivalent of expensing of those expenditures undertaken on behalf of the student by governments and private persons. This treatment (the equivalent of expensing) also is provided for direct transfers to students in the form of qualified scholarships or employer-provided educational assistance, which are excludable from income. Similarly, because forgone wages are never earned, the implicit expenditure incurred by students forgoing present earnings also receives expensing under the present-law income tax.

The present-law treatment of direct payment of tuition and other educational expenses by the student is subject to various tax treatments. With certain exceptions . . . the present-law income tax treats direct payments of tuition and other educational expenses as consumption, neither deductible nor amortizable. . . .

The theoretical income tax would have all expenditures toward investment in human capital capitalized and recovered against the student's future earnings. . . . On balance, the variety and complexity of educational benefits afforded through the tax code, when coupled with expenditures that do not receive favorable tax treatment, make it difficult to determine the extent to which educational expenditures are subsidized by the tax code, relative to investments in physical capital.

2. Defining Deductible Educational Expenses in Practice

The following two cases, in which taxpayers sought to deduct education expenses in connection with their contemporaneous jobs, have opposite outcomes. How clear and easy to apply is the line between them, and how (if at all) does it relate to the underlying theoretical issues?

CARROLL v. COMMISSIONER

418 F.2d 91 (7th Cir. 1969)

CASTLE, Chief Judge . . .

James A. Carroll (hereinafter referred to as the petitioner) was employed by the Chicago Police Department as a detective during the year in question. In his 1964 federal income tax return, he listed as a deduction $720.80 which represented his cost of enrollment in DePaul University. The course of study entered into by plaintiff was stated by him to be in preparation for entrance to law school and consisted of a major in Philosophy. The six courses in which plaintiff was enrolled included two English, two Philosophy, one History and one Political Science course. Petitioner justified the deduction under §162(a), . . . as an expense "relative to improving job skills to maintain [his] position as a detective."

During 1964, the Police Department had in effect General Order No. 63-24, which encouraged policemen to attend colleges and universities by arranging their schedules of duties so as to not conflict with class schedules. Petitioner availed himself of the benefits of this order when he enrolled in DePaul University. . . .

[Reg. §1.162-5] abolished the primary purpose test and established a more objective standard for determining whether the cost of education may be deducted as a business expense. . . . Thus, petitioner in the instant case must justify his deduction under §1.162-5(a)(1), as maintaining or improving skills required by him in his employment. . . .

While the Commissioner concedes that a general college education "hold[s] out the potential for improved performance as a policeman," he argues that petitioner has failed to demonstrate a sufficient relationship between such an education and the particular job skills required by a policeman. Thus, although a college education improves the job skills of all who avail themselves of it, this relationship is insufficient to remove the expense of such education from the realm of personal expenses which are disallowed under §262. Many expenses, such as the cost of commuting, clothing, and a babysitter for a working mother, are related and even necessary to an individual's occupation or employment, but may not be deducted under §162(a) since they are essentially personal expenditures. See Smith v. Commissioner. We are of the opinion that plaintiff's educational expenditure is even more personal and less related to his job skills than the expenditures enumerated above.

Of course, not all college courses may be so classified as nondeductible. Thus, the cost of a course in Industrial Psychology was properly deducted from the income of an Industrial Psychologist, although it led to an advanced degree and the potential of new job opportunities. . . . Similarly, a housing administrator was allowed to deduct the cost of courses in housing administration, . . . and a professional harpist was allowed to deduct the cost of music lessons. . . . The difference between those cases and the instant case is that petitioner's courses were general and basically unrelated to his duties as a policeman. As the Commissioner notes in his brief, a currently employed taxpayer such as petitioner might be allowed to deduct the cost of college courses which directly relate to the duties of his employment. If such courses were taken along with other, more general courses, their cost, or that part of the tuition representing their cost, would be deductible under §162(a). In the instant case, however, petitioner does not claim that any particular course in which he was enrolled in 1964 bears any greater relationship to his job skills than the others.

Therefore, while tax incentives might be employed as an effective tool to encourage such valuable public servants as policemen, as well as others, to acquire a college education so as to improve their general competence, we feel that such a decision should be made by the Congress rather than the courts. To allow as a deduction the cost of a general college education would surely go beyond the original intention of Congress in its enactment of the Internal Revenue Code of 1954. Accordingly, we affirm the judgment of the Tax Court.

Affirmed.

NOTES AND QUESTIONS

1. The cost of a college education, according to the orthodox rationale relied on in *Carroll*, is a personal expense. Mr. Carroll tried to avoid losing on this ground by arguing that his education was helpful to him in his job as a detective. This, however, was difficult to square with his taking classes of such general interest as English, Philosophy (his major), History, and Political Science.

2. Mr. Carroll further said that he went to college in order to prepare to go to law school. Would he have had a stronger case with respect to law school tuition, based on the argument that detectives can make professional use of legal expertise?

3. In the renowned television series *The Wire*, narcotics detective Kima Greggs is studying at night for a law degree. Would her case for deducting the law school tuition have been strengthened or weakened if her reason for seeking the degree had been that it would increase her chances of being promoted to lieutenant and then further rising in the hierarchy of the Baltimore police department?

KOPAIGORA v. COMMISSIONER
Tax Court Summary Opinion 2016-35 (August 2, 2016)

NEGA, Judge . . .

Petitioner began working for Marriott International Corp. in 2002 as an accounting manager. In June 2006 petitioner accepted a position as senior assistant controller for the Marriott hotel in Los Angeles International Airport (Marriott LAX). In his role as senior assistant controller, petitioner was responsible for managing a team of employees, reviewing employee performances annually, participating in hiring activities, and training employees. Petitioner's duties included preparing financial reports, creating budgets, analyzing financial data, producing forecasts to enable reaction to business changes, and monitoring different departments' performances. Additionally, petitioner conducted audits, prepared an accounting of taxes, prepared financial reports according to generally accepted accounting principles (GAAP), enforced internal controls, reconciled balance sheets, and ensured compliance with reporting requirements.

In July 2010 petitioner enrolled in the EMBA degree program at Brigham Young University (BYU) in Utah in order to improve his leadership skills in corporate finance and management. Petitioner would work at Marriott LAX on the weekdays and would travel to Salt Lake City, Utah, every other weekend to attend classes at BYU. Petitioner took the following courses in pursuit of his EMBA degree: Introduction to Management; Introduction to Management 2; Corporate Financial Reporting; Entrepreneurial Management; Leadership; Operations Management; Business Finance; Marketing Management; Management and Information Technology; Human Resources Management; Managerial Accounting 1; Business Ethics; Strategy; Selected Topics in Management; Global Business Negotiations; Strategy Implementation and the General Manager's Role; Foreign Business Excursion; Introduction to Global Management; and Spreadsheets for Business Analysis.

On April 18, 2011, while petitioner was still working towards his EMBA degree, his employment with Marriott International Corp. was terminated for reasons that were later found to be unjustified. After his termination from Marriott International Corp. petitioner continued to pursue his EMBA degree at BYU and look for full-time employment within the corporate finance and accounting field as a controller, assistant controller, senior manager, vice president, or director.

Petitioner graduated from the EMBA degree program in August 2012. On September 2, 2012, petitioner was hired as vice president of finance of Driveit Financial Services (Driveit), a small financing company. As vice president, petitioner was responsible for overseeing department managers, managing and leading a team of employees, supervising employees in daily issues of accounting, cash, risk, and business operations, and participating in hiring and training. Additionally, petitioner was responsible for auditing, accounting for taxes, setting up monthly reporting according to GAAP, and enforcing internal controls.

Petitioner . . . claimed an $18,879 deduction for petitioner's EMBA degree expenses. . . .

Education expenses are deductible if they satisfy the general requirements under section 162 as well as the specific requirements under the regulations. Section 162 requires a taxpayer to be presently engaged in a trade or business in order for education expenses to be deductible. . . . A taxpayer may be engaged in a trade or business, although unemployed, if the taxpayer was previously involved in and actively sought to continue in that trade or business while pursuing a defined degree program related to his or her line of work. . . .

The regulations disallow a deduction for education expenses for: (1) education required to meet the minimum requirements of a taxpayer's trade or business or (2) a program of study leading to the qualification of a taxpayer in a new trade or business. Sec. 1.162-5(b), Income Tax Regs. When evaluating whether education expenses qualify the taxpayer for a new trade or business, the Court uses a "commonsense approach" comparing "the types of tasks and activities which the taxpayer was qualified to perform before the acquisition of a particular title or degree, and those which he is qualified to perform afterwards." Glenn v. Commissioner, 62 T.C. 270, 275 (1974). . . .

If the taxpayer can show that neither of the disqualifying factors applies, the taxpayer can deduct the education expenses if the education maintains or improves skills required by the taxpayer in his or her employment or other trade or business. Sec. 1.162-5(a)(1), Income Tax Regs. Required skills in a taxpayer's employment are those skills that are appropriate or helpful in the taxpayer's employment or trade or business. . . .

Petitioners argue that they are entitled to deductions for petitioner's unreimbursed employee expenses because petitioner was established in the business of corporate finance and management before commencing his pursuit of an EMBA degree, he continued to be established in this business during his temporary unemployment, and his EMBA degree did not qualify him for a new trade or business. . . .

Respondent argues that petitioner did not carry on his trade or business through the 2011 tax year because he was unemployed for an indefinite period, the EMBA degree was a general degree that did not maintain or improve specific skills required for his employment, and the degree qualified him for a new trade or business.

We believe that the facts support petitioners' argument. When petitioner enrolled in the EMBA degree program, he was a well-established finance and accounting business manager at Marriott LAX. He managed the hotel's financial operations and auditing departments, he was responsible for large groups of employees from various backgrounds and specializations, and he made sure the hotel's business practices were in compliance with GAAP. When his employment was abruptly terminated, he continued to take courses at BYU that improved his managerial and leadership skills—skills that were appropriate and helpful to his position as a business manager. The courses petitioner chose to fulfill his degree requirements did not qualify him for a new trade or business because he was not qualified to perform new tasks or activities with the conferral of his degree. Instead, petitioner chose courses in a line of study that he was familiar with—management and finance. Even though petitioner took a few courses that were outside this scope, we do not believe that these courses by themselves could have prepared him to enter a new trade or business.

Finally, petitioner's unemployment did not prevent him from continuing his trade or business as a finance and accounting business manager for purposes of section 162. After petitioner's employment at Marriott LAX was terminated he actively sought employment within the corporate finance and accounting field for the remainder of his time at BYU, and his active job search paid off. Soon after he graduated from the EMBA degree program, petitioner was hired by another company to perform duties that were substantially similar to the duties of his former job. Although petitioner was hired after he graduated, nothing in the record suggests that the degree was a prerequisite for the job. See sec. 1.162-5(b)(2), Income Tax Regs. We hold that petitioner's EMBA degree tuition education expenses are deductible as unreimbursed employee expenses under section 162. . . .

NOTES AND QUESTIONS

1. Suppose that Mr. Kopaigora (a) had been told by his supervisors at Marriott that he should get the EMBA degree to help him meet his responsibilities in the senior assistant controller job, and/or (b) would likely not have been hired at the new company had he not possessed the degree. How would these hypothetical facts have affected the analysis and the outcome in the case?

2. *Additional benefits for education.* A number of tax benefits for college costs have been enacted since 1996.[27] These include the Hope scholarship credit (§25A(a)(1)), the lifetime learning credit (§25A(a)(2)), the deduction for interest on education loans (§221), the tax exemption for qualified tuition programs (§529), and the tax exemption for Coverdell education savings accounts (§530). These provisions employ a bewildering array of income phaseouts, definitions of eligible individuals, and other special features. A felony drug conviction, for example, deprives one of the Hope scholarship credit but not the other benefits.

The §529 "qualified tuition program" has proved to be especially attractive, particularly because it is available to high-income taxpayers while many of the other programs are phased out as income rises above modest levels. Qualified tuition includes public, private, or religious elementary or secondary school tuition, and postsecondary school tuition. The so-called 529 plans are set up by the states, and each of the fifty states has its own plan. Any person can invest in the plan of any state, creating an account for the benefit of a designated beneficiary to pay educational expenses, including room, board, tuition, and certain other expenses. Thus, for example, a wealthy couple living in Maine with grandchildren living in Massachusetts can set up a plan under Colorado law (and it can in effect be administered by their broker in New York). The state plans vary as to the types of available investments, fees, and various other matters, and as to the state income tax treatment of distributions (see www.savingforcollege.com). The amounts contributed to these plans are not deductible, but the income earned while the funds are held in the plan is not taxed, and the distributions are tax free if made for "qualified educational expenses" (otherwise, they are taxable and subject to a 10 percent penalty). The person setting up and funding the plan can retain substantial control over the disposition of the funds by virtue of the freedom to change the beneficiary at any time, so long as the recipient is a member of the "family" of the original designated beneficiary. For this purpose, "family" is broadly defined to include the beneficiary's spouse, siblings, first cousins, descendants, and various other relations identified in §152(a)(1) through (8).

These 529 plans have attracted billions of dollars in investment, which generates fees for the states, which in turn has generated competition among the states. The competition has encouraged some states to engage in anticompetitive measures such as imposition of a state income tax on distributions from

---

27. Section 222, enacted in 2001, provided an above-the-line deduction for "qualified higher education expenses," such as tuition, paid by the taxpayer during a taxable year. However, it expired at the end of 2014.

plans set up under the laws of another state. The 529 plans compete with, but have proved far more popular than, the "Coverdell Educational Savings Accounts" (§530), which limit contributions to $2,000 per year.

3. *More on law school tuition.* Sharon v. Commissioner, 66 T.C. 515 (1976), aff'd, 591 F.2d 1273 (9th Cir. 1978), cert. denied, 442 U.S. 941 (1979), held that a lawyer could not amortize the costs of a legal education or of a bar preparation course but could (under §167) amortize registration, test, and bar admission fees over his expected life. In Kohen v. Commissioner, 44 T.C.M. 1518 (1982), the court denied a deduction of the cost of obtaining an LLM in taxation at NYU immediately following graduation from law school but before entering into practice in any way other than giving free advice to family members. Presumably the costs of a legal education cannot be deducted as a loss when one's legal career ends. See Reg. §1.162-5(b)(1), indicating that the costs "constitute an inseparable aggregate of personal and capital expenditures." Do you agree?

4. *The cost of finding a new business or job.* Rev. Rul. 77-254, 1977-2 C.B. 63, 64 holds:

> Expenses incurred in the course of a general search for or preliminary investigation of a business or investment include those expenses related to the decisions *whether* to enter a transaction and *which* transaction to enter. Such expenses are personal [!] and are not deductible under section 165 of the Code. Once the taxpayer has focused on the acquisition of a specific business or investment, expenses that are related to an attempt to acquire such business or investment are capital in nature and, to the extent that the expenses are allocable to an asset the cost of which is amortizable or depreciable, may be amortized as part of the asset's cost if the attempted acquisition is successful. If the attempted acquisition fails, the amount capitalized is deductible in accordance with section 165(c)(2). The taxpayer need not actually enter the business or purchase the investment in order to obtain the deduction.

Do you agree that the costs of a "general search" for a business or investment opportunity are personal? If not, does the language of the Code require the result that some outlays of this sort will never give rise to a deduction? Compare the treatment of the costs of a law school education. In some circumstances, the costs of investigating a business opportunity may be amortizable under §195, but this provision does not appear to be relevant to the costs of "general search."

5. *Costs of job search within one's current trade or business.* In Cremona v. Commissioner, 58 T.C. 219 (1972), acq., a taxpayer who was employed as an "administrator" paid $1,500 for job counseling and referral services that had not led to a new position by the time of hearing of the case. The Court held the expenses deductible under §162 since the taxpayer was in "the trade or business of being an administrator." Rev. Rul. 77-16, 1977-1 C.B. 37, allowed deduction of the expenses of looking for a new position in the taxpayer's present trade or business, a limit that is quite broad since the Service, like the Tax Court, recognizes such a broad trade or business as being a corporate executive or administrator. See also Rev. Rul. 78-93, 1978-1 C.B. 38, permitting the deduction of expenses for career counseling when the taxpayer, engaged in

the businesses of being both a full-time practicing attorney and part-time law school lecturer, after receiving the counseling secured a position of full-time assistant professor of law. The Service held that since the taxpayer had been engaged in two trades or businesses, he was not changing his trade or business by seeking a full-time teaching job.

8

TAX SHELTERS AND TAX PLANNING

A. THE NATURE OF THE PROBLEM

> The letter kills, but the spirit gives life.
> —*2 Corinthians, from the New Testament*

> I'm looking for loopholes.
> —*W.C. Fields, explaining to a friend why he was leafing through the Bible*

One need not cite either the New Testament or comedians famous for their irreverence to find parallels for both of the ideas expressed above. Consider, for example, the Code of Hammurabi, one of the oldest known legal texts, dating to about 1750 B.C. Among other operative provisions, it (1) authorizes property transactions, such as sales and leases; (2) bans usury, or charging what was deemed excessive interest on a loan; and (3) provides guidance regarding property transactions, such as sales and leases.

Reportedly, even in the days of ancient Babylon, prospective lenders recognized that sales and leases offered a potential loophole permitting avoidance of the usury ban. For example, suppose that *A* wanted to lend *B* 100 shekels at 10 percent annual interest, payable at the end of each year, and with a five-year term. Alas, this would violate the usury ban, which took no account of loans' time periods and thus would have deemed the interest rate to be a usurious 50 percent.

Suppose instead, however, that the parties did the following. *B* would purport to sell farmland to *A* for 100 shekels. *A* would agree to resell the land for 100 shekels in five years. *A* would agree to rent the land back to *B* for ten shekels a year. *B* would commit to buying the land back at the end of five years for 100 shekels.

This approach would leave the two parties in the exact same situation as a loan. *B* would get 100 shekels in Year 1, pay ten shekels each year for five years, and then pay back 100 shekels at the end of the five years. *B* would continue to farm the land throughout the five-year period (and afterwards, given his renewed legal ownership). In short, a sale-leaseback followed by a repurchase can be structured to mimic the terms of a loan! The first sale leads to a cash flow from *A* to *B*, just like a loan. The rent is a cash flow from *B* to *A*, just like paying interest on a loan. The repurchase leads to a cash flow from *B* to *A*, just like the repayment of a loan.

Under a literal reading of the Code of Hammurabi, this meant that the usury ban could be rendered ineffective. So far as we know, this is what actually happened in ancient Babylon. But suppose that Babylon's rulers had wanted to defend the actual effectiveness in practice of the usury ban. Then they would have strong reason to treat the above transaction, although in *form* consisting of two legally permissible sales plus a legally permissible lease, as actually in *substance* a secured loan that violated the usury ban.

Had they taken this stance, further interpretive problems would have arisen. For example, the next move by *A* and *B* might have been to ask their advisors—lawyers did not yet exist—how they might alter the sale-leaseback transaction so as to avoid its being recharacterized by the authorities as a usurious loan. One could even imagine their asking authorities for advance guidance regarding whether or not a given transaction would be deemed a loan, and, if it would, how it might be altered so as to avoid this outcome. And, had ancient Babylon had a modern-style judicial system, one could imagine litigation regarding whether a given transaction, structured as a sale-leaseback, was actually a usurious loan. Finally, one could imagine the authorities issuing clear guidelines regarding when sale-leasebacks would be recharacterized as loans—and then, perhaps, worrying about clever efforts to exploit unanticipated loopholes in the guidelines.

Now consider another possible way of avoiding the usury ban: converting the single five-year loan, with 10 percent annual interest, into five separate one-year loans at 10 percent. Perhaps the parties could find a way to make unnecessary the actual circular flow of cash implied by repaying and then reborrowing the 100-shekel loan principal each year.

Once again, if the parties took too many shortcuts, one could imagine the authorities taking the view that such a transaction was actually a single five-year loan with usurious interest (as it was then calculated), rather than five separate, and legally permissible, one-year loans. Suppose, however, that the authorities realized that it was a bit silly for the Code of Hammurabi to calculate interest rates, for usury purposes, without regard to the time period. If so, then conceivably they would be more tolerant of planning arrangements that aimed to avoid the lack of annual interest calculations than of those that aimed to avoid characterization of a given transaction as a loan.

We know of no evidence that the authorities in ancient Babylon actually made any effort to ascertain whether particular sale-leasebacks were "actually" loans. Trying to do this might have been far beyond their administrative capacity, even if they had wanted to do it. Yet, if they had possessed the capability to apply such an approach, and if they cared about the actual effectiveness in practice of the usury ban, they would have had some motivation to consider it. Otherwise, the usury ban might simply turn into a dead letter, or a trap for the ill-advised and unwary, routinely avoided by lenders and borrowers at the cost of requiring them to make their transactions slightly more complicated.

In modern federal tax law, since at least the 1930s, the courts and the Treasury, with the approval of the U.S. Congress, have applied the view that, to fulfill the "spirit" of the law when in tension with the "letter," in some circumstances taxpayers' transactions should be recharacterized in accordance with their substance, as distinct from their form. However, exactly when this doctrine will apply, and when instead taxpayers will be permitted to arrange their affairs so as to minimize their tax liabilities, can be contested and unclear. Good tax lawyers acquire an instinct for recognizing when "substance over form" and related common-law doctrines are likely to apply to the taxpayer's detriment, as opposed to when such doctrines are unlikely to apply. Of course, this is not to say that they always agree with each other or that they always prove after the fact to have predicted the outcome correctly.

Related conceptually to such doctrines are specific statutory and regulatory requirements that obviate, or at least reduce, the need to apply any of them, by specifying the exact degree of "substance" that a particular transaction must have, in order to achieve a specified tax effect. Here are a couple of related examples. Suppose a taxpayer wanted to realize a loss on property that had declined in value, without actually ceasing to own it. One device she might consider is selling it and immediately repurchasing the same or identical property. A second device she might consider is selling it to a closely related family member or, alternatively, to a corporation that she (perhaps along with family members) wholly owned.

One could imagine the courts developing standards under which particular transactions that involved sales in form were treated as not actually sales, giving rise to allowable losses, in substance. Instead, however—or in addition—the Internal Revenue Code has specific rules defining "wash sales,"[1] in which the sale and repurchase are too close in time to each other and losses thus are disallowed, and applying a similar approach to certain related party transactions.[2]

In this chapter, we will first examine leading cases and examples in which "substance over form" and related common-law doctrines have applied—or not applied—to particular transactions, resulting in a rich body of law that tax lawyers must always keep in mind when advising clients. In addition, we will look at important tax statutes that either relate to or take the place of requiring economic substance, and at the common-law doctrines' impact on tax lawyers' legal and ethical obligations.

---

1. §1091.
2. §267.

B.   THE ORIGIN OF SUBSTANCE-OVER-FORM DOCTRINE

Gregory v. Helvering, 69 F.2d 809 (2d Cir. 1934), aff'd, 293 U.S. 465 (1935), is one of the most famous, influential, and frequently-cited cases in the history of the federal income tax.[3] This eminence extends both to the Second Circuit opinion, by Judge Learned Hand, and to the Supreme Court's unanimous affirmance, by Justice Sutherland. *Gregory* both decisively established substance-over-form doctrine as an important element of federal income tax law and offered eloquent rhetorical road maps both to government attorneys, when they argue that substance-over-form doctrine applies to a particular transaction, and to taxpayers, when they argue that it does not apply. The degree to which it answers the question of what exactly the doctrine means is perhaps less definite.

In the following discussion, don't worry if the facts of the case seem confusing. They related to a subject whose rules have changed and that is covered in classes on corporate income taxation. Focus instead on the bottom line questions: Can a taxpayer rely on the literal words of the statute to reach a result that may be inconsistent with legislative purpose or intent? Does it matter if, to qualify for favorable tax treatment under the literal terms of the statute, the taxpayer structures a transaction that includes wholly meaningless steps?

In *Gregory*, the taxpayer's wholly owned company, United Mortgage Corporation (UMC), held appreciated shares of the Monitor Securities Corporation. Mrs. Gregory wanted to sell the Monitor shares and end up with the cash. She knew, however, that if UMC either just gave her the shares or sold them and gave her the cash, she would have ordinary income from the receipt of a dividend. At the time, unlike under present law, dividends were taxable at the same rate as all other ordinary income.[4]

Other tax rules (still existing today, although in altered form) permitted corporations to engage in tax-free reorganizations. The general idea was that if, for example, taxpayers converted one company into two separate companies, or two separate companies into one, they could qualify (under specified circumstances) for nonrecognition of gain and loss at both the corporate and shareholder levels. The rationale, presumably, was that mere reshuffling of the corporate entity structure, while basically business operations went on as before, did not offer a suitable occasion for recognizing gain or loss.

Mrs. Gregory's lawyers realized that the tax-free reorganization rules offered them an opportunity, albeit one that at least arguably was unintended and unanticipated by Congress, to reduce the tax liability that she would face if UMC simply made a dividend distribution of the Monitor shares. Accordingly, instead of obtaining the shares directly, she caused Monitor to engage in an

---

3. The discussion in this section of Gregory v. Helvering draws on that in Daniel N. Shaviro, "*The Story of* Knetsch: *Judicial Doctrines Combating Tax Avoidance,*" in Tax Stories, Paul L. Caron, ed. (2d ed. 2009).

4. In addition, at the time but unlike today, UMC would not be taxable on the appreciation of the Monitor shares if it distributed them to Mrs. Gregory as a dividend.

apparently tax-free reorganization that created a sister corporation, Averill. Mrs. Gregory got all of Averill's shares (since she owned all of UMC's shares), and Averill got the Monitor stock. Three days later, Mrs. Gregory liquidated Averill and immediately sold the Monitor shares. The result, under a literal interpretation of existing tax law at the time, was that Mrs. Gregory had (1) capital gain upon, in effect, selling her Averill shares via the liquidation, plus (2) basis recovery, reducing the amount of income she realized, since, in the tax-free reorganization, the Averill shares received a portion of prior basis in UMC's shares.

If the plan worked, it could potentially be used by all other taxpayers who wanted to avoid dividend treatment on the receipt of corporate distributions. Even if one was getting cash, rather than property such as the Monitor shares, one could use a divisive reorganization to give the cash to a separate corporation, that would then immediately be liquidated. To be sure, Congress could (and soon did) change the laws defining tax-free divisive reorganizations, so that this prospectively would no longer be possible. But was there any bar to Mrs. Gregory's getting the favorable tax result she sought?

Technically speaking, the transaction had been executed impeccably. All of the explicit statutory requirements pertaining at the time to a specific tax-free reorganization had unambiguously been satisfied. To the Board of Tax Appeals (the predecessor to today's Tax Court), Mrs. Gregory's technical compliance with the rules was good enough to establish that she should win: "A statute so meticulously drafted must be interpreted as a literal expression of the taxing policy and leaves only the small interstices for judicial consideration."[5]

In the Second Circuit, however, Judge Learned Hand, writing for a unanimous three-judge panel, reversed and held for the Commissioner, stating the following:

> We agree with the Board and the taxpayer that a transaction, otherwise within an exception of the tax law, does not lose its immunity, because it is actuated by a desire to avoid, or, if one choose, to evade, taxation. Any one may so arrange his affairs that his taxes shall be as low as possible; he is not bound to choose that pattern which will best pay the Treasury; there is not even a patriotic duty to increase one's taxes. . . . Therefore, if what was done here, was what was intended by [the statute], it is of no consequence that it was all an elaborate scheme to get rid of income taxes, as it certainly was. Nevertheless, it does not follow that Congress meant to cover such a transaction, not even though the facts answer the dictionary definitions of each term used in the statutory definition. It is quite true, as the Board has very well said, that as the articulation of a statute increases, the room for interpretation must contract; but the meaning of a sentence may be more than that of the separate words, as a melody is more than the notes, and no degree of particularity can ever obviate recourse to the setting in which all appear, and which all collectively create. The purpose of the section is plain enough; men engaged in enterprises—industrial, commercial, financial, or any other—might wish to consolidate, or divide, to add to, or subtract from, their holdings. Such transactions were not to be considered as "realizing"

5. Gregory v. Commissioner, 27 B.T.A. 223, 225 (1932), rev'd, 69 F.2d 809 (2d Cir. 1934), aff'd, 293 U.S. 465 (1935).

any profit, because the collective interests still remained in solution. But the underlying presupposition is plain that the readjustment shall be undertaken for reasons germane to the conduct of the venture in hand, not as an ephemeral incident, egregious to its prosecution. To dodge the shareholders' taxes is not one of the transactions contemplated as corporate "reorganizations."

NOTES AND QUESTIONS

1. *Battle of the dueling quotes.* If nothing else, Judge Hand's opinion was eloquent enough to ensure that it would continually be cited by both sides in subsequent litigation and debate exploring the contours of the "substance over form" doctrine that it helped establish. Taxpayer briefs and memos frequently quote his statement that "[a]ny one may so arrange his affairs that his taxes shall be as low as possible; he is not bound to choose that pattern which will best pay the Treasury; there is not even a patriotic duty to increase one's taxes." Pro-government writers note in response that Judge Hand nonetheless held in the government's favor, on the ground that what the taxpayer did was not within the scope of what the statute was "intended" to cover.

2. *What does the holding actually mean?* Judge Hand tells us that "the meaning of a sentence may be more than that of the separate words, as a melody is more than the notes." But what does this actually mean? Perhaps it is best interpreted as saying that transactions within the scope of the tax-free reorganizations statute must serve a company-level business purpose that relates to continuing the company's business operations. An aim of reducing shareholder-level taxes is not disqualifying, but it does not count towards satisfying this implicit requirement—which evidently is deduced from the statute's structure and apparent purpose, given that Congress had not expressly stated it anywhere.

1.   Gregory v. Helvering on Appeal

The Supreme Court affirmed the Second Circuit's holding in *Gregory*, stating in relevant part as follows:

It is earnestly contended on behalf of the taxpayer that since every element required by the [statute] is to be found in what was done, a statutory reorganization was effected; and that the motive of the taxpayer thereby to escape payment of a tax will not alter the result or make unlawful what the statute allows. It is quite true that if a reorganization in reality was effected within the meaning of subdivision (B), the ulterior purpose mentioned will be disregarded. The legal right of a taxpayer to decrease the amount of what otherwise would be his taxes, or altogether avoid them, by means which the law permits, cannot be doubted. . . . But the question for determination is whether what was done, apart from the tax motive, was the thing which the statute intended. The reasoning of the court below in justification of a negative answer leaves little to be said.

. . . Putting aside . . . the question of motive in respect of taxation altogether, and fixing the character of the proceeding by what actually occurred, what do we find? Simply an operation having no business or corporate purpose—a mere device which put on the form of a corporate reorganization as a disguise for concealing its real character, and the sole object and accomplishment of which was the consummation of a preconceived plan, not to reorganize a business or any part of a business, but to transfer a parcel of corporate shares to the petitioner. No doubt, a new and valid corporation was created. But that corporation was nothing more than a contrivance to the end last described. It was brought into existence for no other purpose; it performed, as it was intended from the beginning it should perform, no other function. When that limited function had been exercised, it immediately was put to death.

In these circumstances, the facts speak for themselves and are susceptible of but one interpretation. The whole undertaking, though conducted according to the terms of subdivision (B), was in fact an elaborate and devious form of conveyance masquerading as a corporate reorganization, and nothing else. The rule which excludes from consideration the motive of tax avoidance is not pertinent to the situation, because the transaction upon its face lies outside the plain intent of the statute. To hold otherwise would be to exalt artifice above reality and to deprive the statutory provision in question of all serious purpose.

NOTES AND QUESTIONS

1. *What was the Supreme Court saying?* The Supreme Court lauds and echoes Judge Hand's opinion, likewise concluding that, while tax avoidance motives are entirely permissible, "the determination . . . [of] whether what was done . . . was the thing which the statute intended" depended on more than just full technical compliance. A "business or corporate purpose" was required for the transaction's form to prevail over what the Court found was its substance, even though the statute did not expressly set forth a business purpose requirement.

By one reading, this is merely plain-vanilla statutory interpretation. The tax-free reorganization rules, as viewed by the Court, happened to require a plan by the taxpayer to reorganize an ongoing corporate business, as opposed to simply a reorganization in the narrow state corporate law sense. However, this was not based on, say, those rules' particular legislative history, and much about the opinion could be viewed as supporting a much broader reading.

For example, consider how harshly the Court castigated the transaction. It was a "mere device" that used a "disguise for concealing its real character," not to mention "an elaborate and devious . . . masquerad[e]." The taxpayer was trying to "exalt artifice above reality" and to "deprive the statutory provision in question of all serious purpose." It arguably suggested that courts should in general search assiduously for underlying statutory purposes, at least or especially when they detected insultingly transparent "devices," "disguises," "masquerades," and "artifices."

2. *Evaluating substance over form doctrine.* The substance over form doctrine that Gregory v. Helvering helped to establish is deeply embedded in federal tax law and is widely (though not universally) accepted. The reasons for this may become clearer as we trace its application and development in other transactional settings. For now, however, it is worth noting possible reasons why one

might dislike it. As judicial overreaching? In tension with the rule of law? Too uncertain? Inferior to demanding of Congress that it draft statutes more carefully up front or amend them as needed if unintended applications emerge?

How might one more fully express these criticisms? How might one respond to them? Would it matter to the analysis, for example, if we were to conclude that a taxpayer victory in *Gregory* would have permitted substantially all dividend transactions to get capital gains treatment plus basis recovery, through the use of otherwise pointless extra corporate transactions, until such time as Congress got around to amending the relevant statutes?

3. *The early aftermath of* Gregory. Reflecting its dual character, *Gregory* swiftly came to mean "all things to all men."[6] Courts siding with the taxpayer could easily distinguish it if they were so minded—better still after noting that the Supreme Court had "repeatedly stated that the taxpayer's desire to reduce her taxes was irrelevant."[7] Other courts viewed *Gregory* as a kind of "philosophical pronouncement" mandating application of "an overriding principle in dealing with tax-avoidance plans: If the arrangement departs from normal family or business patterns or contains an element of artificiality, it is to be viewed with skepticism, scrutinized carefully and rejected if some weakness in it can be detected."[8]

Two distinct types of transactions, however, were clearly most likely to face attack under *Gregory*. The first were those where the taxpayer arguably inserted an extra step in an otherwise straightforward transaction, making it more circuitous for tax reasons. The extra step could therefore be attacked as a sham, albeit that something (such as the effective payment of a dividend) had undeniably happened overall. Second, *Gregory* invited attacking transactions in which the IRS could argue that nothing had happened overall because two offsetting steps, each concededly significant if considered in isolation, had left the taxpayer right back where she started. This brings us to the next major Supreme Court case evaluating substance over form and related doctrines.

C.   REQUIRING ECONOMIC SUBSTANCE IN RESPONSE TO LOSS-GENERATING TAX SHELTERS

In *Gregory*, the taxpayer could have done nothing—that is, kept the appreciated Monitor shares in UMC—and paid no tax. Indeed, this presumably is what her tax advisors would have recommended, purely from a tax planning standpoint. All their plan did (or would have done, had it worked) was reduce the tax hit she faced by reason of wanting to sell the Monitor shares and extract the cash.

---

6. Randolph Paul, *Studies in Federal Taxation* 125 (1940).

7. Gilbert v. Commissioner, 248 F.2d 399, 404 (2d Cir. 1957).

8. Walter J. Blum, *Knetsch v. United States: A Pronouncement on Tax Avoidance*, 40 Taxes 296, 302 n.40 (1962).

Suppose, however, that one can engage in a transaction that combines (1) doing nothing (or as close to nothing as possible) from a business and economic standpoint, with (2) generating large losses that one can deduct for tax purposes. Two things that this would change are the following. First, the tax advisors may now be positively enthusiastic. Indeed, they have reason to market such transactions to taxpayers who otherwise would have done nothing, instead of merely trying to mitigate the tax cost. Second, the danger to the federal revenue interest is much greater—and indeed, potentially unlimited.

Suppose the tax advisor comes up with a scheme under which there's basically a circular flow of cash. That is, the taxpayer pays a third party $X, and the third party pays the taxpayer $X. (Actually, the taxpayer is likely to pay the third party $X plus a fee—providing that party's motivation for the transaction.) So far, this sounds pointless. But suppose the tax advisor can show that, under a literal interpretation of existing tax law, the $X (plus fee) that the taxpayer pays out is currently deductible, while the $X that the taxpayer receives need not currently be included in income.

If this works, the end result is that the taxpayer reduces her taxable income by $X plus the fee, despite being out nothing, on balance, except for the fee. And given the nature of circular cash flows—i.e., they don't actually cost you anything net and may not even require actual offsetting fund transfers—the $X that is used in the transaction can be as big as the taxpayer likes. $1 million? $1 billion? $1 trillion? Why not, in the unlikely event that the taxpayer could actually use $1 trillion in deductible losses?

Does this sound fanciful? In fact, it is not. This exact pattern has manifested itself frequently in the history of federal tax law. The following classic Supreme Court case remains the definitive legal analysis of how substance over form, and related doctrines, are deployed in response.

KNETSCH v. UNITED STATES
364 U.S. 361 (1960)

Mr. Justice BRENNAN delivered the opinion of the Court.

This case presents the question of whether deductions . . . of $143,465 in 1953 and of $147,105 in 1954, for payments made by petitioner, Karl F. Knetsch, to Sam Houston Life Insurance Company, constituted "interest paid . . . on indebtedness" within the meaning of . . . §163(a). . . .

On December 11, 1953, the insurance company sold Knetsch ten 30-year maturity deferred annuity bonds, each in the face amount of $400,000 and bearing interest at two and one-half percent compounded annually. The purchase price was $4,004,000. Knetsch gave the Company his check for $4,000, and signed $4,000,000 of nonrecourse annuity loan notes for the balance. The notes bore 3½% interest and were secured by the annuity bonds. The interest was payable in advance, and Knetsch on the same day prepaid the first year's interest, which was $140,000. Under the Table of Cash and Loan Values made part of the bonds, their cash or loan value at December 11, 1954, the end of the first contract year, was to be $4,100,000. The contract terms, however, permitted Knetsch to borrow any excess of this value above his indebtedness without waiting until December 11, 1954. Knetsch took advantage of this provision only five days after the purchase.[9] On December 16, 1953, he received from the company $99,000 of the $100,000 excess over his $4,000,000 indebtedness, for which he gave his notes bearing 3½% interest. This interest was also payable in advance and on the same day he prepaid the first year's interest of $3,465. In their joint return for 1953, the petitioners deducted the sum of the two interest payments, that is $143,465, as "interest paid . . . within the taxable year on indebtedness." . . .

The second contract year began on December 11, 1954, when interest in advance of $143,465 was payable by Knetsch on his aggregate indebtedness of $4,099,000. Knetsch paid this amount on December 27, 1954. Three days later, on December 30, he received from the company cash in the amount of $104,000, the difference less $1,000 between his then $4,099,000 indebtedness and the cash or loan value of the bonds of $4,204,000 on December 11, 1955. He gave the company appropriate notes and prepaid the interest thereon of $3,640. In their joint return for the taxable year 1954 the petitioners deducted the sum of the two interest payments, that is $147,105. . . .

[Roughly the same procedure was followed in December 1955.]

Knetsch did not go on with the transaction for the fourth contract year beginning December 11, 1956, but terminated it on December 27, 1956. His indebtedness at that time totaled $4,307,000. The cash or loan value of the bonds was the $4,308,000 value at December 11, 1956. . . . He surrendered the bonds and his indebtedness was canceled. He received the difference of $1000 in cash.

The contract called for a monthly annuity of $90,171 at maturity (when Knetsch would be 90 years of age) or for such smaller amount as would be produced by the cash or loan value after deduction of the then existing indebtedness. It was stipulated that if Knetsch had held the bonds to maturity and continued annually to borrow the net cash value less $1,000, the sum available for the annuity at maturity would be . . . enough to provide an annuity of only $43 per month.

---

9. [The following summary of the basic transaction may be helpful:

Loan to Knetsch from Ins. Co.	$4,000,000
Interest on loan (at 3½%)	$ 140,000
Investment by Knetsch in annuity	4,000,000
Tax-free return (at 2½%)*	100,000
Net before tax effects	(40,000)
Tax saving from interest deduction, at tax rate of:	
90%	126,000
70	98,000
50	70,000
25	35,000
Net after-tax effects at tax rate of:	
90%	86,000
70	58,000
50	30,000
25	(5,000)

*In the form of loan based on increased value of annuity.

—Eds.]

The trial judge made findings that "[t]here was no commercial economic substance to the . . . transaction," that the parties did not intend that Knetsch "become indebted to Sam Houston," that "[n]o indebtedness of [Knetsch] was created by any of the . . . transactions," and that "[n]o economic gain could be achieved from the purchase of these bonds without regard to the tax consequences. . . ." His conclusion of law . . . was that "[w]hile in form the payments to Sam Houston were compensation for the use or forbearance of money, they were not in substance. As a payment of interest, the transaction was a sham."

We first examine the transaction between Knetsch and the insurance company to determine whether it created an "indebtedness." . . . We put aside a finding by the District Court that Knetsch's "only motive in purchasing these 10 bonds was to attempt to secure an interest deduction."[10] As was said in Gregory v. Helvering: "The legal right of a taxpayer to decrease the amount of what otherwise would be his taxes, or altogether avoid them, by means which the law permits, cannot be doubted. . . . But the question for determination is whether what was done, apart from the tax motive, was the thing which the statute intended."

When we examine "what was done" here, we see that Knetsch paid the insurance company $294,540 during the two taxable years involved and received $203,000 back in the form of "loans." What did Knetsch get for the out-of-pocket difference of $91,570? In form he had an annuity contract . . . which would produce monthly annuity payments of $90,171, or substantial life insurance proceeds in the event of his death before maturity. This, as we have seen, was a fiction, because each year Knetsch's annual borrowings kept the net cash value, on which any annuity or insurance payments would depend, at the relative pittance of $1,000. . . . What he was ostensibly "lent" back was in reality only the rebate of a substantial part of the so-called "interest" payments. The $91,570 difference retained by the company was its fee for providing the facade of "loans" whereby the petitioners sought to reduce their 1953 and 1954 taxes in the total sum of $233,298 [about 80 percent of the "interest deduction"]. . . .

The petitioners contend, however, . . . that §264(a)(2) denies a deduction for amounts paid on indebtedness incurred to purchase or carry a single-premium annuity contract, but only as to contracts purchased after March 1, 1954. The petitioners thus would attribute to Congress a purpose to allow the deduction of pre-1954 payments under transactions of the kind carried on by Knetsch with the insurance company without regard to whether the transactions created a true obligation to pay interest. Unless that meaning plainly appears we will not attribute it to Congress. "To hold otherwise would be to exalt artifice above reality and to deprive the statutory provision in question of all serious purpose." Gregory v. Helvering. . . .

Congress . . . in 1942 denied a deduction for amounts paid on indebtedness incurred to purchase single-premium life insurance and endowment contracts . . . "to close a loophole" in respect of interest allocable to partially exempt income.

___

10. We likewise put aside Knetsch's argument that, because he received ordinary income when he surrendered the annuities in 1956, he has suffered a net loss even if the contested deductions are allowed, and that therefore his motive in taking out the annuities could not have been tax avoidance.

The 1954 provision extending the denial to amounts paid on indebtedness incurred to purchase or carry single-premium annuities appears to us simply to expand the application of the policy in respect of interest allocable to partially exempt income.[11]

Moreover, the provision itself negates any suggestion that sham transactions were the congressional concern, for the deduction denied is of certain interest payments on actual "indebtedness." And we see nothing . . . to suggest that Congress is exempting pre-1954 annuities intended to protect sham transactions. . . .

The judgment of the Court of Appeals is affirmed.

Mr. Justice DOUGLAS, with whom Mr. Justice WHITTAKER and Mr. Justice STEWART concur, dissenting. . . .

It is true that in this transaction the taxpayer was bound to lose if the annuity contract is taken by itself. At least, the taxpayer showed by his conduct that he never intended to come out ahead on that investment apart from his income tax deduction. . . . Yet as long as the transaction itself is not hocuspocus, the interest . . . seem[s] to be . . . as respects annuity contracts made prior to March 1, 1954, the date Congress selected for terminating this class of deductions. . . . The insurance company existed; it operated under Texas law; it was authorized to issue these policies and to make these annuity loans. . . .

Tax avoidance is a dominating motive behind scores of transactions. It is plainly present here. Will the Service that calls this transaction a "sham" today not press for collection of taxes arising out of the surrender of the annuity contract? I think it should, for I do not believe any part of the transaction was a "sham." . . . The remedy is legislative. Evils or abuses can be particularized by Congress. . . .

NOTES AND QUESTIONS

1. *Expenses.* Knetsch's decision to terminate the transaction in 1956 may have reflected his receipt, earlier in that year, of an IRS statutory notice of deficiency covering 1953 and 1954. On his 1956 tax return he claimed a deduction for his out-of-pocket losses, which totaled $137,000. This appears to have been a fallback position, protecting his deduction claim lest 1956 "close" for tax purposes before litigation concerning the earlier years was resolved. Had he computed his taxable income for 1956 in a manner consistent with his previous three years' reporting positions, he would instead have reported gain in the amount of $304,000.[12]

---

11. [In 1964, Congress acted again in this field, by enacting §264(a)(3), which disallows (subject to certain exceptions) any deduction for interest on indebtedness incurred or continued to purchase or carry a life insurance, endowment, or annuity contract pursuant to a plan which "contemplates the systematic direct or indirect borrowing of part or all of the increases in the cash value of such contract."—EDS.]

12. Under Knetsch's view of the transaction, $304,000 was the excess of his amount realized (($1,000 cash plus $4,307,000 discharge of indebtedness) over his cost basis ($4,004,000)) in the annuity contracts.

His attempt to deduct the out-of-pocket losses, as a loss under §165(c)(2) or an expense under §212, subsequently failed, on the ground that he had lacked the requisite profit motive. In effect, he was treated as if the expenses had been for personal consumption—which they surely were not, unless one imagines that he expected and enjoyed the IRS audit and subsequent litigation. Denial of the deduction might, however, be rationalized as an implicit penalty for engaging in a sham transaction (as subsequently held) that presumably was unlikely to be detected on audit.

2. *Turning pretax straw into after-tax spun gold.* For 1953, the first year of the transaction, Knetsch paid the company $140,000 of interest and earned $100,000 in the form of a nontaxable increase in the value of his policy. He was able, in effect, to draw down the $100,000 increase in value by "borrowing" from the insurance company. Thus, he paid out $140,000, received $100,000, and was $40,000 out of pocket (leaving aside the $4,000 fee). However, by deducting the $140,000 interest paid without currently including the $100,000 of loan proceeds, he was able (he thought) to reduce his tax liability for the year by about $110,000. (Marginal rates in 1953 were far higher than today, with a top rate of 91 percent; $110,000 was the tax saving from the $140,000 deduction.) He thus—assuming the transaction worked—converted a $40,000 pretax loss into a $70,000 after-tax gain ($110,000 tax saving less $40,000). While this ignores his expected future tax liability when he would have to take all the deferred income into account, this was not scheduled to happen for at least thirty years. It therefore seemingly made sense for him to borrow $4 million at 3.5 percent in order to invest the same amount at 2.5 percent. Indeed, had he needed the deductions (so long as he had the requisite out-of-pocket cash), he presumably could have borrowed $40 million, $400 million, or for that matter $4 billion with the same spread between his borrowing and lending rates.

3. *Private and not-so-private letter rulings.* Knetsch apparently invested in reliance on a private letter ruling that the IRS had issued to one R.C. Salley, the president and treasurer of the company that sold him the annuity contract. The IRS issues such rulings at its discretion to taxpayers who apply for them, stating that a given transaction, if it conforms to the stipulated facts, will be taxed in a specified way. Private rulings always state on their face that they are not precedent and that no other taxpayer may rely on them, thus permitting the IRS to feel safe in issuing them without high-level review. They nonetheless are frequently treated by taxpayers as precedent, or at the least as evidence of IRS administrative practice.

The IRS refused to publish its private rulings, even with the identity of the taxpayer redacted, until publication was compelled in the 1970s following the enactment of the Freedom of Information Act. Even before publication was compelled, however, the IRS could not prevent enterprising taxpayers such as Mr. Salley from using private rulings in their possession to their advantage and profit.

A Supreme Court amicus brief in *Knetsch* (on behalf of taxpayers who were litigating similar transactions) argued that the IRS practice of allowing the taxpayer who received a private ruling, but no other taxpayer, to rely on it was "monstrous" and equivalent to racial discrimination. The Court declined to address this argument, however, noting that Knetsch had not raised it.

4. *Economic substance.* The trial judge's finding that the transaction offered no prospect of pretax economic gain overlooked the possibility that market interest rates would decline substantially. Knetsch had the right to earn 2 percent annually, but was free to pay off his 3 percent loan to the insurance company and borrow the funds elsewhere. Thus, had the market rate at which he could borrow declined sufficiently below 2 percent, he theoretically could have made money on the deal. He apparently was not aware of this possibility, however, since it was not raised during the litigation.

Arguably, this prospect of pretax profit would have been deemed too remote to change the outcome even if Knetsch's attorneys had raised it. It is highly likely, however, that Knetsch would have won the case if interest rates had recently been fluctuating enough for him to point to a plausible upside, and he had left a "paper trail" suggesting that this upside was relevant to him.

Why wasn't the deal structured to involve greater economic risk? A key reason may be that the insurance company could not have offered Knetsch a greater "upside" without either charging him more for the transaction or requiring him to bear a greater "downside" as well. Taxpayers are often reluctant to accept a significant "downside" in their tax shelter investments, for reasons that are easy to understand. In illustration, suppose you could buy, for $49,000, a chance to win either $100,000 or nothing, depending on the outcome of a fair coin toss. Since you would have a 50 percent probability of winning $100,000 (and thus netting $51,000), the odds would be in your favor. But if you are like most people, you would not want to do this (even assuming you had the $49,000) by reason of being risk-averse. That is, you might mind losing $49,000 a lot more than you would value winning a slightly greater amount.

The economic substance requirement therefore deters taxpayers from making tax-favored investments unless they are willing to accept some economic risk (including "downside" risk if they are reluctant to pay extra for being given just the "upside"). Why, however, should taxpayers be rewarded with tax benefits for accepting a given risk? Why not let their risk positions depend purely on their own preferences as investors? Would Knetsch have benefited the public fisc in any way by betting on changes in the market interest rate? So what might be the point of the economic substance requirement?

5. *Statutory response.* As the Court observed, after 1954, §264 expressly denied deductions for interest on debt of the sort involved in *Knetsch*. The case nonetheless remains important as a broader precedent that the IRS can deploy in combating what it regards as unacceptable tax avoidance.

THE DEVELOPMENT OF THE ECONOMIC SUBSTANCE DOCTRINE

In Goldstein v. Commissioner, 364 F.2d 734 (2d Cir. 1966), cert. denied, 385 U.S. 1005 (1967), the taxpayer, having won $140,000 in the Irish Sweepstakes in 1958, in that year borrowed $465,000 from a bank at 4 percent and prepaid $52,000 of interest. She used the proceeds of the loan to buy (for $465,000) U.S. Treasury notes with a face value of $500,000, bearing interest at 1 percent and due in October 1961. She also entered into another transaction of the same sort with another bank. Her projected economic loss on these two transactions, assuming the bonds were held to maturity, was $18,500. Her expected tax saving was from two sources. First, the interest deduction would reduce her income in 1958 and returns on the Treasury notes would arise in later years. Thus, she would push part of her income from the sweepstakes into later years when it would be taxed at lower rates than if it were all taxed in 1958. Second, the interest deduction was to be an offset to the ordinary income from the sweepstakes, while a large part of the return would be capital gain (the difference between the purchase price of the bonds and notes and proceeds received at maturity). The taxpayer was a retired garment worker living on a modest pension and was totally unsophisticated in financial affairs. She followed the advice of her son, a certified public accountant (whose computation of the projected $18,500 economic loss was introduced by the government). The court upheld the Commissioner's denial of an interest deduction for the loans used to finance these transactions. It refused to follow *Knetsch* and characterize the transactions as "shams," pointing out that the loans were made by independent financial institutions, that the "two loan transactions did not within a few days return all the parties to the position from which they started," that the banks could demand payment at any time, and that the notes were with recourse. In holding for the Commissioner, the court relied instead on the fact that the taxpayer's sole motive (given her son's careful computation) was tax avoidance. The court said that §163 "does not permit a deduction for interest paid or accrued in loan arrangements, like those now before us, that cannot with reason be said to have purpose, substance, or utility apart from their anticipated tax consequences."

Goldstein differs from *Knetsch* because the *Goldstein* transaction concededly was not a "sham." Rather than borrowing and lending the same amount and thus inviting the critique that the transaction amounted to no more than paper-shuffling, the taxpayer actually bought Treasury notes with the proceeds of her own personal debt. However, *Goldstein* is similar to *Knetsch* in that both transactions were entered into solely for tax purposes.

D.   COMMON-LAW AND OTHER RESPONSES TO SALE-LEASEBACKS

1.   Two Distinct Tax Reasons for Engaging in Sale-Leasebacks

We started this chapter with an ancient Babylonian illustration regarding the use of sale-leasebacks to avoid the Code of Hammurabi's usury ban. As it happens, sale-leasebacks are an important tax planning device to this day, albeit, for very different reasons. Of the two main motivations taxpayers today have for using them—or would have today, absent statutory or common law standing in the way—one has a lot in common with the loss-generating transactions, such as that in *Knetsch*, that were discussed above, while the second is somewhat different. Both motivations, however, relate to depreciation deductions, and to the fact that (as we saw in Chapter 4, in relation to the *Crane* and *Tufts* case) only the owner of depreciable property, as determined for federal tax purposes, can claim the deductions.

A sale-leaseback of depreciable property, by a party that continues to use the property, changes that party's legal status from owner to lessee. Thus, if the form of transaction is respected for federal tax purposes, the buyer/lessor becomes entitled to depreciation deductions, in place of the seller/lessee. In addition, however, the putative owner's basis for the property of the property, which is used in determining the amount of depreciation deductions, may change if the transaction is respected. These two aspects—change in who claims the depreciation, and in the amount being claimed—trigger the two main tax motivations for engaging in sale-leasebacks. As we will see, the judicial response to these two types of motivations have been very different.

Motivation #1: Increase the amount that is depreciable. Here we are at least potentially in the realm, not just of *Knetsch*-style tax shelters, but even of overt fraud. Suppose that the pen on your desk (if you still use such archaic objects) was depreciable property, with (say) a three-year useful life under the applicable depreciation tables. While you would then be able to depreciate your cost for it over three years, the amount would undoubtedly be trivial. But suppose a friend, with substantial taxable income to shelter, offered to buy the pen from you for $10 million. Too good to be true (and not worth it to your friend)? There turns out to be a catch. All but $1 of the purchase price is borrowed from you, nonrecourse, secured only by the pen. The nonrecourse "loan" is due in three years, at which point you can be sure that your friend will decline to pay, leaving you just with the pen. So you've made a great "sale" of the pen, for $10 million, although it's worth almost zero, but a terrible "loan," since all you'll get back in three years is legal title to the pen. In the interim, you'll hold onto the pen, owing your friend annual "rent" on it that is equal to the annual "interest" she owes you on the "loan."

Why would your friend want to do this, if there was a chance that it would actually work for tax purposes? The answer is, that while including the "rent" in taxable income and deducting the "interest" would be a wash, in the interim she would get to deduct $10 million of depreciation. (Under *Tufts*, this amount presumably would be recaptured in income when the transaction unwound in three years—but there would still have been deferral, and perhaps a new loss-generating transaction in three years could generate further deferral.)

What about the tax consequences to you? Wouldn't the sale of the pen trigger almost $10 million of gain upon sale (i.e., the $10 million amount realized from the sale, minus the pen's trivial basis)? The answer is no, if you can use the installment method to defer reporting gain until you are paid, which of course will never happen, apart from the $1 up front. So the transaction, during its three-year term, would give your friend $10 million in deductions, without giving you any significant taxable income, if the tax system fully respected it.

Does this example sound too extreme to be true? Perhaps yes, insofar as the sheer degree of the overvaluation is concerned, i.e., the difference between $10 million and the actual fair market value of a pen. But otherwise, it's actually a close match for the *Estate of Franklin* case, discussed infra. Not surprisingly, the courts (as well as the Internal Revenue Code, as discussed later in this chapter) have dealt crisply with sale-leasebacks that appear to be relying on overvaluation.

Motivation #2: Change the identity of the party that is claiming depreciation deductions. Even without overvaluation, sale-leasebacks can serve tax planning objectives that are not quite as dangerous to the federal tax system as the transaction described above.

Favorable depreciation rules are designed to, and presumably to some extent do, stimulate business investment. Suppose, though, that a taxpayer in a low bracket (or one that pays no tax at all, for example, due to having net losses) wishes to expand a trade or business and requires additional depreciable property. How might such a taxpayer take advantage of the generous depreciation allowance?

One alternative for the low-bracket taxpayer is to lease the depreciable property from a high-bracket taxpayer. The high-bracket taxpayer will enjoy the tax advantages associated with the investment and can pass on part of those advantages to the low-bracket taxpayer in the form of lower rent.

In some cases, finding a high-bracket lessor of the desired property is difficult. In that situation, the low-bracket taxpayer may itself buy or construct the depreciable property. Before the property is placed in service, however, a suitable high-bracket lessor may be found, in which case the property may be sold to the high-bracket taxpayer, which in turn leases it back to the low-bracket taxpayer. The high-bracket taxpayer receives the tax benefits of ownership and the low-bracket taxpayer receives either some up-front cash in addition to the amount of its investment or rental payments that are less than they would otherwise be.

Such examples look considerably more benign than sale-leasebacks involving overvaluation, at least, absent some exacerbating factor, such as the migration of all the depreciable assets in the world to nominal ownership by U.S. taxpayers through sale-leasebacks. Thus, it is not surprising that such arrangements have generally fared better, both in the courts, such as in the *Frank Lyon* case, discussed below, and with respect to legislative and regulatory responses.

2. Overvaluation Sale-Leasebacks

ESTATE OF FRANKLIN v. COMMISSIONER
544 F.2d 1045 (9th Cir. 1976)

SNEED, Circuit Judge.

This case involves another effort on the part of the Commissioner to curb the use of real estate tax shelters. In this instance he seeks to disallow deductions for the taxpayers' distributive share of losses reported by a limited partnership[13] with respect to its acquisition of a motel and related property. These "losses" have their origin in deductions for depreciation and interest claimed with respect to the motel and related property. These deductions were disallowed by the Commissioner on the ground either that the acquisition was a sham or that the entire acquisition transaction was in substance the purchase by the partnership of an option to acquire the motel and related property on January 15, 1979. The Tax Court held that the transaction constituted an option exercisable in 1979 and disallowed the taxpayers' deductions. Estate of Charles T. Franklin, 64 T.C. 752 (1975). We affirm this disallowance although our approach differs somewhat from that of the Tax Court.

The interest and depreciation deductions were taken by Twenty-Fourth Property Associates (hereinafter referred to as Associates), a California limited partnership of which Charles T. Franklin and seven other doctors were the limited partners. The deductions flowed from the purported "purchase" by Associates of the Thunderbird Inn, an Arizona motel, from Wayne L. Romney and Joan E. Romney (hereinafter referred to as the Romneys) on November 15, 1968.

Under a document entitled "Sales Agreement," the Romneys agreed to "sell" the Thunderbird Inn to Associates for $1,224,000. The property would be paid for over a period of ten years, with interest on any unpaid balance of seven and one-half percent per annum. "Prepaid interest" in the amount of $75,000 was payable immediately; monthly principal and interest installments of $9,045.36 [$108,544 per year] would be paid for approximately the first ten years, with Associates required to make a balloon payment at the end of the ten years of the difference between the remaining purchase price, forecast as $975,000, and any mortgages then outstanding against the property.

The purchase obligation of Associates to the Romneys was nonrecourse; the Romneys' only remedy in the event of default would be forfeiture of the partnership's interest. The sales agreement was recorded in the local county. A warranty deed was placed in an escrow account, along with a quitclaim deed from Associates to the Romneys, both documents to be delivered either to Associates upon full payment of the purchase price, or to the Romneys upon default.

The sale was combined with a leaseback of the property by Associates to the Romneys; Associates therefore never took physical possession. The lease payments were designed to approximate closely the principal and interest payments with the consequence that with the exception of the $75,000 prepaid interest payment no cash would cross between Associates and [the] Romneys until the balloon payment. The lease was on a net basis; thus, the Romneys were responsible for all of the typical expenses of owning the motel property including all utility costs, taxes, assessments, rents, charges, and levies of "every name, nature and kind whatsoever." The Romneys also were to continue to be responsible for the first and second mortgages until the final purchase installment was made; the Romneys could, and indeed did, place additional mortgages on the property without the permission of Associates. Finally, the Romneys were allowed to propose new capital improvements which Associates

---

13. [For a description of the taxation of partners and partnerships. —EDS.]

would be required to either build themselves or allow the Romneys to construct with compensating modifications in rent or purchase price.[14]

In holding that the transaction between Associates and the Romneys more nearly resembled an option than a sale, the Tax Court emphasized that Associates had the power at the end of ten years to walk away from the transaction and merely lose its $75,000 "prepaid interest payment." It also pointed out that a deed was never recorded and that the "benefits and burdens of ownership" appeared to remain with the Romneys. Thus, the sale was combined with a leaseback in which no cash would pass; the Romneys remained responsible under the mortgages, which they could increase; and the Romneys could make capital improvements.[15] The Tax Court further justified its "option" characterization by reference to the nonrecourse nature of the purchase money debt and the nice balance between the rental and purchase money payments.

Our emphasis is different from that of the Tax Court. We believe the characteristics set out above can exist in a situation in which the sale imposes upon the purchaser a genuine indebtedness within the meaning of section 167(a), Internal Revenue Code of 1954, which will support both interest and depreciation deductions.[16] They substantially so existed in Hudspeth v. Commissioner,

14. [The expected tax benefits are revealed in the following table taken from the Tax Court opinion (64 T.C. 752, 760):

| | Lease Income | Depreciation | | Total Contract Interest | Indicated Income (Loss) | Lease Income |
		Building	Furnishings			
1968 (2 months)	$ 2,800	$8,000	$16,300	$24,300	$75,000	($96,500)
1969	48,800	47,500	92,900	140,400	31,300	(122,900)
1970	108,550	44,700	65,000	109,700	89,550	(90,700)
1971	108,550	42,000	53,600	95,600	88,250	(75,300)
1972	108,550	39,500	53,600	93,100	86,550	(71,100)
1973	108,550	37,100	44,600	81,700	84,850	(58,000)
1974	108,550	34,900		34,900	83,050	(9,400)
1975	108,550	32,800		32,800	81,050	(5,300)
1976	108,550	30,800		30,800	78,950	(1,200)
1977	108,550	29,000		29,000	76,650	2,900
1978 (10 months)	90,500	22,700		22,700	62,000	5,800

During this time period, the only cash changing hands was the $75,000 of interest in 1968; rents precisely equaled debt service (interest and principal), and the lessee paid all expenses and taxes. —Eds.]

15. There was evidence that not all of the benefits and burdens of ownership remained with the Romneys. Thus, for example, the leaseback agreement appears to provide that any condemnation award will go to Associates.

16. Counsel differed as to whether the Tax Court's decision that the transaction was not a sale, but at best only an option, is reviewable by this court as a question of law or of fact. We agree with other circuits that, while the characteristics of a transaction are questions of fact, whether those characteristics constitute a sale for tax purposes is a question of law. . . .

509 F.2d 1224 (9th Cir. 1975), in which parents entered into sale-leaseback transactions with their children. The children paid for the property by executing nonnegotiable notes and mortgages equal to the fair market value of the property; state law proscribed deficiency judgments in case of default, limiting the parents' remedy to foreclosure of the property. The children had no funds with which to make mortgage payments; instead, the payments were offset in part by the rental payments, with the difference met by gifts from the parents to their children. Despite these characteristics this court held that there was a bona fide indebtedness on which the children, to the extent of the rental payments, could base interest deductions. . . .

In none of these cases, however, did the taxpayer fail to demonstrate that the purchase price was at least approximately equivalent to the fair market value of the property. Just such a failure occurred here. The Tax Court explicitly found that on the basis of the facts before it the value of the property could not be estimated. 64 T.C. at 767-768.[17] In our view this defect in the taxpayers' proof is fatal.

Reason supports our perception. An acquisition such as that of Associates if at a price approximately equal to the fair market value of the property under ordinary circumstances would rather quickly yield an equity in the property which the purchaser could not prudently abandon. This is the stuff of substance. It meshes with the form of the transaction and constitutes a sale.

No such meshing occurs when the purchase price exceeds a demonstrably reasonable estimate of the fair market value. Payments on the principal of the purchase price yield no equity so long as the unpaid balance of the purchase price exceeds the then existing fair market value. Under these circumstances the purchaser by abandoning the transaction can lose no more than a mere chance to acquire an equity in the future should the value of the acquired property increase. While this chance undoubtedly influenced the Tax Court's determination that the transaction before us constitutes an option, we need only point out that its existence fails to supply the substance necessary to justify treating the transaction as a sale ab initio. It is not necessary to the disposition of this case to decide the tax consequences of a transaction such as that before us if in a subsequent year the fair market value of the property increases to an extent that permits the purchaser to acquire an equity.[18]

Authority also supports our perception. It is fundamental that "depreciation is not predicated upon ownership of property *but rather upon an investment in property.* Gladding Dry Goods Co., 2 BTA 336 (1925)." *Mayerson, supra* at 350 (italics added). No such investment exists when payments of the purchase price in accordance with the design of the parties yield no equity to the purchaser. . . . In the transaction before us and during the taxable years in question the purchase price payments by Associates have not been shown to constitute an *investment in the property.* Depreciation was properly disallowed. Only the Romneys had an investment in the property.

---

17. The Tax Court found that appellants had "not shown that the purported sales price of $1,224,000 (or any other price) had any relationship to the actual market value of the motel property. . . ." 64 T.C. at 767.

18. These consequences would include a determination of the proper basis of the acquired property at the date the increments to the purchaser's equity commenced.

Authority also supports disallowance of the interest deductions. This is said even though it has long been recognized that the absence of personal liability for the purchase money debt secured by a mortgage on the acquired property does not deprive the debt of its character as a bona fide debt obligation able to support an interest deduction. *Mayerson, supra* at 352. However, this is no longer true when it appears that the debt has economic significance only if the property substantially appreciates in value prior to the date at which a very large portion of the purchase price is to be discharged. Under these circumstances the purchaser has not secured "the use or forbearance of money." See Norton v. Commissioner, 474 F.2d 608, 610 (9th Cir. 1973). Nor has the seller advanced money or forborne its use. . . . Prior to the date at which the balloon payment on the purchase price is required, and assuming no substantial increase in the fair market value of the property, the absence of personal liability on the debt reduces the transaction in economic terms to a mere chance that a genuine debt obligation may arise. This is not enough to justify an interest deduction. To justify the deduction, the debt must exist; potential existence will not do. For debt to exist, the purchaser, in the absence of personal liability, must confront a situation in which it is presently reasonable from an economic point of view for him to make a capital investment in the amount of the unpaid purchase price. . . .

Our focus on the relationship of the fair market value of the property to the unpaid purchase price should not be read as premised upon the belief that a sale is not a sale if the purchaser pays too much. Bad bargains from the buyer's point of view—as well as sensible bargains from buyer's, but exceptionally good from the seller's point of view—do not thereby cease to be sales. . . . We intend our holding and explanation thereof to be understood as limited to transactions substantially similar to that now before us.

Affirmed.

NOTES AND QUESTIONS

1. Estate of Franklin *as an overvaluation shelter.* The transaction in *Estate of Franklin* might have been highly disadvantageous to the Romneys, from a tax standpoint, had they been required to report the supposed gain from the sale. However, due to the installment method of accounting for gain on the sale of property, they did not have to do so. The inconsistency between giving Franklin immediate basis for amounts not yet paid (if the transaction worked) while permitting the Romneys to defer treating the same amounts as recognized was crucial to the tax planning opportunity that the transaction was designed to exploit. Thus, the transaction can be seen as a variety of the overvaluation shelter described.

2. *The option theory.* How important is the difference between the Tax Court's option theory and the Court of Appeals' equity theory? Suppose that you have negotiated to buy a house for $30,000 payable at the time you take title and possession and $70,000 payable one year later. The buyer insists that the transaction take the form of a payment of $30,000 for an option to buy the house one year hence for $70,000. Is this what we would normally think of as a true option? Why?

3. *Continuing relevance of* Estate of Franklin. The transaction in this case predates the at-risk rules (§465), which prevent deductions (e.g., the depreciation and interest deductions at issue here) that exceed a taxpayer's "at risk" amount. Nonrecourse debt is included in the at-risk amount only if the terms of the loan are commercially reasonable. Subsequent to the enactment of the at-risk rules, the Service could attack this transaction as involving a loan that did not meet the commercially reasonable standard. *Estate of Franklin* is still an important case because the issues it addresses—such as whether a transaction should be treated as a sale—are important even after the enactment of the at-risk rules. (For one thing, the at-risk rules generally do not apply to corporate taxpayers.)

3.   Sale-Leasebacks That Change the Tax Owner for Depreciation Purposes

Suppose Yaba Company requires $1 million of depreciable property for its business. Yaba has past operating losses that can be carried over to present and future years; as a result, Yaba is in a zero percent marginal tax bracket and will not benefit from the depreciation deduction on the new investment. Yaba buys the property for $1 million and then sells it to Xenon Corporation for $1 million. Xenon pays $200,000 cash and gives Yaba a note for the remaining $800,000. Xenon then leases the property back to Yaba at an annual rent that is exactly equal to the payments Xenon must make on the $800,000 purchase note. The only money that ever changes hands between Yaba and Xenon is the $200,000 purchase payment.

When the smoke has cleared, Xenon has paid $200,000 for the legal ownership of $1 million of business property. Xenon must make payments on its $800,000 purchase money note, but those payments will be offset by the rental payments it receives from Yaba. If the transaction is respected for tax purposes, Xenon will receive the tax benefits associated with the property. Yaba, on the other hand, receives the property it needs for a net outlay of $800,000 instead of $1 million. Yaba will be required to make annual rental payments to Xenon, but these will be offset by the payments to which it will be entitled on the purchase money note.

Will the transaction be respected for tax purposes? The answer to that question will depend on many considerations, including the motivation of the parties and the incidents of ownership borne by the purported lessor. In Frank Lyon Co. v. United States, 435 U.S. 561 (1978), the Supreme Court upheld a transaction a lot like the Yaba-Xenon example except for two things. First, the lessee, a bank, could point to a business reason for the form of the transaction: essentially, to circumvent banking regulations (with the approval of the regulators) that would have applied if it held legal title to the property. Second, although it has never been clear to any commentator why the Court thought this mattered, the transaction had involved a third party, which helped provide the actual financing on behalf of the parties that were analogous to Yaba and Xenon.

The government had argued in *Frank Lyon Co.* that the sale-leaseback was a sham and that it actually constituted a financing by the taxpayer, which therefore could not claim depreciation deductions. The Court, however, held that this was a "genuine multiple-party transaction with economic substance which is compelled or encouraged by business or regulatory realities, is imbued with tax-independent considerations, and is not shaped solely by tax-avoidance features that have meaningless labels attached." Hence, "the Government should honor the allocation of rights and duties effectuated by the parties [i.e., the assignment of tax ownership, and consequently depreciation deductions, to the putative buyer/lessor]. Expressed another way, so long as the lessor retains significant and genuine attributes of the traditional lessor status, the form of the transaction adopted by the parties governs for tax purposes. What those attributes are in any particular case will necessarily depend upon its facts. It suffices to say that, as here, a sale-and-leaseback, in and of itself, does not necessarily operate to deny a taxpayer's claim for [depreciation] deductions."

Frank Lyon, while an important pro-taxpayer precedent with respect to sale-leasebacks, somewhat narrows its impact by somewhat murkily specifying its reliance on *all* of the transaction's pertinent facts. Accordingly, while taxpayers have considerable discretion to transfer depreciation deductions to high-bracket counterparties through similar arrangements, their discretion is not entirely unlimited. For example, some cases have emphasized the business purpose of the lessor and have disallowed its depreciation deductions if it had no chance of earning a before-tax profit. See Hilton v. Commissioner, 74 T.C. 305 (1980), aff'd per curiam, 671 F.2d 316 (9th Cir. 1982); James v. Commissioner, 87 T.C. 905 (1986).

More recently, some taxpayers have attempted to reap tax benefits with a more aggressive form of sale-leaseback, known as a SILO (sale-in-lease-out). SILOs generally involve the sale and leaseback of existing equipment by a tax-exempt or foreign entity. The SILOs at issue in Wells Fargo v. United States, 641 F.3d 1319 (Fed. Cir. 2011) were typical. Wells Fargo purchased subway cars and trains from tax-exempt transit agencies in New Jersey, California, Texas, and Washington, D.C., and then immediately leased the equipment back to the transit agency. The purpose of the transaction was to give the bank a depreciation deduction for the equipment. The transit agencies, which had never benefited from depreciation (because they were tax-exempt), received a cash payment equal to a portion of the value of the deduction to the bank. The court found that the bank had no nontax business purpose and ruled the transaction failed to meet the standards of either *Frank Lyon* or the economic substance test. Other SILO transactions have involved Swedish paper mills, German sewer systems, and rural electric cooperative power plants. The SILOs differed from *Frank Lyon* and the Yaba/Xenon hypothetical posed above because the equipment had been purchased or built by the low-bracket taxpayer well before the SILO transaction. It could not be argued, therefore, that the transfer enabled the taxpayer to purchase that particular equipment. More important, the transactions (which were generally structured by one or two shelter promoters) were found to transfer no meaningful incidents of ownership to the high-bracket taxpayer.

The IRS has promulgated guidelines under which it will issue advance rulings that certain equipment leases will be respected for tax purposes. These guidelines are set forth in Revenue Procedures 75-21, 1975-1 C.B. 715, and 75-28, 1975-1 C.B. 752. The guidelines are not intended to represent the IRS's position on audit and do not apply to many forms of leases, such as the leases of real property. Nonetheless, the guidelines are generally taken into account when structuring a lease transaction. The guidelines require (among other things) that the lessor have a minimum of 20 percent unconditional at-risk investment in the property and that the lessor must expect to receive a pretax positive cash flow from the transaction. Needless to say, the equipment leases that made up the typical SILO did not meet these guidelines.

E.   TAX SHELTERS MORE GENERALLY

1.   Definition and Elements of a Tax Shelter

So far, we have only sporadically used the term "tax shelter" to describe aggressive tax planning that the IRS may challenge, whether successfully in court or not. While there is no universally accepted definition, the term is most commonly used to describe an investment that is unrelated to a taxpayer's normal trade or business and that is expected (or even certain) to produce a tax loss but is not expected to produce a commensurate (or perhaps any) economic loss. The taxpayer uses the loss from the tax shelter to offset income from other sources. Tax shelters usually rely on some combination of (a) deferral, (b) conversion, (c) tax arbitrage, (d) misattribution of income, and (e) aggressive interpretation of a governing statute or regulation.

Deferral consists of pushing income into the future by incurring costs that are currently deductible and receiving the corresponding return from the investment in some future year. The tax advantage arises from the use of the funds that would otherwise be paid in taxes for the period of deferral. Of course, it is better still if no future income need ever be recognized.

Conversion consists of converting ordinary income into tax-favored income, such as capital gain.

Tax arbitrage involves incurring expenses that are deductible in order to generate income that is tax favored, thus creating a tax loss in excess of any economic loss. In illustration, suppose that you borrow to hold municipal bonds. If not for §265, the transaction might generate deductible interest expense on the one hand and excludable income on the other. The tax loss it generated would therefore exceed any real economic loss. While §265 blocks this particular tax arbitrage transaction (assuming the interest expense is indeed allocated to the bonds for tax purposes), the basic idea of pairing deductible expense against tax-favored income can be implemented in a variety of ways.

Misattribution of income consists of allocating an item of income for tax purposes to a low-bracket taxpayer and an item of expense to a high-bracket taxpayer.

Under this definition, *Gregory* was not a tax shelter case—although the taxpayer nonetheless lost—because it involved attempting to reduce the tax burden on positive taxable income rather than generating loss. All of the other examples discussed in this chapter were tax shelters, but *Frank Lyon* is an example that was legally permissible.

Tax shelters have evolved and changed over time. At least on two occasions—in the 1970s through the early 1980s, and then again in the 1990s and early 2000s—their use became highly widespread and prominent, triggering judicial and/or legislative responses that quieted things down again. These episodes are worth reviewing briefly, because the law that they generated remains relevant today.

2.   Real Estate and Other Tax Shelters of the 1970s and Early 1980s

The real estate shelter was the most typical tax shelter of the 1970s and early 1980s. The operation of the shelter may be illustrated by the following simplified example. Assume that before the enactment of the anti–tax shelter legislation described below, and at a time that depreciation rates for real estate were far more generous than they are today, an investor borrowed $100,000 at 9 percent and used the proceeds to buy an apartment building. In the first year, the investor paid $9,000 interest. Assume further that during the first year, the apartment building produced net rental income of $9,000. The net rental income represented profit after taking into account all expenses except that of the $9,000 interest payment on the loan used to purchase the building. Finally, assume that the building neither increased nor decreased in value. The rental income therefore exactly offset the interest expense and left the investor's wealth unchanged. For tax purposes, the investor recognized rental income and deducted interest expense. In addition, however, the investor was able to deduct approximately $12,000 depreciation. Thus, a break-even economic investment produced a $12,000 tax loss. The investor could use this loss as a deduction to offset income from other sources.

Eventually, the tax and economic consequences of the investment would converge. The $12,000 depreciation deduction taken in the first year would reduce the basis of the building to $88,000. If the building were sold on the first day of the second year for its fair market value of $100,000, the taxpayer would recognize a $12,000 gain. In effect, the taxpayer was required to "give back" the $12,000 of depreciation taken in the previous year.

The investment was nonetheless advantageous because the loss in the first year allowed the investor to defer taxes payable on income from other sources. The investment was even more advantageous if, as was generally the case, the gain recognized on sale qualified for favorable capital gain treatment.

The typical "investor" in the real estate shelter was not an individual, but a partnership that was formed by a promoter, who would serve as general partner. Limited partnership interests would be sold to high-income professionals. The loss recognized by the partnership would flow through to those professionals.

Financial and other tax shelters. Real estate was not the only source of tax shelter investments. Many tax shelters were based on financial investments. These often were variants on *Knetsch*, in that they attempted to combine currently deductible expenses with the deferred accrual of income.

Nonrecourse debt and overvaluation. As in the *Estate of Franklin* case, tax shelters in this era frequently used nonrecourse debt to permit the overvaluation of property, thus increasing the amount of deductions that ostensibly could be claimed.

3.   The Congressional Response to the Tax Shelters of the 1980s

Congress responded to the wave of shelters in this area in part by lengthening the period during which depreciation is taken. As noted above, at the heart of the real estate shelter was the ability to take a depreciation deduction that exceeded any (and in fact was unrelated to) decline in value. By lengthening the depreciation period, Congress reduced the present value of depreciation deductions. Congress also eliminated the distinction between ordinary income and capital gain (only to bring back the distinction in later years). Depreciation and capital gain are discussed.

Congress also adopted an approach to the sheltering problem sometimes called "basketing." Under this approach, deductions from items in a group of transactions (colloquially, a "basket") are allowed only against income from other items in the same group, thus preventing the use of net losses from the basket to offset other taxable income, such as wages. We saw an earlier example of a basketing rule in Chapter 2, concerning gambling losses, which (under §165(d)) are deductible only to the extent of gambling gains from the same taxable year.

Many of the basketing rules that Congress adopted to discourage tax shelter activity are hard to understand other than as responses to specific taxpayer practices that had come to its attention. In addition, these rules may in some cases either overlap or leave gaps in their application. For some taxpayers (including those engaged in straightforward business activity that is not primarily designed to generate tax losses), the result is to make tax planning and compliance more complicated than ever, given the need to steer one's way through the various basketing rules or at least to apply them accurately to tax returns. For other taxpayers, the result is to make tax planning simpler, as sheltering becomes too difficult to justify the effort.

The main basketing rules that Congress has adopted to discourage tax sheltering activity by individuals are described below.

Passive activity loss rules. The classic tax shelter investor often is someone who has a lot of taxable income that unmistakably is earned from work. Consider, for example, a doctor or lawyer who gets a salary, service fees from patients or clients, or a share of the income for services earned by her group medical practice or law partnership. Such a taxpayer might be eager to generate tax losses that are deductible against this income. One way to seek these losses is by investing in some sort of business or rental enterprise (say, an apartment building, cattle farm, or oil well) that can be structured to generate large tax losses in excess of any real economic loss. An investor of this sort is unlikely, however, to be eager or even able to spend a lot of time working on the loss-producing enterprise. Few lawyers in New York or Los Angeles, for example, are likely, even for a sizeable tax advantage, to consider spending a significant portion of the free time that is left to them shoveling cattle manure or handling an oil drill in Texas.

The fact that many tax shelter investors were generating taxable income from businesses in which they did substantial work while trying to deduct losses from those in which they did little or no work encouraged Congress to enact §469, which limits deductions for passive activity losses. A passive activity loss is a loss on an investment (a) that constitutes a trade or business and (b) in which the taxpayer does not "materially participate." See §469(d)(1). In addition, rental activities are passive activities without regard to material participation. See §469(e)(2). A passive loss from one investment may be used to offset passive income from another investment, and net passive losses may be carried forward indefinitely and deducted when the investment that generates the loss is sold, but passive losses may not be used to offset other income from nonpassive investments or activities, wages and salaries, or "portfolio income" (dividends, interest, etc.).

The passive loss rules may be illustrated by again considering the investor who borrows $100,000 at 9 percent and uses the proceeds to buy an apartment building that appreciates at 8 percent a year. (Assume that the rental income is offset by taxes, maintenance costs, and other expenses.) Absent special limitations, in the first year the taxpayer would be able to deduct interest and depreciation. The taxpayer would not pay tax on the appreciation because it is not realized gain. If, however, the investor does not materially participate in the activity and does not qualify for special relief provisions discussed below, the loss from the building will be a passive loss. That loss will be deductible against current or future passive activity income from other sources, or from the building itself (in future years), or it may be deducted at the time the building is sold, but the loss will not be deductible against other current income such as salary or portfolio income.

The concept of material participation is central to the passive loss rules. "Material participation" is statutorily defined as participation that is "regular, continuous, and substantial." §469(h). Under the regulations, a taxpayer will be deemed to materially participate in an activity only if he or she meets one of seven tests. Under one test, the taxpayer must personally spend more than 500 hours on the activity. Under another test, the taxpayer must spend at least 100 hours on the activity and must spend at least as much time on the activity as any other individual. A third test is qualitative: An individual materially participates in an activity if (unspecified) facts and circumstances show material participation. Reg. §1.469-5(a). Section 469 contains many exceptions, special rules, and exceptions to the special rules. For example, limited partnership interests and rental activities are considered passive activities. Rental activities, however, are not passive for individuals in the real property business who meet certain tests (such as performing more than 750 hours of service in connection with a real property rental activity). §469(c)(7). In addition, up to

$25,000 of annual losses may be deducted from real estate rental activities of certain individuals who meet a lesser standard of participation, but this exemption is phased out as income rises from $100,000 to $150,000. §469(i)(6)(A). An apartment building with monthly or annual tenants typically is a rental activity, but a hotel typically is not, due to the higher turnover rate and greater services provided in connection with the occupants' use of the property.

Some observers credit the passive loss rules with a major role in reducing tax shelter activity by individuals other than the super-rich (whose income may come from investments rather than work). The rules may apply, however, to people who do not think of themselves as engaged in tax shelter activity. Suppose, for example, that you decide to invest money in a restaurant that you think (or hope) will be profitable, but you will be little if at all involved in the restaurant's operations. If this is your only passive activity, you may face a "heads the IRS wins, tails I lose" scenario, whereby your share of the profits will be taxable if the restaurant is a success, but, if it loses money, the deductions will be suspended until you sell your interest or the restaurant closes.

Under the passive loss rules, taxpayers benefit from seeking passive status for investments that generate positive taxable income (so the income can be sheltered by other passive losses) and nonpassive status for investments that generate tax losses (so the deductions will not be limited). The IRS, if trying to maximize revenues, has an opposite incentive. Struggle concerning passive versus nonpassive classification typically centers on determining the scope of a distinct "activity" that needs to be tested for passive status, whether the taxpayer has materially participated, and whether a given activity is a rental activity.

Limitations on the deduction of interest on "investment indebtedness." The passive loss rules only restrict losses from investments that constitute a trade or business or a rental activity. Section 163(d), which was adopted in 1969, applies a similar restriction on the deduction of interest on "investment indebtedness," that is, on debt tied to any investment, including stocks and bonds and undeveloped real estate. The role of this provision may be illustrated as follows: Assume that an investor borrows $100,000 at 10 percent and uses the proceeds to buy shares of common stock of a growing electronics company. In the first year, consistent with expectations, the shares increase in value by 15 percent but pay no dividends. There has been an economic gain, but no gain or income for tax purposes. Absent special rules, the $10,000 interest expense would be deductible. Section 163(d) prevents a tax advantage by limiting the amount of the interest deduction to "net investment income." Net investment income includes non-capital gain income from all portfolio investments, so that interest payments incurred in holding one such investment can be deducted to the extent of income from another such investment. Net investment income includes capital gain income only if the taxpayer elects to forgo the lower maximum rate on such income and, in effect, treat capital gain income as ordinary income. Interest disallowed as a deduction by reason of §163(d) may be deducted, subject to the same limitations, in succeeding taxable years. In the present example, there is no investment income, so the $10,000 interest expense would not be currently deductible.

Limitations on deductions to amount of "at risk" investment. Another broadscale approach is the "at risk" rules of §465, first introduced in 1976 and broadened in application in 1978 and 1986. These rules are another form of attack on the leverage (use of borrowed funds) that has been vital to most tax shelters. Section 465 disallows deductions for "*losses*" (i.e., the excess of deductions over income) of an investment in excess of the amount that the taxpayer has at risk in that investment. The amount at risk includes cash invested plus amounts of debt for which the taxpayer is personally liable or which is secured by assets of the taxpayer (other than assets of the tax shelter investment). Thus, if a person purports to buy a motion picture for $2 million but puts up only $200,000 in cash and signs a nonrecourse note for the balance, the maximum loss that can be deducted is $200,000. Losses not currently deductible may be carried forward and deducted against income in later years as the investment produces taxable income or as the at-risk amount increases. Section 465 applies to all investments and business activities. There is an exception, however, for real estate activities that are funded with "qualified nonrecourse financing," a term defined in §465(b) to include loans from unrelated parties and seller financing if made at commercially reasonable rates. Section 465 overlaps with the passive loss rules of §469 because both may apply to investments that constitute a trade or business. Losses on trade or business investments will not be deductible unless they pass muster under both §465 and §469.

The at-risk rules should generally prevent the overvaluation shelter described above, in which a taxpayer purports to purchase property for $50,000 cash and a nonrecourse note for $1 billion. The purported loan of $1 billion, made by the seller, would not meet the commercially reasonable test of §465(b). As a result, it would not qualify for the real estate exception to the at-risk rules and the buyer's deductions would be limited to his at-risk investment of $50,000.

Debt used to purchase or carry tax-favored investments. One of the earliest responses to tax avoidance was to deny deductions for "interest on indebtedness incurred or continued to purchase or carry" tax-exempt bonds. §265(a)(2). See also §265(a)(1), denying deductions for certain expenses "allocable to" tax-exempt income. Absent §265(a)(2), a taxpayer might borrow at 8 percent to buy tax-exempt bonds that pay 7 percent. Interest paid on the loan would be deductible, while the interest on the bonds would be tax free. Under §265, the interest on the loan would be nondeductible.

In a similar vein, §264 denies deductions for interest on indebtedness "incurred or continued to purchase or carry" certain insurance and annuity policies. Section 264, among other things, now expressly covers the type of transaction engaged in by the taxpayer in the *Knetsch* case.

NOTES AND QUESTIONS

1. What do you think of the statutory approach of causing the allowance of a deduction to depend on such considerations as whether the taxpayer spends at least 500 hours working on a given activity or whether she would be personally liable for certain economic losses if they occurred? Are there better ways of trying to discourage unduly tax-motivated investment? Are the passive loss and at-risk rules better than doing nothing?

2. (a) On January 1, 2017, Stan obtains a recourse loan of $200,000 and uses the proceeds to buy shares of common stock. Stan pays $20,000 interest on the loan in 2017 and receives $10,000 in dividends. Stan has no other investments or loans. How much, if any, of the 2017 interest payment is deductible?

(b) The facts are the same as in (a) except that Stan also receives $5,000 of dividends from another stock that he bought with nonborrowed funds. How much, if any, of the 2017 interest payment is deductible?

3. On January 1, 2017, Jamie invests $250,000 of nonborrowed funds in a widget manufacturing enterprise. Jamie does not materially participate in the enterprise, which shows a taxable loss of $50,000 for the year. Jamie is the sole owner of the enterprise.

(a) If Jamie has no other investments, how much, if any, of the loss may she deduct?

(b) Assume Jamie has another trade or business investment in which she does materially participate, and in 2018, this produces taxable income of $40,000. How much, if any, of the loss from the widget enterprise may Jamie deduct for the year?

(c) Assume Jamie has net dividend income of $20,000 from common stocks in 2018. How much, if any, of the loss from the widget enterprise may Jamie deduct?

(d) Assume that in 2017 Jamie has no income or loss from the widget enterprise, but that in 2011 she has income of $30,000 from a different trade or business in which she materially participates. How much, if any, of the 2017 loss from the widget enterprise may Jamie deduct?

4. On January 1, 2017, Rafael borrows $200,000 and uses the proceeds to buy a restaurant. The loan is nonrecourse and does not require repayment of any of the principal until 2018. Rafael rents the building in which the restaurant operates. In 2017, the restaurant shows a net loss of $40,000. In 2018, the restaurant shows a net income of $25,000. Also in 2018, Rafael obtains a recourse loan of $10,000 and uses the proceeds to improve the restaurant. In all years, Rafael materially participates in the management of the restaurant. Is any portion of the 2017 loss deductible? When?

5. On January 1, 2017, Sarah obtains a recourse loan of $100,000 and uses the proceeds to buy Fly Co. common stock. In 2017, Sarah pays $10,000 interest on the loan, and the stock pays dividends of $15,000. Sarah pays $10,000 interest on the loan in 2017 and in 2018. The stock pays no dividends in 2017 and dividends of $15,000 in 2018. Sarah has no other investments. What portion, if any, of Sarah's $30,000 interest expense is deductible? When?

4.   More Recent Corporate and Individual Tax Shelters

The 1986 tax reforms, particularly the passive rules, largely put an end to the real estate and other tax shelters designed to provide ordinary losses to individual investors. The passive loss rules and other anti–tax shelter measures do not apply to corporate taxpayers, however. Nor do those rules limit the ability of individual investors to deduct capital losses against capital gains. It is therefore not surprising that, starting in the 1990s, a new market in tax shelters emerged—one in which corporations and wealthy individuals with capital gains to shelter are the primary investors.

The new tax shelters were much more sophisticated than the older individual tax shelters. They were much more likely to involve financial assets than real assets and much more likely to be based on a hyper-technical (and some might say hyper-aggressive) reading of a relevant statute or regulation. By the early 2000s, however, the IRS and Treasury succeeded in slowing down this wave of shelter activity through a combination of enforcement and litigation. In general, the transactions were subject to attack on such grounds as their lack of economic substance, business purpose, and pretax profit potential.

An example is ACM v. Commissioner, T.C. Memo. 1997-115, aff'd in part and rev'd in part, 157 F.3d 231 (3d Cir. 1998), cert. denied, 119 S. Ct. 1251 (1999). *ACM* involved a tax shelter sold to Colgate-Palmolive by Merrill Lynch. Colgate-Palmolive bought and then soon sold approximately $150 million worth of publicly traded bonds. For accounting purposes, and as a matter of economic reality, the transaction generated no loss. However, the transaction was structured so as to take advantage of a flaw in the then-governing Treasury regulations. Based on a literal reading of one part of one regulation, Colgate-Palmolive claimed a tax loss of over $100 million. Tax Court Judge David Laro held that the transaction would not be respected because it had no "economic substance"—it was not expected to generate a pretax profit or serve any other useful nontax purpose.

Subsequent to Judge Laro's decision in *ACM*, the government has litigated scores of tax shelter cases, with considerable success. Some courts based their decision on a finding that the taxpayer simply did not comply with the best reading of the relevant statutes or regulations; others ruled against the taxpayer on grounds that the transaction was a sham; some based their decision on the economic substance doctrine that grew out of earlier cases, such as *Goldstein*, as well as *ACM*; and still other courts used a combination of the above.

WINN-DIXIE STORES, INC. v. COMMISSIONER
254 F.3d 1313 (11th Cir. 2001), cert. denied, 535 U.S. 986 (2002)

PER CURIAM.

Winn-Dixie Stores, Inc. appeals the tax court's judgment resting on the conclusion that Winn-Dixie was not entitled to deduct interest and fees incurred in borrowing against insurance policies that it owned on the lives of more than 36,000 Winn-Dixie employees. We affirm.

BACKGROUND

In summary, the tax court found the following facts: In 1993, Winn-Dixie embarked on a broad-based company-owned life-insurance (COLI) program whose sole purpose, as shown by contemporary memoranda, was to satisfy Winn-Dixie's "appetite" for interest deductions. Under the program, Winn-Dixie purchased whole life insurance policies on almost all of its full-time employees, who numbered in the tens of thousands. Winn-Dixie was the sole beneficiary of the policies. Winn-Dixie would borrow against those policies' account value at an interest rate of over 11%. The high interest and the administrative fees that came with the program outweighed the net cash surrender value and benefits paid on the policies, with the result that in pretax terms Winn-Dixie lost money on the program. The deductibility of the interest and fees post-tax, however, yielded a benefit projected to reach into the billions of dollars over 60 years. Winn-Dixie participated until 1997, when a change in tax law jeopardized this tax arbitrage, and it eased its way out.

The IRS determined a deficiency because of the interest and fee deductions taken in Winn-Dixie's 1993 tax year. Winn-Dixie challenged the determination before the tax court. The tax court rejected Winn-Dixie's assertions that the COLI program had a business purpose, or that Congress had expressly authorized its tax benefits. See Winn-Dixie Stores, Inc. v. Comm'r, 113 T.C. 254 (1999). The court held that the loans against the policies were substantive shams, and that Winn-Dixie was therefore not entitled to deductions for the interest and fees paid for the loans. Winn-Dixie appeals.

Winn-Dixie's two core arguments here are the same as those it made to the tax court. The first is that Congress, through the Internal Revenue Code, explicitly authorized the deduction of interest and fees incurred in certain borrowing against whole life-insurance policies' account value. This explicit permission, Winn-Dixie says, makes application of the sham-transaction doctrine inappropriate. In the alternative, Winn-Dixie argues that even if the sham-transaction doctrine properly applies here, the tax court misinterpreted the economic-substance and business-purpose prongs of that doctrine and thus "shammed" a transaction that was due respect. Winn-Dixie does not dispute any finding of historical fact; these issues are exclusively ones of law, and our consideration of them is accordingly de novo. . . .

DISCUSSION

Winn-Dixie starts its argument by invoking the special treatment afforded life insurance contracts (as defined in §7702) in general, whose benefits are generally untaxed and whose appreciation is tax-deferred. See §§101(a)(1), 72(e). That treatment extends to loans made against a policy, whose interest . . . is generally not deductible. See §264(a)(3). . . . [Under the law in effect until 1997, however, §264(a)(3) was subject to a special exception permitting the interest on such loans to be deducted.] Winn-Dixie's loans fell within . . . [this] exception, all agree. Because they qualify for the exception, and because the loans are within the specially treated world of life insurance that has obviously been the subject of congressional attention, Winn-Dixie contends, there is no room for application of the sham-transaction doctrine.

This argument may have some force, but it runs into binding precedent. The Supreme Court was faced with a materially similar argument decades ago by a taxpayer who sought to deduct interest payments on loans taken against an annuity contract. Knetsch v. United States, 364 U.S. 361 (1960). Because, as here, the annuity contract was obviously being used as a tax shelter, and as used offered the taxpayer no financial benefit other than its tax consequences, the Court held that the indebtedness was not bona fide, and the interest not deductible under §163(a) See id. at 366. . . . Along the way, the Court rejected an argument based on §264 that is at least a cousin of Winn-Dixie's present contention. Knetsch argued that Congress's failure to close a loophole in §264 (that section's prohibition of deductions on indebtedness to purchase life-insurance policies did not extend to annuities until 1954, the year after the tax year in question) equated to blessing the loophole. The Court declined to attribute such an intention to Congress, because that would "exalt artifice above reality." Id. at 367. . . . *Knetsch* holds, therefore, that the sham-transaction doctrine does apply to indebtedness that generates interest sought to be deducted under §163(a), even if the interest deduction is not yet prohibited by §264. . . .

Winn-Dixie tries to get around *Knetsch* with the argument that we have 33 more years (as of 1993) of congressional regulation of interest deductions in this context, and that 33-year history shows that Congress does not want to look behind facial compliance with, for instance, the . . . exception [relied on by Winn-Dixie]. It may well be that *Knetsch* was then, and this is now, but we are not the court to make that call. *Knetsch*'s holding is at best undermined by congressional action (or inaction) in the intervening decades, and it is up to the Supreme Court, not us, to determine when the Court's holdings have expired. . . . We therefore must conclude that the tax court properly examined the transaction under the sham-transaction doctrine.

That doctrine provides that a transaction is not entitled to tax respect if it lacks economic effects or substance other than the generation of tax benefits, or if the transaction serves no business purpose. . . . The doctrine has few bright lines, but "[i]t is clear that transactions whose sole function is to produce tax deductions are substantive shams." . . . That was, as we read the tax court's opinion, the rule the tax court followed. Nor did the court misapply the rule in concluding that the broad-based COLI program had no "function" other than generating interest deductions.

The tax court found, without challenge here, that the program could never generate a pretax profit. That was what Winn-Dixie thought as it set up the program, and it is the most plausible explanation for Winn-Dixie's withdrawal after the 1996 changes to the tax law threatened the tax benefits Winn-Dixie was receiving. No finding of the tax court suggests, furthermore, that the broad-based COLI program answered any business need of Winn-Dixie, such as indemnifying it for the loss of key employees. Nor could it have been conceived as an employee benefit, because Winn-Dixie was the beneficiary of the policies. . . . [T]herefore, the broad-based COLI program lacked sufficient economic substance to be respected for tax purposes, and the tax court did not err in so concluding.

CONCLUSION

For the foregoing reasons, the judgment of the tax court is affirmed.

NOTES

1. Corporate-owned life insurance, or COLI, policies have long been used to cover key employees, such as high-ranking executives, whose untimely death

might disrupt a company's operations. By the early 1990s, tax planners had
come up with the idea of using debt-financed policies to cover rank-and-file
workers, even though these individuals' deaths would have little impact on
operations. They sought the tax benefit available, at little out-of-pocket cost,
through a *Knetsch*-style arbitrage (borrowing deductibly in order to generate
tax-free income). These policies were known in the business as "dead peas-
ants' insurance" or "janitors' insurance."

2. Not surprisingly, given *Knetsch*, the IRS has been quite successful in arguing
that COLI transactions are shams. See In re CM Holding, Inc., 254 B.R. 578 (D.
Del. 2000); American Electric Power, Inc. v. United States, 136 F. Supp. 2d 762
(S.D. Ohio 2001). Its fortunes in other prominent "corporate tax shelter" cases,
particularly on appeal from the Tax Court, have been more mixed.

While there is as yet no clear-cut circuit split in corporate tax shelter cases,
the differences between the approaches taken in different circuits create a
possibility of Supreme Court intervention at some point. At least until then
and perhaps beyond, however, taxpayers that engage in transactions having
little nontax economic effect or prospect of pretax profit must bear significant
tax law risk, whether or not they need bear other economic risk.

3. Suppose Winn-Dixie had financed its purchase of the insurance policies
by borrowing from a bank on its general credit, or using property other than
the insurance policy to secure the loans. Would the interest paid on the loans
still be nondeductible?

Similarly, suppose Winn-Dixie had used spare cash generated by its operations to buy the insurance policies. Suppose further that an internal memorandum showed the investment in the insurance policies made economic sense,
compared with other alternatives, solely because of the favorable tax treatment
of the insurance. Would the IRS have any way to attack the tax consequences?

Why do you think Winn-Dixie (and other COLI purchasers) engaged in
Knetsch-like transactions that amounted to little more than paper-shuffling,
rather than using separate borrowing or spare cash?

4. Is a "sham" transaction one that amounts to little or nothing more than
paper-shuffling? Why should tax-motivated paper-shuffling be treated less
favorably than equally tax-motivated investment decisions that have affirmatively undesirable net economic consequences in the taxpayer's view, including
too little pretax profit potential to have been worth pursuing in isolation but
that have enough economic substance to withstand scrutiny?

5.   Codification of Economic Substance

In 2010, Congress adopted a strict liability penalty of 20 percent (40 percent if the transaction is undisclosed) for transactions that lack economic substance. §§6662(b)(6), 6664(c)(2). The penalty is keyed to the simultaneously
adopted §7701(o), which provided the first-ever codification of the economic
substance doctrine. Under that section, a transaction has economic substance
only if it changes in a meaningful way the taxpayer's pretax economic position
and has a substantial nontax purpose. Thus, the transaction must meet both
an objective and subjective test. It is not enough for the taxpayer to believe a

transaction has a nontax goal; the transaction must in fact, at least potentially and plausibly, serve that goal. In most cases, the nontax purpose will be (or at least will be claimed to be) profit-related. The statute provides that an expectation of profit meets the subjective and objective tests only if the present value of pretax profit is substantial in relation to the expected net tax benefits.

Codification moderately strengthened the doctrine's significance as a weapon in the government's anti–tax shelter arsenal. First, the statute resolved one previously open issue (whether a transaction must have both subjective and objective substance) in the government's favor. Second, enactment of the statute removed the argument that the doctrine is inconsistent with legislative intent,[19] or contrary to allowable methods of statutory interpretation. Finally, the doctrine is now tied to significant strict liability penalties.

However, codification left unresolved most of the ambiguities that surround the doctrine. First, and most obviously, the statute does not offer guidance as to how much expected profit a transaction must offer (and with what probability) in order to qualify as "substantial" in relation to the expected tax benefits. Pre-existing law is surprisingly unhelpful as a guideline because in virtually all of the cases litigated, after allowing for transaction costs, the shelters challenged offer no expected pretax profits whatsoever. Second, the statute does not (and cannot) resolve the question of what constitutes profit attributable to a "transaction." Suppose, for example, a company purchases equipment that is absolutely needed for its business operations, but goes out of its way to structure the acquisition in a tax-favored manner. Are the tax benefits weighed against all future business profit? Or suppose a company claims that interest earned on a bank account was part of a given transaction, but the IRS disagrees. Finally, the statute was not meant to preclude conventionally accepted tax planning, such as choosing a form of business operations for tax reasons or to rule out tax-motivated transactions (e.g., investments that qualify for the low-income housing tax credit) that are clearly consistent with statutory intent. See §7701(n)(5); Joint Committee on Taxation, Technical Explanation of the Revenue Provisions of the "Reconciliation Act of 2010," JCX-18-10 (2010). Taxpayers can be expected to argue, when at all plausible, that their challenged transactions are permissible on such grounds.

The Treasury announced that it generally would not try to fill in these gaps with regulations or guidance: It leaves that task for the courts. Thus, the economic substance doctrine, which some criticize as too vague while others defend it as necessary,[20] will continue to evolve through case-by-case jurisprudence.

6. Rules Versus Standards

The debate over anti–tax shelter remedies reprises a debate over rules versus standards that most students have encountered in other classes. To give

---

19. See Coltec Industries v. United States, 62 Fed. Cl. 716 (2004) (holding the doctrine inconsistent with legislative intent); rev'd 454 F.3d 1340 (Fed Cir. 2006).

20. For a defense of the doctrine, see Joseph Bankman, *The Tax Shelter Battle in the Crisis in Tax Administration,* Aaron & Slemrod, eds. (Brookings 2004), at 19-20.

a simple example, a 65 mile per hour speed limit is a rule, whereas requiring drivers not to drive unreasonably fast, given all of the relevant circumstances, is a standard. Highway drivers are subject to both the rule and the standard; one may, for example, risk being ticketed if one drives 65 miles per hour on ice or when the road is extremely crowded.

Congress dealt with the tax shelters of the 1980s by adopting rules: the passive loss rules, the at-risk rules, and the limitations on investment interest. Rules give clear guidance (relative to standards). However, they are complex and ill-suited to unforeseen situations. The principal weapon against the newer wave of shelters has been the economic substance doctrine, which (even in codified form) is more of a standard than a rule. The doctrine can be read quickly and is somewhat intuitive. It is flexible. However, it is unavoidably vague.

We see a similar conflict between rules and standards elsewhere in federal tax law. For example, Congress deals with the mix of personal and business use of a vacation home through detailed rules. On the other hand, the question of whether a trip is a vacation or for business is resolved through a standard, involving a primary purpose test.

In some cases, specific statutory provisions might be viewed as a mechanism for requiring economic substance, but via the use of a rule, rather than a standard. For example, suppose a taxpayer wants to realize the loss on particular shares of stock that she holds without actually changing her economic position with respect to the asset in any meaningful way. Suppose further that she wants to accomplish this through a "wash sale," that is, via sale of the stock, immediately preceded or followed by a purchase of the same or substantially identical stock.

In principle, such a transaction could be challenged under §7701(o). After all, it presumably would result in the taxpayer's economic position remaining substantially the same, and it would serve no substantial purpose other than its federal income tax effects. In addition, if the stock was bought and sold for the same price, the taxpayer would presumably lose money overall, given transaction costs (such as paying brokers to engage in the purchase and sale).

However, if the purchase and sale take place within thirty days of each other, the IRS does not need to consider raising any such challenge to the taxpayer's loss claim on selling the stock. Code §1091(a) expressly disallows any loss on a "wash sale," which it defines as a sale or disposition of stock or securities, where, "within a period beginning 30 days before the date of such sale or disposition and ending 30 days after such date, the taxpayer has acquired . . . or has entered into a contract or option so to acquire, substantially identical stock or securities."[21]

Thus, for repurchases within thirty days of the loss sale, a specific statutory rule mandates loss disallowance (albeit, subject to the vagaries of defining "substantially identical"), without regard to whether the transaction had economic substance. In effect, the fact that the purchase and sale took place

---

21. The loss disallowance rule does not apply to dealers in stock or securities who are acting in the ordinary course of that business. Where loss disallowance does apply, the basis of the replacement shares is in effect adjusted so that the taxpayer may eventually get to claim the disallowed loss. See §1091(d).

so close in time to each other—thus limiting the period during which the taxpayer faced any market risk that the stock or securities would change in value—is treated as if it conclusively established a lack of economic substance.

Why can't Congress do this all the time? That is, suppose it attempted fully to define, in advance, all of the circumstances in which a given transaction would be held to lack requisite economic substance. Obviously, this would require writing rules of vast length and intricacy—and even so, Congress would surely fail to anticipate all of the circumstances in which, ex post, it might have been appropriate to find a lack of economic substance. This is why standards, as well as rules, are commonly used everywhere in law, despite the effect on ex ante uncertainty.

7.   Rules Aimed at the Tax Lawyer

Tax lawyers play a crucial role in the tax shelter world. Tax lawyers (together with tax accountants and investment bankers) have helped develop shelters, including some of the most aggressive shelters. Paul Daugerdas headed the Chicago office of the then large and prosperous firm of Jenkins & Gilchrist. Between 1994 and 2004, Daugerdas helped develop and sell shelters that gave shelter purchasers over $7 billion of tax losses. The shelters generated over $200 million in revenue to Jenkins & Gilchrist. Daugerdas received $95 million in compensation, but he used the shelters he had developed to reduce his taxable income to less than $8,000. Ultimately, the shelters were found invalid, and the shelter promoters were found guilty of tax evasion and associated crimes. See *Wilmette Lawyer Guilty in Massive Tax Dodge,* Chicago Sun-Times, May 25, 2011 at 15; http://federaltaxcrimes.blogspot.com/2009/06/daugerdas-indictment-part-1-players.html. Mr. Daugerdas is now living with free room and board at a federally operated facility that does not offer upgrades or luxuries.

More commonly, tax lawyers have been asked by promoters or clients to provide opinions as to whether a tax shelter "works": whether it is likely to be challenged by the Service or, if challenged, upheld by the courts. In the past, a favorable opinion was thought to provide insurance against penalties. The taxpayer would argue that its position had been reviewed by a tax lawyer and so met the "reasonable cause" exception to the understatement penalty.

The fact that a tax lawyer's blessing was thought to insulate a taxpayer from penalties led to a race to the bottom in the legal tax market. Promoters would hire multiple tax lawyers to examine each new shelter. The lawyer who was willing to go on record as stating the shelter worked would be hired to write the opinion. The opinion would be shown to prospective purchasers, and purchasers would be encouraged to hire that same lawyer to write the individualized opinion letter thought to be needed for penalty protection. Eventually, promoters found a relatively few tax lawyers to bless a significant portion of their wares. R. J. Ruble, for example, was a lawyer at Brown & Root and later a partner and member of the management committee at the prestigious firm of Sidley & Austin. Ruble wrote opinions for numerous tax shelters, but he was criminally charged and convicted only for his work on four. Ruble wrote 600 opinions on those shelters, essentially four opinions (one for each shelter), with virtual carbon copies of the opinion given to each of the 600 clients the promoters sent his way. Ruble's law firm charged each client $50,000 (which was a bargain, considering the then-prevailing view that the opinion protected against penalties). Shelter purchasers deducted over $10 billion of shelter losses that were eventually ruled invalid. Ruble took in a relatively modest $13 million from his firm. However, he also received money from promoters on the side, which he reported to neither his firm nor the IRS. See *Three Tied to KMPG Sentenced,* Wall St. Journal, Apr. 2, 2009 at c3; http://www.quatloos. com/kmpg_super_indict_17Oct05.pdf (government indictment).

This state of affairs led Congress to amend the "reasonable cause" exception to the accuracy-related penalty. That section now prevents a taxpayer from relying on an opinion from a "disqualified advisor" to establish reasonable cause for its position. A disqualified advisor is defined to include attorneys who write opinions for the use of shelter promoters or who are referred to clients by shelter promoters. §6662A.

Perhaps a more significant restraint on lawyers' behavior has been the criminal prosecutions of attorneys such as Daugerdas and Ruble. Some firms involved in shelter promotion have paid significant amounts to the government, and virtually all shelter promoters have been sued by clients (who paid millions in fees only to see their claims of losses denied by the IRS).

Finally, the Treasury has changed the rules governing tax practice to require higher standards for so-called covered opinions. Under those rules, adopted in a document known as Circular 230 and made part of the code of federal regulations (31 C.F.R. §10.35), a covered opinion includes any more-likely-than-not opinion on a transaction a significant purpose of which is the evasion or avoidance of tax. The rules specify in considerable detail what types of opinions are covered and what types are not. They then impose standards, including the following:

> (c) *Requirements for covered opinions.* A practitioner providing a covered opinion must comply with requirements that include the following:
>
> > – using reasonable efforts to identify and ascertain all of the relevant facts, including those that pertain to anticipated future events,
> > – not basing the opinion on any unreasonable factual assumptions, such as one that the practitioner knows or should know is incorrect or incomplete. This includes not assuming, on less than a reasonable basis, that a transaction has a business purpose or is potentially profitable apart from tax benefits. In assessing reasonableness, the practitioner cannot simply adopt factual representations, statements or findings of the taxpayer or any other person, without assessing their reasonableness.

Attorneys who do not meet these requirements may face monetary fines or suspension from practice before the IRS.

9

MIXED BUSINESS
AND PERSONAL EXPENSES

As explained in Chapter 7, there are two basic provisions under which individuals may claim deductions for expenses that may be thought of as the cost of generating income. The first is §162(a), which allows a deduction for "ordinary and necessary expenses paid or incurred . . . in carrying on any trade or business." It is under this provision, for example, that a practicing lawyer who heads her own office would claim deductions for office expenses, salaries paid to associates, automobile expenses, entertainment expenses, etc.[1] The other basic deduction provision for individuals is §212,[2] which covers expenses of generating income from sources other than a trade or business. Under this provision a person with investments in stocks and bonds would claim deductions for fees paid to investment advisors, the cost of a subscription to the *Wall Street Journal,* and expenses incurred in attending investment seminars.

The rationale for these deductions is easy to discern. A tax on *net income*—as distinguished from a tax on gross revenue—must allow some sort of deduction for the costs incurred in producing that income. When a taxpayer incurs expenses that are not for the production of income but rather personal in nature, the tax code (again, quite rationally and logically) denies a deduction, since those expenses are not for the production of income. More specifically, §262 provides: "Except as otherwise expressly provided in this chapter, no deduction shall be allowed for personal, living, or family expenses." Chapter 10 will examine the types of personal expenditures for which Congress has expressly provided a deduction, overriding §262's general rule of nondeductibility.

A legal and interpretative conundrum arises when a taxpayer's expense is defined not only in §162 or §212 (expressly allowing a deduction) but also in

---

1. These deductions are taken in arriving at "adjusted gross income" (see §62(a)(1)) and are sometimes called "above-the-line" deductions.

2. Deductions under §212 are "itemized" deductions, which are deducted from adjusted gross income to arrive at taxable income.

§262 (expressly denying a deduction). This is an age-old conflict in the administration of our tax system and an area of the law where taxpayer "ingenuity" kicks into high gear, sometimes with comical effect. For better or for worse (usually the latter), it takes very little imagination to concoct a business rationale for even the most routine personal living expenses.

Take the case of Pennel Irwin, the taxpayer in Irwin v. Commissioner, 72 T.C.M. 1148 (1996). Mr. Irwin had a "day job" with the Defense Department. He was also the author of five unpublished novels, and he took the position that "[f]or fiction writing all personal experiences and observations are all business experiences and observations." Consistent with this position, Mr. Irwin deducted all purchases that, in his opinion, would yield interesting observations for his novels. These purchases included a washing machine, a microwave oven, teeth cleaning, flowers, Costco purchases of clothing and tools, as well as the cost of hiring a "research assistant" (coincidentally, his daughter) to move into a college dorm so that he "would have direct access to dormitory life and she could also, by living there, report back to me her impression as about dormitory living."

It is important to remember that the U.S. income tax is essentially a "self-assessment" system in which only a tiny fraction of taxpayers are audited. In the absence of precise rules policing the borderline between business and personal expenditures, taxpayers willing to take aggressive return positions, such as Pennel Irwin, would be able to shift the overall burden of the U.S. tax system to those who, perhaps feeling a duty of compliance with the law, take the more conservative position of not claiming a deduction for everyday personal expenses. The result would be a tilting of the overall tax burden in favor of those willing to play the audit lottery, an outcome hard to defend on any meaningfully principled basis.

This chapter provides an overview of the legal rules that have developed over the past century to determine when deductions claimed as business expenses should instead be disallowed as personal expenditures. Throughout the chapter you will see legal controversies relating to specific categories of expenditures, each of which might plausibly be understood as either a personal expense or a business expense, for example, clothing, home offices, child-care, or commuting. In every case, you will likely be able to discern some plausible business rationale for the expenditure, even though the amount in question may appear to be a quintessentially "personal, living or family expense" per §262. As you will see, the law's response to these controversies has not been uniform. In many cases, Congress has responded with specific statutory changes (e.g., home offices, hobby losses, travel and entertainment expenses). In evaluating these legislative responses, keep in mind the core dilemma (i.e., how to police the business/personal borderline) and try to develop a conceptual typology of alternative approaches. For example, does the law provide an all-or-nothing solution? Or is there some apportionment of the expense between the two categories? Which approach is better?

As you work your way through this chapter, you should also keep in mind that the resolution of any particular case in favor of deductibility is not necessarily the final step in terms of how a particular expense is reflected on the taxpayer's return. In some cases, even if a deduction is allowed by §162 or §212, some other provision may operate to reduce or even eliminate the deduction. This is especially true in the case of business expenses incurred by *employees*, as distinguished from business owners or independent contractors.

To understand why this is the case, you should review §62, which provides the statutory definition of "adjusted gross income." Of particular importance in this section is the allowance of a deduction for "trade and business deductions." For purposes of determining the taxpayer's AGI, these deductions are only allowed if the taxpayer's trade or business "does not consist of the performance of services by the taxpayer as an employee." Historically, this has meant that otherwise deductible business expenses incurred by an employee must be claimed as a "below-the-line" itemized deduction (i.e., deducted from AGI on Schedule A) rather than an "above-the-line" deduction (i.e., deducted from gross income to arrive at AGI). Until recently, the effect of this treatment was to subject the deductions to the limitation of §67 regarding "miscellaneous itemized deductions," meaning that such deductions were allowed only to the extent that they (along with the taxpayer's other miscellaneous itemized deductions) exceeded 2 percent of the taxpayer's adjusted gross income. Needless to say, this provision had the effect of substantially reducing the value of business expense deductions for employees.

Beginning in 2018, however, unreimbursed employee business expenses are treated even more unfavorably. As part of the Tax Cuts and Jobs Act of 2017, Congress has suspended these deductions completely for tax years 2018-2025. For these years, employees are not allowed *any* deduction for business expenses, even if those expenses fully satisfy the requirements for deductibility under §162. In some cases, this outcome can be avoided, provided that the employer establishes a "reimbursement or other expense allowance arrangement." §62(a)(2)(A).

Keep these statutory provisions in mind as you review the remaining materials in this chapter. In some cases, such as the first case below, Pevsner v. Commissioner, the bottom line outcome for the employee/taxpayer would today be governed by the new temporary disallowance rule for unreimbursed employee business expenses. Even so, the legal standards discussed are still relevant for determining the deductibility of the expense in question for taxpayers other than employees (e.g., sole proprietors, independent contractors). In addition, where an employer reimburses an employee for an expense she incurs, the income tax treatment of that reimbursement may depend on whether the expense would have been deductible by the employee had she incurred it herself. §132(d).

A. CLOTHING EXPENSES

There is perhaps no more "personal" expense than the amounts one incurs to cover the human body for protection, warmth, privacy—or whatever other reasons. For example, it is hard to imagine a legitimate business or investment rationale for the acquisition of pajamas. As poet Sandra Boynton once observed, "they may be stripey, or polka dot. But we can all pajammy in whatever we've got."[3] Boynton's formulation suggests a primary role for personal preference in the selection of nightwear, likely eclipsing any imagined business or investment motivation. On the other end of the spectrum, there would seem to be little or no personal reason for members of a police bomb disposal squad to purchase the protective clothing required to carry out their duties safely. But what about the vast middle ground between these two extremes? The case below illustrates one approach for approaching this question.

PEVSNER v. COMMISSIONER
628 F.2d 467 (5th Cir. 1980)

JOHNSON, Circuit Judge.

This is an appeal by the Commissioner of Internal Revenue from a decision of the United States Tax Court. The tax court upheld taxpayer's business expense deduction for clothing expenditures in the amount of $1,621.91 for the taxable year 1975. We reverse.

Since June 1973 Sandra J. Pevsner, taxpayer, has been employed as the manager of the Sakowitz Yves St. Laurent Rive Gauche Boutique located in Dallas, Texas. The boutique sells only women's clothes and accessories designed by Yves St. Laurent (YSL), one of the leading designers of women's apparel. Although the clothing is ready to wear, it is highly fashionable and expensively priced. Some customers of the boutique purchase and wear the YSL apparel for their daily activities and spend as much as $20,000 per year for such apparel.

As manager of the boutique, the taxpayer is expected by her employer to wear YSL clothes while at work. In her appearance, she is expected to project the image of an exclusive lifestyle and to demonstrate to her customers that she is aware of the YSL current fashion trends as well as trends generally. Because the boutique sells YSL clothes exclusively, taxpayer must be able, when a customer compliments her on her clothes, to say that they are designed by YSL. In addition to wearing YSL apparel while at the boutique, she wears them while commuting to and from work, to fashion shows sponsored by the boutique, and to business luncheons at which she represents the boutique. During 1975, the taxpayer bought, at an employee's discount, the following items: four blouses, three skirts, one pair of slacks, one trench coat, two sweaters, one jacket, one tunic, five scarves, six belts, two pairs of shoes and four necklaces. The total cost of this apparel was $1,381.91. In addition, the sum of $240 was expended for maintenance of these items.

Although the clothing and accessories purchased by the taxpayer were the type used for general purposes by the regular customers of the boutique, the taxpayer is not a normal purchaser of these clothes. The taxpayer and her husband, who is partially disabled because of a severe heart attack suffered in 1971, lead a simple life and their social activities are very limited and informal. Although taxpayer's employer has no objection to her wearing the apparel

3. Sandra Boynton, *Pajama Time!* (2000).

away from work, taxpayer stated that she did not wear the clothes during off-work hours because she felt that they were too expensive for her simple everyday lifestyle. Another reason why she did not wear the YSL clothes apart from work was to make them last longer. Taxpayer did admit at trial, however, that a number of the articles were things she could have worn off the job and in which she would have looked "nice."

On her joint federal income tax return for 1975, taxpayer deducted $990 as an ordinary and necessary business expense with respect to her purchase of the YSL clothing and accessories. However, in the tax court, taxpayer claimed a deduction for the full $1,381.91 cost of the apparel and for the $240 cost of maintaining the apparel. The tax court allowed the taxpayer to deduct both expenses in the total amount of $1,621.91. The tax court reasoned that the apparel was not suitable to the private lifestyle maintained by the taxpayer. This appeal by the Commissioner followed. . . .

The generally accepted rule governing the deductibility of clothing expenses is that the cost of clothing is deductible as a business expense only if: (1) the clothing is of a type specifically required as a condition of employment, (2) it is not adaptable to general usage as ordinary clothing, and (3) it is not so worn. . . .

In the present case, the Commissioner stipulated that the taxpayer was required by her employer to wear YSL clothing and that she did not wear such apparel apart from work. The Commissioner maintained, however, that a deduction should be denied because the YSL clothes and accessories purchased by the taxpayer were adaptable for general usage as ordinary clothing and she was not prohibited from using them as such. The tax court, in rejecting the Commissioner's argument for the application of an objective test, recognized that the test for deductibility was whether the clothing was "suitable for general or personal wear" but determined that the matter of suitability was to be judged subjectively, in light of the taxpayer's lifestyle. Although the court recognized that the YSL apparel "might be used by some members of society for general purposes," it felt that because the "wearing of YSL apparel outside work would be inconsistent with . . . [taxpayer's] lifestyle," sufficient reason was shown for allowing a deduction for the clothing expenditures. . . .

[T]he Circuits that have addressed the issue have taken an objective, rather than subjective, approach. . . . Under an objective test, no reference is made to the individual taxpayer's lifestyle or personal taste. Instead, adaptability for personal or general use depends upon what is generally accepted for ordinary streetwear.

The principal argument in support of an objective test is, of course, administrative necessity. The Commissioner argues that, as a practical matter, it is virtually impossible to determine at what point either price or style makes clothing inconsistent with or inappropriate to a taxpayer's lifestyle. Moreover, the Commissioner argues that the price one pays and the styles one selects are inherently personal choices governed by taste, fashion, and other unmeasurable values. Indeed, the tax court has rejected the argument that a taxpayer's personal taste can dictate whether clothing is appropriate for general use. . . . An objective test, although not perfect, provides a practical administrative approach that allows a taxpayer or revenue agent to look only to objective facts in determining whether clothing required as a condition of employment is adaptable to general use as ordinary streetwear. Conversely, the tax court's reliance on subjective factors provides no concrete guidelines in determining the deductibility of clothing purchased as a condition of employment.

In addition to achieving a practical administrative result, an objective test also tends to promote substantial fairness among the greatest number of taxpayers. As the Commissioner suggests, it apparently would be the tax court's position that two similarly situated YSL boutique managers with identical wardrobes would be subject to disparate tax consequences depending upon the particular manager's lifestyle and "socio-economic level." This result, however, is not consonant with a reasonable interpretation of Sections 162 and 262.

For the reasons stated above, the decision of the tax court upholding the deduction for taxpayer's purchase of YSL clothing is reversed. Consequently, the portion of the tax court's decision upholding the deduction for maintenance costs for the clothing is also reversed.

NOTE

In Nelson v. Commissioner, 1966-224 T.C.M., the taxpayers, husband and wife, were allowed to deduct the cost of the clothing they wore in the television series *The Adventures of Ozzie and Harriet*. The annual costs ranged from $12,341 in 1957 to $6,037 in 1962. In the series, the taxpayers "portrayed an average American family, with certain reasonable exaggerations." While the clothing was suitable for personal use, the court found that some of it was too heavy for use in southern California, where the Nelsons lived, it was subject to heavy wear and tear in production of the show, the Nelsons worked such long hours that they had little chance to wear the clothing off the set, and in fact the personal use was de minimis.

In Mella v. Commissioner, T.C.M. 1986-594, the taxpayer was a tennis professional. He was head professional at two tennis clubs and a nationally ranked player who played in at least a dozen tournaments in the year at issue. He claimed deductions for tennis clothes and shoes. The shoes lasted only two or three weeks. The court denied the deductions, stating:

> The Court observes that it is relatively commonplace for Americans in all walks of life to wear warm-up clothes, shirts, and shoes of the type purchased by the petitioner while engaged in a wide variety of casual or athletic activities. The items are fashionable, and in some cases have the name or logo of designers that have become common in America. Indeed, at trial, it was stated that tennis professionals, such as the petitioner, are clothing style setters for their students.

In Williams v. Commissioner, T.C. Memo. 1991-317, the taxpayer rode a motorcycle in his business as an Amway distributor. He was allowed to deduct the cost of his "leather uniform," which he wore while riding the motorcycle in connection with his business, and which bore the Amway label, but not the cost of the helmet and steel-toe boots that he also wore and that the court considered to be suitable for nonbusiness use.

QUESTIONS

1. (a) Do you think the result in *Pevsner* is unfair to the taxpayer? (b) If so, can you suggest a rule that would allow her a deduction, would be feasible for the Service to administer, and would not lead to abuse?

2. Is the present rule allowing a deduction for the cost of uniforms not suitable for ordinary wear subject to significant abuse?

B.   HOME OFFICES AND VACATION HOMES

Many people have offices in their homes, or at least claim that they do, even though their principal place of work is elsewhere. Where a person does in fact use part of his or her home exclusively, or even primarily, for business, the costs of that part of the home (including a pro rata share of utility bills and depreciation on that part) might properly be regarded as a deductible business expense. It is not difficult, however, to see the opportunities for abuse of any opportunity for deduction. For many years, the Service and the courts tried to curb the abuses, but that was a losing effort. The problem was that it was easy for a dishonest, or at least self-serving, taxpayer to offer his or her own testimony in support of a primary business purpose or use and difficult for the government to rebut that testimony. Not only were some taxpayers winning doubtful cases at the administrative level (within the IRS) and in the courts, but many more were playing, and winning, the audit lottery. Congress finally intervened, in 1976, adopting the stringent restrictions found in §280A.

The approach of §280A is to begin with a general rule denying deductions for any use of a home for business purposes (§280A(a)) and then to list specific, concrete exceptions (§280A(c)), which you should examine briefly. At the same time it addressed offices in the home, Congress dealt with vacation homes, again a source of considerable abuse. In the two sections below, we first introduce the rules that apply to home offices, then follow with an overview of the limitations on deductions for vacation homes.

In reviewing these materials, keep in mind the new provision for employee business expenses enacted by Congress in 2017 and referenced above. For tax years 2018-2025, no deduction is allowed for any *employee* business expense, even if the statutory requirements for the deduction are otherwise satisfied. Thus, at least for as long as this provision remains in the law, the rules described below will chiefly be of interest to taxpayers engaged in a trade or business other than as an employee (e.g., sole proprietors, independent contractors).

1.   Home Offices

To curb the abuse of deductions for offices in the home, Congress used broad language denying a deduction (§280A(a)), followed by a set of specific, relatively concrete exceptions (§280A(c)). Thus, taxpayers cannot base home office deduction claims on general assertions regarding business use, but instead must show that they meet the terms of one of the exceptions.

POPOV v. COMMISSIONER

246 F.3d 1190 (9th Cir. 2001)

This case concerns the continuing problem of the home office deduction. We conclude, on the facts of this case, that a professional musician is entitled to deduct the expenses from the portion of her home used exclusively for musical practice.

FACTS AND PROCEDURAL BACKGROUND

Katia Popov is a professional violinist who performs regularly with the Los Angeles Chamber Orchestra and the Long Beach Symphony. She also contracts with various studios to record music for the motion picture industry. In 1993, she worked for twenty-four such contractors and recorded in thirty-eight different locations. These recording sessions required that Popov be able to read scores quickly. The musicians did not receive the sheet music in advance of the recording sessions; instead, they were presented with their parts when they arrived at the studio, and recording would begin shortly thereafter. None of Popov's twenty-six employers provided her with a place to practice.

Popov lived with her husband Peter, an attorney, and their four-year-old daughter Irina, in a one-bedroom apartment in Los Angeles, California. The apartment's living room served as Popov's home office. The only furniture in the living room consisted of shelves with recording equipment, a small table, a bureau for storing sheet music, and a chair. Popov used this area to practice the violin and to make recordings, which she used for practice purposes and as demonstration tapes for orchestras. No one slept in the living room, and the Popovs' daughter was not allowed to play there. Popov spent four to five hours a day practicing in the living room.

In their 1993 tax returns, the Popovs claimed a home office deduction for the living room and deducted forty percent of their annual rent and twenty percent of their annual electricity bill. The Internal Revenue Service ("the Service") disallowed these deductions, and the Popovs filed a petition for redetermination in the Tax Court.

The Tax Court concluded that the Popovs were not entitled to a home office deduction. Although "practicing at home was a very important component to [Popov's] success as a musician," the court found that her living room was not her "principal place of business." In the court's view, her principal places of business were the studios and concert halls where she recorded and performed, because it was her performances in these places that earned her income. . . .[4]

---

4. The Popovs also challenge the Tax Court's denial of their deductions for long-distance phone calls, meal expenses, and clothing. We find no merit in these claims. The Popovs did not adequately establish the business purpose of the phone calls or the meal expenses. See Welch v. Helvering, 290 U.S. 111, 115 (1933). The Tax Court did not err in finding that most of Katia Popov's concert attire was adaptable to general usage as ordinary clothing. See Pevsner v. Comm'r, 628 F.2d 467, 469 (5th Cir. 1980).

Analysis

The Internal Revenue Code allows a deduction for a home office that is exclusively used as "the principal place of business for any trade or business of the taxpayer." §280A(c)(1)(A). The Code does not define the phrase "principal place of business."

A. THE *SOLIMAN* TESTS

Our inquiry is governed by Commissioner v. Soliman, 506 U.S. 168 (1993), the Supreme Court's most recent treatment of the home office deduction. In *Soliman*, the taxpayer was an anesthesiologist who spent thirty to thirty-five hours per week with patients at three different hospitals. None of the hospitals provided Soliman with an office, so he used a spare bedroom for contacting patients and surgeons, maintaining billing records and patient logs, preparing for treatments, and reading medical journals.

The Supreme Court denied Soliman a deduction for his home office, holding that the "statute does not allow for a deduction whenever a home office may be characterized as legitimate." *Id.* at 174. Instead, courts must determine whether the home office is the taxpayer's principal place of business. Although the Court could not "develop an objective formula that yields a clear answer in every case," the Court stressed two primary considerations: "the relative importance of the activities performed at each business location and the time spent at each place." *Id.* at 174-75. We address each in turn.

1. Relative Importance

The importance of daily practice to Popov's profession cannot be denied. Regular practice is essential to playing a musical instrument at a high level of ability, and it is this level of commitment that distinguishes the professional from the amateur.[5] Without daily practice, Popov would be unable to perform in professional orchestras. She would also be unequipped for the peculiar demands of studio recording: The ability to read and perform scores on sight requires an acute musical intelligence that must be constantly developed and honed. In short, Popov's four to five hours of daily practice lay at the very heart of her career as a professional violinist.

Of course, the concert halls and recording studios are also important to Popov's profession. Without them, she would have no place in which to perform. Audiences and motion picture companies are unlikely to flock to her one-bedroom apartment. In *Soliman*, the Supreme Court stated that, although "no one test is determinative in every case," "the point where goods and services are delivered must be given great weight in determining the place where the most important functions are performed." *Id.* at 175. The Service places great weight on this statement, contending that Popov's performances should be analogized to the "service" of delivering anesthesia that was at issue in

---

5. One who doubts this might consult George Bernard Shaw's famous observation that "hell is full of musical amateurs." George Bernard Shaw, *Man and Superman* act 3 (1903).

Soliman; these "services" are delivered in concert halls and studios, not in her apartment.

We agree with Popov that musical performance is not so easily captured under a "goods and services" rubric. The German poet Heinrich Heine observed that music stands "halfway between thought and phenomenon, between spirit and matter, a sort of nebulous mediator, like and unlike each of the things it mediates—spirit that requires manifestation in time, and matter that can do without space."[6] Or as Harry Ellis Dickson of the Boston Symphony Orchestra explained more concretely:

> A musician's life is different from that of most people. We don't go to an office every day, or to a factory, or to a bank. We go to an empty hall. We don't deal in anything tangible, nor do we produce anything except sounds. We saw away, or blow, or pound for a few hours and then we go home. It is a strange way to make a living!

Harry Ellis Dickson, *Gentlemen, More Dolce Please* (1969), quoted in Drucker v. Comm'r, 715 F.2d 67, 68-69 (2d Cir. 1983).

It is possible, of course, to wrench musical performance into a "delivery of services" framework, but we see little value in such a wooden and unblinking application of the tax laws. *Soliman* itself recognized that in this area of law "variations are inevitable in case-by-case determinations." 506 U.S. at 175. We believe this to be such a case. We simply do not find the "delivery of services" framework to be helpful in analyzing this particular problem. Taken to extremes, the Service's argument would seem to generate odd results in a variety of other areas as well. We doubt, for example, that an appellate advocate's primary place of business is the podium from which he delivers his oral argument, or that a professor's primary place of business is the classroom, rather than the office in which he prepares his lectures.

We therefore conclude that the "relative importance" test yields no definitive answer in this case, and we accordingly turn to the second prong of the *Soliman* inquiry.

2.   Amount of Time

Under *Soliman*, "the decisionmaker should . . . compare the amount of time spent at home with the time spent at other places where business activities occur." *Id.* at 177. "This factor assumes particular significance when," as in this case, "comparison of the importance of the functions performed at various places yields no definitive answer to the principal place of business inquiry." *Id.*[7] In *Soliman*, the taxpayer spent significantly more time in the hospitals than

---

6. Heinrich Heine, *Letters on the French Stage* (1837), quoted in *Words about Music: A Treasury of Writings 2*, John Amis and Michael Rose, eds. (1989).

7. Justices Thomas and Scalia concurred in *Soliman*, but noted that the Court provided no guidance if the taxpayer "spent 30 to 35 hours at his home office and only 10 hours" at the hospitals. 506 U.S. at 184 (Thomas, J., concurring): "Which factor would take precedence? The importance of the activities undertaken at home. . . ? The number of hours spent at each location? I am at a loss, and I am afraid the taxpayer, his attorney, and a lower court would be as well." *Id.*

he did in his home office. In this case, Popov spent significantly more time practicing the violin at home than she did performing or recording.[8]

This second factor tips the balance in the Popovs' favor. They are accordingly entitled to a home office deduction for Katia Popov's practice space, because it was exclusively used as her principal place of business. . . .

C. CONCLUSION

For the foregoing reasons, the Tax Court's denial of the Popovs' home office deduction is reversed.

QUESTIONS

1. Is it likely that the living room in a one-bedroom apartment where three people lived was used exclusively as a place of business, as §280A(c)(1) requires?

2. Why is it, according to the court, that "musical performance is not so easily captured under a 'goods or services' rubric"? Did Judge Hawkins's evident fondness for classical music improperly influence his application of the *Soliman* test?

3. Is there any reasonable basis for denying that the first prong of the *Soliman* test (where services are rendered or goods delivered) supported the Commissioner's position? Wouldn't it also support the Commissioner's position (whatever the overall outcome given the second prong, relative time spent) in the case of an appellate advocate or professor who had no office other than a home office?

4. Given that the first prong of the *Soliman* test supported the Commissioner but the second prong supported the taxpayer, how should the court have tried to resolve the case?

5. Justices Thomas and Scalia, whose concurrence in *Soliman* the court mentions in footnote 7 (originally footnote 5), would have adopted a test under which the first prong would be determinative unless "the home office is one of several locations where goods or services are delivered, and thus also one of the multiple locations where income was generated." Would this test have yielded clearer answers than the one the Supreme Court adopted in *Soliman*? Would it have been less fair?

6. Imagine you are a musician who must spend hours at home practicing and that you are looking for a house or apartment. Would your practice-related

---

8. The Service argues that the evidence is unclear as to "how much time Mrs. Popov spent practicing at home as opposed to the time she spent performing outside of the home." It is true that the evidence is not perfectly clear and that the Tax Court made no specific comparative findings. However, the Tax Court found that she practiced four to five hours a day in her apartment. If we read this finding in the light most generous to the Service and assume that she only practiced four hours a day 300 days a year, Popov would still have practiced 1,200 hours in a year. She testified that she performed with two orchestras for a total of 120 to 140 hours. If she spent a similar amount of time recording, she would still be spending about five hours practicing for every hour of performance or recording. The only plausible reading of the evidence is that Popov spent substantially more time practicing than she did performing or recording.

needs influence your choice of residence? Lead you to spend more for a residence? If so, why shouldn't the tax law allow you to deduct those extra costs? Which of the following considerations is persuasive?

(a) It is difficult to determine extra costs.

(b) It is difficult to determine who must in fact work at home and to what degree.

(c) Allowing deductions in cases such as *Popov* will encourage other taxpayers to take wildly aggressive positions. The expected financial return for these taxpayers will be positive, due to low audit rates, low penalty rates, and the unlikelihood of penalty assessments. How would you resolve this issue?

2.   Vacation Homes

As noted above, §280A covers both home offices and vacation homes. In the past many people acquired resort-area dwelling units largely for personal use, while claiming that the purpose of the acquisition was to make a profit and that the personal use was purely incidental. Since a profit-making objective depends on the investor's state of mind, the opportunity for abuse was, as with offices in the home, great. Real estate developers aggressively exploited the opportunity to sell vacation units intended for mostly personal use by pointing to the tax advantages that could be achieved by claiming investor status. Section 280A deals with this problem, with an arbitrary approach that is severe, though somewhat less so than the approach taken with respect to offices in the home. These rules listed below are quite complex. We present them to illustrate the downside of adopting an approach based on rules rather than standards. As you read the rules, imagine yourself to be a taxpayer with a vacation home who is trying to do his or her own taxes.

(1) The statute covers any "dwelling unit" that is used by the taxpayer for more than a specified amount of time during the year for personal purposes. See §280A(a) and (d). The specified amount of time is the greater of "14 days, or 10 percent of the number of days during [the] year for which [the] unit is rented at a fair rental." See §280A(d)(1).

(2) If the unit is not used at all for personal purposes, the taxpayer is allowed to deduct expenses (utilities, repairs, condominium fees, etc.), depreciation (cost recovery), interest, and taxes, subject to the limitation on deduction of passive activity losses.

(3) If the unit is used for personal purposes for more than the specified amount of time, but is rented out for less than fifteen days, then the owner excludes the rental income and may not claim deductions other than for interest and taxes (which are deductible without regard to profit motive, subject to the §163(h) limits on the interest deduction). See §280A(g), (b). This is obviously intended to be a de minimis exception but has allowed tax windfalls for people who have been able to rent their homes for short periods, at high rents.

(4) If the unit is used for personal purposes for less than the specified amount of time, the disallowance rule of §280A(a) does not apply, but the

deduction other than for taxes is allowed only on a pro rata basis (comparing rental and personal use) (§280A(e)) and, again, is subject to the limitation on deduction of passive activity losses. (Interest cannot be deducted without regard to profit because the unit is not a "second home," since it is occupied less than the required number of days. If a profit motive is lacking, the interest becomes "personal interest," which is not deductible. See §163(h)(1), (h)(3), and (h)(4)(A).)

(5) If the unit is used for personal purposes for more than the specified amount of time, then expenses other than interest and taxes must still be prorated, but the deduction for such prorated expenses cannot exceed the rent received, reduced by an allocable share of the interest and taxes. See §280A(c)(5). This rule is comparable to that found in §183(b), which limits deductions for hobby activities to the income from the activity (see Reg. §1.183-1(d)(3)).

C. CHILD-CARE EXPENSES

The case that follows arose before the adoption of express statutory provisions allowing a credit for certain child- and household-care expenses of working parents. The issue of whether or to what degree the government should provide financial assistance for child-care provision continues to be a subject of frequent debate in policymaking circles. Therefore, we address existing provisions (§§21 and 129) in the notes following this case. Despite these provisions, the following case is still controlling on the question of deductibility of child-care costs as a business expense. Like many of the other cases in this chapter, it reflects an effort to grapple with the question whether certain expenses with personal overtones should be regarded as costs of earning income.

SMITH v. COMMISSIONER
40 B.T.A. 1038 (1939), aff'd without opinion, 113 F.2d 114 (2d Cir. 1940)

Opper, J.

[The Commissioner] determined a deficiency . . . in petitioners' 1937 income tax . . . due to the disallowance of a deduction claimed by petitioners, who are husband and wife, for sums spent by the wife in employing nursemaids to care for petitioners' young child, the wife, as well as the husband, being employed. . . .

Petitioners would have us apply the "but for" test. They propose that but for the nurses, the wife could not leave her child; but for the freedom so secured, she could not pursue her gainful labors, and but for them, there would be no income and no tax. This thought evokes an array of interesting possibilities. The fee to the doctor, but for whose healing service, the earner of the family income could not leave his sickbed; the cost of the laborer's raiment, for how can the world proceed about its business unclothed; the very home which gives us shelter and rest and the food which provides energy, might all by an extension of the same proposition be construed as necessary to the operation of business and to the creation of income. Yet these are the very essence of those "personal" expenses the deductibility of which is expressly denied. [§262.]

We are told that the working wife is a new phenomenon. This is relied on to account for the apparent inconsistency that the expenses in issue are now a commonplace, yet have not been the subject of legislation, ruling, or adjudicated controversy. But if that is true, it becomes all the more necessary to apply accepted principles to the novel facts. We are not prepared to say that the care of children, like similar aspects of family and household life, is other than a personal concern. The wife's services as custodian of the home and protector of its children are ordinarily rendered without monetary compensation. There results no taxable income from the performance of this service and the correlative expenditure is personal and not susceptible of deduction. . . . Here the wife has chosen to employ others to discharge her domestic function and the services she performs are rendered outside the home. They are a source of actual income and taxable as such. But that does not deprive the same work performed by others of its personal character. . . .

We are not unmindful that, as petitioners suggest, certain disbursements normally personal may become deductible by reason of their intimate connection with an occupation carried on for profit. In this category fall entertainment, . . . traveling expenses, . . . and the cost of an actor's wardrobe. . . . The line is not always an easy one to draw nor the test simple to apply. But we think its principle is clear. It may for practical purposes be said to constitute a distinction between those activities which, as a matter of common acceptance and universal experience, are "ordinary" or usual as the direct accompaniment of business pursuits, on the one hand; and those which, though they may in some indirect and tenuous degree relate to the circumstances of a profitable occupation, are nevertheless personal in their nature, of a character applicable to human beings generally, and which exist on that plane regardless of the occupation, though not necessarily of the station in life, of the individuals concerned. See Welch v. Helvering.

In the latter category, we think, fall payments made to servants or others occupied in looking to the personal wants of their employers. . . . And we include in this group, nursemaids retained to care for infant children.

NOTES AND QUESTIONS

1. *Causation.* The court's rejection of the taxpayers' "but for" argument is not convincing: The other expenses to which the court refers would be incurred by people even if they were not employed. It is clear in the *Smith* case that the child-care expense would not have been incurred but for the job. It is equally clear, however, that the expense would not have been incurred but for the child. The Smiths would have you compare them with another couple with a child but with one parent staying home to care for it. The court would have you compare

them with another couple with both spouses employed but with no children. Where does this kind of observation leave (or lead) you?

2. *The statutory language.* However appealing the taxpayers' claim may be, can their outlays sensibly be characterized as "ordinary and necessary expenses paid or incurred . . . in carrying on a trade or business"?

3. *Policy.* (a) Which of the following arguments for some sort of allowance for child-care expenses do you find most appealing?

(i)   In our society, since most married people have children, children should be taken as given. From the perspective of a potential job seeker with children the return from taking a job is the amount available after deduction for unavoidable child-care expenses. "Income" must therefore be defined as the net amount after child-care expenses, both in the interests of fairness and in order to avoid distorting job-taking decisions.

(ii)   Our tax system discourages job-taking by the person who is the secondary worker in a marriage. It does this by taxing the secondary worker's earned income at rates determined by piling that income on top of the income of the primary worker, while at the same time imposing no tax on imputed income from performing household and child-care services. The secondary worker also pays Social Security taxes and incurs a variety of work-related expenses. Most secondary workers are women. Thus, the system tends to discourage job-taking by women. It may at the same time impose psychological and other burdens on women by depreciating the value of services performed outside the home as compared with those performed in the home. An allowance for child-care expenses mitigates these effects.

(iii)   Child-care allowances are necessary in order to permit low-income people to take jobs.

(iv)   Child-care allowances will encourage people to have more children.

(v)   Child-care allowances will lead to child-care jobs and will provide employment to people who might otherwise be unemployed.

(b) What implications does each of these arguments have for whether the allowance should be a deduction of the entire outlay, a deduction of some part of the outlay, or a credit?

4. *Congressional response.* (a) In 1954, Congress responded to the claims of people like the Smiths with a new deduction that had some interesting limitations, reflecting the attitudes of the time toward working mothers. The deduction was initially limited to $600 per year. (Even in 1954 it must have been difficult at best to hire babysitters for $12 a week.) It was available to unmarried women, widows, and divorced men but not to unmarried men. The deduction was liberalized several times over the years and then in 1976 converted to a credit, which is what we find today in §21. The credit is a percentage of the amount spent for household services, up to $3,000 for one child (or other "qualifying individual") and $6,000 for two or more children (or qualifying individuals). The percentage used in determining the amount of the credit declines as income rises. In a household with a wife and husband, both employed, with a total income of $50,000, two children, and expenses of $6,000 or more, the credit (which reduces the amount of tax payable dollar for dollar) would be $1,200 (i.e., 20 percent of $6,000).

(b) Examine §21. Consider the possible rationale for each of the following features:

(i)   The phase-down of the credit from 35 percent to 20 percent of expenses as income rises above $15,000 (§21(a)(2));

(ii)   The importance of having in the home a "qualifying individual" (§21(a)(1) and (b)(1));

(iii) The availability for "expenses for household services" (§21(b)(2)(A)(i));

(iv)   The limitation on the dollar amount of the credit (§21(c)); and

(v)   The limitation of expenses that may be taken into account, in the case of a husband and wife, to the income of the lower earner (§21(d)(1)(B)).

(c) Compare §129, which permits an employer to make available to employees, free of tax, up to $5,000 per year for child-care expenses through a dependent care assistance program, or DCAP. This benefit may be part of a §125 cafeteria plan, so the employee can be allowed, in effect, to treat up to $5,000 of salary as a nontaxable DCAP benefit. But under §21(c), the amount of child-care expenses that can be used to calculate the §21 tax credit is reduced by amounts paid through a DCAP and excluded under §129. Taxpayers are therefore confronted with a tax-planning choice. When the marginal rate of tax on their income is lower than the credit rate on their expenses (which, as we have just seen, ranges from 35 percent to 20 percent), they are better off to forgo the DCAP exclusion and use their expenses to claim a credit under §21. Generally speaking, lower-income taxpayers are likely to be better off claiming the credit (because for them the credit percentage is likely to be higher than their marginal tax rate) whereas higher-income taxpayers will favor the DCAP benefit (since their marginal tax rate will typically exceed their credit percentage). Under current law, the maximum benefit for the lowest income taxpayers is $2,100 (i.e., $6,000 of maximum creditable expenses multiplied by a maximum 35 percent credit at AGI of $15,000), while the maximum benefit for the highest income taxpayers is $1,850 (i.e., $5,000 of excludable DCAP expenses multiplied by a top marginal rate of 37 percent). Most middle-income taxpayers will be entitled to a substantially less generous subsidy because their AGI is too high to qualify for the maximum credit percentage but their marginal tax rate is much lower than the top rate of 37 percent.

D.   COMMUTING EXPENSES

What about expenses in getting from home to work then back home again? The amount of these expenses is a function of how far one's place of work is from one's home. But is that distance—and the expense of getting there and back—the result of one's personal choice of where to live? Or is it instead the result of the location of one's place of business? One could easily say both, or just as correctly answer that commuting expenses are attributable exclusively to one or the other. The material below illustrates how the U.S. tax system has approached these issues.

COMMISSIONER v. FLOWERS
326 U.S. 465 (1945)

Mr. Justice MURPHY delivered the opinion of the Court.

This case presents a problem as to the meaning and application of the provision of [the predecessor of §162(a)(2)], allowing a deduction for income tax purposes of "traveling expenses (including the entire amount expended for meals and lodging) while away from home in the pursuit of a trade or business."

The taxpayer, a lawyer, has resided with his family in Jackson, Mississippi, since 1903. There he has paid taxes, voted, schooled his children and established social and religious connections. He built a house in Jackson nearly thirty years ago and at all times has maintained it for himself and his family. He has been connected with several law firms in Jackson, one of which he formed and which has borne his name since 1922.

In 1906 the taxpayer began to represent the predecessor of the Gulf, Mobile & Ohio Railroad, his present employer. He acted as trial counsel for the railroad throughout Mississippi. From 1918 until 1927 he acted as special counsel for the railroad in Mississippi. He was elected general solicitor in 1927 and continued to be elected to that position each year until 1930, when he was elected general counsel. Thereafter he was annually elected general counsel until September, 1940, when the properties of the predecessor company and another railroad were merged and he was elected vice president and general counsel of the newly formed Gulf, Mobile & Ohio Railroad.

The main office of the Gulf, Mobile & Ohio Railroad is in Mobile, Alabama, as was also the main office of its predecessor. When offered the position of general solicitor in 1927, the taxpayer was unwilling to accept it if it required him to move from Jackson to Mobile. He had established himself in Jackson both professionally and personally and was not desirous of moving away. As a result, an arrangement was made between him and the railroad whereby he could accept the position and continue to reside in Jackson on condition that he pay his traveling expenses between Mobile and Jackson and pay his living expenses in both places. This arrangement permitted the taxpayer to determine for himself the amount of time he would spend in each of the two cities and was in effect during 1939 and 1940, the taxable years in question.

The railroad company provided an office for the taxpayer in Mobile but not in Jackson. When he worked in Jackson his law firm provided him with office space, although he no longer participated in the firm's business or shared in its profits. He used his own office furniture and fixtures at this office. The railroad, however, furnished telephone service and a typewriter and desk for his secretary. It also paid the secretary's expenses while in Jackson. Most of the legal business of the railroad was centered in or conducted from Jackson, but this business was handled by local counsel for the railroad. The taxpayer's participation was advisory only and was no different from his participation in the railroad's legal business in other areas.

The taxpayer's principal post of business was at the main office in Mobile. However, during the taxable years of 1939 and 1940, he devoted nearly all of his time to matters relating to the merger of the railroads. Since it was left to him where he would do his work, he spent most of his time in Jackson during this period. In connection with the merger, one of the companies was involved in certain litigation in the federal court in Jackson and the taxpayer participated in that litigation.

During 1939 he spent 203 days in Jackson and 66 in Mobile, making 33 trips between the two cities. During 1940 he spent 168 days in Jackson and 102 in Mobile, making 40 trips between the two cities. The railroad paid all of his traveling expenses when he went on business trips to points other than Jackson or Mobile. But it paid none of his expenses in traveling between these two points or while he was at either of them.

The taxpayer deducted $900 in his 1939 income tax return and $1,620 in his 1940 return as traveling expenses incurred in making trips from Jackson to Mobile and as expenditures for meals and hotel accommodations while in Mobile.[9] The Commissioner disallowed the deductions. . . .

The portion of [§162(a)] authorizing the deduction of "traveling expenses (including the entire amount expended for meals and lodging) while away from home in the pursuit of a trade or business" is one of the specific examples given by Congress in that section of "ordinary and necessary expenses paid or incurred during the taxable year in carrying on any trade or business." It is to be contrasted with the provision of [§262]. [The Regulations provide] that

> Traveling expenses, as ordinarily understood, include railroad fares and meals and lodging. If the trip is undertaken for other than business purposes, the railroad fares are personal expenses and the meals and lodging are living expenses. If the trip is solely on business, the reasonable and necessary traveling expenses, including railroad fares, meals, and lodging, are business expenses. . . . Only such expenses as are reasonable and necessary in the conduct of the business and directly attributable to it may be deducted. . . . Commuters' fares are not considered as business expenses and are not deductible.

Three conditions must thus be satisfied before a traveling expense deduction may be made under [§162(a)(2)]:

(1) The expense must be a reasonable and necessary traveling expense, as that term is generally understood. This includes such items as transportation fares and food and lodging expenses incurred while traveling.

(2) The expense must be incurred "while away from home."

(3) The expense must be incurred in pursuit of business. This means that there must be a direct connection between the expenditure and the carrying on of the trade or business of the taxpayer or of his employer. Moreover, such an expenditure must be necessary or appropriate to the development and pursuit of the business or trade.

Whether particular expenditures fulfill these three conditions so as to entitle a taxpayer to a deduction is purely a question of fact in most instances. . . . And the Tax Court's inferences and conclusions on such a factual matter, under established principles, should not be disturbed by an appellate court. . . .

---

9. No claim for deduction was made by the taxpayer for the amounts spent in traveling from Mobile to Jackson. . . .

In this instance, the Tax Court without detailed elaboration concluded that "The situation presented in this proceeding is, in principle, no different from that in which a taxpayer's place of employment is in one city and for reasons satisfactory to himself he resides in another." It accordingly disallowed the deductions on the ground that they represent living and personal expenses rather than traveling expenses incurred while away from home in the pursuit of business. The court below accepted the Tax Court's findings of fact but reversed its judgment on the basis that it had improperly construed the word "home" as used in the second condition precedent to a traveling expense deduction under [§162(a)(2)]. The Tax Court, it was said, erroneously construed the word to mean the post, station or place of business where the taxpayer was employed—in this instance, Mobile—and thus erred in concluding that the expenditures in issue were not incurred "while away from home." The court below felt that the word was to be given no such "unusual" or "extraordinary" meaning in this statute, that it simply meant "that place where one in fact resides" or "the principal place of abode of one who has the intention to live there permanently." 148 F.2d at 164. Since the taxpayer here admittedly had his home, as thus defined, in Jackson and since the expenses were incurred while he was away from Jackson, the court below held that the deduction was permissible.

The meaning of the word "home" in [§162(a)(2)] with reference to a taxpayer residing in one city and working in another has engendered much difficulty and litigation. . . . The Tax Court and the administrative rulings have consistently defined it as the equivalent of the taxpayer's place of business. . . . On the other hand, the decision below and Wallace v. Commissioner, 144 F.2d 407 (C.C.A.9), have flatly rejected that view and have confined the term to the taxpayer's actual residence. . . .

We deem it unnecessary here to enter into or to decide this conflict. The Tax Court's opinion, as we read it, was grounded neither solely nor primarily upon that agency's conception of the word "home." Its discussion was directed mainly toward the relation of the expenditures to the railroad's business, a relationship required by the third condition of the deduction. Thus even if the Tax Court's definition of the word "home" was implicit in its decision and even if that definition was erroneous, its judgment must be sustained here if it properly concluded that the necessary relationship between the expenditures and the railroad's business was lacking. Failure to satisfy any one of the three conditions destroys the traveling expense deduction.

Turning our attention to the third condition, this case is disposed of quickly. There is no claim that the Tax Court misconstrued this condition or used improper standards in applying it. And it is readily apparent from the facts that its inferences were supported by evidence and that its conclusion that the expenditures in issue were non-deductible living and personal expenses was fully justified.

The facts demonstrate clearly that the expenses were not incurred in the pursuit of the business of the taxpayer's employer, the railroad. Jackson was his regular home. Had his post of duty been in that city the cost of maintaining his home there and of commuting or driving to work concededly would be non-deductible living and personal expenses lacking the necessary direct relation to the prosecution of the business. The character of such expenses is unaltered by the circumstance that the taxpayer's post of duty was in Mobile, thereby increasing the costs of transportation, food, and lodging. Whether he maintained one abode or two, whether he traveled three blocks or three hundred miles to work, the nature of these expenditures remained the same.

The added costs in issue, moreover, were as unnecessary and inappropriate to the development of the railroad's business as were his personal and living costs in Jackson. They were incurred solely as the result of the taxpayer's desire to maintain a home in Jackson while working in Mobile, a factor irrelevant to the maintenance and prosecution of the railroad's legal business. The railroad did not require him to travel on business from Jackson to Mobile or to maintain living quarters in both cities. Nor did it compel him, save in one instance, to perform tasks for it in Jackson. It simply asked him to be at his principal post in Mobile as business demanded and as his personal convenience was served, allowing him to divide his business time between Mobile and Jackson as he saw fit. Except for the federal court litigation, all of the taxpayer's work in Jackson would normally have been performed in the headquarters at Mobile. The fact that he traveled frequently between the two cities and incurred extra living expenses in Mobile, while doing much of his work in Jackson, was occasioned solely by his personal propensities. The railroad gained nothing from this arrangement except the personal satisfaction of the taxpayer.

Travel expenses in pursuit of business within the meaning of [§162(a)(2)] could arise only when the railroad's business forced the taxpayer to travel and to live temporarily at some place other than Mobile, thereby advancing the interests of the railroad. Business trips are to be identified in relation to business demands and the traveler's business headquarters. The exigencies of business rather than the personal conveniences and necessities of the traveler must be the motivating factors. Such was not the case here.

It follows that the court below erred in reversing the judgment of the Tax Court. Reversed.

Mr. Justice JACKSON took no part in the consideration or decision of this case.

Mr. Justice RUTLEDGE, dissenting.

I think the judgment of the Court of Appeals should be affirmed. When Congress used the word "home" in [§162] of the Code, I do not believe it meant "business headquarters." And in my opinion this case presents no other question. . . .

Respondent's home was in Jackson, Mississippi, in every sense, unless for applying [§162]. There he maintained his family, with his personal, political, and religious connections; schooled his children; paid taxes, voted, and resided over many years. There too he kept hold upon his place as a lawyer, though not substantially active in practice otherwise than to perform his work as general counsel for the railroad. . . .

I agree with the Court of Appeals that if Congress had meant "business headquarters," and not "home," it would have said "business headquarters." When it used "home" instead, I think it meant home in everyday parlance, not in some twisted special meaning of "tax home" or "tax headquarters." . . .

Congress gave the deduction for traveling away from home on business. The commuter's case, rightly confined, does not fall in this class. One who lives in an adjacent suburb or city and by usual modes of commutation can work within a distance permitting the daily journey and return, with time for the day's work and a period at home, clearly can be excluded from the deduction on the basis of the section's terms equally with its obvious purpose. But that is not true if "commuter" is to swallow up the deduction by the same sort of construction which makes "home" mean "business headquarters" of one's employer. If the line may be extended somewhat to cover doubtful cases, it need not be lengthened to infinity or to cover cases as far removed from the prevailing connotation of commuter as this one. Including it pushes "commuting" too far, even for these times of rapid transit.[10] . . .

By construing "home" as "business headquarters"; by reading "temporarily" as "very temporarily" into [§162]; by bringing down "ordinary and necessary" from its first sentence into its second; by finding "inequity" where Congress has said none exists; by construing "commuter" to cover long-distance, irregular travel; and by conjuring from the "statutory setting" a meaning at odds with the plain wording of the clause, the Government makes over understandable ordinary English into highly technical tax jargon. There is enough of this in the tax laws inescapably, without adding more in the absence of either compulsion or authority. The arm of the tax-gatherer reaches far. In my judgment it should not go the length of this case. . . .

NOTES AND QUESTIONS

1. Flowers *and commuting costs.* The deductions at issue in *Flowers* were in large part for the expenses of living in Mobile, but the case has been treated as authority primarily for the proposition that a person cannot deduct transportation costs incurred in commuting to and from work. The view of the majority in *Flowers* was that Mr. Flowers's trips to Mobile and back (usually via New Orleans) were just a long commute. As an employee of the railroad on which he traveled, Mr. Flowers "had a railroad pass [and] paid no train fare but did have to pay seat or berth fare." Flowers v. Commissioner, 3 T.C.M. 803, 805 (1944). The Commissioner did not treat the value of the free train fare as income to Mr. Flowers, though logic would suggest that such treatment would have been appropriate.

2. *Causative analysis.* In *Flowers*, the Court says that the expenses at issue "were incurred solely as a result of the taxpayer's desire to maintain a home in Jackson while working in Mobile." In other words, the expenses would not have been incurred but for the personal decision to live in Jackson. It is equally clear, however, that the expenses would not have been incurred but for the business decision to take the job in Mobile. Compare the earlier discussion of "but for" analysis in connection with the deductions for medical expenses and for child-care expenses. Does it help to try to identify a "proximate" cause

---

10. Conceivably men soon may live in Florida or California and fly daily to work in New York and back. Possibly they will be regarded as commuters when that day comes. But, if so, that is not this case and, in any event, neither situation was comprehended by Congress when [§162] was enacted.

of the expenses? Should it be relevant that the necessary business condition (the job in Mobile) arose after the necessary personal condition (the home in Jackson)? As between the two necessary conditions, which seems relatively more fixed and which relatively more variable in each case?

3. *Two places of employment or business.* What if Mr. Flowers had continued to practice law in Jackson after he took the job in Mobile? The Tax Court would apparently permit his expenses in Mobile to be deducted if the business activity in Jackson were substantial, even though the income therefrom was less than the Mobile income. The Service generally takes the position that the "home" of a taxpayer having two widely separated posts of duty is the "principal business" post, so that the taxpayer is not "away from home" while there but may deduct living expenses while at the minor post. See, e.g., Rev. Rul. 75-432, 1975-2 C.B. 60. This ruling is also applicable to seasonal workers such as baseball players.

COMPARATIVE FOCUS:

A Comparative Perspective: Commuting Expenses Auf Deutschland

Most countries with an income tax follow the U.S. approach of disallowing deductions for commuting expense on the theory that it represents personal consumption rather than a cost of earning income. One notable exception is Germany, which has long allowed such a deduction. The amount of the deduction is a set amount per kilometer for travel between the home and workplace, multiplied by the number of days worked. The deduction has long been criticized for its environmental effects—the farther the taxpayer lived from her place of work, the larger the deduction she would be allowed. In 2007, Germany limited the commuting deduction to distances traveled in excess of twenty kilometers. The ostensible rationale for the limitation was that commuting expenses of twenty kilometers or less were inherently personal in nature, though it is hard to see why one's commute becomes more business-related the farther one lives from home. In any event, the limitation was promptly challenged in court, with taxpayers alleging that it was contrary to the ability-to-pay principle and Article 3(1) of the German constitution, providing that all persons shall be equal before the law. Germany's *Bundesfinanzhof* sided with the taxpayer, concluding that commuting expenses are an unavoidable cost of earning income. In late 2008, the German Federal Constitutional Court affirmed the lower court ruling.

HANTZIS v. COMMISSIONER

638 F.2d 248 (1st Cir.), cert. denied, 452 U.S. 962 (1981)

CAMPBELL, Circuit Judge. . . .

In the fall of 1973 Catharine Hantzis (taxpayer), formerly a candidate for an advanced degree in philosophy at the University of California at Berkeley, entered Harvard Law School in Cambridge, Massachusetts, as a full-time student. During her second year of law school she sought unsuccessfully to obtain employment for the summer of 1975 with a Boston law firm. She did, however, find a job as a legal assistant with a law firm in New York City, where she worked for ten weeks beginning in June 1975. Her husband, then a member of the faculty of Northeastern University with a teaching schedule for that summer, remained in Boston and lived at the couple's home there. At the time of the Tax Court's decision in this case, Mr. and Mrs. Hantzis still resided in Boston.

On their joint income tax return for 1975, Mr. and Mrs. Hantzis reported the earnings from taxpayer's summer employment ($3,750) and deducted [under §162(a)(2)] the cost of transportation between Boston and New York, the cost of a small apartment rented by Mrs. Hantzis in New York and the cost of her meals in New York ($3,204). . . .

The Commissioner disallowed the deduction on the ground that taxpayer's home for purposes of section 162(a)(2) was her place of employment and the cost of traveling to and living in New York was therefore not "incurred . . . while away from home." The Commissioner also argued that the expenses were not incurred "in the pursuit of a trade or business." Both positions were rejected by the Tax Court, which found that Boston was Mrs. Hantzis' home because her employment in New York was only temporary and that her expenses in New York were "necessitated" by her employment there. The court thus held the expenses to be deductible under §162(a)(2).[11]

In asking this court to reverse the Tax Court's allowance of the deduction, the Commissioner has contended that the expenses were not incurred "in the pursuit of a trade or business." We do not accept this argument; nonetheless, we sustain the Commissioner and deny the deduction, on the basis that the expenses were not incurred "while away from home." . . .

II

The Commissioner has directed his argument at the meaning of "in pursuit of a trade or business." He interprets this phrase as requiring that a deductible traveling expense be incurred under the demands of a trade or business which predates the expense, that is, an "already" existing trade or business. Under this theory, §162(a)(2) would invalidate the deduction taken by the taxpayer because she was a full-time student before commencing her summer work at a New York law firm in 1975 and so was not continuing in a trade or business when she incurred the expenses of traveling to New York and living there while her job lasted. The Commissioner's proposed interpretation erects at the threshold of deductibility under section 162(a)(2) the requirement that a taxpayer be engaged in a trade or business before incurring a travel expense. Only if that requirement is satisfied would an inquiry into the deductibility of an expense proceed to ask whether the expense was a result of business exigencies, incurred while away from home, and reasonable and necessary.

11. The court upheld the Commissioner's disallowance of a deduction taken by Mr. and Mrs. Hantzis on their 1975 return for expenses incurred by Mrs. Hantzis in attending a convention of the American Philosophical Association. Mr. and Mrs. Hantzis do not appeal that action.

Such a reading of the statute is semantically possible and would perhaps expedite the disposition of certain cases.[12] Nevertheless, we reject it as unsupported by case law and inappropriate to the policies behind §162(a)(2).

The two cases relied on by the Commissioner do not appear to us to establish that traveling expenses are deductible only if incurred in connection with a preexisting trade or business. . . .

Nor would the Commissioner's theory mesh with the policy behind §162(a)(2). [T]he travel expense deduction is intended to exclude from taxable income a necessary cost of producing that income. Yet the recency of entry into a trade or business does not indicate that travel expenses are not a cost of producing income. To be sure, the costs incurred by a taxpayer who leaves his usual residence to begin a trade or business at another location may not be truly travel expenses, that is, expenses incurred while "away from home," but practically, they are as much incurred "in the pursuit of a trade or business" when the occupation is new as when it is old.

An example drawn from the Commissioner's argument illustrates the point. The Commissioner notes that if a construction worker, who normally works in Boston for Corp. *A*, travels to New York to work for Corp. *B* for six months, he is traveling . . . in the pursuit of his own trade as a construction worker. Accordingly, the requirement that travel expenses be a result of business exigencies is satisfied. Had a construction worker just entering the labor market followed the same course his expenses under the Commissioner's reasoning would not satisfy the business exigencies requirement. Yet in each case, the taxpayer's travel expenses would be costs of earning an income and not merely incidents of personal lifestyle. Requiring that the finding of business exigency necessary to deductibility under section 162(a)(2) be predicated upon the prior existence of a trade or business would thus captiously restrict the meaning of "in pursuit of a trade or business." . . .

III

Flowers [v. Commissioner], construed section 162(a)(2) to mean that a traveling expense is deductible only if it is (1) reasonable and necessary; (2) incurred while away from home; and (3) necessitated by the exigencies of business. Because the Commissioner does not suggest that Mrs. Hantzis' expenses were unreasonable or unnecessary, we may pass directly to the remaining requirements. Of these, we find dispositive the requirement that an expense be incurred while away from home. As we think Mrs. Hantzis' expenses were not so incurred, we hold the deduction to be improper.

---

12. We do not see, however, how it would affect the treatment of this case. The Commissioner apparently concedes that upon starting work in New York the taxpayer engaged in a trade or business. If we held—as we do not—that an expense is deductible only when incurred in connection with an already existing trade or business, our ruling would seem to invalidate merely the deduction of the cost of taxpayer's trip from Boston to New York to begin work (about $64). We would still need to determine, as in any other case under section 162(a)(2), whether the expenses that arose *subsequent* to the taxpayer's entry into her trade or business were reasonable and necessary, required by business exigencies and incurred while away from home.

The meaning of the term "home" in the travel expense provision is far from clear. When Congress enacted the travel expense deduction now codified as §162(a)(2), it apparently was unsure whether, to be deductible, an expense must be incurred away from a person's residence or away from his principal place of business. . . . This ambiguity persists and courts, sometimes within a single circuit, have divided over the issue. . . . It has been suggested that these conflicting definitions are due to the enormous factual variety in the cases. . . . We find this observation instructive, for if the cases that discuss the meaning of the term "home" in §162(a)(2) are interpreted on the basis of their unique facts as well as the fundamental purposes of the travel expense provision, and not simply pinioned to one of two competing definitions of home, much of the seeming confusion and contradiction on this issue disappears and a functional definition of the term emerges.

We begin by recognizing that the location of a person's home for purposes of §162(a)(2) becomes problematic only when the person lives one place and works another. Where a taxpayer resides and works at a single location, he is always home, however defined; and where a taxpayer is constantly on the move due to his work, he is never "away" from home. (In the latter situation, it may be said either that he has no residence to be away from, or else that his residence is always at his place of employment. . . .) However, in the present case, the need to determine "home" is plainly before us, since the taxpayer resided in Boston and worked, albeit briefly, in New York.

We think the critical step in defining "home" in these situations is to recognize that the "while away from home" requirement has to be construed in light of the further requirement that the expense be the result of business exigencies. The traveling expense deduction obviously is not intended to exclude from taxation every expense incurred by a taxpayer who, in the course of business, maintains two homes. Section 162(a)(2) seeks rather "to mitigate the burden of the taxpayer who, *because of the exigencies of his trade or business, must* maintain two places of abode and thereby incur additional and duplicate living expenses." . . . Consciously or unconsciously, courts have effectuated this policy in part through their interpretation of the term "home" in §162(a)(2). Whether it is held in a particular decision that a taxpayer's home is his residence or his principal place of business, the ultimate allowance or disallowance of a deduction is a function of the court's assessment of the reason for a taxpayer's maintenance of two homes. If the reason is perceived to be personal, the taxpayer's home will generally be held to be his place of employment rather than his residence and the deduction will be denied. . . . If the reason is felt to be business exigencies, the person's home will usually be held to be his residence and the deduction will be allowed. . . . We understand the concern of the concurrence that such an operational interpretation of the term "home" is somewhat technical and perhaps untidy, in that it will not always afford bright line answers, but we doubt the ability of either the Commissioner or the courts to invent an unyielding formula that will make sense in all cases. The line between personal and business expenses winds through infinite factual permutations; effectuation of the travel expense provision requires that any principle of decision be flexible and sensitive to statutory policy.

Construing in the manner just described the requirement that an expense be incurred "while away from home," we do not believe this requirement was satisfied in this case. Mrs. Hantzis' *trade or business* did not require that she maintain a home in Boston as well as one in New York. Though she returned to Boston at various times during the period of her employment in New York, her visits were all for personal reasons. It is not contended that she had a business connection in Boston that necessitated her keeping a home there; no professional interest was served by maintenance of the Boston home — as would have been the case, for example, if Mrs. Hantzis had been a lawyer based in Boston with a New York client whom she was temporarily serving. The home in Boston was kept up for reasons involving Mr. Hantzis, but those reasons cannot substitute for a showing by *Mrs.* Hantzis that the exigencies of *her* trade or business required *her* to maintain two homes. Mrs. Hantzis' decision to keep two homes must be seen as a choice dictated by personal, albeit wholly reasonable, considerations and not a business or occupational necessity. We therefore hold that her home for purposes of §162(a)(2) was New York and that the expenses at issue in this case were not incurred "while away from home."

We are not dissuaded from this conclusion by the temporary nature of Mrs. Hantzis' employment in New York. Mrs. Hantzis argues that the brevity of her stay in New York excepts her from the business exigencies requirement of §162(a)(2) under a doctrine supposedly enunciated by the Supreme Court in Peurifoy v. Commissioner, 358 U.S. 59 (1958) (per curiam).[13] The Tax Court here held that Boston was the taxpayer's home because it would have been unreasonable for her to move her residence to New York for only ten weeks. At first glance these contentions may seem to find support in the court decisions holding that, when a taxpayer works for a limited time away from his usual home, §162(a)(2) allows a deduction for the expense of maintaining a second home so long as the employment is "temporary" and not "indefinite" or "permanent." . . . This test is an elaboration of the requirements under §162(a)(2) that an expense be incurred due to business exigencies and while away from home. . . . Thus it has been said:

> Where a taxpayer reasonably expects to be employed in a location for a substantial or indefinite period of time, the reasonable inference is that his choice of a residence is a personal decision, unrelated to any business necessity. Thus, it is irrelevant how far he travels to work. The normal expectation, however, is that the taxpayer will choose to live near his place of employment. Consequently,

13. In *Peurifoy* the Court stated that the Tax Court had "engrafted an exception" onto the requirement that travel expenses be dictated by business exigencies, allowing "a deduction for expenditures . . . when the taxpayer's employment is 'temporary,' as contrasted with 'indefinite' or 'indeterminate.' " 358 U.S. at 59. Because the Commissioner did not challenge this exception, the Court did not rule on its validity. It instead upheld the circuit court's reversal of the Tax Court and disallowance of the deduction on the basis of the adequacy of the appellate court's review. The Supreme Court agreed that the Tax Court's finding as to the temporary nature of taxpayer's employment was clearly erroneous. *Id.* at 60-61. Despite its inauspicious beginning, the exception has come to be generally accepted. Some uncertainty lingers, however, over whether the exception properly applies to the "business exigencies" or the "away from home" requirement. . . . In fact, it is probably relevant to both. . . .

when a taxpayer reasonably expects to be employed in a location for only a short or temporary period of time and travels a considerable distance to the location from his residence, it is unreasonable to assume that his choice of a residence is dictated by personal convenience. The reasonable inference is that he is temporarily making these travels because of a business necessity.

Frederick [v. United States], 603 F.2d at 1294-95 (citations omitted).

The temporary employment doctrine does not, however, purport to eliminate any requirement that continued maintenance of a first home have a business justification. We think the rule has no application where the taxpayer has no business connection with his usual place of residence. If no business exigency dictates the location of the taxpayer's usual residence, then the mere fact of his taking temporary employment elsewhere cannot supply a compelling business reason for continuing to maintain that residence. Only a taxpayer who lives one place, works another and has business ties to *both* is in the ambiguous situation that the temporary employment doctrine is designed to resolve. In such circumstances, unless his employment away from his usual home is temporary, a court can reasonably assume that the taxpayer has abandoned his business ties to that location and is left with only personal reasons for maintaining a residence there. Where only personal needs require that a travel expense be incurred, however, a taxpayer's home is defined so as to leave the expense subject to taxation. Thus, a taxpayer who pursues temporary employment away from the location of his usual residence, but has no business connection with that location, is not "away from home" for purposes of §162(a)(2). . . .

On this reasoning, the temporary nature of Mrs. Hantzis' employment in New York does not affect the outcome of her case. She had no business ties to Boston that would bring her within the temporary employment doctrine. By this holding, we do not adopt a rule that "home" in §162(a)(2) is the equivalent of a taxpayer's place of business. Nor do we mean to imply that a taxpayer has a "home" for tax purposes only if he is already engaged in a trade or business at a particular location. Though both rules are alluringly determinate, we have already discussed why they offer inadequate expressions of the purposes behind the travel expense deduction. We hold merely that for a taxpayer in Mrs. Hantzis' circumstances to be "away from home in the pursuit of a trade or business," she must establish the existence of some sort of business relation both to the location she claims as "home" and to the location of her temporary employment sufficient to support a finding that her duplicative expenses are necessitated by business exigencies. This, we believe, is the meaning of the statement in *Flowers* that "[b]usiness trips are to be identified *in relation to* business demands and the traveler's business headquarters." 326 U.S. at 474 (emphasis added). On the uncontested facts before us, Mrs. Hantzis had no business relation to Boston; we therefore leave to cases in which the issue is squarely presented the task of elaborating what relation to a place is required under §162(a)(2) for duplicative living expenses to be deductible.

Reversed.

KEETON, District Judge, concurring in the result.

Although I agree with the result reached in the court's opinion, and with much of its underlying analysis, I write separately because I cannot join in the court's determination that New York was the taxpayer's home for purposes of §162(a)(2). In so holding, the court adopts a definition of "home" that differs from the ordinary meaning of the term and therefore unduly risks causing confusion and misinterpretation of the important principle articulated in this case. . . .

A word used in a statute can mean, among the cognoscenti, whatever authoritative sources define it to mean. Nevertheless, it is a distinct disadvantage of a body of law that it can be understood only by those who are expert in its terminology. Moreover, needless risks of misunderstanding and confusion arise, not only among members of the public but also among professionals who must interpret and apply a statute in their day-to-day work, when a word is given an extraordinary meaning that is contrary to its everyday usage.

The result reached by the court can easily be expressed while also giving "home" its ordinary meaning, and neither Congress nor the Supreme Court has directed that "home" be given an extraordinary meaning in the present context. . . .

NOTES AND QUESTIONS

1. *The motivation in* Hantzis. Hantzis earned $3,750 and spent $3,204, which means she netted $546 for her ten weeks of work. She could have netted more working part time at a menial job in Boston. So why did she go to New York, and what does your answer tell you about how people like her should be taxed?

2. *Temporary versus indefinite jobs.* The court in *Hantzis* refers to the rule, cited by the Supreme Court in Peurifoy v. Commissioner, 358 U.S. 59 (1958) (per curiam), under which a person who takes a *temporary* job away from his or her home area is allowed to deduct travel and living costs (as, for example, would a lawyer from New York who must spend three months in Chicago trying a case). The costs are not deductible, however, where the job away from the area of the taxpayer's residence is of *indefinite* duration. A new job with an indefinite duration is treated as if it were a permanent new job, like Mr. Flowers's job in Mobile. The temporary-versus-indefinite distinction has given rise to a great deal of litigation. Many of the cases involve construction workers. The legal uncertainty that gave rise to much of this litigation was ended in 1992, when Congress, as part of comprehensive energy legislation, added the final sentence of §162(a), which limits "temporary" jobs to those lasting a year or less.

3. *Split summers.* Catharine Hantzis was not allowed to deduct the travel, meals, and lodging expenses she incurred in connection with her summer employment at a New York law firm because, for tax purposes, her "home" was considered to be the place of her principal employment, New York. Suppose Hantzis had spent the first six weeks of her summer working in New York and then had spent the last five weeks of the summer working in the Los Angeles office of the same New York law firm. Would her expenses in connection with the Los Angeles job have been deductible? What if the job in Los Angeles had been with a firm not affiliated with the New York firm?

4. *Daily transportation expenses.* In Revenue Ruling 99-7, 1999-1 C.B. 361, the IRS held (modifying various earlier rulings) that daily transportation expenses incurred in going between a taxpayer's residence and a work location, while generally nondeductible, may be deducted in the following circumstances:

(a) if the work location is temporary and located outside the metropolitan area where she lives and normally works.

(b) if the work location is temporary and she has one or more regular work locations, away from her residence, in the same trade or business. (Same as (a), except that the distance to the temporary work location does not matter.)

(c) if the taxpayer's residence is her principal place of business and the work location is in the same trade or business. (Same as (b), except that the work location need not be temporary.)

PROBLEMS: TESTING THE RATIONALE

The usual rationale for disallowing a deduction for commuting expenses is that the taxpayer is expected to move as near as possible to the job location. If that is done, the expense is trivial. If the taxpayer chooses to live far from the job, that is regarded as a personal choice. Consider the soundness of that rationale in each of the following hypotheticals. Would a deduction be allowed in any of them (disregarding the effect of §67)? Consider whether the tax outcome in each case seems fair and how that outcome might affect family harmony, job-taking decisions by women, and the rationality of job-taking choices in general.

(1) Taxpayer *A* is a woman who lives on a farm with her husband. She drives each day to town, where she earns $50 per day teaching school. The distance is thirty miles each way and the cost of driving is $10 per day. There is no public transportation.

(2) Taxpayer *B* is a poor woman who lives in the central city and works as a maid in an affluent suburb. The distance from her home to the place where she works is twenty miles. Public transportation is available but would take about two hours each way because of the need to make several transfers and to walk substantial distances. *B*'s employer pays $10 a day to a driver of a van who picks *B* up near her home each morning and drops her off at the place where she works. *B*'s pay is $30 per day. She supports her two young children as well as herself. For purposes of determining eligibility for Medicaid, food stamps, and other welfare, what seems to you to be the proper amount of income? What is the rule for income tax purposes? See §132(f). What do you suppose is the practice? Note that even though the worker is probably below the income threshold for paying taxes, the amount of her income is relevant to calculation of her earned income tax credit.

(3) *C* is a tax lawyer who works in the central business district and lives in the suburbs, twenty-five miles from work. When he first took his job, he lived in an apartment about two miles from the office, but he later decided that he preferred the ambience and the recreational opportunities in the suburbs. He earns $150,000 per year and commutes in a Mercedes that costs $20 a day to drive to and from work each day. On rare occasions he uses the car during the day to drive to a meeting with a client.

(4) *D* is a trial lawyer who lives next door to *C*, works in the same firm, earns the same amount, and drives to work in the same model car. *D* needs his car most days in order to get to the various courts in which he must make appearances or to places where he takes depositions.[14] He says that he brings the car to work only in order to have it available for these business uses, but in fact he drives to work even on those days when he will almost certainly spend the entire day in the office. He could take the bus, which would add about forty-five minutes each way to his commuting time and would cost $4 per day round trip.

(5) *E* is a lawyer who is just like *D* in all respects except that his reason for moving to the suburbs was the "better" schools available there. At the time he moved, a federal court had just issued a desegregation order requiring busing in the city schools. In the suburb where he lives, there are very few minority children, and there is no school busing. He denies that his move to the suburbs had anything to do with desegregation and every year contributes $100 to the NAACP Legal Defense Fund.

(6) *F* is also a lawyer, working at the same firm as *C*, *D*, and *E*. *F* is married to *E*. She would prefer to live in the city and to have her children go to the city schools or to a private school in the city, but she acquiesced in *E*'s decision to move to the suburbs. Because *E* and *F* have different schedules, they cannot drive to work together.

(7) *G* is a construction worker. He has lived in the same home, in the central city, for many years. He works at various job sites, for periods ranging from a month to a year. His commutes range in distance from ten to forty miles each way. Rarely is public transportation available, but when it is *G* takes it (largely because he is an avid reader and likes to have the time on the bus or train for reading).

(8) *H* is a construction worker who cannot find a job in the area in which he has lived and worked for the past twenty years. He takes a job in another city, 200 miles away. He expects that job to last about three months, which it does. His cost of traveling to and from the new job location is $100. His living costs while he is there, including food and lodging, are $25 per day. In addition, he spends $5 per day driving back and forth between the job site and his temporary dwelling place.

(9) *I* is just like *H* except that the new job is expected to last three years.

E.   TRAVEL AND ENTERTAINMENT EXPENSES

1.   The Deductibility of Business Travel

Under the provision discussed above in *Hantzis.* §162(a)(2), if a person travels to another city on business, the cost of getting there and back is deductible. If

---

14. The costs of driving to court or to take depositions plainly are deductible, under §162(a), as "ordinary and necessary expenses." Section 162(a)(2) is irrelevant to this expense, though even in cases where it is relevant it is only an elaboration on the basic operative rule stated in the opening clause of §162(a).

the person stays overnight, the cost of food and lodging also is deductible. In most instances these rules are easily reconciled with sound tax policy objectives, but such reconciliation can become difficult where there are significant personal as well as business benefits from the trip. We properly ignore the fact that a person traveling on business may enjoy traveling. The fact that one enjoys one's job is not a reason for denying a deduction of the costs of getting that job done; purely psychic benefits are not part of the income tax base.

But suppose that a self-employed consultant is going to another city on business, that the person's mother happens to live there, and that the person is anxious to see her. Now we have a substantial personal benefit that is not an inextricable part of the business activity. Suppose that the airfare for the trip is $800, that the person would have been willing to pay this much for the purely business objectives, but that he or she would also have been willing to pay $800 to travel to the same place just to see his or her mother. An appealing argument can be made for including in income the value of the personal satisfaction or (what amounts to the same thing) denying a deduction for the $800. But the practical difficulty of such an approach should be obvious. The rule that the courts purport to apply is that the cost of a trip, or of other activities such as dinner with a customer at a restaurant, is deductible if the "primary purpose" is business. The primary purpose test is based on unrealistic assumptions about how people think and about the ability of the tax authorities to get at the true facts. For example, if you travel to another city on business and see your mother while you're there, do you necessarily engage in a mental process in which you weigh the value of the business objective against that of the personal objective? Of course not. And even if you did, the IRS employee who examines your return would have no practical way of verifying or challenging your assertions about that mental process. Thus, one can reasonably surmise that in practice some other test must be used. In all probability that test is that if there is a *sufficient* business justification for the trip, the deduction will be allowed. Even that test leaves considerable opportunity for cheating, since the tax authorities are properly reluctant, and limited in their ability, to challenge the business judgments of taxpayers.

The business versus personal issue often arises when an individual pays her own expenses and then tries to deduct the outlay. In the example above, a self-employed consultant flies somewhere to attend a business meeting and see her mother. In other cases, an employee might pay an expense that has mixed business and personal motives and is not reimbursable by her employer and then deduct the outlay.

Suppose, though, that an employer pays expenses associated with an employee's travel. The trip has some business rationale and therefore some benefit to the employer; it also provides some personal benefits to the employee. If the trip is characterized for tax purposes as business related, the value of the trip is not treated as income to the employee. Employees are not taxed on whatever personal benefit they receive out of employer-provided business travel. Statutory support for nontaxation is found in §132(d), which provides that an employer-provided benefit is not included in employee income if the benefit would have been deductible as a business expense and the employee paid for it out of her own pocket. If, instead, the trip is characterized as non–business related, then it is treated as a form of salary and included in the employee's gross income. What about the employer? Obviously, the cost of employee business travel is deductible.[15] A non–business-related trip the employer pays for is also deductible for the employer,[16] because such a trip is treated as salary to the employee, and salary is a deductible business expense.

Thus, outlays by an employer that have business benefits to the employer and personal benefits to an employee raise the same question that is raised by outlays of a self-employed person that provide business and personal benefits: whether the outlay is properly characterized as business related. Employer-provided outlays that would have been deductible if paid for directly by the employee do not constitute income to the employee. Outlays that would not have been deductible if paid for by the employee are treated as taxable salary to the employee.

RUDOLPH v. UNITED STATES
370 U.S. 269 (1962)

Per Curiam . . .

An insurance company provided a trip from its home office in Dallas, Texas, to New York City for a group of its agents and their wives. Rudolph and his wife were among the beneficiaries of this trip, and the Commissioner assessed its value to them as taxable income. It appears to be agreed between the parties that the tax consequences of the trip turn upon the Rudolphs' "dominant motive and purpose" in taking the trip and the company's in offering it. In this regard, the District Court, on a suit for a refund, found that the trip was provided by the company for "the primary purpose of affording a pleasure trip . . . in the nature of a bonus reward, and compensation for a job well done" and that from the point of view of the Rudolphs it "was primarily a pleasure trip in the nature of a vacation. . . ." 189 F. Supp. 2, 4-5. The Court of Appeals approved these findings. 291 F.2d 841. Such ultimate facts are subject to the "clearly erroneous" rule, cf. Comm'r v. Duberstein, and their review would be of no importance save to the litigants themselves. The appropriate disposition in such a situation is to dismiss the writ as improvidently granted. . . .

Mr. Justice Frankfurter took no part in the decision of this case.

Mr. Justice White took no part in the consideration or decision of this case.

Separate opinion of Mr. Justice Harlan. . . .

[N]ow that the case is here I think it better to decide it, two members of the Court having dissented on the merits. . . .

Petitioners, husband and wife, reside in Dallas, Texas, where the home office of the husband's employer, the Southland Life Insurance Company, is located.

---

15. If the expense creates or improves a long-term asset, it must be capitalized.

16. Occasionally, deductions will be denied because the expense fails the "ordinary and necessary" test of §162.

By having sold a predetermined amount of insurance, the husband qualified to attend the company's convention in New York City in 1956 and, in line with company policy, to bring his wife with him. The petitioners, together with 150 other employees and officers of the insurance company and 141 wives, traveled to and from New York City on special trains, and were housed in a single hotel during their two-and-one-half-day visit. One morning was devoted to a "business meeting" and group luncheon, the rest of the time in New York City to "travel, sightseeing, entertainment, fellowship or free time." The entire trip lasted one week.

The company paid all the expenses of the convention-trip . . . petitioner's allocable share being $560. . . . The District Court held that the value of the trip being "in the nature of a bonus, reward, and compensation for a job well done," was income to Rudolph, but being "primarily a pleasure trip in the nature of a vacation," the costs were personal and nondeductible.

I

Under §61 . . . was the value of the trip to the taxpayer-husband properly includable in gross income? . . .

[I]t was surely within the Commissioner's competence to consider as "gross income" a "reward, or a bonus given to . . . employees for excellence in service," which the District Court found was the employer's primary purpose in arranging this trip. . . .

II

There remains the question whether, though income, this outlay for transportation, meals, and lodging was deductible by petitioners as an "ordinary and necessary" business expense under §162. . . .

[T]he crucial question is whether . . . the purpose of the trip was "related primarily to business" or was rather "primarily personal in nature." . . . [T]hat certain doctors, lawyers, clergymen, insurance agents or others have or have not been permitted similar deductions only shows that in the circumstances of those cases, the courts thought that the expenses were or were not deductible as "related primarily to business."

The husband places great emphasis on the fact that he is an entrapped "organization man," required to attend such conventions, and that his future promotions depend on his presence. Suffice it to say that the District Court did not find any element of compulsion; to the contrary, it found that the petitioners regarded the convention in New York City as a pleasure trip in the nature of a vacation. . . .

Mr. Justice DOUGLAS, with whom Mr. Justice BLACK joins, dissenting.

I

It could not, I think, be seriously contended that a professional man, say a Senator or a Congressman, who attends a convention to read a paper or conduct a seminar *with all expenses paid* has received "income." . . . Income has the connotation of something other than the mere payment of expenses. . . .

The formula "all expenses paid" might be the disguise whereby compensation "for services" is paid. Yet it would be a rare case indeed where one could conclude that a person who gets only his expenses for attendance at one convention gets "income" in the statutory sense. If this arrangement were regular and frequent or if it had the earmarks of a sham device as a cloak for remuneration, there would be room for fact-finders to conclude that it was evasive. But isolated engagements of the kind here in question have no rational connection with compensation "for services" rendered.

It is true that petitioner was an employee and that the expenses for attending the convention were paid by his employer. He qualified to attend the convention by selling an amount of insurance that met a quota set by the company. Other salesmen also qualified, some attending and some not attending. They went from Dallas, Texas, to New York City, where they stayed two and a half days. One day was given to a business session and a luncheon; the rest of the time was left for social events.

On this record there is no room for a finding of fact that the "expenses paid" were "for services" rendered. They were apparently a proper income tax deduction for the employer. The record is replete with evidence that from management's point of view it was good business to spend money on a convention for its leading agents—a convention that not only kept the group together in New York City, but in transit as well, giving ample time for group discussions, exchanges of experience, and educational training. It was the exigencies of the employment that gave rise to the convention. There was nothing dishonest, illegitimate, or unethical about this transaction. No services were rendered. New York City may or may not have been attractive to the agents and their wives. Whether a person enjoys or dislikes the trip that he makes "with all expenses paid" has no more to do with whether the expenses paid were compensation "for services" rendered than does his attitude toward his job. . . .

III

The wife's expenses are, on this record, also deductible.[17] The Treasury Regulations state in §1.162-2(c):

> Where a taxpayer's wife accompanies him on a business trip, expenses attributable to her travel are not deductible unless it can be adequately shown that the wife's presence on the trip has a bona fide business purpose. The wife's performance of some incidental service does not cause her expenses to qualify as deductible business expenses. . . .

The civil law philosophy, expressed in the community property concept, attributes half of the husband's earnings to the wife—an equitable idea that at long last was reflected in the idea of income splitting under the federal income

---

17. This case arose before the adoption of §274(m)(3), which, beginning in 1994, would expressly deny a deduction by Rudolph's employer of the travel expenses of the spouses.

tax law. The wife's contribution to the business productivity of the husband in at least some activities is well known. . . . Business reasons motivated the inclusion of wives in this particular insurance convention. An insurance executive testified at this trial:

Q: I hand you Plaintiff's Exhibit 15, and you will notice it is a letter addressed to "John Doe"; also a bulletin entitled "A New Partner Has Been Formed." Will you tell us what that consists of?

A: This is a letter addressed to the wife of an agent, a new agent, as we make the contract with him. This letter is sent to his wife within a few days after the contract, enclosing this booklet explaining to her how she can help her husband in the life insurance business.

Q: Please tell us, as briefly as you can and yet in detail, how you as agency director for Southland attempt to integrate the wives' performance with the performance of agents in the life insurance business.

A: One of the important functions we have in mind is the attendance at these conventions. In addition to that communication, occasionally there are letters that will be written to the wife concerning any special sales effort that might be desired or promoted. The company has a monthly publication for the agents and employees that is mailed to their homes so the wife will have a convenient opportunity to see the magazine and read it. At most of our convention program[s], we have some specific references to the wife's work, and in quite a few of the convention programs we have had wives appear on the program.

Q: Suppose you didn't have the wives and didn't seek to require their attendance at a convention, would there be some danger that your meetings and conventions would kind of degenerate into stag affairs, where the whole purpose of the meeting would be lost?

A: I think that would definitely be a tendency.

I would reverse the judgments below and leave insurance conventions in the same category as conventions of revenue agents, lawyers, doctors, businessmen, accountants, nurses, clergymen and all others, until and unless Congress decides otherwise.

2.   Limitations Under §274

In 1962, Congress enacted §274, which superimposes on the basic requirements of §162 additional rules for travel and entertainment (often referred to as T and E). Congress has amended §274 at various times since then. Section 274 is specific and detailed; the regulations, which to a considerable extent pick up ideas and language found in congressional committee reports, are even more so. The principal features of §274 are described below.

Disallowance of entertainment expenses. Section 274(a)(1) provides that no deduction is allowed for any item (a) with respect to an activity that is of a type generally considered to constitute entertainment, amusement, or recreation; or (b) with respect to a facility used in connection with such an activity. This blanket disallowance provision was enacted as part of the 2017 tax act and represents a significant departure from prior law, which allowed taxpayers to deduct entertainment expenses in a variety of circumstances.

Fifty percent limitation on meal deduction. Section 274(n), first adopted in 1986, limits the otherwise allowable deduction for meals to 50 percent of the cost. The remaining 50 percent of the cost is treated as a nondeductible personal expense. The reasons given in Congress in 1986 for the original version of this provision, which limited the deduction to 80 percent of the amount otherwise allowable, are noted in the Report of the Senate Finance Committee in its discussion of the 1986 act (S. Rep. No. 313, 99th Cong., 1st Sess. 68 (1986)):

> The committee believes that present law, by not focusing sufficiently on the personal-consumption element of deductible meal and entertainment expenses, unfairly permits taxpayers who can arrange business settings for personal consumption to receive, in effect, a Federal tax subsidy for such consumption that is not available to other taxpayers. The taxpayers who benefit from deductibility under present law tend to have relatively high incomes, and in some cases the consumption may bear only a loose relationship to business necessity. For example, when executives have dinner at an expensive restaurant following business discussions and then deduct the cost of the meal, the fact that there may be some bona fide business connection does not alter the imbalance between the treatment of those persons, who have effectively transferred a portion of the cost of their meal to the Federal Government, and other individuals, who cannot deduct the cost of their meals.
>
> The significance of this imbalance is heightened by the fact that business travel and entertainment often may be more lavish than comparable activities in a nonbusiness setting. For example, meals at expensive restaurants and season tickets at sporting events are purchased to a significant degree by taxpayers who claim business deductions for these expenses. This disparity is highly visible, and contributes to public perceptions that the tax system is unfair. Polls indicate that the public identifies the deductibility of normal personal expenses such as meals to be one of the most significant elements of disrespect for and dissatisfaction with the present tax system.

Expenses of spouse. Where a person is on a legitimate tax-deductible business trip, no deduction is allowed for the additional travel expenses of the person's spouse (or dependent or any other person accompanying that person), unless (i) the spouse (etc.) is an employee of the person claiming the deduction, (ii) the spouse (etc.) had a bona fide business purpose for going on the trip, *and* (iii) the additional expenses would otherwise be deductible. §274(m)(3) (added by the 1993 act). This provision overrules cases allowing deductions of a spouse's expenses if there was a valid reason for the spouse to come along (such as assisting with the entertainment of clients).

Section 274's substantiation requirements. By virtue of §274(d), no deduction may be taken for traveling expenses, business gifts, or certain "listed property" (e.g., automobiles, computers) unless the taxpayer "substantiates by adequate records or by sufficient evidence corroborating the taxpayer's own statement (A) the amount of such expense or other item, (B) the time and place of the travel or the date and description of the gift, (C) the business purpose of the expense or other item, and (D) the business relationship to the taxpayer of the person receiving the benefit." The Treasury is authorized to dispense with some or all of the substantiation requirements, and this power has been exercised as to some expenditures. For example, the amount of expenditures under $75 (other than for lodging) need not be substantiated by receipts (Reg. §1.274-5T(c)(2)(iii)); per diem and mileage allowances paid by an employer to an employee need not be substantiated if they do not exceed maximum amounts specified from time to time by the Commissioner (Reg. §1.274-5T(g)); employees are not required to substantiate expenses to the Service if they have substantiated those expenses to their employers for purposes of obtaining reimbursement (Reg. §1.274-5T(f)(2)); and taxpayers may claim fixed per diem amounts for meals without substantiation if the time, place, and business purpose of the travel are properly substantiated (but subject to the §274(n) 50-percent limitation on the deduction for meals). See Rev. Proc. 92-17, 92-1 C.B. 679.

Club dues. No deduction is allowed for "amounts paid or incurred for membership in any club organized for business, pleasure, recreation, or other social purpose." §274(a)(3).

Foreign travel. Section 274(c) provides that in certain circumstances, where a person combines business and pleasure on a trip to a foreign country, the air fare is partially disallowed. This provision seems to look to benefit rather than to primary purpose or to the sufficiency of the business objective. As initially adopted in 1962 it applied to domestic as well as foreign travel, but in 1964 it was repealed as to domestic travel. The moral of this bit of history would seem to be that one should not underestimate the political power of the hotel and travel industry and the unions representing all the people who work in that industry.

3.   Business Lunches

MOSS v. COMMISSIONER
758 F.2d 211 (7th Cir. 1985)

POSNER, Circuit Judge.

The taxpayers, a lawyer named Moss and his wife, appeal from a decision of the Tax Court disallowing federal income tax deductions of a little more than $1,000 in each of two years, representing Moss's share of his law firm's lunch expense at the Cafe Angelo in Chicago. The Tax Court's decision in this case has attracted some attention in tax circles because of its implications for the general problem of the deductibility of business meals. . . .

Moss was a partner in a small trial firm specializing in defense work, mostly for one insurance company. Each of the firm's lawyers carried a tremendous litigation caseload, averaging more than 300 cases, and spent most of every working day in courts in Chicago and its suburbs. The members of the firm met for lunch daily at the Cafe Angelo near their office. At lunch the lawyers would discuss their cases with the head of the firm, whose approval was required for most settlements, and they would decide which lawyer would meet which court call that afternoon or the next morning. Lunchtime was chosen for the daily meeting because the courts were in recess then. The alternatives were to meet at 7:00 A.M. or 6:00 P.M. and these were less convenient times. There is no suggestion that the lawyers dawdled over lunch, or that the Cafe Angelo is luxurious.

The framework of statutes and regulations for deciding this case is simple, but not clear. Section 262 of the Internal Revenue Code (Title 26) disallows, "except as otherwise expressly provided in this chapter," the deduction of "personal, family, or living expenses." Section 119 excludes from income the value of meals provided by an employer to his employees for his convenience, but only if they are provided on the employer's premises; and §162(a) allows the deduction of "all the ordinary and necessary expenses paid or incurred during the taxable year in carrying on any trade or business, including—. . . (2) traveling expenses (including amounts expended for meals . . .) while away from home. . . ." Since Moss was not an employee but a partner in a partnership not taxed as an entity, since the meals were not served on the employer's premises, and since he was not away from home (that is, on an overnight trip away from his place of work, see United States v. Correll, 389 U.S. 299 (1967)), neither §119 nor §162(a)(2) applies to this case. The Internal Revenue Service concedes, however, that meals are deductible under §162(a) when they are ordinary and necessary business expenses (provided the expense is substantiated with adequate records, see §274(d)) even if they are not within the express permission of any other provision and even though the expense of commuting to and from work, a traveling expense but not one incurred away from home, is not deductible. Treasury Regulations on Income Tax §1.262-1(b)(5); Fausner v. Commissioner, 413 U.S. 838 (1973) (per curiam).

The problem is that many expenses are simultaneously business expenses in the sense that they conduce to the production of business income and personal expenses in the sense that they raise personal welfare. This is plain enough with regard to lunch; most people would eat lunch even if they didn't work. Commuting may seem a pure business expense, but is not; it reflects the choice of where to live, as well as where to work. Read literally, §162 would make irrelevant whether a business expense is also a personal expense; so long as it is ordinary and necessary in the taxpayer's business, thus bringing section 162(a) into play, an expense is (the statute seems to say) deductible from his income tax. But the statute has not been read literally. There is a natural reluctance, most clearly manifested in the regulation disallowing deduction of the expense of commuting, to lighten the tax burden of people who have the good fortune to interweave work with consumption. To allow a deduction for commuting would confer a windfall on people who live in the suburbs and commute to work in the cities; to allow a deduction for all business-related meals would confer a windfall on people who can arrange their work schedules so they do some of their work at lunch.

Although an argument can thus be made for disallowing *any* deduction for business meals, on the theory that people have to eat whether they work or not, the result would be excessive taxation of people who spend more money on business meals because they are business meals than they would spend on their meals if they were not working. Suppose a theatrical agent takes his clients out to lunch at the expensive restaurants that the clients demand. Of course he can deduct the expense of their meals, from which he derives no pleasure or sustenance, but can he also deduct the expense of his own? He can, because he cannot eat more cheaply; he cannot munch surreptitiously on a peanut butter and jelly sandwich brought from home while his client is wolfing down tournedos Rossini followed by soufflé au grand marnier. No doubt our theatrical agent, unless concerned for his longevity, derives personal utility from his fancy meal, but probably less than the price of the meal. He would not pay for it if it were not for the business benefit; he would get more value from using the same money to buy something else; hence the meal confers on him less utility than the cash equivalent would. The law could require him to pay tax on the fair value of the meal to him; this would be (were it not for costs of administration) the economically correct solution. But the government does not attempt this difficult measurement; it once did, but gave up the attempt as not worth the cost. . . . The taxpayer is permitted to deduct the whole price, provided the expense is "different from or in excess of that which would have been made for the taxpayer's personal purposes." Sutter v. Commissioner, 21 T.C. 170, 173 (1953).

Because the law allows this generous deduction, which tempts people to have more (and costlier) business meals than are necessary, the Internal Revenue Service has every right to insist that the meal be shown to be a real business necessity. This condition is most easily satisfied when a client or customer or supplier or other outsider to the business is a guest. Even if Sydney Smith was wrong that "soup and fish explain half the emotions of life," it is undeniable that eating together fosters camaraderie and makes business dealings friendlier and easier. It thus reduces the costs of transacting business, for these costs include the frictions and the failures of communication that are produced by suspicion and mutual misunderstanding, by differences in tastes and manners, and by lack of rapport. A meeting with a client or customer in an office is therefore not a perfect substitute for a lunch with him in a restaurant. But it is different when all the participants in the meal are coworkers, as essentially was the case here (clients occasionally were invited to the firm's daily luncheon, but Moss has made no attempt to identify the occasions). They know each other well already; they don't need the social lubrication that a meal with an outsider provides — at least don't need it daily. If a large firm had a monthly lunch to allow partners to get to know associates, the expense of the meal might well be necessary, and would be allowed by the Internal Revenue Service. . . . But Moss's firm never had more than eight lawyers (partners and associates), and did not need a daily lunch to cement relationships among them.

It is all a matter of degree and circumstance (the expense of a testimonial dinner, for example, would be deductible on a morale-building rationale); and particularly of frequency. Daily — for a full year — is too often, perhaps even for entertainment of clients, as implied by Hankenson v. Commissioner, 47 T.C.M. 1567, 1569 (1984), where the Tax Court held nondeductible the cost of lunches consumed three or four days a week, 52 weeks a year, by a doctor who entertained other doctors who he hoped would refer patients to him, and other medical personnel.

We may assume it was necessary for Moss's firm to meet daily to coordinate the work of the firm, and also, as the Tax Court found, that lunch was the most convenient time. But it does not follow that the expense of the lunch was a necessary business expense. The members of the firm had to eat somewhere, and the Cafe Angelo was both convenient and not too expensive. They do not claim to have incurred a greater daily lunch expense than they would have incurred if there had been no lunch meetings. Although it saved time to combine lunch with work, the meal itself was not an organic part of the meeting, as in the examples we gave earlier where the business objective, to be fully achieved, required sharing a meal.

The case might be different if the location of the courts required the firm's members to eat each day either in a disagreeable restaurant, so that they derived less value from the meal than it cost them to buy it, . . . or in a restaurant too expensive for their personal tastes, so that, again, they would have gotten less value than the cash equivalent. But so far as appears, they picked the restaurant they liked most. Although it must be pretty monotonous to eat lunch the same place every working day of the year, not all the lawyers attended all the lunch meetings and there was nothing to stop the firm from meeting occasionally at another restaurant proximate to their office in downtown Chicago; there are hundreds.

An argument can be made that the price of lunch at the Cafe Angelo included rental of the space that the lawyers used for what was a meeting as well as a meal. There was evidence that the firm's conference room was otherwise occupied throughout the working day, so as a matter of logic Moss might be able to claim a part of the price of lunch as an ordinary and necessary expense for work space. But this is cutting things awfully fine; in any event Moss made no effort to apportion his lunch expense in this way.

Affirmed.

QUESTIONS

1. Is the court's decision in *Moss* grounded on the theory that a taxpayer should only be able to deduct business meals that are more expensive than the meals the taxpayer would otherwise have consumed? On the theory that a taxpayer should only be able to deduct business meals with clients? On the theory that Congress could not have intended to allow a taxpayer to deduct lunch every day?

2. Do you agree with Judge Posner that eating with clients "reduces the costs of transacting business" by lessening the "frictions and the failures of communication that are produced by suspicion and mutual misunderstanding"? Do you think that disallowance of a deduction for all business meals would significantly reduce business efficiency? How do you suppose it would affect the restaurant business and the people employed in that activity?

3. In which, if any, of the following circumstances will the lunch be deductible?

(a) A lawyer takes her client to lunch to discuss her firm's handling of the client's case.

(b) A client takes her lawyer to lunch to discuss the lawyer's firm's handling of the client's case.

(c) A lawyer takes her client to lunch in order to retain the client's goodwill.

(d) A partner in a law firm takes an associate to lunch to discuss the associate's future with the firm.

(e) A partner in a law firm takes an associate to lunch to discuss a pending case.

(f) Two partners go to lunch once a week to talk about an ongoing case.

F. LEGAL EXPENSES

UNITED STATES v. GILMORE
372 U.S. 39 (1963)

Mr. Justice HARLAN . . .

In 1955, the California Supreme Court confirmed the award to the respondent taxpayer of a decree of absolute divorce. . . . The case before us involves the deductibility for federal income tax purposes of that part of the husband's legal expense incurred in such proceedings as is attributable to his successful resistance of his wife's claim to certain of his assets asserted by her to be community property under California law. The claim to such deduction, which has been upheld by the Court of Claims, 290 F.2d 942, is founded on [§212(2)], which allows as deductions from gross income: . . . ordinary and necessary expenses . . . incurred during the taxable year . . . for the . . . conservation . . . of property held for the production of income.

At the time of the divorce proceedings, instituted by the wife but in which the husband also cross-claimed for divorce, respondent's property consisted primarily of controlling stock interests in three corporations [General Motors dealerships]. . . . As president . . . of the three corporations, he received salaries from them aggregating about $66,800 annually, and in recent years his total annual dividends had averaged about $83,000. . . . His income from other sources was negligible.

As found by the Court of Claims the husband's overriding concern in the divorce litigation was to protect these assets against the claims of his wife. Those claims had two aspects: *First*, that the earnings accumulated and retained by these three corporations during the Gilmores' marriage (representing an aggregate increase in corporate net worth of some $600,000) were the product of respondent's personal services, and not the result of accretion in capital values, thus rendering respondent's stockholdings in the enterprises pro tanto community property under California law; *second*, that to the extent that such stockholdings were community property, the wife, allegedly the innocent party in the divorce proceeding, was entitled under California law to more than a one-half interest in such property.

The respondent wished to defeat those claims for two important reasons. *First*, the loss of his controlling stock interests, particularly in the event of their transfer in substantial part to his hostile wife, might well cost him the loss of his corporate positions, his principal means of livelihood. *Second*, there was also danger that if he were found guilty of his wife's sensational and reputation-damaging charges of marital infidelity, General Motors Corporation might find it expedient to exercise its right to cancel these dealer franchises.

The end result of this bitterly fought divorce case was a complete victory for the husband. He, not the wife, was granted a divorce on his cross-claim; the wife's community property claims were denied in their entirety; and she was held entitled to no alimony.

Respondent's legal expenses in connection with this litigation amounted to . . . a total of $40,611.36. . . . The Commissioner found all of these expenditures "personal" or "family" expenses and as such none of them deductible. [§262.] In the ensuing refund suit, however, the Court of Claims held that 80 percent of such expense (some $32,500) was attributable to respondent's defense against his wife's community property claims respecting his stockholdings and hence deductible under [§212(2)] as an expense "incurred . . . for the . . . conservation . . . of property held for the production of income." . . .

The Government['s] . . . sole contention here is that the court below misconceived the test governing [§212(1) and (2)] deductions, in that the deductibility of these expenses turns, so it is argued, not upon the *consequences* to respondent of a failure to defeat his wife's community property claims but upon the origin and *nature* of the claims themselves. . . . [W]e think the Government's position is sound and that it must be sustained.

I

For income tax purposes, Congress has seen fit to regard an individual as having two personalities: "one is [as] a seeker after profit who can deduct the expenses incurred in that search; the other is [as] a creature satisfying his needs as a human and those of his family but who cannot deduct such consumption and related expenditures."[18] The Government regards [§212(1) and (2)] as embodying a category of expenses embraced in the first of these roles.

Initially, it may be observed that the wording of [§212(2)] more readily fits the Government's view of the provision than that of the Court of Claims. For in context "conservation of property" seems to refer to operations performed with respect to the property itself, such as safeguarding or upkeep, rather than to a taxpayer's retention of ownership in it. But more illuminating than the mere language of [§212(1) and (2)] is the history of the provision.

Prior to 1942 [the Code] allowed deductions only for expenses incurred "in carrying on any trade or business," the deduction presently authorized by [§162(a)]. In Higgins v. Comm'r, 312 U.S. 212, this Court gave that provision a narrow construction, holding that the activities of an individual in supervising his own securities investments did not constitute the "carrying on of a trade or business," and hence that expenses incurred in connection with such activities were not tax deductible. . . . The Revenue Act of 1942 . . . by adding what is now [§212(1) and (2)], sought to remedy the inequity inherent in the disallowance of expense deductions in respect of such profit-seeking activities, the income from which was nonetheless taxable.

---

18. Surrey and Warren, *Cases on Federal Income Taxation*, 272 (1960).

As noted in McDonald v. Comm'r, 323 U.S. 57, 62, the purpose of the 1942 amendment was merely to enlarge "the category of incomes with reference to which expenses were deductible." And committee reports make clear that deductions under the new section were subject to the same limitations and restrictions that are applicable to those allowable under [§162(a)]. Further, this Court has said that [§212(1) and (2)] "is comparable and in pari materia with [§162(a)]," providing for a class of deductions "coextensive with the business deductions allowed by [§162(a)], except for" the requirement that the income-producing activity qualify as a trade or business. Trust of Bingham v. Comm'r, 325 U.S. 365, 373, 374.

A basic restriction upon the availability of a [§162(a)] deduction is that the expense item involved must be one that has a business origin. That restriction not only inheres in the language of [§162(a)] itself, confining such deductions to "expenses . . . incurred . . . in carrying on any trade or business," but also follows from [§262], expressly rendering nondeductible "in any case . . . [p]ersonal, living, or family expenses." In light of what has already been said with respect to the advent and thrust of [§212(1) and (2)], it is clear that the "[p]ersonal . . . or family expenses" restriction of [§262] must impose the same limitation upon the reach of [§212(1) and (2)] — in other words that the only kind of expenses deductible under [§212(1) and (2)] are those that relate to a "business," that is, profit-seeking, purpose. The pivotal issue in this case then becomes: was this part of respondent's litigation cost a "business" rather than a "personal" or "family" expense?

The answer to this question has already been indicated in prior cases. In Lykes v. U.S., 343 U.S. 118, the Court rejected the contention that legal expenses incurred in contesting the assessment of a gift tax liability were deductible. The taxpayer argued that if he had been required to pay the original deficiency he would have been forced to liquidate his stockholdings, which were his main source of income, and that his legal expenses were therefore incurred in the "conservation" of income-producing property and hence deductible under [§212(2)]. The Court first noted that the "deductibility [of the expenses] turns wholly upon the nature of the activities to which they relate" (343 U.S. at 123), and then stated (*id.* at 125-126):

> Legal expenses do not become deductible merely because they are paid for services which relieve a taxpayer of liability. That argument would carry us too far. It would mean that the expense of defending almost any claim would be deductible by a taxpayer on the ground that such defense was made to help him keep clear of liens whatever income-producing property he might have. For example, it suggests that the expense of defending an action based upon personal injuries caused by a taxpayer's negligence while driving an automobile for pleasure should be deductible. Section [212(1) and (2)] never has been so interpreted by us. . . .
>
> [T]he threatened deficiency assessment . . . related to the tax payable on petitioner's gifts. . . . The expense of contesting the amount of the deficiency was thus at all times attributable to the gifts, as such, and accordingly was not deductible.
>
> If, as suggested, the relative size of each claim, in proportion to the income-producing resources of a defendant, were to be a touchstone of the deductibility of the expense of resisting the claim, substantial uncertainty and inequity would inhere in the rule.

In Kornhauser v. U.S., 276 U.S. 145, this Court considered the deductibility of legal expenses incurred by a taxpayer in defending against a claim by a former business partner that fees paid to the taxpayer were for services rendered during the existence of the partnership. In holding that these expenses were deductible even though the taxpayer was no longer a partner at the time of suit, the Court formulated the rule that "where a suit or action against a taxpayer is directly connected with, or . . . proximately resulted from, his business, the expense incurred is a business expense. . . ." 276 U.S. at 153. Similarly, in a case involving an expense incurred in satisfying an obligation (though not a litigation expense), it was said that "it is the origin of the liability out of which the expense accrues" or "the kind of transaction out of which the obligation arose . . . which [is] crucial and controlling." Deputy v. duPont, 308 U.S. 488, 494, 496.

The principle we derive from these cases is that the characterization, as "business" or "personal," of the litigation costs of resisting a claim depends on whether or not the claim *arises in connection with* the taxpayer's profit-seeking activities. It does not depend on the *consequences* that might result to a taxpayer's income-producing property from a failure to defeat the claim, for, as *Lykes* teaches, that "would carry us too far"[19] and would not be compatible with the basic lines of expense deductibility drawn by Congress.[20] Moreover, such a rule would lead to capricious results. If two taxpayers are each sued for an automobile accident while driving for pleasure, deductibility of their litigation costs would turn on the mere circumstance of the character of the assets each happened to possess, that is, whether the judgments against them stood to be satisfied out of income- or non-income-producing property. We should be slow to attribute to Congress a purpose producing such unequal treatment among taxpayers, resting on no rational foundation. . . .

We turn then to the determinative question in this case: did the wife's claims respecting respondent's stockholdings arise in connection with his profit-seeking activities?

II

In classifying respondent's legal expenses the court below did not distinguish between those relating to the claims of the wife with respect to the *existence* of community property and those involving the *division* of any such property. . . . Nor is such a break-down necessary for a disposition of the present case. It is enough to say that in both aspects the wife's claims stemmed entirely from the marital relationship, and not, under any tenable view of things,

---

19. The Treasury Regulations have long provided:

> An expense (not otherwise deductible) paid or incurred by an individual in determining or contesting a liability asserted against him does not become deductible by reason of the fact that property held by him for the production of income may be required to be used or sold for the purpose of satisfying such liability.

Treas. Regs. (1954 Code) §1.212-1(m); see Treas. Regs. 118 (1939 Code) §39.23(a)-15(k).

20. Expenses of contesting tax liabilities are now deductible under §212(3) of the 1954 Code. This provision merely represents a policy judgment as to a particular class of expenditures otherwise nondeductible, like extraordinary medical expenses, and does not cast any doubt on the basic tax structure set up by Congress.

from income-producing activity. This is obviously so as regards the claim to more than an equal division of any community property found to exist. For any such right depended entirely on the wife's making good her charges of marital infidelity on the part of the husband. The same conclusion is no less true respecting the claim relating to the existence of community property. For no such property could have existed but for the marriage relationship.[21] Thus, none of respondent's expenditures in resisting these claims can be deemed "business" expenses, and they are therefore not deductible under [§212(2)]....

Mr. Justice BLACK and Mr. Justice DOUGLAS believe that the Court reverses this case because of an unjustifiably narrow interpretation of the 1942 amendment to the Internal Revenue Code and would accordingly affirm the judgment of the Court of Claims.

NOTES AND QUESTIONS

1. *Causative analysis revisited.* (a) Is the "origins" test in *Gilmore* different from the "but for" test that we have encountered earlier in connection with deductions for medical expenses, child-care expenses, and commuting costs?

(b) Would and should the result in *Gilmore* have been different if Mr. Gilmore had first met Mrs. Gilmore when she came to work for his business?

(c) The Court would presumably have us compare Mr. Gilmore with a taxpayer who had the same property interests but who never married or, having married, never got divorced. Does the Court offer any explanation of why we should not compare Mr. Gilmore with a man who gets divorced but who has no property in jeopardy?

(d) What was Mr. Gilmore's "primary purpose" in incurring the expenses he sought to deduct? Would primary purpose be a better test than "origins"?

(e) Are Mr. Gilmore's fees like casualty losses? Medical expenses? Commuting expenses? Does the answer depend on the incidence of divorce among people like the Gilmores?

2. *The scope of* Gilmore. In a companion case, United States v. Patrick, 372 U.S. 53 (1963), the Supreme Court held nondeductible a husband's payments to his and his wife's attorneys for services in connection with another divorce where there was a private settlement of various property interests. The Court held that *Gilmore* was controlling:

> We find no significant distinction in the fact that [in *Patrick*] the legal fees for which the deduction is claimed were paid for arranging a transfer of stock interests, leasing real property, and creating a trust rather than for conducting litigation. These matters were incidental to litigation brought by respondent's wife, whose claims arising from respondent's personal and family life were the origin of the property arrangements.

372 U.S. at 57. Do you agree that *Gilmore* is controlling?

---

21. The respondent's attempted analogy of a marital "partnership" to the business partnership involved in the *Kornhauser* case, *supra,* is of course unavailing. The marriage relationship can hardly be deemed an income-producing activity.

3. *Addition to basis.* In a subsequent year, Mr. Gilmore sold some of the stock that had been contested in the divorce actions. He added disallowed attorneys' fees to the basis of his stock as capitalized costs of defending title. Prior cases had allowed the addition of such costs to basis. See Gilmore v. United States, 245 F. Supp. 383, 384 (N.D. Cal. 1965). The government contended that the reasoning of the Supreme Court in United States v. Gilmore should also be applied to basis questions. The District Court held for the taxpayer, finding that costs of defending title are capital expenses whether arising in suits primarily business or personal in character. The court conceded that legal expenses may not be added to basis in some personal suits because "as a factual matter, the expenses would not have been primarily to defend title." Suppose that a taxpayer is sued for alleged personal debts and a lien is placed on his personal residence, which is his only asset. May the cost of defending against the suit be added to his basis for the house?

4. *Criminal defense.* In Accardo v. Commissioner, 942 F.2d 444 (7th Cir. 1991), the taxpayer, Anthony Accardo, had successfully defended himself in a criminal prosecution for violation of the Racketeer Influenced and Corrupt Organizations Act (RICO). Accardo was "the reputed head of the Chicago organized crime family." See United States v. Guzzino, 810 F.2d 687, 690 (7th Cir.), cert. denied, 481 U.S. 1030 (1987). He was accused of having taken "kickbacks from a union insurance program." Some of his codefendants were convicted and were allowed to deduct their legal fees as ordinary and necessary business expenses, under §162. Accardo could not claim a deduction under §162 because he was acquitted (and presumably was not willing to argue that the acquittal was a mistake or an artifact of the rules for establishing criminal liability). Because of the acquittal he was not in the trade or business of racketeering, so his legal expenses could not be trade or business expenses. Thus, the guilty criminal defendants were treated better by the tax system than innocent defendants. In reaching this result, which it calls "paradoxical," the Seventh Circuit opinion relies in part on *Gilmore.*

Accardo in effect conceded that he was not entitled to a deduction under §162 and claimed instead that the cost of his legal defense was deductible under §212 as the cost of protecting certain assets from seizure by the government under provisions of RICO for forfeiture of the fruits of criminal activity. The court rejected this claim on the ground that the assets that Accardo claimed he sought to protect were not in fact traceable to any criminal activity and therefore were not subject to forfeiture. The court found Accardo's argument so lacking in merit that it sustained a penalty for negligence and a penalty for substantial underpayment of tax (two separate penalties that are now combined in §6662).

What if the government had alleged that Accardo's assets were in fact traceable to the racketeering activity of which he was accused, but, as in the actual case, he was acquitted?

G.   HOBBY LOSSES

NICKERSON v. COMMISSIONER
700 F.2d 402 (7th Cir. 1983)

PELL, Circuit Judge.

Petitioners appeal the judgment of the United States Tax Court finding that profit was not their primary goal in owning a dairy farm. Based on this finding the tax court disallowed deductions for losses incurred in renovating the farm. The sole issue presented for our review is whether the tax court's finding regarding petitioners' motivation was clearly erroneous.

I.   FACTS

Melvin Nickerson (hereinafter referred to as petitioner) was born in 1932 in a farming community in Florida. He worked evenings and weekends on his father's farm until he was 17. Petitioner entered the field of advertising after attending college and serving in the United States Army. During the years relevant to this case he was self-employed in Chicago, serving industrial and agricultural clients. His wife, Naomi W. Nickerson, was a full-time employee of the Chicago Board of Education. While petitioners were not wealthy, they did earn a comfortable living.

At the age of forty, petitioner decided that his career in the "youth oriented" field of advertising would not last much longer, and he began to look for an alternative source of income for the future. Petitioners decided that dairy farming was the most desirable means of generating income and examined a number of farms in Michigan and Wisconsin. After several years of searching, petitioners bought an 80-acre farm in Door County, Wisconsin for $40,000. One year later they purchased an additional 40 acres adjoining the farm for $10,000.

The farm, which had not been run as a dairy for eight years, was in a run-down condition. What little equipment was left was either in need of repair or obsolete. The tillable land, about 60 acres, was planted with alfalfa, which was at the end of its productive cycle. In an effort to improve this state of affairs petitioners leased the land to a tenant farmer for $20 an acre and an agreement that the farmer would convert an additional ten acres a year to the cultivation of a more profitable crop. At the time of trial approximately 80 acres were tillable. The rent received from the farmer was the only income derived from the farm.

Petitioner visited the farm on most weekends during the growing season and twice a month the rest of the year. Mrs. Nickerson and the children visited less frequently. The trip to the farm requires five hours of driving from petitioners' home in Chicago. During these visits petitioner and his family either worked on their land or assisted neighboring farmers. When working on his own farm petitioner concentrated his efforts on renovating an abandoned orchard and remodeling the farm house. In addition to learning about farming through this experience petitioner read a number of trade journals and spoke with the area agricultural extension agent.

Petitioners did not expect to make a profit from the farm for approximately 10 years. True to their expectations, petitioners lost $8,668 in 1976 and $9,872.95 in 1977. Although they did not keep formal books of account petitioners did retain receipts and cancelled checks relating to farm expenditures. At the time of trial, petitioners had not yet acquired any livestock or farm machinery. The farm was similarly devoid of recreational equipment and had never been used to entertain guests.

The tax court decided that these facts did not support petitioners' claim that the primary goal in operating the farm was to make a profit. We will examine the tax court's reasoning in more detail after setting out the relevant legal considerations.

II. THE STATUTORY SCHEME

Section 162(a) of the Code allows deduction of "all the ordinary and necessary expenses paid or incurred during the taxable year in carrying on any trade or business." Section 183, however, limits the availability of these deductions if the activity "is not engaged in for profit" to deductions that are allowed regardless of the existence of a profit motive and deductions for ordinary and necessary expenses "only to the extent that the gross income derived from such activity for the taxable year exceeds [otherwise allowable deductions]." §183(b)(2). The deductions claimed by petitioners are only allowable if their motivation in investing in the farm was to make a profit.

Petitioners bear the burden of proving that their primary purpose in renovating the farm was to make a profit.[22] . . . In meeting this burden, however, "it is sufficient if the taxpayer has a bona fide expectation of realizing a profit, regardless of the reasonableness of such expectation." . . . Although petitioners need only prove their sincerity rather than their realism the factors considered in judging their motivation are primarily objective. In addition to the taxpayer's statements of intent, which are given little weight for obvious reasons, the tax court must consider "all facts and circumstances with respect to the activity," including the following:

(1) *Manner in which the taxpayer carries on the activity.* The fact that the taxpayer carries on the activity in a businesslike manner and maintains complete and accurate books and records may indicate that the activity is engaged in for profit. . . .

(2) *The expertise of the taxpayer or his advisors.* Preparation for the activity by extensive study of its accepted business, economic, and scientific practices, or

---

22. The Code does provide a presumption that a taxpayer engaged in an activity with a bona fide profit motive when a profit is realized two of five consecutive years. §183(d). Because of petitioners' consistent losses this is not available. [The rule has now been changed from two of five to three of five consecutive years. — EDS.]

consultation with those who are expert therein, may indicate that the taxpayer has a profit motive where the taxpayer carries on the activity in accordance with such practices. . . .

(3) *The time and effort expended by the taxpayer in carrying on the activity.* The fact that the taxpayer devotes much of his personal time and effort to carrying on the activity, particularly if the activity does not have substantial personal or recreational aspects, may indicate an intention to derive a profit. . . . The fact that the taxpayer devotes a limited amount of time to an activity does not necessarily indicate a lack of profit motive where the taxpayer employs competent and qualified persons to carry on such activity.

(4) *Expectation that assets used in activity may appreciate in value.* . . .

(5) *The success of the taxpayer in carrying on other similar or dissimilar activities.* . . .

(6) *The taxpayer's history of income or losses with respect to the activity.* . . .

(7) *The amount of occasional profits, if any, which are earned.* . . .

(8) *The financial status of the taxpayer.* . . .

(9) *Elements of personal pleasure or recreation.* The presence of personal motives in [the] carrying on of an activity may indicate that the activity is not engaged in for profit, especially where there are recreational or personal elements involved. On the other hand, a profit motivation may be indicated where an activity lacks any appeal other than profit. It is not, however, necessary that an activity be engaged in with the exclusive intention of deriving a profit or with the intention of maximizing profits. . . .

Treas. Reg. §1.183-2(b)(1)-(9). None of these factors is determinative, nor is the decision to be made by comparing the number of factors that weigh in the taxpayer's favor with the number that support the Commissioner. *Id.* There is no set formula for divining a taxpayer's true motive, rather "[o]ne struggles in vain for any verbal formula that will supply a ready touchstone. The standard set by the statute is not a rule of law; it is rather a way of life. Life in all its fullness must supply the answer to the riddle." Welch v. Helvering. Nonetheless, we are given some guidance by the enumerated factors and by the Congressional purpose in enacting section 183.

> The legislative history surrounding section 183 indicates that one of the prime motivating factors behind its passage was Congress' desire to create an objective standard to determine whether a taxpayer was carrying on a business for the purpose of realizing a profit or was instead merely attempting to create and utilize losses to offset other income.

Jasionowski v. Commissioner, 66 T.C. 312, 321 (1976). Congressional concern stemmed from a recognition that

> [w]ealthy individuals have invested in certain aspects of farm operations solely to obtain "tax losses"—largely bookkeeping losses—for use to reduce their tax on other income. . . . One of the remarkable aspects of the problem is pointed up by the fact that persons with large nonfarm income have a remarkable propensity to lose money in the farm business.

S. Rep. No. 91-552, 91st Cong., 1st Sess., reprinted in 1969 U.S. Code Cong. & Ad. News 2027, 2376. With this concern in mind we will now examine the decision of the tax court.

III.   Decision of the Tax Court

The tax court analyzed the relevant factors and determined that making a profit was not petitioners' primary goal in engaging in farming. The court based its decision on a number of factors that weighed against petitioners. The court found that they did not operate the farm in a businesslike manner and did not appear to have a concrete plan for improving the profitability of the farm. The court believed that these difficulties were attributable to petitioners' lack of experience, but did not discuss the steps actually taken by Melvin Nickerson to gain experience in farming.

The court found it difficult to believe that petitioners actually believed that the limited amount of time they were spending at the farm would produce a profit given the dilapidated condition of the farm. Furthermore, the court found that petitioners' emphasis on making the farm house habitable rather than on acquiring or repairing farm equipment was inconsistent with a profit motive. These factors, combined with the consistent history of losses borne by petitioners, convinced the court that "petitioner at best entertains the hope that when he retires from the advertising business and can devote his complete attention to the farming operation, he may at that time expect to produce a profit." The court did not think that this hope rose to the level of a bona fide expectation of profit.

IV.   Review of the Court's Findings

Whether petitioners intended to run the dairy farm for a profit is a question of fact, and as such our review is limited to a determination of whether the tax court was "clearly erroneous" in determining that petitioners lacked the requisite profit motive. . . . This standard of review applies although the only dispute is over the proper interpretation of uncontested facts. . . . This is one of those rare cases in which we are convinced that a mistake has been made.

Our basic disagreement with the tax court stems from our belief that the court improperly evaluated petitioners' actions from the perspective of whether they sincerely believed that they could make a profit from their current level of activity at the farm. On the contrary, petitioners need only prove that their current actions were motivated by the expectation that they would later reap a profit, in this case when they finished renovating the farm and began full-time operations. It is well established that a taxpayer need not expect an immediate profit; the existence of "start up" losses does not preclude a bona fide profit motive. . . . We see no basis for distinguishing petitioners' actions from a situation in which one absorbs larger losses over a shorter period of time by beginning full-time operations immediately. In either situation the taxpayer stands an equal chance of recouping start-up losses. In fact, it seems to us a reasonable decision by petitioners to prepare the farm before becoming dependent upon it for sustenance. Keeping in mind that petitioners were not seeking to supplement their existing incomes with their current work on the farm, but rather were laying the ground work for a contemplated career switch, we will examine the facts relied upon by the tax court.

The tax court found that the amount of time petitioners devoted to the farm was inadequate. In reaching this conclusion the court ignored petitioners' agreement with the tenant-farmer under which he would convert 10 acres a year to profitable crops in exchange for the right to farm the land. In this situation the limited amount of time spent by petitioners, who were fully employed in Chicago, is not inconsistent with an expectation of profit. . . .

The court also rested its decision on the lack of a concrete plan to put the farm in operable condition. Once again, this ignores petitioners' agreement with the tenant-farmer concerning reclamation of the land. Under this agreement the majority of the land would be tillable by the time petitioners were prepared to begin full-time farming. The tax court also believed that petitioners' decision to renovate the farm house and orchard prior to obtaining farm equipment evidenced a lack of profit motive. As petitioners planned to live on the farm when they switched careers refurbishing the house would seem to be a necessary first step. The court also failed to consider the uncontradicted testimony regarding repairs made to the hay barn and equipment shed, which supported petitioners' contention that they were interested in operating a farm rather than just living on the land. Additionally, we fail to understand how renovating the orchard, a potential source of food and income, is inconsistent with an expectation of profit.

The tax court took into account the history of losses in considering petitioners' intentions. While a history of losses is relevant, in this case little weight should be accorded this factor. Petitioners did not expect to make a profit for a number of years, and it was clear from the condition of the farm that a financial investment would be required before the farm could be profitable. . . .

The court believed that most of petitioners' problems were attributable to their lack of expertise. While lack of expertise is relevant, efforts at gaining experience and a willingness to follow expert advice should also be considered. Treas. Reg. §1.183-2(b)(2). The court here failed to consider the uncontradicted evidence that Melvin Nickerson read trade journals and Government-sponsored agricultural newsletters, sought advice from a state horticultural agent regarding renovation of the orchard and gained experience by working on neighboring farms. In addition, petitioners' agreement with the tenant-farmer was entered into on the advice of the area agricultural extension agent. To weigh petitioners' lack of expertise against them without giving consideration to these efforts effectively precludes a bona fide attempt to change careers. We are unwilling to restrict petitioners in this manner and believe that a proper interpretation of these facts supports petitioners' claims.

The tax court recognized that the farm was not used for entertainment and lacked any recreational facilities, and that petitioners' efforts at the farm were "prodigious," but felt that this was of little importance. While the Commissioner need not prove that petitioners were motivated by goals other than making a profit, we think that more weight should be given to the absence of any alternative explanation for petitioners' actions. As we previously noted the standard set out by the statute is to be applied with the insight gained from a lifetime of experience as well as an understanding of the statutory scheme. Common sense indicates to us that rational people do not perform hard manual labor for no reason, and if the possibility that petitioners performed these labors for pleasure is eliminated the only remaining motivation is profit. The Commissioner has argued that petitioner was motivated by a love of farming that stems from his childhood. We find it difficult to believe that he drove five hours in order to spend his weekends working on a dilapidated farm solely for fun, or that his family derived much pleasure from the experience. Furthermore, there is no support for this contention in the record. At any rate, that petitioner may have chosen farming over some other career because of fond memories of his youth does not preclude a bona fide profit motive. Treas. Reg. §1.183-2(b)(9). We believe that the absence of any recreational purpose strongly counsels in favor of finding that petitioners' prodigious efforts were directed at making a profit. . . .

If this were a case in which wealthy taxpayers were seeking to obtain tax benefits through the creation of paper losses we would hesitate to reverse. Before us today, however, is a family of modest means attempting to prepare for a stable financial future. The amount of time and hard work invested by petitioners belies any claim that allowing these deductions would thwart Congress' primary purpose, that of excluding "hobby" losses from permissible deductions. Accordingly, we hold that the tax court's finding was clearly erroneous and reverse.

NOTES AND QUESTIONS

1. *Hobby losses and tax losses.* Since the court in *Nickerson* holds that the Nickersons' farm activity was a business and not a hobby, the losses incurred in running the farm are deductible — that is, those losses can be used to offset the Nickersons' salary and other income. Assuming that the Nickersons reasonably and realistically viewed their cash outlays on the farm not as money down the drain (a true economic loss) but rather as an investment in what they hoped would be a valuable asset, their loss can be thought of as an artifact of the tax system, a "tax loss" that is not a true economic loss.

2. *Start-up costs.* Although the Tax Court opinion in *Nickerson* does not describe the outlays that gave rise to the deductible losses, it seems clear that on the court's view of the taxpayers' primary objective, those outlays were made for the purpose of creating a productive farm; they were part of the farm's start-up costs. For purposes of normal accounting, such outlays should be treated as capital expenditures; they are part of the cost of acquisition of a productive farm, not current expenses. For tax purposes, however, the outlays are treated as deductible expenses, at least for a cash method farmer. (The distinction between capital expenditures and current expenses is explored in Chapter 6.) On the government's view of the case, the distinction between capital and current outlays was irrelevant to the outcome of the case it was litigating, since the outlays were simply the personal cost of indulging a desire to play farmer. The distinction would, however, be relevant to basis and thus to gain on disposition. If a person buys a farm for purely personal purposes, the acquisition cost becomes the farm's basis, which affects gain or loss on ultimate disposition. Though a loss would not be deductible, a gain would be taxable. Expenses of maintaining the farm (current outlays) would not be added

to basis and thus would not reduce any gain that might otherwise be realized on disposition, but even for a farm owned for personal purposes, capital outlays would increase basis.

In McCarthy v. Commissioner, 164 F.3d 618 (2d Cir. 1998), the Tax Court had held that, because of a lack of profit motive, McCarthy was not entitled to deduct losses incurred in "managing and promoting his 13-year-old son's motocross racing career." The Second Circuit reversed and remanded on the ground that the Tax Court had improperly reasoned that since the son was an amateur and could not earn prize or endorsement money, no profit motive was possible. The Second Circuit, citing *Nickerson*, stated that "the inability to make a profit in a particular tax year is not dispositive," and held that all the facts bearing on long-term profit motive must be weighed. It went on to state, however, that on remand the Tax Court should consider the "pre-opening expense" doctrine, under which "expenses incurred before a taxpayer begins business operations [must] be capitalized." The court noted that this possibility had been "mentioned in the Commissioner's brief on this appeal." *Nickerson* is distinguishable on this issue because farmers are allowed to deduct currently many outlays that would be treated as capital expenditures in other businesses.

3. *Primary purpose.* (a) The *Nickerson* court follows the typical approach in cases involving activities with both business and personal elements: It seeks to determine the taxpayer's primary purpose. The objectively observed facts reviewed by the court are indirect evidence of purpose. The court insists, however, that the taxpayers "need only prove their sincerity rather than their realism." In other words, a person might establish a sincere intent to make a profit even though the hope or expectation of profit is unrealistic. How important are the nine factors listed in the regulations (§1.183-2(b)) and cited by the court? See the last sentence of Reg. §1.183-2(a).

(b) Is the court's decision too trusting and generous? Why do you suppose the farm had been abandoned eight years before the Nickersons bought it?

4. *An alternative approach.* Is primary purpose the best test? Why not focus on benefit? Suppose, for example, that it could be established that the Nickersons had lost (and had expected to lose) $10,000 per year, that the farm was not as good an investment as other alternatives available to them, but that it became a good investment when they took account of the fact that it provided $6,000 worth of pleasure each year. How much deduction, if any, would you allow? What if the pleasure had been worth only $4,000 per year? Is it feasible to determine the value of the pleasure element? Less so than to determine primary purpose? If you don't like either approach because of the difficulty of the factual determinations, what objective approach would you prefer?

5. *The role of §183.* (a) Does §183 provide much guidance with respect to the basic question of deductibility in cases like *Nickerson*?

(b) Note the presumption rule in §183(d). Where applicable, this rule overcomes the normal presumption of correctness of the Commissioner's determination. Did that presumption seem important in *Nickerson*?

10

PERSONAL DEDUCTIONS, EXEMPTIONS, AND CREDITS

A. INTRODUCTION

In the previous chapters, we have focused on the definition of business expenses, or expenses of earning income. These expenses are properly deducted against gross income to arrive at adjusted gross income, though, as we have seen, that deduction is sometimes limited for administrative or revenue-generating reasons.

But what about expenditures that are unrelated to the production of income? Is there any place in an income tax for deductions for those types of expenses? And if so, what is the rationale for such deductions? In the materials that follow, we will refer to these deductions somewhat generically as "personal deductions," but note that this is not a legal term but rather just shorthand for deductions unrelated to the cost of producing income. A similar set of questions arises from certain exemptions from income, most notably that for employer-provided healthcare. As discussed earlier in the book, the exemption from income for health benefits has the same effect as including that benefit in income and then allowing a deduction for the expenditure. What justifies this exemption?

1. The Basic Structure of Personal Deductions

Once adjusted gross income (AGI) is determined, taxpayers are presented with a choice on their return: They may either take the standard deduction or itemize their personal deductions. The standard deduction varies with the individual's filing status and is indexed for inflation. In 2018, the standard deduction is $12,000 for single individuals and $24,000 for married individuals filing jointly. §63(c)(2). Itemized personal deductions are listed on Schedule A and are discussed in this chapter.

In 2013, almost 95 percent of taxpayers with adjusted gross income of $25,000 or less took the standard deduction, while a majority of taxpayers with adjusted gross income of over $75,000 itemized. The current standard deduction is much higher than the standard deduction effective in 2013, and many of the personal itemized deductions available in 2013 have been reduced. It therefore seems likely that only upper-middle-class and high-income taxpayers will now be itemizing their deductions. Everyone else will be taking the standard deduction.

2.   The Rationale for Personal Deductions

What justifies allowing personal deductions within an income tax? On the one hand, a deduction may be a proper allowance in arriving at a definition of income that accords with attempting to measure ability to pay. On the other hand, a deduction may be intended as an express approval of, or encouragement to, particular kinds of expenditures, in which case the deduction can sensibly be analogized to a direct subsidy. The use of deductions as subsidies is often attacked on the ground that the amount of the subsidy increases as income rises, since a deduction is worth nothing to a poor person and more to a high-bracket person than to a low-bracket person. For this reason, certain personal deductions are sometimes labeled "upside-down" subsidies—subsidies that benefit the most those who need them the least. For whatever it's worth, Henry Simons (of the Haig-Simons definition of income) believed there should be no personal deductions. Personal deductions are also eliminated or cut back under many simplification proposals, including under the so-called flat-tax.[1]

In the materials that follow, we will examine the most significant personal deductions allowed under the U.S. federal income tax. Bear in mind, however, that the availability of a deduction for a particular expenditure does not necessarily reflect a stable consensus in favor of the allowance. For example, until 2018, the tax law allowed "personal exemption" deductions for taxpayers and their dependents. That deduction, which was more valuable to taxpayers with large families, is now suspended until 2026. More generally, the Code contains a set of tax rules—the alternative minimum tax (AMT)—that has for many years reduced the benefit of some otherwise favorable provisions. The AMT's differential treatment of certain expenditures perhaps suggests some ambivalence regarding what sort of adjustments are appropriate within an "income" tax. We discuss the AMT *infra*, at the end of this chapter.

---

1. E.g., Robert E. Hall and Alvin Rabushka, *The Flat Tax* 90 (2d ed. 2007).

SCHEDULE A (Form 1040)	Itemized Deductions	OMB No. 1545-0074
Department of the Treasury Internal Revenue Service (99)	Go to www.irs.gov/ScheduleA for instructions and the latest information. ▶ Attach to Form 1040. Caution: If you are claiming a net qualified disaster loss on Form 4684, see the instructions for line 28.	**2017** Attachment Sequence No. **07**

Name(s) shown on Form 1040: **TIMOTHY J & GWEN L WALZ**   Your social security number

Medical and Dental Expenses

Caution: Do not include expenses reimbursed or paid by others.
1. Medical and dental expenses (see instructions) ... **1**
2. Enter amount from Form 1040, line 38 | **2** | 211,434
3. Multiply line 2 by 7.5% (0.075) ... **3** | 15,858
4. Subtract line 3 from line 1. If line 3 is more than line 1, enter -0- ... **4**

Taxes You Paid

5. State and local (check only one box):
   a [X] Income taxes, or
   b [ ] General sales taxes } ... **5** | 11,802
6. Real estate taxes (see instructions) ... **6** | 2,590
7. Personal property taxes ... **7**
8. Other taxes. List type and amount ▶ ... **8**
9. Add lines 5 through 8 ... **9** | 14,392

Interest You Paid

Note: Your mortgage interest deduction may be limited (see instructions).

10. Home mortgage interest and points reported to you on Form 1098 ... **10** | 10,495
11. Home mortgage interest not reported to you on Form 1098. If paid to the person from whom you bought the home, see instructions and show that person's name, identifying no., and address ... **11**
12. Points not reported to you on Form 1098. See instructions for special rules ... **12**
13. Mortgage insurance premiums (see instructions) ... **13**
14. Investment interest. Attach Form 4952 if required. See instructions. ... **14**
15. Add lines 10 through 14 ... **15** | 10,495

Gifts to Charity

If you made a gift and got a benefit for it, see instructions.

16. Gifts by cash or check. If you made any gift of $250 or more, see instructions ... **16** | 3,200
17. Other than by cash or check. If any gift of $250 or more, see instructions. You **must** attach Form 8283 if over $500 ... **17** | 1,770
18. Carryover from prior year ... **18**
19. Add lines 16 through 18 ... **19** | 4,970

Casualty and Theft Losses

20. Casualty or theft loss(es) other than net qualified disaster losses. Attach Form 4684 and enter the amount from line 18 of that form. See instructions ... **20**

Job Expenses and Certain Miscellaneous Deductions

21. Unreimbursed employee expenses—job travel, union dues, job education, etc. Attach Form 2106 or 2106-EZ if required. See instructions. ▶ ... **21**
22. Tax preparation fees ... **22**
23. Other expenses—investment, safe deposit box, etc. List type and amount ▶ ... **23**
24. Add lines 21 through 23 ... **24**
25. Enter amount from Form 1040, line 38 | **25** | 211,434
26. Multiply line 25 by 2% (0.02) ... **26** | 4,229
27. Subtract line 26 from line 24. If line 26 is more than line 24, enter -0- ... **27**

Other Miscellaneous Deductions

28. Other—from list in instructions. List type and amount ▶ ... **28**

Total Itemized Deductions

29. Is Form 1040, line 38, over $156,900?
   [ ] No. Your deduction is not limited. Add the amounts in the far right column for lines 4 through 28. Also, enter this amount on Form 1040, line 40.
   [X] Yes. Your deduction may be limited. See the Itemized Deductions Worksheet in the instructions to figure the amount to enter. ... **29** | 29,857
30. If you elect to itemize deductions even though they are less than your standard deduction, check here ▶ [ ]

For Paperwork Reduction Act Notice, see the Instructions for Form 1040.   Schedule A (Form 1040) 2017

DAA

B. CASUALTY LOSSES

Until 2018, taxpayers were allowed under §165(c)(3) to deduct certain losses from "fire, storm, shipwreck, or other casualty, or from theft." This so-called casualty loss deduction raised difficult interpretive issues. Could a lost ring constitute a casualty loss? Damage from a fire you set yourself? From a fire your husband set to terrorize you, if you file a joint return with him? See

Kielts v. Commissioner, 42 T.C.M. 238 (1981); Blackman v. Commissioner, 69 T.C. 677 (1987). The casualty loss was limited by a requirement that imposed a $100 deductible, and then only allowed a deduction in the amount that losses exceeded 10 percent of AGI. The 2017 act suspends the casualty loss deduction through the year 2025.[2]

C.   MEDICAL EXPENSES: EXCLUSION FOR EMPLOYER-PROVIDED HEALTHCARE AND DEDUCTION FOR EXTRAORDINARY MEDICAL EXPENSES

1.   Overview and Policy

Americans spent an estimated $2 trillion on healthcare in 2016. At least half of total spending came from employees using their employer-provided health insurance. As discussed in Chapter 2, the value of employer provided insurance, and the receipt of benefits under that insurance, is exempt from both income and payroll tax. The exemption has the effect of a deduction—but without the limitations that come with most deductions (e.g., deductions available only if expenses exceed a certain percentage of AGI or that may be taken only by itemizers).

The exemption of about $1 trillion in employer-provided health insurance from income tax is estimated to cost the government between $150 billion (Joint Committee) and $200 billion (Treasury Department) a year. It is the largest single tax expenditure.

Suppose an individual doesn't have employer-provided insurance but instead buys her own policy or pays for healthcare on a visit-by-visit basis. Section 213 provides a deduction for medical expenses—but only to the extent they exceed 7.5 percent of adjusted gross income in 2018, and 10 percent thereafter. The threshold seems to reflect the same kind of effort to distinguish between extraordinary misfortune and the ordinary vicissitudes of life that was reflected in the now-suspended casualty loss deduction. The deduction is much less generous to taxpayers, and much less costly to the fisc, than the exemption.

Which represents the better policy: the limited deduction or unlimited exemption? Tax policy analysts generally favor the deduction over the exemption; or at the very least, they do not like the exemption. The exemption goes to individuals who are working, and generally working at well-paying jobs. As a result, it goes to individuals who are healthier and wealthier than average. Its effect on health seems to be rather small; it certainly improves health less than an equivalent amount spent in a cost-effective manner on areas of greatest

---

2. There are a few small exceptions to the suspension. For example, the section will still apply to losses suffered in a presidentially declared disaster area and for losses that offset casualty gains.

need.[3] Finally, it appears to significantly drive up health expenditures and costs. This occurs because the tax subsidy reduces the effective cost of health-care, so more is purchased. In addition, the subsidy requires the taxpayer to have health insurance, and once insured, the taxpayer's expense is limited to copays and deductibles. This further increases the amount of health services utilized, which drives up costs.

Three other healthcare tax provisions deserve mention. First, employees whose employers set up "cafeteria plans," discussed briefly in Chapter 2, can set aside up to $2,650 a year to set up flexible health spending accounts. This amount is indexed for inflation. These amounts can and must be spent during the year on medical expenses.[4] The amount set aside for this purpose are exempt from income and payroll taxes. Employees who benefit from these plans, like employees with employer-provided insurance in general, tend to be wealthier than average.

Second, Congress has tried to encourage taxpayers to purchase high-deductible insurance through "Health Savings Accounts." High-deductible insurance is thought desirable because it leads taxpayers to be more careful about incurring medical expenses, since until they reach their deductible, they will be spending their own money. In general, under §223, an individual can contribute an amount equal to her deductible to a Health Savings Account and deduct that amount. She can then use the funds in her Health Savings Account to pay medical expenses.

Unfortunately, §223 is not well designed. It is more generous than it needs to be, and for the well-informed, it can serve as an additional form of tax-deferred savings. At the same time, the provision is too complex for many taxpayers to understand or use.

Finally, many receive medical care that is free or subsidized through government programs such as Medicaid or the Affordable Care Act. As is true of welfare in general, the value of that is not subject to tax.

2. What Is "Medical Care"?

Section 213 allows a deduction for "medical expenses," which are defined in §213(d) to include amounts paid for the diagnosis, cure, mitigation, treatment, or prevention of disease, or for the purpose of affecting any structure or function of the body, as well as for transportation necessary for treatment, and certain long-term care expenses.

At one time, expenses under §213 were allowed without an AGI threshold, giving taxpayers an incentive to recast ordinary (and in some cases, luxury) expenditures as deductible "medical expenses." In one case, a taxpayer

---

3. For discussion of these and other points discussed in this section, see Joseph Bankman et al., *Reforming the Tax Preference for Employer Health Insurance*, 26 Tax Pol'y & Econ. 43 (2012).

4. Employers are allowed to offer one of two limited options for employees who do not use all their benefits during the year. Under one option, employees are allowed to carry over $500 of benefits to the following year; under another option, they are given a two-and-a-half-month grace period in which to use their benefits.

deducted the cost of a four-star hotel and spa on the grounds that it was tied to "[weight] reduction therapy."[5] In another, a taxpayer deducted the cost of trips to Florida on the grounds that a "warm climate" was good for his heart condition.[6] The first case that follows, Taylor v. Commissioner, falls in this category.

The 7.5 percent AGI threshold for 2018 and 10 percent thereafter removes small-stakes litigation under §213. The definition of medical expense is still important with respect to larger items of expense. It is also important in governing the use of cafeteria plans with flexible health spending accounts. As noted immediately above, wages that go to these accounts are exempt from taxation. The exemption is conditioned, however, on the use of the accounts to pay for "medical expenses."

The government rarely, if ever, tries to tax benefits provided under conventional health insurance policies on the grounds that they are not for "medical expenses." Presumably, this reflects the belief that insurers have an incentive to monitor claims and restrict benefits to a core category of medical expenses.

TAYLOR v. COMMISSIONER
54 T.C.M. 129 (1987)

. . . Due to a severe allergy, petitioner's doctor instructed him not to mow his lawn. Petitioner in 1982 paid a total of $178 to have his lawn mowed and claimed a medical expense deduction in that amount for lawn care.

. . . Petitioner contends that since his doctor had advised him not to mow his lawn, he is entitled to a deduction for amounts he paid someone else to do his lawn mowing. Respondent contends the amounts paid by petitioner for lawn mowing are nondeductible personal expenses under section 262 rather than section 213 medical expenses.

Except as otherwise specifically provided, section 262 disallows deductions for personal, living or family expenses. Section 213, however, specifically authorizes a deduction for medical care expenses paid during the taxable year which are not compensated for by insurance or otherwise. . . .

In this case, petitioner, bearing the burden of proof . . . must establish that the apparently personal expense of lawn care is a medical expense. Petitioner has cited no authority to support his position either in general or with respect to lawn care expenses specifically. Petitioner testified that due to a severe allergy his doctor had directed him not to perform lawn care activities but there was no showing why other family members could not undertake these activities or whether petitioner would have paid others to mow his lawn even absent his doctor's direction not to do so himself.

Doctor recommended activities have been held in a number of cases not to constitute deductible medical expenses where the expenses did not fall within the parameters of "medical care." For example, in Altman v. Commissioner, 53 T.C. 487 (1969), this Court held that the expense of playing golf was not

---

5. Murray v. Comm'r, 43 T.C.M. (CCH) 1377, 1378 (1982).
6. Estate of Levine, 43 T.C.M. (CCH) 259, 264 (1982).

a deductible medical expense even though this activity was recommended by the taxpayer's doctor as treatment for his emphysema and provided therapeutic benefits. On this record we conclude that petitioner has not carried his burden of proof with respect to the deduction of lawn care costs as a medical expense and is thus not entitled to include the $178 expended for lawn care in his medical expense deductions.

Decision will be entered for the respondent.

OCHS v. COMMISSIONER
195 F.2d 692 (2d Cir. 1952)

Before AUGUSTUS N. HAND, CHASE and FRANK, Circuit Judges.
AUGUSTUS N. HAND, Circuit Judge. . . .
The Tax Court made the following findings:

> During the taxable year petitioner was the husband of Helen H. Ochs. They had two children, Josephine age six and Jeanne age four.
>
> On December 10, 1943, a thyroidectomy was performed on petitioner's wife. A histological examination disclosed [cancer]. . . . During the taxable year [1946] the petitioner maintained his two children in day school during the first half of the year and in boarding school during the latter half of the year at a cost of [$1,450]. Petitioner deducted this sum from his income for the year 1946 as a medical expense under [§213].
>
> During the taxable year . . . [efforts by Helen] to speak were painful, required much of her strength, and left her in a highly nervous state. . . . Petitioner and his wife consulted a reputable physician and were advised by him that if the children were not separated from petitioner's wife she would not improve and her nervousness and irritation might cause a recurrence of the cancer. Petitioner continued to maintain his children in boarding school [until 1948] . . . having been advised that if there was no recurrence . . . during that time his wife could be considered as having recovered from the cancer.
>
> During the taxable year petitioner's income was between $5,000 and $6,000. Petitioner's two children have not attended private school but have lived at home and attended public school since [1948]. . . .

In our opinion the expenses incurred by the taxpayer were nondeductible family expenses within the meaning of [§262] rather than medical expenses. Concededly the line between the two is a difficult one to draw, but this only reflects the fact that expenditures made on behalf of some members of a family unit frequently benefit others in the family as well. . . . If, for example, the husband had employed a governess for the children, or a cook, the wages he would have paid would not be deductible. Or, if the wife had died, and the children were sent to a boarding school, there would certainly be no basis for contending that such expenses were deductible. The examples given serve to illustrate that the expenses here were made necessary by the loss of the wife's services, and that the only reason for allowing them as a deduction is that the wife also received a benefit. We think it unlikely that Congress intended to transform family expenses into medical expenses for this reason. . . .

The decision is affirmed.

FRANK, Circuit Judge (dissenting). . . .

The Commissioner, the Tax Court, and now my colleagues, are certain Congress did not intend relief for a man in this grave plight. The truth is, of course, no one knows what Congress would have said if it had been faced with these facts. The few paltry sentences of Congressional history for [§213] do not lend strong support—indeed any support at all—to a strict construction theory:

> This allowance is granted in consideration of the heavy tax burden that must be borne by industry during the existing emergency [1942] and of the desirability of maintaining the present high level of public health and morale. . . . The term "medical care" is broadly defined to include amounts paid for the diagnosis, cure, mitigation, treatment, or prevention of disease, or for the purpose of affecting any structure or function of the body. It is not intended, however, that a deduction should be allowed for any expense that is not incurred primarily for the prevention or alleviation of a physical or mental defect or illness.[7]

I think that Congress would have said that this man's expense fell within the category of "mitigation, treatment, or prevention of disease," and that it was for the "purpose of affecting [a] structure or function of the body." . . . The Commissioner seemingly admits that the deduction might be a medical expense if the wife were sent away from her children to a sanitarium for rest and quiet, but asserts that it never can be if, for the very same purpose, the children are sent away from the mother—even if a boarding-school for the children is cheaper than a sanitarium for the wife. "I cannot believe that Congress intended such a meaningless distinction. . . ."[8] The cure ought to be the doctor's business, not the Commissioner's. . . .

In the final analysis, the Commissioner, the Tax Court and my colleagues all seem to reject Mr. Ochs' plea because of the nightmarish spectacle of opening the floodgates to cases involving expense for cooks, governesses, baby-sitters, nourishing food, clothing, frigidaires, electric dish-washers—in short, allowances as medical expenses for everything "helpful to a convalescent housewife or to one who is nervous or weak from past illness." I, for one, trust the Commissioner to make short shrift of most such claims. The tests should be: Would the taxpayer, considering his income and his living standard, normally spend money in this way regardless of illness? Has he enjoyed such luxuries or services in the past?

---

7. Sen. Rep. 1631, 77th Cong., 2d Sess. 95-96 (1942).

8. The Commissioner has, in the past, shown more liberal tendencies in sanctioning somewhat unorthodox kinds of treatment as contemplated by the statute: He has allowed the deduction of fees paid to chiropractors and Christian Science practitioners. I.T. 3598, 1943 C.B. 157. He should not, in this context, lag behind the progress of the medical art. Especially in this case should the Commissioner realize the growing emphasis placed by medical practitioners upon peace of mind as a major factor in the recovery of patients from what were formerly thought to be entirely organic diseases. If the wife here had been recovering from a nervous breakdown, it could not be sensibly argued that the cure did not fit the disease. Are we ready now to discount the uncontroverted evidence of the doctor in this case that peace of mind and body (it takes not only mental but physical gymnastics to keep up with two children aged four and six) was essential to recovery from, and prevention of, a throat cancer? [See Ring v. Commissioner, 23 T.C. 950 (1955) (disallowing cost of trip to shrine at Lourdes).—EDS.]

Did a competent physician prescribe this specific expense as an indispensable part of the treatment? Has the taxpayer followed the physician's advice in the most economical way possible? Are the so-called medical expenses over and above what the patient would have to pay anyway for his living expenses, that is, room, board, etc.? Is the treatment closely geared to a particular condition and not just to the patient's general good health or well-being?

My colleagues . . . would classify the children's schooling here as a family expense, because, they say, it resulted from the loss of the wife's services. . . . The Tax Court specifically found that the children were sent away so they would not bother the wife, and not because there was no one to take care of them. Ochs' expenditures fit into the Congressional test for medical deductions because he was compelled to go to the expense of putting the children away primarily for the benefit of his sick wife. Expenses incurred solely because of the loss of the patient's services and not as a part of his cure are a different thing altogether. . . . I would limit the deductible expense to the care of the children at the times when they would otherwise be around the mother. . . .

Line-drawing may be difficult here as everywhere, but that is what courts are for. See Lavery v. Purssell, 399 Ch. D. 508, 517: ". . . courts of justice ought not to be puzzled by such old scholastic questions as to where a horse's tail begins and where it ceases. You are obliged to say, this is a horse's tail at some time."

NOTES AND QUESTIONS

1. *Causation.* (a) The expenditure in *Ochs* would not have been incurred but for the illness, which suggests that it should be deductible. It is equally true, however, that the expenditure would not have been incurred but for the children, which suggests that it should not be deductible. (Cf. W. Prosser, *The Law of Torts* 236 (4th ed. 1971): "In a philosophical sense, the consequences of an act go forward to eternity, and the causes back to the discovery of America and beyond.") Is it relevant to ask whether Mr. and Mrs. Ochs made a conscious decision to have children; in the language of torts, whether the children were "preventable"? What about the *Taylor* case? What were the significant necessary antecedents to the expense incurred in that case?

(b) In some cases, of course, a court may reject entirely the taxpayer's claimed causative link. In Jacobs v. Commissioner, 62 T.C. 813 (1974), the taxpayer claimed a deduction under §213 for the lawyer's fees and settlement costs for his divorce, claiming that his psychiatrist had recommended the divorce after the taxpayer had experienced severe depression and suicidal tendencies. The Tax Court concluded that the divorce would have been obtained regardless of the psychiatric problems and denied the deduction. The court distinguished Gerstacher v. Commissioner, 414 F.2d 448 (6th Cir. 1969), which allowed a deduction under §213 of legal fees for a commitment proceeding that was necessary in order to render medical treatment, on the ground that the expenses would not have been incurred but for the illness.

2. *The language of the Code.* The claim for a deduction in *Ochs* may appeal strongly to one's sense of compassion or fairness, but how strong is the statutory basis for the deduction? Was the expenditure for the "cure, mitigation,

treatment, or prevention of disease, or for the purpose of affecting any structure or function of the body"? §213(d)(1)(A). Or was it only for dealing with the consequences of disease? If you interpret §213 to allow a deduction in *Ochs,* would a deduction also be allowed in *Taylor?*

3. *Statutory drafting.* How would you draft the language of a Code provision intended to ensure a deduction in a case like *Ochs?* Would you favor extending the deduction to expenses that would have been incurred by someone like Mr. Ochs in raising his children if Mrs. Ochs had died? If so, what about the child-rearing expenses of other single parents? What about a deduction for all expenses incurred as a result of any physical or mental impairment, illness, or disability, including additional living expenses? Would such a provision promote the goal of fairness? If your answer is yes, what does that imply as to societal obligations to people with an impairment, illness, or disability and no income?

4. *Drawing the line.* (a) Rev. Rul. 75-318, 1975-2 C.B. 88, holds that a taxpayer may deduct as a medical expense the excess of the cost of Braille books and magazines, for his blind child, over the cost of regular printed editions. And Rev. Rul. 64-173, 1964-1 C.B. (Pt. 1) 121, allows a deduction for the cost of hiring a person to accompany the taxpayer's blind child while at school "for the purpose of guiding the child in walking throughout the school day." The rationale is that the purpose of the outlay is to "alleviate the child's physical defect of blindness." Has the Service had a change (addition) of heart since *Ochs?*

(b) Deductions were also allowed for face-lifts (Rev. Rul. 76-332, 76-2 C.B. 81) and for electrolysis but not for tattoos and ear piercing (Rev. Rul. 82-111, 1982-1 C.B. 48). Deductions for "cosmetic surgery" are now limited under §213(d)(9).

(c) Outlays for elevators, swimming pools in one's house, etc., are currently deductible if they are necessitated by illness, though only to the extent that they do not add to the value of the house. Reg. §1.213-1(e)(1)(iii).

(d) In 1996, Congress expressly provided that the costs of long-term care for the "chronically ill," including the cost of "maintenance or personal care services," if provided by a "licensed health care practitioner," are treated as medical expenses under §213, as are premiums paid for insurance for such care, subject to certain dollar limits. See §§213(d)(1)(C), 213(d)(10), 7702B(c).

D. CHARITABLE CONTRIBUTIONS AND TREATMENT OF NONPROFITS

1. Overview

The nonprofit sector accounts for over 5 percent of the gross national product and is comprised of over 1.4 million nonprofits.[9] It is supported by fees

9. Brice S. McKeever, Urban Inst., *The Nonprofit Sector in Brief,* 2015 1 (2015).

for services (such as tuition by private schools), government grants, and dona-tions. In 2013, taxpayers took income tax deductions for charitable donations in the amount of $194 billion;[10] those deductions were estimated to cost the government about $40 billion in 2013.[11] The charitable sector, and the amount of annual donations, has been increasing faster than the economy for many years.[12] Not surprisingly, the amount a taxpayer contributes rises with income, both as an absolute matter and as a percentage of income (since the wealthy will have more disposable income). Since contributions are deductible only by itemizers (who as noted above, are wealthier than the average taxpayer) and the tax benefit of itemizing rises with income, the benefit of contributions also rises with income. One study estimated that those in the top 1 percent of adjusted gross income contribute one-quarter of all charitable donations and receive almost 40 percent of all tax benefits.

As noted at the start of this chapter, the standard deduction now in effect is substantially greater than the deduction in effect in prior years, and some item-ized deductions have been eliminated (e.g., personal exemptions) or scaled back (e.g., deductions for state and local taxes). Fewer middle-class individuals will itemize, and to that extent the cost of the deduction to the fisc will fall. The deduction will become even more concentrated among high-income taxpayers.

Taxpayers at different income levels tend to give to different charities.[13] Low- and middle-income taxpayers are most likely to give to religious organizations, while taxpayers in the highest brackets are most likely to give to schools or health-care organizations.[14] In addition to donating property or money, about a quarter of all Americans volunteered at one or more charitable organizations in 2014.[15]

2.   Rules Governing Charitable Contributions

The Code allows individuals and corporations to claim as itemized deduc-tions any "charitable contribution . . . payment of which is made within the taxable year." §170(a)(1). The term "charitable contribution" is defined to be a "contribution or gift to or for the use of" certain enumerated eligible donees. §170(c). These include the United States and any political subdivisions of it or any of the states, organizations that are "organized and operated exclusively for religious, charitable, scientific, literary, or educational purposes," and cer-tain other enumerated donees. In general, these organizations must operate on a nonprofit basis, and none of their profits can "inure to the benefit of any private shareholder or individual."

Section 170 generally limits allowable deductions for individuals to 60 per-cent of the taxpayer's "contribution base" (which is generally adjusted gross

10. IRS, Pub. No. 1304, Individual Tax Return, 2013 33 tbl. 1.2.

11. Joint Committee on Taxation, *Estimates of Federal Tax Expenditures for Fiscal* 2012-2017, 37-39 tbl.1 (2013).

12. McKeever, *supra* note 9, at 2.

13. Cong. Budget Office, *Options for Changing the Tax Treatment of Charitable Giving* 3-4 (2011).

14. *Id.*

15. McKeever, *supra* note 9, at 11.

income).[16] The 60 percent limit, like many other limits, seems to reflect congressional ambivalence about the deduction. In the case of contributions to other organizations, principally "private foundations," and gifts "for the use of" an organization, the allowable deductions for individuals are limited to a maximum 30 percent of adjusted gross income.[17] §170(b)(1)(B). Corporations may deduct charitable contributions only to the extent such contributions do not exceed 10 percent of taxable income. §170(b)(2). If the taxpayer makes gifts that exceed any of these limits, the excess may be carried over to the succeeding five years. See §§170(d), 170(b)(1)(B), 170(b)(1)(C)(ii), and 170(b)(1)(D)(ii).

When a taxpayer makes a gift of property whose sale would produce long-term capital gain, the amount allowed as a deduction is generally the full fair market value of the property. If, for example, a taxpayer in the 37 percent tax bracket owns shares of common stock with a fair market value of $10,000 and a basis of $1,000, has held them for the requisite holding period (generally more than one year), and gives the shares to a charitable organization, no tax is paid on the gain, and the deduction is for the full $10,000 value. The deduction reduces taxes owed by $3,700. In contrast, if the taxpayer had sold the stock and contributed the entire $10,000 proceeds, she would recognize $9,000 income on the same and incur (at a 20 percent capital gain rate) a $1,800 tax. Her net tax benefit would be $3,700 (from deducting the $10,000 proceeds) less $1,800, or $1,900. Obviously, then, the gift of the property itself is more advantageous than the sale of the property followed by a gift of the proceeds. In the case of a gift of property whose sale would produce short-term capital gain or ordinary income, the deduction is limited to the taxpayer's basis in the property; a limit also applies on the deductibility of the value of tangible personal property (e.g., a painting, except when given to certain kinds of organizations). §170(e)(1).

Deductions for gifts of property the sale of which would have generated long-term capital gain are limited to 30 percent of adjusted gross income, or 20 percent if the gift is to a private foundation or for the use of a charitable organization.

3.   Treatment of Nonprofit Organizations

Most well-known charities fall within the definition in 501(c)(3) as "organized exclusively for religious, charitable, scientific, literary or educational purposes." Charities that fall into that definition, such as the Red Cross, the

---

16. The rationale for the 50 percent limit is not obvious. If the first dollar a taxpayer gives to charity is worth subsidizing (through a tax deduction), why isn't the last dollar worth subsidizing? If Congress is worried about the deduction benefiting wealthy donors, or about giving those donors too much say in how the funds get allocated, why not set an absolute limit on the amount of the deduction, rather than base the limit on the proportion of income donated? The AMT, discussed at the end of this chapter, involves a somewhat analogous set of limits on other deductions.

17. Such deductions are also reduced to the extent that deductions to organizations listed in §170(b)(1) exceed 20 percent of adjusted gross income.

Boy Scouts, or most private universities, are generally immune from taxation on donations, investments, or receipts from activities. They are sometimes called "(c)3" organizations. Note §170 uses the same language (organized for religious, charitable . . . purposes") to define organizations to whom donations will generate a tax deduction. So contributions to a (c)3 organization are deductible, and a (c)3 organization generally does not pay tax on the contribution or any of its receipts.

The immunity from tax on receipts does not extend to activities carried on that are unrelated to an organization's exempt purpose. See §§512 et seq. Under the tax law enacted in 2017, there is a 1.4 percent excise tax on net investment of any college university with at least 500 students that has net assets of $500,000 per student. The excise tax is expected to affect a few dozen of the wealthiest universities, such as Harvard, Princeton, Stanford, and Yale.

If an organization engages in lobbying, it may lose its status as an organization to which tax-deductible contributions may be made, although it may remain exempt from taxation. See §§170(c)(2)(D), 501(c)(3), 501(h). Some organizations (such as the Sierra Club) have coped with the prohibition on lobbying by setting up separate but related organizations that limit their activities to such matters as nonpartisan education or litigation.

Some organizations that meet the (c)(3) list of specified purposes are defined as private foundations under §509. In general, these are organizations that get one-third or more of their funding from founders. The Bill and Melinda Gates Foundation, for example, was funded by Gates's Microsoft stock and is a private foundation. Private foundations are subject to special restrictions, including severe restrictions on self-dealing between founder and organization, and they are required to make minimum annual distributions of at least 5 percent of endowment value. §4942.

Section 501(c)4-10 describes other nonprofit organizations, such as fraternal societies or business leagues. In general, while donations to these organizations do not generate a tax deduction, these organizations are not taxed on donations, investment income, or activities related to their exempt function. Section 527 provides separate and detailed rules for the tax treatment of political organizations, making them taxable on their income, but excluding from their income such items as political contributions, income from fundraising events, etc.

4. Policy

Is the tax deduction for charitable gifts a cost-effective way to support charity? The charitable deduction reduces tax revenues by billions of dollars a year. Does the deduction stimulate charitable giving? Or is the deduction just a (deserved?) windfall to those who would give (and give the same amount) anyway? One way to answer these questions is to look at how charitable giving changes as tax rates change. A decline in the marginal tax rates of donors reduces the value of the tax deduction. If the tax deduction is an important factor in charitable giving, then donations should decline with falling marginal rates. Conversely, donations should rise as marginal rates rise, as the

deduction becomes more valuable. Economists who have studied the issue
have generally concluded that the "dollar efficiency" of the deduction is relatively high.[18] Deductions stimulate donations, and most studies find the dollar
gain to the supported organizations equals and in some cases exceeds the
dollar loss to the fisc.

Of course, even if the deduction is efficient, it may not be desirable. Critics
charge that the deduction is undemocratic, because it leaves the decision of
what to subsidize in the hands of the donor. If, as studies suggest, the deduction increases giving on a little more than a dollar-for-dollar basis, then the
$50 billion estimated cost of the deduction in 2016 will stimulate an extra
$50 billion or so giving by donors. In contrast, without the deduction, the
fisc would have an extra $50 billion dollars. Elected representatives, rather
than donors, could decide where to spend that money. Supporters of the
deduction argue that taking the funding decision away from government
leads to social experimentation and better oversight. A similar debate rages
on the tax exemption granted to nonprofits — with exceptions for unrelated
business income and the excise tax (described above) that applies to a few
dozen or so colleges and universities. One way to think about these differences is to compare the spending of wealthy institutions such as Yale, the
Ford Foundation, or the Bill and Melinda Gates Foundation with that of the
State of Connecticut or the United States government.[19] Which type of institution makes the best choice of expenditures or does a better job controlling
expenses?

COMPARATIVE FOCUS:
Canada's Charitable Contribution Credit

In 1988, Canada converted its longstanding deduction for charitable
contributions to a credit. Under pre-1988 Canadian law, individuals were
allowed to claim a deduction for charitable contributions as they are in
the United States. The 1988 law eliminated the deduction and enacted
in its place a "two tier credit" under which taxpayers would be allowed a

---

18. See Jon Bakija, *Tax Policy and Philanthropy: A Primer on the Empirical Evidence for the United States and Its Implications*, 80 Soc. Res. 557, 581 (2013); Brian D. Galle, *How Do Nonprofit Firms Respond to Tax Policy?*, 44 Pub. Fin. Rev. 2017, http://pfr.sagepub.com/content/early/2016/03/18/ 1091142116634850. abstract.

19. Compare Yale, http://provost.yale.edu/budget/dataglance (over $3.2 billion in expenses); Sue Desmond-Hellman, *What If . . . : A Letter from the CEO of the Bill and Melinda Gates Foundation*, Gates Found., http://www.gatesfoundation.org/2016/ceo-letter?wt.mc_id=05_23_2016_5_ceoletter16_gf-gfo_&wt.tsrc=gfgfo (last visited Aug. 9, 2016) (over $225 million spent since 2008 in combating to-bacco); and *Grant Making by Thematic Area in 2016*, Ford Found., https://www.fordfoundation.org/ work/our-grants/grants-database/grants-initiatives (last visited Aug. 9, 2016) (nearly $100 million in grants in 2016) with Office of Mgmt. & Budget, *Budget of the U.S. Government* 115 tbl.S-1 (2016) (bud-geted outlays for FY 2015 of nearly $4.7 trillion); Office of Fiscal Analysis, *Connecticut State Budget: FY 16 & FY 17 Budget 2* (roughly $20 billion of appropriations for FY 2016 and FY 2017); and Andrew Soergel, *7 Stats from Obama's Budget Proposal*, U.S. News & World Report (Feb. 2, 2015), http://www. usnews.com/news/articles/2015/02/02/7-numbers-to-know-from-obamas-2016-budget ("President Barack Obama . . . unveiled a $4 trillion fiscal year 2016 budget").

credit equal to 17 percent for the first $250 in charitable donations and 29 percent for all donations in excess of $250. Because these initial credit percentages were keyed to statutory tax rates in place at the time, the change had little effect on aggregate charitable giving. Note, however, that the credit device allows policymakers substantially greater flexibility in crafting a subsidy. In effect, a credit allows the government subsidy for charitable contributions to be "unhitched" from the marginal rate structure. Subsidy rates can then be modified depending upon any number of factors, including, for example, the amount of the taxpayer's total donations or the nature of the donee institutions.

5.   Gifts with Private Objectives or Benefits

One of the most important legal issues surrounding the deduction for charitable contributions concerns situations where the donor receives something in return for her gift. In many cases, getting something in return has clear and obvious effects. For example, assume that Ava gives $100 to PBS and gets a PBS tote bag, with a value of $20, in exchange for her donation. It is clear that Ava's deduction is $80, not $100. It is as though she purchased a tote bag for $20 and made a donation of $80. In other cases, however, a charitable donation may provide the donor with more indirect benefits. If these benefits are significant, they may even call into question the characterization of the transfer as a charitable gift. The case below offers a good example.

OTTAWA SILICA CO. v. UNITED STATES
699 F.2d 1124 (Fed. Cir. 1983)

[The taxpayer, Ottawa, was in the business of mining, processing, and marketing silica, also known as quartzite. Beginning in 1956 the taxpayer acquired various ranch properties in Oceanside, California, a town located on the ocean, north of San Diego, with a major U.S. Marine Corps base, Camp Pendleton, on its northern border. Initially Ottawa acquired properties for their quartzite deposits; those deposits were found only on a portion of the land, and the rest was of relatively little interest to Ottawa. Before many years had passed, however, it became apparent that the land would ultimately be valuable for residential or commercial development. Silica mining is a dirty process that cannot be carried on close to residential areas, so Ottawa was in no hurry with the development, but in 1965 it hired William L. Pereira & Associates to produce a plan for the use of the properties that Ottawa had acquired. On the recommendation of Pereira, Ottawa bought two additional ranches (the Jones and Talone ranches) for the purpose of permitting it to maximize its land development opportunities; these ranches contained no quartzite deposits.

In the mid-1960s it became apparent that a new high school would be needed for the school district that included Oceanside and its neighbor to the south,

Carlsbad. The Oceanside-Carlsbad Union High School District (OCUHSD), after a survey of possible sites, asked Ottawa whether it would be willing to donate to it about fifty acres on a portion of its property known as the Freeman Ranch. It was plain that if the OCUHSD did build the high school on the taxpayer's site, it would be required to build access roads that would be of benefit to Ottawa. In 1970, after long negotiations, Ottawa contributed the fifty-acre site, plus twenty acres for right-of-way for two access roads, to OCUHSD, and claimed a deduction of $415,000 for the value of the property contributed. It was conceded that OCUHSD was a political subdivision of the State of California within the meaning of §170(c)(1). The government argued that no deduction was allowable because Ottawa had received a substantial benefit from the transfer of the property. The court of appeals agreed, affirming per curiam the Claims Court decision on the basis of the opinion of Judge Colaianni. Portions of that opinion follow.]

The case law dealing with this aspect of a §170 deduction makes clear that a contribution made to a charity is not made for exclusively public purposes if the donor receives, or anticipates receiving a substantial benefit in return. . . .

In Singer [Co. v. United States, 196 Ct. Cl. 90, 449 F.2d 413 (1972)], this court considered whether discount sales of sewing machines to schools and other charities entitled Singer to a charitable deduction. The court found that Singer, which at the time of the sales was in the business of selling sewing machines, had made the discount sales to the schools for the predominant purpose of encouraging the students to use and, in the future, to purchase its sewing machines, thereby increasing Singer's future sales. This purpose colored the discount sales, making them business transactions rather than charitable contributions. Accordingly, the court disallowed the deduction for the sales to the schools. The court allowed deductions for the discount sales made to other charities, however, because Singer had no expectation of increasing its sales by making the contributions and benefited only incidentally from them.

The *Singer* court noted that the receipt of benefits by the donor need not always preclude a charitable contribution. The court stated its reasoning as follows:

> [I]f the benefits received, or expected to be received, [by the donor] are substantial, and meaning by that, benefits greater than those that inure to the general public from transfers for charitable purposes (which benefits are merely *incidental* to the transfer), then in such case we feel that the transferor has received, or expects to receive, a quid pro quo sufficient to remove the transfer from the realm of deductibility under section 170.

Singer Co. v. United States, 196 Ct. Cl. at 106, 449 F.2d 423. The parties to the present case disagree as to the meaning of the above quotation. The plain language clearly indicates that a "substantial benefit" received in return for a contribution constitutes a quid pro quo, which precludes a deduction. The court defined a substantial benefit as one that is "greater than those that inure to the general public from transfers for charitable purposes." Id. at 106, 449 F.2d at 423. Those benefits that inure to the general public from charitable contributions are incidental to the contribution, and the donor, as a member of the general public, may receive them. It is only when the donor receives or expects to receive additional substantial benefits that courts are likely to conclude that a quid pro quo for the transfer exists and that the donor is therefore not entitled to a charitable deduction. . . .

Plaintiff argues that it received no benefits, except incidental ones as defined by *Singer*, in return for its contribution of the site, and it is therefore entitled to a §170 deduction for the transfer of its land to the school district. After having considered the testimony and the evidence adduced at trial, I conclude that the benefits to be derived by plaintiff from the transfer were substantial enough to provide plaintiff with a quid pro quo for the transfer and thus effectively destroyed the charitable nature of the transfer.

To begin, although plaintiff is correct in arguing that it was not the moving party in this conveyance, and that the school district sought plaintiff out for a donation of a high school site, that alone fails to justify a §170 deduction. The record clearly establishes that following the passage of a bonding referendum, which authorized the building of a new high school by the city of Oceanside in 1968, as many as nine sites had been evaluated. Because of the eastward growth of the city, Mr. LaFleur, the superintendent of the OCUHSD, felt that the ideal location for the new high school would be near El Camino Real [the road on the western boundary of plaintiff's property]. Following careful consideration, the city and school district decided that the best location for a high school would be on plaintiff's land. Thus, during the summer of 1968, John Steiger, the vice-mayor of Oceanside, and Mr. LaFleur approached Mr. Thomas Jones to see if plaintiff would consider making a site on the Freeman Ranch available for the new high school.

On September 20, 1968, Mr. LaFleur wrote to plaintiff's president, Mr. Thornton, to ask if plaintiff would be willing to donate 50 acres of its land for a school site. The record also establishes, however, that plaintiff was more than willing to oblige Mr. LaFleur on the basis of its own self-interest. Indeed, the evidence shows that on that same September 20, Mr. Jones also wrote to Mr. Thornton to advise him of the discussions he had participated in regarding a high school site. In his letter Mr. Jones stated that he had met with John Steiger and Larry Bagley, Oceanside's planning director, and had learned that the school district's first choice for a high school site was on land owned by plaintiff. In a most revealing statement, Mr. Jones went on to say:

> I was pessimistic when talking to John and Larry, but this actually could trigger and hasten the development of the whole eastern end of [the] Freeman and Jones [ranches] at no cost to us. The increase in these property values should be substantial if this should go through. . . . In any event, nothing more is to be done on this until the school board writes to you and asks to open negotiations. On the other hand, I recommend that [Ottawa] actively pursue this, since a high school in this location would probably trigger the early development of El Camino Real from the May Co. to Mission Road.

The exact meaning of Mr. Jones' statement will be better understood following a full development of the prevailing circumstances at the time of the transfer. It should be recalled that plaintiff had amassed some 2,300 acres in eastern Oceanside, but only 481 acres had silica reserves. . . . While a portion of the western boundary of the Freeman Ranch ran along El Camino Real, its northernmost boundary was about a mile from all of the major roads. The unavailability of major roads to service the northernmost reaches of the Cubbison and Freeman Ranches ultimately led Pereira to recommend that plaintiff purchase the Jones and Talone Ranches. . . .

The only thing frustrating the implementation of the plan was the inaccessibility of the Jones Ranch from Mission Boulevard. . . .

The construction of a high school on the Freeman Ranch, however, alleviated this problem for plaintiff. State and local officials required that the high school be serviced by two separate access roads. After some discussions, the school district and plaintiff agreed on the general direction of Mesa Drive which would provide the school with access to El Camino Real, and the surrounding topography dictated that the second road run north to Mission Boulevard through the Jones Ranch and parcels of property owned by Mr. Ivey and the Mission of San Luis Rey. This road, Rancho Del Oro Drive, provided plaintiff with access to the Jones Ranch directly from Mission Boulevard. Plaintiff could not have obtained such access to Mission Boulevard on its own unless both Mr. Ivey and the fathers at the mission had agreed to convey part of their land or easements to plaintiff. There is no evidence suggesting that either party was interested in doing so. Mr. Ivey, in fact, had resisted plaintiff's overtures about selling or developing his land. . . .

It is thus quite apparent that plaintiff conveyed the land to the school fully expecting that as a consequence of the construction of public access roads through its property it would receive substantial benefits in return. In fact, this is precisely what happened. Plaintiff obtained direct access to the Jones Ranch via Rancho Del Oro Drive and ultimately sold the ranch to a developer. Plaintiff also sold two parcels of the Freeman Ranch, lying north of Mesa Drive, to other developers. . . . It is my opinion that the plaintiff knew that the construction of a school and the attendant roads on its property would substantially benefit the surrounding land, that it made the conveyance expecting its remaining property to increase in value, and that the expected receipt of these benefits at least partially prompted plaintiff to make the conveyance. Under *Singer*, this is more than adequate reason to deny plaintiff a charitable contribution for its conveyance.

NOTES AND QUESTIONS

1. *What's at stake in* Ottawa Silica Co.*?* Had the taxpayer won, it would have recognized a current deduction equal to the fair market value of the contributed property. Instead, the taxpayer received no current deduction and could only add the basis of the contributed property to its other land. See discussion of capital expenditures in Chapter 7. The taxpayer would, in effect, be able to deduct that basis when and if it sold its other land. The effect of the government victory was twofold. First, the taxpayer was forced to defer any tax benefit for what might turn out to be many years. Second, the eventual tax benefit would be limited to the basis of the contributed property, rather than the fair market value of the contributed property.

(a) *Business versus nonbusiness benefits.* The taxpayer in *Ottawa Silica* received a business-related benefit from its transfer of property to a charity. In the business-related setting, the rule applied by the court was that no charitable deduction was allowable if the business benefit was substantial. An alternative might have been to allow a charitable deduction for the value of the property transferred to the charity reduced by the value of the benefit received by the taxpayer. This alternative would more accurately reflect the amount of the charitable gift and is in fact the approach used for "quid pro quo" contributions that are not business related—as described immediately below.

(b) In DuVal v. Commissioner, T.C. Memo. 1994-603, DuVal was a real estate developer who needed rezoning for a parcel of property he intended to develop. The county authorities from whom DuVal sought the rezoning had in the past "solicited" developers to dedicate land for public use. There was some doubt as to the legal authority to require such dedications, but the county "assumed that it did have such authority." The county's representatives asked DuVal to contribute a portion of his property as a site for a library. DuVal did so. He claimed that his motivation was a desire "to give something back" to the community and his commitment to education. The court found that the gift of the library site was not a "condition precedent to the county's approval of Mr. DuVal's rezoning request." In holding that DuVal was entitled to a charitable deduction for the gift of the land for the library site, the court stated:

> To resolve the question of whether a transfer is a gift for purposes of §170(c), we must determine the taxpayer's primary or dominant intent or purpose in making the transfer. . . . To resolve this question, we do not examine only the taxpayer's statements of his or her subjective intent. Rather, we must make an objective inquiry into the nature of the transaction to determine whether what is labeled a gift is in substance a gift.

How does this test differ from the test applied in *Ottawa Silica*? To what extent, if at all, is the outcome in a case like *DuVal* or *Ottawa Silica* likely to change depending on which test is applied?

6.   More on Private Benefits

a.   *Quid Pro Quo Contributions*

As noted above, it has long been the rule that the amount of any non-business-related deduction for a charitable contribution is limited to the excess of the payment to the charity over the value of any benefit (other than trivial ones) received by the donor. In determining the amount of the reduction, it is the value to the donor that counts. The value to the donor is assumed to be the fair market value of whatever is received by the donor—that is, what the item or service would cost the donor if purchased. The cost to the donee organization is irrelevant. See Rev. Rul. 67-246, 1967-2 C.B. 104; Rev. Proc. 90-12, 1990-1 C.B. 471; Rev. Proc. 92-49, 1992-1 C.B. 987. To ensure compliance, §6115 requires that for any quid pro quo contribution over $75 the charity must provide the donor with a written statement that the entire amount is not deductible and must provide a "good faith estimate of the value of [the] goods or services" received. The $75 threshold for a written statement does not change the rule for contributions of lesser amounts. The deduction is still limited to the excess over the value of any goods or services received, but the charity has no statutory obligation to provide an estimate of that value and the level of compliance with the law seems to be low.

The quid pro quo rationale has never been applied to psychic returns. If an individual contributes money to a university in return for the university's agreement to name a building after him or her, it is plain that the contribution is deductible, despite the obvious psychic benefit to the taxpayer.

b.   *The Complicitous Role of Some Charitable Organizations*

The problem of disentangling individual benefit from charitable donation is exacerbated by the tendency of many §170(c) organizations to adopt fee structures that blur the distinction between donations and the costs of services. As a result, individuals deduct amounts that might be more accurately described as nondeductible fees for services. Consider, for example, the fee structure at one West Coast opera company. The nominal cost of a "Series A" box seat is $1,585. However, such seats are available only after a major donation. The amount of donation that will secure such a box is said to be $20,000—down from $100,000 in the 1980s. In addition, holders of Series A boxes are requested to make a "minimum contribution" of $4,500 a year. It is virtually certain that holders of Series A seats deduct the major donation necessary to get the seats and the annual minimum contribution associated with the seats. Suppose, instead, that the opera company charged (continued to charge?) what the market would bear for the seats but did not tie the seats to donations or term any of the amount paid as a donation. It would then be clear that no portion of the ticket price could be deducted. The after-tax cost of the seats would rise. This would disadvantage ticket holders. It would also make it harder to sell seats and, in that sense, disadvantage the opera company. (Indeed, the most likely result is that the opera company would have to reduce the price of the seats.)

7.   Overvaluation of Contributed Property

One of the major problems with charitable contributions has been the overvaluation of works of art. A good illustration is provided by the case of Isbell v. Commissioner, 44 T.C.M. 1143 (1982). The taxpayer contributed to a public television station, for its annual fund-raising auction, a Han dynasty jar with a crack on one side and a hole in its bottom (made for the purpose of converting the jar to a lamp). Isbell had received the jar as a gift. Initially he claimed a deduction of $15,000 and later, in an amended return, raised this to $50,000, based on an appraisal of all his valuables, done at his request two years before the gift, by a firm that appraised interior furnishings, that had no experience in appraising Asian art objects, whose representatives were not called as witnesses, and whose appraisal was "incorrect in several respects." The jar sold at the auction for $360. A "very impressive" expert who testified for the government placed the value at $800, which the court accepted as the fair market value. In response to the abuse and the enforcement difficulties suggested by this case, the Tax Reform Act of 1984 imposed a requirement that the Treasury issue regulations for substantiation of the amount of the deduction in the case of gifts of property with a value greater than $5,000 (or $10,000 in the case of non-publicly traded stock). See §155 of the act, which was not made part of the Code. Substantiation is not required, however, for publicly traded stock. To meet the substantiation requirement, the donor must obtain a qualified appraisal and attach to his or her return a signed appraisal summary. Along similar lines, §170(f)(11) provides that for contributions of property that is not "readily valued" and for which the deduction is more than $500, the taxpayer must include with the return "a description of such property and such other information as the Secretary [of the Treasury] may require." Section 170(f)(8) requires that taxpayers who claim a deduction for any form of contribution in excess of $250 must be able to substantiate the deduction with a written acknowledgment of the donation by the donee organization. The acknowledgment must state the fair market value, if any, of any services or goods provided by the organization in return for the donation. §170(f)(8).

8.   The Special Case of Collegiate Athletics

In Rev. Rul. 86-63, 86-1 C.B. 88, the IRS ruled on the politically sensitive issue of deductions for contributions to the athletic scholarship programs of colleges and universities, where the contributor becomes entitled to buy tickets for seating at athletic events. The holding, relying on Rev. Rul. 67-246, *supra,* was that where reasonably comparable seating would not have been available in the absence of the contribution, the presumption is that the contribution was the price of a substantial benefit to the taxpayer and no deduction is allowable unless the taxpayer can establish that the amount of the contribution exceeded the value of the benefit received. After considerable whining by universities and the supporters of their athletic (and other) programs, Congress, in 1988, adopted §170(l). For three decades, this provision allowed a deduction for 80 percent of any amount paid to an "institution of higher learning" if the deduction would be allowable "but for the fact that the taxpayer receives (directly or indirectly) as a result of paying such amount the right to purchase tickets for seating at an athletic event in an athletic stadium of such institution." As part of the 2017 act, this provision was amended to disallow the deduction entirely.

9.   Religious Benefits and Services

Rev. Rul. 70-47, 1970-1 C.B. 49, states that "pew rents, building fund assessments, and periodic dues paid to a church . . . are all methods of making contributions to the church, and such payments are deductible as charitable contributions within the limitations set out in section 170 of the Code." Similarly, the IRS has never challenged the deductibility of specified amounts required to be paid for attendance at Jewish High Holy Day services. (The principle underlying these rules is now reflected in §170(f)(8)(B), relating to the $250 substantiation rule described above.) On the other hand, fees for attendance at parochial schools providing mostly secular education are not deductible.

In Hernandez v. Commissioner, 490 U.S. 680 (1989), the Supreme Court upheld the Commissioner's disallowance of a deduction for amounts paid by members of the Church of Scientology for individual "training" (learning of doctrine) and "auditing" (development of "spiritual awareness"). The amounts to be paid were determined by a schedule of prices based on the length of the sessions and their level of "sophistication." A central tenet of the Church was the "doctrine of exchange," under which a person receiving something must pay something in return. Free auditing or training sessions were "categorically barred." For the purposes of the case, the IRS stipulated that the Church was a bona fide religious organization, contributions to which were deductible. The IRS's argument was that the fees at issue were not "contributions." The majority concluded, "As the Tax Court found, these payments were part of a quintessential quid pro quo exchange: in return for their money, petitioners received an identifiable benefit, namely, auditing and training sessions." In reaching this result, the majority rejected the tax-payers' argument that the receipt of consideration in the form of religious or spiritual services is not inconsistent with the notion of gift or contribution. Justice O'Connor, in a dissent joined by Justice Scalia, argued that the disal-lowance of the deductions was inconsistent with the IRS's "70-year practice of allowing [deduction of] fixed payments indistinguishable from those made by petitioners." The majority attempted to avoid this argument by stating that the record was unclear on the precise facts in the allegedly similar situ-ations: "for example, whether payments for other faiths' services are truly obligatory or whether any or all of these services are generally provided whether or not the encouraged 'mandatory' payment is made."

The *Hernandez* decision seemed to resolve the question of whether payments by members of the Church of Scientology for training and auditing could be deducted as charitable contributions. Yet despite the Supreme Court's ruling, the controversy has continued. The taxpayers in the *Hernandez* case were individuals who had made payments to the Church of Scientology in exchange for training and auditing courses, but the Church itself also had several open tax contro-versies with the IRS. In 1997, the *Wall Street Journal* reported that the IRS had entered into a settlement agreement with the Church of Scientology regarding these disputes. Among other things, the *Journal* reported that the agreement "lets Scientologists deduct on their individual tax returns 'auditing' fees as dona-tions, [superseding] the IRS's earlier rule denying such deductions—a position that was backed by the Supreme Court." See Elizabeth MacDonald, *Scientologists and IRS Settled for $12.5 Million,* Wall St. Journal (Dec. 30, 1997).

10.   Voluntariness

In Lombardo v. Commissioner, 50 T.C.M. 1374 (1985), the taxpayer pleaded guilty to a state-law charge of felonious sale and delivery of marijuana. Incident to the taxpayer's arrest, the police seized fourteen tons of marijuana, $148,000 in cash, the land (with improvements) on which he was operating, and various other property. The taxpayer was placed on probation and was able to stay out of prison under an order that required him to pay $145,000 to the county school fund. He made the required payments over two years and claimed charitable deductions. His tax returns for the years at issue (during which he was on probation) showed income from "Business or Profession," without elaboration; in response to a question on the return about the nature of his business, he relied on the Fifth Amendment. The Tax Court upheld the Commissioner's denial of the charitable deduction. It observed that the taxpayer made the payments in order to avoid going to prison and stated, "It would strain our credulity to the breaking point to conclude that petitioner's contributions proceeded even remotely from a charitable impulse." The court viewed as irrelevant the possibility that the state court might have exceeded its authority by requiring a payment of $145,000 for violation of a statute with a maximum fine of $5,000.

11.   Public Policy and Charitable Purpose

BOB JONES UNIVERSITY v. UNITED STATES
461 U.S. 574 (1983)

Chief Justice BURGER delivered the opinion of the Court.

We granted certiorari to decide whether petitioners, nonprofit private schools that prescribe and enforce racially discriminatory admissions standards on the basis of religious doctrine, qualify as tax-exempt organizations under §501(c)(3) of the Internal Revenue Code of 1954.

I . . .

Bob Jones University is a nonprofit corporation located in Greenville, South Carolina. Its purpose is "to conduct an institution of learning . . . , giving special emphasis to the Christian religion and the ethics revealed in the Holy Scriptures." . . . The corporation operates a school with an enrollment of approximately 5,000 students, from kindergarten through college and graduate school. Bob Jones University is not affiliated with any religious denomination, but is dedicated to the teaching and propagation of its fundamentalist Christian religious beliefs. It is both a religious and educational institution. Its teachers are required to be devout Christians, and all courses at the University are taught according to the Bible. Entering students are screened as to their religious beliefs, and their public and private conduct is strictly regulated by standards promulgated by University authorities.

The sponsors of the University genuinely believe that the Bible forbids interracial dating and marriage. To effectuate these views, Negroes were completely excluded until 1971. From 1971 to May 1975, the University accepted no applications from unmarried Negroes, but did accept applications from Negroes married within their race.

Following the decision of the United States Court of Appeals for the Fourth Circuit in McCrary v. Runyon, 515 F.2d 1082 (C.A. 4 1975), aff'd, 427 U.S.

160 (1976), prohibiting racial exclusion from private schools, the University revised its policy. Since May 29, 1975, the University has permitted unmarried Negroes to enroll; but a disciplinary rule prohibits interracial dating and marriage. That rule reads:

There is to be no interracial dating

1. Students who are partners in an interracial marriage will be expelled.
2. Students who are members of or affiliated with any group or organization which holds as one of its goals or advocates interracial marriage will be expelled.
3. Students who date outside their own race will be expelled.
4. Students who espouse, promote, or encourage others to violate the University's dating rules and regulations will be expelled.

The University continues to deny admission to applicants engaged in an interracial marriage or known to advocate interracial marriage or dating.

Until 1970, the IRS extended tax-exempt status to Bob Jones University under §501(c)(3). By the letter of November 30, 1970, that followed the injunction issued in Green v. Kennedy [309 F. Supp. 1127 (D.D.C.), app. dismissed sub nom. Cannon v. Green, 398 U.S. 956 (1970)] the IRS formally notified the University of the change in IRS policy, and announced its intention to challenge the tax-exempt status of private schools practicing racial discrimination in their admissions policies.[20]

The United States District Court for the District of South Carolina held that revocation of the University's tax-exempt status exceeded the delegated powers of the IRS, was improper under the IRS rulings and procedures, and violated the University's rights under the Religion Clauses of the First Amendment. 468 F. Supp. 890, 907 (D.S.C. 1978). . . .

The Court of Appeals for the Fourth Circuit, in a divided opinion, reversed, 639 F.2d 147 (C.A. 4 1980). Citing Green v. Connally, *supra,* with approval, the Court of Appeals concluded that §501(c)(3) must be read against the background of charitable trust law. To be eligible for an exemption under that section, an institution must be "charitable" in the common law sense, and therefore must not be contrary to public policy. In the court's view, Bob Jones University did not meet this requirement, since its "racial policies violated the clearly defined public policy, rooted in our Constitution, condemning racial discrimination and, more specifically, the government policy against subsidizing racial discrimination in education, public or private." *Id.,* at 151. The court held that the IRS acted within its statutory authority in revoking the University's tax-exempt status. Finally, the Court of Appeals rejected petitioner's arguments that the revocation of

---

20. Revenue Ruling 71-447, 1971-2 Cum. Bull. 230, defined "racially nondiscriminatory policy as to students" as meaning that:

> [T]he school admits the students of any race to all the rights, privileges, programs, and activities generally accorded or made available to students at that school and that the school does not discriminate on the basis of race in administration of its educational policies, admissions policies, scholarship and loan programs, and athletic and other school-administered programs.

the tax exemption violated the Free Exercise and Establishment Clauses of the First Amendment. The case was remanded to the District Court with instructions to dismiss the University's claim for a refund and to reinstate the Government's counter-claim. . . .

Goldsboro Christian Schools is a nonprofit corporation located in Goldsboro, North Carolina. Like Bob Jones University, it was established "to conduct an institution of . . . , giving special emphasis to the Christian religion and the ethics revealed in the Holy scriptures." . . . The school offers classes from kindergarten through high school, and since at least 1969 has satisfied the State of North Carolina's requirements for secular education in private schools. The school requires its high school students to take Bible-related courses, and begins each class with prayer.

Since its incorporation in 1963, Goldsboro Christian Schools has maintained a racially discriminatory admissions policy based upon its interpretation of the Bible.[21] Goldsboro has for the most part accepted only Caucasians. On occasion, however, the school has accepted children from racially mixed marriages in which one of the parents is Caucasian.

[A district court decision in favor of the government's denial of exemption was affirmed by the Fourth Circuit on the authority of *Bob Jones University*.][22]

II

In Revenue Ruling 71-447, the IRS formalized the policy first announced in 1970, that §170 and §501(c)(3) embrace the common law "charity" concept. Under that view, to qualify for a tax exemption pursuant to §501(c)(3), an institution must show, first, that it falls within one of the eight categories expressly set forth in that section, and second, that its activity is not contrary to settled public policy.

Section 501(c)(3) provides that "[c]orporations . . . organized and operated exclusively for religious, charitable . . . or educational purposes" are entitled to tax exemption. Petitioners argue that the plain language of the statute guarantees them tax-exempt status. They emphasize the absence of any language in the statute expressly requiring all exempt organizations to

21. According to the interpretation espoused by Goldsboro, race is determined by descendance from one of Noah's three sons—Ham, Shem and Japheth. Based on this interpretation, Orientals and Negroes are Hamitic, Hebrews are Shemitic, and Caucasians are Japhethitic. Cultural or biological mixing of the races is regarded as a violation of God's command. . . .

22. After the Court granted certiorari, the Government filed a motion to dismiss, informing the Court that the Department of Treasury intended to revoke Revenue Ruling 71-447 and other pertinent rulings and to recognize §501(c)(3) exemptions for petitioners. The Government suggested that these actions were therefore moot. Before this Court ruled on that motion, however, the United States Court of Appeals for the District of Columbia Circuit enjoined the Government from granting §501(c)(3) tax-exempt status to any school that discriminates on the basis of race. Wright v. Regan, No. 80-1124 (C.A.D.C. Feb. 18, 1982) (per curiam order). Thereafter, the Government informed the Court that it would not revoke the revenue rulings and withdrew its request that the actions be dismissed as moot. The Government continues to assert that the IRS lacked authority to promulgate Revenue Ruling 71-447, and does not defend that aspect of the rulings below. [The Court appointed special counsel to argue in support of the Court of Appeals decision.]

be "charitable" in the common law sense, and they contend that the disjunctive "or" separating the categories in §501(c)(3) precludes such a reading. Instead, they argue that if an institution falls within one or more of the specified categories it is automatically entitled to exemption, without regard to whether it also qualifies as "charitable." The Court of Appeals rejected that contention and concluded that petitioners' interpretation of the statute "tears section 501(c)(3) from its roots." United States v. Bob Jones University, *supra*, 639 F.2d, at 151. . . .

Section 501(c)(3) . . . must be analyzed and construed within the framework of the Internal Revenue Code and against the background of the Congressional purposes. Such an examination reveals unmistakable evidence that, underlying all relevant parts of the Code, is the intent that entitlement to tax exemption depends on meeting certain common law standards of charity—namely, that an institution seeking tax-exempt status must serve a public purpose and not be contrary to established public policy.

This "charitable" concept appears explicitly in §170 of the Code. That section contains a list of organizations virtually identical to that contained in §501(c)(3). It is apparent that Congress intended that list to have the same meaning in both sections. In §170, Congress used the list of organizations in defining the term "charitable contributions." On its face, therefore, §170 reveals that Congress' intention was to provide tax benefits to organizations serving charitable purposes. The form of §170 simply makes plain what common sense and history tell us: In enacting both §170 and §501(c)(3), Congress sought to provide tax benefits to charitable organizations, to encourage the development of private institutions that serve a useful public purpose or supplement or take the place of public institutions of the same kind.

Tax exemptions for certain institutions thought beneficial to the social order of the country as a whole, or to a particular community, are deeply rooted in our history, as in that of England. The origins of such exemptions lie in the special privileges that have long been extended to charitable trusts.[23] . . .

A corollary to the public benefit principle is the requirement, long recognized in the law of trusts, that the purpose of a charitable trust may not be illegal or violate established public policy. . . .

When the Government grants exemptions or allows deductions all taxpayers are affected; the very fact of the exemption or deduction for the donor means that other taxpayers can be said to be indirect and vicarious "donors." Charitable exemptions are justified on the basis that the exempt entity confers a public benefit—a benefit which the society or the community may not itself choose or be able to provide, or which supplements and advances the work of public institutions already supported by tax revenues. History buttresses logic to make clear that, to warrant exemption under §501(c)(3), an institution must fall within a category specified in that section and must demonstrably

---

23. The form and history of the charitable exemption and deduction sections of the various income tax acts reveal that Congress was guided by the common law of charitable trusts. See Simon, The Tax-Exempt Status of Racially Discriminatory Religious Schools, 36 Tax L. Rev. 477, 485-489 (1981) (hereinafter Simon).

serve and be in harmony with the public interest.[24] The institution's purpose must not be so at odds with the common community conscience as to undermine any public benefit that might otherwise be conferred.

We are bound to approach these questions with full awareness that determinations of public benefit and public policy are sensitive matters with serious implications for the institutions affected; a declaration that a given institution is not "charitable" should be made only where there can be no doubt that the activity involved is contrary to a fundamental public policy. But there can no longer be any doubt that racial discrimination in education violates deeply and widely accepted views of elementary justice. Prior to 1954, public education in many places still was conducted under the pall of Plessy v. Ferguson, 163 U.S. 537 (1896); racial segregation in primary and secondary education prevailed in many parts of the country. See, e.g., Segregation and the Fourteenth Amendment in the States (B. Reams & P. Wilson, eds. 1975). This Court's decision in Brown v. Board of Education, 347 U.S. 483 (1954), signalled an end to that era. Over the past quarter of a century, every pronouncement of this Court and myriad Acts of Congress and Executive Orders attest a firm national policy to prohibit racial segregation and discrimination in public education.

An unbroken line of cases following Brown v. Board of Education establishes beyond doubt this Court's view that racial discrimination in education violates a most fundamental national public policy, as well as rights of individuals. . . . In Norwood v. Harrison, 413 U.S. 455, 468-469 (1973), we dealt with a nonpublic institution:

> [A] private school—even one that discriminates—fulfills an important educational function; *however, . . . [that] legitimate educational function cannot be isolated from discriminatory practices. . . . [D]iscriminatory treatment exerts a pervasive influence on the entire educational process.*

(Emphasis added.) See also Runyon v. McCrary, 427 U.S. 160 (1976); Griffin v. County School Board, 377 U.S. 218 (1964). . . .

Petitioners contend that, regardless of whether the IRS properly concluded that racially discriminatory private schools violate public policy, only Congress can alter the scope of §170 and §501(c)(3). Petitioners accordingly argue that the IRS overstepped its lawful bounds in issuing its 1970 and 1971 rulings.

Yet ever since the inception of the tax code, Congress has seen fit to vest in those administering the tax laws very broad authority to interpret those laws. In an area as complex as the tax system, the agency Congress vests with administrative responsibility must be able to exercise its authority to meet changing conditions and new problems. . . .

The actions of Congress since 1970 leave no doubt that the IRS reached the correct conclusion in exercising its authority. It is, of course, not unknown

---

24. The Court's reading of §501(c)(3) does not render meaningless Congress' action in specifying the eight categories of presumptively exempt organizations, as petitioners suggest. See Brief of Petitioner Goldsboro Christian Schools 18-24. To be entitled to tax-exempt status under §501(c)(3), an organization must first fall within one of the categories specified by Congress, and in addition must serve a valid charitable purpose.

for independent agencies or the Executive Branch to misconstrue the intent of a statute; Congress can and often does correct such misconceptions, if the courts have not done so. Yet for a dozen years Congress has been made aware—acutely aware—of the IRS rulings of 1970 and 1971. As we noted earlier, few issues have been the subject of more vigorous and widespread debate and discussion in and out of Congress than those related to racial segregation in education. Sincere adherents advocating contrary views have ventilated the subject for well over three decades. Failure of Congress to modify the IRS rulings of 1970 and 1971, of which Congress was, by its own studies and by public discourse, constantly reminded; and Congress' awareness of the denial of tax-exempt status for racially discriminatory schools when enacting other and related legislation make out an unusually strong case of legislative acquiescence in and ratification by implication of the 1970 and 1971 rulings. . . .

The evidence of Congressional approval of the policy embodied in Revenue Ruling 71-447 goes well beyond the failure of Congress to act on legislative proposals. Congress affirmatively manifested its acquiescence in the IRS policy when it enacted the present §501(i) of the Code. . . .

III

Petitioners contend that, even if the Commissioner's policy is valid as to nonreligious private schools, that policy cannot constitutionally be applied to schools that engage in racial discrimination on the basis of sincerely held religious beliefs. As to such schools, it is argued that the IRS construction of §170 and §501(c)(3) violates their free exercise rights under the Religion Clauses of the First Amendment. This contention presents claims not heretofore considered by this Court in precisely this context. . . .

The governmental interest at stake here is compelling. . . . [T]he Government has a fundamental, overriding interest in eradicating racial discrimination in education[25]—discrimination that prevailed, with official approval, for the first 165 years of this Nation's history. That governmental interest substantially outweighs whatever burden denial of tax benefits places on petitioners' exercise of their religious beliefs. The interests asserted by petitioners cannot be accommodated with that compelling governmental interest, . . . and no "less restrictive means" . . . are available to achieve the governmental interest.

The judgments of the Court of Appeals are, accordingly,

Affirmed.

Justice POWELL concurring in part and concurring in the judgment. . . .

I . . . concur in the Court's judgment that tax-exempt status under §§170(c) and 501(c)(3) is not available to private schools that concededly are racially discriminatory. I do not agree, however, with the Court's more general

---

25. We deal here only with religious *schools*—not with churches or other purely religious institutions; here, the governmental interest is in denying public support to racial discrimination in education. . . .

explanation of the justifications for the tax exemptions provided to charitable organizations. . . .

With all respect, I am unconvinced that the critical question in determining tax-exempt status is whether an individual organization provides a clear "public benefit" as defined by the Court. Over 106,000 organizations filed §501(c)(3) returns in 1981. Internal Revenue Service, 1982 Exempt Organization/Business Master File. I find it impossible to believe that all or even most of those organizations could prove that they "demonstrably serve and [are] in harmony with the public interest" or that they are "beneficial and stabilizing influences in community life." Nor am I prepared to say that petitioners, because of their racially discriminatory policies, necessarily contribute nothing of benefit to the community. It is clear from the substantially secular character of the curricula and degrees offered that petitioners provide educational benefits.

Even more troubling to me is the element of conformity that appears to inform the Court's analysis. The Court asserts that an exempt organization must "demonstrably serve and be in harmony with the public interest," must have a purpose that comports with "the common community conscience," and must not act in a manner "affirmatively at odds with [the] declared position of the whole government." Taken together, these passages suggest that the primary function of a tax-exempt organization is to act on behalf of the Government in carrying out governmentally approved policies. In my opinion, such a view of §501(c)(3) ignores the important role played by tax exemptions in encouraging diverse, indeed often sharply conflicting, activities and viewpoints. . . .

The Court's decision upholds IRS Revenue Ruling 71-447, and thus resolves the question whether tax-exempt status is available to private schools that openly maintain racially discriminatory admissions policies. There no longer is any justification for Congress to hesitate—as it apparently has—in articulating and codifying its desired policy as to tax exemptions for discriminatory organizations. Many questions remain, such as whether organizations that violate other policies should receive tax-exempt status under §501(c)(3). These should be legislative policy choices. . . . The contours of public policy should be determined by Congress, not by judges or the IRS.

Justice Rehnquist, dissenting.

The Court points out that there is a strong national policy in this country against racial discrimination. To the extent that the Court states that Congress in furtherance of this policy could deny tax-exempt status to educational institutions that promote racial discrimination, I readily agree. But, unlike the Court, I am convinced that Congress simply has failed to take this action and, as this Court has said over and over again, regardless of our view on the propriety of Congress' failure to legislate we are not constitutionally empowered to act for them. . . .

With undeniable clarity, Congress has explicitly defined the requirements for §501(c)(3) status. An entity must be (1) a corporation, or community chest, fund, or foundation, (2) organized for one of the eight enumerated purposes, (3) operated on a nonprofit basis, and (4) free from involvement in lobbying activities and political campaigns. Nowhere is there to be found some additional, undefined public policy requirement.

I have no disagreement with the Court's finding that there is a strong national policy in this country opposed to racial discrimination. I agree with the Court that Congress has the power to further this policy by denying §501(c)(3) status to organizations that practice racial discrimination. But as of yet Congress has failed to do so. Whatever the reasons for the failure, this Court should not legislate for Congress.

NOTES AND QUESTIONS

1. *Drawing the line.* The actions by the government described in n. 22 of *Bob Jones* reflected the Reagan Administration's discomfort with the exercise of IRS discretionary authority to withhold tax-exempt status on public policy grounds. It offered legislation that would have provided express statutory authority for the result in the case, by denying §501(c)(3) treatment to any school that practiced racial discrimination. The legislation was effectively mooted by the Supreme Court's decision in *Bob Jones*.

During Senate Finance Committee hearings to consider this legislation, the question arose whether the legislation would deny tax-exempt status to a yeshiva (an Orthodox Jewish religious school) that had no black students as a foreseeable consequence of its admitting only Orthodox Jews. Everyone seemed to agree that the legislation would not deny tax-exempt status to the yeshiva, by reason of the absence of an intent to discriminate against blacks.

Is this distinction persuasive? Does the decision in *Bob Jones* permit such a yeshiva to be tax exempt?

2. *Public policy.* Once the Court in *Bob Jones* decides that §§501(c)(3) and 170 include a public policy limitation, it turns to the question whether racial discrimination in private schools violates public policy. The Court cites Brown v. Board of Education. How is that case relevant to racial discrimination in private education? Note that if the Court had been willing to treat tax deductibility as a form of governmental support or subsidy, Brown v. Board of Education would have been not only relevant but dispositive. But what would that approach have done to the deduction for contributions to religious organizations?

Norwood v. Harrison, also cited by the Court, held that the equal protection and due process rights of minority citizens were violated by a state textbook lending program for private schools to the extent that it included schools that engaged in racial discrimination. In addition, Runyon v. McCrary, also cited, held that the protection of the right of contract under the Civil Rights Act of 1866 (now 42 U.S.C. §1981) applied to private schools.

3. *"Charitable" versus "educational."* Given the Court's interpretation of §170(c)(2)(B), does the word "educational" have any function? That is, could the provision be amended, without losing anything, to cover "charitable purposes" as opposed to "charitable or educational purposes"?

4. *Where there's a will.* Examine §501(i). Note its limited applicability and its failure to include discrimination based on gender. What does that tell us about public policy concerning such discrimination?

12.   Loss of Exemption Due to Private Inurement

Bob Jones University lost its tax-exempt status because the relevant statutory provisions were held to incorporate the requirement that an organization's activities be consistent with public policy. A more common reason for loss (or denial) of tax-exempt status is that an organization benefits donors, employees, or other persons and therefore serves a private, rather than a public, purpose. See §503; Reg. §1.501(c)(3).

In United Cancer Council v. Commissioner, 165 F.3d 1173 (7th Cir. 1999), reversing 109 T.C. 326 (1997), the IRS challenged the taxpayer's status as a §501(c)(3) charity. The taxpayer, an offshoot of the American Cancer Society, entered into a no-risk arrangement with a fund-raising company. Under that arrangement, nearly 80 million solicitations for donations were mailed, at a cost of almost $30 million. The arrangement netted the charity less than $3 million, but netted the fundraising companies about $8 million. The rest of the donations went to pay for postage and other expenses. The Tax Court upheld the denial of exempt status on the rationale that the fundraising companies were insiders. The appellate court reversed but remanded the case for a hearing on whether the charity had violated its duty of care and, through negligence, had ended up conferring a benefit upon a private party. The parties ended up settling, with the charity agreeing not to solicit donations and distribute its assets to other §501(c)3 organizations.[26]

E.   INTEREST

1.   The Rules

Interest is the cost of borrowing money. Imagine a taxpayer who expects to have $10,000 in cash one year from now but wants to be able to use that $10,000 today. By borrowing $10,000, he can make current use of money he expects to receive later. Thus, interest can be thought of as the price one pays for accelerating access to financial resources that would otherwise only be available in the future. Should interest costs be deductible within an income tax? U.S. tax law offers a familiar answer: It depends.

Business or investment interest—that is, interest incurred in a trade or business or for the production of income—is generally deductible. See Chapters 7 and 8 for discussion of limits on that deduction. By contrast, the tax treatment of interest on debt incurred for personal purposes has undergone some important changes over the past quarter century. Until 1987, all personal interest was deductible. Today, however, personal interest is deductible only if it is "qualified residence interest" within the meaning of §163(h)(3). All other

---

26. *United Cancer Council Closing Agreement*, Planned Giving Design Ctr. http://www.pgdc.com/pgdc/united-cancer-council-closing-agreement (last updated May 18, 2011).

interest not incurred for business or investment purposes is nondeductible. §163(h)(2).

"Qualified residence interest" is "home acquisition debt" incurred to buy, build, or improve a personal residence, and that it is secured by the residence. There is a limit of $1 million on debt principal that can generate deductible interest; the limit is $750,000 for debt incurred after 2017. §163(h)(3)(B). (For years after 2025, the $750,000 limit applies regardless of when debt is incurred.) Along with the nontaxation of imputed rent from living in one's own home, these rules form the core of the U.S. tax system's subsidy for homeownership.

Until 2018, individuals were also allowed to deduct the first $100,000 interest on so-called home equity loans. These were loans secured by a residence, but the proceeds of which were not used to buy or improve the residence. Thus, a taxpayer could borrow out some of the equity in her home, use the proceeds for other purposes (e.g., a new car, trip around the world), and deduct the interest on that loan.

The following examples illustrate the operation of these rules. In each example assume that the house is used as the taxpayer's personal residence.

Example A

In 2018, A buys a house for $1.2 million, with a down payment of $200,000 and a loan of $1 million. Acquisition indebtedness accounts for $750,000 (which is the limit) of the loan. A may deduct interest attributable to that amount of the loan.

Example B

B buys a house for $300,000, with a loan of $150,000 and the remaining $150,000 from her savings. A month later she borrows $100,000, secured by the house. She uses the proceeds of the second loan to replenish her savings. Only the first loan ($150,000) is acquisition indebtedness. If B had borrowed the entire $250,000 at the time of the purchase of the house, the entire amount of the loan would have been acquisition indebtedness. Can you think of any sound justification for this difference in result?

2.   Asymmetrical Treatment of Interest Income and Expense

One widely held view about interest on personal indebtedness is that it is a cost of consuming sooner rather than later, part of the cost of achieving personal satisfaction, and as such represents a form of consumption expense and should not be deductible.

This view is consistent with a present value analysis of consumption. The cost of paying interest is balanced, for the marginal borrower, by the advantage of earlier consumption. Once this cost is taken into account, the borrower is no poorer. It would be improper to allow her to deduct consumer interest. Suppose, however, we used the same type of analysis to look at the marginal investor, that is, someone who saves instead of spends. On a present value basis, the deferred consumption is worth less than current consumption. For the saver, the receipt of interest is offset by the disadvantage of later consumption. If we were truly serious about this sort of present value analysis, perhaps we would neither permit deduction of interest expense nor tax receipt of interest income. (See discussion of consumption tax in Chapter 2.)

Of course, while we deny the deduction for consumer interest expense, we do not exempt interest income. As a result, a taxpayer who incurs $10,000 of consumer interest expense and realizes $10,000 of interest income has net taxable interest of $10,000—even though her economic interest income is zero.

3. Policy Justification and Transition Issues

The Senate Finance Committee Report on the 1986 bill[27] justifies the mortgage interest on the ground that "encouraging home ownership is an important policy goal." Do you agree? Why should Congress encourage people to own rather than rent their homes or to buy homes rather than cars, other consumer durables, or investments in assets such as stocks?

Most proponents of tax reform believe the home mortgage interest deduction ought (eventually) to be eliminated. They believe that the special treatment of home ownership is inefficient. One difficulty with this reform is persons have purchased homes on the assumption that they would be able to deduct their mortgage interest. Repeal might significantly reduce home values, in some cases to less than the outstanding mortgage balance. It would be possible, of course, to grandfather persons with existing loans but repeal the deduction for new mortgage indebtedness. This more limited reform would not affect current homeowners who keep their present homes and do not increase the size of their mortgages. The reform would, however, reduce the value of homes to new purchasers, who could no longer deduct mortgage interest. This in turn would reduce the price existing homeowners could get when and if they decide to sell their home. Do the reliance interests of current homeowners offer a persuasive argument against reform? Would you take a different view of the reliance interests if the reason existing homes lost value was that the Federal Reserve Board had raised interest rates? If so, then on what ground?

As noted above, beginning in 2018, the cap for acquisition indebtedness falls from $1 million to $750,000 for newly purchased homes. Beginning in 2026, the $750,000 cap applies to all homes, whenever purchased. In addition, as noted above, effective 2018, taxpayers can no longer deduct interest on so-called home equity loans, which were not used to buy or improve their residence. Do these limitations on deductibility represent a reasonable compromise between efficiency and reliance interests?

---

27. S. Rep. No. 313, 99th Cong., 2d. Sess. 804 (1986).

4.   Tracing

The differing treatment of interest on personal and business loans raises a number of difficult tracing issues. Suppose, for example, that business property is used to secure a loan that is used for personal purposes. Is the loan a personal or a business loan? Under Treas. Reg. §1.163-8T,[28] interest generally is allocated according to the *use* of the loan proceeds. Thus, interest on a loan that is used for personal purposes is characterized as personal interest; the fact that the loan may be secured by business property is irrelevant. Reg. §1.163-8T(c). As noted earlier, however, special rules apply to interest incurred in connection with a principal residence.

Suppose borrowed funds are commingled with nonborrowed funds, with some of the commingled funds used for business purposes and some to finance personal consumption. No portion of the loan is incurred in connection with a principal residence. Is the loan a business loan, a personal loan, or a combination of both? What portion of interest on the loan is deductible? Treas. Reg. §1.163-8 provides a complicated set of tracing rules for that situation. A review of those rules is left to the curious student.

5.   Interest on Student Loans

Section 221 allows a deduction for interest on indebtedness used to pay higher education expenses of the taxpayer, the taxpayer's spouse, or a dependent of the taxpayer. The maximum amount deductible is $2,500. The deduction is phased out as income rises, and in 2017 it is phased out completely for taxpayers with modified adjusted gross income in excess of $80,000 ($165,000 in the case of a joint return). The phase-out thresholds are adjusted annually for inflation.

F.   TAXES

Under §164, a taxpayer may claim a deduction for certain taxes paid to state, local, and foreign governments. Our focus here will be on the deduction for taxes paid to state and local governments. Like the various provisions already discussed above, the deduction for state and local taxes (SALT) is an itemized deduction that appears on Schedule A. The deduction is not available to those who choose to claim the standard deduction instead of itemizing their deductions.

Under the 2017 act, the individual SALT deduction is capped at $10,000. This cap significantly affects high-income taxpayers in high-tax states. For example, the top individual marginal income tax rate in California is approximately 13 percent. High-income taxpayers might pay $50,000 or more in income taxes (and pay property taxes as well). In the past, this payment was

---

28. The regulation was promulgated as temporary (that's what the "T" stands for) in 1987, but it appears in fact to be permanent.

entirely deductible, reducing the effective income tax rate from around 13 percent to about 8 percent. Now most of that tax will be nondeductible, leaving the effective marginal tax rate at 13 percent. An open issue in tax policy is whether the new, high effective tax rates will cause some high-income individuals to locate or relocate out of high-tax states.

Corporations may continue to deduct state and local taxes without limitation.

1. Rationale for the SALT Deduction

The policy issue presented by §164 is similar in many ways to the issue raised by other deductions considered in this chapter: Should the deduction be regarded as an adjustment necessary to arrive at a proper definition of net income or, if not, is it simply a device for achieving some desirable goal extraneous to the income tax system, in this case support of state and local governmental operations?

On the question of properly defining income, one argument commonly offered in favor of the §164 deduction is that taxes are involuntary and do not buy personal consumption. They may, however, help to pay for the benefits provided by state and local governments, including police and fire protection, education, medical benefits, a legal infrastructure for the enforcement of contracts, etc. While the value that individual taxpayers derive from these benefits may not precisely (or even approximately) equal the state and local taxes they pay, the value is unlikely to be zero, and it may not otherwise be subject to inclusion. Given the difficulty of measuring the exact value received and then computing a net inclusion or deduction given its variance from the amount of tax paid, simply denying the deduction may be the best one can do from an ability-to-pay standpoint.

An alternative rationale for the deduction is that a good portion of state and local government funding is on education. Education may be seen as generating positive externalities and under some theories of the tax base the cost of education may be an appropriate offset against income. See Chapter 7.

2. The Basic Structure of U.S. State and Local Taxation

The most important of the taxes listed as personal deductions in §164 are state and local income, sales, and real property taxes. The deduction for sales taxes was actually repealed as part of the Tax Reform Act of 1986. In 2004, however, Congress reintroduced the deduction for sales taxes in a modified form primarily for the benefit of people in states with no income tax. §164(b)(5). Under this new provision, taxpayers may elect to deduct state and local general sales taxes in lieu of state and local income taxes. These three taxes—income taxes, property taxes, and sales taxes—make up the vast majority of state and local governments' tax revenues in the United States. As shown in Figure 10-1, revenues from these three sources accounted for 92 percent of all state and local tax revenue for 2013.

Of course, not all taxes paid to state and local governments will be deducted on a federal income tax return. The deduction is available only to itemizers and, as noted above, those who do itemize must choose between deducting either income or sales taxes. Because of these features, the amount of the federal subsidy available under §164 varies greatly depending on the type of tax. For example, note from Figure 10-1 that approximately $496 billion in sales taxes were paid in 2013. According to IRS data, however, taxpayers claimed only $17 billion of sales taxes on individual tax returns in 2013. The disparity between these two numbers is likely due to the fact that those paying sales taxes are either not itemizing their deductions or are claiming the deduction for income taxes instead of the deduction for sales taxes. By contrast, taxpayers claimed $304 billion in property tax deductions and $174 billion in income tax deductions for tax year 2013.

The $10,000 cap on individual SALT deductions, combined with the higher standard deductions effective 2018, is expected to greatly reduce the aggregate amount of SALT deductions.

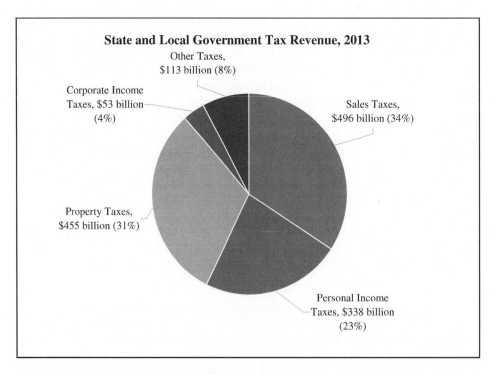

FIGURE 10-1.
State and Local Government Tax Revenue, 2013

G.   PERSONAL EXEMPTIONS

Prior to 2018, taxpayers received a personal exemption deduction for themselves and each of their dependents. In 2017, the deduction was $4,050 for both the taxpayer and his or her spouse filing a joint return, and each dependent. Thus, a married couple with two dependent children would receive personal exemptions totaling $16,200. Personal exemptions are now suspended until 2026. The higher standard deduction, described at the start of this chapter, is intended to serve as a rough substitute.

The suspension of personal exemptions makes it unnecessary to review the definition of a dependent, which was (and is, since the definition is still in the Code) quite complex. In general, the term "dependent" includes children under age 19 (24 if students) who live at home and do not provide more than half their support. It also includes certain other individuals who are supported by the taxpayer.

H.   THE ALTERNATIVE MINIMUM TAX

1.   The Individual Alternative Minimum Tax

The alternative minimum tax (AMT) imposes a tax at a reduced rate on a broader base. Broadly speaking, the AMT starts with taxable income, adds to that amount certain tax preferences the taxpayer has taken advantage of, subtracts an exemption amount subject to a phase-out, and imposes a tax on the resulting figure at a reduced rate—presently between 26 and 28 percent for individuals. The taxpayer pays the greater of the AMT or his tax liability as determined under normal tax.[29]

Consider this simplified AMT calculation for a single individual:

Taxable income
+ Tax preferences
− $70,300 exemption amount for single individuals[30]
= Alternative minimum taxable income (AMTI)
Tax due = AMTI * 26% (28% above $95,750)

The exemption is subject to phase out, which for single individuals begins when adjusted gross income reaches $500,000; it is phased out completely at $781,200. The AMT is indexed for inflation: The above brackets and exemption amount apply in 2018.

Most taxpayers will find their AMT tax liability less than their liability under the normal tax and thus won't pay anything under the AMT. The AMT won't apply to them because of some combination of the following three factors:

---

29. To the extent the amount of the AMT attributable to timing rules (as opposed to exclusions such as tax-exempt interest) exceeds the regular tax, the excess is treated as a credit that can be used in subsequent years to reduce the excess of the regular tax over the AMT. The credit provides relief where an AMT timing rule includes an item in AMT income in one year and the same item in regular income under the regular-tax rules in a later year.

30. $109,400 for married individuals filing jointly.

They don't have many tax preference items; the exemption amount reduces the AMTI to a low figure, or the AMT tax rate of 26 or 28 percent is lower than the rate their income is subject to under the regular income tax.

The AMT was adopted as a response to news that a small number of very high-income taxpayers had taken advantage of tax preferences to eliminate their tax liability altogether. The AMT was designed to ensure that these taxpayers, and other high-income taxpayers, paid at least some tax—however they organized their financial affairs. The AMT has always been controversial, and generally disfavored by tax policy scholars. Preferences that gave rise to the AMT (and that have been added back into income to produce AMTI) included the deduction for state and local taxes, personal exemptions that helped individuals with large families, capital gains, and interest on municipal bonds. Most tax policy scholars believe that if these preferences are not a good idea, they should be eliminated; if they are justified, taxpayers should be allowed to benefit from them.

The 2017 tax act significantly reduces the scope of the AMT. First, as noted above, the SALT deduction is now capped at $10,000. In the past, that deduction has been most responsible, on the margin, for pushing taxpayers into the AMT. Now that the deduction is capped, the amount of the preference that is added to taxable income will be less. Taxpayers no longer get much of a SALT deduction, but as a result will not have to worry as much about being subject to the AMT. Second, personal exemption deductions, another preference item, have been eliminated. Third, as noted above, the deduction for interest on home equity loans, another preference item, has been eliminated. Finally, the exemption amounts and thresholds at which the exemptions are phased out have been raised.

Perhaps the major tax preference remaining for individuals that can trigger the AMT is incentive stock options.

2.   Corporate AMT

For many years, there was a corporate AMT, as well as an individual AMT. However, the corporate AMT never raised as much money as the individual AMT. The outline of the Corporate AMT was similar to the outline of the individual AMT. Income was increased by tax preferences and then taxed at a lower rate. The major tax preference was accelerated depreciation.

The corporate AMT was eliminated by the 2017 tax act.

11

TAX AND POVERTY: THE EARNED
INCOME TAX CREDIT

A. INTRODUCTION

The Census Bureau estimated that in 2016 over 40 million Americans were living in poverty.[1] That translates into about 13 percent of the population, a figure that has remained remarkably constant over the years. See Figure 11-1, *infra.*

The Census Bureau's figures represent an annual snapshot, measuring how large the poverty rate is at any given point in time. The figures do not tell us anything about the movement of individuals in and out of poverty, but studies of income mobility do measure that movement. These studies show that poverty tends to be persistent, not just through an adult's life but through the life of his or her children. Children born in poverty are likely to have below-average incomes,[2] and rags-to-riches stories are rare. One recent study found that only about one in twelve children born to parents in the bottom income quintile will wind up in the top income quintile; only about one in five hundred will wind up in the top 1 percent.[3] International comparisons of poverty are difficult to make, in part because each jurisdiction defines poverty

---

1. Jessica L. Semega, Kayla R. Fontenot, and Melissa A. Kollar, *U.S. Census Bureau, Income and Poverty in the United States: 2016*, 12, fig. 4 (2017), https://www.census.gov/content/dam/Census/library/publications/2017/demo/P60-259.pdf. The Census Bureau defines poverty, generally, as earning less than three times the cost of a minimum food diet. See *How Is Poverty Measured in the United States?* Ctr. for Poverty Res., U.C. Davis (last updated Dec. 17, 2018), http://poverty.ucdavis.edu/faq/how-poverty-measured-united-states.

2. *Id.*

3. Raj Chetty, Nathaniel Hendren, Patrick Kline, Emmanuel Saez, and Nicholas Turner, *Is the United States Still a Land of Opportunity? Recent Trends in Intergenerational Mobility,* fig. 3, Nat'l Bureau of Econ. Res., Working Paper No. 19844, 2014, http://www.nber.org/papers/ w19844.pdf; Downloadable Data from Chetty and Hendren, tbl. 1 (2015), *The Equality of Opportunity Project,* http://www.equality-of-opportunity.org/index.php/data (last visited Sept. 7, 2016).

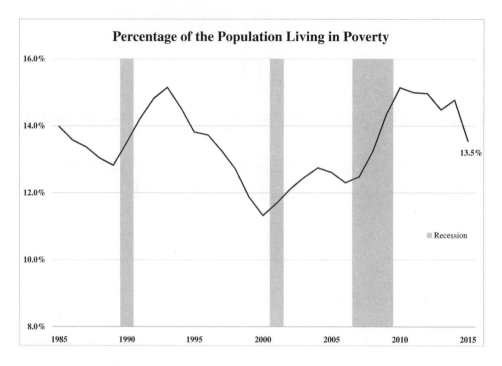

FIGURE 11-1.

differently. In general, though, the United States has greater inequality and less intergenerational mobility than other OECD nations.[4]

The primary way in which the federal government addresses poverty is through the direct or indirect provision of goods and services. The federal government spends over $800 billion a year subsidizing health care as part of the Affordable Care Act, Medicaid coverage for disabled individuals, and Medicare.[5] Medicare is an age-based program, but it is highly progressive in its distribution of benefits.[6] Food assistance programs include SNAP, or food

4. Chetty, Hendren, Kline, Saez, and Turner, *Is the United States Still a Land of Opportunity? Recent Trends in Intergenerational Mobility*, 146 (Nat'l Bureau of Econ. Res., Working Paper No. 19844, 2014), http://www.nber.org/papers/w19844.pdf. *See also* Miles Corak, *Income Inequality, Equality of Opportunity, and Intergenerational Mobility*, 27 J. Econ. Perspectives, 82, fig. 1 (2013), http://pubs. aeaweb.org/doi/pdfplus/10.1257/jep.27.3.79.

5. Dep't of Health and Human Servs., *Fiscal Year 2018 Budget in Brief*, 1, https://www.hhs.gov/about/budget/fy2018/budget-in-brief/index.html; Juliette Cubanski and Tricia Newman, *The Facts on Medicare Spending and Financing*, Kaiser Family Foundation (July 18, 2017), https://www.kff.org/medicare/issue-brief/the-facts-on-medicare-spending-and-financing/; Bds. of Trs. of the Fed. Hosp. Ins. and Fed. Supplementary Med. Ins. Tr. Funds, *2017 Annual Report* 7 (2017), https://www.cms. gov/Research-Statistics-Data-and-Systems/Statistics-Trends-and-Reports/ReportsTrustFunds/Downloads/TR2017.pdf ; Cong. Budget Office, *Federal Subsidies for Health Insurance Coverage for People Under Age 65:* 2017-2027, 3 (2017), https://www.cbo.gov/system/files/115th-congress-2017-2018/reports/53091-fshic.pdf.

6. The overall program remains very progressive even though, as noted earlier, it is funded in part through a somewhat regressive payroll tax.

stamps, at a cost of over $70 billion a year and subsidized school lunch programs, at a cost of about $10 billion a year.[7] The Department of Education has an annual budget of over $60 billion, most of which goes to pay for programs for special education, programs for economically disadvantaged students, or financial aid.[8] The Department of Housing and Urban Development is budgeted at about $50 billion a year, and Temporary Assistance to Families in Need provides over $30 billion a year in cash benefits and services to low-income families.[9]

In addition to these and many other programs, the federal government distributes more than $900 billion a year in social security benefits. In 2017, about $150 billion of this distribution was for individuals who suffered from physical or mental disabilities.[10] The remainder was paid to retired individuals or their beneficiaries under a formula that is highly progressive with respect to past earnings.[11]

The above figures should help put the tax measures cited below in perspective. They also illustrate a broader point made in Chapter 1. Tax is only half of our fiscal system; the other half is spending. Both tax and spending ought to be considered when evaluating a policy objective or existing program or provision.

B.   THE INCOME TAX AND THE EARNED INCOME TAX CREDIT

1.   Features of the Tax Law That Reduce Liability to Zero

One obvious way in which the income tax addresses poverty is that it does not levy a tax on low-income individuals. The law accomplishes this primarily through the standard deductions and personal exemptions, discussed in the previous chapter. In addition, the law has a series of other provisions, ranging from child-care credits to exclusion from income of scholarships and welfare payments, designed to benefit low-income taxpayers. These and other provisions are discussed throughout this book. Finally, the rate structure ensures that taxpayers with small amounts of positive income pay tax at low rates.

7. Dep't of Agric., *2018 Budget Summary*, 40 (2017), https://www.usda.gov/sites/default/files/documents/USDA-Budget-Summary-2018.pdf; Cong. Budget Office, *Child Nutrition Programs, Spending and Policy Options*, 3 (2015), https://www.cbo.gov/sites/default/files/114th-congress-2015-2016/reports/50737-ChildNutrition.pdf.

8. Dep't of Educ., *Education Department Budget History* (2017), https://www2.ed.gov/about/overview/budget/history/edhistory.pdf.

9. Dep't of Hous. and Urban Dev., *Overview of FY 2017 President's Budget*, 1 (2017), https://www.hud.gov/sites/documents/PROPOSEDFY17FACTSHEET.pdf; Cong. Budget Office, *Temporary Assistance for Needy Families: Spending and Policy Options* (2015) 1, https://www.cbo.gov/publication/49887.

10. Soc. Sec. Admin., *Fast Facts and Figures About Social Security*, 15-35 (2017), https://www.ssa.gov/policy/docs/chartbooks/fast_facts/2017/fast_facts17.pdf.

11. *Id.*

In considering these features, students should recognize that other federal taxes, including payroll taxes and excise taxes on gasoline, alcohol, and cigarettes, apply with full force to low-income taxpayers. Still other federal taxes, such as corporate income taxes, might be shifted in part to low-income taxpayers. A similar analysis might be done at the state and local level, with state sales taxes in particular imposing significant burdens on low-income taxpayers.

2.　Overview of the EITC

The Earned Income Tax Credit, or EITC, is the feature of the income tax most directed at poverty and one of the most significant anti-poverty provisions or programs in the federal system. In 2016, the EITC generated payments of around $64 billion to low-income households.[12] The EITC is the largest source of cash (as opposed to in-kind) transfers to the working poor.

The EITC is best understood as an alternative to traditional welfare. Traditional welfare has the unfortunate effect of discouraging labor force participation and work effort. One reason for this is that benefits are reduced as work increases and income rises. The reduction in benefits has the effect of a tax, and some workers will respond to this tax like any other tax, by reducing work effort. This is the substitution effect of the tax: Workers substitute untaxed leisure for taxed labor. In addition, welfare benefits increase wealth, albeit from almost nothing to very little. This creates a so-called income or wealth effect, as workers become a little less desperate for jobs, leading some workers to reduce effort by some amount. The substitution and income effects are discussed in Chapter 2.

The Earned Income Tax Credit, or EITC, is designed to provide benefits to low-income workers without a net decrease in work effort or labor force participation. Under the EITC, benefits are given in the form of a refundable credit to low-income taxpayers with labor income. To get the credit, the taxpayer must work and, at low levels of total income, the credit increases as wages increase. Under the rate structure in effect in 2016, the credit reaches a maximum of $.40 for every dollar earned. The EITC thus encourages labor force participation and work effort for low-income taxpayers. The EITC is eventually phased out, and the phaseout acts in the same manner as described above, as an implicit tax.

Thus, while traditional welfare discourages both labor force participation and work effort, the EITC encourages work-force participation and both favors (at low income levels) and discourages (as it is phased out) work effort.

---

12. Elaine Maag, *Refundable Credits: The Earned Income Tax Credit and the Child Tax Credit*, Tax Policy Center (2017), https://www.urban.org/sites/default/files/publication/89171/2001197-refundable-credits-the-earned-income-tax-credit-and-the-child-tax-credit_0.pdf.

The EITC, which grew out of experiments with a negative income tax in the late 1960s, was originally enacted in 1975 and was substantially expanded during the Reagan and Clinton years.

3.   Operation of the EITC

Under §32, a taxpayer is entitled to claim a credit equal to a specified percentage of "earned income" up to a certain level. Several features of the EITC deserve mention:

- The amount of the credit depends on the number of the taxpayer's children. In 2018, taxpayers with no children receive a very small credit (a maximum of $519), while substantially larger maximum amounts are available for taxpayers with one child ($3,461), two children ($5,716), or three or more children ($6,431).
- The EITC is a "refundable" credit, which means that it does not just offset any tax liability but, far more important, results in a payment from the government to the extent that the credit exceeds tax liability.
- The credit is phased in; that is, over a certain income range, the credit rises as earned income rises, so it can be thought of as a form of wage subsidy or supplement.
- At a specified higher level of adjusted gross income (or earned income, if higher), the credit is phased out as income rises, which is consistent with the objective of providing benefits only to people with low incomes.
- The point at which the credit begins to phase out is slightly higher for a married couple than it is for a single taxpayer, reflecting an effort to reduce the marriage penalty inherent in the credit's design.

Each of these features can be seen in Figure 11-2, which shows the amount of the EITC available to taxpayers in different circumstances for the tax year 2016.[13]

Figure 11-2 helps to illustrate the EITC's chief incentive effects. First, take note of the steep line that represents the phase-in range of the credit. In that income range, the taxpayer can substantially increase her EITC payment by increasing her earned income. As an example, for a single taxpayer with two children, every one-dollar increase in earned income over the phase-in range (up to a maximum of $14,320) increases the taxpayer's EITC by 40 cents. Thus, an increase in earned income from, say, $5,000 to $15,000 will increase the EITC payment from $2,000 to the maximum credit allowable of $5,716 for 2016 (that is, 40 percent multiplied by $14,320).

---

13. Please note that, with respect to married taxpayers, we have included a dotted line only for taxpayers with three or more children. Lines showing the amounts available for married taxpayers with no children, one child, or two children were omitted to avoid excessive clutter in the chart.

Federal Earned Income Tax Credit
Single or Head-of-Household Filers, Tax Year 2016

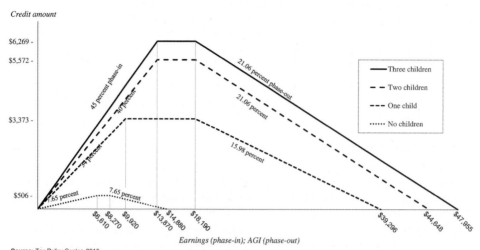

Source: Tax Policy Center, 2016.
Note: Amounts are for taxpayers filing a single or head-of-household tax return. For married couples filing a joint tax return, the credit begins to phase out at income $5,550 higher than shown.

FIGURE 11-2.
Structure of the Earned Income Tax Credit: Tax Year 2016

Continuing with the example of a single parent with two children, the credit amount remains the same over the range of $14,320 to $18,700 and then begins to phase out as the taxpayer's adjusted gross income or earned income (whichever is higher) exceeds $18,700 ($24,400 for married taxpayers filing a joint return). Note that in this phase-out range, the declining credit amount has incentive effects similar to the imposition of a positive tax. That is, for every one-dollar increase in income over the range from $18,700 to $45,898, the taxpayer loses 21 cents of the credit. Here the incentive effects are exactly the opposite of those in the phase-in range. The more the taxpayer earns, the smaller the credit she will receive. This work disincentive is in addition to numerous other taxes and phaseouts that create work disincentives in this same range: for example, payroll taxes, the federal income tax, and housing subsidy phaseouts. This kind of "piling on" of taxes and benefit reductions, resulting in high marginal rates of "taxation" of earnings, is common in welfare programs.

Finally, it should be noted that, because of the way the EITC is made available to single people and to married couples, it can also result in a significant "marriage penalty." Consider two single taxpayers, Mike and Carol, each of whom earns $15,000 and has three children. Because he has three boys and earned income in the plateau range of the EITC, Mike will be entitled to the maximum credit of $6,431. Carol, with three girls and the same income, will also be entitled to a credit of $6,431. Thus, assuming they remain single, the two families combined will be entitled to an EITC payment of $12,862. If Mike and Carol get married, however, their combined earned income will be $30,000, which entitles them to a total credit of $5,235: $7,627 less than they were receiving when single.

On the other hand, the EITC can sometimes produce significant marriage bonuses. For example, consider a taxpayer with three children and no earned income who marries someone with no children and $15,000 of income. Before getting married, this couple would be entitled to no EITC payments (see Figure 11-2). After marrying, the couple will be entitled to an EITC payment of $6,431.

4.   Efficiency of the EITC

The EITC appears to be extremely effective in helping individuals escape poverty, both by paying out $60 plus billion dollars a year and by increasing the number of low-income individuals in the labor force. One study estimated that a $1,000 per family increase in EITC payouts increases labor participation by about 7 percent and leads to about a 9 percent reduction in the number of individuals below the poverty level.[14] The EITC has also been found to provide ancillary benefits, such as increased school performance and health outcomes for children in families receiving EITC payments.[15]

As noted above, the EITC might be expected to increase lower-income individuals' employment and hours worked but to reduce hours worked by individuals in the phase-out range. Economists have found, however, that while the EITC does substantially increase employment, it has relatively little effect on the average number of hours worked by those subject to the phase-in and phase-out.[16] One possible explanation for this unexpected effect is that participants recognize that the EITC rewards work-force participation (thus leading to an increase in employment) but they may not respond to the phase-in and phase-out rules by reducing hours worked because those rules are more complicated to understand.[17]

5.   Reform Proposals

The EITC has been criticized on three main points. First, it is complex not only in operation (see Figure 11-2) but also in its qualification requirements, foremost in its methods for determining who can claim a child in

---

14. Hilary W. Hoynes and Ankur Patel, *Effective Policy for Reducing Inequality: The Earned Income Tax Credit and the Distribution of Income,* 29, Nat'l Bureau of Econ. Res., Working Paper No. 21340, 2015, http://www.nber.org/papers/w21340.

15. Hilary W. Hoynes, Douglas L. Miller, and David Simon, *Income, the Earned Income Tax Credit, and Infant Health,* 30, Nat'l Bureau of Econ. Res., Working Paper No. 18206, 2012, http://www.nber.org/papers/w18206.pdf; Raj Chetty, John N. Friedman, and Jonah Rockoff, *New Evidence on the Long-Term Impacts of Tax Credits,* 2-3 (I.R.S., 2011), https://www.irs.gov/pub/ irs-soi/11rpchettyfriedmanrockoff.pdf.

16. Hoynes and Patel, *Effective Policy for Reducing Inequality: The Earned Income Tax Credit and the Distribution of Income,* 10, Nat'l Bureau of Econ. Res., Working Paper No. 21340, 2015, http://www.nber.org/papers/w21340. This paper argues that the EITC has no effect at the phase-out range but some effect at the phase-in range. See the reference in *infra* note 18 for a paper maintaining there is little effect at either range.

17. This suggestion is made by the authors in Raj Chetty and Emmanuel Saez, *Teaching the Tax Code: Earnings Responses to an Experiment with EITC Recipients,* 6-7, Nat'l Bureau of Econ. Res., Working Paper No. 14836, 2009, http://www.nber.org/papers/w14836.pdf.

a divorced, separated, multigenerational, or nontraditional family.[18] Because of its complexity, about one in five taxpayers who qualify for the EITC do not claim it,[19] and some claimants do not qualify. A second perceived weakness of the EITC is that it provides virtually no benefits to childless individuals living in poverty. And third, it overlaps with other provisions with similar aims, such as the dependent tax credit and the head of household filing status.

To address these concerns, some policymakers have recommended that the EITC be expanded to provide work incentive for all individuals, including those without children, and that the various child benefit provisions be combined into one unitary provision.[20] Another reform suggestion is that the IRS, working with existing data (from tax returns or third-party employer reports), provide EITC payments to taxpayers it finds eligible, regardless of whether those taxpayers request the EITC on their tax returns.[21] While the EITC has been found to be an extremely effective antipoverty program, its reach is, by definition, limited to those who have jobs. Consider two individuals, A and B, each of whom are looking for a job. A finds employment, but B does not. The benefits of the EITC go to A, even though B is the needier of the two. B's support must then come from more traditional forms of government transfers, or possibly from programs that go further in supporting employment.

Reformers have also suggested changing the way the EITC is distributed to help low-income families maintain savings and liquidity throughout the year. Coming as a lump sum refund at tax time, the EITC provides many families a much-needed financial boost to pay bills, make repairs, and deal with unexpected expenses. To better serve as a "rainy day" savings resource throughout the year, some reformers recommend allowing EITC recipients to opt in to a program that offers them a modest savings if they choose to defer a portion of their refund for six months.[22] This provides them with another liquidity boost to handle financial shocks that have arisen later in the year.

18. Robert Greenstein, John Wancheck, and Chuck Marr, *Reducing Overpayments in the Earned Income Tax Credit,* Ctr. on Budget & Pol'y Priorities (Dec. 1, 2015), http://www.cbpp.org/research/federal-tax/reducing-overpayments-in-the-earned-income-tax-credit.

19. Jacob Goldin, *Tax Benefit Complexity and Take-Up: Lessons from the Earned Income Tax Credit* (Feb. 2018) (draft), http://www.law.nyu.edu/sites/default/files/upload_documents/Tax%20Benefit%20Complexity%20and%20Take-Up%20-%20Goldin.pdf.

20. Chuck Marr, Chye-Ching Huang, Cecile Murray, and Arloc Sherman, *Strengthening the EITC for Childless Workers Would Promote Work and Reduce Poverty,* Ctr. on Budget & Pol'y Priorities (Apr. 11, 2016), http://www.cbpp.org/research/federal-tax/strengthening-the-eitc-for-childless-workers-would-promote-work-and-reduce.

21. The IRS currently does some of this, using tax return data to notify some taxpayers who have not requested it that they seem to qualify for the EITC. For a proposal that the IRS complete the returns of low-income taxpayers, see *The Simple Return: Reducing America's Tax Burden Through Return-Free Filing,* The Brookings Institution (July 2006), http://www.hamiltonproject.org/assets/legacy/files/downloads_and_links/The_Simple_Return-_Reducing_Americas_Tax_Burden_Through_Return-Free_Filing_Brief.pdf. Encouraging the use of Assisted Preparation Methods (AMPs) would also likely increase take-up. See Goldin, *supra* note 19.

22. Sarah Halpern-Meekin, Sara Sternberg Greene, Ezra Levin, and Kathryn Edin, *The Rainy Day Earned Income Tax Credit: A Reform to Boost Financial Security by Helping Low-Wage Workers Build Emergency Savings,* 4 Russell Sage Foundation J. Soc. Sci. 161, 172 (2018).

12

CAPITAL GAINS AND LOSSES

In this final chapter, we examine in further detail a topic that has surfaced throughout the book: the federal income tax treatment of capital gains and losses. Most students are generally aware that the U.S. tax system offers preferential treatment of capital gains in some circumstances. The materials that follow are designed to help you supplement that general awareness with substantive and detailed legal knowledge. As you might suspect, the availability of a preferential rate for capital gains, as well as the law's special rules for capital losses, has put substantial pressure on the legal system to define the term "capital asset." The resulting body of law will be the primary focus of this chapter. We begin, however, with some basic background and an introduction to the statutory framework for capital gains and losses.

A. BACKGROUND AND STATUTORY FRAMEWORK

Throughout most of the history of income taxation in this country, a distinction has been drawn between ordinary income (e.g., salaries, interest, and profits from running a business) and "capital gain"—usually for the purpose of taxing the latter at lower rates. In loose, nonlegal terms, one might describe "capital gain" as gain from the sale of property such as real estate, stocks, and bonds. As you know by now, however, the Internal Revenue Code rarely relies on loose, nonlegal terms. The Code's reputation for linguistic precision is especially well deserved when it comes to capital gains and losses, an area bursting with defined terms.

1. Net Capital Gain

We begin our examination of the statutory framework with §1(h), the subsection that specifies the maximum statutory capital gains tax rates. In reviewing this provision, take note that it begins with the language, "If a taxpayer has a *net capital gain* for any taxable year, the tax imposed by this section for such taxable year shall not exceed the sum of—" (emphasis added); it then goes on to specify the preferential statutory capital gains rates for different types of capital gain. The key point here for our purposes is that these preferential rates are not available unless the taxpayer has a "net capital gain." Thus, the key to unlocking the preferential rate structure is having "net capital gain," a term defined in §1222(11) as "the excess of the net long-term capital gain for the taxable year over the net short-term capital loss for such year." But this is just the beginning of the defined terms. Like nesting dolls, the phrases "net long-term capital gain" (§1222(7)) and "net short-term capital loss" (§1222(6)) themselves contain multiple defined terms, which in turn contain further defined terms. Take a moment to review these provisions and how they fit together.

In a nutshell, these rules require a netting process involving short-term capital gains and losses (i.e., those arising from the sale of capital assets held for one year or less) and long-term capital gains and losses (i.e., those arising from the sale of capital assets held for more than one year). Only after netting the short-term gains with the short-term losses and the long-term gains with the long-term losses will the taxpayer be able to determine if she has any "net capital gain." If she does, then the preferential rates set forth in §1(h) will apply. The resulting tax liability—that is, the tax derived from the imposition of these special rates to the taxpayer's net capital gain—is then included as part of the taxpayer's federal income tax liability. It is not, as those unfamiliar with the law sometimes mistakenly believe, a separate tax; it is, rather, simply a component of the income tax owed by the taxpayer.

Once you take the time to master the netting rules just described, along with the underlying definitions, you may find yourself bristling at casual statements by family and friends that "long-term capital gains are taxed at a lower rate." This is true as far as it goes. For example, if a taxpayer's sole transaction for the year is the sale for $30,000 of stock purchased several years ago for $20,000, then her "long-term capital gain" (assuming the stock is a capital asset in her hands) is $10,000, as are her "net long-term capital gain" and her "net capital gain." The result would be a lower tax rate—a maximum of 20 percent under current law—for that portion of the taxpayer's gross income. But this simple outcome requires a simple set of facts (one transaction for the year) and no need to contend with the netting rules.

Here's an example of how the netting rules apply when taxpayers have multiple transactions for the year. Assume that Cathy and her husband Jason sold the following four blocks of stock during the year: (1) *W* stock at a long-term gain of $10,000, (2) *X* stock at a long-term loss of $3,000, (3) *Y* stock at a short-term gain of $4,000, and (4) *Z* stock at a short-term loss of $9,000. In this scenario, Cathy and Jason have a net long-term capital gain of $7,000 (after netting the longs with the longs) and a net short-term capital loss of $5,000 (after netting the shorts with the shorts). As a result, assuming that these four transactions make up all of their sales of capital assets for the year, Jason and Cathy's "net capital gain" would be $2,000. This is the amount that would be taxed at the preferential rate.

But now suppose that it's December 15 and Jason and Cathy, having sold the four blocks of stock in the manner described above, are deciding whether to sell for $15,000 some Q stock that they bought just a few weeks earlier for $10,000. In isolation, this transaction would generate $5,000 of short-term capital gain, which, according to a loose, informal understanding of the rules, would not benefit from the preferential rate structure. When added to the four transactions above, however, this short-term gain is absorbed by the outstanding net short-term capital loss, resulting in an increase of the couple's "net capital gain" from $2,000 to $7,000. In other words, the sale of an asset giving rise to $5,000 of short-term capital gain increases the amount of income subject to the preferential rate.

2.   Statutory Tax Rates for Net Capital Gain

Under current law, the maximum nominal rate for individuals on most types of net capital gain is 20 percent, while ordinary income is now subject to a maximum marginal rate of 37 percent. Depending on the taxpayer's taxable income, it is possible for an even lower capital gains rate to apply — either 15 percent or even 0 percent. §1(h)(1)(B). In effect, Congress is attempting to introduce marginal rate progressivity to the taxation of capital gains, but with breakpoints between the brackets determined by reference to the taxpayer's total taxable income. The political impulse underlying these changes is understandable: Republicans generally prefer lower capital gains rates, while Democrats generally favor reducing taxes for lower-income households. However, the resulting rules, together with the rules described below for special categories of capital gain, require a maddeningly complex, difficult to understand, statutory provision (§1(h)) and a correspondingly complex tax return form. The fault for the complexity lies not with the IRS but with Congress. Until recent years the rules, as well as the tax form, were far simpler.

As just noted, in addition to applying different capital gains rates for taxpayers of different incomes, Congress has adopted different tax rates for different types of assets. For example, gain from the sale of collectibles, such as art (or baseball cards), that would otherwise qualify for the preferential capital gains rates described above is taxed at a maximum rate of 28 percent. Long-term gain from the sale of real property that would otherwise be treated as capital gain is taxed at a maximum rate of 25 percent to the extent of previously taken depreciation. More possible maximum rates are created by the interaction of the capital gain rates and the alternative minimum tax. Because of the different rates for different categories of net long-term gain, §1(h) must, and does, provide rules for "stacking" the gains; this is part of the reason why that provision is difficult to understand, even after multiple readings. Fortunately, the calculations can be done by computer programs, but although the tax return itself is ingeniously devised, and yields the correct result to a person with the patience to follow its directions, its logic is beyond the grasp of all but the most sophisticated and experienced tax expert.

There is an additional advantage, apart from the favorable tax rates, to characterization of income as capital gain. Capital gain is gain from the sale of property. If a transaction is characterized as one involving the sale of property (as opposed, for example, to the rental of property), the gain is not only capital in nature, but before it is calculated a deduction is allowed for the basis of the property. In other words, cases focusing on the capital gain issue often decide implicitly what may be a difficult timing question: namely, whether some of the amount received should be treated as a recovery of investment (basis).

3.   Net Capital Loss

Of course, taxpayers sometimes have capital losses that exceed their capital gains for the year. If this is the case, the resulting loss may be used to offset $3,000 of ordinary income. Any net loss above this $3,000 figure is defined as a "net capital loss" and may be carried forward to subsequent years, when it may be used to offset capital gains or, again, up to $3,000 of ordinary income. For example, assume that Dev sells stock for $10,000 that he purchased several years ago for $17,000, resulting in a long-term capital loss of $7,000. Assume further that Dev has $50,000 of salary income and no other capital asset sales for the year. Dev may deduct $3,000 of his capital loss from ordinary income as an above-the-line deduction, reducing his gross income to $47,000. The remaining $4,000 of "net capital loss" may be carried forward to the following year.

Capital gains and losses are reported on Schedule D, which a taxpayer would include with his completed Form 1040. While there is no substitute for reading and understanding the statute, a review of Schedule D (the latest version of which can be found easily online) provides a helpful illustration of how gains and losses are netted. In particular, note that the form asks the taxpayer to list "Short-Term Capital Gains and Losses—Assets Held One Year or Less" in Part I and "Long-Term Capital Gains and Losses—Assets Held More Than One Year" in Part II. The form then directs the taxpayer to use the resulting figures to calculate any "net capital gain" for the year. Of course, all of these calculations are relevant only for gains and losses derived from selling a "capital asset"—a central legal question to which we now turn.

B.   THE DEFINITION OF "CAPITAL ASSET"

As you may have noted from reviewing §1222, capital gain or loss arises from the "sale or exchange of a capital asset." Note the two elements: "sale or exchange" and "capital asset." Most of the problems in distinguishing between capital gain and ordinary income involve interpretation of the term "capital asset." "Capital asset" is defined in §1221(a) as all "property," with eight listed exceptions. "Property" is, of course, a broad and vague term. We will see that the courts have interpreted "property" narrowly in an effort to avoid extending capital gain treatment to transactions for which such treatment seems plainly inappropriate. The major function of the exceptions is to deny capital gain treatment for the ordinary gains and losses from operating a trade or business. The first five statutory exceptions (paraphrased) are:

1. The inventory, or stock in trade, of a business (either retail or manufacturing), and property held primarily for sale to customers in the ordinary course of a trade or business;
2. Real property or depreciable property used in a trade or business;
3. A patent, invention, model, or design (whether or not patented), a secret formula or process, as well as copyrights and similar property held by the creator or those whose basis in the property is determined by reference to the creator's basis (e.g., acquired by gift);
4. Accounts receivable acquired in the ordinary course of a trade or business; and
5. U.S. government publications held by someone who received them free or at reduced cost (e.g., a member of Congress).

A limitation on §1221(a)(2), however, virtually swallows it up. The limitation is found in §1231, which seems more a response to economic or political forces than to tax logic. The rule embodied in §1221(a)(2) seems logically correct, since it is difficult to see any good reason for distinguishing, for tax purposes, between gains or losses arising from normal business operations and gains or losses from disposing of assets used in the business. Nonetheless, at the beginning of World War II, Congress became concerned that people were being compelled to sell property for wartime uses, which subjected them to high income and excess-profits taxes on their gains. Apparently, it was thought unfair to impose these high taxes on windfalls generated by wartime conditions, at least when other taxpayers were able to escape such taxes by not selling. Moreover, it was feared that the potential tax liability would inhibit people from selling property such as factory buildings, machinery, and ships to others who might be able to put them to better use in the war effort. These concerns led to the adoption of the predecessor of §1231, which preserves the §1221(a)(2) taxpayer benefit of ordinary loss treatment where the taxpayer has a net loss, but provides for capital gain treatment where there is a net gain. All sales or exchanges of assets described in §1221(a)(2) (depreciable property and real property used in a business), plus certain other transactions, are covered by §1231. A complex set of rules covers netting out of §1231 gains and losses and the carryover of losses.

Various other provisions govern whether certain specified assets or transactions are accorded capital-gain or capital-loss treatment. For example, §1244 provides that loss on the sale of "small business stock" is treated as an ordinary loss, even though it is plain that such stock is a capital asset within the contemplation of §1221 and therefore that any gain on its sale is capital gain. Section 631 provides capital-gain treatment for the proceeds of certain sales of timber and coal. In addition, §1221(b)(3) allows taxpayers to treat self-created musical works and copyrights in musical works as capital assets—a provision championed by the country music industry.

Sections 165 and 166 contain special provisions dealing with loans made by the taxpayer. If a loan is evidenced by a bond, the bond is a capital asset under §1221, so its sale gives rise to capital gain or loss. Section 1271(a)(1) ensures that the result is the same where the bond is retired by the issuer, and §165(g) does the same where the bond becomes worthless. But suppose that the loan does not take the form of a bond. Suppose, for example, that an individual who is not in the finance business lends money to the corner grocer, as an investment. That is a "nonbusiness debt," and if it is not repaid, the loss is treated as a short-term capital loss under §166(d). If, on the other hand, a wholesaler sells produce to the grocer on credit and that debt is not repaid, the loss is from a business debt and is treated as an ordinary loss.

C. POLICY CONSIDERATIONS

1. Rationale for Favorable Treatment of Capital Gain

The following paragraphs briefly describe and respond to the major arguments that have been used to justify favorable treatment of capital gain. It should be apparent that some of the arguments had more force in past years when the maximum marginal rate exceeded 50 percent.

Bunching. Capital gains often accrue over many years. If capital gain were taxed as ordinary income along with the taxpayer's other income, the effect could be to subject all, or almost all, of the taxpayer's gain to the maximum rate even though it might have been taxed at a lower rate if it had been realized ratably over the period of ownership of the asset. This argument has little force because under the current rate structure most individuals and corporations realizing substantial capital gains will have been paying tax at the maximum rate at all relevant times.

Lock-in. A tax on capital gains tends to induce people to hold assets when they might otherwise sell and reinvest the proceeds in some other way. This effect is exacerbated by §1014, under which basis is stepped up to fair market value at death, thus eliminating the potential tax liability on such gain. Suppose, for example, an elderly entrepreneur owns a business with a fair market value of $1 million and a basis of $10,000. In the absence of taxation, the business might be worth more to another person than to the entrepreneur. The entrepreneur might wish to sell her business, use some of the proceeds to purchase an annuity, and give the remainder of the proceeds to her children. Another person might have better ideas (or think she has better ideas) on how to manage the business and might be willing to put more time into the business. Present law discourages sale, since it triggers a tax that can be entirely avoided if the entrepreneur holds onto the business until her death. The lock-in effect leads to immobility of capital and inefficient uses of capital: Assets are not held by those who will put them to best use. Some supporters of preferential treatment for capital gain believe the lock-in effect is so strong that a reduction in tax rates would actually increase tax revenue by dramatically increasing the number of investors who chose to sell appreciated assets.

Inflation. Favorable treatment of capital gain mitigates the possible unfairness of taxing gains attributable to inflation rather than to "real" gain. Capital-gain treatment is, however, an inaccurate solution to the inflation problem. It provides relief in some cases where inflation may have had little, if any, impact, and it fails to provide relief in other cases where inflation may have taken a heavy toll. An alternative approach that Congress could consider would be to index the taxpayer's basis for inflation, that is, increasing the basis of assets to reflect increases in an index of prices. This would likely entail considerable complexity, especially in the case of depreciable property. Given this complexity, one might regard a preferential rate for capital gains as an imperfect alternative to the (even more) imperfect solution of basis indexation.

General incentive. Favorable rates of taxation of capital gains reduce the aggregate tax burden on returns on investments and thus arguably provide an incentive (or reduce the disincentive) for saving, investment, and economic growth. Of course, to provide constant tax revenue, other forms of taxes must be raised, and these taxes may reduce economic growth. For example, a cut in the capital gain tax rate may require an increase in the tax rate on labor income, and that increase might reduce work effort. Supporters of favorable rates of taxation on capital income sometimes claim that the efficiency gains from reducing the tax on investment gains outweigh such efficiency losses. Again, there appear to be other, more accurate (and perhaps fairer) solutions to the problem (if it is one) of excessive tax burdens on returns on investments. Moreover, it may be that collectively we should save and invest less rather than more. Increased saving necessarily implies decreased consumption. This trade-off implies a transfer of consumption from the current generation to subsequent generations. The consumption that is forgone might be the private consumption of taxpayers or that of poor people to whom welfare payments might be made; or it might be public consumption for park services, public television, crime prevention, or national defense; or it might be any other private or public consumption.

Incentive to new industries. Since new industries tend to generate capital gain, favorable treatment of such gain tends to stimulate investment in such industries, and many people seem to take it for granted that such stimulation is a good thing. One can question whether new industries that need special tax breaks in order to flourish ought to be encouraged. It is one thing to say that the tax structure is too onerous for business and quite another to say that it is too onerous for new businesses but not for established businesses. Moreover, the capital gain preference is not, in fact, limited to new industries. If such industries do warrant favorable tax treatment, a more narrowly designed measure may be preferable. (In fact, such a measure exists: the §1202 exclusion for small business stock.)

Unrealized gains are not taxed. The favorable rate of taxation of capital gains reduces the disparity in treatment of realized and unrealized gains. If that disparity is the problem, however, the more appropriate solution would be to expand provisions allowing tax-free exchanges, taking us down a path likely, ultimately, to lead to a consumption tax.

Double tax on corporate earnings. Corporate income is in some sense taxed twice: once when earned by the corporation (currently at a rate of 21 percent), and again when distributed to shareholders in the form of dividends or corporate repurchase of shares. The rationale for this treatment of corporate profits is unclear. A capital gain preference reduces the tax paid by shareholders on sale of their stock. Many observers support maintaining or expanding the break shareholders get on stock sales as an indirect way of ameliorating the double tax on corporate income. One difficulty with this argument is that the capital gains preference is not limited to investments in corporate stock; it also applies to individual investments in land and other assets.

2.   Rationale for Limiting the Deductibility of Capital Losses

As noted above, capital losses are subject to an unfavorable set of tax rules. Individuals may deduct capital losses from capital gain, but individuals with capital losses in excess of capital gain may deduct only $3,000 of such losses in any year. Corporations may only deduct capital losses from capital gain. The fact that capital losses are treated unfavorably when capital gains are treated favorably may seem odd. The limitation on deductibility of capital losses certainly works against some of the policy goals that support the favorable treatment of capital gain. For example, the limitation on deductions of capital losses presumably discourages, rather than encourages, capital investment, especially in new, innovative, and risky activities.

Arguably, the limitation is necessary to prevent taxpayers from manipulating the recognition of gains and losses to recognize "false" losses. Absent the limitation, a taxpayer could buy two sets of investments that are expected to move in opposite directions. For example, the taxpayer could buy some investments (such as gold) that are expected to rise with inflation and other investments (such as long-term bonds) that are expected to decline with inflation. If inflation rose, the decline in the value of one set of investments would be offset by the rise in the value of the other set of investments, and the taxpayer would suffer no economic loss. However, the taxpayer could sell the investments that declined in value and retain the appreciated investments, thereby recognizing a tax loss. The offsetting gain on the appreciated investments would not be recognized until those assets were sold.

Relatedly, suppose a taxpayer has invested over the years in a diversified portfolio of common stocks and that some have risen in value while others have declined. Without the limitation on the deduction of losses, the taxpayer would have a strong incentive to sell the loss assets and retain the gain assets. In the aggregate, over the long run, the result would be a substantial advantage to investors and a corresponding disadvantage to the Treasury (that is, to other taxpayers, who would be required to pick up the slack). By imposing a limitation on the deduction of losses, Congress in effect says to taxpayers, "If you want to recognize your losses, you should also recognize a similar amount of gains."

One obvious objection to using the capital-loss limitation to prevent manipulation of the realization requirement is that it applies even in cases where the taxpayer owns no appreciated assets and thus the feared manipulation does not occur. In such scenarios, the government is in a "heads-I-win-tails-you-lose" position: It shares in gains but bears none of the burden of losses.

COMPARATIVE FOCUS:
South Africa's Decision to Tax Capital Gains

With the collapse of apartheid and the subsequent election of Nelson Mandela as president in April 1994, South Africa embarked on an ambitious reform of its social, political, and legal institutions. The country's new constitution, approved by the Constitutional Court of South Africa in 1996, took effect in February 1997.

Among the many areas of South African law reform in the post-apartheid era was taxation, including the question of whether and how the country's income tax should treat capital gains. Historically, South Africa had not taxed capital gains; rather, it explicitly excluded from the definition of gross income "receipts or accruals of a capital nature." As noted by two U.S. economists involved in the South African tax-reform process in the late 1990s, the "absence of a capital gains tax provide[d] huge opportunities to avoid tax by characterizing labor or business income as capital gains." See Henry Aaron and Joel Slemrod, *The South African Tax System: A Nation in Microcosm, Tax Notes* (Dec. 6, 1999).

After extensive study, including an examination of the tax treatment of capital gains and losses in nearly every country in the world, South Africa amended its Income Tax Act in 2001 to include a new Capital Gains Tax (CGT). Under the terms of the new CGT law, individual taxpayers must include 25 percent of capital gains (less an annual exclusion of R10,000, or about $1,000) as taxable income subject to the normal tax rates applicable to other sources of income. With a top marginal rate of 40 percent, the result is an effective rate on capital gains of no more than 10 percent.

Like the United States, South Africa provides for the nonrecognition of gain or loss in several situations, known as "roll-overs," including, for example, involuntary disposals (similar to U.S. §1033) and transfers between spouses (similar to U.S. §1041). In addition, South African law includes a provision, similar to §121, providing for the exclusion of gain from the sale of a primary residence. Unlike the United States, however, South Africa applies its capital gains tax to transfers (other than transfers to a spouse) at death.

D.   PROPERTY HELD "PRIMARILY FOR SALE TO CUSTOMERS"

1.   Sale to "Customers"

BIELFELDT v. COMMISSIONER
231 F.3d 1035 (7th Cir. 2000)

Before POSNER, COFFEY, and KANNE, Circuit Judges.

POSNER, Circuit Judge.

Gary Bielfeldt (and his wife, but she is a party only by virtue of having filed a joint return with her husband), a large trader in U.S. Treasury notes and bonds, seeks to overturn a decision by the Tax Court denying him the right to offset immense trading losses that he incurred in the 1980s against all but $3,000 a year in ordinary income. He claims to be not a trader but a dealer and that the losses he incurred in the sale of the Treasury securities were losses connected with his dealer's "stock in trade"; such losses, even when they result as his did from the sale of a capital asset, are treated as ordinary rather than capital losses and can therefore be fully offset against ordinary income. In contrast, capital losses, while they can be fully offset against capital gains, can be offset against ordinary income only up to $3,000 a year. §1211(b). Although the amount is arbitrary, the rationale for limiting such offsets is not; it is to reduce taxpayers' incentives to so structure their capital transactions as to realize losses today and defer gains to the future. If Bielfeldt's characterization of his status is sound, he is entitled to some $85 million in refunds of his federal income tax.

The standard distinction between a dealer and a trader is that the dealer's income is based on the service he provides in the chain of distribution of the goods he buys and resells, rather than on fluctuations in the market value of those goods, while the trader's income is based not on any service he provides but rather on, precisely, fluctuations in the market value of the securities or other assets that he transacts in. . . . This is not to deny that a trader, whether he is a speculator, a hedger, or an arbitrageur, serves the financial system by tending through his activities to bring prices closer to underlying values, by supplying liquidity, and by satisfying different preferences with regard to risk; he is not a parasite, as the communists believed. But he is not paid for these services. His income from trading depends on changes in the market value of his securities between the time he acquired them and the time he sells them.

Although one thinks of a dealer's inventory or stock in trade as made up of physical assets, it can be made up of securities instead. A stockbroker who owned shares that he sold to his customers at market price plus a commission would be a bona fide dealer. The example of a recognized "dealer" in securities that is closest to Bielfeldt's self-description because it blurs the distinction between deriving income from providing a service in the purchase or sale of an asset and deriving income from changes in the market value of an asset is a floor specialist on one of the stock exchanges. The specialist maintains an inventory in a specified stock in order to maintain liquidity. If its price soars, indicating that demand is outrunning supply, he sells from his inventory to meet the additional demand, and if the price of the stock plunges, he buys in the open market in order to provide a market for the people who are trying to sell. He is not paid by the stock market for this service, but is compensated by the income he makes from his purchase and sales and by commissions on limit orders (orders contingent on a stock's price hitting a specified level) placed with him by brokers. The Internal Revenue Service treats his gains and losses as ordinary income because the Internal Revenue Code classifies him as a dealer.

Treasury securities, at least the ones in which Bielfeldt transacted, are not sold on an organized exchange, and so there are no floor specialists—there is no floor. The market for Treasury securities is an over-the-counter market, like the NASDAQ. But the economic function that the specialists on the organized exchanges perform is independent of the form of the market, and dealers who specialize in Treasury securities (called "primary dealers," and discussed in the next paragraph) are close analogues of the floor specialists, just as NASD market makers are. There is even a new law that requires the primary dealers in Treasury securities, with some exceptions, to register with the SEC or the NASD.

Bielfeldt claims that he performs this function too, though he is not a registered or primary dealer. The securities in question are used to finance the national debt. During the period in which he incurred losses, there was no talk of paying off the debt—on the contrary, the debt was growing. To finance growth and redemptions, the Treasury would periodically auction large quantities of bonds and notes, which would be underwritten by a relative handful of primary dealers. Bielfeldt would buy in huge quantities from these dealers and resell in smaller batches, often to the same dealers, a few weeks later. His theory, which worked well for a few years and then turned sour, was that the Treasury auctions were so large that each one would create a temporary glut of Treasury securities, driving price down. He would buy at the depressed price and hold the securities off the market until, the glut having disappeared (because he was hoarding the securities), price rose, and then he would sell. He argues that had it not been for this service that he performed in the marketing of Treasury securities, the price the Treasury got at its auctions would have been depressed, with the result that interest on the national debt would be even higher than it is.

What he is describing is simply the social benefit of speculation. Think back to the Biblical story of Joseph. During the seven fat years, years of glut, Joseph "hoarded" foodstuffs so that there would be an adequate supply in the seven lean years that he correctly predicted would follow. In a money economy, he would have financed the program by buying cheap, which would be easy to do in a period of glut, and selling dear, which would be easy to do in a period of scarcity and would help to ration supplies in that period. He would buy cheap yet pay higher prices than people who were buying for consumption, since he would anticipate a profit from the later sale during the period of scarcity. Similarly, Bielfeldt hoarded Treasury securities during the fat weeks immediately after an auction so that there would be an adequate supply in the lean weeks (the weeks between auctions) that followed. That activity may have been socially beneficial, as he argues, but it is no different from the social benefits of speculation generally. His argument if accepted would turn every speculator into a dealer for purposes of the Internal Revenue Code. . . .

Unlike a floor specialist, Bielfeldt undertook no obligation to maintain an orderly market in Treasury securities. He did not maintain an inventory of securities; and because he skipped auctions that didn't seem likely to produce the glut that was the basis of his speculative profits, there were months on end in which he could not have provided liquidity by selling from inventory because he had no Treasury securities. In some of the tax years in question he participated in as few as 6 percent of the auctions, and never did he participate in more than 15 percent. As a result, he was out of the market for as much as 200 days a year. He was a speculator, period. As the Federal Reserve Bank of New York, which kept track of Bielfeldt's trading in Treasury securities and sent updates to the IRS, put it, "his activities are in most cases outright speculation of interest rate movements."

In saying that Bielfeldt was not a specialist, we don't mean to imply that the Internal Revenue Service would be required to recognize as a dealer a trader who structured his operation to resemble that of a floor specialist but was not a floor specialist as defined in §1236(d)(2). That issue is not before us. Nor is the bearing of . . . §475(f), which allows a securities trader to treat paper gains and losses as ordinary rather than capital income by marketing to market the securities he owns at the end of the tax year, that is, by pretending they had been sold then. We note finally that Bielfeldt's alternative argument, that Treasury securities are "notes receivable acquired in the ordinary course of trade or business" and therefore are not capital assets within the meaning of §1221(4), is frivolous. It implies that no bonds, government or private, are capital assets, since a bond, like a note receivable, is a promise to pay the holder of the instrument.

Affirmed.

NOTES AND QUESTIONS

1. *The general thrust of §1221(a)(1): Non-capital characterization of ordinary business profits.* As stated above, §1221(a)(1) excludes from the definition of capital asset "stock in trade of the taxpayer or other property of a kind which would properly be included in the inventory of the taxpayer . . . or property held by the taxpayer primarily for sale to customers in the ordinary course of his trade or business." The broad intent of this section is clear (even if the underlying rationale for capital gain and loss treatment is not): Ordinary business activities generate ordinary income and loss. Unfortunately, it is often difficult to determine exactly what constitutes the form of ordinary business activities that should fall into §1221(a)(1) and out of capital gain and loss. This case, and the remaining cases in this Section D, all examine this question.

2. *The meaning of the term "to customers."* The term "to customers" was added to the statute in 1934. It was designed to prevent "a stock speculator trading on his own account" from claiming ordinary losses on his transactions and thus canceling out his income from dividends, interest, etc., by what were

apparently thought by Congress often to be economically insignificant transactions. H.R. Rep. No. 1385, 73d Cong., 2d Sess., 1939-1 C.B. (Pt. 2) 627, 632. In enacting the restriction, Congress seems to have overlooked the possibility that, in another part of the business cycle, "traders" might realize profits and would be able to report them as capital gains.

Judge Posner does not refer to the history behind the 1934 amendment in his decision. Does the fact that Congress specifically intended to exclude from capital asset gains from stock speculation support the decision? Relieve the pressure on the "trader v. dealer" distinction that underlies Posner's decision?

3. *Section 475.* Section 475 now requires securities dealers to mark-to-market any securities that are not properly treated as inventory or held for investment. Mark-to-market tax accounting requires a taxpayer to treat each security as if it is sold at the end of the year. Gain or loss is recognized as ordinary income or loss and then basis adjusted. Section 475(e) allows traders in securities (and dealers in commodities) to elect into mark-to-market accounting. The election applies to the taxable year in which it is made and may not be revoked without consent of the Service.

Do you imagine many traders elect mark-to-market? Why or why not? Under what circumstances would such an election be desirable?

4. *Investment securities held by dealers.* Section 1236 provides that if a securities dealer segregates securities in an investment account, those securities are treated as capital assets. This provision was obviously designed to allow firms dealing in securities to take advantage of the favorable treatment of capital gain. May a firm anxious to escape the capital loss restrictions avoid capital asset treatment simply by avoiding compliance with §1236? Even if it is clear that some securities are held as investments for the benefit of the members of the firm? What advice would you give to securities dealers on how to handle the firm's investments? See Stephens, Inc. v. United States, 464 F.2d 53 (8th Cir. 1972), cert. denied, 409 U.S. 1119 (1973), holding that an investment company was not a dealer when it acquired shares of corporations, drew off large cash dividends, then sold the stock at a loss because it had reduced the net assets of the companies by the dividends. The court found that the investment house was not entitled to an ordinary loss deduction on the sale of the stock.

2.   "Primarily for Sale"

BIEDENHARN REALTY CO. v. UNITED STATES
526 F.2d 409 (5th Cir.), cert. denied, 429 U.S. 819 (1976)

[Before the court, en banc, thirteen judges: seven agreeing with the majority opinion, one concurring, and five dissenting.]

GOLDBERG, Circuit Judge.

[The facts, much abbreviated, are as follows: Taxpayer corporation, organized in 1923 to hold and manage family investments, held in the relevant years substantial investments in commercial real estate, a stock portfolio, a motel, warehouses, a shopping center, residential real property, and farm property. Among the last was a plantation purchased for $50,000 in 1935, totaling 973

acres, which was said to have been bought for farming and as a good investment. It was farmed for a few years and then leased for farming. The land was
close to Monroe, Louisiana, and from 1939 through 1966, three basic residential subdivisions covering 185 acres were carved from the plantation. Although
the plantation was named "Hardtimes," for Biedenharn Realty it was a good
investment; 208 lots were sold in 158 separate sales at an $800,000 profit. In
a pre-1964 settlement with the government it was apparently agreed that 60
percent of the gain would be reported as ordinary income and 40 percent as
capital gain for the years of the settlement. The taxpayer then reported its
gains for the years 1964 through 1966 on the same basis. The IRS asserted a
deficiency, arguing that all the gains were ordinary income, and the taxpayer
filed for refund claiming all the gains to be capital.

In addition to the subdivision sales, the taxpayer also sold approximately
275 other acres from the plantation in twelve separate sales starting in 1935.
From other land that it owned, the company in the years 1923 through
1966 sold 934 lots, 249 before 1935 and 477 in the years 1935 through 1966.
Improvements—streets, drainage, water, sewerage, and electricity—were
made in the plantation subdivisions, at an aggregate cost of about $200,000.

The District Court found that the plantation was originally bought for
investment and that the intent to subdivide arose later when the city of Monroe
expanded in the direction of the plantation. Sales by the taxpayer largely
resulted from unsolicited approaches by individuals, except that in the years
1964 through 1966 about 75 percent of the sales were induced by independent
brokers with which the company dealt. The issue before the court as to all of
the 1964 through 1966 sales from the subdivisions was whether the lots constituted property held by the taxpayer primarily for sale to customers in the
ordinary course of its trade or business under §1221(1).]

II . . .

The problem we struggle with here is not novel. We have become accustomed to the frequency with which taxpayers litigate this troublesome question. . . . The difficulty in large part stems from ad-hoc application of the
numerous permissible criteria set forth in our multitudinous prior opinions.[1]
Over the past 40 years, this case by case approach with its concentration
on the facts of each suit has resulted in a collection of decisions not always
reconcilable. . . .

Assuredly, we would much prefer one or two clearly defined, easily employed
tests which lead to predictable, perhaps automatic, conclusions. However, the
nature of the congressional "capital asset" definition and the myriad situations
to which we must apply that standard make impossible any easy escape from
the task before us. . . .

---

1. One finds evidence of the vast array of opinions and factors discussed therein by briefly pe-
rusing the 24 small-type, double column pages of Prentice-Hall's Federal Taxation ¶32,486 which
lists the cases involving subdivided realty. See also 33 Mertens, The Law of Federal Income Taxation
§§22.138-22.142 (Malone Rev.). The Second Circuit has called these judicial pronouncements
"legion." Gault v. Comm'r, 2 Cir. 1964, 332 F.2d 94, 95.

Yet our inability to proffer a panaceatic guide to the perplexed with respect to this subject does not preclude our setting forth some general, albeit inexact, guidelines for the resolution of many of the §1221(1) cases we confront. . . . [W]e more precisely define and suggest points of emphasis for the major *Winthrop* delineated factors[2] as they appear in the instant controversy. . . .

III

We begin our task by evaluating in the light of Biedenharn's facts the main *Winthrop* factors—substantiality and frequency of sales, improvements, solicitation and advertising efforts, and brokers' activities—as well as a few miscellaneous contentions. A separate section follows discussing the keenly contested role of prior investment intent. Finally we consider the significance of the Supreme Court's decision in Malat v. Riddell 383 U.S. 569 (1966).

A. FREQUENCY AND SUBSTANTIALITY OF SALES

Scrutinizing closely the record and briefs, we find that plaintiff's real property sales activities compel an ordinary income conclusion. In arriving at this result, we examine first the most important of *Winthrop*'s factors—the frequency and substantiality of taxpayer's sales. Although frequency and substantiality of sales are not usually conclusive, they occupy the preeminent ground in our analysis. The recent trend of Fifth Circuit decisions indicates that when dispositions of subdivided property extend over a long period of time and are especially numerous, the likelihood of capital gains is very slight indeed. . . .

On the present facts, taxpayer could not claim *isolated* sales or a passive and gradual liquidation. . . .

The frequency and substantiality of Biedenharn's sales go not only to its holding purpose and the existence of a trade or business but also support our finding of the ordinariness with which the Realty Company disposed of its lots. These sales easily meet the criteria of normalcy set forth in *Winthrop*, supra at 912.

Furthermore, . . . one could fairly infer that the income accruing to the Biedenharn Realty Company from its pre-1935 sales helped support the purchase of the Hardtimes Plantation. Even if taxpayer made no significant acquisitions after Hardtimes, the *purpose, system, and continuity* of Biedenharn's efforts easily constitute a business. . . .

[T]he District Court sought to overcome this evidence of dealer-like real estate activities and property *primarily held for sale* by clinging to the notion

---

2. In U.S. v. Winthrop, 5 Cir. 1969, 417 F.2d 905, 910, the Court enumerated the following factors: (1) The nature and purpose of the acquisition of the property and the duration of the ownership; (2) the extent and nature of the taxpayer's efforts to sell the property; (3) the number, extent, continuity and substantiality of the sales; (4) the extent of subdividing, developing, and advertising to increase sales; (5) the use of a business office for the sale of the property; (6) the character and degree of supervision or control exercised by the taxpayer over any representative selling the property; and (7) the time and effort the taxpayer habitually devoted to the sales. The numbering indicates no hierarchy of importance.

that the taxpayer was merely liquidating a prior investment. We discuss later the role of former investment status and the possibility of taxpayer relief under that concept. Otherwise, the question of liquidation of an investment is simply the opposite side of the inquiry as to whether or not one is holding property primarily for sale in the ordinary course of his business. In other words, a taxpayer's claim that he is liquidating a prior investment does not really present a separate theory but rather restates the main question currently under scrutiny. . . .

B.   IMPROVEMENTS

Although we place greatest emphasis on the frequency and substantiality of sales over an extended time period, our decision in this instance is aided by the presence of taxpayer activity—particularly improvements—in the other Winthrop areas. Biedenharn vigorously improved its subdivisions, generally adding streets, drainage, sewerage, and utilities. . . .

C.   SOLICITATION AND ADVERTISING EFFORTS

Substantial, frequent sales and improvements such as we have encountered in this case will usually conclude the capital gains issue against taxpayer. Thus, on the basis of our analysis to this point, we would have little hesitation in finding that taxpayer held "primarily for sale" in the "ordinary course of [his] trade or business." "[T]he flexing of commercial muscles with frequency and continuity, design and effect" of which *Winthrop* spoke, *supra* at 911, is here a reality. This reality is further buttressed by Biedenharn's sales efforts, including those carried on through brokers. Minimizing the importance of its own sales activities, taxpayer points repeatedly to its steady avoidance of advertising or other solicitation of customers. Plaintiff directs our attention to stipulations detailing the population growth of Monroe and testimony outlining the economic forces which made Hardtimes Plantation attractive residential property and presumably eliminated the need for sales exertions. We have no quarrel with plaintiff's description of this familiar process of suburban expansion, but we cannot accept the legal inferences which taxpayer would have us draw.

The Circuit's recent decisions . . . implicitly recognize that even one inarguably in the real estate business need not engage in promotional exertions in the face of a favorable market. As such, we do not always require a showing of active solicitation where "business . . . [is] good, indeed brisk." . . . In cases such as *Biedenharn*, the sale of a few lots and the construction of the first homes, albeit not, as in *Winthrop*, by the taxpayer, as well as the building of roads, addition of utilities, and staking off of the other subdivided parcels constitute a highly visible form of advertising. Prospective home buyers drive by the advantageously located property, see the development activities, and are as surely put on notice of the availability of lots as if the owner had erected large signs announcing *residential property for sale*. We do not by this evaluation automatically neutralize advertising or solicitation as a factor in our analysis. This form of inherent notice is not present in all land sales, especially where the property is not so valuably located, is not subdivided into small lots, and is not improved.

Moreover, inherent notice represents only one band of the solicitation spectrum. Media utilization and personal initiatives remain material components of this criterion. When present, they call for greater Government oriented emphasis on *Winthrop*'s solicitation factor.

D. BROKERAGE ACTIVITIES

In evaluating Biedenharn's solicitation activities, we need not confine ourselves to the . . . *Winthrop* theory of brisk sales without organizational efforts. Unlike in . . . *Winthrop* where no one undertook overt solicitation efforts, the Realty Company hired brokers who, using media and on site advertising, worked vigorously on taxpayer's behalf. We do not believe that the employment of brokers should shield plaintiff from ordinary income treatment. . . . Their activities should at least in discounted form be attributed to Biedenharn. To the contrary, taxpayer argues that "one who is not already in the trade or business of selling real estate does not enter such business when he employs a broker who acts as an independent contractor. Fahs v. Crawford, 161 F.2d 315 (5 Cir. 1947); Smith v. Dunn, 224 F.2d 353 (5 Cir. 1955)." Without presently entangling ourselves in a dispute as to the differences between an agent and an independent contractor, we find the cases cited distinguishable from the instant circumstances. In both *Fahs* and *Smith*, the taxpayer turned the entire property over to brokers, who, having been granted total responsibility, made all decisions including the setting of sales prices. In comparison, Biedenharn determined original prices and general credit policy. Moreover, the Realty Company did not make all the sales in question through brokers as did taxpayers in *Fahs* and *Smith*. Biedenharn sold the Bayou DeSiard and Biedenharn Estates lots and may well have sold some of the Oak Park land. In other words, unlike *Fahs* and *Smith*, Biedenharn's brokers did not so completely take charge of the whole of the Hardtimes sales as to permit the Realty Company to wall itself off legally from their activities.

E. ADDITIONAL TAXPAYER CONTENTIONS

Plaintiff presents a number of other contentions and supporting facts for our consideration. . . . Taxpayer emphasizes that its profits from real estate sales averaged only 11.1% in each of the years in controversy, compared to 52.4% in *Winthrop*. Whatever the percentage, plaintiff would be hard pressed to deny the substantiality of its Hardtimes sales in absolute terms (the subdivided lots alone brought in over one million dollars) or, most importantly, to assert that its real estate business was too insignificant to constitute a separate trade or business.

The relatively modest income share represented by Biedenharn's real property dispositions stems not from a failure to engage in real estate sales activities but rather from the comparatively large profit attributable to the Company's 1965 ($649,231.34) and 1966 ($688,840.82) stock sales. The fact of Biedenharn's holding, managing, and selling stock is not inconsistent with the existence of a separate realty business. . . .

Similarly, taxpayer observes that Biedenharn's manager devoted only 10% of his time to real estate dealings and then mostly to the company's rental properties. This fact does not negate the existence of sales activities. Taxpayer had a telephone listing, a shared business office, and a few part-time employees. Because, as discussed before, a strong seller's market existed, Biedenharn's sales required less than the usual solicitation efforts and therefore less than the usual time. Moreover, plaintiff . . . hired brokers to handle many aspects of the Hardtimes transaction — thus further reducing the activity and time required of Biedenharn's employees.

Finally, taxpayer argues that it is entitled to capital gains since its enormous profits (74% to 97%) demonstrate a return based principally on capital appreciation and not on taxpayer's "merchandising" efforts. We decline the opportunity to allocate plaintiff's gain between long-term market appreciation and improvement related activities. . . . Even if we undertook such an analysis and found the former element predominant, we would on the authority of *Winthrop*, supra at 856, reject plaintiff's contention which, in effect, is merely taxpayer's version of the Government's unsuccessful argument in that case.

IV

The District Court found that "[t]axpayer is merely liquidating over a long period of time a substantial investment in the most advantageous method possible." 356 F. Supp. at 1336. In this view, the original investment intent is crucial, for it preserves the capital gains character of the transaction even in the face of normal real estate sales activities.

The Government asserts that Biedenharn Realty Company did not merely "liquidate" an investment but instead entered the real estate business in an effort to dispose of what was formerly investment property. Claiming that Biedenharn's activities would result in ordinary income if the Hardtimes Plantation had been purchased with the intent to divide and resell the property, and finding no reason why a different prior intent should influence this outcome, the Government concludes that original investment purpose is irrelevant. Instead, the Government would have us focus exclusively on taxpayer's intent and the level of sales activity during the period commencing with subdivision and improvement and lasting through final sales. Under this theory, every individual who improves and frequently sells substantial numbers of land parcels would receive ordinary income.[3]

While the facts of this case dictate our agreement with the Internal Revenue Service's ultimate conclusion of taxpayer liability, they do not require our acquiescence in the Government's entreated total elimination of *Winthrop*'s first criterion, "the nature and purpose of the acquisition."

---

3. The Government suggests that taxpayer can avoid ordinary income treatment by selling the undivided, unimproved tract to a controlled corporation which would then develop the land. However, this approach would in many instances create attribution problems with the Government arguing that the controlled corporation's sales are actually those of the taxpayer. . . . Furthermore, we are not prepared to tell taxpayers that in all cases a single bulk sale provides the only road to capital gains.

We reject the Government's sweeping contention that prior investment intent is always irrelevant. There will be instances where an initial investment purpose endures in controlling fashion notwithstanding continuing sales activity. We doubt that this aperture, where an active subdivider and improver receives capital gains, is very wide; yet we believe it exists. We would most generally find such an opening where the change from investment holding to sales activity results from unanticipated, externally induced factors which make impossible the continued preexisting use of the realty. . . . Acts of God, condemnation of part of one's property, new and unfavorable zoning regulations, or other events forcing alteration of taxpayer's plans create situations making possible subdivision and improvement as a part of a capital gains disposition. . . .

The distinction drawn above reflects our belief that Congress did not intend to automatically disqualify from capital gains bona fide investors forced to abandon prior purposes for reasons beyond their control. At times, the Code may be severe, and this Court may construe it strictly, but neither Code nor Court is so tyrannical as to mandate the absolute rule urged by the Government. However, we caution that although permitting a land owner substantial sales flexibility where there is a forced change from original investment purpose, we do not absolutely shield the constrained taxpayer from ordinary income. . . .

Clearly, under the facts in this case, the distinction just elaborated undermines Biedenharn's reliance on original investment purpose. Taxpayer's change of purpose was entirely voluntary and therefore does not fall within the protected area. Moreover, taxpayer's original investment intent, even if considered a factor sharply supporting capital gains treatment, is so overwhelmed by the other *Winthrop* factors discussed supra, that that element can have no decisive effect. However wide the capital gains passageway through which a subdivider with former investment intent could squeeze, the Biedenharn Realty Company will never fit.

V

The District Court, citing Malat v. Riddell, supra, stated that "the lots were not held . . . primarily for sale as that phrase was interpreted . . . in *Malat*. . . ." 356 F. Supp. at 1335. Finding that Biedenharn's primary purpose became holding for sale and consequently that *Malat* in no way alters our analysis here, we disagree with the District Court's conclusion. *Malat* was a brief per curiam in which the Supreme Court decided only that as used in Internal Revenue Code §1221(1) the word "primarily" means "principally," "of first importance." The Supreme Court, remanding the case, did not analyze the facts or resolve the controversy which involved a real estate dealer who had purchased land and held it at the time of sale with the dual intention of developing it as rental property or selling it, depending on whichever proved to be the more profitable. . . . In contrast, having substantially abandoned its investment and farming intent, Biedenharn was cloaked primarily in the garb of sales purpose when it disposed of the 38 lots here in controversy. With this change, the Realty Company lost the opportunity of coming within any dual purpose analysis. . . .

VI . . .

We cannot write black letter law for all realty subdividers and for all times, but we do caution in words of red that once an investment does not mean always an investment. A simon-pure investor forty years ago could by his subsequent activities become a seller in the ordinary course four decades later. The period of Biedenharn's passivity is in the distant past; and the taxpayer has since undertaken the role of real estate protagonist. The Hardtimes Plantation in its day may have been one thing, but as the plantation was developed and sold, Hardtimes became by the very fact of change and activity a different holding than it had been at its inception. No longer could resort to initial purpose preserve taxpayer's once upon a time opportunity for favored treatment. The opinion of the District Court is reversed.

[Four judges joined in a dissent written by Judge Gee stating that the majority summarily discounted a critical trial court fact finding that taxpayer was still farming a large part of the land, that neither the plaintiff nor the court claimed any dual purpose, and that the majority placed preeminent emphasis on sales activities and improvements, effectively eliminating the other factors in *Winthrop*.]

NOTES AND QUESTIONS

1. *Continuing relevance of* Biedenharn. Biedenharn was a corporate taxpayer. Under current law, there is no corporate capital gain preference. Capital gains may still be preferable to a corporation, however, if it has an otherwise unusable capital loss. Of course, there is a considerable capital gain preference for individuals. *Biedenharn* is a useful case to examine because it illustrates the kinds of factors a court might look to when interpreting the "primarily for sale" language of the statute.

2. *Standard of review.* In *Biedenharn*, the Fifth Circuit treated the "ultimate" issue of holding purpose as a question of law. In Byram v. United States, 705 F.2d 1418 (1983), however, responding to the Supreme Court decision on standard of review in Pullman-Standard v. Swint, 456 U.S. 273 (1982), the Fifth Circuit changed its position and held that the question of holding purpose is one of fact, subject to the "clearly erroneous" standard of review. In *Byram*, the court sustained a district court judgment for the taxpayer, who had, "during a three-year period, sold 22 parcels of real estate for over $9 million, netting approximately $3.4 million profit." In the taxpayer's favor, the court cited these facts: Byram made no personal effort to initiate the sales; buyers came to him. He did not advertise, he did not have a sales office, nor did he enlist the aid of brokers. The properties at issue were not improved or developed by him. The district court found that Byram devoted minimal time and effort to the transactions.

3. *Real estate "dealers."* (a) Compare the taxpayer in *Biedenharn* with the taxpayer in *Bielfeldt*. Is there any reason of policy why one should realize ordinary income and losses while the other has capital gains and losses? If the

persons to whom Biedenharn sold land were "customers," as that term is used in §1221(a)(1), why were not the persons who bought securities from Bielfeldt also "customers"? Neither taxpayer had a regular clientele of the kind enjoyed by a department store or other dealer in merchandise. How do the taxpayers in each of these two cases compare with a television manufacturer that sells to distributors? With the distributors, which sell to retailers? With an importer of television sets, which buys from distributors in Japan and sells to distributors in the United States?

(b) While the relevance of most of the factors discussed by the court in *Biedenharn* is easy enough to see, the effect of the use of agents may be puzzling. To what extent should the activities of others be attributed to the owner? What if the owner of the property enters into a contract with a real estate firm in which the latter is paid a fixed fee plus a percentage of gain above a certain level and is given complete control of selling price and methods, with permission to subdivide and make improvements out of its fee? What if the owner subdivides and improves and then contracts with an agent to sell the lots, with the owner to receive a fixed price for each lot, regardless of the selling price? See Fahs v. Crawford, 161 F.2d 315 (5th Cir. 1947), distinguished in *Biedenharn* as a case where the broker made all sales and was given full responsibility over the project so that the taxpayer could wall himself off legally from the activities of the broker; Voss v. United States, 329 F.2d 164 (7th Cir. 1964), where the owner of farm land authorized a real estate dealer to arrange for subdividing and selling property for a fee; held, capital gain.

(c) All of the leading real estate development cases are like *Biedenharn* in that the taxpayer realized gain and argued for status as an investor rather than a dealer. For the tax planner, the challenge in such cases is to figure out how far one can go with development and sales activities without becoming a dealer. Roughly speaking, the answer is not far at all. Where real estate prices have declined, by contrast, real estate investors will want to know how much activity is necessary in order to qualify as a dealer so that losses will be ordinary. Suppose you represent a group of investors who bought a parcel of farm land several years ago and intended to hold it for investment until it became attractive to developers. Unfortunately, the value of the land has declined. They are ready to sell. The investors are doctors, lawyers, and other such professionals who have no inclination to become involved in the business of development and sales. Yet they would like to be able to treat their losses as ordinary losses. What advice would you give them?

E.   TRANSACTIONS RELATED TO THE TAXPAYER'S BUSINESS

While Congress, in §1221, broadly defined capital assets as *all* "property," the word "property" cannot be given a broad, or even a plain-language, definition without violating informed notions of the congressional purpose in providing special treatment for capital gain or loss, however dimly perceived that purpose may be. For example, even though a landlord's rights to receive rent under a lease or an insurance agent's rights to renewal commissions might be thought of as "property," most knowledgeable people would agree that the landlord's sale of the leasehold or the insurance agent's sale of the rights to the renewal commissions should not produce capital gain. The cases that follow in this section, and most of the cases in the remainder of the chapter, reflect the efforts of the courts to narrow the concept of "capital asset."

The first case is Corn Products Refining Co. v. Commissioner, which appears immediately below. For the purpose of understanding and discussing the case, consider the following hypothetical and its description of the use of corn futures contracts. Suppose that *CP* is in the business of manufacturing corn syrup, which is made from corn, and that *CP* is committed to the sale of $1,200,000 worth of syrup six months hence. Suppose further that the price at which the syrup will be sold, the $1,200,000, will not vary with the price of corn but the price of the corn itself may change considerably between now and five months from now, when it must be acquired in order to make the syrup. *CP* is anxious to avoid the risk associated with a possible rise in the price of corn. Fortunately for *CP*, there is an active market in corn "futures." A corn future is a contract for the purchase (and delivery) of a specified amount of corn at a specified date in the future for a specified price. A person who buys a contract for such future delivery of corn is said to buy futures (that is, corn futures contracts) or to be "long" in futures. The seller of the contract is sometimes said to have taken a "short" position. (The holder of the short position could be a speculator who anticipates a decline in the price of corn or a person who is hedging against such a decline.) Suppose that *CP* buys futures contracts for the amount of corn it needs, that the price to be paid on delivery is $800,000, and that the cost of buying these contracts, plus all other expenses of manufacture of the syrup, will be $220,000; the total costs of production are thus $1,020,000, and *CP* can expect to make a profit of $180,000. Now suppose that five months later, when the time has come for *CP* to take delivery of the corn and make the syrup, the price of corn for immediate delivery on the market — the so-called spot price — is $980,000. *CP* can follow either of two routes. Under Route A, *CP* would take delivery of the corn that it has contracted to buy under its futures contracts, paying $800,000. The result would be a total cost of $1,020,000 and a profit of $180,000, which plainly would be ordinary income, from its normal operations. Under Route B, *CP* would not take delivery on the corn but would instead sell the futures contracts. Ordinarily, this is the more convenient way to do business. The profit on the sale of the corn futures contracts should be $180,000: the difference between the spot price of the corn ($980,000) and the price at which the corn can be bought by a person holding the contracts ($800,000). Having sold the contracts, *CP* would buy the corn it needs on the spot market for $980,000. Disregarding the profit on the sale of the futures contracts, the production of the corn syrup would now be a break-even activity. See Table 12-1.

TABLE 12-1
Illustration of Use of Corn Futures Contracts
Route A (CP takes delivery under futures contracts)

Revenue		$1,200,000
Costs		
Corn	$800,000	
Other	220,000	
		1,020,000
Net profit		$180,000

Route B (CP sells contracts and buys spot corn)

Revenue		$1,200,000
Costs		
Corn	$980,000	
Other	220,000	
		1,020,000
Net profit, operations		-0-
Gain from sale of futures contracts		$180,000
Total gains and profits		$180,000

CORN PRODUCTS REFINING CO. v. COMMISSIONER
350 U.S. 46 (1955)

Mr. Justice CLARK delivered the opinion of the Court.

This case concerns the tax treatment to be accorded certain transactions in commodity futures. In the Tax Court, petitioner Corn Products Refining Company contended that its purchases and sales of corn futures in 1940 and 1942 were capital-asset transactions under [§1221]. . . .

Petitioner is a nationally known manufacturer of products made from grain corn. It manufactures starch, syrup, sugar, and their byproducts, feeds and oil. Its average yearly grind of raw corn during the period 1937 through 1942 varied from thirty-five to sixty million bushels. Most of its products were sold under contracts requiring shipment in thirty days at a set price or at market price on the date of delivery, whichever was lower.

In 1934 and again in 1936 droughts in the corn belt caused a sharp increase in the price of spot corn. With a storage capacity of only 2,300,000 bushels of corn, a bare three weeks' supply, Corn Products found itself unable to buy at a price which would permit its refined corn sugar, cerealose, to compete successfully with cane and beet sugar. To avoid a recurrence of this situation, petitioner, in 1937, began to establish a long position in corn futures "as a part of its corn buying program" and "as the most economical method of obtaining an adequate supply of raw corn" without entailing the expenditure of large sums for additional storage facilities. At harvest time each year it would buy futures when the price appeared favorable. It would take delivery on such contracts as it found necessary to its manufacturing operations and sell the remainder in early summer if no shortage was imminent. If shortages appeared, however, it sold futures only as it bought spot corn for grinding.[4] In this manner it reached a balanced position with reference to any increase in spot corn prices. It made no effort to protect itself against a decline in prices.

In 1940 it netted a profit of $680,587.39 in corn futures, but in 1942 it suffered a loss of $109,969.38. . . . It now contends that its futures were "capital assets" under [§1221] and that gains and losses therefrom should have been treated as arising from the sale of a capital asset. In support of this position, it claims that its futures trading was separate and apart from its manufacturing operations and that in its futures transactions, it was acting as a "legitimate capitalist." U.S. v. New York Coffee & Sugar Exchange, 263 U.S. 611, 619. It denies that its future transactions were "hedges" or "speculative" dealings as covered by the ruling of General Counsel's Memorandum 17322, XV-2 C.B. 151, and claims that it is in truth "the forgotten man" of that administrative interpretation.

Both the Tax Court and the Court of Appeals found petitioner's futures transactions to be an integral part of its business designed to protect its manufacturing operations against a price increase in its principal raw material and to assure a ready supply for future manufacturing requirements. . . .

We find nothing in this record to support the contention that Corn Products' futures activity was separate and apart from its manufacturing operation. On the contrary, it appears that the transactions were vitally important to the company's business as a form of insurance against increases in the price of raw corn. Not only were the purchases initiated for just this reason, but the petitioner's sales policy, selling in the future at a fixed price or less, continued to leave it exceedingly vulnerable to rises in the price of corn. Further, the purchase of corn futures assured the company a source of supply which was admittedly cheaper than constructing additional storage facilities for raw corn. Under these facts, it is difficult to imagine a program more closely geared to a company's manufacturing enterprise or more important to its successful operation.

Likewise the claim of Corn Products that it was dealing in the market as a "legitimate capitalist" . . . exercising "good judgment" in the futures market, . . . ignores the testimony of its own officers that in entering that market the company was "trying to protect a part of [its] manufacturing costs"; that its entry was not for the purpose of "speculating and buying

---

4. The disposition of the corn futures during the period in dispute were as follows:

	Sales of futures thousand bushels	Delivery under futures thousand bushels
1938	17,400	4,975
1939	14,180	2,865
1940	14,595	250
1941	2,545	2,175
1942	5,695	4,460

and selling corn futures" but to fill an actual "need for the quantity of corn [bought] . . . in order to cover . . . what [products] we expected to market over a period of fifteen or eighteen months." It matters not whether the label be that of "legitimate capitalist" or "speculator"; this is not the talk of the capital investor but of the far-sighted manufacturer. For tax purposes, petitioner's purchases have been found to "constitute an integral part of its manufacturing business" by both the Tax Court and the Court of Appeals, and on essentially factual questions the findings of two courts should not ordinarily be disturbed. . . .

Petitioner also makes much of the conclusion by both the Tax Court and the Court of Appeals that its transactions did not constitute "true hedging." It is true that Corn Products did not secure complete protection from its market operations. Under its sales policy petitioner could not guard against a fall in prices. It is clear, however, that petitioner feared the possibility of a price rise more than that of a price decline. It therefore purchased partial insurance against its principal risk, and hoped to retain sufficient flexibility to avoid serious losses on a declining market.

Nor can we find support for petitioner's contention that hedging is not within the exclusions of [§1221]. Admittedly, petitioner's corn futures do not come within the literal language of the exclusions set out in that section. They were not stock in trade, actual inventory, property held for sale to customers or depreciable property used in a trade or business. But the capital-asset provision of [§1221] must not be so broadly applied as to defeat rather than further the purpose of Congress. Burnet v. Harmel, 287 U.S. 103, 108. Congress intended that profits and losses arising from the everyday operation of a business be considered as ordinary income or loss rather than capital gain or loss. The preferential treatment provided by [§1221] applies to transactions in property which are not the normal source of business income. It was intended "to relieve the taxpayer from . . . excessive tax burdens on gains resulting from a conversion of capital investments, and to remove the deterrent effect of those burdens on such conversions." Burnet v. Harmel, 287 U.S., at 106. Since this section is an exception from the normal tax requirements of the Internal Revenue Code, the definition of a capital asset must be narrowly applied and its exclusions interpreted broadly. This is necessary to effectuate the basic congressional purpose. This Court has always construed narrowly the term "capital assets" in [§1221]. See Hort v. Commissioner.

The problem of the appropriate tax treatment of hedging transactions first arose under the 1934 Tax Code revision. Thereafter, the Treasury issued G.C.M. 17322, *supra,* distinguishing speculative transactions in commodity futures from hedging transactions. It held that hedging transactions were essentially to be regarded as insurance rather than a dealing in capital assets and that gains and losses therefrom were ordinary business gains and losses. The interpretation outlined in this memorandum has been consistently followed by the courts as well as by the Commissioner. While it is true that this Court has not passed on its validity, it has been well recognized for 20 years; and Congress has made no change in it though the Code has been re-enacted on three subsequent occasions. This bespeaks congressional approval. . . .

Furthermore, Congress has since specifically recognized the hedging exception here under consideration in the short-sale rule of §1233(a) of the 1954 Code.[5]

We believe that the statute clearly refutes the contention of Corn Products. Moreover, it is significant to note that practical considerations lead to the same conclusion. To hold otherwise would permit those engaged in hedging transactions to transmute ordinary income into capital gain at will. The hedger may either sell the future and purchase in the spot market or take delivery under the future contract itself. But if a sale of the future created a capital transaction while delivery of the commodity under the same future did not, a loophole in the statute would be created and the purpose of Congress frustrated.

The judgment is affirmed.

Mr. Justice HARLAN took no part in the consideration or decision of this case.

ARKANSAS BEST CORPORATION v. COMMISSIONER
485 U.S. 212 (1988)

Justice MARSHALL delivered the opinion of the Court.

The issue presented in this case is whether capital stock held by petitioner Arkansas Best Corporation (Arkansas Best) is a "capital asset" as defined in §1221 of the Internal Revenue Code regardless of whether the stock was purchased and held for a business purpose or for an investment purpose.

I

Arkansas Best is a diversified holding company. In 1968 it acquired approximately 65% of the stock of the National Bank of Commerce (Bank) in Dallas, Texas. Between 1969 and 1974, Arkansas Best more than tripled the number of shares it owned in the Bank, although its percentage interest in the Bank remained relatively stable. These acquisitions were prompted principally by the Bank's need for added capital. Until 1972, the Bank appeared to be prosperous and growing, and the added capital was necessary to accommodate this growth. As the Dallas real estate market declined, however, so too did the financial health of the Bank, which had a heavy concentration of loans in the local real estate industry. In 1972, federal examiners classified the Bank as a problem bank. The infusion of capital after 1972 was prompted by the loan portfolio problems of the bank.

---

5. Section 1233(a) provides that gain or loss from "the short sale of property, other than a hedging transaction in commodity futures," shall be treated as gain or loss from the sale of a capital asset to the extent "that the property, including a commodity future, used to close the short sale constitutes a capital asset in the hands of a taxpayer." The legislative history recognizes explicitly the hedging exception. H.R. Rep. No. 1337, 83d Cong., 2d Sess., p. A278; S. Rep. No. 1622, 83d Cong., 2d Sess., p. 437: "Under existing law bona fide hedging transactions do not result in capital gains or losses. This result is based upon case law and regulations. To continue this result, hedging transactions in commodity futures have been specifically excepted from the operation of this subsection."

Petitioner sold the bulk of its Bank stock on June 30, 1975, leaving it with only a 14.7% stake in the Bank. On its federal income tax return for 1975, petitioner claimed a deduction for an ordinary loss of $9,995,688 resulting from the sale of the stock. The Commissioner of Internal Revenue disallowed the deduction, finding that the loss from the sale of stock was a capital loss, rather than an ordinary loss, and that it therefore was subject to the capital loss limitations in the Internal Revenue Code.[6]

Arkansas Best challenged the Commissioner's determination in the United States Tax Court. The Tax Court, relying on cases interpreting Corn Products Refining Co. v. Commissioner, held that stock purchased with a substantial investment purpose is a capital asset which, when sold, gives rise to a capital gain or loss, whereas stock purchased and held for a business purpose, without any substantial investment motive, is an ordinary asset whose sale gives rise to ordinary gains or losses. . . . The court characterized Arkansas Best's acquisitions through 1972 as occurring during the Bank's "'growth' phase," and found that these acquisitions "were motivated primarily by investment purpose and only incidentally by some business purpose." . . . The stock acquired during this period therefore constituted a capital asset, which gave rise to a capital loss when sold in 1975. The court determined, however, that the acquisitions after 1972 occurred during the Bank's "'problem' phase," . . . and, except for certain minor exceptions, "were made exclusively for business purposes and subsequently held for the same reasons." . . . These acquisitions, the court found, were designed to preserve petitioner's business reputation, because without the added capital the Bank probably would have failed. . . . The loss realized on the sale of this stock was thus held to be an ordinary loss.

The Court of Appeals for the Eighth Circuit reversed the Tax Court's determination that the loss realized on stock purchased after 1972 was subject to ordinary-loss treatment, holding that all of the Bank stock sold in 1975 was subject to capital-loss treatment. 800 F.2d 215 (1986). The court reasoned that the Bank stock clearly fell within the general definition of "capital asset" in Internal Revenue Code §1221, and that the stock did not fall within any of the specific statutory exceptions to this definition. The court concluded that Arkansas Best's purpose in acquiring and holding the stock was irrelevant to the determination whether the stock was a capital asset. We granted certiorari . . . and now affirm.

II

Section 1221 of the Internal Revenue Code defines "capital asset" broadly, as "property held by the taxpayer (whether or not connected with his trade or business)," and then excludes five specific classes of property from capital-asset status. Arkansas Best acknowledges that the Bank stock falls within the literal definition of capital asset in §1221, and is outside of the statutory exclusions. It

---

6. Title 26 U.S.C. §1211(a) states that "[i]n the case of a corporation, losses from sales or exchanges of capital assets shall be allowed only to the extent of gains from such sales or exchanges." Section 1212(a) establishes rules governing carrybacks and carryovers of capital losses, permitting such losses to offset capital gains in certain earlier or later years.

asserts, however, that this determination does not end the inquiry. Petitioner argues that in Corn Products Refining Co. v. Commissioner, *supra,* this Court rejected a literal reading of §1221, and concluded that assets acquired and sold for ordinary business purposes rather than for investment purposes should be given ordinary-asset treatment. Petitioner's reading of *Corn Products* finds much support in the academic literature and in the courts.[7] Unfortunately for petitioner, this broad reading finds no support in the language of §1221.

In essence, petitioner argues that "property held by the taxpayer (whether or not connected with his trade or business)" does not include property that is acquired and held for a business purpose. In petitioner's view an asset's status as "property" thus turns on the motivation behind its acquisition. This motive test, however, is not only nowhere mentioned in §1221, but it is also in direct conflict with the parenthetical phrase "whether or not connected with his trade or business." The broad definition of the term "capital asset" explicitly makes irrelevant any consideration of the property's connection with the taxpayer's business, whereas petitioner's rule would make this factor dispositive. . . .

In the end, petitioner places all reliance on its reading of Corn Products Refining Co. v. Commissioner—a reading we believe is too expansive. In *Corn Products*, the Court considered whether income arising from a taxpayer's dealings in corn futures was entitled to capital-gains treatment. The taxpayer was a company that converted corn into starches, sugars, and other products. After droughts in the 1930's caused sharp increases in corn prices, the company began a program of buying corn futures to assure itself an adequate supply of corn and protect against price increases. . . . The company "would take delivery on such contracts as it found necessary to its manufacturing operations and sell the remainder in early summer if no shortage was imminent. If shortages appeared, however, it sold futures only as it bought spot corn for grinding." . . . The Court characterized the company's dealing in corn futures as "hedging." . . . As explained by the Court of Appeals in *Corn Products*, "[h]edging is a method of dealing in commodity futures whereby a person or business protects itself against price fluctuations at the time of delivery of the product which it sells or buys." 215 F.2d 513, 515 (C.A.2 1954). In evaluating the company's claim that the sales of corn futures resulted in capital gains and losses, this Court stated:

> Nor can we find support for petitioner's contention that hedging is not within the exclusions of [§1221]. Admittedly, petitioner's corn futures do not come within the literal language of the exclusions set out in that section. They were not stock in trade, actual inventory, property held for sale to customers or depreciable property used in a trade or business. But the capital-asset provision of [§1221] must not be so broadly applied as to defeat rather than further the purpose of Congress. Congress intended that profits and losses arising from the everyday operation of a business be considered as ordinary income or loss rather than capital gain or loss. . . . Since this section is an exception from the normal

---

7. See, e.g., Campbell Taggart, Inc. v. United States, 744 F.2d 442, 456-458 (C.A.5 1984); Steadman v. Commissioner, 424 F.2d 1, 5 (C.A.6), cert. denied, 400 U.S. 869 (1970); Booth Newspapers, Inc. v. United States, 157 Ct. Cl. 886, 893-896, 303 F.2d 916, 920-921 (1962); W. W. Windle Co. v. Commissioner, 65 T.C. 694, 707-713 (1976).

tax requirements of the Internal Revenue Code, the definition of a capital asset must be narrowly applied and its exclusions interpreted broadly. . . .

The Court went on to note that hedging transactions consistently had been considered to give rise to ordinary gains and losses, and then concluded that the corn futures were subject to ordinary-asset treatment. . . .

The Court in *Corn Products* proffered the oft-quoted rule of construction that the definition of capital asset must be narrowly applied and its exclusions interpreted broadly, but it did not state explicitly whether the holding was based on a narrow reading of the phrase "property held by the taxpayer," or on a broad reading of the inventory exclusion of §1221. In light of the stark language of §1221, however, we believe that *Corn Products* is properly interpreted as involving an application of §1221's inventory exception. Such a reading is consistent both with the Court's reasoning in that case and with §1221. The Court stated in *Corn Products* that the company's futures transactions were "an integral part of its business designed to protect its manufacturing operations against a price increase in its principal raw material and to assure a ready supply for future manufacturing requirements." . . . The company bought, sold, and took delivery under the futures contracts as required by the company's manufacturing needs. As Professor Bittker notes, under these circumstances, the futures can "easily be viewed as surrogates for the raw material itself." 2 B. Bittker, Federal Taxation of Income, Estates and Gifts, para. 51.10.3, p.51-62 (1981).

III

We conclude that a taxpayer's motivation in purchasing an asset is irrelevant to the question whether the asset is "property held by a taxpayer (whether or not connected with his business)" and is thus within §1221's general definition of "capital asset." Because the capital stock held by petitioner falls within the broad definition of the term "capital asset" in §1221 and is outside the classes of property excluded from capital-asset status, the loss arising from the sale of the stock is a capital loss. Corn Products Refining Co. v. Commissioner, *supra,* which we interpret as involving a broad reading of the inventory exclusion of §1221, has no application in the present context. Accordingly, the judgment of the Court of Appeals is affirmed.

It is so ordered.

NOTES AND QUESTIONS

1. *What is a hedge?* (a) Despite the Court's restrictive reading of §1221, limiting the *Corn Products* exception to substitutes for inventory, the Treasury regulations adopted after the decision in *Arkansas Best* allow ordinary gain or loss treatment for a broad variety of hedging transactions, including hedges used to protect against the risk of changes in interest rates or in currency exchange rates. Reg. §1.1221-2. The regulations address the potential abuse identified by the Court (that is, taxpayers treating gain as capital and loss as ordinary) by providing for taxpayer advance identification of hedging transactions. Reg. §1.1221-2(e).

(b) What if the taxpayer in *Corn Products* had been unwilling for some reason to buy corn futures and, as an alternative hedge against a rise in the price of corn, had bought contracts for some other commodity, such as hogs, whose price fluctuations were closely correlated to fluctuations in the price of corn? See Reg. §1.1221-2(b)(1), (c), (c)(1).

(c) What if the taxpayer had concluded that the price of corn futures contracts was low and had bought contracts for more corn than it normally used in its operations?

2. *Source of supply cases.* Some of the cases applying the *Corn Products* doctrine, or similar analysis, to allow ordinary deductions for losses on investments involved investments made to ensure a source of supply. For example, in *Booth Newspapers,* cited by the Court in *Arkansas Best,* the taxpayer, a newspaper publisher, bought shares of stock of a paper manufacturing corporation to protect its source of newsprint in a time of shortage. How would such a case be decided under the rule of *Arkansas Best?* Under the current regulations? See Reg. §1.1221-2(c)(5)(ii). What is the likely effect of taxpayer identification of the transaction as a hedging transaction? See Reg. §1.1221-2(e), (f). What if an airline hedges against the risk of an increase in the price of jet fuel?

3. *What is inventory?* The regulations provide that the taxpayer's inventory "should include all finished or partly finished goods and, in the case of raw materials and supplies, only those which have been acquired for sale or which will physically become a part of merchandise intended for sale." Reg. §1.471-1. Is this provision applicable not only to §471 (use of inventories in determining income) but also to §1221(a)(1)? If a business sells an excess stock of supplies that were not to be physically incorporated in its merchandise (e.g., office supplies, cleaning materials, or repair parts for machinery), do they come within §1221(a)(1)? Should the fact that their cost was deducted (from ordinary income) as a business expense be relevant in determining whether a sale produces ordinary income or capital gain?

F.   SUBSTITUTES FOR ORDINARY INCOME

The next two cases (*Hort* and *McAllister*) focus on the question of whether the taxpayer is entitled to a recovery of basis, but they are also treated as authority on the issue of capital gain versus ordinary income.

1.   Payment for Cancellation of a Lease

HORT v. COMMISSIONER
313 U.S. 28 (1941)

Mr. Justice MURPHY delivered the opinion of the Court.

We must determine whether the amount petitioner received as consideration for cancellation of a lease of realty in New York City was ordinary gross income as defined in [§61(a)], and whether, in any event, petitioner sustained a loss through cancellation of the lease which is recognized in [§165(a)].

Petitioner acquired the property, a lot and ten-story office building, by devise from his father in 1928. At the time he became owner, the premises were leased to a firm which had sublet the main floor to the Irving Trust Co. In 1927, five years before the head lease expired, the Irving Trust Co. and petitioner's father executed a contract in which the latter agreed to lease the main floor and basement to the former for a term of fifteen years at an annual rental of $25,000, the term to commence at the expiration of the head lease.

In 1933, the Irving Trust Co. found it unprofitable to maintain a branch in petitioner's building. After some negotiations, petitioner and the Trust Co. agreed to cancel the lease in consideration of a payment to petitioner of $140,000. Petitioner did not include this amount in gross income in his income tax return for 1933. On the contrary, he reported a loss of $21,494.75 on the theory that the amount he received as consideration for the cancellation was $21,494.75 less than the difference between the present value of the unmatured rental payments and the fair rental value of the main floor and basement for the unexpired term of the lease. He did not deduct this figure, however, because he reported other losses in excess of gross income.

The Commissioner included the entire $140,000 in gross income, disallowed the asserted loss, made certain other adjustments not material here, and assessed a deficiency. The Board of Tax Appeals affirmed. 39 B.T.A. 922. The Circuit Court of Appeals affirmed per curiam on the authority of Warren Service Corp. v. Commissioner, 110 F.2d 723. 112 F.2d 167. Because of conflict with Commissioner v. Langwell Real Estate Corp., 47 F.2d 841, we granted certiorari limited to the question whether, "in computing net gain or loss for income tax purposes, a taxpayer [can] offset the value of the lease canceled against the consideration received by him for the cancellation." 311 U.S. 641.

Petitioner apparently contends that the amount received for cancellation of the lease was capital rather than ordinary income and that it was therefore subject to [the provisions of the Code] which govern capital gains and losses. Further, he argues that even if that amount must be reported as ordinary gross income he sustained a loss which [§165(a)] authorizes him to deduct. We cannot agree.

The amount received by petitioner for cancellation of the lease must be included in his gross income in its entirety. . . . [Section 61(a)] reached the rent paid prior to cancellation just as it would have embraced subsequent payments if the lease had never been canceled. It would have included a prepayment of the discounted value of unmatured rental payments whether received at the inception of the lease or at any time thereafter. Similarly, it would have extended to the proceeds of a suit to recover damages had the Irving Trust Co. breached the lease instead of concluding a settlement. . . . That the amount petitioner received resulted from negotiations ending in cancellation of the lease rather than from a suit to enforce it cannot alter the fact that basically the payment was merely a substitute for the rent reserved in the lease. So far as the application of [§61(a)] is concerned, it is immaterial that petitioner chose to accept an amount less than the strict present value of the unmatured rental payments rather than to engage in litigation, possibly uncertain and expensive.

The consideration received for cancellation of the lease was not a return of capital. We assume that the lease was "property," whatever that signifies abstractly. Presumably the bond in Helvering v. Horst and the lease in Helvering v. Bruun were also "property," but the interest coupon in *Horst* and the building in *Bruun* nevertheless were held to constitute items of gross income. Simply because the lease was "property" the amount received for its cancellation was not a return of capital, quite apart from the fact that "property" and "capital" are not necessarily synonymous in the Revenue Act of 1932 or in common usage. Where, as in this case, the disputed amount was essentially a substitute for rental payments which [§61(a)(5)] expressly characterizes as gross income, it must be regarded as ordinary income, and it is immaterial that for some purposes the contract creating the right to such payments may be treated as "property" or "capital."

For the same reasons, that amount was not a return of capital because petitioner acquired the lease as an incident of the realty devised to him by his father. Theoretically, it might have been possible in such a case to value realty and lease separately, and to label each a capital asset. . . . But that would not have converted into capital the amount petitioner received from the Trust Co., since [§102(b)(1)] would have required him to include in gross income the rent derived from the property, and that section, like [§61(a)], does not distinguish rental payments and a payment which is clearly a substitute for rental payments.

We conclude that petitioner must report as gross income the entire amount received for cancellation of the lease, without regard to the claimed disparity between that amount and the difference between the present value of the unmatured rental payments and the fair rental value of the property for the unexpired period of the lease. The cancellation of the lease involved nothing more than relinquishment of the right to future rental payments in return for a present substitute payment and possession of the leased premises. Undoubtedly it diminished the amount of gross income petitioner expected to realize, but to that extent he was relieved of the duty to pay income tax. Nothing in [§165(a)] indicates that Congress intended to allow petitioner to reduce ordinary income actually received and reported by the amount of income he failed to realize. . . . We may assume that petitioner was injured insofar as the cancellation of the lease affected the value of the realty. But that would become a deductible loss only when its extent had been fixed by a closed transaction. Regulations [§1.165-1(b)]. . . .

The judgment of the Circuit Court of Appeals is affirmed.

NOTES AND QUESTIONS

1. *Background: Prepaid leases.* (a) Suppose *L* buys land for $100,000 and can rent it out for $10,000 per year net of all expenses. For the sake of simplicity, assume further that there is no inflation, that the rent is expected to remain $10,000, and that the value of the land remains $100,000 for the foreseeable future. If *L* rents the land for one year and receives a rent payment of $10,000 at the end of that year, plainly the $10,000 is fully taxed as ordinary income. Note two elements in this statement of tax consequences. First, no part of *L*'s basis is offset against the $10,000 receipt. This is as it should be, since at the end of the year she still has the land, which is not a wasting asset and which is therefore presumed for tax purposes still to be worth $100,000. (If the land in fact changes in value, that change is unrealized gain or loss.) Second, the $10,000 is ordinary income. It is rent, not the proceeds of the sale of property.

(b) Suppose that L rents the land for two years with the tenant paying $17,355 in advance. (The figure $17,355 is the present value of the right to receive $10,000 at the end of each year for two years, discounted at the rate of 10 percent. Assume here and in the subsequent questions in this note that 10 percent is the appropriate market rate.) Is the entire amount taxable at the time received? Is it still ordinary income?

(c) What if the lease is for ten years and the advance payment is $61,000 (the approximate present value of $10,000 at the end of each year for ten years, discounted at 10 percent)? If the value of the leasehold is $61,000, the value of the reversion should be $39,000. As time passes, the value of the leasehold declines and the value of the reversion rises. See Chapter 2, Section C.6. Does this observation help to explain why it may be appropriate to treat the receipt of the advance rent as income, with no basis offset? Does it help explain why the amount received is ordinary income rather than capital gain?

(d) What if the lease is for ninety-nine years and the advance payment is $99,992 (the present value, at a 10 percent discount rate)? Compare Reg. §1.1031(a)-1(c) (leasehold for thirty years or more is like a fee for purposes of like-kind exchange rules).

(e) By way of review, what are the tax consequences for the tenant in each of the above situations, assuming the property is used in the tenant's business? See Chapter 6, Section A.

(f) If the property is depreciable, how is L's deduction for depreciation affected by the fact that L receives two or more years' rent in advance?

2. *The legal doctrine of* Hort. Is the holding of *Hort* that there was no "sale or exchange" or that what was sold was not a "capital asset" (that is, "property" not within one of the exceptions of §1221)?

3. *Inherited property.* Suppose that L owns property worth $100,000, leases it for $10,000 per year (payable at the end of each year) for ten years, and immediately dies, leaving the property, subject to the lease, to her son, S. At the time of L's death the leasehold is worth $61,000, and the remainder $39,000. Before any time passes, S talks the tenant into paying $60,000 to S in full payment for the use of the property for the remaining ten years of the lease. What are the tax consequences to S under *Hort*? Is that result consistent with sound tax policy? Suppose S argues that he inherited a leasehold worth $61,000, sold it immediately for only $60,000, resulting in a loss of $1,000.[8] How would you respond?

4. *Premium leases.* Suppose that L, the owner of land worth $100,000, leases it for $10,000 per year for ten years and that a year later the value of the land has

---

8. In essence this was the position taken by the taxpayer in *Hort*. The taxpayer claimed that the right to receive rent of $25,000 per year for the remaining thirteen years of the lease was worth $257,000, that he received a cash payment of $140,000, plus the right to the use of the property for the fourteen years (worth $96,000), so he gave up $257,000 and received a total of only $236,000 and was entitled to deduct the difference of $21,000. To this, the Court of Appeals (112 F.2d 167 (2d Cir. 1940)) responded by citing its earlier decision in Warren Service Corp. v. Commissioner, 110 F.2d 723 (1940), in which it had said that the taxpayer's claimed loss was "merely a diminution of expected income," which produces "no loss of property in the income-tax sense." 110 F.2d at 724. This may dispose of the taxpayer's claim to a loss deduction, but it does not resolve the question of how the receipt of the $140,000 should be treated. Apart from the defect in the taxpayer's position noted by the Court of Appeals in *Hort*, it is not the value of the property sold but rather its basis that determines the amount of a gain or loss. See §1001(a).

fallen to $60,000 and the rent that could be earned if now leased for nine years would be $6,000 per year. The existing lease for $10,000 per year is a valuable asset; it calls for a premium rent and is called a premium lease. The value of the premium is the present value of the difference, for nine years, between the rent payment called for in the lease ($10,000) and the rent that could be earned if the property were rented at market rates ($6,000). That difference on our facts is $4,000 per year. The present value of $4,000 per year for nine years, discounted at 10 percent, is approximately $23,000. Thus, *L*'s wealth includes the land, independent of the lease, worth $60,000. The $60,000 can be divided into two segments, one consisting of the right to $6,000 per year for nine years (worth $34,554), and the other consisting of the right to $60,000 at the end of nine years (worth $25,446). Adding to this the $23,000 (approximate) present value of the right to the $4,000 premium for nine years, we arrive at the total value of $83,000.

Suppose that *L* dies and leaves the land, subject to the lease, to her son, *S*. The property, with the lease, is worth $83,000. At the end of the remaining nine-year term of the lease it will be worth only $60,000 (all other things equal). The premium lease is a wasting asset. A forceful argument can therefore be made that *S* should treat the premium value of the lease as a separate asset with a basis of $23,000, to be taken into account in determining gain or loss on disposition, or through a deduction for amortization if *S* retains the property and collects the annual rent. But see Schubert v. Commissioner, 286 F.2d 573, 580 (4th Cir.), cert. denied, 366 U.S. 960 (1961) (discussing a conflict in other circuits and denying a deduction for failure of proof of premium). The position of a purchaser of property subject to a premium lease is different. See World Publishing Co. v. Commissioner, 299 F.2d 614 (8th Cir. 1962), where the taxpayer bought property subject to a lease with twenty-eight years remaining and a building constructed by the lessee, with a useful life less than twenty-eight years and a value of $300,000. The taxpayer's purchase price was $700,000, and there was testimony that the land was worth $400,000. The court allowed depreciation on the building, with a basis of $300,000. The court commented sympathetically on the alternative possibility, not urged by the taxpayer, that a deduction for the premium value of the lease should be allowed. In any event, in *Hort* it seems unlikely that the lease was a premium lease at the time the property was inherited by the taxpayer.

5. *Leases as capital assets of lessees.* We now turn our attention from the lessor with an advantageous (premium) lease to the lessee with an advantageous (premium) lease.

(a) Suppose *T* is the tenant under a lease calling for annual rental payments of $10,000 and having a remaining term of ten years and that *T* is able to sell the leasehold interest to a third person for $25,000. Is the $25,000 capital gain? The answer is yes, regardless of whether the property has been used for personal purposes, and is therefore covered by §1221, or has been used in the taxpayer's business, and thus is §1231 property. See Rev. Rul. 72-85, 1972-1 C.B. 234. How can this result be reconciled with *Hort*? What if *T* had sold the next three years of the remaining ten years of use of the leasehold for $10,000?

(b) Suppose *T* pays $60,000 in advance for the use of the land for ten years and one year later sells the leasehold interest for $75,000. What is the amount of gain? Is it capital gain? What if the leasehold had been sold for $40,000? Does the result depend on whether the property was used in *T*'s business? Rev. Rul. 72-85 states that a tenant's leasehold interest in land is "real property."

6. *The relevance of §61(a).* The reliance in the *Hort* opinion on the fact that §61(a)(5) "expressly characterizes [rental payments] as gross income" reflects a common misunderstanding about capital gain and the meaning of gross income. Section 61(a) defines gross income. Capital gain is part of gross income; §61(a)(3) expressly includes in gross income "gains derived from dealings in property." Section 61(a) provides no guidance in distinguishing between capital gain and ordinary income.

7. *The "substitute for ordinary income" theory.* The suggestion in the *Hort* opinion that an amount can be characterized as ordinary income because it is a "substitute for" ordinary income, such as rental payments, is also misguided. If Mr. Hort had sold his entire interest in the land, the amount he received would be a substitute for the rents he otherwise would have received in perpetuity. A fundamental principle of economics is that the value of an asset is equal to the present discounted value of all the expected net receipts from that asset over its life.

What, then, is the rule of the *Hort* case? Does the following case help you in answering this question?

2. Sale of Interest in a Trust

McALLISTER v. COMMISSIONER
157 F.2d 235 (2d Cir. 1946), cert. denied, 330 U.S. 826 (1947), acq.

Before Swan, Clark, and Frank, Circuit Judges.
Clark, Circuit Judge.

This petition for review presents the question whether the sum of $55,000 received by petitioner on "transfer" or "surrender" of her life interest in a trust to the remainderman constitutes gross income under [§61(a)], or receipts from the sale of capital assets as defined in [§1221]. . . . Petitioner contends that the life estate was a capital asset, the transfer of which resulted in a deductible capital loss, leaving her with no taxable income for the year. A majority of the Tax Court agreed with the Commissioner that the receipt in question was merely an advance payment of income. . . .

The will of Richard McAllister established a trust fund of $100,000, the income of which was to be paid to his son John McAllister for life and, on the latter's death without children, to John's wife, the petitioner herein. On her death, the trust was to terminate, the residue going to the testator's wife and his son Richard. The testator died in 1926, his widow in 1935, and John in 1937. Except for stock in the R. McAllister corporation, not immediately salable at a fair price, John left assets insufficient to meet his debts; and in order to obtain immediate funds and to terminate extended family litigation according to an agreed plan, petitioner brought suit in the Court of Chancery of New Jersey to end the trust. The parties then agreed upon, and the court in its final decree ordered, a settlement by which the remainderman Richard, in addition to taking over the stock for $50,000, was to pay petitioner $55,000, with accumulated income and interest to the date of payment, in consideration of her release of all interest in the trust and consent to its termination and cancellation. For the year 1940, she reported a capital loss on the transaction of $8,790.20, the difference between the amount received and the value of the estate computed under [Reg. §1.1014-5].[9]

The issue, as stated by the Tax Court and presented by the parties, reduces itself to the question whether the case is within the rule of Blair v. Commissioner, or that of Hort v. Commissioner. In the *Blair* case, the life beneficiary of a trust assigned to his children specified sums to be paid each year for the duration of the estate. The Supreme Court held that each transfer was the assignment of a property right in the trust and that, since the tax liability attached to ownership of the property, the assignee, and not the assignor, was liable for the income taxes in the years in question. The continued authority of the case was recognized in Helvering v. Horst, although a majority of the Court thought it not applicable on the facts, and in Harrison v. Schaffner, 312 U.S. 579 (1941), where the Court very properly distinguished it from the situation where an assignor transferred a portion of his income for a single year. We think that its reasoning and conclusion support the taxpayer's position here. . . .

Petitioner's right to income for life from the trust estate was a right in the estate itself. Had she held a fee interest, the assignment would unquestionably have been regarded as the transfer of a capital asset; we see no reason why a different result should follow the transfer of the lesser, but still substantial, life interest. As the Court pointed out in the *Blair* case, the life tenant was entitled to enforce the trust, to enjoin a breach of trust, and to obtain redress in case of breach. The proceedings in the state chancery court completely divested her of these rights and of any possible control over the property. The case is therefore distinguishable from that of Hort v. Commissioner, *supra,* where a landlord for a consideration cancelled a lease for a term of years, having still some nine years to run. There the taxpayer surrendered his contractual right to the future yearly payments in return for an immediate payment of a lump sum. The statute expressly taxed income derived from rent [§61(a)(5)]; and the consideration received was held a substitute for the rent as it fell due. It was therefore taxed as income.

What we regard as the precise question here presented has been determined in the taxpayer's favor on the authority of the *Blair* case by the Eighth Circuit in Bell's Estate v. Commissioner, 8 Cir., 137 F.2d 454, reversing 46 B.T.A. 484. . . .

The Tax Court and the government have attempted to distinguish both the *Bell* and the *Blair* cases on grounds which seem to us to lack either substance or reality. The principal ground seems to be the form the transaction assumed between the parties. Thus the Court says that petitioner received the payment for "surrendering" her rights to income payments, and "she did not assign her interest in the trust, as did petitioners in the *Bell* case." But what is this more than a distinction in words? Both were cases where at the conclusion of the transaction the remaindermen had the entire estate and the life tenants had a substantial sum of money. . . .

---

9. [The court apparently uses "value of the estate" to mean "basis."—Eds.]

Setting the bounds to the area of tax incidence involves the drawing of lines which may often be of an arbitrary nature. But they should not be more unreal than the circumstances necessitate. Here the line of demarcation between the *Blair* and the *Hort* principles is obviously one of some difficulty to define explicitly or to establish in borderline cases. Doubtless all would agree that there is some distinction between selling a life estate in property and anticipating income for a few years in advance. . . . The distinction seems logically and practically to turn upon anticipation of income payments over a reasonably short period of time and an out-and-out transfer of a substantial and durable property interest, such as a life estate at least is. See 57 Harv. L. Rev. 382; 54 Harv. L. Rev. 1405; 50 Yale L.J. 512, 515. Where the line should be finally placed we need not try to anticipate here. But we are clear that distinctions attempted on the basis of the various legal names given a transaction, rather than on its actual results between the parties, do not afford a sound basis for its delimitation. More rationally, to accept the respondent's contention we ought frankly to consider the *Blair* case as overruled, 50 Yale L.J. 512, 518, a position which, as we have seen, the Supreme Court itself has declined to take.

The parties are in conflict as to the valuation of the life estate; and we are returning the case to the Tax Court for computation, without, of course, assuming that there will necessarily be some tax.

Reversed and remanded.

FRANK, Circuit Judge (dissenting). . . .

We must . . . ascertain the intention of Congress expressed in those provisions—specially [§1221]—in the light of the language it employed and the policy there embodied. . . .

My colleagues avoid a direct discussion of that problem. Instead, they rely on Blair v. Commissioner, which they hold to be controlling. But the court in the *Blair* case had no occasion to, and did not, consider [§1221]. . . . The only question was whether thereafter the donor, notwithstanding the gift, should be regarded, under [§61(a)], as the recipient annually of that part of the income which was the subject of the gift and, consequently, should be taxed each year thereon. In other words, no capital gain or loss was involved, and the one issue was whether the donor or donee was annually taxable.

The policy of the capital gains provisions is not in doubt: Congress believed that the exaction of income tax on the usual basis on gains resulting from dispositions of capital investments would undesirably deter such dispositions. To put it differently, Congress made an exception to [§61(a)], in order to give an incentive to the making of such transfers. Having regard to that purpose, the courts have been cautious in interpreting the clauses creating that exception. They have refused to regard as "capital" transactions for that purpose divers sorts of transfers of "property," especially those by which transferors have procured advance payments of future income.

Those cases and Hort v. Commissioner, seem to me to render it somewhat doubtful whether any transfer of a life estate for a valuable consideration is within [§1221]. The consideration paid for such a transfer is a substitute for future payments which would be taxable as ordinary income, and resembles the advance payment of dividends, interest, or salaries. . . .

I think it most unlikely that Congress intended by [§1221] to relieve such a taxpayer of the ordinary tax burdens to supply an incentive for the demolition of such a trust. . . .

NOTES AND QUESTIONS

1. *Treatment of the life tenant.* The court decided two issues in *McAllister*: first, that a life estate is a capital asset falling within the general statutory definition of §1221, and second, that a life tenant has basis in a life estate. In accord with the characterization of a life estate as a capital asset is Allen v. First National Bank & Trust Co., 157 F.2d 592 (5th Cir. 1946), which held *Hort* not applicable because the taxpayer in *Hort* did not sell all his rights in the property he owned.

Under the rule applied in Irwin v. Gavit, 268 U.S. 161 (1925), if Mrs. McAllister had retained her life estate and collected the income, she would have been taxable on the entire amount received; no part of the basis of the property held in trust would have been allocated to her in this situation. On the other hand, under the *McAllister* decision, when she in fact sold, part of the basis in the property was allocated to her (see *infra* Note 2) and she reported a loss. She could then have taken the $55,000 and used it to buy an annuity for her life. Disregarding the costs of servicing the annuity, the payments she should receive under it should be about the same as the payments she would have received from the life estate. But part of the payments received under the annuity would be excluded from income. Meanwhile, the purchaser of the life estate would be entitled to amortize, over Mrs. McAllister's life, the cost of buying it from her,[10] even if the purchaser was also the holder of the remainder interest. See Bell v. Harrison, 212 F.2d 253 (7th Cir. 1954), and Rev. Rul. 62-132, 1962-2 C.B. 73 (acquiescence in Bell v. Harrison, limited to transactions that are bona fide and not for tax avoidance purposes). Even though part of the basis for the property had been used by the life tenant, when the life estate ultimately terminated, the remainder holder's basis would be the entire basis for the property, so the effect is a double use of part of the property's basis. This set of rules gave rise to tax avoidance opportunities that were ended in 1969 with the adoption of §1001(e), which provides that where a life tenant sells the life interest, unless the remainder holder sells at the same time, the basis for the life interest is zero. Thus, under present law, Mrs. McAllister would have recognized a gain of $55,000. It would still have been capital gain.

2. *Uniform basis.* At the time of *McAllister,* and under present law if the life tenant and the remainder holder sell at the same time, to allocate the total basis in the property between the life interest and the remainder interest, one starts with the adjusted basis for the property (the uniform basis) and allocates that basis between the two interests in accordance with the relative actuarial values of each at the time of sale. Thus, the basis of the life estate declines as the life expectancy of the life tenant declines and the basis of the remainder

---

10. If the life estate continued past the expected life, the purchaser's entire basis would be exhausted, and the full amounts received would be taxable. If, on the other hand, the life estate terminated before the entire cost had been recovered through amortization deductions, the purchaser would be entitled to a deduction for the remaining basis.

rises correspondingly. See Reg. §1.1014-5. The same rule determines the basis for the remainder where the remainder holder sells his or her interest, regardless of whether the life tenant sells at the same time.

3. *The consequences of accelerating income.* Under present law, if a life tenant sells a life interest in a trust and the remainder holder does not sell, the entire amount of the proceeds is taxable, at the capital-gain rate. Suppose that a life tenant sells because of a concern for the nature of the investment held by the trust, and uses the proceeds to buy a life annuity. If the rate of return of the trust and of the company selling the annuity are comparable, it would take the full amount of the proceeds of the sale of the life interest to buy an annuity with annual income equal to the income of the trust. But the proceeds of the sale of the trust will be reduced by the tax on those proceeds, so the life tenant who changes the source of his or her income stream will experience a reduction in income, both before and after tax.[11] Does this outcome argue for allowing the exchange of a life interest for an annuity to be accomplished tax free under a provision like §1031? If not, does it argue for a favorable rate of taxation of the proceeds of the sale of the life interest?

4. *Sale of a payment from the life estate.* Suppose that in return for a present payment of $30,000, Mrs. McAllister had "sold" the right to the next $30,000 worth of income from the trust plus an increment equal to 5 percent of the unrecovered balance. Assuming that §1001(e) applies, her gain would be $30,000. Should that be treated as ordinary income or capital gain? Reserve a decision on this question until you have read the next case.

3. Lottery Winnings

WOMACK v. COMMISSIONER
510 F.3d 1295 (11th Cir. 2007)

This is an appeal by Florida State Lottery winners from the United States Tax Court's decision that proceeds from the sale of the rights to future installment payments from lottery winnings ("Lottery Rights") are taxable as ordinary income, rather than at the lower tax rate applied to the sale of a long term capital asset. The Tax Court specifically held that Lottery Rights are not capital assets as defined in [§1221], under the judicially established substitute for ordinary income doctrine. We affirm.

I. BACKGROUND

Roland Womack won a portion of an $8,000,000 Florida State Lottery ("Florida Lotto") prize on January 20, 1996. At the time, the prize was payable only in twenty annual installments of $150,000. Mr. Womack received four such annual installments from 1996 to 1999, and he reported those payments as ordinary income on the federal tax returns he filed jointly with his wife, Marie Womack.

---

11. This effect will be mitigated but not eliminated by the fact that the annuity will have a basis equal to its cost and, consequently, part of each annuity payment will be nontaxable.

In 1999, Florida amended its law to permit lottery winners to assign Lottery Rights. . . . Mr. Womack subsequently sold the right to receive the remaining sixteen payments to Singer Asset Finance Company ("Singer") in exchange for a sum of $1,328,000. The total face value of the remaining payments was $2,400,000. The Womacks reported the amount received from Singer on their 2000 joint federal income tax return as proceeds from the sale of a long-term capital asset.

[Another couple, the Spiridakoses, who were in essentially the same tax position as the Womacks, were also parties; the two couples are referred to by the court as "Taxpayers." Another 57 "Florida Lotto winners . . . agreed to be bound by the decision in the case."]

. . .

III. Discussion

The question before us is whether Lottery Rights are "capital assets" as defined by . . . §1221. . . . Taxpayers held their Lottery Rights for more than one year before selling them, so Taxpayers may report the lump sum payment they received in consideration as a [long term] capital gain if Lottery Rights are considered a capital asset.

The Tax Court and the four U.S. Circuit Courts to consider the question have concluded that Lottery Rights are not a capital asset within the definition set forth in §1221. E.g., Prebola v. Comm'r, 482 F.3d 610 (2d Cir. 2007); Watkins v. Comm'r, 447 F.3d 1269 (10th Cir. 2006); Lattera v. Comm'r, 437 F.3d 399 (3d Cir. 2006), cert. denied, [549] U.S. [1212], 127 S. Ct. 1328 (2007); United States v. Maginnis, 356 F.3d 1179 (9th Cir. 2004); Davis v. Comm'r, 119 T.C. 1, 2002 WL 1446631 (2002). These decisions are based on the so-called substitute for ordinary income doctrine, which provides that when a party receives a lump sum payment as "essentially a substitute for what would otherwise be received at a future time as ordinary income" that lump sum payment is taxable as ordinary income as well. Commissioner v. P.G. Lake, Inc., 356 U.S. 260, 265 (1958). We agree that the substitute for ordinary income doctrine applies to Lottery Rights, and therefore that proceeds from the sale of Lottery Rights are taxable as ordinary income.

A.   THE SUBSTITUTE FOR ORDINARY INCOME DOCTRINE

The statutory definition of capital asset "has . . . never been read as broadly as the statutory language might seem to permit, because such a reading would encompass some things Congress did not intend to be taxed as capital gains." *Maginnis*, 356 F.3d at 1181. Congress intended ordinary income to be the default tax rate, with capital gains treatment an exception applicable only in appropriate cases. In fact, "the term 'capital asset' is to be construed narrowly in accordance with the purpose of Congress to afford capital-gains treatment only in situations typically involving the realization of appreciation in value accrued over a substantial period of time." Commissioner v. Gillette Motor Transp., Inc., 364 U.S. 130, 134 (1960). This interpretation prevents taxpayers from circumventing ordinary income tax rates by selling rights to future ordinary income payments in exchange for a lump sum. . . .

[Each of the prior circuits to review] the precise legal question we face here [did so] under materially identical circumstances. Each Circuit has concluded that Lottery Rights are substitutes for ordinary income, but came to this conclusion in different ways. The Ninth Circuit used a case-by-case analysis, but focused on two factors in particular: that the taxpayer "(1) did not make any underlying investment of capital in return for the receipt of his lottery right, and (2) the sale of his right did not reflect an accretion in value over cost to any underlying asset [he] held." *Maginnis*, 356 F.3d at 1183. Though the *Maginnis* court noted that these factors would not be dispositive in all cases, the Third Circuit in *Lattera*, 437 F.3d at 404-09, found the factors problematic, and instead formulated its own approach, which it termed the "family resemblance" test. Within the confines of this test, the Third Circuit analyzed the nature of the sale and the character of the asset, specifically, whether the payment was for the future right to *earn* income or for the future right to *earned* income. Id. at 409. The Second and Tenth Circuits did not explicitly adopt the *Maginnis* reasoning or the *Lattera* test, but held that "whatever the [substitute for ordinary income] doctrine's outer limits, this case falls squarely within them." *Prebola*, 482 F.3d at 612; see *Watkins*, 447 F.3d at 1273 ("[W]e need not formulate any specific test regarding the appropriate limits of the doctrine's application"); Wolman v. Comm'r, 180 Fed. Appx. 830, 831 (10th Cir. 2006) ("For the same reasons stated in *Watkins*, we reject the Wolmans' argument and hold that the lump sum payments were taxable as ordinary income").

We agree with our sister circuits that Lottery Rights are a clear case of a substitute for ordinary income. A lottery winner who has *not* sold the right to his winnings to a third party must report the winnings as ordinary income whether the state pays him in a lump sum or in installments. . . . Thus, when a lottery winner sells the right to his winnings, he replaces future ordinary income. In defining "capital asset," Congress did not intend for taxpayers to circumvent ordinary income tax treatment by packaging ordinary income payments and selling them to a third party. . . .

There are important differences between Lottery Rights and the typical capital asset. The sale of a capital asset captures the increased value of the underlying asset. Perhaps the most common example occurs when a taxpayer purchases shares of stock, owns the shares for longer than a year, and then sells them at a higher price. The taxpayer makes an underlying investment in a capital asset when he purchases the stock. When he sells the shares at a higher price, the gain represents an increase in the value of the original investment. As the Ninth Circuit noted in *Maginnis*, 356 F.3d at 1183, Lottery Rights lack these characteristics emblematic of capital assets—Lottery Rights involve no underlying investment of capital. Furthermore, any "gain" from their sale reflects no change in the value of the asset. It is simply the amount Taxpayers would have received eventually, discounted to present value.[12]

---

12. As they are stated in *Maginnis*, these factors are obviously imperfect. For example, relying on the taxpayer's underlying investment ignores legitimate capital assets obtained through gifts or inheritances, and consideration of accretion in value excludes capital assets that typically depreciate, such as cars. See *Lattera*, 437 F.3d at 405. The *Maginnis* court properly observed that the factors would not be dispositive in every case. *Maginnis*, 356 F.3d at 1183. A court would have no occasion to evaluate these factors where the asset sold is something other than a claim to ordinary income, such as a car. The factors do, however, serve to emphasize the essence of a capital transaction: "that the sale or exchange of an asset results in a return of a capital investment coupled with realized gain or

Furthermore, when a lottery winner sells Lottery Rights, he transfers a right to income that is already earned, not a right to earn income in the future. See *Lattera,* 437 F.3d at 407-09. . . .

A capital asset has the potential to earn income in the future based on the owner's actions in using it. Lottery winners, by contrast, are "entitled to the income merely by virtue of owning the property." Note, Thomas G. Sinclair, Limiting the Substitute-for-Ordinary-Income Doctrine: An Analysis Through Its Most Recent Application Involving the Sale of Future Lottery Rights, 56 S.C. L. Rev. 387, 406 (2004). . . . Income need not be accrued for tax purposes to be "earned" in this sense. . . . Thus, income from a lottery payment is earned income despite the fact that it does not accrue until the scheduled annual payment date. Proceeds from the sale of Lottery Rights are a clear substitute for ordinary income and are taxable as ordinary income.

1.   *Effect of Arkansas Best*

The court next addressed the taxpayers' argument that *Arkansas Best* requires construing exceptions to capital gains treatment narrowly. The court rejected this argument on the ground that *Arkansas Best* addresses statutory exceptions to capital gain status and has a footnote expressly distinguishing the "substitute for ordinary income" doctrine from the scope of its analysis.

This is not to say that the substitute for ordinary income doctrine applies upon the sale of *every* asset that produces ordinary income. Taken to its logical extreme, the substitute for ordinary income doctrine would obliterate capital gains treatment altogether because a capital asset's present value is often based on its future ability to produce revenue in the form of ordinary income. *Maginnis,* 356 F.3d at 1182. We acknowledge that the doctrine has its outer limits, but we do not define them here. We merely recognize that *Arkansas Best* did not circumscribe the substitute for the ordinary income doctrine. . . .

IV.   CONCLUSION

For the foregoing reasons, we hold that proceeds from the sale of Lottery Rights should be taxed as ordinary income under the substitute for ordinary income doctrine. The Tax Court's decision is AFFIRMED.

QUESTIONS

1. (a) Suppose Lois buys 100 lottery tickets for $1 each, or a total of $100. A week later, one of the tickets proves to be a winner, in the amount of $100,000, payable a week later. She sells the ticket for $99,000. Is the ticket "property" within the meaning of §1221? If so, could all lottery winnings (including those providing for immediate payment) be transformed into capital gain simply by selling the ticket before collecting the winning amount? (Note that the gain

---

loss." Holt v. Comm'r, 303 F.2d 687, 691 (9th Cir. 1962). . . . We also note that the tax treatment of gifts, inheritances, and sales of automobiles is well established and neither relevant to nor affected by the issues in this case.

would be short term but would still be capital gain, with the advantage that it could be offset by capital losses.)

(b) Suppose Susan buys 100 shares of stock of an Internet start-up company for $1 each, or a total of $100. The company proves to be wildly, and quickly, successful and six months later Susan sells the 100 shares for $100,000. Does she have $99,900 of short-term capital gain?

(c) How can you reconcile your answers to parts (a) and (b)?

2. Imagine a lottery that occurs in two stages. Suppose Tyrone buys a ticket for $10 in round one and that his ticket is one of the few that survives to round two. Tyrone then sells the ticket to Ida for $5,000. Ida holds the ticket until the winner is determined, and the ticket is a winner, to the tune of $1 million, but a week before she would have been entitled to collect the money, she sells the ticket to Betty for $995,000. A week later Betty receives the $1 million. Is Tyrone entitled to treat his $4,990 gain as capital gain? What about Ida's $990,000 gain and Betty's $5,000 gain? Does it, and should it, matter that Betty sells the ticket to Ida rather than turning in the ticket and selling her claim to a payment that is due a week later? Would it matter if the delay between the selection of the winning ticket and the entitlement to payment were a year rather than a week?

3. The court's opinion indicates that the Womacks sold their lottery payments to Singer Asset Finance Company (see http://www.singerasset.com). In addition to offering lump sum cash payments to lottery winners, Singer describes itself as "an industry leader in buying structured settlements," which are generally excluded from the recipient's gross income under §104, provided they are received on account of personal physical injury or physical sickness. Suppose Katia was injured in a car accident and recovered damages from the negligent driver in the form of a right to receive $20,000 per year for the next ten years. After two years, she sells the remaining payments to Singer in exchange for a lump sum payment of $100,000. How, if at all, should Katia be taxed on the receipt of that $100,000? Does your answer to that question provide any further insight regarding the proper tax treatment of the Womacks? What if the driver defaults on his obligation before Katia is able to sell the remaining payments? Should Katia be entitled to a bad debt deduction under §166? (See Diez-Arguelles v. Commissioner.)

4. Oil Payments

COMMISSIONER v. P. G. LAKE, INC.
356 U.S. 260 (1958)

Mr. Justice DOUGLAS delivered the opinion of the Court.

We have here, consolidated for arguments, five cases involving an identical question of law. . . . The cases are here on petitions for certiorari which we granted because of the public importance of the question presented. 353 U.S. 982.

The facts of the *Lake* case are closely similar to those in the *Wrather* and *O'Connor* cases. Lake is a corporation engaged in the business of producing oil and gas. It has a seven-eighths working interest[13] in two commercial oil and gas leases. In 1950 it was indebted to its president in the sum of $600,000 and in consideration of his cancellation of the debt assigned him an oil payment right in the amount of $600,000, plus an amount equal to interest at 3 percent a year on the unpaid balance remaining from month to month, payable out of 25 percent of the oil attributable to the taxpayer's working interest in the two leases. At the time of the assignment it could have been estimated with reasonable accuracy that the assigned oil payment right would pay out in three or more years. It did in fact pay out in a little over three years.

In its 1950 tax returns Lake reported the oil payment assignment as a sale of property producing a profit of $600,000 and taxable as a long-term capital gain.[14] . . . The Commissioner determined a deficiency, ruling that the purchase price (less deductions not material here) was taxable as ordinary income, subject to depletion.

[The Court here describes the facts in the companion cases, all of which present the same issue raised by the *P. G. Lake* facts.]

[A]s to whether the proceeds were taxable as long-term capital gains . . . or as ordinary income subject to depletion, [t]he Court of Appeals started from the premise, laid down in Texas decisions, . . . that oil payments are interests in land.

We too proceed on that basis; and yet we conclude that the consideration received for these oil payment rights (and the sulphur payment right) was taxable as ordinary income, subject to depletion.

The purpose of [the capital gains provisions] was "to relieve the taxpayer from . . . excessive tax burdens on gains resulting from a conversion of capital investments, and to remove the deterrent effect of those burdens on such conversions." See Burnet v. Harmel, 287 U.S. 103, 106. And this exception has always been narrowly construed so as to protect the revenue against artful devices. See Corn Products Refining Co. v. Commissioner.

We do not see here any conversion of a capital investment. The lump sum consideration seems essentially a substitute for what would otherwise be received at a future time as ordinary income. The pay-out of these particular assigned oil payment rights could be ascertained with considerable accuracy.

---

13. An oil and gas lease ordinarily conveys the entire mineral interest less any royalty interest retained by the lessor. The owner of the lease [that is, the lessee] is said to own "the working interest" because he has the right to develop and produce the minerals. In Anderson v. Helvering, 310 U.S. 404, we described an oil payment as "the right to a specific sum of money, payable out of a specified percentage of the oil, or the proceeds received from the sale of such oil, if, as and when produced." *Id.*, at 410. A royalty interest is "a right to receive a specified percentage of all oil and gas produced" but, unlike the oil payment, is not limited to a specified sum of money. The royalty interest lasts during the entire term of the lease. *Id.*, at 409.

14. [It would seem that the proceeds of the sale of the oil payment would be the amount of debt discharged rather than the amount to be received by the assignee. For purposes of analysis, one can assume that the taxpayer sold the oil payment for $600,000 cash. The taxpayer's treatment of the entire $600,000 as capital gain raises the question of why there was no reduction for the adjusted basis of the property. Presumably the answer is that the basis had started out small because of the deduction of intangible drilling costs, and what there was had been exhausted by depletion allowances.—Eds.]

Such are the stipulations, findings, or clear inferences. In the *O'Connor* case, the pay-out of the assigned oil payment right was so assured that the purchaser obtained a $9,990,350 purchase money loan at 3 percent interest without any security other than a deed of trust of the $10,000,000 oil payment right, he receiving 4 percent from the taxpayer. Only a fraction of the oil . . . rights were transferred, the balance being retained.[15] [C]ash was received which was equal to the amount of the income to accrue during the term of the assignment, the assignee being compensated by interest on his advance. The substance of what was assigned was the right to receive future income. The substance of what was received was the present value of income which the recipient would otherwise obtain in the future. In short, consideration was paid for the right to receive future income, not for an increase in the value of the income-producing property.

These arrangements seem to us transparent devices. Their forms do not control. Their essence is determined not by subtleties of draftsmanship but by their total effect. See Helvering v. Clifford, 309 U.S. 331; Harrison v. Schaffner, 312 U.S. 579. We have held that if one, entitled to receive at a future date interest on a bond or compensation for services, makes a grant of it by anticipatory assignment, he realizes taxable income as if he had collected the interest or received the salary and then paid it over. That is the teaching of Helvering v. Horst and Harrison v. Schaffner, *supra;* and it is applicable here. As we stated in Helvering v. Horst, "The taxpayer has equally enjoyed the fruits of his labor or investment

---

15. Until 1946 the Commissioner agreed with the contention of the taxpayers in these cases that the assignment of an oil payment right was productive of a long-term capital gain. In 1946 he changed his mind and ruled that "consideration (not pledged for development) received for the assignment of a short-lived in-oil payment carved out of any type of depletable interest in oil and gas in place (including a larger in-oil payment right) is ordinary income subject to the depletion allowance in the assignor's hands." G.C.M. 24849, 1946-1 C.B. 66, 69. This ruling was made applicable "only to such assignments made on or after April 1, 1946," I.T. 3895, 1948-1 C.B. 39. In 1950 a further ruling was made that represents the present view of the Commissioner. I.T. 4003, 1950-1 C.B. 10, 11, reads in relevant part as follows:

> After careful study and considerable experience with the application of G.C.M. 24849, *supra,* it is now concluded that there is no legal or practical basis for distinguishing between short-lived and long-lived in-oil payment rights. It is, therefore, the present position of the Bureau that the assignment of any in-oil payment right (not pledged for development), which extends over a period less than the life of the depletable property interest from which it is carved, is essentially the assignment of expected income from such property interest. Therefore, the assignment for a consideration of any such in-oil payment right results in the receipt of ordinary income by the assignor which is taxable to him when received or accrued, depending upon the method of accounting employed by him. Where the assignment of the in-oil payment right is donative, the transaction is considered as an assignment of future income which is taxable to the donor at such time as the income from the assigned payment right arises.

> Notwithstanding the foregoing, G.C.M. 24849, *supra,* and I.T. 3935 *supra,* do not apply where the assigned in-oil payment right constitutes the entire depletable interest of the assignor in the property or a fraction extending over the entire life of the property.

The pre-1946 administrative practice was not reflected in any published ruling or regulation. It therefore will not be presumed to have been known to Congress and incorporated into the law by re-enactment. . . . Moreover, prior administrative practice is always subject to change "through exercise by the administrative agency of its continuing rule-making power." See Helvering v. Reynolds, 313 U.S. 428, 432. . . .

and obtained the satisfaction of his desires whether he collects and uses the income to procure those satisfactions, or whether he disposes of his right to collect it as the means of procuring them." There the taxpayer detached interest coupons from negotiable bonds and presented them as a gift to his son. The interest when paid was held taxable to the father. Here, even more clearly than there, the taxpayer is converting future income into present income. . . .

NOTES AND QUESTIONS

1. *Analysis.* (a) Note that the Court cites *Horst*, in which a father gave bond coupons to his son, and not *Hort*. Which of the two cases seems to you to be more relevant? In its brief, the government cited *Hort* (and other cases) for the proposition that "in any case where the lump sum consideration is essentially a substitute for what would otherwise be received in the future as ordinary income, the lump sum consideration is taxable as ordinary income even though, in a sense, a transfer of 'property' is involved." Does this statement go too far? Earlier in its brief the government describes *Horst* as holding that even though the coupons given to the son were "property," they were a type of property that "amounted only to a right to receive future income from the income-producing property (the bond)," that the label attached by the state law of property should not be controlling for tax purposes, and that the state-law characterization of oil payments as "interests in land" should be irrelevant for tax purposes. Is this argument sound? Is it dispositive?

(b) Suppose a taxpayer owns a farm whose boundaries are formed in part by streams and ridges and whose size is about 1,000 acres. The taxpayer sells a rectangular portion of the central part of the farm, consisting of 600 acres. Plainly, the taxpayer has sold a capital asset, with the consequence that any gain is treated as capital gain and the taxpayer is entitled to offset against the proceeds of the sale some portion of his or her total basis in the property. If the taxpayer's oil interest in *P. G. Lake* had been valued at $1 million and the taxpayer had sold an undivided 60 percent share in that oil interest for $600,000, the transaction would no doubt have been treated as a sale of a capital asset. How do these transactions differ from the actual transaction in the case?

(c) Suppose a taxpayer owns the right to take half of the water flowing along a river and sells this right for the next ten years for a lump sum payment of $60,000. Has the taxpayer sold a capital asset? How does this case differ from *P. G. Lake*?

(d) Suppose a taxpayer pays $60,000 for the right to use as lessee certain business premises for ten years and then subleases those premises for six years for $40,000 paid in advance. What are the tax consequences? How does this case differ from *P. G. Lake*?

2. *Advantages to taxpayers from* P. G. Lake *and the enactment of §636.* In certain situations, the *P. G. Lake* decision proved advantageous to taxpayers. For example, if a taxpayer with a producing mineral property had a net loss from other transactions or was restricted in the amount of percentage depletion it could claim by reason of the 50 percent of taxable income limit (§613), it could boost current depletable income by carving out and selling an oil payment.

Another taxpayer ploy was called the *ABC* transaction. *A*, the owner of a mineral property, would sell *B* the entire interest less a carved-out, retained mineral payment, which *A* would then sell to *C*. *A* would have capital gain, having disposed of all that he or she owned. The amounts received by *C* were treated as *C*'s income, but *C* was entitled to offset the receipts with an amortization deduction. The payments to *C* were not treated as *B*'s income and, to that extent, *B* was able, in effect, to acquire the property with before-tax dollars.

Under §636, enacted in 1969, these taxpayer opportunities are eliminated by treating the transactions in most instances as a financing device, with the buyer of the oil payment treated as a lender. Thus, in the *ABC* transaction, *B* is treated as the purchaser of both the working interest and the oil payment, with the latter used as security for a nonrecourse loan from *C*.

G.   OTHER CLAIMS AND CONTRACT RIGHTS

1.   Termination Payments

BAKER v. COMMISSIONER

---

118 T.C. 452 (2002)

PANUTHOS, Chief Special Trial Judge:

[T]he issue for decision is whether the termination payment received by petitioner upon retirement as an insurance agent of State Farm Insurance Cos. is taxable as capital gain or ordinary income.

BACKGROUND

I.   PETITIONER'S AGREEMENT WITH STATE FARM

A.   General

[P]etitioner conducted his business as the Warren L. Baker Insurance Agency (the agency). He sold policies exclusively for State Farm. When he began his relationship with State Farm, he was not assigned customers. Instead, he developed a customer base. He selected the location of his office with State Farm's approval. He also hired and paid employees. He was responsible for paying the expenses of an office such as rent, utilities, telephones, and other equipment. He was obligated to establish a trust fund into which he deposited premiums collected on behalf of State Farm.

Petitioner entered into a series of contracts with State Farm known as agent's agreements. The agent's agreement at issue was executed on March 1, 1977. While the agreement contains approximately 6 pages, there are numerous attachments including schedules of payments, amendments, addenda, and memoranda that total 61 pages. The agreement was prepared by State Farm. Petitioner did not have the ability to change the terms of the agreement, but he had the option to refuse a new or revised agreement.

The preamble to the agreement reads, in part, as follows: "The Companies believe that agents operating as independent contractors are best able to provide the creative selling, professional counseling, and prompt and skillful service essential to the creation and maintenance of successful multiple-line companies and agencies."

Section I of the agreement, Mutual Conditions and Duties, provides that petitioner was an independent contractor of State Farm. As a State Farm agent, petitioner agreed to write policies exclusively for State Farm, its affiliates, and government and industry groups. Paragraph C, section I of the agreement states that State Farm "will furnish you, without charge, manuals, forms, records, and such other materials and supplies as we may deem advisable to provide. All such property furnished by us shall remain the property of the Companies [State Farm]." Further, State Farm considered any and all information regarding policyholders to be its property, as follows:

> D. Information regarding names, addresses, and ages of policyholders of the Companies; the description and location of insured property; and expiration or renewal dates of State Farm policies acquired or coming into your possession during the effective period of this Agreement, or any prior Agreement, except information and records of policyholders insured by the Companies pursuant to any governmental or insurance industry plan or facility, are trade secrets wholly owned by the Companies. All forms and other materials, whether furnished by State Farm or purchased by you, upon which this information is recorded shall be the sole and exclusive property of the Companies.

Essentially, any data relating to a policyholder recorded by an agent on any paper was the property of State Farm.

Petitioner's compensation was based on a percentage of the net premiums....

B. Termination

Section III of the agreement addresses termination. Either party could terminate the agreement by written notice. The agreement also provided for termination upon the death of petitioner. Within 10 days after termination of the agreement, "all property belonging to the Companies shall be returned or made available for return to the Companies or their authorized representative."

Petitioner was required to abide by a covenant not to compete for a period of 12 months following termination. The covenant not to compete provides as follows:

> E. For a period of one year following termination of this Agreement, you will not either personally or through any other person, agency, or organization (1) induce or advise any State Farm policyholder credited to your account at the date of termination to lapse, surrender, or cancel any State Farm insurance coverage or (2) solicit any such policyholder to purchase any insurance coverage competitive with the insurance coverages sold by the Companies.

Pursuant to section IV of the agreement, petitioner qualified for a termination payment if he met certain requirements. First, he must work for 2 or more continuous years as an agent. Second, within 10 days of termination, he must return or make available for return all property belonging to State Farm.

The amount of the termination payment [depended on the policies in force during the 12 months preceding termination]. . . .

State Farm and petitioner did not negotiate the amount or conditions of the termination payment. State Farm agreed to pay petitioner a termination payment over either a 2- or 5-year period.

Section V of the agreement provides for an extended termination payment if petitioner worked for State Farm for at least 20 years, of which 10 years were consecutive. The extended termination payment would begin 61 months after termination and continue until petitioner's death. The extended termination payment is also based on policies personally produced by petitioner during his last 12 months as an agent for State Farm. . . .

II.   PETITIONER'S RETIREMENT

Petitioner retired and terminated his relationship with State Farm on February 28, 1997. At that time, he held approximately 4,000 existing policies generated from 1,800 households. Approximately 90 percent of the policies were assigned to one successor agent. . . .

Petitioner returned State Farm's property, such as policy and policyholder descriptions, which he gathered in master folders that he purchased, claim draft books, rate books, agent's service texts, and a computer. He maintained much of the information regarding the policies and policyholders on the computer. He fully complied with the provision in the agreement for return of property to State Farm.

The successor agent hired the two employees previously employed by petitioner and assumed petitioner's telephone number. The successor agent also worked with petitioner on occasion prior to petitioner's retirement to meet policyholders and to ask questions. The successor agent opened an office in the vicinity of petitioner's office. When the termination was completed, petitioner had returned all of the assets used in the agency to State Farm and the successor agent. . . .

III.   TAX RETURN AND NOTICE OF DEFICIENCY

Petitioners timely filed their 1997 Federal income tax return. They reported the income of $38,622 from the termination payment which petitioner received in 1997 as long-term capital gain on Schedule D, Capital Gains and Losses. . . .

In a notice of deficiency, respondent determined that the termination payment from State Farm was ordinary income and did not qualify for capital gain treatment.

DISCUSSION

I.   POSITIONS OF THE PARTIES

Respondent argues that petitioner did not sell any property to State Farm because all of the property was owned by State Farm and reverted to State Farm when petitioner terminated his relationship with State Farm. Respondent contends that the agreement does not evidence a sale because the contract does not list a seller or purchaser. Respondent also argues that petitioners failed to establish that the termination payment represents proceeds from the sale of a business, business assets, or goodwill. Respondent also suggests that the termination payment is in the nature of income from self-employment, but hedges that position in arguing that the payment is "similar to an annuity" and a "retirement benefit." We note that respondent did not determine that petitioners were liable for self-employment tax with respect to the termination payment.

Petitioners argue that the termination payment was for the sale or buyout of a business resulting in capital gain. They assert that petitioner developed a customer base and the termination payment was designed to protect the existing customer base for the successor agent as well as compensate petitioner for the goodwill and going business concern he developed. Petitioners rely on the concurring opinion in Jackson v. Commissioner, 108 T.C. 130, 141 (1997), which characterizes a termination payment similar to the one at issue as a buyout of the taxpayer's business.

The Coalition of Exclusive Agent Associations, Inc. (CEAA), filed with leave of the Court an amicus brief pursuant to conditions specified in the Court's order. The CEAA's argument is similar to the arguments made by petitioners: State Farm purchased the goodwill generated by petitioner; therefore, petitioner is entitled to capital gain treatment. . . .

[Sections II and III of the discussion, dealing with Burden of Proof and Evidentiary Issues, respectively, are omitted—EDS.]

IV.   SALE OR EXCHANGE OF A CAPITAL ASSET

We must decide the proper characterization of the termination payment made by State Farm to petitioner. We first consider whether petitioner owned a capital asset and whether petitioner sold or exchanged a capital asset for Federal income tax purposes. We also consider whether petitioner sold a business to which goodwill attached. If petitioner did not sell or exchange a capital asset, then the termination payment is taxable as ordinary income.

Long-term capital gain is defined as gain from the sale or exchange of a capital asset held for more than 1 year. §1222(3). A "capital asset" means property held by the taxpayer (whether or not connected with his trade or business) that is not covered by one of five specifically enumerated exclusions. §1221.

In Schelble v. Commissioner, T.C. Memo. 1996-269, aff'd 130 F.3d 1388 (10th Cir. 1997), we considered whether the taxpayer received gain from the sale or exchange of a capital asset. Pursuant to the terms of the agreement with the insurance company for which he was an agent, the taxpayer was required to return all records, manuals, materials, advertising, and supplies or other property of the company. Id. We concluded that there was no evidence of "vendible business assets," and the record did not support a finding of a sale of assets of a business.

The Court of Appeals in Schelble v. Commissioner, 130 F.3d at 1394, held that there was "no evidence in the record of vendible assets to support the sale of Mr. Schelble's insurance business." It observed the following:

By transferring policy records to . . . [the insurance company] pursuant to the Agreement, . . . [the taxpayer] maintains he transferred insurance business goodwill developed by him. . . . [The taxpayer] has failed, however, to show a sale of assets occurred.

Id.

In Foxe v. Commissioner, 53 T.C. 21, 26 (1969), we considered whether payments made to an insurance agent were made pursuant to the sale or exchange of a capital asset to his former insurance company upon the cancellation of his employment contract. The taxpayer claimed that in the course of his business he built up "something of value, an organization" that the insurance company acquired. Moreover, his personal contacts with customers, which were important to the insurance company, were "something of real value."

We concluded that even if the taxpayer had "built up an organization of value," it was not his to sell since . . . [the insurance company] under the contract owned all the property comprising such organization. As to the customer contacts . . . [t]hey were not his to sell. It was held that the taxpayer did not sell or exchange a capital asset, and the payments were taxable as ordinary income.

Section 1001(c) provides that gain is recognized upon the sale or exchange of property. "The word 'sale' means 'a transfer of property for a fixed price in money or its equivalent.' " Schelble v. Commissioner, *supra* at 1394 (quoting Five Per Cent. Cases, 110 U.S. 471, 478, 28 L. Ed. 198, 4 S. Ct. 210 (1885)); see also Commissioner v. Brown, 380 U.S. 563, 570, 14 L. Ed. 2d 75, 85 S. Ct. 1162 (1965). "Exchange" means an exchange of property for another property that is materially different either in kind or in extent. Regs. §1.1001-1, Income Tax Regs.

The key to deciding whether there has been a sale for Federal income tax purposes is whether the benefits and burdens of ownership have passed. Highland Farms, Inc. v. Commissioner, 106 T.C. 237 (1996); Grodt & McKay Realty, Inc. v. Commissioner, 77 T.C. 1221, 1237 (1981). Among the many factors we may consider in deciding whether there has been a sale are the following: Whether legal title passes; how the parties treat the transaction; whether an equity was acquired in the property; whether the contract creates a present obligation on the seller to execute and deliver a deed and a present obligation on the purchaser to make payments; whether the right of possession is vested in the purchaser; which party pays the property taxes; which party bears the risk of loss or damage to the property; and which party receives the profits from the operation and sale of the property. Levy v. Commissioner, 91 T.C. 838, 860 (1988); Grodt & McKay v. Commissioner; *supra* at 1237-1238.

Cases addressing whether there has been a sale or exchange of a capital asset often combine the issue of whether the taxpayer owned a capital asset with the issue of whether the taxpayer sold the asset. For example, in Erickson v. Commissioner, T.C. Memo. 1992-585, aff'd 1 F.3d 1231 (1st Cir. 1993), we concluded that there was no sale of the taxpayer's assets to his former insurance company because there was nothing in the facts showing that there was a sale of "vendible tangible assets" of a business. In *Erickson*, the Court stated:

[The taxpayers] maintain that . . . certain indicia of a sale exist. They assert that employees who formerly worked for . . . [the taxpayer] went over to Union Mutual and that all records, supplies, and equipment were turned over to Union Mutual. . . . [H]owever, the individuals who had worked with . . . [the taxpayer] had always been salaried employees of Union Mutual. . . . And by his own admission, . . . [the taxpayer] had owned very little in the way of supplies and equipment. . . .

Id.

Respondent cites Jackson v. Commissioner, 108 T.C. 130 (1997), Milligan v. Commissioner, T.C. Memo. 1992-655, rev'd 38 F.3d 1094 (9th Cir. 1994), and similar cases for the proposition that the taxpayer did not sell or exchange the assets in his business. These cases bear a factual resemblance to the case at hand in that the taxpayer, a former insurance agent, received a termination payment after the termination of his agreement with the insurance company. But these cases focus on whether the taxpayer was subject to self-employment tax under sections 1401 and 1402.

The holdings by the Court of Appeals in *Milligan* and by this Court in *Jackson* do not require a conclusion that the termination payment paid to petitioner represents proceeds from the sale or exchange of a capital asset. Both *Jackson* and *Milligan* left open the question of whether termination payments constitute the sale or exchange of capital assets subject to capital gain treatment or whether they should be treated as ordinary income (other than income subject to self-employment tax).

V.   THE CONTROLLING FACTS OF THIS CASE

We now apply the above discussion to the facts before us in this case. Upon his retirement, petitioner returned all assets used in the daily course of business, including a computer, books and records, and customer lists to State Farm pursuant to the agreement. Thus, much like the taxpayers in Foxe v. Commissioner, *supra,* and Schelble v. Commissioner, 130 F.3d 1388 (10th Cir. 1997), petitioner did not own these assets and, therefore, could not have sold them to State Farm.

Petitioner argues that the successor agent assumed his telephone number and hired the two employees of the agency, and that petitioner taught the successor agent about the agency and introduced him to policyholders, all of which support the argument that he sold the agency to State Farm.

The successor agent obtained the right to use the telephone number utilized by petitioner's agency. Petitioner did not argue, and we do not conclude, that the telephone number was a capital asset in the hands of petitioner. Additionally, there are no facts in the record that indicate that petitioner received any portion of the termination payment as payment for the successor agent's use of the telephone number.

There are no facts in the record that indicate that there was an employment contract between petitioner and the employees who worked for the agency or that the successor agent was required to hire the employees. Petitioner did not argue, and we do not conclude, that the employees constitute capital assets in the hands of petitioner. There is nothing in the record that indicates that petitioner received any portion of the termination payment as payment for the successor agent's hiring of the employees. The fact that the successor agent hired petitioner's former employees does not support petitioner's argument that he sold his agency.

Petitioner may have taught the successor agent about the agency and introduced him to policyholders when the successor agent visited petitioner's office, but there are no facts in the record that indicate that petitioner received the termination payment as payment for teaching the successor agent about the agency and introducing him to policyholders.

We conclude that petitioner did not own a capital asset that he could sell to State Farm. He did not receive the termination payment as payment for any asset. Accordingly, the termination payment does not represent gain from the sale or exchange of a capital asset.

Petitioner also argues that State Farm purchased goodwill. To qualify as the sale of goodwill, the taxpayer must demonstrate that he sold " 'the business or a part of it, to which the goodwill attaches.' " Schelble v. Commissioner, 130 F.3d at 1394 (quoting Elliott v. United States, 431 F.2d 1149, 1154 (10th Cir. 1970)). Goodwill is "the expectancy of continued patronage, for whatever reason." Boe v. Commissioner, 307 F.2d 339, 343 (9th Cir. 1962), aff'g 35 T.C. 720 (1961); see also VGS Corp. v. Commissioner, 68 T.C. 563, 590 (1977).

Nevertheless, because petitioner, for the reasons already explained, did not own and sell capital assets in his agency to State Farm, we conclude that petitioner did not sell goodwill.

VI.   NATURE OF ORDINARY INCOME

Respondent does not clearly explain his position as to the nature of the termination payment other than to argue that it is not taxable as capital gain. In the notice of deficiency, respondent determined that the termination payment was ordinary income. In his brief, respondent primarily argues that petitioners did not satisfy their burden of proof to establish that the termination payment was proceeds of a sale and thus subject to capital gain treatment.

Having concluded above that the termination payment was not received for the sale or exchange of a capital asset and is not entitled to treatment as a capital gain, we conclude that the termination payment is taxable as ordinary income. Ordinary income treatment is accorded to a variety of payments. See, e.g., Hort v. Commissioner, 313 U.S. 28, 85 L. Ed. 1168, 61 S. Ct. 757 (1941) (income received upon cancellation of lease derived from relinquishment of right to future rental payments in return for a present substitute payment and possession of premises); Elliott v. United States, *supra* (payment for termination of insurance agency contract was ordinary income); Foxe v. Commissioner, 53 T.C. at 25 (payment to insurance agent upon cancellation of employment contract was ordinary income); General Ins. Agency, Inc. v. Commissioner, T.C. Memo. 1967-143 (payment for agreement not to compete was ordinary income), aff'd 401 F.2d 324 (4th Cir. 1968).

VII.   COVENANT NOT TO COMPETE

An amount received for an agreement not to compete is generally taxable as ordinary income. Banc One Corp. v. Commissioner, 84 T.C. 476, 490 (1985), aff'd without published opinion 815 F.2d 75 (6th Cir. 1987); Warsaw Photographic Associates, Inc. v. Commissioner, 84 T.C. 21 (1985); Ullman v. Commissioner, 29

T.C. 129 (1957), aff'd 264 F.2d 305 (2d Cir. 1959); General Ins. Agency, Inc. v. Commissioner, *supra*.

Petitioners reported the sale of a covenant not to compete on Form 8594 attached to the return. The agreement provides that, after retiring, petitioner would not solicit State Farm's policyholders for 1 year, or petitioner would forfeit the termination payment. If petitioner had competed against State Farm after retiring, he would not have received a termination payment. We find that petitioner entered into a covenant not to compete with State Farm and that a portion of the termination payment was paid for the covenant not to compete.

Proceeds allocable to a covenant not to compete are properly classified as ordinary income. . . . Petitioner did not allocate any portion of the termination payment to the covenant not to compete, and it is unnecessary for us to make such an allocation because the termination payment is classified as ordinary income. . . .

NOTES AND QUESTIONS

1. *The importance of legal title.* The court held that no portion of the termination payment constituted capital gain because the taxpayer had neither owned nor sold any capital assets. Suppose that taxpayer had been given title to all books and records connected with the insurance business, but the agreement required the taxpayer to transfer title if for any reason he had ceased performing duties as an agent. Suppose, further, that the agreement between taxpayer and State Farm required a termination payment in exchange for "all assets connected with taxpayers' insurance business, including all books and records and all goodwill." If the court's opinion is taken at face value, the decision would have then gone for the taxpayer. Does that make sense?

2. *Were the payments best characterized as renewal commissions?* The court in the present case characterized part of the termination payment as received in exchange for a covenant not to compete. What about the remaining portion of the payment? There are really only two possibilities: Either that portion of the payment was received in exchange for capital assets or it was received in exchange for personal service income—here, Baker's right to renewal commissions. The court held that no portion of the payments was received in exchange for capital assets. The court did not, however, take what would seem to be the logical step and attribute the remainder of the payment to Baker's right to renewal commissions. It obviously felt that such a holding would be inconsistent with the position it had taken in the employment tax context. Instead, the court simply refused to opine on the source of that portion of the termination payment.

2. Theatrical Production Rights

COMMISSIONER v. FERRER
304 F.2d 125 (2d Cir. 1962)

FRIENDLY, Circuit Judge.

This controversy concerns the tax status of certain payments received by José Ferrer with respect to the motion picture "Moulin Rouge" portraying the

career of Henri de Toulouse-Lautrec. The difficulties Mr. Ferrer must have
had in fitting himself into the shape of the artist can hardly have been greater
than ours in determining whether the transaction here at issue fits the rubric
"gain from the sale or exchange of a capital asset held for more than 6 months,"
[§1221(3)], as the Tax Court held, 35 T.C. 617 (1961), or constitutes ordinary
income, as the Commissioner contends. We have concluded that neither party
is entirely right, that some aspects of the transaction fall on one side of the line
and some on the other, and that the Tax Court must separate the two.

In 1950 Pierre LaMure published a novel, "Moulin Rouge," based on the life
of Toulouse-Lautrec. He then wrote a play, "Monsieur Toulouse," based on the
novel. On November 1, 1951, LaMure as "Author" and Ferrer, a famous actor
but not a professional producer, as "Manager" entered into a contract, called a
Dramatic Production Contract, for the stage production of the play by Ferrer.

The contract was largely on a printed form recommended by the Dramatists
Guild of the Authors League of America, Inc. However great the business
merits of the document, which are extolled in Burton, Business Practices in
the Copyright Field, in C.C.H., 7 Copyright Problems Analyzed (1952) 87, 109,
for a court, faced with the task of defining the nature of the rights created, it
exemplifies what a contract ought not to be. Its first six pages include eleven
articles, some introduced by explanatory material whose contractual status is,
to say the least, uncertain. Here the last of these pages was preceded by three
single-spaced typewritten pages of "Additional Clauses," one with a still further
insert. Finally come 15 pages of closely printed "Supplemental Provisions,"
introduced by explanatory material of the sort noted. We shall thread our way
through this maze as best we can.

By the contract the Author "leased" to the Manager "the sole and exclusive
right" to produce and present "Monsieur Toulouse" on the speaking stage in
the United States and Canada, and gave certain rights for its production elsewhere. Production had to occur on or before June 1, 1952, unless the Manager
paid an additional advance of $1,500 not later than that date, in which event
the deadline was extended to December 1, 1952. Five hundred dollars were
paid as an initial advance against Author's royalties; the Manager was required
to make further advances of like amount on December 1, 1951, and January
1, 1952. Royalties were to be paid the Author on all box-office receipts, on a
sliding scale percentage basis.

Article Seventh said that "In the event that under the terms hereof the
Manager shall be entitled to share in the proceeds of the Motion Picture and
Additional Rights hereafter referred to, it is agreed that the Manager shall
receive 40% for the first ten years and diminishing percentages thereafter."
Among the additional rights so described were "Radio and Television."

For the beginning of an answer whether the Manager would be so entitled,
we turn to Article IV, §2, of the Supplemental Provisions. This tells us that "In
the event the Manager has produced and presented the play for the 'Requisite
Performances and Terms,' the Negotiator shall pay the Manager" the above
percentages "of the proceeds, from the disposal of the motion picture rights."
Article VI, §3, contains a similar provision as to payment by the Author of the
proceeds of the "additional rights" including radio and television. . . .

Further provisions put flesh on these bones. Article IV, §1(a), says that
"the title" to the motion picture rights "vests in the Author, as provided in

Article VIII hereof." Article VIII says, even more broadly, "The Author shall retain for his sole benefit, complete title, both legal and equitable, in and to all rights whatsoever (including, but not by way of limitation, the Motion Picture Rights . . . Radio and Television Rights . . .)," other than the right to produce the play. . . .

Finally, . . . [an] "Additional Clause" prescribes that "All dramatic, motion picture, radio and television rights in the novel Moulin Rouge shall merge in and with the play during the existence of this contract," and if the Manager produces and presents the play for a sufficient period, "throughout the copyright period of the play."

Shortly after signature of the Dramatic Production Contract, John Huston called Ferrer to ask whether he would be interested in playing Toulouse-Lautrec in a picture based upon "Moulin Rouge." On getting an affirmative indication, Huston said he would go ahead and acquire the motion picture rights. Ferrer replied, in somewhat of an exaggeration, "When you get ready to acquire them talk to me because I own them."

Both Huston and Ferrer then had discussions with LaMure. Ferrer expressed a willingness "to abandon the theatrical production in favor of the film production, provided that, if the film production were successful, I would be recompensed for my abandoning the stage production." On the strength of this, LaMure signed a preliminary agreement with Huston's corporation. In further negotiations, Huston's attorney insisted on "either an annulment or conveyance" of the Dramatic Production Contract. LaMure's lawyer prepared a letter of agreement, dated February 7, 1952, whereby Ferrer would cancel and terminate the Contract. Ferrer signed the letter but instructed his attorney not to deliver it until the closing of a contract between himself and the company that was to produce the picture; the letter was not delivered until May 14, 1952.

Meanwhile, on May 7, 1952, Ferrer entered into a contract with Huston's company, Moulin Productions, Inc. ("Moulin"), hereafter the Motion Picture Contract. This was followed by an agreement and assignment dated May 12, 1952, whereby LaMure sold Huston all motion picture rights to his novel, including the right to exploit the picture by radio and television. Under this agreement LaMure was to receive a fixed sum of $25,000, plus 5% and 4% of the Western and Eastern Hemisphere motion picture profits, respectively, and 50% of the net profits from exploitation by live television.

The Motion Picture Contract said that Romulus Films Limited, of London, proposed to produce the picture "Moulin Rouge," that Moulin would be vested with the Western Hemisphere distribution rights, and that Moulin on behalf of Romulus was interested in engaging Ferrer's services to play the role of Toulouse-Lautrec. Under clause 4(a), Ferrer was to receive $50,000 to cover 12 weeks of acting, payments to be made weekly as Ferrer rendered his services. Ferrer's performance was to begin between June 1 and July 1, 1952. By clause 4(b), Ferrer was to receive $10,416.66 per week for each additional week, but this, together with an additional $50,000 of salary provided by clause 4(c), was "deferred and postponed" and was payable only out of net receipts. Finally, clauses 4(d) and (e) provided "percentage compensation" equal to stipulated percentages of the net profits from distribution of the picture in the Western and Eastern Hemispheres respectively—17% of the Western Hemisphere net profits until Ferrer had received $25,000 and thereafter 12-¾% (such payments to "be made out of sixty-five (65%) percent of the net profits," whatever that may mean), and 3-¾% of the Eastern Hemisphere net profits. If Ferrer's services were interrupted by disability or if production of the picture had to be suspended for causes beyond Moulin's control, but the picture was thereafter completed and Ferrer's "acts, poses and appearances therein" were recognizable to the public, he was to receive a proportion of the compensation provided in clauses 4(c), (d), and (e) corresponding to the ratio of his period of acting to 12 weeks. The same was true if Ferrer failed to "conduct himself with due regard to public conventions and morals" etc. and Moulin cancelled on that account. The absence of any similar provision with respect to termination for Ferrer's wilful refusal or neglect to perform services indicates that all his rights, except that for compensation already due under clause 4(a), would be forfeited in that event. Over objections by the Commissioner, Ferrer offered testimony by Huston's attorney, who was also president of Moulin, that in the negotiation "it was said that the ultimate percentage payment to be made to Ferrer would be his compensation for giving up his interest in the dramatization guild," and a letter from the same attorney, dated March 3, 1953, confirming that in the negotiations with Ferrer's attorney "for the sale of the dramatic rights held by you to the property entitled 'Monsieur Toulouse' and the novel 'MOULIN ROUGE,' it was understood that the consideration for such sale price was the payments due, or to become due, to you under Clause 4(d) and Clause 4(e)," and also that LeMure "refused to sell the motion picture rights for the production of the motion picture known as 'MOULIN ROUGE' unless you sold the aforesaid dramatic rights." Ferrer's agent testified, again over objection, that the largest salary Ferrer had previously received for a moving picture appearance was $75,000.

Moulin's books showed $109,027.74 as a salary payment to Ferrer in August, 1953, and $178,751.46 at various later dates in 1953 as the payment of "Participating Interests" under clause 4(d). Ferrer's 1953 return reported the former as ordinary income, and the latter, less expenses of $26,812.72, as a long-term capital gain. The Commissioner determined a deficiency on the basis that the difference, $151,938.74, constituted ordinary income; from the Tax Court's annulment of that determination he has taken this appeal.

Section . . . 1221 tells us, not very illuminatingly, that "capital asset" means property held by the taxpayer (whether or not connected with his trade or business), but does not include four (now five) types of property therein defined. However, it has long been settled that a taxpayer does not bring himself within the capital gains provision merely by fulfilling the simple syllogism that a contract normally constitutes "property," that he held a contract, and that his contract does not fall within a specified exclusion. . . . This is easy enough; what is difficult, perhaps impossible, is to frame a positive definition of universal validity. Attempts to do this in terms of the degree of clothing adorning the contract cannot explain all the cases, however helpful they may be in deciding some, perhaps even this one; it would be hard to think of a contract more "naked" than a debenture, yet no one doubts that is a "capital asset" if held by an investor. Efforts to frame a universal negative, e.g., that a transaction can never qualify if the taxpayer has merely collapsed anticipation of future income, are equally fruitless; a lessor's sale of his interest in a 999 year net lease and an investor's sale of a perpetual bond sufficiently illustrate why. . . .

Two issues can be eliminated before we do this. We need no longer concern ourselves, as at one time we might have been obliged to do, over the alleged indivisibility of a copyright; the Commissioner is now satisfied that sales and exchanges of less than the whole copyright may result in capital gain. . . . Neither do we have in this case any issue of excludability under . . . §1221(1); Ferrer was not in the "trade or business" of acquiring either dramatic production rights or motion picture rights.

When Huston displayed an interest in the motion picture rights in November 1951, Ferrer was possessed of a bundle of rights, three of which are relevant here. First was his "lease" of the play. Second was his power, incident to that lease, to prevent any disposition of the motion picture rights until June 1, 1952, or, on making an additional $1,500 advance, to December 1, 1952, and for a period thereafter if he produced the play, and to prevent disposition of the radio and television rights even longer. Third was his 40% share of the proceeds of the motion picture and other rights if he produced the play. All these, in our view, Ferrer "sold or exchanged," although the parties set no separate price upon them. To be sure, Moulin had no interest in producing the play. But Ferrer did, unless a satisfactory substitute was provided. Hence Moulin had to buy him out of that right, as well as to eliminate his power temporarily to prevent a sale of the motion picture, radio and television rights to liquidate his option to obtain a share of their proceeds.

(1) Surrender of the "lease" of the play sounds like the transactions held to qualify for capital gain treatment in [Commissioner v. Golonsky, 200 F.2d 72 (3d Cir. 1952), cert. denied, 345 U.S. 939 (1953); Commissioner v. McCue Bros. & Drummond, Inc., 210 F.2d 752 (2d Cir.), cert. denied, 348 U.S. 829 (1954)], see §1241. Such cases as Wooster v. Crane & Co., 147 F. 515 (8 Cir. 1906), . . . are a fortiori authority that courts would have enjoined LaMure, or anyone else, from interfering with this, unless the Dramatic Production Contract dictated otherwise. None of its many negations covered this basic grant. Ferrer thus had an "equitable interest" in the copyright of the play.

The Commissioner did not suggest in the Tax Court, and does not here, that this interest or, indeed, any with which we are concerned in this case, fell within . . . §1221(3), excluding from the term "capital asset" "a copyright; a literary, musical, or artistic composition; or similar property; held by—(i) a taxpayer, whose personal efforts created such property. . . ." He was right in not doing this. In one sense the lease of the play was "created" simply by the agreed advance of $1,500. If it be said that this is too narrow an approach and that we must consider what Ferrer would have had to do in order to make the lease productive, the result remains the same. Although the Dramatic Production Contract demanded Ferrer's personal efforts in the play's production, much else in the way of capital and risk-taking was also required. Yet the legislative history, . . . shows that [§1221(3)] was intended to deal with personal efforts and creation in a rather narrow sense. . . . Ferrer's role as producer, paying large sums to the theatre, the actors, other personnel, and the author, is not analogous to that of the writer or even the "creator" of a radio program mentioned by the Committee. Moreover, the dramatic producer does not normally "sell" the production to a single purchaser, as an author or radio program "creator" usually does—he offers it directly to public customers.

We see no basis for holding that amounts paid Ferrer for surrender of his lease of the play are excluded from capital gain treatment because receipts from the play would have been ordinary income. The latter is equally true if a lessee of real property sells or surrenders a lease from which he is receiving business income or subrentals; yet *Golonsky* and *McCue Bros. & Drummond* held such to be the sale or exchange of a capital asset, as §1241 now provides. Likewise we find nothing in the statute that forbids capital gain treatment because the payment to Ferrer might be spread over a number of years rather than coming in a lump sum; although prevention of the unfairness arising from applying ordinary income rates to a "bunching" of income may be one of the motivations of the "capital gains" provisions, the statute says nothing about this. . . . Finally, with respect to the lease of the play, there was no such equivalence between amounts paid for its surrender and income that would have been realized by its retention as seems to lie at the basis of the Tenth Circuit's recent refusal of capital gain treatment in Wiseman v. Halliburton Oil Well Cementing Co., 301 F.2d 654 (1962), a decision as to which we take no position.

(2) Ferrer's negative power, as an incident to the lease, to prevent any disposition of the motion picture, radio and television rights until after production of the play, was also one which . . . would be protected in equity unless he had contracted to the contrary, and would thus constitute an "equitable interest" in this portion of the copyright. . . . As a practical matter, this feature of the Dramatic Production Contract "clouded" LaMure's title, despite the Contract's contrary assertion. Huston would not conclude with LaMure and LaMure would not conclude with Huston unless Ferrer released his rights; Huston's attorney testified that a contract like Ferrer's "imposes an encumbrance on the motion picture rights." Ferrer's dissipation of the cloud arising from the negative covenant seems analogous to the tenant's relinquishment of a right to prevent his landlord from leasing to another tenant in the same business, held to be the sale or exchange of a capital asset in *Ray*. What we have said in (1) with respect to possible grounds for disqualification as a capital asset is a fortiori applicable here.

(3) We take a different view with respect to the capital assets status of Ferrer's right to receive 40% of the proceeds of the motion picture and other rights if he produced "Monsieur Toulouse."

We assume, without deciding, that there is no reason in principle why if the holder of a copyright grants an interest in the portion of a copyright relating to motion picture and other rights contingent on the production of a play, or, to put the matter in another way, gives the producer an option to acquire such an interest by producing the play, the option would not constitute a "capital asset" unless the producer is disqualified by . . . §1221(1). Although the copyright might not be such an asset in the owner's hands because of that section or . . . §1221(3)(A), the latter disqualification would not apply to the producer for reasons already discussed, and the former would not unless the producer was a professional. However, it is equally possible for the copyright owner to reserve the entire "property" both legal and equitable in himself and agree with the producer that a percentage of certain avails shall be paid as further income from the lease of the play—just as the lessor of real estate might agree to pay a lessee a percentage of what the lessor obtained from other tenants attracted to the building by the lessee's operations. In both instances such payments would be ordinary income. If the parties choose to cast their transaction in the latter mold, the Commissioner may take them at their word.

Here the parties were at some pains to do exactly that. LaMure was to "retain for his sole benefit, complete title, both legal and equitable, in and to all rights whatsoever" other than the right to produce the play. Ferrer was to "have no right, title or interest, legal or equitable, in the motion picture rights, other than the right to receive the Manager's share of the proceeds"; even as to that, he was to have "no recourse, in law or in equity" against a purchaser, a lessee, or the Negotiator, but only a right to arbitration against the Author. We cannot regard all this as mere formalism. The Contract is full of provisions designed to emphasize the Negotiator's freedom to act—provisions apparently stemming from a fear that, without them, the value of the motion picture rights might disintegrate in controversy. . . .

It follows that if Ferrer had produced the play and LaMure had sold the motion picture, radio and television rights for a percentage of the profits, Ferrer's 40% of that percentage would have been ordinary income and not the sale or exchange of a capital asset. The decisions in *Hort* and [Holt v. Commissioner, 303 F.2d 687 (9 Cir. 1962) (producer receives profit percentage in return for future services; liquidation of claim for lump sum payment treated as ordinary income)] point to what would seem the inevitable corollary that if, on the same facts, Ferrer had then sold his rights to a percentage of the profits for a lump sum, that, too, would have been ordinary income. . . . The situation cannot be better from Ferrer's standpoint because he had merely a contingent right to, or an option to obtain, the 40% interest. . . .

The situation is thus one in which two of the rights that Ferrer sold or exchanged were "capital assets" and one was not. Although it would be easy to say that the contingent contract right to a percentage of the avails of the motion picture, radio, and television rights was dominant and all else incidental, that would be viewing the situation with the inestimable advantage of hindsight. In 1952 no one could tell whether the play might be a huge success and the picture a dismal failure, whether the exact opposite would be true, whether both would succeed or both would fail. We cannot simply dismiss out of hand the notion that a dramatic production, presenting an actor famous on the speaking stage and appealing to a sophisticated audience, might have had substantial profit possibilities, perhaps quite as good as a film with respect to a figure, not altogether attractive and not nearly so broadly known then as the success of the picture has made him now, which presumably would require wide public acceptance before returning production costs. At the very least, when Ferrer gave up his lease of the play, he was abandoning his bet on two horses in favor of a bet on only one.

In such instances, where part of a transaction calls for one tax treatment and another for a different kind, allocation is demanded. . . . If it be said that to remand for this purpose is asking the Tax Court to separate the inseparable, we answer that no one expects scientific exactness; that however roughly hewn the decision may be, the result is certain to be fairer than either extreme; and that similar tasks must be performed by the Tax Court in other areas. . . .

Still we have not reached the end of the road. The Commissioner contends that, apart from all else, no part of the payments here can qualify for capital gain treatment, since Ferrer could receive "percentage compensation" only if he fulfilled his acting commitments, and all the payments were thus for personal services. [T]he Commissioner says it was error for the Tax Court to rely on extrinsic evidence to vary the written contract.

Although the parties have taken opposing positions on the applicability of the "parol evidence rule" to a dispute involving a stranger to the contract, . . . no such issue is here presented. No one argued the contract provided anything other than what was plainly said. Huston's attorney did not assert that Ferrer would become entitled to the percentage compensation without fulfilling his acting commitment; what the attorney said in his testimony, as he had earlier in his letter, was that Ferrer was selling two things to Moulin—his services as an actor and his rights under the Dramatic Production Contract—and that the parties regarded the payments under clauses 4(a), (b) and (c) as the consideration for the former and those under clauses 4(d) and (e) as the consideration for the latter.

On the basis of this evidence the Tax Court found that the percentage compensation was not "to any extent the consequence of, or consideration for, petitioner's personal services." In one sense, this is hardly so. Under the Motion Picture Contract, Ferrer would receive no percentage compensation if he wrongfully refused to furnish acting services, and none or only a portion if, for reasons beyond his control, he furnished less than all. Since that must have been as plain to the Tax Court as to us, we read the finding to mean rather that Ferrer and Moulin adopted the percentage of profits formula embodied in clauses 4(d) and (e) as an equivalent and in lieu of a fixed sum payable in all events for the release of the Dramatic Production Contract. If they had first agreed on such a sum and had then substituted the arrangement here made, it would be hard to say that although payments under their initial arrangement would not be disqualified for capital gain treatment, payments under the substituted one would be. Ferrer was already bound to play the role of Toulouse-Lautrec, at a salary implicitly found to constitute fair compensation for his services; adoption of a formula whereby his receipt of percentage compensation for releasing his rights was made contingent on his fulfilling that undertaking does not mean that the percentage compensation could not be solely for his release of the Contract. The Tax Court was not bound to accept the testimony that this was the intent—it could lawfully have found that the percentage compensation was in part added salary for Ferrer's acting services and in part payment for the release. However, it found the contrary, and we cannot say that in doing so it went beyond the bounds to which our review of its fact findings is confined [under] §7482(a). Since, on the taxpayer's own evidence, the percentage compensation was for the totality of the release of his rights under the Dramatic Production Contract, allocation is required as between rights which did and rights which did not constitute a "capital asset."

We therefore reverse and remand to the Tax Court to determine what portion of the percentage compensation under clauses 4(d) and (e) of the Motion

Picture Contract constituted compensation for Ferrer's surrendering his lease of the play and his incidental power to prevent disposition of the motion picture and other rights pending its production, as to which the determination of deficiency should be annulled, and what part for the surrender of his opportunity to receive 40% of the proceeds of the motion picture and other rights as to which it should be sustained. . . .

NOTES AND QUESTIONS

1. *Fragmentation.* Why did the court break up the set of rights for which Ferrer had bargained? Does it seem likely that Ferrer himself saw the rights as independent of one another?

2. *Drafting around the decision.* Could the contract between Ferrer and LaMure have been written so that all of Ferrer's gain would have been capital gain? Would that have required significant changes in LaMure's substantive rights? Would such changes have had any adverse tax effect for LaMure?

3. *The significance of profit sharing.* Note that the fact that Ferrer was to receive a share of the profits of the film, rather than a fixed amount, did not preclude a finding of a "sale" for purposes of allowing capital-gain treatment. This result is consistent with the position taken by the Service (after a long battle) as to licenses of patents (Rev. Rul. 58-353, 1958-2 C.B. 408)[16] and copyrights (Rev. Rul. 60-226, 1960-1 C.B. 26, regardless of whether the amounts "are payable over a period generally coterminus with the grantee's use of the copyrighted work").

3.   Right of Publicity or Commercial Exploitation

MILLER v. COMMISSIONER
299 F.2d 706 (2d Cir.), cert. denied, 370 U.S. 923 (1962)

Before WATERMAN, KAUFMAN and MARSHALL, Circuit Judges.

KAUFMAN, Circuit Judge.

Petitioner is the widow of Glenn Miller, a band leader who achieved world fame about twenty-five years ago. Although Glenn Miller died in 1944, petitioner has been able to engage in a number of enterprises actively exploiting his continuing popularity. . . .

Thus, in 1952, she entered into a contract with Universal Pictures Company, Inc. (Universal) in connection with the production of a motion picture film entitled "The Glenn Miller Story"; and in the calendar year 1954, she received $409,336.34 as her share of the income derived from that theatrical venture. According to the terms of the 1952 contract, petitioner had purportedly granted to Universal "the exclusive right to produce, release, distribute and exhibit . . . one or more photoplays based upon the life and activities of Glenn Miller throughout the world"; and had warranted that she was "the sole and exclusive owner of all the rights" conveyed by her.

---

16. Section 1235, enacted in 1954, allows royalties received by the inventor or other "holder" to be treated as capital gains.

Petitioner now contends that the payment . . . should be considered . . . "gain from the sale or exchange of a capital asset held for more than 6 months. . . ." [T]he conflict is narrowed to the meaning of the word "property" for purposes of [§1221].

The Internal Revenue Code does not define "property" as used in §1221. . . . Therefore, we must look outside the eight corners of the Code for some elucidation. The ordinary technique is to refer to principles of state property law for, if not an answer, at least a hint. Since ultimately it is the Congressional purpose which controls, such nontax definitions are certainly not binding on us. . . . On the other hand, Congress may be presumed to have had ordinary property concepts in mind so they are relevant to our inquiry.

Most people trained in the law would agree that for many purposes one may define "property" as a bundle of rights, protected from interference by legal sanctions. Cf. Restatement, Property §§1-5. This concept is behind one prong of petitioner's attack. She cites several cases, claiming they indicate that if Universal had made its motion picture without contracting with her, it would have been the victim of a substantial lawsuit.

Even if this were so, those cases would not compel this court to recognize, for income tax purposes, a "property right" in Glenn Miller himself if he were still alive. However, it is not necessary for us to reach a determination upon such an assertion. Those cases do not even remotely bear on the question whether such a property right, if it existed, could pass to the sole beneficiary under his will; and certainly they lend no support to petitioner's theory that the reputation or fame of a dead person could give rise to such "property rights." In fact, in the only case cited in which the rights of a dead man were considered at all, the court held against the claimant. . . .

Undeterred by her failure to find case authority which would substantiate the existence of "property rights" petitioner invokes the authority of logic. With considerable ingenuity, she argues:

(1) Universal paid petitioner $409,336.34 in 1954, which is a great deal of money.
(2) Universal was a sophisticated corporate being to which donative intent would be difficult to ascribe.
(3) If there was no danger in free use of Glenn Miller material, why did Universal pay?

Petitioner appears to find this question unanswerable unless it is conceded that there was a sale of "property right." Petitioner is wrong.

It is clear to this Court, at least, that many things can be sold which are not "property" in any sense of the word. One can sell his time and experience, for instance, or, if one is dishonest, one can sell his vote; but we would suppose that no one would seriously contend that the subject matter of such sales is "property" as that word is ordinarily understood. Certainly no one would contend that such subject matter was inheritable. We conclude, therefore, that not everything people pay for is "property."

In the instant case, "something" was indeed sold. And the expedient business practice may often be to sell such "things." But the "thing" bought, or more appropriately "bought off," seems to have been the chance that a new theory of "property" might be advanced, and that a lawsuit predicated on it might be successful. . . . Because Universal feared that it might sometime in the future be held to have infringed a property right does not mean, however, that a court presently considering whether that property right *did* exist in 1952 must realize Universal's worst fears. That does not mean that Universal's payment was foolish or illusory. It got what it contracted for in 1952 and what it later paid Mrs. Miller for: freedom from the danger that at a future date a defensible right constituting "property" *would* be found to exist. But it didn't pay for "property."[17]

It may be helpful to compare this situation with one which involves the settlement of a tort claim, e.g., a negligence lawsuit. No one doubts the existence of a legal principle creating liability for negligence. If the facts are as a plaintiff contends, and they come within that principle, the defendant's liability exists. Even if they do not, the defendant, for his own reasons, may agree to make a payment in settlement of his alleged liability. Moreover, the Commissioner, for purposes of taxation, may accept that settlement as an implied affirmation that the *facts* were substantially as the plaintiff contended, and treat the recovery accordingly. But no two individuals can, by agreement between themselves, create a *legal* principle, binding upon everyone else, including the Commissioner, where none existed before. This is the exclusive domain of the legislature and the courts as repository of the public will. . . . Petitioner concedes that at the time of the "sale" there had been no authoritative decision holding that a decedent's successors had any "property right" to the public image of a deceased entertainer; and therefore it follows that their bargain was not, at that time, a bargain that both parties knew involved a "property right." . . . "[I]t is evident that not everything which can be called property in the ordinary sense and which is outside the statutory exclusions qualifies as a capital asset. . . ." Commissioner v. Gillette Motor Transport, Inc., 364 U.S. 130, 134 (1960). . . . Gains which result from the sale or exchange of capital assets receive preferential tax treatment. Therefore, "The definition of a capital asset must be narrowly applied," Corn Products Refining Co. v. Commissioner, in order to effectuate the basic Congressional purpose "to relieve the taxpayer from . . . excessive tax burdens on gains resulting from a conversion of capital investments, and to remove the deterrent effect of those burdens on such conversions." Burnet v. Harmel, [287 U.S. 103, 106 (1932)]; Corn Products Refining Co. v. Commissioner, *supra.* We do not believe that for income tax computation purposes beneficiaries of the estate of a deceased entertainer receive by descent a capitalizable "property" in the name, reputation, right of publicity, right of privacy or "public image" of the deceased; or that in this case the petitioner, for tax purposes, owned any "property" which came into existence after Glenn Miller's death. Therefore, income received by Mrs. Miller from contractual arrangements made by her with Universal dealing with deceased's intangible rights of the nature above specified is "ordinary" income as opposed to capital gain or loss under §1221.

Affirmed.

---

17. One must remember that, the techniques of advertising and promotion being what they are, timing is very important and a successful motion for a preliminary injunction made by one who *claims* a "property right" might be as disastrous as a final award of damages. One can easily find wisdom in this payment by Universal without finding that it paid for "property."

QUESTION

Suppose that at the time of the decision in the *Miller* case there had been clear precedent that a person like Glenn Miller has the exclusive right to exploit his own name and fame and that this right is enforceable by injunction and passes by inheritance to his heirs at his death.[18] Would the result in *Miller* have been different? Should it be? Would Mrs. Miller be entitled to capital gain treatment even if Mr. Miller would not have been? Compare the treatment of holders of copyrights, discussed in the next section.

4. Patents and Copyrights

Before 1950, a patent or copyright was treated as a capital asset if the taxpayer could show that it was neither property held for sale to customers in the regular course of trade or business nor depreciable property used in his or her business. In general, capital gain treatment was confined to "amateur" authors, and inventors, who had not made more than one or two sales. In 1950, Congress added §§1221(a)(3) and 1231(b)(1)(C), depriving authors of the possibility of capital-gain treatment for the fruits of their efforts. In the 2017 act, Congress extended this non-capital treatment beyond copyrights to "a patent, invention, model or design (whether or not patented), a secret formula or process." Thus, from 2018 onward, the term "capital asset" includes neither copyrights nor patents for either (1) a taxpayer whose personal efforts created such property, or (2) a taxpayer whose basis in such property is determined by reference to the basis of the property in the hands of the creator (e.g., acquired by gift). Note that this latter provision ensures that capital treatment is preserved for persons who acquired the copyright or patent by purchase. These rules are generally consistent with the notion that gains from one's efforts are ordinary income while gains or losses from passive investments are capital gains or losses.

The "letter or memorandum" language was added to §§1221(a)(3) and 1231(b) (1)(C) in 1969, apparently in an effort (in conjunction with §170(e)(1)(A)) to prevent politicians from claiming charitable deductions for contributions of their papers to libraries, museums, etc. The addition of this language helped bring about the impeachment of President Richard Nixon, who, having signed

---

18. In Lugosi v. Universal Pictures, 25 Cal. 3d 813, 160 Cal. Rptr. 323, 603 P.2d 425 (1979), the California Supreme Court held that the heirs of Bela Lugosi did not have any protected rights in his special depictions of the character Dracula, even though he might have had such rights during his lifetime. In 1984, the California legislature added Cal. Civ. Code §990, which provides a cause of action for damages for unauthorized commercial use of "a deceased person's name, voice, signature, or likeness" and stating that the rights established are "property rights, freely transferable." Cal. Civ. Code §3344 provides a similar cause of action in respect of living persons. Compare Factors, Etc., Inc. v. Creative Card Co., 444 F. Supp. 279 (S.D.N.Y. 1977); Factors, Etc., Inc. v. Pro Arts, Inc., 44 F. Supp. 288 (S.D.N.Y. 1977); and Memphis Dev. Found. v. Factors, Etc., Inc., 441 F. Supp. 1323 (W.D. Tenn. 1977) — all recognizing property rights in the name and likeness of Elvis Presley; the rights had been exploited by him during his lifetime and survived his death.

the legislation, later filed a tax return claiming a deduction based on back-dated documents of transfer of his own papers.[19]

The reference in §1221(a)(3) to "similar property" includes "theatrical productions, a radio program, a newspaper cartoon strip, or any other property eligible for copyright protection. . ." Reg. §1.1221-1(c)(l). The term "similar property" has also been applied to the format of a radio quiz program "Double or Nothing," on which participants could progressively double their winnings by electing to answer an additional question. Cranford v. United States, 338 F.2d 379 (Ct. Cl. 1964). Even if not entitled to copyright protection, the idea was held to be similar to the items explicitly listed in §1221(a)(3) because it was a type of artistic work resulting from personal effort and skill. The same fate befell the author of "Francis," a talking army mule figuring in a series of novels, when he sold his rights to the character and the novels to a motion-picture company. Stern v. United States, 164 F. Supp. 847 (E.D. La. 1958), aff'd per curiam, 262 F.2d 957 (5th Cir.), cert. denied, 359 U.S. 969 (1959).

The tax treatment of patents has followed a somewhat different and less coherent evolution than that of copyrights. As noted above, the 1950 amendment removing copyrights from the definition of capital asset did not change the treatment of inventors, thus preserving (until 2017) the characterization of patents as capital assets. While Congress amended §1221(a)(3) in 2017 to include patents alongside copyrights, seemingly denying capital-asset treatment, it left unchanged another provision that provides special rules for the sale or exchange of patents. This provision, §1235, was enacted in 1954 and provides that gain from the transfer of patents will be taxed as long-term capital gain even if received by a professional inventor. With the amended §1221(a)(3) and the old §1235 both in effect, the statute now provides that the term "capital asset" does *not* include a patent held by a taxpayer whose personal efforts created the patent (i.e., the §1221(a)(3) rule), but the transfer of a patent by such person (and other qualifying "holders") will nevertheless be treated as the sale of a capital asset held for more than one year (i.e., the §1235 rule). Whether Congress actually intended this result is not clear.

H. CORRELATION WITH PRIOR RELATED TRANSACTIONS

MERCHANTS NATIONAL BANK v. COMMISSIONER
199 F.2d 657 (5th Cir. 1952)

STRUM, Circuit Judge. . . .

On January 1, 1941, the petitioner held notes of Alabama Naval Stores Company, representing loans made by the bank to the Naval Stores Company,

---

19. For background on this fascinating chapter in American history, see Joseph J. Thorndike, *JCT Investigation of Nixon's Tax Returns* (February 2016) (available at https://uschs.org/wp-content/uploads/2016/02/USCHS-History-Role-Joint-Committee-Taxation-Thorndike.pdf).

on which there was an unpaid balance of $49,025.00. In 1941 and 1943, at the direction of national bank examiners, the bank charged these notes off as worthless, thereafter holding them on a "zero" basis. Deductions for the charge-offs, as ordinary losses, were allowed in full by the Commissioner on petitioner's income tax returns in 1941 and 1943. In 1944, petitioner sold the notes to a third party for $18,460.58, which it reported on its return for 1944 as a long term capital gain and paid its tax on that basis. The Commissioner held this sum to be ordinary income. . . .

The rule is well settled, and this Court has held, that when a deduction for income tax purposes is taken and allowed for debts deemed worthless, recoveries on the debts in a later year constitute taxable income for that year to the extent that a tax benefit was received from the deduction taken in a prior year. . . .

When these notes were charged off as a bad debt in the first instance, the bank deducted the amount thereof from its ordinary income, thus escaping taxation on that portion of its income in those years. The amount subsequently recovered on the notes restores pro tanto the amount originally deducted from ordinary income, and is accordingly taxable as ordinary income, not as a capital gain. When the notes were charged off, and the bank recouped itself for the capital loss by deducting the amount thereof from its current income, the notes were no longer capital assets for income tax purposes. To permit the bank to reduce its ordinary income by the amount of the loss in the first instance, thus gaining a maximum tax advantage on that basis, and then permit it to treat the amount later recovered on the notes as a capital gain, taxable on a much lower basis than ordinary income, would afford the bank a tax advantage on the transaction not contemplated by the income tax laws.

The fact that the bank sold these notes to a third party, instead of collecting the amount in question from the maker of the notes does not avoid the effect of the rule above stated. . . .

As the recoveries in question were ordinary income, not capital gains, the 1944 deficiency was properly entered.

Affirmed.

ARROWSMITH v. COMMISSIONER
344 U.S. 6 (1952)

Mr. Justice BLACK delivered the opinion of the Court.

. . . In 1937 two taxpayers, petitioners here, decided to liquidate and divide the proceeds of a corporation in which they had equal stock ownership. Partial distributions made in 1937, 1938, and 1939 were followed by a final one in 1940. Petitioners reported the profits obtained from this transaction, classifying them as capital gains. They thereby paid less income tax than would have been required had the income been attributed to ordinary business transactions for profit. About the propriety of these 1937-1940 returns, there is no dispute. But in 1944 a judgment was rendered against the old corporation. . . . The two taxpayers were required to and did pay the judgment for the corporation, of whose assets they were transferees. . . . Classifying the loss as an ordinary business one, each took a tax deduction for 100% of the amount paid. Treatment of the loss as a capital one would have allowed deduction of a much smaller amount. . . . The Commissioner viewed the 1944 payment as part of the original liquidation transaction requiring classification as a capital loss, just as the taxpayers had treated the original dividends as capital gains. . . .

[Section 165(f)] treats losses from sales or exchanges of capital assets as "capital losses" and [§331(a)(1)] requires that liquidation distributions be treated as exchanges. The losses here fall squarely within the definition of "capital losses" contained in these sections. Taxpayers were required to pay the judgment because of liability imposed on them as transferees of liquidation distribution assets. And it is plain that their liability as transferees was not based on any ordinary business transaction of theirs apart from the liquidation proceedings. It is not even denied that had this judgment been paid after liquidation, but during the year 1940, the losses would have been properly treated as capital ones. For payment during 1940 would simply have reduced the amount of capital gains taxpayers received during that year.

It is contended, however, that this payment which would have been a capital transaction in 1940 was transformed into an ordinary business transaction in 1944 because of the well-established principle that each taxable year is a separate unit for tax accounting purposes. United States v. Lewis, North American Oil Consolidated v. Burnet. But this principle is not breached by considering all the 1937-1944 liquidation transaction events in order properly to classify the nature of the 1944 loss for tax purposes. Such an examination is not an attempt to reopen and readjust the 1937 to 1940 tax returns, an action that would be inconsistent with the annual tax accounting principle. . . .

Affirmed.

Mr. Justice DOUGLAS, dissenting.

I agree with Mr. Justice JACKSON that these losses should be treated as ordinary, not capital, losses. There were no capital transactions in the year in which the losses were suffered. Those transactions occurred and were accounted for in earlier years in accord with the established principle that each year is a separate unit for tax accounting purposes. See United States v. Lewis. I have not felt, as my dissent in the *Lewis* case indicates, that the law made that an inexorable principle. But if it is the law, we should require observance of it—not merely by taxpayers but by the Government as well. We should force each year to stand on its own footing, whoever may gain or lose from it in a particular case. We impeach that principle when we treat this year's losses as if they diminished last year's gains.

Mr. Justice JACKSON, whom Mr. Justice FRANKFURTER joins, dissenting.

This problem arises only because the judgment was rendered in a taxable year subsequent to the liquidation.

Had the liability of the transferor-corporation been reduced to judgment during the taxable year in which liquidation occurred, or prior thereto, this problem, under the tax laws, would not arise. The amount of the judgment rendered against the corporation would have decreased the amount it had available for distribution, which would have reduced the liquidating dividends proportionately and diminished the capital gains taxes assessed against the stockholders. Probably it would also have decreased the corporation's own taxable income.

Congress might have allowed, under such circumstances, tax returns of the prior year to be reopened or readjusted so as to give the same tax results as would have obtained had the liability become known prior to liquidation. Such a solution is foreclosed to us and the alternatives left are to regard the judgment liability fastened by operation of law on the transferee as an ordinary loss for the year of adjudication or to regard it as a capital loss for such year.

I find little aid in the choice of alternatives from arguments based on equities. One enables the taxpayer to deduct the amount of the judgment against his ordinary income which might be taxed as high as 87%, while if the liability had been assessed against the corporation prior to liquidation it would have reduced his capital gain which was taxable at only 25% (now 26%). The consequence may readily be characterized as a windfall (regarding a windfall as anything that is left to a taxpayer after the collector has finished with him).

On the other hand, adoption of the contrary alternative may penalize the taxpayer because of two factors: (1) [limitations on the deductibility of capital losses against ordinary income]; and (2) had the liability been discharged by the corporation, a portion of it would probably in effect have been paid by the Government, since the corporation could have taken it as a deduction, while here the total liability comes out of the pockets of the stockholders.

Solicitude for the revenues is a plausible but treacherous basis upon which to decide a particular tax case. A victory may have implications which in future cases will cost the Treasury more than a defeat. This might be such a case, for anything I know. Suppose that subsequent to liquidation it is found that a corporation has undisclosed claims instead of liabilities and that under applicable state law they may be prosecuted for the benefit of the stockholders. The logic of the Court's decision here, if adhered to, would result in a lesser return to the Government than if the recoveries were considered ordinary income. Would it be so clear that this is a capital loss if the shoe were on the other foot?

Where the statute is so indecisive and the importance of a particular holding lies in its rational and harmonious relation to the general scheme of the tax law, I think great deference is due the twice-expressed judgment of the Tax Court . . . [which] is a more competent and steady influence toward a systematic body of tax law than our sporadic omnipotence in a field beset with invisible boomerangs. I should reverse, in reliance upon the Tax Court's judgment more, perhaps, than my own.

NOTES

In United States v. Skelly Oil Co., 394 U.S. 678 (1969), the taxpayer was required to refund amounts that it had received in an earlier year from the sale of natural gas and that had been the basis for a 27 percent depletion allowance. The Court held that the deduction for the refund was limited to 72 percent of the amount refunded, since it was only this amount that had been taxed. In reaching this result, the Court referred to the problems created by the principle of annual accounting and, citing *Arrowsmith*, said that "the annual accounting concept does not require us to close our eyes to what happened in prior years." 394 U.S. at 684. The Court went on to say (at 685):

> The rationale for the *Arrowsmith* rule is easy to see; if money was taxed at a special lower rate when received, the taxpayer would be accorded an unfair tax windfall if repayments were generally deductible from receipts taxable at the higher rate applicable to ordinary income. The Court in *Arrowsmith* was unwilling to infer that Congress intended such a result.

Four Circuit Court decisions have addressed the tax problem that arises from the repayment of insider profits. In each case, an employee stockholder made a profit on employer stock purchased and sold (or sold and purchased) allegedly in violation of the securities laws regarding trading restrictions on insiders. None of the employees admitted liability, but each decided to repay the profits to the corporation to preserve his business position and reputation. In all four cases, the Tax Court held the amount repaid was a deduction from ordinary income rather than a capital loss since the taxpayers made the sales in their capacities as shareholders rather than as employees, while the repayments arose from their status as employees. The Circuit Courts reversed all four decisions and held that the deduction must take its character from the income item in which it had its genesis, which was the purchase and/or sale of a capital asset. Mitchell v. Commissioner, 428 F.2d 259 (6th Cir. 1970), cert. denied, 401 U.S. 909 (1971); Anderson v. Commissioner, 480 F.2d 1304 (7th Cir. 1973); Cummings v. Commissioner, 506 F.2d 449 (2d Cir. 1974), cert. denied, 421 U.S. 913 (1975); Brown v. Commissioner, 529 F.2d 609 (10th Cir. 1976).

I.   REQUIREMENT OF A SALE OR EXCHANGE

Section 1222 defines capital gains and losses as those recognized from the "sale or exchange" of a capital asset. Suppose a capital asset simply becomes worthless? If the asset is a security, such as stock or a corporate bond, §165(g)(1) treats the loss as one that arises from sale or exchange. Similarly, under the holding of Helvering v. Hammel, 311 U.S. 504 (1941), the foreclosure of property is treated as a sale or exchange. The sale or exchange requirement is also relaxed in situations that do not involve worthless property. For example, §1271 treats amounts realized from the retirement of a bond as having been realized from sale or exchange. Insurance or other proceeds from involuntary conversions may generate capital gain under §1231.

In general, the sale or exchange requirement comes into play in situations in which there is a dispute about whether the taxpayer has parted with ownership. For example, an issue in *Ferrer* was whether the taxpayer retained or sold a copyright; an issue in *Baker* was whether the taxpayer parted ownership with enough business assets to characterize the proceeds as arising from the sale or exchange of those assets. Occasionally, the sale or exchange require-ment comes into play in situations in which there is no dispute about what was retained or transferred. For example, suppose in Year 1 a grocer borrows $10,000 from a commercial lender and then runs into financial difficulties. The commercial lender sells its claim to the taxpayer for $6,000. In Year 2, the grocer regains its financial footing and later that year repays the debt in full. If the taxpayer resells the debt for $10,000 shortly before repayment, any gain recognized will be capital gain. But if the taxpayer retains the debt until it is repaid, the gain recognized will be ordinary income. Capital gain is unavail-able because there has been no sale or exchange.

APPENDIX

THE FEDERAL TAXING
AND SPENDING POWERS

It is possible to enjoy a long and successful career as a tax professional without dwelling on the constitutional foundations of the tax statutes one analyzes. Nonetheless, the constitutional limits of Congress's taxing and spending powers have featured prominently in recent policy and political debates. It therefore might be helpful to offer a brief summary of the constitutional limits imposed on Congress's taxing authority. Students unfamiliar with the area will be surprised to see how limited are the constraints on Congress's authority to tax and to spend. In most cases, the principal remedy for harsh, oppressive, or stupid tax legislation is to vote the rascals out, not to appeal to some imagined list of constitutional dos and don'ts.

Previous editions of this casebook made short work of any constitutional law discussion. But the area was particularly reanimated in 2012, when a divided Supreme Court upheld the constitutionality of the core element of the Patient Protection and Affordable Care Act of 2010 (now universally known as Obamacare) — the law's "mandate" that certain individuals either obtain health insurance or pay a penalty, codified as §5000A of the Internal Revenue Code.[1] The Court did so, not on the grounds that the mandate was a valid exercise of the Congress's power to regulate interstate commerce, but rather on the basis that the mandate was an instance of Congress's constitutional taxing power.

NFIB v. Sebelius triggered a great deal of controversy. Some commentators lamented that the Court had opened a back door to the Constitution, through which Congress could exercise new regulatory powers by fashioning future legislation as exercises in taxing and spending. There is truth in that assertion, except that there is no novelty about these powers or strategy. For more than 100 years, the Supreme Court has consistently held that Congress possesses extremely broad powers to spend as it sees fit in order to enhance "the general welfare," and to collect taxes to pay for that spending.

---

1. Nat'l Federation of Independent Businesses v. Sebelius, 132 S. Ct. 2566 (2012) (hereinafter NFIB v. Sebelius).

This Appendix briefly summarizes some of the relevant landmarks along the way. Constitutional experts will find our summary simplistic, and some scholars may feel that our presentation overclaims the scope of congressional authority. Students interested in pursuing the subject should look to some of the material referenced in the footnotes.[2]

As Chief Justice Roberts reminded readers at the outset of his opinion in NFIB v. Sebelius, the Constitution created a federal government with "enumerated powers"; powers not enumerated were reserved to the States. One of those enumerated powers is found in Article I, §8, cl. 1, which grants to Congress the "Power to lay and collect taxes, duties, imposts, and excises, to pay the debts and provide for the common defense and general welfare of the United States." In addition, Article I, §8, cl. 18 grants Congress the authority to "make all laws which shall be necessary and proper for carrying into execution" the powers enumerated in Article I, §8.

Chief Justice Roberts in NFIB v. Sebelius neatly summarized the fundamental reach of the congressional power to spend and to tax under Article I, §8 as follows: "Put simply, Congress may tax and spend. This grant gives the Federal Government considerable influence even in areas where it cannot directly regulate. The Federal Government may enact a tax on an activity that it cannot authorize, forbid, or otherwise control. And in exercising its spending power, Congress may offer funds to the States, and may condition those offers on compliance with specified conditions. These offers may well induce the States to adopt policies that the Federal Government itself could not impose."[3]

---

2. There is a vast literature on the scope of the taxing power, reinvigorated by the decision in NFIB v. Sebelius. What follows is a very short list of a few relevant contributions; omissions are not intended to convey disapprobation.

One recent book in this area is Jasper L. Cummings, Jr., *The Supreme Court, Federal Taxation, and the Constitution* (2013). Another, predating NFIB v. Sebelius, is Erik M. Jensen, *The Taxing Power: A Reference Guide to the United States Constitution* (2005). Books focusing on the history of the Constitution's framing of the taxing power include Calvin H. Johnson, *Righteous Anger at the Wicked States: The Meaning of the Founders' Constitution* (2005); W. Elliot Brownlee, *Federal Taxation in America* (2d ed. 2004); Max Edling, *A Revolution in Favor of Government: Origins of the U.S. Constitution and the Making of the American State* (2003); Roger H. Brown, *Redeeming the Republic: Federalism, Taxation, and the Origins of the Constitution* (1993).

Erik Jensen is a prolific author whose interpretation of the taxing and spending power is much narrower than that presented here. In addition to the book just referenced, see Erik M. Jensen, *Did the Sixteenth Amendment Ever Matter? Does It Matter Today?*, 108 Nw. U. L. Rev. 799 (2014); *Post*-NFIB: *Does the Taxing Clause Give Congress Unlimited Power?*, 136 Tax Notes 1309 (Sept. 10, 2012); and *The Individual Mandate and the Taxing Power*, 134 Tax Notes 97 (Jan. 2, 2012). Another recent article that takes a narrower view than that which we adopt here is Bret N. Bogenschneider, *The Taxing Power After* Sebelius, 51 Wake Forest L. Rev. 941 (2016). See also Jasper L. Cummings, Jr., *Cost of Goods Sold and the Constitution*, 156 Tax Notes 77 (July 3, 2017), including the material gathered in his footnote 2.

Articles putting NFIB v. Sebelius into a larger constitutional law context include Jonathan H. Adler, *The Conflict of Visions in NFIB v. Sebelius*, 62 Drake L. Rev. 937 (2014); Lawrence B. Solum, *How NFIB v. Sebelius Affects the Constitutional Gestalt*, 91 Wash. U. L. Rev. 1 (2013); Mark D. Rosen and Christopher W. Schmidt, *Why Broccoli: Limiting Principles and Popular Constitutionalism in the Health Care Case*, 61 UCLA L. Rev. 66 (2013); Gillian E. Metzger, *To Tax, to Spend, to Regulate,* 126 Harv. L. Rev. 83 (2012).

3. 132 S. Ct. (citations omitted).

Chief Justice Roberts's opinion in NFIB v. Sebelius in this respect was consistent with many prior Supreme Court cases. For example, the Supreme Court in 1983 observed that "Congress' power to tax is virtually without limitation." United States v. Ptasynski, 462 U.S. 74, 79 (1983). And over 100 years

What this basically means is that Congress can spend money any way it sees fit to advance our collective "general welfare," so long as in doing so it does not violate some fundamental individual right or express prohibition contained elsewhere in the Constitution (for example, by funding a national church). And Congress in turn has the plenary power to raise taxes to pay for that spending, subject only to some limitations that usually are trivial in practice (like not taxing exports). For example, even before NFIB v. Sebelius, Congress unquestionably could have enacted a single-payer national healthcare program—it would have needed only to determine that spending money on healthcare advanced the general welfare, and then would have been free to enact whatever taxes were required to fund that program. That is the constitutional basis for Medicare.

It is natural to have a visceral reaction that the individual mandate of §5000A should not properly be characterized as a tax, because it is not primarily designed to collect revenue, but rather to compel behavior. Since 1937, however, the Supreme Court has rejected any invitation to distinguish between taxes designed to influence behavior and taxes designed to raise revenue, so long as the tax legislation "has some reasonable relation to the exercise of the taxing authority conferred by the Constitution."[4] This principle applies even when the revenue raised is "negligible."[5]

---

ago, in Spencer v. Merchant, 125 U.S. 345 (1888), the Court acknowledged the broad power of the Congress to impose taxes, even oppressive taxes:

> The judicial department cannot prescribe to the legislative department limitations upon the exercise of its acknowledged powers. The power to tax may be exercised oppressively upon persons; but the responsibility of the legislature is not to the courts, but to the people by whom its members are elected.

As one final example, an 1867 Supreme Court opinion by Chief Justice Chase summarized the "very extensive" federal power to tax as follows:

> [The power to tax] is given in the Constitution, with only one exception and only two qualifications. Congress cannot tax exports, and it must impose direct taxes by the rule of apportionment, and indirect taxes by the rule of uniformity. Thus limited, and thus only, it reaches every subject, and may be exercised at discretion.

License Tax Cases, 72 U.S. 462 (1868), quoted by Bittker, *Constitutional Limits on the Taxing Power of the Federal Government*, 41 Tax Law. 3, 4 (1987). To this list might be added the origination clause (Article I, §7, cl. 1), which provides that tax legislation must originate in the House of Representatives. Tax bills originating in the Senate are "blue slipped" by the House, and not further considered. Michael W. Evans, *"A Source of Frequent and Obstinate Altercations": The History and Application of the Origination Clause*, 105 Tax Notes 1215 (Nov. 29, 2004).

4. Sozinsky v. United States, 300 U.S. 506 (1937) (upholding federal license tax on dealers in firearms). In *Sozinsky*, the Court stated that "every tax is in some measure regulatory. . . . But it is not any less a tax because it has a regulatory effect. . . . Inquiry into the hidden motives which may move Congress to exercise a power constitutionally conferred upon it is beyond the competency of the courts." *Id.* at 513 (citations omitted). See also Bittker, *supra* note 3, at 11-12.

Citing pre-*Sozinsky* case law to the contrary (e.g., United States v. Butler, 297 U.S. 1 (1936)) misses the point that the Supreme Court changed its mind and reversed its substantive due process line of cases beginning in 1937. Bob Jones University v. Simon, 416 U.S. 725, 741 n.12 (1974) ("It is true that the Court [in early cases] . . . drew what it saw at the time as distinctions between regulatory and revenue-raising taxes. But the Court has subsequently abandoned such distinctions.").

5. United States v. Sanchez, 340 U.S. 42, 44 (1950) ("It is beyond serious question that a tax does not cease to be valid merely because it regulates, discourages, or even definitely deters the activities

In light of this hoary and consistent history, one might be left wondering why the outcome in NFIB v. Sebelius with respect to the individual mandate was at all controversial. The answers are, first, the government in arguing the case relied principally on the commerce clause, and only secondarily on the taxing power; second, Congress in enacting §5000A (the individual mandate) went out of its way to make the case for invoking the taxing power a bit more difficult by consciously avoiding the use of the term "tax" in §5000A to describe the financial charge imposed on affected taxpayers who choose not to obtain health insurance (preferring terms like "penalty" and "shared responsibility payment" instead); and third, the tax (for such it was, regardless of labels) had to overcome the claim that it was a "direct tax" that had not properly been "apportioned among the states."

As to the second point, there is no question but that Congress in 2010 wanted to have its cake and eat it too—to impose a tax without the political consequences of acknowledging that this is what it had done. Critics can call the 2010 Congress craven in this regard, but congressional cravenness by itself is not a constitutional infirmity. Section 5000A (that is, the mandate) functions as an income tax. It is a section of the Internal Revenue Code. Low-income taxpayers are exempt (§5000A(e)(1)), the amount collected in fact is measured as a percentage of income (§5000A(c)(2)(B)) (subject to a floor and a ceiling), and the amount is includable on a taxpayer's federal income tax return. Chief Justice Roberts therefore concluded that the label used by Congress did not determine the constitutional category under which the exaction should be analyzed, and that §5000A in fact operated as a tax in the constitutional understanding of the term.[6] Responding to the argument that a tax imposed on individuals must relate to some activity to constitute a tax, but that here the exaction was on simply existing, Roberts observed that "it is abundantly clear the Constitution does not guarantee that individuals may avoid taxation through inactivity. A capitation, after all, is a tax that everyone must pay simply for existing, and capitations are expressly contemplated by the Constitution."[7]

The "direct tax" argument requires more explication, as it figures prominently in the history of the income tax, as laid out in the next section. Article I, §2 of the Constitution provides that "direct taxes shall be apportioned among the several states," and Article I, §9 further provides that no "capitation, or other direct, tax shall be laid, unless in proportion to the census or enumeration herein before directed to be taken."[8] What this means is that a federal "direct tax" must be apportioned to each state based on the population of that

---

taxed. The principle applies even though the revenue obtained is obviously negligible, or the revenue purpose of the tax may be secondary. Nor does a tax statute necessarily fall because it touches on activities which Congress might not otherwise regulate.") (citations omitted).

6. In operation, the individual mandate is just another income tax (subject to various exemptions and limitations, just like any other income tax), with a twist: You can claim a tax credit (a dollar-for-dollar offset against your tentative tax bill) if you provide proof that you have purchased qualifying private insurance. Since the tax itself can be seen as funding some of government's costs of providing medical care for the uninsured, the tax-and-credit mechanism makes good logical sense: It prevents what otherwise would be effective double taxation—once when you pay the tax, and once when you buy private insurance that duplicates to some extent the minimal coverage of the government emergency care safety net.

7. 132 S. Ct.

8. The requirement of apportionment with respect to direct taxes and uniformity with respect to imposts, duties, and excises, are "not so much a limitation upon the complete and all-embracing

state, and the tax then imposed such that the activity within the state yields the apportioned amount.

For example, if California has 10 percent of the country's population, then an apportioned direct tax would require that Californians pay 10 percent of the total federal tax. In any case other than a pure capitation tax (a "head" tax imposed on all individuals at a fixed rate), this requirement would mean that the tax rate paid by Californians and the tax rate paid by Texans might differ, if the underlying activity were conducted in different proportions in the two states. In practice, this means that a federal "direct tax" is wholly impractical, as different rates would apply to residents of different states. In fact, some have argued that the very impracticality of the apportionment requirement argues for an extremely narrow reading of what exactions should be construed to constitute direct taxes.[9]

While there have been many articles in recent years on what constitutes a "direct" tax, and whether the apportionment requirement still survives,[10] it is interesting to note that virtually all of the debate relates to taxes that are laid on property or an incident of property ownership. The only example offered by the Supreme Court of a direct tax whose nominal objects are natural persons is the simple capitation tax (that is, a tax imposed on every person simply by virtue of existing), because that tax alone is imposed "without regard to property, profession or any other circumstances."[11] The other category of direct tax usually offered by the Supreme Court — putting to one side the infamous

---

authority to tax, but in their essence [are] simply regulations concerning the mode in which the plenary power [is] to be exerted." Brushaber v. Union Pacific Railroad Co., 240 U.S. 1, 13 (1916).

9. Calvin N. Johnson, *Apportionment of Direct Taxes: The Foul-Up in the Core of the Constitution*, 7 Wm. & Mary Bill Rts. J. 1 (1998).

10. An extremely important — if controversial — contribution here is Bruce Ackerman, *Taxation and the Constitution*, 99 Colum. L. Rev. 1 (1999).

11. Hylton v. United States, 3 U.S. 171, 175 (1796) (Chase, J.) (emphasis supplied). In NFIB v. Sebelius, Chief Justice Roberts summarized the law as follows:

> Even when the Direct Tax Clause was written it was unclear what else, other than a capitation (also known as a "head tax" or a "poll tax"), might be a direct tax. See Springer v. United States, 102 U.S. 586, 596-598 (1881). Soon after the framing, Congress passed a tax on ownership of carriages, over James Madison's objection that it was an unapportioned direct tax. Id., at 597. This Court upheld the tax, in part reasoning that apportioning such a tax would make little sense, because it would have required taxing carriage owners at dramatically different rates depending on how many carriages were in their home State. See Hylton v. United States, 3 Dall. 171, 174 (1796) (opinion of Chase, J.). The Court was unanimous, and those Justices who wrote opinions either directly asserted or strongly suggested that only two forms of taxation were direct: capitations and land taxes. . . .
>
> That narrow view of what a direct tax might be persisted for a century. In 1880, for example, we explained that "direct taxes, within the meaning of the Constitution, are only capitation taxes, as expressed in that instrument, and taxes on real estate." *Springer*, supra, at 602. In 1895, we expanded our interpretation to include taxes on personal property and income from personal property, in the course of striking down aspects of the federal income tax. Pollock v. Farmers' Loan & Trust Co., 158 U.S. 601, 618 (1895). That result was overturned by the Sixteenth Amendment, although we continued to consider taxes on personal property to be direct taxes. See Eisner v. Macomber, 252 U.S. 189, 218-219 (1920).

132 S. Ct.

Chief Justice Robert's passing reference to Eisner v. Macomber has itself been the subject of great controversy, as many scholars had come to the view that this case, including in particular its "realization" doctrine, involved rules of convenience rather than constitutional constraint. This is an issue that will remain for another day.

Pollock v. Farmers' Loan & Trust Co., discussed *infra*, were land taxes imposed on the value of that property. There was a famous exchange on the floor of the Constitutional Convention when one delegate asked for the meaning of the phrase "direct tax," and no one answered.

The defendants in NFIB v. Sebelius argued that if the individual mandate at issue in the Affordable Care Act case constituted a tax, it must be a "direct tax" in the constitutional sense, which in turn was not apportioned in the manner required by the Constitution. Chief Justice Roberts responded by pointing out that the tax "does not fall within any recognized category of direct tax. It is not a capitation. . . . The payment is also plainly not a tax on the ownership of land or personal property." Instead, he concluded, "The whole point of the shared responsibility payment is that it is triggered by specific circumstances — earning a certain amount of income but not obtaining health insurance."[12]

One other interesting modern case on the meaning of "direct" taxes is Murphy v. Internal Revenue Service,[13] a 2007 D.C. Circuit opinion, set out in Chapter 2, with much of the constitutional argumentation redacted for brevity. In that case, the D.C. Circuit held that the Internal Revenue Code character- ized a damage award received for emotional distress as gross income, and fur- ther held that, while the award might not constitute income in the Sixteenth Amendment sense, it nonetheless could be *labeled* gross income and taxed as such, because the resulting levy was not a "direct" tax in the constitutional sense. The case is relevant here because the *Murphy* court concluded that a tax imposed directly on a person, without regard to any profession or other commercial activity, nonetheless did not constitute a direct tax. Instead, the court concluded that the tax either was on a transaction (the involuntary con- version of Murphy's human capital) or an excise laid on the proceeds received from vindicating a statutory right through the medium of the legal system.[14] Under either theory, *Murphy* fits squarely within the long history of case law that adopts a very narrow reading of the apportionment requirement.[15]

Article I, §8 requires all "duties, imposts and excises" to be "uniform throughout the United States." The Supreme Court has interpreted this clause to exact "only a geographical uniformity,"[16] meaning "if a particular item is subject to tax, it must be taxed at the same rate throughout the United States, wherever it may be found."[17] As a result, the clause does little to limit the taxing

---

12. 132 S. Ct.

13. 493 F.3d 170 (D.C. Cir. 2007).

14. 493 F.3d at 185-186. The *Murphy* court relied in part in this respect on Steward Mach. Co. v. Davis, 301 U.S. 548 (1937) (employer's share of employee wage taxes is a valid excise), and quoted a passage that has some relevance here: "[N]atural rights, so called, are as much subject to taxation as rights of less importance. An excise is not limited to vocations or activities that may be prohibited altogether. . . . It extends to vocations or activities pursued as of common right." (footnote omitted). 301 U.S. at 580-581, quoted at 493 F.3d at 186.

15. In doing so, the *Murphy* court roundly rejected the argument, developed by Erik Jensen in particular, that indirect taxes are only those that can be shifted to others. 493 F.3d at 183-184.

16. Brushaber v. Union Pacific Railroad Co., 240 U.S. 1, 24 (1916).

17. Bittker, *supra* note 3, at 3, 9 (citing Knowlton v. Moore, 178 U.S. 41, 83-106 (1900)); see also Laurence H. Tribe, *American Constitutional Law* 842 (2000) ("This requirement is one of geographic uniformity only; so long as the tax structure does not discriminate among the states, it does not

power, and a provision that "might have dramatically influenced the structure of the federal income tax . . . has shriveled away to a mere flyspeck."[18]

An additional limitation on "taxes and duties" is found in Article I, §9, which provides that no "tax or duty shall be laid on articles exported from any state." This means that Congress can impose taxes on imports, but not exports. One of the few modern cases to hold that a federal tax was unconstitutional did so on this basis. A "harbor maintenance tax" was found to burden exports, and therefore to be unconstitutional.[19]

Indeed, with the exception of Eastern Enterprises v. Apel[20] (technically, not a tax case) and the export clause case referenced above, we are not aware of *any* instance in the last fifty years where the Supreme Court has struck down any federal tax or comparable levy on the ground that the levy unconstitutionally burdened a taxpayer's claim to his income, property, or similar economic rights as an unapportioned direct tax, impermissibly retroactive, excessively narrowly targeted to an identifiable set of taxpayers, or as arbitrary and irrational.[21]

Nonetheless, the Constitution's other general checks on the powers of Congress can, in extremely unusual cases, limit the taxing powers of Congress. A century ago, the Supreme Court explained that

> if a case was presented where the abuse of the taxing power was so extreme as to be beyond the principles which we have previously stated, and where it was plain to the judicial mind that the power had been called into play not for revenue

---

matter that a tax may not be 'uniform' as it applies to particular individuals."). In United States v. Ptasynski, 462 U.S. 74 (1983), the Supreme Court upheld an exemption under the Crude Oil Windfall Profit Tax Act for certain oil produced in particular geographic locations, primarily (but not exclusively) in Alaska. The Court stated that the uniformity clause "does not require Congress to devise a tax that falls equally or proportionately on each state"; nor does it "prevent Congress from determining the subject of a tax by drawing distinctions between similar classes." 462 U.S. at 82.

18. Bittker, *supra* note 3, at 9. Bittker may have been too quick to dismiss the uniformity clause. For example, Congress from time to time has considered regional cost of living adjustments to various allowances, such as the cap on home mortgage debt whose interest can be deducted on individual returns. Different views have been expressed as to whether such regional adjustments would pass constitutional muster. See, e.g., Written Testimony of the Staff of the Joint Committee on Taxation Regarding H.R. 3244, The District of Columbia Economic Recovery Act, JCX 45-96 (July 31, 1996).

19. United States v. U.S. Shoe, 523 U.S. 360 (1988). The case in turn triggered years of controversy over whether taxpayers could obtain refunds of unconstitutionally collected tax, and interest thereon, when the statute of limitations to claim tax refunds had expired.

20. 524 U.S. 498 (1998) (new obligation to fund retiree health benefits attributable to plan from which appellant had withdrawn decades earlier held unconstitutional; plurality relied on takings clause).

21. The Supreme Court has, however, invalidated certain taxes on commercial activities where the design of those taxes burdened other fundamental rights. See, e.g., Marchetti v. United States, 390 U.S. 39 (1960) (registration requirement connected with excise tax on bookmakers violated Fifth Amendment privilege against self-incrimination; information made available to state authorities); accord, Grosso v. United States, 390 U.S. 62 (1968).

Lower courts in recent years have considered some interesting constitutional issues in noncommercial settings. *Murphy*, of course, is one example. Another is Moritz v. Commissioner, 469 F.2d 466 (10th Cir. 1972), which held that the tax code's limitation of the dependent care deduction (as then in effect) in a manner that denied the deduction to men who had never married was unconstitutional as a violation of equal protection. And as discussed, the Defense of Marriage Act's ban on same-sex marriages has been declared unconstitutional, and the Internal Revenue Service now accepts joint returns filed by same-sex married couples.

but solely for the purpose of destroying rights which could not be rightfully destroyed consistently with the principles of freedom and justice upon which the Constitution rests, that it would be the duty of the courts to say that such an arbitrary act was not merely an abuse of a delegated power, but was the exercise of an authority not conferred.[22]

Examples of such general constitutional constraints that might in theory be invoked to constrain the legislature's taxing power in extraordinary cases include the Fifth Amendment's due process clause, the prohibition on bills of attainder (basically, arrest warrants issued by the legislature), and the Eighth Amendment's restriction on "excessive fines." For example, at the height of the financial crisis in 2008-2009 some suggested that Congress impose penalty taxes on a small universe of specific individuals who had received bonuses from one or more financial institutions that had been recipients of federal "bailouts." That idea at a minimum raised a bill of attainder issue.

It might seem that retroactive tax legislation must necessarily be unconstitutional, but it is not, provided that the retroactive period is not very long and is "supported by a legitimate legislative purpose furthered by rational means."[23] Indeed, the first income tax act following the passage of the Sixteenth Amendment applied retroactively to income beginning seven months prior to the law's enactment. In an extraordinary case, the due process or takings clauses of the Constitution might be relevant. In practice, however, both parties in Congress have been extremely averse to retroactivity in tax legislation, and almost never come anywhere close to a constitutional question in this area.[24]

In sum, the power of the Congress to tax and to spend is extremely broad. Congress can basically spend money anyway it pleases, so long as there is some colorable claim that in doing so it is advancing the general welfare, and Congress can withhold spending as a device to encourage the states to adopt rules that Congress cannot legislate directly. Congress can impose taxes to pay for all this spending, subject only to some minor constraints (like not taxing exports or imposing unapportioned head taxes). Congress can design taxes that have a very large incentive effect (the polite term for nudging behavior in a direction that Congress wishes to encourage). All this can be distressing to those who believe that surely the framers of the Constitution could not possibly have granted so much power to Congress. But the framers did, and left us

---

22. McCray v. United States, 195 U.S. 27, 64 (1904).

23. United States v. Carlton, 512 U.S. 26 (1994). *Carlton* addressed an amendment to the Internal Revenue Code enacted in December 1987 to correct an oversight in legislation adopted in 1986. For a rare case holding a retroactive exaction (in that case, an obligation to fund a pension plan from which the taxpayer had withdrawn decades earlier) to be unconstitutional, see Eastern Enterprises v. Apfel, 524 U.S. 498 (1998).

24. Retroactivity is closely bound up to the notion of fair notice of the new tax provision, so that taxpayers can elect to order their affairs to avoid its reach. This is perhaps why a series of cases from the 1920s held newly enacted estate and gift taxes to be unconstitutional in their retroactive impact: The taxes themselves were unprecedented. Conversely, retroactive technical corrections or loophole closing measures usually are easily justified. Over the years, the relevant tax-writing committees (the House Ways and Means Committee and the Senate Finance Committee) have relied on informal measures, such as a joint press release from the two committee chairmen, to put taxpayers on notice that retroactive legislation would be proposed that would reach back to the date of that informal measure.

with a simple remedy for congressional overreach in taxing or spending, which is the ballot box.

HISTORY

The current federal income tax is a creature of the twentieth century. From the time of the Jefferson Administration until the Civil War, tariffs (whose burden Jefferson thought was borne by the rich) were the backbone of the federal tax system. Tariffs not only produced revenues but also protected developing industries, mostly in the North. Congress levied the country's first income tax in 1861 at the outset of the Civil War with a single rate of 3 percent on all incomes over $800 per year. Initially, Treasury Secretary Salmon Chase did little to enforce or even collect the tax. As the war progressed, however, the demand for revenue escalated dramatically. Faced with financial calamity and widespread calls for the rich to sacrifice more for the war effort following the New York draft riots, Congress in 1864 amended the rate structure to impose a tax of 5 percent on income from $600 to $5,000, 7.5 percent on income from $5,000 to $10,000, and 10 percent on income above $10,000. By comparison with the present law, the statute then was almost unbelievably short and simple. The Confederacy also employed an income tax.

After the Civil War, the federal income tax was repealed and tariffs again became the most important source of federal revenue, supplemented by excises on tobacco and liquor. Throughout the 1870s and 1880s, agrarian and labor groups called for reductions in the tariff and for a revival of the income tax. Leading the opposition were Eastern businessmen, for whom the income tax meant "confiscation," "spoliation," and "communism." Throughout this period the Republican Party was able to hold the fort against the enactment of an income tax, but the task became more difficult with the rise of the Populist movement after the Panic of 1893.

In 1894, during Grover Cleveland's second administration, a federal income tax, based largely on the Civil War statute, passed Congress after a bitter struggle, a notable feature of which was the oratory of William Jennings Bryan. A tax of 2 percent was imposed on individual incomes over $4,000 and on the entire income of business corporations. In 1894, eggs sold for twenty cents a dozen and round steak for twelve cents a pound,[25] and the average annual earnings of non-farm employees was $420.[26] Adjusted to take account of inflation (by applying the Consumer Price Index) the $4,000 threshold of 1894 would have been about $100,000 in today's terms. Thus, the income tax was a tax on the well-to-do.

The victory of the Democrats and the Populists was soon to be snatched away, however, by the Supreme Court. The tax became law on August 28, 1894, to take

---

25. See U.S. Department of Commerce, Historical Statistics of the United States, Colonial Times to 1970, at 213 (1975).

26. *Id.* at 165.

effect as of January 1, 1895, and by January 29, 1895, the Supreme Court had agreed to hear a test case challenging its constitutionality. Pollock v. Farmers' Loan & Trust Co., 157 U.S. 429, aff'd on rehearing, 158 U.S. 601 (1895). The attack was based on the theory that a tax on rental income and on dividends and interest was in effect a tax on the underlying property interest, and because it was not levied on states in proportion to population, it violated the prohibition on unapportioned "direct" taxes. The Court heard argument, involving several notable attorney-orators, for five days. The public interest was intense. After a rehearing, the Court, in a five-to-four decision, sustained the constitutional challenge to the imposition of the tax on rents, dividends, and interest and further held that since the provisions taxing those receipts were inseparable from the other provisions of the law, the entire income tax law was invalid.

The Court also stated that progressive tax rates, where the average tax rate goes up as income does, were an unconstitutional violation of due process. Today we often think about the design of progressive income taxes as relying primarily on increasing marginal tax rates, where income is divided into different layers, and the top layers are taxed at higher rates than income in the lower layers. But it also is the case that a "flat" tax with an exemption for a specified first layer of income ($4,000, in Pollock v. Farmers' Loan & Trust Co.) operates as a progressive tax, because the more income you have, the greater the proportion of your income that is subject to the flat tax, and the less important the exemption becomes. (It might help here to think of the exemption as a "zero rate bracket" sitting below the tax rate applied to income above that threshold.)

After Pollock v. Farmers' Loan & Trust Co., advocates of an income tax turned their efforts to amendment of the Constitution. Those efforts bore fruit in 1913 with the adoption of the Sixteenth Amendment, which provides: "The Congress shall have the power to lay and collect taxes on incomes, from whatever source derived, without apportionment among the several States, and without regard to any census or enumeration."

Congress reacted quickly, adopting in 1913 a tax law modeled after the 1894 act. Like its 1894 predecessor, the 1913 tax was imposed only on the well-to-do, but the rates were modest. There was an exemption of $3,000 for an individual and of an additional $1,000 for a married person living with his or her spouse. The rate was 1 percent with a "surtax" ranging from 1 percent on net income from $20,000 to $50,000 up to 6 percent on that part of net income exceeding $500,000. The revenue needs created by World War I led to dramatic expansion of the tax, however, leading to "the discovery of how easily and quickly large sums or revenue could be raised through the income tax."[27] The reach of the tax was broadened by reducing personal exemptions and its impact was increased by raising rates, with individual rates reaching a maximum of 77 percent in 1918. Despite the lowering of exemptions, the major burden of the tax fell on people with high incomes.[28]

---

27. See J. Witte, *The Politics and Development of the Federal Income Tax* 81 (1985). This book is an excellent source of facts and analysis and is relied on heavily in the account that follows in the text.

28. *Id.* at 86.

Following World War I, as federal expenditures declined and budget surpluses arose, rates were gradually reduced, reaching a maximum individual rate of 24 percent. During World War II, the income tax became, and since then has remained, a mass tax (that is, one imposed on people across a broad range of the income spectrum), although, as noted above, high-income individuals continue to pay a substantial share of the total tax. Maximum marginal rates have gone as high as 91 percent (for some forms of income, in the early 1960s), back down to 28 percent in 1986, and gradually back up to 39.6 percent by the end of the twentieth century.

The so-called Bush tax cuts, enacted in 2001, temporarily lowered the top rate to 35 percent. The top rate reverted to 39.6 percent as of January 1, 2013 through what was known as the "fiscal cliff" tax deal; in addition, "net investment income" above a high-income threshold ($250,000 in 2013 for a married couple filing a joint return) became subject to an additional 3.8 percent tax (§1411). Prior to 2013, an individual's labor income had been subject to a hospital tax of 2.9 percent, either as self-employment income or wage income (with the nominal incidence of the tax in the latter case shared equally between employee and employer). §§1401, 3101, and 3111. The fiscal cliff tax deal added 0.9 percent to the hospital tax, again for income above the same high-income threshold. As a result, the basic idea is that all income above the threshold will be subject to an incremental 3.8 percent tax, although some room for gamesmanship remains at the margins.

TABLE OF CASES

Principal cases are indicated by italics.

TABLE OF INTERNAL REVENUE
CODE SECTIONS

TABLE OF TREASURY
REGULATIONS

TABLE OF IRS REVENUE RULINGS

TABLE OF MISCELLANEOUS IRS PRONOUNCEMENTS

INDEX